Interact with your textbook

→ **each book in the complete** series offers free teaching and learning solutions online

www.oxfordtextbooks.co.uk/orc/complete/

complete: law solution

 online resource centre
www.oxfordtextbooks.co.uk/orc/webley_complete2e/

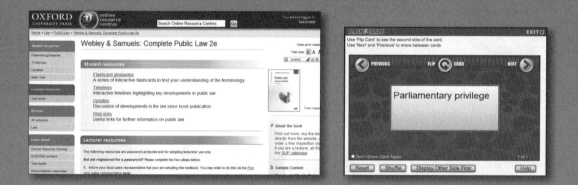

Visit the website for access to the following resources:

For lecturers

→ A test bank of 150 multiple choice questions with answers and feedback

For students

→ Twice-yearly updates
→ Web links
→ A flashcard glossary
→ A timeline of key events

See the **Guide to the Online Resource Centre** on p. viii for full details.

complete

Public Law

Text, Cases, and Materials

Second Edition

Lisa Webley
Professor of Empirical Legal Studies, University of Westminster

Harriet Samuels
Reader in Law, University of Westminster

OXFORD
UNIVERSITY PRESS

OXFORD
UNIVERSITY PRESS

Great Clarendon Street, Oxford, OX2 6DP,
United Kingdom

Oxford University Press is a department of the University of Oxford.
It furthers the University's objective of excellence in research, scholarship,
and education by publishing worldwide. Oxford is a registered trade mark of
Oxford University Press in the UK and in certain other countries

© Oxford University Press 2012

The moral rights of the authors have been asserted

First Edition published 2009

Impression: 1

Public sector information reproduced under Open Government Licence v1.0
(http://www.nationalarchives.gov.uk/doc/open-government-licence/
open-government-licence.htm)

Crown Copyright material reproduced with the permission of the
Controller, HMSO (under the terms of the Click Use licence)

British Library Cataloguing in Publication Data
Data available

Library of Congress Cataloging in Publication Data
Library of Congress Control Number: 2012933282

ISBN 978–0–19–969456–3

Printed in Great Britain by
Ashford Colour Press Ltd, Gosport, Hampshire

To Jan, Paul, Jemma, Caitlin, and Natasha with love
LCW

To Annette, Andy, Abi, and Esther-Rose
HS

Guide to using the book

Complete Public Law: Text, Cases, and Materials includes a number of different features that have been carefully designed to enrich your learning and help you along as you develop your understanding of criminal law.

● *United Kingdom v. Iceland* [1973] ICJ REP 3 [the *Fisheries Jurisdiction Cas*

Iceland claimed the authority to extend its fishing zone unilaterally from miles. It gave notice of its intention to the UK in 1971, but went ahead wi zone despite the UK's objection. This notice was in accordance with the between Iceland and the UK to the effect that the former would not exten without giving the latter at least six months' notice. The 1961 agreemer in an exchange of notes between the two countries, which also entitled t to confer jurisdiction on the Court if a dispute arose between the two. Th (at 6) that:

Cases and materials

Cases play an integral role in shaping the relationship between the citizen and the state, so it is important to read first-hand reports in order to fully understand the subject. This book includes extracts from a wide range of cases, legislation, and academic material, which complement the authors' commentary.

thinking point
How do you refer to the UK? Do you refer to it as a state, a kingdom, a realm, a country or the Crown?

the 'state', and you will see the terms used interchan law texts.

So, what is the Queen's role in UK? The Queen's role similar to president in some countries, although she do political decision-making in government as a presider stitutional arrangements in a country). In the domestic process through the mechanism of royal assent to leg also presides over the state opening of Parliament ea in so far as she may offer advice to the **Prime Ministe** copies of all state papers. Honours are granted throu

Thinking points

Should the UK have an elected head of state? Should the voting age be lowered? Thinking points throughout the text draw out topical issues and encourage you to approach the subject critically.

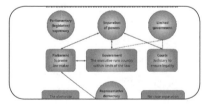

Diagrams

Helpful diagrams appear at key points throughout the book, helping to make constitutional structures and legal procedures as clear as possible.

NOTE

You may wish to do some research on other areas of law that are cov law'. The Public Law Project, a national charity that provides advice ar law matters for those whose access to advice and effective remedies restricted, may be a good place to start: see online at http://www.pu index.html

Public law is not a static concept and it has changed over time. As in

Notes

Useful notes throughout the text clarify and emphasise particular facts or points of law to help you in your studies.

should be exercised in a way that is politically neutral,
appointed representatives rather than the monarch.
rules according to the constitution and there are limits
In other words, her exercise of power is subordinate to
laterally to override the constitution as an absolute m
have greater constitutional power than the constitutio

cross reference
For more on the development of the monarchy, see Chapters 4 and 5, both of which chart the development of our present constitutional framework.

Why would a monarch be in a strong position to adv
sets out the rationale for retaining this power withir
monarch, as a constant and stable force in the UK, r
of benefit to a Prime Minister, even if the Prime Mir
the advice.

Cross reference notes

These helpful notes make navigation quick and easy by
pointing you to a different section or chapter where a
topic is discussed in more detail.

---

summary points

What is the Crown and is this the same as the Queen?

* The Crown is the name given to the coronation crown th
  to the monarch herself, and to the state.
* In most instances, you will need to distinguish between
  monarch or to the state as a whole.
* The Queen is the head of state for the United Kingdon
  Ireland, and heads the three branches of the state: the l
  judiciary.

Summaries

Short summaries appear throughout the book to
reinforce your knowledge. At the end of each chapter is
a longer summary that reiterates the key topics covered
in the chapter. You should use these to check your
understanding and return to any areas that aren't yet
completely clear.

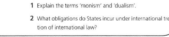

❓ Questions

Self-test questions

1 Explain the terms 'monism' and 'dualism'.

2 What obligations do States incur under international treatie
  tion of international law?

Reflective questions

The questions at the end of each chapter provide the
ideal opportunity for you to test your understanding of
a topic. They challenge you to apply your knowledge,
either by preparing a full answer to a question, or by
debating the issues with your fellow students.

📖 Further reading

Lord Bingham of Cornhill, 'Dicey revisited' [2002] Public Law 39

This article explains how Dicey's approach to public law remains
theories are often a starting point for academic debate.

Blackburn, R. W., 'Dicey and the teaching of public law' [1985] P

This article sets out how Dicey's approach to definition public la

Further reading

These suggestions for additional reading have been
carefully selected to highlight key areas and to help you
deepen your knowledge of the subject.

Guide to the Online Resource Centre

The Online Resource Centre that accompanies this book provides students and lecturers with ready-to-use teaching and learning resources. They are free of charge, and are designed to complement the book and maximise the teaching and learning experience.

www.oxfordtextbooks.co.uk/orc/webley_complete2e/

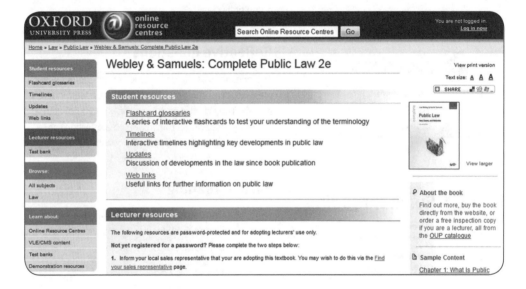

For students

These resources are available to all, enabling students to get the most from their textbook; no registration or password is required.

---

want to look at the updates in relation to constitutional conve[n]
Minister, in the chapter 12 updates.

6.4.3 The dismissal of the government

One of the challenges for a coalition government is that so m
system (and the constitutional system that underpins it)
government. There are some who are concerned that coalition
weak government as it may be more difficult for government to b
must co-operate to run the country. Some of the proposals for
may address these concerns include: fixed term Parliaments: F
2010 (published 22 July 2010); and the proposal that 55% of

Regular updates

The authors regularly update this section of the site to account for recent cases and developments in public law that have occurred since publication of the book. These updates are accompanied by page references to the textbook, so you can easily see how the new developments relate to the existing law.

Web links

Links to useful websites enable you to instantly look at reliable sources of online information, and efficiently direct your online study.

Flashcard glossary

This edited version of the full glossary that appears in the book can be easily downloaded to an iPod or other portable device, and is a great way to test your knowledge of key terms and definitions.

Timeline

This interactive timeline provides an easy way for you to trace the key events and decisions that have shaped the UK's constitutional landscape.

For lecturers

These resources are password protected to ensure only adopting lecturers can access the resource; each registration is personally checked to ensure the security of the site.

Registering is easy: simply click on 'Lecturer Resources' on the Online Resource Centre, complete a simple registration form which allows you to choose your own username and password, and access will be granted within three working days (subject to verification).

Test bank

Containing 150 multiple choice questions with answers and feedback, this is a fully customisable resource of ready-made revision assessments which you can use to test your students. It can be easily downloaded onto your Virtual Learning Environment.

Summary contents

Detailed contents

Chapter 16   Illegality   479

Chapter 17   Irrationality and Proportionality   517

Chapter 18   Procedural Impropriety   549

Chapter 19   Remedies   594

Preface

The developments in Public Law since the first edition of this book have ensured that the production of a second edition has not been a boring task. The book has been updated to include a discussion of the formation of the Coalition government in May 2010 and the subsequent constitutional and legislative developments. We have added a new chapter on the law on terror to illustrate many of the public law principles we discuss throughout the book.

During the writing of the second edition we have incurred many debts along the way. We wish to thank all our colleagues, past and present, who gave particular help and encouragement including: Sylvie Bacquet, Andy Boon, Liz Duff, Steve Greenfield, Andrea Jarman, Kim Marshall, Emma McClean, Danny Nicol, Guy Osborn, and Stephanie Roberts. Some provided help with constitutional and administrative matters in relation to this book, others have shaped our teaching practice over the years, others have contributed to the public law courses on which we have taught, and others have provided support, encouragement, and belief in our ability. Many others, too numerous to mention, have helped us over the years. Our students have also challenged us to rethink our understanding of received wisdom on teaching and learning constitutional and administrative law. Their enthusiasm for their teachers' book and their gentle feedback has helped us shape the second edition. We should particularly like to thank some of them: Aruj Aman, Siobhan Duncan, Alistair Henwood, and John McCrea for their research assistance over the summer of 2011. We should like to thank Tom Young, from Oxford University Press, for his great patience during the lifetime of this project. And last, but of course not least, we should like to thank our family and friends for allowing us to be absent at many important times, so as to worry about, read for, and write the book. Lisa would like to thank Paul, Jan, and Jemma Webley, Ruth Baxter, Sarah Turnbull, and Christina Howard. Harriet would again like to thank Lisa Webley for generously asking her to be part of this project, Annette Samuels, Andrew Raffell, and Abi and Esther-Rose for allowing her to spend a part of their summer holiday in the library and for their encouraging refrain of 'haven't you finished that second edition yet'.

Lisa Webley & Harriet Samuels
School of Law, University of Westminster, London, February 2012

Acknowledgements

Grateful acknowledgement is made to all the authors and publishers of copyright material which appears in this book, and in particular to the following for permission to reprint material from the sources indicated:

Crown copyright material is reproduced under Class Licence Number C2006010631 with the permission of the Controller of HMSO and the Queen's Printer for Scotland. Parliamentary copyright material is reproduced with the permission of the Controller of Her Majesty's Stationery Office on behalf of Parliament.

Lord Bingham of Cornhill: extract from 'The Rule of Law' 6th Sir David Williams Lecture

Centre for Public Law 16 November 2006.

Cambridge Law Journal and the authors: extracts from *Cambridge Law Journal:* N W Barber: 'Prelude to the Separation of Powers', 60 (1) CLJ 59 (2001), David J Feldman: 'None, One or Several? Perspectives on the UK's Constitution(S)', 64 (2) CLJ 329 (2005), and H W R Wade: 'The Basis of Legal Sovereignty', CLJ 172 (1955).

The Constitution Unit: extract from Robert Hazell (with contributions from Mark Glover, Akash Paun, and Meg Russell): *Towards a New Constitutional Settlement: An Agenda for Gordon Brown's First 100 days and Beyond* (The Constitution Unit, UCL, 2007).

Fergal F Davis: extract from 'Extra-Constitutionalism, The Human Rights Act and the "Labour Rebels": Applying Professor Tushnet's theories in the UK', 4 *Web Journal of Current Legal Issues* (2006).

Incorporated Council of Law Reporting: extracts from the *Law Reports: Appeal Cases* (AC), *Chancery Division* (Ch), *Queen's Bench Division* (QB), and *Weekly Law Reports* (WLR).

Liberty Fund, Inc: extract from M J C Vile: *Constitutionalism and the Separation of Powers* (2e, Liberty Fund, 1998) Part III.

Melbourne University Law Review: extract from John Goldring: 'Administrative Law: Teaching and Theory 15 *Melbourne University Law Review* 489 (1986).

Peter Morton: extracts from P A Morton: 'Conventions of the British Constitution', 15 *Holdsworth Law Review* 114 (1991–2).

New Zealand Journal of Public and International Law and the author: extract from Jeffery Goldsworthy: 'Is Parliament Sovereign? Recent Challenges to the Doctrine of Parliamentary Sovereignty', 3 *New Zealand Journal of Public and International Law* 7 (2005).

Oxford University Press: extracts from Eric Barendt: *An Introduction to Constitutional Law* (OUP, 1998); Peter Cane: *Administrative Law* (4e, OUP 2004); Martin Loughlin: *Public Law* (Clarendon Press, 1992); Colin Munro: *Studies in Constitutional Law* (2e, Butterworths, 1999); Adam Tomkins: *Public Law* (OUP, 2003); and Gavin Drewry: 'The Executive: Towards Accountable Government and Effective Governance', J Jowell: 'The Rule of Law and its Underlying Values', Anthony Lester QC and Kate Beattie: 'Human Rights and the British Constitution', and Dawn Oliver: 'The "Modernization" of the United Kingdom Parliament', in Jeffrey Jowell and Dawn

Oliver (Eds.): *The Changing Constitution* (6e, OUP, 2007); also extracts from *Parliamentary Affairs*: Tony Benn: 'The Case for a Constitutional Premiership', 33 (1) PA 7, F F Ridley:'There is no British Constitution: A Dangerous Case of the Emperor's New Clothes', 41 (3) PA 340, and Dawn Oliver: 'Written Constitutions: Principles and Problems' 45(2) PA 132; from *Current Legal Problems:* Danny Nicol: 'Britain's Transnational Constitution', in C O'Cinnedie & J Holder with C Campbell-Holt (Eds.): 61 *Current Legal Problems* (2008); and from *Statute Law Review*: Sir John Laws: 'Constitutional Guarantees', 29(1) SLR 1.

Sebastian Payne: extract from 'A Critique of Prerogative Powers', Institute of Advanced Studies Workshop: *The Crown and Public Law*, 21 January 1994.

Reed Elsevier (UK) Ltd trading as LexisNexis: extracts from *New Law Journal*: Seamus Burns: 'When is an Act of Parliament not an Act of Parliament?', 156 NLJ 191 (2006), and 'An Incoming Tide', 158 NLJ 44 (2008); from *Justice of the Peace*: Glenna Robson: 'The Slow March to Constitutional Reform', 169 JP 112 (2005); and from *All England Law Reports* (All ER).

Sweet & Maxwell Ltd: extracts from Gabriele Ganz: *Understanding Public Law* (3e, Sweet & Maxwell, 2001); and from *Public Law*: Rodney Brazier: 'Choosing a Prime Minister', *Public Law* 395 (1982), David McKeever: 'The Human Rights Act and anti-terrorism in the UK: one great leap forward by Parliament, but are the courts able to slow the steady retreat that has followed?' *Public Law* 110 (2010), Danny Nicol: 'Original Intent and the European Convention on Human Rights', *Public Law* 152 (2005).

Katherine Swinton: extracts from Katherine Swinton: 'Challenging the Validity of an Act of Parliament: The Effect of Enrolment and Parliamentary Privilege' 14(2) *Osgoode Hall Law Journal* 345 (1976).

Taylor & Francis Books UK: extract from Susan Millns & Noel Whitty: *Feminist Perspectives on Public Law* (Cavendish Publishing, 1999).

Wiley-Blackwell Publishing Ltd: extracts from *British Journal of Politics and International Relations*: extract from Alexandra Kelso: 'The House of Commons Modernization Committee: Who Needs It?, 9 (1) *BJPIR* 138 (2007); from *Modern Law Review*: J L Hiebert: 'Parliamentary Review of Terrorism Measures', MLR 676 (2005), and R Kirkham: 'Challenging the Authority of the Ombudsman:The Parliamentary Ombudsman's Special Report on Wartime Detainees', (69) 5 MLR 792 (2008); from *Political Quarterly*: Vernon Bogdanor: ''Reform of the House of Lords: A Sceptical View'. PQ 375 (1999); and from

Political Studies: Matthew Flinders: 'Shifting the Balance? Parliament, the Executive and the British Constitution', 50 POST 23 (2000).

Every effort has been made to trace and contact copyright holders prior to going to press but this has not been possible in every case. If notified, the publisher will undertake to rectify any errors or omissions at the earliest opportunity.

Table of cases

Table of statutes

Table of statutory instruments

Table of treaties and conventions

Table of international legislation

Part 1
Introduction and Constitutional Principles

1

What is Public Law?

Key points

This chapter will cover:

- What is public law and how does it differ from private law?
- What is the constitutional and administrative law distinction?
- Why is public law of relevance today?
- What are the key principles of public law?
- How can you make use of this book in your study of public law?

Introduction

Welcome to *Complete Public Law: Text, Cases, and Materials.* This chapter aims to explain the structure of the book. It will introduce you to public law and set out how public law differs from private law, as many students have not thought in terms of 'public' and 'private' law until they study public law. It will also clarify constitutional and administrative law, because some of you will study modules or courses that use these terms in their titles, and may study the two separately. The chapter also aims to explain the importance of public law to everyday life, as it can seem rather abstract and removed from students' experience of the world. It will set out the key principles, in very general terms, so that you are familiar with how these fit together before you come across them in subsequent chapters. It will also provide some guidance on how to make use of the book and how the book is structured to help your learning.

1.1 What is public law and how does it differ from private law?

Most of the law subjects that you will study, and the legal situations with which you come into contact, will be based in private law. Private law regulates relationships between people, organisations, and companies. Examples include contract, tort, land, company, and employment law. Public law, on the other hand, regulates the relationships between individuals (and organisations) with the **state** and its organs. Examples include criminal and immigration law, and human rights-related matters. Broadly speaking, 'private law' is an umbrella term for all areas of law that are essentially horizontal in nature, whereas 'public law' is the term that covers all areas of law that bring us into contact with state power and its application. Public law is essentially vertical in nature, as Figure 1.1 illustrates.

Figure 1.1

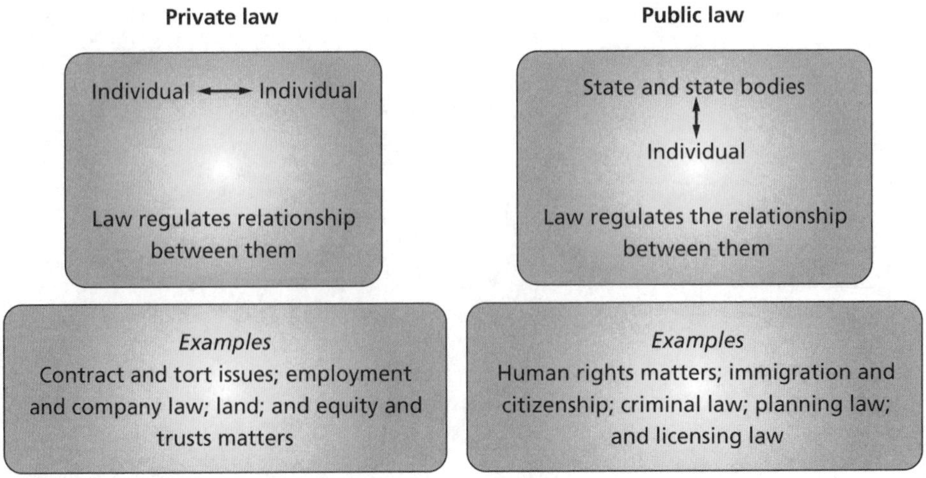

Private law

Individual ←→ Individual

Law regulates relationship between them

Examples
Contract and tort issues; employment and company law; land; and equity and trusts matters

Public law

State and state bodies
↕
Individual

Law regulates the relationship between them

Examples
Human rights matters; immigration and citizenship; criminal law; planning law; and licensing law

If a case involves only individuals, companies, and other private organisations then it is likely to be a private law matter. If it involves any of these along with a local authority, a public body or **public authority**, a **government** department, the police, or any other public official, then it may be a public law matter depending on the nature of the facts. The distinction between public and private law is sometimes rather difficult to make in the UK because we do not have a distinctive public law system. Some countries, such as France, have a separate administrative or public law system, including a separate court system for this type of law. Indeed, it was argued by Dicey in the nineteenth century that the UK has no system of public law (although he recognised constitutional law as a type of law), and other academics continue to discuss whether public law exists, if so, whether it differs from private law, and if so, how.

● M. Loughlin, *Public Law and Political Theory* (Oxford: Clarendon Press, 1992), pp. 2–4

What is it, then, that is distinctive about public law? Is public law a discipline? ...

For some, it is sufficient to identify a particular set of institutional arrangements which may be treated as forming a discrete object of analysis. This seems to be the approach adopted by Professor Birks when he suggests that 'few lawyers would deny that administrative law has a unity and an internal anatomy of its own, made explicit by many textbooks'.[1] What is being suggested here, however, is simply that public law may be identified anatomically as a separate branch of legal study. While, as a result, particular concepts such as *ultra vires* or natural justice may have been developed, there is nothing in this argument which necessarily challenges this idea of the unity of law [that all law is similar—public and private alike].

Others, however, have gone further and have intimated that public law can be placed on an acceptable footing only by laying bare the skeleton of principle that provides it with a conceptual unity.[2] This constitutes a more radical claim, since it implies that the subject possesses distinctive juristic foundations. Claims of this nature are sometimes made in conjunction with the argument ... that the tradition of ordinary law has cast a long shadow over the study of public law ... that public law is still secreted within ... private law and has yet to develop its own philosophy and methodology.

...

This is not, however, the method I propose to adopt ... There is, I believe, a more interesting premise from which to commence this inquiry. This is to start from the assumption that public law is simply a sophisticated form of political discourse; that controversies within the subject are simply extended political disputes. Since many argue that public law is rooted in its social, political, economic, and historical context this approach should ensure that our inquiry is embedded in the realities of the times ...

1 P. Birks, An Introduction to the Law of Restitution (Oxford: Oxford University Press, 1983), p. 3.

2 See, e.g., T. R. S. Allan, 'Legislative supremacy and the rule of law: democracy and constitutionalism' (1985) 44 Cambridge Law Journal 111.

This extract is quite complicated because it is comparing and contrasting different ways in which academics have come to view public law. The first is as a set of laws that relate to the state and thus must be public law. The second is as a subset of private law, when in fact it is a distinct area with distinctive concepts underpinning it. The third, Loughlin's view, is that public law is really a product of political negotiation and political ideologies. Many students studying public law say that they find the constitutional law part of the course or module to be similar to their previous politics studies; others ask why they are studying politics within a law degree, because there seems to be very little 'hard law' in the constitutional law course. This may be because constitutional law, in particular, and many branches of administrative law too are inherently political and are evidence of what different groups believe to be the role of the state, the extent of individual self-determination, and the differing values of groups within society. It is possible to organise and run a country in many different ways, and the choices that are made in founding and running a state are the product of political decisions. Consequently, law and political theory are inherently intertwined in most public law courses, as are individuals' and groups' values and beliefs.

Constitutional law is also a product of a state's historical development and, in many courses, history plays an important role in the constitutional law section of the course. The scholar Dicey was of the view that the history of constitutional law was not of much use to students or lawyers. Indeed, he commented:

● **R. W. Blackburn, 'Dicey and the teaching of public law'** [1985] Public Law 679, 681–2

...that the function of a trained lawyer is not to know what the law was yesterday...or what it ought to be tomorrow, but to explain what are the principles of law actually existing in England...

Lord Bingham of Cornhill disagrees with this view.

● **Lord Bingham of Cornhill, 'Dicey revisited'** [2002] Public Law 39, 41

In the field of constitutional law such an approach seems to me not only anti-intellectual, but plainly misguided. Happily, as I think, it has increasingly come to be recognised that a lawyer without history, as well as literature, is a mechanic, and probably not a very good mechanic at that.

Consequently, we shall address historical issues in this book as and when they are relevant.

summary points

What is public law and how does it differ from private law?

- *Public law is the study of the law that regulates the relationship between the individual and the state, and organisations and the state.*
- *There are different views on what the term 'public law' means.*
- *Public law is linked to politics, history, and other disciplines, such as economics and sociology, and cannot be studied by merely referring to the text of the law.*
- *You will come across competing theories in your studies and there is no one right answer—although there may be a number of wrong ones!*

1.2 What is the constitutional and administrative law distinction?

In the past, the term 'public law' was used to describe all law that related to administrative law. In modern usage and on some degree courses, 'public law', as a phrase, is sometimes used as a short cut for the longer expression 'constitutional and administrative law'. In this book, we use it to mean both constitutional and administrative law. It may be useful to explain what constitutional and administrative law are. '**Constitutional law**' is the law that relates to the structure or framework of the state, and the political and **judicial** institutions of the state. It includes the theories and principles that underpin the state. We cover constitutional law in the first fourteen chapters of this book. '**Administrative law**' is the body of law that deals with the workings of the state, along with the statutory and common law powers and duties of government departments, local authorities, and public bodies and public authorities, which assist in the everyday life of the country. Constitutional law is the law that establishes the state and its institutions; administrative law is the law that these institutions use to run the country.

· ·

constitutional law

The law that provides the framework of the state and establishes the state's principal institutions, e.g. Parliament, the government, the courts, and devolved legislatures and executives.

administrative law

The law that provides the legal power and the legal duties of individual public bodies and public authorities, e.g. local authority powers and duties, government departments, HM Revenue and Customs (HMRC), and the Student Loans Company.

· ·

Without constitutional law, it is difficult to see how we could have administrative law, because administrative law is the law made by the state in order to allow it to run the country. But that presupposes that the state exists. Constitutional law must come first, so that there is a legitimate state—and this assumes that there is a state that is recognised by the people. In most instances, the state will include **legislative**, executive, and judicial organs that are imbued with power. Thereafter, they are involved in making the law, implementing the law, and enforcing the law, so that the state functions. But where does the power to establish the state come from, so that we may make constitutional law to establish it?

There are many different political and jurisprudential theories as to what power has been delegated by individuals (or taken from them), or who has the authority to rule, and under what circumstances and for what purposes. There are different schools of thought on the extent to which the individual's delegation of power is for all time or is time-limited (whether we can ever get our power back from the state), and what we may expect from the state in return for handing over some of our power to it. Whole books have been written on these questions. There are two main political ideologies that underpin many of the explanations, the first being conservatism and the second being liberalism, and these ideologies shape the way in which one views the role and powers of the rulers or the state.

· ·

● M. Loughlin, *Public Law and Political Theory* (Oxford: Clarendon Press, 1992], p. 63

...

Conservatism as a form of thought is traditionalist, is primarily concerned with the issue of authority and views the individual organically, as part of a social order. Liberalism is a rationalistic theory which has little regard for the past, is primarily concerned with liberty and is constructed on the assumption of the autonomy of the individual. Despite such important differences, these two political ideologies nevertheless share certain affinities with respect to their vision of law and government. It is the common core of shared understanding about law and government that provides us with an insight into the normativistic style in public law...

Our ideas about the relationship between the individual and the state, and consequently about public law, are shaped by our political ideology. Put crudely: do you believe in the authority of the state to regulate individuals' behaviour according to a set of values (conservatism)? Or do you believe that the state has a duty to leave the individual to make his or her own moral decisions on appropriate behaviour in all but a small set of situations, even if that means that he or she is free to act in ways that you may find unpleasant or consider to be immoral (liberalism)? Your answer to this will determine some of your reactions to public law and to constitutional theory.

We are still little nearer to answering how states are established, however. Some states have been set up after a period of turbulence (war, revolution, independence) and have been founded after a process of consultation with the population or sections of the population. Others appear to have developed over time, without any individual having been asked to make a decision on how the state is to be set up, what values (if any) it should embody, and for what purpose it has been developed. It is not possible to say for certain whether constitutional law results from individuals in a country delegating some of their power to a central point on the basis that they believe that they are stronger as a collective rather than as individuals. Similarly, we cannot deduce whether individuals have entered into an explicit or an implicit social contract with a sovereign or with parliamentarians to provide power to them and to respect their authority to rule in return for certain protections or services. Equally, it may be argued that no decision was ever made to delegate or to hand over, or to assume power for particular purposes, because in reality constitutional law has developed gradually over the centuries. This development may be the product of historical, political, social, and economic processes that have resulted in a form of law—constitutional law—being generally accepted and respected by citizens and by state bodies in some countries.

For undergraduate purposes, it is probably sufficient to understand that there are many views on how constitutional law was born and what its purpose is. Jurisprudence and legal theory courses will probably address this issue in much more detail. But you may want to consider this: can you imagine what life would be like in a place where there were no organised state? What do you think would be the strengths and the weakness, if you and everyone else were to have total power over your own lives (with no laws to be enforced against you and no recourse to the law either)? Constitutional law provides the building blocks of the state, while administrative law provides the power to make it run according to the political proclivities of those in power and their values and beliefs. Between them, they give, legitimise, and limit the use of power, and our rights and duties as citizens.

summary points

What is the constitutional and administrative law distinction?

- *Constitutional law is the study of the law that founds the state and sets up its institutions. It also regulates the relationships between the organs of the state.*

- *Administrative law is the law that provides the power and imposes the duties on government departments and public bodies, so that they may fulfil the tasks that have been designated to them by the state.*

- *Constitutional and administrative law are inherently political, because they are based on different notions of how states should run and for what purpose.*

1.3 Why is public law of relevance today?

'Public law' is a wide term that covers many disparate areas of law. At its highest level, it relates to the special powers that the state has to run the country—that is:

- the power to make law, amend law, and repeal law;
- the power to implement the law; and
- the power to apply and enforce the law against us all (including against the state itself).

The power to implement the law—or perhaps, more specifically, to use the powers that have been bestowed on the state through legislation and the common law—is extremely wide-ranging. In UK terms, these include the power to deprive people of their liberty (in most instances as a result of a criminal conviction or pending a criminal trial of relating to a serious offence), to require individuals to do certain things as set out in law, to require us not to do certain things that are contrary to the law, to pay taxes, to make our children attend school or to be home schooled up to the age of 16 (or the age of 17 for pupils recently entering secondary education), to enter and remain in the UK only if we have the appropriate entry clearances or we have been granted citizenship, etc. Figure 1.2 sets out a few of the areas that fall under the term 'public law' with which you may have come into contact so far.

As you can see, public law pervades many areas of our lives. You will certainly have come into contact with public law issues already. We often take many areas for granted, such as human rights, the availability of welfare benefits, and the education and health services, perhaps because most of the time the state broadly respects human rights (sometimes a contested point, but as a general rule the UK government has a good human rights record when compared worldwide), we have a legal right to access educational services to the age of 16 or 17, and British citizens have a legal right to health care via the National Health Service (NHS).

Figure 1.2

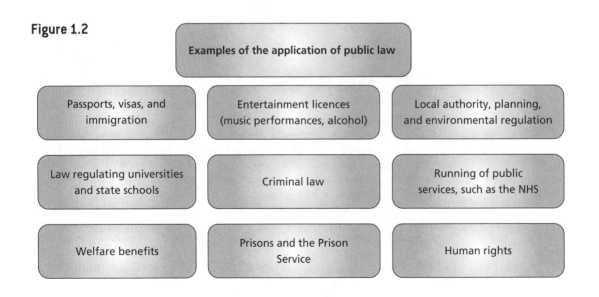

NOTE

You may wish to do some research on other areas of law that are covered by the term 'public law'. The Public Law Project, a national charity that provides advice and assistance on public law matters for those whose access to advice and effective remedies from elsewhere is restricted, may be a good place to start: see online at http://www.publiclawproject.org.uk/index.html

Public law is not a static concept and it has changed over time. As indicated in the first section, Dicey was of the view that we did not have a system of public law per se in the UK, although it would be difficult to find a serious commentator now who agreed with that proposition. Indeed, the public sector arena changes as different political administrations come and go in government. This affects the way in which public law is framed and the theories that underpin it. It has been argued by some commentators that public law today is very different from public law prior to the election of the Conservative government in 1979. As a result of reforms linked to a theory known as 'new public management' (NPM), it has changed the way in which some people view public law and the relationship between the individual and the state.

● **G. Drewry, 'The executive: towards accountable government and effective governance', in J. Jowell and D. Oliver (eds)** *The Changing Constitution*
(6th edn, Oxford: Oxford University Press, 2007), pp. 185–206, at 193–5

Modernising Government: From Public Administration to Public Management

The election of the Thatcher Government in 1979 marked the beginning of a period of rapid and radical change in UK public administration. The process continued under...John Major—and was further developed and repackaged by Tony Blair's Labour Government. Public administration has been displaced—at least in part—by a 'new public management' (NPM) which rejects traditional bureaucratic methods and structures in favour of market-based and business-like regimes of public service.[1] The radical nature and extent of the NPM phenomenon is summarized by Owen Hughes:

> ...This is not simply a matter of reform or a minor change in management style, but a change in the role of government in society and the relationship between government and citizenry.[2]

...NPM has seen the growth of new relationships between the public sector and the private and voluntary sectors...The transformative process culminated, in 1988, in the launch of the radical Next Steps initiative...The Next Steps initiative has effected a transformation of the structure and the culture of the civil service, and has had a massive impact upon the organizational arrangements of government departments.[3] It is only one aspect of the much wider NPM agenda...

...It might of course be argued that the arrangements for delivering public services—such as welfare, education, and health—are not a 'constitutional' matter at all, being concerned with administrative superstructure rather than with fundamental principles of government that are the essence of constitution. The Next Steps white paper, for instance, was not itself regarded as, or presented as, a 'constitutional' document, neither was the Blair Government's *Modernising* Government white paper. However, both these documents...have important implications for 'the changing constitution'...The *Modernising Government* proposals consolidated and developed changing ideas about the relationship between the citizen, as a consumer of public services, and the state as service provider...And of course the Blair Government's wider programme has featured major items of constitutional reform that both form a blackcloth to and feed into the micro-agenda of public service and public management reform: devolution, for instance...; the Freedom of Information Act 2000...

1 There is a very large literature on the nature and development of NPM. See, in particular, O. Hughes, *Public Management and Administration* (3rd edn, Basingstoke: Palgrave Macmillan, 2003).

[Other references omitted]

2 Hughes, n.1, p. 1.

3 See P. Dunleavy, 'The architecture of the British central state' (1989) 67(3) Public Administration 249 and 67(4) Public Administration 391.

Why does this matter? Shifts in the relationship between the individual and the state affect citizens' rights and responsibilities, and public bodies' powers and duties. In turn, these shifts affect the nature of public services, their content and delivery, as well as the way in which the courts address judicial review questions (administrative law cases). The purpose of administrative law has been hotly debated, and differences in viewpoint have been categorised by Harlow and Rawlings (2006; see the end-of-chapter 'Further reading') as 'red-light', 'green-light', and 'amber-light' theories of administrative law. Each colour corresponds to a different set of theoretical assumptions about the purpose of administrative law, the executive and public body powers and duties, and the extent to which the courts should determine public law disputes. One's understanding of whether the red-light, green-light or amber-light theory outlines the most appropriate role of administrative law will colour the way in which you approach the study and practice of public law.

Goldring explains the basic distinction between red and green-light theorists as follows.

● **J. Goldring, 'Administrative law: teaching and theory'** (1986) 15 Melbourne University Law Review 489, 495–6

(3) The Operation of Administrative Law

Harlow and Rawlings[1] group those who have tended to theorize about administrative law into 'red light' and 'green light' theorists, though they concede the existence of 'amber light' theory. This characterization can be seen as a device to assist in understanding the effect of various approaches to administrative law. Dicey is a 'red light' theorist, in that he sees administrative law as placing restraints on what officialdom may do. To the extent that a theorist sees administrative law as establishing a system of limits on the exercise of governmental power, she/he is a 'red light' theorist. A 'green light' theorist, by contrast, perceives the law as an instrument by which policy can be implemented. McAuslan, in this taxonomy, is probably a 'green light' theorist. Others would be harder to classify...

These theories centre around the theorists' perceptions of how the rules, practices and institutions operate. A major failing of many lawyers in the common law tradition is that they perceive administrative law solely from the standpoint of the private lawyer whose task it is to vindicate the right of the individual, or to protect the collective interest against those who, for reasons based on their interest of property, profit or ideology, seek to assert an individual right against it. Neither McAuslan,[2] nor Harlow and Rawlings, fall into this trap: they are respectively aware that the interest which is asserted by the State is not necessarily a collective interest but may just as easily be the interest of a private person or group on whose behalf the State has intervened. Therefore they do not see administrative law in terms solely of rights or interests but rather of a system in which various forces have some influence. While cases (and, to a lesser extent, statutes) which seek to enforce or protect rights are an important part of administrative law, they are not the only part. They are merely the part that is emphasized by the private law orientation of our legal culture...

Since administrative law deals with what might, in broad terms, be called 'the administration' (including, but not limited to, the state), it is important that lawyers realize that in addition to the legal culture with which they are most familiar there is also an 'administrative culture' which, in terms of forming 'administrative law' . . . is probably more important. Lawyers often tend to see rules, practices and institutions in the light of results in individual cases. Administrators are more likely to see them in terms of either policy implementation or mass decision-making, which may amount to the same thing . . .

1 *Law and Administration* (London: Weidenfeld & Nicolson, 1984), ch. 1.

[2] P. McAuslan, 'Administrative law, collective consumption and judicial policy' (1983) 46 Modern Law Review 1.

The extract explains that red-light theorists consider the purpose of administrative law to be a means of controlling the state's exercise of power to protect individual liberty. Green-light theorists consider administrative law to be a means of permitting the state to develop its policy agendas. Amber-light theorists, whom Goldring mentions, but whom he does not characterise, tend towards the view that law should control the exercise of executive **discretion** when that discretion has an impact on individuals' constitutional rights. Some consider this to be a new direction for judges in judicial review cases in the UK, and particularly relevant to cases that involve the Human Rights Act 1998. This will be considered in more detail in Chapter 14. Administrative law is part law, part procedural rules, and part policy. Some argue that this places administrative law in a very different category from private law, and that it should be treated differently by lawyers as a result.

Tomkins' (2002; see 'Further reading') provides a more detailed explanation of the red, green, and amber-light theories of public law. Harlow and Rawlings' book provides an extremely detailed analysis, to which you may wish to refer if you wish to consider and develop your own view of the purpose of administrative law. However, it is probably sufficient for most undergraduate and graduate diploma students to know that there are fundamental differences in understanding the purpose of constitutional and administrative law, and that these in turn affect the way in which people approach politics and law, and the application of legal rules in individual cases. These differences have an impact on the way in which public services are delivered and indeed whether a particular area is considered to be a public law or a private law matter. They also have an effect on the way in which judicial review judgments are framed, as you will see in later chapters, as judges try to balance the interests of different groups and to determine the appropriate limits on the exercise of public power.

summary points

Why is public law of relevance today?

• *Public law is a term that covers many different areas of law.*

• *It pervades many aspects of our everyday lives, from health and education, to immigration and the environment.*

• *There are different understandings about the purpose of constitutional and administrative law, linked to different political ideologies about the purpose of the state and the relationship between the individual and the state.*

• *The different theories are evidenced by changes in public administration and changes in the way in which public services are delivered.*

• *Recent governmental reforms have made changes to the structure of the state, which in turn have had an impact on public law.*

• *The red-light, green-light, and amber-light labels are useful ways of categorising some of these differences to help us to understand the interplay between law and politics, the individual and the state, policy and law.*

1.4 What are the key principles of public law?

Public law is made up of a number of key principles, doctrines, or theories that are designed to ensure a healthy, representative, law-abiding country that has a balance between the needs of the state and the needs of its citizens. These principles will be discussed in detail in subsequent chapters. This section will introduce you very briefly to the main theories and how they fit together, as follows.

- *The UK's 'unwritten' constitution*   This is less straightforward in a UK context than in many other countries, because the UK has a constitution that has developed and evolved over many, many centuries. It is uncodified, in so far as we do not have one document of higher constitutional importance that sets out our rights and the constitutional structure and under-pinnings of the state. It is heavily reliant on political mechanisms to constrain the executive, in the form of **constitutional conventions**. These are non-legal rules that are consequently not enforceable via the courts. Indeed, the constitution is made up of a range of legal and non-legal sources, and is defined differently by different commentators. Some suggest that it is made up of European Union (EU) law (which is considered by some to be hierarchically superior to UK law), the **European Convention for the Protection of Human Rights and Fundamental Freedoms**, or **European Convention on Human Rights (ECHR)**, UK primary and secondary legislation, the **royal prerogative**, the common law precedent, constitutional conventions, and authoritative academic and practitioner sources. Others consider it to be restricted to domestic law and precedent. This is considered in detail in Chapter 3.

- *The **rule of law***   All are subject to law regardless of their status; in other words, no one is beyond the reach of the law even if he or she is a state official. We all owe a duty to respect the law, both individuals and the state. The rule of law also covers a second concept, which is that the state should not exercise its power in an arbitrary fashion. This means that a public body should be consistent in its exercise of power and should not use any discretion unfairly to favour one individual or group of individuals over another. This is discussed in Chapter 4.

- *The **separation of powers***   There is some form of division between the three main powers of the state to ensure that a form of dictatorship cannot become established and abuse the power entrusted to the state by the people. Leaders with absolute power are considered to be more at risk of abusing their power than are leaders who are checked or limited by other branches of the state as they exercise public power. The independence of the **judiciary** is seen as particularly important to safeguard citizen's rights and to ensure limited government. This is discussed in Chapter 5.

- *We live in a representative democracy*   Our elected officials represent our views (and if you choose not to vote, then you choose to hand over your power to decide on your repre-sentatives to everyone else). Our elected representatives in **Parliament**—that is, members of Parliament (MPs)—determine the law that is passed, and the executive develops policy so that it may implement its political agenda. In turn, MPs and appointed peers call the execu-tive to account for its actions. This is discussed in Chapter 7 in relation to Parliament. Chapter 10 addresses **devolution**, the Scottish Parliament, and the Welsh and the Northern Ireland Assemblies.

- *The supremacy of Parliament*   Because the law is supreme and Parliament is the supreme law-making body, then the Westminster Parliament is supreme and may change or make any law that it so wishes. (Parliament should not be confused with the government, which is subject to Parliament and to the courts.) Countries that operate a pure system of legislative parliamentary supremacy do not have a written constitution of higher constitutional importance against which primary legislation can be compared to review whether the primary legislation is constitutional and valid, or unconstitutional and invalid or void. Such countries, including the UK, do not have an **entrenched bill of rights** that can be asserted against Parliament. In other words, human rights may be restricted by Parliament and the courts cannot prevent Parliament from doing this, because Parliament is legislatively supreme. This is in contrast to countries with written constitutions, which restrict the legislature's power to enact law by delineating particular legal rights as 'constitutional' and therefore susceptible to amendment only if the constitution itself is amended. This is known as 'constitutional supremacy' rather than parliamentary supremacy. In states that operate a system of constitutional supremacy, it is usually for the courts to determine whether legislation is valid or invalid as compared against the constitution. The UK attempts to preserve parliamentary supremacy and to protect individuals' ECHR rights through the operation of the Human Rights Act 1998. This is discussed in Chapters 7–10 and also in Chapter 14.

- *Limited and responsible government* This is coupled with accountability to our representatives (parliamentarians) and to the electorate. This is one of the key mechanisms that limits the state's opportunity to abuse its power. uncodified British constitution is heavily reliant on political mechanisms to limit and restrain the government's exercise of power, and to call it to account for its actions. Constitutional conventions—non-legal rules that seek to limit the legal power conferred on the executive—are of particular importance. In addition, we shall consider the role of Parliament in calling the government to account for its exercise of power, as well as the role of the Parliamentary Commissioner for Administration (PCA). This is discussed in Chapters 11–13.

- *The judicial review of executive action by the courts* This is used to ensure that the executive's use of power is legal, rational (and proportionate in the case of human rights issues), procedurally proper, and conforms to the requirements of **natural justice** (and does not breach the terms of the Human Rights Act 1998). Parliament is legislatively supreme, but it is important not to confuse this with the requirement that the executive must act within its power, either as provided by statute or by royal prerogative. The courts may review the executive's exercise of power via a mechanism known as 'judicial review'. This is discussed in Chapter 14 in overview, and then in detail in Chapters 15–20.

Figure 1.3 oversimplifies the relationships between these theories and the state institutions, as you will discover during your study of public law. However, it illustrates that the key doctrine is the rule of law, which presupposes that the state is founded on the principle that the law prevails, and that the state and citizens must act within the law or face court sanction. This is extremely important, because, without this, the separation of powers would be largely ineffective: how does one ensure that different bodies stay within their legal remits if they do not respect the law that limits their powers and roles? Equally, the supremacy of Parliament would be relatively worthless if the law were not considered to be authoritative and legitimate: what use would it be for Parliament to make law if the population and the state organs were to ignore it and do what they wish according to their own sets of rules or moral precepts? Limited and accountable government would also be difficult to achieve if the government were not to recognise the law as limiting what it could do, when, and under what circumstances. Consequently, although you may learn each of the theories in turn in separate chapters, lectures, and tutorials, it is important to bear in mind that they all overlap and support each other. It is also important to remember that there are different views on each of them: there is no conclusive right answer, because theories or doctrines are made up of competing arguments based on a series of assumptions (with evidence to support them), rather than clear-cut descriptions of a set of accepted facts.

Figure 1.3

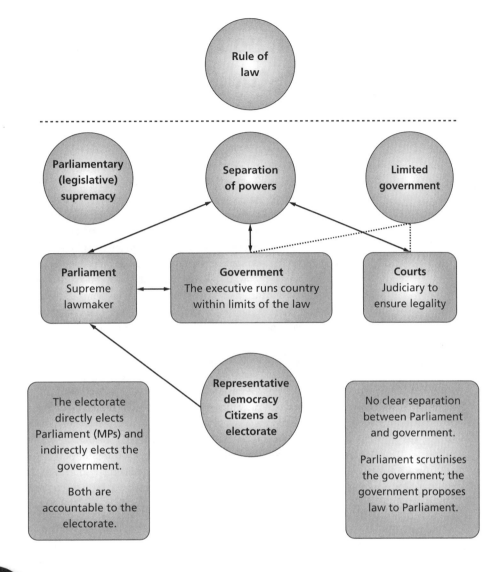

summary points

What are the key principles of public law?

- *The first key principle is the rule of law, which means that the state is founded on the assumption that the law will be respected and that any individual or official may be brought before the court if there is evidence that he or she has broken the law.*

- *The separation of powers means that the organs of the state are sufficiently separate so that the power of the state is not abused to the detriment of citizens.*

- *Representative democracy indicates that parliamentarians have the power to make the law and to scrutinise the workings of government, because the electorate has elected MPs to perform these functions on our behalf (as its representatives).*

- *Parliamentary legislative supremacy means that Parliament has the supreme power to make, amend, and repeal laws on our behalf.*

- *Finally, limited and responsible government means that the executive must obey the law and may be judicially reviewed and held to account by the courts if it is believed that the executive has acted illegally, irrationally, or procedurally improperly, has broken the rules of natural justice, or has breached the Human Rights Act 1998.*

1.5 How can you make use of this book in your study of public law?

We hope that this book will provide you with a clear understanding of each of the topics that it seeks to address. We have tried to keep the content as simple as possible, while balancing simplicity with the need for sufficient detail to allow you to reach an appropriate level of understanding at undergraduate or graduate diploma level. Many of the chapters have a common structure: they provide some background on the area, an insight into its historical development, and an explanation of the competing theories or judgments, as well as evidence of them in the extracts that we have chosen. Each chapter will set out the general principles of the topic and address each one in turn. Extracts provide you with the evidence that backs up the points that are being made. Sometimes, the evidence will be the text of the law; sometimes, it will be judicial opinion on the law; sometimes, it is academic opinion. In other instances, you will read extracts from interest groups, or we will have included extracts from government proposals that indicate areas of concern or propositions for change. Some of the extracts are quite long and they are, at times, complicated. You will usually find an explanation after an extract that highlights the salient points to be considered. In addition, the chapters are organised a little like a diamond: at the beginning of each chapter, you are told what will be covered and the general principles that relate to the topic. The middle (and wider part) of the chapter is split down so that each of the general principles has a section dedicated to it. At the end of the chapter, we return to a summary of the key principles as a form of revision. Most of the chapters contain bullet-point summary boxes at the end of long sections to summarise the essential points that have been made, and there is a summary at the end of each of the substantive chapters that highlights the main points for the topic. We hope that this structure will help you to see both the overview and the detail of each of the areas that you are studying. There are self-test questions at the end of each chapter, and there are additional resources on the Online Resource Centre so that you may practise and test your knowledge further, if you so wish.

We have often been asked by students how they should approach their reading, which is a difficult question to answer, because there are as many approaches as there are people. However, in response to repeated questions on this, we have set out a few different ways in which you may wish to make use of this book, in case any of them are helpful to you.

- One approach might be to write down the key principles that are set out in the summary box at the end of each chapter, and then add in the detail for each of the principles underneath each one, once you have read each section that relates to the principle.

- Another approach might be to draw a diagram of how the general principles fit together, along with each principle's components—a little like Figure 1.3 of the key principles of public law that appeared earlier in the chapter.

- Another, more traditional way of approaching your reading is simply to make notes as you go along and largely to ignore the material that we have put in the summary boxes, but to develop your own instead. The summary boxes contain our views on what we consider to be important, but you may come to different conclusions. Also, the process of developing your own summary boxes or bullet-point lists may be a form of revision that helps you to make the links between the topics and between the principles, and which deepens your understanding.

Good luck with your public law studies, however you choose to make use of this book.

Questions

1 Draft a brief definition of the term 'constitutional law' and one for 'administrative law'.

2 Make a list of areas of public law with which you think you have come into contact.

3 What are the key principles of public law and how do these link together?

4 How will you make use of this book as part of your public law/constitutional and administrative law studies?

Further reading

Lord Bingham of Cornhill, 'Dicey revisited' [2002] Public Law 39

This article explains how Dicey's approach to public law remains relevant today and why his theories are often a starting point for academic debate.

Blackburn, R. W., 'Dicey and the teaching of public law' [1985] Public Law 679

This article sets out how Dicey's approach to defining public law and his mode of teaching public law has shaped our current understanding of what is public law even today.

Drewry, G., 'The executive: towards accountable government and effective governance', in J. Jowell and D. Oliver (eds) *The Changing Constitution* (7th edn, Oxford: Oxford University Press, 2011), ch. 7

This edited-collection chapter explains the changing face of public administration, the less than clear-cut separation between the executive, legislative, and judicial functions, and the influence that NPM has had on the way in which public services are delivered and the approach to government and governance.

Harlow, C. and Rawlings, R., *Law and Administration* (2nd edn, Cambridge: Cambridge University Press, 2006)

This book provides a very detailed explanation of the red-light/amber-light/green-light theories of administrative law and how these structure our understanding of what is administrative law.

Tomkins, A., 'In defence of a political constitution' (2002) 22(1) Oxford Journal of Legal Studies 157

This article provides an explanation of the importance of politics within the British constitution, and also the political mechanisms that check and balance the legal power that has been conferred through the legal sources of the constitution.

Constitutional Organisations, Institutions, and Roles

Key points

This chapter will cover:

- What are the main UK-wide constitutional bodies or offices in the UK?

- What is the Crown and is this the same as the Queen?

- What is Parliament and its role?

- What is the executive and how does this differ from the government?

- What are the courts and what is their role?

- Who may be involved in electing UK representatives and through what mechanisms are UK representatives elected?

Introduction

This chapter considers the constitutional significance of a number of key UK-wide bodies and offices. They form the basis of more theoretical and practical discussions in subsequent chapters and will, where relevant, be discussed in detail there. You may already be familiar with much of the material, or you may be more familiar with the key institutions in another country or countries. Either way, it is important that you have a firm foundation upon which to build your deepening understanding of constitutional and administrative law. Please do take the time to read through this chapter, even if only as a revision aid. This chapter, like the others, is organised with summary boxes at the end of each section, as a guide to the key issues of importance. There are also resources on the Online Resource Centre to allow you to test and apply your knowledge. Institutions particular to England, Wales, Scotland, and Northern Ireland are mentioned only briefly in this chapter, as they are principally discussed in Chapter 10.

2.1 What are the main UK-wide constitutional bodies or offices in the UK?

The institutions and offices that run through the **state** are linked to the three main powers at work within it, as follows.

- The *legislative* power is embodied in the legislature that enacts and reforms law. In a UK context, this is linked to the theory of parliamentary supremacy, as discussed in Chapters 7–9, as well as **parliamentary privilege**, which is examined in Chapter 7. **Devolution** and legislative power is discussed in Chapter 10.

- The *executive* power is embodied in the **government** and the civil service, along with related institutions such as the armed forces and police. The executive implements the law, and has day-to-day control of the state and its relations with other countries. In a UK context, this is linked to notions of limited and responsible government, discussed in Chapters 11–13. Devolution and executive power are discussed in Chapter 10.

- The *judicial* power is embodied in the **judiciary**, who may be called upon to review the executive's actions, omissions, and decisions to ensure that the law is respected at all levels of the state. This is the **rule of law** in operation, as discussed in Chapters 4 and 14.

However, the three powers do not map perfectly onto three distinct bodies, as discussed further in Chapter 5 on the **separation of powers**; instead, there are a number of bodies and offices that make use of the state's three powers. We shall consider these in turn. We shall begin by considering the complex issue of the **Crown** and the Crown's relationship with the **Queen**.

2.2

What is the Crown and is this the same as the Queen?

The Crown is quite a complicated concept. It relates to the actual object: the crown that is placed on the **monarch**'s head as part of the ritual of coronation. It is also the symbol used to describe the state. The Crown is also used to describe the physical representation of the state by the monarch. Figure 2.1 provides an illustration of the different definitions given to the term 'The Crown'.

2.2.1 Composition of the government

To make matters even more complicated, the Queen, as the representative of the Crown, is also at the head of all branches of the state, hence the terms 'Queen in **Parliament**', 'Her Majesty's Government' and 'Her Majesty's Ministers', the 'Royal Courts of Justice' and the 'Queen's courts', and 'Queen's Counsel'. It is clear that the term 'Crown' is, at times, used interchangeably with 'Queen', although this can lead to some confusion between the Queen as a person, the monarch as an office, and the notion of the state. Consequently, you may need to consider when reading, whether the Crown is the physical embodiment of the state (the Queen) or the state itself. This is explained further in the following extract.

● **S. Millns and N. Whitty,** *Feminist Perspectives on Public Law* (London: Cavendish Publishing, 1999), pp. 48–9

> **The Crown as nation, state and executive power**
>
> My second example concerns the range of uses of the concept of 'the Crown' in relation to state authority and executive power. Significantly, most constitutional law texts do not spend much time explaining why there is no concept of the state in British public law. In contrast to other democracies, the Crown is the legal entity which takes the place of the state, and to which allegiance is owed. As Jacob attempt to clarify in The Republican Crown:
>
> > In Britain [sic] the Crown is the sovereign. For other nations, those which have post-Enlightenment constitutions, that sovereignty is the State itself. But there, the State also manages the nation's business. Political theory which seeks to describe

Figure 2.1

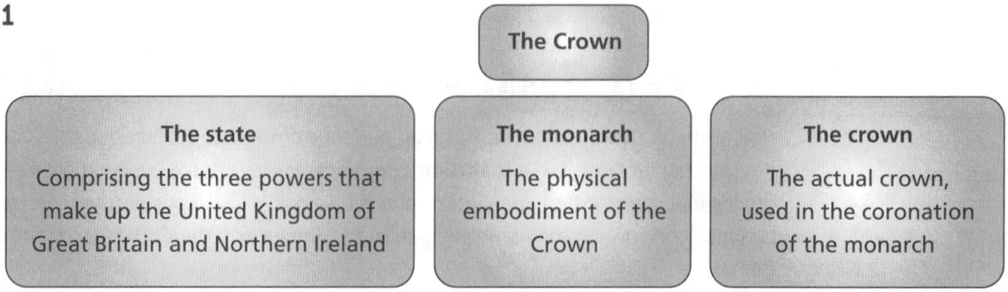

The Crown

The state	The monarch	The crown
Comprising the three powers that make up the United Kingdom of Great Britain and Northern Ireland	The physical embodiment of the Crown	The actual crown, used in the coronation of the monarch

Britain as a state forgets that the formal structure of our constitution predates the Enlightenment. Our sovereign Crown becomes equated with statehood.[1]

The crucial importance of theorising the late 20th century state, and revealing its gendered nature, is spelt out fully in Murphy's chapter in this volume.[2] My interest here is in highlighting the role of the Crown terminology in depoliticising and distorting the concept of the state. I will focus on two important aspects.

First, if, as suggested in constitutional texts, the Crown equals the state—and the state is taken to refer to the political organisation of people and territory—there is immediate confusion. As Nairn points out, in naming the state:

> ...none of the existing handles quite fit: we live in a State with a variety of titles having different functions and nuances—the UK (or 'Yookay', as Raymond Williams relabelled it), Great Britain (imperial roles), Britain (boring lounge suit), England (poetic but troublesome), the British Isles (too geographical), 'This Country' (all-purpose within the Family), or 'This Small Country of Ours' (defensive Shakespearean).[3]

The legally correct title, the one that constitutional lawyers are supposed to use in their lectures to avoid confusing the students, is the United Kingdom of Great Britain and Northern Ireland. And the key word here is 'Kingdom'; not a state or republic but a kingdom, or what some constitutional lawyers quaintly refer to as 'a realm'. So the Crown as state is equated with the United Kingdom, which is taken to represent the 'whole nation'.[4]

The 'whole nation' mentality has further implications for the construction of British identity. As will be discussed below in relation to subjecthood, I do not want to suggest that 'Britishness' cannot, and does not, have multiple and inclusive meaning; in fact, its potential as an umbrella identity is valued by many racial and ethnic groups within the UK. My point is that public law's blurring of the boundaries between 'the Crown' as state, nation and monarchy has consequences for the construction of national identities and limits the debate about the new constitutionalism in the UK.

1 J. Jacob, *The Republican Crown: Lawyers and the Making of the State in 20th Century Britain* (Aldershot: Dartmouth, 1996), p. 1.

2 See T. Murphy, 'Cosmopolitan feminism: towards a critical reappraisal of the late modern British state', in S. Millns and N. Whitty, *Feminist Perspectives on Public Law* (London: Cavendish Publishing, 1999), pp. 19–40.

3 T. Nairn, *The Enchanted Glass: Britain and its Monarchy* (London: Hutchinson Radius, 1988), p. 93.

[Further notes omitted]

4 See, e.g., E. Breitenbach, A. Brown, and F. Myers, 'Understanding women in Scotland' (1998) 58 Feminist Review 44.

Millns and Whitty explain very effectively the difficulties associated with the term 'Crown'. The British 'state' is a kingdom, rather than a republic or a civic state, and at its head we have a constitutional monarch, rather than a president. The state as an entity cannot be separated from the Queen as long as the state is a kingdom: a kingdom belongs to a queen (or a king) and the state is represented by the monarch, who pervades all aspects of it. The *Oxford English Dictionary* (OED) demonstrates that even the definition of 'the state' is a difficult and contested one. Definitions range from a country's government and constitution (with no reference to their type), to types of constitution and formats of constitutional rule, including republics and non-monarchial commonwealths, to states royal, which are headed by a monarch. Another definition in the OED suggests that any form of organised political system that has supreme governmental power may be considered to be a state, as may a territory or land that is ruled over by a sovereign. In short, the difficulties that we have with 'Crown' are no less evident in

thinking point

How do you refer to the UK? Do you refer to it as a state, a kingdom, a realm, a country, or the Crown?

cross reference

For more on the development of the monarchy, see Chapters 4 and 5, both of which chart the development of our present constitutional framework.

the 'state', and you will see the terms used interchangeably in some constitutional and public law texts.

So, what is the Queen's role in UK? The Queen's role is as head of state. She has the position similar to president in some countries, although she does not actively participate in day-to-day political decision-making in government as a president often would (depending on the constitutional arrangements in a country). In the domestic arena, she is involved in the legislative process through the mechanism of royal assent to legislative Acts and Orders in Council. She also presides over the state opening of Parliament each year. She is involved in the executive in so far as she may offer advice to the **Prime Minister** at their weekly meetings. She receives copies of all state papers. Honours are granted through the exercise of her **royal prerogative**, and the appointment to many offices of the state (Prime Minister, ministers, the senior judiciary, etc.) is also dependent on her exercising her royal prerogative. Having said that, the face value of the power that this gives her is lessened by the operation of **constitutional conventions**. One such convention is that she exercises her royal prerogative on advice—usually the advice of the Prime Minister. In truth, she has very few remaining personal prerogative powers. This is discussed further in Chapter 6 on the Crown and royal prerogative, as well as in Chapters 3 and 12, which examine constitutional conventions. In the external arena of foreign affairs, she receives heads of state and other foreign dignitaries in a diplomatic capacity, and she also represents the UK abroad. Treaties between the UK and other countries are signed under her royal prerogative power.

How does the monarch's power differ from the power enjoyed by an absolute monarch? After all, the UK does have a Parliament as well as a political government. Absolute monarchs rule the kingdom according to their own will or wishes. In other words, the monarch has total power, unfettered by an independently elected Parliament and government. A constitutional monarch is the ceremonial head of state, who may also exercise real constitutional powers. These should be exercised in a way that is politically neutral, and politics are conducted by elected and appointed representatives rather than the monarch. In a constitutional monarchy, the Queen rules according to the constitution and there are limits placed on her power by the constitution. In other words, her exercise of power is subordinate to the constitution—she cannot chose unilaterally to override the constitution as an absolute monarch may choose to do. She does not have greater constitutional power than the constitution.

Why would a monarch be in a strong position to advise a Prime Minister? The extract below sets out the rationale for retaining this power within the constitution. It suggests that the monarch, as a constant and stable force in the UK, may have a long range view that may be of benefit to a Prime Minister, even if the Prime Minister chooses not to act on the basis of the advice.

● **The Official Website of the British Monarchy, 'The role of the monarchy: history and background'** (undated), available online at http://www.royal.gov.uk/ MonarchUK/HowtheMonarchyworks/History and background.aspx

From the point of view of political power, according to Bagehot, the main influence of the Sovereign was during a political ministry, for the Sovereign had three rights: 'the right to be consulted, the right to encourage, the right to warn'. According to Bagehot, a Sovereign would, over the course of a long reign, accumulate far more knowledge and experience than any minister. Bagehot's views of how monarchy works proved influential, and by the reign of King George V, the principle of constitutional monarchy was firmly established in Britain.

As the extract indicates, the role of the monarch has changed over time. One can understand why an absolute monarchy may, in time, develop into a constitutional monarchy. But why has

Parliament in modern times not chosen to sweep away the monarchy and replace it with an appointed, or an indirectly or a directly elected, president, or even to dispense with the role altogether? Australia has considered replacing the Queen as head of state with an indirectly elected president (elected by Parliament rather than the people). The **referendum** did not succeed, but it is widely considered that were the referendum to give the Australian people a choice of a monarch as their head of state or a president whom they may elect themselves, it is likely that the referendum would be carried, paving the way for a directly elected president in Australia.

There has been little popular support for wholesale reform of the office of head of state in the UK. A directly elected presidential office is difficult to reconcile with a Westminster-style parliamentary executive tradition. Some countries do combine parliamentary and presidential systems—Germany, for example—but these tend to be based on indirectly elected presidents who do not compromise the power of a prime minister and his or her government drawn from the parliament. Countries that have adopted a directly elected presidential model have tended towards presidential executives—a government selected by the president rather than chosen from parliamentarians. This mitigates against the difficult power relationship that may exist between a president as head of the executive and a second form of executive drawn from the parliament. France is the exception in some respects. France has a directly elected president, as well as a parliament from which the Prime Minister and government ministers are drawn. The interesting twist is that the president selects the Prime Minister and then the Prime Minister selects his or her Cabinet from the elected parliamentarians. These parliamentarians then step away from their parliamentary (legislative) role and concentrate solely on their executive role. This would be difficult to achieve in the UK within our current constituency-based system of parliamentary representation, as discussed further below.

cross reference
See Chapter 6 for more on the royal prerogative.

This still does not answer the question of why Parliament has not given serious consideration to reform of the monarchy. The limitations placed on the royal prerogative by constitutional conventions and the gradual increase in power that the Prime Minister has come to enjoy (as de facto political head of the executive) may go some way towards explaining this. The office of Prime Minister is discussed in more detail below and the royal prerogative is discussed in Chapter 6.

thinking point
Would you rather elect a political head of state with real power, or elect a politically neutral ceremonial head of state, or would you rather keep the status quo? And do you believe that the Queen wields great power?

summary points

What is the Crown and is this the same as the Queen?

- *The Crown is the name given to the coronation crown that is used to crown the monarch, to the monarch herself, and to the state.*
- *In most instances, you will need to distinguish between whether the Crown refers to the monarch or to the state as a whole.*
- *The Queen is the head of state for the United Kingdom of Great Britain and Northern Ireland, and heads the three branches of the state: the legislative; the executive; and the judiciary.*
- *The Queen is a constitutional monarch and her power is subject to constitutional limits.*
- *The Queen's legal power, termed the 'royal prerogative', is exercised subject to constitutional conventions.*

What is Parliament and its role?

2.3.1 An overview of Parliament

Parliament is the body charged with the roles of law-making, the scrutiny of Bills, and holding the executive to account. The former two functions are common to all parliaments; the latter function is generally reserved for parliamentary executive systems in which the executive (or government) is drawn from the parliament and is thus not directly elected by the electorate. Parliament, made up of directly elected as well as appointed representatives, calls the indirectly elected executive to account. The UK Parliament is located in Westminster in London and is made up of a lower chamber, known as the House of Commons, the members of which are elected by local voters in general elections, and an upper chamber, known as the House of Lords. Parliament has retained this **bicameral** structure since the fourteenth century. The final piece of the jigsaw is the Queen, who is also part of Parliament as its head. The two chambers, when taken together and coupled with the legislative role of the monarch (through royal assent), are said to constitute the Queen in Parliament—or Parliament, for short.

2.3.2 Membership of Parliament

NOTE This House of Lords is not the same as the appellate court, which has recently been renamed the Supreme Court.

Members of the House of Commons are directly elected. Elections must, by law, be held at least once every five years, although the timing of the election has not historically been fixed by statute. The Prime Minister has had the **discretion** within that period to ask the Queen to dissolve Parliament so that a general election may be held at the most favourable time for his or her party. The general election in 2010 led to a hung Parliament. This meant that no one political party had a majority of seats (half of the total seats plus one additional seat) in the House of Commons. One of the reforms that the resulting Conservative–Liberal Democrat **coalition government** introduced was the Fixed-term Parliaments Bill to remove this discretion and to fix the election date at five-yearly intervals, so as to provide stability to the coalition and make it more likely to succeed given the fact that the Prime Minister alone could not trigger an early election. The Fixed-term Parliaments Act 2011 provides that elections may be called mid-cycle only if the government loses a vote of confidence and no alternative government can be formed, or if at least two-thirds of members of Parliament (MPs) approve an early general election. The Bill proved controversial given the fact that the proposal was introduced by the coalition and given the fact that elections have usually been called at around the four-year point rather than at five years. The fixed-term system will be subject to review in 2020, which was a compromise accepted in the light of proposed amendments to include a **sunset clause** in the Bill.

sunset clause
A clause that has the effect of bringing the terms of an Act to an end at a specified date, unless Parliament chooses to renew the terms of the Act.

NOTE You will find an explanation of hung parliaments online at http://www.youtube.com/watch?v=wJA02BOggWs

NOTE The next general election will take place on the 7 May 2015, but the Prime Minister may move the date by up to two months by Order in Council.

The second and upper, although less powerful, chamber is made up of peers. The total membership of the House is currently 827 (646 men and 181 women), although only 788 members are eligible to sit in the House (for example, thirteen are not permitted to do so because they hold senior judicial posts and, as a result of the Constitutional Reform Act 2005, they may no longer be members of the House). The vast majority of members of the Lords have been appointed to **life peerages** in recognition of their distinction in other areas of life (professional or other work, philanthropic activities, political service, other state service, or other achievement or expertise). Since the Life Peerages Act in 1958, life peers have been entitled to sit in the House of Lords and to remain members for their lifetimes. This was also the point at which women were allowed to take up membership of the House of Lords as life peers. The House of Lords also contains ninety-two **hereditary peers**, who hold a peerage by virtue of inheritance. They remain members of the House for their lifetimes. These hereditary peers have been elected by the House (seventy-five by all hereditary peers, to represent the then party-political balance; fifteen were elected by the whole House; and two office holders remained in post) to represent their views in the House of Lords, during this period of constitutional reform. Until the House of Lords Act 1999 came into force, all hereditary peers were entitled to sit in the House of Lords and they far outnumbered the life peer members. This was viewed as problematic by many on the left and centre of politics, because there were far more Conservative hereditary peers than there were Labour, Liberal, or cross-bench (independent) ones. This meant the House of Lords had an inbuilt Conservative majority that could make it difficult for Labour and Liberal governments to pass their legislation. The Labour Party came to power in 1997 with an electoral mandate to reform the membership of the House of Lords, although its term in office ended at the halfway stage in this process. The coalition government has signalled its intention to continue with House of Lords' reform. Its proposal is for a 300-member House, 80 per cent of whom will be elected through a system of proportional representation (for single fifteen-year terms) and 20 per cent of whom will be appointed. However, for the time being, there remain ninety-two hereditary peers, along with the far larger life peer element of the House. The House of Lords also contains twenty-six bishops and archbishops of the Church of England who do not hold peerages, but who sit in the House until they retire from their Church positions. This is a historic oddity linked to the established status of the Church of England within the British constitution. The coalition proposals do not appear to remove this element from the Lords.

2.3.3 Representatives and their role in Parliament

cross reference
House of Lords reform is discussed in more detail below.

NOTE Life peers do not pass on their peerages to their heirs when they die, although hereditary peers do—hence the terms 'life' and 'hereditary' peers.

The House of Commons is the representative assembly for the UK and, as such, it has been the subject of some criticism. The three main criticisms levelled are that:

- the current electoral system does not represent all parties equally in Parliament;
- the House of Lords is unrepresentative and unelected, and yet forms an important part of Parliament; and
- the composition of MPs is unfairly biased against women and against ethnic minorities.

Your views on this will depend, to a certain extent, on how you view the role of a representative assembly and the type of representation that you expect.

There are a number of underlying assumptions about the role that MPs fulfil, some of which are accepted and others of which are contested. First, it is argued that MPs fulfil a representative role—that they stand in the shoes of the electorate when debating and enacting legislation, and when calling the government to account for its actions.

The second assumption is that the electoral process is fair and inclusive, and gives rise to a result that is considered to be appropriate given the votes polled. This is considered in the elections section towards the end of this chapter. Even within systems that are considered to be relatively

25

free from corruption, there are different views about the extent to which particular electoral processes are considered to be representative and fair.

The third principle underpinning the role of MPs is that they have the power to reform the law and to enact new law. This is certainly the case in the UK, although it should be noted that devolution has had an impact on the role of Westminster MPs in this regard, the corollary of which is that members of the Scottish Parliament and Assembly members for Wales and Northern Ireland now have legislative powers when, once, all of the power was vested in an English-dominated Westminster Parliament.

Two other assumptions remain: that MPs are free from outside interference in the performance of their duties, and that MPs do not perform their parliamentary functions in a way that is corrupt or dishonest. These two are linked, although the first suggests that an MP may be the subject of external pressure or undue influence, and the second that the MP has chosen to give in to his or her own dishonesty. When combined, these two assumptions require parliamentary protection: first, to ensure that an MP is able to speak freely during proceedings in Parliament without fear of court action that may cause him or her to act other than according to his or her representative status (party-political influence and constituency influence are both considered to be appropriate rather than inappropriate, because they go to the heart of the MP's role); and second, it amounts to a protection of Parliament's integrity through the operation of parliamentary privilege, its investigatory and disciplinary mechanisms, as well as the operation of the criminal law in some instances. These have come under pressure in recent years given the MPs' expenses scandal and the criminal conviction of some former MPs in relation to expense claims that they submitted.

Members of the Commons (MPs)

MPs hold their offices as our representatives, that much is clear. But there are different types of representative: a representative who acts on behalf of the people whom he or she represents by putting forward their views, and a representative who has been elected to put forward his or her own views because he or she is trusted by the electorate to act wisely and fairly. There is no agreement about which of these two models (and shades in between) our MPs should follow. The following extract illustrates this point neatly.

● **C. J. Carman, 'Public preferences for parliamentary representation in the UK: an overlooked link?'** (2006) 54 Political Studies 105, 107 and 116

... in the representation literature, representation style refers to the extent that a legislator acts on public demands alone (often referred to as a delegate, or mandate model) or bases their legislative decisions on their perception of what is best for their constituents (referred to as a trustee or independence model). Even a casual perusal of the representation literature finds critiques and criticisms of this approach...

So what do we know? First and foremost, the system of Westminster representation in the UK is, at best, a 'complicated' triad between MPs, political parties and constituents. In terms of policy, the strongest link tends to tie together political parties and MPs (as members of the parties). Yet, as Norton and Wood[1] point out, constituents think of their MP as a vehicle to advance their (that is, constituent) policy goals. This last point would seem to indicate that constituents have expectations about the sort of representational relationship they should have with their MPs. On the other hand, Norton and Wood also state that constituents know that MPs are more likely to vote with their party, even at the risk of upsetting their constituents. This leaves us with an empirical puzzle: how do individuals in the UK envision their relationship with their MP?

This suggests that there is no real consensus on how MPs should represent their constituents. It is an oversimplification to suggest that an MP is there to represent what the majority (or even minority) of his or her constituents believe. It is also an oversimplification to say that constituents hand over their decision-making power to the MP and ask the MP to use his or her own judgement to determine the most appropriate way in which to vote or to participate in debates in Parliament. However, the 'mandate' approach to representation, whereby an MP is required to do the bidding of his or her constituents even if this is contrary to his or her own judgement, has been strongly criticised. Burke explains why.

● **E. Burke, Rt Hon, 'Speech to the Electors of Bristol, 3 November 1774', in *The Works of the Right Honourable Edmund Burke, Vol. 1*** (London: Henry G. Bohn, 1854), pp. 446–7

…[I]t ought to be the happiness and glory of a representative to live in the strictest union, the closest correspondence, and the most unreserved communication with his constituents. Their wishes ought to have great weight with him; their opinion, high respect; their business, unremitted attention. It is his duty to sacrifice his repose, his pleasures, his satisfactions, to theirs; and above all, ever, and in all cases, to prefer their interest to his own. But his unbiased opinion, his mature judgment, his enlightened conscience, he ought not to sacrifice to you, to any man, or to any set of men living. These he does not derive from your pleasure; no, nor from the law and the constitution. They are a trust from Providence, for the abuse of which he is deeply answerable. Your representative owes you, not his industry only, but his judgment; and he betrays, instead of serving you, if he sacrifices it to your opinion.

…If government were a matter of will upon any side, yours, without question, ought to be superior. But government and legislation are matters of reason and judgment, and not of inclination; and what sort of reason is that, in which the determination precedes the discussion; in which one set of men deliberate, and another decide; and where those who form the conclusion are perhaps three hundred miles distant from those who hear the arguments?

To deliver an opinion, is the right of all men; that of constituents is a weighty and respectable opinion, which a representative ought always to rejoice to hear; and which he ought always most seriously to consider. But authoritative instructions; mandates issued, which the member is bound blindly and implicitly to obey, to vote, and to argue for, though contrary to the clearest conviction of his judgment and conscience, these are things utterly unknown to the laws of this land, and which arise from a fundamental mistake of the whole order and tenor of our constitution.

Different people have different views on the relationship between constituents, MPs, and political parties, and your view on this will colour your understanding of MPs and also future reform of the Lords. However, the prevailing view is that MPs are elected to use their judgement in reaching decisions and acting in their role as our representatives in the Commons.

Member of the Lords (peers)

The situation is further complicated when we introduce the House of Lords, because members of the Lords are either appointed, through the system of life peerages, or have their positions in the House of Lords as a result of being selected by the peers to represent hereditary peers who formerly sat in the House. They have not been directly elected by **universal suffrage**, they cannot be removed by the electorate, and they do not in any meaningful way represent territorial areas. So are they supposed to be performing a representative function? This is a moot point, because the upper chamber is a reviewing and revising chamber rather than an initiating one. This means that the House of Lords has a distinct role from the Commons; it is not a second lower chamber. The House of Lords is undergoing a long-term process of reform, which is altering its composition and which also raises questions about its function and the role of its members. Some of these issues are illustrated in the next extract, which addresses House of Lords' reform and the consequences of different models of reform.

- ● **V. Bogdanor, 'Reform of the House of Lords: a sceptical view'** (1999) 70(4) Political Quarterly 375, 375

There are, broadly, three methods of constructing a second chamber: through nomination, through election (whether direct or indirect) and through some combination of the two methods, i.e. a mixed chamber. The White paper *Modernising Parliament: Reforming the House of Lords* proposes a 'more democratic and more representative' second chamber.[1] This would seem to require the introduction of an elected element into the House of Lords. Indeed, the removal of the right of the hereditary peers to sit and vote in the Lords has been justified, not only because of the large Conservative majority among the hereditary peers, but also because hereditary peers, are, by definition, unrepresentative.

But what electoral method should be used to secure a 'more democratic and more representative' second chamber? The problem is one of finding a valid principle of representation upon which the second chamber might be based, and an alternative principle to that used for electing the House of Commons. The principle of representation for the second chamber, moreover, must be of a lesser validity to that upon which the House of Commons is based, given that the royal commission is required, by its terms of reference, to have regard 'to the need to maintain the position of the House of Commons as the pre-eminent chamber of Parliament'.

Were the principle of representation to be *more* valid than that used for the Commons, then in any clash between the two chambers it will be argued that the second chamber, rather than the Commons, should prevail. That might be the case, for example, were the Commons to continue to be elected by the first past the post system, while the second chamber were elected by some form of proportional representation: for many would regard proportional representation as the more legitimate method of election and thus the second chamber, and not the Commons, as best representing the will of the people.

The second chamber, moreover, being elected presumably at a different time from the House of Commons, might come to be regarded as representing a more recent manifestation of the will of the people, and for this reason more legitimate that the Commons. Thus a second chamber elected, for example, in 1994, by proportional representation, would almost certainly have contained a Labour/Liberal Democrat majority. The Commons, it would then be said, represented the will of the people as it had been in 1992, while the second chamber represented that will as expressed two years later, in 1994, and therefore deserved to be listened to with more respect that the Commons. Again, then, in any clash with the Commons it would be suggested that the wishes of the Lords should prevail.

...

[380] It must, of course, be recognised that a second chamber composed entirely of nominated members, of the life peers, which will be the situation once all the hereditary peers lose their right to sit and vote in the House of Lords, is deeply offensive to many people. The upper house would then become the largest quango in the land. Such a house would hardly be a 'more democratic and more representative' one. For life peers, being primarily men and women who have achieved distinction in some sphere of life, are, almost by definition, unrepresentative; and also undemocratic, in that they have not been elected.

1 *Modernising Parliament: Reforming the House of Lords* (Cm 4183, London: HMSO, 1999).

Bogdanor considers a number of possible modes of direct and indirect election to the House of Lords, ranging from direct election of regional (rather than constituency) representatives—as in the Senate in Australia and the United States—or a quasi-federal system of directly or indirectly elected representatives from the four countries that make up the United Kingdom, as in Germany. However, all have difficulties associated with them. Some challenge the supremacy of the Commons; others challenge the electoral mechanism in operation in the UK; others highlight the confusion over the function of the House of Lords. These difficulties have been widely debated by both chambers of the House, and are set out in the 2007 White Paper on *The House of Lords: Reform* (see the end-of-chapter 'Further reading').

Bogdanor explains that there is no simple solution to House of Lords' reform.

● **V. Bogdanor, 'Reform of the House of Lords: a sceptical view'** [1999] 70(4) Political Quarterly 375, 380–1

> There is, then, no ideal solution to the problem of reforming the second chamber, once one departs from the notion of a prescriptive House of Lords. Perhaps the solution with the fewest disadvantages, and involving the least upheaval, would be for the reformed second chamber to combine the nominated element with the ninety-two hereditary peers, selected as provided for by the Weatherill amendment. These hereditary peers would leaven the element of patronage in the new second chamber.
>
> It cannot be pretended that this is in any sense a wholly satisfactory solution. First, it constitutes no advance towards making the second chamber 'more democratic and more representative'. Second, it would not fulfil Labour's manifesto commitment to remove the hereditary element entirely from the House of Lords. Third, there is the problem of how each of the selected ninety-two hereditary peers would be replaced after death. Fourth, there is the fact that such a house would be a mixed chamber, so giving rise to the various problems outlined above.
>
> A solution of this kind, moreover, would have to be accompanied by severe restrictions on the power of patronage so as to prevent the swamping of the house by the Prime Minister …
>
> Yet there is at least one compensating advantage in the solution suggested here. It is that the second chamber so constituted cannot undermine the legitimacy of the government of the day. It would not be able, as an elected chamber might do, to threaten legislative deadlock, nor would it have the potential of paralysing the everyday work of government. It could moreover, continue to play a 'modest' role in the revision of legislation, especially legislation involving a constitutional or human rights element; and it could continue with the important work of scrutinizing European legislation and delegated legislation, as well as the ad hoc select committee activity which the House of Lords does so well.

Updates on House of Lords' reform are available on the Online Resource Centre.

In March 2007, in response to the government's White Paper, Parliament voted on a number of proposals for composition of the House of Lords that ranged from a fully elected upper chamber to a fully appointed one. The vote was a **free vote** and members could vote on multiple proposals. The Commons voted in favour of two options: an 80 per cent elected upper chamber and a 100 per cent elected upper chamber. By contrast, the House of Lords voted in favour of an entirely appointed chamber. With this level of deadlock, the second phase of House of Lords' reform did not proceed under the Labour government. The coalition government has announced its plans for a 300-strong 80 per cent elected House of Lords. We shall see whether these proposals suffer the same fate as did those of the previous Labour governments.

What is clear from the texts above is that there is no one clear definition of what our representatives are required to do: are they required to represent us by standing in our shoes and giving our views, or are they there as our nominated representatives to use their own

thinking point

Do our representatives in the Commons truly represent us and do we share in the making of political decisions? If so, how?

judgement to make important policy decisions? Further, is it important that Parliament is composed of members who, when considered together, reflect the range of viewpoints on religion, culture, lifestyle, etc., that may be found within the population? Or is the composition of Parliament supposed to be in keeping with the population's demographic characteristics: if there are 52 per cent women in the population, should 52 per cent of our representatives be women instead of the current 144:506 female-to-male MP ratio, and likewise in relation to ethnicity, religion, age, and background? Should our representatives have the same knowledge base as us, or do we need a chamber or a portion of a chamber that includes people with expertise in the medical and veterinary professions, law, construction, the service industries, people with caring responsibilities, religious leaders? Your answers to these questions will fundamentally affect your views on whether both Houses should be elected, or whether some representatives should be nominated, and how we should elect people if elections are to be used. Differing election mechanisms are discussed later in the chapter. For now, however, it is important that you consider your views on representatives and their role in Parliament.

2.3.4 Functions of Parliament

The House of Common's Select Committee on Procedure (First Report, Session 1977–78, HC 588–1, London: HMSO, 1987), p. viii, reported that the major tasks of the Commons were fourfold: enacting law, scrutinising the executive, controlling expenditure, and redressing constituents' grievances—the last two arguably being part of the second task of scrutinising the executive. Parliament is empowered to consider, review, and enact primary and secondary legislation. This provides the executive with the power that it needs to run the country, as well as to effect change for others such as interest groups and sections of society, all of whom are sometimes referred to as **stakeholders**. Parliament needs to strike a balance between providing power and limiting power by putting in place checks and balances to restrain those who attempt consciously or unconsciously to extend their power beyond Parliament's intention. Parliament may also delegate some of its legislative power to others, to the devolved parliaments and assemblies of Scotland, Wales, and Northern Ireland, to local authorities, to government ministers, and at a lower level to professional and other bodies.

cross reference

See Chapter 20 for more on concerns about the Prevention of Terrorism Act 2005.

cross reference

There is a further discussion on the Parliament Acts in Chapter 7.

The House of Lords does not perform the same legislative function as the House of Commons. But why have two chambers that perform different functions? Some jurisdictions operate a **unicameral** system; others, a bicameral system with two chambers that perform similar functions, but with representatives who represent different constituencies or different constituency interests. The UK system is based on the two chambers performing different functions. The House of Lords acts as a check on the power of the executive, which may largely dominate the Commons if the party in power has a large majority in the lower chamber. It is charged with the responsibility of counterbalancing political-party dominance by, at times, requiring the Commons to think again, such as when concerns were raised about proposed anti-terrorism legislation that introduced **control orders** considered by some to infringe human rights unduly (the Prevention of Terrorism Act 2005). But, ultimately, the House of Lords is not empowered to block legislative proposals that are initiated by the government and introduced first in the Commons, particularly if the proposals were part of the government's election commitment. The House of Lords may delay legislation, but, under the operation of the Parliament Acts of 1911 and 1949, it cannot prevent legislation from being passed if it is the will of the House of Commons that it be enacted.

The second main function of Parliament is to scrutinise the executive.

● **John Stuart Mill,** *Representative Government* (1861), available online at http://ebooks. adelaide.edu.au/m/mill/john_stuart/m645r/, ch. 5

> ...the proper office of a representative assembly is to watch and control the government; to throw the light of publicity on its acts; to compel a full exposition and justification of all of them which anyone considers questionable; to censure them if found condemnable, and if the men who compose the government abuse their trust, or fulfil it in a manner which conflicts with the deliberate sense of the nature, to expel them from office...

This indicates that Parliament has a substantial role to play in overseeing the actions undertaken, and the decisions made, by the executive. To what extent is Parliament to act as a control on government and to what extent is Parliament supposed to act as a support to it? The next extract sets out two different conceptions of the Parliament–executive relationship.

● **M. Flinders, 'Shifting the balance? Parliament, the executive and the British constitution'** (2000) 50 Political Studies 23, 23–6

> Fundamentally, parliament has two inherently contradictory roles—first, to sustain the executive, which it would appear to do well, and second, to hold the executive to account between elections, which it does rather less well. Lord Nolan (1996) noted, 'The role of sustaining the government does not sit well with the task of challenging it and holding it to task'.[1] ...
>
> This tension stems from a critical period in British political history between the mid and late nineteenth century. Bagehot famously referred to the convention of ministerial responsibility as the 'buckle' of the British constitution—the lynch-pin in the Whitehall/Westminster model. The convention of ministerial responsibly antedates the modern party system and was designed in a period when the role of government was limited and it was reasonable to assume that a competent minister would have personal control over a small department. The mid-Victorian state was modest in both size and ambition. There was no pretence that the government could do much on its own to remedy or compensate for social ills...
>
> Crucially, this period convinced parliament that ministerial responsibility was a workable convention on which to base the relationship between parliament and the executive. Parliament severely underestimated the subsequent effect that the evolving state and mass parties would have on the convention and so it became the political rationale and procedural logic around which an expanding system of government was structured...
>
> The effect of the growth of parties and the state was seriously miscalculated. By the time the problems associated with the convention were apparent the dominant position of the executive had been stabilised.[2] The convention of ministerial responsibility provided the critical link in the Westminster/Whitehall model, and yet the executive's majority within the House insulated ministers from effective scrutiny. Moreover, the position of the executive allowed it to dictate the rules, resources and information flows through which it would be held to account. It is clear that throughout the twentieth century the balance of power has shifted to the executive.
>
> However, debates about the relationship between parliament and the executive and the need for reform depends on the view taken on what the British constitution should ensure and deliver—representative or responsible government. This was a distinction made by Birch[3] in respect to his 'liberal' and 'Whitehall' views of the constitution. Beattie[4] offers a more precise framework with his historical analysis of two distinct views of the role of the convention of ministerial responsibility. Beattie distinguishes two views—a more representative 'Whig' view which stressed the need for political control to be paramount and for the government to be held responsible for state actions; and the 'Peelite' view, which defines ministerial responsibility as a way of limiting democratic control to ensure strong, coherent and stable

government...In practice, the two views have combined to elevate the role of ministers and justify the unlimited notion of parliamentary sovereignty.

[1] Lord Nolan, 'Parliament' (First Radcliffe Lecture, Warwick University, 7 November 1996).

[2] P. Fraser, 'The growth of ministerial control in the nineteenth century House of Commons' (1960) 75 English Historical Review 444.

[3] A. Birch, *Representative and Responsible Government* (London: Unwin, 1964), pp. 65–81.

[4] A. Beattie, 'Ministerial responsibility and the theory of the British state', in R. Rhodes and P. Dunleavy (eds) *Prime Minister, Cabinet and Core Executive* (Basingstoke: Macmillan, 1995), pp. 158–81.

To what extent is Parliament achieving the Peelite or the Whig view of the function of governmental scrutiny set out by Flinders? A Whig commentator would probably consider that Parliament's powers have been eroded over the years as the prime ministerial role has strengthened and governments have been returned with large majorities, thus rendering Parliament's powers useless in the face of a House of Commons dominated by the party in power that is more likely to support, rather than to oppose, the executive. This commentator may also point to the influence that big business and the media have on the executive and also on individual MPs, along with concerns about the power of the European Union (EU) and other supranational organisations. All of these would appear to weaken Parliament's control over the government.

The Peelite commentator may be more sanguine. Modern-day parliaments have presided over a period of stable and strong governmental action. Peelites encourage support for, rather than control of, government action, within the context of a system that permits the electorate to change its government if it ceases to meet the electorate's expectations. Consequently, a Peelite may be more relaxed about the Parliament–executive relationship, and consider that a strong government is better able to achieve its electoral promises and to act decisively.

2.3.5 Scrutiny of Parliament

We have discussed the fact that Parliament acts as a point of scrutiny over the government, but whom or what scrutinises Parliament? Parliament sets its own rules and privileges, so that it can function effectively. This includes rules and legislation to regulate party-political funding, for example the Political Parties, Elections and Referendums Act 2000, which established the Electoral Commission to oversee this area among others. However, much of the regulation and oversight of Parliament is undertaken by Parliament itself. This is termed 'parliamentary privilege' and it is part of the law and the custom of Parliament. The courts do not oversee or adjudicate matters relating to the internal operation of privilege, but will consider the nature and extent of privilege where it affects those outside Parliament. The case of *Edinburgh & Dalkeith Railway v Wauchope* (1842) 8 Cl & Fin 710 is evidence for this point and is considered in more detail in Chapter 7. Parliament is therefore not accountable to the courts, but remains accountable to the electorate at least in respect of the Commons.

There are a number of key privileges. The most striking is the freedom of speech during the debates and proceedings in parliament, which stems from article 9 of the Bill of Rights 1689. In real terms, this provides immunity from the law of defamation for words spoken in parliamentary proceedings, although it may also, in some circumstances, limit an MP's ability to sue in defamation as well. In turn, this means that members should use this freedom to perform their functions effectively, and to work for the good of their constituents and the country, rather than to further their own agendas or in return for personal advancement. This is examined in more detail in Chapter 13, when we consider the Parliamentary Commissioner for Administration (PCA) and her role. As with all privileges and immunities, there are responsibilities associated with them. Parliamentary privilege is designed so that the House can function effectively. It creates immunities and privileges that extend to members so that they can fulfil their responsibilities in the House. As noted in a memorandum from Sir Barnett Cocks (Session 1966–67, HC 34): 'The sole justification for the present privileges of the House of Commons is that they are essential for the conduct of its business and maintenance of its authority.' Parliament remains the guardian of parliamentary privilege, and exercises investigatory and disciplinary powers over members, staff, and visitors to Parliament with the purpose of safeguarding Parliament's ability to represent the people, to enact legislation, and to scrutinise the government.

NOTE

You will need to be aware in broad terms of the nature and role of parliamentary privilege, because it explains, in part, the nature of parliamentary supremacy and the relationship between the courts and Parliament. Key issues concern Parliament's self-governing status (see Chapter 7), the role of Parliament in regulating its members, including the financial interests of MPs and the Lords and the Register of Members' Interests, issues associated with party funding, and the role of the PCA (see Chapter 13). You will find it useful to keep up with current affairs in this regard, as this will help you to develop your knowledge and provide you with some current examples that illustrate the areas under discussion.

It may help to read a broadsheet newspaper regularly, to listen to Radio 4's *Today in Parliament*, and/or to watch Prime Minister's Questions (PMQs) on *BBC Parliament* on Wednesdays.

summary points

What is Parliament and its role?

- *Parliament is made up of the House of Commons and the House of Lords, and is headed by the Queen.*
- *Parliament has two main functions: to reform and to enact legislation; and to scrutinise the government and the the wider executive.*
- *Members of Parliament (MPs) represent their constituents in the House of Commons, the lower chamber, and are directly elected by the electorate.*
- *A combination of life and hereditary peers sit in the House of Lords, the upper chamber, and act as a point of scrutiny and review. Life peers are appointed to positions for life; the remaining hereditary peer members also hold their positions for life.*
- *The House of Lords is undergoing a process of reform and its composition may change to incorporate a proportion of directly or indirectly elected representatives.*
- *Parliament is self-regulating, through the medium of parliamentary privilege. This means that the Parliament has its own internal rules and disciplinary procedures, and that the courts do not enquire into the workings of Parliament—the body, rather than the individuals who work in it.*

2.4 What is the executive and how does this differ from the government?

2.4.1 An overview of the executive

The executive is an umbrella term that is used to describe two different entities: the political government, sometimes referred to as the 'political executive'; and the wider machinery of government. The political executive is relatively easy to sum up, because it contains the Prime Minister and government ministers. This is considered in the remainder of this section. The wider machinery of government is the collection of people who, together, keep the country running. These include the civil service, the police, the armed forces, members of executive agencies such as the Prison Service, the welfare benefits system, and the Passport Agency, to name but a few. The executive, in its broad definition, includes all public servants who are involved in running the country; the political executive, by contrast, is what we usually think about when someone mentions the word 'government'. However, 'the executive', as it is often discussed in the media, is often the political executive—that is, the government, along with the civil servants who work with the government to run the country. The devolved administrations have their own executives too, as discussed in Chapter 10.

2.4.2 The civil service

It may be useful to consider the politically neutral part of the executive to begin with, because the UK system is somewhat different from many others. Civil servants are required to act in a way that is politically neutral. That is not to say that they do not have political views, but instead that they must work for whichever political administration is in power at the time. It is often referred to as the 'Westminster model', or the 'permanent civil service model', as laid down in the Northcote–Trevelyan Report.

. . . .

● **Sir Stafford Northcote and Sir Charles Trevelyan,** *Report on the Organisation of the Permanent Civil Service* (London: House of Commons, 1854) (The Northcote–Trevelyan Report), p. 2

> It cannot be necessary to enter into any lengthened argument for the purpose of showing the high importance of the Permanent Civil Service of the country in the present day. The great and increasing accumulation of public business, and the consequent pressure upon the Government, need only to be alluded to; and the inconveniences which are inseparable from the frequent changes which take place in the responsible administration are matters of sufficient notoriety. It may safely be asserted that as matters now stand, the Government of the country could not be carried out without the aid of an efficient body or permanent officers, occupying a position duly subordinate to that of the Ministers who are directly responsible to the Crown and to Parliament, yet possessing sufficient independence, character, ability, and experience to be able to advise, assist, and, to some extent, influence those who are from time to time set over them.

This contrasts with the civil service in some other countries, for example the US, where the civil service is appointed to serve a particular administration (by the President) and leaves office when the President leaves office. A politically neutral and enduring civil service provides some stability even at the point of a change in government, because these public servants stay even as the ministers are replaced. Equally, there are concerns that an enduring service may stifle change and institutionalise certain characteristics of government that are difficult for the political executive to overturn. Further, the distinction between a politically neutral civil service and a civil service that overtly serves a political regime is not as clear-cut as it once was, at least in the UK context. There has been an increase in the appointment of political advisers by government, from the Thatcher government to the present, who are political appointees who work at a very senior level within the civil service—Alistair Campbell's appointment as Prime Minister Tony Blair's press spokesperson was one of the more notable. This has led to the charge that the civil service is becoming politicised, within a context in which it is expected to be apolitical. This will be examined in more depth in Chapter 11.

The Constitutional Reform and Governance Act 2010 provides a statutory basis for the management of the civil service. It establishes a Civil Service Commission, provides the power to manage the civil service, provides a civil service code of conduct, and provides for the appointment to the civil service. The reforms aim to counter criticism that the civil service has become less independent and more at the political service of the government. It is too early to say, at this stage, whether the reforms will achieve their aims.

NOTE

You will find the Constitutional Reform and Governance Act 2010 online at http://www.legislation.gov.uk/ukpga/2010/25/contents

You will find information about the changes brought in by the 2010 Act online at http://webarchive.nationalarchives.gov.uk/+/http://www.justice.gov.uk/publications/constitutional-reform.htm

You will find commentary on the changes from the Civil Service Commissioners online at http://www.civilservicecommissioners.org/legislation/

2.4.3 The composition of the government

NOTE You may wish to refresh your memory of the breakdown of the general election results online at http://news.bbc.co.uk/1/hi/uk_politics/election_2010/default.stm

The May 2010 general election resulted in a hung Parliament at Westminster. This meant that no political party had won at least half of the seats in the House of Commons and so no single party could form a majority government. As a result, two parties joined together to form a coalition government—their combined number of seats (when one adds up the seats won by the Conservative Party and those won by Liberal Democrats) making up more than half of the total number of seats in the House of Commons, meaning that they were able to form a government that would be likely to be able to pass legislation through the Commons and to command the confidence of the majority of MPs.

David Cameron, as leader of the party with the most seats in the Commons (the Conservative Party), became the Prime Minister and he invited Nick Clegg, leader of the Liberal Democrats, to join him as Deputy Prime Minister within a coalition government. Government ministers were drawn from the Conservative and Liberal Democrat parties, with the former being the party with the most seats. One of the challenges for a coalition government is that so much of the British political system (and the constitutional system that underpins it) is set up for one-party government. The coalition had to work out a way of bringing together the two parties' policies so as to permit them to be able to work together in government. This was set out in the Coalition Agreement for Stability and Reform (London: HMSO, May 2010).

NOTE For a list of positions and party affiliation, see online at http://www.parliament.uk/mps-lords-and-offices/government-and-opposition1/her-majestys-government/

NOTE

You may wish to look at the Coalition Agreement, and at *The Coalition: Our Programme for Government* (London: HMSO, May 2010), both of which are available online at http://www.cabinetoffice.gov.uk/news/coalition-documents

The political executive is made up of the Prime Minister (who is the political head of the government) and his or her team of senior ministers who make up the Cabinet, junior ministers or ministers of state, and parliamentary private secretaries. The Cabinet is made up of between twenty and twenty-five senior ministers who have been chosen by the Prime Minister, who, by constitutional convention, exercises the decision-making power that is legally vested in the Queen. It is the Queen who has the legal power to select her ministers and, indeed, her Prime

What is the executive and how does this differ from the government?

35

Minister. By the terms of another constitutional convention, the majority of senior ministers are drawn from the Commons rather than the Lords (all must be drawn from one or other of the two chambers). This convention is logical, because only the Commons contains the UK's elected representatives, no member of the Lords is permitted in the Commons chamber, and consequently if a senior minister were to be a member of the Lords, then he or she could not be directly questioned and held to account by MPs; instead, this would be left to the upper, unelected chamber in the absence of an effective method of scrutiny via the Commons. The government also contains junior ministers (the level below Cabinet ministers) and parliamentary private secretaries (the lowest level of political office within the government), all selected by and answerable to the Prime Minister. Figure 2.2 provides an illustration of the composition of the political executive.

All members of the government, in the true political sense of the word, are drawn from the Commons and the Lords, and all retain their parliamentary office as well as acquire a governmental role. In other words, members of the government have two jobs: a parliamentary one and a governmental one. That is not to say that a Prime Minister cannot select someone who is neither a member of the Commons nor of the Lords. However, that person would, by convention, be ennobled, so that he or she would become a member of the House of Lords. A recent example of this was the appointment of Peter Mandelson as the Secretary of State for Business, Enterprise and Regulatory Reform (BERR). He was not an MP at the time, nor was he a member of the House of Lords, and so he was granted a life peerage and became Baron Mandelson of Foy (shortened to Lord Mandelson) so as to take up his place in the Labour government. Members of the government who are MPs must answer to their constituents and their political parties in relation to their jobs as parliamentarians. They must account to the Prime Minister, other members of the government (through the constitutional convention of collective responsibility), and to Parliament (through individual ministerial responsibility) for their governmental one. This multilayered approach to accountability is a difficult one to manage and, as discussed above in relation to MPs and their role, is fraught with conceptual difficulties: how can a minister serve so many masters (or mistresses)?

NOTE

For more information on this, see B. Yong and R. Hazell, *Putting the Goats Amongst the Wolves: Appointing Ministers from Outside Parliament* (London: The Constitution Unit University College London, 2011), available online at http://www.ucl.ac.uk/constitution-unit/publications/tabs/unit-publications/151-cover.pdf

Figure 2.2

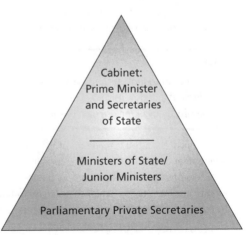

Cabinet:
Prime Minister
and Secretaries
of State

Ministers of State/
Junior Ministers

Parliamentary Private Secretaries

In relation to her government role, the minister is ultimately responsible to the Prime Minister and holds the role only as long as the Prime Minister has confidence in him or her. The Prime Minister may remove the minister from office by reshuffling him or her out of the post, asking the minister to resign, or by simply sacking the minister at any time. Government positions are not covered by employment protection and the Prime Minister does not need to justify the decision in legal terms. However, it should also be said that prime ministers retain their positions only while they retain the confidence of the parliamentary party and wider party members. They too are subject to summary dismissal according to the rules governing their party. On this basis, prime ministers are wise to limit their exercise of discretion in hiring and firing ministers, because the more enemies they create, the more vulnerable they become to challenge. This is particularly the case in a coalition government, in which the survival of the government is dependent on the continued cooperation not only of the members of one party, but also members of another. It has been indicated that, during the life of the coalition, the Prime Minister (a Conservative) will be responsible for the discipline of Conservative ministers and the Deputy Prime Minister (a Liberal Democrat) will be responsible for Liberal Democrat ministers. Further, arrangements have been put in place to allow discipline issues to be addressed in a cooperative manner between the two parties. As Brazier notes, in the context of one-party government, the Prime Minister is really a creation of his or her own party's choice of leader, and it could be argued that his or her position is evern more tenuous in a coalition government.

. . . .

● **R. Brazier, 'Choosing a Prime Minister'** [1982] Public Law 395, 395

The appointment by the Sovereign of a Prime Minister[1] is an act done by virtue of the royal prerogative. In theory the Queen could commission anyone she pleased to form a government. But in practice such a notion is entirely removed from reality, because of course today the royal discretion is subject to several limiting factors, the most important of which is that in making an appointment she should commission that person who seems able to command a majority in the House of Commons. There are other restraints too.[2] It is possible to go further than noting these limitations and to argue that, although the formal *appointment* of a Prime Minister is a prerogative act, the actual *choice* no longer normally rests with the Queen at all: in the sense the election of a new Prime Minister does not depend upon any prerogative power. For, the argument runs, in most cases (say after a general election) the identity of the politician who is to remain or is to become the Prime Minister is obvious. Further, the political parties each now has machinery for electing its Leader,[3] so that, on the assumption for the moment that Labour's new rules have changed nothing as far as the British Constitution is concerned, there should be no repetition of controversial events like those in 1957 and (particularly) of 1963, when the Queen had to become involved in the actual evolution of a new Prime Minister[4] as distinct from his formal appointment to office. Today the party election machinery would make the choice, in consequence of which the Queen would properly be insulated from the contenders and from having to prefer (or seem to prefer) one man or women rather than any other.

The present purpose is to try to demonstrate that this restrictive view of the prerogative is generally correct, but that the royal prerogative of choice, as distinct from that of appointment, of a new Prime Minister is not dead, but dormant. There could still be far from fanciful instances in which the Queen would have to act without the protection of any prior party election of a Leader . . .

1 It can be argued that, even by the end of the nineteenth century, the sovereign had been reduced in many circumstances to a cypher in the choice of a Prime Minister, partly because of the combined efforts of Gladstone and Disraeli.

[Further notes omitted]

2 They are that he must be a member of Parliament (or be about to occupy his seat as an MP when a change of Prime Minister is necessary after a general election), not a peer (unless

he can disclaim his peerage under the Peerage Act 1963 and seek a seat in the Commons), and usually be elected Leader of his party [...]

3 [Notes omitted as relating to the political parties' modes of elections, which have since been reformed.]

4 In 1957, when Sir Anthony Eden resigned, the Queen consulted Sir Winston Churchill (presumably as former Conservative Prime Minister) and the Marquess of Salisbury (Lord President of the Council and Leader of the House of Lords in Eden's government). Both recommended Mr Macmillan rather than the only other candidate, Mr Butler. Lords Salisbury and Kilmuir had polled individual members of Eden's Cabinet. In the ferocious 1963 battle, there were at various times a number of candidates to succeed Mr Macmillan. He tried to ensure (in his words) that 'the customary processes of consultation' about the leadership were carried out as widely as possible within the Conservative Party, but the controversy over the methods and the result remains. Lord Home 'emerged'.

The last paragraph indicates that the Queen may have to choose a Prime Minister from a range of possible candidates if, for example, a general election were to result in a hung Parliament in which no one party held a majority. This is considered in brief below and is considered in more detail in Chapter 12 in the light of the coalition government. On a final note, it is also worth remembering that if a minister is sacked by the Prime Minister, he or she does not lose the parliamentary role at the same time. MPs who are members of the party that is in power, but who do not have a government position, are referred to as **backbench MPs** (because government members and shadow government members sit on the front benches in the Commons and the Lords, and those with only parliamentary roles sit towards the back). They can still use their parliamentary power from the back benches, albeit to a lesser extent than an MP who is also a government member.

2.4.4 The role of the government

The government has the power to run the country in so far as it has been provided with the legal power to do so by legislation or the royal prerogative. It also has the power to propose law to Parliament to aid it in running the country. Backbench MPs may also propose legislation, but because the government dominates the legislative timetable of the Commons, the vast majority by far of Bills are introduced by the government. Senior government ministers also represent the country abroad in foreign policy terms. This gives the government a lot of day-to-day power, but with power comes responsibility, including abiding by the law when exercising legal power (a basic rule of law requirement) and exercising power fairly so that any exercise of discretion is not arbitrary. There is also a duty to report honestly to Parliament, keeping Parliament informed (to keep the public informed), so that Parliament may check that the power it has conferred on the government is being properly executed.

The government is made accountable for its exercise of power and discretion (its choice of how to exercise its power) through a number of mechanisms. Some of these mechanisms are legal ones, such as judicial review of executive action by the courts, and civil and criminal accountability by virtue of the Crown Proceedings Act 1947 and related legislation. Others are political ones via parliamentary processes, such as through Question Time, parliamentary debates, and select and standing committees. These are all considered in much more detail in Chapters 11 and 12. At this stage, it is enough to know that the government is scrutinised by parliament, by the courts, and also, of course, by the electorate, in some instances via the media.

2.4.5 The role of the Prime Minister

The Prime Minister of the UK government, unlike a president, is not directly elected by the electorate and does not have security of office. By that, we mean that the Prime Minister may be removed from prime ministerial office during the course of a government term, according to the rules in place within the political party of which he or she is a member. This is what happened recently when Tony Blair stepped down as leader of the Labour Party and Prime Minister, and Gordon Brown was elected unopposed as leader of the party and thus was asked by the Queen to become the Prime Minister. The Prime Minister is appointed by the monarch under the royal prerogative, although there are constitutional conventions associated with the Queen's role in selecting the Prime Minister that strictly limit her choice of candidate. These will be examined in Chapter 6. However, it is important to note that the Prime Minister is not elected by the whole electorate. Instead, in recent years, the Prime Minister has been appointed by the Queen by virtue of having been elected as the leader of his or her political party and that party having won more seats than any other party in the House of Commons. The party leader's election is made by a combination of his or her political party members, and MPs and others (for example trade unions), rather than through the general electorate. Some commentators view this as a strength of the UK system, whereas others consider this to be a weakness—particularly at a time when the Prime Minister appears to be developing greater and broader powers more akin to those held by a directly elected president.

● **T. Benn, 'The case for a constitutional premiership'** (1979) 33(1) Parliamentary Affairs 7, 7–8

> My argument can be very simply summarised. The wide range of powers exercised at present by a Prime Minister, both in that capacity and as party leader, are now so great so as to encroach up on the legitimate rights of the electorate, undermine the essential role of parliament, usurp some of the functions of collective cabinet decision making and neutralise much of the influence deriving from the internal democracy of the Labour party. In short, the present centralisation of power into the hands of one person has gone too far and amounts to a system of personal rule in the very heart of our parliamentary democracy. My conclusion is that the powers of the prime minister, and party leader, must be made accountable to those over whom they are exercised, so that we can develop a constitutional premiership in Britain. To transform an absolute premiership into a constitutional premiership would involved making such fundamental changes in its functions comparable to those made over the years, when the crown was transformed from an absolute monarchy to a constitutional monarchy.
>
> ...
>
> Britain's political history has been marked by a long series of struggles to wrest powers away from the centre and redistribute them to a wider group of interests. From the truly absolutist monarchy of William the Conqueror, there was a succession of bitter battles from which the monarchy emerged with its powers trimmed, first by the feudal barons at Runneymede, then by the House of Lords itself and, later by the revolution of the gentry at the time of Cromwell. The growing power of the House of Commons after 1688, and the development of cabinet government in the century that followed, led to the situation under which the crown's own ministers were required to command a majority in the elected chamber. After the 1832 Reform Act the processes of extending the franchise were carried to the point which we have reached today, when ministers are accountable to a House of Commons chosen following an election at which all adults may vote. Under this textbook version of the development of our constitutional monarchy, within a parliamentary democracy, the powers of the prime minister can be seen as a great achievement because they have been wrested away from the throne, and are now only exercised at the will of the electorate—but the analysis leaves out of account the impact that the powers of the prime minister may have on the rights of those in parliament, in the

What is the executive and how does this differ from the government?

39

NOTE You may wish to consider Benn's view in the light of your knowledge of the role of the monarch in the UK, and also your understanding of parliamentary executive systems contrasted with presidential executive ones.

thinking point
Do you consider that the Prime Minister should be directly elected? If so, how would that work in a UK context? Should we move away from a parliamentary executive constitution?

NOTE You may wish to read more about the history, membership, and work of the Privy Council online at http://privycouncil. independent.gov.uk

political parties and on the electorate as a whole. The establishment of an 'elected monarchy' may reproduce, in a significant sense, the very system of personal rule which earlier struggles were intended to end. Indeed, it is quite legitimate to ask whether we have not, accidentally, made a very good job are reproducing feudalism, complete with a whole new generation of barons, who owe their positions of power to a new 'monarch' dispensing power and status of a much more significant kind, as well as the old honours. This is not to suggest that all the very real achievements of British democracy have been eroded by these tendencies. The ultimate power of the House of Commons to topple a prime minister remains unaffected, as does the even greater power of the voters to get rid of both governments and the MPs who support them: the very fact that this power is there operates to restrain the exercise of all powers by prime ministers and their ministers. Within the broad framework of public and parliamentary consent, however, there has certainly been a greater centralisation of personal power in the hands of one man or women that outward appearances would suggest.

Benn argues that the absolutist power of the monarch (now curtailed as a constitutional monarch) has been replaced by a similar strand of absolute power enjoyed by the Prime Minister. He proposes that either prime ministerial power should be limited via a redistribution to other parts of the UK (through devolution—which has since been introduced, albeit on a lesser scale than Benn considered necessary), or that prime ministers should be accountable to the electorate via direct elections.

2.4.6 Other government institutions: the Privy Council

You may also come across the Privy Council in your constitutional law studies. The Privy Council is an ancient part of the government that has been in existence since the Middle Ages. At one time, it answered directly to the monarch, but over time it has adapted to meet the demands of a constitutional monarchy and an elected parliamentary system of government. The monarch appoints Privy Counsellors and appointment is for life. All Cabinet members are appointed as Privy Counsellors, and it is possible to work out who is a Privy Counsellor by whether he or she is accorded the title 'The Right Honourable' before his or her name and the designation 'PC' after his or her name. However, only ministers serving in the current government are permitted to take part in developing Privy Council policy. The Privy Council works within the framework of royal prerogative and statutory powers. Parliament may assign functions to the Queen and Privy Council via Act of Parliament, including the power to make a form of law known as Orders in Council. These Orders are considered by Privy Counsellors and, if approved, are given to the Queen for her formal approval. Many bodies, such as universities, were established by royal charter, and the Privy Council oversees the grant and amendment of royal charters, as well as the affairs of some professions, such as the medical and veterinary professions. The Privy Council may be required to appoint some of the members of the boards of these bodies, and to approve the bodies' rules and procedures. The Privy Council has a second part to it, known as the Judicial Committee of the Privy Council, which will be discussed very briefly below.

summary points

What is the executive and how does this differ from the government?

- *The executive is split into the political executive (the government) and the wider machinery of government (the civil servants and others who assist in running the country).*

- *The political executive is headed by the Prime Minister, who is appointed by the monarch exercising her royal prerogative, but in reality he or she is the MP who leads the party that has a working majority in the House of Commons.*

- *The remainder of the political executive is made up of MPs and peers who have been selected by the Prime Minister and who serve as government ministers (Cabinet minister, junior minister, and parliamentary private secretaries) for as long as the Prime Minister remains in office and wishes the minister to serve in the government. In strict law, it is the Queen who appoints ministers; however, her royal prerogative is exercised by the Prime Minister on her behalf by virtue of constitutional convention.*
- *The executive uses the power conferred on it by Parliament and via the royal prerogative to run the country.*
- *In real terms, the political executive is also responsible for the UK's relationships with other countries.*
- *Although the monarch is the head of state in legal terms, the Prime Minister is the de facto head of state in political negotiations.*

2.5 What are the courts and what is their role?

We have devoted a whole chapter of the book (Chapter 14) to the constitutional role of the courts; there are, however, a number of points that it may be useful to note at this stage. The courts are usually considered for their private law role, which is to adjudicate in disputes between private citizens, or between individuals and companies. The **Supreme Court** is the final court of appeal for civil law matters for England, Northern Ireland, Scotland, and Wales. We are also familiar with the courts' public law criminal case work, and the Supreme Court is also the final court of appeal in criminal law cases for England, Northern Ireland, and Wales (although see below), but not Scotland, which has the High Court of Justiciary as its highest criminal court of appeal. Since the Appellate Jurisdiction Act 1876, the former appellate House of Lords and now Supreme Court is made up of professional judges, and not the life peers and hereditary peers who are members of the House of Lords legislative chamber. There are twelve Supreme Court justices; the first female appointee was Baroness Hale of Richmond, who was appointed in 2004.

. . . .

Supreme Court
The court comprising the most senior judiciary in the UK. It was formerly known as the Appellate Committee of the House of Lords, which, although the two shared a name, was not the same body as the legislative chamber containing life and hereditary peers.

. . . .

The courts have an important constitutional and administrative role to play too, which is less well known by the public. The courts may not be involved in scrutinising the day-to-day running of Parliament, but they do review the day-to-day actions, omissions, and decisions of government to ensure that they are within the law, that they are rational, that they meet statutory procedural requirements and the common law rules of **natural justice**, and that they adhere to the requirements of the Human Rights Act 1998. In short, the courts act as a legal check on government through the mechanisms of judicial review, initiated in the administrative division of the High Court, with appeal mechanisms to the Court of Appeal and the Supreme Court.

There are some important differences in the powers of the courts in the UK when compared with other jurisdictions. The Supreme Court does not have the power to strike down primary legislation on grounds that it is considered to be unconstitutional. Parliament's legislative

41

power is supreme, which means that it may pass any law that it wishes, assuming that it has the requisite votes in the Commons and the Lords to allow it to pass to the Queen for royal assent. We consider the nature of the British constitution in the next chapter and this sheds some light on the relationship between Parliament and the courts. We consider it further in Chapter 5, which addresses the separation of powers, and further still in Chapter 7, which focuses on the theory of parliamentary supremacy. At this stage, however, it is enough to know that the courts have the power to review the executive's actions, but not the power to review those of Parliament.

The Supreme Court is also charged with overseeing disputes related to devolution matters. This will be considered in more detail in Chapter 10. The Judicial Committee of the Privy Council is the final court of appeal for the Commonwealth nations that retain this appeal mechanism and it also an appeal court for the purposes of some of the professional body disciplinary systems, such as the veterinary and medical professions. It also has a role in some ecclesiastical (Church of England) matters. The Judicial Committee of the Privy Council is made up of judges from the Supreme Court, as well as some of the senior judiciary from the Commonwealth nations that retain the Privy Council as an appellate body.

summary points

What are the courts and what is their role?

- *The courts have an important constitutional role to play.*

- *They oversee the operation of the rule of law by reviewing actions, omissions, and decisions taken by the executive to ensure that they are legal, rational, and procedurally proper, and that they do not breach the terms of the Human Rights Act 1998.*

- *The courts may make orders against the executive in the event that the executive has acted illegally, procedurally improperly, or irrationally, and in some instances they may order that the executive comply with an individual's human rights.*

- *The courts do not have the legal power to overturn primary legislation, although there are circumstances in which Parliament requires the courts to give effect to European law in preference to domestic law.*

- *Consequently, the courts do not perform the function of a constitutional court: Parliament remains supreme, but the executive is required to act within the law.*

2.6 Who may be involved in electing UK representatives and through what mechanisms are UK representatives elected?

The final section in this chapter addresses elections to the Westminster Parliament—the mechanism through which MPs are elected and other ways in which those elections could be run. This is particularly topical in the light of discussions about whether members of the House of Lords should be directly or indirectly elected, and if so, what this would mean in relation to the balance of power between the Commons and the Lords. The first extract in this section explains who is entitled to vote in parliamentary elections. This may now seem a settled and relatively

NOTE Consider your own views as you read Ganz's description of who may and who may not participate in the democratic process.

uncontroversial topic given the recent 'no' vote in the national referendum on whether to change the voting system from 'first past the post' to an alternative voting (AV) system, but the more one considers different groups who are included and excluded from the electoral process, the more complex it becomes. After all, it is only ninety years since women were first permitted to vote in parliamentary elections! And there remain some sections of society still excluded from the electoral process.

● **G. Ganz,** *Understanding Public Law* [3rd edn, London: Sweet & Maxwell, 2001], p. 4

Electoral System

Historically the electoral system is based on the representation of communities. This is still reflected in the qualification for voting and the method of voting. Everyone who is 18, a Commonwealth citizen (who is legally in the UK) or a citizen of Eire, not a peer who is entitled to sit in the House of Lords ... and not serving a sentence of imprisonment or held in a mental institution as a consequence of criminal activity is entitled to be placed on the electoral register in a constituency where he is resident. Residence does not now involve a qualifying period or residence on a particular date (formerly October 10). It may not even now require a degree of permanence, which was sufficiently manifested by the women protesting at Greenham Common (*Hipperson v. Newbury Electoral Registration Officer*, 1985). A person can be resident where he is staying at a place otherwise than on a permanent basis, if he has no home elsewhere (Representation of the People Act 2000, s.3). This could apply, for example, to travellers. Similarly, a homeless person, who is not resident at any address, can be registered, if he gives an address of a place where he spends a substantial part of his time. Patients in mental hospitals, other than those detained there for criminal activity, can now be treated as resident at the mental hospital and those remanded in custody, who have not been convicted of an offence, can be treated as resident at the place of detention. Those who cannot satisfy the residence qualification may be entitled to be registered in a constituency where they were resident, e.g., if they are absent because they are members of the armed forces or British citizens living abroad who have been registered there within the preceding 20 years (Representation of the People Act 1989). In such cases entitlement to vote is based on citizenship rather than residence to which lip-service is paid through registration in the constituency where the citizen was previously registered. Such a notional residence is essential as all voters much be on an electoral register in a constituency.

As Ganz explains, life and hereditary peers who are members of the House of Lords are not permitted to vote, and yet MPs are. Convicted criminals serving time in prison are excluded from the electoral process—although this has been criticised by the European Court of Human Rights (ECtHR) and the UK remains in breach of the **European Convention on Human Rights (ECHR)** through its continued blanket ban on prisoners exercising the right to vote, as discussed in Chapter 9—and yet British citizens who have emigrated to other countries may still participate in parliamentary elections. EU citizens may not vote in parliamentary elections even if they have lived in the UK for many years (they may vote in European elections, devolved parliament/assembly elections, and local elections) and yet Commonwealth citizens resident in the UK may vote in parliamentary elections. It is now possible for the homeless, the mentally ill, and those of no fixed address to vote, as may those on remand in prison, but who are not convicted of an offence. And non-UK nationals who are legally entitled to live in the UK and who are Commonwealth or Eire citizens may also vote in parliamentary elections. The electorate is now very wide, and yet only just over 70 per cent of those on the electoral register choose to exercise their right to participate in choosing their parliamentary representative.

thinking point

To what extent do you agree with the type and range of people who are eligible to vote? Should people be entitled to vote at the age of 16? Should criminals be permitted to vote? How about people who live abroad? Consider your views carefully: for example women were only given the vote in 1918 and it was generally accepted until the early 1900s that women were not capable of making a proper decision about whom to elect! Should we exclude people on grounds of capacity (as were women), or on grounds of residence, or as a punishment—or on all or none of the above grounds?

The second consideration is the mechanism used to elect representatives. There are a number of options, including named individuals on the ballot paper, or political parties, which then have lists of people who will be elected if their party gains enough votes. There are also systems described as 'first past the post' (FPTP) and 'proportional representation'.

The next extract provides an example of the way in which the FPTP system in UK parliamentary elections leads to the distribution of seats between the main political parties.

● **G. Ganz, Understanding Public Law** [3rd edn, London: Sweet & Maxwell, 2001], pp. 4–6

The constituency is the linchpin of our electoral system. Its origin lies in the representation of communities which is still an important part of an M.P.'s work. There is, however, a constant pressure between this concept of representation and the modern party system which affects so many facets of our representative democracy.

…

The crucial importance of constituency boundaries to the outcome of elections is the result of our electoral system, called first past the post, under which an M.P. is elected for a constituency if he receives one vote more than his nearest rival however small his percentage of the total vote. This not only enables M.P.s to be elected on a minority vote [312 M.P.s in 1997] but on two occasions since the war [1951 and February 1974] the party gaining the most seats polled fewer votes that the main opposition party. Most disadvantaged by our electoral system are the Liberal Democrats, whose support is fairly evenly spread throughout the country and who come second in a large number of seats but only win a handful of seats where their support is concentrated. In 1997 they gained 46 seats for 17 per cent of the vote, whilst Labour gained 418 seats for 43 per cent and the Conservatives 165 seats with 31 per cent of the vote. It is this glaring discrepancy between seats and votes since the revival of the Liberal party in 1974 which has fuelled the pressure for electoral reform. The rest of the 2001 election has left this situation virtually unchanged.

As these figures illustrate the system can also be unfair to the major parties. Labour obtained over 60 per cent of the seats with 43 per cent of the vote whilst the Conservatives gained 25 per cent of the seats with 31 per cent of the vote.

Ganz notes that, under the FPTP system, voter turnout and a party's willingness to target key marginal seats—ones for which the vote is close rather than those safe seats for which there is a large majority in favour of one party—are likely to have a major impact on the national results. She argues that the Labour Party won the election from the Conservatives in 1997 by targeting 100 key marginal seats rather than focusing the party's campaigning attention on the remaining 559. It is interesting to note, therefore, that it is not simply the people whom you permit to vote who may make a difference to the election result, but also how the constituency boundaries are drawn (which determines which voters are in which voting area) and also the method used to determine the winner of each constituency ballot. There is a process under way that will see the number of seats in the House of Commons reduced from 650 to 600 and constituency boundaries are being redrawn so as to make this possible. There are concerns in some quarters that this may skew the constituencies so as to favour one party over another (although, interestingly, these concerns have been voiced by all sides in the political debate).

There are a number of other electoral systems, many of which are used in other elections in the UK. Both the Scottish Parliament and the Welsh Assembly employ an additional member system that asks electors to vote for a constituency MP (in the same way as general elections via a FPTP system) and then to vote for an additional representative using proportional representation from a party list. This makes it less likely that one party will obtain an overall majority in the chamber and is likely to lead to coalition government, whereby two or more parties are required to cooperate and work together to have a large enough working majority in the Parliament or Assembly to permit legislation to be passed. The Northern Ireland Assembly uses another form of proportional representation known as the 'single transferable vote' (STV) system, and members of the European Parliament (MEPs) are elected using yet another form in which individuals vote for a party rather than an individual and representatives are chosen from a list of party names in proportion to the votes cast for each party. 'First past the post' has the benefit of being very simple in comparison with some forms of proportional representation, and it regularly returns parties to power who have a large majority and which thus may put their electoral mandates into operation. This is considered to be an electoral system that promotes strong government. Systems that promote a plethora of parties that gain a small proportion of the vote and which are required regularly to form coalitions with other parties in order to form a government, as is the case in Italy, are less likely to have a strong platform from which to run the country, because coalition partners may not be able to agree on policy and direction, and one small party may exert a disproportionate influence over its coalition partners because it holds the balance of power in a weak government that is struggling to stay united.

However, the FPTP system does suffer some disadvantages too. It is considered to lead to a distribution of seats within the Commons that is not as representative of the proportions of voters who have selected individuals from particular parties than would be the case with a system of proportional representation. Parties, such as the Liberal Democrats, which would gain far more seats under a system of proportional representation, will continue to campaign for electoral reform; parties such as the Labour and Conservative Parties, which benefit from the current system, will continue to resist change. For now, however, the issue of electoral reform has been put to one side. The recent referendum on the alternative voting system was rejected by the electorate and it is unlikely that any party in power will put the issue of electoral reform on the agenda for a number of decades, as a consequence of this. It will be interesting to see, too, how the electorate views coalition government as a model at the end of the Conservative–Liberal Democrat coalition government.

Further details and illustrations of preference for particular parties are available on the Online Resource Centre.

summary points

Who may be involved in electing UK representatives and through what mechanisms are UK representatives elected?

- *All seats in the House of Commons are subject to re-election whenever a general election is called. This means that MPs must contest their seats; all seats are contested at the same time.*

- *By law, the electorate has the opportunity to vote for a constituency MP at least every five years and the Fixed-term Parliaments Act 2011 has provided more certainty regarding the date of the next general election.*

- UK parliamentary elections are conducted using the 'first past the post' mechanism. This may be contrasted with other voting systems that are based on proportional representation, which is used to elect members of the devolved assemblies and the Scottish Parliament.

- The electorate for the purposes of parliamentary elections is made up of adults who are British citizens, as well as Commonwealth citizens and citizens of the Republic of Ireland who meet residence requirements. There are groups of people within these categories who are not entitled to vote in parliamentary elections, including persons serving prison sentences, members of the House of Lords upper chamber, and people convicted of electoral fraud or corruption in the previous five years.

◉ Summary

cross reference
Overlaps between the legislative, executive, and judicial functions are considered in Chapter 5.

Figure 2.3 illustrates how the institutions fit together. The three main institutions of the state—Parliament, the government, and the courts—are all headed by the monarch. Parliament is responsible for law-making and scrutinising the executive, and is a body charged with representing the electorate through the workings of the House of Commons. The government is responsible for implementing the law in order to run the country. It creates policy with the purpose of achieving its political objectives in the country and to provide a measure of consistency while implementing policy. It proposes legislative reform in order to meet its policy objectives. The courts apply and interpret the law, and review the executive's exercise of power through the doctrine of the rule of law. The courts also play an important role in hearing disputes from individuals who believe that the state has infringed their legal or human rights. Judicial review actions, as they are called, examine the executive's actions, decisions, or failures to act in accordance with law, rationality, the proper procedure, and the operation of the Human Rights Act 1998.

Figure 2.3

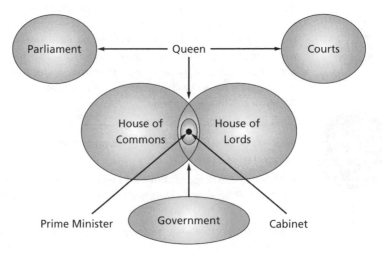

Questions

1 What are the main institutions of the UK?

2 What are their roles and their memberships?

3 How do they relate to each other?

4 To what extent are the people involved in the state?

5 How do the various House of Lords' reform proposals affect the relationship between the two parliamentary chambers and what consequence may that have for the electoral system?

Further reading

Feldman, D., 'Parliamentary scrutiny of legislation and human rights' [2002] Public Law 323

This article sets out the way in which Parliament scrutinises legislation so as to check whether it conforms to human rights provisions. It is useful as a means of learning about the parliamentary legislative processes.

Gay, O. 'Fixed-term Parliaments Act 2011' (House of Commons Library Standard Note SN/PC/6111, 3 November 2011) available online at http://www.parliament.uk/briefing-papers/SN06111

This factsheet sets out the way in which elections are triggered, including the role of motions of confidence since the introduction of fixed-term parliaments. It covers both general elections and by-elections. It is quite detailed, but also clear and readily understandable.

Hazell, R., Paun, A., Chalmers, M., Yong, B., and Haddon, C., *Making Minority Government Work: Hung Parliaments and the Challenges for Westminster and Whitehall* (London: The Constitution Unit University College London, 2009)

This report illustrates the challenges faced by minority and coalition governments, with reference to recent examples here and in other similar jurisdictions. It also sets out the challenges that parliaments face in this situation too.

HM Government, *The House of Lords: Reform* (Cmd 7027, London: HMSO, February 2007), available online at http://www.official-documents.gov.uk/document/cm70/7027/7027.pdf

This provides detail about House of Lords Reform proposed by the previous government. Although a little out of date in relation to current proposals, it is useful in that it sets out the advantages and disadvantages of different models that could be adopted.

Maer, L. and Gay, O., 'The Royal Prerogative' (House of Commons Library Standard Note SN/PC/03861, 30 December 2009) available online at http://www.parliament.uk/commons/lib/research/briefings/snpc-03861.pdf

This note sets the nature of the royal prerogative, as well as recent reform proposals. It provides a really good overview and is well worth reading.

Malleson, K. and Moules, R., *The Legal System* (Oxford: Oxford University Press, 2010)

This book provides much more detail about many of the issues that have been addressed in brief in this chapter. It both provides overview material and more detail than it was possible to provide in a single chapter in this book.

Tyrie, A., Young, G., and Gough, G. *An Elected Second Chamber: A Conservative View* (London: The Constitution Unit University College London, 2009)

This publication provides exactly what it says in the title: a Conservative view of the proposal to reform the House of Lords so as to be an elected body. This gives us some insight into how a majority Conservative government may have reformed the Upper Chamber had there not been a hung Parliament and thus a coalition government.

3

The Nature of the British Constitution

Key points

This chapter will cover:

- What is a constitution?
- How do written and unwritten constitutions compare?
- How might we classify the British constitution compared with others?
- What are the sources of the British constitution?
- What is the hierarchical position of the British constitution and how is it amended?
- Proposed reforms to the British constitution

The term 'constitution' means many different things to different people. This chapter will consider the nature and role of constitutions, comparing and contrasting different types of constitution and the ways in which they may be amended. It will also address the concept of unconstitutionality, which has been brought into focus by comments (albeit erroneous) in the media about the effects of the operation of the Human Rights Act 1998 in the UK. The chapter will examine in detail the British constitution and briefly consider how it differs from a range of others. It will examine past and present reform proposals. The chapter ends with a summary and questions.

3.1 What is a constitution?

Many people, when asked to describe a constitution, would describe it as a single and important document that sets out citizens' rights. They would point to a document such as the US Constitution as the template. In a lot of respects, they would be right, because many constitutions are made up of a single document that contains a **bill of rights**. However, in reality, constitutions come in many shapes and sizes. Some are a single document, such as the constitutions of the United States, Canada, and France; others are formed from a collection of legal and non-legal sources, such as those in the UK, Israel, and New Zealand. These are sometimes referred to as 'uncodified', or 'unwritten', constitutions even though they are made up of a range of sources, including written ones. Some commentators go so far as to say that constitutions that do not appear in formal written form in the same way as does the US Constitution, for example, are not real constitutions at all. However, it is probably more accurate to describe a constitution as a set of laws and other sources or principles that explains the way in which the **state** is established, and which provides a degree of legitimacy to the state and its institutions. It delineates the powers of the different branches of the state, and the restrictions placed on the institutions and on state power. In short, a constitution is a framework that defines the structure of the state and its powers.

But constitutions do more than just describe the way in which the state is set up and should function: a constitution also seeks to confer power and to provide legitimacy for the state's use of power. It provides an implicit explanation as to why the state is empowered to operate some control over individuals' lives in contrast to private citizens, who are not legally empowered to forbid other adults from behaving in certain ways. It also legitimises the state's requirement that people and bodies must behave in certain ways, backed by sanctions for non-compliance administered according to the law and courts' judgments.

The use of state power must be the subject of some form of overarching principles, to which the state yields, in order for it to be considered as a legitimate exercise of power. In other words, the constitution marks out the principles upon which the country is founded and it gives power to state officials to ensure that the country operates within those principles. As Thomas Paine explained:

● **T. Paine,** *Rights of Man* (Whitefish, MT: Kessinger Publishing, 1998), p. 29

> A constitution is not a thing in name only, but in fact. It has not an ideal, but a real existence; and whenever it cannot be produced in a visible form there is none. A constitution is a thing antecedent to a government, and a government is only the creature of a constitution. The constitution of a country is not the act of its government, but of the people constituting its government.

He further argues that a 'government without a constitution, is a power without a right'. Power is conferred for a reason, not only so that officials may have power and make use of it as and how they wish. If it is not legitimised by reference to some form of constitution, the state's use of power amounts to the use of force rather than a legal expression of its will.

FUNCTIONS

Consequently, constitutions have multiple functions—of which we have so far considered two: setting up a framework for the state; and conferring and legitimating state power. There have been many attempts to categorise the functions of the constitution. Professor Feldman has used a series of humorous analogies to attempt to do just that in the context of the UK constitution. He suggests that there are four main functions of a constitution and that these functions are more important than the way in which the constitution is expressed, or set out.

● **D. Feldman, 'None, one or several? Perspectives on the UK's constitution(s)'** (2005) 64(2) Cambridge Law Journal 329, 335–6

> From this, we can identify four roles for constitutions. The first is institutionalization. The constitution establishes institutions within the body politic, allocates functions to them, and confers on them the powers and duties appropriate to those functions, ensuring that so far as possible the limits of each institution's powers and duties are indicated (although not necessarily defined). The second role is to prevent institutions from acting improperly by providing ways of ensuring that they adhere to their powers and duties, or are held accountable for any lapse. Bits of the body politic, like parts of human bodies, can sometimes expand in undesirable directions, and need to be restrained. We can call this the 'corsetry' function, the corset taking the form of such procedures as judicial review and parliamentary or electoral accountability.
>
> The first two roles feed into the third, namely the conferral of a particular kind of respectability or legitimacy by cloaking in appropriate garb those features of the body politic that might, if left exposed, be regarded as improper or even indecent. This is done by the conscious adoption of principles of government designed to appeal to the morality of both the elites and the masses within the state. These elements turn an act of naked aggression into an arrest or lawful imprisonment, the refusal of support to the indigent into an act of state prudence, and the conspiracy of a cabal into an exercise of responsible government by a cabinet accountable to a more or less representative legislature. They fulfil for the state purposes similar to those of good clothes, hiding what cannot be revealed in polite company and presenting the body politic in such a way as to avoid public embarrassment or discomfort. We can call this the decency-preserving or legitimating function, and its importance can be seen analogically in the tale of the Emperor's new clothes.
>
> Finally, the clothes (including the corset) must be sufficiently comfortable and adaptable to avoid the need for a completely new wardrobe each time the body politic changes its shape. This flexibility is provided by a number of mechanisms which, for want of a more descriptive name, we can call the knicker-elastic function. This elasticity cannot be unlimited, or the constitution would be unable to perform its first two roles, but it must be sufficient to allow adaptation to the pressures that arise naturally from the dynamic development of an organic state structure.

Professor Feldman argues that the constitution fulfils four basic roles:

- it establishes the institutions of the state, and provides them and their members with sufficient powers so that they may carry out their missions;

- it puts checks and balances in place to limit the abuse of power, and to provide mechanisms to uncover and to restrain or punish abuse, if it occurs;

- it then provides some legitimacy for the use of power—it provides a set of basic principles that explain the moral principles of the state and thus the purpose to which state power may be put; and

- it provides a certain degree of flexibility to allow the state to evolve as it will over time, without allowing it to change out of all recognition without conscious effort on the part of those in power and the public.

But constitutions also say something about the values that underpin the nation. A constitution is not a value-neutral political document, but gives effect to the principles upon which the state is founded. Tomkins explains it as follows.

● **A. Tomkins, *Public Law*** (Oxford: Oxford University Press, 2003), p. 5

What is missing is the sense that constitutions . . . also embody something of a nation's values. Consider the following famous account of what a constitution is, which comes from the early eighteenth century Tory politician, Viscount Bolingbroke:

> By constitution we mean, whenever we speak with propriety and exactness, that assemblage of laws, institutions and customs, derived from certain fixed principles of reason, directed to certain fixed objects of public good, that compose the general system, according to which the community hath agreed to be governed.[1]

There are at least two elements present in this definition which are missing from the functional account offered above. The first is the notion that constitutional laws and institutions are derived from certain fixed principles of reason and are directed to certain fixed objects of public good. Leaving aside the now rather out-moded Enlightenment idea that principles of reason are fixed, what Bolingbroke is getting at here is that constitutions not only have functions, they also have goals. They are underpinned and indeed shaped by values, by certain visions of what is in the public good (or public interest), by political ideas. What he is suggesting is that you cannot understand what a constitution is for unless you first understand what values it is based on, and what policies it is seeking to promote. Constitutions are not value-neutral legal documents, dry as dust and dull as ditchwater: they are living representations of the politics which made them and which consume them. Lawyers can find this uncomfortable and embarrassing. It is as if our subject (public law) is somehow to be regarded as being above all this, that law is not only autonomous from but also superior to and purer than mere politics. Such lawyers need to lose their inhibitions. Let us not be ashamed of it: ours is inescapably and deeply a political subject.

1 Bolingbroke wrote these words in 1734; for a modern edition, see D. Armitage (ed.) *Bolingbroke's Political Writings* (Cambridge: Cambridge University Press, 1997), p. 88.

Therefore, in order to understand a country's constitution, one needs to examine the country's values at the time that the constitution was drafted. There is much agreement on the basic functions of constitutions, but thereafter there is disagreement about the principles that they should embody, the form that a constitution should take, and the way in which it ought to be amended in order for it to be deemed a constitution. We will consider the values that the British constitution embodies as we work our way through the study of public law in this book.

What is a constitution?

- *Constitutions have multiple purposes.*
- *Commentators agree that constitutions generally define the institutions and powers of the state.*
- *A constitution usually also sets out the limits of state power.*
- *A constitution may provide legitimation for the use of state power, within those defined limits.*
- *The constitution may also set out the principles upon which the state is founded.*
- *It may also provide a bill of rights for citizens or subjects.*
- *In short, it establishes the framework of the state.*

3.2 How do written and unwritten constitutions compare?

We have considered the purpose of a constitution, which appears to be relatively straightforward, but what does a constitution look like and do constitutions follow an agreed structure? The simple answer to these questions is that there is no one model of a constitution and that no, there is no agreed structure for them. Constitutions come in all shapes and sizes: some are very detailed; others contain little more than a statement of principles upon which the state is founded or a bill of rights that individuals within the state enjoy. Some contain a body of constitutional law in a single document and are referred to as 'written' constitutions; others are made up from a collection of different sources and are referred to as 'unwritten', or 'uncodified', constitutions. There is no one way of drawing up a constitution, although it is fair to say that newer or more recent constitutions are more likely to be written rather than unwritten or uncodified.

cross reference
The historical development of the UK constitution is considered in Chapters 4 and 5.

Historically, all constitutions were unwritten—that is, they were not contained in one single document. Oliver Cromwell's regime in 1653 established an early forerunner to a written constitution, 'the articles of government', but that regime lasted only a year before military rule overtook it. The Glorious Revolution in 1688 was in part won on the principle of restoration of the old way of doing things rather than a drive towards new constitutional innovation and England returned to its unwritten constitutional roots. Magna Carta remained the central bill of rights, but there was no real attempt to bring together other elements of constitutional law into one document to be entitled the 'constitution of England'. Written constitutions began to spring up around the world from the late eighteenth century onwards, usually after events such as revolutions or when countries gained independence from colonial powers. The earliest known examples of Western written constitutions (although admittedly these are relatively recent in historical terms and early civilisations such as the Ancient Greeks had written constitutions) are the US Constitution, dating from 1787, and the French Declaration of the Rights of Man (*Déclaration des Droits de l'Homme et du Citoyen*, or DDHC), dating from 1789, both of which followed revolutions and a change of political regime. The documents set out the founding principles of the new state and included a set of basic rights for some sections of society (the US Constitution had the Bill of Rights added later, by amendment, rather than in the original document). It is important to note that these bills of rights were not universal: the US Constitution conferred rights on citizens and excluded slaves (and all people of colour and minority ethnic groups); the DDHC excluded those who had been part of the old regime—those associated with the aristocracy were excluded from the terms of the constitutional document. A wave of constitutions followed these two, as a number of European empires began to crumble and countries were granted independence or were granted home rule after a period of colonial rule. The Australian Constitution in 1901 marked the creation of the Commonwealth of Australia, for example. Many marked their independence, or a change of structure and powers, with a new written constitution that set out the terms of the new state and some founding principles, established the institutions and their powers, and ascribed a set of rights to their citizens.

Tomkins explains the English roots of codified constitutions in the extract below.

● **A. Tomkins, *Public Law*** (Oxford: Oxford University Press, 2003), p. 7

...The reason the English constitution takes this unusual unwritten nature is simple. It is because of England's historical development. Written constitutions do not happen by accident. A country acquires a written constitution deliberately, and in direct consequence of a certain political event: either revolution...; acquiring independence from colonial rule...; or following defeat in war, when victorious conquerors may impose a new constitution on the defeated enemy... It would be an historical inaccuracy to suggest that these events have not occurred in England: there were successful invasions (or defeats at war) in 55 BC and in 1066, and there was a revolution in 1649. But written constitutions are creatures of political fashion. In their modern form they were invented in the radicalism of the political Enlightenment, in the late seventeenth and early eighteenth centuries. England experienced its moments of greatest political turmoil well before Enlightenment thinking took hold (indeed the English political situation of the 1640s and subsequent reaction to it was one of the principal inspirations behind Enlightenment political philosophy), and was not therefore able to benefit from it. If there had been revolution in England, or in Britain, in the late 1700s rather than in the mid 1600s, our constitution would almost certainly look extremely different now.

The oldest and probably the most revered example in the western world of a written constitution is that of the United States of America whose constitution dates from 1787 (although significant amendments were added both in 1791- the 'Bill of Rights'—and again after the American civil war in the 1860s as well as on other occasions). Yet even a cursory glance at the American constitutional text suffices to illustrate that notwithstanding its almost sacred status in the USA it does not contain a complete code of all America's constitutional rule, nor even of all the important ones. Take for example the impeachment proceedings against President Clinton in the mid 1990s: easily the most important constitutional event in recent American history.[1]... What this example shows in that written constitutions are not complete codes capable of answering all constitutional questions. Indeed no written constitution could ever be. Constitutional questions, which change over time, are too varied and too unpredictable for any single legal instrument to be capable of answering them all.

1   It could be argued that the Supreme Court's decision in *Bush v Gore* 121 S Ct 525 (2000) to award the presidency to George W. Bush rather than to Al Gore following the apparently indecisive election of November 2000 has overtaken the Clinton impeachment proceedings as the most important constitutional event in recent American history. As it turns out, however, the same argument could be made of *Bush v Gore* as is here made of the Clinton impeachment: the text of the Constitution was silent on the critical question of whether hanging chads were to be counted as lawful votes or not. As with the impeachment hearings in Congress, the text itself played only a minimal role in the decision of the Court.

Consequently, it could be argued that there are fewer differences between written and unwritten constitutions than one may think at first glance. Not all constitutional 'rules' are generally included in written constitutions—not even very developed written constitutions—due to the need to keep constitutions sufficiently brief so as to be workable. Equally, just because something is written in a constitution does not mean that the state necessarily follows the terms to the letter. Some principles are mandatory; others are there as expressions of intent. Some constitutions were developed through a process of consultation with the population; others were imposed by new regimes; others were developed by the **judiciary**, who set out the guiding principles of **natural justice** and fundamental freedoms. Written versus unwritten, codified versus uncodified, judge-made versus people-made—these are all dichotomous phrases that are used to try to categorise constitutions, and yet the face-value differences between the words in each phrase are less obvious when one considers the purpose of constitutions and the content and operation of individual constitutions. There is much diversity even within written constitutions, and thus the form matters less than the substance and its operation.

As Professor Feldman explains, the more important debates relate to the provisions within constitutions rather than to their form, and even more importantly how the substance translates into action in a country.

● **D. Feldman, 'None, one or several? Perspectives on the UK's constitution(s)'** (2005) 64(2) Cambridge Law Journal 329, 335–6

> When one widens the angle to look at the constitution of the United Kingdom, rather than just of England, we encounter a sea of conflicting visions. The constitution, as a single set of rules, is very hard to pin down. I should make it clear at the outset that I am not talking about the absence of a codified constitutional document. That is a relatively trivial, formal matter. I am concerned not with the form but with the substance and function of constitutional rules: what they require and what they do. In the UK's constitution, as in all constitutions, what appears on the surface is often an illusion, and what appears to be absent is sometimes present (although often in an unexpected form).

Instead, one needs to consider what the constitution says and how that translates into what happens within a country. Are the constitutional rules applied? If so, how are they enforced—by political means or through **judicial** means? What rights do citizens or subjects have against state power? Who gets to make amendments to the constitution and how? These are all more important questions than that relating to the way in which the constitution is evidenced in a country. The next section will, however, consider how we might classify the British constitution before turning to these more fundamental issues.

summary points

How do written and unwritten constitutions compare?

- *Lawyers and political commentators often refer to constitutions as 'written', or 'unwritten' or 'uncodified'.*
- *The term 'written constitution' is usually used to refer to a single constitutional document that contains a bill of rights and the constitutional law that sets out the structure of the state.*
- *The term 'unwritten constitution', or 'uncodified constitution', is used to refer to constitutions that are made up from multiple documents or sources.*
- *Many written constitutions in recent times were developed by the need to restructure the country after a revolution, a major change of regime, or a granting of independence.*
- *The term is, however, less important than the content and enforcement mechanism that the constitution contains.*

3.3 How might we classify the British constitution compared with others?

The UK constitution is a difficult constitution to classify and also to assess at any given time. It is in a constant state of change and much of the detail is not written in traditional legal texts. Consequently, it is not easy to explain the exact nature of the UK constitution, as Bagehot explained in his book on the English constitution.

● **W. Bagehot, 'Introduction to the second edition', in *The English Constitution*** (2nd edn, 1873; New York: Cosimo Classics, 2007), p. 5

There is a great difficulty in the way of a writer who attempts to sketch a living constitution,—a Constitution that is in actual work and power. The difficulty is that the object is in constant change. An historical writer does not feel this difficulty: he deals only with the past; he can say definitely, the Constitution worked in such and such a manner in the year at which he begins, and in a manner in such and such respects different in the year at which he ends; he begins with a definite point of time and ends with one also. But a contemporary writer who tries to paint what is before him is puzzled and perplexed; what he sees is changing daily.

The UK constitution is often referred to by what it is *not*: it is not a traditional written constitution and so it is defined as an 'unwritten' constitution, although the term 'uncodified' is perhaps more apposite, because much of our constitutional law is written—it is just not written in a single document. The fact that it is not a written constitution that is hierarchically superior to all other law in the country is itself a difficulty for some commentators, who doubt that the UK even has a constitution on this basis. Ridley discusses this in the following article.

● **F. F. Ridley, 'There is no British constitution: a dangerous case of the Emperor's clothes'** (1988) 41(3) Parliamentary Affairs 340, 343–4

The characteristics of a constitution are as follows.

(1) It establishes, or constitutes, the system of government. Thus it is prior to the system of government, not part of it, and its rules can not be derived from that system.

(2) It therefore involves an authority outside and above the order it establishes. This is the notion of the constituent power ('pouvoir constituant'—because we do not think along these lines, the English translation sounds strange). In democracies that power is attributed to the people, on whose ratification the legitimacy of a constitution depends and, with it, the legitimacy of the governmental system.

(3) It is a form of law superior to other laws—because (i) it originates in an authority higher than the legislature which makes ordinary law and (ii) the authority of the legislature derives from it and is thus bound by it. The principle of hierarchy of law generally (but not always) leads to the possibility of judicial review of ordinary legislation.

(4) It is entrenched—(i) because its purpose is generally to limit the powers of government, but also (ii) again because of its origins in a higher authority outside the system. It can thus only be changed by special procedures, generally (and certainly for major change) requiring reference back to the constituent power.

James Bryce made all these points at the turn of the century. Defining a constitution as a framework of political society organised through law, he distinguished between 'statutory' and 'common law' types of constitutions. Of the former, he wrote:

'The instrument in which a constitution is embodied proceeds from a source different from that whence spring other laws, is regulated in a different way, and exerts a sovereign force. It is enacted not by the ordinary legislative authority but by some higher and specially empowered body. When any of its provisions conflict with a provision of the ordinary law, it prevails and the ordinary law must give way.'

Bryce's alternative, the idea of a common-law constitution, is perhaps another way of saying that the British 'constitution' just grew, as the common law itself. His definition of a statutory constitution does, however, allow us to distinguish constitutional law from other law by clear criteria, thus giving the term not just a specific meaning, but a meaning with consequences. Though he, too, declared the distinction between written and unwritten constitutions old-fashioned, it is a pity that his summary has not served as a starting point for subsequent commentaries on the British 'constitution'.

Ridley argues that the classification of the UK constitution as an unwritten constitution may not be an important issue, but that the fact that the constitution does not rank higher than other forms of law is a problem, to which we shall return later on in this chapter.

However, it is possible to classify the UK constitution with the help of some general terms that explain some of its features. The UK constitution is a constitutional monarchical one, rather than a republican one, as mentioned in Chapter 2. Some people are also surprised to learn that it is also religious rather than secular, in that the **Queen** is head of the Church of England and the Church of England is the state Church. Ceremonies such as the coronation take place in Westminster Abbey, as part of this tradition, and the **monarch** must be a good standing member of the Church of England. The constitution may also be defined as one based on the principles of liberal democracy. Hopefully, the term 'democracy' is relatively self-evident, but 'liberal democracy' may not be so easily understood. This does not mean that the party in power is a party that espouses liberal politics; instead, it denotes that the constitution is founded on the principles that there should be limited **government**, according to law, which recognises and respects individual rights. The movement has its roots in the European age of Enlightenment, during which rule by monarchy according to God's law (as interpreted by the monarch) was replaced by notions of reason, the equality of all people, and the need for legitimate rulers. The UK constitution is one in which there is **universal suffrage**. The **executive** must act within the law, and it may be subject to court sanction if it does not. Individual rights are largely respected and protected within the constitution.

The UK constitution has also been called a 'unitary constitution', which is a little confusing when one considers that the UK is a union of four countries (England, Northern Ireland, Scotland, and Wales) and three legal jurisdictions (England and Wales are a single legal jurisdiction, Northern Ireland, and Scotland). The word 'unitary' relates to the fact that there is one primary source of legal power—the Westminster **Parliament**—which has ultimate **legislative** competence in relation to domestic law (leaving aside issues of EU law, for example), rather than a federal system in which there are two or more sources of independent legal power. Federal systems such as those operated in Australia, Canada, Germany, and the US are systems in which there are two distinct legal systems operating to meet different objectives—a local objective for each individual state, and a separate countrywide objective for the overarching federal system that has another type of legal power. Both are self-contained and separated sources of law and jurisdiction. Figure 3.1 provides an explanation of how a federal system operates.

Figure 3.1

Federal level

Has a legislature, an executive, and a court system to deal with federal level legal issues

Not a higher level, but free from interference by the state level

State level

| **State A** Legislature, executive, and courts | **State B** Legislature, executive, and courts | **State C** Legislature, executive, and courts | **State D** Legislature, executive, and courts |

Not a lower-level jurisdiction, but free from interference by the federal level

The difference between unitary and federal states is considered in much more detail in Chapter 10 on parliamentary supremacy and **devolution**, so we shall not consider it in much more detail here. Suffice to say, in the UK, there is only one source of legal power—the Parliament in Westminster—and there is one ultimate government and one ultimate court—the Supreme Court. It deals with disputes that arise from the devolution of power to the Scottish Parliament and the Welsh and Northern Ireland Assemblies. The Westminster Parliament may legislate on any matters and may take back the legislative power that it has delegated to Scotland, to Wales, and to Northern Ireland—at least in legal terms, even if politically that would be more difficult in some situations. Consequently, the UK does not have a federal constitution in which there are separate sources of legislative power that cannot be overridden by the state or federal-level legislatures.

NOTE In some situations, European Union (EU) law has primacy, as discussed in Chapter 8. Consequently, it might be argued that the Westminster Parliament is not the ultimate source of power.

cross reference
See Chapter 2 for more on the structure of the executive or government.

Other terms used in connection with the UK constitution are 'parliamentary executive constitution' and 'flexible constitution'. The former relates to the way in which we obtain our executive or government. Our executive is drawn out of our parliamentary personnel and so our constitution—or, more accurately, our structure—is defined as a parliamentary executive. Some countries, such as the US, elect a president and then she or he appoints the remainder of the executive. This form of constitutional settlement is referred to as a 'presidential executive' instead. In relation to the tag of flexible, as opposed to rigid, the word 'flexible' refers to how easy it is to amend the constitution. The UK constitution is relatively easy to amend by comparison with many others and, on this basis, it is termed 'flexible'. The amendment mechanism is considered in more detail later on in this chapter.

summary points

How might we classify the British constitution compared with others?

- *The UK constitution is unwritten or uncodified.*
- *It is a unitary, rather than a federal, constitution.*
- *It is a parliamentary executive, rather than a presidential executive, constitution.*
- *It is a constitutional monarchy, rather than a republican, constitution.*
- *It is religious, rather than secular.*
- *It is flexible, rather than rigid.*
- *It is a liberal democracy.*
- *It is rather unusual in terms of form by comparison to most others.*
- *In fact, some argue that it does not even exist!*

3.4 What are the sources of the British constitution?

As stated previously, the British constitution is made up of a range of sources. Some of these sources are legal, while others are non-legal; some of them are written, while others are unwritten; some are domestic and others are international. Figure 3.2 indicates the sources of the constitution and also groups them by type of source. The first oval contains sources of international and European law that have an impact on the structure of the UK and its power map. The second oval contains UK legal sources, and the third contains lower-level, non-legal sources—or rather sources that do not have the full force of law.

Figure 3.2

International/European law
Treaty provisions (*if ratified*)
Applicable EU law
Applicable international law
including ECHR

Domestic law
Acts of Parliament
Secondary legislation
Legislation from the devolved
Parliament and assemblies
Common law (*including the*
royal prerogative)

Non-legal sources
Constitutional conventions
Authoritative opinions
(*academics, practitioners,*
officials, or extrajudicial
opinion)

Judicial interpretation of all of the sources
With reference to binding precedent and persuasive authority, including case
law from other similar jurisdictions and from the EU and Council of Europe

Figure 3.3

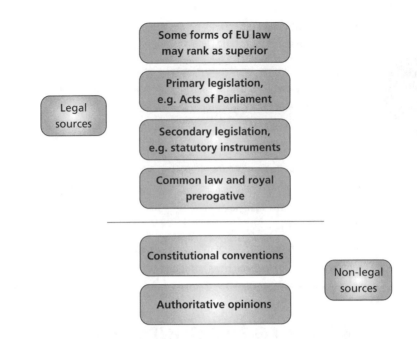

cross reference

See Chapters 8 and 9 for a discussion of dualism and parliamentary supremacy in the context of EU law and the ECHR.

thinking point

Read the definitions of 'monism' and 'dualism' in Chapter 8, and consider how you would describe the hierarchy of sources in the UK constitution.

It is not the purpose of this chapter to explain each of the sources to you: most of the sources are discussed in more detail elsewhere in the book and there is more detail on the Online Resource Centre to test your knowledge of the different sources. However, it may be helpful to provide some brief explanations here, after setting out the hierarchy of domestic sources in Figure 3.3

The highest form of domestic law in the UK constitution is Acts of Parliament, sometimes referred to as 'statutes', or 'primary legislation'. Below Acts is secondary legislation, sometimes known as 'subordinate legislation', or 'delegated legislation'. Further down still is the **royal prerogative** and the common law, which may be overriden by Acts of Parliament. Because the UK is a **dualist state**, law from the EU and international law to which the UK is a party may also have an impact on the UK's constitutional arrangements. Where this is the case, these sources also form part of the constitution to the extent that Parliament has so provided in the Act that brings these forms of law into the domestic arena. On this basis, it could be argued the EU and international law that address constitutional issues are not hierarchically superior, in strict terms, in our constitution, although there are differences of opinion on this.

The non-legal sources of the constitution are more difficult to understand, because it is hard to imagine why things that are not law can be considered to be part of something as important as a constitution. The main non-legal constitutional source is **constitutional conventions**. Constitutional conventions are non-legal rules that set out relatively stable practices that should be followed by those who have been given specific constitutional legal powers to exercise. They have developed in order to ensure that the power is used proportionately or sparingly. The British constitution gives those in executive roles, along with the monarch, extensive legal power. If you were to read the terms of the constitution without knowing about constitutional conventions, you would believe the UK to be close to a true dictatorship rather than a representative majoritarian democracy. For example, the Queen is given the legal power to assent to or to reject any Bill that has been passed by the House of Commons and the House of Lords. The royal prerogative provides her with that power. On the face of it, this suggests that the Queen has the ultimate legislative power: she may choose to say 'yes' and the Bill will become law; she may choose to say 'no' and the Bill will fall. One person would control the whole future of the country. However, there is a corresponding constitutional convention that sets out how the Queen should use her royal prerogative power. Legally, she may use it as she wishes, but the

cross reference

The royal assent is considered in detail in Chapter 6.

non-legal convention is that she will not refuse her assent (agreement) to any Bill that has been passed by the Commons and the Lords in all but the most exceptional of circumstances. The current monarch never has withheld her assent and neither has any other monarch since Queen Anne in 1708. Although they all have had the legal power to do so, they have felt bound by the constitutional convention to exercise their power according to the convention.

There is much debate about constitutional conventions, not least because they are not written down and because the courts cannot enforce them (because they are not legal sources). So why do those in power chose to abide by them? Why not simply use the legal power that they have been given if there is no legal sanction that could be used if they were to break the terms of a convention? The next extract suggests that constitutional conventions embody the UK's moral principles rather than are simply a form of political restraint on those in power. Morton argues that conventions are largely obeyed not because the political consequences of breaking them may be serious (those in power could come under sustained political pressure to resign, for example), but because conventions contain the values to which most of us subscribe and thus breaking them would mean acting against our moral code.

cross reference

Constitutional conventions are considered more in Chapter 12.

● **P. A. Morton, 'Conventions of the British constitution'** (1991–92) 15 Holdsworth Law Review 114, 125–7

Conventions as essentially principled norms are simply misrepresented in so far as they are regarded as being no more than descriptive of generally accepted political practices with a record of successful applications or precedents;[1] or as lubricants oiling the wheels of government;[2] or as being merely the flesh on the legal bones;[3] or as the rules of an ethical code for governors and politicians;[4] or as rules of political practice which are regarded as binding by those to whom they apply,[5] or as no more than the result of the gradual hardening of usages over a period of time.[6] And something is clearly lacking if their emergence and establishment is thought to be explicable, not as a commitment to a principled tradition, but by reference to a general craving of the human psyche for certainty and predictability.[7] ...But the conventions of the British constitution are something more than footpath conventions;[8] they are not merely contingently related to the moral values of a democratic tradition; they are an inextricable, strategically important, part of that tradition...And in insisting on their relation to the political and moral values of a tradition... it is to insist that this is a connection which must be made if we are, as objective observers, to understand them at all...and see why they are to be distinguished from a host of other non-legal norms in our own constitutional arrangements.

1 J. Mackintosh, *The British Cabinet* (3rd edn, London: Stevens & Sons, 1977), p. 13.

2 W. I. Jennings, *The Law and the Constitution* (5th edn, London: University of London Press, 1959), p. 136.

3 Ibid, p. 81. See also de Smith's comments that they are 'forms of political behaviour regarded as obligatory': S. A. de Smith, *Constitutional and Administrative Law* (5th edn, Harmondsworth: Penguin, 1985), p. 52.

4 E. C. S. Wade and A. W. Bradley present conventions as a subset of the non-legal norms of the constitution that regulate the conduct of those holding public office: *Constitutional and Administrative Law* (10th edn, London: Longman, 1985), p. 24. E. A. Freeman described them as 'A whole code of precepts for the guidance of public men': *Growth of the English Constitution* (London: Macmillan, 1872), p. 109, quoted in A. V. Dicey, *The Law and the Constitution* (3rd edn, London: Macmillan, 1889), p. 342.

5 O. Hood Phillips, *Constitutional and Administrative Law* (7th edn, London: Sweet & Maxwell, 1987), p. 113.

6 C. Turpin, *British Government and the Constitution* (2nd edn, London: Weidenfeld and Nicolson, 1990), p. 98.

7 H. Calvert, *An Introduction to British Constitutional Law* (London: Stevens, 1985), p. 42.

8 Statements such as that of Munro (*Studies in Constitutional Law*, London: Butterworths, 1987, p. 38)—that it is simply a natural process for the rules and practices to develop alongside the laws of the constitution—or of Griffiths—that conventions are essentially ways of carrying on business if things are not to degenerate into chaos—would be applicable to the conventions of corruption.

thinking point
Why do you think the people with constitutionally significant roles largely obey constitutional conventions? Would you do so if you were in their place? Why, or why not?

Morton suggests that constitutional conventions have developed from our views, as a nation, on what is appropriate behaviour and what is not, when it is permissible to make use of far-reaching legal powers, and when one should temper one's use of that power. Whatever the reason, constitutional conventions are an important source of the constitution, and go a long way towards explaining why the great legal power that is conferred by the constitution is not used and abused more readily by those who run the country.

summary points

What are the sources of the British constitution?

- *The British constitution is made up of a wide range of sources.*
- *Some sources are legal, such as Acts of Parliament, secondary legislation, and the common law.*
- *Some sources are international legal sources, such as EU law and the **European Convention on Human Rights (ECHR)**.*
- *Other sources are non-legal, such as constitutional conventions.*
- *Constitutional conventions cannot be enforced through the courts, but they do limit the use of legal power that has been given to those in power via the constitution.*
- *They are sometimes referred to as a political mechanism for restraining the excessive use of power.*

3.5 What is the hierarchical position of the British constitution and how is it amended?

It may perhaps be useful to set out the more usual position with respect to constitutional hierarchy before tackling the issue in relation to the UK constitution, which is more complex. When most of us think of a constitution, we think of it as the highest form of law in a country. Written constitutions are nearly always hierarchically superior to other forms of legislation. This means that all other forms of domestic law are inferior to the constitution and should abide by principles contained within the constitution. Judges within a country with such a constitution may be empowered by the constitution to check the legality of any law against the superior constitution, and if the law does not conform to the constitution, then it may be nullified (US) or declared to be unconstitutional, or referred back to the legislature for further consideration (France). This role is usually performed by a constitutional court—the Supreme Court in the US, the *Conseil Constitutionnel* ('Constitutional Council') in France, and the High Court of Australia. This suggests that the legislative body does not have legislative supremacy in all areas, because the constitution will limit the legislature's power to enact only legislation that falls within the terms of the constitution. The situation in France is, however, a little more complicated, because power rests with the legislature even if the matter is referred back for consideration by the *Conseil*. In addition, any executive Act that does not conform to the constitution may be constrained by the judiciary. In this way, there are judicial controls on the legislature and the executive, rather than political controls. However, not all written constitutions have all of these provisions and nor does the UK constitution.

We considered the sources of the UK constitution in the section above. This highest source of constitutional law is contained in Acts of Parliament. Other than *obiter* comments in *Thoburn v Sunderland City Council* [2002] 4 All ER 156, a case known as the *Metric Martyrs* case, there are no solid judicial pronouncements that suggest that there is a hierarchy within Acts of Parliament—an order of importance that would make certain types of Act superior to other types of Act. In *Thoburn*, Lord Justice Laws did indicate that he believed there to be a special form of statute—a constitutional statute—that ranks above standard statutes and which cannot be impliedly repealed. The implications of this case will be discussed later in relation to parliamentary supremacy. We also have evidence that all Acts of Parliament are viewed as of equal rank:

● **Lord Wilberforce** (Hansard, HL 53, 5 July 1966), p. 73

> In strict law there may be no difference in status...as between one Act of Parliament and another, but I confess to some reluctance in holding that an Act of such constitutional significance as the Union with Ireland Act is subject to the doctrine of implied repeal or of obsolescence.

cross reference

The Metric Martyrs case is discussed in Chapters 7 and 8.

If one follows Lord Wilberforce's reasoning, it is not possible for the UK constitution to be hierarchically superior to other forms of law, because the highest source in the constitution is an Act of Parliament and, by virtue of the doctrine of implied repeal (that is, that a later contradictory Act will replace those sections of an earlier Act that it contradicts), any later Act will repeal or amend an earlier Act. Thus the UK constitution may be amended by the passing of an Act of Parliament. There is nothing superior (other than the possibility of constitutional statutes that must be expressly repealed by Parliament) that is fixed or **entrenched** against which a court could judge an Act and rule it to be illegal and invalid.

Figure 3.4

Written constitution superior rank	UK constitution's highest source
Comparison	Act of Parliament 1 Act of Parliament 2
Lower levels of law Inferior rank Is each law consistent with the constitution? If not, then in some countries the lower law may be ruled unconstitutional, or it may be disapplied.	**Ranked equally No comparison possible** In cases of contradiction, the most recent Act is applied and the earlier one is overridden.

cross reference

The difference between parliamentary supremacy and constitutional supremacy is discussed in more detail in Chapter 9.

cross reference

See Chapter 7 for further details of parliamentary supremacy and **parliamentary privilege** *in this respect.*

Questions that are often posed in connection with the UK constitution include: how can an 'unwritten' constitution be superior to Acts of Parliament when it is made up of Acts of Parliament? And: can law be declared 'unconstitutional'? Parliamentary supremacy means that Parliament can make, amend, or repeal any law it wishes, at least in theory, assuming that the proper procedure is followed. In addition, we do not at present have a document of higher constitutional importance against which primary legislation is compared to consider whether it is constitutional in the traditional sense, because all Acts rank on the same level (as illustrated in Figure 3.4). As a result, no Act of Parliament can be declared to be unconstitutional and thus invalid, because there is nothing against which to compare an Act and judge it to be so. It is certainly true that the High Court, Court of Appeal, and Supreme Court may declare UK primary legislation to be incompatible with the ECHR, and some argue that this is a signal that it is unconstitutional. However, those courts cannot invalidate the law on that basis. Secondary legislation can be declared invalid, although not unconstitutional in the strictest sense if it does not conform to primary legislation, because secondary legislation is subordinate to primary legislation; instead, such secondary legislation will simply be invalid on the grounds that it does not conform to the relevant primary legislation.

The following extract illustrates the supremacy of Parliament and our lack of a constitution of higher standing than Acts of Parliament.

● ***Madzimbamuto v Lardner-Burke*** [1969] 1 AC 645

Lord Reid at 723:

> It is often said that it would be unconstitutional for the United Kingdom Parliament to do certain things, meaning that the moral, political and other reasons against doing them are so strong that most people would regard it as highly improper if Parliament did these things. But that does not mean that it is beyond the power of Parliament to do these things. If Parliament chose to do any of them, the courts could not hold the Act of Parliament invalid.

The UK does not currently have a constitutional court unlike many countries, and Figure 3.4 illustrates why it does not. A constitutional court is charged with interpreting the constitution, but also making sure that all aspects of the state respect the constitution, including the legislature. However, in view of the hierarchical position of the UK constitution and the fact that Parliament has legislative supremacy, the Supreme Court cannot be given that function unless the UK constitution is reformed to give it higher constitutional status than any other Act of Parliament. This would require a major reform. There have been many discussions about how the UK constitution could be reformed, and if so, what shape that reform would take. The debate includes whether a formal constitutional court should be established.

cross reference

See Chapter 14 for more on judicial review.

The fact that the UK does not have a constitutional court does not mean that it is not possible to enforce the constitution against the executive. As explained earlier, some constitutions are enforceable against the legislature (although not that of the UK, as discussed) and some against the executive. The UK's constitution is enforceable against the executive via a mechanism known as 'judicial review'. The executive must act within its legal powers; if it does not, the administrative court system may require the executive and other public bodies to act, or to cease to act, as the law dictates. As a consequence, the UK constitution is justiciable (that is, it can be enforced through the courts) as regards the executive if not the legislature.

The next extract considers the issues of justiciabilty.

• **D. Oliver, 'Written constitutions: principles and problems'** (1992) 45(2) Parliamentary
Affairs 132, 142–4

> The principal provisions of the constitutions of the USA, Germany, France and many other
> Western democracies are 'justiciable' in the sense that issues about the constitutionality or
> legality in constitutional terms of acts of state bodies can be taken to the courts, or a special
> Supreme or Constitutional Court, and adjudicated upon.
>
> …
>
> But not all provisions of Western democratic constitutions are 'justiciable' in this way. Under
> the French Fifth Republic Constitution legislation before the Parliament can be subjected to
> scrutiny by the Constitutional Council which may report to the parliament if in its view pro-
> posed legislation is 'unconstitutional'; but if the Parliament insists on passing the law despite
> such a report, there is no jurisdiction in the courts or any other body to hold it invalid. Other
> examples of 'non-justiciable' laws or actions include what in the USA are known as 'political
> questions'. In the UK certain decisions of a highly sensitive political nature in fields such as
> relations with foreign states, diplomacy, and may issues to do with national security are not
> justiciable. In the UK there is also the doctrine of parliamentary privilege which means that the
> courts will not seek to inquire into or control parliamentary procedure …

As Oliver illustrates, the UK constitution is not alone in being a constitution that is only partially justiciable: the constitutions of France and the US are also partially justiciable, although
the US Constitution does allow the Constitution to be enforced against the legislature and
the executive for matters that are not deemed to be political issues. In contrast, the French
DDHC is not justiciable against the legislature and nor is the UK constitution in relation to
primary legislation. These differences mark out different understandings or conceptions of
constitutionalism—that is, the process through which individual rights and freedoms may
be asserted against the state through the courts. One reason given for why it is undesirable
to make a constitution justiciable against a legislature is that legislatures are usually directly
elected, whereas the judiciary seldom are. Some commentators argue that if one were to
make a constitution justiciable against the legislature, then that would raise unelected judges
to a position in which they would be hierarchically superior to elected politicians, who have
been given their power and are accountable to the population. Others argue that it is safer to
make judges, rather than politicians, the guardians of our rights, even if they are not elected:
at least judges are less likely to pander to public opinion in the event of, say, a terrorist attack
and to permit citizens' human rights to be easily and quickly removed in response to a short-
term outrage.

cross reference
*Human rights will
be considered
in more detail in
Chapter 9.*

65

**summary
points**

What is the hierarchical position of the British constitution and how is it amended?

• *The UK constitution is not hierarchically superior to primary legislation.*

• *This means that Acts of Parliament cannot be compared with the constitution by judges
and be declared to be unconstitutional and invalid, even if an Act can be declared incompatible with the ECHR.*

• *The UK constitution cannot be enforced against the legislature as a result, and nor is the
UK constitution entrenched and protected, because it can always be changed by Act of
Parliament.*

• *However, the UK constitution can be legally enforced by the mechanism of judicial review
against the executive, meaning that the executive may legally act only within its legal
power.*

Proposed reforms to the British constitution

Talk of constitutional reform is not a recent phenomenon: there have been calls for constitutional reform through the centuries. However, there have been a plethora of reform proposals over recent decades, and this section will look at three from the 1990s, along with former **Prime Minister** Brown's recent proposals for reform and the present **coalition government**'s proposals. Most of the proposals take the opportunity of developing at least part of the UK constitution into a written document, even if this is only an entrenched, or semi-entrenched, bill of rights. 'Entrenched' means that the bill of rights has been constitutionally protected, usually by making it hierarchically superior to other forms of law and subject to amendment only as the culmination of an arduous process of law reform (with the use of a popular **referendum**, for example). 'Semi-entrenched' is a word used to explain that the bill of rights has some protection from amendment or repeal, albeit lesser than that given to fully entrenched provisions. Both words denote that the bill of rights cannot be amended in the same way as ordinary law. Reform proposals also address the way in which the UK is structured—whether this relates to the House of Lords, the role of the monarchy, whether we become a Commonwealth or federal system, etc. The extracts below provide a little detail on previous reform proposals before we turn to the present government's proposals.

Oliver has set out the three main proposals for reform in the 1990s. The first is known as the 'Macdonald constitution', because it was written by John MacDonald QC on behalf of the Liberal Democrats' Working Group on Constitutional Reform. It was published in 1990.

. . . .

● **D. Oliver, 'Written constitutions: principles and problems'** (1992) 45(2) Parliamentary Affairs 132, 136–7

Three Constitutions

THE MACDONALD CONSTITUTION

The first of these three constitutions to be produced . . . It has 79 articles, each very brief, and it runs to only some ten sides of A4 paper.

The principal reforms that the Macdonald Constitution includes are: the introduction of proportional representation, specifying the single-transferable vote; the replacement of the House of Lords by an elected Senate with power to delay legislation other than money bills; power in Parliament to establish and recognise Parliaments for Scotland, Wales and Northern Ireland and Assemblies for the regions of England; the incorporation of the European Convention on Human Rights as a Bill of Rights into UK law; and the creation of a Supreme Court. The constitution is entrenched by a requirement that it can only be amended by a bill passed by two-thirds majorities of the two House of Parliament sitting separately. European Community law would prevail over UK law . . .

This proposal was not simply an attempt to develop a single written constitutional text, but also to make far-reaching changes to the House of Lords, to the electoral system, to the legislative competence of Parliaments for Scotland, Wales, and Northern Ireland, and to incorporate a bill of rights. The constitution would have been hierarchically superior to all other forms of domestic law, and could have been amended only if the House of Commons and the Senate (the replacement for the House of Lords) were to vote in favour of any amendment with a two-thirds majority. A new Supreme Court would have been created to ensure that the constitution was respected. This would have brought the UK constitution much closer to a more generally accepted written constitution of the type that we have considered elsewhere in this chapter.

The second constitutional proposal in the 1990s was Tony Benn's Commonwealth of Britain Bill in 1991. It was much lengthier than the previous constitution and, as you will see from the extract below, it is far more radical than the Macdonald proposal, including a great many proposals to change the structure of the UK.

● **D. Oliver, 'Written constitutions: principles and problems'** (1992) 45(2) Parliamentary Affairs 132, 137–8

TONY BENN'S CONSTITUTION

...

Under this constitution, the United Kingdom would become a Commonwealth. The monarchy as head of state would be replaced by a President elected by a two-thirds majority of the Houses of the Commonwealth parliament sitting together, for a three-year term, renewable once; the royal prerogative powers would be transferred to the President who is to act on the advice of the Prime Minister or on a resolution of the Commons. Certain civil, political, social and economic 'rights' are entrenched, but they are only enforceable by pressure from a Human Rights Commissioner and judicial review of an administrative act of the executive. The House of Lords would be replaced by a second chamber or 'House of the People' elected so as to represent England, Scotland and Wales (not Northern Ireland) in proportion to their populations. This House may delay legislation for one year and statutory instruments for one month.

...

The Prime Minister is to be elected by the House of Commons and should present the government to the House of Commons for approval before he or she takes office. There is provision for all official information to be published, subject to specific exceptions. The powers of the House of Commons in relation to European matters are enhanced. Appointments to the High Court are subject to confirmation by a select committee of the House of Commons. Magistrates are to be elected for four year terms. There would be national Parliaments for England, Scotland and Wales, with legislative powers in all matters save defence, foreign affairs and Commonwealth finance. However, the Commonwealth parliament would have power to legislate on all matters and its legislation would prevail over inconsistent legislation passed by the national parliaments...The jurisdiction of Britain in Northern Ireland would cease two years after the passage of the Bill. Any amendment to the constitution must have the agreement of both House of the Commonwealth Parliament and is subject to approval by a referendum.

Under the terms of this constitution, the monarchy would be replaced by an elected president who would be the head of state in place of the Queen. Great Britain would become a commonwealth (a form of federation) like Australia, so England, Scotland, and Wales would have legislative power, and the Commonwealth would have a separate overarching legislative jurisdiction for the Union (similar to the illustration in Figure 3.1). Tony Benn drafted the constitution in such a way that Northern Ireland would cease to be part of the Union. The proposals also envisaged major constitutional reforms—not least a change in the way in which the Prime Minister and executive were appointed, fixed terms for the Commons, and changes to the House of Lords to become the 'House of the People'. More importantly for the purposes of our present discussion, the constitution could be amended only with the agreement of Parliament and also the people via a referendum. This would mean that the voting population would be asked to vote 'yes' or 'no' in favour of any change, and that the constitution could not be altered unless a majority of the voting population were to vote in favour. Benn made provision for a form of bill of rights, although the Supreme Court would not have been a full constitutional court in the traditional sense. His proposals were extremely radical in some senses and yet relatively conservative in others.

The third proposal is that which was drafted by the Institute for Public Policy Research (IPPR), a think tank that has been linked to the Labour Party. This text was published in 1991 as the 'Constitution of the United Kingdom' and, at 125 pages containing 129 articles, it is longer than the Macdonald constitution, but shorter than the text developed by Tony Benn.

● **D. Oliver, 'Written constitutions: principles and problems'** (1992) 45(2) Parliamentary Affairs 132, 138

THE IPPR CONSTITUTION

...

The constitution retains the monarchy but removes most of its power...It contains a Bill of Rights which consists of a combination of the European Convention on Human Rights and the International Covenant of Civil and Political Rights. The constitution establishes the Parliament of the United Kingdom and Assemblies for Scotland, Wales, Northern Ireland and the regions of England. The Prime Minister is to be elected by the House of Commons. Individual ministerial responsibility is spelt out in the constitution as a duty. A Code of Conduct for Ministers...is to be laid before Parliament. An Integrity Commission will investigate any alleged breach of the Code of Conduct. A Constitution Commission of the two houses is established to keep under review the working of the constitution and to prepare guidelines and Codes of Conduct for holders of public offices...The assemblies have powers, some of which Parliament also has and can use concurrently if appropriate. In the event of conflict, Parliament will normally prevail if the matter is within its jurisdiction. The House of Commons is to be elected by the Additional Members system and the Second Chamber by STV [single transferable vote]. The Assemblies have wide legislative powers...There is to be a Minister of Justice, a Judicial Services Commission and a Supreme or Constitutional Court. There is provision for entrenchment of the provisions of the constitution by a variety of methods. The general requirement is a two-thirds majority of both Houses of Parliament; in some instances two-thirds of those present and voting, if that is not less than half of all members, is sufficient. Where the Assemblies are affected, the ratification of two-thirds of the Assemblies is required.

This text would also make a number of constitutional changes, including to the nature of the Union between the four countries that make up the UK and to the electoral system. It would strengthen Parliament and increase oversight of the executive. This text includes a bill of rights, which incorporates the rights from the ECHR (now incorporated into UK law via the Human Rights Act 1998) and the UN International Covenant of Civil and Political Rights (UN ICCPR) to which the UK is a signatory. Certain parts of the constitution, including the bill of rights, would be entrenched, while others would not, and there would be different ways of amending the constitution depending on whether the provision was deemed to be extremely important—in which case, it would be more difficult to amend the constitution than currently—or relatively routine—in which case, the mechanism for amendment would be less onerous. In short, it attempts to blend the benefits of a flexible constitution along with the certainty and protection of a more rigid one. In addition, it provides for a constitutional court, as did the Macdonald constitution.

None of these three texts was taken forward by the Conservative government of the day, although calls for constitutional reform persisted. That is not to say that there has not been extensive constitutional reform, however, since the Labour Party swept into power in 1997 with a large majority in the Commons and manifesto commitments to constitutional reform. Since 1997, we have seen reform of the House of Lords, devolution (following referenda in three of the four nations), elected mayors in some cities, and the Constitutional Reform Act 2005, including the new Supreme Court. But a written constitution was not one of the Labour Party's manifesto commitments. The Human Rights Act 1998 was passed, which did introduce a quasi-bill of rights into the domestic legal system, but not in a form that meant that it had overriding authority over other forms of legislation. Citizens cannot enforce this against the legislature and the Supreme Court cannot hold UK primary legislation to be invalid because it breaches the rights contained in the ECHR, which the Human Rights Act 1998 incorporated. Consequently, it appeared that the impetus towards a written constitution had dissolved.

However, when Gordon Brown became Prime Minister, he made a number of announcements that suggested that he would like to see changes made to the UK constitutional framework, including the inclusion of a limited 'written' element. His statement to Parliament on constitutional reform on 3 July 2007 appeared to indicate that the former Prime Minister wished that the UK adopt a bill of rights, with the potential implication that this would override law that was inconsistent with the bill of rights (otherwise it is hard to see how this differs from the current arrangements through the Human Rights Act 1998), or would further the possibility of a written constitution. However, later statements suggested otherwise. These proposals were not included in the Constitutional Renewal Bill, although the Bill did address many of the other reforms set out in the speech, such as reform of the office of the Attorney General, pre-scrutiny hearings by parliamentary committees for certain public appointments, civil service reform, reform of certain parts of the royal prerogative, and yet more changes to the judicial appointments system.

cross reference

The proposed British bill of rights is discussed in more detail in Chapter 9.

However, the coalition government is now considering the introduction of a British bill of rights.

. . . .

● **HM Government, *The Coalition: Our Programme for Government*** (London: HMSO, May 2010) available online at http://www.direct.gov.uk/prod_consum_dg/groups/dg_ digitalassets/@dg/@en/documents/digitalasset/dg_187876.pdf

...

3. CIVIL LIBERTIES

We will be strong in defence of freedom. The Government believes that the British state has become too authoritarian, and that over the past decade it has abused and eroded fundamental human freedoms and historic civil liberties. We need to restore the rights of individuals in the face of encroaching state power, in keeping with Britain's tradition of freedom and fairness.

...

We will establish a Commission to investigate the creation of a British Bill of Rights that incorporates and builds on all our obligations under the European Convention on Human Rights, ensures that these rights continue to be enshrined in British law, and protects and extends British liberties. We will seek to promote a better understanding of the true scope of these obligations and liberties.

...

The Commission and its work will be considered in more detail in Chapter 9 when we examine human rights issues. The Commission has yet to report on its findings and thus it is difficult to know the kind of document that is being envisaged. The coalition's proposals appear to indicate that the UK will retain parliamentary supremacy rather than move in the direction of a full written constitution, even given the proposal that we may introduce a British bill of rights.

It may help to consider how a more traditional written constitution would change the UK's constitutional landscape. University College London's Constitution Unit explains the pros and cons of a move to a written constitution in this country.

● R. Hazell, with contributions from M. Glover, A. Paun, and M. Russell, *Towards a New Constitutional Settlement: An Agenda for Gordon Brown's First 100 Days and Beyond* (London: The Constitution Unit University College London, 2007), pp. 12–15

3.1 The Argument for a Written Constitution

The main argument for a written constitution is one of political literacy: to make it clear what the constitution is, and to educate the public by setting out the constitution in a relatively short and simple document. It would provide an organisation chart of the main institutions of the British state, the relationships between them, and the rights of its citizens. It would lay to rest the common error that the UK does not have a constitution, just because it is not brought together in a single codified document.

If the main purpose is political literacy, there are short written guides to the UK constitution already available...

3.2 The Politics of a Written Constitution

The potential political difficulties of embarking on a written constitution include the following.

3.2.1 No Strong Public Demand

When asked if they want a written constitution, the public say that they do by majorities of around 80 per cent (State of the Nation poll 2004 Q2). But the question is a typical 'cost-free' polling question, all upside and no downside. Nor does the question provide any guide to the salience of the issue. Philip Gould's polls for the Labour party which asked voters to rank issues in order of importance regularly found that the constitution came bottom in voters' order of priorities.

3.2.2 Stronger Judiciary and Weaker Parliament

If it is entrenched..., a written constitution inevitably goes with a stronger judiciary to interpret that constitution. In essence, power is taken away from Parliament. Constitutions circumscribe majoritarian democracy because they create rules to constrain political majorities. MPs who are asked to vote for a written constitution will be aware that they are reducing their own power.

3.2.3 Approval by Referendum

New constitutions are generally submitted to the public for approval in a referendum. Approval cannot be taken for granted. If turnout is low this can threaten the legitimacy of the new constitution. Rejection would be devastating for the project and for the government which initiated it. So the reservations of critics and opponents must be taken seriously from the start: if they are ignored they can come back with a vengeance later in the process.

3.2.4 Reaching Consensus

Reaching agreement on defining the present constitution would not be easy, even amongst a group of experts. There are intrinsically subjective and difficult decisions to be made in deciding what belongs in the constitution and what does not. The difficulties in agreeing a constitution are spelt out below.

3.3 Difficulties in Agreeing a Written Constitution

Drafting a written constitution would require agreement on the following:

3.3.1 Scope and Length

What is to be included and excluded? In the absence of a written constitution, there is no agreed boundary of what is 'constitutional' and what is not. Should the electoral system be defined in the constitution? Should the national flag? Most written constitutions define the flag, but not the electoral system. But the electoral system is vastly more important in determining the nature of the political system.[1]

A related issue is the tension between brevity and detail. For political literacy, a short and simple constitution is much better. But the shorter the document, the greater the scope for interpretation by the courts.

3.3.2 Descriptive or Prescriptive

Is this to be a purely descriptive exercise, defining the constitution as it is; or prescriptive, defining the constitution as people would wish it to be? Most drafters will not be able to resist glosses or small improvements to the constitution as they write it down. Once you allow some improvements it is hard to draw the line...

3.3.3 Entrenchment and Amendment

Entrenchment would involve giving the constitution superior legal status and priority over ordinary legislation. A fully entrenched constitution would become the fundamental source of legal authority in the state, superseding the traditional doctrine of the sovereignty of Parliament. If that was too radical a step, qualified entrenchment could create an elevated status in law for the constitution, while allowing Parliament to legislate in contradiction to the constitution if it expressly chose to do so. The constitution would contain a declaration of primacy over other law, as in the European Communities Act 1972 or the Human Rights Act 1998; but much would depend on how the courts chose to interpret the status of the new constitution in relation to other Acts of Parliament...

A related question is whether the constitution should lay down some special legislative process to govern future amendments. This could take the form of special majorities (such as two thirds) in both Houses of Parliament, and/or a requirement for a referendum, which could apply to all of the constitution, or just certain key provisions.

3.4 Options Short of a Written Constitution

3.4.1 A Statement of Principles

This could help to fill the gap, by explaining the fundamental principles on which the British constitution is based. But it would encounter some of the same difficulties as a written constitution... But the more detail that was applied to give the principles some context and meaning (eg in providing a statement of rights and responsibilities), the closer the exercise would come to drafting a written constitution.

...

[1] A. King, *Does the United Kingdom Still Have a Constitution?* (Hamlyn Lectures, London: Sweet & Maxwell, 2001).

It may be that the move towards a written constitution would be less profound than would be adopting an entrenched bill of rights, along with a constitutional court to enforce the change. The real issue is the extent to which the courts may prevent law from coming into force or from continued operation because it breaches the terms of a constitution. It will be interesting to see whether the current proposals for reform are implemented, unlike those earlier in this section.

summary points

Proposed reforms to the British constitution

- *There have been a number of recent proposals for reform of the form, as well as the substance, of the UK constitution.*

- *The Macdonald Constitution, Tony Benn's Commonwealth of Britain Bill, and the IPPR's Constitution of the United Kingdom have all included proposals that were picked up by the previous Labour government in some form and have come into force, even if the UK has yet to adopt a written constitution.*

- *The Coalition Agreement of the present government contains a number of constitutional reform proposals, including a commission to examine a British bill of rights.*

- *The substance of the reforms is likely to have more far-reaching consequences than merely the form that any new constitution takes.*

Summary

A constitution sets out the framework of the state and the institutions of the state, and sets out the power and the limits on state power. It also provides legitimacy for the state in its exercise of power and the way in which individuals may seek recourse if the state acts beyond its power. Constitutions often contain a bill of rights, which provides protection to citizens or subjects. Constitutions come in many shapes and sizes, and may be classified in different ways: written or unwritten/uncodified; unitary or federal; parliamentary executive or presidential executive; rigid or flexible. The UK constitution is an uncodified, unitary, parliamentary-executive, flexible constitution. It is made up of a range of sources: some are domestic legal sources, while others are international or European sources; some are legal, while others are non-legal, including constitutional conventions. The UK constitution is not hierarchically superior to other forms of law, because it is made up of all forms of law. Consequently, the Supreme Court has no power to declare primary legislation to be unconstitutional, in the traditional sense, in contrast to some other countries' constitutional provisions. The UK constitution continues to be the subject of much reform speculation.

Questions

1   In no more than 150 words, explain the purpose of a constitution.

2   List the ways in which a constitution may be classified and define what each of the terms means.

3   To what extent is it more accurate to describe a constitution as the founding document of the state than as the principles and laws that underpin and legitimise the state?

4   To what extent do you agree that the mode of the constitution is less important than its content?

5   To what extent do political and legal mechanisms to enforce constitutions differ? Which do you consider to be more effective and why?

6   Explain the main proposals for reform of the British constitution since 1990. What difference, if any, do you think each of these would make in real terms?

Further reading

Brown, G., 'Speech on Liberty and Constitutional Reform' (University of Westminster, 25 October 2007), available online at http://webarchive.nationalarchives.gov.uk/+/number10.gov.uk/page13630

You may wish to read through the speech to review the extent to which the former government's vision of constitutional reform (as set out by the then Prime Minister) was achieved.

HM Government, *The Coalition: Our Programme for Government* (London: HMSO, May 2010) available online at http://www.direct.gov.uk/prod_consum_dg/groups/dg_digitalassets/@dg/@ en/documents/digitalasset/dg_187876.pdf

You may wish to read through the coalition agreement and consider the extent to which it is fulfilling its promises for government. You will note the extensive constitutional reform agenda set out in the document.

Wheare, K. C., 'Does it really exist? Some reflections upon the contemporary British constitution' (1978) 31(2) Parliamentary Affairs 213

This article is now relatively dated in some respects, but it is a classic that sets out some of the theoretical, as well as practical, issues associated with the British constitution. It is also useful to read to see how far the British constitution has evolved since the 1970s.

It is also worth reading many of the sources of the extracts that have been set out in this chapter. References are provided so that you may find them easily either via GoogleScholar or through your university library catalogue or database (in most instances).

The Rule of Law

4

Key points

This chapter will cover:

- What is the rule of law and what is its significance?
- What is the history of the rule of law?
- What are the main similarities between different theories of the rule of law?
- What are the main differences between different theories of the rule of law?
- How have recent legal reforms affected the operation of the rule of law in the UK?
- How have the courts interpreted the rule of law?
- What is the relevance of the rule of law today?

Introduction

This chapter considers the differing theories and meanings of the rule of law, and how the rule of law functions in the UK. It will also consider the extent to which recent legislative reforms have affected the nature and extent of the rule of law in the UK constitution. The case extracts and other materials found in this chapter illustrate the main theories, and provide evidence of the context and also of recent reforms. The chapter will conclude with a series of questions that should test whether you have understood this topic and have evidence to back up the points that you would make in answer to questions on this area.

4.1 What is the rule of law and what is its significance?

The **rule of law** is a theory or a doctrine that describes the extent to which certain features are present within a country, or legal system. T. R. S. Allan has explained it as follows.

• T. R. S. Allan, Law, *Liberty, and Justice: The Legal Foundations of British Constitutionalism* (Oxford: Oxford University Press, 1995), p. 143

> In the mouth of a British constitutional lawyer, the term the rule of law seems to mean primarily a corpus of basic principles and values, which together lend some stability and coherence to the legal order.

There is a difference of opinion about what those basic principles and values are, although many theorists agree on a core set of principles that ought to be present before it may be claimed that a **state** is based on the rule of law. This core relates to how the law is made and applied within the state. A smaller group of theorists argue that the content of the law must also meet some basic minimum standards for the rule of law to be present in a meaningful way.

The rule of law explains the legitimacy of law, and why law should be applied and upheld. It provides at least some answers to the following questions.

• Why should individuals abide by the law when some laws appear to be against their interests, and in some instances also against their view of what is right and what is wrong?

• Why should the state be permitted, via the courts, to punish wrongdoers and why are individuals not permitted to set up lynch mobs to punish people suspected of terrible crimes?

• Why do the courts have the power to adjudicate in disputes between individuals and between companies?

• Why are people entitled to go to court to enforce their legal rights against the **executive** and **public authorities**?

The rule of law is the explanation for why the law is treated as legitimate, and thus why it overrides personal and other interests. It reinforces to those in power that they too are subject to legal restraint. It reminds the executive that it may act only if it has the legal power to do so and that its actions are subject to **judicial** review to examine whether they are legal. And if the actions are illegal, the courts have the power to require the executive to act within the law. The rule of law is, above all, the guarantee to everyone living in a state based upon it that people and organisations may not act illegally with impunity, and that those who have done no wrong should not be punished by the state. It prohibits arbitrary **government** by preventing the law from being used as a tool with which to reward supporters and to punish lawful opposition. It provides legitimacy for state action, but at the same time limits the power of officials to that which is provided by law or other legal norms. In short, it limits the excessive and arbitrary use of power. That is why some argue that the rule of law means 'government under the law', because the government is subject to the law. Dicey summed it up as follows.

● **A. V. Dicey, *The Law of the Constitution*** (9th edn, London: Macmillan, 1959), p. 194

> ...every official from the Prime Minister down to a constable or collector of taxes, is under the same responsibility for every act done without legal justification as any other citizen. The Reports abound with cases in which officials have been brought before the courts, and made, in their personal capacity, liable to punishment, or to the payment of damages, for acts done in their official character but in excess of their lawful authority...And all subordinates, through carrying out the commands of their official superiors, are as responsible for any act which the law does not authorise as is any private and unofficial person.

We have evidence for this within the UK legal system. In the case of *M v Home Office* [1994] 1 AC 377, the Home Secretary was held to be legally accountable for the actions of his department when the Court found that the minister had acted contrary to a court order. The Court went a stage further to explain that a government minister may even be held to be personally liable for his own actions even if they were actions performed as part of his office. This case is discussed in more detail in section 4.6, which addresses how the courts have interpreted the rule of the law. It is evidence for Dicey's point that the rule of law means that government must be performed according to the law.

The rule of law is not an absolute standard. It exists to a greater or lesser extent within all countries rather than being something that a country either has or has not. As Finnis has written, the term 'the rule of law' is:

● **J. Finnis, *Natural Law and Natural Rights*** (Oxford: Oxford University Press, 1980), p. 270

> ...the name commonly given to the state of affairs in which a legal system is legally in good shape.

The strength or weakness of the rule of law may also vary over time within any given state. Just because a country appears to have a strong commitment to the rule of law does not mean that it cannot be eroded through **legislative** changes or the actions of those in positions of authority. It should not be taken for granted, as evidenced by Germany under Nazi rule in the early to mid twentieth century, or currently in Zimbabwe and Iraq, for example.

There are two main schools of thought as regards the rule of law, although this oversimplifies the similarities and the differences between different theories. In general terms, **the formal school** describes a state as abiding by the rule of law if:

1 the law is made by a predetermined procedure;

2 the law is clear, stable, and certain (it is not changing so frequently that it is impossible to know what is the applicable law);

3 no one is punished by the state other than for a breach of the law; and

4 the law is applied equally to all regardless of their status.

This is the traditional view of the rule of law. It is perhaps useful to consider this school as largely procedural—because the procedure through which the law is made and the way in which it is applied determines the extent to which the rule of law is respected.

The substantive school considers that the formal conditions must have been met (the proper procedure has been followed to enact the law and that the law is applied equally to all, including to those in power—similar to the formal school). But, in addition, the content or substance of the law must meet certain conditions. For some substantive theory commentators, the condition is that the law must uphold human rights. For other substantive-rule-of-law theorists, it is that the law is moral. The substantive theory consequently builds on the formal school, rather than directly contradicts it. The differences have been explained as follows.

● **P. Craig, 'Formal and substantive conceptions of the rule of law: an analytical framework'** [1997] Public Law 467, 467

> Those who espouse substantive conceptions of the rule of law seek to go beyond this. They accept that the rule of law has the formal attributes mentioned above, but they wish to take the doctrine further.

The similarities and differences between different understandings of the rule of law will be considered later in more detail.

summary points

What is the rule of law and what is its significance?

- *It is a theory or doctrine that is open to numerous different interpretations.*
- *The rule of law is founded on the principle that the law is above all, and consequently that all people within the state are subject to the law regardless of their rank, financial status, gender, or race.*
- *It is the explanation for why the law should be respected: all are subject to the law, and the law is of higher authority than the authority of any person.*
- *It is the basis of legal justice, because legal justice may be achieved only if all are legally accountable for their actions and no one may be punished unless he or she has broken the law.*
- *It provides a mechanism for law to be enacted and implemented equally in the state.*
- *It provides legitimacy to the legal system.*
- *It provides legitimacy to law itself.*
- *There are broadly two main schools of thought on the rule of law: the formal school, which is the traditional school; and the substantive school, which builds upon the formal school.*
- *The formal school considers the way in which the law is enacted, its stability, its clarity, and its non-arbitrary application to all people as being the essential features of a state that is governed by the rule of law.*
- *The substantive school also looks to the content of the law, including the extent to which the law furthers conceptions of morality and/or human rights, when judging the extent to which the rule of law applies in a state.*
- *For those who believe that the rule of law dictates that the content of law must comply with minimum standards of morality and human rights, it also provides a guarantee that the content of the law is moral and/or humane.*

4.2 What is the history of the rule of law?

Much of the literature on the rule of law begins with its relatively recent history; however, the rule of law has much more distant roots. It was discussed by the Ancient Greeks in the fourth century BC by Plato, who sought to determine the most effective way in which to govern a state so as to promote a model society. He pondered whether the rule of good men was preferable to rule through law. His preference was the rule by good men, assuming that good men could be found, as the means to instil altruism into the population. However, in the absence of that, then rule by law was preferable to other forms of governance. Aristotle took this further, considering that rule by law was probably the better of the two options, because it is difficult to ensure that rule by men will lead to virtue. Aristotle believed that society as a whole, and individuals in particular, could be shaped through law, which would then create a virtuous society. Plato stated in *The Laws* that the law would act as a constraint on government, as well as on judges, who would have to decide cases according to the law. However, the Platonic and Aristotelian theories of the rule of law later gave way to an understanding that the **monarch** ruled by divine right—in other words, that the King had the right to rule, because he had been chosen by God for this purpose. This placed the King above the law, because it was believed that the King was divinely authorised. Therefore Plato and Aristotle's conceptions of the rule of law lost some of their potency.

. . . .

● D. Clark, 'The many meanings of the rule of law', in K. Jayasuriya (ed.) *Law, Capitalism and Power in Asia: The Rule of Law and Legal Institutions* (London: Routledge, 1999), p. 25

... [Y]et the view took hold in the late Roman period that the Prince was above the law,[1] though by the Christian era he might be subordinate to God, but not to other men. In other words, laws existed to order and regulate human affairs and to allow citizens to make choices or face punishments for transgressions. There was little indication until the medieval period that kings should be subordinate to the law, and even when this was suggested, there was little said about what institutional arrangements might be appropriate to achieve this.[2] In fact, the impulse to obey the law was said to come only from the monarch's sense of moral obligation; for no man, and certainly no judge, could enforce this.[3] In short, despite doctrinal assertion that the king was subject to the law[4] and the argument that no Prince should rule without laws,[5] the translation of this idea into an institutional arrangement whereby it may actually be enforceable took several centuries, during which there were notable reverses of course, and also powerful voices opposed to limit a sovereign, particularly a monarch, by law.[6]

1 A. Wallace-Hadrill, '*Civilis princeps*: between citizen and king' (1982) 72 Journal of Roman Studies 32, 39; G. Post, 'Bracton on kingship' (1968) 42 Tulane Law Review 519, 520.

2 C, J. Nederman, 'Bracton on kingship revisited' (1984) 5(1) History of Political Thought 61.

3 Ibid, at 63.

4 For a review of these doctrines, see C. C. Weston, 'English constitutional theories from Sir John Fortescue to Sir John Eliot' (1960) 75 English Historical Review 410.

5 H. J. Berman, *Law and Revolution* (Cambridge, MA: Harvard University Press, 1983), pp. 292–4; Marsilius of Padua, *Defensor Pacis*, trans. A. Gewirth (New York: Harper Collins, 1967).

6 Thomas Hobbes, *Leviathan*, ed. C. B. MacPherson (Harmondsworth: Penguin, 1968), p. 232.

Clark's article mentions that the path to the institutionalisation of the rule of law in many countries has not been linear—that the rule of law advanced and then at times was weakened. This has certainly been true in UK history. The rule of law was asserted in Magna Carta in 1215, which enshrined the principle that even the King was not above the law. Magna Carta came about after a period of domestic unrest, in part caused by the King's focus on foreign war and his need to raise taxes to finance the war with France. Some of the barons demanded that King John accept the charter (Magna Carta), which they had drafted with the aid of the Church, drawing upon the documents of previous kings who had ruled in England. During the period of civil war, the barons seized London in mid 1215. The King entered into negotiations with the barons via the Archbishop of Canterbury at Runneymede, the result of which was a peace treaty between the two sides that later became known as Magna Carta. The King subsequently sought to have the document annulled by the Pope on the basis that divine rule put the King above man-made laws, to which request the Pope agreed. The result was further civil war; thus Magna Carta was in force only briefly before it appeared to have been set aside. However, the King died suddenly in 1216 and the nobles reissued the document, with further amendments. Magna Carta was accepted as law in 1225 when it was reissued, although the final version to which we refer today dates from 1297. The following extract from Magna Carta sets out the provisions that are particularly relevant to the development of the rule of law.

Magna Carta 1215

...

38. No bailiff, on his own simple assertion, shall henceforth put any one to his law, without producing faithful witnesses in evidence.

39. No freeman shall be taken, or imprisoned, or disseized, or outlawed, or exiled, or in any way harmed—nor will we go upon or send upon him—save by the lawful judgment of his peers or by the law of the land.

40. To none will we sell, to none deny or delay, right or justice.

...

45. We will not make men justices, constables, sheriffs, or bailiffs unless they are such as know the law of the realm, and are minded to observe it rightly.

...

52. If any one shall be been disseized by us, or removed, without a legal sentence of his peers, from his lands, castles, liberties or lawful right, we shall straightaway restore them to him. And if a dispute shall arise concerning this matter it shall be settled according to the judgment of the twenty-five barons who are mentioned below as sureties for the peace...

...

55. All fines imposed by us unjustly and contrary to the law of the land, and all amerciments made unjustly and contrary to the law of the land, shall be altogether remitted, or it shall be done with regard to them according to the judgment of the twenty-five barons mentioned below as sureties for the peace...

...

60. Moreover all the subjects of our realm, clergy as well as laity, shall, as far as pertains to them, observe, with regard to their vassals, all these aforesaid customs and liberties which we have decreed shall, as afar as pertains to us, be observed in our realm with regard to our own.

Magna Carta provided that the law must be respected by law enforcement officials—the justices, the bailiffs, and the sheriffs, which were the magistrates and the police of their day. It was made clear that justice must be done, rather than bought and sold. It provided that no freeman (a particular and relatively small section of society rather than the whole population) should be imprisoned without trial or fined unless he had broken the law. Finally, it stated that all subjects were to have the freedom of liberty. Magna Carta is a landmark legal document that places the law above the King. It appears, therefore, that the rule of law was clearly established in England in 1215, even though, by modern standards, it was largely unenforceable and not all of the chapters (some refer to them as 'articles') applied equally to all subjects. Three of the chapters remain in force in England and Wales today: the first, which confirms the rights and liberties of subjects; the ninth, which confirms the liberties of the City of London; and the twenty-ninth, which states that there should be no imprisonment without trial, as well as includes the most famous phrase associated with Magna Carta—'To none will we sell, to none deny or delay, right or justice'. The remainder of the chapters were repealed between the early nineteenth and mid twentieth centuries, to be replaced by more recent legal guarantees.

As Clark's article suggested, the development of the rule of law did not stop here; nor were its principles consistently accepted and applied. The Petition of Right, enacted four centuries after Magna Carta, would have been largely unnecessary if the rule of law, as described in Magna Carta, had been enforced. Indeed, in the case entitled *Prohibitions del Roy* (1607, published 1656 (1572–1616) 12 Co Rep 63), Sir Edward Coke diplomatically, but firmly, asserted that the King could not act as a judge using his own reason to reach decisions, but instead that cases were to be tried by legally knowledgeable judges who were to apply to law rather than common reason in order to determine the decision in the case. Instead, the barons in the 1600s were forced to issue a petition to the King to demand that martial law (a form of military rule) be suspended, and that civilian law and standards of justice be applied throughout the country. They reminded the King of promises made in Magna Carta (the Great Charter of the Liberties of England) by earlier monarchs, including: the right for a citizen not to be punished, including imprisoned, unless it is demonstrated that he or she has broken the law; the right for a citizen to know the charge against him or her; and the right to a fair trial to determine guilt, which includes the right to be presumed innocent until proven guilty (that is, the right not to be 'fore-judged', as it is termed in the Petition).

Petition of Right, 1628

. . . .

To the King's Most Excellent Majesty . . .

. . .

III. And whereas also by the statute classed 'The Great Charter of the Liberties of England', it is declared and enacted, that no freeman may be take or imprisoned or be disseized of his freehold or liberties, or his free customs, or be outlawed or exiled, or in any manner destroyed, but by the lawful judgment of his peers, or by due process of law.

IV. And in the eight-and twenty-year of the reign of King Edward III it was declared and enacted by authority of parliament, that no man, of what estate or condition that he be, should be put out of his land or tenements, nor taken, nor imprisoned, nor disinherited nor put to death without being brought to answer by due process of law.

V. Nevertheless, against the tenor of the said statutes, and other good laws and statutes of your realm . . . , divers of your subjects have of late been imprisoned without any cause showed; and when for their deliverance they were brought before your justices by your Majesty's writs of habeas corpus, there to undergo and receive as the court should order, . . . no cause was certified, but [except] that they were detained by your Majesty's special command, . . . and yet were returned back to several prisons, without being charged with anything to which they might make answer according to the law.

VII. And whereas also by authority of parliament, in the five-and-twentieth year of the reign of Kind Edward III, it is declared and enacted, that no man shall be forejudged of life or limb against the form of the Great Charter and the law of the land; and…no man ought to be adjudged to death but by the laws established in this your realm…and whereas no offender of what kind soever is exempted from the proceedings to be used, and punishments to be inflicted by the laws and statues of this your realm; nevertheless…certain persons have been assigned and appointed commissioners with power and authority to proceed within the land, according to the justice of martial law…to proceed to the trial and condemnation of such offenders, and them to cause to be executed and put to death according to the law martial.

NOTE To learn more about Magna Carta, visit the Magna Carta Trust online at http://www. magnacartatrust. org.uk/

Interestingly, as Lord Bingham—former **Lord Chief Justice**, then Senior Law Lord—has commented, many of the provisions that the barons claim were made in Magna Carta were not mentioned in the earlier document even though they have long been implied into the terms of the charter. They may be part of the spirit of Magna Carta, but the goals of the thirteenth-century law were more modest than has later been suggested. Indeed, the Petition of Rights was far more extensive in providing for the rule of law and due proess rights even if it suggests that the petition is merely restating rights that had already been accepted in England.

● **Lord Chief Justice Lord Bingham (1996), cited in St Edmundsbury Borough Council (undated) 'Magna Carta in modern times',** available online at http://www.stedmundsbury. gov.uk/sebc/visit/mcartamodern.cfm

…
Historically the constitutional significance of Magna Carta has depended much less on what the charter said, than on what it was thought to have said. What it was thought to have said was the subject of constant development, with the aid of some statutory reinforcement, over succeeding centuries. It was this process which led to the English Bill of Rights, the heavy reliance placed on Magna Carta by the American colonies with their battles with the Crown, the constitution of the United States and, more recently, the constitution of the Republic of India.

Indeed, the famous right of **habeas corpus** (considered to be an essential feature of the rule of law) was not explicitly mentioned in Magna Carta and was the subject of much subsequent legislation, but did not mature in legal terms until after the Petition of Right. The Act was required because the King had asserted his right to answer the court's request by stating that the prisoner was held at his command, without presenting the prisoner or providing other legal justification for the prisoner's detention. This circumvented clause 39 of Magna Carta, which provided that no one should be punished or detained except by law, and thus offended under one of the fundamental principles of the rule of law.

habeas corpus

Latin meaning 'let you have the body', habeas corpus is a legal action by writ to ask the court to order that a detainee be brought before the court so that the court can determine whether his or her detention is lawful and consequently whether the prisoner must be released.

Habeas Corpus Act 1679

An act for the better securing the liberty of the subject, and for prevention of imprisonments beyond the seas.

What is the history of the rule of law?

81

Whereas great delays have been used by sheriffs, gaolers and other officers, to whose custody, any of the King's subjects have been committed for criminal or supposed criminal matters, in making returns of writs of habeas corpus to them directed, by standing out an alias and pluries habeas corpus, and sometimes more, and by other shifts to avoid their yielding obedience to such writs, contrary to their duty and the known laws of the land, whereby many of the King's subjects have been and hereafter may be long detained in prison, in such cases where by law they are bailable, to their great charges and vexation.

II. For the prevention whereof, and the more speedy relief of all persons imprisoned for any such criminal or supposed criminal matters;

...

(2) be it enacted...That whensoever any person or persons shall bring any *habeas corpus* directed unto any sheriff or sheriffs, gaoler, minister or other person whatsoever, for any person in his or their custody, and the said writ shall be served upon the said officer...that the said officer...or their under-officers...shall within three days after the service...(unless the commitment aforesaid were for treason or felony, plainly and specially expressed in the warrant of commitment) [longer periods in other listed circumstances such as if the prisoner was being held a long way away] upon payment...of the charges of bringing the said prisoner, to be ascertained by the judge or court...and upon security given by his own bond to pay the charges of carrying back the prisoner, if he shall be remanded by the court or judge...and that he will not make any escape by the way, make return of such writ;

(3) and bring or cause to be brought the body of the party so committed or restrained, unto or before the lord chancellor, or lord keeper of the great seal of *England*...or the judges or barons of the said court...

(4) and shall then likewise certify the true causes of his detainer or imprisonment...

The principle remained that a detainee was entitled to be brought before a court to have his or her detention subject to judicial, and thus legal, scrutiny. This is the principle that was invoked by campaigners who were concerned about the detention without trial of terrorist suspects for up to twenty-eight days (although judicial **permission** is required for a suspect to be detained for this period and that may not always be forthcoming).The maximum period of pre-charge detention has recently be lowered to fourteen days. It is also one of the principles referred to by campaigners against the continued detention of prisoners in Guantanamo Bay without full judicial oversight, because they believe that continued detention without trial (a non-military tribunal) offends against the rule of law. The Habeas Corpus Act 1679 re-established the authority of the court even over the will of the King and gave all persons the opportunity to have the legality of their detention determined by a judge. Later statutory provisions, such as the Bill of Rights 1689, strengthened the role of the courts in determining the legality of the actions of the executive, as did numerous judicial pronouncements and judge-made rules, such as the rules of **natural justice**. However, judges did not have security of tenure (and thus a degree of employment protection) until the Act of Settlement, and security of tenure is considered to be one of the essential safeguards for an independent **judiciary**.

cross reference
See Chapter 20 for a discussion of the law in this area, as well as of legal challenges to detention without trial.

Bill of Rights 1689

...

And thereupon the said Lords Spiritual and Temporal and Commons...Do in the first place (as their ancestors in like case have usually done) for the vindicating and asserting their ancient rights and liberties declare:

> That the pretended power of suspending the laws or the execution of laws by regal authority without consent of Parliament is illegal;
>
> That the pretended power of dispensing with laws or the execution of laws by regal authority, as it hath been assumed and exercised of late, is illegal;
>
> That the commission for erecting the late Court of Commissioners for Ecclesiastical Causes, and all other commissions and courts of like nature, are illegal and pernicious;
>
> ...
>
> That it is the right of the subjects to petition the king, and all commitments and prosecutions for such petitioning are illegal;
>
> ...
>
> That excessive bail ought not to be required, nor excessive fines imposed, nor cruel and unusual punishments inflicted;
>
> ...
>
> That all grants and promises of fines and forfeitures of particular persons before conviction are illegal and void;
>
> ...

The Bill of Rights went a stage further than previous legislation. It spelled out that: law could not be made, repealed, or suspended without the consent of **Parliament**; the court system could not be manipulated by the **Crown**; subjects could bring an action against the King; and the courts and the King could not circumvent the requirements of habeas corpus by setting excessively high bail or fines, or by resorting to cruel or unusual punishment of those who have been found guilty. Finally, it reiterated that subjects could not be punished unless they had been convicted. In short, it set out the procedures through which law must be made and applied, and the basic and fundamental principles that determine the operation of the rule of law.

The concept of the rule of law remained vaguely defined. Although the procedures were delineated, a number of important questions still remained. The writings of theorists and scholars from the late nineteenth century onwards went some way towards explaining both the underpinning of the doctrine and also some of the points of detail.

One of the scholars credited with being at the forefront of developing the doctrine of the rule of law in the UK is A. V. Dicey, who enumerated its essential features. Although Dicey's theory of the rule of law was criticised by Jennings on the basis that it represented only 'his [Dicey's] own subjective notions', Jennings and other theorists have frequently used Dicey's theory as the basis of their own critique. Dicey's theory became the basis of the rule-of-law discussion in British legal theory and is often used as the starting point for a modern definition of the rule of law today. As Lord Bingham commented:

● **Lord Bingham of Cornhill, 'Dicey revisited'** [2002] Public Law 39, 50

> ...whether as the late Professor Lawson wrote, Dicey 'coined' the phrase 'the Rule of Law'[1] or whether he merely popularised it,[2] he was effectively responsible for ensuring that no discussion of modern democratic government can properly omit reference to it.
>
> 1 F. H. Lawson *The Oxford Law School 1850–1965* (Oxford: Clarendon Press, 1968), p. 72.
>
> 2 H. W. Arandt, 'The origin of Dicey's concept of the rule of law' (1957) 31 Australian Law Journal 117: 'I am not myself aware that anyone before Dicey used the expression "the rule of law", although the meaning he gave to it was not itself novel.'

The final principal part of the rule of law jigsaw came much later, when the courts held that the exercise of the **royal prerogative** is capable of judicial review. It was well established that the exercise of statutory power—one of two strands of legal power—was capable of judicial oversight and review; however, the executive's exercise of the royal prerogative was considered to be exempt from full legal scrutiny. Lord Denning commented *obiter* in the case of *Laker Airways Ltd v Department for Trade* [1977] QB 643 that he did not see any reason why the exercise of the royal prerogative should not be reviewed by the courts in a similar way to the exercise of statutory power; however, it was later in the case of *Council of Civil Service Unions and others v Minister for the Civil Service* [1985] AC 374 that this principle was finally settled by the courts. Subsequently, actions, omissions, and decisions by the executive and other public bodies have been susceptible to judicial review, regardless of the source of the power relied upon. Consequently, the courts now have full oversight of the exercise of all power, regardless of its source, thus ensuring that the executive and all public bodies are acting in accordance with the law. There are, however, areas of the royal prerogative that are not considered to be justiciable, such as the grant of honours. These are discussed further in Chapter 6.

summary points

What is the history of the rule of law?

- *Discussions about the rule of law versus the rule of man date back many centuries.*
- *They are embedded in the search for legitimacy for rules and for systems of governance.*
- *Once attained, the rule of law may be weakened or strengthened over time. Its development is rarely linear within a state.*
- *The rule of law appeared in England through Magna Carta, which enshrined the principle that even the ruler—the King—was subject to the law and legal restraint. It was, however, many centuries before the principle became fully embedded in the legal system.*
- *The rule of law was subsequently dismissed, but then strengthened over the intervening centuries, until it became largely accepted that even those in power were also subject to the law.*
- *The courts established full oversight through judicial review of the royal prerogative, which was the final main strand of power that had not been subject to scrutiny by the courts, in 1984 in the Council of Civil Service Unions case. This firmly established that the legality of all executive action may be examined by the courts.*

4.3 What are the main similarities between different theories of the rule of law?

Dicey set out a series of principles that he believed were essential for the rule of law to be present in a state. The principles may be summarised as:

- 'no person may be punished by the state except for a breach of the law'—sometimes cited in Latin as *nulla poeana sine lege*;
- the law should not be applied arbitrarily or retrospectively;
- the law should be made according to established procedure; and
- cases involving the state as a party should be heard in the ordinary courts rather than specialist administrative courts.

Other commentators have criticised some of these principles or added to them.

● **A. V. Dicey,** *Introduction to the Study of the Law of the Constitution* [5th edn, London: Macmillan, 1897), pp. 179, 185, and 187

> We mean, in the first place, that no man is punishable or can be lawfully made to suffer in body or goods except for a distinct breach of the law established in the ordinary legal manner before the ordinary Courts of the land.
>
> ...
>
> We mean in the second place, when we speak of the 'rule of law' as a characteristic of our country, not only that with us no man is above the law, but [what is a different thing) that here every man, whatever be his rank or condition, is subject to the ordinary law of the realm and amenable to the jurisdiction of the ordinary tribunals.
>
> ...
>
> We may say that the constitution is pervaded by the rule of law on the ground that the general principles of the constitution [as for example the right to personal liberty, or the right of public meeting) are with us as the result of judicial decisions determining the rights of private persons in particular cases before the Courts; whereas under many foreign constitutions the security (such as it is) given to the rights of individuals results, or appears to result, from the general principles of the constitution.

In the later tenth edition, Dicey summed this up even more clearly.

● **A. V. Dicey,** *Introduction to the Study of the Law of the Constitution* [10th edn, London: Macmillan & Co, 1959), pp. 202–3

> It means, in the first place, the absolute supremacy or predominance of regular law as opposed to the influence of arbitrary power ... Englishmen are ruled by the law, and by the law alone; a man may with us be punished for a breach of the law, but he can be punished for nothing else. It means, again, equality before the law or the equal subjection of all classes to the ordinary law of the land administered by the ordinary law courts; the 'rule of law' in this sense excludes the idea of any exemption of officials or others from the duty of obedience to the law which governs other citizens or from the jurisdiction of the ordinary tribunals.

We shall consider each of these propositions in turn, briefly.

4.3.1 No one may be punished by the state except for a breach of the law

Dicey believed that no one should be subject to criminal or civil penalty unless he or she had been convicted of an offence through a court process. This has been discussed in detail in the previous section and is considered to be the cornerstone of the doctrine of the rule of law. It is widely accepted in democratic nationals that actively seek to abide by the rule of law.

4.3.2 Government under the law: equality before the law

Secondly, Dicey stated that no one is above the law, because the law is supreme even over government, creating equality before the law. Linked to this, the law should not be arbitrary—that is, the law should not be applied in differing ways to different people. Most theorists also accept that the rule of law requires the law to be applied equally to all. F. A. von Hayek would argue that this does not mean that it is not possible to enact law that differentiates between different groups in society: those who have broken the law may be imprisoned (assuming that there has been a fair trial and that imprisonment is the sentence for the particular type of crime, etc.); those who have not may not.

· ·

● **F. von Hayek, *The Road to Serfdom*** (Chicago, IL: University of Chicago Press, 1944), p. 42

> Stripped of all technicalities this means that government in all its actions is bound by rules fixed and announced beforehand—rules which make it possible to foresee with fair certainty how the authority will use its coercive powers in given circumstances and to plan one's individual affairs on the basis of this knowledge.

It means that no one is exempt from the law. Some students find this concept difficult, pointing to members of Parliament (MPs) and commenting that MPs are treated differently from others in the UK in that they are permitted to vote on new legislation, whereas the rest of the population is not. This is not evidence of unequal treatment, however, because MPs have been elected to perform that task in an official capacity as our representatives. However, if the police were not to take action against MPs or officials whom they found to be acting illegally, then that would be evidence of one group being above the law. Officials should be—and have been—subject to police investigation after a serious allegation of criminal wrongdoing has been made against them. It has previously been alleged that some officials may have given preferential treatment for recommendations for honours to donors of large sums of money to political parties, which allegations were investigated and arrests made (although no charges were brought). Even more recently, a small number of (former) MPs and also peers have been convicted of offences relating to their parliamentary expense claims. Both of these examples demonstrate that investigations are conducted against those in positions of power, who are not exempt from the reach of the law, and that in some instances they have not only been charged and tried, but also convicted and imprisoned. This would tend to indicate that all are subject to the law.

cross reference
See Chapter 7 for more detail about the expenses scandal.

4.3.3 Individuals' rights are protected through the ordinary law and the ordinary court system

Thirdly, and most controversially, Dicey wrote that the rights and protections for individuals are contained in the ordinary law of the land, judged by ordinary courts. This is a difficult feature to understand. What Dicey meant was that rights' protection against the state is afforded by the common law, which is developed and applied by judges through the same courts as all other forms of law. Dicey believed that it was important that cases involving the state as a party were heard by the same judges, using similar modes of interpretation, as those that were between individuals and companies. He did not consider that a separate system of administrative justice, as is employed in France, afforded adequate protection to the rule of law. This part of his theory has been criticised by many theorists, including Sir Ivor Jennings, who considered that Dicey's third principle of the rule of law was more a reflection of his bias for the British system than it was a necessary condition for the rule of law to flourish. Lord Bingham, while noting the criticism particularly in respect of Dicey's knowledge of the French system of *droit administratif*, explains that Dicey's third principle has some merit.

● **Lord Bingham of Cornhill, 'Dicey revisited'** [2002] Public Law 39, 51

> I would myself view with suspicion any body outside the province of the ordinary courts, deciding rights between the citizen and the state in any of its manifestations, unless the lawfulness of its decisions were reviewable by the ordinary courts.

Jennings considered that Dicey had not addressed the issue of wide discretionary powers that were used by government and which may offend against the **injunction** against arbitrary exercise of power. He did, however, agree with much of Dicey's conception of the rule of law.

4.3.4 Legal certainty and non-retrospectivity

Most theorists agree with Jennings that the rule of law requires that there must be a relatively stable system in place that allows for legislative reform—in other words, that there must be a system for making law, repealing law, and amending law, and that the system must be followed. If the system in place were that a parliament must vote on all propositions of law, but if instead the president or the monarch were to announce new 'law' without a vote in parliament, and if the law were then applied by the police and the security forces in the country, this would be evidence that the rule of law was not being respected in that country.

Another reason why it is important to have a stable system of laws is that the law must be relatively constant so as to allow the population the opportunity to know the law. This does not mean that everyone has to be aware of every law, nor that the law cannot be changed; instead, it means that it must be possible for individuals to know the law and to decide whether to act in accordance with the law, or to break the law. It is very difficult to respect the law in a country in which behaviour that is legal one day is made illegal without warning the next day. As Lord Diplock commented:

● *Black-Clawson International Ltd v Papierwerke Waldhof-Aschaffenberg AG* [1975] AC 591

Lord Diplock at 638:

> The acceptance of the rule of law as a constitutional principle requires that a citizen, before committing himself to any course of action, should be able to know in advance what are the legal consequences that will flow from it.

Frequent changes mean that even law-abiding citizens may inadvertently find themselves breaking the law. This has the consequence of bringing the law into disrepute, because either many law-abiding citizens will find themselves being punished for actions they did not know to be wrong, or the law will be incapable of application because the law-enforcement officials will not be able to know and apply the law in an effective manner. Retrospective laws are also considered to offend against the rule of law because laws that are backdated may lead to people being punished for breaking a law that did not exist at the time that they acted. Consequently, retrospective laws—in particular, retrospective criminal laws—have the effect of punishing lawful rather than unlawful behaviour.

4.3.5 Fair hearing by an independent judiciary

Finally, to ensure the legality of action and equality before the law, most commentators believe that a prerequisite for the rule of law is an independent judiciary that employs a system of fair hearings to review the operation of the law. This has been discussed in the previous section, which considered the history of the rule of law, and will be discussed in a later section that provides evidence of how the courts have interpreted the rule of law.

The key common features of the doctrine have been developed and are effectively summarised by Joseph Raz, as follows.

● **J. Raz, 'The rule of law and its virtue'** (1977) 93 Law Quarterly Review 195, 198–201

> 1. All laws should be prospective, open, and clear; 2. Laws should be relatively stable; 3. The making of particular laws ... must be guided by open, stable, clear, and general rules; 4. The independence of the judiciary must be guaranteed; 5. The principles of natural justice must be observed (i.e., open and fair hearing and absence of bias); 6. The courts should have review powers ... to ensure conformity to the rule of law; 7. The courts should be easily accessible; and 8. The discretion of crime preventing agencies should not be allowed to pervert the law.

In summary, Raz considers that the rule of law requires that the law be made according to the proper procedure and that procedure should be open, stable, and clear. The law itself should be available to be known by the public and should be clear. The law should also be relatively stable, meaning that it should not be in a state of such constant change that individuals may inadvertently break the law owing to frequent amendments about which they are unlikely to have been in a position to know. Judges must be independent from the other branches of the state and other outside interests, beccause they are the guarantors of the rule of law. The principles of natural justice are designed to permit fair hearings and trials, and the courts' review powers permit the courts to review the legality of the executive's actions, and the proper application of the law. T. R. S. Allan (1999: 223) goes a stage further to suggest that the rule of law 'encompasses principles of procedural fairness and legality, equality and proportionality', which the courts should oversee. Raz further explains that individuals must be able to bring cases before the courts to allow for judicial review. Finally, Raz believes that the police and other law enforcement agencies must act within the law, which forms part of the requirement that all are subject to the law.

Fuller (1969) also provides an efficiency model of the rule of law, by stating in his book *The Morality of Law* (see the 'Further reading' listed at the end of the chapter) that eight principles must be met in order for a legal system to function according to the rule of law:

1 there should be law to govern action, and law should be obeyed by all, including officials;

2 the laws must be published so that they are capable of being known;

3 the laws must have prospective and not retrospective effect;

4 the law should be clear so that it can be applied fairly;

5 laws should be free of contradictions;

6 it must be possible for the people to fulfil the terms of the law rather than for it to make impossible demands on them;

7 law should remain relatively stable over time, although revised when required; and

8 officials should act in accordance with the law.

These look very similar to many of the elements outlined by Raz in his assessment. However, while many scholars agree on these features of the rule of law, there are also differences in view. These are discussed in more detail below.

summary points

What are the main similarities between different theories of the rule of law?

- *Law must be enacted according to the proper procedure and, once enacted, it must be available to the public rather than secret.*

- *The law must be clear and precise.*

- *The law must be relatively stable, so that it can become known.*

- *The law must be applied equally to all—no one is above and beyond the reach of the law, including the officers of the state and state institutions.*

- *An individual should not be punished by the state except for a breach of the law, and even then only as a result of a finding against him or her by a court. This principle is usually interpreted to mean that indefinite detention without trial (as opposed to being held on remand, or being kept for a finite defined period for the purpose of answering police questions) offends against the rule of law.*

- *Legal disputes and the interpretation of the law should be decided by independent judges.*

- *Many commentators also argue that implied in the notion of the rule of law is that everyone with a legal dispute should have access to the courts.*

- *Linked to equal access to the courts is the view that trials must be conducted according to the principles of natural justice to ensure fair trials.*

4.4

What are the main differences between different theories of the rule of law?

The main differences between commentators on the rule of law relate to the substance of the law rather than the principles set out above. Some scholars have implied a number of other features within the concept of the rule of law: for example T. R. S. Allan adds substantive features to Dicey's formal conception—namely, that the law should promote the common good. Lord Woolf argues that the rule of law implies some form of basic minimum standards of human rights. All of these are disputed by Raz.

● **J. Raz, 'The rule of law and its virtue'** [1977] 93 Law Quarterly Review 195, 211

> The rule of law is a political ideal which a legal system may lack or may possess to a greater or lesser degree. That much is common ground. It is also to be insisted that the rule of law is just one of the virtues which a legal system may possess and by which it is to be judged. It is not to be confused with democracy, justice, equality (before the law or otherwise), human rights of any kind or respect for persons or the dignity of man. A non-democratic legal system, based on the denial of human rights, on extensive poverty, on racial segregation, sexual inequalities, and religious persecution may... conform to the requirements of the rule of law...

Raz rejects the notion that the system of law must be based on morality in order for the legal system to be based on the rule of law. He also rejects the belief that the law should promote and serve the interests of all who are subject to it, and that the rule of law implies a notion of basic human rights. Finally, he makes it clear that the rule of law is a constitutional principle that is part of the legal order, rather than a political principle that demands adherence to democratic principles or certain forms of political ideology. We shall consider each of these issues in turn, in brief.

4.4.1 The law should promote the common good

T. R. S. Allan believes that the rule of law demands that the state must be able to justify the law and its actions towards individuals based on principles of the common good. Barber sets out Allan's position very clearly.

● **N. W. Barber, 'Must legalistic conceptions of the rule of law have a social dimension?'** (2004) 17(4) Ratio Juris 474, 481–2

Non-legalistic conceptions of the rule of law include rights which are not directly related to the structure of law or the processes of the legal system…Perhaps the broadest example of a non-legalistic conception of the rule of law was advanced by the International Congress of Jurists in 1959: This understanding incorporated social, political, and economic rights.[1] More modestly, T.R.S. Allan has claimed that the core of the rule of law is a demand that the state be able to justify its treatment of individuals by reference to the common good.[2] The common good includes 'the basic liberties of thought, speech, conscience and association', coupled with broader considerations of equal dignity, fair treatment, and respect for citizens.[3] Allan's rule of law purports to be a principle implicit in all common law legal systems that judges may invoke to strike down government, and even legislative, action.[4] Similar modes of the rule of law have proved attractive to members of the British judiciary: both Sir John Laws and Lord Woolf have conjured wide conceptions of the rule of law.[5] Allan's conception of the rule of law demonstrates the potential breadth of non-legalist conceptions; conceptions that amount to strong theories of how the state is required to treat its citizens.

1 J. Raz, 'The rule of law and its virtue', in J. Raz *The Authority of Law* (Oxford: Oxford University Press, 1979), pp. 210–29, at 211; N. Marsh, 'The rule of law as a supra-national concept', in A. G. Guest (ed.) *Oxford Essays in Jurisprudence* (Oxford: Oxford University Press, 1961), pp. 223–64.

2 T. R. S. Allan, *Constitutional Justice* (Oxford: Oxford University Press, 2001); critique in T. Poole, 'Dogmatic liberalism? T. R. S. Allan and the common law constitution' [2002] 65 Modern Law Review 463, and P. P. Craig, 'Constitutional foundations, the rule of law and supremacy' [2003] Public Law 92.

3 Allan, n. 2, p. 2.

4 Ibid, pp. 4–5; M. Loughlin, *Public Law and Political Theory* (Oxford: Oxford University Press, 1992), pp. 149–50.

5 J. Laws, 'The constitution, morals and rights' [1996] Public Law 622; H. Woolf, 'Droit public: English style' [1995] Public Law 56; critiqued by J. A. G. Griffith, 'The brave new world of Sir John Laws' [2000] 63 Modern Law Review 159.

Allan's view rests on the assumption that the freedoms of thought, expression (speech), conscience, and association are so fundamental to law that without them it could not be argued that there is rule by law. He has argued that these are prerequisites for the rule of law.

4.4.2 The rule of law implies basic human rights

Both Lords Woolf and Bingham go a stage further than Allan in their assertion that at least a minimum standard of human rights' protection is implied in the rule of law. Lord Woolf addresses the issue by stating that were Parliament to enact legislation that was so unthinkable in its denial of human rights, then the courts may be forced to disapply that particular law to protect the whole system of law and rule by law in the country. Although he considers this to be contrary to the general norms of both the **separation of powers** and democratic systems, he believes that this may be the only way in which the legal system can retain legitimacy and be in a position to enforce all of the other laws in existence.

● **Sir Harry Woolf, 'Droit public: English style'** [1995] Public Law 56, 69

> If Parliament did the unthinkable, then I would say that the courts would also be required to act in a manner which would be without precedent. Some judges might chose to do so by saying that it was an unrebuttable presumption that Parliament could never intend such a result. I myself consider that there were advantages in making it clear that ultimately there are even limits on the supremacy of Parliament which it is the courts' inalienable responsibility to identify and uphold. They are limits of the most modest dimensions which I believe any democrat would accept. They are no more than necessary to enable to rule of law to be preserved.

Lord Bingham agrees with Lord Woolf that human rights form part of the rule-of-law doctrine, but again finds it difficult to define what the human rights are in concrete terms. He recognises that human rights instruments are separate legal documents, and that even internationally negotiated human rights conventions and treaties also suffer from a lack of agreement about what the rights mean in real terms. This makes it difficult to pinpoint the rights that are essential for the rule of law to flourish.

● **Lord Bingham of Cornhill, 'The Rule of Law'** (The Sixth Sir David Williams Lecture Centre for Public Law, 16 November 2006, Cambridge), pp. 17–21

> I turn to my fourth sub-rule, which is that the law must afford adequate protection of fundamental human rights. This would not be universally accepted as embraced within the rule of law. Dicey, it has been argued, gave no such substantive content to his rule of law concept. Professor Raz has written:
>
> > 'A non-democratic legal system, based on the denial of human rights, on extensive poverty, on racial segregation, sexual inequalities, and racial persecution may, in principle, conform to the requirements of the rule of law better than any of the legal systems of the more enlightened Western democracies...It will be an immeasurably worse legal system, but it will excel in one respect: in its conformity to the rule of law...The law may...institute slavery without violating the rule of law.
>
> On the other hand, as Geoffrey Marshall has pointed out, chapters V to XII of Dicey's Introduction to the Law of the Constitution in which he discusses what would now be called civil liberties, appear within part II of the book entitled 'The Rule of Law', and, as Marshall observes, 'the reader could be forgiven for thinking that Dicey intended them to form part of an account of what the rule of law meant for Englishmen'. The preamble to the Universal Declaration of Human Rights 1948 recites that 'it is essential, if man is not to be compelled to have recourse, as a last resort, to rebellion against tyranny and oppression, that human rights should be protected by the rule of law'. The European Court of Human Rights has referred to 'the notion of the rule of law from which the whole Convention draws its inspiration'. The European Commission has consistently treated democratisation, the rule of law, respect for human rights and good governance as inseparably interlinked.

While, therefore, I recognise the logical force of Professor Raz's contention, I would not myself accept it. A state which savagely repressed or persecuted sections of its people could not in my view be regarded as observing the rule of law, even if the transport of the persecuted minority to the concentration camp or the compulsory exposure of female children on the mountainside were the subject of detailed laws duly enacted and scrupulously observed. So to hold would, I think, be to strip the existing constitutional principle affirmed by section 1 of the 2005 [Constitutional Reform] Act of much of its virtue and infringe the fundamental compact which, as I shall suggest at the end, underpins the rule of law. But this is a difficult area, for I would agree with Professor Jowell that the rule of law

> 'does not, for example, address the full range of freedoms protected by bills of rights in other countries or in international instruments of human rights, or those now protected by our recently enacted Human Rights Act 1998, as set out in the European Convention on Human Rights (such as the right not to suffer torture, or the right to freedom of expression or rights of privacy or sexual freedom).'

There is not, after all, a standard of human rights universally agreed even among civilised nations. We may regret the United States' failure to ratify the UN Convention on the Rights of the Child 1989, which forbids the imposition of capital punishment for offences committed by persons under 18, and the Supreme Court's decision upholding the imposition of capital punishment for a murder committed at the age of 16½, but accession to any international convention is a matter of national choice, and different countries take different views on the morality as well as the efficacy of the death penalty. It is open to a state to acknowledge, as some have, that a penalty is cruel and unusual treatment or punishment within the meaning of its Constitution, and nonetheless to assert that it is authorised by that Constitution as lawful. There is, I would accept, an element of vagueness about the content of this sub-rule, since the outer edges of fundamental human rights are not clear-cut. But within a given state there will ordinarily be a measure of agreement on where the lines are to be drawn, and in the last resort (subject in this country to statute) the courts are there to draw them. The rule of law must, surely, require legal protection of such human rights as, within that society, are seen as fundamental.

NOTE

For the full text of Lord Bingham's speech, visit the University of Cambridge Centre for Public Law online at http://www.cpl.law.cam.ac.uk/past_activities/the_rule_of_law_text_transcript.php

Lord Bingham's discussion highlights the difficulty that all commentators have in defining the substantive norms that the rule of law requires. Formal school scholars argue that the great strength of their conception is that it provides certainty, and a set of basic principles for the state to follow and for citizens to enforce. However, substantive school scholars argue that the formal school is too limited to be of use in the face of a regime that is prepared to pass legislation that is contrary to basic dignity and rights. Without a minimum standard of rights protection, the rule of law may prove relatively useless against a determined executive.

summary points

What are the main differences between different theories of the rule of law?

- *Some commentators believe that the system of law must be based on morality; if the system is not based on morality, then the system is not a legal system in the true sense of the word.*
- *Some believe that the law should promote and serve the interests of all who are subject to it, and thus this implies a notion of basic human rights.*

- *Some believe that the state must be run along democratic principles and that certain liberal conditions must be evidenced in the country in order for the rule of law to be strong.*

- *Some scholars do not believe that any of these conditions need to be met as long as the system of governance and of law and order meet the conditions set out by the formal school.*

- *Judicial opinion is also divided on this issue.*

4.5 How have recent legal reforms affected the operation of the rule of law in the UK?

The rule of law requires that no person may be punished expect for a breach of the law. Reforms such as the introduction of antisocial behaviour orders (ASBOs) fall into a difficult legal grey area in this regard, because they are civil actions that may lead on to criminal sanctions without the need for a full criminal trial with its related standards of procedure and evidence. A civil court may make an order to require an individual to stop acting in a way that it is claimed is antisocial, but is nonetheless lawful. A breach of this court order is, however, unlawful and may lead to imprisonment. But there is no list of antisocial behaviour that an individual may consult to examine whether actions that he or she is considering may be subject to an ASBO. A person may be subject to an order banning him or her from behaving in certain ways, even though his or her behaviour is lawful, but for the order that bans him or her from doing it. Some would consider that this offends against a traditional view of the rule of law. Others would argue that it is unlikely that a case would go to court prior to some form of warning from the police or other agency, and that this would give the individual the opportunity to change his or her behaviour prior to a case proceeding to court. This may mean that the individual has been made aware that the behaviour is unacceptable and has had notice that legal action may be taken to prevent him or her from pursuing it (similar to in a criminal matter). And if this were argued, then the rule of law may not have been breached by this reform.

Other reforms, such as the extension of detention without trial (discussed previously), also concern some commentators. However, one reform that has been aimed at strengthening the rule of law is the Constitutional Reform Act 2005, which reinforces the importance of the independence of the judiciary and puts measures in place to attempt to strengthen the separation of the courts from the other arms of the state—principally, the executive. This is explained in detail in Chapter 5, which considers the separation of powers.

summary points

How have recent legal reforms affected the operation of the rule of law in the UK?

- *The use of ill-defined civil measures, such as antisocial behaviour orders (ASBOs), which may lead to a criminal sanction has provoked some criticism that punishment without a breach of the law (other than a breach of a court order) may offend against (at least conservative) notions of the rule of law. Supporters claim that it would be highly unlikely that an individual would be imprisoned unless he or she had repeatedly broken court orders and thus had been made aware that his or her behaviour was unlawful. Opponents consider that ASBOs take the legal system in a dangerous direction.*

- *Detention without trial for up to twenty-eight days has also been criticised on similar grounds (it currently stands at fourteen days in the UK), although again there is judicial oversight of this in the UK, even if not in all countries.*
- *The Constitutional Reform Act 2005 reinforces the independence of the judiciary, particularly from the reach of executive influence.*

4.6 How have the courts interpreted the rule of law?

The courts have had many opportunities to consider the operation of the rule of law in cases that have involved individuals taking action against the executive or a public body. Any case in which a court rules on the legality of the actions of the executive and other public bodies is evidence of the rule of law in operation, because those cases apply the principle of equality before the law. Cases that consider the certainty of the law, and whether it has retrospective effect, are also evidence of the application of the rule of law, beccause they apply the principles of certainty, the prospectivity of the law, and no punishment without a breach of the law. This section considers judicial interpretation of the rule of law through a selection of cases that have examined the legality, the **irrationality**, or the **procedural impropriety** of the actions of the executive or public bodies, or whether their actions conform to the Human Rights Act 1998.

4.6.1 No one may be punished by the state except for a breach of the law

Punishment without trial is an extremely topical issue and has been brought back into the spotlight as a result of recent anti-terror legislation in the UK. One of the recent and important cases in this field is the case of *A and others v Secretary of State for the Home Department* [2004] UKHL 56. The appellants in this case were foreign nationals who had all been certified by the Home Secretary under section 21 of the Anti-Terrorism, Crime and Security Act 2001 (now repealed), and were thus being detained without trial on grounds that they were suspected of involvement in terrorist activity and were alleged to be a danger to the public. All were free to leave the country, but the appellants claimed that they could not return to their country of origin, because they had a well-founded fear of persecution if they were to do so—and there was even the possibly that they may be killed. If they were to remain in the UK, then, under the terms of the 2001 Act and the Home Secretary's certification, they would be detained without trial for an indefinite period. They brought an action to challenge the legality of their detention. This judgment illustrates that indefinite detention without trial in all but the most exceptional of circumstances is considered by the House of Lords (now the Supreme Court) to offend against the rule of law, as evidenced Lord Nicholls's statement.

● ***A and others v Secretary of State for the Home Department*** [2004] UKHL 56

Lord Bingham of Cornhill:

> [3] The appellants share certain common characteristics which are central to their appeals. All are foreign (non-United Kingdom) nationals. None has been the subject of any criminal charge.

> In none of their cases is a criminal trial in prospect. All challenge the lawfulness of their detention...They duty of the House, and the only duty of the House in its judicial capacity, is to decide whether the appellants' legal challenge is soundly based.
>
> [38] ...Judicial control of interferences by the executive with the individual's right to liberty is an essential feature of the guarantee embodied in article 5[3], which is intended to minimise the risk of arbitrariness and to ensure the rule of law.

Lord Nicholls of Birkenhead:

> [74] My Lords, indefinite imprisonment without charge or trial is anathema in any country which observes the rule of law. It deprives the detained person of the protection a criminal trial is intended to afford. Wholly exceptional circumstances must exist before this extreme step can be justified.

The case addressed a number of issues, not least the fact that the UK had sought to derogate from the **European Convention on Human Rights (ECHR)** under Article 15. This will not be discussed here, but instead in Chapter 9. In relation to the current point, although the Law Lords did not rule that indefinite detention without trial was always illegal, they did note that the circumstances required to justify had to be utterly exceptional. In this instance, the House of Lords ruled that the fact that the measures differentiated between non-UK citizens (the appellants) and UK citizens, who could not be detained in this way under the terms of the legislation, was discriminatory and therefore unjustifiable. It was this ground, rather than arguments related to the rule of law, which led the government to introduce a Bill to amend this legislation and to end this practice. This is discussed in greater detail in Chapter 20.

4.6.2 Government under the law: equality before the law

A case from the eighteenth century that is often cited to provide evidence that even the government is subject to the law and to the authority of the courts is the case of *Entick v Carrington* (1765) 19 State Tr 1029. This case involved the King's men entering Mr Entick's premises without his permission, searching his home, and seizing documents that were considered to constitute a seditious libel. The defendants claimed that they were acting under the terms of a warrant issued by the Secretary of State through the power of the Constables Protection Act 1750, and that this had been common practice since the Glorious Revolution. However, the court held that only a justice of the peace had the power to issue a warrant and not the Secretary of State. The court also found that the grounds for issuing a warrant were not present. Consequently the search was illegal, as was the seizure of property, which had been undertaken as the result of a trespass. The court reiterated that even state officials needed to have the legal power to act and must abide by the law.

A more recent case that is often cited in support of the operation of the rule of law in the UK is *M v Home Office and another* [1994] 1 AC 337, HL. It is used as evidence for the proposition that government ministers are also subject to the law and to the operation of court orders—government under the law. M was a citizen of Zaire, who sought political asylum in the UK in 1990. His claim was rejected, as was his application for **leave** (permission) to apply for judicial review of that decision. M was informed that he would be deported on 1 May 1991 and his legal team immediately made an application to the Court of Appeal. This application was rejected and M immediately appointed new solicitors, who issued another application for leave based on new grounds. The High Court judge wanted time in which to consider the application and thus asked for M's deportation to be postponed. Garland J believed that counsel for the Home Secretary had given an undertaking (a form of promise made between legal professionals) that M would not be removed from the country pending consideration of the application. However, counsel for the Secretary of State did not have the authority to give that undertaking and nor were they aware that they had. In the meantime, M was on a plane bound for Zaire, via Paris. The judge was informed of the situation on the evening of 1 May and made an interim order for the return of M. Officials from the Home Office made arrangements for the return of M, and informed the Secretary of State of the situation on the afternoon of 2 May, whereupon he cancelled the return arrangements, because he believed that he had acted legally in ordering the deportation of M. The Secretary of State was also of the opinion, as was his legal team, that the judge did not have the legal power to make an interim order against a minister of the Crown. On 3 May, the judge set aside the interim order. M's counsel instituted legal proceedings against the Secretary of State, in part seeking the return of M. The judge held that the Crown was immune from injunctions, and also that ministers of the Crown and their officials could not be held in contempt of court for actions that they performed as part of their duties. The judge consequently dismissed the proceedings. The legal team appealed. On appeal, it was held that whilst a government department does not have a legal personality and so cannot be held to be in contempt of court, ministers and officials do have legal personality and can be held in contempt for actions that they have undertaken. In this instance, there had been a genuine misunderstanding, and consequently even though the Home Secretary was held to be in contempt of court, no penalty other than the finding of contempt was to be imposed. The House of Lords stated as follows.

● *M v Home Office and another* [1994] 1 AC 337, HL

Lord Templeman at 395:

My Lords, Parliament makes the law, the executive carry the law into effect and the judiciary enforce the law. The expression 'the Crown' has two meanings; namely the monarch and the executive. In the 17th century Parliament established its supremacy over the Crown as monarch, over the executive and over the judiciary…The judiciary enforce the law against individuals, against institutions and against the executive. The judges cannot enforce the law against the Crown as monarch because the Crown as monarch can do no wrong but judges enforce the law against the Crown as executive and against the individuals who from time to time represent the Crown. A litigant complaining of a breach of the law by the executive can sue the Crown as executive bringing his action against the minister who is responsible for the department of state involved, in the present case the Secretary of State for Home Affairs. To enforce the law the courts have power to grant remedies including injunctions against a minister in his official capacity. If the minister has personally broken the law, the litigant can sue the minister, in this case Mr. Kenneth Baker, in his personal capacity. For the purpose of enforcing the law against all persons and institutions, including ministers in their official capacity and in their personal capacity, the courts are armed with coercive powers exercisable in proceedings for contempt of court.

In the present case, counsel for the Secretary of State argued that the judge could not enforce the law by injunction or contempt proceedings against the minister in his official capacity. Counsel also argued that in his personal capacity Mr. Kenneth Baker the Secretary of State for Home Affairs had not been guilty of contempt.

My Lords, the argument that there is no power to enforce the law by injunction or contempt proceedings against a minister in his official capacity would, if upheld, establish the proposition that the executive obey the law as a matter of grace and not as a matter of necessity, a proposition which would reverse the result of the Civil War. For the reasons given by my noble and learned friend, Lord Woolf, and on principle, I am satisfied that injunctions and contempt proceedings may be brought against the minister in his official capacity and that in the present case the Home Office for which the Secretary of State was responsible was in contempt.

I am also satisfied that Mr. Baker was throughout acting in his official capacity, on advice which he was entitled to accept and under a mistaken view as to the law. In these circumstances I do not consider that Mr. Baker personally was guilty of contempt. I would therefore dismiss this appeal substituting the Secretary of State for Home Affairs as being the person against whom the finding of contempt was made.

The principle that the executive is subject to full judicial oversight was reinforced by this case. The case of *R v Mullen* [2000] QB 520, CA, went a stage further. The appellant had been deported to the UK to face criminal charges, but the deportation was not legal. Instead, Mullen claimed that he had been forcibly brought to this jurisdiction rather than extradited according to the law. He was arrested in Zimbabwe, immediately placed on a plane to London, and then arrested when he arrived in the country. He was tried and convicted of conspiracy to cause explosions likely to endanger life or to cause serious injury to property, and he was sentenced to thirty years in prison. This case sought to determine whether this rendered Mullen's conviction unsafe, to the extent that it should be quashed. The trial itself was considered to be fair, but the nature of the deportation was in issue. Ten years into Mullen's original sentence, Lord Justice Rose considered the case law on abuse of process, citing a number of previous cases on this point, as follows.

● *R v Mullen* [2000] QB 520, CA

Rose LJ, at 529, citing authority:

(QC for appellant) Mr MacKay accepted that the burden of proving abuse of process is on the Appellant and that knowledge on the part of the English authorities that local or international law was broken must be shown. He relied on *R v Horseferry Road Magistrates' Court, ex parte Bennett* [1994] 1 AC 42, [1993] 3 All ER 138. At p 62G of the former report Lord Griffiths said:

'In my view your Lordships should now declare that where process of law is available to return an accused to this country through extradition procedures our courts will refuse to try him if he has been forcibly brought within our jurisdiction in disregard of those procedures by a process to which our own police, prosecuting or other executive authorities have been a knowing party.'

At p 67G Lord Bridge said:

'When it is shown that the law enforcement agency responsible for bringing a prosecution has only been enabled to do so by participating in violations of international law and of laws of another state in order to secure the presence of the accused within the territorial jurisdiction of the court, I think that respect for the rule of law demands that the court take cognisance of that circumstance ... Since the prosecution could never have been brought if the defendant had not been illegally abducted, the whole proceeding is tainted.'

...

At p 76G Lord Lowry said:

'It may be said that a guilty accused finding himself in the circumstances predicated is not deserving of much sympathy, but the principle involved goes beyond the scope of such a pragmatic observation and even beyond the rights of those victims who are or may be innocent. It affects the proper administration of justice according to the rule of law and with respect to international law.'

In *R v Latif* [1996] 1 All ER 353, [1996] 1 WLR 104 at p 112H of the latter report Lord Steyn said:

'The law is settled. Weighing countervailing considerations of policy and justice, it is for the judge in the exercise of his discretion to decide whether there has been an abuse of process, which amounts to an affront to the public conscience and requires

> the criminal proceedings to be stayed...*Ex parte Bennett* was a case where a stay
> was appropriate because a defendant had been forcibly abducted and brought to
> this country to face trial in disregard of extradition laws...But it is possible to say
> that in a case such as the present the judge must weigh in the balance the public
> interest in ensuring that those who are charged with grave crimes should be tried
> and the competing public interest in not conveying the impression that the court
> will adopt the approach that the end justifies any means.'
>
> ...
>
> Decision:
>
> It follows that, in the highly unusual circumstances of this case, notwithstanding that
> there is no criticism of the trial judge or jury, and no challenge to the propriety of the
> outcome of the trial itself, this appeal must be allowed and the Appellant's conviction
> quashed.

This case, and the cases that are cited, are evidence that the state is required to act according to the law. The means do not justify the ends—in other words, the fact that the state believes someone to have committed a crime does not justify the state engaging in illegal activity to bring him or her before a court. One alleged crime does not justify the state acting outside the law. In this case, the judge made it clear that the judge who had presided over the criminal case that had led to Mullen's conviction and the jury that had heard the case had all acted properly. However, because the defendant had apparently been brought to the UK in contravention of the law, the conviction that flowed from that illegal act had to be quashed even though it was not in itself unsafe.

4.6.3 Individuals' rights are protected through the ordinary law and the ordinary court system

It has long been a feature of the UK constitution that if an individual believes that the executive has acted outside of its legal power in reaching a decision, or if he or she believes that the decision is wrong in law, then he or she may challenge the decision through the courts. The next case to be considered challenges that understanding. G and M had had their asylum applications rejected by the Secretary of State and they sought to challenge those decisions. They first took their case to the Adjudicator, who rejected their appeal; they then went to the Immigration Appeal Tribunal, which also rejected their appeals. Thereafter they would previously have had access to judicial review; this had, however, been replaced by a statutory review procedure that was in the form of a review of written submissions by a single High Court judge. The following extract is from the later judicial review case and sets out the section of the judgment that deals with whether Parliament's restriction on the use of judicial review constitutes an infringement of the rule of law.

● *R (on the application of G) v Immigration Appeal Tribunal and another; R (on the application of M) v Immigration Appeal Tribunal and another* [2005] 2 All ER 165, CA

> Lord Phillips MR at 171:
>
> [12] It is the role of the judges to preserve the rule of law. The importance of that role has long
> been recognised by Parliament. It is a constitutional norm recognised by statutory provisions
> that protect the independence of the judiciary, such as ss 11 and 12 of the Supreme Court Act
> 1981. It is recognised by statutory provisions that define the jurisdiction of the judges, such
> as s 15 of the 1981 Act. It is recognised by a large number of statutory provisions which confer
> on the citizen the right to appeal to a court against decisions of tribunals.
>
> [13] These rights are additional to the common law right of the citizen to have access to the
> courts. In particular, they are additional to the right of the citizen, subject to the permission of

the court, to seek judicial review by the High Court of administrative decisions. The common law power of the judges to review the legality of administrative action is a cornerstone of the rule of law in this country and one that the judges guard jealously. If Parliament attempts by legislation to remove that power, the rule of law is threatened. The courts will not readily accept that legislation achieves that end–see *Anisminic Ltd v The Foreign Compensation Commission* [1969] 1 All ER 208, [1969] 2 AC 147.

…

[16] It is obvious that a review by a High Court judge on paper is a less comprehensive protection than the four-stage process of judicial review, including as it does two opportunities for oral submissions.

…

[19] Mr Fordham submitted that this was an exceptional case, because the statutory procedure was less satisfactory than the procedure of judicial review…

[20] We consider that Mr Fordham was correct to concede that, in principle, the court is right to consider whether an alternative remedy is proportionate when deciding whether to exercise its power of judicial review. The consideration of proportionality involves more than comparing the remedy with what is at stake in the litigation. Where Parliament enacts a remedy with the clear intention that this should be pursued in place of judicial review, it is appropriate to have regard to the considerations giving rise to that intention. The satisfactory operation of the separation of powers requires that Parliament should leave the judges free to perform their role of maintaining the rule of law but also that, in performing that role, the judges should, so far as consistent with the rule of law, have regard to legislative policy.

[21] …In the present case it is the clear intention of Parliament, as explained by Collins J, that statutory review under s 101 of the 2002 [Nationality, Immigration and Asylum Act] Act, [now repealed by the Asylum and Immigration (Treatment of Claimants) Act 2004, section 26(5)(a) and additional sections] should be used in place of judicial review. The reason for that intention is the wish to process asylum applications with expedition. That is a legitimate objective and Mr Fordham and Mr Husain recognised that this was so. It is right to have regard to that objective, but this cannot justify refraining from the use of judicial review if the alternative of statutory review will not provide a satisfactory safeguard for those who are, or may be, entitled to asylum.

Immigration decisions have traditionally been reviewed by the courts through the process of judicial review that permits the review of the legality, rationality, and procedural propriety of the decision, along with a review of whether the decision is in conformity with the ECHR through the operation of the Human Rights Act 1998. However, judicial review was replaced by a statutory procedure for review, which is conducted by a High Court judge, but which provides for less scrutiny of the decisions in relation to asylum applications. In this instance, the Court held that the statutory scheme, although not as extensive as judicial review, did provide access to judicial scrutiny and oversight of executive action, and so did not constitute an infringement of the rule of law or of Article 6 ECHR. But some critics have argued that this reform reduced the rights of individuals to seek full review of executive decisions in court and that this may weaken the courts' powers to protect individuals' rights through ordinary court processes.

4.6.4 Legal certainty and non-retrospectivity

The joined cases *R v Rimmington*; *R v Goldstein* [2006] 2 All ER 257, HL, are evidence that supports the principle that the rule of law demands the criminal law to be prospective rather than retrospective, as well as unambiguous in its terms. The courts consider the operation of precedent to assist in clarifying the law and promoting its consistent application in subsequent cases. Interestingly, this case deals with the thorny issue of the common law, which is the unwritten form of law that pre-dates statutory forms of (written) law and which is arguably more difficult for the public to grasp, because it is not easy to identify without reading through many court judgments. As explained in the judgment, common law is still considered to meet the requirements of clarity and stability that form part of the doctrine of the rule of law.

● **R v Rimmington; R v Goldstein** [2006] 2 All ER 257, HL

Lord Bingham of Cornhill:

Definition

[32] The appellants submitted that the crime of causing a public nuisance, as currently interpreted and applied, lacks the precision and clarity of definition, the certainty and the predictability necessary to meet the requirements of either the common law itself or art 7 of the convention. This submission calls for some consideration of principle.

[33] . . . The relevant principles are admirably summarised by Judge LJ for the Court of Appeal (Criminal Division) in *R v Misra* [2004] EWCA Crim 2375, [2005] 1 Cr App R 328, in a passage which I would respectfully adopt:

> The approach of the common law is perhaps best encapsulated in the statement relating to judicial precedent issued by Lord Gardiner LC on behalf of himself and the Lords of Appeal in Ordinary on 26 July 1966. *Practice Statement (Judicial Precedent)* (1986) 83 Cr App R 191, [1966] 1 WLR 1234.

> 'Their Lordships regard the use of precedent as an indispensable foundation upon which to decide what is the law and its application to individual cases. It provides at least some degree of certainty upon which individuals can rely in the conduct of their affairs, as well as a basis for orderly development of legal rules.'

In allowing themselves (but not courts at any other level) to depart from the absolute obligation to follow earlier decisions of the House of Lords, their Lordships expressly bore in mind:

> '. . . the danger of disturbing retrospectively the basis on which contracts, settlements of property and fiscal arrangements have been entered into and also the especial need for certainty as to the criminal law.'

[34] No further citation is required. In summary, it is not to be supposed that prior to the implementation of the Human Rights Act 1998, either this Court, or the House of Lords, would have been indifferent to or unaware of the need for the criminal law in particular to be predictable and certain. Vague laws which purport to create criminal liability are undesirable, and in extreme cases, where it occurs, their very vagueness may make it impossible to identify the conduct which is prohibited by a criminal sanction. If the court is forced to guess at the ingredients of a purported crime any conviction for it would be unsafe. That said, however, the requirement is for sufficient rather than absolute certainty. There are two guiding principles: no one should be punished under a law unless it is sufficiently clear and certain to enable him to know what conduct is forbidden before he does it; and no one should be punished for any act which was not clearly and ascertainably punishable when the act was done. If the ambit of a common law offence is to be enlarged, it 'must be done step by step on a case by case basis and not with one large leap': *R v Clark (Mark)* [2003] EWCA Crim 991, [2003] 2 Cr App R 363, at [13].

This judgment makes the link between the prohibition on legal sanctions being applied to someone unless he or she has breached the law and the principle that the law has to be capable of being known—in short, that the law is clear, unambiguous, relatively stable, and prospective. These two principles of the rule of law are brought together in these cases.

4.6.5 Fair hearing by an independent judiciary

There are many cases that may be cited in support of the proposition that the rule of law demands that cases be heard by a fair and independent judiciary. Two such cases are *Matthews v Ministry of Defence* [2003] 1 All ER 689, HL, and *R (on the application of Anderson) v Secretary of State for the Home Department* [2002] 4 All ER 1089, HL, both heard by the then House of Lords. The first case related to an action brought by a former member of the Navy, who claimed personal injury as a result of exposure to asbestos during his time in the forces. The Ministry of Defence (the government department responsible for the armed forces) claimed that it was not liable, because section 10(1) of the Crown Proceedings Act 1947 gave immunity to the Crown. This provision was repealed in 1987, but the Ministry of Defence argued that Matthews served between 1955 and 1968, which was before section 10 had been repealed, and that consequently the immunity stood. The following extract considers whether the executive may legally restrict and prevent its liability for a tortious act, in the light of Article 6(1) ECHR, which provides for the right to a fair trial.

● *Matthews v Ministry of Defence* [2003] 1 All ER 689, HL

Lord Hoffmann:

> [28] ... In the great case of *Golder v UK* (1975) 1 EHRR 524 the Strasbourg court decided that the right to an independent and impartial tribunal for the determination of one's civil rights did not mean only that if you could get yourself before a court, it had to be independent and impartial. It meant that if you claimed on arguable grounds to have a civil right, you had a right to have that question determined by a court. A right to the independence and impartiality of the judicial branch of government would not be worth much if the executive branch could stop you from getting to the court in the first place. The executive would in effect be deciding the case against you. That would contravene the rule of law and the principle of the separation of powers.
>
> [29] ... But provided one holds onto the underlying principle, which is to maintain the rule of law and the separation of powers, it should not matter how the law is framed. What matters is whether the effect is to give the executive a power to make decisions about people's rights which under the rule of law should be made by the judicial branch of government.
>
> ...
>
> [35] The purpose for which the distinction [between substance and procedure] being used in applying art 6 is that stated with force and clarity by the Strasbourg court in *Golder v UK* and subsequent cases, namely to prevent contracting states from imposing restrictions on the right to bring one's dispute before the judicial branch of government in a way which threatens the rule of law and the separation of powers. But the requirement of the certificate in s 10 is not to give the government an arbitrary power to stop proceedings. The circumstances in which Parliament intended that no action should be brought are fully defined ... The certificate of the Secretary of State cannot prevent the bringing of an action which does not fall within the terms of those subsections. Its purposes it to protect the service man by ensuring that he will not fall between two stools and be denied both damages and a pension.

The courts did not find in favour of Mr Matthews. It was held that section 10(1) did not offend against the right to a fair trial, because this section did not bar the courts from considering the case, at least not in procedural terms, even if that was the substantive result of that section. Lord Hoffmann considered that a procedural bar that restricted access to the courts would threaten the rule of law and the separation of powers, but that this was not the situation in this instance. The Crown was permitted to limit liability for its tortious acts and this did not amount to a denial of a fair trial. However, a restriction on access to the courts would breach Article 6 and may also breach the rule-of-law doctrine, although that was less clear. Lord Hoffmann cautioned against the distinction that is increasingly being drawn in these cases and warned that it was difficult to make a clear-cut distinction between the two.

Anderson involved an offender who was convicted by a court of murder and was given a mandatory life sentence. A mandatory life sentence is accompanied by a tariff, which is the period of time that must be served before the prisoner may be considered for release on licence. At this time, prior to the reforms discussed in Chapter 5, the Home Secretary held the power to set the tariff, even though it was the court that convicted and sentenced the accused. This case considered whether the Home Secretary's power was a breach of Article 6(1) ECHR through the operation of the Human Rights Act 1998.

● *R (on the application of Anderson) v Secretary of State for the Home Department* [2002] 4 All ER 1089, HL

Lord Steyn:

[51] The power of the Home Secretary in England and Wales to decide on the tariff to be served by mandatory life sentence prisoners is a striking anomaly in our legal system. It is true that Parliament has the power to punish offenders by imprisonment. This power derives from the medieval concept of Parliament being, amongst other things, a court of justice (see *Erskine May Treatise on the Law, Privileges, Proceedings and Usages of Parliament* [22nd edn, 1997] p 131 et seq]. Subject to this qualification, there is in our system of law no exception to the proposition that a decision to punish an offender by ordering him to serve a period of imprisonment may only be made by a court of law [see *Blackstone's Commentaries on the Laws of England* [2001] vol 1 p 102 [para 137]). It is a decision which may only be made by the courts. Historically, this has been the position in our legal system since at least 1688. And this idea is a principal feature of the rule of law on which our unwritten constitution is based. It was overridden by Parliament by virtue of s 29 of the 1997 Act. Now the duty to decide on the compatibility of that statutory provision with art 6(1) has been placed by Parliament on the courts under the 1998 Act.

Lord Steyn ruled that an accused may be tried and convicted only by the courts, not only as a matter of law, but also on the basis of the rule of law since 1688. However, the setting of the tariff had been left in the hands of the Home Secretary. Parliament had conferred the duty on the courts to review whether UK law and actions of the executive were compatible with the ECHR and this included a review of whether the setting of the tariff by a member of the executive breached Article 6, which provides for the right to a fair trial. This issue, and the subsequent reforms, will be discussed in more detail in the next chapter, but this extract is evidence of the courts' role in delivering and upholding the rule of law.

4.6.6 The rule of law and substantive judgments

Thus far, the judgments that we have considered in this section have been that that have re-emphasised the rule of law doctrine as understood by scholars of the formal school. The next case discusses whether the courts are now required to review the substance of the executive's decision in matters related to human rights. Traditionally, judicial review has been restricted to the legality, rationality, and procedural propriety of the executive's action, omission, or decision rather than a review of the content of the decision.

● **R (on the application of Al Rawi and others) v Secretary of State for Foreign and Commonwealth Affairs and another** [2006] EWCA Civ 1279

Lord Justice Laws:

[146] A recurrent theme of our public law in recent years has been the search for a principled means of disentangling the functions of these different arms of government. The reach of the executive's role has sometimes been described by reference to the 'deference' accorded to it by the courts, though the term was somewhat disapproved by Lord Hoffmann in *R (ProLife) v BBC* [2004] 1 AC 185 at para 75... He said:

> 'In a society based upon the rule of law and the separation of powers, it is necessary to decide which branch of government has in any particular instance the decision-making power and what the legal limits of that power are. That is a question of law and must therefore be decided by the courts.'

We think a difficulty in deciding this question of law (at least in a fair number of cases) arises from the fact that, particularly since the HRA came into force, our conception of the rule of law has been increasingly substantive rather than merely formal or procedural. Thus the rule of law requires not only that a public decision should be authorised by the words of the enabling statute, but also that it be reasonable and (generally in human rights cases) proportionate to a legitimate aim. But reasonableness and proportionality are not formal legal standards. They are substantive virtues, upon which, it may be thought, lawyers do not have the only voice: nor necessarily the wisest. Accordingly the ascertainment of the weight to be given to the primary decision-maker's view (very often that of central government) can be elusive and problematic.

[147] For present purposes, we would approach the matter as follows. The courts have a special responsibility in the field of human rights. It arises in part from the impetus of the HRA, in part from the common law's jealousy in seeing that intrusive State power is always strictly justified. The elected government has a special responsibility in what may be called strategic fields of policy, such as the conduct of foreign relations and matters of national security. It arises in part from considerations of competence, in part from the constitutional imperative of electoral accountability. In *Secretary of State for the Home Department v Rehman* ... [2003] 1 AC 153... Lord Hoffmann said at para 62:

> 'It is not only that the executive has access to special information and expertise in these matters. It is also that such decisions, with serious potential results for the community, require a legitimacy which can be conferred only by entrusting them to persons responsible to the community through the democratic process. If the people are to accept the consequences of such decisions, they must be made by persons whom the people have elected and whom they can remove.'

[148] This case has involved issues touching both the government's conduct of foreign relations, and national security: pre-eminently the former. In those areas the common law assigns the duty of decision upon the merits to the elected arm of government; all the more so if they combine in the same case. This is the law for constitutional as well as pragmatic reasons, as Lord Hoffmann has explained. The court's role is to see that the government strictly complies with all formal requirements, and rationally considers the matters it has to confront...

In this case, it is clear that the Court of Appeal believed that the role of the courts has expanded in human rights cases to consider proportionality of the decision, as well as its strict compliance with the law. The court in *Al Rawi* believed this to be a necessary development resulting from the Human Rights Act 1998, but did also acknowledge that this led to an assessment that was not restricted to a review of legal issues. This tends more towards the substantive school of thought, and hints at the views expressed by Lords Woolf and Bingham. In other matters—such as those related to matters of public policy, as opposed to human rights—the judicial role remains to review the legality of executive action, in keeping with the formal school of thought.

This is the more traditional view of the judicial role, and one that many judges will feel more comfortable in fulfilling.

summary points

How have the courts interpreted the rule of law?

- *Some judges have linked the rule of law with the separation of powers, as the two basic foundations for the UK constitution and consequently of the legal system.*

- *The cases of* Entick v Carrington *and* M v Home Office, *many years apart, both make it clear that the executive is subject to the law even though it exercises the power of the state. It is clear that the state is not exempt from the law.*

- *This is linked to the principle of legality: the actions of the executive and its officials must be legally grounded. To this end, the actions of the state and public authorities are susceptible to judicial review.*

- *The case of* A v Secretary for the Home Department *is evidence that intrinsic to the UK courts' interpretation of the rule of law is the right to a fair trial.*

- *The case law also links the right to a fair trial with the independence of the judicial function and thus with the separation of powers.*

4.7 What is the relevance of the rule of law today?

The rule of law continues to face many challenges, not least the difficulty of balancing the basic principles of the rule of law with the first duty of the state to keep its citizens safe and secure. The climate of fear of terrorism, whether the threat is real or imagined, has led the state to bring in legal measures that, until recently, would have been considered draconian and in breach of established rule-of-law principles. Some claim that twenty-eight-day detention without charge or trial (but with judicial oversight) was dangerously close to breaching the basic principles upon which our society is founded (the current fourteen-day limit remains too long for some). Others consider that the state has always adapted to meet the demands of terrorist threats, as it did during many years of the Troubles in Northern Ireland. As the threat has diminished, so have the legal measures put in place to counter it. History will make that judgement on the current situation.

Other, less obvious, threats have been cited as attacks on the rule of law. One is the move towards increased, and in some instances semi-mandated, alternative dispute resolution (ADR) mechanisms in the context of public law disputes. Some disputes between individuals and the state are now being diverted away from courts—from adjudication by a judge in a public forum—towards a private mediation away from public scrutiny. There are strengths to mediation and other forms of ADR, and indeed some individuals may prefer to make use of these methods of dispute resolution rather than to go to court to seek a resolution to their cases. However, there are some matters that are so important that public knowledge of the case, judicial oversight of the actions of government, and a judgment requiring the executive or other public body to act within the law are integral to the rule of law. These cases need to be judged in the ordinary courts by the judiciary, rather than be the subject of a deal brokered behind closed doors. It is difficult to know whether ADR will remain a useful option for public law cases, or whether increasing numbers of cases will be funnelled away from courts and into less formal settings.

Summary

The rule of law is a doctrine that forms an essential part of the UK constitution. There are different views on the nature of the doctrine. Some argue that it is political and others that it is legal; there are also two broad groups or schools of thought—the formal and the substantive. The formal school sets norms about the way in which the law is enacted, its stability, clarity, and its non-arbitrary application, and argues that no one is above the law and that no one may be punished other than as the law provides. The substantive school also looks to the content of the law, including the extent to which the law furthers conceptions of morality, the common good, and/or human rights, when judging the extent to which the rule of law applies in a state. The vast majority of commentators agree that the rule of law is present and is the fundamental principle within the UK constitution.

Questions

1   What are the key components of the formal theory of the rule of law?

2   What are the key components of the substantive theory of the rule of law?

3   To what extent are the two rule-of-law schools similar and different, and to what extent do you agree with each of the two schools?

4   What is the purpose of the rule of law, and what indicators would you look for to determine the extent to which a country respects the rule of law?

5   To what extent do you believe that the rule of law is present in the UK constitution? What evidence do you have for your answer?

6   What evidence do you have that the rule of law has been strengthened or weakened in the UK over recent years?

Further reading

Allan, T. R. S., 'The rule of law as the rule of reason: consent and constitutionalism' (1999) 115 Law Quarterly Review 221

This is a complex article that pulls together a lot of competing strands of the rule of law into Allan's explanation of what the doctrine encompasses and protects. It is certainly not an easy article to read, but it is very thought-provoking if you are able to persevere with it.

Craig, P., 'Formal and substantive conceptions of the rule of law: an analytical framework' [1997] Public Law 467

This article focuses on the similarities and differences between the two main schools of thought on the rule of law. Like Allan's article, it is quite complex and contains a lot of theory. But it is also very helpful when trying to work through one's own understanding of the rule of law.

Finnis, J., *Natural Law and Natural Rights* (Oxford: Oxford University Press, 1980)

This is a particularly challenging, philosophical book that considers what is the essence of law. It is likely to be a set text on any jurisprudence course and, were you willing to challenge yourself by reading it, it would broaden your view of law, legality, and the rule of law no end. It is, however, not for the faint-hearted!

Fuller, L. L., *The Morality of Law* (rev'd edn, New Haven, CT: Yale University Press, 1969)

This is a relatively challenging book to read, but it is considered to be one of the canons of legal theoretical works to which many of the academics mentioned in this chapter refer. It is well worth reading at some point in your legal career.

Jennings, W. I., *Law and the Constitution* (5th edn, London: University of London Press, 1959)

This book is a classic in constitutional law terms. It is very detailed and it does delve into theory in some depth. However, it is not as much of a challenge to read as is Finnis's work and it is one of the definitive works on constitutional law even if it is, now, somewhat out of date as regards the detailed arrangments of the British constitution.

The Separation of Powers

5

Key points

This chapter will cover:

- What is the separation of powers?
- What is the history of the separation of powers in the UK?
- What is the purpose of the separation of powers?
- What are the similarities and differences between different theories of the separation of powers?
- How has recent constitutional reform affected the operation of the separation of powers in the UK?
- How have the courts interpreted the separation of powers?
- What is the relevance of the separation of powers today?

Introduction

This chapter, rather like the previous chapter on the rule of law, considers the theories that seek to define and explain the doctrine of the separation of powers. It examines why it may be desirable to have a separation of powers within a state and it provides examples of the operation of the separation of powers in the UK. It will also consider the extent to which recent constitutional reforms have affected the nature and extent of the separation of powers in the UK constitution. The extracts in this chapter provide evidence of theories and their realisation, and of reforms that have changed the way in which the separation of powers applies. The chapter will conclude with a series of questions that should test whether you have understood the doctrine and whether you have evidence to back up the points that you would make in answer to questions on this area.

5.1 What is the separation of powers?

The **separation of powers** is a theory or a doctrine that describes the way in which a **state** organises the distribution of power and function between its different branches. Although some suggest that it is a legal theory, others maintain that its origins are political rather than legal. It is usually used as an umbrella term to denote the extent to which the three 'powers' in, or branches of, the state are fused or divided—that is, the **legislative**, the **executive**, and the **judicial** powers. Theorists do not agree on how separated these powers need to be, or even on whether it is possible or desirable to have a total separation of powers. The basics of the theory, and the similarities and differences between theories, will be considered in detail below. You may wish to skip subsection 5.1.1 if you are already familiar with the three powers or functions of the state, as set out in section 1.4, and how they link together as set out in Figure 2.3 in the summary at the end of Chapter 2.

5.1.1 What are the three powers and branches?

Because the doctrine of the separation of powers has at its heart the relationship between the legislative, the executive, and the judicial functions, you may wish to refresh your memory of **Parliament**, the **government**, and the courts by rereading the relevant sections in Chapter 2. The legislative function encompasses the power to consider new propositions of law and existing law, and to amend, repeal, and enact legislation. The legislature may also have the function of scrutinising the executive branch of the state, depending on the nature of the constitutional settlement in place in a given country. For example, in the UK, Parliament (the legislature) has the power to enact primary legislation and to authorise secondary legislation. It also has the power—and some would say the duty—to scrutinise the actions of the government (the executive) to ensure that the executive branch acts within the power conferred on it by the legislature and fulfils its electoral mandate. In the United States, Congress (the legislature) has the power to scrutinise the operation of the president and the secretaries of state (the executive) on behalf of the people of the US. These two examples are illustrative of systems that rely on a system of checks and balances between the legislature and the executive within their constitutions—a mechanism that will be discussed in more detail below.

The executive function is often described as the power to govern the country. It involves having day-to-day control of the state by implementing the law made by the legislature and exercising any executive powers that are inherent in the role of the executive. In a UK context, this means that the government may run the country in accordance with the law that Parliament has enacted, but also as the **royal prerogative** so permits. As discussed in Chapter 6, the royal prerogative is a form of executive power enjoyed by the **monarch** and by **constitutional convention**, in many instances exercised by the **Prime Minister** and other ministers on her behalf.

The executive is charged with responding to current events in the country and has the power to bring forward the propositions of law that are required to extend or alter the executive's power to act. It is then for the legislature to consider whether it will enact the law as drawn by the executive, or enact it in an amended form, or reject it. The executive function also includes the formulation of policy to ensure consistent decision-making and the exercise of **discretion**. The policy must be legal—in other words, it must respect the limits of the law and the rules of **natural justice**. The executive function extends further than the domestic sphere, unlike the legislative function in most countries, because it is the executive that represents the country internationally. The monarch, as head of state, is the UK's representative in international affairs; it is, however, the Prime Minister or the delegate of the Prime Minister, such as the Secretary of State for Foreign Affairs, rather than the **Queen** herself who enters into detailed political negotiations with other countries. The presidents of the US and France hold this function in their respective countries: they are both heads of state and heads of the executive branch.

cross reference
See Chapter 14 for more detail on judicial scrutiny of the executive's use of power and formulation of policy.

The third branch of the state is largely made up of the **judiciary**. The judicial function is the administration of justice through the courts and tribunals, and the interpretation and application of law, and the finding of fact, in cases brought before the courts and tribunals. The judiciary is charged with the responsibility of ensuring that the **rule of law** is respected—that the executive acts within its legal power. In some countries (although not in the UK), the judiciary may also have the power to consider the constitutional standing of legislation as compared with the country's constitution. The judiciary also has a private law function in that it adjudicates legal disputes between individuals and companies. Its public law function relates to disputes between individuals and the state and/or public bodies. The latter falls under the umbrella term 'administrative law'.

cross reference
The institutions of the European Union (EU) also have legislative, executive, and judicial powers. See Chapter 8 for more information.

To sum up, the legislature scrutinises the law, amends, enacts, and repeals the law, and may also scrutinise the exercise of power by the executive. In the UK, the legislation enacted by the legislature (along with the royal prerogative) gives the executive the power to run the country. In some countries, the executive has a more clearly defined and regulated set of executive powers that are largely independent of the need for cooperation with the legislature. Where necessary, the executive may seek new or amended legislation to provide it with the power it believes it needs to fulfil its mandate. The judiciary considers the exercise of power by the executive, as well as finds fact and interprets the law more widely, in legal disputes between the state and individuals, but also in cases between private bodies. When taken together, the three powers make up the power of the state.

5.1.2 How does the theory relate to the three functions?

How does the theory of the separation of powers operate within those three functions? The theory, in its traditional form, is based, in simple terms, on the principle that the powers to legislate, to implement the law and to run the country, and to interpret the law and to call people to account for the legality of their actions should not be held by the same people or the same body. This is premised on the assumption that, without separation of power, one person or body would have access to too much power, which may lead to its abuse. Some theorists consider that the functions should be held by different *bodies*—in other words, that the legislature should hold the legislative function, that the executive should hold the executive function, and that the judiciary should hold the judicial function. Others consider that the powers to legislate, to implement the law, and to adjudicate on the law should not be held by the same *people*—that is, that one individual should not be permitted to exercise both executive and judicial powers, for example. For others, it means that the executive should not interfere with the legislature, nor the judiciary with the legislature, nor the executive with judiciary—in other words, that none of the three branches of the state should interfere with the operation of the others. Different theorists have very different views on whether complete or partial separation of powers is possible, or indeed even desirable. This will be considered in more detail after we have examined the history of the separation of powers within the UK.

summary points

What is the separation of powers?

- *It is a theory or doctrine that explains how power is to be distributed within a state to prevent its abuse.*
- *It is based on the principle that the power to legislate, the power to implement the law and to run the country, and the power to interpret the law and to call people to account for their actions should not be held by the same people, nor by the same bodies.*
- *There is disagreement about whether separation of powers should be complete or only partial.*
- *The theories have developed over time and continue to develop; likewise the UK constitutional position on the separation of powers continues to change.*

5.2 What is the history of the separation of powers in the UK?

The origins of the theory of separation of powers can be traced back to Ancient Greece and Aristotle in his work *Politics*. The origins of the theory in the UK are, however, considered to date from much later, as a result of Magna Carta of 1215. Magna Carta established the division of power between the **Crown** and an early form of Parliament, albeit not one that we would recognise as such today. Magna Carta was a groundbreaking legal document that established that a council of barons had an independent power base from that of the monarch. The King of England recognised that (some of) his subjects had liberties that he was required to respect, which limited his previously absolute power within the state. The King's exercise of his newly limited power was to be overseen by the council of barons, who were given the power to enforce the liberties of his subjects against the King. The extract below sets out the relevant sections.

Magna Carta 1215

...

60. Moreover all the subjects of our realm, clergy as well as laity, shall, as far as pertains to them, observe, with regard to their vassals, all these aforesaid customs and liberties which we have decreed shall, as far as pertains to us, be observed in our realm with regard to our own.

61. Inasmuch as, for the sake of God, and for the bettering of our realm, and for the more ready healing of the discord which has arisen between us and our barons, we have made all the aforesaid concessions,—wishing them to enjoy for ever entire and firm stability, we make and grant to them the following security: that the barons, namely, may elect at their pleasure twenty five barons from the realm, who ought, with all their strength, to observe, maintain and cause to be observed, the peace and privileges which we have granted to them and confirmed by this our present charter. In such wise, namely, that if we, or our justice, or our bailiffs, or any one of our servants shall have transgressed against anyone in any respect, or shall have broken one of the articles of peace or security, and our transgression shall have been shown to four barons of the aforesaid twenty five: those four barons all come to us, or, if we are abroad, to our justice, showing to us our error; and they shall ask us to cause that error to be amended without delay. And if we do not amend that error, or, we being abroad, if our justice do not amend it within a term of forty days from the time when it was shown to us or, we being abroad, to our justice: the aforesaid four barons shall refer the matter to the remainder of the twenty five barons, and those twenty five barons, with the whole land in common, shall distrain and oppress us in every way in their power,—namely, taking our castles, lands and possessions, and in every other way that they can, until amends shall have been made according to their judgment. Saving the person of ourselves, our queen and our children. And when the amends shall have been made they shall be in accord with us as they have been previously.

This is a difficult text to read because it is not written in contemporary English and it is difficult to imagine a time when one person had absolute power in the state. However, the extract indicates that the King (referred to as 'we' in the text) agreed that the barons were permitted to elect twenty-five representatives to ensure that the exercise of power by the King and his representatives would respect subjects' liberties. The baron representatives were permitted to enforce the operation of Magna Carta against the King and his representatives. If the barons brought evidence of a breach of the law to the King and that breach was not remedied within forty days, the King was liable to have his possessions and land taken from him until such time as he did. While this appears to be a small step in today's terms, it did establish that there was a body that was able to scrutinise the operation of the King's power and to enforce the law against the King. The power of barons was different from, but nonetheless equal to, that of the King. This was the start of a representative Parliament, and also the limitation on a monarch's power to make law and to govern the country. While Magna Carta paved the way for the concept of separation of powers in the UK, the separation between Crown and Parliament was not settled until towards the end of the seventeenth century.

Although Magna Carta attempted to enshrine the protection of subjects' liberties against the monarch and to establish a body of representatives (albeit of nobles) to oversee this, the process of **entrenching** this protection was less successful than the wording of Magna Carta would suggest. As late as 1628, Parliament (in a form that more closely resembles Parliament today rather than the council of nobles) had need to petition the King in respect of subjects' rights and to remind the monarch of his legal duty to limit his exercise of power to that provided by law. The Petition of Right emphasises the importance of the rule of law and the role of the courts in overseeing its respect—a role that is independent of the executive branch of the state.

Petition of Right 1628

...

III. And whereas also by the statute classed 'The Great Charter of the Liberties of England', it is declared and enacted, that no freeman may be taken or imprisoned or be disseized of his

111

freehold or liberties, or his free customs, or be outlawed or exiled, or in any manner destroyed, but by the lawful judgment of his peers, or by due process of law.

...

VII. And whereas also by authority of parliament...it is declared and enacted, that no man shall be forejudged of life or limb against the form of the Great Charter and the law of the land; and by the said Great Charter and other the laws and statutes of this your realm, no man ought to be adjudged to death but by the laws established in this your realm...and whereas no offender of what kindsoever is exempted from the proceedings to be used, and punishments to be inflicted by the laws and statues of this your realm; nevertheless of late time divers commissions under your Majesty's great seal have issued forth, but which certain persons have been assigned and appointed commissioners with power and authority to proceed...according to the justice of martial law, against such soldiers or mariners, or other...as should commit any murder, robbery, felony, mutiny, or other outrage of misdemeanour whatsoever, and by such summary course and order as is agreeable to martial law, and is used in armies in time of war, to proceed to the trial and condemnation of such offenders, and them to cause to be executed and put to death according to the law martial.

...

cross reference
You will find a longer version of this extract in the previous chapter.

cross reference
An extract from the Bill of Rights 1689 is set out in Chapter 4.

As this extract illustrates, there were concerns that subjects were being imprisoned and penalised without a court hearing of any kind, and that the King was invoking martial law (a form of executive rule) to permit people to be tried and executed outside the normal legal system. These court hearings were not considered to constitute a fair trial, because they operated under martial law rather than through an independent judicial hearing. There were also concerns that the rights and liberties of subjects were not being respected by the monarch and his representatives in the country. The Petition of Right reiterated the requirement that the monarch operate within the limits of his power, and respect the power base of Parliament in making law and of the judiciary in adjudicating legal disputes and trying defendants who were charged with criminal offences. This is a restatement of the liberties of subjects—of the operation of the rule of law—but it is also a restatement of the doctrine of the separation of power between the different institutions of the state. It also re-emphasises that the raising of taxes is a matter for Parliament (which is why the Budget has to this day to be debated and voted upon by Parliament, rather than simply be implemented by the executive through the Chancellor of the Exchequer). Tax-raising powers are extremely important, because a state cannot function without the capital to finance its initiatives, and consequently without the legislature and the executive working in tandem. The Petition of Right reminds the King that the ability to raise taxes is a power that requires the agreement of the legislature rather than a power granted to the executive acting alone. Thus there is a statement of some separation of power, rather than a statement of fusion of powers in the hands of the King.

The Petition of Right 1628 was followed later in the seventeenth century with another legal statement on the separation of powers, the Bill of Rights 1689, which addressed many of the same issues, but in more forceful terms. The Bill of Rights set out the many illegalities that Parliament believed the King and his officers to have perpetrated. It identified a lack of due process through the courts for those accused of crimes. It highlighted situations in which the King had breached the division of power between the monarch and Parliament, by establishing courts other than through enacted legislation, by levying of taxes without the legal basis to do so, and even by suspending law enacted by Parliament. Parliament once more reasserted the separation of powers between the monarch and Parliament, and underlined the operation of the rule of law in the state as protected by the judiciary. This form of separation was finally accepted and attention then turned to the detail of separation of powers between the legislature, the executive, and the judiciary. The recent debates on separation have been largely theoretical rather than legal, in that they have been conducted in the writing of legal and political theorists rather than by parliamentary petitions to the monarch. These debates will be discussed in more detail in subsequent sections after we examine the purpose of the separation of powers.

summary points

What is the history of the separation of powers in the UK?

- *The history in the UK is dominated by the limitation of the power of the Crown by the division of power between the Crown and Parliament.*

- *The process began with Magna Carta, but was not finally settled until the late seventeenth century. Some say it continues to be refined to this day.*

- *This process also assisted in establishing conceptions of the legislative, executive, and judicial powers and functions, although much of the debate prior to the late seventeenth century did not use those terms.*

- *It had the benefit of highlighting that subjects had liberties that were to be recognised within the state, and consequently did not only separate power, but also limited the absolute power of the monarch.*

- *Thereafter discussions turned to what we would now recognise as a separation-of-powers debate, encompassing the legislative, executive, and judicial branches.*

5.3 What is the purpose of the separation of powers?

As the previous section began to demonstrate, the purpose of the separation of powers is to limit the potential for abuse of power by any of the state organs or state actors. It has long been believed that the power to legislate, the power to govern, and the power to judge guilt and innocence, when held by the same person, may result in partial and unjust outcomes for some, if not all. It may be too much of a temptation for those who have the power to make law and to implement law also to judge whether a law has been broken. They may be tempted to apply the law differently in relation to others from the way in which they apply it to themselves unless there is either a separation of the power into different hands, or there are sufficient and effective checks and balances that limit abuse. Some commentators have gone so far as to suggest that the separation of powers is a necessary precondition for the rule of law within a society. Others believe that a pure separation of powers is undesirable and unworkable.

● **E. G. Henderson**, *Foundations of English Administrative Law: Certiorari and Mandamus in the Seventeenth Century* [Cambridge, MA: Harvard University Press, 1962], p. 5

> This threefold division of labour between a legislator, an administrative official, and an independent judge, is a necessary condition for the rule of law in modern society and therefore for democratic government itself.

This sentiment was expressed as early as the seventeenth century by John Locke and later by many other theorists—amongst them, Montesquieu in the eighteenth century, Jennings and Bagehot in the nineteenth century, Barendt and Munro in the twentieth century, and Barber in the twenty-first century. Barendt explains the sentiment very clearly, indicating that an independent judiciary, separate from interference from the other organs of the state, operates as a brake on arbitrary decision-making and application of the law by the executive.

● **E. Barendt,** *An Introduction to Constitutional Law* (Oxford: Oxford University Press, 1998), p. 129

The Courts & Judicial Power

1. The Separation of Judicial Power

Alexander Hamilton, one of the authors of the *Federalist Papers*, described the judiciary as the 'least dangerous' branch of government.[1] He meant that it cannot significantly damage the rights of citizens. The courts do not enjoy the wide law-making power of the legislature or the capacity of the executive to implement political policies. They are dependent on the government for financial support. Further, they may not be able to enforce their judgments without the assistance of bailiffs and other executive officials. Hamilton shared Montesquieu's view that judges are relatively weak, it is, however, more interesting that he also agreed with the French jurist's opinion that 'there is no liberty, if the judicial power be not separated from the legislative and executive'.[2] Otherwise there might be arbitrary government; Parliament or the executive would be able to determine when its laws had been broken. Hamilton concluded that an independent judiciary, was 'essential in a limited Constitution', so anticipating the conclusions reached by the Supreme Court in *Marbury v. Madison*.[3] There is general agreement in the United Kingdom on the importance of the independence of the judiciary, if not over the wisdom of constitutional review of legislation. But it is unclear what independence of the judiciary really means.

...

1 'The Judiciary Department' (Federalist Paper No. 78, *Independent Journal*, 14 June 1788). The description provided the title for one of the great books on US constitutional law: A.Bickel, *The Least Dangerous Branch: The Supreme Court at the Bar of Politics* (Indianapolis, IN: Bobbs-Merrill, 1962).

2 *The Spirit of the Laws* [De L'Esprit de Lois], Book XI, ch. 6 (in translation, New York: Free Press, 1949), p. 152.

3 [5 US (1 Cranch) 137 (1803).]

However, the theorists differ substantially on the desirability of separation and the model to be adopted, in part because there is disagreement about whether the separation of powers is capable of preventing abuse of power. It is a theory that is predicated on the assumption that separating the very real power in the constitution will prevent its abuse. However, if separation were not able to deliver this outcome, or if another mechanism were better able to do so, then the separation of powers may be ineffective or unnecessary. Consequently, it could be argued that the separation of powers is not an end in itself, but instead is a process that seeks to regulate the exercise of state power. This was Jennings's position—that checks and balances were needed to limit power rather than that there should be a rigid separation of powers for its own sake.

There is a school of thought that believes that the separation of powers is not entirely based on the assumption that separation leads to limited government and the protection of liberty, but that a certain amount of separation may also lead to efficient government. Balanced constitutions, which include an element of separation along with checks and balances that require the executive and the legislature to work together, may improve the government of a country. This is known as 'partial separation' by some and 'fused power' by others. Barber explains the efficiency position as follows.

● **N. W. Barber, 'Prelude to the separation of powers'** (2001) 60(1) Cambridge Law Journal 59, 59–64

The essence, though not the whole, of separation of powers lies in the meeting of form and function; the matching of tasks to those bodies best suited to execute them. The core of the doctrine is not liberty, as may writers have assumed, but efficiency...

Barendt, following Vile,[1] distinguishes between 'pure' and 'partial' versions of the doctrine. The pure theory calls for complete separation of the three branches of the state; a strict delineation of functions between the executive, the legislature and the judiciary. The division of power acts as a restraint on the power of the state.[2] An alternative vision of the doctrine, the 'partial' version, instead emphasises the significance of checks and balances within the constitution. Each of the institutions of state is given some power over the others, their functions are deliberately constructed so that they overlap. Friction is consequently created between the branches of the state; no one institution has absolute autonomy. Both of these versions of the doctrine make two critical assumptions. First, that it is possible to identity and group certain powers as 'legislative', 'executive' or 'judicial'.[3]... Secondly, that there is a natural connection between these powers and the corresponding state institution...

Barendt argues that the purpose of separation of powers is to protect the liberty of the individual. It does this by making state action more difficult... The purpose of the doctrine, according to Barendt, is not, primarily, to identify the best, or natural, holder of a particular power. The doctrine rather aims to protect liberty through division of power. The precise delineation of this division is not of great significance; all that separation of powers requires is that some division of power be decided upon and adhered to...

There is much to be gained from classical writings on separation of powers. A clue may be found in the persistence of a second possible aim of separation of powers: the claim that the purpose of the doctrine is to promote efficient state action.[4] Writers on separation of powers have frequently contrasted the claims of efficiency and liberty. These have been treated as rival justifications for the doctrine, bordering on contradiction. John Locke is sometimes read as advocating separation of powers in order to ensure the efficiency of government action.[5] Vile has strongly attacked this characterisation of Locke's work, and has convincingly demonstrated that Locke was also concerned with the protection accorded to individual liberty by the doctrine.[6] However, this should not blind us to the significant role that efficiency plays in Locke's Second Treatise... Locke was attempting to fashion a vision of civil society that would be so great an improvement on individuals' rights within a state of nature that they would voluntarily surrender these rights in order to participate in the common good.[7] He crafted a constitution that took account of human frailty. Limits were placed on institutions to protect against abuse... Locke was advocating a form of separation of powers not in order to slow down the running of the state but in order to ensure that it ran well. Powers were divided in order to facilitate the purposes for which the state existed.

1 M. Vile, *Constitutionalism and the Separation of Powers* (2nd edn, Indianapolis, IN: Liberty Fund, 1998), ch. 1; W. B. Gwyn, *The Meaning of the Separation of Powers* (Tulane Studies in Political Science Vol. 9, New Orlean, FL: Tulane University 1965), ch. 1.

2 Vile, n. 1, p. 14.

3 Barendt does not investigate the nature of these types of power at any length. On Montesquieu's definition of these powers, see generally Vile, n. 1, ch. 4, and Montesquieu, *The Spirit of the Laws* [De l'Esprit de Lois], trans. A. Cohler, B. Miller, and H. Stone (Cambridge: Cambridge University Press, 1989), Book 11, ch. 6. Morgan explores the division as reflected in case law in D. Morgan, *Separation of Powers in the Irish Constitution* (Dublin: Round Hall Sweet & Maxwell, 1997).

4 Gwyn, n. 1, pp. 32–4.

5 E. Barendt, 'Separation of powers and constitutional government' [1995] Public Law 599, 602; Morgan, n. 3, p. 4; editor P. Laslett, in J. Locke, *Two Treatises of Government* (Cambridge:

Cambridge University Press, 1988), pp. 118–20, provides qualified and indirect support for this view. See also W. Gwyn, 'separation of powers and modern forms of democratic government', in R. Goldwin and A. Kaufman (eds) *The Separation of Powers: Does it Still Work?* (Washington, DC: American Enterprise Institute, 1986), p. 70.

6 Vile, n. 1, pp. 63–74.

7 Locke, n. 5, para. 1–123.

Barber suggests that the division of powers between different organs of the state has been misunderstood by many commentators, not least Bagehot. Barber did not accept claims that overlaps of power may lead to inefficiency in government. His article explains that the division and overlap of power may result in critical, yet innovative, friction, which is of benefit in law-making and governance. Indeed, it may be undesirable to have total separation, because this would reduce efficiency and creativity. This degree of overlap may be beneficial as long as power is sufficiently limited to preserve citizens' liberty. The balance between separation and overlap is a difficult one to strike. This tension has dogged theorists through the ages and will be discussed further in the next section.

summary points

What is the purpose of the separation of powers?

- *The theory of the separation of powers seeks to regulate and limit the exercise of power by state institutions or organs to prevent abuse of power or the arbitrary application of power.*

- *As such, it is not an end in itself, but a mechanism by which power may be limited.*

- *Some theorists consider that total separation of powers is a necessity in order to prevent arbitrariness in the exercise of power.*

- *Other theorists consider that a combination of checks and balances on the exercise of power would perform this function more effectively than separation.*

- *Yet others consider that a mixed model, or partial separation with checks and balances, may deliver this outcome.*

5.4 What are the similarities and differences between different theories of the separation of powers?

To what extent is there agreement amongst theorists about the doctrine of the separation of powers? The classic conception of separation requires an independent judiciary. An independent judiciary is viewed as the guardian of individual liberty and the rule of law. The extract from Barendt's book *An Introduction to Constitutional Law*, cited earlier, illustrates the importance of the separation of judicial power from that of the other functions so as to prevent the abuse of power. Locke and Montesquieu also believed in an independent judiciary, as did Jennings and Dicey. In fact, it is difficult to find a mainstream theorist who believes that the existence of an independent judiciary is an undesirable constitutional position. Such is the importance placed on the need for an independent judiciary that it is one of the characteristics

cross reference

See Chapter 18 for more on the right to have a judge free from bias—i.e. the natural justice rule associated with an independent judiciary—as well as Article 6 ECHR on this point.

considered to be inherent in the right to a fair trial provided by the rules of natural justice and also Article 6 of the **European Convention on Human Rights (ECHR)**. Some of the case law, which will be considered in a later section, underlines the need for an independent judiciary.

The separation between legislature and executive is similarly considered to be a mechanism with which to reduce the arbitrary operation of the law within a country, by isolating the power to make law from the power to apply it. Separation between the legislature and the executive is more controversial, and there is less agreement between the theorists on this point. Locke was of the belief that some separation between these two bodies—the legislature and the executive—was desirable. However, he divided the executive in two—domestic execution and policy, and foreign execution and policy; the former, he properly termed 'the executive', and the latter he referred to as 'the federative'. He did not believe that separation of these two parts of the executive was appropriate. Locke's *Two Treatises of Government* explains the differences between the powers, as well the case for separation and fusion.

· ·

● **J. Locke,** ***Two Treatises of Government*** (1689), available online at http://www. gutenberg.org/etext/7370, pp. 167–9

> 143. The legislative power is that which has a right to direct how the force of the commonwealth shall be employed for preserving the community and the members of it. Because those laws . . . may be made in a little time, therefore there is no need that the legislative should be always in being, not having always business to do. And because it may be too great a temptation to human frailty, apt to grasp at power, for the same persons who have the power of making laws to have also in their hands the power to execute them, whereby they may exempt themselves from obedience to the laws they make, and suit the law, both in its making and execution, to their own private advantage, and thereby come to have a distinct interest from the rest of the community, contrary to the end of society and government. Therefore in well-ordered commonwealths, where the good of the whole is so considered as it ought, the legislative power is put into the hands of divers persons who, duly assembled, have by themselves, or jointly with others, a power to make laws, which when they have done, being separated again, they are themselves subject to the laws they have made; which is a new and near tie upon them to take care that they make them for the public good.
>
> 144. But because the laws . . . have a constant and lasting force, and need a perpetual execution, or an attendance thereunto, therefore it is necessary there should be a power always in being which should see to the execution of the laws that are made, and remain in force. And thus the legislative and executive power come often to be separated.
>
> . . .
>
> 146. . . . the power of war and peace, leagues and alliances, and all the transactions with all persons and communities without the commonwealth, and may be called federative if any one pleases . . .
>
> 147. These two powers, executive and federative, though they be really distinct in themselves, yet one comprehending the execution of the municipal laws of the society within itself upon all that are parts of it, the other the management of the security and interest of the public without with all those that it may receive benefit or damage from, yet they are always almost united . . .
>
> 148. Though, as I said, the executive and federative power of every community be really distinct in themselves, yet they are hardly to be separated and placed at the same time in the hands of distinct persons. For both of them requiring the force of the society for their exercise, it is almost impracticable . . . that the executive and federative power should be placed in persons that might act separately, whereby the force of the public would be under different commands, which would be apt some time or other to cause disorder and ruin.

Locke was clear on the need for a separation between the legislature and the executive, but not on the fusion between the two branches of the executive. His reasoning was that there was a potential for an abuse of power, of partiality, if the legislature also got to implement the law. He believed that it was too tempting for people who had the power to make the law to then exempt themselves from its application, were they to also have an executive role. He advocated separation of power between people: the same people should not have legislative and executive power. This is in contrast to the parliamentary executive constitution that operates in the UK, in which the executive is drawn from the legislature. However, were the rule of law to be strong in a country, this would not necessarily pose the problems that Locke envisaged. Locke did not consider it necessary to separate the fields of domestic and foreign policy. He considered that it would be impractical to do so—and that it may also lead to confusion between the two power bases.

cross reference

Refer back to Chapter 2 if you are unsure on this point.

Montesquieu's views on the separation of powers also went a stage further than the partial separation model. He believed that the state should have an independent judiciary separate from the legislature and the executive, as well as a legislature and executive independent of each other. Montesquieu suggested that total separation provided citizens with further protection from the excessive use of power by the state machinery, which, if left unchecked, may be detrimental to personal liberty. He set out his theory in *De l'Esprit de Lois* [The Spirit of the Laws].

• **Baron de Montesquieu, *The Spirit of the Laws [De l'Esprit des Lois]: Book XI, Of the Laws Which Establish Political Liberty, with Regard to the Constitution*** (1748), available online at http://www.constitution.org/cm/sol_11.htm#006

6. Of the Constitution of England

In every government there are three sorts of power: the legislative; the executive in respect to things dependent on the law of nations; and the executive in regard to matters that depend on the civil law.

By virtue of the first, the prince or magistrate enacts temporary or perpetual laws, and amends or abrogates those that have been already enacted. By the second, he makes peace or war, sends or receives embassies, establishes the public security, and provides against invasions. By the third, he punishes criminals, or determines the disputes that arise between individuals. The latter we shall call the judiciary power, and the other simply the executive power of the state.

The political liberty of the subject is a tranquillity of mind arising from the opinion each person has of his safety. In order to have this liberty, it is requisite the government be so constituted as one man need not be afraid of another.

When the legislative and executive powers are united in the same person, or in the same body of magistrates, there can be no liberty; because apprehensions may arise, lest the same monarch or senate should enact tyrannical laws, to execute them in a tyrannical manner.

Again, there is no liberty, if the judiciary power be not separated from the legislative and executive. Were it joined with the legislative, the life and liberty of the subject would be exposed to arbitrary control; for the judge would be then the legislator. Were it joined to the executive power, the judge might behave with violence and oppression.

...

Montesquieu was concerned that some basic human rights could be infringed if too much power were to be concentrated in the hands of people who were lawmakers and members of the executive. It should be noted, however, that Montesquieu was writing at a time when the systems of democracy in Europe were less well developed than they are now and when there was no **universal suffrage** to act as a check on the power of the state. He believed that the constitution needed to act as a check in the absence of an effective check by the people. The

US system is more closely modelled on Montesquieu's conception of the separation of powers than is the UK system, or the relatively recently formed post-unification German system. In the US, the executive function is held in the hands of the elected President and the legislative function is held in the hands of the elected Congress. This system is known as a 'presidential executive constitutional system'. The two sets of personnel have their own functions and are kept separate, although both are involved in the process of making law (other than when the legislature is able to override a presidential veto on legislation). The three branches of the state are described as 'co-equal' in the US and are designed to provide a power-balanced constitution. The German system is closer to the UK system, because it operates on a partial fusion model: Germany follows a parliamentary system of government. The German Chancellor performs a similar role to the Prime Minister as political head of the executive, whereas the role of the German President is largely non-political. The legislature acts as a check on the executive and scrutinises its workings through a committee system similar to that adopted by the Westminster Parliament. There is no clear separation between the legislature and the executive. Consequently, there are modern democratic states that follow both systems of partial separation and clearer separation between legislature and executive.

Why is there a difference of opinion about the appropriate separation of powers within the state? If Locke and Montesquieu both believed that there was a need to separate the legislative and the executive branches, and the US has arranged its constitutional settlement to comply with this (in general terms), then why do other commentators consider relatively complete separation to be less than desirable? Why have many countries adopted a parliamentary system of constitutional settlement that relies on some overlaps between the legislature and executive?

Vile charts the development of the balanced government theory, which is modelled on the British constitutional position. In this, the powers of the legislature and executive overlap as the personnel of government are drawn from the legislature. This is viewed as a strength of the constitutional settlement rather than as a weakness, although commentators insist on the need for an independent judiciary. The legislature (sometimes referred to as the 'deliberative') provides a check on the power of the executive through parliamentary mechanisms that encourage accountability such as ministerial responsibility. It is argued that the power of the executive is checked and balanced by the power of the legislature to oversee it. Vile explains this in his work *Constitutionalism and the Separation of Powers*.

. . . .

● **M. J. C. Vile, *Constitutionalism and the Separation of Powers*** [1967; 2nd edn, Indianapolis, IN: Liberty Fund, 1998], p. 147

> The idea of government by King, Lords, and Commons was recognized by many as merely the formal theory of the Constitution; the reality was very different . . . James Mill in his *Essay on Government* rejected the old classification of mixed and simple forms of government altogether. The *Essay* is in fact a sustained argument for the view that the old theory of the Constitution must be replaced by one the basis of which would be the two functions of 'governing' and 'the control of government'. Just as the idea of balanced government was being reassessed and reformulated, so the role of the separation of powers in the new system was being explored. No crude definition of the separation of powers, such as Bagehot's, would do for a system of government so complex and so delicately balanced. This concern with the relation of the separation of powers to the new theory can be clearly seen in the *Essay on the History of the English Government and Constitution*, which Lord John Russell published in 1821.
>
> Lord John Russell believed that the highest stage in the development of civilization and the perfection of civil society was achieved by a system of government which had for its aim the union of liberty with order. The merit and value of differing systems of government are to be measured in relation to the proportions in which these two qualities are combined.[1] The

function of the modern English system of government was, therefore, to produce harmony between the hitherto jarring parts of the Constitution, in order that they might act 'without disturbance or convulsion'.[2] This was achieved in practice by the system of ministerial responsibility, and by the mutual checks that Crown and Parliament exerted upon each other. But how could this system be reconciled with the principle of the separation of powers insisted upon by earlier writers, asked Lord John. In fact, he answered, the three powers never had been, and never could be completely separated with the exception of the judicial power, whose function was merely to apply general rules to particular cases.[3] As for the other two powers, best styled deliberative and executive, in every constitution they continually influenced and acted upon each other.[4] A few years later Austin, in his lectures at University College, London, criticized the idea that the legislative and executive powers were exercised separately in the British system of government, or indeed that they could even be precisely distinguished, as 'too palpably false to endure a moment's examination.'[5]...

The lack of enthusiasm in the British middle classes for the doctrine of the separation of powers may well have been due to the fact that even before 1832 they realized that the extension of the franchise would give to them the control of *all* of the functions of government, so that there was no need for a revolutionary theory. Furthermore, after 1832 the idea of the separation of powers was associated in their minds with universal suffrage on the American pattern. Certainly there was an outpouring of comparisons derogatory to the United States system of government which emphasized the virtues of the greater harmony of the British system. Nevertheless, although they rejected the extreme doctrine of the separation of powers, the strong emphasis upon balanced government remained, and, therefore, the role of a separation of powers and functions continued to be an important element in constitutional thought. What were reformulated, however, were the concepts of power and function, and just how they were to be separated. The model for this reformulation was not that of Montesquieu, but that of James Mill.

1 Lord John Russell, *Essay on the History of the English Government and Constitution* (2nd edn, London: Longman, Hurst, Rees, Orme, and Brown, 1823).

2 Ibid., pp. 94 and 162.

3 Ibid., pp. 148 and 157–9.

4 Ibid., p. 151.

5 J. Austin, *The Province of Jurisprudence Determined* (London: Weidenfeld and Nicolson, 1954), p. 235.

For some commentators, the notion of complete separation could lead to a fragmented and inefficient state, because no person or body may inquire into the workings of the other, reducing the opportunity for collaboration for the public good. The extract below from Bagehot's book, *The English Constitution*, considers the strengths of fusion between the legislative and executive branches of the state. Bagehot argues that a balanced constitution provides a more realistic explanation of the way in which complex states operate, as well as a method of preventing arbitrary government. Bagehot believes that the doctrine is a means to an end—the prevention of abuse of power—rather than an end in itself. The three functions of the state are functions that have been created by commentators to describe the roles played by state organs, rather than fixed functions that may be neatly attributed to distinct bodies.

● **Bagehot, W.,** *The English Constitution* (2nd edn, 1873), available online at http://socserv.mcmaster.ca/econ/ugcm/3ll3/bagehot/constitution.pdf, pp. 48–53

The efficient secret of the English Constitution may be described as the close union, the nearly complete fusion, of the executive and legislative powers. No doubt by the traditional theory, as it exists in all the books, the goodness of our constitution consists in the entire separation of the legislative and executive authorities, but in truth its merit consists in their singular approximation. The connecting link is the cabinet. By that new word we mean a committee of the legislative body selected to be the executive body...

...

But a cabinet, though it is a committee of the legislative assembly, is a committee with a power which no assembly would—unless for historical accidents, and after happy experience—have been persuaded to intrust to any committee. It is a committee which can dissolve the assembly which appointed it; it is a committee with a suspensive veto, a committee with a power of appeal. Though appointed by one parliament, it can appeal if it chooses to the next. Theoretically, indeed, the power to dissolve parliament is intrusted to the sovereign only; and there are vestiges of doubt whether in all cases a sovereign is bound to dissolve parliament when the cabinet asks him to do so. But, neglecting such small and dubious exceptions, the cabinet which was chosen by one House of Commons has an appeal to the next House of Commons. The chief committee of the legislature has the power of dissolving the predominant part of that legislature—that which at a crisis is the supreme legislature. The English system, therefore, is not an absorption of the executive power by the legislative power; it is a fusion of the two. Either the cabinet legislates and acts, or else it can dissolve. It is a creature, but it has the power of destroying its creators. It is an executive which can annihilate the legislature, as well as an executive which is the nominee of the legislature. It was made, but it can unmake; it was derivative in its origin, but it is destructive in its action.

This fusion of the legislative and executive functions may, to those who have not much considered it, seem but a dry and small matter to be the latent essence and effectual secret of the English Constitution; but we can only judge of its real importance by looking at a few of its principal effects, and contrasting it very shortly with its great competitor, which seems likely, unless care be taken, to outstrip it in the progress of the world. That competitor is the Presidential system. The characteristic of it is that the President is elected from the people by one process, and the House of Representatives by another. The independence of the legislative and executive powers is the specific quality of Presidential Government, just as their fusion and combination is the precise principle of Cabinet Government.

...

In England, on a vital occasion, the cabinet can compel legislation by: the threat of resignation, and the threat of dissolution; but neither of these can be used in a presidential state. There the legislature cannot be dissolved by the executive government; and it does not heed a resignation, for it has not to find the successor. Accordingly, when a difference of opinion arises, the legislature is forced to fight the executive, and the executive is forced to fight the legislative; and so very likely they contend to the conclusion of their respective term...

Barendt agrees that the three functions of the state are normative—in other words, they are descriptions based on one view about the way in which power is used within a state, rather than the only way in which to describe the use of power. He too believes that the separation of powers is a way of preventing the abuse of power, or the arbitrary use of power, rather than a good in itself. If the state is able to prevent the abuse of power through other means, then strict adherence to the separation of powers may not be necessary.

● **E. Barendt, 'Separation of powers and constitutional government'** [1991] Public Law 599, 608–9

The argument in the previous section has shown that the separation of powers should not be explained in terms of a strict distribution of *functions* between the three branches of government, but in terms of a network of rules and principles which ensure that power is not concentrated in the hands of one branch. (In practice the danger now is that the executive has too much power, although it is worth remembering that another times there was more anxiety about self-aggrandizement of the legislature.[1]) That does not mean that the allocation of functions is wholly irrelevant...But that the importance of a correct definition and allocation of functions should not be exaggerated...What is important is that there is a system of checks and balances between institutions which otherwise might exercise excessive power. As Madison put it in *Federalist Paper 51*, the structure of government should be so arranged 'that its several constituent parts may, by their mutual relations, be the means of keeping each other in their proper places'.

1 The Founding Fathers of the US Constitution were primarily concerned by the extensive powers exercised by state assemblies.

To conclude, the separation of powers is a doctrine that aims to explain how the powers of the state should be arranged so as to minimise the potential for abuse of power while allowing for effective government. Commentators largely agree that there should be some separation of the powers to make law, to implement the law and to run the country, and to judge the legality of actions and to interpret the law. The independence of the judiciary is universally accepted. However, there are differences between the relative weight given to the need for separation between the legislature and the executive. The people of modern democratic countries have come to different conclusions about the separation or fusion of the legislative and executive functions, and the theories that underpin these decisions have been greatly influenced by the history of those countries. The UK's history indicates that the separation between the Crown and Parliament was the first in a series of decisions about the allocation of the power in the state. The independence of the judiciary was also an early indicator of the need to protect the population from the power of the state. However, as Vile indicates, the role of the electorate should not be forgotten as a check on the legislature's and the executive's exercise of power.

summary points

What are the similarities and differences between different theories of the separation of powers?

- *Most commentators agree that an independent judiciary is a positive contribution within a state. Some argue that this is a necessary condition for a constitution based on the separation of powers; others argue that this is a necessary condition for a state that is based on the rule of law regardless of whether the constitution is based on the principle of separation.*

- *There is less agreement about the extent to which there should be separation between the executive and legislative functions.*

- *Many commentators consider that some separation between the executive function and the legislative function is desirable.*

- *Other commentators consider that fusion of power between the executive and the legislature is desirable because it leads to cooperation and constructive government.*

5.5 How has recent constitutional reform affected the operation of the separation of powers in the UK?

It is perhaps useful to consider in detail the extent to which the separation of powers is apparent within the UK constitution. The theory of the separation of powers has become topical within the political arena, with attention focusing on anomalies within the system. This has led to a number of constitutional reforms, some the result of findings against the UK by the European Court of Human Rights (ECtHR); others at the government's own initiative. The reforms have led to some wide-ranging changes to constitutional arrangements, some of which have been heralded as a major advance towards a more delineated separation of functions between the three arms of the state; others have been viewed by some as unnecessary and largely cosmetic (such as the establishment of a Supreme Court to replace the House of Lords Appellate Committee).

At the beginning of the latest wave of constitutional reform early in the last decade, executive involvement in the setting of the tariff for criminals who have been sentenced to life in prison was transferred to the judiciary, after a series of cases that criticised executive involvement in sentencing. The Home Secretary had the power to determine how long a criminal who had been sentenced to life in prison had to remain incarcerated before being considered for release on licence. In both the cases of *McGonnell v United Kingdom* (2000) 30 EHRR 289 and *R (Anderson) v Secretary of State for the Home Department* [2003] 1 AC 837, the ECtHR and the British judiciary, respectively, criticised the executive's role in the sentencing of prisoners. Both argued that executive involvement in sentencing amounted to the executive exercising a judicial function. This in itself was not necessarily problematic—but the Home Secretary may have been influenced by public opinion and may have taken a political, rather than a judicial, decision as a result. Judges are expected to make their decisions free from bias. The case of *V v United Kingdom* [1999] 30 EHRR 121, in which the Home Secretary set the tariff for the juvenile offenders Thompson and Venables (found guilty of murdering Jamie Bulger), highlighted this predicament. The reform of decision-making in sentencing, though an amendment introduced by section 60 of the Criminal Justice and Court Services Act 2000, transferred the power to set and review tariffs from the executive to the judiciary. This brought the UK constitution a small step closer to the formal separation of powers.

Adherence to the theory of the separation of powers formed part of the government's rationale for the Constitutional Reform Act 2005. It was discussed in a 2004 report of the House of Lords' Select Committee on the Constitutional Reform Bill (HL Paper 125, 2 July) and is implicit within the text of the Act. The Act enshrines in law the duty of the government to uphold the independence of the judiciary, although this duty has been implied for centuries. It reforms the office of **Lord Chancellor** by transferring the judicial functions that he or she enjoyed until recently to the President of the Courts of England and Wales. In addition, the Act has established an independent **Judicial Appointments Commission (JAC)**, which is charged with the responsibility of selecting potential judges and recommending their appointment to the Justice Secretary and Lord Chancellor (one person holds both positions), rather than the selection being made by him or her alone. It is argued that this will provide more guarantees of a judiciary free from political interference and bias than the previous system of appointments.

Constitutional Reform Act 2005

. . . .

CHAPTER 4

CONTINUED JUDICIAL INDEPENDENCE

3   Guarantee of continued judicial independence

(1) The Lord Chancellor, other Ministers of the Crown and all with responsibility for matters relating to the judiciary or otherwise to the administration of justice must uphold the continued independence of the judiciary.

(2) Subsection (1) does not impose any duty which it would be within the legislative competence of the Scottish Parliament to impose.

(3) A person is not subject to the duty imposed by subsection (1) if he is subject to the duty imposed by section 1(1) of the Justice (Northern Ireland) Act 2002 (c. 26).

(4) The following particular duties are imposed for the purpose of upholding that independence.

(5) The Lord Chancellor and other Ministers of the Crown must not seek to influence particular judicial decisions through any special access to the judiciary.

(6) The Lord Chancellor must have regard to—

(a) the need to defend that independence;

(b) the need for the judiciary to have the support necessary to enable them to exercise their functions;

(c) the need for the public interest in regard to matters relating to the judiciary or otherwise to the administration of justice to be properly represented in decisions affecting those matters.

(7) In this section the "judiciary includes" the judiciary of any of the following—

(a) the Supreme Court;

(b) any other court established under the law of any part of the United Kingdom;

(c) any international court.

...

REPRESENTATIONS BY SENIOR JUDGES

5 Representations to Parliament

(1) The chief justice of any part of the United Kingdom may lay before Parliament written representations on matters that appear to him to be matters of importance relating to the judiciary, or otherwise to the administration of justice, in that part of the United Kingdom.

(2) In relation to Scotland those matters do not include matters within the legislative competence of the Scottish Parliament, unless they are matters to which a Bill for an Act of Parliament relates.

(3) In relation to Northern Ireland those matters do not include transferred matters within the legislative competence of the Northern Ireland Assembly, unless they are matters to which a Bill for an Act of Parliament relates.

As you will see from the extract above, the independence of the judiciary is mentioned repeatedly, and the **Lord Chief Justice** and the chief justices of all parts of the UK are given the right to make representations to Parliament on issues relating to the administration of justice. This provision aims to allay fears that the executive may dismiss the judiciary's concerns on a matter of judicial importance that may, in turn, lead to an erosion of the system of justice, and ultimately to the independence of the judiciary.

The 2005 Act also established the Supreme Court (replacing what was the Appellate Committee of the House of Lords) and mandated that it would be housed in a building separate from Parliament. These reforms were introduced in order to strengthen the impression of the judiciary's independence. There were fears that because the House of Lords' Appellate Committee shared a building with the House of Lords' legislative chamber, this may create the perception that the judiciary was not independent of the legislature and the executive, even though this perception would have been baseless. In addition, appointments to the Supreme Court are independent of the political system, and the Court will benefit from having its own budget and staff, which it is argued further adds to its independence. In turn, the justices of the Supreme Court are not permitted to sit in the legislative chamber of the House of Lords (unlike the former Law Lords). This adds further distance between the judicial and legislative processes and personnel. Further extracts from the Constitutional Reform Act 2005 are set out below.

Constitutional Reform Act 2005

. . . .

CHAPTER 4

PART 3   THE SUPREME COURT

The Supreme Court

23   The Supreme Court

(1) There is to be a Supreme Court of the United Kingdom.

(2) The Court consists of 12 judges appointed by Her Majesty by letters patent.

. . .

(6) The judges other than the President and Deputy President are to be styled "Justices of the Supreme Court".

. . .

24   First members of the Court

On the commencement of section 23–

(a) the persons who immediately before that commencement are Lords of Appeal in Ordinary become judges of the Supreme Court,

. . .

Appointment of judges

. . .

27   Selection process

. . .

(2) As part of the selection process the commission must consult each of the following–

(a) such of the senior judges as are not members of the commission and are not willing to be considered for selection;

(b) the Lord Chancellor;

(c) the First Minister in Scotland;

(d) the Assembly First Secretary in Wales;

(e) the Secretary of State for Northern Ireland.

. . .

(5) Selection must be on merit.

(6) A person may be selected only if he meets the requirements of section 25.

[Qualification of judges]

(7) A person may not be selected if he is a member of the commission.

(8) In making selections for the appointment of judges of the Court the commission must ensure that between them the judges will have knowledge of, and experience of practice in, the law of each part of the United Kingdom.

(9) The commission must have regard to any guidance given by the Lord Chancellor as to matters to be taken into account (subject to any other provision of this Act) in making a selection.

...

28   Report

(1) After complying with section 27 the commission must submit a report to the Lord Chancellor.

...

(5) When he receives the report the Lord Chancellor must consult each of the following–

  (a) the senior judges consulted under section 27(2)(a);

  (b) any judge consulted under section 27(3);

  (c) the First Minister in Scotland;

  (d) the Assembly First Secretary in Wales;

  (e) the Secretary of State for Northern Ireland.

...

30   Exercise of powers to reject or require reconsideration

(1) The power of the Lord Chancellor under section 29 to reject a selection at stage 1 or 2 is exercisable only on the grounds that, in the Lord Chancellor's opinion, the person selected is not suitable for the office concerned.

(2) The power of the Lord Chancellor under section 29 to require the commission to reconsider a selection at stage 1 or 2 is exercisable only on the grounds that, in the Lord Chancellor's opinion-

  (a) there is not enough evidence that the person is suitable for the office concerned,

  (b) there is evidence that the person is not the best candidate on merit, or

  (c) there is not enough evidence that if the person were appointed the judges of the Court would between them have knowledge of, and experience of practice in, the law of each part of the United Kingdom.

(3) The Lord Chancellor must give the commission reasons in writing for rejecting or requiring reconsideration of a selection.

...

These provisions are designed to ensure that the senior members of the judiciary are appointed in a transparent way, free from any impression of party-political bias, or 'cronyism'. The system has been designed to place the greatest power in the hands of the independent JAC, but to provide appropriate consultation with interested parties. Ultimately, the judiciary must be appointed by the state if judges are to be part of the constitutional process. The appointment procedure is now more visibly distanced from the charge that appointment is based on secret criteria that privilege judges from a very narrow cross-section of society. Over time, it will be interesting to see whether the new appointment process appears to change the type of people who take up senior judicial office. There continues to be controversy about the gender balance in the Supreme Court (the justices comprising eleven men and only one woman), as well as the lack of racial or ethnic diversity.

thinking point

To what extent do you consider that the rule of law requires the judiciary—particularly the senior judiciary—to comprise a group of suitably qualified judges who have backgrounds that are broadly representative of society as a whole, with reference to gender, ethnicity, religion, sexual orientation, class background, etc.?

summary points

How has recent constitutional reform affected the operation of the separation of powers in the UK?

- *Recent reforms have removed some of the more obvious anomalies in the UK constitution that appear to undermine the traditional view of the separation of powers.*

- *The executive no longer has a role in setting the length of time for which a life prisoner is required to stay in prison before being considered for parole. This power has been placed in the hands of the judiciary.*

- *The Lord Chancellor, who previously performed legislative, executive, and judicial functions, has relinquished all judicial functions and has also handed the position of speaker of the House of Lords to the House to elect its own speaker. The Lord Chancellor retains legislative and executive functions, as do all other ministers.*

- *The judiciary has lost any involvement in the legislative process in the House of Lords, but in turn has had its independence from interference from the executive guaranteed by statute.*

- *The Appellate Committee of the House of Lords has been replaced by the Supreme Court, housed in new premises outside the Palace of Westminster (the home of Parliament), and granted an independent budget and staff, as well as an appointments process that is farther removed from the political process.*

- *Judges are selected and recommended for appointment by an independent Judicial Appointments Commission that is one step removed from the Secretary of State for Justice (a government minister).*

5.6 How have the courts interpreted the separation of powers?

The courts more usually interpret the common law and legislation, and apply the doctrine of precedent, rather than consider doctrines such as the separation of powers. But because this

cross reference

See Chapters 17 and 18 for details on the rules of natural justice and the operation of Article 6 ECHR.

cross reference

See Chapter 7 for details on parliamentary sovereignty.

doctrine forms a fundamental part of our constitution (as do the rule of law and the doctrine of parliamentary sovereignty), it plays a role in judicial decision-making. The separation of powers rarely forms the basis of a case in its pure form, but the doctrine is apparent in the right to a fair trial (Article 6 ECHR, which may be argued in the domestic courts through the Human Rights Act 1998) and in the rules of natural justice, which require that a judge should be independent and free from bias. In addition, cases that consider the powers and duties of the institutions of the state, as well as the relationship between those institutions, also draw upon the doctrine of the separation of powers.

The courts have developed case law relating to the separation between the legislature and the judiciary. Contrary to what one may consider on first examination, these cases indicate that the legislature is free from interference by the judiciary, rather than the other way around. These cases enshrine **parliamentary privilege**, which is the power of Parliament to self-regulate so as to preserve parliamentary sovereignty. Cases such as *Davis v Johnson* [1979] AC 264 and *Pepper v Hart* [1993] AC 593 reserve the legislative functions to Parliament, as well as Parliament's power to self-govern. This may be contrasted with a case such as *R v R* [1991] 4 All ER 481, which is often cited as a case in which the judiciary moved beyond judicial interpretation to judicial legislation by finding that it was a criminal offence for a husband to have non-consensual sex with his wife. The judiciary did not act in flagrant breach of a clearly worded statute to find the husband guilty of the rape of his wife, but it did have to use its powers of interpretation expansively in order to make such a finding in law. Some have argued that this was a breach of the separation of powers, in that the judiciary performed a legislative function in broadening the scope of the criminal law; others argue that the judiciary did what it was required to do—that is, it made a finding based on rather confused and antiquated legal provisions, and then left it to Parliament to clarify the law through new legislation, were the judiciary's interpretation to have been contrary to the legislature's intention. Lord Diplock addressed this issue in the case of *Dupont Steel Ltd.*

● *Dupont Steels Ltd and others v Sirs and others* [1980] 1 All ER 529, HL

Lord Diplock at 541–2:

> My Lords, at a time when more and more cases involving the application of legislation which gives effect to policies that are the subject of bitter public and parliamentary controversy, it cannot be too strongly emphasised that the British Constitution, though largely unwritten, is firmly based on the separation of powers: Parliament makes the laws, the judiciary interpret them. When Parliament legislates to remedy what the majority of its members at the time perceive to be a defect or a lacuna in the existing law (whether it be the written law enacted by existing statutes or the unwritten common law as it has been expounded by the judges in decided cases), the role of the judiciary is confined to ascertaining from the words that Parliament has approved as expressing its intention what that intention was, and to giving effect to it. Where the meaning of the statutory words is plain and unambiguous it is not for the judges to invent fancied ambiguities as an excuse for failing to give effect to its plain meaning because they themselves consider that the consequences of doing so would be inexpedient, or even unjust or immoral. In controversial matters such as are involved in industrial relations there is room for differences of opinion as to what is expedient, what is just and what is morally justifiable. Under our Constitution it is Parliament's opinion on these matters that is paramount.
>
> ...
>
> It endangers continued public confidence in the political impartiality of the judiciary, which is essential to the continuance of the rule of law, if judges, under the guise of interpretation, provide their own preferred amendments to statutes which experience of their operation has shown to have had consequences that members of the court before whom the matter

comes consider to be injurious to the public interest ... But, except by private or hybrid Bills, Parliament does not legislate for individual cases. Public Acts of Parliament are general in their application; they govern all cases falling within categories of which the definitions are to be found in the wording of the statute. So in relation to s 13(1) of the 1974 Act, for a judge (who is always dealing with an individual case) to pose himself the question, 'Can Parliament really have intended that the acts that were done in this particular case should have the benefit of the immunity?' is to risk straying beyond his constitutional role as interpreter of the enacted law and assume a power to decide at his own discretion whether or not to apply the general law to a particular case. The legitimate questions for a judge in his role as interpreter of the enacted law are, 'How has Parliament, by the words that it has used in the statute to express its intentions, defined the category of acts that are entitled to the immunity? Do the acts done in this particular case fall within that description?'

Lord Diplock considers the paradox of the judicial role. A judge is required to interpret the law, but the law is general in nature and the judge must apply it to the specific context. Sometimes, the Act makes provision for a category of situations within which the facts of the case fall squarely, in which case the judge need only discern the meaning of the law and then apply it to the facts. There are other situations in which the law does not appear to address the situation in question, and it is then for the judge to attempt to interpret the law beyond its apparent scope so as to give judgment in the case. The judge does not have the options of asking Parliament to clarify its position or of choosing not to give judgment, because there appears to be a legal lacuna; instead, the judge must interpret the law as written, as best as he or she can, to reach a conclusion in the case. Cases such as *Pickin v British Railways Board* [1974] AC 765 and others that are discussed in Chapter 7 on parliamentary sovereignty are evidence of the judiciary deferring to the legislative power of Parliament in general terms. In individual cases, in which there are badly worded statutes or competing provisions in multiple laws, or which do not fall neatly into the statutory framework, the judicial interpretation–judicial legislation divide may be less easy to distinguish. This line is even more blurred in the context of judges developing the common law, which many argue is a form of judicial legislation.

The mechanism of judicial review is in part based on the principle that the courts have the power to examine whether the executive is acting within its power and its constitutional role, or whether it is acting **ultra vires** (outside of its power). This mechanism fuses the court's power to ensure that the rule of law be upheld with its power to ensure that the executive does not exercise a legislative function other than that which has been delegated to it by Parliament. Parliament does delegate the power to make secondary legislation to the executive (often called 'delegated legislation', because the power to make the law has been delegated to a government minister or to a particular body)—but the executive is permitted to do so only under the terms set by Parliament. Consequently, the courts may be asked to review a piece of secondary legislation so as to check whether it is legal—to examine whether it conforms to the requirements set out in the parent Act, which is the Act of Parliament that delegates the power to make secondary legislation in this instance. The courts scrutinise the executive's exercise of delegated legislative power to ensure that the separation of functions is maintained according to the balance set by Parliament in the given situation. This is yet more evidence of a parliamentary system of government in which there is not a total separation of power between the legislature and the executive, but a complex system of checks and balances that seek to provide for efficient government without abuse of power.

The courts are also called upon to review the exercise of power by the executive to consider if the executive has the legal power to do what it has done. The courts will respect the executive's exercise of power as long as the power is exercised within the limits of the law. The case of *M v Home Office* [1994] 1 AC 377, discussed in the previous chapter in the context of the rule of law, is evidence for the proposition that the courts require the role of the judiciary to be respected as both independent of the other arms of the state and also binding on the executive. This is necessary so, to prevent the abuse of power by an executive that could otherwise act without legal power and thus could subvert the division of power. The recent case of *Bapio Action Ltd* succinctly summarises the constitutional position, with the aid of Lord Scarman's speech in *Notts County Council v Secretary of State for the Environment* [1986] AC 240.

● *R (on the application of Bapio Action Ltd and another) v Secretary of State for the Home Department and another* [2007] EWHC 199 (QB)

Mr Justice Stanley Burnton, citing Lord Scarman, at 520:

> The present case raises in acute form the constitutional problem of the separation of powers between Parliament, the executive, and the courts. In this case, Parliament has enacted that an executive power is not to be exercised save with the consent and approval of one of its Houses.
>
> … If Parliament legislates, the courts have their interpretative role: they must, if called upon to do so, construe the statute. If a minister exercises a power conferred on him by the legislation, the courts can investigate whether he has abused his power. But if, as in this case, effect cannot be given to the Secretary of State's determination without the consent of the House of Commons and the House of Commons has consented, it is not open to the courts to intervene unless the minister and the House must have misconstrued the statute or the minister has—to put it bluntly—deceived the House. The courts can properly rule that a minister has acted unlawfully if he has erred in law as to the limits of his power even when his action has the approval of the House of Commons, itself acting not legislatively but within the limits set by a statute. But, if a statute, as in this case, requires the House of Commons to approve a minister's decision before he can lawfully enforce it, and if the action proposed complies with the terms of the statute (as your Lordships, I understand, are convinced that it does in the present case), it is not for the judges to say that the action has such unreasonable consequences that the guidance upon which the action is based and of which the House of Commons had notice was perverse and must be set aside.

This extract and the discussion in the *Bapio* case show that the courts have limited power in relation to executive action and parliamentary decision-making. They indicate that the courts' role is limited to a review of the legality of actions, and in cases in which Parliament does not insist on giving its consent as a means of overseeing the exercise of power, the courts may review whether the action or decision is manifestly unreasonable. The earlier case *Council of Civil Service Unions v Minister of State for Civil Service* [1985] AC 374 indicates that the courts have the power to review whether the power upon which the executive relies in order to act or to decide in a particular way both exists and is sufficiently broad to cover the executive's actions. The legislature provides the legal power to the executive, through legislation (with the exception of the operation of the royal prerogative), and the executive uses the legal power to run the country. However, the executive may not act beyond its legal power—to do so would either offend against the rule of law, or indicate that the executive was exercising the legislative function without the permission of the legislature via delegation.

NOTE This is both a separation-of-powers point and a rule-of-law point, because an independent judiciary is essential for the effective operation of both doctrines.

Equally, the judiciary is not permitted to replace the executive's decision with its own if it considers that a better decision could have been reached. The judiciary's power is limited to reviewing the executive's decision or action to ensure that it is legal, rational, and has been reached in a way that conforms to the rules of natural justice and in a way that is procedurally proper. It may also review the executive's action or decision to consider whether it conforms to the Human Rights Act 1998. It cannot offer an alternative decision, or change the policy that the executive has developed (unless Parliament has so provided). The judiciary's role is limited to a review of the legality of the executive's actions (in broad terms) rather than the merits of

cross reference
Parliamentary privilege is discussed in Chapter 7.

its actions or decision. The courts abide by parliamentary privilege in order to uphold the legislative supremacy of Parliament. Judges are also limited to judicial interpretation rather than judicial legislation—although this line is a blurred one, particularly in view of the development of the common law, which is judge-made rather than statutory. The courts will also respect the exercise of power, as long as it remains within the prescribed legal and procedural limits. Thus the separation of powers is implied daily through the courts system, even though the doctrine is not regularly used as the basis of judicial decision-making.

summary points

How have the courts interpreted the separation of powers?

- *Cases pre-reform of the sentencing powers of the Home Secretary highlighted the judicial function of a member of the executive in setting the tariff for a life prisoner. This long-standing anomaly to the doctrine of the importance of an independent judiciary has now been resolved.*

- *The courts have distinguished between their power to interpret the law and their power to legislate, although this is an extremely difficult line to draw.*

- *The courts respect parliamentary privilege so as to preserve parliamentary sovereignty and the legislative supremacy of Parliament, although there have been situations in which the courts' interpretation of the law has bordered on law-making, albeit in the absence of clear guidance from Parliament on a particular area of law.*

- *Judicial review is a mechanism through which the judiciary ensures that the executive is not acting beyond its legal power, or legislating beyond the terms of any delegation of power by Parliament.*

- *The judiciary respects the executive's power to run the country and does not supplant the executive's decision-making power with its own through judicial review cases. Instead, it is required to respect the executive's action or decision as long as it is legal, rational, and has been made according to the rules of natural justice, and in a procedurally proper way.*

- *Human rights cases do, however, draw judges into discussions about the proportionality of the executive's actions, and some argue that this could erode the executive's exclusive policy jurisdiction.*

5.7 What is the relevance of the separation of powers today?

cross reference
See Chapter 20 for recent counter-terrorism developments.

Have we now resolved the debate about the separation of powers within our constitution through recent constitutional reform? Is the position relatively settled? Recent terrorist events have put the theory of separation to the test, not least as regards the need for an independent and robust judiciary. At a similar time to the drafting of the Constitutional Reform Bill, which became the Constitutional Reform Act 2005, while the executive was reiterating the need for an increased separation of powers in the UK constitution, elsewhere the theory was coming under threat within other legislation. As the extract below demonstrates, anti-terror legislation such as the Prevention of Terrorism Act 2005 was eroding the distinction between the executive and the judiciary by permitting the state to subject terrorist suspects (not yet convicted of any crime) to restrictions on their liberty without a court determination of their guilt. Interestingly, this takes us back to where we started the history of the separation of powers in the UK: to Magna Carta, which sought to protect subjects from being punished without being convicted of a crime, through the excessive use of power by the executive.

● *J. L. Hiebert*, **'Parliamentary review of terrorism measures'** [2005] Modern Law Review 676, 678–9

The bill sought to authorise the Secretary of State to make 'control orders' that would allow a suspected terrorist to be placed under house arrest, and thereby derogate from the right to liberty under Article 5 of the ECHR, without prior judicial authorisation. The bill would also authorise a wide range of restrictions on suspects' movements, association, expression, and travel again without prior judicial involvement. The JCHR [Joint Committee on Human Rights] conducted a rigorous rights-review of the proposed measures within days of the bill's introduction. It questioned why house arrest was being contemplated, particularly in the light of the Home Secretary's admissions that 'there is currently no need' to derogate from Article 5 of the ECHR. The JCHR also expressed doubt about the legitimacy of denying liberty without prior judicial involvement [Ninth Report of the JCHR, Session 2004–5, *Prevention of Terrorism Bill: Preliminary Report*, HL 61/HC 389, paras 5–13, 15–17]. The reason given for refusing to authorise prior judicial authorisation was that the government has 'prime responsibility to protect the nation's security' and that to abdicate this responsibility to the judiciary would be inappropriate. [Charles Clarke, Secretary of State for the Home Department, HC Deb vol 431 co. 153–155 22 February 2005]. The JCHR characterised this explanation as an 'eccentric interpretation of the constitutional doctrine of the separation of powers', and reminded the government that the 'judiciary's responsibility for the liberty of the individual' has long been accepted and respected. Therefore, to 'invoke national security to deny the role' would be to 'subvert' the nation's 'traditional constitutional division of powers'. [Ninth Report of the JCHR, para. 12].

The bill was subject to a political ping-pong match between the House of Commons and the House of Lords. After surviving an initial vote in the Commons (albeit with a greatly reduced majority), the government agreed to make modest amendments because of speculation of a possible defeat in the Lords. These were assessed by the JCHR in it second report on the bill within a week, in which it expressed concerns about the unprecedented scope of the powers contained in the bill..., the JCHR reminded parliament that such political intentions reinforce the importance of having 'independent safeguards for individual liberty'. The JCHR asserted that while the intention not to be accused of being vigorous enough to protect the public interest is a sentiment that is 'entirely understandable in elected representatives' it demonstrates why politicians should not be in charge of determining when to deprive an individual of his or her liberty...Despite the JCHR's critical report, the Commons passed the amended bill. But the House of Lords was still not persuaded that rights would be adequately protected...after a marathon session, the House of Lords agreed to pass the bill, but only when the government promised that the legislation would be reviewed in a year.

At times when national security may be deemed to be at risk, the theory of the separation of powers frequently returns to the spotlight. The executive, charged with governing the nation and protecting the public, may attempt to increase its powers to defend the state. What a political party rejected while in opposition or during its first few weeks of office may later be championed as events appear to indicate that 'robust' policing may be in order. The recent UK riots and political indications of ongoing or increased terror threats may lead to the introduction of measures that once seemed unthinkable, unless the electorate is prepared to argue strongly against them. Such legislation has the potential to restrict individuals' liberties and rights disproportionately, and to lead the judiciary to reassert its role as guardian of individual liberty through the operation of the common law. An independent judiciary that is permitted to review the exercise of executive power is a protection against its excessive use.

However, the judiciary has also been criticised for using its powers so as to develop (or some would say create) new law on privacy. Others go even further and suggest that the judiciary is trying to usurp the power of Parliament altogether by stifling debate of this issue in the House by its use of super-**injunctions**. This has led to an investigation into the use of super-injunctions (discussed in Chapter 9). The debate is set out, neatly, in the extract below.

· ·

● **R. Benwell and O. Gay, 'The Separation of Powers'** (House of Commons Library Standard Note SN/PC/06053, 16 August 2011) available online at http://www.parliament.uk/briefing-papers/SN06053, pp. 10–11

4 Super-Injunctions

In 2011, the question of separation of powers has arisen in relation to the use of injunctions. An injunction is a court order that requires a party to do or refrain from doing certain acts. For example, it may order that certain identifies, facts or allegations may not be disclosed. Standard Note 5978 *Privacy* provides background as to the development of a new type of injunction whose very existence may not be disclosed. In some cases, known as 'super injunctions', the court has provided for anonymity and a prohibition on publishing or disclosing the very existence of the order. Restrictions may also be placed on access to documents on the court file.[1] Professor Zuckerman has argued that super-injunctions created a new kind of procedure for an 'entire legal process ... conducted out of the public view' of which the very existence is 'kept permanently secret under pain of contempt'.[2]

In April 2011, David Cameron said that he felt 'uneasy' about super-injunctions and that judges were developing a privacy law without Parliamentary approval.[3] The Human Rights Act 1998 imposed a duty on the judges to interpret legislation 'as far as possible' in a manner to make it compatible with the European Convention on Human Rights. Article 8 of the Convention sets out respect for privacy and family life, which the courts have developed as part of the common law in the absence of statutory privacy laws in the UK. Those developments have led some to argue that the courts have gone beyond their power to develop common law to introduce a right of privacy into English law.[4] Others have suggested that the enactment of the Human Rights Act effectively created the right of privacy, so the foundations were, in fact, laid by Parliament.[5]

Parliamentarians have criticised the judiciary for their use of a novel legal instrument. MPs have used parliamentary privilege to circumvent the injunctions, naming recipients in the House.[6] On the other hand, members of the judiciary have argued that Parliamentarians have used privilege to defy the law and that this could undermine the role of judges. Lord Judge suggested that it may not be advisable for MPs to 'flout a court order' even if they did not agree with it. He insisted that 'there has never been any question, in any of these orders, not in any single one of them, of the court challenging the sovereignty of parliament ... We are following the law, as best we understand it'.[7]

Some MPs have criticised the use of privilege to name those protected by injunction. Chuka Ummana said that 'if MPs and peers use parliamentary privilege to flout Court injunctions, that is a serious breach of the separation of powers'.[8] Mr Speaker has said that he strongly deprecated 'the abuse of parliamentary privilege to flout an order or score a particular point'.[9] The Attorney General announced on 23 May 2011 that a joint committee of both Houses would be established to examine the issues on privacy and the use of anonymity injunctions.[10]

1 Master of the Rolls, *Report of the Committee on Super-Injunctions: Super-Injunctions, Anonymised Injunctions and Open Justice* (London: HMSO, May 2011) (the Neuberger Report)

2 A. Zuckerman, 'Super injunctions: curiosity-suppressant orders undermine the rule of law' (2010) 29 Civil Justice Quarterly 134.

3 D. Casciani, 'Q&A: superinjunctions', BBC News, 20 May 2011, available online at http://www.bbc.co.uk/news/mobile/uk-13473070

4 Master of the Rolls, n. 1, section 1.4.

5 *The Telegraph*, 'Injunction review: judges only implementing Parliament's privacy laws, says Lord Justice', 20 May 2011, available online at http://www.telegraph.co.uk/news/uknews/law-and-order/8525556/Injunctions-review-judges-only-implementing-parliaments-privacy-laws-says-Lord-Justice.html

6 John Hemming [HC Deb, 23 May 2011], col. 638.

7 *The Independent*, 'Judges accused of gagging bid', 20 May 2011, available online at http://www.independent.co.uk/news/uk/home-news/judges-accused-of-gagging-bid-2286874.html

8 Ibid.

9 Hemming, n. 6, col. 653.

10 Ibid, col. 635.

Consequently, the separation of powers remains a live issue in British political and legal life, and is likely to continue to remain so for some time.

summary points

Of what relevance is the separation of powers today?

- *The separation of powers often comes under pressure at times of national emergency or civil disobedience, as the executive strives to maintain control of the country.*

- *There are also particular concerns that the use of super-injunctions may breach fundamental principles associated with the separation of powers, because many MPs subvert super-injunctions by using parliamentary privilege to name those who have been protected by them.*

- *Further, relatively recent legislation such as the Constitutional Reform Act 2005 has sought to strengthen the separation of powers in the UK, demonstrating that it remains a live issue in British political and legal life.*

Summary

The separation of powers is a theory or doctrine that describes the relationship between the three branches of the state: the law-making branch known as the legislature; the governing and policymaking branch known as the executive; and the legal interpretation and application branch known as the judiciary. The doctrine is premised on the assumption that if one group of people, or one body, is able to exercise the powers of the three branches of government, then individuals' rights may be adversely affected and the rule of law may be damaged. Different theorists have offered alternative views about how the potential for an abuse of power may be reduced or prevented, and these are based on the concept of separation of power. Some theorists, such as Montesquieu, believed that the separation of powers needs to be absolute, and consequently that the people and the bodies that make the law, implement the law in running the country, and adjudicate on legal disputes must be different. Other theorists, such as Jennings, are of the opinion that it may be impossible—and indeed undesirable—for there to be a total separation of powers between the legislative and executive branches of the state. All do agree, however, on the need for an independent judiciary, and consequently separation of the judicial arm is considered to be a prerequisite for a society that operates under the rule of law.

 # Questions

1   What are the different functions of the three main powers of the state?

2   What is the essence of the doctrine of the separation of powers?

3   What are the main similarities and differences in key theorists' views on the separation of powers?

4   How would you explain the separation of powers in a UK context?

5   How have the courts applied the separation of powers and what does this indicate about the operation of the separation of powers in the UK?

6   To what extent could it be argued that the Constitutional Reform Act 2005 has tipped the British constitution closer to the traditional conception of the separation of powers, and farther away from that of a balanced constitution with checks and balances?

Further reading

Barber, N. W., 'Prelude to the separation of powers' (2001) 60(1) Cambridge Law Journal 59

This is an interesting article that is written in an engaging style and yet is extremely academic. Its focus is on the differing interpretations of the separation of powers and it is well worth reading if you want to learn more.

Barendt, E., 'Separation of powers and constitutional government' [1991] Public Law 599

This, too, is an excellent article. It positions the separation of powers within the concept of constitutional government and governance, and examines the way in which the different conceptions of the theory affect our understanding of appropriate institutional frameworks. It examines the extent to which the British constitution is fundamentally grounded in the doctrine.

Benwell, R. and Gay, O., 'The Separation of Powers' (House of Commons Library Standard Note SN/PC/06053, 16 August 2011), available online at http://www.parliament.uk/briefing-papers/SN06053

This is a very clear guide to the essential features of the separation of powers, its history and development, and how it is evidenced in the British constitution. It considers recent reforms and also touches upon challenges brought about by super-injunctions.

6

The Crown and Royal Prerogative

Key points

This chapter will cover:

- What is the history of the role of the Crown and the royal prerogative?
- What is the royal prerogative?
- What is the relationship between the royal prerogative and Acts of Parliament?
- To what extent does the Queen exercise prerogative powers?
- To what extent does the political executive exercise prerogative powers?
- What control, if any, does Parliament have in relation to the exercise of prerogative powers?
- How have the courts reviewed the operation of prerogative powers?
- What is the relevance of the royal prerogative today and is it in need of reform?

Introduction

This chapter will examine the nature and extent of prerogative powers. It will consider the history and development of the royal prerogative, and the role of the Crown in the exercise of these powers. It will address the division between prerogative powers that are personally exercised by the Queen and those that are exercised on her behalf by the political executive. We shall then turn to the respective roles of Parliament and the courts in the operation and development of prerogative powers, before turning to the relevance of those powers today and proposals for reform. As in previous chapters, this will be followed by a summary and self-test questions.

There are two strands of legal power that may be used by the state: one emanating from Parliament (statute and related secondary legislation) and the other from the common law. The doctrine of the rule of law dictates that the Crown may not act unless it has the legal power to do so, either as a result of statute or the common law The case of *Entick v Carrington* (1765) 19 State Tr 1029 established that the executive (in the form of the King's men at that time) had to be able to demonstrate the legal power under which it acts. The royal prerogative is a special form of common law that may be exercised by the Crown, either through the Queen as monarch (her personal prerogative) or through the executive as Her Majesty's government (the political prerogative). Royal prerogative powers are similar to presidential powers in some other jurisdictions. You will sometimes see the royal prerogative referred to as 'Crown powers' and sometimes as 'prerogative powers'.

cross reference
Chapter 2 provides an overview of the monarch and the government.

137

6.1 What is the history of the role of the Crown and the royal prerogative?

Chapters 4 and 5 provide a detailed account of the changing nature of the relationship between the **monarch** and **Parliament**. The key events are also displayed on the historical timeline that you will see on the Online Resource Centre that accompanies this book. Magna Carta 1215 marked a turning point in the relationship between the feudal barons and the monarch. The monarch was required to recognise that his subjects (or at least a portion of his subjects) had rights. This acted as a limit on the monarch's power. There followed a series of struggles between the barons and the King, which included Richard II being removed from the throne (or abdicating, depending on your point of view) in 1399 for a failure to rule under the law. Subsequently, the Statute of Proclamations in 1539 removed the monarch's power to rule by use of proclamation, and a series of cases in the early 1600s, including the *Prohibitions del Roy* [the Case of Prohibitions], spelled out the limits on the King's power. The civil war and the restoration of the monarchy in 1660 paved the way for a clearer division of power between the King exercising the **royal prerogative** and Parliament enacting written law via **legislative** procedures. The culmination of the ongoing dispute between the monarch and the Parliament was the Bill of Rights in 1689. However, Parliament remained reliant on the King to call Parliament to permit it to meet. Unless it could meet, it could not exercise its power. The monarch's power to call Parliament was, and remains, a prerogative power. Some of the historical kings and queens had a better record at calling Parliament than did others. Their record on calling Parliament to meet was, in part, dependent on the extent to which the monarch required Parliament to approve tax increases so as to provide the monarch with funds. With such a chequered history between Parliament and the monarch, it is perhaps surprising that Parliament did not remove the royal prerogative that endows the monarch with the power to call and dissolve Parliament. Indeed, it is perhaps surprising that Parliament has not sought to remove the royal prerogative altogether and to replace it with statutory **executive** powers, which are transparent, can be more easily overseen by Parliament, and can be reviewed by the courts.

Parliament may have limited the monarch's power leading to the development of a constitutional, rather than an absolutist, monarch, but it did not list the royal prerogative powers in a clear and concise form for the avoidance of doubt or ambiguity. Why was this? Payne explains that one of the reasons for this lack of definition can be found in the way in which the royal prerogative developed and the justifications for it. He argues that most commentators begin their discussion by providing a description of the powers rather than looking behind them. He suggests that it is easier to define the powers once one has considered their justifications and ancestry. But he also considers the prerogative to be a somewhat murky area that may violate some principles of the **rule of law** on grounds of lack of certainty.

cross reference
You may wish to refresh your memory by rereading the history sections of Chapters 4 and 5.

cross reference
See Chapter 2 for an overview of the royal prerogative.

- **S. Payne, 'A critique of prerogative powers'** (Institute of Advanced Legal Studies Workshop: The Crown and Public Law, 21 January 1994, London), pp. 1–3

> The Crown exercises power under statute and the prerogative. In analysing the existence and use made of prerogative powers, there are two very different approaches which I shall call the traditional and the radical approach. The traditional approach espouses the harmlessness of the present position. Most of the prerogative powers relate to trivial matters such as University charters. Where the prerogative deals with more important matters, then Parliament gets a look in, witness for example the Ponsonby rules with regard to treaties [Parliament gets to discuss the treaty, by kind permission].
>
> The Radicals would describe this approach as the Establishment smugly patting itself on the back at the status quo. On the contrary, they would say, the status quo is not benign at all. It is bad in both theory and practice. The prerogative is a feudal, monarchical power. What is absurd is that whilst the personal power of the Sovereign has shrunk to almost nothing, the executive powers of the sovereign have remained but have been transferred to the Prime Ministers and ministers. Feudalism in the guise of democracy...
>
> Put another way, every description of what the legal political system is has within it an argument or set of assumptions about how we should organise our society... [an] explanation of how the world works... This is a significant issue in dealing with the powers of the prerogative. 'Is such a distribution of power justifiable' may look like a separate question from 'What are the powers that the Crown has'. But these questions may be closely connected for the following reasons.
>
> A. The powers of the prerogative, as the case law suggests, are vague.

B. The answer to the question 'what powers exist' may be resolved by the concept of necessity. Prerogative powers are those powers that inhere by necessity in the Crown. For instance, the power to secure the safety of the realm. Everyone appreciates that the powers of the prerogative are the result (or residue) of an historical process, feudal in original some suggest. But is there something odd in the acceptance of the transmission of such powers across the centuries? ...

An elaboration of the indeterminacy of the class of prerogative powers

...

The existence of the Royal prerogative in the seventeenth century was set in the context of the King being the Chief Executive ... The relation between ruler and ruled was deemed to be based on a form of contract. The King entered into a contract when he swore his Coronation oath. As well as privileges and powers he had obligations to the people. The people assented to be ruled on the basis that there were advantages accruing to them as well as obligations. In England the Chief Executive was also the spiritual head of the Church.

The religious element was clearly an essential ingredient. Whereas the King ruled by the grace of God, such grace also implied that the ruler would behave in a manner consonant with Christian belief and obligations. Hence sixteenth century debate on the circumstances in which a people were freed from their obligations to a 'bad' King. Furthermore there was a belief in Fundamental Law ... which imposed overarching limitations on what a monarch might do and on the authority of man made law. The judges in 1610 stated that they could strike down legislation for going against natural law (*Dr. Bonham's case*).

Prerogative powers were developed so that the King could rule effectively; in return, he owed obligations of protection to his people. His legal power sprang from his role as chief executive and protector, as presidential prerogative powers do in the United States (which followed a British model of executive powers). Payne argues that there are two distinct views of prerogative powers:

- that they are relatively harmless and so have been left in place substantially the same through the centuries; and

- that they are a set of far-reaching powers, now mostly used by the executive, and as such should have been reformed as the constitutional system developed into a democracy.

He suggests that one of the reasons that prerogative powers have not been reformed is that many people do not question their historical background and their underlying purposes. We have got so used to them being there that we do not question why we retain a set of powers that relate to the times of absolute monarchy when the monarch ruled according to what was considered to be God's will.

Current prerogative powers can be explained as the powers that Parliament has not removed from the monarch (or her political executive) by statute, but which remain available to conduct international relations and to defend the realm and public safety, as well as to facilitate the proper functioning of the **state**. Some prerogative powers have been placed on a statutory footing at a point at which the prerogative power has become problematic, has needed to be narrowed or broadened, or has needed to be updated to meet current conditions. The remaining prerogative powers remained pretty much intact, and remain wide and relatively ill-defined so as to be flexible to respond to urgent, unexpected, and sometimes dangerous situations.

summary points

What is the history of the role of the Crown and the royal prerogative?

- *The royal prerogative is derived from the historic personal power of the monarch, who ruled as an absolute monarch until his (or her) power was challenged and eroded by an early form of Parliament.*

- *The royal prerogative has remained vague and somewhat obscure because Parliament has not sought to codify it or to set out the remaining powers of the monarch.*

- *Parliament has not sought to do this in part because it has intervened to remove individual prerogative powers on a case-by-case basis to meet specific concerns.*

- *In addition, Parliament may not have placed the remaining prerogative powers onto a statutory footing so as to ensure that they remain flexible and available for urgent atypical situations.*

6.2 What is the royal prerogative?

6.2.1 The key features of the royal prerogative

There are a number of key features of prerogative powers. Personal and political prerogative powers cover those areas that the monarch used to be able to conduct in person without further authorisation or consultation. They are linked to the monarch's status as head of state and ruler. This is reflected in the areas that are covered by prerogative powers: foreign affairs, including relationships with other countries, entering into treaties, and the granting of passports for foreign travel; national defence (sometimes called 'defence of the realm'), which is to protect the country and its subjects from outside aggression, including war powers; and national security, linked to internal threats to the safety of the nation and the need to preserve the confidentiality of state secrets. In addition, prerogative powers also encompass appointing certain office holders and granting honours. The dissolution of Parliament is also a royal prerogative power. The areas covered by the prerogative reflect their historical roots.

cross reference

The nature of constitutional conventions is discussed more in Chapter 12, as are parliamentary and governmental recommendations that some of them be put on a statutory footing.

Prerogative powers are based in the common law and so are not written down in a codified form. As a result, their extent is not easy to discern, because it is not possible to read a definitive text that sets out each of the powers. **Constitutional conventions** have developed over time to regulate and place limits on the exercise of prerogative powers. There are many constitutional conventions that indicate how the powers should be used, and when Parliament should be informed and consulted about their use by the executive. Constitutional conventions, in contrast to prerogative powers, are not law at all, but are instead binding principles that, if broken, may incur severe political consequences. Suffice to say that constitutional conventions are an area ripe for reform in some people's eyes, and a distinctive and positive contribution to Britain's relatively eccentric constitution in others'.

cross reference

This is an example of parliamentary supremacy, as discussed in Chapter 7.

Unlike statutory powers, no new prerogative powers may now be created. All new constitutional and administrative powers are created by statute instead. This means that the royal prerogative is residual—that is, what is left in the hands of the monarch (or her delegate), which has not yet been removed by Parliament through statute. However, existing prerogative powers may be interpreted to meet the needs of modern-day situations and this has led to considerable development of the prerogative powers far beyond instances that they had been designed to meet. In keeping with their residual status, a power may be abolished, restricted, or suspended by statute.

Parliament could replace all prerogative powers by statutory powers, should it wish to do so. Why may Parliament consider this to be desirable? Parliament cannot control or direct the exercise of prerogative powers, although it may scrutinise the executive's use of some prerogative powers as it would scrutinise the executive's use of statutory power. It may ask a **government** minister to account for his or her department's actions that rely on prerogative power, through parliamentary mechanisms such as questions and debates, ministerial statements to the House, and select committee investigations. Some areas are, however, exempt from full scrutiny by reason of national security considerations, for example. Consequently, Parliament has more control over the executive if the executive is using statutory powers than it does if it is using prerogative powers. In the event of a dispute, it is for the courts to determine the extent and existence of prerogative powers. It is suggested that the courts may also examine the exercise of the prerogative to ensure that the powers are being used legally, rationally, and procedurally properly, as they would any other acts of the executive through **judicial** review. Traditionally, prerogative powers have not been susceptible to review by the courts to the same extent as the exercise of statutory power, although this position has changed over time, as discussed later in the chapter.

cross reference

Parliament's scrutiny of the executive is considered in Chapters 11–13.

6.2.2 The scope of the royal prerogative

So far, we have considered the royal prerogative in general terms, but we have not really attempted to define the scope of prerogative powers. A number of commentators have sought to define the royal prerogative, including leading scholars such as Blackstone and Dicey. The two extracts that follow illustrate core definitions of prerogative powers, as well as some differences in opinion about them. The first extract—the older of the two—demonstrates that Blackstone took a restrictive approach to the definition of the royal prerogative.

● **Blackstone's Commentaries on the Laws of England** (8th edn, Oxford: Clarendon Press, 1778), p. 232

> ...in its nature singular and eccentrical that it can only be applied to those rights and capacities which the king enjoys alone...and not to those which he enjoys in common with any of his subjects.

The extract explains that, in Blackstone's view, the royal prerogative is the common law legal power that the monarch holds because he (or she) is the monarch. It is a special branch of the common law that is unique to the monarch and can be distinguished from the general common law that the rest of us enjoy. In other words, the royal prerogative is a group of powers that are clearly defined and available to the **Crown**, to be exercised by the head of state. They are also limited in their extent—they do not comprise a general power that permits the Crown to do as it wishes in the absence of other statutory authority.

As one would expect in an area of law that remains largely uncodified, there are other interpretations of the royal prerogative. Blackstone may have had a narrow approach to prerogative powers, but at the other end of the spectrum lies Dicey's much broader approach. He argued that the royal prerogative was a term that encompassed all of the residual powers retained by the Crown other than those reserved to Parliament. If this were accurate, the powers of the Crown would be quite extensive, because they would include all of the powers that the monarch had prior to Magna Carta, but which Parliament had not removed or restricted subsequently by statute.

● A. V. Dicey, *The Law of the Constitution* (10th edn, London: MacMillan, 1959), pp. 424–5

> The prerogative appears to be both historically and as a matter of actual fact nothing else than the residue of discretionary or arbitrary authority, which is at any given time legally left in the hands of the Crown…Every Act which the executive government can lawfully done without the authority of an Act of Parliament is done in virtue of this prerogative.

This extract suggests that the royal prerogative is actually rather broad and covers any legal power that Parliament did not remove, and has not subsequently removed, from the monarch. This will encompass a wide range of powers, because at one time the monarch ruled absolutely rather than as a constitutional monarch. The courts have tended to adopt a relatively broad definition more in keeping with Dicey's stance, although the position is by no means settled. There is consequently some disagreement about the nature and extent of prerogative powers in the UK. Although it is sometimes difficult to reconcile differing views, the debate is largely theoretical (other than for specialist constitutional and administrative law practitioners and scholars), and for the purposes of this book it is more important to know that there are different views than it is to be able to assess the extent to which you consider them to be a reflection of current practice.

Such disagreements are not confined to countries like the UK, which have a constitutional monarch and an uncodified constitution. There are debates about the nature and extent of executive (prerogative) powers exercisable by the US President. It may appear odd at first glance that prerogative powers provoke similar definitional concerns in a country that has a clear delineation of responsibilities and competencies between the three branches of the state spelled out in a written constitution. But in the US, prerogative powers are also not defined in specific terms by law. The areas covered by prerogative powers are not clearly expressed and the way in which they may be used is subject to some debate. It is interesting to note that the subject areas covered by US prerogative powers are similar to those in the UK. In addition, Congress (the closest UK equivalent would be the Westminster Parliament) and the courts have a role to play in checking the use of prerogative powers, but some argue that the checks are insufficiently rigorous and that the US President may use the power with little watchful scrutiny. Furthermore, some commentators express concern that 'national security' may be used as a mechanism with which to stifle scrutiny and debate about the exercise of particular powers in specific situations. In short, many of the concerns expressed about the UK's royal prerogative, or prerogative powers, are also raised in a very different context in the US.

It may be helpful at this stage to consider in more detail the areas covered by the royal prerogative in the UK, to illustrate the powers in more detail. As indicated above, the areas covered by the royal prerogative have been fixed and new prerogatives cannot be established. These broad headings have been discussed in Parliament, by academics and practitioners, and in the courts. The often-quoted passage that illustrates this point comes from one of the leading cases on the royal prerogative.

● *British Broadcasting Corporation v Johns (Inspector of Taxes)* [1965] Ch 32, CA

Lord Justice Diplock at 79:

> …[I]t is 350 years and a civil war too late for the Queen's courts to broaden the prerogative. The limits within which the executive government may impose obligations or restraints on citizens of the United Kingdom without any statutory authority are now well settled and incapable of extension.

Table 6.1

Examples of royal prerogative

....

The legislature and legislation: The monarch summons, prorogues, and dissolves Parliament (hence the state opening of Parliament). She is involved in making law through royal assent.

....

Appointments to certain state offices and the award of honours: These include high judicial office, the office of Prime Minister and other ministers, as well as appointment of civil servants and regulation of the civil service.

....

Courts and justice system: These include the pardoning of convicted criminals through the prerogative of mercy and the Attorney General's role as representative of the Crown in legal proceedings.

....

Foreign affairs: These include the issuing of passports, treaty negotiations and signature, the acquiring of new territories, the recognition of foreign states, and the recognition of diplomats.

....

Defence: The sovereign is commander in chief of the armed services, can make a declaration of war, and is responsible for making of peace, commissioning officers, and deploying forces abroad.

....

Emergency powers related to national security.

....

Creating of bodies by charter: (This applies to some) universities, (some) professional bodies, and corporations.

What areas were reserved to the monarch at the point at which Parliament required that all new legal powers were made by statute rather than through an extension of the royal prerogative? The case of *BBC v Johns* does not shed much light on the powers, rights, and immunities that are encompassed by the royal prerogative—and it is difficult to know with any certainty what is the extent of the royal prerogative, due to its lack of documentation. Table 6.1 provides examples of prerogative powers, grouped by subject area. The executive attempted to define them after a request was made by the House of Commons Public Administration Select Committee in 2003.

Some of these are personal prerogatives reserved to the **Queen**; others are delegated to the political executive. Some of the monarch's powers are in all real terms formal or ceremonial in nature. In other words, they are so tightly regulated by constitutional convention that her choice of action is largely illusory. There is an ongoing debate about this. Brazier recognises greater scope for monarchical activism than does Blackburn, who considers that modern constitutional practice largely removes the monarch's **discretion** even in the use of personal prerogatives. This will be discussed in more detail later in the chapter.

There are also certain immunities and privileges associated with the royal prerogative. These too may be removed by Parliament. Markesinis explains this as:

....

● **B. S. Markesinis, 'The royal prerogative revisited'** (1973) 32(2) Cambridge Law Journal 287, 309

...the residue of executive powers, immunities or other attributes which the government possesses without the authority of Parliament, but which can be withdrawn—expressly or impliedly—by Parliament.

The Crown is not bound by statute unless the wording in the statute expressly provides for this or the content of the Act is such that the Crown's liability may be necessarily implied. In other words, the Crown is exempt from the law unless the law states that the Crown is bound by it or the content of the law is such that it must be bound by it. This was firmly established in the case of *Mersey Docks and Harbour Board v Cameron* (1865) 29 JR 483 and has been further illustrated in the subsequent case of *BBC v Johns*.

The case of *BBC v Johns* involved a discussion of the royal prerogative, because the BBC was set up under royal charter, which is a form of legal instrument that is executed through the operation of the royal prerogative. The case is complicated. It sought to consider the extent to which the BBC was liable to pay income tax on any surplus that it made on its broadcasting activity. It also considered whether that financial surplus could be deemed to be profit in the true sense (rather than a surplus that could be ploughed back into broadcasting activities), because the BBC was not permitted to make a profit under the terms of its royal charter and licence. Of particular relevance to our examination of the royal prerogative is Lord Justice Wilmer's discussion towards the end of this extract, in which he explains the way in which Crown immunity operates and how it extends to Crown servants that are carrying out certain Crown functions under the royal prerogative.

● ***British Broadcasting Corporation v Johns (Inspector of Taxes)*** [1965] Ch 32, CA

Lord Justice Willmer at 59–60:

> ... Mr. Bucher, in opening the appeal on behalf of the B.B.C., formulated his argument under six propositions, as follows: (1) the Sovereign personally is immune from the operation of any statute unless named in the statute. (2) Servants or agents of the Crown are equally immune unless named in the statute. (3) Persons who are not Crown servants or agents are immune if they are in consimili casu with Crown servants or agents. (4) Persons are to be regarded as being in consimili casu with servants or agents of the Crown if they are appointed to carry out government purposes. (5) Government purposes include the traditional provinces of government (for instance, the making of war or peace, the administration of justice, or the maintenance of law and order). (6) Government purposes also include non-traditional provinces of government if the Crown has constitutionally asserted that they are to be within the province of government.
>
> Nobody, I think, could quarrel with propositions (1) to (4) ...
>
> In my judgment, however, the argument for the B.B.C. breaks down in relation to proposition (6), because I find it impossible to accept the contention that the Crown has ever asserted that broadcasting should be within the province of government. I do not find it necessary to express any view as to whether it would be within the prerogative of the Crown to assert any such claim ...

These immunities have been reiterated by Lord Keith in *Lord Advocate v Dumbarton District Council* [1990] 2 AC 580. These immunities and privileges are also a product of the royal prerogative's historic roots. Crown servants undertaking certain activities of state are immune from the law, unless the law specifically applies to them. This does not mean that Crown servants, or civil servants and the executive, are above the law. When acting in their personal capacity, they are as answerable in law as you or I: as private citizens, they are subject to the law in the normal way. Instead, it means that the law does not apply to the state, the Crown, unless the legislation specifically so provides.

It may be useful to consider the relationship between the royal prerogative and Parliament in more detail to consider why these immunities have developed.

What is the royal prerogative?

- *The royal prerogative covers the subject areas that were reserved to the monarch by Parliament.*
- *It is not well defined.*
- *We rely on case law and academic works to determine the extent of the royal prerogative.*
- *It is constantly reinterpreted to fit current situations.*
- *Examples of the exercise of royal prerogative can be seen in:*
  - *the legislature and legislation, including the sovereign's power to summon, prorogue, and dissolve Parliament (hence the state opening of Parliament) and to assent to Acts of Parliament;*
  - *the courts and justice system, including the pardoning of convicted criminals and the Attorney General's role as representative of the Crown in legal matters before the court;*
  - *foreign affairs, including passport issuing, negotiating and making treaties, acquiring new territories, or granting independence to (soon to be) British colonies;*
  - *defence, including going to war and making peace (the sovereign is commander in chief of the armed forces);*
  - *appointments and honours, including appointment to certain official offices of the state and also the granting of honours; and*
  - *immunities and privileges, including that statutes do not bind the Crown except by express words or by necessary implication.*
- *Emergency powers have traditionally been rooted in the royal prerogative, although in recent years the state has sought to extend these through statute.*

thinking point

Do you think that the lack of precision in the royal prerogative is a strength or weakness, given the fact that it covers powers related to defence and national security?

6.3 What is the relationship between the royal prerogative and Acts of Parliament?

In this section, we shall consider the relationship between prerogative powers and Acts of Parliament. There is some debate about whether prerogative powers can become extinct if they are not used. This process is known as 'desuetude'. However, it is generally accepted that, in all but the most rare of circumstances, prerogative powers continue to exist unless they are abolished or restricted by statute. In a situation in which Parliament enacts a statute on the same area as a prerogative power, the prerogative power is suspended (held in abeyance) until such time as the legislation is repealed and the prerogative power is required. In other words, the prerogative power yields to statute while the statute subsists. It is possible for statute and prerogative powers to coexist, assuming that the Act amplifies or expands on the prerogative power rather than restricts, suspends, or removes it. We shall take each of these issues in turn.

6.3.1 Prerogative powers remain unless they have been abolished or restricted by statute

Prerogative powers are enduring, other than in very limited circumstances that come under the preserve of the rule of desuetude. However, Acts of Parliament are the highest form of domestic law in the UK and they are consequently hierarchically superior to prerogative powers. This means that if a statute is enacted on the same area as the prerogative power, and there is a contradiction between the Act and the prerogative, the Act will be applied by the courts. In effect, an Act overwrites the prerogative power, either expressly or by implication. Parliament may state in the Act that it is abolishing the prerogative power by statute. There is a debate as to whether it is ever possible for Parliament to extinguish a prerogative power or whether an Act suspends its operation only until such time as the Act or Acts are repealed. In most instances, the debate is relatively academic, because while the Act remains in force, the prerogative ceases to have any legal implications. More important for the purposes of this book is that Parliament is supreme and an Act of Parliament overrides a contradictory prerogative power. But, from now on, we shall refer to this process as 'abolition' (rather than 'abolition or suspension') so as to simplify the debate.

Why would Parliament wish to legislate to abolish the royal prerogative, having left it in place for so many centuries? There are circumstances under which the Crown may find that, in exercising a prerogative power, it is bound by certain duties associated with the power. The royal prerogative cannot be amended by the executive; instead, any change must be made by statute by placing the power on a statutory footing via Act of Parliament. This may lead to some confusion about whether the Crown is acting under the original prerogative power, or whether this has been superseded by a statutory power. The case of *Burmah Oil Co Ltd v Lord Advocate* [1965] AC 75 is a good illustration of the confusion that can arise from the use of an unwritten power, and also the relationship between prerogative and statute. In this case, Burmah Oil brought an action against the Crown for a **declaration** that the company was entitled to compensation for the destruction of its property by British armed forces. The British army destroyed the company's oil refinery in Burma in 1942, to slow the advance of the enemy, the Japanese, in the Second World War. British forces did not want the refinery and its products to fall into the hands of the enemy, because if they were to do so, they would be likely to assist the Japanese war effort. It was asserted that the actions were lawful by virtue of prerogative powers and this was largely accepted. However, the issue that arose was the extent to which the Crown was liable to pay compensation for the damage under the terms of the royal prerogative. We shall pick up the case at this point.

· ·

● *Burmah Oil Co Ltd v Lord Advocate* [1965] AC 75

Sir Milner Holland QC (of the English Bar), Henry Keith QC (of the English Bar), QC (of the Scottish Bar), J. Hobhouse (of the English Bar), and J. J. Clyde (of the Scottish Bar) for the appellant companies, at 78–80:

> ...The following questions arise: (1) Whether a deliberate planned act of destruction of an entire industry in order to deny it to the enemy is (a) something done in exercise of the prerogative power for the benefit of the whole country or (b) an act of necessity which the Crown and the subject alike could lawfully perform and which is therefore not actionable, by reason of the defence of necessity. It is submitted that this case falls within the first alternative. (2) Whether, assuming that what was done was an exercise of the royal prerogative, compensation was payable. It is submitted that all deliberate acts of the taking of the property of the subject and all acts of destruction of his property for the prosecution of a war and the safety of the realm attract compensation; this includes the deliberate destruction of property which may be of advantage to the enemy. The only exception is accidental destruction in the course of battle in the sense that it is accidental on whom the loss falls. (3) If such a principle exists that compensation is due in those circumstances, is it payable where the destruction was done under pressure of extreme necessity? It is submitted that it is...
>
> In the matter of necessity, the rights of private individuals have nothing to do with the rights of States, since the acts of the former are limited to their own necessity, but those of the latter are not. The prerogative right of the State to take the citizen's property is founded on necessity. There is a distinction between this and the right of every citizen to defend his own property. The fact that the State may be under the necessity to take property for the public need does not justify a taking without compensation... In time of war the commander of the armed forces on the spot conducts a campaign as if it were being conducted by the prince in the medieval sense. Parliament has nothing to do with it. So where there is no question of the supremacy of Parliament authorising a taking without compensation, compensation is payable in respect of a sacrifice required of the individual for the benefit of the State. The appellants put forward the broad principle that full compensation is payable for the taking of the subject's property by the State. On this point the unanimity of the civilians and commentators is remarkable and therefore of considerable force as authority. Where there is no modern authority one must go back to the civilians and to Justinian and, if there is virtually complete unanimity among them, that is at least strongly persuasive, though one cannot say that any particular passage is binding.
>
> ...

This judgment reiterates the vagueness of many royal prerogative powers and the difficulty faced by lawyers and judges in their interpretation of them. In this case, the **judiciary** sought to establish whether the royal prerogative had been replaced by statutory powers, and if not, the extent of the continuing prerogative and duties associated with it. After consideration at great length of historical precedents, a majority of the Law Lords found that the prerogative had been engaged, and that Burmah Oil and related companies were entitled to compensation under the terms of the royal prerogative. But that was not the end of the story: Parliament was asked to pass the War Damages Bill, which became the War Damages Act 1965. This was a controversial piece of legislation not least because it had retrospective effect. This means that its terms were backdated to a date before the Act was passed. The Act removed the possibility of compensation for certain types of war damage inflicted by the Crown, thus removing Burmah Oil's right to compensation. It did not change the House of Lords' judgment, because

cross reference
The rule-of-law issues associated with this case are considered in Chapter 4.

this would be a direct breach of the **separation of powers**, but it did frustrate its effect. Not only is this a challenge to the rule of law, but it is also evidence of the superiority of legislation over the royal prerogative.

6.3.2 Whilst a statute is in force in similar terms to the prerogative, the executive cannot use the prerogative power

Prerogative powers, being residual in nature, have to give way to Parliament and parliamentary supremacy. A statute that addresses the subject matter of the prerogative power in specific terms will override the prerogative power if it contradicts it rather than enlarges upon it. The case of *Attorney General v De Keyser's Royal Hotel* [1920] AC 508 illustrates the confusion that can arise in situations in which there is an Act and a prerogative power in similar terms, but with some substantive differences. In this case, the London hotel was commandeered by the state during the Second World War to house troops. The government, in the form of the War Office, attempted to negotiate a contractual deal with the hotel; when that appeared to hit an impasse, it chose to commandeer the hotel for use in the war effort. It was contended that there was legislation—the Defence of the Realm Regulations—that could have formed the legal basis of this action. There was also a prerogative power related to the defence of the realm that could provide legal authority for such an action. But the two forms of law would lead to different levels and liabilities of compensation to be paid by the executive to the hotel owner, who had not had the use of his premises while the hotel had been commandeered. The executive argued that it had made use of the prerogative power, for which only voluntary **damages (ex gratia)** had to be paid, as opposed to the statutory scheme, which provided for a right to compensation. This is where we join the case.

• •

● *Attorney General v De Keyser's Royal Hotel Ltd* [1920] AC 508

Lord Dunedin at 508:

> The prerogative is defined by a learned constitutional writer as 'The residue of discretionary or arbitrary authority which at any given time is legally left in the hands of the Crown'. Inasmuch as the Crown is a party to every Act of Parliament it is logical enough to consider that when the Act deals with something which before the Act could be effected by the prerogative, and specially empowers the Crown to do the same thing, but subject to conditions, the Crown assents to that, and by that Act, to the prerogative being curtailed.
>
> ...

Lord Atkinson at 539–40:

> It is quite obvious that it would be useless and meaningless for the Legislature to impose restrictions and limitations upon, and to attach conditions to, the exercise by the Crown of the power conferred by a statute, if the Crown were free at its pleasure to disregard these provisions, and by virtue of its prerogative do the very thing the statutes empowered it to do. One cannot in the construction of a statute attribute to the Legislature (in the absence of compelling words) an intention so absurd. It was suggested that when a statute is passed empowering

> the Crown to do a certain thing which it might therefore have done by virtue of the prerogative, the prerogative is merged in the statute. I confess I do not think the word 'merged' is happily chosen. I should prefer to say that when such a statute, expressing the will and intention of the King and of the three estates of the realm, is passed, it abridges the Royal Prerogative while it is in force to this extent: that the Crown can only do the particular thing under and in accordance with the statutory provisions, and that its prerogative power to do that thing is in abeyance. Whichever mode of expression be used, the result intended to be indicated is, I think, the same—namely, that after the statute has passed, and while it is in force, the thing it empowers the Crown to do can thenceforth only be done by and under the statute, and subject to all the limitations, restrictions and conditions by it imposed, however unrestricted the Royal Prerogative may theretofore have been.

The question before the Court was whether the hotel had housed troops by virtue of a contract between the Crown and the hotel owner, and whether it had been commandeered by virtue of a statutory power or under the royal prerogative. In all instances, the Court was to determine whether the owner was entitled to a form of rent or monetary compensation. The House of Lords held that the Crown was not permitted by prerogative or statute to take possession or to make use of another's property for the purposes outlined in the case without paying some form of compensation. The Lords concluded that the Crown acted by virtue of statutory and not prerogative powers. The prerogative was not open to the Crown, because it had been superseded by statutory provisions. Where there is both a statutory power and a prerogative power, the statutory power must be used. This is further evidence that the prerogative must yield to statute.

6.3.3 Statutes and prerogative power may coexist

So far, we have focused on situations in which a prerogative power has been overridden by statute. There are situations in which an Act may provide additional power to the executive, to amplify or to complement the prerogative power, rather than to remove or restrict it. One such controversial case is *R v Secretary of State for the Home Department, ex p Northumbria Police Authority* [1989] QB 26. This provides a somewhat confusing addition to the case law on prerogative powers, indicating that the area remains the subject of some judicial, as well as practitioner and academic, debate.

In this case, the police authority sought to challenge the legality of the government's decision to provide chief constables with rounds of plastic bullets and CS gas in the event that they were needed to quell public disturbances. Public disturbances were (as now) much in the news at the time: the late 1980s were a time of political and social unrest, after a period of national strikes (the miners' strike), poll tax demonstrations, and related incidents. The Home Secretary decided to equip the police to be able to deal robustly with any future problems. There was provision for these materials to be provided in some instances even without the consent of the local police authority that regulates each police force. The court at first instance held that the Home Secretary's power was derived from the royal prerogative. The Court of Appeal held that the Home Secretary's decision was legally grounded in both statute and the prerogative, which would appear to contradict some commentators' views of the exclusivity of jurisdiction between legislation and prerogative. The following extract is taken from the first-instance judgment of Mann J, who explains how the prerogative and statute can coexist in this instance.

● *R v Secretary of State for the Home Department, ex p Northumbria Police Authority* [1989] QB 26

Mann J at 33—4:

Experience of events of many kinds in recent years has demonstrated beyond any doubt that serious breaches of the peace can suddenly erupt and can sorely test the ability of the police to control disorder. The availability to a chief constable of suitable equipment for the purpose of maintaining or restoring the peace ought not in our view to depend upon the outcome of an application for judicial review unless there is a most compelling reason in law for such a dependency.

In our judgment, the prerogative powers of themselves were adequate to empower the supply of equipment where the equipment was necessary to meet either an actual or an apprehended threat to the peace. The critical question is whether the power (otherwise than in regard to a grave emergency) survived the Act of 1964. It is plain that where a statute covers the same power as is enjoyed under the prerogative then the prerogative power is no longer exercisable. Thus, in *Attorney-General v De Keyser's Royal Hotel Ltd* [1920] A.C. 508 Lord Dunedin said, at p. 526:

'Inasmuch as the Crown is a party to every Act of Parliament it is logical enough to consider that when the Act deals with something which before the Act could be effected by the prerogative, and specially empowers the Crown to do the same thing, but subject to conditions, the Crown assents to that, and by that Act, to the prerogative being curtailed.'

Lord Parmoor said, at p. 575:

'The constitutional principle is that when the power of the executive to interfere with the property or liberty of subjects has been placed under parliamentary control, and directly regulated by statute, the executive no longer derives its authority from the Royal Prerogative of the Crown but from Parliament, and that in exercising such authority the executive is bound to observe the restrictions which Parliament has imposed in favour of the subject.'

The familiar principle was more recently applied in *Laker Airways Ltd. v Department of Trade* [1977] Q.B. 643 which was a case where reliance upon the prerogative would by necessary implication have been inconsistent with a statutory regime.

Mr. Keene submitted that a prerogative power to supply (other than in grave emergency) was inconsistent either expressly or by implication with the statutory power to equip conferred upon police authorities. We cannot accept that submission. The prerogative power is not the subject of a statutory equivalent as it was in *De Keyser's case* nor does section 4(4) of the [Police] Act of 1964, in our judgment, confer a monopoly power so as to limit the prerogative by implication. The subsection is not drawn so as to create a monopoly and even granted the different statutory functions of a police authority and of the Secretary of State we see no cause to imply that the conferred power is to be a monopoly. Granted the possibility of an authority which declines to provide requisite equipment, there is every cause not to imply a Parliamentary intent to create a monopoly. The Secretary of State's power to supply equipment to meet actual or apprehended breaches of the peace is neither by the terms of the Act of 1964 nor by implication from it, placed in abeyance.

It was not entirely clear which prerogative power was being invoked to provide the legal grounding for the decision. If the Defence Secretary had armed British troops to repel a foreign invader, then the basis in prerogative would have been clear: the defence of the realm. However, it is less certain in relation to internal threats and perceptions of internal threats: after all, the difficulty had not yet occurred—and may not have occurred—to warrant the supply of rounds of plastic bullets and CS gas. The court acknowledged this difficulty, but asserted the legality of this particular exercise of prerogative power. This remains a difficult decision to integrate into the other case law on prerogative powers, because it appears to lack a firm connection with a known prerogative power. However, the court believed that, by implication, the Home Secretary must have such a power at his disposal. In the event of a dispute relating to the relationship between an Act and a prerogative power, it is for the court to determine the extent to which a prerogative power is still in force.

This case had been the subject of a great deal of criticism, including the following.

● **A. Tomkins,** *Public Law* (Clarendon Law Series, Oxford: Oxford University Press, 2003), p. 82

> That the courts are prepared to grant to the Crown such elastic and ill-defined powers, and to subject their exercise to such modest—even superficial—review, constitutes the second way in which the executive will find the rule of law a much less onerous check on its powers than might first have seemed.

This is not the only case that has attracted criticism. The case of *R v Secretary of State for the Home Department, ex p Fire Brigades Union* [1995] 2 AC 513 also considered the relationship between an Act that had not yet been brought into force and a prerogative that would have been suspended by the operation of the Act if it had been. The controversy related to the judicial reasoning at the Court of Appeal and House of Lords stages, in which all judges involved provided different legal reasons for their decisions. It is not necessary to go into detail in this chapter about the case, but it is good evidence for the proposition that the relationship between statute and the prerogative is not as clear-cut as many of the precedents may suggest.

The next two sections will consider the division of prerogatives between the Queen and the executive, as well as the constitutional conventions that have been established over time to regulate the exercise of this power.

151

summary points

What is the relationship between the royal prerogative and Acts of Parliament?

* *Acts of Parliament are hierarchically superior to prerogative powers.*
* *An Act of Parliament may overwrite a prerogative power and abolish it.*
* *An Act of Parliament may overwrite a part of a prerogative power and restrict it.*
* *An Act of Parliament may suspend the operation of the prerogative power for the time being, until the Act is repealed or amended to that effect.*
* *An Act of Parliament may amplify or complement a prerogative power.*
* *In the event of a dispute, the courts will have to determine the extent to which the prerogative power remains available to the executive to use.*

6.4

To what extent does the Queen exercise prerogative powers?

This is an issue that sometimes causes confusion on comparative constitutional law courses in other countries. The confusion relates to who is able to exercise the royal prerogative: the monarch as sovereign, or the executive. Sometimes, it is suggested that it is in the Queen's legal gift to take the UK to war, to send troops abroad, to grant us our passports, and to pardon convicted criminals. And in some respects this is true, at least on a stark legal level, even if not in practice. But the division of prerogative powers between the monarch and the executive is not what at first it seems. We shall try in this section to demystify some of the unnecessary complexity that dogs this area. But first we shall see from where some of the confusion has arisen. Bagehot outlines some of the areas that give rise to misconceptions.

● **W. Bagehot, The English Constitution, Vol. III: The Monarchy** (2nd edn, 1873), available online at http://socserv.mcmaster.ca/econ/ugcm/3ll3/bagehot/constitution.pdf, pp. 74–5

> The House of Commons has inquired into most things, but has never had a committee on 'the Queen'. There is no authentic blue-book to say what she does. Such an investigation cannot take place; but if it could, it would probably save her much vexatious routine, and many toilsome and unnecessary hours.
>
> The popular theory of the English Constitution involves two errors as to the sovereign. First, in its oldest form at least, it considers him [the monarch] as an 'Estate of the Realm', a separate co-ordinate [legislative] authority with the House of Lords and the House of Commons. This and much else the sovereign once was, but this he is no longer. That authority could only be exercised by a monarch with a legislative veto...But the Queen has no such veto. She must sign her own death-warrant if the two Houses unanimously send it up to her. It is a fiction of the past to ascribe to her legislative power. She has long ceased to have any. Secondly, the ancient theory holds that the Queen is the executive. The American Constitution was made upon a most careful argument, and most of that argument assumes the King to be the administrator of the English Constitution, and an unhereditary substitute for him [president]...—to be...necessary. Living across the Atlantic, and misled by accepted doctrines, the acute framers of the Federal Constitution...did not perceive the Prime Minister to be the principal executive of the British Constitution, and the sovereign a cog in the mechanism. There is, indeed, much excuse for the American legislators in the history of that time. They took their idea of our Constitution from the time when they encountered it...Inevitably, therefore, the American Convention believed the King, from whom they had suffered, to be the real executive, and not the Prime Minister, from whom they had not suffered.
>
> If we leave literary theory, and look to our actual old law, it is wonderful how much the sovereign can do. A few years ago the Queen very wisely attempted to make life peers, and the House of Lords very unwisely, and contrary to its own best interests, refused to admit her claim. They said her power had decayed into non-existence; she once had it...but it had ceased by long disuse. If any one will run over the pages of Comyn's Digest or any other such book, title 'Prerogative', he will find the Queen has a hundred such powers which waver between reality and desuetude, and which would cause a protracted and very interesting legal argument if she tried to exercise them. Some good lawyer ought to write a careful book to say which of these powers are really usable, and which obsolete. There is no authentic explicit information as to what the Queen can do, any more than of what she does.

Bagehot's extract, in rather complicated language, attempts to dispel some myths. The Queen has a wide range of legal powers that originate in history, some of which have been superseded by statute and some of which appear to have become extinct because they have not been used in centuries. Some of them have been delegated to the **Prime Minister** and other ministers; others remain within her personal power. Jennings refers to these as personal prerogatives; Bogdanor refers to them as reserve powers for or to the monarch.

Table 6.2

Personal prerogatives of the monarch

....

Summon, prorogue, and dissolve Parliament

....

Dismiss the government

....

Appoint the Prime Minister

....

Give her royal assent to Bills so that they may become Acts

There are four main prerogative powers that the monarch is free to exercise personally: the summoning, proroguing, and dissolution of Parliament (usually to trigger a general election and to summon Parliament after an election); the appointment of the Prime Minister; the dismissal of the government; and the granting of royal assent to Acts of Parliament. The monarch has very wide legal powers in each of these four instances. She may dissolve Parliament whenever she chooses and for whatever reason (or none). She may appoint whomever she wishes to be Prime Minister regardless of whether he or she is a politician or a member of a political party: she is legally entitled to choose you or me, if she so wishes. She may dismiss the government from office at the stroke of a pen. And she may choose to override the will of Parliament and refuse to give her royal assent to any Bill, thus preventing it from becoming law. Her legal powers really are extensive, as illustrated in Table 6.2.

However, as with many forms of prerogative, a series of constitutional conventions has developed so as to limit, in all but the most extreme cases, the exercise of the monarch's choice. The choice remains open to her, in legal terms, but constitutional conventions provide that she should use that choice in its fullest form only in the most extreme, exceptional circumstances. In all other instances, constitutional conventions have been developed that explain how she is to act in the exercise of her power. These effectively bind her in all but the most unusual of circumstances. This is illustrated clearly by Feldman in the next extract.

153

● **D. Feldman, 'None, one or several? Perspectives on the UK's constitution(s)'** (2005)
64(2) Cambridge Law Journal 329, 331–3

In every constitution there are gaps between appearance and reality . . . Formally, legislation is made by Her Majesty. The relationship between her and the two Houses of the Westminster Parliament is summed up in the words of enactment at the beginning of each Act as follows:

'BE IT ENACTED by The Queen's most Excellent Majesty, by and with the advice and consent of the Lords Spiritual and Temporal and Commons, in this present Parliament assembled, and by the authority of the same, as follows: . . .'

[We can pause, parenthetically, to note a curious feature of this formulation: the mention of the Queen's most excellent majesty summons a picture of Her Majesty looking through her wardrobe, saying, 'Now should one wear one's most excellent majesty, or the old one that one uses for pottering round the garden? No, one has to enact legislation today; it must be the most excellent one, with all the velvet and ermine.' Does the monarch have a range of different qualities of majesty to choose between?]

Where an Act is passed under the authority of the Parliament Acts 1911 and 1949, like the Hunting Act 2004, the words are different:

'BE IT ENACTED by The Queen's most Excellent Majesty, by and with the advice and consent of the Commons in this present Parliament assembled, in accordance with the provisions of the Parliament Acts 1911 and 1949, and by the authority of the same, as follows: …'

Now the appearance that the enacting of the legislation is done by the Queen is correct as a matter of legal theory, but we know that the initiative usually lies with the Government, and that the legislative process is under the control of the two Houses and the Government, working together (or sometimes against each other). The Hunting Act 2004 is not the result of a decision by Her Majesty to clothe herself in her most Excellent Majesty and visit Parliament to suggest that, in the light of representations by the royal corgis that foxhounds and beagles were wasting too much of their time chasing wild mammals round the countryside when they could be better employed studying to become sheepdogs or legal philosophers, it was expedient for Parliament to prohibit the hunting of wild mammals with dogs. The Act was the product of long, difficult and acrimonious debates conducted along three axes: between different members of the Government; between the Government, the Parliamentary Labour Party and other politically aligned and non-aligned elements in the two Houses; and between the two Houses as collective bodies. To this extent, the words of enactment at the beginning of the Hunting Act 2004 do less than justice to the work done by the House of Lords: the statutory formula hides the fact that the Lords Spiritual and Temporal offered their advice, although in the event most of it was rejected by the House of Commons.

We all know that, in reality, the Queen enacts what the two Houses have approved (or, in the case of a Bill presented for royal assent under the Parliament Acts 1911 and 1949, the House of Commons has approved). There is a constitutional convention that Her Majesty exercises her prerogative power as legislator only on the advice of her Prime Minister and in accordance with the text approved by Parliament. This is the result of a long battle between the Crown and Parliament, reaching a climax in the civil war of the mid-seventeenth century, and effectively sealed by the Bill of Rights 1689. The convention makes it possible to speak of legislation as a process with some representative legitimacy, and, since the extension of the electoral franchise in the century or so following 1832, also a degree of electoral legitimacy. If Her Majesty were to exercise her legislative power in a way that failed to comply with the convention she might commit no legal wrong, but she would be acting unconstitutionally. There is no doubt about this. The gap between the appearance and the reality gives rise to no uncertainty in relation to this matter, unless one is a newly-arrived visitor from another planet. Yet it is a major gap, and it is important that it should be there. It allows a formal, legal process of monarchical legislation that would be unacceptable today on account of its clash with values of democratic constitutionalism to operate in accordance with those values and to be regarded as being consistent with them.

The gap is important for practical and theoretical reasons relating to the nature of constitutions. All constitutions deal with the business of governing, a dynamic and, to a great extent, political and pragmatic process. As a result constitutional law is political, in that it is concerned with the allocation of public power and has to explain or rationalise the allocation and exercise of that power, even when the practical day-to-day operation of government has moved away from the formulae embodied in formal rules and texts. Conventions of the constitution are means of holding in check the tension between the formal, legal appearance of the constitution and the current practice. By framing the practices in terms of rules of the political elite and theorising their relationship to legal rules, both the political elites and the legal elites can recognise and accommodate to each other the competing demands of law and politics…

Feldman argues that the gap between the theory and practice of the Queen's exercise of personal prerogative power is great. The power is given through the prerogative free from restriction and yet it is restricted through the operation of a constitutional convention that is not a form of law, is thus not legally binding, and so cannot be enforced by the courts. He concedes that may appear to leave a certain degree of uncertainty about how the Queen will exercise her power, but that in practice it is clear to all of us that she believes herself to be bound by the convention almost as if it were law. In this way, the piecemeal, ever-changing British constitution holds two seeming contradictory systems in place: a monarchy in the age of democracy. It also provides a final check on the power of Parliament in a system of parliamentary supremacy. Were Parliament to do the unthinkable and pass a law so morally reprehensible that it would bring the rule of law into disrepute, the monarch would have the legal power to delay and even refuse to provide her assent, thus preventing its enactment. What would be the consequences of such an act would depend largely on the views of the public at the time. With popular support, she may be lauded as a check on the power of Parliament. Without popular support, such an action would likely precipitate the demise of the constitutional monarchy. It is difficult to say for certain what would be the implications, because no monarch has refused royal assent since 1708.

6.4.1 Summoning, proroguing, and dissolving Parliament

The Queen is charged with the power to summon Parliament and to prorogue Parliament. The operation of these powers is described in Chapter 2, but to summarise in brief: the monarch has the power to call Parliament back to session after a general election and for the new parliamentary sitting, to call the parliamentary sitting to a close at the end of the parliamentary year, and to dissolve Parliament so as to trigger a general election. In strict law, she may do this at will, but in reality the exercise of power is tightly constrained by the operation of constitutional conventions. The following special parliamentary note drafted to aid parliamentarians and their advisers suggests that the exercise of this personal prerogative is relatively certain in nature, although the end of the extract highlights the academic discussion between Blackburn and Brazier about the extent to which the monarch has real power in exercising this prerogative power.

● **L. Maer and O. Gay, 'The Royal Prerogative'** (House of Commons Library standard note SN/ PC/03861, 30 December 2009), p. 5

> Secondly, the dissolution of Parliament, in the absence of a regular term for the life of Parliament fixed by statute, the Sovereign may by the prerogative dissolve Parliament and cause a general election to be held. The sovereign normally accepts the advice of the Prime Minister and grants dissolution when it is requested; a refusal would probably be treated by the Prime Minister as tantamount to a dismissal. These areas of the prerogative are the subject of continuing academic debate.[1]
>
> 1 R. Blackburn, 'Monarchy and the personal prerogatives' [2004] Public Law 546; R. Brazier '"Monarchy and the personal prerogatives": a personal response to Professor Blackburn' [2005] Public Law 45.

The controversy is in part related to the extent to which the Queen is required to follow the advice of the Prime Minister in relation to the dissolution of Parliament. The Westminster Parliament has not historically been subject to fixed terms, meaning that there has been no set date on which a general election must be called as long as an election is called within the five-year term of Parliament, as required by law. The choice of general election date was, until 2011, left to the Prime Minister. He or she, with or without the consent of Cabinet, chose when the time was right to call an election and then asked the Queen to exercise her prerogative to trigger that election. Recent legislation has severely limited the Prime Minister's power in this

cross reference
See Chapter 2 for a discussion of the position after the Fixed-term Parliaments Act 2011.

regard, as discussed in Chapter 2. However, the monarch retains the prerogative power nonetheless, albeit subject to the provisions of the Fixed-term Parliaments Act 2011. The legislation was introduced with the stated intention of providing stability to the current **coalition government**, but it has effect until such time as the legislation is amended or repealed, and so is likely to continue to operate into the next single-party government.

6.4.2 The appointment of the Prime Minister

cross reference
You may wish to reread the extract from Brazier's article in Chapter 2 to refresh your memory of this.

The Queen also has the legal power to appoint the Prime Minister and, in law, she may select whomever she chooses to form a government and lead the country. Once again, her apparently free choice is restricted through the operation of constitutional conventions to such an extent that, in recent decades, there have been no surprises in relation to her choice. In each case, she has asked the leader of the party with the most seats in the House of Commons (and who may command a majority either on the basis of his or her party alone or in coalition with others) to become the Prime Minister. Party leadership has been determined by each of the political parties in accordance with their party rules and so the choice of party leader is not within her gift. However, selection of the next Prime Minister has not always been that straightforward. Indeed, but for the senior civil service drawing up guidance to assist in the event of a hung Parliament and working with the political parties after the most recent general election, the choice of the Prime Minister may have been more controversial than it was at the point at which no one party was able to command a majority of seats in the House of Commons.

6.4.3 The dismissal of the government

The Queen also has the legal power to dismiss the government and thus to force a general election. At face value, it does appear to strike at the heart of democratic principles for a monarch to dismiss our elected representatives and to require an election to be fought. This could have the effect of changing the political complexion of the country, including the direction of policy and law. However, this power is also subject to constitutional convention and public scrutiny. Were the Queen to decide to dismiss a government on a relative whim, then a public debate may ensue about whether the monarch should be permitted to hold such a power or any power for that matter. Like many aspects of the British constitution, this power remains uncurtailed because its exercise has not posed sufficient concern to justify the parliamentary time required to debate its reform. But that has not been the case in all countries: a particularly controversial exercise of the royal prerogative in this respect was the dismissal of the Australian Prime Minister and government by the Governor General of Australia, who is the Queen's representative in the country. Australia retains Queen Elizabeth II as its head of state, although there has been a national debate and even a **referendum** in 1999 to vote on whether the monarch should be replaced as head of state by a president and whether Australia should become a republic. The Queen's prerogative powers in Australia are exercised on her behalf by someone whom she appoints on the advice of the Prime Minister to become the Governor General. In this instance, the Australian constitutional convention that operated in similar circumstances to the British one did not seem to have been followed as many expected.

summary points

To what extent does the Queen exercise prerogative powers?

- *The monarch retains four personal prerogative powers: the dissolution of Parliament; the dismissal of the government; the appointment of the Prime Minister; and the granting of royal assent to Bills.*

- *The monarch's legal powers are extremely wide, with no legal restrictions placed on her exercise of power.*

- *Constitutional conventions have developed over time to restrict the exercise of power to a level that retains certainty and aids the rule of law.*

- *However, constitutional conventions are not legal rules, are not legally binding, and cannot be enforced through the courts.*

- *Breach of a constitutional convention may trigger grave political consequences, but not legal ones.*

- *The exercise of these forms of prerogative powers are generally considered to be exempt from judicial review.*

6.5 To what extent does the political executive exercise prerogative powers?

There are a wide range of prerogative powers of which the political executive makes use. The most often discussed and hotly debated relate to negotiating and entering into treaties with other countries, declaring war and deploying troops abroad, and recognising foreign states and their diplomats—for example Kosovo, which has recently declared independence from Serbia, and also the newest-formed state South Sudan. However, there are others that affect our daily lives on a regular basis, including prerogative powers associated with national security matters that prevent us from being informed of some of our state's actions in the UK and abroad. The next two subsections will consider treaty-making powers, and declarations of war and deployment of troops abroad—two topical issues at present.

6.5.1 Treaty-making powers and prerogative powers

The power to negotiate and enter into treaties with other countries, including treaties relating to the European Union (EU), is based in the royal prerogative. Under the Ponsonby rule, Parliament was given the opportunity to comment on treaties before they are ratified, but this is not a legal requirement and, in law, the executive could enter into a treaty without Parliament's consent. The Constitutional Reform and Governance Act 2010 provides a statutory basis for the House of Commons and House of Lords to scrutinise treaties prior to ratification. Thus the Act provides Parliament with the legal right to scrutinise treaties prior to their ratification. Indeed, the European Union Act 2011 makes it a legal requirement for there to be a referendum prior to a decision to ratify a treaty that would lead to a delegation of UK power to the EU—a stage further than parliamentary scrutiny of new treaties.

Why has parliamentary scrutiny of treaties proved so controversial? The executive may use royal prerogative to enter into a legally binding treaty that has far-reaching consequences for UK citizens. Parliament is involved in the treaty-making process only in so far as the executive permits it the right to comment on treaties before they are ratified. This may give rise to difficulties in relation to domestic implementation of the treaty, because the UK is a **dualist state**. Unless Parliament agrees to implement the terms of the treaty into the domestic sphere, the UK will remain bound by the treaty provisions in international law, but will have difficulty in meeting those obligations without Parliament's consent.

cross reference
See Chapter 8 for an explanation of dualism.

Are the courts willing to examine the exercise of prerogative power in respect of treaty-making? It may be helpful to consider the case of *Blackburn v Attorney General* [1971] 1 WLR 1037 in this respect, which relates to the European Community (EC) Treaty. The case was brought around the time that the UK entered the European Community. To join the EC, the UK was required to sign and implement the Treaty of Rome. Mr Blackburn sought to challenge the exercise of prerogative power on the grounds that it would erode parliamentary supremacy. Because Parliament is supreme and the royal prerogative is subservient to the will of Parliament, Mr Blackburn sought a declaration that the exercise of power would be unlawful.

● ***Blackburn v Attorney General*** [1971] 1 WLR 1037, CA

Lord Denning MR at 1039:

> In this case Mr Blackburn—as he has done before—has shown eternal vigilance in support of the law. This time he is concerned about the application of Her Majesty's government to join the Common Market and to sign the Treaty of Rome. He brings two actions against the Attorney General, in which he seeks declarations to the effect that, by signing the Treaty of Rome, Her Majesty's government will surrender in part the sovereignty of the Crown in Parliament and will surrender it for ever. He says that in so doing the government will be acting in breach of the law. The Attorney General has applied to strike out the statements of claim on the ground that they disclose no reasonable cause of action. The master and the judge have struck them out. Mr Blackburn, with our leave, appeals to this court. He thinks it is important to clear the air.
>
> ...
>
> The general principle applies to this treaty as to any other. The treaty-making power of this country rests not in the courts, but in the Crown; that is, Her Majesty acting on the advice of her Ministers. When her Ministers negotiate and sign a treaty, even a treaty of such paramount importance as this proposed one, they act on behalf of the country as a whole. They exercise the prerogative of the Crown. Their action in so doing cannot be challenged or questioned in these courts.
>
> ... [T]hese ... courts will not impugn the treaty-making power of Her Majesty, and on the ground that in so far as Parliament enacts legislation, we will deal with that legislation as and when it arises.
>
> I think the statements of claim disclose no cause of action, and I would dismiss the appeal.
>
> ...

Stamp LJ at 1040:

> I agree that the appeal should be dismissed; but I would express no view whatsoever on the legal implications of this country becoming a party to the Treaty of Rome. In the way Mr Blackburn put it I think he confused the division of the powers of the Crown, Parliament and the courts. The Crown enters into treaties; Parliament enacts laws; and it is the duty of this court in

> proper cases to interpret those laws when made; but it is no part of this court's function or duty to make declarations in general terms regarding the powers of Parliament, more particularly where the circumstances in which the court is asked to intervene are purely hypothetical. Nor ought this court at the suit of one of Her Majesty's subjects to make declarations regarding the undoubted prerogative power of the Crown to enter into treaties.

This case sets out the courts' reluctance to become involved in what is essentially a political decision—to enter into a treaty with another country. Similarly, in the later case of *R v Secretary of State for Foreign Affairs, ex p Lord Rees-Mogg* [1994] QB 552, the court was once again unwilling to question the use of the prerogative power to sign and ratify the Treaty on European Union. This prerogative power is one that appears to be non-justiciable, although it is likely that the European Union Act 2011 will create a justiciable right to a referendum and that consequently the denial of a referendum could be challenged via the courts.

6.5.2 Declarations of war and peace, deployment of troops, and prerogative powers

The prerogative powers relating to declarations of war and peace, and the deployment of troops, are firmly established in the hands of the executive and in particular the Cabinet. However, over time, these prerogative powers appear to have become restricted by what began as an early form of constitutional convention that is developing to give Parliament greater say in the decision to deploy troops and to go to war. In 1982, Parliament was informed that the government intended to send a task force of troops to the Falkland Islands, and Parliament was permitted to debate this before troops were sent. It is difficult to know what Prime Minister Thatcher would have done had Parliament strongly expressed its disapproval of her proposed cause of action. Would she have considered the government bound by Parliament's view(s)? Just under a decade later, Parliament was recalled during the summer recess (the holidays) in early September 1990 to be informed about and to debate the sending of troops to the Gulf after Iraq had invaded Kuwait. An advance party of troops had already been dispatched at this point, but not the main force. In January 1991, the government gave time for a parliamentary debate prior to troops being sent into action on the expiry of a United Nations Resolution requiring Iraq to comply with the requirement to withdraw from Kuwait. This was further evidence that Parliament's views would be sought by the executive before troops would be sent into a battle. However, it appeared to stop short of a duty to seek approval; instead, it was framed more as a duty to inform and at most to consult. Further, it must be noted that although it is a royal prerogative power that permits the deployment of the armed forces, Parliament's power is needed in so far as it is Parliament that authorises funding for the maintenance of the armed forces, which is renewable annually. Without funds to feed and equip the armed forces, it would not be possible to mount an effective (and indeed acceptable) military campaign. This is why Parliament included this provision in the Bill of Rights 1689, so as to curtail the monarch's powers to fight wars.

It was former Prime Minister Tony Blair's decision to provide Parliament with opportunities to debate and then to vote on whether to go to war with Iraq in 2003 that added weight to assertions that there is a developing constitutional convention that the executive must consult and seek Parliament's approval prior to declaring war. It is certainly not yet the case that the executive is bound by Parliament's views—there is no legal mechanism to review this type of prerogative power. And we do not know what Tony Blair would have done had Parliament not voted in favour of the war, as it did. He has since said that were Parliament to have voted against, he would not have taken the country to war and he would have felt duty-bound to resign. One instance of Parliament being given a vote on whether to go to war hardly constitutes a convention. But subsequently both Parliament and government have expressed an interest in reforming this prerogative power. Interestingly, on this occasion, the Prime Minister gave Parliament the power to determine whether the UK was to embark on a war, and yet the decision to go to war has provoked great controversy and calls for the power to enter into wars to be removed from the executive! However, the extent to which the House of Commons should be given a debate prior to a decision to deploy troops abroad is a moot one, as explained in the extract below, because there are a number of different points at which the Commons could be consulted.

● **Political and Constitutional Reform Committee, 'Parliament's role in conflict decisions: Written evidence submitted by Sebastian Payne, University of Kent'**
(28 March 2011), available online at http://www.publications.parliament.uk/pa/cm201012/cmselect/cmpolcon/923/11033104.htm

PRELIMINARY POINTS

Has a convention now been established requiring the approval of the House of Commons?

Bearing in mind the consensus across the political spectrum that Parliament should have a greater role with regard to war powers there is clearly a change of expectations on the part of this Government and indeed the last Government as to what is appropriate.

What appears to be emerging is the expectation that the House of Commons will be consulted and that there will be a division but not necessarily prior to the deployment decision.

This could be seen as a three stage process:

1. Government makes an informal assessment of the mood of the House.
2. On the basis that there is believed to be substantial support the Government makes a statement as to what it is planning to do or indeed has decided to do.
3. A debate and division is held.

This new approach implies that it would be difficult to sustain operations without a fairly early formal approval of the House.

In the case of Libya, the Government took the decision to act and then made a statement on the 18 March 2011, deployed the armed forces on the 19 March and held a full debate and division on the 21 March 2011.

Both Parliament and the Government have to confront a paradox:

Parliament's influence is maximised by an early debate and division on the plans to deploy troops but there may be sound reasons why the Government in some scenarios needs to act prior to approval from the House.

Early consultation allows the House to extract clarification from the Government as to the purpose of the operation, troop numbers, allies to be involved, duration of operation and international mandate. But at an early stage it may be impossible for the Government to give answers to all those questions as is evident from the Libyan scenario with the Government having to engage in persuasion and coalition building with international allies.

A vote after the deployment has occurred weakens the influence of the House as those who vote against an existing deployment can be accused of undermining the morale of the armed forces. Nonetheless Governments may need to act prior to a vote.

What are the circumstances in which forces could reasonably be committed before a debate and vote in the House of Commons, as happened recently in the case of Libya?

The Libyan deployment presents an example of an occasion which justifies acting prior to a vote. The justification is to avert an imminent humanitarian disaster.

Other examples would be where immediate action is needed to defend the United Kingdom or its overseas territories.

Conceptually, one needs to separate the debate question from the 'debate and vote'. There may be circumstances that allow for an early debate to inform the House and for the House to influence the Government. A vote may not be appropriate at the early stage because the Government is still developing its policy and engaged in negotiation with its allies and trying to pressure the enemy. Indeed strong support from the House may act as a warning to the enemy and influence the shape of events.

Is a detailed parliamentary resolution needed to clarify Parliament's role, as proposed by the last Government, or should the role of Parliament in conflict decisions be enshrined in law, as the current Foreign Secretary has suggested?

A detailed resolution is highly desirable. The last Government produced a detailed draft resolution that covered many of the issues of concern. That resolution needs refining to enhance the role of Parliament.

A convention embodied in a resolution will allow the House and the Government the opportunity to develop an appropriate modus operandi. There is still much that needs to be changed to allow Parliament to effectively influence the policy cycle. There needs to be a re-thinking of the boundaries between the executive and the legislature part of which should include the Government seeking input from the House at an earlier stage of policy formation. Parliament is extending its authority and influence through Select Committees. Indeed the demand for more influence over war powers is testimony to the growth of Parliamentary influence on the executive. It is too early to crystallise these arrangements in legislation which will bring with it the risk of judicial review of government action.

The developing constitution has solidified to such an extent that it appears to have developed into a duty to consult the House of Commons as soon as possible given the exigencies of the situation. This duty has been included in a (draft) House of Commons Resolution as a result of the Constitutional Reform and Governance Act 2010.

NOTE A brief history of the discussion is provided in ch. 7, 'War Powers', in the First Report of the Joint Committee on the Draft Constitutional Renewal Bill (Session 2007–08, 31 July 2008, London: HMSO), available online at http://www.publications.parliament.uk/pa/jt200708/jtselect/jtconren/166/16602.htm

Thus, at present, it appears that the favoured approach is for the need for a Commons' resolution prior to deployment of troops, plus a number of statutory definitions to clarify the area. However, we shall see what happens as the legislative process unfolds.

thinking point

What are your views on this reform? Did the constitutional convention operate effectively without the need for statutory recognition and a House of Commons resolution, or did we need reform and, if so, of what type?

To what extent does the political executive exercise the royal prerogative?

- *Many of the prerogative powers have been delegated by the monarch to the political executive.*

- *This provides a greater degree of legitimacy and accountability to the exercise of prerogative powers in a modern democratic society.*

- *The principal prerogative powers in use by the government relate to: international affairs and foreign relations, including negotiation and signing treaties with other countries, such as EU treaties and the European Convention on Human Rights (ECHR); defence of the realm, including declarations of war and peace, and the deployment of armed forces abroad; and national security and related emergency powers.*

- *The executive's exercise of many, but not all, of these powers is susceptible to judicial review in similar ways to the exercise of statutory power.*

- *Some of these powers have recently been curtailed, to an extent, by statute.*

6.6 What control, if any, does Parliament have in relation to the exercise of prerogative powers?

Parliament has the duty to scrutinise the executive through the mechanisms of parliamentary questions (oral and written), and in particular Prime Minister's and Ministers' Question Time, parliamentary debates, and through the workings of select committees. However, Parliament is heavily reliant on the executive to inform its members about government action, and any problems associated with government policy and operational initiatives. This places Parliament at a disadvantage, because it means that Parliament has to know which questions to ask in order to receive the information that it needs to scrutinise the government. There are constitutional conventions governing how the executive has to behave in relation to Parliament and its duty to inform and to account for its actions. But these remain non-legal rules—binding, but sanctioned by political consequences rather than legal ones. This may have the effect of reducing Parliament's ability to scrutinise the use of prerogative powers when coupled with their vague limits and poor definition. In addition, Parliament has adopted resolutions that have limited its power to debate and criticise the monarch. This has the effect of limiting Parliament's ability to oversee the monarch's exercise of prerogative power except in certain situations for which there are statutory protections, such as Parliament's power to authorise expenditure for the maintenance of the armed forces. But it has also been argued that because the monarch exercises her power on the advice of the Prime Minister, whom Parliament may seek to scrutinise, Parliament may have more power than it may at first appear for many of the prerogative powers. Feldman explains this further.

cross reference
This is discussed further in Chapter 11 on responsible government.

. . . .

● **D. Feldman, 'None, one or several? Perspectives on the UK's constitution(s)'** (2005)
   64(2) Cambridge Law Journal 329, 331–3

In the United Kingdom the prerogative is no longer a set of powers and duties special to the monarch. Because of the convention that nearly all prerogatives are exercised in accordance with the advice of the Prime Minister, prerogative power is now almost wholly an instrument of executive government. In a way this makes the prerogative more democratically legitimate than before, as the Prime Minister is, by convention, always an elected member of the House of Commons, and is accountable to that House for the use made of the prerogative. On the other hand, that accountability is not by any means perfect, and, even when there is accountability, the House does not always have control over decision-making. For example, the power to enter into treaties is normally exercised without reference to Parliament [now subject to the Constitutional Reform and Governance Act 2010], and the decision to go to war does not require parliamentary assent as a matter of law (although it is just possible that, following the parliamentary debates that preceded the second Gulf War in 2003, there is now a constitutional convention that no military invasion of another country will be initiated without parliamentary approval).

The prerogative can sometimes be used to legislate without recourse to Parliament. This reflects an executive-centred vision of the policy-making and implementation elements in the constitution, and can be hard to reconcile with a vision of the constitution in which the Crown in Parliament holds the key legislative place.

cross reference
The GCHQ case is discussed in Chapter 17, as well as later in the chapter.

This is a particular concern when one considers that the making of treaties and the deployment of troops fall into categories of prerogative power that the courts have not historically recognised as justiciable—in other words, that the courts have not reviewed how the power is exercised in these instances. Lord Roskill's quote from the *GCHQ* case is instructive in this regard.

● **Council of Civil Service Unions v Minister for the Civil Service** [1985] AC 374

Lord Roskill at 418:

> The courts are not the place wherein to determine whether a treaty should be concluded or the armed forces disposed in a particular matter or Parliament dissolved on one date rather than another.

If Parliament believes itself to be ill-equipped to scrutinise certain types of exercise of prerogative powers and the courts do not consider themselves able to review a subset of prerogative power, then there are likely to be powers that are not subject to adequate oversight or scrutiny. This is particularly true in relation to certain types of law (Orders in Council) executed under the royal prerogative, although in a later section you will see that the courts are beginning to make inroads into this area after the recent case of *Bancoult*.

cross reference
Bancoult is discussed in detail in Chapter 19, as well as later in the chapter.

Parliament is particularly concerned about powers exercised within the category of national security, because these are less susceptible to meaningful enquiry than many executive actions. After all, who decides whether, in providing X or Y answer to a parliamentary question, there may be potential for a breach of national security? It is the government that has the information upon which to judge a national security issue and that information is largely secret. There are protocols by which a small group of senior members of Parliament (MPs) and peers (some of the Privy Counsellors) may be provided with a confidential briefing or sight of classified documents on the condition that they are treated in the strictest of confidence on Privy Council Rules, but these are rare occurrences, such as in 2003 in the lead-up to the war with Iraq. Consequently, were a MP or peer to ask a question of a minister and the minister to say that he or she was unable to answer it on grounds of national security, the MP or peer would not be in a position to judge whether this was a true reflection of a real concern for the safety of the nation or whether it was a smokescreen. This may in part explain why there has been increasing discussion about the need for reform, including Parliament's ultimate power to replace the prerogative power with a statutory one that is more readily reviewable by the courts and also by Parliament. This will be discussed in the final section of the chapter.

summary points

What control, if any, does Parliament have in relation to the exercise of prerogative powers?

- *It is difficult for Parliament to exercise effective control over the political executive's exercise of prerogative power and, as a result of parliamentary resolutions, it does not question the monarch's exercise of power (although Parliament is supreme and may amend a resolution if it so chooses).*

- *Parliament has the power to ask ministers to account for their exercise of power to permit parliamentary scrutiny. This is true for the exercise of statutory and prerogative powers.*

- *However, certain powers are considered to be personal to the monarch and to the Prime Minister (such as asking for the dissolution of Parliament), and these are not subject to meaningful parliamentary or judicial scrutiny.*

- *Scrutiny is limited in the context in which the government has national security concerns, because the government is not required to provide information that would put national security at risk. This is understandable, on the one hand, but defeats the possibility of effective scrutiny, on the other.*

- *Parliament may ultimately take away the prerogative powers by enacting a statute that provides for a statutory replacement for the prerogative.*

6.7 How have the courts reviewed the operation of prerogative powers?

Historically, the courts ruled only on whether a royal prerogative existed and to what extent, not on the way in which it was exercised. Its approach to prerogative powers was similar to its approach to constitutional conventions (which are used in part to restrict the exercise of power). The traditional approach meant that the courts could check that the executive was indeed acting legally in relying on prerogative powers, but not the substance of the exercise of that power. The detail of the exercise of the power was outside the courts' powers of review. Cases such as *R v Criminal Injuries Compensation Board, ex p Lain* [1962] 2 QB 864 are evidence of this traditional approach, although also a foreshadowing of the greater court scrutiny of the prerogative. Without this power of oversight, there would be no other way in which to ensure that the executive was acting within its power, which would be a breach of the doctrine of the rule of law, because the executive must have the legal power to act and must act within its power.

The courts have gradually increased their scrutiny of prerogative powers through the mechanism of judicial review. It may perhaps be useful to chart this development through a series of cases from the 1970s to the present day. In *Laker Airways Ltd v Department of Trade and Industry* [1977] QB 643, Lord Denning stated that the prerogative could be examined by the courts in the same way as any other executive act. This was viewed as a departure from previous practice, whereby the courts had exercised a supervisory jurisdiction over the existence and use of prerogative powers rather than developed an approach more akin to scrutiny. The other Court of Appeal judges did not endorse Denning's radical stance. It may be unsurprising that Lord Denning was involved in this landmark judgment: he was known as a reforming judge.

Laker Airways is an interesting case. It was brought by Mr Laker, who had set up the first UK-based cheap air carrier at a time when most of the population had never been on a plane. His plan was for it to operate like a Skytrain: people would not be able to purchase tickets in advance, but instead would turn up at the airport, buy a ticket, and get on the next plane to New York rather like one would catch a train. The fares were to be much cheaper than those of the single British carrier that had a London–New York route: British Airways. In order to take the project forward, Laker Airways needed to be a designated air carrier, which meant that it had to get a series of permissions from the UK and US authorities. Mr Laker got a long way through this process before the Secretary of State in the UK withdrew one of his earlier permissions, which effectively prevented him from ever flying the Skytrain service even though he had spent a considerable amount of money buying planes, training crews, and setting up his service. The detail of the case is not important in relation to this topic, but the legal point in issue was whether the Secretary of State had power under the prerogative or statute to withdraw the permission. We join Lord Denning's discussion at the point at which he is explaining whether, were the Secretary of State to have relied on a prerogative, the Court could review the exercise of power. If you remember, the traditional position was that it could not examine and review the exercise of power, only whether the power existed and applied to the situation in question.

● ***Laker Airways Ltd v Department of Trade and Industry*** [1977] 2 All ER 182, CA

Lord Denning at 192–3:

> Much of the modern thinking on the prerogative power of the executive stems from John Locke's treatise, *True End of Civil Government*[1] . . . It was the source from which . . . Blackstone drew in his *Commentaries*[2] and on which Lord Radcliffe based his opinion in *Burmah Oil* . . . The prerogative is a discretionary power exercisable by the executive government for the public good, in certain spheres of governmental activity for which the law has made no provision, such as the war prerogative . . . or the treaty prerogative . . . The law does not interfere with the proper exercise of the discretion by the executive in those situations; but it can set limits on defining the bounds of the activity; and it can intervene if the discretion is exercised improperly or mistakenly. This is a fundamental principle of our constitution. It derives from two of the most respected of our authorities. In 1611 when the King, as the executive government, sought to govern by proclamations, Sir Edward Coke declared: 'The King hath no prerogative but that which the law of the land allows him': see the *Proclamations Case* [(1611) 12 Co Re 74 at 76]. In 1765 Sir William Blackstone added his authority:
>
> > 'For prerogative consisting (as Mr Locke has well defined it) in the discretionary power of acting for the public good, where the positive laws are silent; if the discretionary power be abused to the public detriment, such as prerogative is exerted in an unconstitutional manner.'
>
> Quite recently the House of Lords set a limit to the war prerogative when it declared that, even in time of war, the property of a British subject cannot be requisitioned or demolished without making compensation to the owner of it: see *Burmah Oil* . . . It has also circumscribed the treaty prerogative by holding that it cannot be used to violate the legal rights of a British subject, except on being liable for any damage he suffered: see *Attorney General v. Nissan* . . .
>
> Seeing that the prerogative is a discretionary power to be exercised for the public good, it follows that its exercise can be examined by the courts just as any other discretionary power which is vested in the executive. At several times in our history, the executive have claimed that a discretion given by the prerogative is unfettered: just as they have claimed that a

How have the courts reviewed the operation of prerogative powers?

165

discretion given by statute or a regulation is unfettered. On some occasions the judges have upheld these claims of the executive, notably in *R v. Hampden*, *Ship Money case*, and in one or two cases during the Second World War, and soon after it, but the judges have not done so of late. The two outstanding cases are *Padfield v. Minister of Agriculture, Fisheries and Food*... and Secretary of State for *Education and Science v. Metropolitan Borough of Tameside*, where the House of Lords have shown that when discretionary powers are entrusted to the executive by statute, the courts can examine the exercise of those powers, so as to see that they are used properly and not improperly or mistakenly. By mistakenly, I mean under the influence of misdirection in fact or in law. Likewise, it seems to me that, when discretionary powers are entrusted to the executive by the prerogative—in pursuance of the treaty-making power—the courts can examine the exercise of them so as the see that they are not used improperly or mistakenly...

(1) 1764 Edn, pp. 239–348.

(2) Commentaries [8th Edn 1778], vol 1, p. 252.

cross reference

Laker Airways Ltd *is discussed in detail in Chapters 18 and 19.*

The Court found in favour of Laker Airways on the ground that a licence granted under statute could not be withdrawn through the use of prerogative, but only by a lawful exercise of power under the Act that gave rise to the grant of the licence. It was to be decades before Lord Denning's far-sighted approach to the review of the prerogative was to be accepted as the position in British law. Indeed, it is only in recent judgments such as the Court of Appeal judgment in the case of *Bancoult* that the courts have been willing to consider review in hitherto-protected areas such as treaty-making powers. Interestingly, the House of Lords' ruling in *Bancoult* is much more restrictive.

There was little change in court practice until the courts addressed this issue in another leading case: *Council for Civil Service Union v Minister for the Civil Service* [1985] AC 374—sometimes referred to as the *CCSU* case and at other times named the *GCHQ* case in reference to the government listening centre that was at the centre of the controversy. The case concerned a ban imposed on employees at this national security centre preventing them from being members of a union. The case was brought by the union on behalf of its members, challenging the decision taken by the executive through its prerogative powers. This decision was taken on the grounds that trade union membership may lead to industrial action that jeopardised or disrupted the secret intelligence operations in GCHQ, with a potentially detrimental effect on national security.

The case was a very complicated one that shaped judicial review in general and the review of prerogative powers in particular. The House of Lords held that some prerogative powers could be reviewed by the courts. The key word is 'review' rather than oversight. Review means that the courts may look at whether the prerogative power exists (as previously), what it covers, and its extent (as previously), but also the detail of how it has been used, taking into account issues of legality and rationality. This is a similar form of review as for discretionary executive acts executed by virtue of statutory power. The House of Lords emphasised that if the government exercises a prerogative power that affects citizens' rights and interests, it should be subject to judicial review. The government should not be able to claim immunity from judicial review just because it is exercising a prerogative power. In this instance, however, the interests of national security meant that the Council for Civil Service Unions was not successful even given the fact that the prerogative power was deemed to be reviewable.

• **Council of Civil Service Unions v Minister for the Civil Service** [1985] AC 374

Lord Fraser at 398:

> As *De Keyser's case* shows, the courts will inquire into whether a particular prerogative power exists or not, and, if it does exist, into its extent. But once the existence and the extent of the power has been established to the satisfaction of the court, the court cannot inquire into the propriety of its exercise. That is undoubtedly the position as laid down in the authorities to which I have briefly referred...

Lord Scarman at 407:

> ...I believe that the law relating to judicial review has now reached the stage where it can be said with confidence that, is the subject matter in respect of which prerogative power is exercised is justiciable, that is to say if it is a matter upon which the court can adjudicate, the exercise of the power is subject to review in accordance with the principles developed in respect of the review of the exercise of statutory power...

Lord Diplock at 410:

> ...My Lords, I see no reason why simply because a decision-making power is derived from a common law and not a statutory source, it should for that reason only be immune from judicial review.

Lord Roskill at 418:

> ...But I do not think that the right of challenge can be unqualified. It must, I think, depend upon the subject matter of the prerogative power which is exercised. Many examples were given during the argument of prerogative powers which as at present advised I do not think could properly be made the subject of judicial review. Prerogative powers such as those relating to the making of treaties, the defence of the realm, the prerogative of mercy, the grant of honours, the dissolution of Parliament and the appointment of ministers as well as others are not, I think, susceptible to judicial review because their nature and subject matter as such are not to be amenable to the judicial process. The courts are not the place wherein to determine whether a treaty should be concluded or the armed forces disposed in a particular matter or Parliament dissolved on one date rather than another.
>
> ...

Whether or not a prerogative power is subject to judicial review depends on the nature of the power in question. Some prerogatives are unlikely ever to be reviewable by the courts, such as the decision of the monarch to summon and dissolve Parliament. They are similar to 'political questions', as they are defined in the US, which are not justiciable. Other prerogative powers, which are similar to statutory powers, will be reviewable. The House of Lords said that the powers to be reviewable would be decided through the development of the case law. Subsequent cases, such as *R v Secretary of State for Foreign and Commonwealth Affairs, ex p Everett* [1989] QB 811 and *Abassi v Foreign Secretary* [2002] EWCA Civ 1598, illustrate this development. In *Everett*, Lord Justices O'Connor, Nicholls, and Taylor had to determine whether decisions relating to the issue or refusal to issue a passport to a British citizen were capable of judicial review. Passports are issued under the royal prerogative and the prevailing view at the time was that the nature of this type of prerogative power, relating as it did to foreign affairs, meant that it was not susceptible to judicial review. Everett was a British citizen living in Spain. His passport would shortly expire and so he applied for a new one. This was refused, but the

British embassy was prepared to issue Everett with travel documents to permit him to return to the UK. After pressing the Foreign and Commonwealth Office for the reasons for the refusal of the passport, he was told that there was a warrant for his arrest in the UK and it was not the Secretary of State's policy to issue passports in such situations. At a later stage, he was provided with the details of the alleged offence and of the warrant. Everett sought a judicial review of the decision. The Court of Appeal held, in respect of its power to review the exercise of pre-rogative, that whether the prerogative in question was susceptible to judicial review depended on the subject of the case.

The prerogative in this instance was related to foreign affairs, which normally would put it beyond judicial review. However, the decision to refuse a passport to a British citizen raised questions of individual rights and liberties. On this basis, the Court of Appeal held that it had the power to review the exercise of the prerogative power. It further stated that the Secretary of State was entitled to refer to the policy that he had developed, but that he had to commu-nicate the reasons for his decision at the point at which he reached the decision. The decision to deny Mr Everett a passport could have been quashed on this basis but for the facts that the applicant had been given the relevant information in the intervening time, that his situation was not exceptional as regards the application of the policy, and that he had not been unduly prejudiced by having to wait to receive the information about the offence and the warrant. For these reasons, the Secretary of State's appeal was allowed and Mr Everett did not receive his passport. This is further evidence of the courts' increased surveillance of the exercise of pre-rogative powers in areas that have been considered taboo by the courts until recently.

The judges in *Abassi* reached a similar conclusion. Abassi argued that the UK had done insuf-ficient to safeguard his rights as a British citizen while he was being held by the US authorities in Guantanamo Bay. The Court of Appeal held that the Foreign Office had a discretion as to whether to protect a British citizen in this kind of situation and that the Foreign Office had provided guidance about what someone may expect from it in such a situation. In this instance, there was no legal duty to protect a British citizen. The Court held that it may be possible to review such an exercise of discretion in some situations, but reiterated that it was not empow-ered to review foreign policy decisions. So the case of *Abassi* may have broadened the focus of judicial review a little, but it is unclear to what extent.

To what extent have the courts continued to expand their powers of review in respect of pre-rogative powers? The recent case of *R (on the application of Bancoult) v Secretary of State for Foreign and Commonwealth Affairs* provides ample evidence that the courts may be willing to broaden their approach to the prerogative, including the categories of review that they may examine. The legal question in issue in this case was whether legislation enacted under the royal prerogative was subject to judicial review. Moules (2008), in his article on prerogative orders (see the 'Further reading' list at the end of the chapter), explains the issue before the Court of Appeal very clearly. He describes the two types of Order in Council (a type of legisla-tion): one type is made under statutory powers, is classed as a form of delegated legislation, and is subject to parliamentary scrutiny; the other is enacted under the royal prerogative and is classed as primary legislation, yet is not subject to parliamentary scrutiny. Instead, these latter types of Order in Council are approved by the Queen and the Privy Council. The question in this case was whether this latter form of Order in Council enacted by virtue of the prerogative may be subject to judicial review. The order was made in relation to the Chagos Islands, situated in the Indian Pacific. It had the effect of requiring the Chagossian islanders to leave their islands permanently, so that the British Indian Ocean Territory of Diego Garcia, one of the Chagos Islands, could be used as a US military base. The islanders sought to challenge the legality of the order, and thus their exile from their homes and their island.

● *Secretary of State for Foreign and Commonwealth Affairs v R (on the Application of Bancoult) (No 2)* [2007] EWCA Civ 495; [2008] QB 365

Lord Justice Sedley:

> [46] It can be observed without disrespect, particularly since Lord Roskill was careful to express himself tentatively, that a number of his examples could today be regarded as questionable: The grant of honours for reward, the waging of a war of manifest aggression or a refusal to dissolve Parliament at all might well call in question an immunity based purely on subject matter.

The Court of Appeal was unanimous in deciding that the courts may review all forms of royal prerogative including Orders in Council. The Court held that even a foreign policy exercise of royal prerogative was not immune from judicial review per se. Indeed, the Court found in favour of the Chagossians. The quote from Lord Justice Sedley indicates that he believes that the categories of power that are now subject to review are more numerous than was suggested by Lord Roskill, albeit with a number of caveats, in the *GCHQ* case in 1985. Therefore it depends on the circumstances, as well as the power, whether the exercise of the prerogative may be reviewed. A manifest abuse of power or an extreme exercise of power that affects citizens' rights may bring that prerogative power under the judicial spotlight. It may also call the power into question to such an extent that there are calls for reform. Having said that, when the case of *Bancoult* was heard in the House of Lords, it was clear that their Lordships were minded to adopt an extremely conservative approach to reviewing this type of royal prerogative power: they stated that this prerogative power was open to review, before finding in favour of the state and against the Chagossians. This case is discussed in much more detail, as is the judgment, in subsequent chapters.

summary points

How have the courts reviewed the operation of the royal prerogative?

• *The courts have historically been reluctant to review the operation of prerogative powers other than to establish whether the power exists in law and its extent.*

• *Lord Denning opened the prospect of full judicial review of the operation of the royal prerogative in the case of* Laker Airways *in the 1970s.*

• *The* CCSU/GCHQ *case in the 1980s took this a stage closer to reality, when Lord Roskill explained that the courts could review the operation of certain types of prerogative power similar in type to statutory powers.*

• *Other prerogative powers were excluded from review, including treaty-making powers, the defence of the realm, the prerogative of mercy, the dissolution of Parliament, the appointment of ministers, and the granting of honours, although this list is not definitive and more recent cases suggest that this list may be shrinking over time.*

• *The case of* Bancoult *in 2008 indicates that prerogative powers that have previously been considered to be exempt from judicial review are now being reviewed by the judiciary, suggesting that the courts are becoming bolder in their approach. However, the House of Lords also applied a relatively conservative approach in relation to the standard to which the state is held. Consequently, the range of justiciable prerogative powers may be broader, but the way in which they are reviewed may be relatively deferential to the executive.*

6.8 What is the relevance of the royal prerogative today and is it in need of reform?

This chapter has sought to outline the nature and extent of prerogative powers in brief, as well as the way in which their use is subject to political and legal scrutiny. The royal prerogative remains the basis of many executive actions that have a fundamental impact on people both at home and abroad. As one would expect, unwritten powers that remain relatively unclear without extensive research of history and legal precedents have been subject to repeated calls for reform. These calls have become increasingly frequent in recent years not least as a result of the war in Iraq (which was approved by Parliament) and Parliament's concern about a lack of time in which to scrutinise the Lisbon Treaty. The extracts that follow provide a snapshot of Parliament's views on the need for reform. Of course, without government support, it is un-likely that all of the parliamentary committees' proposals will make it on to the statute book. However, some parliamentary scrutiny mechanisms as regards the use of the royal prerogative have been introduced, as indicated above (the European Union Act 2011; the Constitutional Reform and Governance Act 2010).

The first extract is from the report of the Select Committee for Public Administration, which focused on reforming the prerogative as exercised by ministers so as to afford Parliament a greater opportunity for oversight.

● **Select Committee on Public Administration,** *Taming the Prerogative: Strengthening Ministerial Accountability to Parliament* (First Special Report, Session 2003–04, HC 422, London: HMSO, March 2004), available online at http://www.publications.parliament.uk/pa/cm200304/cmselect/cmpubadm/1262/126202.htm

> This report considers the prerogative powers of ministers. These include some of the most important functions of government, such as decisions on armed conflict and the conclusion of international treaties. The report describes how such powers have, over many years, come to be delegated by Sovereigns to ministers, and notes that they may be exercised without par-liamentary approval or scrutiny. They are therefore best described as ministerial executive powers.
>
> While recognising that such powers are necessary for effective administration, especially in times of national emergency, the report considers whether they should be subject to more systematic parliamentary oversight. It examines the arguments for scrutiny of some of the most significant prerogative powers, and concludes that the case for reform is unanswer-able. There is discussion of the merits of various ways of dealing with this question, including a continuation of the current approach, by which individual prerogative powers are made subject to parliamentary control on a case-by-case basis as the necessity for such control is demonstrated.
>
> The report concludes that a different approach is needed, and that comprehensive legisla-tion should be drawn up which would require government within six months to list the pre-rogative powers exercised by Ministers. The list would then be considered by a parliamentary committee and appropriate legislation would be framed to put in place statutory safeguards where necessary. A paper and draft Bill appended to the Report, prepared by Professor Rodney Brazier, the specialist adviser to the inquiry, contain these provisions as well as proposals for early legislative action in the case of three of the most important specific areas covered by

> prerogative powers: decisions on armed conflict, treaties and passports. The Report recommends that the Government should, before the end of the current session, initiate a public consultation exercise on the prerogative powers of Ministers.

In his *Cambridge Law Journal* article, Brazier (2007) notes that there is little appetite for major change in the scope and exercise of the monarch's powers, not even from the Fabian Society (a left-leaning political group), although the Society does suggest defining the scope and exercise of the monarch's powers. Brazier explains that most major changes to the monarch's position have been brought about on the initiation of the monarch rather than that of the government of the day. It is interesting to note, although there is no suggestion that this has held back Bills that would otherwise have reformed the monarch's prerogatives, that the Queen's consent is required in advance of Bills being passed that affect the prerogative power. However, because the Queen acts on the advice of ministers, it would be unlikely that the Queen would refuse her consent that the Bill proceed through Parliament unless the Bill were sponsored by a **backbench MP** and the government were not prepared to provide support to it. The rule that requires the Queen's consent in advance of the Bill passing through the latter stages of debate and vote is made by Parliament, and may be changed by Parliament on its own volition in keeping with parliamentary supremacy.

The government replied to the Committee's proposals for reform of the prerogative in July 2004. It did not agree that codification of prerogative powers in statute would be an improvement on the current position. Further, the government argued that ministers were already accountable to Parliament for their exercise of both statutory and prerogative powers, and that the proposed changes would thus be unlikely to garner major improvements in that respect. However, it did concede that, from time to time, it will be necessary for Parliament to replace an individual prerogative power with a statutory one, because situations arise that require different powers and liabilities. These were to be considered by the government on a case-by-case basis and supported where possible.

Shortly after this, the House of Lords Select Committee on the Constitution began its investigation into, and then published its findings on, the prerogative power to declare war and deploy troops abroad. The following extract from the report sets out the Committee's main recommendations.

● **House of Lords Select Committee on the Constitution,** *Waging War* [Fifteenth Report, Session 2005–06, HL 236, London: HMSO, 2006], paras 96–110

> 96. It has been the purpose of this inquiry to consider the nature of the executive's powers in relation to the fundamentals of peace and war, and to consider whether, and if so how, Parliament can play a fuller part as the voice of Ernest Bevin's 'common man'.[1] ...
>
> 98. The Royal Prerogative reflects two of the constitutional features outlined above: it is rooted in the common law and its exercise is governed by convention ... its extent has been reduced over time through the enactment of statute law. Furthermore, its exercise has been progressively refined by the evolution of the conventions surrounding it and by the willingness of the courts to supervise the exercise of some prerogative powers. In the nineteenth century governments could—and on occasion did—engage in military adventures with little or no reference to Parliament. Today, as the Prime Minister himself has said, there are unlikely to be any circumstances in which a government could go to war without the support of Parliament. The precise meaning of 'support' is, of course, elusive: it could be implicit, as the Lord Chancellor would have it, in the sense that in the absence of disapproval, the support can be assumed; or it could be explicit, through a more formal parliamentary process. Many would agree with the inference to be drawn from Gordon Brown's 2005 remarks that the House of Commons vote on

171

18 March 2003 (endorsing the decision to invade Iraq[2]) marked a new stage in the evolution of the convention governing parliamentary oversight of the deployment power. He was, unfortunately, unable to take up our invitation to appear before us, but we note the close similarity between his conclusion in January 2006, that 'a case now exists for a further restriction of executive power and a detailed consideration of the role of Parliament in the declaration of peace and war', and that of David Cameron, leader of the Opposition, that '... the time has come to look at those [prerogative] powers exercised by Ministers ... Giving Parliament a greater role in the exercise of these powers would be an important and tangible way of making government more accountable'.[3] Mr Cameron's conclusions were in turn echoed by Jack Straw.

...

101. Although there have been exceptions, such as emergencies, recent history shows that the processes leading up to deployments are generally protracted, allowing plenty of time not only to evaluate and plan for the action but to obtain parliamentary support. The fact that it might be inconvenient for the Government to seek this support is hardly a justification for denying it. The Government's preparations have also been conducted under full media coverage, rendering the arguments about security and secrecy more theoretical than real. The Government also argues that it is in any case accountable to Parliament; but it seems to us that if substance is to be given to the glib cliché that 'Parliament can decide' then significant adjustment needs to be made to the processes that are employed to enable it to do so.

102. As for the potential problem of politicisation of military decision making, we do not believe that constraints on the deployment power will affect the freedoms which military commanders have and should continue to enjoy. We fully acknowledge that controversy at home could have a deleterious effect on the morale of the troops in the field and agree the importance of guarding against it, but note that that would be so whatever process was followed. More to the point, we believe strongly that the balance of the argument falls in favour of ensuring that those troops know that Parliament is behind them rather than be left to speculate. We can do no better than repeat Lord Bramall's view that '... the armed forces need to be reassured ... that they had the support of the country ... Parliament represents the will of the people and if Parliament supports the action ... the Armed Forces can take heart that constitutionally the country supports it'.[4]

103. ... Our conclusion is that the exercise of the Royal prerogative by the Government to deploy armed force overseas is outdated and should not be allowed to continue as the basis for legitimate war-making in our 21st century democracy. Parliament's ability to challenge the executive must be protected and strengthened. There is a need to set out more precisely the extent of the Government's deployment powers, and the role Parliament can— and should— play in their exercise.

1 'There never has been a war yet which, if the facts had been put calmly before the ordinary folk, could not have been prevented ... The common man, I think, is the greatest protection against war': Ernest Bevin, Foreign Affairs debate (HC Hansard, 23 November 1945), col. 786.
2 Among other things, the resolution 'supports the decision of Her Majesty's Government that the United Kingdom should use all means necessary to ensure the disarmament of Iraq's weapons of mass destruction'.
3 The Rt Hon. David Cameron, MP, Speech on 6 February 2006, launching the Democracy Task Force.
4 Volume II: Evidence, Q109.

There is no need to rehearse the points explained very clearly by the Committee, but it is evident that the Committee felt strongly that the position was in need of reform. This was accepted, in part, by the government in a Green Paper, *The Governance of Britain* (Cmnd 7870), in July 2007, in which a proposal was announced that the House of Commons should develop a convention that required Parliament's view to be sought prior to a declaration of war being made. The proposal suggested further that the convention could then be put before Parliament to be formalised as a resolution that would bind the executive. Then Prime Minister Gordon Brown, in his constitution speech at the University of Westminster on 27 October 2007, announced that he—and by implication the government—was in favour of reform of the prerogative in relation to the executive's power to declare war (in keeping with the extract above from the Select Committee report), the power of the executive to ratify international treaties without Parliament's decision, and the power to appoint judges to be reformed in such a way as to ensure the independence of the judiciary. Government proposals were published in this respect and, as discussed above, were later included in the Constitutional Reform and Governance Act 2010. The Act also addresses calls for the Ponsonby rule to be placed on a statutory footing.

Would placing a number of the prerogative powers on a statutory footing lead to clarity, limit the potential for abuse of power, and provide concerned citizens with an opportunity to seek review of the government's exercise of power? Possibly—but it would rather depend on whether the royal prerogative itself were replaced by statute or simply regulated by statute. And it depends too on whether judges consider themselves to have the power to review the exercise of such powers. This is a more difficult issue than at first it may appear, because many prerogative powers may be considered to be political. Do we really want judges to become involved in weighing up and regulating highly political decisions? Are not our political representatives in Parliament better placed to do this and to allow the judiciary to stand one step removed from party politics? There are different views on the desirability of judicial involvement in political decisions, even though many commentators would welcome some form of codification or elucidation of royal prerogative powers. A taxonomy—or detailed list—of which powers exist, when they may normally be used and by whom, is considered to be the answer by some. For others, nothing short of complete reform is sufficient.

cross reference

See the extract above for details of the Joint Committee's response to the Bill.

summary points

What is the relevance of the royal prerogative today and is it in need of reform?

- *The royal prerogative continues to provide extensive power, and some of the most fundamental powers, to the Crown.*

- *The power to declare war and to enter into international treaties are just two of the powers available to the Crown, and neither is subject to full judicial review.*

- *Reform proposals have encompassed codifying prerogative powers in statutory form, or limiting prerogative powers by adopting parliamentary resolutions with binding force that will permit Parliament to restrict the exercise of prerogative powers.*

- *Recent proposals include reforms of the power to declare war without the legal requirement for parliamentary approval and reform of the Ponsonby rule. A number of these powers are now subject to parliamentary oversight or approval as a result of the Constitutional Reform and Governance Act 2010.*

- *Parliament has also raised concerns about its lack of ability to scrutinise the operation of the executive prerogative in other areas, although there is less of a consensus about the need for reform in this regard.*

Summary

The royal prerogative is a series of powers, duties, and immunities enjoyed by the Crown, and exercised by the monarch and/or the political executive. Royal prerogative powers are a special branch of the common law. As such, they may be abolished, restricted, or suspended by statute. They remain somewhat vague and there is no clear record of all of the powers in existence, who may exercise them, and under what circumstances. Some prerogative powers are enjoyed by the monarch herself, although most are exercised by the executive. Some powers are subject to review by the courts, although there are others that are not susceptible to review. The case law does not entirely clarify which powers are subject to full judicial scrutiny, although over time it appears that the courts have become increasingly willing to review the exercise of royal prerogative powers. The Constitutional Reform and Governance Act 2010 has provided Parliament with greater powers of scrutiny over some aspects of the royal prerogative, such as deploying the armed forces in combat situations and the powers of Parliament in respect of treaty scrutiny prior to ratification. Some commentators are keen to see prerogative powers placed on a statutory footing, whereas others consider the current nature of prerogative powers to be ideally suited to the areas that they were largely designed to address, such as matters of national security and the defence of the realm.

Questions

1 In more no more than 100 words, how would you define the royal prerogative?

2 What are the royal prerogative powers, who has the legal power to exercise them, and who, by constitutional convention, is given the power to make use of them?

3 To what extent is the royal prerogative similar to statutory powers given to the executive, and to what extent does it differ from them?

4 To what extent do you think that the royal prerogative should be reformed, in what way, and why?

5 To what extent does parliamentary sovereignty mean that concerns about the royal prerogative could be eradicated relatively easily? Provide examples and reasons for your answer.

Further reading

Blackburn, R., 'Monarchy and the personal prerogatives' [2004] Public Law 546

This article provides an interesting difference of perspective from Brazier's as regards the monarch and her personal prerogatives (as opposed to those exercised by the government on her behalf).

Brazier, R., '"Monarchy and the personal prerogatives": a personal response to Professor Blackburn' [2005] Public Law 45

This article provides a discussion about the monarch's royal prerogative and the way in which constitutional conventions have assisted in developing the use of the prerogative, so as to minimise the politicisation of the monarchy.

Brazier, R., 'Legislating about the monarchy' (2007) 66(1) Cambridge Law Journal 86

This article is a response to Blackburn's article above and is well worth reading in conjunction with that article, to provide a different perspective on Blackburn's points.

Maer, L., 'Governance of Britain: An Update' (House of Commons Library Standard Note PC/04703, 16 October 2009), available online at http://www.parliament.uk/commons/lib/research/briefings/snpc-04703.pdf

This note provides a detailed description of reform proposals in this area, including the thinking behind them.

Maer, L. and Gay, O., 'The Royal Prerogative' (House of Commons Library Standard Note PC/03861, 30 December 2009), available online at http://www.parliament.uk/commons/lib/research/briefings/snpc-03861.pdf

This note is a clear account of the royal prerogative, setting out its development and use. It is well worth reading to clarify the essential features of this power base. It is regularly updated. It has links to short briefing notes on areas of the prerogative that have recently been amended.

Markesinis, B. S., 'The royal prerogative revisited' (1973) 32(2) Cambridge Law Journal 287

This is a classic article that sets out the debates about the extent of the royal prerogative. It is more theoretical than many of the other sources listed above, but is also clearly written.

Moules, R., 'Judicial review of prerogative Orders in Council: recognising the constitutional reality of executive legislation' (2008) 67(1) Cambridge Law Journal 12

This article contains a clear explanation of how the royal prerogative permits the executive to legislate through Orders in Council. It is very useful in the context of the *Bancoult* case discussed in this chapter and later in the administrative law section of this book.

Part 2
Parliamentary Supremacy

Parliamentary Supremacy: the theory

Key points

This chapter will cover:

- What does 'parliamentary supremacy' mean?
- What is the history leading to parliamentary supremacy?
- What are the theories behind the doctrine of parliamentary supremacy?
- Are there any restrictions on the power of Parliament?
- Who or what regulates Parliament if not the courts?
- How does parliamentary supremacy compare with constitutional supremacy?
- How does parliamentary supremacy fit with the separation of powers and the rule of law?
- If lost, can supremacy be regained?

Introduction

In this chapter, we shall consider the theory and the reality of parliamentary supremacy. We shall examine the differing theories of parliamentary supremacy, as well as any restrictions that may be placed on Parliament's power by the executive, the courts, and supranational organisations. This will cover the extent to which any restrictions are legal or political, real or perceived. We shall also explore how parliamentary supremacy differs from constitutional supremacy, which is the system that operates in many other countries. And we shall examine whether the UK is moving towards a system that is a hybrid between parliamentary and constitutional supremacy. This chapter will not consider the detail of the UK's membership of the European Union and the Council of Europe, because this will be examined in Chapters 8 and 9, respectively.

7.1 What does 'parliamentary supremacy' mean?

Parliamentary supremacy is an expression that explains that the Westminster **Parliament** is legally entitled to pass, amend, or repeal any law it wishes. Consequently, if the House of Commons and the House of Lords (unless the Parliament Acts of 1911 and 1949 are being relied upon) pass the legislation and the **monarch** gives her royal assent, then no court or other body is said to have the legal power to declare the legislation invalid. This explains why the term 'parliamentary supremacy' has been coined: (the **Queen** in) Parliament holds the supreme law-making power in the UK. This is a statement of law rather than politics, meaning that although Parliament is, in law, entitled to pass any legislation that it wishes, it may not be politically possible to enact that legislation. The proposed legislation may not have sufficient support from the electorate for it to be politically sensible to enact it as it stands. Table 7.1 provides a basic working definition of parliamentary supremacy.

Table 7.1

Parliamentary supremacy means that:
Parliament has supreme law-making powers in the UK
Therefore
Parliament may pass or amend or repeal any primary legislation it chooses
and
No body in the UK (including the executive and the courts) may challenge its legal validity

Some commentators use the term 'parliamentary sovereignty' in preference to parliamentary supremacy. A supreme ruler is often termed a sovereign and so using the word 'sovereign' denotes Parliament's supreme power. 'Sovereign' is understood to mean 'ultimate' in some usages; in others, it is considered to mean 'all powerful'. Supremacy, by contrast, indicates more powerful than others, rather than all powerful. And so there are subtle differences in interpretation between the two phrases, according to some commentators. There has also been a change of usage over time and the word 'supreme' has overtaken 'sovereign'. You will see both used to denote substantially the same concept in some instances; in others, you will find that they are used to denote different understandings of the theory. Although there are academic debates about the difference between the two, it is unlikely that you will need to address these to any great extent for the purposes of legal study. In most courses and modules, the phrases will be used interchangeably.

7.2 What is the history leading to parliamentary supremacy?

Much of the historical development of constitutional law has been discussed in detail in Chapters 4 and 5—on the **rule of law** and the **separation of powers**—and you may wish to refresh your memory of that by rereading those sections again. This section will consider the later stages of history, from 1600 onwards, in so far as it sheds light on the relationship between Parliament (the legislature) and the King (the **executive**), and the developing theory of parliamentary supremacy. It will also examine the role that the courts have played in recognising the supremacy of Parliament and the limitations of executive power. It is, however, a rather simplified view of the historical events that led to the **legislative** supremacy of Parliament.

The fact that the King and the courts recognised Parliament's legislative supremacy is the reason why Parliament came to be regarded as legislatively supreme. They did not always recognise Parliament's legislative supremacy, however, and a series of cases throughout the seventeenth century provides an insight into the differing **judicial** views on the King's powers and Parliament's powers. The King's legislative supremacy was doubted by Chief Justice Coke in *The Case of Proclamations* (1611) 12 Co Rep 74, as indicated in the extract below, although the later cases of *R v Hampden* (1687) 3 State Tr 825 and *Godden v Hales* (1686) 11 St Tr 1166 suggested that the King's prerogative allowed the King to levy tax without parliamentary consent in contradiction to Parliament's Petition of Right. In short, the extent and the supremacy of the King's powers were rather confused at this time.

cross reference
See Chapter 4 for more details on the history leading to the monarch's acceptance of the supremacy of Parliament.

. . . .

● ***The Case of Proclamations*** [1611] 12 Co Rep 74; 77 ER 1352

Chief Justice Coke at 1353–4:

> ...the King by his proclamation or other ways cannot change any part of the common law, or statute law, or the customs of the realm.
>
> ...the King cannot create any offence by his prohibition or proclamation, which was not an offence before, for that was to change the law, and to make an offence which was not.
>
> Also, it was resolved that the King hath no prerogative but that which the law of the land allows him.

But then Parliament's legislative supremacy had also been doubted by Coke CJ in *Dr Bonham's Case* (1610) 8 Co Rep 114. Instead, Coke appeared to be suggesting that it was the common law, as developed via the **judiciary**, which was the ultimate legal protection for the people. Prior to the Glorious Revolution of 1688 and the constitutional settlement of 1689, there had been a series of cases that indicated that Parliament was subject to the common law (some argued that this was natural law that comes from God; others that it was the fundamental law of man). England was a very different society at that time. Cases such as *Dr Bonham's Case* illustrate this point.

● *Dr Bonham's Case* [1610] 8 Co Rep 114

Coke CJ at 118:

> ...when an Act of Parliament is against common right and reason, or repugnant, or impossible to be performed, the common law will control it, and adjudge such an Act to be void.

Other cases, such as *Day v Savadge* (1614) Hob 85, concurred with Coke's statement in *Dr Bonham's Case* that an Act of Parliament would be invalid if it were 'made against natural equity'. Judges variously appeared to be asserting the authority of the common law over the King and over Parliament. This may be contrasted with the following more recent statement by the courts on their role vis-à-vis Acts of Parliament.

● *M v Home Office and another* [1994] 1 AC 377

Lord Templeman at 395:

> Parliament makes the law, the executive carry the law into effect and the judiciary enforce the law...In the seventeenth century Parliament established its supremacy over the Crown as monarch, over the executive and over the judiciary. Parliamentary supremacy over the Crown as executive stems from the fact that Parliament maintains in office the Prime Minister, who appoints the ministers in charge of the executive. Parliamentary supremacy over the judiciary is only exercisable by statute. The judiciary enforce the law against individuals, against institutions and against the executive.

The generally accepted position, which we shall use as a basis for further critique later on in the chapter, is that, from the late seventeenth century onwards, the judiciary accepted Parliament's legislative supremacy and has subsequently enforced Acts of Parliament through the courts.

Parliament's legislative supremacy really began to take hold at the time of the Glorious Revolution of 1688 more than twenty years after the Civil War (1642–49), the execution of Charles 1 (1649), after the reinstatement of the monarch Charles II in 1660, and after a brief republic under Oliver Cromwell. Charles I had asserted his exclusive power to rule and to legislate, which he believed to be derived from God as previous monarchs had believed. He did not recognise Parliament's power or its attempts to limit his power. In the intervening period, Charles II and James II, his successor, had continued the struggle for power with Parliament. But only a few years later Parliament was in a much stronger position to negotiate with the new King, when William of Orange was invited to take the throne (William's wife was James II's sister) and James II fled to France. The throne was offered to William and Mary subject to their recognition of Parliament's legislative supremacy, which was then enshrined in the Bill of Rights. The Bill of Rights provided for Parliament's supremacy—or at least the recognition of its authority via article 9: '... the freedom of speech and debates or proceedings in Parliament ought not to be impeached or questioned in any court or place out of Parliament.' This is the root of **parliamentary privilege** today, as discussed briefly later on in this chapter. The relationship between Parliament and the King was largely settled: the King's power to have a standing (regular) army was subject to Parliament's consent via statute, and the King did not have the power to override an Act of Parliament. The negotiations also determined that the King needed Parliament to consent to taxation before tax could be levied, which is important because, in order for the **Crown** to govern, it needs the funds to operate—the monarch had lost the ability to raise taxes and thus to derive an income. The King became dependent on Parliament's support. The case of *Bowles v Bank of England* [1913] 1 Ch 57 is more recent evidence for this point.

The Bill of Rights in 1689 set out the relationship and power bases of the King and Parliament, and from this document was born the concept of Parliament's legislative supremacy. This meant that the 'King in Parliament' (the term for the threefold consent to legislation—the Commons, the Lords, and the monarch) was assured over the King's personal legislative supremacy. Some commentators argue that this was the point at which our first true representative Parliament was born, and at which the power of the monarch was finally and fundamentally restricted. Others point to the fact that, at the time, Parliament was not the democratically elected institution that it is today (at least in respect of the lower chamber), because the electorate and their representatives were drawn from a very narrow section of the population. The powers of Parliament and of parliamentary privilege are clear in the Bill of Rights of 1689, but although the principle of parliamentary supremacy appears from this account to have been largely accepted, it was an incremental development over quite a period of time, as Lord Reid asserted in the following case.

cross reference

The Bill of Rights is discussed in detail in Chapter 4.

● *British Railways Board v Pickin* [1974] AC 765

Lord Reid at 782:

> In earlier times many learned lawyers seem to have believed that an Act of Parliament could be disregarded in so far as it was contrary to the law of God or the law of nature or natural justice, but since the supremacy of Parliament was finally demonstrated by the Revolution of 1688 any such idea has been obsolete.

Indeed, one cannot point to a legal document that confers legislative supremacy on Parliament, for who would have the power to execute such a document? Parliament could not draw up a document that gave itself such power unless it already had the power to do so. Jennings asserted that parliamentary supremacy is rooted in a legal rule that the courts accept the legislation that Parliament enacts as law. The legal theorist and jurist Dicey, in his leading work *An Introduction to the Study of the Law of the Constitution*, could not point to any such text and maintained that the legislative supremacy of Parliament was contained within the common law, as did Wade. It appears that it was the common law proponents, including some sections of the judiciary, who chose the give up their claim of supremacy in order to ensure that the King's claim to supremacy was finally overridden by that of Parliament's, as Swinton suggests in the next extract.

● K. Swinton, 'Challenging the validity of an Act of Parliament: the effect of enrolment
   and parliamentary privilege' [1976] 14[2] Osgoode Hall Law Journal 345, 363

> The principal characteristic of the British constitution, parliamentary supremacy or sovereignty, evolved through the seventeenth century struggles of Parliament and the Crown, which

climaxed in 1688 with the Glorious Revolution. Parliament's legislative supremacy had been proven by the end of the fifteenth century, although there was still some debate as to whether its Acts were subject to review to ensure consistency with natural law (or common law).[1] With the Glorious Revolution it was recognized that no such doctrine of fundamental law could exist in Britain. To have subjected Parliament to constraints in the common law would have been to concede a distinct advantage to the royal prerogative, which was founded in common law. The theory of parliamentary sovereignty was thus an invention of common law lawyers to solve the problem of the locus of power.

1 Coke's dictum in *Bonham's Case* inspired the debate. C. H. McIlwain, *The High Court of Parliament and Its Supremacy* (Hamden, CN: Archon Books, 1962), pp. 148–9, believes that a limitation on Parliament existed, but see contra T. Plucknett, '*Bonham's Case* and judicial review' (1926) 40 Harvard Law Review 30 and J. Gough, *Fundamental Law in English Constitutional History* (Oxford: Clarendon Press, 1955). Gough argues convincingly, at pp. 35–6, that seventeenth-century courts were using 'natural law' as an aid in the construction of statutes, and assuming that Parliament would not violate the common law rights to freedom and property. The courts would not necessarily refuse to enforce a statute contrary to these values.

Much more recently, Lord Steyn agreed with this assessment in the case of *R (on the application of Jackson) v Attorney General* [2005] UKHL 56. H. L. A. Hart, in his book *The Concept of Law*, suggests the parliamentary sovereignty is the UK's rule of recognition. A 'rule of recognition' is the *ultimate* rule in a legal system that establishes the criteria for identifying whether a rule is valid or not. The rule of recognition, unlike other rules, is binding because it is accepted by the community, and in particular its judges and officials. Its origin lies in politics and ideology. Hart argues that because the rule relies on general acceptance, it is possible that judges might, in some instances, reject it. Extrajudicial writing by judges such as Lord Woolf, Lord Justice Sedley, and Lord Justice Laws has challenged the notion that Parliament can make any law whatsoever and that the courts will respect it. These speculative writings concern potential limits to Parliament's power should Parliament abrogate basic requirements of the rule of law and fundamental rights. *Jackson* also raises this issue, which will be discussed later.

summary points

What is the history leading to parliamentary supremacy?

- *The early historical developments leading to the monarch recognising the supremacy of Parliament were discussed in Chapters 4 and 5.*

- *It is generally accepted that, from the late seventeenth century onwards, the judiciary accepted Parliament's legislative supremacy.*

- *The judiciary has subsequently enforced Acts of Parliament, although there is debate about whether parliamentary supremacy is a legal fact that the courts respect, or whether it is a political pact between the courts and Parliament.*

- *Parliamentary supremacy is one of the fundamental constitutional principles of the UK's constitution, although its precise definition remains subject to debate.*

What are the theories behind the doctrine of parliamentary supremacy?

Parliamentary sovereignty, as Dicey termed it, meant that Parliament was the supreme law-maker, whereas political sovereignty rested with the electorate who elected their parliamentary representatives. The theory, developed by other theorists such as Hobbes, Paine, and Locke, was that the people gave their consent to be governed as part of a social contract that provided them with safety and security. They thus gave up some of their freedom in return for living in a state of order. However, were the **government** to fail to meet its side of the social contract, the people would remain politically sovereign to topple the government and take back the freedom, so as to seek an alternative form of government that could fulfil the terms of the contract. As a result of this, it has been argued that Parliament's sovereignty is the power that has been given to that body by the people to allow it to make law so as to permit a stable form of government that achieves the requirements of the social contract. There are other theories of why Parliament has been imbued with such supreme law-making power, but this was the dominant theory developed during the seventeenth and eighteenth centuries, when Parliament's legislative supremacy became assured. There are many theoretical perspectives on parliamentary supremacy, but by far the most quoted even now is Dicey's *Introduction to the Study of the Law of the Constitution* of 1885. A. V. Dicey, writing in the nineteenth century, set out three main principles underpinning Parliament's legislative supremacy, as illustrated in Table 7.2.

Table 7.2

Dicey's three main principles of parliament supremacy

1 Parliament is the supreme law-making body and it may enact laws on any subject matter.

2 No Parliament may be bound by a predecessor (a previous Parliament) or may bind a successor (a future Parliament).

3 No person or body—including a court of law—may question the validity of Parliament's enactments.

Some students find the first principle and the third principle relatively straightforward, but struggle with the second. The first simply confirms what we have said thus far in this chapter—that the Parliament of the day may pass any law, amend any law, and repeal any law it chooses. There is no area of life on which Parliament cannot legislate, should it be able to command a majority in the Commons, in the Lords (subject to the Parliament Acts), and the assent of the monarch. The third principle is similarly straightforward: once Parliament has enacted a law and it has been brought into force, it is the law. Neither any institution nor any individual has the power to challenge the legal validity of an Act of Parliament. An Act of Parliament is the highest form of law in the UK, which cannot be overridden by the monarch or by the common law. It remains in force until such time as a future Parliament chooses to amend it or repeal it. The second principle, however, does look a little peculiar in any discussion about supremacy. If Parliament is supreme, how can it be prevented from binding a future Parliament? Is that not a restriction on Parliament's power? As Tomkins explains, it is the most modest of restrictions, put in place to ensure that Parliament does not diminish its supremacy over time.

...if Parliament may make or unmake any law whatsoever, surely this must include the ability to make (or unmake) a law that altered the doctrine of legislative supremacy. Such simplicity is in this instance deceptive, however. A law that altered the doctrine of legislative supremacy would be a law that reduced it: after all, the doctrine could hardly be further expanded! Herein lies the problem. If Parliament passes an Act that reduces the legislative competence of a future Parliament, then the future Parliament will no longer be legislatively supreme. Some commentators—most notably Dicey and Wade—have strongly argued that Parliament does not possess this power. That is to say that the only law that Parliament may not make is one that reduces supremacy of future Parliaments: Parliament 'may not bind its successors'. According to this interpretation it is not only the present Parliament that enjoys legislative supremacy, it is all Parliaments, present and future.

But this is not a universally held view. Other theorists, among them Jennings and Heuston, consider that Parliament may **entrench** legislation under some circumstances so as to bind future parliaments. Marshall also subscribes to this view. This perspective is often referred to as the 'manner and form' rule (not actually a rule, but rather a theory), which indicates that although Parliament may not limit a future Parliament's competence in terms of the areas of law upon which it may legislate (the content), it may alter the way in which future parliaments may make, amend, or repeal law. Parliament remains free to pass law on whatever area it chooses, but many argue that a previous Parliament may bind a future Parliament as to the manner and the form of (that is, the way in which the law is enacted and the appearance of) the new law. 'Manner and form' is the phrase used to suggest that Parliament may be permitted to change the way in which future parliaments must make law, usually to denote that a current Parliament may make it more difficult for a future Parliament to amend or repeal existing legislation by requiring a greater majority of votes in favour of the change than the standard simple majority, or by requiring the consent of the electorate to a fundamental legal change by way of a **referendum**. The current Parliament may decide to change the current three readings in the Commons and the Lords, followed by royal assent from the Queen, to introduce a new legislative stage—perhaps a fourth reading—or to remove the requirement of royal assent. We shall consider Jennings's view as an illustration of the manner-and-form point.

Jennings's challenge to Dicey's theory is more a redefinition of Dicey's theory. He argued that sovereignty is not the best way of describing Parliament's power and that supremacy is a more accurate description of Parliament's legislative competence. He argued that Parliament's power was derived from the fact that the courts acknowledge Parliament's legislative supremacy in instances in which it enacts law according to the proper procedures, whatever they are at the time the law comes into force. Were Parliament to enact a law that permitted law to be entrenched (fixed), then the courts would accept that as the new basis for parliamentary supremacy. Jennings describes this very simply, by explaining that parliamentary supremacy is a legal concept that describes the relationship between Parliament and the courts. He argued that 'It means that the courts will always recognise as law the rules which Parliament makes as legislation' (1959: 149). For him, parliamentary supremacy is the recognition that the courts give to Parliament's enactments and ongoing legislative power. But it is unclear whether Parliament is sovereign for all time, or whether it may limit its supremacy by placing hurdles in the way of future parliaments' enactments through changing the manner and form of subsequent legislation or by entrenching key constitutional provisions. In the next extract, Jennings explains something of a conundrum: is Parliament's power without limit, so as to permit Parliament the power to limit future parliaments, or is Parliament's power illimitable but for the fact that it cannot limit the power of a future Parliament?

· ·

● **I. Jennings,** *The Law of the Constitution* (5th edn, London: London University Press, 1959), pp. 152–3

> …Legal sovereignty is merely a name indicating that the legislature has for the time being power to make laws of any kind in the manner prescribed by law. That is, a rule expressed to be made by the Queen, 'with the advice and consent of the Lords spiritual and temporal, and the Commons, in this present Parliament assembled …' will be recognised by the courts *including a rule which alters this law itself*. If this is so, the 'legal sovereign' may impose legal limitations upon itself, because its power to change the law includes the power to change the law affecting itself.

Other scholars have offered different explanations about the nature of parliamentary supremacy. Heuston asserted that the 'new view' of sovereignty had overtaken Dicey's in many quarters and consisted of the following.

· ·

● **R. F. V. Heuston,** *Essays in Constitutional Law* (2nd edn, London: Stevens & Sons, 1964), pp. 6–7

> (1) Sovereignty is a legal concept: the rules which identify the sovereign and prescribe its composition and functions are logically prior to it.
>
> (2) There is a distinction between rules which govern, on the one hand, (a) the composition, and (b) the procedure, and, on the other hand, (c) the area of powers, of a sovereign legislature.
>
> (3) The courts have jurisdiction to question the validity of an alleged Act of Parliament on grounds 2(a) and 2(b) but not on ground 2(c).
>
> (4) This jurisdiction is exercisable either before or after the Royal Assent has been signified—in the former case by way of injunction, in the latter by way of declaratory judgment.

Heuston's understanding of parliamentary supremacy makes it possible for Parliament to change the way in which legislation is enacted and to provide for legislation to be entrenched. Entrenchment means that legislation is fixed and thus will bind future parliaments unless and until the law may be changed following the special procedure mandated by the earlier Parliament. For example, it would be possible, according to Heuston, for Parliament to enact a **bill of rights** that could be amended only following a special majority of two-thirds in favour in the House of Commons and the House of Lords, as well as royal assent, rather than the traditional simple majority vote in favour in the Houses. Alternatively, it could provide that a new bill of rights could be amended only with the consent of the electorate evidenced by way of a referendum. Dicey's formulation of the theory of parliamentary supremacy did not address this issue.

Wade considered that he had found a way around this problem, by arguing that parliamentary supremacy was not a legal rule, but a common law one that existed for as long as the judiciary believed it to reflect the political reality of the constitution. He argued that the rule of recognition (the ultimate rule) that has developed, whereby the courts will apply Parliament's primary legislation on the basis of parliamentary supremacy, is deeply rooted in our constitution. He argued that it grew out of the constitutional settlement that resulted in 1689, and it would take a major constitutional shift for this rule of recognition to change and for the courts to recognise and apply primary law on a different basis. Redefinition would result only from fundamental constitutional reform that was recognised by the courts. And thus parliamentary supremacy results from the courts' recognition of the legislative supremacy of Parliament through the operation of the common law. This provides us with an odd challenge to overcome, because if Parliament's enactments are above the common law and Parliament may change any law it wishes, does that not mean that Parliament is beyond the reach of the common law and yet subject to it at one and the same time? Wade attempts to explain this by saying that the common law rule that judges recognise the legislative supremacy of Parliament is the ultimate political fact upon which the whole constitutional system of law-making is based and is a special rule in the common law that is above all others.

● **H. W. R. Wade, 'The basis of legal sovereignty'** [1955] Cambridge Law Journal 172, 187–8

Once this truth is grasped, the dilemma is solved. For if no statute can establish the rule that the courts obey Acts of Parliament, similarly no statute can alter or abolish that rule. The rule is above and beyond the reach of statute ... because it is itself the source of the authority of statute.[1] This puts it into a class by itself among rules of common law, and the apparent paradox that it is unalterable by Parliament turns out to be a truism. The rule of judicial obedience is in one sense a rule of common law, but in another sense—which applies to no other rule of common law—it is the ultimate political fact upon which the whole system of legislation hangs. Legislation owes its authority to the rule: the rule does not owe its authority to legislation. To say that Parliament can change the rule, merely because it can change any other rule, is to put the cart before the horse.

For the relationship between the courts of law and Parliament is first and foremost a political reality. Historical illustrations of this are plentiful. When Charles I was executed in 1649 the courts continued to enforce the Acts of the Long Parliament ... and the other Commonwealth legislatures. For a revolution took place, and the courts (without any authority from the previous sovereign legislature) spontaneously transferred their allegiance from the King in Parliament to the kingless Parliaments. In other words, the courts altered their definition of 'an Act of Parliament' and recognised that the seat of sovereignty had shifted. This was a political fact from which legal consequences flowed. But in 1660 there was a counter-revolution: Charles II was restored, and it was suddenly discovered that all Acts passed by the Commonwealth Parliaments were void for want of the royal assent. The courts, again without any prior authority, shifted their allegiance back to the King in Parliament, and all the Commonwealth legislation was expunged from the statute book.[2] The 'glorious revolution' of 1688 was, in its legal aspect if in no other, much like the revolution of 1649, for the courts, recognising political realities but without any legal justification, transferred their obedience from James II to William and Mary ...

What Salmond calls the 'ultimate legal principle' is therefore a rule which is unique in being unchangeable by Parliament—it is changed by revolution, not by legislation; it lies in the keeping of the courts, and no Act of Parliament can take it from them. This is only another way of saying that it is always for the courts, in the last resort, to say what is a valid Act of Parliament; and that the decision of this question is not determined by any rule of law which can be laid down or altered by any authority outside the courts.[3] It is simply a political fact. If this is accepted, there is a fallacy in Jennings' argument that the law requires the courts to obey any rule enacted by the legislature, including a rule which alters this law itself. For this law itself is ultimate and unalterable by any legal authority.

1 The same point is made by Professor E. C. S. Wade, following Mr R. T .E. Latham, in the ninth edition of A. V. Dicey, *Introduction to the Law of the Constitution* (London: Macmillan, 1939), p. xxxviii.

2 F. W. Maitland, *The Constitutional History of England* (Reprint edn, Cambridge: Cambridge University Press, 1955), p. 282: 'In *Heath v. Pryn* (1670) 1 Vent. 14, counsel had the hardihood to challenge an Act of the Restoration Parliament: "The plaintiff's counsel would have

denied the Act of 12 Car. to be an Act of Parliament because they were not summoned by the King's writ; but the judges would not admit it to be questioned, and said, that all the judges resolved, that the Act being made by King, Lords and Commons they ought not now to pry into any defects of the circumstance of calling them together …"'

3 The same point is well put by K. C. Wheare, *The Statute of Westminster and Dominion Status* (5th edn, Oxford: Oxford University Press, 1953), pp. 155–6.

If Wade is right, then we have a system of parliamentary supremacy not because Parliament has so willed it, but because the courts have recognised parliamentary supremacy as the ultimate political reality of the UK legal system. And were there to be a fundamental constitutional re-form that the courts recognised to be the new political reality, then that would be the basis on which future law would be accepted by judges. This is a long way from Dicey's classic statement of parliamentary supremacy, although in some respects the two are not entirely inconsistent. Dicey was talking about the political reality in existence in his time, while Wade was projecting forward to hypothesise on the relationship between the courts and Parliament given a different set of political circumstances. Both were theories—Dicey had little empirical evidence to back up his theory at the time he published it and Wade's projection on how the legal system may develop operates on a similar basis. We do, however, have evidence that this debate persists.

● *AXA General Insurance Ltd and others v Lord Advocate and others* [2011] UKSC 46

Lord Hope:

[50] The question whether the principle of the sovereignty of the United Kingdom Parliament is absolute or may be subject to limitation in exceptional circumstances is still under discussion. For Lord Bingham, writing extrajudicially, the principle is fundamental and in his opinion, as the judges did not by themselves establish the principle, it was not open to them to change it: *The Rule of Law*, p 167. Lord Neuberger of Abbotsbury, in his Lord Alexander of Weedon lecture, Who are the masters Now? (6 April 2011), said at para 73 that, although the judges had a vital role to play in protecting individuals against the abuses and excess of an increasingly powerful ex-ecutive, the judges could not go against the will of Parliament as expressed through a statute. Lord Steyn on the other hand recalled at the outset of his speech in *Jackson*, para 71, the warning that Lord Hailsham of St Marylebone gave in *The Dilemma of Democracy* (1978), p 126 about the dominance of a government elected with a large majority over Parliament. This process, he said, had continued and strengthened inexorably since Lord Hailsham warned of its dangers. This was the context in which he said in para 102 that the Supreme Court might have to consider whether judicial review or the ordinary role of the courts was a constitutional fundamental which even a sovereign Parliament acting at the behest of a complaisant House of Commons could not abolish.

[51] We do not need, in this case, to resolve the question how these conflicting views about the relationship between the rule of law and the sovereignty of the United Kingdom Parliament may be reconciled. The fact that we are dealing here with a legislature that is not sovereign [the Scottish Parliament] relieves us of that responsibility.

cross reference

See Chapters 3 and 9 for further discussion of parliamentary supremacy in the context of the changing nature of the UK constitution.

We shall examine this case in a little more detail in Chapter 10. In the meantime, its importance for the purposes of the study of parliamentary supremacy is that there are judges who believe that parliamentary supremacy is respected by the courts as long as Parliament respects the rule of law. If Parliament steps away from upholding the rule of law, then the courts may not be willing to recognise Parliament's enactment as legal.

The next section will explore how parliamentary supremacy has operated in the UK and con-sider the extent to which the different conceptions of parliamentary supremacy are supported by the evidence.

summary points

What are the theories behind the doctrine of parliamentary supremacy?

- *The theorists discussed in this section consider that Parliament has legislative supremacy.*

- *Some argue that parliamentary supremacy is a legal fact that the courts respect, even though there is no legal text that confers this power on Parliament. Others argue that it is a political one.*

- *Dicey and Wade consider that Parliament cannot bind future parliaments; this is the only limit on the power of Parliament so as to ensure that Parliament's power does not diminish over time.*

- *Jennings, Heuston, and Marshall consider that it may be possible for Parliament to entrench (fix) legislation so that the nature of parliamentary supremacy changes over time. One example used is that Parliament could enact a Bill of Rights that could be semi-entrenched.*

7.4 Are there any restrictions on the power of Parliament?

We have considered the basic theory of parliamentary supremacy, but we have not examined the evidence in favour of Dicey or Wade's interpretation as compared with that of Jennings, Marshall, and Heuston. We shall take each of Dicey's three principles in turn and explore the evidence.

7.4.1 May Parliament enact law on any subject matter it chooses?

The simple answer to the above question is 'yes': in law, it may (subject to the discussion in the section above as regards some judicial thought that legislation enacted contrary to the rule of law may not be upheld by the courts)—but politically it may not be easy or expedient to pass laws drafted in certain terms. In theory, it would be perfectly possible for Parliament to pass a law that removes the vote from women and from men who do not own property, returning the electoral system back to its Victorian roots. However, in political terms, this would be so outrageous and subject to so much opposition that Parliament would be exceptionally unlikely to do so. But we have seen Parliament enact retrospective legislation—that is, legislation that has its effects backdated to before the Act was passed—such as the War Damages Act 1965, which sidestepped a rather inconvenient judgment in *Burmah Oil v Lord Advocate* [1965] AC 75. This demonstrates that Parliament has the power to backdate legislation, even if this is frowned upon when such legislation diminishes, rather than enhances, legal rights and freedoms. Indeed, Article 7 of the **European Convention on Human Rights (ECHR)**, to which the UK is a signatory, outlaws retrospective legislation that may lead to criminal sanction. Parliament has also enacted legislation, such as the War Crimes Act 1991, which applies extraterritorially, in that people who are alleged to have committed war crimes abroad may be tried in UK courts for those offences if they live in the UK or hold British citizenship. More recent legislation, such as the Criminal Justice and Immigration Act 2008, sought to outlaw child sex tourism by extending current UK sexual offences against children beyond the UK's borders. A British citizen who commits overseas what would be an offence in the UK is liable to prosecution on his or her return to Britain. Equally, Parliament could choose to pass law that operates in a different country, such as France, Canada, Zimbabwe, or the United States, but it would be of little use unless those countries were to chose to recognise Parliament's legislative supremacy in relation to them. Again, there is little prospect of that. British courts would be able to apply the law in cases working their way through the British court system, but that would have little local effect in other countries unless the courts there were to recognise and apply the law. A series of cases towards the end of the British Empire illustrated the practical limitations on Parliament's legislative competence, even though in strict law it is without restriction.

cross reference
Burmah Oil *was discussed in Chapter 6.*

· ·

● *British Coal Corporation v R* [1935] AC 500

Lord Sankey LC at 520:

> It is doubtless true that the power of the Imperial Parliament to pass on its own initiative any legislation it thought fit extending to Canada remains in theory unimpaired: indeed the Imperial Parliament could, as a matter of abstract law, repeal or disregard section 4 of the Statute. But that is theory and has no relation to realities.

This judgment of the Judicial Committee of the Privy Council related to the Statute of Westminster, by which legislative independence was given to Dominions such as Canada and Australia. Section 4 of the Colonial Laws Validity Act 1865 provided that the Imperial Parliament (in Westminster) would pass legislation for the Dominions only with their consent.

· ·

● *Madzimbamuto v Lardner-Burke* [1969] 1 AC 645

Lord Reid at 723:

> It is often said that it would be unconstitutional for the United Kingdom Parliament to do certain things, meaning that the moral, political and other reasons against doing them are so strong that most people would regard it as highly improper if Parliament did these things. But that does not mean that it is beyond the power of Parliament to do such things. If Parliament chose to do any of them the courts could not hold the Act of Parliament invalid.

Madzimbamuto provides an illustration of the classic formulation of Parliament's legislative supremacy, but the context is a little more nuanced. This case involved Parliament's enactment of the Southern Rhodesia Act 1965, which asserted the Westminster Parliament's legislative supremacy over Southern Rhodesia, as part of the Empire, after Ian Smith's government had issued a unilateral declaration of independence. Parliament's assertion of the right to rule did not change the local legislature's view of its legislative independence or the Southern Rhodesian courts' recognition of the legislature's law. Southern Rhodesia became Zimbabwe. Parliament may be able to enact law, but that is not the same as being able to enforce it against a people who are not willing to bow to its supremacy. Other examples of Parliament enacting legislation that relates to other countries are the Canada Act 1982 and the Australia Act 1986, both of which transferred the remaining legislative competence to Canada and to Australia. The Australia Act 1986 makes this very clear.

Australia Act 1986

Section 1

No Act of the Parliament of the United Kingdom passed after the commencement of this Act shall extend, or be deemed to extend, to the Commonwealth [of Australia], to a State or to a Territory as part of the law of the Commonwealth, of the State or of the Territory.

Both are thus examples of the Westminster Parliament enacting legislation for other countries, but in this situation, they are also evidence that the Westminster Parliament has effectively restricted its future legislative competence as regards those countries. It could be argued that a future Westminster Parliament could attempt to regain this power and so has not restricted its ultimate law-making power forever, but only for the time being. But as Lord Denning put it in *Blackburn v Attorney General* [1971] 1 WLR 1037, 1040: 'Can anyone image that Parliament could or would reverse these laws and take away their independence? Most clearly not. Freedom once given cannot be taken away.' And that is an important distinction between apparent legal sovereignty and political sovereignty.

Are there no areas beyond the reach of the Westminster Parliament? Some scholars argue that Acts such as those that established the United Kingdom—the Act of Union with Scotland 1707, for example—are of such fundamental constitutional importance that they could not be amended or repealed using the same procedure as a standard Act of Parliament. Indeed, in *McCormick v Lord Advocate* (1953) SC 396, the Lord President indicated that parliamentary sovereignty in its traditional formulation was an English, rather than a Scottish, constitutional doctrine. He argued that the 1707 Act provided for amendment or repeal of certain sections by the Westminster Parliament, but not for that of all sections, and thus it is unclear how, if at all, those reserved sections could be amended or repealed. In practical terms, it is likely that a substantial renegotiation would take place between the peoples of Scotland and England and/or their representatives before such a momentous change were effected. It may be that there would be a referendum, as was the case in relation to **devolution**. However, in strict law, we do have evidence of a potential problem in relation to the Scottish position, but not evidence of a problem from the English side. Indeed, the traditional doctrine of parliamentary supremacy is based on the assumption that an Act of Parliament is the highest form of law and that there is none higher. It does not provide for two classes of Act: those of standard importance and those of constitutional significance. Yet this was suggested by *obiter dicta* in the following case.

● *Thoburn v Sunderland City Council* [2002] 4 All ER 15, QBD DC

Lord Justice Laws at 183–5:

Third conclusion: the 1972 Act is a constitutional statute which by force of the common law cannot be impliedly repealed

[60] The common law has in recent years allowed, or rather created, exceptions to the doctrine of implied repeal: a doctrine which was always the common law's own creature. There are now classes or types of legislative provision which cannot be repealed by mere implication...

[62] ... In the present state of its maturity the common law has come to recognise that there exist rights which should properly be classified as constitutional or fundamental ... And from this a further insight follows. We should recognise a hierarchy of Acts of Parliament: as it were 'ordinary' statutes and 'constitutional' statutes. The two categories must be distinguished on a principled basis. In my opinion a constitutional statute is one which (a) conditions the legal

relationship between citizen and state in some general, overarching manner, or (b) enlarges or diminishes the scope of what we would now regard as fundamental constitutional rights; (a) and (b) are of necessity closely related: it is difficult to think of an instance of (a) that is not also an instance of (b). The special status of constitutional statutes follows the special status of constitutional rights. Examples are ... Magna Carta, the Bill of Rights 1689, the Act of Union, the Reform Acts which distributed and enlarged the franchise, the Human Rights Act 1998, the Scotland Act 1998 and the Government of Wales Act 1998. The 1972 Act clearly belongs in this family. It incorporated the whole corpus of substantive Community rights and obligations, and gave overriding domestic effect to the judicial and administrative machinery of Community law. It may be there has never been a statute having such profound effects on so many dimensions of our daily lives. The 1972 Act is, by force of the common law, a constitutional statute.

[63] Ordinary statutes may be impliedly repealed. Constitutional statutes may not. For the repeal of a constitutional Act or the abrogation of a fundamental right to be effected by statute, the court would apply this test: is it shown that the legislature's actual—not imputed, constructive or presumed—intention was to effect the repeal or abrogation? I think the test could only be met by express words in the later statute, or by words so specific that the inference of an actual determination to effect the result contended for was irresistible. The ordinary rule of implied repeal does not satisfy this test. Accordingly, it has no application to constitutional statutes ...

cross reference

See Chapter 8 for more information about the European Union Act 2011.

This case did not go beyond the Divisional Court and so we do not have further judicial evidence on this matter. However, regardless of whether Laws LJ's views have substantial judicial support, he did not argue that Parliament did not have the legal power to amend or repeal Acts of Parliament of constitutional significance; he argued instead that any such amendment or repeal should be made expressly rather than by implication. He did not argue that a change could be made only in conjunction with a referendum, as some have suggested. Politically, however, it may be difficult to make fundamental constitutional changes without clear electoral support, either on the basis of a successful manifesto commitment or via the use of a referendum, as employed during the devolution reforms.

What this principle does denote is that the UK does not have a written constitution that sets out the areas reserved for the people (or other institutions) to determine as compared with the areas reserved for Parliament. When you read Chapter 10, which addresses parliamentary supremacy and devolution, you will see that the Scottish Parliament, and the Welsh and Northern Ireland Assemblies all have restrictions placed on their legislative competence, with certain legislative powers reserved to the Westminster Parliament. In contrast, the Westminster Parliament has no such restrictions. In legal, rather than political terms, Dicey's first principle appears to be correct.

7.4.2 May Parliament bind subsequent parliaments?

The courts have developed rules to assist them in interpreting law. Some you will know about already—the rules of statutory interpretation; the ones in issue here are the rules of the doctrine of express and implied repeal. These are used when the courts are faced with two Acts of Parliament on the same subject matter that contradict each other. Which one is the court to apply? Parliamentary privilege is such that the courts cannot contact the current Parliament and ask which of the two it considers to be the more appropriate. The courts instead have to imply repeal of the earlier statute by the later. In simple terms, a section in a later Act of Parliament will repeal a section in a former Act of Parliament when the later contradicts the earlier, whether or not Parliament expressly states so in the later Act of Parliament.

The doctrine of express repeal is one of the most obvious ways in which Parliament continues to use its legislative supremacy: a later Parliament cannot be bound by an earlier Parliament. Implied repeal is used by the courts to give further effect to the principle that each new Parliament is free to enact any law it wishes—an earlier Parliament's Act that is contradicted by a later Parliament's Act will be amended or repealed according to the terms of the later Act, regardless of whether the later Parliament says that it expressly wishes that to be done. This is evidenced by the case of *Vauxhall Estates v Liverpool Corporation* [1932] 1 KB 733, in which there were contradictions between the Acquisition of Land (Assessment of Compensation) Act 1919 and the Housing Act 1925. The earlier Act contained a provision that its compensation assessment was to apply over any other such provision either passed or to be passed in the future. However, the courts held that the provision was overridden by the terms of the later Housing Act 1925, because an earlier Parliament cannot bind a future one under the terms of parliamentary supremacy. The following case is also evidence for this proposition.

● *Ellen Street Estates Ltd v Minister of Health* [1934] 1 KB 590

Maugham LJ at 597:

> The legislature cannot, according to our constitution, bind itself as to the form of subsequent legislation, and it is impossible for Parliament to enact that in a subsequent statute dealing with the same subject-matter there can be no implied repeal. If in a subsequent Act Parliament chooses to make it plain that the earlier statute is being to some extent repealed, effect must be given to that intention just because it is the will of the Legislature.

thinking point

What are your views on parliamentary supremacy so far? To what extent do you consider Parliament to be the supreme lawmaker and why?

However, it is clear that Parliament may change the way in which future legislation is to be made, or can be made. The Parliament Acts of 1911 and 1949 are evidence for this proposition, because a Bill may become law without the consent of the House of Lords if the terms of the Parliament Acts are met. This will remain the situation until such time as Parliament wishes to change the law again in respect of parliamentary law-making. It is difficult to see how a Parliament that is legislatively supreme can be prevented in law from changing the way in which legislation is to be enacted in future. And indeed the Parliament Acts contradict this position, as we will see later in the chapter.

NOTE

Some of you may be wondering whether Parliament's enactment of the European Communities Act 1972, sections 2 and 3, and the UK's membership of the European Union (EU) may conflict with this view of parliamentary supremacy. Others of you may wonder about the Human Rights Act 1998, which brings the ECHR into effect through domestic courts. Do these British Acts of Parliament conflict with the theories of parliamentary supremacy? We'll look at both of these issues in the two subsequent chapters, and consider the extent to which EU law and the ECHR have become entrenched within the UK system, including in our discussion the landmark case of *Thoburn v Sunderland City Council* [2002] EWHC 195 Admin.

7.4.3 No body or person may question the legal validity of an Act of Parliament

Earlier in this chapter, we considered the case law that developed and then enshrined the courts' recognition of Parliament's power to legislate on any subject matter. Thus it is generally accepted that an Act cannot be ruled as invalid on grounds of substance. The classic statement of Dicey's proposition that no body or person may question the legal validity of an Act of Parliament is set out in the following case.

● *Manuel v Attorney General* [1983] Ch 77

Sir Robert Megarry VC at 86:

> …nothing in this case to make me doubt the simple rule that the duty of the court is to obey and apply every Act of Parliament, and that the court cannot hold any such Act to be ultra vires. Of course there may be questions about what the Act means, and of course there is power to hold statutory instruments and other subordinate legislation ultra vires. But once an instrument is recognised as being an Act of Parliament, no English court can refuse to obey it or question its validity.

However, what about as regards manner and form? When is an Act of Parliament recognised as being a valid Act of Parliament in procedural terms? This case indicates that the courts are not entitled to consider any defects in parliamentary procedure leading to the enactment of the legislation; instead, Parliament's supremacy is reinforced. It is for Parliament to regulate itself (and the electorate as well, of course), rather than the courts. This is in stark contrast to the courts' powers to review the legality of executive action.

As indicated above, in the case of *Bowles v Bank of England* [1913] 1 Ch 57, the courts recognised an Act of Parliament as supreme, but that does not mean that all of Parliament's pronouncements are accorded that status. Thus, in *Bowles*, a resolution of the House of Commons' Ways and Means Committee was not held to be sufficient authorisation for the imposition of tax, even if Parliament does have the power to impose tax via Act of Parliament. A resolution is not the same as an Act and the court required an Act to be passed before it would recognise Parliament's exercise of power. The next case is also evidence for this proposition

● *Stockdale v Hansard* (1839) 9 Ad & E 1; 112 ER 1112

Lord Denham CJ at 1153–4:

> The House of Commons is not Parliament but only a co-ordinate and component part of the Parliament. That sovereign power can make and unmake the laws; but the concurrence of the three legislative estates is necessary; the resolution of any one of them cannot alter the law, or place anyone beyond its control.

Consequently, a resolution of the House of Commons was insufficient to trigger the courts' recognition for the purposes of parliamentary supremacy. It should be noted that this case was determined prior to the enactment of the Parliament Acts of 1911 and 1949, which have changed the way in which legislation may be made in certain circumstances (as will be discussed below). Finally, it is also important to bear in mind that although Acts of Parliament are hierarchically superior, delegated legislation is, by definition, of a lower order. This means that the courts may be required to invalidate it if the delegated legislation is deemed to be **ultra** *cross reference*

See the discussion of dualism in Chapter 8 for further details.

vires—that is, beyond its legal power, as designated by the Act of Parliament that gave rise to the power to make delegated legislation in that area.

Parliament does recognise some limits on the exercise of its supremacy, although it is arguable that, because these are not legal limits but relate to political limitations drawn up to assist in good governance, they do not in real terms affect Parliament's legislative supremacy. An example would be the Sewel Convention, which provides that, with respect to Scotland, the Westminster Parliament will not legislate on devolved matters without the consent of the Scottish Parliament. Parliament could consequently be viewed as having restricted its law-making powers in the areas devolved to the Scottish Parliament. Having said that, as explained in Chapter 10, the Westminster Parliament retains the legal right to legislate on all matters affecting the four countries that make up the United Kingdom and so it could be argued that its legislative supremacy remains intact.

What if a statute contradicts a provision of international law? Would that render the British Act void? The short answer to this is 'no', because, in general terms, international law is not binding within the domestic sphere unless Parliament so provides by enacting a statute to that effect. A case such as *Cheney v Conn* [1968] 1 All ER 779 asserts the hierarchical superiority of Acts of Parliament even over international law. However, the courts operate on the principle that Parliament does not intend to legislate contrary to a provision of international law in circumstances in which there is ambiguity of meaning between the two. In this situation, the courts use statutory interpretation so as to give the Act a consistent meaning with that of the international provision. Where there is a direct conflict between the two, the UK law will prevail.

NOTE

Some of you may be thinking that this is not your impression of how the system works vis-à-vis EU law and UK law, because cases such as *Factortame* appear to contradict Dicey's assertion that no one may question the validity of an Act of Parliament and no court may refuse to apply it. EU law is in a slightly different category from standard international law and this will be discussed in the next chapter in detail. The case of *Factortame*, in which certain provisions of a UK Act could not be applied because they breached European law, certainly challenges Dicey's conception of parliamentary sovereignty, at least in its most traditional formulation. By contrast, Jennings's redefinition of parliamentary supremacy is less affected by this legal development.

7.4.4 May Parliament bind future parliaments in relation to the way it enacts future Acts of Parliament?

Is Parliament able to change the way in which it enacts law and, in effect, bind a future Parliament as to the manner and form of future legislation? Some theorists have argued 'no', such as Dicey and Wade; others have argued 'yes', such as Jennings, Heuston, and Marshall. It has been argued that, were Dicey and Wade to be correct, Parliament would never have been able to introduce the Parliament Act 1911, which in turn gave rise to the Parliament Act 1949, because in effect that changes the way in which Parliament may make law in the future. We have evidence from case law to assist us with this.

The Parliament Act 1911 restricted the power of the House of Lords to veto money Bills and some other public Bills. It was introduced after the House of Lords rejected the Finance Bill 1909, which would have had the effect of limiting the funds open to the government of the day to run the country. The Parliament Act 1911 was used to make a further change to the legislative powers of the House of Lords—the Parliament Act 1949. These provisions, and their effect, are discussed in a little more detail below, but it may help to consider the standing orders of the House of Lords in relation to these Acts.

● **R. Kelly, 'The Parliament Acts'** (House of Commons Library Standard Note PC/675, 23 March 2007), available online at http://www.parliament.uk/briefing-papers/SN00675.pdf, p. 4

> The House of Lords Companion to the Standing Orders sets out in detail the application and procedures of the Parliament Acts:
>
> **Parliament Acts 1911 and 1949**
>
> 6.174 Under the Parliament Acts 1911 and 1949 certain public bills may be presented for Royal Assent without the consent of the Lords. The Acts do not apply to bills originating in the Lords, bills to extend the life of a Parliament beyond five years, provisional order bills, private bills or delegated legislation. The conditions which must be fulfilled before a bill can be presented for Royal Assent under the Acts vary according to whether or not the bill is certified by the Speaker as a money bill.
>
> **Money bills**
>
> 6.175 A money bill is a bill endorsed with the signed certificate of the Speaker that it is a money bill because in the Speaker's opinion it contains only provisions dealing with national, but not local, taxation, public money or loans or their management. If a money bill, which has been passed by the Commons and sent up to the Lords at least one month before the end of a session, is not passed by the Lords without amendment within a month after it is sent to them, the bill shall, unless the Commons direct to the contrary, be presented for Royal Assent without the consent of the Lords. This does not debar the Lords from amending such bills provided they are passed within the month, but the Commons are not obliged to consider the amendments. On a few occasions minor amendments have been made by the Lords to such bills and have been accepted by the Commons.
>
> **Other public bills**
>
> 6.176 If the Lords reject any other public bill to which the Acts apply which has been sent up from the Commons in two successive sessions, whether of the same Parliament or not, then that bill shall, unless the Commons direct to the contrary, be presented for Royal Assent without the consent of the Lords. The bill must be sent up to the Lords at least one calendar month before the end of each session; and one year must elapse between second reading in the Commons in the first session and the passing of the bill by the Commons in the second. The Lords are deemed to have rejected a bill if they do not pass it either without amendment or with such amendments only as are acceptable to the Commons. The effect of the Parliament Acts is that the Lords have power to delay enactment of a public bill until the session after that in which it was first introduced and until not less than 13 months have elapsed from the date of Second Reading in the Commons in the first session.[1]
>
> While the Parliament Acts are fairly short, simple statutes, there are various aspects of the procedure that are open to interpretation.
>
> 1 (London: HMSO, 2010), paras 8.195–7, also available online at http://www.publications. parliament.uk/pa/ld/ldcomp/compso2010/compso.pdf [updated version added].

197

As the extract indicates, Parliament has indeed already changed the way in which law may be enacted. But the Parliament Acts do not make any claims to be entrenched and thus the procedure could be changed again in future.

This is a fundamental question that goes to the very core of the courts' ability to recognise what is a valid Act of Parliament: what procedure must be followed in order for law to be passed, and when should the courts accept that an Act is the law? The courts have developed a principle known as the 'enrolled Act rule', sometimes referred to as the 'enrolled Bill rule'. This means that as long as Parliament has entered the Act on to its official Roll, the courts infer that it has been properly enacted. The courts do not look at how it was introduced or what went on during its passage through Parliament, as the following case explained.

● *Edinburgh & Dalkeith Railway v Wauchope* (1842) 8 Cl & Fin 710

Lord Campbell at 725:

> ...all that a court of justice can look to is the Parliamentary Roll; they see that an Act has passed both Houses of Parliament, and that it has received the Royal Assent, and no court of justice can inquire into the manner in which it was introduced into Parliament, what was done previously to its being introduced, or what passed in Parliament during the various stages of its progress through both House of Parliament.

Lord Campbell's statement suggests that this is relatively easy. All that the courts have to do is to look at the Parliamentary Roll—the official record of Acts—and if the legislation appears on that, then it is a valid Act and must be applied. However, we have evidence to the contrary in a persuasive Australian case from some thirty years earlier: *Attorney General for New South Wales v Trethowan* [1932] AC 526. This case concerned an Act from another jurisdiction—the legislature of New South Wales (NSW) in Australia. At that time, the Judicial Committee of the Privy Council was the highest appeal court for determining this case. The case concerned the attempt to pass a law to abolish the NSW Parliament's Upper Chamber. The Constitution (Legislative Council Amendment) Act 1929 provided that the NSW Upper Chamber could be abolished only if, prior to a Bill being placed before the Governor-General (the Queen's representative in Australia) for royal assent, there had been a referendum that had endorsed the terms of the Bill. The NSW Parliament sought to enact two Bills: the first to restrict the need for a referendum in the instant case; the second to abolish the Upper Chamber of Parliament. However, neither Bill was subject to a referendum. The case resulted from a challenge to the validity of the Act on the grounds that it had not been enacted following the proper procedure—that is, that there had been no referendum, as was required. The High Court of Australia and the Privy Council both agreed that there was a requirement for a referendum before the Bill could become law. It was held that section 5 of the Colonial Laws Validity Act 1865 provided that the Act would be valid only if it complied with any manner-and-form requirements, meaning that it would have to respect the proper procedure when being enacted in order for it to have the force of the law. The fact that the 1929 Act required a referendum meant that the new legislation would have to be passed using such a mechanism, and that removing the need for a referendum could only be achieved by first using the then current procedure (the use of a referendum) to agree the change to the manner and form of legislation. Why is this important? The reason that NSW was held to the need for a referendum at that time was that the Westminster Parliament's provisions were supreme—the Colonial Laws Validity Act 1865 was a Westminster Act of Parliament, which was binding on the Dominions. The High Court of Australia and the Judicial Committee of the Privy Council deemed that its provisions restricted the NSW legislature as to the manner and form of its legislation. This Act was repealed in respect of Australia by the Australia Act 1986, discussed above. The case is also important, because it is evidence that there was an accepted manner-and-form rule that flowed from a UK Act of Parliament.

● K. Swinton, 'Challenging the validity of an Act of Parliament: the effect of enrolment and parliamentary privilege' (1976) 14(2) Osgoode Hall Law Journal 345, 345–7

A. INTRODUCTION

...

> Within a study of parliamentary sovereignty, reference is normally made to the enrolled bill principle or rule. This precept, regarded by some as an aspect of sovereignty and by others simply as a rule of evidence, states that the parliamentary roll is conclusive—an

Act passed by Parliament and enrolled must be accepted as valid on its face and cannot be challenged in the courts on grounds of procedural irregularity. Because of the complexity of the issues involved in the definition of 'parliamentary sovereignty', most commentators have focussed their attention on an elaboration of the nature of sovereignty and the ability of Parliament to bind its successors, with the result that only passing reference has been made to the enrolment issue.

Yet the enrolled bill rule is a significant factor in the analysis of sovereignty, and one meriting study. Even if it were proven that Parliaments can bind their successors by mandatory procedural requirements, the enrolled bill rule, along with a second neglected aspect of constitutional law, that of parliamentary privilege, may render such binding effect nugatory in practice. Depending on the answers to questions such as what constitutes the parliamentary roll, whether the enrolled bill principle is a rule of law, and whether royal assent is curative of irregularities in the passage of a bill, the binding effect of manner and form legislation could be non-existent.

Similarly, parliamentary privilege could prevent any enforcement of procedural provisions. Parliament has long held the right to control its internal proceedings, free from outside interference. Yet a defect in procedure may only be provable through resort to the records of proceedings of the Houses of Parliament or of a provincial legislature. Would such practice be a violation of privilege? More importantly, should the courts be able to question and over-rule Parliament's interpretation of a given procedure? These are very real questions which must be dealt with if one is to decide that manner and form legislation is effective.

Privilege and enrolment, while inter-related, are separate questions. Many commentators and judges confuse the two, perhaps understandably, since the enrolment question is inextricably linked to privilege, while both may be related to parliamentary sovereignty. Within this study of the origins and scope of privilege and enrolment, reference must necessarily be made to the various types of procedural rules governing the passage of a bill and their differing effects in constitutional law, for it is clear that the courts have enforced and will continue to enforce some types of rules even though they leave others to Parliament alone to uphold.

B. ENROLMENT—THE RULE AND ITS SCOPE

Edinburgh and Dalkeith Ry. Co. v. Wauchope is the case most frequently cited to support the proposition that the parliamentary roll is conclusive. Lord Campbell made a statement in his judgment which has often been repeated:

All that a Court of Justice can do is to look to the Parliamentary roll: if from that it should appear that a bill has passed both Houses and received the Royal assent, no Court of Justice can inquire into the mode in which it was introduced into Parliament, nor into what was done previous to its introduction or what passed in Parliament during its progress in its various stages through both Houses.[1]

The words appear clear and categorical: a bill must be passed by both Houses of Parliament, receive Royal assent, and be inscribed on the parliamentary roll. Once these events have occurred, the resulting Act's validity is incontestable. Yet the words are deceptively simple, for Lord Campbell makes no effort to elaborate what constitutes the 'roll' to which one looks, nor does he deal with what constitutes 'passage' through the Houses, nor does he examine the issue of error on the face of the record...

1. Parliamentary Records

The term 'parliamentary roll' is anachronistic, as an historical discussion will show, for the roll per se was eliminated in England in 1849. Up to that date, all bills passed by Parliament were engrossed on parchment rolls. These rolls constituted the official copy of the Acts of Parliament, although the original Acts, those which bore the monarch's signature, were also retained after 1487.[2] Since 1849, the British practice with regard to official copies of statutes has changed. Two vellum copies are made of each Act passed and are endorsed with the words of royal assent and signed by the Clerk of the Parliaments. They are kept in the Public Records Office and the House of Lords. These Acts, printed as they are from the same type face as the copies available for public purchase, differ from those documents only in the quality of their paper and the fact of the signature. Therefore, they are unlike the original 'enrolled bills', which had been transcribed onto the roll, while public copies were printed just as they are today.

1 (1842), 8 Cl & F 710, 8 ER 279, 285 (HL).

2 S. Edgar (ed.) *Craies on Statute Law* (7th edn, London: Sweet & Maxwell, 1971), p. 39; *Claydon v Green* (1868) 3 CP 511, 522; B. Cocks (ed.) *May's Parliamentary Practice* (18th edn, London: Butterworths, 1971), p. 558.

However, the extent to which it would be applied against a UK Act is a difficult one to judge. We do know from cases such as *Manuel v Attorney General* [1983] Ch 77 that there is judicial reluctance to intervene in the workings of Parliament in order to establish whether the proper parliamentary procedure was followed. In *Manuel*, the Native Canadian nations sought to challenge the Canada Act 1982, which they claimed had not been enacted according to section 4 of the Statute of Westminster 1931. The Statute provided that the Westminster Parliament would not legislate for a Dominion 'unless it is expressly stated in the Act that the Dominion has requested, and consented to, the enactment'. The challenge was unsuccessful, with their Lordships stating that the Statute of Westminster required only that the Act states that it has been requested and consented to, not that the Dominion had indeed done so. The Canada Act 1982 did contain a form of words that met those requirements in its Preamble. The House of Lords also restated the traditional formulation of Parliament's legislative supremacy.

This was further underlined in *Pickin*.

● *British Railways Board v Pickin* [1974] AC 765

Lord Reid at 787:

The function of the court is to construe and apply the enactments of Parliament. The court has no concern with the manner in which parliament or its officers carry out its standing orders.

This flows at least in part from the Bill of Rights and parliamentary privilege, but to what extent would the judiciary be prepared to ignore a serious error in parliamentary procedure that appeared to undermine its legitimacy? It may become pertinent, however, as a result of the European Union Act 2011 and the requirement for a referendum prior to any powers being transferred from the UK to the European Union.

However, Swinton's extract, above, suggests that for parliamentary supremacy to be truly meaningful, the courts should surely check that Parliament has actually enacted the legislation properly, because this would protect the long-term standing of Parliament? A piece of legislation that provoked much controversy was the Hunting Act 2004, which was passed with the aid of the Parliament Acts. The legislation was controversial, not least because there was a real division of opinion between the pro-hunting and anti-hunting lobbies, and also between the prevailing views in the Commons and the Lords. And there were even strong differences of opinions within the political parties. In the end, the Hunting Act was passed after there had been strong support for it in the House of Commons, both when it had first been introduced and after its reintroduction. The Bill had been defeated in the Lords until the point at which the Lords was bypassed by the use of the Parliament Acts. There followed a case brought by the Countryside Alliance, one of the key interest groups in the pro-hunt lobby, along with others who sought to challenge the validity of the Hunting Act on the grounds that it was not validly enacted. The Countryside Alliance argued that the use of the Parliament Act 1949 was unconstitutional, because the Parliament Act 1949 had not itself been validly enacted. The Alliance argued that the Parliament Act 1911 required that the House of Lords' consent be acquired before the 1949 Act could be passed, and yet it was not. This, it was contended, was contrary to the legislative supremacy of Parliament. The Crown asserted that the Parliament Act 1911 allowed legislation to be passed even if the House of Lords refused to consent, as long as the procedure in section 2 was complied with. The Crown argued that the Parliament Act 1949 was validly enacted on that basis and thus so was the Hunting Act 2004. Burns provides an explanation of the legal interpretative and theoretical difficulties arising from the case in relation to parliamentary supremacy:

· ·

● **S. Burns, 'When is an Act of Parliament not an Act of Parliament?'** [2006] 156 New Law Journal 191, 191–3

The House of Lords decision

The law lords agreed with the decision of the lower courts, concluding that PaA 1949, and therefore HuA 2004, were indeed enacted Acts of Parliament with full legal effect. It is worth emphasising that PA 1911, introduced by the then liberal government, was itself passed by both Houses of Parliament—their Lordships knew that the King would otherwise appoint a sufficient number of new peers to guarantee its passage through the House of Lords, although this would be the monarch's last resort. PA 1911, s 1(1) prevented the House of Lords rejecting or amending money Bills, thus emphasising the primacy and predominance of the elected chamber—the House of Commons—even in 1911.

Section 2(1) provides:

'If any public Bill . . . is passed by the House of Commons (in three successive sessions) . . . and . . . is rejected by the House of Lords in each of those sessions, that Bill shall, on its rejection (for the third time) by the House of Lords . . . be presented to His Majesty and become an Act of Parliament on the Royal Assent . . . notwithstanding that the House of Lords have not consented to the Bill . . .'

Thus, the House of Lords' delaying power for non-money bills is strictly limited and precisely demarcated. PA 1911 also facilitates the enactment of valid legislation, without the usual requirement that it be approved by the second chamber—a radical departure from the traditional concept of Royal standing within Parliament.

. . .

Courts since 1911 have effectively been given an alternative rule of legal recognition, ie a new and equally legitimate way, on occasions, of identifying a valid Act of Parliament. PA 1911, therefore, resulted in a major constitutional development . . . Lord Bingham stated:

'. . . this, of course is a further example of the supremacy of Parliament—namely it has the power to alter how and even by whom, it passes legislation. Dicey, in 1885, enunciated the classical statement of parliamentary supremacy, namely . . . that Parliament . . . has, under the English constitution, the right to make or unmake any law whatever; and, further, that no person or body is recognised by the law of England as having a right to override or set aside the legislation of Parliament.'

However, their Lordships were emphatic that PA 1911 could not be viewed as a delegation of legislative authority by either the House of Lords or by Parliament to the House of Commons. The overall purpose of PA 1911 was to reduce the powers of the House of Lords, not to increase those of the House of Commons.

. . .

Finally, Lord Bingham agreed with the claimants that the change following PaA 1949 was not '. . . as the Court of Appeal described it "relatively modest" but . . . substantial and significant'.

However, he agreed with the government that the breadth and scope of the power given to the House of Commons by virtue of s 2(1) '... cannot depend on whether the amendment in question is or is not relatively modest'. Thus, the government could misuse PA 1911 and PaA 1949 to curtail legitimate criticism and scrutiny of its proposed Bills by the House of Lords, on areas of enormous public significance. By the same token, said Lord Bingham, both Acts had been invoked on several occasions to '... achieve objects of more minor or no constitutional import ...' such as, of course, banning fox-hunting, which was one of the aims of HuA 2004.

Lord Nicholls said there was one instance for which the PA 1911, s 2(1) procedure could not be invoked, and that was when the purpose of a Bill from the House Commons was to extend the duration of Parliament—bearing in mind the danger of an unpopular government clinging on to power by Machiavellian means.

Redefinition theory

Lord Steyn correctly identified two distinct questions concerning whether HuA 2004 was a valid Act of Parliament:

> '(1) what Parliament may do by legislation, and (2) what the constituent elements of Parliament must do to legislate. The first question involves the domain of the supremacy or sovereignty of Parliament...The focus of the appeal is the second question ...'

PA 1911, s 2(1) and later PaA 1949 answer the second question—generally all three components must consent to a Bill before it is enacted, which is the case on the majority of occasions. However, as Lord Steyn said, in some circumstances, Parliament may functionally redistribute legislative power in different ways, as here where the second chamber is deliberately thwarting proposed government Bills.

Parliament has redefined its constituent elements for the purpose of passing certain legislation, and so long as the proposed legislation is enacted in accordance with the prescribed method at the time, as stipulated by PA 1911 and PaA 1949, then its legislation will not be susceptible to legal challenge in the courts. This notion of legislation being passed in a certain 'manner or form', sometimes referred to as the 'redefinition theory', before that legislation is deemed to be validly and constitutionally enacted, has been specifically endorsed in several cases, including *AG New South Wales v Trethowan* [1932] AC 526 PC—albeit referring to subordinate legislation.

Lord Steyn warns that the implications of the use of PA 1911 and PaA 1949 could potentially be used as a Trojan horse, on the pretext of overriding objections from reactionary peers, but in reality and as a means to introduce:

> '... oppressive and wholly undemocratic legislation. For example, it could theoretically be used to abolish judicial review of flagrant abuse of power by a government or even the role of the ordinary courts in standing between the executive and citizens.'

Conclusions

For most, the arguments over the merits of the HuA 2004, and indeed the issues raised in the House of Lords, may appear of marginal significance. However, Lord Hailsham, a former Lord Chancellor and senior cabinet member, as far back as 1978, warned the public about the dangers posed by an over-powerful executive—'an elective dictatorship'. The reality in 2006 is that Parliament (the House of Commons) has become largely, though not entirely—noting the government's recent defeat in the House of Commons over proposals to detain terrorist suspects up to 90 days without charge—a rubber-stamp for government policy.

Overuse and arguably misuse of PA 1911 and PaA 1949 to ram through government legislation may conform to strict legalism, but at the cost of weakening the constitutional checks on government. It has been stated that the theory of parliamentary sovereignty is a rule of legal recognition, ie one created and currently accepted by the courts, and therefore one that could be reconsidered and changed by the judges—'not unthinkable', said Lord Steyn, if the government, 'in exceptional circumstances', were, for example, trying to prevent judicial review or passing oppressive laws.

The deference of the courts to the supremacy of laws of Parliament, even if they are critical of the theory, is still evident in the words of Lord Steyn:

> 'The classic account given by Dicey of the doctrine of the supremacy of Parliament, pure and absolute as it was, can now be seen to be out of place in the modern United Kingdom. Nevertheless, the supremacy of Parliament is still the general principle of our constitution.'

This extract provides good evidence in support of Jennings' and others' contention that Parliament may change the manner and form by which legislation is passed in the future, but not the legislative competence of Parliament. Burns quotes Lord Steyn's demarcation between the content of a Bill and the way in which it is enacted, and refers to the redefinition theory of parliamentary supremacy, which is another way of explaining the manner-and-form rule. It is clear that the Law Lords agreed that Parliament may bind future parliaments as regards how legislation is to be enacted, but that future parliaments may also once again change the legislative process. Were Parliament to object to the way in which the Parliament Acts operate, Parliament could seek to change the way in which future legislation was enacted. It would have to use the current procedure to amend the Parliament Acts, but once amended the new procedure would be used. Consequently, the Parliament Acts are in force only until such time as a future Parliament chooses to enact law to amend or repeal them. In some respects, this is a logical position. The British constitution is an organic and evolving one; were Parliament to be unable to change the way in which it makes law, then the UK constitutional position would be rigidly fixed for all time, in direct contradiction to its historical reality.

summary points

Are there any restrictions on the power of Parliament?

- *In law, Parliament may pass any law it wishes to pass; in politics, this may be less easy.*

- *The courts assume that when then are two contradictory provisions in Acts of Parliament, the later is the current will of Parliament and the earlier is repealed by implication.*

- *Parliament should use the proper procedure when enacting law, but as a result of parliamentary privilege, the courts have been reluctant to enquire into the passage of legislation and have instead left this for Parliament to determine.*

- *When UK law appears both ambiguous and yet potentially to contradict international law, the courts make the assumption that Parliament intended to legislate in conformity with international law. Direct conflicts are more difficult to deal with, as discussed in the next chapter.*

- *The Parliament Acts suggest that Parliament is able to change the way in which legislation is enacted. However, future parliaments would also be free to change the procedure further, or to revert back to the original procedure for enactment, assuming that they make use of the current procedure to do so.*

203

7.5 Who or what regulates Parliament if not the courts?

We have mentioned parliamentary privilege on a number of occasions in this chapter, which is the mechanism through which Parliament operates free from outside interference. Parliament sets its own rules and privileges so that it can function effectively.

● **Memorandum from Sir Barnett Cocks** (HC 34, 1966–67)

> The sole justification for the present privileges of the House of Commons is that they are essential for the conduct of its business and maintenance of its authority.

Privilege is part of the law and the custom of Parliament. The courts do not interpret the internal operation of privilege, but will consider the nature and extent of privilege where it affects those outside Parliament. As Lord Browne-Wilkinson explained in *Pepper v Hart* [1993] AC 595, 645: '... it is for the courts to determine whether a privilege exists and for the House to decide whether such a privilege has been infringed.' Parliament has internal regulatory mechanisms that permit it to investigate complaints that there has been a breach of privilege and to sanction any such breach.

● **O. Gay, 'Parliamentary Privilege and Individual Members'** (House of Commons Library Standard Note PC/04905, 10 February 2010), pp. 2–3

1. Parliamentary privilege

Parliamentary privilege has two main components:

- Freedom of speech, which is guaranteed by Article IX of the Bill of Rights 1689
- The exercise by Parliament of control over its own affairs, known technically as 'exclusive cognisance'.

The privilege of freedom of speech protects what is said in debate in either House. As Article IX states:

> That the freedom of speech and debates or proceedings in Parliament ought not to be impeached or questioned in any court or place out of Parliament.

The Joint Committee on Parliamentary Privilege set out the modern interpretation of Article IX in 1999, as follows:

> ...The modern interpretation is now well established: that article 9 and the constitutional principle it encapsulates protect members of both Houses from being subjected to any penalty, civil or criminal, in any court or tribunal for what they have said in the course of proceedings in Parliament.[1]

The Joint Committee considered that this protection extended to preparations for debates and questions, citing the conclusions reached by the Select Committee on Official Secrets in the Duncan Sandys case in 1939...

Exclusive cognisance enables Parliament to have control over all aspects of its own affairs, to determine its procedures and to discipline its own members for misconduct. The Joint Committee on Parliamentary Privilege set out the justification as follows:

> 13. The other main component of parliamentary privilege is still called by the antiquated name of **'exclusive cognisance'** (or 'exclusive jurisdiction'). Parliament must have sole control over all aspects of its own affairs: to determine for itself what the procedures shall be, whether there has been a breach of its procedures and what then should happen. This privilege is also of fundamental importance. Indeed, acceptance by the executive and the courts of law that Parliament has the right to make its own rules, and has unquestioned authority over the procedures it employs as legislator, is of scarcely less importance than the right to freedom of speech. Both rights are essential elements in parliamentary independence.

> 14. Parliament's right to regulate its own affairs includes the **power to discipline its own members** for misconduct and, further, **power to punish anyone,** whether a member or not, for behaviour interfering substantially with the proper conduct of parliamentary business. Such interference is known as contempt of Parliament. This falls within the penal jurisdiction exercised by each House to ensure it can carry out its constitutional functions properly and that its members and officers are not

obstructed or impeded, for example by threats or bribes. The sanctions available are reprimand, imprisonment for the remainder of the session and, possibly in the House of Lords but probably not in the House of Commons, a fine of unlimited amount. Even in the House of Lords the power to impose a fine has not been used in modern times. Members of the House of Commons are also liable to suspension for any period up to the remainder of the Parliament (though there is no modern case of suspension for anything like this length). Members so suspended usually forfeit their salaries for the period of their suspension. Members of the House of Commons can be expelled, although it is over 50 years since the power of expulsion was last used.

2. The Joint Committee's report in 1999

A joint committee of both Houses was established in 1997 as part of the new Government's initiative to modernise Parliament, with a brief to review parliamentary privilege and make recommendations. The Joint Committee reported in March 1999 and among other recommendations, argued that the meaning of 'proceedings in Parliament' and 'place out of Parliament' set out in Article IX should be clarified and defined; it also recommended a new Parliamentary Privileges Act.[3] It recommended that 'the absolute privilege accorded by article 9 to proceedings in Parliament should not be extended to include communications between members and ministers'.[4] The Australian Parliament had enacted an Australian Parliamentary Privileges Act in 1987, following court cases in New South Wales which appeared to give judgements contrary to the usual interpretation of Article IX.

The Joint Committee also recommended clarification of 'exclusive cognisance'; it suggested the enactment of a provision to the effect that the privileges of each House to administer its own affairs in its precincts apply only to activities directly and closely related to proceedings in Parliament. In addition, it suggested a principle of statutory interpretation that Acts of Parliament bind both Houses unless there was a contrary expression of intention.

The report was debated in the House of Commons on 27 October 1999.[5] No legislative action has followed the Joint Committee report. *Erskine May* remains the authoritative guide to precedent.[6]

1 *Report of the Joint Committee on Parliamentary Privilege* (First Report, Session 1998–99, HL Paper 43/HC 214-I, April 1999), para. 37, available online at http://www.publications. parliament.uk/pa/jt199899/jtselect/jtpriv/43/4305.htm

2 [Passage omitted]

3 See n. 1.

4 Ibid, para. 112.

5 (HC Deb, 29 October 1999) vol. 336, cols 1020–74.

6 M. Hutton, A. G. Sandall, M. Robertson, S. Patrick, W. Mackay, and R. Wilson (eds) *Erskine May on Parliamentary Practice* (23rd edn, London: Lexis Nexis Butterworths, 2004).

NOTE

Please read this note in full, available online at http://www.parliament.uk/documents/commons/lib/research/briefings/snpc-04905.pdf, if you want to learn more about parliamentary privilege and recent controversies that relate to its use.

One notable privilege is freedom of speech during the debates and proceedings in Parliament (under article 9 of the Bill of Rights 1689), as mentioned in the extract. This protection was sought so that parliamentarians had the right to speak freely, rather than having to self-censor so as not to be charged with a civil or a criminal offence. There were concerns that any potential criticism of the King could lead to court action. *Eliot's Case* (1629) 3 St Tr 294 provides evidence that three parliamentarians were convicted of sedition as a result of things said during proceedings in the House of Commons. As a result, the courts were not permitted to consider words spoken during proceedings in Parliament, thus protecting parliamentarians from action. But that freedom is provided to members of Parliament (MPs) so that they may properly represent their constituents and also hold the executive to account. Similar protections apply to witnesses in court (although this is obviously not a form of parliamentary privilege), so that courts can function effectively.

NOTE

See the Report of the Committee on Super-injunctions, available online at http://www.judiciary.gov.uk/Resources/JCO/Documents/Reports/super-injunction-report-20052011.pdf

This privilege has sparked some controversy recently in view of its use by an MP to name a footballer whose identity was protected by a super-**injunction** that had been granted in the light of an application to prevent alleged details about his private life from being revealed by the press and others. A super-injunction both prevents publication of the allegations made about the person and also about the existence of the injunction itself, thus protecting the identity of the person as well as the details of the allegations that cannot be published. A further recent example of freedom of speech during proceedings in Parliament relates to the comments made by Louise Mensch MP about a former newspaper editor's alleged knowledge of telephone hacking at the time of his editorship. Piers Morgan denied the allegations, but indicated that he was unable to take action against Louise Mensch, because her comments were protected by parliamentary privilege. Ms Mesch has since clarified her comments and offered an apology to Mr Morgan during proceedings in the Department for Culture Media and Sport Committee, which has been investigating allegations of phone hacking.

In real terms these days, this privilege means that MPs have immunity from the law of defamation for words spoken in parliamentary proceedings (as discussed in cases such as *Dillon v Balfour* (1887) 20 LR IR 600 and *Church of Scientology of California v Johnson-Smith* [1972] 1 QB 522). But, until recently, this also limited MPs' ability to bring defamation proceedings against someone if the defendant would be unable to mount a full defence on the basis that doing so would require the court to consider material from proceedings in Parliament (see *Prebble v Television New Zealand Ltd* [1995] 1 AC 321). Since the early 1980s, the courts have been permitted to consider words spoken during proceedings in Parliament, as evidenced in Hansard, but not as an aid to statutory interpretation. And this relaxation required the permission of the House before each reference and use of words spoken in proceedings in Parliament. The rule against reference to Hansard for the purpose for statutory interpretation was relaxed by the courts as a result of *Pepper v Hart*, but only in relation to certain sections of Hansard. In the light of a political scandal engulfing Neil Hamilton MP, in which it was alleged that he had received 'cash for questions' (that is, that he had been paid to raise certain matters during proceedings in Parliament), Parliament changed the Defamation Act 1996 so as to allow a person to waive parliamentary privilege in relation to what he or she has said in Parliament, and thus to permit a defamation action to be sought. Neil Hamilton waived his privilege so that he could sue *The Guardian* newspaper and also Mohammed Al-Fayed (*Hamilton v Al-Fayed* [2001] 1 AC 395) in relation to some of the allegations made against him.

Many courses will not require an in-depth knowledge of the case law in parliamentary privilege, while others will—but a good general knowledge with examples may be important. We shall not consider this in much detail in this chapter, but you may wish to consider the House of Commons Library Standard Note (mentioned in the further reading section and available online), which provides an excellent exposition of the area. You may also want to include parliamentary privilege in the light of the MPs' expenses scandal. Recent concerns about MPs' (and Lords') expenses have meant that parliamentary privilege has come under greater scrutiny.

Parliament has passed legislation to tighten up the expenses scheme and to introduce independent oversight of their expenses. Part 3 of the Constitutional Reform and Governance Act 2010 amends the Parliamentary Standards Act 2009 so as to change the powers and functions of the Independent Parliamentary Standards Authority (IPSA) to implement Part 4 of the Parliamentary Standards Act 2009, which requires MPs and Lords Temporal (members of the House of Lords) to be ordinarily resident and domiciled in the UK for the purposes of income tax, capital gains tax, and inheritance tax.

NOTE

You may wish to visit IPSA's online at http://www.ipsa-home.org.uk to read up on its remit. You will see details of the new MPs' expenses regime on that site. You will find details of MPs' and Lords' expenses online at http://www.parliament.uk/mps-lords-and-offices/members-allowances/

There is some evidence that Parliament has and does, via parliamentary privilege, impose sanctions against MPs and Lords whom it considers to have fallen below the standards expected of them. Three peers were suspended from the House of Lords on 21 October 2010 as a result of findings made by the House of Lords' Subcommittee on Lords' Conduct. The Subcommittee found against the peers as regards expenses claims that they had made under the former expenses regime. Three former MPs were charged with offences in respect of expenses claims that they made while serving as MPs, as was one peer. The MPs and peers argued, unsuccessfully, that they should not be subject to prosecution in court, but instead by the High Court of Parliament. They claimed that they were protected from prosecution in a normal criminal court due to the operation of parliamentary privilege. Subsequent prosecutions led to convictions and prison sentences for some of those charged with criminal offences related to fraudulent expenses claims.

summary points

Who or what regulates Parliament if not the courts?

- *Parliament asserts parliamentary privilege, which provides it with protection from outside interference so as to permit it to function effectively.*

- *Parliamentary privilege asserts Parliament's power to self-regulate.*

- *Parliament has mechanisms in place to set its own privileges, to investigate alleged breaches of privilege, and to sanction breaches of privilege by members and non-members of the House.*

- *The courts may examine whether a privilege exists and how broadly it is drawn, but thereafter it is for Parliament to enforce privilege.*

- *Recent reforms have relaxed the rule that no words spoken during proceedings in Parliament may be considered in court, but only in limited circumstances and for particular reasons.*

- *What this means, in relation to parliamentary supremacy, is that the courts have no power to regulate Parliament, ensuring that Parliament remains supreme.*

- *This section has provided only a very brief introduction to the topic and you may wish to read the House of Commons Library Standard Note detailed in the further reading at the end of the chapter for more information.*

How does parliamentary supremacy compare with constitutional supremacy?

Many countries do not have parliamentary supremacy as a feature of their constitutions; instead, many operate a system of constitutional supremacy, meaning that legislation passed by the legislature may be invalidated by the courts if the legislation breaches the constitution. The legislature has to bow to the constitution and so is not entirely supreme in its law-making powers. Instead, it is the guardians of the constitution—usually constitutional or supreme court judges—who determine whether the legislature has respected or breached the constitution by enacting the legislation in those terms. This is the case in the US, for example, where the written US Constitution is the rule of recognition. The landmark case of *Marbury v Madison* 5 US (1 Cranch) 137 (1803) clearly states this principle. It is also the rule of recognition for the European Union—not a country, but a new form of legal entity—in which treaties, as interpreted by the European Court of Justice (ECJ), are the rule of recognition and are considered to be supreme in respect of EU matters.

Figure 7.1 aims to provide a simplified picture of the differences between a pure form of parliamentary supremacy and a pure form of constitutional supremacy. It demonstrates how the courts interpret and apply primary legislation in both systems.

Some countries, such as Canada and South Africa, have moved from a system or parliamentary supremacy to one of constitutional supremacy at the time when they have adopted a written or a new written constitution that altered the country's constitutional settlement. Both countries have changed their systems relatively recently: Canada in the 1980s; South Africa in the 1990s. Other countries, such as France, have recently modified their approach to constitutional supremacy. The French *Conseil Constitutionnel* ('Constitutional Council') can be asked to rule on the constitutionality of primary legislation before it is fully enacted. It is also now possible for anyone before a court to make an application that allows the *Conseil Constitutionnel* to examine whether primary legislation infringes constitutional rights and to repeal the legislation, if that is required. The German *Bundesverfassungsgericht* ('Constitutional Court') is a more traditional constitutional court, which may strike down legislation of all levels (as well as executive and judicial Acts) on the ground that they violate the German *Grundgesetz* ('Basic Law') of the Federal Republic of Germany, which has the status of a constitution even if that word is not used in its title.

There are examples of countries that adopt a hybrid approach to supremacy, having elements of parliamentary and constitutional supremacy. One such country is Australia. Australia combines parliamentary supremacy with a (partially) written constitution (the Constitution of the Commonwealth). The Constitution of the Commonwealth is not the only source of constitutional law, because Australia was not established by this document, but by royal proclamation in 1900, and a number of Acts of constitutional importance also form an integral part of the Constitution, as do resolutions of Parliament and **constitutional conventions**. All legislation must comply with the Constitution of the Commonwealth and the High Court of Australia (Australia's highest court) has the responsibility for deciding constitutional disputes. Chapter I, Part V, of the Constitution lays out Parliament's legislative competence. In that sense, the Constitution performs its traditional function. However, the Constitution does not contain a Bill of Rights against which legislation may be compared to ensure that the legislation is

Figure 7.1

Pure form of parliamentary supremacy	Pure form of constitutional supremacy
1. Do the courts recognise this as a valid piece of primary legislation? *There may be rules about what the courts recognise as a valid piece of primary legislation. The courts may take Parliament's recognition of the legislation as sufficient proof of its validity. In the UK, this is known as the enrolled Bill/Act rule.*	**1. Has the piece of primary legislation (equivalent to an Act of Parliament for that country) been subject to the proper legislative process?** *There may be rules about what constitutes a valid piece of primary legislation. These may be set out in the constitution. If it is not valid, it will be invalidated.*
2. Is it the most recent expression of Parliament's will on the topic? *That is, there a later Act of Parliament that must be applied in preference to this one?* *In UK terms, the doctrines of express and implied repeal.*	**2. Does the content of the primary legislation conform to the constitution?** *The courts will have to look at the content of the legislation to make sure that it does not infringe any constitutional principles.*
3. If yes to 1 and 2, the courts must apply the Act of Parliament. *The courts cannot declare the Act of Parliament invalid and refuse to apply it.* *In UK terms, the courts must apply the law according to the rules laid down by Parliament as regards EU law and the ECHR.*	**3. If either 1 or 2 demonstrate that the legislation does not conform to the constitution, the constitutional court will invalidate the legislation.** *In some countries, the constitutional court may not invalidate the legislation, but may disapply it and return it to the legislature for amendment.*

constitutional. In this regard, Australia is much more similar to the UK system than to, say, that of the US. Because the Constitution is a relatively narrowly focused document by comparison with many written constitutions, the Australian Parliament's legislative supremacy is largely unrestricted. And, like the UK, many of the constitutional 'law' or 'rules' are not contained in written legal texts, but instead in constitutional conventions.

Is the British system an example of pure parliamentary supremacy? Some commentators such as Chief Justice Dickson have argued that it is, while others argue that Britain is moving from a system of parliamentary supremacy to a midway point between the two as a result of the UK's membership of the European Union and the Council of Europe. Others argue that not only is this debate a dangerous one, because it ascribes more power to the judiciary than is wise, but it also introduces uncertainty into what has been a relatively settled constitutional system. Judges in the UK have to consider the UK law in the light of certain types of EU law that are considered to be hierarchically superior and also the ECHR. In relation to the hierarchically superior EU law, UK judges must apply EU law and disapply UK law in a

cross reference

We shall consider the ECHR and the Human Rights Act 1998 in more detail in Chapters 8 and 9.

situation in which there is a direct contradiction between the terms of the EU and the terms of the UK law. This is not true in relation to a direct contradiction between UK law and the ECHR, because the Human Rights Act 1998 explicitly preserves parliamentary supremacy in this regard.

However, this is not the only challenge to parliamentary supremacy, according to some academics and legal practitioners. It is also argued that increasing judicial activism in the field of common law rights verges on constitutional reform and may lead to a slow creep from parliamentary supremacy to constitutional supremacy, but without the introduction of a written constitution. Others see it as a natural progression towards constitutionalism. Two extracts illustrate this point. The first is taken from a Court of Appeal case and explains one view of the development from parliamentary to constitutional supremacy.

● *International Transport Roth GmbH and others v Secretary of State for the Home Department* [2002] EWCA Civ 158

Lord Justice Laws:

[69] In *Vriend* [1998] 1 SCR 493, in the Supreme Court of Canada, Iacobucci J stated at 563:

'When the Charter [the Canadian Charter of Rights and Freedoms] was introduced, Canada went, in the words of former Chief Justice Brian Dickson, from a system of parliamentary supremacy to constitutional supremacy...Simply put, each Canadian was given individual rights and freedoms which no government or legislature could take away.'

[70] Not very long ago, the British system was one of Parliamentary supremacy pure and simple. Then, the very assertion of constitutional rights as such would have been something of a misnomer, for there was in general no hierarchy of rights, no distinction between 'constitutional' and other rights. Every Act of Parliament had the same standing in law as every other, and so far as rights were given by judge-made law, they could offer no competition to the status of statutes. The courts evolved rules of interpretation which favoured the protection of certain basic freedoms, but in essence Parliament legislated uninhibited by claims of fundamental rights.

[71] In its present state of evolution, the British system may be said to stand at an intermediate stage between parliamentary supremacy and constitutional supremacy, to use the language of the Canadian case. Parliament remains the sovereign legislature; there is no superior text to which it must defer (I leave aside the refinements flowing from our membership of the European Union); there is no statute which by law it cannot make. But at the same time, the common law has come to recognise and endorse the notion of constitutional, or fundamental rights. These are broadly the rights given expression in the European Convention on Human Rights and Fundamental Freedoms ('ECHR'), but their recognition in the common law is autonomous: see for example *Derbyshire County Council v Times Newspapers Ltd* [1993] AC 534, *Leech* [1994] QB 198, *Witham* [1998] QB 575, *Pierson v Secretary of State* [1998] AC 539, *Reynolds* [1999] 3 WLR 1010, and with respect perhaps especially *Simms* [2000] 2 AC 115 *per* Lord Hoffmann at 131. The Human Rights Act 1998 ('HRA') now provides a democratic underpinning to the common law's acceptance of constitutional rights, and important new procedural measures for their protection. Its structure, as has more than once been observed, reveals an elegant balance between respect for Parliament's legislative supremacy and the legal security of the Convention rights.

[72] This being our constitution's present nature, there exists a tension between the maintenance of legislative sovereignty and the vindication of fundamental, constitutional rights. How are their respective claims to be reconciled? Where is the point of escape if the legislature tramples on the territory of rights? This tension is hardly to be found in a system of pure parliamentary supremacy, and is less acute in a system of constitutional supremacy. In the former,

fundamental rights are not recognised as such. The majoritarian principle, expressed and made good by a sovereign Parliament, comes first. In the latter, the majoritarian principle gives way to fundamental rights. In practice, the constitutions and jurisprudence of sovereign States in the civilised world show that this distinction is by no means always clear-cut; and to the extent in any concrete instance that it is not clear-cut, the tension to which I refer will arise.

Lord Justice Laws explains that, in his view, the difference between systems that operate under parliamentary supremacy and those that rely on constitutional supremacy is not that pronounced in respect of the difficult balance between legislative supremacy and the protection of rights. He argues that the balance needs to be struck between freedom to legislate and the protection of the individual, although where the balance is drawn between the two may differ according to which system is employed. But there are those who disagree with this proposition—who believe that there are important differences between the two systems and that the boundaries should not be blurred by judicial activism. Commentators who ascribe to this view explain that constitutional reform should not be the product of judges alone and that active participation by all branches of the **state** (and perhaps also the population) would be required to effect proper change. The next extract provides an indication of some of the criticism levelled at the slow march towards constitutional supremacy.

· ·

● **J. Goldsworthy, 'Is Parliament sovereign? Recent challenges to the doctrine of parliamentary sovereignty'** (2005) 3 New Zealand Journal of Public & International Law 7, 8 and 33–5

Today, a number of our judges and legal academics in Britain and New Zealand are attempting a peaceful revolution, aimed a toppling the doctrine of parliamentary sovereignty and replacing it with a new constitutional framework in which Parliament shares ultimate authority with the courts. They describe this framework as 'common law constitutionalism', 'dual' or 'bi-polar' sovereignty or as a 'collaborative enterprise' in which the courts are in no sense subordinate to Parliament.[1] But they deny that there is anything revolutionary, or even unorthodox, in their attempts to establish this new framework. They claim to be defending the 'true' constitution; properly understood, from misrepresentation and distortion. And they sometimes accuse their opponents, the defenders of parliamentary sovereignty, of being the true revolutionaries.[2]

It is rather audacious to portray the doctrine of parliamentary sovereignty, which for hundreds of years has been generally accepted as fundamental to the British constitution, as 'a latter-day-myth' that 'Conceals the true locus of political power' in the constitution.[3]

…

D Increasing Recognition of 'Constitutional' Principles

If the sovereignty of Parliament is faced with a serious challenge in the near future, it is most likely to arise from further development of the tendency to describe important common law principles—and now statutes—as having constitutional status, which entitles them to special protection when statutes that might otherwise impinge on them are interpreted.[5] Joseph and Dame Sian both advert to this phenomenon.[6]

Jeffery Jowell, for example, discusses what he calls the 'new constitutional litigation', in which:[7]

> Without the aid of the Human Rights Act [1998] … [UK] courts have begun to short their boundaries of administrative law into the constitutional realm by explicitly endorsing a higher order of rights inherent in our constitutional democracy … A live question is the extent to which the courts will continue their search for constitutional principle outside of the sometimes limited scope of Convention rights.

The direction in which some judges would like to take this idea is clearly implied in a recent judgment of Laws LJ:[8]

> In its present state of evolution, the British system may be said to stand at an intermediate stage between parliamentary supremacy and constitutional supremacy...Parliament remains the sovereign legislature...But at the same time, the common law has come to recognise and endorse the notion of constitutional or fundamental rights. These are broadly the rights given expression in the European Convention [on Human Rights], but their recognition in the common law is autonomous.

A few years earlier, he wrote that parliamentary sovereignty:[9]

> ...remains the plainest constitutional fundamental at the present time, a departure from it will only happen, in the tranquil development of the common law, with a gradual re-ordering of our constitutional priorities to bring alive the nascent idea that a democratic legislature cannot be above the law.

As Lord Irvine has observed, this may be 'a prediction that we are only half-way on a constitutional journey and that in the fullness of time, we will leave parliamentary supremacy behind altogether'.[10]

It is impossible to predict with any confidence whether or not the judiciary will try to push this far, or if it does, whether Parliament will allow it to succeed. That is why, I suggest, neither Dame Sian, Justice Thomas nor Professor Joseph is currently willing to make any stronger claim than that it is 'possible' that the courts might hold that Parliament cannot effectively abrogate fundamental rights.[11] I take their uncertainty to be due partly to their realising that it is not yet clear that the courts could get away with it. But one further point should be made.

Judges are often keen to dispel any impression that they are engaged in changing the constitution...

1 P. A. Joseph 'Parliament, the courts, and the collaborative enterprise' (2004) 15 Kings College Law Journal 321, 333–4.

2 Judicial repudiation of parliamentary sovereignty 'would not be at all revolutionary. What is revolutionary is to talk of the omnipotence of Parliament': R. A. Edwards, '*Bonham's Case*: the chose in the constitutional machine' (1996) Denning Law Journal 63, 76.

3 Joseph, n. 1, at 321.

4 [Passage omitted]

5 This tendency was extended to statutes by Laws LJ in *Thorburn v Sunderland City Council*.

6 Joseph, n. 1, at 341–2: S. Elias, 'Sovereignty in the 21st century: another spin on the merry-go-round' (2003) 14 PLR 148, 161.

7 J. Jowell, 'Beyond the rule of law: towards constitutional judicial review' [2000] Public Law 671, 675 and 683 (footnote omitted).

8 *International Transport Roth GmbH v Secretary of State for the Home Department* [2002] EWCA Civ 158, [2002] 3 WLR 344, [71].

9 Sir John Laws, 'Illegality and the problem of jurisdiction', in M. Supperstone and J. Goldie (eds) *Judicial Review* (2nd edn, London: Butterworths, 1997), para. 4.17.

10 Lord Irvine of Lairg, 'The impact of the Human Rights Act: Parliament, the courts and the executive' [2003] Public Law 308, 310.

11 Elias, n. 6, at 160; Hon. E. W. Thomas, 'The relationship of Parliament and the courts' (2000) Victoria University of Wellington Law Review 5, 8; Joseph, n. 1, at 342.

The extract from Goldsworthy's article gives a flavour of the different views on modern-day parliamentary supremacy, and the role that judges should perform with respect to fundamental rights and primary legislation that appears to undermine perceived common law rights and principles. There is some evidence to suggest that some UK judges believe that were Parliament to legislate in an entirely repugnant fashion, with flagrant disregard for basic and fundamental human rights, the courts would be duty-bound to intervene and to disapply any such legislation. For example, Lord Woolf's often-quoted extrajudicial comment in his article in *Public Law* is good evidence for Goldsworthy's contention that some judges believe that their role may be to invalidate legislation if Parliament attempts to legislate in contravention of common law rights.

● **Lord Woolf, *'Droit public*: English style'** [1995] Public Law 57, 69

> If Parliament did the unthinkable, then I would say that the courts would also be required to act in a manner which would be without precedent. Some judges might chose to do so by saying that it was an unrebuttable presumption that Parliament could never intend such a result. I myself consider that there were advantages in making it clear that ultimately there are even limits on the supremacy of Parliament which it is the courts' inalienable responsibility to iden-tify and uphold. They are limits of the most modest dimensions which I believe any democrat would accept. They are no more than necessary to enable to rule of law to be preserved.

There are other judges who believe that they are pointing out the obvious when they state that the courts can recognise as law only legislation that is not so absurd that, were it to be enforced, the population would singularly reject it.

● ***R (on the application of Jackson and others) v Attorney General*** [2005] UKHL 56

Lord Hope of Craighead:

> [120] Professor Sir William Wade, too, observed that sovereignty is a political fact for which no purely legal authority can be constituted even though an Act of Parliament is passed for the very purpose of transferring sovereign power: 'The Basis of Legal Sovereignty' [1955] CLJ 172 at 196. The open texture of the foundations of our legal system which Professor HLA Hart discusses in Ch VI of *The Concept of Law* (1961), especially at pp 107–114, defies precise ana-lysis in strictly legal terms. More recently other commentators have asserted that the rule of parliamentary supremacy is ultimately based on political fact: Peter Mirfield 'Can the House of Lords Lawfully be Abolished?' (1979) 95 LQR 36 at 42–44 and George Winterton 'Is the House of Lords Immortal?' (1979) 95 LQR 386 at 388. It is sufficient to note at this stage that a con-clusion that there are no legal limits to what can be done under s 2(1) does not mean that the power to legislate which it contains is without any limits whatever. Parliamentary sovereignty is an empty principle if legislation is passed which is so absurd or so unacceptable that the populace at large refuses to recognise it as law.

cross reference

We shall consider human rights protection in more detail in Chapter 9.

This is a direct challenge to many of the theories of parliamentary supremacy that we have considered thus far. However, other commentators argue that Dicey always contended that British judges were the guardians of common law rights and that they would protect the population against excessive use of power by the state. These commentators argue that judges today are, in their dicta and extrajudicial writings, talking about nothing more than Dicey's interpretation of the rule of law. This is countered by those concerned about judi-cial activism in this area, who argue that Dicey's theory of the rule of law was to protect the people against the executive and not to limit the power of Parliament. The debate will no doubt continue, but it is interesting to note that, until quite recently, parliamentary su-premacy appeared to be a relatively settled proposition in judicial, other legal, and academic circles, whereas there appears to be a developing discussion about its proper scope. This may be a short-lived phase, but, as Goldsworthy states, it is not clear what the outcome of that debate will be.

How does parliamentary supremacy compare with constitutional supremacy?

- *Parliamentary supremacy accords the legislature with supreme law-making power.*

- *This means, in UK terms, that primary legislation cannot be invalidated by the courts on the ground that it does not conform to the constitution.*

- *Constitutional supremacy means that the constitution is the highest form of law in the state.*

- *If primary legislation does not conform to the requirements of the constitution, it may be deemed to be invalid law and have no legal effect.*

- *There are hybrid systems that have elements of both systems. It is argued by some commentators that the UK may be moving in this direction in view of the operation of EU law and also the way in which Parliament is responding to declarations of incompatibility. This will be considered in more detail in the next chapter.*

7.7 How does parliamentary supremacy fit with the separation of powers and the rule of law?

So how does parliamentary supremacy fit with the separation of powers and the rule of law? The previous section raised some of the controversies as regards a potential or perceived move away from the traditional doctrine of the supremacy of parliament—but what of the traditional concept and its relationship with two key doctrines of the UK constitution? As seen in the discussion of *M v Home Office and another* [1994] 1 AC 337, HL, in Chapter 4 and later in Chapter 5, the traditional view of the British constitutional position is that Parliament makes the law, the executive runs the country with the power conferred on it by Parliament through legislation and through the Crown's **royal prerogative**, and the courts ensure that the executive remains within its power. There is no mention of the courts seeking to restrict Parliament's use of power by striking down Acts of Parliament. Indeed, this is contrary to any pure form of parliamentary supremacy. Stevens argues that there is lack of judicial activism in Britain because one of the consequences of the system of parliamentary supremacy is that judges have not historically been called upon to mediate between different competing quasi-political claims in the arena of rights.

. . . .

● **R. Stevens, 'A loss of innocence? Judicial independence and the separation of powers'** (1999) 19 Oxford Journal of Legal Studies 365, 376–7

The tenure of English judges since 1714 has been relatively peaceful. The closest that a judge has come to being dismissed after addresses by both Houses was Mr Justice Barrington, an Irish judge, for alleged bribery. Mr Justice Grantham,[1] one of the undistinguished political appointments to the High Court bench by Lord Halsbury, the Conservative Lord Chancellor at the turn of the century, was nearly dismissed after a particularly partisan decision in the Yarmouth By-Election case in the first decade of this century. The most noted recent near example was that of Sir John Donaldson, a High Court judge sitting as the President of the Industrial Relations Court. In December 1973, 187 Labour MPs called for his removal for 'political prejudice and partiality'. The move failed and, as we shall see, Donaldson ended as Master of the Rolls (President of the Civil Division of the Court of Appeal).[2] In short, Grantham and Donaldson survived. The fact that there were so few ripples to disturb the peace of judicial independence over 300 years is mainly a tribute to the staid quality of the English judiciary and the political process which has protected it. Secondarily, however, the advent of parliamentary supremacy, confirmed under Georges I and II, and only marginally challenged under George III, meant a diminishing, and therefore less controversial, role for the judges. Moreover, with the arrival of a reformed and more democratic House of Commons after 1832, in whom virtually all legitimate power resided, the creative role of the courts was increasingly limited by the political culture as well as the galloping reforms engendered by Utilitarianism.

1 R. Stevens, 'Judges, politics and the confusing role of the judiciary', in K. Hawkins (ed.) *The Human Face of Law: Essays in Honour of Donald Harris* (Oxford: Oxford University Press, 1997), pp. 245 and 257. See also R. Stevens, *The Independence of the Judiciary: The View from the Lord Chancellor's Office* (Oxford: Clarendon Press, 1993), pp. 171–2. And see also J. Griffiths, *Judicial Politics since 1920: A Chronicle* (Oxford: Blackwell, 1993), pp. 129 et seq.

2 R. Jackson, *The Chief: Biography of Gordon Hewart—Lord Chief Justice of England, 1922–40* (London : Harrap, 1959), pp. 126–44.

It is argued that this has provided a stable system of governance, which has not been subject to much controversy or call for reform. This may have protected the British judiciary from the politicisation and thus public distrust that can be found in some other systems. Whether one agrees with that or not, this is stated to be one of the strengths of parliamentary supremacy systems. The population must live with the consequences of its electoral decisions (electing new representatives at the next election, if needs be), rather than seek to charge the judiciary with remedying any legislative concerns it may have. The public are responsible for their representatives in the Commons. Parliamentary supremacy falls back on democratic majoritarian principles, but in turn it does not afford obvious mechanisms for protecting minority groups should their needs conflict with those of a powerful majority.

What of the relationship between parliamentary supremacy and the rule of law? This is a difficult question to answer, not least because, as we have seen in Chapter 4 and in this chapter, both the theories of the rule of law and the legislative supremacy of parliament are subject to some debate. Is the rule of law a separate legal concept that is of higher constitutional significance than that of parliamentary supremacy, and if so, may the courts invalidate an Act of Parliament if it clearly breaches the rule of law? Is the rule of law subordinate to parliamentary supremacy, and thus can an Act of Parliament never be invalidated on the ground that it infringes a concept that is of lesser weight than parliamentary supremacy? Or are they on the same level, in which case how are judges to deal with these twin concepts of similar importance? This discussion was played out during the passage of the Constitutional Reform Bill, which became the Constitutional Reform Act 2005. The judiciary was concerned that if the office of **Lord Chancellor** were fundamentally reformed and the Law Lords were removed from the House of Lords legislative chamber, there would be little opportunity for the Lord Chancellor, as head of the judiciary sitting in Cabinet, and the Law Lords to make their views known were a Bill to appear to offend against the rule of law. This pre-enactment constitutional check on parliamentary supremacy was said to be of great value. The question then arose, assuming that the pre-enactment constitutional check on parliamentary supremacy did in fact assist in strengthening the rule of law without weakening parliamentary supremacy, what would happen if it were removed? Would the Law Lords feel that they had to perform this function once the legislation had been enacted and, if so, would this not call into question the notion of the legislative supremacy of Parliament? The next extract illustrates some of the discussion.

● **G. Robson, 'The slow march to constitutional reform'** (2005) 169 Justice of the Peace 112, 112–14

...

As the Bill entered the Report stage in the Lords an interesting contrast of emphasis emerged from the speeches of the Lord Chancellor and the Lord Chief Justice. The former, plainly trying to ride the twin horses of politician and purveyor of legal gravitas, proposed an amendment which would insert a new clause affirming 'the existing constitutional principle of the rule of law' at the beginning of the Bill. In a lengthy speech he sought to answer those critics who feared that the change in the office of Lord Chancellor would remove some ill-defined cover for that mysterious concept 'the rule of law'.[1]

> 'First, the notion of the rule of law cannot be expressed in the form of an ordinary legal rule. Such a rule cannot itself determine whether the law in general always prevails. There is a paradox in trying to formulate a legal rule that determines the status of the law. Such a rule must be open to the interpretation that it is referring to standards that lie outside—and, in a sense, above—the law. That leaves open the question of which prevails when the two come into conflict.

> If we are not careful, we could be taken as seeking to create a special rule with a higher status than that of the law itself, including primary legislation. That would be to limit the sovereignty of Parliament by reference to the rule of law. The question of which prevailed in the event of conflict would have to be resolved by the courts. That is something that we cannot contemplate. A rule of law can never, in our constitution, enable individual cases to be decided by the courts in such a way as to invalidate an Act of Parliament validly passed. Such a radical and fundamental constitutional change surely must not be enacted by Parliament in a Bill devoted to limited reforms relating to the Lord Chancellor and the judiciary.'

Although plainly devised to soothe those critics who had spoken with such vehemence about the 'rule of law' in the ongoing debate about the Constitutional Reform Bill this statement only serves to confuse the issue still further since it appears to want to maintain both parliamentary supremacy and a 'rule of law' which is 'referring to standards that lie outside—and, in a sense, above—the law'.

By contrast, the Lord Chief Justice was more single minded: basically his speech was that of a strong Trade Union leader concerned with the rights of his members—

> '... The first principle is that the independence of the judiciary must be preserved. This is essential, not for the benefit of the judiciary, but for the benefit of the public. A healthy parliamentary democracy cannot function satisfactorily without an independent judiciary. That principle is a long-established part of our unwritten constitution.

> However, it is important that the House should hear the views of the Judges' Council on this Bill in its present form. After all, the Judges' Council is the one body that consists of members from, and representing, every level of the judiciary, including the Master of the Rolls ... Even though it is for the protection of the public that we value the independence of the judiciary so highly, the serving judiciary's collective view on how the Bill will affect its independence is surely worthy of close attention.'

The support of the Judges' Council was called in aid as a reason for wanting the Lord Chancellor to be a respected lawyer and preferably a member of the House of Lords. They also wanted a clear statement on the face of the Bill that the Lord Chief Justice will be the head of the judiciary. Apparently this was to be the subject of a further agreed amendment so that there could be no confusion about the role of the Lord Chief Justice in the future ... Equally interesting was the proposed amendment concerning the right of the Lord Chief Justice of England and Wales, the Lord President in Scotland and the Lord Chief Justice of Northern Ireland to lay written representations before Parliament which are, in the opinion of the Judge laying the paper, matters of importance relating to the judiciary or the administration of justice. Speaking to this the Lord Chief Justice approached the 'rule of law' debate from another angle:

'My Lords, we have had several useful debates on the rule of law. Perhaps I may summarize the position which I think we reached. We all agreed that we do not want to change the Lord Chancellor's existing role in relation to the rule of law. That role goes further than simply respecting the rule of law in discharging his ministerial functions. It includes being obliged to speak up in Cabinet or as a Cabinet Minister against proposals that he believes offend the rule of law. That role does not require him proactively to police every act of government. The role is not one that is enforceable in courts.

This is an attempt to square the circle between the present position, where as Lord Chief Justice I can address the House directly, and the position in the future, if the Bill continues in his present form, when I will not have the privilege of appearing before your Lordships.'

Leaving aside the interesting idea that the 'rule of law' is handed like the Mosaic tablets from one Lord Chancellor to another this too goes no further in helping to define the 'rule of law'.

1 (2004) 168 Justice of the Peace 332.

The relationship between the rule of law and parliamentary supremacy remains somewhat vague. That is perhaps how it will remain while the debate continues about whether the rule-of-law concept requires that the state follow the proper procedure in order to enact clear transparent and reasonably stable prospective law, or whether it imputes the need for the law to respect some form of fundamental value, such as rights or morality. The courts currently recognise as law Acts that conform to the enrolled Act rule, and as such that implies that Parliament has used the proper procedure to enact law and consequently that the rule of law has been respected at least in terms of the procedure used to enact it. A number of judges have argued that were Parliament to pass law that appeared to them to be in direct contradiction to commonly held views of morality (*per* Lord Woolf above), or to be absurd (*per* Lord Steyn), or to breach fundamental common law rights (*per* Lord Justice Laws), then they may invalidate the Act in question or refuse to apply it. This suggests that there are some judges, at least, who consider that the concept of the rule of law is superior to that of Parliament's legislative supremacy. However, we have yet to reach a point at which this is tested in the courts. In modern times, the courts have broadly respected Parliament's legislative supremacy and have not ruled that an Act so contradicts the rule of law that it cannot be permitted to stand.

summary points

How does parliamentary supremacy fit with the separation of powers and the rule of law?

- *In UK terms, parliamentary supremacy, the separation of powers, and the rule of law are all extremely important doctrines that pervade the constitution.*

- *Parliamentary supremacy reserves law-making powers (as regards statute rather than common law) to Parliament or Parliament's delegates (secondary legislation).*

- *The courts are not permitted to trespass on the internal workings of Parliament so that Parliament may be free from undue interference. This is parliamentary privilege in operation.*

- *It appears that Parliament may change the way in which it makes law, as it did, for example, by enacting the Parliament Acts of 1911 and 1949, according to the manner-and-form rule.*

- *It remains unclear whether Parliament may truly bind its successors. There is little evidence at present that it may, although the redefinition theory would suggest that it were possible.*

- *The courts also cannot invalidate Acts of Parliament on grounds that they are unconstitutional, although they can declare that a piece of primary legislation is incompatible with the European Convention on Human Rights.*
- *However, in keeping with the doctrine of the rule of law, the courts can review the actions of the executive to ensure that they are legal. They can also review secondary legislation to ensure that it is in conformity with primary legislation; if it is not, it is invalid.*
- *However, the relationship between parliamentary supremacy and the rule of law remains somewhat vague.*

7.8   # If lost, can supremacy be regained?

Parliamentary supremacy is often in the news in relation to EU law and in relation to human rights instruments such as the European Convention on Human Rights. Many sections of the British press, and also the British people, believe that Parliament has lost much of its power by giving that power to international or supranational bodies such as the European Union and the Council of Europe. Media stories about the legislative influence of the EU and the Council of Europe rarely go into much detail about the complexity of the arguments both that support the view that Parliament has lost some of its legislative power to outside institutions or to the British courts (as discussed in the previous section), or that Parliament has delegated some of its powers to those institutions for the time being. The next two chapters will consider these arguments in detail, so that you may reach your own conclusions.

But if Parliament were to lose its legislative supremacy, could it regain it? This is an interesting question that goes to the heart of the history and development of parliamentary supremacy. As we considered earlier in the chapter, there is no legal text that definitively confers legislative supremacy on the Queen in Parliament; instead, this developed as a result of negotiations between the different arms of the state at a time of some turbulence. Eventually, the King and Parliament appear to have reached an accommodation among them that was recognised and enforced by the courts. It could be argued that Parliament and the courts have had to re-negotiate this position as representative democracy emerged, not in formal terms, but as an incremental process. On this basis, it could be argued that if supremacy were to be lost and if Parliament, the executive, the courts, and the people were able to reach a new consensus about the supremacy of Parliament, then it could be restored or reinvented to meet the requirements of the times—it would become Britain's new rule of recognition. We shall consider its development in the next chapter.

summary points

If lost, can supremacy be regained?

- *Parliamentary supremacy was a product of political negotiations between the monarch and Parliament and recognition of a broad agreement by the courts.*
- *Parliamentary supremacy has developed over time to take into account the changing nature of Parliament and its burgeoning democratic legitimacy.*
- *Theories of parliamentary supremacy have been reworked following Britain's membership of the European Union and the Council of Europe.*

- *Assuming that a political consensus could be reached between any Parliament, executive, and monarch (were there to be a monarch) that was accepted by the people and by the courts, it would seem possible that even if lost, parliamentary supremacy may be regained.*
- *Parliamentary supremacy is the expression of a rule of recognition.*

Summary

Parliamentary supremacy is the courts' recognition of Parliament's supreme law-making power. Parliament may make, amend, or repeal any law it wishes and the courts will accept as law any Act that appears on the parliamentary Roll. The courts may use techniques of statutory interpretation so as to interpret the law and these now include reference to certain sections of Hansard. However, as a general rule, words spoken in proceedings in Parliament may not be referred to in court, which is an expression of parliamentary privilege. And the courts cannot regulate Parliament, although individual MPs and peers are subject to criminal and civil law other than in very limited circumstances relating to proceedings in Parliament. The courts must apply the latest will of Parliament (the doctrine of implied repeal) as required by Parliament (subject to the interpretive duties imposed on them by the European Communities Act 1972 and the Human Rights Act 1998).

Questions

1 Who has ultimate power to decide on the law in the country?

2 From where does this body derive its power?

3 Is the power ever open to challenge?

4 If so, under what circumstances and by whom?

5 Can the body divest itself of the power and, if so, can it do so on a permanent or merely a temporary basis?

6 What is our evidence of this?

Further reading

Barber, N. W., 'Sovereignty re-examined: the courts, Parliament, and statutes' (2000) 20 Oxford Journal of Legal Studies 131

This is a classic article that explains the relationship between Parliament and the courts, and the courts' powers to interpret statutes in the light of parliamentary supremacy.

Bowers, P., 'The Sewel Convention' (House of Commons Library Standard Note PC/2084, 25 November 2005), available online at http://www.parliament.uk/commons/lib/research/briefings/snpc-02084.pdf

This note provides a clear explanation about the relationship between the UK Parliament and the Scottish Parliament, and the convention that governs that relationship.

Gay, O., 'Parliamentary Privilege and Individual Members' (House of Commons Library Standard Note PC/04905, 10 February 2010), available online at http://www.parliament.uk/commons/lib/research/briefings/snpc-04905.pdf

This note is a clearly written and comprehensive guide to parliamentary privilege and how it relates to MPs. It has been updated in the light of the arrest of Damian Green and the police search of his parliamentary office.

Gay, O. and Horme, A., 'Parliamentary Privilege and Qualified Privilege' (House of Commons Library Standard Note PC/02024, 24 May 2011), available online at http://www.parliament.uk/commons/lib/research/briefings/snpc-02024.pdf

This note is a very useful guide to parliamentary privilege and qualified privilege that has been updated in the light of recent events, including super-injunctions, which prevent the reporting of court cases, and the extent to which these injunctions bind MPs and peers during proceedings in Parliament.

Kelly, R., 'The Parliament Acts' (House of Commons Library Standard Note PC/675, 23 March 2007), available online at http://www.parliament.uk/briefing-papers/SN00675.pdf

This note explains the operation of the Parliament Acts.

Lakin, S., 'Debunking the idea of parliamentary sovereignty: the controlling factor of legality in the British constitution' (2008) 28 Oxford Journal of Legal Studies 709

This is a challenging academic article. It considers some of the more theoretical aspects of parliamentary sovereignty, but is well worth reading. It considers that parliamentary supremacy rests on the principle of legality and government under the law.

Wade, H. R. W., 'The basis of legal sovereignty' (1955) 13 Cambridge Law Journal 172

Wade's article examines the basis for parliamentary supremacy. It too is an important, if challenging, article, but it does form one of the foundations of the current debate on parliamentary supremacy.

Winterton, G., 'The British grundnorm: parliamentary supremacy re-examined' (1976) 92 Law Quarterly Review 591

Winterton's article critiques the various explanations for parliamentary supremacy. It examines the relationship between Parliament and the courts, and posits that parliamentary supremacy forms part of the complex foundation of the British constitution.

8

Membership of the European Union

Key points

This chapter will cover:

- What is the European Union (EU)?
- What are the sources of EU law?
- How does membership of the EU affect the UK legal order?
- What does membership of the EU mean for parliamentary supremacy?
- Reform of the EU and parliamentary supremacy

Introduction

This chapter follows on from the previous one outlining the doctrine of parliamentary supremacy. It aims to provide you with an overview of the relationship between the European Union and the UK, and the impact that this relationship has on Parliament's legislative supremacy. We shall consider, in brief, the nature of the EU and the sources of EU law. We shall examine how the UK's membership of the EU affects the UK legal order and how EU law is applied within the domestic sphere. We shall then turn our attention to what membership of the EU means for parliamentary supremacy, and ask whether, if lost, supremacy can be regained. This chapter will not examine the workings of the EU or EU law in any detail, because its primary focus is on UK constitutional law and, in particular, parliamentary supremacy.

8.1 What is the European Union (EU)?

The European Union is a membership organisation that, at present, consists of twenty-seven member **states**. It continues to enlarge as more European countries seek membership; the forty-year history of the EU has been one of development and growth. The European Economic Community (EEC) was established by the Treaty of Rome in 1957. There were two other European communities—the European Atomic Energy Community (Euratom) and the European Coal and Steel Community (ECSC)—and the three together were known as the European Community (EC). The UK became a signatory to the Treaty of Rome in 1972 and became a member of the EC in 1973. It may help to have some background to the EU, as it became, and the history of the UK membership. Munro's summary is particularly instructive.

● C. Munro, *Studies in Constitutional Law* (2nd edn, London: Butterworths, 1999), pp. 174–6

> The origins of the Communities and some other European organisations lie in the devastation suffered by the continent in the 1939–45 war.[1] After the war, the United States and the Soviet Union seemed to be on the verge of world domination, while the countries of Europe were struggling to emerge from the ruins. To those countries, the consequences of unbridled nationalism were only too obvious. The time was ripe for a new and more effective form of internationalism, when Mr Winston Churchill, in a speech at Zurich in 1946, suggested that the remedy was 'to recreate the European family, or as much of it as we can, and provide it with a structure under which it can dwell in peace, in safety and in freedom...we must build a kind of United States of Europe'. In this, he added, a partnership between France and Germany was essential.
>
> Churchill's vision of European unity struck a chord among those nations yearning for security, harmony and recovery. One result was the formation of the Council of Europe, inaugurated in 1949 at Strasbourg.[2] On the economic front, the Organisation for European Economic Co-operation was created in 1948 to administer the Marshall Plan, under which American aid was offered to assist in the economic reconstruction of Europe by means of a common programme. In the same year, the Benelux countries (Belgium, the Netherlands, Luxembourg) established a free trade area as a step on the way to a full customs union.

Then, under the inspiration of Jean Monnet and Robert Schuman, the French government in 1950 proposed 'to place the whole Franco-German coal and steel production under one joint High Authority, in an organisation open to the participation of other countries of Europe'. According to Schuman, this would constitute the 'first stage of the European Federation'. The French plan was accepted in principle by Germany, the Netherlands, Belgium, Luxembourg and Italy, but the United Kingdom declined to join in. In 1951 those six countries concluded a treaty at Paris, establishing the European Coal and Steel Community (ECSC), which became operative in 1952 upon ratification by the national legislatures.

The Treaty of Paris[3] created three political institutions along with a court to settle disputes arising out of the Treaty or actions under it. The institutional structure was novel, as was the 'supranational' character of the creation. The signatories had not merely accepted mutual obligations in international law. They had invested institutions outside the state with continuing powers to act and to alter their laws, without the intervention of national legislature or governments, in ways which would bind them and could affect their citizens. They had created a new legal system, the law of the Community.

This model, and the experience of it, were to be influential when the member states involved, the 'Six', entered into further co-operation. Attempts to create a European Defence Community and a European Political Community foundered in 1954 (although they foreshadowed the eventual development of the Union). However, in 1955 the Benelux countries suggested to their partners in the Coal and Steel Community that further steps be taken towards economic integration. The Spaak Report, from a committee chaired by the Belgian statesman, led to negotiations for treaties which would provide for a common market and for the common development of nuclear energy. These were successfully concluded, and the two Treaties of Rome were signed in 1957.[4] In 1958 the European Economic Community (EEC), often known as the Common Market, and the European Atomic Energy Community (Euratom) came into being.

Thus, from 1958 there were three Communities, with the same six member states participating in each. A single Court of Justice and a single Assembly served all the Communities, as a result of arrangements made in 1957,[5] but the Treaties of Rome provided for Commissions and Councils of Ministers on a different pattern from the ECSC's equivalent bodies. In practice, this separation of institutions was found to be unsatisfactory in view of the overlapping interests of the three Communities, and in 1965 a treaty[6] (the 'Merger Treaty') was concluded which established a single Council and Commission. From 1967, when it became effective, there was one Council, one European Commission, one Court of Justice, and one European Parliament or Assembly. As a consequence of the institutional merger, the three Communities were increasingly referred to in the singular as 'the European Community'.[7] In strictly juristic terms, there are still different Communities.

Unlike the ECSC and Euratom, which were limited to particular sectors of the economy, the EEC was general in its scope. Its basic objectives were economic development and the improvement of standards of living.[8] To these ends, its policies included the establishment of a customs union between the member states and common commercial policy towards other countries; free movement of persons, services, and capital within the Community; a common agricultural policy; a common transport policy; and fair competition.

1 See D. Weigall and P. Stirk (eds) *The Origins and Development of the European Community* (Leicester: Leicester University Press, 1992); J. Pinder, *European Community: The Building of a Union* (Oxford: Oxford University Press, 1995), chs 1–3.

2 See F. E. Dowrick 'Juristic activity in the Council of Europe: 25th year' (1974) 23(3) International and Comparative Law Quarterly 610. As a political entity, the Council of Europe has remained in embryonic form. Its principal achievements lie in the protection of human rights, through the European Convention on Human Rights and Fundamental Freedoms, and its associated enforcement machinery.

3 *Treaty establishing the European Coal and Steel Community, Paris, 18 April 1951* (Cmnd 5189, London: HMSO, 1973). The more important treaties are also collected in B. Rudden and D. Wyatt (eds) *Basic Community Laws* (6th edn, Oxford: Oxford University Press, 1996).

4 *Treaty establishing the European Atomic Energy Community, Rome, 25 March 1957* (Cmnd 5179-II, London: HMSO, 1973).

5 Convention relating to Certain Institutions Common to the European Communities (Rome, 25 March 1957).

6 Cmnd 5179-II.

7 A resolution of the European Parliament on 16 February 1978 was to the effect that they should be so designated.

8 Under the EEC Treaty, Arts 2 and 3 (as it was, before amendment).

But if the Communities appeared to be so successful and had been encouraged by the British political classes after the Second World War, why then did the UK not join until much later, when the structures of the Communities were set and their mission well developed? Munro's explanation of the history of the UK membership continues.

· ·

● C. Munro, *Studies in Constitutional Law* (2nd edn, London: Butterworths, 1999), pp. 176–7

Through the 1950s, United Kingdom governments remained aloof from the infant Communities. Politically, the special relationship with the United States was thought more important than links with the European countries. In economic and cultural matters, the closest ties were with the countries of the British Empire and Commonwealth. Besides, the supranational character of the Communities' structure was regarded as unacceptable, or at least viewed with some suspicion.

Attitudes began to change when the success of the Common Market was demonstrated by the six countries' economic performance and rising standards of living. In 1959 the government entered into the European Free Trade Association (EFTA) with six other countries which were outside the EEC, in an attempt to obtain similar benefits. The arrangement was not very successful, and in 1961 Mr Macmillan's government despatched Mr Edward Heath to enter into negotiations with the Six. These were at an advanced stage when the French President, General de Gaulle, concerned that British entry to the Community would diminish his country's influence, exercised a veto. He did the same in 1967, when a Labour government applied for membership.

De Gaulle's resignation cleared the way, and in 1969 the Six agreed to commence negotiations with the states which had applied to join. The successful culmination of these was in the Treaty of Brussels,[9] signed in January 1972, which allowed for the accession of the United Kingdom, Ireland, Norway and Denmark to the three Communities. In fact, it became a Community of nine, for Norway, as a result of a referendum on entry, did not ratify the Treaty. There was no referendum concerning entry in this country, but one was held in 1975 to confirm that the British people wished to remain in.[10] Labour's leader, Harold Wilson, had promised a 're-negotiation' of the terms of British membership and a referendum as an election ploy (which serviced to paper over cracks within his party).

9 Cmnd 5179-I.

10 There was a 67 per cent vote in favour of continued membership. See A. King, *Britain Says Yes* (Washington, DC: American Enterprise Institute, 1977); D. E. Butler and U. Kitzinger, *The 1975 Referendum* (London: Macmillan, 1976).

In time, the European Community developed into the European Union in 1992 through the Treaty on European Union (TEU, or the 'Maastricht Treaty'), which came into force in 1994. The Treaty of Amsterdam further amended the TEU in 1997 and came into force in 1999. The

European Community did not disappear at this stage, because the original legal order and legal institutions remain in place. Instead, we continued to use the term 'European Community' to describe the institutional framework and the law that is derived under the original treaties, and we used the term 'European Union' for the areas of law that were added through the newer treaties and which did not form part of the original Community. The Maastricht Treaty provided that the European Community phase of the European project is known as the first pillar, and later phases as the second and third pillars. The recently signed and ratified Lisbon Treaty aimed, in part, to rationalise all of the existing legal provisions into one consolidating treaty, as well as to make some significant changes to the way in which the EU is run, and to the relationship between member states and the Union. The Lisbon Treaty amended the previous European treaties without replacing them, and came into force on 1 December 2009. The European project is now referred to as the 'European Union', and the distinctions between EC and EU terminology have been removed. However, you will see the phrase 'Community law' used from time to time in this chapter, where it is appropriate to the historical discussion. References to 'EU law' as overriding in this chapter relate to EU first pillar, and not second pillar and third pillar, provisions.

8.1.1 The development of the EU

The European Community and then the European Union's mission has also changed over time. It was primarily concerned with economic matters and free trade in the early years, but its role and focus has broadened. The TEU extended freedoms and rights for individuals and for business, based on the European economic project. These included: free movement of persons; free movement of goods; free movement of capital; and free movement of services. The later treaties dealt with European Union and integration, including monetary union (including the euro), as well as employment and social protections, and included a Charter of Fundamental Rights. Some countries have negotiated 'opt-outs' from certain parts of the later treaties—for example, the UK did not join the euro—whereas the tenets of the Treaty of Rome are mandatory for all who wish to be EU member states. The UK has also opted out of the Charter in so far as it would extend the competence of the European Court of Justice (ECJ) or allow individuals to assert Charter rights against the UK. However, the Charter will shape the development of EU law and thus will have some effect within the UK. Figure 8.1 at the end of this section sets out the three main pillars of the European Union.

First pillar matters are considered to be binding on member states, whereas there is discussion about the extent to which second and third pillar matters are strictly binding or whether are a form of international cooperation. The difference is important, because if they are binding, then a member state will be required to take whatever action is needed so as to comply with their terms. If the second and third pillar matters are a matter of international cooperation, then each member state will choose the extent to which it is able to cooperate with other member states at any one time. This is a moot point, although it is clear that, at the time when second and third pillar matters were under negotiation, then **Prime Minister** John Major believed that they were to be cooperative rather than binding. The extract below is taken from comments made by him to the House of Commons during a debate on the TEU, prior to its ratification.

● **[Former] Prime Minister John Major** (Hansard, HC Deb, 20 May 1992), vol. 208 col. 267

In foreign and security policy, and in justice and interior matters, the Member States will work together when it is in their common interest to do so . . . [We] cannot be forced into policies

> we do not approve of. We keep our ability to act on our own where we need to do so. We shall co-operate within a framework of international law but outside a framework of Community law. For instance, any dispute would go to the International Court of Justice, not the European Court of Justice. I believe that that marks a vital and important change in direction for the Community.

John Major's views are clear at the time he was negotiating the TEU, but the later Treaty of Amsterdam made the position less clear. As an organisation set up through international law, the EU has only the power conferred on it by the member states through the treaties that they have negotiated and signed. It may be helpful to think of a treaty as a contract that has been negotiated by all parties and agreed on terms that they are prepared to accept. Once signed, the terms of the contract must be respected, or else there are applicable legal sanctions. Treaties operate in a similar way—but treaty negotiations are largely confined to pre-treaty stages. This means that accession states—that is, those that are in the process of joining, but have not yet joined, the EU—do not have the same power to negotiate terms in relation to existing treaties, because their terms have been largely fixed by the original contracting countries who devised the treaties.

Figure 8.1

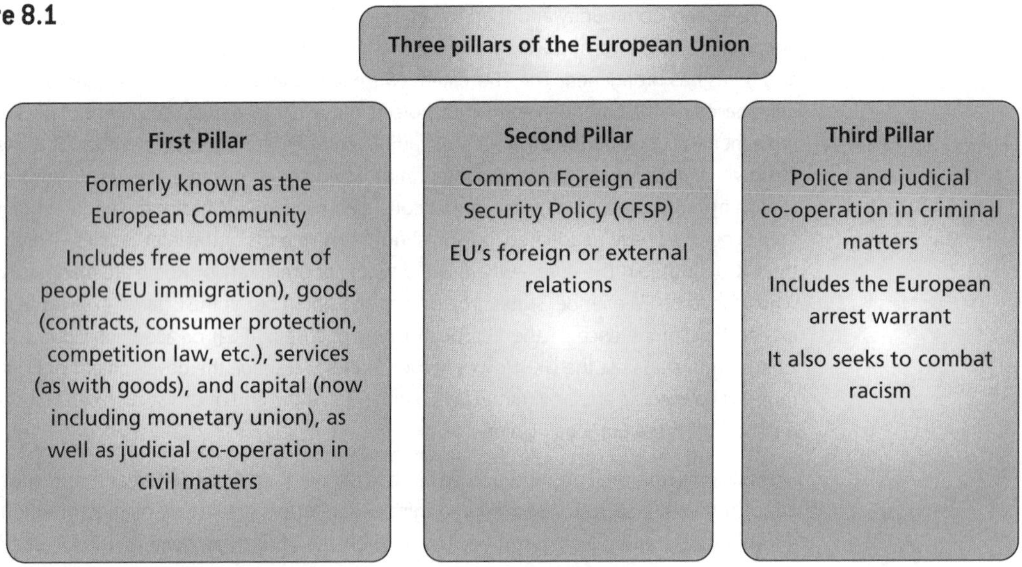

Three pillars of the European Union

First Pillar	Second Pillar	Third Pillar
Formerly known as the European Community	Common Foreign and Security Policy (CFSP)	Police and judicial co-operation in criminal matters
Includes free movement of people (EU immigration), goods (contracts, consumer protection, competition law, etc.), services (as with goods), and capital (now including monetary union), as well as judicial co-operation in civil matters	EU's foreign or external relations	Includes the European arrest warrant It also seeks to combat racism

8.1.2 The structure of the EU

It may help to have a brief explanation of the main institutions of the EU before we move on to consider sources of EU law. Figure 8.2 is a simplified depiction of the main EU institutions.

The EU has many of the institutions that one would expect a state to have, such as a courts structure and a **Parliament**, but in other respects it looks rather different from a traditional state. At the top of the figure is the European Council, which guides the direction of the EU. It is made up of the heads of state or **government** of each of the member states, along with the European Council President (Herman Van Rompuy, at time of writing) and the President of the European Commission; the EU's High Representative for Foreign Affairs and Security Policy,

Figure 8.2

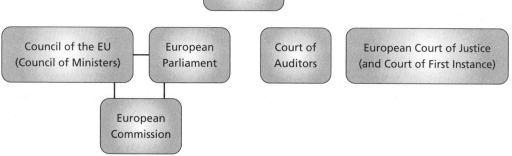

who is also Vice-President of the European Commission (Catherine Ashton, at time of writing, who is British), also participates in European Council meetings, which are really meetings of the heads of each of the members states. In UK terms, it is the British Prime Minister who attends meetings of the European Council. On the left-hand side of the figure are three bodies linked together; these are the EU's decision-making and law-making bodies. Law-making and decision-making differ depending on whether the matter is a first pillar, or a second or third pillar, matter.

- The Council of the European Union is made up of member states' governmental representatives. In UK terms, it is the Home Secretary who would attend the Council of the European Union were the matter under discussion to relate to his or her portfolio, along with his or her counterparts from the other member states; it would be the Secretary of State for Environment, Food, and Rural Affairs were it to be a Common Agricultural Policy (CAP) issue, for example. The Council of the European Union is the body that represents member states.

- The European Parliament contains representatives—members of the European Parliament (MEPs)—elected by the citizens of each of the member states to represent them within the EU.

- The European Commission is the body that represents the EU itself and comprises appointees, rather than elected representatives.

These bodies together operate a 'co-decision' procedure rather than a Westminster parliamentary **executive** model.

On the right-hand side of the figure are the ECJ and the lower court, the Court of First Instance (CFI). The ECJ is the highest court for the purposes of European law. The Court of Auditors is charged with the responsibility of overseeing EU funds and expenditure. The European Central Bank (ECB) plays a pivotal role for countries that have adopted the euro as their currency. There are other bodies and offices as well, which together make up the European Union.

Having sketched the basics of the European Union, we shall turn our attention to the sources of EU law and how they apply within member states.

NOTE
See http://europa.eu/about-eu/institutions-bodies/index_en.htm; for explanations about the work of the EU, see http://ec.europa.eu/publications/booklets/eu_glance/79/index_en.htm

What is the European Union?

- *The European Union is a membership body, currently made up of twenty-seven member states from western, central, and eastern Europe.*

- *The EU has developed over time, from a free trading zone to an economic, political, and social union of member states.*

- *The body is based in international law and is founded on a series of treaties.*

- *Areas of EU competence referred to as 'first pillar' were, before the Lisbon Treaty, often referred to as 'European Community law' and are largely binding on member states. Second and third pillar areas of competence are closer to a model of international cooperation than binding law.*

- *The EU comprises a set of institutions, the main ones being:*

  - *the European Council, which guides the direction of the EU;*

  - *the Council of the European Union, made up of member state representatives—usually members of each state's government with responsibility for the issue under discussion;*

  - *the European Parliament, made up of MEPs elected by citizens of each of the member states, who represent individuals living within the EU;*

  - *the European Commission, which contains appointees and represents the interests of the EU;*

  - *the European Court of Justice (and the lower court, the Court of First Instance), which determine matters of European law; and*

  - *the Court of Auditors, which oversees the use of EU funds.*

- *The EU operates a co-decision model, which means that the Council of the European Union, the European Parliament, and the European Commission are all involved in law-making.*

8.2 What are the sources of EU law?

The EU is an entity set up through international law, the highest form of which is the treaty. However, EU law is a special branch of law that has its roots in international law, but which has become a new legal order. The EU is able to enter into certain types of international agreement on behalf of the member states by way of international agreements. It has this power as a result of provisions in the treaties. The EU also has the power to make law itself, again, only in so far as the EU has been given this power by the member states through the terms of the treaties. Regulations, directives, and decisions are binding on member states—but they may be made only in the areas for which the EU has **legislative** competence. Figure 8.3 sets out, in a simplified form, the hierarchy of the main forms of law. It is important to note that this oversimplifies the actual position, which is really quite complicated. However, this should be sufficient for our purposes in a chapter designed to consider EU membership and parliamentary supremacy.

There are five main sources of EU law: treaties; regulations; directives; decisions; and recommendations. Treaties and regulations may be directly applicable within member states, meaning that once they are ratified by the member states, nothing more needs to be done in order to translate some of their provisions into, for example, UK law. Once they are in force, some of their provisions may be applied within a member state without further enactment. However,

Figure 8.3

Simplified hierarchy of EU law

Treaties

The highest form of international law, referred to as first-level or first-order law in the EU, negotiated by member states.

Regulations

EU law that is derived from the treaties. This kind of law applies directly within member states. It is sometimes referred to as derivative or second-level law, but is similar in nature to what we consider to be primary legislation in the UK. Regulations are binding.

Directives

Again, these are a form of derivative law, or second-level law. They are framed as outcome statements. It is for each member state to bring about the outcome via whatever legislative means it deems fit (if indeed it needs to change domestic law). Directives are binding.

Decisions

These are also derivate law, or second level law.
They are binding on the member states to which they apply.

There are also non-binding recommendations and opinions made under the EC Treaty.

This figure provides only a simplified picture of the main types of EU law. For more information, you may wish to refer to the Europa website: http://www.europa.int.

There are also international agreements
These are negotiated by the Community and/or between the Community and members states. They are agreements on particular areas of cooperation or international trade, etc. These relate to the second and third pillars of the EU rather than to the European Community.

not all treaty provisions are of a type that can be directly applicable. Again, this is relatively complicated, but for the purposes of this chapter, we shall leave the complexity to one side. The other three main sources of EU law—directives, decisions, and recommendations—are not directly applicable, but may be directly effective. How does **direct effect** differ from **direct applicability**? In simple terms, it means that, as a general rule, member states will choose how to translate these forms of law into their own legal order. This type of EU law is phrased more like an outcome statement rather than a text to be adopted. The EU states what result must be achieved (for example, that all member states should have the same retirement age for men and women in their countries, rather than different ages for the two sexes) and then it is for the member state to enact law to achieve that result. Should a member state not comply with the terms of the directive by the deadline, then the directive may be applied directly in the member

cross reference
You may now wish to return to Chapter 3 and reconsider your views on the British constitution in the light of your understanding about the UK–EU relationship.

state against the state, if it is considered to be sufficiently clear and unconditional to permit it to be applied this way. In this way, a member state cannot ignore these forms of EU law with impunity: it must either introduce its own law to achieve the results required, or else risk the EU law provisions taking direct effect until such time as it does.

Second and third pillar measures do not enjoy the same status as do first pillar ones, and the ECJ does not have full jurisdiction in relation to second and third pillar matters in quite the same way as it does for first pillar EU law. It is generally considered that, at present, they are not supreme over domestic provisions. The next section will consider how membership of the EU affects the UK domestic legal order and how EU law interacts with UK law.

summary points

What are the sources of EU law?

- *EU law is split into three pillars. The first pillar is binding on member states.*

- *The five principal forms of EU law are: treaties; regulations; directives; decisions; and recommendations.*

- *Treaties and regulations may be directly applicable in member states. In relation to treaties, once they have been ratified by member states, some of their provisions may take effect in domestic jurisdictions without further enactment by national legislatures.*

- *Directives and decisions are not directly applicable, but may have a direct effect. This means that if a member state does not comply with the requirements of those types of law, the provision may be applied within domestic courts until such time as the member state enacts its own legislation to achieve the result specified in the directive or decision.*

- *Recommendations are not legally binding, although they have political, persuasive force.*

230

8.3 How does membership of the EU affect the UK legal order?

How does membership of the EU affect the UK domestic legal order? Many of you will have heard a lot about this via the media, but many of the reports that you see and read will be relatively ill-informed. This section will, we hope, provide you with a little more information about the relationship between the EU and the UK to allow you to judge some of the Europhile and Eurosceptic comments for yourself.

Before we can turn to the specifics of the EU–UK relationship, we need to consider the UK's relationship with international law, because the European Community was born out of international law. International law does not automatically apply in the UK, because the UK is a **dualist state**. The UK is bound by international law only once it has been signed and once it has been recognised by Parliament; however, the UK would be bound only in international law and not in domestic law if Parliament were not to implement the international law into the UK legal system. Consequently, the UK could break international law and be subject to international sanction, but an individual in the UK would not be able to rely on the international legal provision in a British court were the international law not pulled down into the domestic legal system by Parliament. Figure 8.4 provides a simplified comparison of monist and dualist states, **monist states** being those in which ratified international law automatically applies in the domestic jurisdiction and dualist states being those in which it does not.

It may help if we consider an international treaty and how it applies in the UK. The **European Convention on Human Rights (ECHR**; not EU law), is an international treaty that the UK signed

Figure 8.4

How does membership of the EU affect the UK legal order?

231

Monist states	Dualist states
International and domestic law are part of one sphere	**International and domestic law are separate spheres**
International law becomes part of the domestic jurisdiction once fully ratified by the state. Ratification may involve the executive and legislative branches agreeing on the treaty or convention.	When a dualist state fully ratifies a piece of international law, treaty, or convention, then it becomes bound by its terms.
Once the treaty or convention is ratified, it becomes part of the domestic legal system.	However, because the international sphere is separate from the domestic one, the state can be challenged for breach of the treaty only via the international court system that applies to that treaty.
Its provisions, if of a kind that are directly enforceable, may be enforced via the domestic courts.	Its provisions are not enforceable via the domestic courts.
In other words, it may be possible for individuals to take the state to court in their own country, to argue that the state has breached a directly enforceable treaty provision. The court will apply the international law.	In order for its provisions to be directly enforceable via the domestic courts, a domestic provision (in the UK, an Act of Parliament) would need to be passed to bring the international legal provisions down into the domestic sphere.
	The domestic courts will be able to apply the international provisions only according to the terms of the Act that has brought them into force.

in the 1950s. That treaty (the Convention) contained no provision that required the UK to implement it into the domestic jurisdiction as long as the UK respected its terms. In other words, as long as the UK abided by the spirit of the Convention, it was not necessary to take the actual provisions and make them enforceable via the UK courts. As a result, the UK's failure to incorporate the treaty into the domestic legal order until 2000 posed no legal consequences. Indeed, individuals were permitted to take the UK to the European Court of Human Rights (ECtHR) in Strasbourg if they believed that the UK had breached their Convention rights. But because the Convention was not implemented in the UK, individuals were not able to rely on the Convention in British courts. This changed when Parliament incorporated the Convention into the domestic sphere by passing the Human Rights Act 1998.

However, the Treaty of Rome was drafted so as to require member states to incorporate (then) Community law into their domestic jurisdictions, with penalties attached (via the ECJ) for member states that failed to do so. Were the UK to have signed and ratified the EC Treaty, and yet failed to have incorporated Community law, then it would have been subject to sanction under the terms of the treaty, rather like being in breach of contract. However, British judges in British courts would not have been able to apply Community law within the domestic sphere unless authorised to do so by Parliament via an Act of Parliament. The Act would set out how the international law is to be applied—persuasive, binding, subordinate to UK domestic law, or hierarchically superior and overriding. When the UK signed the EC Treaty, it agreed to give effect to Community law; to fulfil this obligation, Parliament enacted the European Communities Act 1972 (ECA 1972). The Act provides as follows.

cross reference

We shall consider the differences between the way in which EU law and the ECHR were incorporated in the UK in detail in the next chapter.

European Communities Act 1972

. . . .

Section 2

(1) All such rights, powers, liabilities, obligations and restrictions from time to time created or arising by or under the treaties, as in accordance with the Treaties are without further enactment to be given legal effect or used in the United Kingdom shall be recognised and available in law, and be enforced, allowed, and followed accordingly; and the expression 'enforceable Community right' and similar expressions shall be read as referring to one to which this subsection applies.

...

(4) The provision that may be made under subsection (2) includes, subject to Schedule 2 to this Act, any such provision (of any such extent) as might be made by Act of Parliament, and any enactment passed or to be passed..., shall be construed and have effect subject to the foregoing provisions of this section...

As is the case with any legislation, the ECA 1972 took precedence over all legislation passed before it. It remains in force until such time as Parliament repeals it by later Act of Parliament. To date, it has not been repealed and consequently certain types of EU law (first pillar legislation) are overriding within the domestic sphere. Importantly, and somewhat unusually in the case of a British statute, the ECA 1972 is also prospective. Section 2 requires that any domestic legislation passed in the future should also be read in such a way so as to give effect to EU law. It is clear from section 2(4) that all future enactments of Parliament should be read in the light of the ECA 1972 and Community law, until such time as the ECA 1972 is amended or repealed. This means that British judges are required to interpret UK law, including Acts of Parliament, in such a way as to make them compatible with applicable EU law. In some instances, this may mean straining the interpretation of UK law so as to make it comply with the relevant EU law provisions.

. . . .

● *Garland v British Rail Engineering Ltd* [1983] 2 AC 751

Lord Diplock at 771:

> It is a principle of construction of United Kingdom statutes, now too well established to call for citation of authority, that the words of a statutes passed after the Treaty has been signed and dealing with the subject matter of the international obligation of the United Kingdom, are to be construed if they are reasonably capable of bearing such a meaning, as intended to carry out the obligation, and not to be inconsistent with it.

In effect, the Westminster Parliament changed the way in which all UK law was to be interpreted from the inception of the 1972 Act. This is not a difficulty if UK law complies with Community law, because judges will simply apply the UK law. If there appear to be minor inconsistencies between UK law and EU law, judges will use techniques of statutory interpretation, in the light of section 2 of the ECA 1972, to reread and reinterpret UK law so that it can be applied in conformity with the EU provisions. The difficulty arises, however, when there is a direct contradiction between a UK Act of Parliament and high-level EU law: then what are judges to do? If it is not possible to reinterpret UK law so as to give effect to EU law, British judges are required to apply the EU law rather than the UK law, because EU law is hierarchically superior for as long as the ECA 1972 remains in force.

> **European Communities Act 1972**
> ....
>
> **Section 3**
>
> (1) For the purposes of all legal proceedings any question as to the meaning or effect of any of the Treaties, or as to the validity, meaning or effect of any Community Instrument, shall be treated as a question of law (and if not referred to the European Court), be for determination as such in accordance with the principles laid down by and any relevant decision of the European Court or any court attached thereto.
>
> ...

As indicated by section 3, where there is doubt about EU law—its meaning or its applicability within a member state—the question is treated as a question of law, and it is ultimately for the ECJ to determine the meaning and validity of the application of European law. One thing that often trips up students and others is the impression that the ECJ interprets the law of member states and, for example, makes rulings on UK law. The ECJ does not consider domestic law, because to do so would mean that the Court would have to have expertise in the law of all of the member states and their methods of statutory interpretation. The ECJ does include a judge from each member state on its panel, but its role is not to be a final court of appeal for domestic law. In addition, because much of European law is hierarchically superior to domestic law, all that is necessary is for the ECJ to check that the relevant EU law is being applied in the right way in the member state rather than for it to address the domestic law points. The highest court for determining points of UK law is the Supreme Court. However, the ECJ is the highest court in relation to European law and its decisions are binding on all member states. It is argued that, if the Union is to work, each member state must apply EU law in the same way—otherwise we would get 'French EU law' and 'British EU law', which would lead to inconsistencies. If there is a lack of clarity about the meaning or application of EU law, the domestic courts should therefore turn to the case law of the ECJ; if the question of law remains, they should refer the matter to the ECJ for a ruling.

This is the important issue as regards parliamentary supremacy, and the issue that divides scholars, practitioners, commentators, and members of the public. To what extent does this mean that the Westminster Parliament has lost its supremacy in matters covered by the EU? To what extent does it mean that the Westminster Parliament has merely delegated some of its supremacy to the EU for as long as it is prepared to retain the ECA 1972 in force? This will be discussed more in the next section. However, it is important to note that the EU does not cover all areas of life and so there are swathes of domestic law that are not affected at all by the EU. It is easy to receive the impression from the media that the EU has the power to legislate in all areas rather than only those areas that are so provided by the treaties that have been negotiated by the member states. We shall consider this is more detail in the next section.

summary points

How does membership of the EU affect the UK legal order?

- *One of the conditions for membership of the European Community was that Community law would be incorporated into domestic law.*
- *The UK is a dualist state and so, to incorporate Community law, it passed the European Communities Act 1972 (ECA 1972).*
- *The ECA 1972 provides that all legislation passed prior to its introduction should be read in conformity with its provisions and that inconsistent provisions will be impliedly repealed. This is in keeping with the UK legal tradition.*

233

- However, the ECA 1972 also provides that all future legislation passed while the ECA 1972 remains in force should be interpreted in such a way so as to comply with European Community law.
- Where UK law complies with EU law, then British judges will apply UK law.
- Where UK law appears to have some inconsistencies with EU law, then judges will reinterpret UK law so that it may be applied in terms that conform to EU law.
- Where UK law directly contradicts some higher form of EU law, then EU law must be applied and UK law disapplied.

8.4 What does membership of the EU mean for parliamentary supremacy?

The interrelationship between membership of the EU and Parliament's legislative supremacy has preoccupied politicians, scholars, and commentators since even before the UK joined the European Community. Some have welcomed it, pointing to the economic prosperity (at least until recently) and the lack of wars between member states during its lifetime Others in the UK—and in other member states too—have expressed concern about the increasing dominance and spread of the EU's reach. These concerns are not new: one individual in the UK even went as far as to challenge the UK's signature of the Treaty of Rome through the British courts, at the inception of the UK's membership. Mr Blackburn considered that, by signing the Treaty, the UK Parliament would lose its legislative supremacy for good.

. . . .

● **Blackburn v Attorney-General** [1971] 1 All ER 567, CA

Lord Denning MR at 1381–3:

> In this case Mr Blackburn—as he has done before—has shown eternal vigilance in support of the law. This time he is concerned about the application of Her Majesty's government to join the Common Market and to sign the Treaty of Rome. He brings two actions against the Attorney General, in which he seeks declarations to the effect that, by signing the Treaty of Rome, Her Majesty's government will surrender in part the sovereignty of the Crown in Parliament and will surrender it for ever. He says that in so doing the government will be acting in breach of the law . . .
>
> Much of what Mr Blackburn says is quite correct. It does appear that if this country should go into the Common Market and sign the Treaty of Rome, it means that we will have taken a step which is irreversible. The sovereignty of these islands will thenceforward be limited. It will not be ours alone but will be shared with others. Mr Blackburn referred us to a decision by the European Court of Justice, *Costa v ENEL* in February 1964, in which the court in its judgment [reported at [1964] CMLR 425, 455] said:
>
>> '... the member-States, albeit within limited spheres, have restricted their sovereign rights and created a body of law applicable both to their nationals and to themselves.'
>
> Mr Blackburn points out that many regulations made by the European Economic Community will become automatically binding on the people of this country; and that all the courts of this

country, including the House of Lords, will have to follow the decisions of the European Court in certain defined respects, such as the construction of the treaty.

I will assume that Mr Blackburn is right in what he says on those matters. Nevertheless, I do not think these courts can entertain these actions. Negotiations are still in progress for us to join the Common Market. No agreement has been reached. No treaty has been signed. Even if a treaty is signed, it is elementary that these courts take no notice of treaties as such. We take no notice of treaties until they are embodied in laws enacted by Parliament, and then only to the extent that Parliament tells us ...

...

Mr Blackburn takes a second point. He says that, if Parliament should implement the treaty by passing an Act of Parliament for this purpose, it will seek to do the impossible. It will seek to bind its successors. According to the treaty, once it is signed, we are committed to it irrevocably. Once in the Common Market, we cannot withdraw from it. No Parliament can commit us, says Mr Blackburn, to that extent. He prays in aid the principle that no Parliament can bind its successors, and that any Parliament can reverse any previous enactment. He refers to what Professor Maitland said about the Act of Union between England and Scotland. Professor Maitland in his *Constitutional History of England* wrote (At p 332):

'We have no irrepealable laws; all laws may be repealed by the ordinary legislature, even the conditions under which the English and Scottish Parliaments agreed to merge themselves in the Parliament of Great Britain.'

...

So, whilst in theory Mr Blackburn is quite right in saying that no Parliament can bind another, and that any Parliament can reverse what a previous Parliament has done, nevertheless so far as this court is concerned, I think we will wait until that day comes. We will not pronounce on it today.

A point was raised whether Mr Blackburn has any standing to come before the court. That is not a matter which we need rule on today. He says that he feels very strongly and that it is a matter in which many persons in this country are concerned. I would not myself rule him out on the ground that he has no standing. But I do rule him out on the ground that these courts will not impugn the treaty-making power of Her Majesty, and on the ground that insofar as Parliament enacts legislation, we will deal with that legislation as and when it arises.

I think the statements of claim disclose no cause of action, and I would dismiss the appeal.

...

Appeals dismissed.

The courts do not have jurisdiction over the prerogative of treaty-making, as demonstrated by the case, and nor do they address politically contentious questions. On this basis, Mr Blackburn's appeal was dismissed and there was no **injunction** to prevent the UK from becoming a member of the European Community. As we can see, though, Lord Denning did wonder whether the UK would be able to leave the Community were it to join. And he did also point to ECJ case law, demonstrating that the ECJ, at least, considered that member states had limited their legislative supremacy on joining the Community. It may be useful to consider what other ECJ rulings have said about this issue.

8.4.1 Lessons from European Court of Justice cases

Prior to the UK joining the European Community, issues of the legislative supremacy of certain types of EC law had already been addressed by the ECJ. By looking at these cases, we can, firstly, examine what the ECJ had said about the direct applicability of Community law before the UK became a member, and secondly, gain an understanding about the way in which different types of EU law are to be applied within the domestic jurisdiction.

One of the key cases in relation to the applicability of Community law within the domestic legal order was C-26/62 *NV Algemene Transport—en Expeditie Onderneming van Gend en Loos v Nederlandse Administratie der Belastingen* [1963] ECR 1 (known simply as *van Gend en Loos*). The case concerned a conflict between national customs regulations and the EC Treaty. The ECJ was asked to determine the law that was to be applied. It held that Article 12 of the Treaty had 'direct effect' and that an individual could rely on it within his or her domestic jurisdiction through its national court. Direct effect in this context means that a piece of EU (non-domestic) law can be applied directly within the member state without the need for further action on the part of the member state. The Court further explained that the European Community was not simply another international legal body, but instead 'the Community constitutes a new legal order of international law for the benefit of which the States have limited their sovereign rights, albeit within limited fields'. In addition, even where treaties do not expressly state that they impose obligations or effects, they can have direct effect and therefore create rights for individuals that national courts will be required to uphold. Consequently, even in 1962, there was evidence that European law could apply directly within a member state and that member states may have limited their sovereignty or legislative supremacy in some way.

The second case that is often cited is C-6/64 *Flaminio Costa v ENEL* [1964] ECR 585, because it provides an insight into the way that the ECJ viewed the European Community, and its relationship with member states and their domestic jurisdictions. The passage that is often cited is as follows.

● **C-6/64 *Flaminio Costa v ENEL*** [1964] ECR 585, 593–4

> By creating a Community of unlimited duration, having its own institutions, its own personality, its own legal capacity and capacity of representation on the international plane and, more particularly, real powers stemming from a limitation of sovereignty or transfer of powers from the States to the Community, the Member States have limited their sovereign rights, albeit within limited fields, and thus have created a body of law which binds both their nationals and themselves.
>
> …
>
> The integration into the laws of each Member State of provisions which derive from the Community [in the UK by the terms of the European Communities Act 1972, section 2] and more generally the terms and the spirit of the Treaty, make it impossible for the States, as a corollary, to accord precedence to a unilateral and subsequent measure over a legal system accepted by them on a basis of reciprocity.

The case of *Costa v ENEL* established the precedence of Community law. It also explained that regulations are to be binding (as provided by the Treaty) and directly applicable within member states. This was a bold statement, because it is not clear from the Treaty text that direct applicability was provided by that Article, even if the binding nature of regulations was assured. Indeed, there have been a number of instances in which the ECJ appears to have extended the terms of European law supremacy beyond that which was understood during treaty negotiations and in political statements in ratification debates.

We posed a question earlier about what would happen if domestic law were directly to contradict EU law. The following case provides some evidence of the way in which the ECJ understands the primacy of EU law—albeit in relation to treaty provisions.

● C-11/70 *Internationale Handelsgesellschaft mbH v Einfuhr- und Vorratsstelle fur Getreide und Futtermittel* [1970] ECR 1125, 1134

> Recourse to the legal rules or concepts of national law in order to judge the validity of measures adopted by the institutions of the Community would have an adverse effect on the uniformity and efficacy of Community law. The validity of such measures can only be judged in the light of Community law. In fact, the law stemming from the Treaty, an independent source of law, cannot because of its very nature be overridden by rules of national law, however, framed, without being deprived of its character as Community law.

This case demonstrates a couple of things. Firstly, it is clear that the European treaties, signed by each of the member states, are considered to be hierarchically superior to all domestic law; secondly, it is clear that any EU law derived from that treaty is also accorded supremacy. In addition, this judgment provides that ECJ rulings on EU law must be considered to be authoritative, and that UK judges are therefore required to consider ECJ judges' interpretations and consider themselves bound by the case law of the ECJ. This is in keeping with Parliament's provisions in section 3(1) of the ECA 1972, as discussed above. A landmark case in 1977— C-106/77 *Amministrazione delle Finanze dello Stato v Simmenthal SpA* [1978] ECR 629 (known as *Simmenthal*)—subsequent to the UK becoming a member state, reinforced the 'principle' of precedence of European law. It established that national courts are under a duty to give full effect to European Community law 'if necessary refusing of its own motion to apply any conflicting provision of national legislation, even if adopted subsequently'. These two cases, taken together, posed a real challenge to those determined to cling on to traditional notions of parliamentary supremacy, because a later domestic provision would be overridden by an earlier EU provision were there to be a direct conflict.

We have seen that the terms of the ECA 1972 challenge the traditional view of the sovereignty of Parliament in two ways: firstly, by purporting to bind future parliaments to legislate in keeping with EU law obligations; and secondly, by incorporating the principle of the 'supremacy' of certain forms of EU law into domestic law. We shall now consider some of the instances in which the UK courts have interpreted UK law so as to comply with EU law obligations and also those in which UK law has been overridden by EU law entirely.

8.4.2 Instances in which UK courts have interpreted UK law so as to comply with EU law

As discussed in Chapter 7, the traditional doctrine of parliamentary supremacy ensures that an Act of Parliament is the highest form of law and cannot be set aside or overruled by the **judiciary** on the grounds that it is invalid or inapplicable other than via the doctrine of implied repeal. But, as we have discovered during this chapter, membership of the EU challenges this position, as *Halsbury's Laws* summarises.

● *Halsbury's Laws of England Administrative Law: Vol. 1(1)* [2001 Reissue], Introduction

> **Introduction; sub-section: 4. Organs and Functions of Government**
>
> 4 In general, Parliamentary (or primary) legislation may not be challenged in the courts...However, this rule does not apply in circumstances where primary legislation conflicts with a directly effective provision of European Union law. In these circumstances, the courts will override conflicting provisions within the primary legislation in order to give effect to the European Union legislative provision...In contrast, subordinate (or secondary) legislation may generally be challenged in the courts since that subordinate legislation is necessarily

> subject to the principles of ultra vires...The Human Rights Act 1998, which incorporates the majority of rights guaranteed under the Convention for the Protection of Human Rights and Fundamental Freedoms (Rome, 4 November 1950; TS 71 (1953) Cmd 8969), further entrenches the general principle that, save where a directly effective provision of European Union law is in issue, the judiciary's powers to strike down legislation extends only to secondary and not to primary legislation...

The ECA 1972 charged judges with an interpretive power that they should use in situations in which UK law appeared to contradict EU law, so that any ambiguity in the domestic law could be ironed out by use of statutory interpretation techniques. That way, UK law could be applied and no one needed to become too concerned about much of the European law by which the UK was bound. Indeed, we have evidence of cases of conflict between national and European law that were rectified through clever **judicial** interpretation: for example, *Pickstone v Freemans plc* [1989] AC 66, in which the House of Lords applied a mode of statutory construction that permitted treaty obligations to be fulfilled. A year later, they were called upon again to undertake a similar task in *Litster v Forth Dry Dock and Engineering Co Ltd* [1990] 1 AC 546, in which the Law Lords interpreted domestic law in such a way so as to implement a European directive and to comply with the ECJ's interpretation of the directive, even though in doing so it fundamentally changed the meaning of the law. As you will see, over time, it was becoming increasingly difficult for judges to be able to use their interpretative obligations under the ECA 1972 so as to render UK law compliant with European law. Sooner or later, judges were going to find it impossible to strain the interpretation of a UK statute so as to apply it in conformity with UK law. And in this section we shall consider two such cases.

In some cases, it was plainly not possible to read UK law so as to give effect to European law. What is the court to do in such a situation? The House of Lords was faced with such a decision in *Factortame Ltd and others v Secretary of State for Transport* [1990] 2 AC 85, HL, which became a landmark case, because the courts were required to disapply part of a UK Act of Parliament so as to comply with the UK's Community obligations. Another case, *R v Secretary of State for Employment, ex p Equal Opportunities Commission* [1995] 1 AC 1, similarly challenged notions of the UK Parliament's legislative supremacy. The *Factortame* cases related to provisions in the Merchant Shipping Act 1988 and regulations that flowed from it. The provisions were challenged on the ground that they offended against what were then Articles 7 and 52 of the EEC Treaty. It was argued that the provisions made it more difficult for Spanish-owned vessels to apply for licences to fish than it did for British-owned ones—an apparently deliberate decision by the UK Parliament so as to attempt to ring-fence fishing quotas for UK fishermen. There followed a series of cases. The first led the European law to be referred to the ECJ so that it could rule on its meaning and extent. The Spanish fishermen wanted the provision of the UK Act to be suspended, while waiting for the ECJ to rule, so that they could continue to operate until such time as the matter was determined. Opposing counsel stated that this would offend against parliamentary supremacy and that the Court had no power to set aside the provisions of a UK Act of Parliament. The Court of Appeal agreed that interim relief should not be granted, as did the House of Lords.

. . . .

● *Factortame Ltd and others v Secretary of State for Transport [on appeal from R v Secretary of State for Transport, ex p Factortame Ltd and others]* [1990] 2 AC 85, HL

Lord Bridge at 143:

> If the applicants fail to establish the rights they claim before the ECJ, the effect of the interim relief would be to have conferred upon them rights directly contrary to Parliament's sovereign will and correspondingly to have deprived British fishing vessels, as defined by parliament, of

> the enjoyment of a substantial portion of the United Kingdom quota of stocks of fish protected by the common fisheries policy. I am clearly of the opinion that, as a matter of English law, the court has no power to make an order which has these consequences.

The ECJ did not agree with this position and stated that if the only thing standing in the way of granting interim relief is a rule of national law, it should be set aside so as to permit Community law to be effective. Interim relief was eventually granted by the House of Lords in *Factortame (No 2)* [1991] 1 AC 603 and the area was looked at again by the Divisional Court, which, in *Factortame (No 3)* [1992] QB 680, ruled that the treaty Article had been infringed. Thus it is clear that EU law is hierarchically superior to UK law and that UK law must be set aside, if necessary, so as to give effect to its provisions.

What does this mean for our understanding of parliamentary supremacy and also for the UK constitution? Some scholars argue that our constitutional settlement has been changed over time and with little consultation with the people—or, for that matter, with national politicians. They point to the creep of EU supremacy via the case law of the ECJ as evidence for this.

● **D. Nicol, 'Britain's transnational constitution'** (2008) 61(1) Current Legal Problems 125, 127–8

> Intuitively a British public lawyer might object to regarding international agreements as forming part of the British constitution. After all, we are ostensibly a dualist state and our sovereign Parliament can legislate contrary to EU law, so the story goes, provided, it expresses an explicit intention so to do.[1] Yet, the Westphalian era where the national state reigned supreme (always over-exaggerated) has drawn to a close as the world's politicians have transformed international law.[2] Gone are the days when international law presented a picture of universal weakness in the face of national sovereignty... [I]nternational law presents a spectrum: some international law regimes remain weak and can be flouted with impunity by sufficiently powerful states... —whilst others are stronger.
>
> The EU, WTO and ECHR fall on the stronger side of the spectrum, with EU law the strongest of all. Only EU law enjoys a quasi-federal status vis-à-vis national law. The doctrines of supremacy and direct effect... compel our domestic courts and tribunals to enforce EU law even if this conflicts with our own national provision, including United Kingdom Acts of Parliament.[3] Thus EU law has a unique interpenetration into the domestic legal order, and therefore a unique constitutional impact. This was the result of the revolution effected by the European Court of Justice (ECJ) after the Treaty of Rome came into force. When the original Member States designed the legal machinery in the 1950s, it was intended to be weak: a system 'where few cases would make it to the Court, and in which the largest infractions could easily and without repercussion persist until a political will to rectify the situation emerged'.[4] Indeed, the system was chiefly designed to keep the Community institutions within the limits of their powers. But in the early 1960s the ECJ created its doctrines of direct effect and supremacy, effectively recruiting the national courts as the policemen of EU law in the Member States, to prevent national governments and national parliaments from violating EU rules. The stories of the developments are well known.[5] Half of the original Member States intervened in the landmark case of *van Gend en Loos* to oppose the creation of direct effect, but were overridden by an ECJ desirous of a new legal order which would limit national sovereignty.[6] Direct effect and supremacy meld EU law into the national legal systems, making every national court a EU court, every national judge a EU judge.[7] The preliminary reference system, not originally intended to monitor national laws for their compatibility with EU law, has been extensively deployed for this very purpose.[8]
>
> 1 *Macarthys Ltd v Smith* [1979] ICR 685, 789, *per* Lord Denning MR. See A. Young, *Parliamentary Sovereignty and the Human Rights Act 1998* (Oxford: Hart, 2008), ch. 2; cf. D. Feldman

(2005) 'None, one or several? Perspectives on the UK's constitution(s)' (2005) 64(2) Cambridge Law Journal 329–51.

2 According to Krasner, the Westphalian model was based on territoriality and the exclusion of external actors from domestic authority structures. Westphalian sovereignty is violated when external actors influence or determine domestic authority structures: S. Krasner, *Sovereignty: Organized Hypocrisy* (Princeton, NJ: Princeton University Press, 1997), p. 20.

3 Case 26/62 van Gend en Loos v Nederlandse Administratie Belastingen [1963] ECR 1; Case 6/64 Costa v ENEL [1964] ECR 585, [1965] CMLR 425; Case 106/77 Amministratizione della Finanze dello Stato v Simmenthal SpA (II) [1978] ECR 629, [1978] CMLR 263; R v Secretary of State for Transport, ex p Factortame Ltd (No. 2) [1991] 1 AC 603; R v Secretary of State for Employment, ex p Equal Opportunities Commission [1994] ICR 317.

4 K. Alter, *Establishing the Supremacy of European Law* (Oxford: Oxford University Press, 2001), p. 1.

5 For an insightful analysis, see P. P. Craig, 'Once upon a time in the West: direct effect and the federalization of EEC law' (1992) 12(4) Oxford Journal of Legal Studies 453.

6 See n. 3 above and [1963] CMLR 105. As Craig and de Búrca put it, 'the ECJ's vision of the EEC was very different from that advanced by the Member States': P. Craig and G. de Búrca, *EU Law: Text Cases and Materials* (4th edn, Oxford: Oxford University Press, 2007), p. 274.

7 These doctrines have since been joined by additional doctrines that further reinforce the effective enforcement of EU law rights: indirect effect, state liability, and the principles of equivalence and effectiveness in the sphere of national court remedies and procedural rules where EU law rights are being exercised.

8 Enforcement proceedings brought by the Commission play a lesser, although important, role. See A. Tomkins, 'Of institutions and individuals: the enforcement of EC law', in P. Craig and R. Rawlings (eds) *Law and Administration in Europe* (Oxford: Oxford University Press, 2003), pp. 273–95.

Is the position settled, and does this mean that EU law is overriding and that the UK has limited its parliamentary supremacy for all times? It rather depends on your point of view—on whether you believe that, in real terms, the Westminster Parliament is likely to repeal the ECA 1972. We have judicial evidence on this point as a result of the case *Thoburn v Sunderland City Council* [2002] EWHC 195 Admin. The *Metric Martyrs cases* (as the case is known) provided an excellent opportunity for the constitutional position of EU membership and the UK's dualist status to be considered at length. It is a case well worth reading in full, because it provides a comprehensive discussion of the case law pertinent to parliamentary supremacy in general and in relation to EU membership in particular. At issue in *Thoburn* was the validity of the legislation that gave effect to the EU policy to introduce a compulsory system of metric weights and measures.

....

● ***Thoburn v Sunderland City Council*** [2002] EWHC 195 Admin (the *Metric Martyrs cases*)

Counsel for Mr Thoburn argued at 37:

> The rule is that if Parliament has enacted successive statutes which on the true construction of each of them make irreducibly inconsistent provisions, the earlier statute is impliedly repealed by the later. The importance of the rule is, on the traditional view, that if it were otherwise the earlier Parliament might bind the later, and this would be repugnant to the principle of Parliamentary sovereignty.

It was argued that, on that basis, certain provisions of the ECA 1972 had been impliedly repealed.

Counsel for Sunderland City Council argued at 56:

> that . . . the supremacy of EC law became part of the law of England by force of the ECA . . . that by the ECA Parliament entrenched EC law in the domestic law of the United Kingdom, subject only . . . to

> the possibility of withdrawal from the EU by express repeal of the ECA. And ... though it was done by means of the ECA, EC law is said to have been entrenched, rather than merely incorporated, not by virtue of any principle of domestic constitutional law, but by virtue of pnciples of Community law already established in cases such as *Van Gend en Loos* and *Costa v ENEL*.

Both positions reflect different stances that have been taken in debates surrounding parliamentary supremacy and membership of the EU.

Lord Justice Laws held that there was no conflict that triggered the doctrine of implied repeal. The doctrine of implied repeal is engaged only where a provision of a later Act contradicts that of an earlier one, in which instance the courts apply the later as the most recent expression of the will of Parliament. This means that the inconsistent sections of the earlier Act are repealed by implication. Laws LJ considered that Thoburn's counsel's argument of implied repeal was without merit, because the later legislation was not legislation on the topic of the UK's membership of the EU and the way in which EU law, in general, was to apply in the UK. He also rejected the argument of Sunderland City Council's counsel that the ECA 1972 has been effectively **entrenched** within the UK constitution and thus could not be repealed. Instead, Laws LJ provided a detailed and helpful history of the development of parliamentary supremacy, and set out a series of propositions that could be advanced in relation to the relationship between UK and EU law, as follows.

cross reference

See Chapter 7 for more details on express and implied repeal.

- All the specific rights and obligations created by first pillar EU law are incorporated in UK domestic law as a result of the ECA 1972. They are hierarchically superior, and thus any UK law provision that is inconsistent with any of these EU rights and obligations must be set aside, or must be amended, so as to avoid the inconsistency. This is true even where the inconsistent municipal/domestic provision is contained in primary legislation.

- The ECA 1972 is a constitutional statute. Laws LJ considers that statutes that have heavy constitutional import should be treated a little differently from all other statutes and should be capable of repeal by Parliament only through express (stated) repeal rather than via the court-developed mechanism of implied repeal.

- Laws LJ argued that the special status of constitutional statutes is recognised by the common law and has nothing to do with EU law or arguments about the entrenchment of EU law.

- The fundamental legal basis of the UK's relationship with the EU rests with the domestic, not the European, legal powers.

Law LJ's judgment therefore recognises the supremacy of EU law within the UK domestic order. But the next part of his judgment explains that such supremacy persists only for as long as the UK Parliament wishes it to do so. The supremacy of EU law is recognised by judges in the UK only as a result of a British Act of Parliament that states that this be so. Were Parliament to repeal that Act (the ECA 1972), then EU law would no longer be supreme, or even applicable, in the UK legal sphere.

241

● ***Thoburn v Sunderland City Council*** [2002] EWHC 195 Admin (the *Metric Martyrs cases*)

Lord Justice Laws:

> [70] I consider that the balance struck by these four propositions gives full weight both to the proper supremacy of Community law and to the proper supremacy of the United Kingdom Parliament. By the former, I mean the supremacy of *substantive* Community law. By the latter, I mean the supremacy of the legal *foundation* within which those substantive provisions enjoy their primacy. The former is guaranteed by propositions (1) and (2). The latter is guaranteed by propositions (3) and (4). If this balance is understood, it will be seen that these two supremacies are in harmony, and not in conflict. [Counsel for the appellants'] argument is

> wrong because it would undermine the first supremacy; [counsel for respondents] because it would undermine the second.

In law, it appears that the ECA 1972 is capable of repeal; if so, then *Factortame* is simply an expression of the ordinary rule of parliamentary supremacy—that Parliament retains supremacy and a future Parliament may change the Acts of any previous Parliament. In legal terms, a future Parliament would be entitled to repeal or amend the ECA 1972. By doing so, the UK constitutional settlement would alter, and EU law would no longer be applicable in the domestic jurisdiction and would not be applied by British judges. However, the UK would remain bound by EU law unless and until it could negotiate an exit from the European Union and be released from its international legal obligations. This would depend on the political will of the UK and the EU (and member states), and also the terms that the UK would have to accept on leaving the Union. Would UK citizens living aboard in EU member states be required to return to the UK? Would they have to sell their holiday homes, and give up their businesses and their jobs in those countries? What would happen in relation to free trade and free movement of people? Would UK citizens be prepared to accept the travel and work restrictions that leaving the Union would bring? All of these are political, rather than legal, questions and attempts to answer them are mere conjecture. But, in legal terms, were the Westminster Parliament to repeal the ECA 1972, then EU law would cease to have domestic effect even if the UK would remain bound by it through the treaties it has signed. But is it possible for the UK to leave the European Union, in the light of Denning's statements in *Blackburn*, above? We shall consider this in the context of the newly negotiated Lisbon Treaty.

summary points

What does membership of the EU mean for parliamentary supremacy?

- *It very much depends on your understanding of whether the UK could or would ever leave the EU.*

- *If the UK were to repeal the ECA 1972, then it is argued by Laws LJ that EU law would no longer have any application in the UK.*

- *However, even then, until such time as the UK left the EU, the UK would remain bound by its treaty obligations and thus would be in breach of international law for failure to comply with the obligations into which it entered.*

- *If the UK were to be able to leave the EU, then it is argued by many that it has only delegated certain areas of its legislative supremacy to the EU until such time as it decides to leave and retrieve those areas for the Westminster Parliament.*

- *The ease with which the UK could withdraw from the EU, were it to wish to do so, is difficult to establish given that no members state has used the explicit exit clause within the Lisbon Treaty.*

- *Some politicians suggest that the UK could renegotiate its terms of membership in the EU—although, as with all treaty negotiations, this would have to be agreed by all member states.*

8.5 Reform of the EU and parliamentary supremacy

The EU member states have recently negotiated and ratified a new treaty, which is making fundamental changes to the European project. The European Parliament has increased legislative powers and increased powers in relation to the EU budget. It has equal power with the Council as regards policymaking. The concept of subsidiarity has been strengthened, meaning that decisions should be taken at the EU level only if this will yield better outcomes than if the decisions were to be taken at a national level. The Lisbon Treaty has drawn a clearer line between the competencies of member states and those of the EU, so as to clarify what is a matter for individual member states and what rests with the EU. EU citizens may call upon the European Commission to bring forward a policy or policies, assuming that 1 million citizens (from a number of member states) support such a policy. This is referred to as the 'Citizens' Charter'. Qualified majority voting (QMV) in the Council of the European Union has been extended to new areas. It has introduced the European Charter of Fundamental Rights (from which the UK negotiated an opt-out). The EU now has a unified legal personality, rather than a number of distinct legal personalities drawn from different treaties. The extract below sets out a summary of some of the main changes that have ensued.

● **S. Burns, 'An incoming tide'** (2008) 158 New Law Journal 44, 44–6

> Lord Denning once famously likened the impact of EU law, which originated under the aegis of the Treaty of Rome 1957, to an incoming tide flowing up the UK legal system, and incontrovertibly having a profound impact on the sovereignty of Westminster (see *Bulmer (HP) Ltd v J Bollinger SA* [1974] Ch 401 at 418–19).
>
> If he were surveying the legal horizon today in the light of the Treaty of Lisbon (the reform treaty), and casting his judicial eyes over the past 33 years, he might have to revise his image of EU law being like an incoming tide permeating our existing legal order, and more realistically compare it to a tsunami, enveloping everything in its path with irresistible force.
>
> **Union of Member States**
>
> The reform treaty, signed by the prime minister, Gordon Brown, on 13 December 2007 amends the Treaty on European Union (TEU) and the Treaty establishing the European Community, ie the Treaty of Rome 1957, which created the EEC, the precursor of the EU. It amends TEU in a number of important ways, eg Art 1 of TEU is amended to read 'the Union shall replace and succeed the European Community', emphasising that the EU is a union of member states, with a concomitant pooling and transfer of sovereignty, and not just an economic free-trading block.
>
> The new Art 3 of TEU loftily states 'the Union's aim is to promote peace, its values and the well-being of its peoples' and an area of freedom 'without frontiers, in which the free movement of persons is ensured'. It also states that 'the Union shall establish an internal market' and will 'work for the sustainable development of Europe based on balanced economic growth and price stability, a highly competitive social market economy, aiming at full employment and social progress, and a high level of protection and improvement of the quality of the environment', and generally it shall promote economic, social and territorial cohesion, and solidarity among member states.
>
> Article 3, not surprisingly, also states that 'the Union shall establish an economic and monetary union whose currency is the euro'. However, the UK still retains its currency, the prime minister not being satisfied that his five economic tests for joining the single currency have been met.
>
> **Red Lines**
>
> The government might refer to the new Art 4 of TEU as evidence of its success in negotiating the reform treaty, preserving the so-called red lines, ie fundamental and exclusive law-making powers in critical areas that must remain at Westminster and not be transferred to the EU. In accordance with Art 5, competences not conferred upon the EU in the treaties remain with the member states:
>
>> 'The Union...shall respect their essential State functions, including ensuring the territorial integrity of the State, maintaining law and order and safeguarding national security. In particular, national security remains the sole responsibility of each Member State.'

That said, the Article proceeds to emphasise that member states must still 'facilitate the achievement of the Union's tasks and refrain from any measure which could jeopardise the attainment of the Union's objectives', and that member states 'shall take any appropriate measure, general or particular, to ensure fulfilment of the obligations arising out of the Treaties or resulting from the acts of the institutions of the Union'—clearly flagging up how crucial it is that EU law is applied consistently, uniformly and fully in all member states, which echoes the approach of the European Court of Justice (ECJ).

Limits

Under Art 5 of the amended TEU, it is stated 'the limits of Union competences are governed by the principle of conferral', which entails that 'the Union shall act only within the limits of the competences conferred upon it by the Member States in the Treaties to attain the objectives set out therein'. Importantly, it then clearly states 'competences not conferred upon the Union in the Treaties remain with the Member States'.

...

Withdrawal

Interestingly, a new Art 35 provides that 'any Member State may decide to withdraw from the Union in accordance with its own constitutional requirements', which is fully in accordance with the Diceyean concept of Parliamentary supremacy, namely that Parliament has the:

'Right to make or unmake any law whatever; and further, that no person or body is recognised by the law of England as having a right to override or set aside the legislation of Parliament.'

Hence the UK Parliament could pass an Act tomorrow repealing the European Communities Act 1972, pulling the country out of the EU—albeit a highly improbable scenario—and our courts would have to give effect to and follow such a major constitutional Act.

The ECJ will continue to comprise and consist of one judge from each member state.

...

What does this mean in relation to our discussion in this chapter? One thing that is very clear is that the new Article 35 provides a mechanism through which a member state may withdraw from the EU if it were to wish to do so. This means that Lord Denning's concern that the UK may not be able to leave the EU (formed in the early days of the UK's membership of the EC) may be laid to rest. That also must mean, in logical terms, that the British Parliament can, via withdrawal from the Union, regain its legislative supremacy in areas currently covered by the EU. This adds weight to the contention that the Westminster Parliament has delegated, rather than lost, its legislative supremacy in first pillar areas. What the Treaty of Lisbon does not and cannot do, however, is answer the big political questions that underpin any member state's decision to remain within or to leave the Union and whether the price of staying or going is too high for the majority of the population to accept. Once again, it is politics rather than law that would determine that issue.

The European Union Act 2011, recently passed by the UK Parliament, effectively retains the UK–EU balance of power at a status quo. The Act requires that any proposal that seeks to transfer power from the UK to the EU be put to a **referendum** of the UK electorate (and be passed) before the UK government will be empowered to enter into such a treaty. This is an interesting development, because it is the first time that an ongoing right to referendum has been included in a British Act of Parliament. It does not, however, give a right to a referendum on the vexed question of whether the UK should remain within or leave the EU. There have been calls for this from politicians from all sides of politics, and also from the media and the electorate. David Cameron has ruled this out for the time being, until such time as the eurozone situation stabilises. It will be interesting to see what happens in due course.

summary points

What does reform of the EU mean for parliamentary supremacy?

- *The EU continues to evolve as the European project moves in different directions, as evidenced by the Lisbon Treaty. The Treaty contains a provision that allows a member state to leave the EU in certain circumstances.*

- *The UK's relationship with the EU has also developed over time, in keeping with the political agenda of the party in power at Westminster, and the public's perception of the relationship between the UK and the EU.*

- *The European Union Act 2011 effectively retains the balance of power between the UK and the EU as it stands according to the current Treaty provisions, unless the British electorate votes in a referendum in favour of ceding more powers to the EU. The Act does not, however, require a referendum on whether the UK should remain a member of the EU.*

- *The exit provision in the Lisbon Treaty provides clear evidence in law that a member state could leave the EU under certain circumstances. On that basis, it is probably more correct to say that any power that the Westminster Parliament has given to the EU has been delegated rather than ceded for all time.*

Summary

This chapter has provided a brief overview of the European Union (EU) and its development. You should now understand the supremacy of certain types of EU law within the UK domestic legal order, as provided by the European Communities Act 1972 (ECA 1972). You should also be aware that treaty provisions and regulations may be directly applicable within the UK, and that directives, decisions, and recommendations may, under certain circumstances, take direct effect. Case law of the European Court of Justice (ECJ) demonstrates that the EU is a new legal order and that each member state has (while remaining a member of the EU) delegated some of its legislative supremacy to the EU; this is confirmed by the UK case law. There is UK case law that indicates that if the UK were to repeal the ECA 1972, European law would no longer apply within the UK even though, in international law terms, the UK would remain bound by, and in breach of, EU law until such time as it negotiated an exit from the Union. On this basis, some scholars suggest that the UK Parliament remains legislatively supreme, because it has the power to repeal the ECA 1972. Others argue that as long as the UK remains bound by EU law in the international sphere, the UK Parliament cannot claim to have legislative supremacy. The Lisbon Treaty has made express provision for the first time for a mechanism that allows a member state to leave the EU. On this basis, one may conclude, in legal terms at least, that it is possible for a member state to leave the Union and thus regain its legislative supremacy. Whether this is possible in practical terms—and whether this would be desirable—is outside the scope of this chapter.

Questions

1 Explain in your own words what is the nature and role of the European Union.

2 What are the main EU institutions and who are the personnel involved in them?

3 How would you describe monist and dualist states to a friend interested in international law?

4 In no more than 300 words, explain the UK's relationship with the EU.

5 Chart the development of UK and EU case law, which has an impact on parliamentary supremacy. What does each tell you about the changing nature of parliamentary supremacy, if anything? What does this mean in relation to your own understanding of parliamentary supremacy?

6 To what extent has parliamentary supremacy been lost? If lost, can it be regained?

Further reading

Albi, A. and Van Elsuwege, P., 'The EU constitution, national constitutions and sovereignty: an assessment of a "European constitutional order"' (2004) 29 European Law Review 741

This article provides a discussion of the European Constitutional Treaty, which was the forerunner to the Lisbon Treaty. This treaty was not ratified by all member states and so did not come into force.

Biskup, P., *Conflicts Between Community and National Laws: An Analysis of the British Approach* (Sussex European Institute Working Paper No. 66, Brighton: University of Sussex, 2003), available online at http://www.sussex.ac.uk/sei/documents/sei-working-paper-no-66.pdf

This paper is a clear guide to the way in which the UK has approached compliance with EU law. It is slightly out of date, but is nonetheless useful.

Miller, V., 'The UK Parliament and European Business: Recent Reforms and Scrutiny Issues' (House of Commons Library Standard Note SN04977, 24 February 2009), available online at http://www.parliament.uk/briefing-papers/SN04977

This note examines the scrutiny procedures for EU law, government practice, and Parliament's role in this process. It is a clear and comprehensive account.

Thorp, A., 'Parliamentary Scrutiny of Treaties up to 2010' (House of Commons Library Standard Note 04693, 8 February 2011), available online at http://www.parliament.uk/briefing-papers/SN04693

This note provides an analysis of the role of Parliament in scrutinising EU treaties signed by the government under the **royal prerogative**. It explains the limited power that Parliament had—up until 2010, when the Constitutional Reform and Governance Act was enacted—to scrutinise treaties prior to ratification.

Human Rights

Key points

This chapter will cover:

- What are human rights?

- What is the link between human rights protections and parliamentary supremacy?

- What is the history of the European Convention on Human Rights (ECHR) in a UK context and what is the ECHR's legal standing?

- What is the Human Rights Act 1998 (HRA 1998) and how does it operate in the UK?

- How do the ECHR and the HRA 1998 affect parliamentary supremacy?

- How does the human rights context differ from the EU context as regards parliamentary supremacy?

- Is the current system of human rights protection in need of reform, or does parliamentary supremacy appear to provide adequate protection?

Introduction

This chapter will address parliamentary supremacy from yet another angle: the legislative supremacy of the UK Parliament and the effect that may have on the protection of human rights (and vice versa). The chapter will address membership of the Council of Europe, a different body from that which we considered in the previous chapter (the European Union). It will also consider the operation of the Human Rights Act 1998 and any impact that the Act has on parliamentary supremacy. Finally, it will provide some analysis on the way in which parliamentary supremacy may be inconsistent with, or may buttress, human rights protection.

9.1 What are human rights?

Before we go any further, it may be helpful to consider what human rights are. This may appear to be an obvious and rather simplistic question, but in a UK context human rights development has been relatively slow and there are a number of myths disseminated through the media about what human rights are. Human rights are generally considered to be minimum legal protections and freedoms to which individuals are entitled by virtue of being human. They are inherent to all people regardless of nationality or citizenship and are considered necessary in a civilised society. They are inalienable, meaning that the **state** cannot remove these basic rights. This may be contrasted with other legal rights, which are rights that the state may confer, and which the state may remove or give to individuals, groups, or companies subject to their fulfilling certain conditions.

What has been the UK's position vis-à-vis human rights? As we shall discover, the UK has championed basic protections in the form of civil liberties. However, civil liberties are residual, meaning that citizens may do anything that is not legally forbidden. Civil liberties are relatively precarious legal concepts, in that they may be removed by express provisions that override them in a statute. Consequently, many commentators would argue that human rights afford greater protection than do civil liberties. Rights discourse (a focus on human rights rather than civil liberties) has gained ground in the UK since the 1940s and culminated in the passing of the Human Rights Act 1998, which brought into the UK domestic jurisdiction an international human rights treaty that the UK had helped to draft back in the late 1940s and early 1950s. This has moved the discussion on from the protection of civil liberties from restriction by the state to the protection of human rights from limitation by it.

Human rights are often discussed in terms of 'waves', which explain the type of rights that are under discussion. The first wave of rights comprised civil and political rights and freedoms necessary to ensure respect for basic citizenship requirements linked to security, liberty, and equality. Civil and political rights are seen by some as foundations for the **rule of law** to flourish. For some, they are the essentials of any functioning democratic state; for others, they are not requirements for any particular kind of political system, but are the essential safeguards needed to protect the dignity and autonomy of each person. In countries that have a written constitution that contains a **bill of rights**, it is the civil and political rights that usually make up the statement of rights. As we shall see later in the chapter, the **European Convention on Human Rights (ECHR)**, to which the UK is a signatory, is a statement of civil and political rights,

cross reference
The rule of law is discussed in detail in Chapter 4.

as are some other regional systems' human rights treaties; likewise the Universal Declaration of Human Rights (UDHR) of 1948 and the International Covenant on Civil and Political Rights (ICCPR) of 1966.

This first wave of rights is sometimes referred to as comprising negative rights, meaning that they are rights that explain what the state should not be permitted to take away from an individual or to do to an individual. This is in contrast to second-generation or second-wave rights, which are economic and social rights that require the state to provide something or to guarantee something in an active sense. Further, third-wave or third-generation rights are those through which the state accords rights to communities rather than simply to individuals. We are going to focus on the first wave of rights in this chapter, because these are the ones that are more easily actionable in the UK domestic sphere.

● **L. Loughlin, *The Idea of Public Law*** (Oxford: Oxford University Press, 2004), p. 114

This contemporary 'rights revolution'[1] is linked to the triumph of social power over political power, to the emergence of a more individualistic conception of society, and at least in an ideological sense, to the formation of a political order built on the foundation of the rights-bearing individual... The traditional focus of political thought—on the rights of sovereigns and the duties of subjects[2]—has been inverted, the emphasis now being placed on the rights of citizens and the obligations of government. Since rights and duties are twin aspects of a reciprocal relationship,[3] this looks like a distinction without a difference. But in practice, this inversion has had an important effect on the way governmental authority is constituted. It is when rights are given positive institutional effect that this effect is disclosed...

1 C. R. Epp, *The Rights Revolution: Lawyers, Activists, and Supreme Courts in Comparative Perspective* (Chicago, IL: University of Chicago Press, 1998); M. Ignatieff, *The Rights Revolution* (Toronto, ON: Anansi, 2000).

2 See, e.g., Thomas Hobbes, *On the Citizen* (1647), ed. and trans. R. Tuck and M. Silverhorne (Cambridge: Cambridge University Press, 1998), pp. 7 and 10: 'This book sets out men's duties, first as men, then as citizens and lastly as Christians' and is intended to investigate 'the right of a commonwealth and the duties of its citizens'.

3 See, e.g., B. Bailyn, *The Ideological Origins of the American Revolution* (Cambridge, MA: Belknap Press, 1967), p. 27: 'In pamphlet after pamphlet the American writers cited Locke on natural rights and on the social and governmental contract.'

This extract provides a brief insight into the changing face of the relationship between the individual and the state. In the past, it was argued that the individual owed a duty of allegiance to the sovereign in return for protection. Over time, this relationship led to the development of civil liberties, otherwise known as freedoms, which were permitted to individuals in the absence of formal law that placed restrictions on those freedoms. These freedoms allowed individuals autonomy to the extent that the law allowed. However, over time, these negative freedoms have been reworked into positive rights that the state must respect in its dealings with individuals. Loughlin argues that the state now owes the individual a duty to respect his or her human rights, as opposed to the classical statement of duty that imposes responsibilities and duties on the individual and right in the hands of the sovereign. This development accelerated after the Second World War, and led to the formation of a number of international bodies and human rights treaties designed to protect individual human rights, including the United Nations and the Council of Europe. The next section will consider the Council of Europe and its human rights treaty, the ECHR.

What are human rights?

- *Human rights are basic, minimum protections or guarantees that each individual has by virtue of being alive. They do not require individuals to meet other special conditions before they can be deemed worthy of these protections.*

- *Human rights are sometimes referred to in terms of 'generations' or 'waves'. The first wave comprises civil and political rights, the second, social and economic rights; and the third, community rights.*

- *The UK has gradually moved in the direction of a rights-based system from its roots as a system based on civil liberties.*

9.2 What is the link between human rights protections and parliamentary supremacy?

We considered parliamentary supremacy in Chapter 7, in which we learnt that **Parliament** can make and unmake any law it wishes as a result of its **legislative** supremacy. How does that fit with minimum human rights protections, which are considered to be inalienable (that is, rights that cannot be removed)? If Parliament can make, repeal, or change any law and yet human rights are considered to be fixed and irremovable, how can the two systems be reconciled? This remains a difficult issue, and there are a number of different theories that seek to explain the contradictions between them and/or to demonstrate how the two may live in harmony. Some equate human rights with the rule of law; others equate human rights with the common law protection afforded by judges (Dicey, for example); yet others see overriding human rights protection as a basic moral principle by which Parliament abides out of a moral, rather than a legal, duty. Finally, there are those who say that the two systems cannot be aligned, but that, in any event, as a result of the UK's signature of the European Convention on Human Rights (and other international human rights instruments), there is little prospect of the Westminster Parliament making major incursions into human rights protections. We shall consider some of these points further below. At this stage, it is sufficient to know that the two systems appear to be in contradiction: on the one hand, human rights protection is designed to protect individuals from the state to ensure that legislation and **executive** action do not remove basic and fundamental rights; on the other hand, parliamentary supremacy appears to accord total freedom to the Westminster Parliament to legislate on any matter in any way. By contrast, the executive must stay within its legal (and prerogative) powers.

Sir John Laws illustrates the issues of parliamentary supremacy versus human rights protection, or what he calls constitutional guarantees (of human rights), in the following extract.

cross reference

Parliamentary supremacy is discussed in Chapter 4.

● **J. Laws, 'Constitutional guarantees'** [2008] 29(1) Statute Law Review 1, 1–2

What I am going to talk about in this lecture is prompted by a very old chestnut. It consists in two linked questions: how, if at all, can special status be given in the law of England to constitutional guarantees, and are they anyway a good thing? The theme is an old one sure enough, but also contemporary. For this there are several reasons. Here are two. First, six years after its coming into force, we can begin to see the true constitutional setting of the Human Rights Act 1998 more clearly. Secondly, we are living through a time when opinion about what our constitutional arrangements should be seems particularly unsettled.

...

First I should explain what I mean by a constitutional guarantee. I take the expression 'constitutional guarantee' to refer to a legal measure which has two characteristics.

(1) The first is that it protects basic or fundamental rights against intrusion or subversion by the State. What in this context is to be regarded as a basic or fundamental right is of course itself a question, but it means at least a right which is understood to belong to everyone. There are some measures which, though they do not directly safeguard rights belonging to every individual, are of such an overarching nature that it seems appropriate to describe them as offering constitutional protection: see for example section 9 of the Bill of Rights 1688 ...

(2) The second characteristic of a constitutional guarantee is that it is in some sense entrenched—that is, it is proof against being changed, or abrogated, by those legal mechanisms which are deployed to change ordinary laws. One could in theory postulate a constitutional guarantee which the law does not allow to be changed in any circumstances whatever. I think there is jurisprudence of the Supreme Court of India recognizing such a state of affairs. More usual, however, is the kind of provision which requires a special majority of the legislature—say two-thirds—before it can be altered or abrogated ...

The law of England has included measures or principles having the first of these characteristics—the protection of rights—for centuries. Take the presumption of innocence; and alongside it, section 39 of the Magna Carta. Or section 1 of the Habeas Corpus Act 1679 ...

However, English law runs into difficulty with the second characteristic of constitutional guarantees: entrenchment—at least where the putative guarantee is offered by statute: I shall come to common law constitutional guarantees. The truth is that entrenchment is the very feature which marks out a constitutional guarantee from the general body of law. Here we encounter the first part of our old chestnut: how, if at all, can special status be given in the law of England to statutory constitutional guarantees? ...

cross reference
Thoburn *is discussed in Chapters 7 and 8.*

As discussed in Chapter 3, in many countries there are rights and freedoms ring-fenced within a bill of rights of a written constitution. These rights and freedoms usually cannot be amended without additional hurdles being overcome, such as the consent of the people at **referendum**, or a higher-majority support (rather than a simple majority) from the legislature and the consent of the executive. However, under the UK constitutional settlement, this is not the case, because no Act of Parliament is deemed to be higher than any other (subject to *obiter* comments made in the case of *Thoburn*) and there is no law higher than an Act within the domestic hierarchy of norms (subject to overriding EU law provisions, of course).

NOTE

You may wish to refresh your memory of this by looking again at Chapter 3 on the nature and sources of the British constitution, and Chapter 7 on the theory of parliamentary supremacy, if you remain unsure.

So, is parliamentary supremacy always inconsistent with a system of **entrenched** or semi-entrenched human rights? The answer is 'not necessarily'. It would be possible under the manner-and-form rule set out by Jennings and examined in Chapter 7 for Parliament to provide that statutes that restrict human rights and fundamental freedoms can be passed by Parliament only if the Commons and the Lords vote in support, with a 'yes' vote from at least 60 per cent, or 70 per cent, or even 75 per cent of members, and a relatively large quorum of members present in the chambers to vote. However, at present, the system in the UK requires only that one member more votes 'yes' than votes 'no' in order for a Bill to be carried, regardless of its subject matter or impact.

summary points

What is the link between human rights protections and parliamentary supremacy?

- *Human rights protections aim to limit the state from passing law or acting in a way that threatens individuals' basic and fundamental human rights.*

- *Parliamentary supremacy provides Parliament with supreme legislative powers, to prevent Parliament from being restricted in its legislative function, subject to EU law requirements.*

- *Human rights protection and parliamentary supremacy seem, on the face of it, to be contradictory norms. On the one hand, there is the desire to restrict legislatures and executives; on the other, the desire to protect legislative competence.*

- *Some have argued that parliamentary supremacy operates within a restricted environment because Parliament seeks to uphold the rule of law and the rule of law demands that basic human rights are protected.*

- *Others argue that the rule of law does not demand that rights be protected, only that the law be made in a way that is procedurally proper and leads to clear, transparent, and relatively stable law, in a legal system that upholds law above all else.*

- *The mechanics of parliamentary supremacy and human rights are discussed in later sections.*

9.3 What is the history of the European Convention on Human Rights (ECHR) in a UK context and what is the ECHR's legal standing?

cross reference
Dualism was discussed in Chapter 8.

The main human rights document that has an impact on human rights protection in the UK is the European Convention on Human Rights—or, in full, the European Convention for the Protection of Human Rights and Fundamental Freedoms—which results from membership body the Council of Europe. In this section, we shall look at the history and development of the Council of Europe, before turning our attention to the nature of the ECHR itself and the way in which the Convention rights operate. It is important to remember that the UK is a **dualist state** and that consequently international law does not have **direct effect** within the UK, unless Parliament so provides by law.

9.3.1 The Council of Europe

The Council of Europe is an international body, founded in 1949 to promote individual human rights protection by sovereign states. It should not be confused with the institutions of the European Union: while the EU respects the Council of Europe's ECHR and each of the EU member states is also a member of separate membership body the Council of Europe, the EU and the Council of Europe are totally different bodies that operate very differently. The Council of Europe was established after the Second World War—a war that saw wide-scale, catastrophic abuse of human rights. The body's aim was—and is—to promote and protect individual human rights, democracy, and the rule of law among all member countries, and to promote human rights more widely. The original members of the Council of Europe included the UK, along with Belgium, Denmark, France, Greece, Ireland, Italy, Luxembourg, the Netherlands, Sweden, and Turkey. It is a membership body, meaning that countries that are governed by human rights protections have agreed to join the Council of Europe, and to sign and ratify the ECHR. Member countries may also have signed up to one or more of the optional protocols that address other human rights issues, such as the prohibition on the use of the death penalty. There are now forty-seven member countries that have signed up to the Convention, the UK being one of the first in 1950 (as ratified by the UK Parliament in 1951); the ECHR came into force in 1953. Each country is represented in the Council of Europe at the Council's decision-making body, the Committee of Ministers. Each of the forty-seven contracting countries sends a minister representative—usually the foreign minister for the state.

cross reference

The European Union is discussed in Chapter 8.

When first established, the Council of Europe provided a means whereby one sovereign state could take legal action against another member sovereign state for breach of the terms of the ECHR. The European Court of Human Rights (ECtHR) in Strasbourg (not to be confused with the European Court of Justice, or ECJ, in Luxembourg) was established for this purpose. The ECtHR judges are drawn from each of the member states of the Council of Europe. They are 'elected' for six years from a list of three nominees put forward by each member state, one being elected from the three names proposed by each member country. However, judges do not act as state representatives and must act independently of their state sponsor. Originally, the Court heard complaints from one country about another's alleged breached of the ECHR; in time, the Council of Europe introduced the right of individual petition, meaning that an individual could bring an action against the member country believed to be breaching his or her Convention rights. In international law, it is usually one country that seeks action against another country, whereas the right to individual petition is more usually associated with domestic legal routes to redress. The UK finally permitted individual petition in 1966; up until then, it had not been possible for an individual to seek direct enforcement of his or her rights.

cross reference

Refer back to Chapter 8 if you need to remind yourself about dualism and how this affects the way in which international law operates within the UK.

Some countries went a stage further in keeping with Article 13 of the ECHR, which requires a state to provide an effective remedy to a breach of a Convention right, by allowing individuals to enforce their ECHR rights directly via the domestic court system. Courts in the UK could not initially apply international law directly, because the UK is a dualist state; rights would be directly enforceable only if the UK Parliament were to make them so by passing an Act of Parliament to instruct judges to apply the ECHR in British courts. This did not happen until the enactment of the Human Rights Act in 1998 and its entry into force in May 1999 in Scotland, and October 2000 in the rest of the UK. Consequently, until then, in the UK individuals' human rights were protected by virtue of the ECHR, but they were enforceable only via the ECtHR in Strasbourg and not by British courts. This is important, because the ECtHR operates in the international sphere and as such can neither strike down any domestic law nor override domestic policy. Its judgments are extremely persuasive, and, of course, member countries have agreed to abide by their international legal responsibilities by virtue of joining the Council of Europe and signing the Convention. However, it is not possible for the body to force a sovereign state to change its law or practice. Ultimately, its most forceful sanction against a sovereign state would be expulsion from the body. This would be counterproductive in many ways, because expulsion would take the country outside the continuing oversight of the Council of Europe and remove the right of petition from individuals to take action against the country concerned. Instead, the Council of Europe relies upon countries to abide by its judgments, or to bow to international pressure and negative publicity about its human rights record in the long term, even if unwilling to do so in the short term. Just as most of us consider ourselves under a moral obligation to fulfil our commitments, so do most countries—particularly in the face of public condemnation and recriminations for continued non-compliance.

thinking point

This is not always the situation, however. The UK remains in breach of an ECtHR judgment ruling that the blanket removal of prisoners' rights to vote in elections was contrary to the ECHR. What are your views on this? Should the UK government introduce legislation to Parliament so as to change the law, or should it allow UK law to remain in breach the ECHR?

9.3.2 The nature of the ECHR rights and how they operate

The rights in the ECHR are creatures of international law, meaning that they are interpreted using the methods adopted under international law and the Vienna Convention on the Law of Treaties 1969. They are not interpreted in the same way as domestic provisions would be, because otherwise there may be forty-seven different countries' interpretations of each right. Instead, the ECtHR has developed its own approach to interpreting the rights and provides member states with a margin of appreciation. This is particularly true in cases that relate to perceptions of morality, such as *Handyside v United Kingdom* (1976) 1 EHRR 737. The margin of appreciation is really a certain amount of flexibility given to member states to permit legitimate national differences of view to be accommodated within the international framework.

The ECHR is designed to encourage each country to comply with rights to the greatest extent that they can, while providing a minimum protection or base line under which member states should not fall. The rights contained in the ECHR reflect conceptions of civil and political rights—namely, those that individuals are entitled to assert against the state. Rights are broadly vertical rather than horizontal in nature, and therefore apply in respect of individuals against the state and against public bodies (see section 6(1) of the Human Rights Act 1998 in this regard). States have a duty to ensure human rights protection within the country. This means that the state should have legislation in place that seeks to protect fundamental rights and freedoms throughout the country.

Few Convention rights are absolute, meaning that they cannot be restricted in some way, and this is why the restrictions placed on rights by the state may be considered to be legitimate and legal. Any restrictions placed on rights will be considered against the list of lawful categories of restriction contained within the Convention Articles. Restrictions placed on the rights, even if lawful, will also have to be considered against standards of proportionality. Restrictions must be both lawful and proportionate. Proportionality means that the restriction must be no greater than is necessary to meet the required lawful aims. The rights are as follows.

European Convention on Human Rights (as amended by Protocol No. 11)

· ·

Article 1 Obligation to respect human rights

The High Contracting Parties shall secure to everyone within their jurisdiction the rights and freedoms defined in Section I of this Convention.

...

Article 2 Right to life

1 Everyone's right to life shall be protected by law. No one shall be deprived of his life intentionally save in the execution of a sentence of a court following his conviction of a crime for which this penalty is provided by law.

2 Deprivation of life shall not be regarded as inflicted in contravention of this article when it results from the use of force which is no more than absolutely necessary:

A in defence of any person from unlawful violence;

B in order to effect a lawful arrest or to prevent the escape of a person lawfully detained;

C in action lawfully taken for the purpose of quelling a riot or insurrection.

Article 3 Prohibition of torture

No one shall be subjected to torture or to inhuman or degrading treatment or punishment.

Article 4 Prohibition of slavery and forced labour

1 No one shall be held in slavery or servitude.

2 No one shall be required to perform forced or compulsory labour.

3 For the purpose of this article the term 'forced or compulsory labour' shall not include:

A any work required to be done in the ordinary course of detention imposed according to the provisions of Article 5 of this Convention or during conditional release from such detention;

B any service of a military character or, in case of conscientious objectors in countries where they are recognised, service exacted instead of compulsory military service;

C any service exacted in case of an emergency or calamity threatening the life or well-being of the community;

D any work or service which forms part of normal civic obligations.

Article 5 Right to liberty and security

1 Everyone has the right to liberty and security of person. No one shall be deprived of his liberty save in the following cases and in accordance with a procedure prescribed by law:

A the lawful detention of a person after conviction by a competent court;

B the lawful arrest or detention of a person for non-compliance with the lawful order of a court or in order to secure the fulfilment of any obligation prescribed by law;

C the lawful arrest or detention of a person effected for the purpose of bringing him before the competent legal authority on reasonable suspicion of having committed an offence or when it is reasonably considered necessary to prevent his committing an offence or fleeing after having done so;

D the detention of a minor by lawful order for the purpose of educational supervision or his lawful detention for the purpose of bringing him before the competent legal authority;

E the lawful detention of persons for the prevention of the spreading of infectious diseases, of persons of unsound mind, alcoholics or drug addicts or vagrants;

F the lawful arrest or detention of a person to prevent his effecting an unauthorised entry into the country or of a person against whom action is being taken with a view to deportation or extradition.

2 Everyone who is arrested shall be informed promptly, in a language which he understands, of the reasons for his arrest and of any charge against him.

3 Everyone arrested or detained in accordance with the provisions of paragraph 1.c of this article shall be brought promptly before a judge or other officer authorised by law to exercise judicial power and shall be entitled to trial within a reasonable time or to release pending trial. Release may be conditioned by guarantees to appear for trial.

4 Everyone who is deprived of his liberty by arrest or detention shall be entitled to take proceedings by which the lawfulness of his detention shall be decided speedily by a court and his release ordered if the detention is not lawful.

5 Everyone who has been the victim of arrest or detention in contravention of the provisions of this article shall have an enforceable right to compensation.

Article 6 Right to a fair trial

1 In the determination of his civil rights and obligations or of any criminal charge against him, everyone is entitled to a fair and public hearing within a reasonable time by an independent and impartial tribunal established by law. Judgment shall be pronounced publicly but the press and public may be excluded from all or part of the trial in the interests of morals, public order or national security in a democratic society, where the interests of juveniles or the protection of the private life of the parties so require, or to the extent strictly necessary in the opinion of the court in special circumstances where publicity would prejudice the interests of justice.

2 Everyone charged with a criminal offence shall be presumed innocent until proved guilty according to law.

3 Everyone charged with a criminal offence has the following minimum rights:

A to be informed promptly, in a language which he understands and in detail, of the nature and cause of the accusation against him;

B to have adequate time and facilities for the preparation of his defence;

C to defend himself in person or through legal assistance of his own choosing or, if he has not sufficient means to pay for legal assistance, to be given it free when the interests of justice so require;

D to examine or have examined witnesses against him and to obtain the attendance and examination of witnesses on his behalf under the same conditions as witnesses against him;

E to have the free assistance of an interpreter if he cannot understand or speak the language used in court.

Article 7 No punishment without law

1 No one shall be held guilty of any criminal offence on account of any act or omission which did not constitute a criminal offence under national or international law at the time when it was committed. Nor shall a heavier penalty be imposed than the one that was applicable at the time the criminal offence was committed.

2 This article shall not prejudice the trial and punishment of any person for any act or omission which, at the time when it was committed, was criminal according to the general principles of law recognised by civilised nations.

Article 8 Right to respect for private and family life

1 Everyone has the right to respect for his private and family life, his home and his correspondence.

2 There shall be no interference by a public authority with the exercise of this right except such as is in accordance with the law and is necessary in a democratic society in the interests of national security, public safety or the economic well-being of the country, for the prevention of disorder or crime, for the protection of health or morals, or for the protection of the rights and freedoms of others.

Article 9 Freedom of thought, conscience and religion

1 Everyone has the right to freedom of thought, conscience and religion; this right includes freedom to change his religion or belief and freedom, either alone or in community with others and in public or private, to manifest his religion or belief, in worship, teaching, practice and observance.

2 Freedom to manifest one's religion or beliefs shall be subject only to such limitations as are prescribed by law and are necessary in a democratic society in the interests of public safety, for the protection of public order, health or morals, or for the protection of the rights and freedoms of others.

Article 10 Freedom of expression

1 Everyone has the right to freedom of expression. This right shall include freedom to hold opinions and to receive and impart information and ideas without interference by public authority and regardless of frontiers. This article shall not prevent States from requiring the licensing of broadcasting, television or cinema enterprises.

2 The exercise of these freedoms, since it carries with it duties and responsibilities, may be subject to such formalities, conditions, restrictions or penalties as are prescribed by law and are necessary in a democratic society, in the interests of national security, territorial integrity or public safety, for the prevention of disorder or crime, for the protection of health or morals, for the protection of the reputation or rights of others, for preventing the disclosure of information received in confidence, or for maintaining the authority and impartiality of the judiciary.

Article 11 Freedom of assembly and association

1 Everyone has the right to freedom of peaceful assembly and to freedom of association with others, including the right to form and to join trade unions for the protection of his interests.

2 No restrictions shall be placed on the exercise of these rights other than such as are prescribed by law and are necessary in a democratic society in the interests of national security or public safety, for the prevention of disorder or crime, for the protection of health or morals or for the protection of the rights and freedoms of others. This article shall not prevent the imposition of lawful restrictions on the exercise of these rights by members of the armed forces, of the police or of the administration of the State.

Article 12 Right to marry

Men and women of marriageable age have the right to marry and to found a family, according to the national laws governing the exercise of this right.

Article 13 Right to an effective remedy

Everyone whose rights and freedoms as set forth in this Convention are violated shall have an effective remedy before a national authority notwithstanding that the violation has been committed by persons acting in an official capacity.

Article 14 Prohibition of discrimination

The enjoyment of the rights and freedoms set forth in this Convention shall be secured without discrimination on any ground such as sex, race, colour, language, religion, political or other opinion, national or social origin, association with a national minority, property, birth or other status.

Article 15 Derogation in time of emergency

1 In time of war or other public emergency threatening the life of the nation any High Contracting Party may take measures derogating from its obligations under this Convention to the extent strictly required by the exigencies of the situation, provided that such measures are not inconsistent with its other obligations under international law.

2 No derogation from Article 2, except in respect of deaths resulting from lawful acts of war, or from Articles 3, 4 (paragraph 1) and 7 shall be made under this provision.

3 Any High Contracting Party availing itself of this right of derogation shall keep the Secretary General of the Council of Europe fully informed of the measures which it has taken and the reasons therefor. It shall also inform the Secretary General of the Council of Europe when such measures have ceased to operate and the provisions of the Convention are again being fully executed.

Article 16 Restrictions on political activity of aliens

Nothing in Articles 10, 11 and 14 shall be regarded as preventing the High Contracting Parties from imposing restrictions on the political activity of aliens.

Article 17 Prohibition of abuse of rights

Nothing in this Convention may be interpreted as implying for any State, group or person any right to engage in any activity or perform any act aimed at the destruction of any of the rights and freedoms set forth herein or at their limitation to a greater extent than is provided for in the Convention.

Article 18 Limitation on use of restrictions on rights

The restrictions permitted under this Convention to the said rights and freedoms shall not be applied for any purpose other than those for which they have been prescribed.

There are three broad categories of right: some rights are absolute; others are derogable (meaning that a state may place limits on them in times of national emergency); and others are qualified rights, which must be balanced against other rights.

- An **absolute right** is a right that cannot be restricted: for example, there are no circumstances under which the UK may torture someone (subject to discussions about what constitutes torture). But absolute rights may be subject to limitations, as contained within the text of the right: for example, the right to life does not prevent the armed forces from killing someone in the heat of battle as a matter of self-defence and where the use of force was no more than was necessary to achieve that aim.

- **Derogable rights** are those that, under normal circumstances, cannot be restricted. However, in a time of national emergency, the ECHR provides that a contracting state may derogate, limiting the operation of the right for the duration of the national emergency, subject to meeting certain procedural requirements as set out in the Convention.

- **Qualified rights** are different: they are rights that have to be balanced against a set of circumstances to determine the extent to which they may be lawfully and proportionately restricted. For example, the right to freedom of thought, conscience, and religion is not absolute—it may be lawfully restricted if the circumstances so require, as may rights such as the freedom of expression, and the right to the respect of one's private and family life, one's home, and one's correspondence (which also includes basic privacy protection).

The European Convention contains all three broad categories of rights, as indicated in Figure 9.1.

NOTE

This is where many students get a bit stuck, because some think that all rights are absolute and cannot be restricted under any circumstances. It is important to understand the differences between the three types of right and which ones fall into which category.

The UK has also ratified optional Protocols 1, 6, and 13, which provide additional rights.

Figure 9.1

Absolute rights in the ECHR	Derogable rights in the ECHR	Qualified rights in the ECHR
Art 2: Right to life Art 3: Freedom from torture or inhuman or degrading treatment or punishment Art 4: Freedom from slavery (Art 4(1) only) Art 7: No punishment without law (the prohibition on retroactive law)	Art 4: Freedom from compulsory labour (Art 4(2) only) Art 5: Right to liberty and security Art 6: Right to a fair trial	Art 8: Right to respect for private and family life, home, and correspondence Art 9: Freedom of thought, conscience, and religion Art 10: Freedom of expression Art 11: Freedom of peaceful assembly and association with others, including the right to join trade unions Art 12: Right to marry (men and women) and to found a family (although not easily qualified)

It may help if we consider the operation of a qualified right in practice. The next subsection will illustrate the operation of a qualified right—Article 8, the right to respect for private and family life, home, and correspondence—in a little more detail.

9.3.3 The right to respect for private and family life, home, and correspondence: an example

One of the most frequently discussed rights on undergraduate and graduate diploma courses is the right to respect for private and family life, sometimes referred to as the right to privacy. This freedom is one that has to be balanced against other rights and freedoms so as to maximise everyone's rights. Respect for Article 8 is considered to be one of the hallmarks of a free and democratic society, coupled with Article 10, the right to freedom of expression. The two often come into apparent conflict. Why would the state wish to restrict either of these two rights? In relation to the right to a private and family life, the police may believe that they need to keep an individual under surveillance in order to collect intelligence information to thwart a potential crime or to solve a crime that has already been committed. The state may also believe that it needs to access someone's medical records or to hold someone in quarantine in a situation in which that person is deemed to be a real threat to public health owing to the virulence of an infectious disease with which he or she is infected. In relation to Article 10, freedom of expression, the state may have a legitimate interest in restricting certain types of broadcast and publication, in order to protect the population from harm. This leads policymakers into difficult territory, because assessment of harm in this respect can be very difficult and value-laden. Over time, the UK has liberalised its policies on freedom of expression—but certain categories of material (such as child pornography) remain banned, as do other images and words that may be deemed to corrupt, deprave, or injure. The courts have the right to restrict publication and broadcast of certain material so as to protect a person's Article 8 right. As you will see, there are circumstances in which, in order to maximise the rights of one group of people, the rights of another group may be subject to restriction. However, any restriction must be lawful and no greater than is necessary to secure the outcome required. The text of Article 8 is as follows.

European Convention on Human Rights

. . . .

Article 8

1. Everyone has the right to respect for his private and family life, his home and his correspondence.

2. There shall be no interference by a public authority with the exercise of this right except such as is in accordance with the law and is necessary in a democratic society in the interests of national security, public safety or the economic well-being of the country, for the prevention of disorder or crime, for the protection of health or morals, or for the protection of the rights and freedoms of others.

thinking point

To what extent do you consider privacy to be more important than the public's right to know, and to be able to say and publish, information about people or entities other than themselves? What sort of information is it in the public's interest to know even if it breaches someone's privacy for it to be known? And is your decision affected by whether the information relates to people whom you know or to strangers?!

cross reference

The proportionality test is considered in some detail in Chapter 18.

As you will see from the text, Article 8(1) indicates the nature of the right and Article 8(2) indicates lawful restrictions that may be placed on the right. But even restrictions deemed to be lawful, falling under the terms of Article 8(2), will need to be proportionate. The proportionality test is not contained within the text, although it is an integral part of interpreting restrictions placed on each qualified right.

Our discussion of an ECHR right would not be complete without considering it within the context of the UK's dualist status. As we have discussed previously, some states take a *monist* approach to international law. In those states, international obligations entered into by the state, such as the ECHR, automatically become a part of national law. The UK adopts a *dualist* approach to international law under which treaties have no effect in domestic law unless they are 'incorporated' into domestic law by an Act of Parliament. Consequently, the ECHR has no effect within the domestic jurisdiction unless and until Parliament so decides through parliamentary enactment. Parliament did not pass law to permit UK courts to apply ECHR rights until 1998, with the passage of the Human Rights Act. One case that addressed the application of Article 8 in the UK prior to the introduction of that Act is *Malone v Metropolitan Police Commissioner (No 2)* (1979) Ch 344, which is useful in this context because it demonstrates the way in which the domestic courts referred to the ECHR prior to the Human Rights Act 1998, and also the role of the ECtHR in this regard. It also provides evidence of what would happen as regards the ECHR were the 1998 Act to be repealed. In this case, Malone argued that his right to a private and family life had been breached by the police, whom he claimed had unlawfully tapped (that is, bugged) his telephone. The extract below illustrates the courts' position prior to the incorporation of the ECHR into the domestic sphere via the Human Rights Act 1998.

● ***Malone v Metropolitan Police Commissioner (No 2)*** [1979] Ch 344

Sir Robert Megarry VC at 362:

> With that, I turn to Mr. Ross-Munro's second main contention, based on the Convention. As I have mentioned, there were two limbs: first, that the Convention conferred direct rights on citizens of the United Kingdom, and, second, that the Convention should be applied as a guide in interpreting and applying English law in so far as it is ambiguous or lacking in clarity...

He continued at 365–6:

> I have devoted some space to setting out a summary of the *Klass* decision because Mr. Ross-Munro placed so much weight on it, and because of the background that it provides for the present case. The main thrust of his argument, which had a number of facets to it, was that although a treaty forms no part of the law of this country, it might nevertheless have some effect in English law. In this case, he said, the Convention, as construed in the *Klass* case, could and should have a significant effect in determining what the law was on a point which, like this, was devoid of any direct authority. On this, he put before me a number of recent authorities in the Court of Appeal. In these, the high water mark for his purpose was, I think, the judgment of Scarman L.J. in *Pan-American World Airways Inc. v. Department of Trade* [1976] 1 Lloyd's Rep. 257, 261. After stating that the treaty there in question was 'no part of the law of England',

Scarman L.J. referred to a situation where it would be proper for the courts to take note of an international convention. That arose when two courses were reasonably open to the court, but

'one would lead to a decision inconsistent with Her Majesty's international obligations under the convention while the other would lead to a result consistent with those obligations. If statutory words have to be construed or a legal principle formulated in an area of the law where Her Majesty has accepted international obligations, our courts—who, of course, take notice of the acts of Her Majesty done in the exercise of her sovereign power—will have regard to the convention as part of the full content or background of the law. Such a convention, especially a multilateral one, should then be considered by courts even though no statute expressly or impliedly incorporates it into our law.'

There was then a reference to two of the cases which were cited to me, both of which concerned the Convention now before me ...

It is not for me, sitting at first instance, to resolve the variant shades of meaning in the dicta, and I do not attempt to do so. For the present, all that I say is that I take note of the Convention, as construed in the *Klass* case, and I shall give it due consideration in discussing English law on the point. As for the direct right which the Convention confers, it seems to me to be plain that this is a direct right in relation to the European Commission of Human Rights and the European Court of Human Rights, the bodies established by the Convention, but not in relation to the courts of this country. The Convention is plainly not of itself law in this country, however much it may fall to be considered as indicating what the law of this country should be, or should be construed as being.

Sir Robert Megarry acknowledged that the Convention may act as a guide to what the UK state had intended by way of its domestic law. Where there is ambiguity of meaning in UK law, judges assume that Parliament intended to pass law so as to meet the UK's international obligations. However, Sir Robert noted that the Convention had no force of law in the UK and could not confer directly enforceable rights on individuals via the British courts. In this case, the application was dismissed. Malone took his case on to the ECtHR, which found that the UK had indeed breached his Article 8 right through the use of telephone-tapping powers that were not authorised by a clear and transparent legal procedure. This is necessary to fulfil the Article 8(2) text: 'There shall be no interference by a public authority with the exercise of this right except such as is in accordance with the law.' Communications may be intercepted as long as the interception is of a type that would be deemed 'necessary in a democratic society', and for at least one of the reasons listed in the text thereafter, such as 'the prevention of disorder or crime', and as long as domestic law so provides. Note that, in the domestic case, Malone took action against the police, but at the ECtHR, the action was against the UK. This is because the ECHR is a treaty to which states subscribe. Consequently, any legal action must be made against the contracting party—the state—rather than against another public body. This illustrates the vertical nature of human rights protection under this international mechanism.

As a result of this judgment, the UK enacted new legislation, the Interception of Communications Act 1985, which provided a statutory basis for telephone tapping by the state with the aim of countering the ECtHR's criticisms of its common law scheme. The new law set out the circumstances under which a person may lawfully tap a telephone, and the offence and potential penalties for those who intercept communications, including phone calls, unlawfully. These fulfilled the Article 8(2) requirements for the procedures to be 'authorised by law'. As you will see, there are a number of factors that must be considered before it is possible to say with certainty whether a qualified human right has been breached. This will be considered in much more detail in Chapters 17 and 20 on administrative law.

This legislation gave power to the state to intercept communications. It did not authorise interception by private bodies and legislation has since been enacted to render this activity by private bodies illegal—hence the controversy, at the time of writing, around the newspaper 'Hackgate' scandal.

summary points

What is the history of the European Convention on Human Rights in a UK context and what is the ECHR's legal standing?

- *The ECHR is an international treaty associated with membership of the Council of Europe.*

- *The ECHR is made up of civil and political rights.*

- *These human rights and fundamental freedoms may be categorised as absolute, derogable, and qualified.*

- *The rights do not form part of UK law, because they are a form of international rather than domestic law.*

- *However, individuals may assert these rights against the UK, if necessary in the European Court of Human Rights in Strasbourg.*

- *With the introduction of the Human Rights Act 1998, the rights may also be asserted in domestic courts.*

9.4 What is the Human Rights Act 1998 (HRA 1998) and how does it operate in the UK?

So far, we have examined human rights in general and the ECHR in particular, but we have noted that because the UK is a dualist state, the Convention does not in and of itself have any force of law within the UK. The next extract charts the mounting pressure to give effect to Convention rights within the UK and the attempts to bring forward legislation that would require the UK courts to interpret UK law so as to give effect to Convention rights. Early attempts focused on according the ECHR similar status to European law, whereas the final text of the Human Rights Act 1998 was more of a compromise so as to ensure broad support for the proposal.

● **A. Lester QC and K. Beattie, 'Human rights and the British constitution', in J. Jowell and D. Oliver (eds)** *The Changing Constitution* (6th edn, Oxford: Oxford University Press, 2007), pp. 59–83, at 66–8

The first public call for the incorporation of Convention rights by statute was made in 1968.[1] In 1974, Lord Scarman gave his great authority to the campaign to make the Convention directly enforceable, in his radical Hamlyn Lecture.[2] In 1976, the Home Secretary, Roy Jenkins, published a little-noticed discussion paper on the subject,[3] and gave his personal support for incorporation. In 1977, the Northern Ireland Standing Advisory Committee on Human

Rights published a report unanimously recommending incorporation.[4] In 1978, a Lords Select Committee also recommended incorporation.[5] However, the only political force in favour of incorporation was the Liberal Party.

During the 1980s, especially after the emergence of Charter 88 an influential political movement, support for incorporation became more widespread, not least among senior judges. The Conservative and Labour Parties remained opposed to incorporation.[6]

On 1 March 1993, the then Leader of the Labour Party, John Smith, QC, gave a lecture under the auspices of Charter 88, entitled 'A Citizen's Democracy'. It represented a turning point in Labour Party policy on human rights in the UK, calling for statutory incorporation of the Convention, and a Human Rights Commission to advise on and bring human rights cases. The 1993 Labour Party Conference adopted a policy document[7] supporting a two stage process on human rights in the UK: first, the incorporation of the Convention and, secondly, the establishment of an all-party commission to consider and draft a home-grown Bill of Rights.

In 1994, Lord Lester of Herne Hill introduced in the House of Lords the first of two Private Member's Bills to incorporate the Convention into UK law.[8] The first Bill adopted a strong form of incorporation; it sought to give the Convention a similar status in UK law as is given to directly effective European Community law under the European Communities Act 1972, empowering the courts to disapply inconsistent existing and future Acts or Parliament, and creating effective remedies for breaches of Convention rights. The Bill had a turbulent passage through the Lords, and was mutilated by wrecking amendments supported by Conservative ministers.

By then, the most senior judges, including the Lord Chief Justice, Lord Taylor of Gosforth, Lord Brown-Wilkinson, and Lord Woolf of Barnes supported the Bill, but given a political climate of concern about threats to parliamentary sovereignty perceived to come from the supremacy of European Community law, they suggested that it would be prudent to adopt a model that did not give the courts an express power to disapply or strike down inconsistent legislation. Their advice was heeded.

Lord Lester's second Bill, introduced in 1996[9] ... was to be influential in shaping what became the Human Rights Act 1998 ...

In December 1996 Jack Straw MP, the then Shadow Home Secretary, and Paul Boateng MP, produced a consultation paper, *Bringing Rights Home*,[10] which set out the Labour Party's proposals for incorporation. In March 1997, the Labour and Liberal Democrat Joint Consultative Committee on Constitutional Reform ... published its report. The joint report closely reflected the model of incorporation adopted in Lester's second Private Member's Bill ...

On 1 May 1997, Tony Blair's New Labour Party was returned to office. In October 1997 the Government published a White Paper, *Rights Brought Home: The Human Rights Bill*,[11] together with the Bill itself. The Human Rights Act 1998 received the Royal Assent on 9 November 1998. It was brought fully into force on 2 October 2000.

1 A. Lester, *Democracy and Individual Rights* (Fabian Tract No. 390, London: Fabian Society, November 1968).

2 Lord Scarman, *English Law: The New Dimension* (London: Hamlyn Trust, 1974).

3 R. Jenkins, '*Legislation on Human Rights*', with Particular Reference to the European Convention on Human Rights (London: HMSO, June 1976).

4 Northern Ireland Standing Advisory Committee on Human Rights, *The Protection of Human Rights in Northern Ireland* (Cmnd 7009, London: HMSO, 1977).

5 Report of the Select Committee on a Bill of Rights (HL 176, London: HMSO, 1978). There was a bare majority in favour caused by Baroness Gaitskell's refusal to adopt the negative Labour Party line.

6 The Fundamental Freedoms and Human Rights Bill, introduced by Lord Broxbourne in 1985, was passed by the Lords and later introduced into the Commons by Sir Edward Gardner, QC, MP. The Bill received broad cross-party support from the Liberal Democrat front bench and the Conservative and Labour back benches, but it was opposed by the government and Labour front benches, and failed to obtain a sufficient majority to be given a Second Reading (109 HC Official Report, 6 February 1987, cols 1223–89).

7 Labour Party Policy Commission, *A New Agenda for Democracy: Labour's Proposals for Constitutional Reform* (London: Labour Party, 1993).

8 Human Rights Bill, Second Reading Debate (560 HL Official Report, 25 January 1995), col. 144.

9 Human Rights Bill, Second Reading Debate (568 HL Official Report, 5 February 1997), cols 1725–30.

10 J. Straw MP and P. Boateng MP, *Bringing Rights Home: Labour's Plans to Incorporate the European Convention on Human Rights into UK Law* (London: HMSO, December 1996), the text of which was published in [1997] EHRLR 71.

11 Cm 3782 (London: HMSO, 1997).

We pick up the story at the point at which the Human Rights Act, as it became, was proposed in the White Paper that preceded it. The White Paper provides useful evidence about the purpose of the Act and the way in which it was structured so as to attempt to protect parliamentary supremacy. The HRA 1998 incorporates into UK law the rights guaranteed by UK signature of the ECHR. Its purpose, as stated in the White Paper, was to enable:

● **Home Office, *Rights Brought Home: The Human Rights Bill*** (Cm 3782, London: HMSO, October 1997), para. 1.18

> …people to enforce their Convention rights against the State in British courts, rather than having to incur delays and expense which are involved in taking a case to the European Human Rights Commission and the court in Strasbourg.

Thus the HRA 1998 does not provide a new set of rights, but instead provides a new mechanism for enforcement of existing rights through the domestic courts. It did not incorporate the rights into a Bill of Rights in the UK with overriding effect.

● **Home Office, *Rights Brought Home: The Human Rights Bill*** (Cm 3782, London: HMSO, October 1997), para. 2.13

> [The] courts should not have the power to set aside primary legislation, past or future, on the ground of incompatibility with the Convention. This conclusion arises from the importance which the Government attaches to parliamentary sovereignty.

cross reference

Contrast the HRA 1998 provisions with the ECA 1972 provisions that led to the Factortame decision, set out in Chapter 8.

The basic features of the Act are that the courts in the UK are required to take the Act (and therefore Convention rights) into account, as stated in section 3. They are required to use techniques of statutory interpretation so as to render UK law compatible with Convention rights, unless this is not possible without a strained interpretation of UK primary legislation. This may be contrasted with the terms of the European Communities Act 1972 (ECA 1972) in respect of EU law, which does have overriding effect in some circumstances, even if this means disapplying a UK statute so as to give effect to EU law. Judges are also required to take into account the case law of the ECtHR when interpreting the scope of the right in issue (see section 2 of the HRA 1998).

Human Rights Act 1998

Section 3 Interpretation of legislation

(1) So far as it is possible to do so, primary legislation and subordinate legislation must be read and given effect in a way which is compatible with Convention rights.

265

(2) This section—

   (a) Applied to primary legislation and subordinate legislation whenever enacted;

   (b) Does not affect the validity, continuing operation or enforcement of any incompatible primary legislation; and

   (c) Does not affect the validity, continuing operation or enforcement of any incompatible subordinate legislation if (disregarding any possibility of revocation) primary legislation prevents removal of the incompatibility

cross reference

Entrenchment is discussed in Chapters 3 and 7.

The HRA 1998 has not been entrenched and therefore can be repealed, as with any other Act of Parliament (subject to *obiter* comments in *Thoburn*, as discussed in Chapter 7). However, Convention rights are not in themselves part of the HRA 1998 and therefore cannot be repealed by Act of Parliament. The UK would still be bound by the rights in international law unless it were able to negotiate a withdrawal from the ECHR and the Council of Europe.

Because Convention rights are not embedded in our legal system and do not have higher constitutional importance, later primary legislation may prevent the courts from directly enforcing Convention rights through national law. Where UK primary legislation contradicts an ECHR right, judges in UK courts are required to apply UK law. Where a conflict between UK law and the ECHR arises, the judge in the High Court or above must invite the **Crown** to take part in the case (section 5 of the HRA 1998). If a conflict remains between the ECHR right and UK law, then the judge may declare the primary legislation incompatible with the ECHR (section 4 of the HRA 1998). However, the judge may not set aside the legislation, but instead must decide the case according to the domestic primary legislation (section 4 of the HRA 1998). This may not be the end of the story, however: the declaration of incompatibility triggers a referral of the matter to the government. The government may then choose to take remedial action via a fast-track amendment route, which makes use of delegated legislation so as to speed up the process to bring an end to the incompatibility (section 10 of the HRA 1998).

thinking point

What do you think about this? Should these rights be overriding? And if so, how do you think this should be achieved? You may want to revisit Chapter 7 for help with your answer.

Human Rights Act 1998

. . . .

Section 4 Declaration of incompatibility

(1) Subsection (2) applies in any proceedings in which a court determines whether a provision of primary legislation is compatible with a Convention right.

(2) If the court is satisfied that the provision is incompatible with a Convention right, it may make a declaration of that incompatibility.

(3) Subsection (4) applies in any proceedings in which a court determines whether a provision of subordinate legislation, made in the exercise of a power conferred by primary legislation, is compatible with a Convention right.

(4) If the court is satisfied—

    (a) that the provision is incompatible with a Convention right, and

    (b) that (disregarding any possibility of revocation) the primary legislation concerned prevents removal of the incompatibility,

it may make a declaration of that incompatibility.

(5) In this section 'court' means—

    (a) the Supreme Court;

    (b) the Judicial Committee of the Privy Council;

    (c) the Courts-Martial Appeal Court;

    (d) in Scotland, the High Court of Justiciary sitting otherwise than as a trial court or the Court of Session;

    (e) in England and Wales or Northern Ireland, the High Court or the Court of Appeal.

(6) A declaration under this section ("a declaration of incompatibility")—

    (a) does not affect the validity, continuing operation or enforcement of the provision in respect of which it is given; and

    (b) is not binding on the parties to the proceedings in which it is made.

At the time of writing, there have been twenty-seven declarations of incompatibility in the UK, of which nineteen were upheld in whole or in part. Details of the action taken may also be found in the Annex to *Responding to Human Rights Judgments: Report to the Joint Committee on Human Rights on the Government's Response to Human Rights Judgments 2010–11* (Cm 8162, London: HMSO, September 2011). But there will be circumstances in which UK law is not at odds with the ECHR and it is a **public authority** that has chosen to breach an ECHR right. In this circumstance, a judge does have the power to require the breach to be remedied. Section 8 sets out the remedies open to the judges if they conclude that there has been a breach of the HRA 1998 by a public authority. The judge may award **damages** for a breach of an ECHR right by a public authority, although this remedy is discretionary and may be given only subject to the following.

Human Rights Act 1998

. . . .

Section 8

. . .

(3) No award of damages is to be made unless, taking account of all the circumstances in the case, including—

    (a) any other relief or remedy granted, or order made, in relation to the act in question (by that or any other court) and

    (b) the consequences of any decision (of that or any other court in respect of that act) the court is satisfied that the award is necessary to afford just satisfaction to the person in whose favour it is made.

There is no direct remedy in respect of primary legislation being incompatible with an ECHR other than a declaration of incompatibility. The only route open to the applicant in this situation would be to take the case to the ECtHR in Strasbourg, which will decide the case on the basis of the ECHR right rather than give overriding effect to domestic law. The next extract explains the operation of section 4 of the HRA 1998 and provides an assessment of its relationship with parliamentary supremacy.

● **F. F. Davis, 'Extra-constitutionalism, the Human Rights Act and the "labour rebels": applying Prof Tushnet's theories in the UK'** [2006] 4 Web Journal of Current Legal Issues, available online at http://webjcli.ncl.ac.uk/2006/issue4/davis4.html

Extra-constitutionalism and the HRA

The HRA, which was passed as part of the New Labour agenda of constitutional reform, incorporates the ECHR into UK law. It is a highly significant piece of legislation since it allows UK citizens to enforce their Convention rights in the domestic courts (s.6 HRA, 1998). S.3(1)of the HRA provides that all primary and secondary legislation must, so far as is practical, be interpreted in a way which is compatible with the HRA. This is the nearest thing the UK has to an enforceable Bill of Rights. However, the HRA was drafted in such a way as to respect the UK constitutional doctrine of Parliamentary Supremacy. It achieves this balance through s.4 which allows the courts to make a declaration of incompatibility where legislation contravenes Convention rights and the primary legislation prevents the removal of that incompatibility. Significantly, unlike a judgment of the US Supreme Court to the effect that legislation is unconstitutional, a declaration of incompatibility 'does not affect the validity, continuing operation or enforcement of the provision in respect of which it is given' (s.4(6)(a) HRA, 1998). Following a s.4 declaration where 'a minister of the Crown considers that there are compelling reasons for proceeding under this section, he may by order make such amendments to the legislation as he considers necessary to remove the incompatibility' (s.10(2) HRA, 1998). Importantly, however, the minister and Parliament are not compelled to amend the legislation. The reason for this is because any element of compulsion would be an attempt to fetter future Parliaments and would, as such, violate the concept of Parliamentary Supremacy.

In *Ghaidan v. Godin-Mendoza* [2004] UKHL 30 Lord Steyn analysed the application of s.3 and s.4 of the HRA. He concluded that the courts were over utilising the declaration of incompatibility function of s.4. According to Lord Steyn the primary objective of the HRA was to give domestic effect to Convention rights. As such s.3 must be the 'prime remedial measure, and s. 4 a measure of last resort' [2004] UKHL 30, 46. Lord Steyn was concerned that the s.4 was being over utilised because the courts were unwilling to exercise their function under s.3 for fear of breaching Parliamentary Sovereignty. He dismissed this argument noting that 'if Parliament disagrees with an interpretation by the courts under s.3(1), it is free to override it by amending the legislation and expressly reinstating the incompatibility' [2004] UKHL 30, 43. Lord Steyn's final conclusion was 'to emphasise that interpretation under s.3(1) is the prime remedial remedy and that resort to s.4 must always be an exceptional course' [2004] UKHL 30, 50.

...

If s.4 of the HRA provides an example of extra-constitutionalism in operation why have the media and the government reacted to s.4 declarations as if they were judicial rulings of unconstitutionality? Following the initial ruling of the House of Lords in *A & others v. Secretary of State for the Home Department* [2004] UKHL 56 the UK *Daily Telegraph* announced that the judgment had 'left the government's policy on how to deal with foreign terrorists in...a giant mess'.[1] Two days earlier, the same newspaper said that 'the government is caught between a rock and a hard place. The rock is the threat from international terrorists and what to do about them; the hard place is that European human rights laws make it very difficult to do anything'.[2] Furthermore, in a letter to his new Home Secretary, John Reid, Prime Minister Tony Blair, referring to the HRA, stated: 'we will need to look again at whether primary legislation is needed to address the issue of court rulings which overrule the government'.[3] Such reactions appear to misunderstand the power of the courts in HRA cases.

[1] A. Palmer, 'It's a giant mess', *Daily Telegraph*, 19 December 2004.

[2] P. Johnston, 'Terrorism v. human rights', *Daily Telegraph*, 17 December 2004.

[3] N. Temko and J. Doward, 'Revealed: Blair attack on human rights law', *The Observer*, 14 May 2006.

This extract indicates that section 4 declarations of incompatibility do not, at least in legal terms, undermine parliamentary supremacy. Parliament is free to choose whether to leave the Act in force unamended or to bring it into line with the Convention. In political terms, it appears that, thus far, the government and Parliament have felt compelled to amend legislation declared to be incompatible with a Convention right or rights. This is an interesting development, and somewhat at odds with reported discussions by government ministers and senior members of the official Opposition that it may be better to amend the HRA 1998 so as to remove any obligation that Parliament feels it has to change the law following a declaration of incompatibility.

But how are Convention rights interpreted by judges? When may a breach be remedied? The following box lists considerations when interpreting Convention rights.

Considerations when interpreting Convention rights

1 Identify the right in issue.

2 How has the right been interpreted by the courts in the past? What is its extent? For example, the phrase 'freedom of expression' is not very revealing in itself—what has previous ECtHR case law to say on the nature, extent, and range of the right in issue?

3 Has the public authority appeared to act in a way that would be contrary to the right (when considering the case law) and therefore breached section 6(1) of the HRA 1998, unless section 6(2) applies (see point 4 below)? If section 6(2) does not apply, then the public authority has acted in breach of the HRA 1998 if case law indicates that the public authority's behaviour would be a breach of the Convention right.

4 Is there UK law in place that authorises or requires the public authority to act in a way that appears to be contrary to the Convention right? If so, reconsider the Convention right in light of any lawful restrictions permitted within the Article. Does the UK legislation fall within those restrictions?

5 If the restrictions placed on the right by UK law are lawful, are they proportionate?

6 Finally, conclude whether UK law is incompatible with the Convention right or not.

In short, a breach of a Convention right may be remedied if the breach was committed by a public authority exercising a public function and if the breach was not authorised by primary legislation. However, there is no domestic remedy for a breach that is authorised by primary legislation incompatible with the Convention right. This will be discussed in much more detail in Chapters 17 and 19 on administrative law.

summary points

What is the Human Rights Act 1998 (HRA 1998) and how does it operate in the UK?

• *Courts can review executive and public authority action against the HRA 1998 to ensure that they are not acting contrary to the HRA 1998 by unlawfully breaching* a Convention right. Any unauthorised breach of the HRA 1998 may be remedied by the courts.

- The HRA 1998 requires judges to interpret UK law so as to give effect to the ECHR, as far as it is possible to do so (under section 3).

- Primary legislation that is in direct conflict with one or more Convention rights cannot be held to be invalid or disapplied. Instead, the higher courts may issue a declaration of incompatibility to indicate that the legislation is incompatible with the terms of the ECHR (under section 4 of the HRA 1998).

- The executive and then Parliament have the final say on whether or not incompatible UK law should be amended via **remedial order** or Act of Parliament so as to bring it into line with the ECHR. Thus parliamentary supremacy is preserved.

- Where the UK law remains in breach of the ECHR and Parliament does not change the law, an individual whose ECHR rights have not been capable of remedy via the British courts may take his or her case to the ECtHR in Strasbourg, although the ECtHR's judgment is not overriding in the UK.

- However, it is argued that if Parliament always changes UK law as a matter of course so as to ensure that it meets the requirements of the ECHR, then in all practical terms parliamentary supremacy has, at least while the HRA 1998 remains in force, been restricted.

9.5 How do the ECHR and the HRA 1998 affect parliamentary supremacy?

The ECHR is not superior to domestic statutes. Judges have to 'take into account' the judgments, decisions, declarations, and advisory opinions of organs of the Council of Europe, but are not bound by them. They do not affect the validity or operation of any statute; nor do they affect the position of the parties before the court. The court may issue a declaration of incompatibility in respect of a statute if domestic law is incompatible with the ECHR. A fast-track procedure is adopted for changing legislation that is declared incompatible. As a matter of domestic law, it is open to ministers and Parliament not to change incompatible legislation (under section 6(6) of the HRA 1998).

The **victim** may take his or her case to the ECtHR not as an *appeal* (actions before the ECtHR are not appeals), but as an action in international law under the Convention. If the ECtHR agrees that there has been a breach of the ECHR, the government will be liable to remedy the violation as a matter of international law. However, as discussed above, it is not possible to enforce an ECtHR judgment in the domestic sphere and so the individual is reliant on the state's willingness to abide by the Strasbourg Court's ruling. Parliamentary sovereignty is thus preserved, although the UK would face continued pressure from the Court until such time as it did abide by the Court's judgment and the ECHR. This is the case, at present, in respect of ECtHR judgments against the UK as regards the continuing ban on prisoners' rights to vote in breach of the ECHR, such as *Hirst v the United Kingdom (No 2)* [2005] ECHR 681.

There is an ongoing debate about whether human rights protections are being strengthened over time and whether the original drafters of the ECHR really intended human rights minimum protections to become so strong. The next extract explains this debate, and also provides some evidence in support of and against the proposition that human rights have changed from minimum protections to stronger political and legal protections that limit the state's power.

● **D. Nicol, 'Original intent and the European Convention on Human Rights'** [2005] Public Law 152, 152–4 and 170–2

…It has often been assumed that the ECHR founders only intended to guarantee the rights already protected by the contracting states back in the 1950s.[1] Their aim, in other words, was solely to prevent the descent into dictatorship threatened by a fascist revival or pro-Soviet coup. This widespread belief has led national politicians and judges to attack the European Court of Human Rights for disregarding the ECHR's origins, arguing that the history of the Convention's negotiations favours a restrictive interpretation of its provisions. They accuse the Court of imposing upon Europe a US-style Bill of Rights wholly unintended by the ECHR founding fathers. British opponents of the Court's interpretative strategy have particularly frequent recourse to this argument, and their frustration is understandable in view of the misconceptions entertained by the UK government of the day…

These expectations have long since been dashed by the case law of the Court, which both rejects the strictures of the ECHR text in favour of a teleological emphasis on effectiveness,[2] and also treats the ECHR as a living instrument, the interpretation of which it can update in response to changing social conditions.[3] Nonetheless, the conviction that the framers only ever meant to establish an anti-Nazi, anti-Stalinist charter, designed to have little impact on states in no danger of succumbing to dictatorship, continues to damage the Court's legitimacy, certainly in the United Kingdom. The argument focuses on the ECHR's substantive content: the Court is accused of going beyond the basic 'core' of human rights in a way which was never intended. Thus, for example, Michael Howard, in the wake of the *Thompson and Venables* judgment[4] argued that anyone who had signed the ECHR in the wake of the Second World War's unspeakable horrors would have reacted with utter disbelief at the Court's 'insatiable compulsion' to intervene.[5] Similarly, in the aftermath of *Osman v UK*,[6] Lord Hoffmann accused the Court of straying beyond the undisputed minimum content of human rights upon which the ECHR negotiations were premised, thereby submerging Britain's own hierarchy of moral values and sense of fairness under a pan-European jurisprudence:

> When we joined, indeed, took the lead in the negotiation of the European Convention, *it was not because we thought it would affect our own law*, but because we thought it right to set an example for others and to help to ensure that all the Member States respected those *basic* human rights which were not culturally determined but reflected our common humanity.[7]

Lord Scott advanced essentially the same argument in *Harrow LBC v Qazi* when he appealed to original intent reasoning to justify a restrictive interpretation of ECHR rights in the field of local authority housing:

> The Universal Declaration and the Convention were the product of the horrors of fascism which led to World War II and the Holocaust. One of the recitals to the former records that 'disregard and contempt for human rights have resulted in barbarous acts which have outraged the conscience of mankind'. The intention of these instruments was to enshrine fundamental rights and freedoms. It was not the intention to engage in social engineering in the housing field.[8]

The charge levied against the Strasbourg Court is potentially deeply damaging. Critics contend that the ECHR was not meant to curb the freedom of action of nation states save for their 'freedom' to become dictatorships. Accordingly the Court is accused of restricting the political liberty of the states (and their electorates) not merely when it comes to true, 'core' fundamental rights, but also in the case of matters which constitute the ordinary stuff of democratic politics, and which accordingly should be allowed to vary from state to state. The ECHR, it is argued, was never intended to intrude into such matters, which should rather be resolved through the democratic process. One consequence is that the Court is undermining precisely the political democracy it was designed to protect.

This accusation implicitly assumes, however, that the other framers broadly shared the British view. Fifteen states signed the ECHR in 1950. Let us accept the finding that most of the British contingent at the negotiations never wanted the Convention to go beyond an antitotalitarianism measure. The question remains whether the same was true of those representing the other contracting states...

...

In fact, analysis of the travaux préparatoires goes nowhere near establishing the existence of such a consensus. To be sure, the British and certain others wanted the ECHR to be just an exercise in conservation,[9] designed to censure only a 'flagrant violation of a principle on which all the world is agreed'.[10] But the desire to limit the ECHR to an anti-dictatorship device cannot be considered as representing the general view. Rather, the negotiators were split into two camps with competing ideologies. One camp believed that the ECHR should indeed only serve to protect existing rights, the other camp pursued the more ambitious goal of a cross-frontier Bill of Rights... [An]... explanation relates to constitutional culture. Countries with a strong faith in a written constitution enshrining supra-legislative rights were pitted against countries where the political culture did not favour review of parliamentary legislation.[11]...

Once the ECHR was in force, the negotiators merely passed the baton to the judges to continue the disagreement. Thus the same argument was played out in the European Court of Human Rights, in which a majority treated the ECHR as a 'living' Bill of Rights whilst a minority maintained that the ECHR was intended solely to prevent European countries becoming one-party states...

1   See, e.g., A. Drzemczewski, *The European Human Rights Convention in Domestic Law* [Oxford: Clarendon Press, 1983], pp. 6–7; L. Sohn and T. Buergenthal, *International Protection of Human Rights* [Indianapolis, IN: Bobbs-Merrill, 1973], p. 1149; Travaux Préparatoires (TP) IV, p. 252 [Belgium, Denmark, France, Ireland, Italy, Luxembourg, Norway, Sweden, and Turkey].

2   See, e.g., *Golder v UK* [1975] 1 EHRR 524. This was produced by the UK; TP V, p. 68.

3   See, e.g., *Tyrer v UK* [1978] 2 EHRR 1; TP V, p. 114. Once again, such declarations could be made for a specific period.

4   *T v UK; V v UK* [2000] 30 EHRR 121; H. Rolin, 'Has the European Court of Human Rights a future?' [1965] 11 Howard Law Journal 442.

5   Hansard [16 December 1999], vol. 341, col. 403; C. Morrisson Jr, *The Dynamics of Development in the European Human Rights Convention System* [The Hague: Martinus Nijhoff, 1981], p. 19.

6   [2000] 29 EHRR 245; *Golder v UK* [1975] 1 EHRR 524.

7   Lord Hoffmann, 'Human rights and the House of Lords' [1999] 62 Modern Law Review 159 [emphasis added]; *Tyrer v UK* [1978] 2 EHRR 1.

8   [2003] UKHL 43, [2004] 1 AC 983, [123]. See further I. Loveland, 'The impact of the Human Rights Act on security of tenure in public housing' [2004] Public Law 594, 601–2. The passage appears to have the approval of Lord Hope in *Harrow LBC v Qazi* [2003] UKHL 43, [2004] 1 AC 983, [48].

9   TP V, p. 326 [Mr Beaufort, Netherlands]; B. Simpson, *Human Rights and the End of Empire* [Oxford: Oxford University Press, 2001], p. 5.

10 Article 1(b); TP II, p. 262 [Mr Philip, France].

11 For example, TP I, pp. 2, 4, 6, 8, 16, 22, 28, and 86, TP IV, p. 1, and TP V, p.34. Similarly, the Committee of Ministers discussed the 'definition, safeguarding and development of human rights and fundamental liberties', the word 'development' again indicating forward movement as opposed to simply safeguarding those rights already guaranteed by governments at the time: TP I, p. 10. This reading would explain, for example, the strong support of Irish politicians for an interventionist ECHR, despite Ireland's common law legal system. Similarly, Dutch negotiators sided with the British on such issues as the establishment of the Court, the right of petition, and the need for detailed definition of the rights, even though the Netherlands is a civil law country.

Nicol concludes that there were two distinct views about the purpose of the ECHR: one, the British view, that it was a minimum protection regime; and the other that it was to advance the political movement of individual rights. Just as the Convention drafters disagreed on its purpose, so have ECtHR judges. This debate remains live. Nicol, in his later 2006 article (see the further reading list at the end of the chapter), goes further to argue that we should recognise the political nature of rights, and allow Parliament to engage in this political debate, and to discuss and to reach decisions about the content of rights. He suggests that British judges are currently placed in this position as a result of their interpretive duty under the terms of the HRA 1998, and that this masks the political dimension of rights and the legitimate debates about morality, scope, and the public good. This view is interesting, because it is in contrast to the debate about the need to entrench human rights in a document of higher constitutional importance beyond the reach of Parliament. It reasserts the importance of Parliament's legislative supremacy by arguing that the current formulation of human rights goes beyond basic and fundamental rights that provide minimum protections, but instead institutionalises one view of the way in which the individual and the state should relate. Further, this masks the very real differences of opinion about expression, religion, and ideology that have to be balanced in any complex state, and provides one possible interpretation as *the* only interpretation on how those competing views should be resolved. This not only limits parliamentary supremacy, but also political and public discussion about the appropriate balance of rights for this society. This is in contrast to Lester's human rights discussion in the extract above, which highlights the introduction of a (later defeated) private member's Bill that would have introduced an EU-style implementation of the ECHR that would have had overriding effect in UK law had it been passed. The next section will consider the differences between the way in which the ECHR and the EU law have been incorporated into the UK domestic sphere, and the effect of these arrangements.

summary points

How do the ECHR and the HRA 1998 affect parliamentary supremacy?

- *There are disagreements about the extent to which membership of the Council of Europe, signature of the ECHR, and the enactment of the HRA 1998 affect parliamentary supremacy.*

- *In legal terms, the HRA 1998 does not affect the continuing operation of any Act of Parliament and therefore it could be argued that it does not affect parliamentary supremacy.*

- *In political terms, recent governments and Parliament appear to have felt compelled to amend statutes that are declared incompatible with the ECHR.*

- *Some scholars and practitioners argue that the tension set up between judges and Parliament as a result of the HRA 1998 is a positive one, because it requires all sides to consider human rights and politicians to have strong reasons for restricting rights if they deem it to be necessary.*

- *Others argue that the HRA 1998 has placed judges in a difficult political position, and that politicians should be prepared to take back the political responsibility for interpreting and developing human rights in the UK.*

9.6

How does the human rights context differ from the EU context as regards parliamentary supremacy?

Treaties are negotiated by the executive as an exercise of the **royal prerogative**, but ratification is a matter for Parliament. The Constitutional Reform and Governance Act 2010 gives

Parliament the opportunity to scrutinise treaties prior to ratification. In order for a treaty or other international obligation to have effect in national law in the UK, it must be 'incorporated' by an Act of Parliament. UK judges may not apply international law in the domestic courts until such time as an Act of Parliament authorises them to do so. This is illustrated in the following brief extract.

● **Cheney v Conn** [1968] 1 WLR 242

Mr Justice Ungoed-Thomas at 245:

> First, International Law is part of the law of the land but it yields to statute. That is made clear by *Inland Revenue Commissioners v Collco Dealings Ltd* where Lord Simmonds quoted with approval, and in accordance with the decision of the House of Lords in that case, *Maxwell on the Interpretation of Statutes*. I quote the 10th ed. (1953) at p 148: 'But if the statute is unambiguous, its provisions must be followed even if they are contrary to international law.' ... Secondly, conventions which are ratified by an Act of Parliament are part of the law of the land. And, thirdly, conventions which are ratified but not by an Act of Parliament, which thereby gives them statutory force, cannot prevail against a statute in unambiguous terms ...

He continued at 247:

> What the statute itself enacts cannot be unlawful, because what the statute says and provides is itself the law, and the highest form of law that is known in this country. It is the law which prevails over every other form of law, and it is not for the court to say that a parliamentary enactment, the highest law in this country, is illegal.
>
> ...

The decision to incorporate an international obligation will often depend on the terms of the international treaty itself. Some treaties require that their terms be incorporated into domestic law; others require the contracting state to respect the terms of the treaty, but do not require direct incorporation. The UK has taken different approaches in respect to incorporation of EU law into the domestic sphere and the ECHR. There is an essential difference between European Union law and the European Convention on Human Rights: it is a requirement of membership of the European Union that member states give priority to directly effective EU law in their own legal systems, but there is no such explicit requirement in the Convention. The impact on parliamentary supremacy consequently differs. Figure 9.2 sets out the similarities and differences in respect of EU law and the ECHR.

thinking point

What do you think of the differences between the effect of EU law and Convention rights in the UK? Would it be better to adopt the same system for both? If yes, why? If not, why not? And which of the two systems do you favour and why?

What does this mean in real terms? Some EU law provisions are overriding in UK law and primary legislation may have to be set aside in order to allow the EU provisions to be given effect. This does not happen in relation to Convention rights, because they do not have overriding status. Were the EU Charter of Rights to be given overriding status in the UK, this would mean that these rights (similar in nature, in some respects, to those in the ECHR) would be overriding. The UK has opted out of the Charter in so far as it would extend the competence of the European Court of Justice or allow individuals to assert Charter rights against the UK. However, the Charter will shape the development of EU law and thus will have some effect within the

Figure 9.2

Incorporation of European Union Law (Membership of the European Union)	**Incorporation of the European Convention on Human Rights** (Membership of the Council of Europe)
Domestic legislation that effected incorporation: **European Communities Act 1972**	Domestic legislation that effected incorporation: **Human Rights Act 1998**
Under s 2 ECA 1972, judges are under a duty where there is ambiguity in the meaning of UK law: **to interpret UK law ambiguity, where possible, so as to give effect to EU law* and the case law of the ECJ (and related courts).**	Interpretive duty on UK judges where ambiguity in the meaning of UK law: **to interpret UK law ambiguity, where possible, so as to give effect to the ECHR and case law of the ECtHR (and related courts).**
Interpretive duty on UK judges where UK law conflicts with the provisions of EU law: **in most instances, to apply EU law (treaty provisions, regulations, and in some circumstances directives), and if necessary to disapply UK law.**	Interpretive duty on UK judges where UK law conflicts with the provisions of ECHR: **to apply UK law and possibly to issue a declaration of incompatibility.**
In this instance, a domestic remedy may be provided.	**In this instance, no domestic remedy.**
Appeals on points of EU law to the ECJ and related courts.	Appeals in relation to UK conformity to the ECHR to the ECtHR and related courts.

* Not all EU law is overriding in the UK: most of the overriding EU legislation is first pillar law. This issue may be covered in more detail in your EU law course.

UK. What does this all mean for parliamentary supremacy? The next extract is taken from a case heard in the Court of Appeal. It sets out Lord Justice Laws' views on the changes being made to parliamentary supremacy.

. . . .

● *International Transport Roth GmbH and others v Secretary of State for the Home Department* [2002] EWCA Civ 158

Lord Justice Laws:

> [71] In its present state of evolution, the British system may be said to stand at an inter-mediate stage between parliamentary supremacy and constitutional supremacy, to use the language of the Canadian case. Parliament remains the sovereign legislature; there is no su-perior text to which it must defer (I leave aside the refinements flowing from our membership of the European Union); there is no statute which by law it cannot make. But at the same time, the common law has come to recognise and endorse the notion of constitutional, or funda-mental rights. These are broadly the rights given expression in the European Convention on Human Rights and Fundamental Freedoms ('ECHR'), but their recognition in the common law is autonomous:... The Human Rights Act 1998 ('HRA') now provides a democratic underpin-ning to the common law's acceptance of constitutional rights, and important new procedural

> measures for their protection. Its structure, as has more than once been observed, reveals an elegant balance between respect for Parliament's legislative supremacy and the legal security of the Convention rights.

Laws LJ appears to be arguing that, in relation to human rights protection, we may be moving in the general direction of EU law towards overriding protection of rights. He argues that we may be at a halfway house at the moment, where parliamentary supremacy is largely still intact, but Parliament feels bound by the ECHR and also common law human rights protections. We shall see how this develops over time, but there is still evidence to suggest that Parliament is free, at least in law, to legislate in contravention of the ECHR (although this would be a breach of international law). Whether Parliament feels politically compelled to respect the terms of the Convention is less clear—but we do have evidence that Parliament has enacted law that has been declared to be incompatible with the ECHR even after the entry into force of the HRA 1998.

summary points

How does the human rights context differ from the EU context as regards parliamentary supremacy?

- *Where a UK Act of Parliament conforms to EU law and the ECHR, the Act will be applied as written.*
- *Where an Act of Parliament is ambiguous in its meaning, it will be interpreted (under the terms of the ECA 1972 and the HRA 1998) so as to give effect to the relevant EU legal provision or Convention right.*
- *The difference becomes apparent when an Act contradicts either a provision of EC law or an Convention right.*
  - *Some provisions of EU law have overriding effect. The courts are required to apply the EU legal provision and dto isapply the Act.*
  - *The ECHR has no overriding effect in the UK. The courts are required to apply the UK statute if there is a direct contradiction with an ECHR right. The judge may issue a declaration of incompatibility. The alleged victim may take the case to the ECtHR.*

9.7 Is the current system of human rights protection in need of reform, or does parliamentary supremacy appear to provide adequate protection?

Thus far, we have considered that the ECHR does not form part of UK law, although domestic judges are under a duty to apply UK law so as to conform to the UK's commitments under the ECHR where it is possible for them to do so. This suggests that judges are faced with the unenviable task of reinterpreting UK law using techniques of statutory interpretation so as to strain the meaning of British Acts of Parliament, in order to protect the rights of British citizens. It also implies that if a judge were unable to do this, then he or she would be powerless in the face of the breach of a human rights unless the executive and Parliament were to agree to change the law. This troubles many law students, perhaps understandably, because it suggests that there is little domestic human rights protection. Others may be worried that the courts have too much power and Parliament too little. However, there have been relatively few declarations of incompatibility since the entry into force of the Human Rights Act in 1999 in Scotland and 2000 in the rest of the UK. And although there are calls to strengthen our human rights protection, there are others who consider that the current balance between parliamentary supremacy and human rights protection is about right; others, including senior members of the Conservative Party (such as David Cameron and Theresa May) consider that the HRA 1998 should be repealed so as to rebalance the powers of the courts and Parliament in favour of Parliament. This has led to the establishment of a British Bill of Rights Commission. In the extract below, Professor Harlow provides evidence to the Joint (Parliamentary) Committee on Human Rights on this point. The extract is a relatively long one, but sets out the complexity of the arguments with some clarity.

● **Joint Committee on Human Rights, 'Written Evidence: 14. Memorandum from Carol Harlow, Emeritus Professor of Law, London School of Economics'** (20 June 2007), available online at http://www.publications.parliament.uk/pa/jt200708/jtselect/jtrights/165/165we15.htm

1. Is A British Bill of Rights Needed?

Britain already has a Bill of Rights: the European Convention. To add something further would in all probability merely be confusing, especially as the European Union has approved a further text, which although not binding is likely to prove influential: the ill conceived and badly drafted Charter of Fundamental Rights and Freedoms (ECFR).

The main purpose of a specifically British Bill of Rights would be to provide 'ownership' of the document, which would add something positive to the current debate about the nature of British citizenship. Since the content would be controversial (see below) the effects might, however, be less positive than anticipated.

A further important function for a British Bill of Rights would be to act as a defence against incursions by transnational jurisdictions . . . The absence in the United Kingdom of a Bill of Rights at a time when the Convention was not incorporated created a suspicion that the United Kingdom did not recognise human rights. Steps were taken (of which arguably the Human Rights Act was one) to remedy this problem . . . A British Bill of Rights would in this way strengthen the position of the United Kingdom before international courts.

On the other hand, there is a very real danger in a proliferation of texts on human rights (and more especially of jurisdictions concerned to enhance their competence) that protection will be watered down because signatories and the judiciary will be able to 'cherry pick' between the texts . . .

If we were to add a further text to what we already have, the United Kingdom would be subject to the ICCR and specific UN conventions; the European Convention as implemented by the Human Rights Act and interpreted by the ECtHR and domestic courts; the ECFR as interpreted in binding judgements of the ECJ; and a British Bill of Rights as interpreted by our Supreme Court. There is considerable variance between the texts.

. . .

3. Constitutional Relationships

Although in theory a Bill of Rights strengthens the hand of the judiciary against the executive, in practice much depends on culture and the relative power of the two institutions. Whether the judges possess a 'strike down' power is also a significant factor . . . This is certainly the Canadian experience.

Is the current system of human rights protection in need of reform?

277

In the British constitution, the primacy of parliamentary legislation necessarily raises the question of entrenchment, the legal niceties of which are too complex to deal with in this short response. Assuming, however, that a Bill of Rights could be entrenched, would this really be desirable? Serious problems arise with updating entrenched Bills of Rights—such as the argument in the United States over 'gun law'. (See T Macklem, 'Entrenching Bills of Rights' (2006) 26 Oxford Journal of Legal Studies 107).

...Changing the Convention would not be easy; topping it up through the medium of domestic law is much easier as we can see from the experience of anti-discrimination legislation, easily amended to take inside (eg) religious discrimination or with abortion law to take on board medical progress. To put this differently, the common law method combines with parliamentary sovereignty to make law much easier to update. The argument of those who favour an entrenched or semi-entrenched Bill of Rights is, of course, precisely that rights may be swept away too easily, as they have been recently in a series of criminal justice and public order measures; to put this differently, updating is not always what it seems. Which risk can more safely be taken is largely a matter of opinion. (Consider the debate between Lord Lester of Herne Hill and Professor Keith Ewing: K Ewing, 'The Futility of the Human Rights Act' [2004] Public Law 829; A. Lester, 'The Utility of the Human Rights Act: A Reply to Keith Ewing' [2005] Public Law 249).

What appears to be emerging in the common law countries of Australia, New Zealand and the United Kingdom is a more nuanced position in which legislature, courts and administration all feel obligations and join in the attempt to strike appropriate balances between individual human rights protection and interests of the collectivity...Nicol has argued that Parliament, arguably the most representative forum for the discussion of human rights, deserves its own 'voice' independent from government. Arguably, recent institutional changes, including the emergence of new Select Committees is bringing about this effect. The number of committees that now scrutinise draft legislation with human rights in mind is increasing.

This 'dialogue model' of human rights is the one which I am firmly convinced best fits common law countries. We have a powerful media and civil society organisations are already able to join in the media debate and by giving evidence to select committees. It is very desirable that new machinery should be set in place to encourage ordinary people to join in, if only electronically, through 'blogs' and so on...The taking of evidence from the public by parliamentary general committees is another step forward.

...

In conclusion, I believe that the Human Rights Act is working relatively well and should be left to 'bed in'. It is by and large an adequate basis for the protection of human rights in what is inherently a 'political constitution'. There are of course grave weaknesses but where the weaknesses lie is a contentious issue. In recent years, it has been the areas of pre-trial and trial procedure, sentencing and treatment of prisoners and asylum-seekers that have stimulated the loudest calls for reform: but whether the liberties in issue are to be maintained, extended, shored up or curtailed are hotly contested and very political questions. Human rights are not written in stone. They are as controversial as any other area of politics and have, if they are to be truly effective, to be fought for in the same way as all political and social rights. In our political system, discussion tends to crystallise around projected laws or focus on high visibility court cases. Whether a Bill of Rights would change this situation is, I feel, unlikely.

Harlow indicates that there are difficulties with the current position, but there are also difficulties with the perceived solutions. It is not as simple as saying that the UK should have its own Bill of Rights, because these rights may be difficult to amend and may conflict with the other human rights instruments by which the state is bound. This may lead the UK to adopt a relatively toothless version of a Bill of Rights so as to ensure that home-grown legislation does not contradict other provisions from the Council of Europe and the EU, in particular. Or the UK could take the alternative position and adopt an extremely protective mode of human rights protection—but that would seem to be at odds with current public opinion. The **coalition government** (at the instigation of the Conservative Party) has set up a British Bill of Rights Committee to consider the adoption of such a text; the composition of the Commission and its remit have proved controversial. It is still taking evidence at the time of writing, so it is difficult to say whether the Committee will recommend the status quo or the repeal of the HRA 1998 and the introduction of a Bill of Rights. Indeed, it is unclear whether the Bill would take the form of a standard Act of Parliament or would introduce a higher level of law into the UK constitution and thus move the UK in the direction of constitutional supremacy, although that seems unlikely if Parliament's power is to be preserved.

NOTE

You may wish to check the Commission's work and progress. The UK Constitutional Law Group has a good blog that regularly includes information on the Commission's work: http://ukconstitutionallaw.org/blog/

This is an extremely complex debate, which will continue for some time and will involve many different viewpoints. Consider what you believe to be the best position: do nothing and let the HRA 1998 and the ECHR develop over time; work to limit their increasing influence; or work towards a greater degree of domestic human rights protection via a Bill of Rights that is strong and protects minorities, but which restricts Parliament, or one that is weaker, protects Parliament's power, and is more likely to work in favour of dominant public opinion?

summary points

Is the current system of human rights protection in need of reform, or does parliamentary supremacy appear to provide adequate protection?

- *Arguments in favour of a British Bill of Rights include that it may:*
  - *provide more ownership of human rights protections in the UK;*
  - *be politically more acceptable to some;*
  - *protect the UK against the influence of other legal systems;*
  - *give British judges more power, particularly if they were given the power to strike down inconsistent primary legislation, or less power if the Bill of Rights is narrower than the ECHR;*
  - *be difficult to amend, if entrenched, which could lead to greater human rights protection;*
  - *offer more protection of minorities (if strong), or less protection of minorities and more protection of the majority and of Parliament's supremacy (if weak).*
- *Arguments against a British Bill of Rights include that:*
  - *adding another human rights document may create confusion, given that the UK would still be bound by the terms of the ECHR and other international human rights treaties that it has signed;*
  - *it may give judges more power and thus weaken parliamentary supremacy, or it may give them less power and leave minorities less protected;*
  - *it would be difficult to amend, if entrenched, which could lead to undesirable consequences such as unpopular or outdated provisions being difficult to remove.*

Summary

The European Convention on Human Rights (ECHR) is an international treaty that seeks to provide minimum human rights standards in all contracting member states. The UK was one of the countries that founded the Council of Europe and helped to draft the ECHR. The ECHR provides a right of individual petition to the European Court of Human Rights (ECtHR) in Strasbourg. If an individual believes that the UK has breached one or more of his or her ECHR rights, he or she may take a case to the ECtHR. However, since the introduction of the Human Rights Act 1998 (HRA 1998), the alleged victim of the human rights breach must first take his or her claim through the domestic courts. The HRA 1998 requires judges to enforce ECHR rights in the UK, as long as there is no Act of Parliament that authorises a breach of the Convention right in question. Where a public authority has committed an unauthorised breach of the HRA 1998 and an ECHR right, the judge may require the breach to be remedied (and stopped). Where UK law authorises the breach, there is no real remedy that the judge may provide; instead, the judge may issue a declaration that the Act in question is in breach of—incompatible with—the Convention right. It is then for the government and Parliament to decide whether to amend the law to bring it into line with the Convention, or to leave the legislation as originally drafted. This is said to preserve parliamentary supremacy, while at the same time providing a measure of human rights protection from authorised breaches by public authorities.

Questions

1 What do you understand by the term 'human rights'? How do they differ from civil liberties?

2 What are the different waves of human rights?

3 What is the European Convention on Human Rights (ECHR) and how does it operate?

4 What is the Human Rights Act 1998 (HRA 1998) and how does that operate?

5 To what extent does the HRA 1998 allow an effective enforcement of ECHR rights in the UK?

6 How do the terms of the European Communities Act 1972 (ECA 1972) and the HRA 1998 compare and contrast in relation to the application of EU law and the ECHR in the domestic jurisdiction?

7 To what extent would it be better to adopt the ECA 1972 regime in relation to human rights and the HRA 1998 regime in relation to EC law provisions? Why do you believe this and what evidence do you have in support of and against your arguments?

Further reading

Black-Branch, J. L., 'Parliamentary supremacy or political expediency? The constitutional position of the Human Rights Act under British law' (2002) 23 Statute Law Review 59

This article is a good one to read if you want to understand the way in which the Human Rights Act 1998 operates and why.

Evans, C. and Evans, S., 'Legislative scrutiny committees and parliamentary conceptions of human rights' [2006] Public Law 785

This article provides information about how parliamentary committees have scrutinised the protection of human rights in the UK.

Feldman, D., 'The impact of human rights on the UK legislative process' (2004) 25 Statute Law Review 91

This article examines how law-making in the UK has changed in the light of the introduction of the Human Rights Act 1998.

Hiebert, J., 'Parliamentary bills of rights: an alternative model?' (2006) 69 Modern Law Review 7; 'Interpreting a bill of rights: the importance of legislative rights review' (2005) 35 British Journal of Political Studies 235; 'A hybrid approach to protect rights? An argument in favour of supplementing Canadian judicial review with Australia's model of parliamentary scrutiny' (1998) 26 Federal Law Review 115

These articles are useful as a comparative perspective on how a bill of rights operates in Canada, and thus what we could expect in the UK were we to adopt a similar model following the British Bill of Rights Commission.

Klug, F. and Wildbore, H., 'Breaking new ground: the Joint Committee on Human Rights and the role of parliament in human rights compliance' (2007) 3 European Human Rights Law Review 231

This article explains the way in which Parliament's Joint Committee (Commons and Lords) on Human Rights operates and the extent to which it plays a role in scrutinising the government's human rights' record.

Ministry of Justice, *Responding to Human Rights Judgments: Report to the Joint Committee on Human Rights on the Government's Response to Human Rights Judgments 2010–11* (Cm 8162, London: HMSO, September 2011), available online at http://www.justice.gov.uk/downloads/publications/policy/moj/responding-to-human-rights-judgments.pdf

This report gives the government's view on human rights protection, its approach to the European Convention on Human Rights and the Human Rights Act 1998, and also provides a detail of how declarations of incompatibility have been approached since the inception of the Act.

Nicol, D., 'Law and politics after the Human Rights Act' [2006] Public Law 722

This article provides an explanation of the changing face of politics and law-making at Westminster since the introduction of the Human Rights Act 1998.

Simpson, S., *Human Rights and the End of Empire: Britain and the Genesis of the European Convention* (Oxford: Oxford University Press, 2001)

This book details the history of the European Convention and its development, as well as Britain's involvement in the drafting of the Convention.

10

Devolution

Key points

This chapter will cover:

- What is devolution?
- What is the history of devolution?
- In what ways can power be devolved?
- What are the role and powers of the Scottish Parliament?
- What are the role and powers of the Welsh Assembly?
- What are the role and powers of the Northern Ireland Assembly?
- Should there be an English Parliament?
- What effect has devolution had on parliamentary supremacy?

Introduction

This chapter considers devolution and parliamentary supremacy to provide you with a basic understanding of the different devolved institutions. It examines different models of devolution and considers the topical question of whether there should be an English Parliament to complement the Scottish Parliament, and the Northern Ireland and Welsh Assemblies. It concludes by addressing the impact that devolution has had, and may have, on the doctrine of parliamentary supremacy in the UK.

10.1 What is devolution?

In general terms, the process of devolving powers involves the transfer of competence or functions from a central governing administration to a regional body within its jurisdiction. All three main powers of the **state**—the **legislative**, **executive**, and **judicial** powers—may be devolved, either together or separately. The important point about **devolution** that distinguishes it from federal systems (such as in Australia, Canada, Germany, or the United States, for example) is that the central administration does not concede its legislative supremacy. In federal systems, a region may be given its own legislative, executive, and judicial functions in certain policy areas, while the nation's central, federal **government** will have its own legislative, executive, and judicial functions in other policy areas. The two power bases remain separate and are usually outlined in a constitution. The two power bases are also protected via the constitution, which sets out whether the power to do X or Y is held at the federal level or the regional level. At no point can the regional or the federal legally take the power of the other. However, devolution does not work in that way. It may be useful to think of devolution as a way of lending power to another institution: the devolved institution gets to use the power as lent to it, but there is always the possibility, in legal terms at least, that the power may have to be given back to (or may be taken back by) the lending institution. This means that the national-level bodies (legislature, executive, and **judiciary**) retain the legal right to use their power, but they lend elements of the power to regional bodies. The UK operates a form of devolution.

Terminology can be difficult in this area because different states have different ways of describing their overarching structure and their regional or local structures. For example, it is difficult to use the word 'national' in the UK context, because the UK is made up of four separate countries that are described as nations in their own right. In Figure 10.1, the word 'national' has been used to describe the whole nation state, or collection of countries that have come together under some form of unified legislature, executive, and judiciary. The word 'regional' has been used to describe the individual nations, states, or countries within the unified system. The first example, which is of a form of a federal state, is similar in structure to the US. The second example, which is of a devolved state, is similar in structure to the UK. However, neither example is a perfect representation of either, but instead illustrates the difference between the two types of system.

In the UK context, the process of establishing such regional or national devolved bodies began with the holding of successful **referenda** in Scotland, Wales, and Northern Ireland in 1997–98. The results of these referenda led directly to the passing of the Devolution Acts of 1998, whereby three of the four countries of the United Kingdom of Great Britain and Northern Ireland—Scotland, Northern Ireland, and Wales—were granted their own directly elected

Figure 10.1

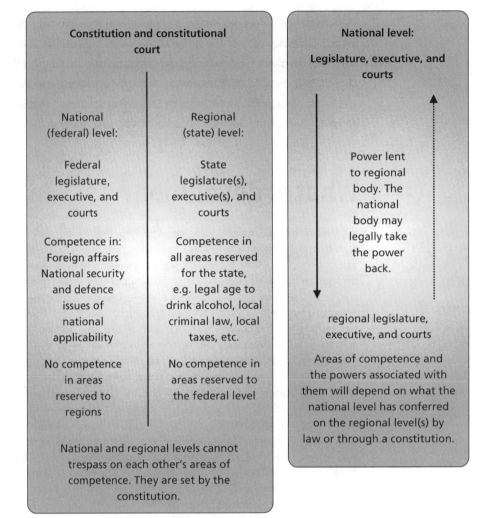

An example of a type of federal system	An example of a devolved system

Constitution and constitutional court

National (federal) level:	Regional (state) level:
Federal legislature, executive, and courts	State legislature(s), executive(s), and courts
Competence in: Foreign affairs National security and defence issues of national applicability	Competence in all areas reserved for the state, e.g. legal age to drink alcohol, local criminal law, local taxes, etc.
No competence in areas reserved to regions	No competence in areas reserved to the federal level

National and regional levels cannot trespass on each other's areas of competence. They are set by the constitution.

National level:

Legislature, executive, and courts

Power lent to regional body. The national body may legally take the power back.

regional legislature, executive, and courts

Areas of competence and the powers associated with them will depend on what the national level has conferred on the regional level(s) by law or through a constitution.

representative bodies. England was the only country of the UK not to be offered such an institution.

By enacting the so-called Devolution Acts—the Scotland Act 1998, the Government of Wales Act 1998, and the Northern Ireland Act 1998—the Westminster **Parliament** established or, in the case of Northern Ireland, reinstated devolved administrations, each with varying degrees of power to formulate and execute policy for the nation in question. There are numerous differences between the settlements created for all three nations, especially in terms of legislative powers, but there are also some notable similarities. One unifying factor is that the Westminster Parliament retains its overall legislative supremacy under each of these devolution settlements. In other words, the Westminster Parliament has reserved the legal right to take back its legislative power by repealing the Devolution Acts if it so chooses. It has also reserved the right to legislate on any matter, notwithstanding that is has devolved power to the three bodies. We shall consider whether it is politically possible or practical for the Westminster Parliament to do this, even though it is within its legal power to do so.

So far, we have talked about powers being devolved, but why have we chosen to use that term rather than the term 'delegated'? In general terms, institutions exercising powers that have been devolved to them have more power to create and execute their own distinct policies, and to do so in their own names (under their own authority), than do bodies that have had powers delegated to them. Therefore although devolved powers are clearly distinguishable from delegated powers, on the one hand, it is also vital that they are distinguished from federal powers, on the other. Federal states, including the most often-quoted examples of such systems, the US and Germany, have distinct constitutional arrangements that differ greatly from that currently seen in the post-devolution UK, as illustrated in Figure 10.1. The essence of federal states is that the central, federal government shares legislative supremacy with the states that constitute the federation. In such a system, the central government will retain complete legislative supremacy in certain policy fields. It will share supremacy with the states in other fields, and in some, supremacy is granted to the state government. Such arrangements and distribution of functions are set out in the country's codified constitution, and the existence and powers of the individual state governments are also set out and protected in the constitution. Indeed, such is the importance of the constitution in such systems that it is debatable whether a federal state can actually exist without a written, codified constitution. As has been discussed in Chapter 3, the UK has no such codified document.

cross reference
Refer back to Chapter 3 on the nature of the British constitution, if necessary.

Thus devolved powers differ greatly from those granted under federal systems, chiefly because of the way in which the central institution—in the UK, for example—has retained legislative supremacy over all matters, irrespective of the amount of power conferred on the newly established national legislatures in Scotland, Wales, and Northern Ireland. Of course, allied to this is the fact that the UK has no single codified constitution that could seek to establish and sustain such a federal state.

● **V. Bogdanor, *Devolution in the United Kingdom*** [Oxford: Oxford University Press, 2001], pp. 2–3

> Devolution involves the transfer of powers from a superior to an inferior political authority. More precisely, devolution may be defined as consisting of three elements: *the transfer to a subordinate elected body, on a geographical basis, of functions at present exercised by ministers and Parliament.* These functions may be either legislative, the power to make laws, or executive, the power to make secondary laws—statutory instruments, orders, and the like—within a primary legal framework still determined at Westminster.
>
> Devolution involves the creation of an elected body, subordinate to Parliament. It therefore seeks to preserve intact that central feature of the British Constitution, the supremacy of Parliament. Devolution is to be distinguished from federalism, which would divide, not devolve, supreme power between Westminster and various regional or provincial parliaments. In a federal state, the authority of the central or federal government and the provincial governments is co-ordinate and shared, the respective scope of the federal and provincial governments being defined by an enacted constitution as, for example, in the United States or the Federal Republic of Germany. Devolution, by contrast, does not require the introduction of an enacted constitution...
>
> Devolution has profound implications for the way in which we are governed, and for the kind of society in which we are to live.

To sum up, devolution is the process whereby the central governing institution confers powers to create legislation (primary and/or secondary) and to execute policies on regional or national administrations within its jurisdiction. It does so without relinquishing its overall legislative supremacy over all fields for all regions or nations that have received devolved powers. As a result, legally at least, it retains the right to legislate for those territories or to revoke the powers in their entirety. This differs considerably from a federal system such as the one used in Germany, under which the constitution of the country establishes and protects the functions and competences of the federal states, and the states share legislative supremacy with the central governing institution, by each having their own topics over which they have legislative supremacy.

In the UK context, the recent process of devolving powers from Westminster was begun by the enactment of the Devolution Acts of 1998, which established directly elected Assemblies for Wales and Northern Ireland and a Parliament for Scotland. The various powers of these institutions will be examined later in the chapter, as will the ways in which the Westminster Parliament ensured that it would remain the supreme law-making institution in the UK.

summary points

What is devolution?

- *Devolution can be defined as the conferral of powers by a central governing institution on a regional or national governing body, without the central institution having to concede legislative supremacy.*

- *Such devolved powers can be administrative, executive, or legislative in nature.*

- *The process of devolving such powers to three of the UK's four nations—Scotland, Wales, and Northern Ireland—was begun by the passing of the Devolution Acts of 1998.*

- *Devolved powers are to be distinguished from ordinary delegated powers by reference to the amount of autonomy granted to the institution exercising the power and by the fact that a devolved body exercises such powers in its own name.*

- *Devolved systems of government are differentiated from federal systems by:*
  - *the lack of constitutional protection to the existence and powers of a devolved body; and*
  - *the way in which federal states share supremacy with the federal government.*

10.2 # What is the history of devolution?

The concept of devolving powers from a supreme political institution to a subordinate body is by no means a new one. As was seen in Chapter 5, legal and political theorists have been debating for many centuries the importance of ensuring that no single governing institution becomes excessively powerful—the essence of the principle of the **separation of powers**. In this respect, the devolution or transfer of powers from a dominant institution to a subordinate one is but one means used over the last few centuries of ensuring that no single institution accumulates too much power. However, devolution is also a product of different peoples' needs to be ruled by those who acknowledge, understand, and respect their cultural and religious identities and their traditions. Devolution may make it possible for these different peoples to remain together in a state that retains popular legitimacy, while allowing peoples to be governed in a manner in keeping with their traditions and identities. While accepting that a devolved administration must always remain subordinate to the power-conferring institution, devolution nevertheless remains a credible way of ensuring that different institutions exercise different functions—that no single body becomes excessively powerful. It is also a method of ensuring local autonomy.

cross reference
This is discussed in Chapter 5 on the separation of powers.

10.2.1 Devolution debates and the American colonies

Devolution can also be used in a number of different contexts, to confer powers and/or functions from a state's central government on a national or regional governing institution, or even to transfer functions from an empire's seat of power to inferior legislatures within its territories. Britain trialled different forms of devolution around the world during the operation of its Empire. Indeed, it is under these circumstances that we find some of the first references to devolutionary schemes as we know them today—those coming from the debates on the political situation in pre-independence America towards the end of the eighteenth century.

Despite not expressly using the term 'devolution' itself, one example of a reference to the existence of such 'devolved' administrations comes from a speech delivered by member of Parliament (MP) and political theorist Edmund Burke to the House of Commons in 1774. Speaking on the issue of taxation in the American colonies, Burke not only acknowledged the existence of the colonial legislatures, but also actively encouraged the transfer of functions to them, including taxation powers. The power to raise taxes is important, because without finance it is virtually impossible for a government to do anything meaningful for its people in a practical sense. Burke noted that, in a situation in which it was impractical to have physical representation of the colonies in Parliament (in this case, in Westminster), it was both acceptable and advantageous for people in the colony to have their own suitably local legislature, provided that that body accepted Westminster's supremacy. He argued that such a body should have tax-raising powers of its own, for the purpose of furthering government in America, rather than the Westminster Parliament raising tax revenue from America.

Although primarily concerned with Westminster's taxation policy in the colonies, Burke delivered a stark general warning to Parliament that if it sought to disregard the will of the people and their regional governing bodies, the natural consequence would be that they would question the very supremacy of the Westminster Parliament. Two things are therefore clear: firstly, that the colonies did have their own representative bodies at that time and that those institutions had significant functions; and secondly, that Parliament failed to heed Burke's warning— the American War of Independence started within a year of Burke delivering his speech, which directly led to America's rejection of the sovereignty of the British Parliament.

. . . .

● E. Burke, Rt Hon, 'American taxation', in *Speeches and Letters on American Affairs* (London: J. M. Dent & Sons Ltd, 1908), pp. 57–61

> Again and again revert to your own principles—seek peace and ensure it—leave America, ... to tax herself ... Do not burden them by taxes; you were not used to do so from the beginning. Let this be your reason for not taxing ...
>
> But if, intemperately, unwisely, fatally, you sophisticate and poison this very source of government, by urging subtle deductions and consequences odious to those you govern, from the unlimited and illimitable nature of supreme sovereignty, you will teach them by these means to call that sovereignty itself in question ... If that sovereignty and their freedom cannot be reconciled, which will they take? They will cast your sovereignty in your face. Nobody will be argued into slavery ...
>
> If this is the case, ask yourself this question, Will they be content in such a state of slavery? If not, look to the consequences. Reflect how you are to govern a people who think they ought to be free and think they are not. Your scheme yields no revenue, it yields nothing but discontent, disorder, disobedience; and such is the state of America, that after wading up to your eyes in blood, you could only end just where you begun; that is, to tax where no revenue is to be found ...

> ...The Parliament of Great Britain sits at the head of her extensive empire in two capacities: one as the local legislature of this island [the UK], providing for all things at home...; the other, and I think her nobler capacity, is what I call her *imperial character*, in which, as from the throne of heaven, she superintends all the several inferior legislatures [around the world], and guides and controls them all, without annihilating any. As all these provincial legislatures are only co-ordinate to each other, they ought all to be subordinate to her [Parliament of Great Britain]; else they can neither preserve mutual peace, nor hope for mutual justice, nor effectually afford mutual assistance. It is necessary to coerce the negligent, to restrain the violent, and to aid the weak and deficient by the overruling plenitude of her power. She is never to intrude into the place of others, whilst they are equal to the common ends of their institution...
>
> Such, Sirs, is my idea of the constitution of the British empire, as distinguished from the constitution of Britain; and on these grounds I think subordination and liberty may be sufficiently reconciled through the whole...

This extract is not an easy one to read, but it illustrates an important point about local legislatures and their powers, as well as their need for finance. It also demonstrates the link between devolution and parliamentary supremacy, and between the legal right of a sovereign Parliament (in this case, the Westminster Parliament) to legislate and the political consequences of it disregarding a subordinate legislative body. Constitutional law is not only about the legal, but also about the political, and, as Burke explains, a legal right enforced by a sovereign Parliament contrary to the wishes of a subordinate legislature and its electorate may have serious political consequences. In this instance, it led to the American War of Independence and finally the forced independence of the Americas from British control.

10.2.2 Home Rule, devolution, and Ireland

The concept of devolving power is therefore far from a new one. However, it was not until the late nineteenth and early twentieth centuries that the term 'devolution' began to be used in today's context, when it was used to describe the various 'Home Rule' schemes that were proposed for Ireland. We shall consider the history of devolving powers to Scotland, Wales, and Northern Ireland later in this chapter; at this stage, it is important to consider in brief the attempts of the UK government to introduce a form of self-government for Ireland between 1886 and 1914, because it is here that the roots of today's devolutionary schemes lie.

The history of Ireland is contested, not least because it was subject to military incursions for many centuries by different peoples. However, Ireland did not become a formal part of the United Kingdom until the enactment of the Act of Union of 1800, despite the fact that Britain had been asserting influence over Ireland for many centuries through Protestant settlement at the expense of the majority Catholic population. Nationalist sentiments in Ireland gained momentum in the second half of the nineteenth century. Direct rule from Westminster gave rise to developing resentment amongst the Irish. This resentment often manifested itself in violent outbursts and in a consistent lack of respect for the laws imposed by the British Parliament. This was especially true in relation to the legislation concerning land tenure. Such legislation had, for many years, ensured the dominant position of the wealthy, mainly Protestant, landowners at the expense of the poorer Catholic majority. This in turn led to a massive surge in support for political parties that called for Irish self-government and Irish independence.

The British government headed by **Prime Minister** William Gladstone responded by legislating to remove or to limit some of the practices that were fuelling Catholic Irish resentment. However, support for a scheme of self-government grew rapidly, so much so that, in the 1885 General Election, eighty-five so-called 'Home Rulers' were returned as members of Parliament to Westminster. The term 'Home Ruler' was used to denote those representatives who supported a form of Irish self-government. This meant that, in effect, Irish Home Rulers held the balance of power at Westminster and could influence the legislative agenda in the House—a situation that Gladstone promptly recognised as one that needed to be given the highest possible political priority.

In order both to satisfy the demands of the MPs in favour of Home Rule and to combat the perceived problem of increasing nationalism in Ireland, Gladstone introduced a Bill to establish Home Rule for Ireland in 1886. The intention of the Government of Ireland Bill 1886 was to establish a legislature in Dublin in which the Irish constituency MPs would sit to legislate on Irish matters. However, the Bill, which was ultimately defeated in the House of Commons, also reserved so-called imperial matters, such as defence and foreign affairs, to Westminster. This meant that only Westminster, and not Dublin, would have had the right to debate and to decide on such matters. In spite of the 1886 scheme being rejected by the House of Commons, Prime Minister Gladstone largely reintroduced his reworked proposals by means of the Government of Ireland Bill 1893. In this Bill, it was envisaged that the Irish constituency MPs would have been permanently based at Westminster, albeit in lesser numbers. In other respects, the final version of the 1893 Bill was very similar in principle to its predecessor. The second Bill also failed; this time, it was the House of Lords and not the Commons that finally rejected it. In doing so, the more conservative House of Lords had very heated discussions on whether it was at all justifiable that MPs representing Irish constituencies would have the right to debate and vote on matters affecting only England (and therefore Wales and Scotland). They were concerned that even though there were very few Irish constituency MPs and that number was set to be reduced were the Bill to be passed, these MPs could still be decisive in debates about domestic matters for England, Scotland, and Wales even though MPs for those constituencies would not have a similar influence over Irish matters devolved to Ireland. Interestingly, this concern is still being debated in the context of devolution to Scotland, Wales, and Northern Ireland, but not England.

In truth, the representation problem was never conclusively resolved. The same solution, that of reducing the number of members representing Ireland, was again preferred in the third Home Rule Bill, introduced to Parliament in 1912. However, despite the fact that the Bill was relatively unchanged from the 1893 one in most respects, its passage through the House of Commons proved relatively straightforward. The resolve of the Commons on the issue of Home Rule had become so strong by 1912 that the government relied upon the provisions of the Parliament Act 1911 so as to pass the Bill when the Lords defeated it again. Therefore the Government of Ireland Act 1914 should have introduced a scheme of devolution to early twentieth-century Britain. There was to be a devolved legislative body based in Dublin, which had legislative control over all Irish domestic affairs and had a completely separate membership from Westminster. Westminster, meanwhile, was to remain supreme, to retain imperial functions at all times, and to be financed via Irish taxes for that purpose. These are all features that are clearly reflected in each and every one of today's devolution settlements in the UK.

Devolution, however, was never to happen in the whole of Ireland. The outbreak of the First World War led to the postponement of the Act's implementation and, by the end of hostilities in 1918, the political situation in Ireland had changed dramatically. In reality, devolution of the kind imagined in 1886–1914 was no longer feasible. On the one hand, the Unionists' opposition to a single Home Rule scheme for the whole of Ireland had strengthened during the war years; on the other hand, the Nationalists, under the guidance of the dominant political party, Sinn Féin (which means 'we ourselves' in Irish Gaelic, although it has also been translated as 'ourselves alone'), had turned its sights towards complete independence. It seemed that no one wanted the Home Rule of 1914. As a result, a second Government of Ireland Act was passed in 1920, providing for two distinct Home Rule regions: one in the north and one in the

cross reference

Refer back to Chapter 7 on the Parliament Acts, if necessary.

south of the country. Despite the amendments, the new Act was also far from welcomed. The Nationalists, sometimes referred to as the Republicans, argued that the whole of the island should be granted independence. They continue to argue for the reunification of Northern Ireland with the Republic of Ireland (that is, Éire) today. The Unionists, sometimes referred to as the Loyalists because they are loyal to the **Crown**, argued that the whole of Ireland should remain part of the United Kingdom. They continue to argue that Northern Ireland should remain part of the UK.

The 1920 Act eventually paved the way for the Northern Ireland Parliament, which remained in existence until 1972. The Southern Ireland Parliament, however, never became a reality. Due to the opposition of the Nationalists, it met only to approve the Anglo-Irish Treaty of 1922, which in effect established the Irish Free State and consequently brought the notion of Southern Ireland and its Parliament to an end. In so doing, it also brought to an end Gladstone's dream of keeping a unified, devolved Ireland as part of Britain. We continue to live with consequences of this time today, with Éire as an entirely independent country and Northern Ireland being part of the United Kingdom of Great Britain and Northern Ireland.

10.2.3 How historical devolution debates have influenced devolution in the UK today

Despite its ultimate failure, much of the discussion on Home Rule in Ireland from 1886 to 1920 is extremely valuable in identifying key aspects of today's devolution settlements. It is clear, for instance, that the Liberal Party's reasoning for attempting to establish Home Rule for Ireland at the end of the nineteenth century was similar in many respects to the reasoning behind devolving powers to Scotland, Wales, and Northern Ireland at the end of the twentieth century. It is also clear that many of the problems that were faced between 1886 and 1920 are still applicable today, albeit in different parts of the UK. Indeed, one could perhaps argue that had devolution happened in the whole of unified Ireland a century ago, many of the difficult questions that we still face would be at least partly solved. Gladstone's primary reasons for suggesting such a Home Rule scheme were twofold. His intention, firstly, was to pacify the Nationalists, or even to stunt the remarkable growth in their support, by offering a form of self-government. However, his other great hope was that allowing Ireland to have its own legislature would strengthen the union with the rest of Britain. Of course, both of these intentions were also present when devolution was on offer for Scotland, Wales, and Northern Ireland in the 1970s and 1990s.

However, as has already been mentioned, the proposals of the second and third Bills were severely criticised for granting the MPs representing Irish constituencies a say in matters that did not directly involve them, because they were also to have a voice in relation to all other matters coming before the Westminster Parliament. Once again, this argument is one that is continuously raised with reference to today's devolution settlements, especially with regard to Scotland, since Scottish constituency MPs retain a say in all Westminster parliamentary business.

In fact, so fierce was the debate at the turn of the twentieth century about the role of the MPs from Irish constituencies that some suggested that devolution of this nature should happen in Ireland only if it were also to happen in all of the other nations of the UK, including England. Under this notion—what Vernon Bogdanor today terms 'federal devolution'—all nations would have their own legislatures for domestic affairs. As a result, the UK Parliament would legislate only on matters of imperial importance. Consequently, the representatives from Ireland would have had a role to play only in domestic affairs and in matters common to all nations. Parliament would retain its legislative supremacy in the background, in relation to matters individual to all four nations, but in practice would leave those issues to the four devolved bodies. Instead, it would exercise its day-to-day legislative supremacy in respect of matters that affected all four countries together. This model is distinguishable from a true federal constitution model, because, in a true federal model, the individual countries would have a protected sphere for legislative competence in that their power could not be removed by the central Westminster Parliament. The federal devolution debate and the federal constitution debate are still raging today in the discussion surrounding the calls for an English Parliament, an issue that will be addressed later in the chapter.

To sum up, it is important to remember that devolution is far from being a new concept. In fact, the earliest ancestors of today's settlements are to be seen in the relationship between Britain and its American colonies, over 200 years ago. However, the more recent, refined, examples of proposed devolutionary schemes come from the discussions on Irish Home Rule at the turn of the twentieth century. Despite the fact that Irish devolution ultimately failed, the debates that surrounded the proposals are highly informative and provide valuable insights into the discussions that surround devolution nowadays. Questions addressed later in the chapter on whether there should be an English Parliament and whether or not devolution has had any effect on parliamentary supremacy are far from new. In order to understand them properly, one must first of all understand their historical basis.

thinking point

To what extent do you agree that history has had an enormous impact on the legal and political development of our constitutional settlement?

summary points

What is the history of devolution?

- *Its roots lie in Britain's relationship with the American and other colonies. Edmund Burke, amongst others, advocated the transfer of power to regional legislatures in America.*

- *Burke felt that recognising such legislatures was the most effective way of pacifying the colonies.*

- *The first examples of devolution within the UK emanate from the Irish Home Rule debates of the late nineteenth century.*

- *Despite never becoming reality in the whole of Ireland, many of the principles applied to the Irish question have been reapplied to the debate surrounding devolution in Scotland, Wales, and Northern Ireland.*

10.3 In what ways can power be devolved?

cross reference

If you are unsure what these terms mean, you may wish to refer back to Chapter 5 on the separation of powers.

An institution can receive its powers in many different ways. The nature of these powers and the method of conferral determines whether a devolved body exercises administrative, executive, or legislative power. Before one can go on to establish the true nature of the devolutionary schemes introduced in Scotland, Wales, and Northern Ireland, it is essential briefly to examine the main features of administrative, executive, and legislative devolution. The extract below provides a short discussion of the different types of devolution that will be examined in this section.

● C. Munro, *Studies in Constitutional Law* (2nd edn, London: Butterworths, 1999), pp. 33–4

'Devolution' is an inexact term. The Royal Commission on the Constitution, which reported in 1973, defined it as 'the delegation of central government control powers without the relinquishment of sovereignty'.[1] That description, apart from its exclusion of federalism, was advisedly imprecise. There are different kinds of powers which might be distributed, and different ways of distributing them.[2] It is a type of devolution when powers with regard to a particular function or service are distributed, as for example to the Post Office or to the Arts Council. But, in this country recently, devolution has normally been used to describe a distribution of powers on a geographical basis to the different parts of the United Kingdom.

In that context, the Royal Commission went on to describe and discuss three models of devolution.[3] Under 'legislative devolution', the power to legislate, to settle policies and to administer might be devolved on elected assemblies in respect of specified subjects, with the central legislature retaining ultimate power to legislate on all matters. Under 'executive devolution', directly elected regional assemblies might be responsible for devising regional policies and administering regional affairs, in accordance with laws and general policies made by the legislature and central government. A third type 'administrative devolution',[4] would involve the central government, without the creation of new regional institutions of government, arranging for aspects of its work to be conducted on a regional framework or in a regional setting.

These were only working definitions, but they suffice to show something of the variety of possible arrangements. The Royal Commission would have had in mind that Scotland and Wales already had measures of administrative devolution. The Commission also sat against the backcloth of a disintegrating system of legislative devolution in Northern Ireland, where home rule from Stormont was proving unsustainable.

1 *Report of the Royal Commission on the Constitution 1969–1973* (Cmnd 5460, London: HMSO, 1973) (the Kilbrandon Report), Pt X1, para. 543.

2 See H. Calvert, 'Devolution in perspective', in H. Calvert (ed.) *Devolution* (London: Professional Books, 1975).

3 Kilbrandon Report, para. 546 and chs 17, 18, and 21.

4 The phrase has been criticised as a misnomer: see A. W. Bradley, 'Devolution of government in Britain: some Scottish aspects', in Calvert (ed.), op. cit.

We shall consider legislative devolution, followed by executive devolution and administrative devolution, before we consider the devolution settlements in Scotland, Wales, and Northern Ireland.

10.3.1 Legislative devolution

In the context of devolution in the UK, it is probably sensible to begin with legislative devolution, because it is the most advanced form of power transfer within a system based on parliamentary supremacy. This is the form of devolution that was proposed for Ireland at the start of the twentieth century and it is also the most relevant to today's discussions of devolution in the UK. In essence, legislative devolution involves conferring power on a devolved institution to allow it to formulate policy in selected fields, to legislate (pass primary legislation) on those specific policy areas, and to execute and administer the policy. Of course, as was emphasised in the section on Home Rule in Ireland, the power-conferring institution, Westminster, retains its supremacy at all times. It also retains numerous functions that are deemed to be better suited to be centrally governed—the so-called 'reserved matters'.

Setting aside for now the issue of which policy fields can be devolved, most of the major questions in this respect arise in relation to the way in which the dominant institution retains its supremacy. In the UK context, the Kilbrandon Commission Report of 1973 stated that, in the case of legislative devolution, not only was supremacy retained by virtue of the fact that Parliament could at any time repeal the primary legislation that devolves powers to a body (known as the enabling legislation), but legally it could also choose to legislate on any issue, including devolved matters, even if the enabling legislation remained in force. This means that, despite conferring full legislative power in a particular field on a devolved administration, Westminster could still choose to legislate on the field in question. Indeed, in legal terms, it could even do so contrary to the wishes of the devolved institution.

However, there remains a distinction between legal rights, on the one hand, and political reality, on the other. Westminster has legally retained its right to legislate on all matters for all nations; however, one must also recognise that this is not the whole story. In its report, in which it recommended legislative devolution for Scotland, the Kilbrandon Commission stressed the importance of a good working relationship between both devolving and devolved administrations. As part of that relationship, it was felt that the general rule should be that, ordinarily, Parliament would not legislate contrary to the wishes of the devolved region, nor would it seek to 'block' legislation passed by the devolved body for a non-legal reason. It could be argued that, in practical terms, the Westminster Parliament's sovereignty has been limited during the operation of devolution unless the people in a given country are willing to have power taken from their regional body and returned to Westminster. Alternatively, one could argue that Westminster is sufficiently secure in the knowledge that it retains legal sovereignty that it is willing to devolve some of its legislative power to a local body.

Devolved administrations are usually formed by the enactment of primary legislation that establishes a new institution, sets out the mechanisms for the election of members, and prescribes the functions that are to be exercised by it. This piece of legislation is normally referred to as the 'enabling legislation'. There are two main ways of transferring power to a devolved body. The first is to list the policy areas in which powers have been reserved for central government. This is the option that transfers most functions to the devolved institution—that is, the devolved administration can legislate on any matter not listed in the legislation. The second option would be to list only the fields in which the devolved administration has powers; the remaining fields would be reserved for the central administration. Clearly, this would be more limiting for the devolved body. In both cases, it is assumed that functions would be devolved in fields such as education, health, local government, and transport, whereas fields such as the administration of justice would be more controversial and dependent on the strength of support for devolution. We shall consider this in the context of the individual devolution settlements for the three devolved bodies, as well as the way in which disputes about legislative competence are to be resolved. The next extract explains legislative devolution.

. . . .
● **Royal Commission on the Constitution 1969–73, _Report: Vol. I_** (Cm 5460, London: HMSO, 1973), pp. 234–5

768. We envisage, therefore, that any scheme of legislative devolution would involve the transfer to the region of power to determine policy in prescribed subjects and to enact legislation to give effect to it, and that, while there would be some restrictions on the powers of the region in relation to finance...there would otherwise be no restrictions on the use of the devolved powers. The sovereign powers of Parliament would be retained in full, but there would be a [constitutional] convention that those powers would not ordinarily be used to legislate on a transferred matter without the consent of the region. The powers would, however, be available for use in exceptional circumstances...United Kingdom Ministers would also have a

power, exercisable perhaps only with the approval of Parliament, to veto regional legislation considered to be unacceptable. But this power, like that of securing Parliamentary legislation without the agreement of the region, would in practice have to be regarded as a weapon of last resort. Frequent recourse to either of them would be bound to undermine regional autonomy and the smooth working relationship between central and regional authorities which would be essential to good government.

769. In examining the scope for legislative devolution it has therefore to be assumed that these reserve powers could not often be used to veto regional policies or to impose central government policies on an unwilling region.

770. Any form of devolution which involves the sharing of powers between two levels of government will work only if there is a readiness on both sides to co-operate in making it work. In the case of legislative devolution, this means that the central government must be prepared to allow maximum freedom to the region in respect of the transferred matters, to accept that in a clash of views on which a compromise does not prove possible the regional view will generally have to prevail, and to use its reserve powers only when the issue at stake is such that it is left with no possible alternative.

771. If it is not accepted that both central and regional authorities could be relied upon to strive to administer a scheme of legislative devolution in this spirit of co-operation, legislative devolution is not to be contemplated. But if it is accepted, there would in our view be considerable scope for devolution.

In short, legislative devolution involves a devolved institution receiving power to create and execute policies by means of both primary and secondary legislation. As the above extract emphasises, the power-conferring institution retains its supremacy at all times, but these supreme powers are not ordinarily to be used contrary to the wishes of the devolved institution. The next section will consider a different model of devolution, executive devolution and administrative devolution, before examining the devolution settlements in Scotland, Wales, and Northern Ireland.

10.3.2 Executive devolution

The main differences between executive and legislative devolution all relate to the devolved institution's legislative powers. The key characteristic of executive devolution is that the power-conferring institution (Westminster, in a UK context) devolves no primary legislative power to the devolved body and retains the power to create general policies in all fields for that country or region. This means that the Westminster Parliament would retain its power to form general policy for the devolved region. It would also retain the *only* powers to pass framework legislation—pieces of primary legislation that set out the government's general policies. But the primary legislation would remain relatively vague, with detail being supplied by secondary legislation that could be enacted by the devolved body. In effect, the devolved body would be granted the same powers as are delegated to members of the executive, the secretaries of state in government, but over a much wider range of issues than are given to an individual minister. The main framework would be set by Westminster and the detail would be left to the devolved body. As you can see, this is a more restrictive approach than in relation to legislative devolution, through which the devolved institution is also given some primary law-making powers.

The main issues regarding executive devolution arise in relation to the split between responsibility for the general policy and responsibility for its implementation. At face value, it is easy to conclude that the power-conferring institution is the one responsible for general policy and primary legislation, and the devolved body is the one responsible for its execution and administration. In reality however, this is much too simplistic a distinction. As the Kilbrandon Commission Report illustrated (1973: 252), policies are often set out in secondary legislation, not in Parliament's primary legislation. This would mean that the devolved administration would have responsibility for forming general policies in certain fields, as well as for executing and administering them, even though the devolution model appears to suggest the contrary. If this is the case, then the appearance of day-to-day control by Westminster would belie that actual day-to-day control by the devolved body. This leads to a number of potential problems. The first is that where *any* executive functions have been transferred to a devolved institution, then so have at least some policy functions. This could well lead to conflict between the institutions in circumstances in which either the dominant institution considers that the devolved administration has assumed some responsibility for policy that it believes to be its own, or vice versa, in which the devolved government resents the fact that so little responsibility for policy had been devolved to it. This would be particularly likely were the national and regional bodies to be controlled by different political parties with different policy objectives. To have any hope of succeeding, executive devolution is nearly completely reliant on a good working relationship between the governments of the two institutions. This is difficult even where the relationship between the two bodies is clearly defined and policy objectives are aligned. The situation would be worsened significantly if the functions of the devolved institution were unclear and debatable, and if the difference in opinion in policy terms were coupled with a difference in opinion about which body had the power to make the policy.

The second major problem linked to this is that it would be practically impossible for the enabling legislation to set out conclusively the executive functions of the devolved body. In attempting to do so, it could choose to do one of two things: it could transfer *all* executive functions in a certain field to the devolved administration; or it could attempt to provide an exhaustive list of the transferred executive functions. By definition, therefore, if an executive function were not to appear in such a list, it would be reserved for the central government. The two options may be better illustrated by way of hypothetical example.

example

Let us say that the enabling piece of primary legislation lists 'Health Services' as a field in which executive functions *could* be devolved. The enabling legislation, or subsequent secondary legislation, would then either:

1 state that, in effect, 'All executive functions in the field of Health Services are to be transferred to the devolved administration'; or

2 provide a long, exhaustive list of executive functions within health services that are to be transferred. This would usually take the form of a list of hundreds or thousands of statutory sections and subsections that had previously delegated powers to the secretary of state.

As one can imagine, the second option would be extremely complex and would lead to much uncertainty within both institutions as to the limits of the devolved body's powers. The first option could lead to discontent within Parliament that the devolved body had been granted so much executive power; the second could also lead to debates on whether a specific power had been devolved in the first place. It would not be inconceivable under such a scheme that the devolved institution itself would be uncertain of its powers. This would, in turn, lead to confusion amongst the general public as to the limits of the institution's powers. This issue will be considered later in the context of Welsh devolution.

10.3.3 Administrative devolution

Administrative devolution is considered in less detail because it is of reduced relevance to today's discussions of devolution in the UK. Administrative devolution is primarily concerned with the central government exercising its functions in a more regionally responsive capacity, and so it is often more about central government spreading out across a country rather than about it devolving power to independent local entities. In the UK context, it can refer to any situation in which a central government department is represented outside Whitehall in London, the traditional home of government. It can range from a government department having a regional office in, say, the north-east of England, to the existence of powerful secretaries of state for Scotland, Wales, and Northern Ireland. In this respect, it could be said that administrative devolution in the UK reached its zenith before the passing of the 1998 devolution legislation, when all three nations had their own relatively powerful national offices. The Scottish Office, the Welsh Office, and the Northern Ireland Office not only had the power to administer government policies within the respective countries, but also held executive power to form detailed separate policies for the individual nations. Although the three nations still have their own representative offices, the majority of their executive and administrative functions are now exercised by the devolved institutions.

The essence of administrative devolution means that the formation of new, directly elected regional or national bodies is not required. However, devolved institutions that exercise executive or legislative functions will also have administrative powers by default.

summary points

In what ways can power be devolved?

- *Legislative devolution involves devolving the power to create policy in certain fields, to legislate on such policy areas, and to execute and administer the policy once formed.*

- *The main issues with legislative devolution relate to the way in which parliamentary supremacy is retained and the question of the fields over which the devolved institutions have power.*

- *Executive devolution involves devolving of power to create, execute, and administer detailed policies within the general framework legislation enacted by Parliament. It includes the power to enact secondary legislation.*

- *The main problems with executive devolution relate to the distinction between responsibility for policy and responsibility for its execution, and the question of which executive functions should be conferred on the institution.*

- *Administrative devolution involves the establishment of representative offices of central government in regions or nations within its territory to administer government policy.*

- *Legally, all devolution schemes retain parliamentary supremacy.*

10.4 What are the role and powers of the Scottish Parliament?

The history of the union between Scotland and England helps to explain the role and powers of today's Scottish Parliament. After all, it is this history that mainly accounts for the differences in the legislative powers granted to the respective devolved legislatures established by the enactment of the 1998 Devolution Acts.

10.4.1 A history of the union between England and Scotland

England and Scotland have shared a sovereign since the death of Elizabeth I in 1603 brought the Tudor dynasty to an end and James VI of Scotland became James I of England. However, despite sharing a **monarch**, the two countries did not begin to share a Parliament until over a century later, when they were united by the enactment of the Acts of Union of 1706 and 1707. The Treaty of Union was passed by both English and Scottish Parliaments, and this is doubtless one of the main reasons for the union's relative success and longevity. The two countries came together in a partnership as two countries in union (a little like two individuals in a committed relationship), rather than one country taking over the other. When one considers that England and Scotland had been sworn enemies, at war as recently as 1513, the fact that both countries voluntarily agreed to the union is nothing short of an astounding achievement. Much of that success is down to the very fact that the union was voluntary for both countries. It was also vital that the Scottish Parliament was offered sufficient assurances that Scotland would remain a separate nation with its own institutions so as to convince the Scottish that it was in their interests to join such a union.

NOTE

You may wish to refer to 'The Scottish Parliament: Past and Present', available online at http://www.scottish.parliament.uk/PublicInformationdocuments/TimelineEnglish.pdf, for more information about the route to the current Scottish Parliament and the history of England and Scotland.

As a result, the Treaty of Union made it explicitly clear that both countries were to be joined together as equal partners in a political and economic union (in much the same way, many people would argue, as member states accede to or join the European Union today). Article I of the Treaty provided for the forming of Great Britain and Article III stated that both countries were to be served by a single Parliament, based at the Palace of Westminster. Scotland was then to send its own elected representatives to the newly formed Parliament. Importantly, the Treaty also ensured that Scotland maintained a separate educational system, legal system, and Church. This has remained the case to this day and the two countries still retain separate legal jurisdictions, as provided for by Articles XVIII and XIX of the Treaty of Union.

For the years between 1707 and 1999, Scotland was served solely by the Westminster Parliament. However, that is not to say that it did not have influence in its own domestic affairs. Firstly, MPs have been returned to Westminster to represent Scottish constituencies in relatively high numbers ever since the Union. Secondly, there have been numerous 'Scottish' committees within Parliament, particularly from the end of the nineteenth century onwards, and these focused on Scottish matters. Thirdly, and most significantly, Scotland has had its own office of Secretary for Scotland (a senior government minister) since as early as 1885. Established at a time when Home Rule was becoming an increasingly hot political topic, it seems that the original intention of Parliament in establishing the office was quite a straightforward one: in brief, it aimed to pacify the Scots, who felt aggrieved with direct parliamentary rule from Westminster. It was in Parliament's interests to be seen to take positive action to give Scotland a louder voice—or, as Gladstone subtly put it, 'a little mouthful of Home Rule'.

However, the new office began life far from being powerful. It had only a handful of functions, mostly in peripheral matters, and was of more symbolic significance than of practical importance. Nevertheless, the office did accumulate significant executive and administrative powers, and by 1926 the post was upgraded to a full secretary of state exercising functions in a wide range of fields such as education, the administration of justice, agriculture, and health. Its responsibilities developed even further during the latter half of the twentieth century, when it assumed executive and administrative functions in practically all Scottish affairs. Its responsibility was not only to represent Scottish interests at Westminster and Whitehall, but also to develop, execute, and administer distinctly Scottish policies within the prescribed limits of Westminster's primary legislation. It was also entrusted with the task of guiding Scotland-only primary legislation through Parliament in two different contexts.

The nature of the union between Scotland and England meant that, on some occasions, it was necessary for Parliament to pass primary legislation that applied only to Scotland—so-called 'Scotland-only legislation'. This was especially true when central government wished to make changes to the law in relation to matters for which the terms of the union had kept distinctly Scottish institutions or administrations. This could be done either via the enactment of a Scotland-only Act of Parliament or via a series of sections that applied only to Scotland set out within a UK-wide Act of Parliament. Scotland-only Bills were the responsibility of the Secretary of State for Scotland. The Secretary of State was responsible for introducing the Bill to Parliament and guiding it through the legislative procedure. He acted as the agent of central government, responsible for introducing and executing the changes that central government requested and enacted.

Secondly, particularly from the middle of the twentieth century onwards, the Scottish Office headed by the Secretary of State for Scotland was also actively seeking to establish its own distinctly Scottish policies rather than to rely on or accept the policies determined by central government. The Secretary of State quickly realised that, as *the* 'Scottish' Minister, there was a perceived duty on his office to establish policies that benefited Scotland, regardless of whether or not they differed from those in operation in the rest of the UK. When such policies required an amendment to primary legislation, the Secretary would then have to convince his Cabinet colleagues of the need for change. It is apparent that this was no easy task, but the sheer number of enacted Scotland-only pieces of legislation suggests that it was possible. Therefore, despite the fact that by the 1960s the Scottish Office had accumulated a great deal of executive and administrative power, Westminster retained the only primary legislative powers for Scotland. Indeed, even if the Secretary of State for Scotland happened to be successful in his attempts to have Scotland-only Bills introduced at Westminster, their successful passage through Parliament was far from guaranteed, because the Bills were dependent on English constituency MPs' votes.

10.4.2 The path to Scottish devolution

Prior to devolution, the legislative procedure for any Scotland-only Bills was identical to that for all other Bills introduced at Westminster. This meant that they would be debated and voted upon by the whole House of Commons and House of Lords, according to the procedure set out in Chapter 2. Despite the fact that the Bills would affect only Scotland, MPs representing England, Wales, and Northern Ireland would all have a vote. In effect, this gave representatives from the other three nations a power of veto over the proposed legislation and a right regularly to determine what would happen in Scotland even though it had no impact on them or their constituents. Needless to say, this situation was heavily criticised north of the border. It was considered to have severe implications for the democratic legitimacy of Parliament, in that the wishes of a Scottish executive (the Scottish Office) could be easily rejected by those representing English, Welsh, and Northern Irish constituencies. Whilst accepting that the 'executive', the Secretary of State for Scotland and his office, were not directly elected by the Scottish voters, it was still perceived as being unwarranted. Such a point was made in reverse in Parliament on 14 November 1977 by Tam Dalyell, MP for West Lothian, in a speech that gave rise to the popular

NOTE For more information, you may wish to visit the Scottish Parliament online at http://www.scottish.parliament.uk/

cross reference
See Chapter 2 for more on proposals to reduce the number of seats in the House of Commons from 650 to 600.

name for the issue—'the West Lothian question'. He questioned how long people living in English constituencies would be willing to permit Scottish, Welsh, and Northern Irish MPs to vote on English matters, were Scotland, Wales, and Northern Ireland to be granted devolved legislative powers over which English constituency MPs would have no say.

As will be seen later in the chapter, since the legislative devolution process began in 1998, the West Lothian question has been thrown into sharp relief. Members of Parliament representing Scotland, Wales, and Northern Ireland can all regularly vote on matters affecting only England—practically a mirror image of the situation prior to 1999. However, it must also be recognised that, in terms of pure numbers, it is less of an imbalance, since, at present, England has 529 MPs in Westminster, Scotland fifty-nine, Wales forty, and Northern Ireland eighteen. Without going into a lot of detail, it is difficult to give a comprehensive account of the reasons for the increase in calls for devolution to Scotland in the latter half of the twentieth century. However, the reverse situation was a significant factor in Scottish disquiet about its governance from Westminster.

Having said that, it must be acknowledged that calls for devolution or Home Rule for Scotland are by no means new. At the time of Home Rule discussions for Ireland, a total of thirteen Scottish Home Rule Bills appeared before Parliament. They were all ultimately unsuccessful, partly because of the increasing importance of the office of Secretary of State for Scotland, but the issue was firmly back on the political agenda by the late 1960s and early 1970s. At that time, dissatisfaction with numerous elements of direct parliamentary rule from Westminster manifested itself in Wales and Scotland in a significant rise in the support for the nationalist parties. In Scotland, for example, general discontent with what became the West Lothian question, and the fact that the executive could not directly and effectively be held to account by the Scottish public, had led to notable gains for the Scottish National Party (SNP) at both local and national levels, which sought Scottish self-government. The SNP's manifesto commitment did not go unnoticed by Harold Wilson's Labour government. Accordingly, in spring 1969, it appointed the Royal Commission on the Constitution, the Kilbrandon Commission.

The Commission interpreted its terms of reference very broadly and investigated the possibilities of establishing devolved administrations for all of the UK's nations and regions, including the English regions. In its report, published in 1973, it proposed the establishment of a legislative Assembly for Scotland. If established, the Assembly would have had primary legislative powers in fields such as health, education, the environment, and legal services. Of course, as noted in the section on legislative devolution above, the Westminster Parliament would have reserved some matters and retained its overall legislative supremacy. The majority of the Kilbrandon Commission's recommendations finally found their way on to the statute book through the enactment of the Scotland Act 1978. The Act provided that the institution would be established if over 40 per cent of the registered Scottish voters were to vote in favour of the Assembly in a referendum held on 1 March 1979. It is important to emphasise that 40 per cent of the total electorate needed to vote 'yes', not only 40 per cent of those who turned out to vote on referendum day. As the history books show, the referendum was unsuccessful. Despite the fact that 51.6 per cent of those who voted on voted in favour of the Assembly, the overall 40 per cent threshold was not reached and the new body was not established. As provided for in the Scotland Act 1978 itself, the legislation was repealed later in 1979 by the incoming Conservative government.

Despite the devolution issue dropping off the UK government's radar for the subsequent eighteen years, the question of legislative devolution for Scotland was never forgotten, especially north of the border. Scotland consistently voted Labour at general elections, but since it was a Conservative government in power at Westminster, the Scottish executive—that is, the Secretary of State for Scotland and his office—were Conservative MPs. This served only to strengthen the feeling of discontent with the political situation and the perceived democratic deficit. If anything, the situation worsened during the 1980s, when the Conservative secretaries not only had to contend with an increased workload, but also with receiving less money from central government.

- **V. Bogdanor, *Devolution in the United Kingdom*** (Oxford: Oxford University Press, 2001), p. 114

> His position became particularly embarrassing during the years of Conservative government between 1979 and 1997, when he enjoyed the support of only a minority in Scotland. It was hard for him to represent Scottish opinion effectively in Westminster, and he became, in reality, more like the ambassador of a hostile power than Scotland's spokesman in the Cabinet.

As a result, in the early 1990s, the Labour and Liberal Democrat parties backed the Scottish Constitutional Convention's calls for the establishment of a full legislative body for Scotland. They also pledged their support to such a scheme in their 1997 general election manifestos, provided that a successful result was had in a referendum on the issue.

10.4.3 Devolution and the Scottish Parliament

Within four-and-a-half months of its landslide general election victory in 1997, the Labour government had made good its promise. It had not only outlined its vision for the new Scottish Parliament in a White Paper, *Scotland's Parliament* (Cm 3658, London: HMSO, 1997), but it had also held a successful referendum on the proposals. Held under the Referendums (Scotland and Wales) Act 1997 in September of that year, the poll showed strong support for introducing a devolution settlement to Scotland—74 per cent of the voters voted in favour of a legislative body and 63.5 per cent voted in favour of establishing a legislative body with slight tax-varying powers. Fourteen months later, on 19 November 1998, the Scotland Act 1998 received its royal assent, thus establishing the Scottish Parliament.

The 1998 Act itself is comparatively straightforward, or at least as uncomplicated as such a piece of legislation could ever be. As a result, the powers of the Scottish Parliament are relatively easy to define. Section 28 of the Act establishes the Parliament's right to pass legislation termed 'Acts of the Scottish Parliament', but also reserves the UK Parliament's right to legislate for Scotland (section 28(7)). Rather than list the fields in which the Scottish Parliament *has* legislative competence, the Act chooses rather to list the fields in which it does *not* have competence—the so-called reserved matters. As mentioned in the section on legislative devolution above, this method grants more extensive power to the institution in question. Section 29 in effect states that an Act of the Scottish Parliament is law unless it is outside the Parliament's legislative competence. Firstly, it must not involve the reserved matters listed in Schedule 5 to the Act (sections 29(2)(b) and 30(1)). Secondly, the Act must not form part of the law of another country. Thirdly, the Act must not conflict with European Union law or with the **European Convention on Human Rights (ECHR)**. As will be seen below, there are other restrictions on the Parliament's powers in this respect.

Scotland Act 1998

Section 28 Acts of the Scottish Parliament

(1) Subject to section 29, the Parliament may make laws, to be knows as Acts of the Scottish Parliament.

(2) Proposed Acts of the Scottish Parliament shall be known as Bills; and a Bill shall become an Act of the Scottish Parliament when it has been passed by the Parliament and has received Royal Assent.

...

(5) The validity of an Act of the Scottish Parliament is not affected by any invalidity in the proceedings of the Parliament leading to its enactment.

(6) Every Act of the Scottish Parliament shall be judicially noticed.

(7) This section does not affect the power of the United Kingdom to make laws for Scotland.

Section 29 Legislative competence

(1) An Act of the Scottish Parliament is not law so far as any provision of the Act is outside the legislative competence of the Parliament.

(2) A provision is outside that competence so far as any of the following paragraphs apply—

   (a) it would form part of the law of a country or territory other than Scotland, or confer or remove functions exercisable otherwise than in or as regards Scotland,

   (b) it relates to reserved matters,

   (c) it is in breach of the restrictions in Schedule 4,

   (d) it is it is incompatible with any of the Convention rights or with Community law,

   (e) it would remove the Lord Advocate from his position as head of the systems of criminal prosecution and investigation of deaths in Scotland.

(3) For the purposes of this section, the question whether a provision of an Act of the Scottish Parliament relates to a reserved matter is to be determined, subject to subsection (4), by reference to the purpose of the provision, having regard (among other things) to its effect in all the circumstances.

(4) A provision which—

   (a) would otherwise not relate to reserved matters, but

   (b) makes modifications of Scots private law, or Scots criminal law, as it applies to reserved matters, is to be treated as relating to reserved matters unless the purpose of the provision is to make the law in question apply consistently to reserved matters and otherwise.

Section 30 Legislative competence: supplementary

(1) Schedule 5 (which defines reserved matters) shall have effect.

...

301

Schedule 5 to the Act provides a lengthy list of reserved matters under six headings: the constitution; political parties; foreign affairs; public service; defence; and treason. It also provides for specific reservations under eleven subheadings, including financial and economic matters, home affairs, and trade and industry. A recent case heard by the Supreme Court has considered the extent to which an Act of the Scottish Parliament is invalid on the grounds that it falls outside the Scottish Parliament's legislative competence. The Damages (Asbestos-related Conditions) (Scotland) Act 2009 was challenged on a number of grounds, including the fact that it was incompatible with the ECHR's first optional protocol. The *AXA* case is a complex one, but for our purposes it is important to note that the Supreme Court did review the Act for conformity to the ECHR. It considered that it did have the power to do this, but it did not find that the Act was outside the Scottish Parliament's competence. The judgment by Lord Hope provides an explanation of the relationship between the UK Parliament and the Scottish Parliament, and the fact that the Scottish Parliament's legislative powers are circumscribed.

● **AXA General Insurance Ltd and others v Lord Advocate and others** [2011] UKSC 46

Lord Hope:

[1] The Appellants are insurance companies, whose business includes the writing of employers' liability insurance policies. They undertake to indemnify the employer in respect of any liability incurred by it for harm or injury arising out of the employer's negligence. They have brought these proceedings to challenge the lawfulness of an Act of the Scottish Parliament which was passed on 11 March 2009, received the Royal Assent on 17 April 2009 and came into force on 17 June 2009. It is the Damages (Asbestos-related Conditions) (Scotland) Act 2009 ('the 2009 Act') which provides that asymptomatic pleural plaques, pleural thickening and asbestosis shall constitute, and shall be treated as always having constituted, actionable harm for the purposes of an action of damages for personal injury.

...

[45] Devolution is an exercise of its law-making power by the United Kingdom Parliament at Westminster. It is a process of delegation by which, among other things, a power to legislate in areas that have not been reserved to the United Kingdom Parliament may be exercised by the devolved legislatures. The Scotland Act 1998 sets out the effect of the arrangement as it affects Scotland with admirable clarity. Section 1(1) of the Act declares: 'There shall be a Scottish Parliament'. Its democratic legitimacy is enshrined in the provisions of s 1(2) and s 1(3), which provide for the election of those who are to serve as its members as constituency members and by a system of proportional representation chosen from the regional lists. Section 28(1) provides that the Parliament may make laws, to be known as Acts of the Scottish Parliament, and s 28(2) provides for them to receive the Royal Assent. Section 28(5) provides that the validity of an Act of the Scottish Parliament is not affected by any invalidity in the proceedings of the Parliament leading to its enactment. Although s 28(7) provides that that section shall not affect the power of the United Kingdom to make laws for Scotland, in practice the Scottish Parliament enjoys the same law making powers for Scotland as the Westminster Parliament except as provided expressly for in s 29 which, in certain closely defined respects, limits its legislative competence. Section 29 does not, however, bear to be a complete or comprehensive statement of limitations on the powers of the Parliament. The Act as a whole has not adopted that approach: see *Somerville v Scottish Ministers (HM Advocate General for Scotland intervening)* [2007] UKHL 44, 2008 SC (HL) 45, [2007] 1 WLR 2734, para 28.

[46] The carefully chosen language in which these provisions are expressed is not as important as the general message that the words convey. The Scottish Parliament takes its place under our constitutional arrangements as a self-standing democratically elected legislature. Its democratic mandate to make laws for the people of Scotland is beyond question. Acts that the Scottish Parliament enacts which are within its legislative competence enjoy, in that respect, the highest legal authority. The United Kingdom Parliament has vested in the Scottish Parliament the authority to make laws that are within its devolved competence. It is nevertheless a body to which decision making powers have been delegated. And it does not enjoy the sovereignty of the Crown in Parliament that, as Lord Bingham said in *Jackson*, para 9, is the bedrock of the British constitution. Sovereignty remains with the United Kingdom Parliament. The Scottish Parliament's power to legislate is not unconstrained. It cannot make or unmake any law it wishes. Section 29(1) declares that an Act of the Scottish Parliament is not law so far as any provision of the Act is outside the legislative competence of the Parliament. Then there is the role which has been conferred upon this court by the statute, if called upon to do so, to judge whether or not Acts of the Parliament are within its legislative competence: see s 33(1) and paras 32 and 33 of Sch 6, as amended by s 40 and paras 96 and 106 of Sch 9 to the Constitutional Reform Act 2005. The question whether an Act of the Scottish Parliament is

within the competence of the Scottish Parliament is also a devolution issue within the meaning of para 1(a) of Sch 6 to the Scotland Act in respect of which proceedings such as this may be brought in the Scottish courts.

...

[49] The dominant characteristic of the Scottish Parliament is its firm rooting in the traditions of a universal democracy. It draws its strength from the electorate. While the judges, who are not elected, are best placed to protect the rights of the individual, including those who are ignored or despised by the majority, the elected members of a legislature of this kind are best placed to judge what is in the country's best interests as a whole. A sovereign Parliament is, according to the traditional view, immune from judicial scrutiny because it is protected by the principle of sovereignty. But it shares with the devolved legislatures, which are not sovereign, the advantages that flow from the depth and width of the experience of its elected members and the mandate that has been given to them by the electorate. This suggests that the judges should intervene, if at all, only in the most exceptional circumstances. As Lord Bingham of Cornhill said in *R (Countryside Alliance) v A-G* [2007] UKHL 52, [2008] 1 AC 719, para 45, [2008] 2 All ER 95, the democratic process is liable to be subverted if, on a question of political or moral judgment, opponents of an Act achieve through the courts what they could not achieve through Parliament.

...

cross reference
Judicial review is discussed in Chapter 14 et seq.

Lord Hope's, and later Lord Reed's, judgments consider whether it is open to the Court to review the exercise of legislative power through the medium of judicial review. They reject this argument on the basis that the Scottish Parliament is a plenary body and can legislate for whatever purpose it wishes, assuming that the exercise of its legislative power is within its competence. However, Lord Reed kept open the possibility that the courts could review Acts of the Scottish Parliament and other devolved assemblies on common law grounds—that is, on the ground that they offend against the **rule of law** and fundamental rights not protected through Convention rights. The Damages (Asbestos-related Conditions) (Scotland) Act 2009 was not considered to breach any such provisions and consequently the question of whether this is within the courts' powers remains moot.

303

Further key provisions of the Scotland Act 1998

Part I

- Section 1—Establishes the Parliament.

- Sections 2–3—Establish the electoral system—general elections held every four years using the additional member system. Of the 129 members of the Scottish Parliament (MSPs), seventy-three are elected through the simple majority element, while fifty-six are elected as 'additional members' through party lists.

- Sections 15–18—Provide for disqualification from standing for election.

- Section 19—Establishes the office of the Presiding Officer.

- Sections 22–27—Provide for the Parliament's standing orders and powers to call for witnesses and documents.

- Section 31—Establishes that the minister responsible for a Bill must declare it to be within Parliament's competence.

- Section 33—Provides that the Supreme Court can consider the legitimacy of a Bill. See also Schedule 6, which provides that where an Act's legitimacy is raised during court proceedings, the issue may be referred to a superior court. Final appeals are heard by the Supreme Court.

Part II

- Section 44—Establishes the Scottish Executive.

- Sections 45–48—Note that the Executive comprises the First Minister, appointed by the Queen, the Scottish Ministers, appointed by the First Minister with the Queen's approval, and the Law Officers.

- Sections 52–58—Set out the Executive's duties and responsibilities. Generally, it exercises executive functions in areas relating to the Parliament's legislative power (much the same as the executive powers exercised by the Scottish Office prior to 1999).

- Sections 45(2), 47(3)(c), and 48(2)—Provide for a vote-of-confidence mechanism to hold the Executive to account by the rest of the Parliament.

Parts III and IV—The Parliament's finances and tax-varying powers.

Parts V and VI—Catch-all, general parts of the Act.

There is no doubt that the Scottish Parliament is a powerful institution with significant legislative functions in practically all areas of Scottish life. Equally, there is no doubt that the Scottish Parliament is more than willing to use the powers granted to it by the Scotland Act 1998. In fact, at the time of writing, the Parliament had enacted 181 Acts of the Scottish Parliament. One must not forget that legislation is only a means to the overall end of implementing policy changes. Clearly, the substantial number of Acts is testament to the fact that the Scottish Executive and Parliament have been relatively prolific in formulating and executing distinctly Scottish policies. The Barnett formula, which provides Scotland with a financial block grant, also assists Scotland in developing its own policy initiatives—but reductions in the block grant arising from public spending cuts at the time of writing may put a brake on this phenomenon.

Despite the clearly defined limitations to its legislative powers, it is apparent that the Scottish Parliament has had more than a purely symbolic effect on law and politics in the UK. It was hugely symbolic for Scotland to be granted its own Parliament for the first time in nearly three centuries, but the real impact of its establishment has been much more concrete. In short, it has meant not only that the law of Scotland is different from the law of England and Wales, but that it is also continuously becoming more so. But it has not stemmed support for full Scottish independence from the UK, as evidenced by the SNP's overall majority in the Scottish Parliament in an assembly that was designed to promote **coalition government** and plans to hold a referendum on independence.

thinking point

What are your views on the current form of Scottish devolution? Should Scotland be given further power? If so, of what type? If you are in favour of a more limited devolution settlement, what type do you favour and why?

summary points

What are the role and powers of the Scottish Parliament?

- *England and Scotland's parliaments were united by the Acts of Union 1706–1707. The treaty was a voluntary one for both nations. Scotland retained its own legal system and institutions.*

- *Scotland has had its own executive office since 1885, when the office of Secretary of State for Scotland was established. By 1999, the office had significant executive power in all areas of Scottish life.*

- *Calls for devolving legislative power to Scotland began at the same time as the calls for Irish Home Rule. They gathered pace during the second half of the twentieth century, when concerns were raised about democratic deficit in Scotland.*

- *Following a successful referendum in 1997, the Scotland Act 1998 was enacted, thus establishing the Scottish Parliament.*

- *The Parliament has significant primary legislative power in all matters, except those specifically reserved to Westminster. Westminster has also reserved the right to legislate on all devolved issues.*

- *The Scottish Parliament has consistently used its powers to implement distinctly Scottish policies.*

10.5 What are the role and powers of the Welsh Assembly?

The Right Honourable Ron Davies, former Secretary of State for Wales, once famously said that devolution was a process, not an event. Perhaps it is therefore fitting that it is the Welsh devolution settlement more than any other that proves his statement. A brief introduction to the history of Welsh devolution may well shed light on why this is the case.

NOTE You may want to refer to the information made available by the Welsh Assembly online at http://www.assemblywales.org/

10.5.1 A history of Wales' union with England

The history of Wales' union with England is markedly different from Scotland's. Whilst Scotland's Parliament voluntarily agreed to join England in union, much of Wales was conquered by the English Crown in 1282. This took its toll on Welsh unity and on the possibilities of having united 'Welsh' institutions. Ultimately, it also partly accounts for current differences between the powers of the Scottish Parliament and those of the National Assembly for Wales.

Wales is one of four countries that makes up the United Kingdom, but it is difficult to pinpoint when Wales became recognised as the country that it is, with a fixed border. Wales' last prince, Llywelyn, was killed in December 1282. His death, along with the enactment of the Statute of Rhuddlan 1284, secured the English conquest of Llywelyn's kingdom and brought it under the control of the Crown. The Act established five new administrative shires in his former lands, mainly located on the western seaboard of Wales. It also introduced the English common law to these regions. However, some native Welsh civil law customs survived and the Welsh language continued to be used in the courts. The remainder of today's Wales—that is, the areas located adjacent and close to today's English border—continued to be controlled by individual local leaders, the Marcher lords, who had been governing the region since the Norman conquest of 1066. The 1284 Act had no effect in these individual lordships, and the lords retained the right to create and execute their own laws for another two-and-a-half centuries. Both pre- and post-1284, the laws of the Marches were distinct combinations of English and Welsh laws. Despite a briefly successful rebellion led by lawyer Owain Glyndŵr in the early 1400s, Wales never experienced the same degree of unity as Scotland had. In truth, the fact that so much of the land was controlled by different Marcher lords meant that Wales did not have a single set of common institutions that could have survived the conquest.

Somewhat ironically, the first full geographical definition of Wales was provided by the enactment of Henry VIII's Laws in Wales Acts of 1535 and 1542, commonly referred to today as the Acts of Union. These Acts abolished the Marcher lordships and created the last of Wales' five new administrative divisions, thus creating a thirteen-county Wales. All thirteen shires were permitted to return elected representatives to the English Parliament at Westminster. The Acts also established a distinct court structure for Wales. Perhaps unwittingly, by establishing the Courts of the Great Session, the Acts of Union established a 'Welsh' institution, one that would continue to be source of great pride until its final abolition in 1830.

These provisions were initially welcomed in Wales, or at least by some members of the Welsh gentry, but section 20 of the 1535 Act was universally hated in Wales. The clause outlawed the use of the Welsh language in all court proceedings and public office in Wales—a provision that could have had a terrible effect on the fate of the language, one of the single biggest symbols of Welshness at that time. The Crown's intention in doing so was to foster a sense of a common identity between the Welsh and the English, and to break any latent nationalism or cultural pride within the minority group, the Welsh, that could eventually call for independence from England.

In fact, it is probable that the so-called 'language clause' *would* have led to the death of the language and killed cultural pride were it not for the Bible being translated into Welsh in 1588. However, as matters transpired, the language's continued survival, the developing Welsh literary culture, the Courts of the Great Session, and religion all played their part in ensuring that the Welsh nation survived culturally, even if not officially. Indeed, so established was the notion of Welsh nationhood by the end of the nineteenth century that calls were made for Welsh Home Rule, alongside the Irish and Scottish campaigns.

10.5.2 The rise of Welsh nationalism

The political impetus for Welsh Home Rule fizzled out more rapidly than it did for the other two countries, but it is clear that the notion of nationhood did not. Wales was finding its own voice and wanted to administer its own distinct policies. It had succeeded in exerting pressure on Parliament to enact Wales-only legislation. It also succeeded in securing a measure of administrative devolution as early as 1907, when the Welsh Department of the Board of Education was established, and 1919, when similar boards were established for health and agriculture. By the end of the Second World War in 1945, there were fifteen such offices in Wales dealing with Welsh policy and administration.

Partly in order to coordinate these somewhat piecemeal administrative offices, the Conservative government of Winston Churchill established the office of Minister for Welsh Affairs in 1951 to oversee Welsh affairs, roughly sixty-five years after its Scottish equivalent. However, the office was rarely popular and never powerful. From its inception, it had no executive powers and its popularity was hardly helped by originally being headed by an Englishman representing an English constituency in Parliament, Home Secretary Sir David Maxwell-Fyfe. Its esteem in the eyes of the Welsh public plummeted even further in 1957 when, under the leadership of Henry Brooke, the office approved the drowning of the Tryweryn valley (and thus people's homes in a completely Welsh-speaking community) in Meirionnydd to supply drinking water to the north-west of England. This was despite extremely strong local opposition and the fact that thirty-five of Wales' thirty-six MPs voted against the Bill. Needless to say, this served only to increase the calls for a full-time Welsh representative at governmental level.

The Conservative government consistently rejected such demands throughout the 1950s and it was not until the Labour general election victory of 1964 that the office of Secretary of State for Wales was established. Initially, however, the office had executive powers in only two fields—housing and local government. It had significant administrative functions in practically all Welsh matters—but it was not until 1968 that the office was granted executive powers in health matters; 1970 for powers in the field of education. Nevertheless, other executive functions soon followed and, by the mid 1970s, the Welsh Office had become a relatively powerful executive body, exercising a wide range of functions in most areas of Welsh affairs.

As discussed above, at this time, partly as a result of the perceived increased 'threat' of na-tionalism, the Kilbrandon Commission had been appointed in spring 1969 to enquire into the possibility of devolving further powers to Scotland and Wales. As in Scotland, difficult eco-nomic conditions and a so-called democratic deficit had led to a surge in the support for the nationalist party, Plaid Cymru (meaning 'the Party of Wales' in Welsh). Although its support did not grow at the same rapid rate as the support for the SNP in Scotland, Gwynfor Evans *did* capture the party's first parliamentary seat as early as July 1966. By October 1974, twelve months after the Commission reported, it had a total of three MPs returned to Westminster. Welsh nationalism was visibly gaining ground.

In its report, the Kilbrandon Commission noted that the strength of public support in Wales for a scheme of self-government was not as great as it was in Scotland. The opinion of the majority of its members therefore was that Wales should be granted its own directly elected executive Assembly, responsible for roughly the same functions as were exercised by the Welsh Office. Of course, the main difference would be that Wales could then hold its executive to account directly and it would have more resources, so that it could develop distinctly Welsh policy. A large minority, six of the Commission's thirteen members, recommended a different model of a full legislative Assembly with competence in the majority of the areas that had been proposed for conferral on the Scottish Assembly. The recommendation of the majority, an ex-ecutive Assembly, found its way on to the statute book by virtue of the Wales Act 1978. Had the referendum result been a positive one, an elected Assembly would have been established in Cardiff, with strong executive power in a relatively wide range of Welsh matters. However, the referendum was anything but successful. The hugely successful 'no' campaign, led by Labour's 'gang of six' MPs, ensured that the motion was soundly defeated. On 1 March 1979, St David's Day (St David being the patron saint of Wales), 79.8 per cent of the Welsh voters voted 'no' to having their own directly elected political body. Margaret Thatcher's incoming Conservative government quickly repealed the Wales Act 1978 in July 1979 and devolution sank without trace from the central government's political agenda.

However, as was the case in Scotland, this did not mean that the devolution issue was com-pletely forgotten on the Welsh side of the border. In fact, the calls for a democratically elected Welsh political institution only strengthened during the eighteen years of Conservative rule. During that time, the worsening Welsh economy and the fact that the powers of the Secretary of State for Wales were continuously increasing, without a corresponding increase in the demo-cratic legitimacy of his office, all contributed to a feeling of general discontent. The situation was exacerbated by the fact that, in eighteen years of Conservative government, Wales had only one secretary of state representing a Welsh constituency. In effect, Wales was being partly executively governed by a member of a political party that it did not elect in any way, shape, or form.

10.5.3 A commitment to devolution in Wales

As a direct result of these concerns, the Labour Party committed itself in the early 1990s to establishing a directly elected Welsh political body to replace the outdated, undemocratic Welsh Office. It incorporated this promise in its manifesto for the 1997 general election and, once elected in May of that year, it moved rapidly to implement the pledge. The new government published its White Paper, *A Voice for Wales* (Cm 3718, London: HMSO), in July and held a referendum on the issue in September. The result was far from the resounding 'yes' vote heard in Scotland, but the effect was the same (50.1 per cent of the voters voted in favour of establishing the National Assembly for Wales). The Government of Wales Act 1998 received royal assent on 31 July of that year, thus establishing the National Assembly for Wales.

If the Scotland Act 1998 can be regarded as being relatively straightforward, the Government of Wales Act 1998 is positively complex in comparison. It has since been the subject of reform. The devolution settlement introduced to Wales was fundamentally different from the one established in Scotland. Scotland was granted full legislative powers in all areas except the matters reserved to Westminster; Wales was to be granted only limited executive powers—a far less extensive form of devolution. What does this mean in essence? To say that the provisions of the Government of Wales Act 1998 provided the Assembly with teething difficulties would be a massive understatement. The transfer of *some* executive powers, but not all powers in all fields, certainly allowed the fledgling institution to grow and to develop its power, but it also proved to be a massive hindrance. Not only did the general public fail to comprehend the Assembly's powers, but in many cases so did the Assembly members themselves. The powers were extremely piecemeal, conferring powers in some areas and failing to do so in others, apparently without good reason.

Numerous other problems arose from the 1998 legislation, one of which was the institutional framework that provided no real institutional distinction between the legislature and the executive branches. Central government's intention in creating such an Assembly was to move away from the gladiatorial battle of Westminster politics and towards a consensus-seeking model in which all parties would work together for the benefit of the country. However, not only did the concept seemingly breach the doctrine of the separation of powers (see Figures 10.2 and 10.3 for the situation pre- and post-Government of Wales 2006), but it also prevented the executive committee from working to its full capacity since it did not have the necessary resources.

This situation was remedied in spring 2002 when a de facto Welsh Assembly government was established, thus moving the Assembly towards Westminster-style opposition politics. Although universally accepted, the government had no legal basis whatsoever. This solved some of the major issues, but many problems remained. As a result, a Commission was established in July 2002 under the chairmanship of Lord Ivor Richard to enquire into the possibility of amending the Assembly's powers and procedures. A significant number of the 2004 Richard Commission Report's recommendations were accepted by the central government.

10.5.4 A developing model of Welsh devolution

The Government of Wales Act 1998 proved to be extremely unsatisfactory. It did not provide a workable system of government. The powers conferred were limited, complex, and did not provide for accountable government. You will find more detail on this in the further reading suggested at the end of the chapter. As a consequence of the criticisms, the government published a second White Paper on Welsh devolution, *Better Governance for Wales* (Cm 6582, London: HMSO), in June 2005. In it, the government followed the Richard Commission's suggestion in proposing the formal separation of the Assembly as a legislature and its executive government. It also outlined minor changes to some of the electoral arrangements. However, the most significant development by far was the changes that were proposed to the Assembly's legislative power. In short, it agreed with the Richard Commission that the Assembly had served its apprenticeship of exercising executive functions and that it had reached the limit of what realistically could be achieved with such powers. In a comparatively short period of time, the White Paper's recommendations were put on a statutory footing in the Government of Wales Act 2006. In reality, the 2006 Act repealed most of the 1998 Act. Part I of the 2006 Act established the Assembly as a parliamentary body (section 1), not as a 'body corporate'. Part II of the Act formally established the Welsh Assembly government and prescribed its functions, thus legally separating the executive and legislative powers. In effect, this meant that, as from the 2006 Act's implementation in May 2007, the Welsh Assembly government was responsible for all executive functions.

The reforms not only changed the institutional structure, but they also made amendments to the legislative competence of the Welsh Assembly. Parts III and IV of the Government of Wales Act 2006 set out the Assembly's current and future legislative powers. Sections 93–102 provided for the Assembly's new legislative provisions, termed **Assembly Measures**, which have the same effect as primary legislation, but which needed to be 'switched on' one by one by the UK Parliament. In order for an Assembly Measure to be lawful, it had to relate purely to Wales, not breach the restrictions in Part 2 of Schedule 5, and not be incompatible with Convention rights or European Union law. Most importantly, the measure must also have related to one of the twenty areas listed in Part 1 of Schedule 5. However, there was also the prospect of more extensive legislative power within the Government of Wales Act 2006. Sections 103–109 provided that if the people of Wales were to vote in favour of primary law-making powers in a referendum, the Welsh Assembly would have the power to enact Assembly Acts within the fields set out in Schedule 7 without the need for approval from the UK Parliament.

Figure 10.2 sets out the institutional framework under the Government of Wales Act 1998.

Figure 10.2

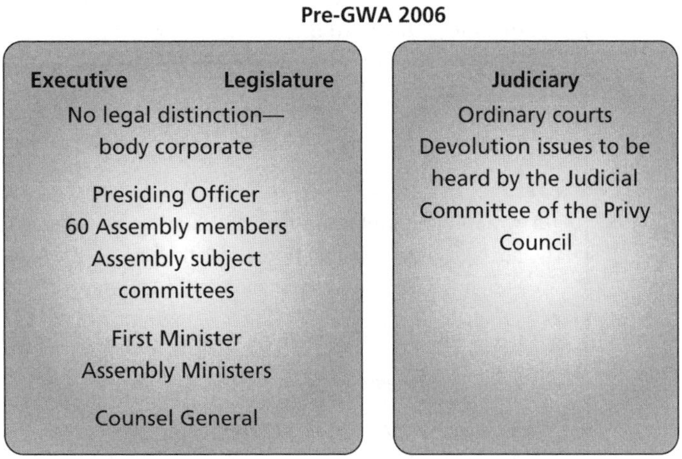

Pre-GWA 2006

Executive Legislature	Judiciary
No legal distinction— body corporate	Ordinary courts Devolution issues to be heard by the Judicial Committee of the Privy Council
Presiding Officer 60 Assembly members Assembly subject committees	
First Minister Assembly Ministers	
Counsel General	

Figure 10.3

Post-GWA 2006

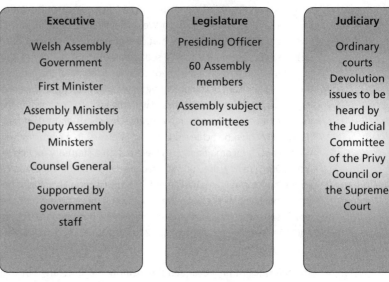

Executive	Legislature	Judiciary
Welsh Assembly Government	Presiding Officer	Ordinary courts
First Minister	60 Assembly members	Devolution issues to be heard by the Judicial Committee of the Privy Council or the Supreme Court
Assembly Ministers Deputy Assembly Ministers	Assembly subject committees	
Counsel General		
Supported by government staff		

Figure 10.3 illustrates the position after reform by the Government of Wales Act 2006.

Government of Wales Act 2006

. . . .

Section 103 Referendum about commencement of Assembly Act provisions

(1) Her Majesty may by Order in Council cause a referendum to be held throughout Wales about whether the Assembly Act provisions should come into force.

(2) If the majority of the voters in a referendum held by virtue of subsection (1) vote in favour of the Assembly Act provisions coming into force, the Assembly Act provisions are to come into force in accordance with section 105.

(3) But if they do not, that does not prevent the making of a subsequent Order in Council under subsection (1).

(4) No recommendation is to be made to Her Majesty in Council to make an Order in Council under subsection (1) unless a draft of the statutory instrument containing the Order in Council has been laid before, and approved by a resolution of, each House of Parliament and the Assembly.

(5) But subsection (4) is not satisfied unless the resolution of the Assembly is passed on a vote in which the number of Assembly members voting in favour of it is not less than two-thirds of the total number of Assembly seats.

(6) A draft of a statutory instrument containing an Order in Council under subsection (1) may not be laid before either House of Parliament, or the Assembly, until the Secretary of State has undertaken such consultation as the Secretary of State considers appropriate.

(7) For further provision about referendums held by virtue of subsection (1) see Schedule 6.

(8) In this Act "the Assembly Act provisions" means—

(a) sections 107 and 108, and

(b) sections 110 to 115.

On 3 March 2011, a referendum was held in Wales with the question: 'Do you want the Assembly now to be able to make laws on all matters in the twenty subject areas for which it has powers?' In favour were 63.5 per cent of voters; against, 36.5 per cent. The UK Parliament thus transferred the power to the Welsh Assembly to make Assembly Acts, as provided for in the Government of Wales Act. The Assembly can now make laws for Wales on subjects for which the Welsh Assembly and government have competence without the need for permission from the UK Parliament. The list of fields for which the Assembly has competence is as follows, although it should be noted that most of these fields contain exceptions and you should refer to Schedule 7 so as to see the limits of the Assembly's powers in this regard:

- agriculture, fisheries, forestry, and rural development;
- ancient monuments and historic buildings;
- culture;
- economic development;
- education and training;
- the environment;
- the fire and rescue services, and the promotion of fire safety;
- food;
- health and health services;
- highways and transport;
- housing;
- local government;
- the National Assembly for Wales;
- public administration;
- social welfare;
- sport and recreation;
- tourism;
- town and country planning;
- water and flood defence; and
- the Welsh language.

The Assembly is now a full legislative body in its own right. The only differences between the Scottish Parliament and the Welsh Assembly are the wider range of fields in which the Scottish Parliament is able to legislate. The Scottish system gives legislative competence to the Scottish Parliament except for those listed areas reserved for the UK Parliament; the Welsh system gives legislative competence to the Welsh Assembly in twenty fields, and reserves all others to the UK Parliament.

To complete the picture, Part IV of the 2006 Act relates to the Assembly's finances and Part V is the catch-all section containing miscellaneous provisions. As was the case with the Scotland Act, the Government of Wales Act 2006 also provides for resolving devolution issues. Section 149 and Schedule 9 establish the mechanism for the resolution of disputes in cases in which a question is raised in court proceedings as to the legitimacy of an Assembly Measure or Act. Final appeals are to be heard by the Supreme Court. Trench comments that although the 2006 Act resolves some of the problems of the 1998 Act, it does not provide a complete solution. This is because the 2006 Act is a political compromise between those who want Wales to assume more devolved powers and those who are against such further developments.

● A. Trench, 'The Government of Wales Act 2006: the next steps on devolution for Wales' [2006] Public Law 687, 695

Towards a constitutional settlement?

It has long been clear that the Government of Wales Act 1998 was a transitional measure, creating arrangements that were cumbersome in benign conditions and which would have been unworkable in the face of serious political differences between Cardiff and London. The 2006 Act resolves some of the problems that the 1998 Act presented, but not all of them, and it creates new ones. Many of these lie in the 2006 Act's origin, as a carefully-crafted political tool, designed to maximise support for increased devolution while not going beyond what was acceptable to anti-devolutionists in the Labour Party.[1] The result was a set of proposals that offered something for everyone. For supporters of devolution, there was the prospect of substantially enhanced legislative powers for the Assembly, and legislation setting out a powerful legislature for Wales for the first time in over 500 years. For anti-devolutionists, there was the promise that nothing could happen without Labour's consent, enforced partly through the office of the Secretary of State, and partly by the need for many steps to have a two-thirds majority in the National Assembly. (While it is quite conceivable that Labour will never attain a majority in the Assembly, it would need to do extraordinarily badly to fall beneath a third of the seats.) This masterful political ambiguity comes at the price of legal certainty, with the result that now legislation has been passed that clearly means something—but it is impossible to say exactly what.

1 It is worth noting that the key features of the 2005 White Paper were set out in a document approved at a special conference of the Welsh Labour Party in August 2004. This even bore the same name as the later White Paper. See Wales Labour Party, *Better Governance for Wales: A Welsh Labour Policy Document* (Cardiff: Wales Labour Party, 2004).

thinking point

What are your views on the current form of Welsh devolution? To what extent do you agree that the previous model was too restrictive?

Welsh devolution has come an extraordinarily long way in a relatively short time frame. Less than a decade ago, the Assembly was exercising piecemeal executive functions in a limited range of fields. The 2011 referendum has activated the Assembly Act provisions, thus making the Assembly a full legislative body, able and willing to formulate and execute its own distinctly Welsh solutions to distinctly Welsh issues.

summary points

What are the role and powers of the Welsh Assembly?

- *Differently from Scotland, much of Wales was conquered by England. The remaining parts were incorporated by the Acts of Union of 1535 and 1542.*

- *A measure of administrative devolution was granted to Wales at the start of the twentieth century. Executive powers were granted to a Secretary of State for Wales from the mid 1960s onwards.*

- *The Government of Wales Act 1998 established the National Assembly for Wales, a directly elected body with executive powers. Owing to many problems, most of the Act was eventually repealed by the Government of Wales Act 2006.*

- *The 2006 Act establishes that the Assembly can pass pieces of primary legislation, Assembly Measures, provided that it has the legislative competence to do so.*

- *The 2006 Act also provides for the possibility that the Assembly may be granted full legislative powers in the form of Assembly Acts. The positive vote in the 2011 referendum on the issue has made this a reality.*

What are the role and powers of the Northern Ireland Assembly?

Northern Ireland is no stranger to devolution. As was noted previously, the peculiar history of the Irish Home Rule campaign meant that it had its own Parliament from 1921 until 1972. A quick recap of the history of that Parliament's establishment and development will serve as a useful introduction to the current Assembly's powers.

Ireland first came under English control in 1171, when Henry II declared himself to be 'Lord of Ireland'. Nevertheless, as Henry's title implies, the English Crown's role was limited to that of an overlord. Provided that the Irish princes and lords paid homage to the English Crown on a regular basis, they would retain relative autonomy. Indeed, by the end of the thirteenth century, Ireland even had its own Parliament, albeit one that represented only the English immigrants. However, from 1494 onwards, the Irish Parliament's legislative initiatives were subject to a power of veto by the English Crown. Poynings' Law provided that Irish Bills would be enacted only if approved by the King and his Council in London. Needless to say, this severely restricted the Parliament's powers, but perhaps not as much as it would have done if the Parliament had consisted of any native Irishmen. This is especially true of the period between 1542 and the first decades of the seventeenth century. In that time, not only did the Irish Parliament pass the Crown of Ireland Act in 1542, proclaiming Henry VIII as King of Ireland, but it also supported the stream of English and Scottish immigrants who flowed into the north of the country from 1603. It is unlikely that a Parliament representing the Irish would have allowed either of these developments at least without some protection for the native Irish Catholic majority, whose situation only worsened after the Protestant William of Orange came to power in 1690.

England's control remained thus until 1782, when its power of veto over Irish legislation was repealed. As a result, further Irish legislation was passed in 1793 to allow Catholics to vote in general elections, but they still were not permitted to sit in Parliament. In any event, seven years later, both the English and Irish parliaments enacted legislation uniting the two kingdoms and establishing a single Parliament for the United Kingdom of Great Britain and Ireland, thereby abolishing the Irish Parliament (the Westminster Parliament enacted the Union With Ireland Act 1800; the Irish Parliament enacted the Act of Union (Ireland) Act 1800). This situation remained the case until the enactment of the Government of Ireland Act in 1920.

There is no need to repeat the facts already laid out in the section on the history of devolution, but we need to consider the powers of the Northern Ireland Parliament in brief. As explained previously, the 1920 Act provided for two legislative institutions: one in the south; the other serving six northern counties. However, owing to the foundation of the Irish Free State in the south, which later would become the Republic of Ireland, the Northern Ireland Parliament was the only one actually to be established. In operation between June 1921 and March 1972, the institution was a powerful one. It had a **bicameral** structure (that is, it was a two-chamber legislature, like the Westminster Parliament), with an executive controlled by its Prime Minister and Cabinet. The government had considerable functions in all Northern Irish matters and had practically full executive control over those areas in which the parliamentary body had primary legislative powers. These fields of competence covered practically all Northern Irish affairs. Matters such as the Crown, war and peace, defence, foreign relations, and treason were either excepted or reserved to the Westminster Parliament. Section 75 of the Act also retained Westminster's overall legislative supremacy and the right to legislate for all devolved matters.

The year 1972 saw an escalation in the civil unrest in Northern Ireland, with claims that the minority nationalist/Catholic community was experiencing discrimination as a result of the majority unionist/Protestant community's exercise of power in the state. Despite starting in earnest as early as 1969, the Troubles reached a low point in 1972, when as many as 500 people died. As a result, the Northern Ireland Parliament was initially suspended and then permanently abolished by the Northern Ireland Constitution Act 1973. The institution's significant executive powers were taken over by the Secretary of State for Northern Ireland and the conferred legislative powers returned to Westminster. Owing to the continued difficulties, direct rule from Westminster continued until the late 1990s. The enactment of the Northern Ireland Act 1998 was the culmination of a decade's hard negotiation between those involved in the Troubles. Discussions between the various political parties had begun in the late 1980s and led indirectly to the Downing Street Agreement of 1993. This was followed in summer 1994 by one of the largest paramilitary organisations, the Provisional Irish Republican Army (PIRA), declaring a ceasefire. Despite the fact that its official suspension of hostilities came to an end in February 2006, by the time the Labour government was elected in May 1997, moves had been made to attempt to secure cross-party negotiations. These discussions gathered pace under the leadership of Tony Blair and the PIRA announced a second ceasefire in July of that year. Eventually, after Sinn Féin had been allowed to join the negotiations, the political parties came to the Good Friday, or Belfast, Agreement on 10 April 1998 (Cm 3383, London: HMSO).

● C. McCrudden, 'Northern Ireland and the British constitution since the Belfast Agreement', in J. Jowell and D. Oliver (eds) *The Changing Constitution* (6th edn, Oxford: Oxford University Press, 2007), pp. 227–67, at 228

> Since the time when it was finalized, on Good Friday, 10 April 1998, the Belfast Agreement[1] has dominated the political life, and constitutional development, of Northern Ireland. It was, and remains, an enormously ambitious attempt to establish a constitutional process that will enable both sides of the Northern Ireland dispute—the nationalists, who prefer a united Ireland independent of the UK, and unionists, who prefer continued membership of the UK—to participate in government together. To enable this to occur, it is necessary to address (not to solve, but to address) all of the major contentious issues in Northern Ireland politics and constitutional debate. The Belfast agreement can be seen as having two major functions: first, as a major part of a peace process aimed at securing a permanent move away from the use of armed force as an ever-present element of Northern Ireland politics; and, second, as a detailed framework for a form of devolved government in Northern Ireland that would differ considerably from that in Scotland and Wales. The first aim is further along the road of being achieved than the second, which still hangs in the balance...
>
> 1 'The Belfast Agreement': An Agreement Reached at the Multi-Party Talks on Northern Ireland, 10 April 1998 (Cm 3383, London: HMSO, 1998).

NOTE You may wish to refer for more information to the Northern Ireland Assembly online at http://www.niassembly.gov.uk/

The agreement provided that Northern Ireland would remain a part of the UK until such time as the population of the North would vote otherwise in a referendum on the issue. It also dealt with the issue of decommissioning of arms and prisoner release. Significantly for these purposes, the Agreement also provided for the establishing of a 108-member Northern Ireland Assembly. All of the Agreement's recommendations were subject to positive votes in separate referenda held in the Republic of Ireland and Northern Ireland. Held on 22 May 1998 under powers granted to the Secretary of State for Northern Ireland under the Northern Ireland (Entry to Negotiations etc) Act 1996, the Northern Ireland referendum provided a strong 'yes' vote, with 71.1 per cent of the voters voting in favour. The Northern Ireland Act 1998 was subsequently enacted to give effect to the provisions of the Agreement. It received its royal assent on 19 November 1998.

Somewhat surprisingly, considering its difficult history, the Northern Ireland Act 1998 itself is relatively straightforward and its powers are quite easy to comprehend. The Northern Ireland Assembly has the power to pass primary legislation, termed 'Acts of the Northern Ireland Assembly', in all fields, except for those reserved to Westminster (Schedule 3) or excepted (Schedule 2). The reserved matters include such things as the Post Office, disqualification from Assembly office, the criminal law, and civil defence. Excepted matters include the Crown and its succession, defence of the realm, international relations, and the UK Parliament. Section 5(6) also provides that the Act does not affect the UK Parliament's right to legislate on the devolved matters.

Northern Ireland Act 1998

Section 5 Acts of the Northern Ireland Assembly

(1) Subject to sections 6 to 8, the Assembly may make laws, to be known as Acts.

(2) A Bill shall become an Act when it has been passed by the Assembly and has received Royal Assent.

...

(5) The validity of any proceedings leading to the enactment of an Act of the Assembly shall not be called into question in any legal proceedings.

(6) This section does not affect the power of the Parliament of the United Kingdom to make laws for Northern Ireland, but an Act of the Assembly may modify any provision made by or under an Act of Parliament in so far as it is part of the law of Northern Ireland.

Section 6 Legislative competence

(1) A provision of an Act is not law if it is outside the legislative competence of the Assembly.

(2) A provision is outside that competence if any of the following paragraphs apply—

  (a) it would form part of the law of a country or territory other than Northern Ireland, or confer or remove functions exercisable otherwise than in or as regards Northern Ireland;

  (b) it deals with an excepted matter and is not ancillary to other provisions (whether in the Act or previously enacted) dealing with reserved or transferred matters;

  (c) it is incompatible with any of the Convention rights;

  (d) it is incompatible with Community law;

  (e) it discriminates against any person or class of person on the ground of religious belief or political opinion;

  (f) it modifies an enactment in breach of section 7.

Summarised below are the other key further provisions as regards devolution and Northern Ireland.

Further key provisions of the Northern Ireland Act 1998

Part I

- Section 1—Provides that Northern Ireland is to remain part of the UK until such time as the people of Northern Ireland vote otherwise.

- Section 2—Repeals the Government of Ireland Act 1920 in its entirety.

- Section 3—Provides that an elected Assembly was to be formed at such a time as the Secretary of State for Northern Ireland saw fit.

- Section 4—Sets out the legislative procedure where 'cross-community support' is required. A certain percentage of both the Nationalist and Unionist members must vote in favour of the proposed legislation in order for it to be carried. This should give the Assembly its democratic legitimacy.

Part II

- Sections 9–13—Provide for the scrutiny of Bills and the legislative procedure.

- Section 14—Detail the royal assent.

Part III—The Northern Ireland Executive

- Sections 16A—16C, 16—Provide for a First Minister and a deputy First Minister. They are to be approved by the Nationalist and Unionist members as a single unit, which ensures that they are to come from different political parties, representing both sides of the divide.

- Section 17–19—Provide for Northern Ireland Ministers. They too must be representative of the Assembly as a whole.

- Section 20—Provides for the Executive Committee, comprising the First Minister and deputy, and the other Ministers.

- Sections 21A—21C—Provide for Northern Ireland departments and policing.

- Section 22–28E—Set out the functions of the Executive.

Part IV

- Sections 31–35—Establish the procedures for the Assembly's elections and constituencies. Each constituency is to return six Assembly members through the single transferrable vote in quadrennial Assembly elections. The Assembly has 108 members.

- Sections 36–38—Provide for disqualification from office.

- Sections 39–40—Provide for the office of the Presiding Officer and Commission.

- Section 41—Sets out the Assembly's standing orders.

- Sections 47–48—Provides for members' remuneration.

Part VI—The Assembly's finances

Part VII—Human rights and equal opportunities

Parts VIII and IX—Miscellaneous and supplemental

- Schedule 10—Provides that, in the event of a devolution issue being raised in court proceedings, the power to determine final appeals will lie with the Judicial Committee of the Privy Council (or Supreme Court once established).

Therefore, the Belfast Agreement, as implemented by the provisions of the Northern Ireland Act 1998 seen above, has established a powerful legislative institution, with powers in practically all domestic affairs. It also established a multi-party government, responsible for exercising a wide range of executive functions. However, the new institution has faced many difficulties.

In fact, in the early years of its existence, the amount of time that it has spent in suspension has far exceeded the time that it has spent in operation. Owing to political problems, mainly arising from the issue of arms decommissioning, the Assembly was suspended during February–May 2000, twice in 2001 (for 24 hours), and a fourth time from October 2002 until May 2007. In effect, the very fact that the Westminster Parliament *has* suspended the Assembly so very recently underlines the way in which it has retained its supremacy. Nevertheless, the section of the chapter does finish on a positive note. Thanks to the St Andrews Agreement of 2006, power has been returned to Stormont and has thus far remained there.

summary points

What are the role and powers of the Northern Ireland Assembly?

- *Northern Ireland had its own Parliament from 1921 until 1972. Established under the provisions of the Government of Ireland Act 1920, it had substantial legislative power over domestic affairs.*

- *The Troubles made it impossible to devolve power to Northern Ireland between 1972 and 1998. However, the Good Friday Agreement of 1998 paved the way for the establishment of a new Northern Ireland Assembly. The terms of the Agreement were accepted by the people of Northern Ireland in a 1998 referendum.*

- *The Northern Ireland Act 1998 established the 108-member Assembly and conferred full legislative competence in most areas of domestic policy.*

- *Its executive consists of members of both sections of the Northern Ireland community— the so-called power-sharing structure. The hope is that this will increase the government's democratic legitimacy in the eyes of the public.*

- *Despite a difficult first few years, the Assembly has been restored since May 2007 and indications for the future are positive.*

10.7 Should there be an English Parliament?

We have now discussed devolution for three of the four countries that make up the United Kingdom of Great Britain and Northern Ireland, along with the supremacy of the Westminster Parliament, the UK's Parliament. However, one country has been missing from our discussion so far. As was noted in the section on the history of devolution, calls for an English Parliament are by no means new. Indeed, a question was raised during the Home Rule debates of the early twentieth century on whether legislative power could be devolved to all the UK's nations, not only to Ireland. In effect, this would have meant that all four countries would have had their own individual parliaments, but with the UK Parliament at Westminster retaining power in the 'imperial' matters. Of course, the fact that the issue was first raised a century ago does not mean to say that it has been at the top of the political agenda ever since. In reality, it has resurfaced only in the years after devolution was introduced to Scotland and Wales, and reintroduced to Northern Ireland.

Nevertheless, the Kilbrandon Commission of 1969–73 did consider the possibility of devolving executive or legislative powers to either England as a whole or to its regions. However, it decided that there was no need for such an administration and found that there were certainly no calls from the general public for such institutions. At that time, most changes in the law affecting England also applied to Wales and Scotland, and because the Parliament was mainly made up of representatives of English constituencies, England's voice would be heard loudly enough. There was simply no room for another level of bureaucracy. This remained the case until the coming to power of the Labour government in May 1997.

Tony Blair's government was elected on a manifesto that pledged to introduce devolved administrations not only to Scotland and Wales, but also to the English regions. However, with the exception of the London Assembly and its powers relating to transport, environmental matters, etc, England has yet to receive any such devolved administrations. That is not to say that they have not been offered. Put simply, it seems that the English still do not want regional assemblies. The only local referendum held on the issue thus far was conducted in the region in which it was expected that the calls for a regional assembly would be at their strongest—the north-east. However, the November 2004 referendum provided an extremely strong 'no' vote, with 78 per cent of the voters voting against the notion of an Assembly for the North East. The fact that (these) English voters do not want regional devolved institutions does not automatically mean that they do not want a national devolved administration. In this respect, there is at least some evidence to suggest that support for such an institution is increasing. To understand why, one must return to the West Lothian question of 1977.

Prior to the Scotland Act 1998, Scottish voters thought it unjust that MPs representing English, Welsh, and Northern Irish constituencies held a power of veto over Scotland-only legislation. The MPs in question could reject the perceived wishes of the Scottish electorate without the proposed legislation having any affect whatsoever in their constituencies and countries. However, since the establishment of the Scottish Parliament, this is no longer the case. Scottish domestic policies that once had to be executed through Scotland-only Acts of Parliament are now enacted through Acts of the Scottish Parliament in Edinburgh. Members of the Westminster Parliament (the bulk of whom will represent English constituencies) now have practically no say in the matters within the legislative competence of the Scottish Parliament. The same is now true for Wales and Northern Ireland. However, this is not true vice versa. In effect, the West Lothian question has been turned on its head and, in fact, today it is more commonly known as the 'English question'.

To fully understand the current debate, it is worth having a quick recap of the Westminster Parliament and its members. Each constituency (in England, Northern Ireland, Scotland, and Wales) sends a representative to act as a member of the Westminster Parliament. However, the people living in Scotland, Wales, and Northern Ireland also have a second set of representatives who are elected to that country's Parliament or Assembly. This is in contrast to those living in England, who are still only represented by the members of the Westminster Parliament, owing to the fact that England has no separate executive/legislative body of its own. Some claim that this is unfair on those resident in England (as will be shown later in this section). It is vital to note at this juncture that this discussion has never been about the separate peoples in a nationalist sense as such (that is, about whether an individual considers himself or herself to be English, Welsh, Scottish, or Northern Irish), but rather about the people living in the UK's four different countries (that is, where in the UK he or she happens to be living). By way of illustration, there are many English people living in Scotland. The fact that these people are English by birth does not mean that they are not affected by the Acts of the Scottish Parliament or that they are not represented in it; quite the opposite is true in fact—they *are* affected by, and represented in, the Scottish Parliament by virtue of the fact that they permanently live in Scotland, as are those Welsh and Northern Irish people who also live there. The same is clearly true vice versa: the many Scottish people who live in England are represented only by members of the Westminster Parliament and are directly affected only by the Acts of that Parliament. Obviously, this is also true of the Welsh and Northern Irish people living in England. Therefore the vital point to remember is that it is one's place of residence that affects the law and policy that shape daily life, not 'national identity' per se.

Owing to the devolution process, English policies are becoming increasingly distinct from those in operation in Scotland and Northern Ireland, and to a lesser extent, Wales. As a result, the central government will occasionally wish to enact legislation that applies only to England, or to England and Wales. In such circumstances, as things currently stand, the MPs that represent Northern Irish, Scottish, and Welsh constituencies all have the right to vote on such measures. Thus if a controversial Bill were to come before Parliament (that is, one for which it is expected that a vote would be close), MPs for Scottish, Northern Irish, and Welsh constituencies for whom the legislation has no effect could hold a power of veto over English legislation. In the same manner, a government could depend on the votes of MPs from Scottish, Northern Irish, and Welsh constituencies to pass a controversial motion, despite the fact that the measure would have no effect outside of England. The most often-quoted example of such a situation is the one that arose in relation to the Labour government's controversial Higher Education Bill, in which instance despite the fact that seventy-one Labour MPs voted against the government's proposals in January 2004, the motion was carried owing to the support of Labour MPs representing Scottish constituencies. This was despite the fact that higher education was a matter devolved to the Scottish Parliament and that the Act would have absolutely no affect on the Scottish constituencies.

One solution offered at the time of the vote on higher education reform and since then was to prevent MPs representing any constituencies outside England from voting on English-only matters. A second option would be to establish an English Parliament, set up specifically to legislate on English-only matters. The UK Parliament would remain in existence to legislate for all the issues common to all four nations.

A more controversial argument for establishing an English Parliament is that, as things stand, English taxpayers are contributing to facilities in Scotland and Wales via the Barnett formula that are not on offer to them in England. Such an argument is outlined below by former government minister, Frank Field MP. If his point were to be taken through to its logical conclusion, all of the UK's nations would have their own legislative bodies with tax-raising powers and relative autonomy in how they would choose to spend such revenues.

. . . .

● **Frank Field MP, 'The strange death of Labour England? Revisiting Bagehot's English constitution'** (The Chancellor's Lecture, University of Hertfordshire, 3 June 2008)

Pressures have been building up to revisit the devolution settlement. The English feel that the settlement is unfair both constitutionally and financially. Scottish Members vote on legislation that does not affect their constituents but it does mine. Likewise, the fiscal disadvantages devolution places on my constituents compared with Scottish and Welsh voters, will also ensure that there is inevitably a second great Devolution Act. The fiscal discriminations cover, for example:

- frail citizens in Scotland not facing residential care home fees as they do in England;
- Scottish citizens being treated with the Lucentis drug for macular degeneration of the eye while English citizens simply lose their sight awaiting action from NICE;
- Scottish students going to University not paying top-up fees of £3,000.00 per year as do English students going to University; and,
- most English citizens paying prescription charges while none face such charges in Wales.

These advantages would be entirely acceptable if they were funded by Scottish and Welsh taxpayers. Yet the Scottish Parliament has resolutely refused to use any of its fundraising powers and, of course, the Welsh Assembly has no such powers to employ.

If Mr Field's suggestion were accepted and if all of the UK's nations were granted full legislative bodies, it is possible that the union would have to become a federal system (rather like

Australia, Germany, or the United States) in order to survive. Alternatively, the union could break up, leading to the death of the UK. That is certainly one of the concerns that has been used as an argument both for and against greater devolution of power. It is also an argument attributed to a number of current senior Cabinet officials who have rejected an English Parliament out of concern that it would hasten the demise of the union. Instead, they argue that, because the vast majority of seats in the Westminster Parliament are held by MPs representing English constituencies, the balance of power is actually strongly in favour of those living in England and any move to tip the power more in favour of those in England would jeopardise the union as a whole.

It is, of course, impossible to give a definite answer to the question of whether there will be an English Parliament. However, one can state with certainty that there is an issue to be resolved, and that the so-called English question will become more and more apparent as the devolution process develops in the other three nations.

summary points

Should there be an English Parliament?

- *The question is not a new one—but it has become much more apparent since the devolution process began in 1998.*
- *Most of the calls for an English Parliament stem from the fact that the West Lothian question has been turned on its head and that MPs from the other home nations can now dictate what happens in England.*
- *Other solutions would include preventing Scottish (and Northern Irish and Welsh) members of Parliament from voting on England-only issues.*

10.8 # What effect has devolution had on parliamentary supremacy?

As has been shown throughout the chapter, the devolution process in the UK has led to the Westminster Parliament conferring a substantial amount of power on three devolved institutions. However, as has also been shown, Parliament has completely retained its legislative supremacy in all areas for all countries. Legally, the Westminster Parliament is still sovereign. The devolution statutes all include the caveat that the Westminster Parliament's power to legislate for the nations in question remains unaffected by the passing of the 1998, and subsequent, legislation. Additionally, one must also recognise that, in legal terms, Westminster has the right to repeal all of the enabling Acts, thus abolishing the three institutions. As was shown in Chapter 7, the traditional doctrine of parliamentary supremacy establishes that no Parliament has the power to bind a future Parliament. In relation to the devolution statutes, this means that, theoretically and legally, the Westminster Parliament could choose to reclaim all devolved powers.

One further example that illustrates the full extent of Westminster's continued supremacy is the fact that all three devolved institutions are legally prevented from legislating contrary to the ECHR. If they were to do so, the legislation in question would be open to be struck down by the courts. However, this is not the case with the Westminster Parliament. As illustrated in Chapters 7 and 9, if it were to wish to do so, Westminster could pass legislation that contradicts the ECHR, and if it were to do so, the courts could only issue a declaration of incompatibility. Its legislative supremacy thus remains intact.

. . . .

- ● **B. Hadfield, 'Devolution and the changing constitution: devolution in Wales and the unanswered English question', in J. Jowell and D. Oliver (eds) *The Changing Constitution*** (6th edn, Oxford: Oxford University Press, 2007), pp. 271–92, at 291–2

The UK constitution has not been changed by devolution. Certainly *de facto* the work of the Westminster Parliament is less extensive geographically, although the pressures on its time are stated to be as intense as ever. Certainly intergovernmental processes have been put in place, but they have not really been tested, given the absence of party difference among the UK, Scottish and Welsh Governments, although this is not to state that their policies or ethos have been identical.[1] The constitutions of the three devolved nations have been changed by devolution but not the English constitution (except negatively) and not the UK constitution.[2] Indeed the capacity of devolution to develop in Wales and Scotland is in many ways held back by the elision of 'English' and 'United Kingdom' at the heart of the UK's legislative and executive structures. No new thinking has there emerged to counteract or diminish the assumptions of the 'rightness' of Government dominance and of the manipulation of constitutional questions for partisan advantage. Devolution shows how much change is possible and how little is likely for as long as the Government dominates a sovereign Parliament.

1 See, e.g., M. Keating, L. Stevenson, and J. Loughlin, *Devolution and Public Policy: Divergence or Convergence* (Edinburgh: ESCR Devolution and Constitutional Programme, March 2005).

2 See further D. Feldman, 'None, one or several: perspectives on the UK's constitution(s)' (2005) 64 Cambridge Law Journal 329.

However, having said all of that, it is misleading to think of the situation in legal terms alone. In reality, political considerations also have a significant part to play. For example, a brief look at the argument that Parliament has retained its right to legislate for all matters, devolved or otherwise, for all nations quickly demonstrates that the issue is much more complex. As the Kilbrandon Commission report stressed in 1973, when Parliament confers legislative powers in certain fields on a devolved institution, there is a strong presumption that Westminster will not choose to legislate on those issues contrary to the wishes of the devolved nation or region. This has proved to be an entirely accurate summary of the situation in the post-devolution United Kingdom. Indeed, the Sewel Convention has developed so as to provide that Westminster will not legislate contrary to the wishes of the devolved Parliament and Assemblies on matters relating to their jurisdiction. One must remember that any UK government is still partly reliant on support from the devolved regions. Whilst it is true that, even combined, the number of MPs for Scottish, Welsh, and Northern Irish constituencies (117) is significantly less than the number of MPs for England (529), it is still a substantial number. Only a foolhardy government would seek to incur the wrath of the three devolved nations by consistently legislating against their wishes. In the extract below, Little explains, in relation to Scotland, that supremacy remains with the Westminster Parliament and has not been transferred to Scotland. However, since devolution, Scotland has assumed greater political power and this fact may lead Scotland to be less willing, in the future, to accept the traditional doctrine of the supremacy of Parliament.

. . . .

- ● ***G. Little, 'Scotland and parliamentary sovereignty'*** (2004) 24(4) Legal Studies 540, 557–60

In this context, the significance of devolution as a long-term constitutional and political process should not be underestimated. Although, as discussed above, the Scotland Act observed the constitutional orthodoxy that the sovereignty of the UK Parliament remains undiminished, Westminster is, in reality, disappearing from significant areas of Scottish political life quickly and with remarkable little mourning. Whilst the powers reserved under the Scotland Act to Westminster and the UK government in key areas such as macro economic policy, the constitution, foreign policy, defence, taxation and broadcasting are clearly very substantial, Scotland has already started to diverge in important devolved areas of domestic policy such as health, education criminal justice, social policy and the environment...

...

With the above arguments in mind, it seems likely that the authority of the doctrine of parliamentary sovereignty in Scotland may face serious political challenges in the years to come. More specifically, if it is accepted that parliamentary sovereignty should correspond with wider reality if it is to maintain its political and therefore ultimately its constitutional status, there must be doubt as to whether it can continue to do so in the long term in post devolution Scotland.

In terms of practical examples from the UK context, one can look both to the history of the Parliament of Northern Ireland 1921–72 and the early history of the new Scottish Parliament from 1999 to the present day. The reality is that the Westminster Parliament has never legislated on a devolved issue without the request and/or consent of the devolved legislature. Of course, that is not to say that the devolved administrations are hesitant in any way to ask Parliament for legislative assistance when they need it. In fact, the Scottish Parliament has made a substantial number of legislative consent orders—so-called Sewel motions—giving the Westminster Parliament its 'consent' to legislate on a devolved area.

The same principle applies to the second point—that Parliament could choose to abolish the devolved institutions at any time, without the request and consent of the region or nation's public. It has done so in the past in Northern Ireland, in very difficult political circumstances. But it seems very unlikely that Parliament would choose to do so in ordinary circumstances. To use the Scottish example again, one would suspect that it would be verging on political suicide for central government to repeal the Scotland Act 1998 without the express consent of the Scottish people. Indeed, it could be argued that the Scotland Act was in part motivated by the desire to stem calls for the total independence of Scotland from the United Kingdom, and that as such a unilateral end to devolution would only serve to increase those calls substantially.

The question of Parliament's continued supremacy is therefore quite a complex one. On the one hand, Parliament has the legal right to legislate on all devolved fields for all devolved nations. It also has the ultimate power to repeal a devolved institution in its entirety. However, owing to political pressures, one must also recognise that it appears highly unlikely that any central government would wish to do so contrary to the wishes of the general public, except in the most extraordinary of circumstances.

summary points

What effect has devolution had on parliamentary supremacy?

- *Legally, Parliament's supremacy is retained. It can choose to legislate on any issue devolved to Scotland, Wales, or Northern Ireland. It can also vote to repeal the Devolution Acts, thereby abolishing the devolved institutions.*

- *Parliament's superiority is emphasised by the very fact that some matters are reserved to it and by virtue of its ability to legislate contrary to the European Convention on Human Rights.*

- *However, political considerations also play their part. Any government is partly reliant on the support of the devolved nations. In this context, it is therefore unlikely that any government would legislate contrary to the wishes of the nations in question, except in the most unusual of circumstances. The Sewel Convention underlines this.*

 # Summary

Devolution is not a new concept. It was first introduced in its current form over a century ago, when Prime Minister William Gladstone attempted to establish a devolved government for Ireland. Although ultimately unsuccessful, the proposals did illustrate what is meant by 'legislative devolution'. Put simply, it is the conferral of power to create policies and to legislate on such matters. It also includes the power to execute and to administer those policies once formed. By definition, therefore, it confers more significant powers than any executive or administrative devolution settlement, because these deal exclusively with the execution and administration of central government policy. The Scotland Act 1998 and the Northern Ireland Act 1998 are prime examples of Acts that create legislative bodies. Both the Scottish Parliament and the Northern Ireland Assembly have the legal competence to create primary legislation in a wide range of domestic fields. The Government of Wales Act 2006 *does* establish the National Assembly for Wales' power to pass primary legislation, but in a narrower range of areas. The devolution agenda has had an effect on the traditional doctrine of parliamentary supremacy. Political reality means that Westminster will not legislate on devolved matters contrary to the wishes of the devolved nations, and neither will it choose to abolish the institutions without the consent of the people either. In effect, this means that devolution is here to stay and that the legislative competence of all three institutions will only increase with time. The question that remains unanswered is whether or not England will also receive such a devolved institution.

 # Questions

1   What is the history of devolution? When did 'devolution', as currently understood, first appear on the political landscape?

2   What are the different ways of conferring power? In what way is legislative devolution more advanced than other forms?

3   What is the history of devolving power to Scotland, Northern Ireland, and Wales? What are the legislative powers of the three institutions?

4   Why do some want to see the establishment of an English Parliament?

5   What effect has devolution had on the doctrine of parliamentary supremacy, both legally and politically?

 # Further reading

Bowers. P., 'The Sewel Convention' (House of Commons Library Standard Note PC/2084, 25 November 2005), available online at http://www.parliament.uk/commons/lib/research/briefings/snpc-02084.pdf

This note provides an explanation of the workings of the Sewel Convention. It is written in clear language and explains, in comprehensive terms, the main issues associated with the Convention.

Gay, O., Holden, H., and Bowers, P., 'The West Lothian Question' (House of Commons Library Standard Note PC/02586, 23 March 2011), available online at http://www.parliament.uk/commons/lib/research/briefings/snpc-02586.pdf

This note examines the issue of the 'West Lothian Question' in the light of the devolution settlements in Scotland, Wales, and Northern Ireland from 1999. It is very comprehensive, but is written in clear language and is a very useful guide to this topic.

Hadfield, B., 'Devolution: a national conversation', in J. Jowell and D. Oliver (eds) *The Changing Constitution* (7th edn, Oxford: Oxford University Press, 2011), pp. 213–36

This chapter provides a detailed and interesting account of devolution and the continuing debates that surround it. It has been recently updated and so is more current than many chapters on devolution that are available at present.

Part 3
Responsible Government

11

Executive Power and Accountability

Key points

This chapter will cover:

- What is executive power, from where is it derived, and who may exercise it?
- Through what mechanisms can the executive be called to account for its exercise of power?
- To what extent may Parliament hold the government accountable?
- To what extent may the courts hold the government accountable?

Introduction

This is the first of a series of chapters on responsible and accountable government. We have entitled this part of the book 'responsible government', because the purpose of calling the government to account is to ensure that it uses its powers lawfully and rationally, and in some senses also in conformity with its electoral mandate. This part will focus primarily on the central government in Westminster, although mention will be made of the committee structures in the devolved Parliament and Assemblies to illustrate different approaches to the Westminster system. We shall consider the nature of the power that the executive uses to run the country, from where it is derived, and who gets to make use of that power. We shall briefly examine the history and development of governmental power, including changes over recent decades, such as the rise of a phenomenon known as 'new public management' (NPM). We shall also consider the institutions and mechanisms through which the government may be held to account through political, legal, and electoral means, and we shall assess their strengths and weaknesses. Over the next three chapters, we shall focus in particular on political mechanisms, before turning to the detail of legal mechanisms for much of the remainder of the book. However, the political will be juxtaposed against the legal to provide some balance and some contrast to the nature of political accountability. Finally, we shall address calls for reform of the accountability structures currently in place. This chapter will focus on the institutions and mechanisms through which the executive may be called to account; the next chapter will focus on the role that constitutional conventions play in making the government accountable via these mechanisms. The third chapter in this part will examine the role that the Parliamentary Commissioner for Administration (PCA) plays in this respect. We shall begin by examining some of the more important mechanisms by which the government may be called to account and to take responsibility for its actions, omissions, and decisions.

11.1 What is executive power, from where is it derived, and who may exercise it?

In some respects, the question posed in the title of this section is something of a misnomer and Dicey would not recognise it at all. He would argue that there is no such thing as public law or administrative power in the UK, because there is no separate system of administrative law, unlike countries such as France. However, times have changed, and most scholars and practitioners would recognise that administrative law comprises a special form of law distinct from private law, which is the preserve of the **executive** and **public authorities** more generally. We discussed this right at the beginning of the book in Chapter 1 and you may wish to refresh your memory of that debate if you are in any way unsure about it. The executive is free to make use

cross reference

*Executive accountability is discussed in Chapter 4 in the context of **the rule of law**.*

of private law powers as well and is also subject to private law liability unless the **Crown** has been excluded from liability via statute. However, we shall not consider private law issues in any detail here, not because this is not an important element of executive legal authority, but because private law does not, in general terms, operate in a different way in respect of the executive from how it does in respect of the rest of society. You will see later in this chapter that there are concerns that there is insufficient scope for the review of governmental initiatives based on private law, for example in the field of **government** contracts. We provide further reading on this point at the end of the chapter, if you wish to consider this aspect of government accountability in more detail.

11.1.1 The executive and public law powers

cross reference

*See Chapter 6 for further details on executive power by virtue of the **royal prerogative**.*

It is a basic requirement of the rule of law that all are subject to the law, even government. The executive needs to have legal authority for its decisions, its actions, and its failures to act. This legal authority will come from **Parliament**, via the enactment of Acts of Parliament and through delegated legislation that is enacted with Parliament's authority. Legal authority may also be given via the Crown's royal prerogative, which is a special form of the common law available to the executive. The royal prerogative is similar in nature to presidential powers that exist in other countries. In order for the executive's actions to be deemed lawful, it must be possible to point to a statutory or a prerogative power that authorises or justifies them. The Crown also has access to normal common law powers, which we all enjoy, such as the power to make contracts, to own, and to dispose of property. This includes the power to do things that have not been prohibited by law too. The sources of executive public law power are set out in Figure 11.1.

One important point to note is that the executive may need to ask Parliament whether it is willing to enact new legislation or to amend existing legislation in order to give the executive the power to run the country as it wishes. Most **legislative** proposals come from the government for that reason, because the government needs the law to be changed to permit it to act according to its policy objectives. As long as the government can command a sufficient majority in the House of Commons (and usually in the House of Lords) in support of its Bill, then it can gain the power that it wants. Parliament is supreme, and thus if Parliament is prepared to pass legislation, then government is authorised to act. However, the situation is less easy in

Figure 11.1

Sources of executive public law power

Statutory power	Royal prerogative
Acts of Parliament and delegated legislation	**A special form of the common law**
Power is via Parliament	**Power is via the Crown**
Exercise of this power is open to scrutiny by the courts through the mechanism of judicial review	Exercise of this power is also open to scrutiny by the courts through judicial review
Some areas are considered to be non-justiciable, on the grounds that they are political rather than legal questions, for example.	Some areas are considered to be non-justiciable, on the grounds that they relate to the personal prerogatives of the monarch, or that they relate to certain areas of foreign policy, such as the executive's treaty-making powers, etc.

cross reference

See Chapter 7 for a brief explanation of the Parliament Acts 1911 and 1949.

respect of the royal prerogative, because royal prerogative powers are residual. This means that no new powers can be created. The executive cannot ask the **monarch** to extend its power through this route. Having said that, this is less of an issue than it may appear, because statutory powers override the royal prerogative. As long as the executive can convince Parliament to pass legislation to give it the power that it needs and the executive acts within the terms of the legislation, then the executive's actions will be legally authorised.

11.1.2 Who holds and exercises public law powers?

At first glance, this probably looks like a question with an obvious answer: who holds and exercises public law powers? 'The executive.' But, as we discussed in Chapter 2, the executive is more extensive than simply the political executive known as the government. The executive includes the civil servants who support the government and put its policy objectives into practice. Moreover, the government may confer public law powers on other bodies and individuals so that they may exercise a public function on its behalf. And so the answer is not quite as straightforward as it would first appear. Institutional reform of the public services since the early 1980s, with a programme of Next Step agencies and the contracting out of public services to private contractors, has altered the public service landscape and widened the range of bodies that—and thus the people who—may be charged with exercising public functions and public law powers.

● G. Drewry, 'The executive: towards accountable government and effective governance?', in J. Jowell and D. Oliver (eds) *The Changing Constitution* (6th edn, Oxford: Oxford University Press, 2007), pp. 185–206, at 186

> ...
>
> The familiar word 'executive' which features in the title of this chapter is more problematical that [sic] might at first be supposed. Much constitutional discourse still revolves around traditional 'separation of powers' distinctions between executives, legislatures, and judiciaries. But ... in an age in which traditional notions of 'government' have given way to the broader and more flexible concept of 'governance', and as policy making is seen as a complex and evolving process, conducted in an array of specialized policy networks with varied and shifting memberships, it has become unfashionable to depict the modern executive function as being confined merely to presidents, prime ministers, and cabinets and (by extension) their civil servants.
>
> This shift in the terminology is linked to the growing complexity of the relationship between political and bureaucratic office holders—ministers and civil servants. The comfortingly democratic idea that the 'policy' decisions that matter are taken by ministers, accountable to citizens via the ballot box (and in the UK, to Parliament), while civil servants merely play a subordinate 'administrative' role has long been recognized as a myth. The constitutional doctrine of ministerial responsibility suggests that ministers should account to Parliament for all the actions of their officials, but in an era of 'big government' in which ministries are large, fragmented, and decentralized, this too is largely a mythical aspiration. This gap between fact and fiction has ... been exacerbated (or at least consolidated) in recent years by 'new public management' (NPM) developments, such as the Next Steps agency programme.
>
> So today ... the meaning of the terms 'executive', and the constitutional character of the executive function, have become afflicted by much doubt and confusion. And this ambiguity poses particular difficulty when we seek to determine who is responsible for what, and who is to be held accountable, and by what means, for the deeds and misdeeds of a government.

This is discussed in the next chapter in more detail, but it is important to note at this stage that public law powers are not only the preserve of government ministers and senior civil servants; there is now a web of executive agencies that exercise these powers at the initiative of government, but are in some ways separate from it. Some of these agencies, such as the Benefits Agency and the Passport Office, remain situated within the government departments that address the policy areas linked to them. The chief executives of these agencies are accountable for the operation of the policy objective; the ministers, for the resources that flow to those agencies and the objectives that are set for them. The relationship is outlined through a framework agreement. Other agencies sit outside government departments. These agencies are known as Next Step agencies—which is relatively easy to remember if one considers that they are one step removed from government. They are charged with putting the government's policy initiatives into practice. It is increasingly difficult for Parliament to use traditional means for scrutinising the executive so as to ensure that it is fulfilling its electoral mandate, and making good use of its legal powers and effective use of public funds, because much of the detailed work of the executive is now being performed by other agencies. Ministerial responsibility has had to adapt to this new environment, as have Parliament and the courts. We shall consider recent reforms of Parliament's processes in an attempt to keep pace with public service changes. We shall also consider some of the challenges faced by Parliament in the next chapter.

summary points

What is executive power, from where is it derived, and who may exercise it?

- *The executive, just as the rest of society, must have the legal authority to act. This is a fundamental tenet of the rule of law.*

- *The executive may benefit from private law powers, just as we do. It may also be subject to private law liabilities, such as breach of contract and tortious liability.*

- *It also benefits from public law powers, which are derived from statute and the royal prerogative.*

- *Public law powers are those that are required to enable to government to run the country.*

- *The government may seek wider powers from Parliament, by proposing new legislation. It is for Parliament to decide whether to pass that legislation, to pass it in a modified form, or to reject it.*

- *Public law powers may be delegated to those outside government, so that they may exercise public functions and provide public services. There has been much recent reform in this area.*

11.2 Through what mechanisms can the executive be called to account for its exercise of power?

There are two principal means through which the executive may be held to account: the political and the legal. There is a third means, administrative accountability, through mechanisms such as the Ombudsman, discussed in Chapter 13. By 'political', we usually mean through parliamentary scrutiny mechanisms; by 'legal', we usually mean through the mechanism of **judicial** review. However, there is another broadly political mechanism through which the government may be scrutinised and challenged, and that is through the electorate, with the assistance of the media. We shall consider this one too, albeit briefly. Before we turn to the first two of these in detail, it may help to explain the rationale behind each of them in summary form in this section. This should provide some context for the sections that follow.

11.2.1 What is the rationale for parliamentary scrutiny?

Parliamentary scrutiny of the executive is relatively focused, in that it seeks to hold the government to account, via government ministers, rather than seeks to hold the wider web of public bodies and authorities to account. It is charged with the responsibility of requiring ministers to account, and in some circumstances to take responsibility, for things that have been done in the name of the government while carrying out government policy and also, in some cases, in their private capacities. Why has Parliament been charged with this role and why is its role relatively narrow? In Chapter 2, we discussed the representative role of members of Parliament (MPs) and the extent to which they operate under a mandate from the electorate, or whether they are elected to exercise their judgement to the best of their ability for the good of their constituents. We considered the way in which some members of the House of Commons and House of Lords are called upon to form the government. We also discussed the role that Parliament plays in supporting the government for as long as the government retains its confidence. The importance of the parliamentary confidence in government is also considered in more detail in the next chapter.

As an essential part of Parliament's role to act as a check on and balance to the power of the government, it needs to scrutinise the executive to determine whether it should provide its continued support to the government policy and legislative agenda. MPs seek to raise issues of concern that have come to their attention from communications with their constituents and through the media. These concerns may not otherwise be brought to the attention of government ministers, who would not then consider whether government policy needed to reflect the difficulties that some of the population may be experiencing. Ministers are normally obliged to answer questions raised by parliamentarians, even if they are not required to answer media questions. In reality, most ministers also respond to media questions, because to do otherwise might provoke a media firestorm if the topic were a particularly controversial or topical one. Parliament is also the major forum for party-political debates about the way in which the country should be ordered and the people assisted, supported, and punished for wrongdoing. It is the main nationally recognised debating chamber in which different ideologies, beliefs, and evidence bases may be considered, criticised, thought through, and ultimately accepted or rejected by our politicians. These ideological and pragmatic clashes allow for creative thinking, policy development, and legal changes. And through this process Parliament seeks to check the power of the executive, while individual members of both Houses get to air their views, and also, in some instances, further their constituents' needs and their own political ambitions.

11.2.2 What is the rationale for judicial scrutiny?

Judicial scrutiny of the executive is one of the fundamental principles associated with the rule of law. The **judiciary** should be able to hold the executive to account for its exercise of power in much the same way as it can members of the public. The government and public bodies are also liable in private law through the courts for breach of contract and for the tort of negligence, for example. Dicey believed it important that the executive be judged in the ordinary courts by ordinary judges in much the same way as the rest of us. However, as public law powers have developed, so has an additional form of judicial oversight known as judicial review. This is a mechanism through which the judiciary, in the **Administrative Court** of the High Court (and on appeal to the Court of Appeal and the Supreme Court) may scrutinise executive and public body decisions, actions, and omissions to ensure that they have been taken in accordance with the law. Private individuals are not subject to judicial review, because we do not employ public law powers; only the executive, public bodies, and public authorities may be scrutinised in this way by the courts. In the event that a judge discovers that the executive is acting illegally, irrationally, procedurally improperly, in breach of the rules of **natural justice**, or in breach of the Human Rights Act 1998, it may quash a decision, require action, or prohibit certain forms of action. It is also important to bear in mind that there is a tribunal system, to which social security, tax disputes, etc., may be brought. These tribunals are under the auspices of the HM Courts and Tribunals Service, established in 2011 (formerly the Tribunals Service, established in 2006), which is an executive agency of the Ministry of Justice. They too oversee the executive, public bodies, and public authorities.

NOTE You may wish to visit the HM Courts and Tribunals Service online at http://www.justice.gov.uk/about/hmcts/index.htm

11.2.3 What is the rationale for scrutiny by the electorate?

Ultimately, the government and Parliament are charged with the responsibility of running the country for the betterment of the population who live within it. The electorate has the legal right to choose parliamentary representatives every five years (at the very least). The media plays a vital role in bringing issues to voters' attention, although many would argue that the largely London-based media are obsessed with covering stories about the government, government ministers, and public services, rather than focusing on local constituency MPs. Thus general elections have become distorted into contests between political parties and their leaders, rather than between local candidates and local issues. Voters do not vote, technically, for a government, but for a local constituency MP to represent them in Parliament. And yet the media circus around general election time is, on the whole, focused squarely on the party leaders and their senior team and on central party-political messages. There have been a few exceptions to this, such as where a local issue has caused such an outcry from constituents that they were prepared to eschew national politics in favour of electing an independent candidate (one not linked to one of the major national political parties) who was elected on a single issue mandate that had great meaning to the local population. Thus Neil Hamilton MP was unseated by the independent candidate Martin Bell, who was elected on an anti-sleaze manifesto after links were uncovered suggesting that Neil Hamilton was too closely linked to Mohammed Al-Fayed and allegations of political sleaze were made against him. The other main parties chose not to campaign against Martin Bell and even withdrew their candidates so that the field was free for him. A long-running defamation case followed in which Neil Hamilton sought to disprove the allegations that had been made by Al-Fayed, but to no avail. On this occasion, the local electorate focused on a matter of local importance, but in many instances individuals will vote on the basis of party loyalty and a desire to see the party that they support form the next government. As a consequence, the electorate does call the government to account at each general election and gives its verdict on the government's performance in its previous term of office. And the threat of the ultimate sanction, losing the next election to one of the opposition parties, is enough to make the government of the day focus on media reports and seek good press for their initiatives in the hope that they will carry the electorate along with them. Why else would they employ media consultants, or 'spin doctors'? Opinion polls also have a role to play in gauging the temperature of electoral opinion, particularly towards the latter stages of any government's term.

summary points

Through what mechanisms can the executive be called to account for its exercise of power?

- *The government is subject to political scrutiny by Parliament. Parliament is charged with the responsibility of supporting the government, as long as Parliament retains confidence in the government. It uses its powers of scrutiny to ask questions of the government to gain answers to any concerns it may have on its own account or on behalf of MPs' constituents.*

- *The government is subject to legal scrutiny in its use of public law power through judicial review. The judiciary examines the legality of governmental action (as well as the actions of public bodies more widely) and may require action or prohibit actions that it holds to be illegal, irrational, procedurally improper, a breach of the rules of natural justice, or in breach of the Human Rights Act 1998.*

- *The electorate, with the assistance of the media, determines the make-up of the House of Commons through general elections and, as a consequence, the next government to hold office. The government, conscious of the need for electoral support, is increasingly focused on the need to retain public confidence and to put in place popular policies that will garner support from the public.*

11.3 To what extent may Parliament hold the government accountable?

Parliament has recently been undergoing a process of modernisation, much of which has occurred since 1997 when New Labour was elected to government, in part on a modernisation agenda. One of its first acts was to set up the Modernisation Committee of the House of Commons, to be chaired by the Leader of the House, to consider the reforms that were required in order to make the Commons more effective. Part of the reasoning behind this decision was that the Labour Party had voiced concern during its time in opposition (echoed by the other opposition parties) that Parliament had become too dominated by the executive and was no longer able to call the executive to account in any meaningful way. The Modernisation Committee was thus asked to consider how Parliament's role could be strengthened, as well as to suggest ways in which it could be reformed so as to attract MPs from a wider cross-section of the population, and to make it more streamlined and efficient. The (admittedly long) extract that follows sets out a summary of the main reforms from 1997 to 2005, as well as some of the criticisms that were levelled at the Committee's composition, its focus, and the results that it has achieved.

● L. Maher, *Modernisation of the House of Commons 1997–2005* House of Commons Research Paper 05/46 (London: HMSO, June 2005), available online at http://www.parliament. uk/documents/commons/lib/research/rp2005/rp05–046.pdf

Summary of Main Points

The Select Committee on Modernisation of the House of Commons was established in June 1997 with a remit to 'consider how the practices and procedures of the House should be modernised' After two Parliaments, during which the Committee has put forward proposals for reform many of which have been adopted by the House, assessments of the Modernisation process are beginning to be made...

The establishment of the Modernisation Committee had been one of the proposals of the Joint Consultative Committee on Constitutional Reform agreed by the Labour and Liberal Democrat parties before the 1997 general election, and its creation was a Labour Party manifesto commitment. The Committee was to be chaired by the Leader of the House of Commons. It has been argued that this has been crucial to its approach, its recommendations, and their relative success at being adopted by the House of Commons. However, it is also argued that having a Cabinet Minister on the Committee has proven to be a 'double edged sword': although the recommendations have a good chance of being agreed to by the House, the nature of the Committee's recommendations could be seen as reflecting the will of the Government to pass its business through the House efficiently rather than aiming to strengthen Parliament's scrutiny role.

A number of changes to the practices and procedures of the House of Commons have occurred following recommendations of the Modernisation Committee. The way the House processes legislation has been altered with more Bills subject to pre-legislative scrutiny, the introduction of carry-over for some public bills, the programming of legislation and the introduction of deferred divisions also giving more certainty to the legislative schedule. Parliamentary questions have been reformed to allow them to be more topical. There have been a number of changes to the way that select committees operate including the agreement of core tasks for select committees. A parallel debating chamber has been established in Westminster Hall. There have also been changes to the sitting hours of the House, and the Parliamentary week and year with sitting days announced in advance. The practices of the House have also been changed in order to remove some procedures considered to be outdated and to make more use of technology and to encourage parliamentary reporting by the media. Initiatives to improve communication with the general public have been taken.

It has been argued that the sum of these reforms has done little to address what is considered to be the trend towards executive dominance of Parliament. Others have suggested that the changes were the result not of a desire to redress this balance, but to enable Members to carry out their role as constituency representatives and caseworkers more effectively. Some changes to the way Parliament conducts its business have been argued for on the basis that they would make Parliament more understandable and reportable by the media, and hence help to address the fall in turnout witnessed at the 1997 and 2001 general elections. For others, more importance has been placed on the working lives of Members and their ability to spend time with their families, thereby making a Parliamentary career more attractive. The failure to define 'modernisation' has led the term being interpreted differently by different people. At times, arguments have been put for and against the same proposal, with both sides arguing that they would 'modernise' Parliament.

However, the Modernisation Committee's interpretation of 'modernisation' has, it is argued, been affected by the chair being held by a Cabinet Member. It has been suggested that proposals to strengthen the scrutiny role of Parliament have not generally emerged from the Modernisation Committee. Proposals to reform select committees were originally made by the Liaison Committee and were at first rejected by the Government. Proposals for the Prime Minister to give evidence to a select committee were likewise proposed by various individual select committees and the Liaison Committee, and were at first rejected on the basis that there was no precedent. But the individuals who have chaired the Modernisation Committee have also had different approaches; reforms to select committees and the Prime Minister's agreement to give evidence to the Liaison Committee both occurring whilst Robin Cook was Leader of the House.

The extract explains that the Committee was subject to criticism because it was chaired by a government minister, the Leader of the House, and yet that too may also have been one of its strengths. In order to move from reform proposals to concrete reform, a House that has been dominated by the executive (not least because it controls most of the Commons timetable) needs the support of the executive to effect change. Some of the Committee's successes will be discussed below, along with some of the criticism that it has attracted. The Committee secured pre-legislative review of Bills, or at least some Bills, which acts as a means of improving legislation and shaping government thinking at an earlier stage than would otherwise be possible through the standard law-making procedures. The debating function of the House has been enlarged through the use of the Westminster Hall debates, which allows for parallel debates to take place in Westminster Hall. This has the effect of increasing the time available for the discussion and debate of matters of political topicality. The procedure for tabling parliamentary questions has also been reformed so as to allow more topical questions to be tabled and answered. The Committee was also able, in the face of initial government opposition, to reform select committees to provide them with more powers and thus a greater ability to scrutinise the executive. The subsequent subsections will consider pre-legislative and legislative review, parliamentary debates, parliamentary questions, and parliamentary committees to examine the extent to which they provide effective mechanisms for calling the government to account for its policy initiatives, decisions, and actions. There are other scrutiny mechanisms, some of which are mentioned in subsequent chapters, others in the further reading listed at the end of this chapter.

11.3.1 To what extent may Parliament scrutinise the government pre-legislatively and legislatively?

Parliament has an important role to play in scrutinising the government pre-legislatively in relation to draft Bills. Draft Bills are usually scrutinised by at least one committee in the Commons and one in the Lords. Some are scrutinised by a joint committee of both Houses. The committees report to the House(s) and the government may choose to accept or reject any suggestions that they have made, or to compromise on the proposals. This may seem like an odd way in which to act as a point of scrutiny, because this is prior to legislation being passed and thus also prior to executive action that flows from that legislation. At this stage, Parliament has a good opportunity to determine the executive's motives for wanting legislative reform. It also has the power to determine whether the executive should be given the additional powers and in the terms requested. It may also consider how effective the government has been thus far in this particular policy area, and provide comment and guidance to the executive on future policy actions. The government may be more inclined to take suggestions on board at this stage, before the Bill attracts a lot of publicity and also before the matter has reached the floor of the House, rather than at a later stage of the Bill's passage. On this basis, the move towards pre-legislative scrutiny of the government's legislative proposals has been welcomed both by Parliament and by many commentators outside.

The First Report of the Select Committee on Modernisation of the House of Commons, an extract from which follows, welcomed the pre-legislative scrutiny of draft Bills and hailed it as one of the most successful parliamentary innovations of the last ten years. The Select Committee argued that this practice should become more widespread and, indeed, that it should be broadened, so as to give outside bodies and individuals a chance to have their say before a Bill is introduced. It was suggested that this would improve the quality of the Bills that are presented to Parliament and permit Parliament more time to focus on the detail of each Bill. This raises two issues, as follows.

1 There is concern that large swathes of some Bills go unconsidered in the Commons phase of the passage of legislation, and that the Lords have to spend a good deal of time acting not as a revising chamber (the House of Lords' mission in this regard), but as an initial stage in the scrutinising process.

2 The more that interest groups, as well as Parliament, may provide their views on the draft Bill, the more likely it is that the final Act, if passed, will be effective and comprehensive in scope and reach.

Having said that, there are criticisms of the current system of pre-legislative scrutiny, and it is by no means universally applauded, perhaps because it is considered to be somewhat unsystematic. Some commentators consider that pre-legislative consultation is not as pervasive as is often suggested. And the Modernisation Committee was inclined to agree, although it sees evidence of improvement:

● **Modernisation Committee, *The Legislative Process*** (First Report, Session 1997–98, HC 1097, London: HMSO, July 2006), paras 5–6

> [T]here has hitherto been little, if any, consultation with Members or with the House as a whole before Bills are formally introduced. In recent years some draft Bills have been produced prior to consultation, and the present Government has specifically undertaken in the Queen's Speech to extend this process. The House itself has however made no attempt to undertake any systematic consideration of such draft Bills. There has as a result been no formal channel to allow time and opportunity for Members to receive representations from interested parties. Consultations between Government and those outside parliament with a legitimate concern in the legislation has also be criticised as patchy and spasmodic.

There are approximately forty to fifty Bills introduced per parliamentary year. All Bills are considered by the Joint Committee on Human Rights, which scrutinises the Bill for any human rights implications that it may have. The legislative procedure was discussed in Chapter 7, and so we shall not consider it further here; however, the role of general committees (formerly known as standing committees) is instructive at this point with regard to their role in scrutinising legislation. Public Bill committees do not restrict their work to government-sponsored Bills, but because the vast majority of legislation is sponsored by the executive, their role is pivotal in overseeing the government's legislative intentions. They have an important role to play by way of suggesting amendments to the text and this, in turn, may have an impact on the powers that the government will acquire as a result of the legislation. Each public Bill committee is named after the Bill that it considers. For example, a committee considering a Bill entitled the 'Climate Bill' would be called the 'Climate Bill Committee'. The main role of public Bill committees is to consider proposed legislation, mostly public Bills, in detail. This committee system allows faster processing of Bills and is unique to the House of Commons; the Lords meet as a whole House in this function, known as the Committee of the Whole House. The committees reflect the political make-up of the House, so the government will usually have a majority in the House of Commons, although it is less likely in the House of Lords.

To what extent are these committees able to provide a point of real scrutiny? To what extent may government sidestep them by means of the party whip system, use of the guillotine, and programming motions? Does the government ever lose a vote on legislation? There are occasional rebellions by **backbench MPs** who do not follow the whip and vote against a government Bill. One such example was the Higher Education Bill 2004, which the government won by a very narrow majority of 316 votes to 288. The guillotine is a technical device by which the Bill's sponsor may force the fate of the Bill to be determined by a given date. It is usually invoked towards the later stages of the legislative process and Ganz (1990; see the end-of-chapter 'Further reading' list) argues that it should be used as a weapon of last resort if the opposition tries to delay a Bill by attempting to talk it out (that is, keep debating it until the time allowed is up). In short, it cuts off debate and forces a vote regardless of whether all points have been discussed by that stage. It was used by the Labour government between 1945 and 1951 on only three occasions, by the Conservative governments between 1979 and 1990 on thirty-four occasions, and by the Labour government between 1997 and 2000 on twenty occasions, suggesting that its use is increasing over time. A programme motion is similar to the guillotine, but it is a motion agreed with the opposition at an earlier stage of the legislative process and, in effect, it seeks to agree the timetable of the passage of the Bill through the process. It is usually agreed at the end of the second reading stage of the Bill. Its use is controversial, although less so than the use of the guillotine. The programming motion has been found to be useful and is used more frequently than the guillotine. So in the 2002–03 session, the guillotine was used three times and the programming motion seventy-one times. This has the effect of limiting debate, on the one hand, but also focusing the debate, on the other.

NOTE

More information is provided in R. Kelly, 'Modernisation: Revitalising the Chamber' (House of Commons Library Standard Note SN/PC04542, 12 December 2007), available online at http://www.parliament.uk/documents/commons/lib/research/briefings/snpc-04542.pdf

There is recent evidence that ministers have sought to restrict amendments to draft legislation, through the use of technical devices. *The Guardian* reported, on 22 October 2008, that ministers were blocking abortion amendments to the Fertilisation Bill by permitting only four-and-a-half hours for debate on the proposed amendments to the Bill, thus limiting discussion time and the ability to vote on each one. This was so controversial that then Speaker of the House Michael Martin told the House that it could vote down the programme motion if it so chose. One other key area of controversy is the Legislative and Regulatory Reform Act 2006, which allows a minister to amend primary legislation using secondary legislation. The stated aim of this Act is to lighten the burden imposed by legislation on anyone carrying on a trade, business, or profession. However, this may have the effect of changing the balance of power between the executive and Parliament, because the level of scrutiny required of primary legislation is far higher than that of secondary legislation. Evidence from the **coalition government** period is that programming motions are being used on most government Bills, although the guillotine motion is being used rarely. There is much disquiet about the widespread use of programming motions because they restrict the opportunity for amendments to be tabled and voted upon. The House of Lords has even sat through the night (a highly unusual step for the Upper Chamber) so as to keep the debate from the day before alive and to buy time to continue to scrutinise Bills it has considered to be particularly problematic, such as the Fixed-term Parliaments Bill (now the Fixed-term Parliaments Act 2011).

NOTE

See Hélène Mulholland, 'Ministers attacked for blocking abortion debate', *The Guardian*, 22 October 2008, available online at http://www.guardian.co.uk/politics/2008/oct/22/health-health

NOTE

You may wish to visit http://www.saveparliament.org.uk/information.html for information on the problems with the Fixed-term Parliaments Act 2011.

The Wright Report made some recommendations on the legislative process in relation to the report stage. The Committee noted that there was insufficient time devoted to this stage.

● **Reform of the House of Commons Select Committee,** *Rebuilding the House* [First Report, London: HMSO, November 2009] [the **Wright Report**], para. 33, available online at http://www.publications.parliament.uk/pa/cm200809/cmselect/cmrefhoc/1117/111702.htm

The single greatest cause of dissatisfaction which we have detected with current scheduling of legislative business in the House arises from the handling of the report stage of government bills—technically the 'consideration' stage when a Bill has been reported back to the House from a public bill committee.... Effective scheduling of business at report stage of many bills would often require nothing more than the allocation of a sufficient total time. It is too often insufficient at present.

The Committee suggested that the House of Commons Business Committee should determine the length of the report stage, that all groups of amendments should be debated, that government amendments should have priority, and that there should be restrictions on the length of speeches so that a Bill could not be 'talked out'.

The government does not, however, have the legislative process all its own way: there have been government defeats, such as the Terrorism Bill in November 2005 when the government was defeated over the ninety-day detention clause, and another problematic Bill was the Incitement to Religious Hatred Bill of February 2006. Amendments were made in the House of Lords, which then had to be considered by the House of Commons. The government was not in favour of the amendments and yet the Commons voted for them in the face of government opposition. And the Education Bill 2006 was passed only after the government made concessions to ensure that it was not defeated in the House of Commons. So we have evidence to suggest that there are occasions on which the government is able to pass its legislation by use of guillotine motions, the Parliament Acts, and programming motions; on other occasions, it is forced to amend its proposed legislation or face defeat. The House of Lords can be particularly persuasive in this regard, and the Parliament Acts 1911 and 1949 reflect the House of Lords' long history of legislative revision and government challenge.

· ·

● D. Oliver, 'The "modernization" of the United Kingdom Parliament?', in J. Jowell and D. Oliver (eds) *The Changing Constitution* (6th edn, Oxford: Oxford University Press, 2007), pp. 161–84, at 161

A major problem over the scrutiny of legislation on the floor of the House of Commons or in its standing committees is that it is not conducted according to any particular criteria, but at large. Scrutiny tends to be highly politically partisan, aimed only partly towards improving the Bill and largely towards drawing attention to weaknesses in the Bill and opposing and harassing ministers.[1] As Feldman has pointed out, scrutiny should include the examination of measures against certain standards that are independent of the terms or subject matter of the measure itself.[2] These standards should include matters such as clarity of drafting, compatibility with international obligations and the Human Rights Act, and respect for various constitutional principles such as the independence of the judiciary, legal certainty, non-retroactivity, proportionality of penalty, and so on. This kind of scrutiny is not done well by the House of Commons,[3] dominated as it is by party.

A number of supposedly modernizing measures have been taken both to improve House of Commons scrutiny of legislation and to facilitate the passage of government legislation. The two objectives are commonly in tension with one another. The scrutiny of legislation has been improved by publication of explanatory notes with Bills and the introduction of pre-legislative scrutiny of some draft Bills. Acceptance of the carry-over of some Bills from one session to the next[4] would take the time pressure off scrutiny and could thus enable it to be done thoroughly if the will to do so existed among backbenchers. However, very few Bills have been carried over and the norm remains for scrutiny to be completed to enable Bills to receive Royal assent before the end of the session. The establishment in 2002 of a Joint Committee on Human Rights[5] (on an initiative from the House of Lords) with the specific responsibility for scrutiny of legislation for compatibility with the Human Rights Act 1998 and the European Convention on Human Rights and for other human rights implications has produced focused, expert, and independent scrutiny of bills.

1 See Select Committee on Procedure, *Public Bill Procedure* (Second report, Session 1984–85, HC 49, London: HMSO, 1984), para. 30.
2 See D. Feldman, 'Parliamentary scrutiny of legislation and human rights' [2002] Public Law 323.
3 [Footnote omitted]
4 See HC Deb, 29 October 2002, cols 688–828. Normally, if a Bill does not complete its parliamentary passage by the end of the parliamentary session each year, it is 'lost'. The

government will have to reintroduce the Bill in the following session and start the parliamentary process over again. 'Carry over' enables the Bill to continue its parliamentary passage from one session to the next.

5 [Footnote omitted]

Perhaps, then, it is unsurprising if, at times, the government, with the electoral mandate, seeks to stifle debate and press a vote on MPs and Lords as swiftly as it can. However, that does not aid open government nor does it engender cross-party or even backbench support. And the introduction of the Joint Committee on Human Rights (so-called because it is a joint House of Commons and House of Lords committee) does appear to provide an effective and important point of scrutiny in relation to legislative proposals that may have human rights implications.

11.3.2 To what extent do parliamentary debates assist?

A parliamentary debate is a formal discussion on a Bill or a topic. Parliamentary debates on Bills usually take place at the second reading stage. Other debates will be on policy initiatives, the public services, or other issues of national or local concern. There are also special debates that take place every year, such as the debate in reply to the **Queen**'s Speech, moved by the opposition, and the debate that follows the Budget. Debates are introduced by a member of the House through a device known as 'moving a motion'. The Speaker then repeats the motion by way of a question and the debate begins. Debates follow the rules of the House, which are known as 'standing orders'. They are controlled by the Speaker in the Commons, although in the Lords peers, rather than the Lords Speaker, control their own debates. MPs must catch the eye of the Speaker, often by standing or half-standing up as the last person speaking provides his or her closing comments, so to attract the Speaker's attention. A member may contact the Speaker in advance in writing to indicate his or her wish to speak in the debate, but this will not necessarily guarantee that the member will be called to do so. The rules that govern debates are very similar to those used in university debating societies up and down the country: in the Commons, members address their comments to the Speaker or his or her deputy; in keeping with the different ethos and structure of the Lords, peers address the other peers instead. The member who tabled the motion (that is, started the debate) has the right to reply to speeches. The question posed at the beginning of the debate is then put to the vote. The results are published in Hansard. Controversial subjects may lead to very tight votes, for example the debate on the proposed war in Iraq in February 2003 resulted in 122 Labour MPs rebelling against the government position. In March 2003, 139 Labour MPs voted against the government. However, the government won the vote 412 to 129 with the aid of opposition votes (these were, on the whole, Conservative votes). There are mechanisms to permit emergency debates under Standing Order 24, which have been used recently in relation to the war in Afghanistan (in March 2002) and in relation to the UK–US extradition treaty in July 2006.

The House of Commons also has a mechanism to hold debates that do not require a vote. These are known as 'adjournment debates' and are used as a way of having a general debate on an issue, or as a way in which backbench MPs can raise issues with a minister and receive answers to constituency concerns. They take place Monday to Thursday during the last half-hour of the parliamentary sitting. The Speaker chooses the topic for debate on Thursdays, but the other three debates on Monday, Tuesday, and Wednesday are chosen through a ballot procedure from among the topics put forward by members to the Speaker. The House of Lords does not have adjournment debates, but instead use 'questions for short debate', which allow for short debates similar in nature to adjournment debates. There have been attempts to put more power in the hands of backbench MPs: see, for example, Leader of the House of Commons,

Governance of Britain: Revitalising the Chamber—The Role of the Back-Bench Member (Cm 7231, Session 2006–07, London: HMSO, October 2007). The House agreed to changes to its standing orders to provide for topical debates to be piloted in the 2007–08 Session.

NOTE

The report is available online at http://www.official-documents.gov.uk/document/ cm72/7231/7231.pdf and details of other sources are in the further reading listed at the end of this chapter.

There is now more opportunity for debate in Parliament since the Westminster Hall debates were instituted in 1999 following recommendations made by the Modernisation Committee. There are two 90-minute debates on Tuesdays and Wednesdays, as well as three 30-minute debates. Each government department will respond to the debates, but on a rota rather than on the request of members. Members apply to the Speaker for the opportunity to debate their chosen area and are selected, once again, by ballot; debates are chaired by one of the Deputy Speakers. Westminster Hall has been much praised as a venue that permits lively and probing debate on a regular basis, in a less partisan fashion than on the floor of the House of Commons. This has gone some way to meeting the criticism that Parliament had become dominated by the executive's programme of business. However, Westminster Hall debates take place at the same time as sessions in both chambers; they are parallel sessions. This has been criticised on the grounds that members may not be able to participate fully in the business of the House, or for that matter in important debates in Westminster Hall, because the sessions run concurrently rather than consecutively.

Debates provide an opportunity for members of both Houses to question government policy and to seek justifications and explanations from ministers. They allow MPs to raise constituency concerns and also to demonstrate that they are performing their representative function. This may enhance their reputation, although a poor performance may have the opposite effect. Debates also draw matters to the public's attention, as well as ministers', because they may be covered by the media and broadcast on the news. They are one of the few opportunities that backbench MPs have to demonstrate their disapproval of government policy or legislative direction, and backbench rebellions, although relatively infrequent, send powerful messages to the government and in particular to the **Prime Minister**. They may force a change in government policy or secure important concessions in relation to legislation. Rebellions happen infrequently, because MPs will normally follow the party whip, meaning that they will vote the way in which their party requires them to vote.

Debates are not universally successful. The parliamentary timetable is largely controlled by the executive, and therefore debates usually take place at a time of the executive's choosing and on the topics that it is willing to debate. The opposition parties have twenty opposition days per year in the House of Commons that they may use for the purpose of debate. There is often insufficient time to debate a matter fully, and even then it is often the well-known senior front-bench MPs who get to participate. Moreover, debates in the Commons, if not in the Lords, are greatly influenced by party politics and the adversarial cut-and-thrust that this brings. Debates may impact on government policy, but it is difficult to gauge the extent to which debates do have a major influence on the way in which the government operates. They may have less of an influence than other mechanisms, such as lobbying by campaign and lobby groups or business interests, and media reporting. Of course, the executive would wish to avoid negative publicity, but this any such media attention usually relatively short-lived and few people in the country follow parliamentary debates with real enthusiasm. Debates may not attract many members to the Chamber. In short, they are a useful mechanism with which to permit Parliament to scrutinise the executive, but with executive domination of the House of Commons and a strong party-political system in place too, debates in the Commons are more ritualistic than those in the Lords, which do offer a less partisan, more sophisticated examination of the issues even if they gain far less coverage in the media.

11.3.3 To what extent do parliamentary questions and Question Time provide a mechanism for scrutiny and accountability?

Parliamentary questions take a number of forms at Westminster. There are oral questions that may be asked during Prime Minister's Question Time and Ministers' Question Time. There are also written questions that may be tabled, and which are answered via the House of Commons or the House of Lords official journals—Hansard Commons and Hansard Lords. There are differing views as to the success and utility of oral and written questions.

Oral questions are normally not notified to ministers or the Prime Minister in advance; instead, they are asked at the regular Prime Minister's Questions (PMQs) or Ministers' Questions (MQs) slot. PMQs take place in the House of Commons every Wednesday for around half an hour at noon, during the parliamentary term. The Prime Minister, or his or her deputy if he or she is away from Parliament on business, is asked questions by his or her opposite number(s), the Leader of the Labour Party (during the coalition government at time of writing), as well as by backbench MPs. One of the strengths of PMQs is that the Prime Minister may be asked topical questions on a regular basis and be required to provide his or her answers to the House of Commons. However, because questions are not notified to the Prime Minister in advance, his or her ability to answer questions is limited to his or her knowledge base at the time the question is posed (as well as any briefing papers that he or she may have brought along with him or her just in case). There may be questions that he or she cannot answer, or that he or she cannot answer well. This limits the quality of the answers he or she is likely to be able to provide. In addition, PMQs is a relatively robust, adversarial party-political contest in which the leaders of the main parties attempt to weaken their opponent(s), and to display their own oral dexterity and their political prowess. It is less an opportunity to scrutinise the government via the Prime Minister, and more an opportunity for the Leader of the Opposition to appear strong and the Prime Minister weak on the evening news broadcasts.

In addition to PMQs, there is also an opportunity to ask questions of ministers. Ministers' Questions are arranged on a rota basis, so that questions may be put to each government department in the Commons or the Lords on a regular basis. In the House of Commons on Mondays to Thursdays when Parliament is sitting, ministers take it in turns to answer questions. Commons oral questions are tabled at least three days in advance. The strengths that have been identified in relation to Question Time include that the government regularly has to account to Parliament, that there is an opportunity for the opposition parties and for backbenchers to raise issues of concern and to test the effectiveness of the government, that there is an opportunity to put individual ministerial responsibility into practice, and that there is an opportunity for constituency MPs to raise matters of concern to their constituents. Oral questions also make ministers aware of issues affecting the population (although written questions may do this just as well, if not better). But weaknesses have also been identified. For example, Question Time lasts for only 50–60 minutes. Although it does take place four times a week, it still provides a relatively limited time frame within which to ask questions. Senior ministers may not always be available to answer questions and even when questions are answered, they may not be answered in as much detail as the questioner would wish. In addition, some questions may not be answered for reasons of national security and confidentiality, among others.

Question Time in the Lords is a little different from that in the Commons, in that questions are asked of the government rather than individual ministers and Question Time lasts for only

342

NOTE You may wish to watch PMQs online at http://www.parliamentlive.tv

NOTE More detail about the role of Commons questions is available online at http://www.parliament.uk

30 minutes at a time. There are additional opportunities to ask questions. On Mondays to Thursdays when Parliament is sitting, up to four questions may be put to a government spokesperson at the start of the day's business. Peers may also question the government via written questions. Urgent oral questions may be posed via the Leader of the House, although the number that may be asked is limited. Urgent questions are also taken in the House of Commons and are notified via the Speaker of the House in a similar way. Maer and Sandford explain the strengths and weaknesses of oral and written questions in the next extract.

● **L. Maer and M. Sandford,** *The Development of Scrutiny in the UK: A Review of Procedures and Practice* (London: The Constitution Unit University College London, 2004), p. 49

Oral and written questions to ministers are perhaps the oldest form of scrutiny available in Westminster. They were central to obtaining information from ministers throughout much of the 20th century, though their significance has declined comparatively since the introduction of select committees. Oral and written questions cannot oblige Ministers to give answers. Sometimes answers will not be given on the grounds of national security or confidentiality; more often, responses which do not address the questions asked, or omit important information, will be given. Some recent parliamentary 'scandals', such as the arms-to-Iraq affair which led to the Scott Inquiry in 1994–95, and parliamentary questions leading to the *Belgrano* trial in 1985, began with misleading answers to parliamentary questions. However, the ability to ask questions can in itself reveal information which Ministers would rather not reveal: it is a forensic process.

Question times have been less remarked upon in the devolved assemblies, due to the strength of their committees to make and debate policy and to the time spent in committee (much greater than in Westminster). However, they remain important forums of debate, and written questions remain a useful means to information—particularly on members' constituency issues...

Written questions may provide a more detailed answer than do oral ones, because the government has the opportunity to find the information that is required to provide a fuller answer. However, some questions may not be answered fully if at all, because the cost of investigating the issue to provide an answer to the question may be unduly prohibitive. A new form of oral question was introduced in 2003 known as the 'cross-cutting question', which means a question that cuts across or involves more than one government department. These questions take written form.

NOTE

You may wish to refer to House of Commons, 'Brief Guide to Select Committees', available online at http://www.parliament.uk/documents/commons-information-office/Brief-Guides/Select-Committees.pdf

11.3.4 To what extent do select committees perform this function?

Much of the work of Parliament is undertaken through parliamentary select committees. There are a number of types of select committee. House of Commons departmental select committees scrutinise a single government department. They contain at least eleven members, who set their own terms of reference in relation to matters to be considered as regards that department. They report to Parliament and, once a report has been published, the government will normally respond to it within sixty days. There are also a small number of select committees that address issues that are beyond one government department, such as the Public Accounts Committee, and there are other committees, such as the Committee on Standards and Privileges, which address more general issues, such as in respect of behaviour of members of the House, day-to-day business of the House, etc. The House of Lords also has select committees, but these are focused on four areas—the constitution; economic affairs; the European Union; and science and technology—rather than on government departments.

Since the government has accepted the Modernisation Committee's proposals for reform, the core tasks of select committees have now been agreed, as follows.

Select committee objectives

1 To examine and comment on the policy of the department

2 To examine the administration of the department

3 To examine the expenditure of the department

4 To assist the House in debate and decision-making

NOTE

You will find more detail about these objectives in the Appendix to Liaison Select Committee, *The Work of Select Committees 2001* (First Report, Session 2001–02, HC 590, London: HMSO, February 2002).

Oliver explains select committee tasks as follows.

● **D. Oliver, 'The "modernization" of the United Kingdom Parliament?', in J. Jowell and D. Oliver (eds)** *The Changing Constitution* (6th edn, Oxford: Oxford University Press, 2007), pp. 161–84, at 169–70

Some reforms have been designed to increase the influence and powers of the House of Commons' select committees and thus the effectiveness of individual ministerial responsibility. The departmental and other investigative select committee had the function of monitoring the expenditure, administration, and policy of government and its departments. These committees now have an agreed, explicit set of core objectives, extending beyond the long established role of imposing direct ministerial responsibility to tasks such as monitoring performance against targets in public service agreements, taking evidence from independent regulators and inspectorates, considering the reports of Executive Agencies, considering major appointments made by ministers, and examining treaties within their subject areas.[1] However, in practice committees remain autonomous in how they interpret those core tasks. Several have refused to take on scrutiny of draft Bills, for instance.

1 See Modernisation Committee, *Select Committees* (First Report, Session 2001–02, HC 221, London: HMSO, 2002); Liaison Committee, *Select Committees: Modernisation Proposals* (Second Report, Session 2001–02, HC 692, London: HMSO, 2002); approved HC Debs, 14 May 2002, cols 648–730.

She argues that, in truth, many parliamentarians are really not that well equipped to carry out the task of scrutinising Bills, and that it may be preferable to require legal and other advisers to perform this function. However, Tomkins argues otherwise.

● A. Tomkins, *Public Law* (Oxford: Oxford University Press, 2003), p. 169

> ...notwithstanding it being unfashionable to say so Parliament and its committees continue to make an outstanding contribution to the central constitutional task of holding the Crown's government to account.

There is therefore some debate about the extent to which select committees are able to be effective in scrutinising the executive.

The composition of each committee is obviously a key factor in terms of how successful it will be in calling the government department to account. So who decides who is to sit on each of the committees? Selection can be controversial, as demonstrated by the controversy over the whips' decision not to renominate Gwyneth Dunwoody and Donald Anderson in their roles as committee chairs in the previous Parliament. It was alleged that Dunwoody and Anderson had not been put forward by the whips in the new Parliament because they had been involved in a backbench rebellion, which meant that they had not obeyed the party whip. When the whips put forward others to become the committee chairs, the Commons rejected the nominations. The whips bowed to Commons pressure and the two names were put forward for election. This was hailed as a triumph of parliamentary independence. It has been argued that the key to an independent and vigorous select committee is a strong select committee chair. The Modernisation Committee recommended that committee chairs should be paid an additional salary on top of their parliamentary salary, but that they should serve as chair for no more than two parliamentary terms and in any event for a maximum of eight years. It also argued that the standard membership of a committee should be fifteen, supported by way of specialist support staff in a scrutiny unit designed to assist select committees. The reforms have not gone sufficiently far for some, however. Kelso argues that reform of the rules and procedures surrounding committee membership have been stifled by the parties.

● A. Kelso, 'The House of Commons Modernisation Committee: who needs it?' (2007)
  9(1) British Journal of Politics and International Relations 138, 151–2

> **The Effectiveness of the House of Commons: Select Committee Reform**
>
> The Modernisation Committee has spent most of its time looking at issues of procedural efficiency, and effectiveness matters have received limited attention as a result. Only three reports have looked exclusively at enhancing Commons capabilities in terms of executive scrutiny. Two reports have examined scrutiny of European business (HC 719, 1997–98; HC 465, 2004–05), an area that arguably requires much more attention. However, the most notable work done by the Modernisation Committee with regards to scrutiny is that concerning the select committee system.
>
> ...It is fortuitous that criticism of the existing system came to a head just as Robin Cook was appointed Leader of the House. His arrival in the chair of the Modernisation Committee enabled a window of opportunity to open in favour of reform (Norton 2000; Kelso 2003), and the committee's eventual proposals to reform the select committee system (HC 224, 2001–02) attempted to tackle some of the issues that were at the heart of the imbalance in executive–legislative relations, particularly those recommendations geared towards removing whip influence from select committee nominations, which had long been criticised for delimiting the scrutiny abilities of the select committees (Kelso 2003, 62–63)...
>
> However, despite the Commons having the opportunity to engage with reform that would make a significant difference to its scrutiny capabilities, the House did not possess the political will to secure that reform. While a number of the proposals were accepted by the Commons in May 2002, such as core duties for select committees, the most important aspects of the reform

package were defeated, such as those aimed at removing whip influence from the committee selection process (Kelso 2003, 62–66). Reformist arguments failed to sway those MPs who were persuaded by the whips that existing arrangements were best preserved (Kelso 2003, 64–66). Of course, core duties for select committees and payment for committee chairmen may contribute to enhanced scrutiny. However, these reforms were underpinned by the notion that the executive should not make decisions about who scrutinises it. So long as the whips play a central role in choosing those MPs who serve on select committees, the real effectiveness of these other reforms will be constrained. As one Liberal Democrat MP explained, if chairmen are paid while the committee selection process is still controlled by the whips, then it is possible that such positions can be used as 'sweeteners' to place compliant or sympathetic MPs on to certain committees (interview, 12 March 2002).

She suggests that the use of the **whipped vote**, the mechanism through which political parties require their members to vote along party lines, has a negative impact on the composition and working of select committees. She further argues that there is little political will to take the important step of removing the whip system in relation to select committee nominations. Membership of the committees reflects a balance between the parties in the House. Committee members for each party are nominated by the whips, as are the chairs. Members of the Commons get to vote on these nominations to determine committee membership. Now that chairs are paid a salary for performing this function, there has been criticism that these positions could be used by the government to reward party loyalty and to ensure kindly treatment by the select committee chair in the exercise of his or her duties. Having said that, committee membership is viewed by many as an alternative career path to a position in government and committees generally work on a cross-party, rather than party-political, basis—although there have been some notable exceptions to this, such as the Foreign Affairs Committee 1984–85 in relation to the sinking of the ship *General Belgrano* in the Falklands conflict. And it is important to note that one cannot be a member of a select committee as well as a member of the government. This provides a measure of parliamentary independence so as to maximise the opportunity for effective scrutiny of the relevant government department.

What powers do select committees have to compel ministers and civil servants to attend, and to require disclosure of information and of documents? There are examples of ministers failing to attend select committee hearings and/or obstructing the work of the committee. Examples of a few obstructions are set out in the next extract.

. . . .

● **House of Commons Liaison Committee,** *First Report: Appendix 12: Foreign Affairs Committee 1992–97, Report by the Rt Hon David Howell, Chairman of the Committee* (London: HMSO, February 1997), available online at http://www.publications. parliament.uk/pa/cm199697/cmselect/cmliaisn/323i/lc0119.htm

Summoning of witnesses and access to documents

7. The Committee has encountered no general difficulty in the present Parliament over summoning of witnesses and access to documents. Even in the case of the Pergau inquiry, where the Committee sought evidence in two sensitive categories: communications between Governments and communications between Ministers and advice to Ministers from officials, it was able to report to the House that it had 'had adequate responses to most, but not all, of our requests to the Foreign Secretary and other Ministers for written material'.[1]

8. In the same inquiry, though, the Committee was unable to persuade Lady Thatcher to give evidence. She cited 'the convention, established since 1945, that Prime Ministers and former Prime Ministers do not give evidence to Select Committees on specific issues'.[2] That apart, the Committee has encountered only one serious difficulty in the current Parliament over securing the attendance of appropriate witnesses.

9. The one major difficulty with the Government arose from the Committee's inquiry into United Kingdom policy on weapons proliferation and arms control in the post-Cold War era. The Government refused to allow the Intelligence Services either to give formal evidence or informal briefing on their work in combating proliferation of weapons of mass destruction.[3] In its response[4] to the Committee's report, the Government sought to justify this on the grounds that its refusal was 'in accordance with the long-standing policy that the work of the intelligence agencies falls outside the remit of select committees'. The Committee maintains its view, set out in the report, that 'it is essential that departmental select committees should be able to have access to relevant intelligence briefing where . . . it has direct and central bearing on a particular inquiry'. For this reason, the Committee supports the use of the 'crown jewels' procedure (which was used in 1984–85 to enable this Committee's predecessors to consult intelligence material related to the sinking of the *General Belgrano*) in appropriate cases.

1 Foreign Affairs Committee, *Foreign and Commonwealth Office Resources* (Fifth Report, Session 1998–99, HC 271-I, London: HMSO, July 1999), paras 9–11.

2 Ibid, para. 8.

3 See Foreign Affairs Committee, *UK Policy on Weapons Proliferation and Arms Control in the Post-Cold War Era : Observations by the Secretary of State for Foreign and Commonwealth Affairs* (Second Report, Session 1994–95, Cm 2895, London: HMSO, June 1995), paras 108–13.

4 Ibid, para. 26.

As you can see, select committees are reliant on ministers to choose to assist them in their investigations. Ministers may face political pressure, and even opprobrium, if they refuse to attend a select committee hearing or fail to answer questions and provide documents, but there is no legal sanction that can be applied to a minister who fails to cooperate with a committee investigation. Civil servants are encouraged to avoid giving information on controversial matters that would reveal sensitive information, or which relate to matters that are *sub judice*. The 2002 First Report of Select Committee on Modernisation of the House of Commons recommended that there should be a review of whether select committees should be granted the power to require witnesses to give evidence; at the time of writing, they may not compel attendance even though unwillingness to attend is met with great disapproval. Select committees do not have such extensive powers as US congressional committees, as was extremely evident during a review of the arms to Iraq affair in 1993–94 and in relation to the Foreign Affairs Select Committee investigations into the weapons of mass destruction (WMD) claims prior to the more recent Iraq war. However, recent research indicates that select committees may have more influence over government policy that sceptics would suggest. Russell and Benton (2011, see the further reading list at the end of the chapter) found that 40 per cent of select committee recommendations are taken up by the government and result in changes in government policy. The research suggests that government policy may be changed as a result of knowing that a select committee is likely to investigate the matter in the near future (that is, anticipatory change so as to avoid difficult questions in the committee), and that select committees have an ongoing influence on government departments as a result of the evidence base that they collect and publish as part of their investigations.

NOTE

Russell and Benton's research is also a good source of information about the workings of select committees: see the further reading listed at the end of the chapter for more details.

NOTE

The Osmotherly Rules give guidance to civil servants or officials who are to appear before select committees. See the further reading list at the end of the chapter for more information.

11.3.5 To what extent are the committees in the Scottish Parliament, the National Assembly of Wales, and the Northern Ireland Assembly better able to scrutinise the devolved executives?

Thus far, we have concentrated on central government and the Westminster Parliament. **Devolution** provided an opportunity for Scotland, Wales, and Northern Ireland to construct a system of executive scrutiny from scratch rather than to remain at the mercy of centuries of tradition and precedent. To what extent are the devolved Parliament and Assemblies better equipped to scrutinise the executive? Maer and Sandford have conducted research into the operation of these three countries' systems. An extract from their report illustrates their findings in relation to Wales and Northern Ireland, which operate very differently from the Westminster model.

● **L. Maer and M. Sandford, *The Development of Scrutiny in the UK: A Review of Procedures and Practice*** (London: The Constitution Unit University College London, 2004), p. 27

The creation of the three devolved national institutions—The Scottish Parliament, Northern Ireland Assembly, and National Assembly of Wales—represented a step-change in British constitutional politics. As Burrows says, in all three 'it was anticipated that the bulk of the work...would be conducted through committees. It is in their operation that the devolved institutions are self-consciously "modern"'.[1] Committees in each institution are involved in policy making reflecting the desire to make the new institutions inclusive, and legislative scrutiny (secondary legislation only in Wales) as well as the traditional scrutiny role that subject committees have in the Westminster Parliament.

The most movement in the operation of committees has taken place in Wales where there have been three periods of government: May 1999–October 2000, under a Labour minority government; October 2000, under a Labour minority government; October 2000–May 2003, with a Labour–Liberal Democrat coalition with a working majority; and May 2003 onwards, with a Labour majority. Under the minority government there were examples of the Subject Committees being able to frustrate the policy direction of the Executive. This was due both to the lack of an Executive majority and other parties' discontent with Alun Michael's style of leadership, which tended towards not releasing information to subject committees.

Committee structures in Northern Ireland are subject to a number of special circumstances which make direct comparison difficult. The Assembly has only sat for some 50% of the duration of its first term, from 1998 [to] 2003. The remainder of the term has been lost to repeated suspensions of the institution. Secondly, the complex model through which the Northern Ireland executive is selected in order to represent each party in proportion to its share of the seats in the Assembly. Thus the Cabinet contains representatives from four different parties. The precarious nature of the political settlement has meant that it is difficult to oppose or censure a Minister and as such, has affected the behaviour of committees.[2]

1 N. Burrows, *Devolution* (London: Sweet & Maxwell, 2000), p. 46.

2 This was written before the Northern Ireland elections of 26 November 2003.

There is some evidence to suggest that devolution has allowed for different models of scrutiny to develop between the legislative body and the executive. These are still in a state of flux, although the Welsh Assembly, already the subject of reform and having had three administrations since its inception, provides the most compelling evidence of strong scrutiny of the executive by the legislature.

11.3.6 To what extent is the House of Commons able to scrutinise the executive?

There remain concerns that the House of Commons does not have the necessary tools or time to allow MPs to scrutinise the executive effectively.

The Select Committee on Reform has completed its first report, setting out its conclusions and recommendations for change.

NOTE

You may wish to watch A. Wright, the former chair of the Select Committee on Reform, talking about this topic to the Constitution Unit, online at http://vimeo.com/7848190

● **Reform of the House of Commons Select Committee, *Rebuilding the House*** [First Report, London: HMSO, November 2009], paras 22–35, available online at http://www.publications.parliament.uk/pa/cm200809/cmselect/cmrefhoc/1117/111702.htm

CONCLUSIONS AND RECOMMENDATIONS

A Principles

(a) We should seek to enhance the House of Commons' control over its own agenda, timetable and procedures, in consultation with Government and Opposition, whilst doing nothing to reduce or compromise such powers where they already exist;

(b) We should seek to enhance the collective power of the Chamber as a whole, and to promote non-adversarial ways of working, without impeding the ability of the parties to debate key issues of their choosing; and to give individual Members greater opportunities;

(c) We should seek to enhance the transparency of the House's decision making to Members and to the public, and to increase the ability of the public to influence and understand parliamentary proceedings;

(d) We should recognise that the Government is entitled to a guarantee of having its own business, and in particular Ministerial legislation, considered at a time of its own choosing, and concluded by a set date;

(e) We should recognise that time in the Chamber, Westminster Hall and committees is necessarily limited, and therefore should work broadly within the existing framework of sitting days and sitting hours;

(f) Changes should be devised with sensitivity to real-world political constraints, and in a way which maximises the likelihood of achieving majority support in the House.

These principles have informed our deliberations and are reflected in our approach to the specific matters on which we have been asked to report. We aim to make the Commons matter more, increase its vitality, and rebalance its relationship with the executive.

Some of the key recommendations set out in the report include the following.

• The chair of departmental select committees should be elected by the whole of the House of Commons by secret ballot.

- Members of departmental select committees should be elected by secret ballot by political party in accordance with their level of representation in the House.
- A House Business Committee should be created, to comprise government and backbench members, and to be tasked with determining the agenda of the House of Commons.
- A Backbench Business Committee should also be created.
- There should be protected time for backbench business and this should preferably be one day per week.
- In order to enhance the scrutiny of legislation, there should be greater opportunity for debate at the report stage of a Bill.

A number of these recommendations were implemented in the Parliament that commenced May 2010, including electing the chairs and members of departmental select committees, and creating a Backbench Business Committee to organise backbench business.

NOTE

A speech by the coalition Leader of the House of Commons, setting out the changes and the coalition's plans, can be found online at http://www.commonsleader.gov.uk/output/Page3023.asp

summary points

To what extent may Parliament hold the government accountable?

- *Parliament has a number of mechanisms through which to hold the government to account, including: pre-legislative and legislative scrutiny; parliamentary debates in the Houses and in Westminster Hall; oral and written questions; and parliamentary committees.*
- *These mechanisms have all undergone a process of reform, much of which has taken place since 1997.*
- *Day-to-day scrutiny takes places through questions and debates.*
- *Pre-legislative and legislative scrutiny provides the opportunity to examine government policy and future direction.*
- *Select committees provide a more in-depth investigation of governmental policy and action or inaction.*
- *The devolved Parliament and assemblies have adopted at least slightly, and in some cases markedly, different models of executive scrutiny of the executive.*

11.4 # To what extent may the courts hold the government accountable?

11.4.1 Are there areas that are not susceptible to review?

As we have seen, political accountability is focused largely on holding ministers to account for their records and those of their departments. In contrast, the courts have a wider remit, to ensure that, in cases brought before them, the executive or the public body concerned is acting within its legal powers. Most actions involving the review of statutory powers or the exercise of the royal prerogative will be susceptible to judicial review, assuming that the claimant has sufficient **standing** to bring the action (that is, that the claimant is sufficiently closely connected to the case to be permitted to have the matter reviewed by the court), assuming that the body in question is a public body exercising a public function, and that the case appears on the face of it to have some merit. However, the courts' powers are not without limit and there are areas that the courts deem to be non-justiciable, meaning that they do not consider it their role to review the exercise of power in those instances.

● **E. Barendt,** *An Introduction to Constitutional Law* [Oxford: Oxford University Press, 1998], pp. 143–5

4. Non-justiciable Political Questions

Are there some issues which courts should not be prepared to resolve because they are too political and therefore inappropriate for judicial resolution? Or, put more simply, are some issues 'non-justiciable'? This question has surfaced in a number of cases in this country, as well as spawning some compact constitutional law in the United States, where the courts have traditionally abstained from determining what they term 'political questions'. In contrast, the concepts of 'justiciable' and 'non-justiciable' issues are relatively new in this country. But arguably they explain why United Kingdom courts are reluctant to intervene in some cases, despite their general jurisdiction to review unlawful administrative action. For example, they are unwilling to entertain an action, at least when brought by non-British subjects in respect of executive conduct which can be justified as an 'act of state', that is an act of policy in the field of foreign affairs.[1] The courts also do not allow anyone to challenge the exercise by the Crown of its prerogative power to make a treaty with a foreign country or international organization. That is the reason litigants have hand no success in contesting UK accession to treaties with the European Community.[2]

Until recently, the courts also automatically abstained from reviewing the exercise of prerogative [as distinct from statutory] powers in the domestic field.[3] In the *Council of Civil Service Unions [CCSU]* case, the majority of the House of Lords abandoned this position. It held that an individual should be able to challenge in the courts an executive decision which affects his rights, irrespective whether it was taken under statutory or prerogative powers. But this does not apply where the character of the particular power, whether statutory or prerogative, make it unsuitable for review...

Later cases should the difficulty in drawing a sharp line between justiciable and non-justiciable issues...

English courts do not really need to draw a sharp line between justiciable and non-justiciable issues in judicial review cases when a challenge is brought on the ground that the minister has exercised his statutory powers in a grossly unreasonably or irrational way. Judges are particularly hesitant to question the rationality of a government decision involving the formulation of national economic policy; in these circumstances it would be difficult to formulate standards on the basis of which a court could comfortably conclude that the decision was irrational...The courts are only prepared to invalidate decisions of this hind, if they were patently absurd, or were clearly taken in bad faith. A separate doctrine of 'non-justiciable' decisions is redundant in these cases. Furthermore, it would be inappropriate to invoke the doctrine when courts are asked to protect fundamental human rights, except possibly in cases involving genuine national security or emergency considerations.[4] Indeed, the House of Lords scrutinizes administrative decisions impinging on fundamental human rights, such as the right of asylum and freedom of speech, particularly carefully to check whether they have been taken within the powers granted by Parliament.[5]

1 The leading modern case is *Nissan v Attorney-General* [1970] AC 179, which regrettably failed to resolve the question of whether an act of state can be argued where the claim is brought by a British subject.

To what extent may the courts hold the government accountable?

351

2 *Blackburn v Attorney-General* [1979] 1 WLR 1037; *R v Foreign Secretary, ex p Rees-Mogg* [1994] QB 552.

3 [Footnote omitted]

4 [Footnote omitted]

5 See *R v Secretary of State for the Home Department, ex p Bugdaycay* [1987] AC 514; *R v Secretary of State for the Home Department, ex p Brind* [1991] 1 AC 696.

The extract demonstrates that there are areas of executive action that the courts consider to be non-justiciable, meaning that these areas are not susceptible to judicial scrutiny. These include the executive's treaty-making powers, as discussed in Chapter 6. But these areas are extremely limited and are becoming increasingly limited over time. The rationale for non-justiciability is that some issues are a matter of political judgement rather than legal judgment. It is for politicians to answer to our elected representatives and, essentially, to the electorate for their decision-making in those fields. Political questions are likely to be open to a number of different, yet competing, answers and judges are not necessarily better qualified to reach a reasonable decision than are politicians. However, decisions that may be blatantly wrong, or may have been made in bad faith, will be open to judicial scrutiny. But, as the extract illustrates, the divide between justiciability and non-justiciability is not a straightforward divide between the exercise of statutory and royal prerogative powers. The courts may review the executive's reliance on and use of the royal prerogative, as well as the exercise of statutory powers. There are exceptions to this—national security exemptions, for example, although since *Council of Civil Service Unions v Minister for the Civil Service* [1985] AC 374, it has been clear that the courts no longer consider the royal prerogative to be non-justiciable. Ultimately, it is for the courts to determine the extent of their power to review the executive. Over time, the courts have broadened their review powers and are particularly diligent in using them to scrutinise decisions or actions that have an impact on our fundamental human rights.

cross reference
Refer back to Chapter 6 if you are in any way unsure about this point.

11.4.2 To what extent is this an effective mechanism?

Tomkins identifies three main limitations of legal accountability of the executive: capacity; potency; and democracy. The first of these, capacity, is linked to the courts' reluctance to intrude on certain areas of government (as discussed earlier in this section)—in particular the judiciary's exclusion of private law matters from judicial review, its reluctance to challenge national security justifications for action, and the continuing exceptions within the exercise of the royal prerogative. With (both Conservative and Labour) governments' use of NPM and market principles to deliver public services, the public law–private law divide is becoming increasingly anachronistic. More and more public services are being delivered via private law means, and the courts will struggle to hold the executive legally accountable if they hold firm to traditional notions of public law and private law.

Tomkins's potency argument relates to the remedies available to a claimant who succeeds in a judicial review action. He notes that **damages** are rarely awarded and that, in any event, an award of damages against the **state** is unlikely to act as a useful deterrent in relation to future wrongdoing. After all, the state has access to vast wealth by comparison with an individual or even a large company. Further, assuming that the executive loses an action for judicial review and its decision is quashed or it is prohibited from acting in a specified manner, it is always open to government to ask Parliament to amend the law so as to give it the legal power it needs to act in that way in future. Thus the illegal act becomes a legal one through Parliament's acquiescence.

Finally, Tomkins explains the complex relationship between democracy and legal accountability. We take up his argument at this point, in the extract below.

● **A. Tomkins, Public Law** (Oxford: Oxford University Press, 2003), pp. 209–10

In the previous chapter we identified a number of 'fault-lines' of political accountability. Is legal accountability also possessed of a number of fault-lines and, if so, what are they? Three fault-lines may be discerned from our analysis thus far: these we shall call the fault-lines of capacity, of potency, and of democracy.

...

The third fault-line of legal accountability is democracy. Why should it be to the unrepresentative and—still—overwhelmingly old, white, male, upper-middle class judges that we turn when we desire to hold the democratically elected government to account? Why should it be for the judges (and not the people of Leicester) to decide whether or not Leicester City Council acted appropriately in taking action against rugby players who had toured in apartheid South Africa? Why should it be for the judges (and not for Parliament) to decide whether homosexual men and women should be allowed to serve in the armed forces? And why should it be for the judges (and not for the electorate) to decide whether republican political voices should be broadcast or silenced in response to political violence in Northern Ireland? These are not rhetorical questions: they are not posed here as if they have no answers. On the contrary, it is clear that many would find the task of answering these questions relatively straight-forward. The answer would be roughly the same in each case: namely, that it was the constitutional role of the courts to ensure that the minority was not been treated unreasonably by the majority.

On one account, it is undemocratic to have unrepresentative and unelected State officials (judges) deciding constitutional questions such as these. But on another account, it is an essential feature of democracy that, while the majority should govern, it should not be permitted to govern in such a way as to trample upon the rights or interest of minorities. Politics in a democracy is the vehicle through which the will of the majority is identified and given authority. But as majoritarian politics will always find it difficult to accommodate and to protect the interests of minorities, particularly those minorities that the majority finds distasteful or disturbing, such protection as minorities are going to receive may well have to come from sources not under the immediate control of the majority—sources such as the courts of law.

...

The point is simply this: that in assessing the extent to which a fault-line of democracy runs through, or undermines, any system of legal accountability, a great deal of thought will first have to be given to what is meant by, and what importance attached to, the values of democracy. It is not good enough merely to condemn the judges simply because nobody voted for them or because they tend to come from a limited socio-economic class. But equally, we all, and lawyers especially, must guard against complacency. It is unsafe to assume that greater judicial power, even greater judicial power that is ostensibly confined to the enforcement of human rights, is either a good or a democratic thing. And lawyers do tend to make exactly these assumptions: that no constitutional problem is solved unless or until it is judicially solved, and that there is no constitutional problem that cannot be successfully solved by the judiciary. These assumptions dangerously underplay the significant role that political accountability, notwithstanding its imperfections, can and should continue to play while simultaneously they exaggerate the contribution that it is reasonable to expect the law to be able to make.

thinking point

What are your views of Tomkins's extract? Do you think that, ultimately, judges should hold the executive to account, or Parliament, or the electorate, or all three in different ways? Why?

What should we conclude from this section? Judicial review is a special mechanism through which the courts may scrutinise the exercise of public power by the executive (and public authorities more broadly). It permits judges to consider that the power conferred by the Crown (the prerogative) or Parliament (statutory power) is being used legally, rationally, and proportionately. Judges will examine whether the Human Rights Act 1998 has been respected in the exercise of that power. They will also ensure that the proper procedure has been followed in

cross reference

You may want to consider this in the light of your reading on parliamentary supremacy in Chapter 7.

reaching a decision or taking action. However, judicial scrutiny is only as effective as the courts are prepared to make it, meaning that it is the courts that determine the scope of their competence in relation to public law scrutiny. Their reluctance to become involved in questions of high politics and their unwillingness to substitute their decisions for those of the democratically elected politicians are entirely understandable, and are, in a sense, an aspect of the **separation of powers** in operation. However, this does also limit the courts' ability to hold the executive to account through legal means. Tomkins reminds us that law is not the be-all and end-all of accountability mechanisms. The British constitution is largely a creature of politics rather than of law. And in being based so firmly rooted in politics, it places the ultimate responsibility for the direction of government policy in the hands of the electorate via our elected representatives. Democracy requires that we exercise our political voices and hold our representatives to account for their actions. But the courts remain an important safeguard to ensure that the will of the majority does not trample the vulnerable minority under foot. Or at least, that is the theory. Judicial review will be considered in the last part of this book, when the courts' ability to scrutinise the executive's use of power will be examined in detail. You may make up your own minds on reading the relevant case law about the extent to which the courts manage to balance the requirements of democracy with the protection of the minority.

summary points

To what extent may the courts hold the government accountable?

- *The courts may review matters brought before them by claimants with the requisite standing, if the body in question is deemed a public body carrying out some form of public function (or exercising a public law power), assuming that the case appears to have merit and does not fall into a non-justiciable area.*

- *The courts may review the exercise of statutory powers and the exercise of the royal prerogative.*

- *However, judges will not substitute their own judgment for that of the executive and will not trespass on questions of high politics.*

- *They will also not seek to quash ministerial decisions on irrationality grounds unless there is a blatant irrationality or the decision was taken in bad faith.*

- *There are areas of the royal prerogative that are deemed non-justiciable, such as the exercise of the personal prerogatives of the monarch and the treaty-making powers of the executive.*

- *National security considerations may also render the courts' jurisdiction largely impotent.*

Summary

One of the most important roles that Parliament performs is to scrutinise the executive. It does this through a number of mechanisms, including scrutiny of legislative proposals, parliamentary debates, oral and written questions, and the work of select committees. Parliamentary reform has gathered pace since 1997 and the Modernisation Committee has made a number of reform recommendations. These include pre-legislative review and changes to the composition, and working practices and tasks, of select committees. In addition, an additional debating forum has been established in Westminster Hall to permit more parliamentary debates and there have been changes to Prime Minister's Question Time. All of these reforms are aimed at increasing Parliament's ability to scrutinise the executive. However, there remain concerns that more needs to be done to strengthen Parliament's powers. It has been suggested that, to be truly effective, select committees may need the power to compel witnesses to attend and to require documents to be submitted to them to be reviewed during their investigations. This may help to counteract the dominance of the executive in Parliament, at times when one political party has a strong majority in the House of Commons.

Questions

1   Why is Parliament given the role of scrutinising the executive?

2   To what extent do you believe that it has the powers to undertake this role effectively?

3   How have recent reforms strengthened and/or weakened its ability to scrutinise the executive? What examples do you have as evidence for your analysis?

4   To what extent do you believe that further reform is necessary? Why and of what type?

Further reading

Ganz, G.,'Recent developments in the use of guillotine motions' (1990) Public Law 496

This article is now a little out of date, but it does set out the essence of guillotine motions, and explains why they are used and objections to their use.

Gay, O., 'The Osmotherly Rules' (House of Commons Library Standard Note SN/PC 2671, 4 August 2005), available online at http://www.parliament.uk/documents/commons/lib/research/briefings/snpc-02671.pdf

This note sets out the Osmotherly Rules in a comprehensive, but clear, fashion. It is a useful insight into the relationship between civil servants and the ministers whom they serve, as well as between certain types of witness and the select committee that calls them to appear. It includes information about the Scottish parliamentary system, as well as the Westminster system.

Heffernan, R., 'Why the Prime Minister cannot be a president: comparing institutional imperatives in Britain and America' (2005) 58(1) Parliamentary Affairs 53

This is a really good article that sets out differences between presidential and prime ministerial leadership roles and styles. It explains the essential differences (as well as some similarities) between the two.

Kelly, R., 'Modernisation: Revitalising the Chamber' (House of Commons Library Standard Note SN/PC 04542, 12 December 2007), available online at http://www.parliament.uk/documents/commons/lib/research/briefings/snpc-04542.pdf

This note sets out recent reform proposals that aim to strengthen the power of backbench MPs (and thus Parliament) and also outlines ways in which non-legislative time may be used more effectively in the House. It also sets out how the reforms were to be implemented prior to the last election.

Kelso, A., 'The House of Commons Modernisation Committee: who needs it?' (2007) 9 British Journal of Politics and International Relations 138

This article explains the remit of the Modernisation Committee, the reforms that it has proposed, and the extent to which they would be a welcome and useful addition to parliamentary processes. It considers the relationship between Parliament and the executive.

Levy, J., *Strengthening Parliament's Powers of Scrutiny? An Assessment of the Introduction of Public Bill Committees* (London: The Constitution Unit University College London, 2009)

This report explains the extent to which public Bill committees (introduced to scrutinise legislation) strengthen Parliament's ability to scrutinise the executive.

Maer, L. and Sandford, M., *The Development of Scrutiny in the UK: A Review of Procedures and Practice* (London: The Constitution Unit University College London, 2004)

This report is now a little out of date, but it is still useful in so far as it sets out differences in scrutiny mechanisms, as between local and central government, and central government and the devolved administrations.

Oliver, D., 'Reforming the United Kingdom Parliament?', in J. Jowell and D. Oliver (eds) *The Changing Constitution* (7th edn, Oxford: Oxford University Press, 2011), pp. 167–86

This chapter sets out recent changes to the UK Parliament, as well as the history of reform. It is comprehensive and provides analysis about what the reforms have provided by way of strengthening Parliament's power.

Russell, M. and Benton, M., *Selective Influence: The Policy Impact of House of Commons Select Committees* (London: The Constitution Unit University College London, 2011)

This report provides research evidence about the extent to which parliamentary select committees have had an influence over recent years on government policy. It provides an insight into the workings of select committees and their effect on government, but it is also a good source of information about how select committees work.

12

The Role of Constitutional Conventions

Key points

This chapter will cover:

- What are constitutional conventions and how do they relate to executive power?
- How does one know whether a constitutional convention exists?
- What types of behaviour are covered by constitutional conventions?
- How have the courts dealt with constitutional conventions?
- Why would the executive respect constitutional conventions?
- Should constitutional conventions be codified and given the force of law?
- How does individual ministerial responsibility operate?
- How does collective ministerial responsibility operate?

Introduction

This chapter is the second in the part on responsible government, which aims to outline the mechanisms that exist within the constitution to limit the power of the executive and to hold it to account for its exercise of power. It examines the nature of constitutional conventions, one such mechanism. It evaluates their role and relevance within the constitution, as well as considers their strengths and weaknesses as mechanisms to limit the excessive use of executive power. It also provides a general overview of constitutional conventions and focuses on two in some detail—individual and collective ministerial responsibility. It explains how the courts have made use of constitutional conventions and outlines some reform proposals in relation to conventions, before providing a summary and questions.

12.1 What are constitutional conventions and how do they relate to executive power?

cross reference
You may wish to refer back to discussion of the royal prerogative in Chapter 6.

This section will seek to define **constitutional conventions**, or at the very least to provide an explanation of the difficulties in providing such a definition. Legal philosophers and academics have been debating the distinction between constitutional conventions, on the one hand, and so-called legal rules, on the other, for well over 150 years. Conventions are linked with the exercise of the **royal prerogative** and other common law powers used by the **monarch** and by the political **executive**. The royal prerogative and the common law confer great power on the executive, but constitutional conventions seek to regulate and limit that use of power. As with many aspects of the UK constitution, constitutional conventions are relatively difficult to delineate with precision because they are not set down in a formalised written format. Consequently, it is probably no surprise to learn that there are many differing opinions about constitutional conventions and little clear agreement on their precise content.

As with so many other areas of constitutional law, a natural starting point for the discussion is A. V. Dicey. In his 1885 *Introduction to the Study of the Law of the Constitution*, Dicey noted that although the lawyer's main function was the interpretation of legal rules, non-legal rules were also of importance. Despite being subsequently criticised for overemphasising the importance of constitutional laws, as opposed to constitutional conventions, Dicey did accept that the constitutional lawyer could not function without having regard to such conventions. In fact, such a lawyer could not expect to understand properly the British constitution without first understanding that these non-legal rules have a significant part to play in the use of power. Dicey provided the following definition of these two kinds of rules.

● **A. V. Dicey,** *Introduction to the Study of the Law of the Constitution* [9th edn, London: Macmillan, 1959], p. 23

The rules which make up constitutional law, as the term is used in England, include two sets of principles or maxims of a totally distinct character.

> The one set of rules are in the strictest sense 'laws', since they are rules which (whether written or unwritten, whether enacted by statute or derived from the mass of custom, tradition, or judge-made maxims known as the common law) are enforced by the courts; these rules constitute 'constitutional law' in the proper sense of that term, and may for the sake of distinction be called collectively 'the law of the constitution'.
>
> The other set of rules consist of conventions, understandings, habits or practices which, though they may regulate the conduct of . . . officials, are not in reality laws at all since they are not enforced by the courts. This portion of constitutional law may, for the sake of distinction, be termed the 'conventions of the constitution', or constitutional morality.

Dicey distinguished between legal rules—that is, those that are the product of statute or of the common law and are enforceable by the courts—and conventions or practices that are not enforceable by the courts. However, despite providing such a relatively straightforward identification test, Dicey's formulation of the distinction has been criticised to a varying degree by a number of subsequent writers.

Chief amongst Dicey's critics was Sir Ivor Jennings. His basic qualm (in *The Law and the Constitution*, 5th edn, London: University of London Press, 1959, at p. 117) with Dicey's propositions was quite straightforward—that the actual difference between legal rules and the non-legal conventions was so negligible so as to make any attempt to draw a distinction between them futile. He argued that both traditionally defined legal rules and conventions are completely dependent on the compliance of those to whom they apply. In effect, laws that are not respected have the same impact as conventions that are not followed and, conversely, laws that are complied with have the same effect as conventions that are adhered to. As a result, he claimed that there was no practical difference between them. He indicated that, in practice, the courts do not differentiate between both kinds of rule even though they may claim to do so. Consequently, he believed that legal rules and constitutional conventions amounted to much the same thing. Further, he argued (as did J. D. B. Mitchell in *Constitutional Law*, 2nd edn, Edinburgh: W. Green & Son, 1968, at p. 34) that some conventions could be stated with the same degree of certainty and clarity as the more formal legal rules. Indeed, some conventions are written and formal, such as the two resolutions on ministerial responsibility passed by both Houses in 1996 in the wake of the Scott Report.

Why, then, does this chapter appear in this book? Were Jennings' proposition to be accepted, then we would have to say that there are no practical differences between constitutional conventions and legal rules. We could leave the discussion at that and refer you back to the part on the hierarchy of laws. However, the weight of evidence suggests that there are notable differences between conventions and legal rules, as we shall discover later in the chapter. Munro (*Studies in Constitutional Law*, 2nd edn, Oxford: Oxford University Press, 1999) conclusively demonstrates that constitutional conventions cannot be legally enforced by the **judiciary**, even if they are discussed by judges in court proceedings. Secondly, he argues that, in most cases, constitutional conventions cannot be stated with the same degree of certainty as legal rules, despite Jennings' claims to the contrary. By way of example, Munro notes that even the most widely accepted of conventions, that the monarch will not withhold her royal assent to Bills passed by **Parliament**, is capable of being expressed in many different ways. It could, for example, be stated that 'the **Queen** must assent to Bills duly passed' or that 'the Crown cannot refuse assent except on advice' (ibid: 82). Both versions are significantly different, yet both are equally correct, because no court of law has ever adjudicated on the issue. This is in contrast to the laws passed by Parliament, since they are both put in writing and interpreted by the courts. The Act in question then remains law regardless of whether the public complies with it or not. Constitutional conventions, however, exist only as long as they are followed.

Further, Munro refutes Jennings' claims that conventions are akin to traditionally defined laws. Jennings' assertion is based on the fact that past practice plays a role in the formation of both law and convention. Although it is true that customs have been judged to acquire the force of law in the past, and that customs and past practices are also responsible for forming conventions, this explains only the process by which some laws and conventions have been formed rather than their nature once formed. In modern times, customs rarely become laws. As Munro explains, in order for customs to become laws, it must be demonstrated that the custom has existed since 'time immemorial', defined in law as 3 September 1189. Given how much time has passed since then, any customs that could be made law would have been made law by now. Consequently, it seems unlikely that customs and past practices play as important a role now in the formation of law as they do in the creation of conventions.

It is all well and good to show that Dicey's identification test has withstood the test of time, subject to a few minor amendments, but that brings us little nearer to defining or describing what is a constitutional convention. The test merely shows that there is a difference between conventions and legal rules. Sir Kenneth Wheare sought to provide a definition.

● **K. C. Wheare,** *Modern Constitutions* (2nd edn, Oxford: Oxford University Press, 1966), p. 122

> A word must be said about the distinction that is intended by the employment of the two words 'usage' and 'convention'. By 'convention' is meant a binding rule, a rule of behaviour accepted as obligatory by those concerned in the working of the Constitution; by 'usage' is meant no more than a usual practice. Clearly a usage might become a convention. What is usually done comes to be what is done. It is often difficult to say whether a particular course of conduct is obligatory or persuasive only, and it is convenient in such a case to be able to say that it is certainly a usage and probably or doubtfully, as the case may be, a convention.

Wheare defines a convention as a rule that is binding upon those to whom it applies. He does not state here how these rules become binding, but he notes that the binding nature of the rule is accepted. This suggests that the convention is instead a rule of behaviour upon which there is some agreement. Although simplistic in some respects, the definition is a useful one nevertheless. Not only does it describe what conventions are, but it also explains to whom they can apply—'those concerned in the working of the Constitution'. The institutions directly involved in the working of the constitution are the **Crown**, Parliament, the civil service, the judiciary, and, most significantly, the executive. Many of the relationships between these institutions are regulated by convention, not by statute. The issue of why these institutions, and the executive in particular, choose to obey these non-legal rules will be considered later in the chapter.

summary points

What are constitutional conventions and how do they relate to executive power?

- *A. V. Dicey noted, at the end of the nineteenth century, that constitutional conventions were non-legal rules and that, as such, they could not be enforced by the courts.*

- *Dicey's views were subsequently challenged on numerous grounds by writers such as Sir Ivor Jennings, who claimed that constitutional conventions were so similar to constitutional laws that it was pointless to attempt to distinguish between them. Jennings preferred that conventions be grouped under a broader heading of 'constitutional rules' rather than be kept separate.*

- *The modern viewpoint is that there are significant differences between laws and conventions.*

- *Constitutional conventions are regarded as political rules that are binding upon those to whom they apply. They are more than mere practices and apply to the relationships between the Crown, Parliament, the judiciary, the civil service, and the executive, because they are considered to be binding rather than simply advisory practices.*

(12.2) # How does one know whether a constitutional convention exists?

It is comparatively easy to identify whether a written legal rule exists and applies; it is altogether more difficult to prove the existence of a constitutional convention. If one accepts that, in some circumstances, traditional practices do come to form constitutional conventions, the key question is: when exactly does a past practice come to form a convention and under what conditions? We shall focus on this in this section of the chapter. The most often-cited test for the existence of constitutional conventions, sometimes referred to as a 'rule of recognition', comes from the 1959 work of Sir Ivor Jennings, *The Law and the Constitution*. This is the usual starting point for any discussion on these questions.

● **I. Jennings, *The Law and the Constitution*** (5th edn, London: University of London Press, 1959), p. 136

> As in the creation of law, the creation of a convention must be due to the reason of the thing because it accords with the prevailing political philosophy. It helps to make the democratic system operate; it enables the machinery of State to run more smoothly; and if it were not there friction would result. Thus, if a convention continues because it is desirable in the circumstances, it must be created for the same reason. We have to ask ourselves three questions: first, what are the precedents; secondly, did the actors in the precedents believe that they were bound by a rule; and thirdly, is there a reason for the rule? A single precedent with a good reason may be enough to establish the rule. A whole string of precedents without such a reason will be of no avail, unless it is perfectly certain that the persons concerned regarded them as bound by it.

As explained in the previous section, Jennings never questioned the existence of conventions. In fact, to the contrary: he believed them to be so essential to the constitution that it was pointless to attempt to distinguish between them and constitutional laws.

But, even given that, the extract is extremely useful because it attempts to clarify when a constitutional convention exists. Firstly, one must look at any precedents for the practice: has the event in question ever happened before? If so, how many times? Even if it has happened time and time again, has it happened because the people concerned believed that they were required to act in that way and for good reason? It may help to provide a hypothetical example.

example

> Say that tea, coffee, and biscuits are served only at the *end* of Cabinet meetings, and under no circumstances during the last fifty years have refreshments been provided at the beginning. Does this regular occurrence mean that, over the years, the tradition in question has evolved into a convention? The answer would most likely be 'no'. If one were to use Jennings' second requirement, it seems likely that the members of the Cabinet would not consider themselves bound by such a practice or rule. Equally, it seems unlikely that anyone would, or could, claim that there is a good reason for the rule (unless it is to stop people spilling coffee over important Cabinet papers!). The practice would thus fail to satisfy Jennings' second and third requirements.

Although Jennings' test remains the most widely accepted and the only truly practicable one for identifying where and when constitutional conventions exist, it has been criticised in the past for being too vague. Under extremely limited circumstances, conventions may be created without the need for precedents. Examples of this arise when conventions are created either by express agreement—say, of the Cabinet, **government**, or Parliament—or by means of prime ministerial decree or announcement. In these instances, a convention can be created with no past practice to support its existence: it is a new constitutional convention established as a reform. Further, as with all other situations involving precedent (including case law), there is scope for debate as to which precedent should be followed in the event that there appears to be more than one that is relevant to the given situation. One of the most often-quoted examples of such a situation is from 1940, in which despite the fact that there was a seemingly established convention that the **Prime Minister** should be a member of the House of Commons, as opposed to the House of Lords, some argued that those precedents should be disregarded and that Lord Halifax be appointed as Prime Minister, rather than Winston Churchill MP. Although those arguments were ultimately unsuccessful, the very fact that some, the King himself included, even considered the possibility that Halifax could be appointed as Prime Minister is evidence of the uncertainty of surrounding precedent and the first element of Jennings' test. A further criticism of Jennings' requirements is linked to the third element, the condition that there must be a (good) reason in order to enable a practice to become a convention. It may be difficult to deem whether or not the reason for adopting a practice as a convention can be regarded as a good one, particularly given the absence of court involvement in conventions. Different people may legitimately hold different views about the reason for adopting the practice, because these are rarely set out at the time that a practice (and then a convention) is adopted.

Despite these criticisms of Jennings' test, it is useful. It is the only rule of recognition accepted by the courts, albeit the Canadian courts (in *Reference re Amendment of the Constitution of Canada* (1982) 125 DLR (3d) 1). We do not have established precedent on this point from the UK courts and so that Canadian ruling would be persuasive, if not binding, evidence of the test to establish whether a constitutional convention exists. It is accepted that there may be exceptions to the rules and criteria set out by Jennings, and that there are many debatable issues, but the test is as precise and useful as we have at present.

summary points

How does one know whether a constitutional convention exists?

- *The most useful test comes from Sir Ivor Jennings' 1959 work. He sets out three criteria for the existence of a constitutional convention, as follows.*

  1 *Are there any precedents for the practice? If so, how many, etc?*

  2 *Did those who acted in such a way do so believing that they were bound to do act in this way?*

  3 *Is there a (good) reason for the forming of the convention?*

- *The test has been subsequently criticised on numerous grounds, including the fact that conventions can be created without the need for any precedents, that the precedents themselves can be unclear and ambiguous, and that it is difficult to judge when a reason becomes a good one in the absence of court adjudication.*

- *However, the test has been recognised by judges in a legal system very similar to our own, Canada, even if we do not have a ruling on this by the British courts.*

What types of behaviour are covered by constitutional conventions?

The aim of this section is to provide a general overview of the types of behaviour that can be covered by constitutional conventions. In doing so, it will provide a non-exhaustive list of the most important constitutional conventions that exist today. At least some of these are related to the control of executive power, and some show the interaction between statute and convention. This will allow you to develop your understanding of the distinction between legal rules and conventions, as discussed in the first section of the chapter. It should also demonstrate some of the circumstances in which conventions can be created. In turn, this should shed light on how and why such conventions are respected by those to whom they apply.

Some, if not all, constitutional conventions function *alongside* statutory provisions. Nowadays, statutes regulate the vast majority of the relationships between the various branches of **state** and their respective powers. It is extremely rare that a constitutional convention will limit the power granted to an institution by statute, because most statutory provisions also establish the limits of power and so conventions are unnecessary. Thus constitutional conventions usually operate to regulate relationships or to limit the use of powers conferred upon one institution or branch of government by *unwritten* rules or sources of power. An example of such an un-written source of power is the royal prerogative. As was discussed in more depth in Chapter 6, the royal prerogative is a largely unwritten and somewhat nebulous concept that refers to the powers that remain legally vested in the monarch. However, as was also highlighted, the fact that the monarch retains the legal right to act does not mean that she necessarily has the power to do so. Usually, the monarch's prerogative power will be limited by constitutional convention. In such circumstances, as some of the examples below illustrate, constitutional conventions can act as unwritten limits or controls on the use of the power granted to the Crown by the (also unwritten) royal prerogative. They are needed because the source of the power (the preroga-tive) does not set sufficient limits in a modern democratic context on the use of the power. It is also worth noting that it is clear that conventions can limit powers conferred upon institutions by unwritten sources or rules *other* than the royal prerogative.

In general, as with the aforementioned royal prerogative and as has been emphasised in the first two sections of this chapter, it is quite difficult to place examples of constitutional conven-tions into neatly labelled boxes. As was highlighted when evaluating Jennings' identification test, the very nature of conventions make them quite vague. As a result, there may be much debate about how to formulate the wording of a specific convention and how to classify it. Indeed, under some circumstances, a convention's very existence may be subject to some de-bate, as was mentioned with reference to the dispute about the Prime Minister to be appointed in 1940.

Consider the controversies that arose after the May 2010 election, which produced a hung Parliament. A hung Parliament refers to the situation in which no single political party has an overall majority; an overall majority means that a political party has more seats than all of the other political parties added together. So, in May 2010, to obtain an overall majority and to win the election outright, the Conservatives would have had to obtain 326 of the 650 seats in the House of Commons.

The monarch has the prerogative power to appoint the government and the Prime Minister, and by convention she appoints the leader of the party that has gained an overall majority of the seats in the House of Commons in a general election. This is, of course, the party that can command the confidence of the House of Commons. Because, in May 2010, no single party had over 325 seats and could command an overall majority, the Queen could not do this. There was considerable uncertainty about the procedure and the conventions that should be followed in the event of a hung parliament. But, before the election, Cabinet Secretary Sir Gus O'Donnell (a senior civil servant) had produced a manual detailing the procedure. The draft manual was presented to the House of Commons Justice Committee on 23 February 2010, in the light of concerns that there was likely to be a hung Parliament at the upcoming general election. The manual made it clear that the Queen should have no part in any negotiations because she must remain politically neutral. It also made stated that the incumbent Prime Minister (Gordon Brown) should remain in office and not resign until a new government could be formed. In the event, the Conservatives had won 305 seats and the Liberal Democrats had 57 seats, and they formed a **coalition government** within a few days of the election result. Once it appeared highly likely that there would be a coalition between the Conservatives and the Liberal Democrats, Gordon Brown resigned as Prime Minister and the Queen asked David Cameron (who was leader of the Conservatives and the leader of the nascent coalition of parties) to become the Prime Minister.

• **Sir Gus O'Donnell, 'Letter to the Chairman of the Committee from the Cabinet Secretary, 23 January 2010: Cabinet Manual, Elections and Government Formation (Chapter 6)'** available online at http://www.publications.parliament.uk/pa/cm200910/cmselect/cmjust/396/396we02.htm

'Hung' Parliaments

16. Where an election does not result in a clear majority for a single party, the incumbent government remains in office unless and until the Prime Minister tenders his and the Government's resignation to the Monarch. An incumbent Government is entitled to await the meeting of the new Parliament to see if it can command the confidence of the House of Commons or to resign if it becomes clear that it is unlikely to command that confidence. If a Government is defeated on a motion of confidence in the House of Commons, a Prime Minister is expected to tender the Government's resignation immediately. A motion of confidence may be tabled by the Opposition, or may be a measure which the Government has previously said will be a test of the House's confidence in it. Votes on the Queen's Speech have traditionally been regarded as motions of confidence.

17. If the Prime Minister and Government resign at any stage, the principles in paragraph 14 apply—in particular that the person who appears to be most likely to command the confidence of the House of Commons will be asked by the Monarch to form a government. Where a range of different administrations could potentially be formed, the expectation is that discussions will take place between political parties on who should form the next Government. The Monarch would not expect to become involved in such discussions, although the political parties and the Cabinet Secretary would have a role in ensuring that the Palace is informed of progress.

18. A Prime Minister may request that the Monarch dissolves Parliament and hold a further election. The Monarch is not bound to accept such a request, especially when such a request is made soon after a previous dissolution. In those circumstances, the Monarch would normally wish the parties to ascertain that there was no potential government that could command the confidence of the House of Commons before granting a dissolution.

19. It is open to the Prime Minister to ask the Cabinet Secretary to support the Government's discussions with Opposition or minority parties on the formation of a government. If Opposition parties request similar support for their discussions with each other or with the Government, this can be provided by the Cabinet Office with the authorisation of the Prime Minister.

20. As long as there is significant doubt whether the Government has the confidence of the House of Commons, it would be prudent for it to observe discretion about taking significant decisions, as per the pre-election period. The normal and essential business of government at all levels, however, will need to be carried out.

During the aftermath of the May 2010 election, the Queen followed the relevant conventions and stood back whilst the politicians negotiated, and the Conservatives and Liberals managed to form a government.

thinking point

Do these events illustrate the positive nature of the flexible unwritten constitution, or do they show the need either for conventions to be formally codified or for there to be a written constitution?

NOTE

See the Constitution Society's information and discussion on the British constitution online at http://www.re-constitution.org.uk/discover-the-facts/the-government

Having said that, it is generally accepted that the examples of constitutional conventions illustrated in Tables 12.1, 12.2, and 12.3 do exist, and that they are amongst the most important. They have been classified according to the institution that is primarily affected by the convention, although most affect more than one branch of state.

Even in areas partly dependent on statutory regulation, such as the appointment of ministers of the Crown, for example, it is apparent that constitutional conventions still have an important role to play. However, as has been emphasised, where powers have been granted to the institutions of government under statute, those powers will be limited by the statute itself, not by convention. But conventions have key roles to play in prescribing the limits of the powers granted to certain institutions by virtue of non-written legal rules, or sources such as the royal prerogative or common law.

Table 12.1

365

Conventions affecting the monarch

Example (1) Royal assent

The common law rule is that Acts of Parliament are enacted by the King or Queen in Parliament. However, convention prescribes that the King or Queen will not withhold royal assent to Bills duly passed by Parliament, except on the advice of ministers of the Crown (who would have to remain accountable to Parliament). Assent has not been withheld since 1708.

Certain aspects of the assent procedure are regulated by the Royal Assent Act 1967, although the limits on the monarch's power are set out only by convention. The convention clearly regulates one aspect of the relationship between Crown, Parliament, and executive in a legislative context.

Example (2) Appointment of the Prime Minister

The appointment of the Prime Minister is the monarch's prerogative right. However, convention dictates that the King or Queen must appoint the leader of the political party with a majority in the House of Commons. This convention governs one key aspect of the relationship between the Crown and the executive.

Example (3) Right to dissolve Parliament

The dissolution of Parliament is the prerogative right of the monarch. However, convention prescribes that the monarch is to do so only after either a vote of no confidence in the government, or where the Prime Minister (with the support of at least some other government ministers) requests it. The Fixed-term Parliaments Act 2011 removes much of the Prime Minister's discretion to request a dissolution of Parliament. This convention regulates another important aspect of the relationship between Crown, Parliament, and executive.

Table 12.2

Conventions affecting the political executive

....

Example (4) Appointment of the Prime Minister

....

Allied to example (2) in Table 12.1 convention dictates that the Prime Minister must be a member of the House of Commons, as opposed to the House of Lords.

....

Example (5) Confidence in government

....

The government must not lose the confidence of the House of Commons (by means of a vote of no confidence). Connected to example (3) in Table 12.1 if such a vote is carried, Parliament will be dissolved by the monarch (now regulated to an extent by the Fixed-term Parliaments Act 2011).

....

Example (6) Ministers of the Crown

....

All ministers must be in either the House of Commons or the House of Lords. Although many aspects of the appointment of ministers are regulated by various statutes, only convention states that all ministers must be in Parliament.

....

Example (7) Resignation of the Prime Minister

....

After a general election, convention states that the incumbent Prime Minister must resign once it becomes apparent that the leader of one of the opposition parties now controls the majority in the House of Commons.

Table 12.3

Conventions affecting the Parliament and judiciary

....

Example (8) Summoning of Parliament

....

Convention dictates that Parliament must be summoned at least once a year.

....

Example (9) Criticism of the judiciary

....

There is a convention that members of Parliament will not criticise members of the judiciary in Parliament.

....

Example (10) Judges and politics

....

The convention is that judges shall not play an active role in political life once appointed as judges.

---

summary points

What types of behaviour are covered by constitutional conventions?

- *Conventions usually operate to limit the powers granted to institutions of government by unwritten rules or sources. They also regulate key parts of the relationship between the institutions of government.*

- *Generally, they do not limit powers granted to bodies through statutory enactment. The limits to such powers are usually prescribed in the statutes themselves.*

- *There are many examples of key constitutional conventions that operate alongside statutes, but that fulfil quite different roles.*

How have the courts dealt with constitutional conventions?

The issue of court recognition of conventions is at the heart of Dicey's distinction between legal and non-legal rules, and is also of significance in Munro's critique of Jennings' approach to conventions. This section will introduce you to the approach taken by the UK courts as regards legal enforcement of conventions. We have touched upon this already, stating that the courts have declined to give legal effect to such conventions, but we shall now examine how and why this is the case.

A useful starting point is *Attorney General v Jonathan Cape Ltd* [1975] 3 All ER 484, otherwise known as the *Crossman Diaries case*, which considers whether a constitutional convention could be enforced by the courts. In this case, the executors of deceased former Cabinet minister Richard Crossman's estate wished to publish the diaries he had kept whilst a member of the Cabinet between 1964 and 1970. The diaries, which had been kept with at least some intention of subsequent publication, contained details of Cabinet discussions. Under the convention of collective ministerial responsibility, which will be discussed later in the chapter, all Cabinet discussions are confidential. Clearly, the convention would be breached if the diaries were to be allowed to be published. As a result, the Attorney General attempted to have an **injunction** issued to prevent the publication of both the proposed books and the extracts that were to be published in the *Sunday Times*. The court case that followed clearly reinforces the principle that conventions are not legal rules and cannot be enforced as such.

. . . .

● *Attorney General v Jonathan Cape Ltd* [1975] 3 All ER 484 (the *Crossman Diaries case*)

Lord Widgery CJ at 491–3:

> The defendants' main contention is that whatever the limits of the convention of joint cabinet responsibility may be, there is no obligation enforceable at law to prevent the publication of cabinet papers and proceedings, except in extreme cases where national security is involved. In other words, the defendants submit that the confidential character of cabinet papers and discussions is based on a true convention as defined in the evidence of Professor Wade, namely, an obligation founded in conscience only. Accordingly, the defendants contend that publication of these diaries is not capable of control by any order of this court.
>
> If the Attorney General were restricted in his argument to the general proposition that cabinet papers and discussion are all under the seal of secrecy at all times, he would be in difficulty.
>
> ...
>
> It seems to me, therefore, that the Attorney General must first show that whatever obligation of secrecy or discretion attaches to former cabinet ministers, that obligation is binding in law and not merely in morals.

In this case, the defence counsel for Jonathan Cape Ltd and the *Sunday Times*, claimed that since the doctrine of collective or joint ministerial responsibility is based on conscience (that is, convention) not on law, the court cannot issue the injunction unless it is in an 'extreme case where national security is involved'. Counsel relied upon Wade's argument that constitutional conventions are binding as a matter of conscience rather than law. Lord Widgery seemed to agree with this proposition, because he stated that the Attorney General would have to do more than merely claim that Cabinet discussions were to be kept confidential at all on the basis of convention.

As events transpired, the Attorney General did attempt to base his argument on law, as well as on convention. He found some sympathy from the court (at 494) with the legal argument that one should not be allowed to profit from 'the wrongful publication of information received by him in confidence'. This was a legal argument rather than one based solely on convention. However, the court also decided that the outcome of such an argument would vary from case to case, dependent on the circumstances. In *Crossman Diaries* itself, the fact that over ten years had passed since the first of the Cabinet discussions in question led the court to hold that there was no reason why the diaries should not be published on these grounds. The Attorney General's arguments thus failed and the injunction was rejected. The fact that the court did not allow the Attorney General to base his argument solely on convention does not mean that the court undermined the importance of conventions. To the contrary, the court not only expressly confirmed the existence of the convention of joint or collective responsibility, but also emphasised its importance. This is highlighted in the extract that appears in section 12.8 later in the chapter.

Another case that confirms the existence of a constitutional convention, but rejects calls to give legal effect to it, is the aforementioned *Reference re Amendment of the Constitution of Canada* (1982) 125 DLR (3d) 1. In this case, the federal government of Canada (a Commonwealth country) had requested that the UK Parliament (as was necessary under the British North America Act 1867) make a formal change to the Canadian Constitution. This amendment would have changed the relationship between the Canadian federal government and the Canadian provinces. However, in so doing, the federal government had seemingly breached the Canadian constitutional convention that the provincial governments had to be consulted on such changes before they were formally requested. The Supreme Court of Canada used Jennings' test to ascertain (by majority) that such a convention did exist, but went on to hold that, despite the apparent breach, it could make no difference to the legal position. There is no doubt that this decision was at least partly based on English law, and that it still represents the law of both Canada and the UK.

It must again be emphasised that the courts do not expressly challenge the importance of constitutional conventions; they merely state that they cannot be given legal effect. Indeed, as was seen in the *Crossman Diaries* case, under some circumstances, conventions can be regarded as useful to the courts because they provide the background to the law. This is especially true where executive powers are delegated under constitutional convention and where there are no statutory controls upon such delegation. *Carltona v Commissioners of Works* [1943] 2 All ER 560 highlights such a point. In this case, the convention that subsequently became known as the 'doctrine of ministerial responsibility' led to the possibility that a decision under regulation 51(1) of the Defence (General) Regulations 1939 could be made by a civil servant within one of the government departments concerned. Of course, as will be shown later in this chapter, the minister in charge of the government department was to remain legally responsible for the decision.

In *Carltona* itself, the regulation in question provided that a 'competent authority' could make a decision to requisition property during the Second World War on numerous grounds, such as defence of the realm, public safety, etc. The requisition would then happen in the name of the Commissioners of Works. The appellants were served with a letter, signed by a civil servant, noting that their factory was being requisitioned. They appealed on the grounds that, amongst other things, the decision had been reached and communicated by an official, not the Commissioners themselves. The Court of Appeal roundly rejected their arguments, noting inter alia that it was an established convention that executive powers could be delegated to officials within government departments, provided that the decision remained the legal responsibility of the minister in charge of the department. Where power had been delegated under such a convention, provided that the decision-maker did not exceed its authority, the court could not enquire into any aspect of the policy or decision.

● *Carltona Ltd v Commissioners of Works* [1943] 2 All ER 560

Lord Greene MR at 593:

> In the administration of government in this country the functions which are given to ministers (and constitutionally properly given to ministers because they are constitutionally responsible) are functions so multifarious that no minister could ever personally attend to them. To take the example of the present case no doubt there have been thousands of requisitions in this country by individual ministers. It cannot be supposed that this regulation meant that, in each case, the minister in person should direct his mind to the matter. The duties imposed upon ministers and the powers given to ministers are normally exercised under the authority of the ministers by responsible officials of the department. Public business could not be carried on if that were not the case. Constitutionally, the decision of such an official is, of course, the decision of the minister. The minister is responsible. It is he who must answer before Parliament for anything that his officials have done under his authority, and, if for an important matter he selected an official of such junior standing that he could not be expected competently to perform the work, the minister would have to answer for that in Parliament. The whole system of departmental organisation and administration is based on the view that ministers, being responsible to Parliament, will see that important duties are committed to experienced officials. If they do not do that, Parliament is the place where complaint must be made against them.

In this manner, the judges in *Carltona* accepted that (1) a convention existed, and (2), in the absence of any statutory limitation or control to the contrary, the convention of ministerial responsibility provided the only political background against which the actions of the Commissioners of Work could be judged. However, it must also be appreciated that the judges in this case were not expressly enforcing a convention; they were merely recognising its existence in circumstances in which there were no conflicting statutory requirements. This distinction is an extremely important one.

From all that has been said in the chapter thus far, it will be apparent that conventions are key pieces of the constitutional jigsaw. However, as Dicey suggested at the end of the nineteenth century, these important rules are not court-enforceable. This has been consistently confirmed by the UK and Commonwealth courts since that time. Judges have made it absolutely clear that whilst conventions can be of use in understanding the political background to the legal situation, they cannot be legally enforced. This was the situation in all of the cases discussed in this chapter. How, therefore, can conventions be considered binding upon those to whom they apply? It has already been noted that conventions play a significant role in limiting the powers of the Crown and executive. If such institutions are not legally bound to comply with the conventions, there must be some other reason. This will be the focus of the next section of the chapter.

summary points

How have the courts dealt with constitutional conventions?

- *The UK and Commonwealth courts have consistently held that constitutional conventions cannot be legally enforced. This was the situation in* Crossman Diaries, Reference re Amendment of the Constitution of Canada, *and* Carltona.

- *However, the courts do recognise the existence of conventions. In certain circumstances, they will also highlight their importance. This is especially true where they operate in areas without statutory controls or limitations, as was true in the* Carltona *case.*

- *Despite recognising the existence of conventions such as ministerial responsibility, it is vitally important for the student to realise that the courts do not enforce them.*

12.5 Why would the executive respect constitutional conventions?

As has been explained in the previous sections of this chapter, constitutional conventions play an important role in limiting the powers of the Crown and the executive. As an illustration of that fact, it was said that convention limits the powers available to the Crown under the royal prerogative. In reality, many of the powers traditionally vested in the monarch are now purely formal in nature and, in many cases, convention deems that the King or Queen may act only on the advice of the ministers of the Crown. This was the case in examples (1) and (3) in Table 12.1, for example. A further example relates to the prerogative power of the Crown to declare war or to commence military activities. Although the legal right to exercise such powers remains vested in the monarch, convention dictates that it will happen only as and when the monarch is instructed to do so by the government of the day. In turn, it may be claimed that there is a more recently developed convention that the government will not request that the UK's armed forces be committed to any major conflict without allowing Parliament to debate such a deployment. However, what would happen if the Crown were to declare war without the request and support of its government? More realistically perhaps, what would happen if the government were to instruct the Crown to deploy its forces abroad without allowing Parliament to debate such action (assuming that such a convention exists)? Since it is already known that the possible sanctions for non-compliance are not legal in nature, this section will seek to explain why the executive would respect such a convention. Having done so, it may be possible to consider whether or not constitutional conventions are effective in ensuring responsible government.

cross reference
See Chapter 6 for details of reform of the decision-making process for deployment of troops abroad.

The executive may respect constitutional conventions on many different grounds. It is accepted that the most important reasons are related to the political sanctions that could follow from the government's failure to adhere to a certain convention. For example, example (7) in Table 12.2 notes that the Prime Minister must resign as and when he or she realises that the opposition has won a majority in a House of Commons general election. From what has already been said, it is clear that the consequences for failing to do so would be political, rather than legal. In this instance, it would probably mean that increasing amounts of political pressure would be put on the Prime Minister to resign until his or her position would become absolutely untenable. Such pressure could come from all quarters: the media; the general public; politicians (including his or her own political party); and even the monarch. Remember the pressure then Prime Minister Gordon Brown was under while waiting for a coalition to be formed after the 2010 general election? Despite having no legal redress against the outgoing Prime Minister, the combined political weight of the above would ensure that the convention would be respected and that he or she would resign before the reconvening of Parliament.

The same principles would apply if one were to consider the question posed above on the major deployment of troops abroad without having a parliamentary debate on the issue. Again, it is likely that significant pressure would be put on the government to hold such a debate. Recent governments have always chosen to do so, and a draft House of Commons resolution indicates that a vote in the Commons is now required in all but the most exceptional circumstances. One must remember that conventions continually develop to keep the procedures and institutions of government in line with changes to society and its values. As a result, the general public and their representatives in Parliament would put considerable pressure on the government to respect the convention in such a situation. The same would be true of a case involving ministerial responsibility, which will be dealt with in more depth later in the chapter. For now, it suffices to say that it is a recognised convention that, under some limited circumstances, ministers will be expected to take responsibility for certain types of error by resigning from government. As was shown in *Crossman Diaries* and *Carltona*, the courts will only recognise, and not enforce, the convention of ministerial responsibility. However, there are examples of situations in which ministers in such circumstances have been forced to face the ultimate political sanction and have had to resign owing to mounting political pressure. In the most extreme cases, the Prime Minister can dismiss ministers who have failed to resign in the face of such pressure.

One way of explaining the type of sanctions that can exist for failing to comply with conventions is to translate them into more simple, non-political, everyday terms. As an example, we could consider the general convention (as opposed to a constitutional convention) in today's society that people tell the truth, apart from in the most exceptional of circumstances. In law, it is not illegal to lie (with notable exceptions)—so why should an individual choose to tell the truth most (or all) of the time? Certainly, under some circumstances, it may even be to his or her benefit to lie. Even then, most members of society choose to respect the convention and tell the truth. This may partly be the result of the individuals' own moral codes. However, it may also be the case that an individual appreciates that a civil society will choose to alienate or ignore those who are known to persistently lie or cheat. It is not generally advantageous for an individual to be regarded as the convention breaker, the liar, nor is it desirable to be part of a society in which breaking the 'truth convention' is a common occurrence. In reality, society will tolerate lying only in the most exceptional of circumstances. The conventions that have been developed by society, such as that which deems lying to be unacceptable, are informal instruments that have evolved to regulate the individual's behaviour. Breaching such conventions will have non-legal sanctions.

It is relatively easy to modify slightly and use the above principles to illustrate the importance of a government's compliance with constitutional conventions. Regardless of the law, such conventions prescribe the way in which the institutions of government, including the executive, should operate. Using our example, one may be alienated from society for persistently lying, but likewise the executive or one of its members could face similar political alienation and sanctions for breaching a convention. The sanctions for individuals can be severe, including the requirement that one resign or, if he or she does not, face dismissal. As a group, the whole government could face the ultimate penalty of being voted from power at the next general election. Thinking about the situation in terms of a 'truth convention' in everyday life may make it easier to understand why politicians do not use all of the power they have, but instead decide to abide by constitutional conventions.

When one considers the situation in these terms, it is possible to see how and why conventions can operate as effective controls upon the executive. As has been emphasised, many of the most important constitutional conventions in today's political society are concerned with the power of the executive. Considering the nature of the non-legal penalties that can face a person or institution deemed to be in breach of a convention, it is no surprise to learn that conventions are largely respected, despite being non-legal instruments. It is easy to understand why when one considers that, ultimately, an individual's political life and livelihood may be ended by the breach of a convention. In this respect, there is no doubt that they are effective controls. It is clear that, under some circumstances, their effectiveness would be enhanced through having legal redress for an individual or a government's non-compliance, but the flip side of the coin may show that their flexibility is one of their greatest strengths. This will be one of the underlying themes of the next part of the chapter.

summary points

Why would the executive respect constitutional conventions?

- *There are many reasons why a government would comply with conventions, most of which are political.*

- *The political sanctions for the executive's failure to comply with constitutional conventions can be severe. At the most extreme end of the spectrum, they can range from causing an individual politician's resignation to a government's eventual rejection at a general election.*

- *Some commentators note, however, that the executive complies out of moral duty and the acceptance that constitutional conventions reflect contemporary political values.*

- *The reasons why the executive chooses to comply with constitutional conventions could be compared with an individual's reasons for complying with one of society's conventions.*

12.6 Should constitutional conventions be codified and given the force of law?

cross reference
For details of the Ponsonby rule, see Chapter 6.

In considering whether or not constitutional conventions are an effective means of ensuring responsible government, some attention should be given to the argument that conventions ought to be codified and given the force of law. Indeed, this has been considered in relation to certain conventions, such as the Ponsonby rule (now enshrined in the Constitutional Renewal and Governance Act 2010). We shall firstly consider the argument that the present system of conventions should be retained, partly owing to its inherent flexibility. We shall then move on to examine the counter-argument that legally enforceable conventions would be more effective in ensuring compliance by the institutions of government. Topical examples will be used to illustrate these arguments, as and when they may be useful.

However, before we can proceed to discuss such arguments, it is important to explain what exactly is meant by the 'codification' of conventions. Professor Munro (1999: 78) explains that the term can mean one of two things in this context. Firstly, it can refer to the process of recording and gathering all constitutional conventions together in one (or more) written document(s), which still would not have legal effect, but would provide clarity of content. Alternatively, and more commonly, it can refer to the practice of legislating to place conventions on a statutory footing, either collectively or on an ad hoc, individual basis. This means that the conventions then cease to exist, because they have been turned into law. In this section, we shall concentrate mainly on the latter of these two options, in which the conventions are codified *and* given the force of law. Of course, that is not to say that the former option is not useful under some circumstances. Examples of such situations can be seen today in documents, such as the Ministerial Code, in which the most important conventions on acceptable ministerial behaviour have been recorded in a single document issued by the Cabinet Office. This method increased certainty without losing flexibility. Not only does the Ministerial Code set out the relevant conventions in black and white, but it also can be changed at any time at the Prime Minister's request. This happens as and when the standards required of government ministers change.

The more ambitious approach to codifying constitutional conventions would involve recording and making such conventions court-enforceable. In effect, it would mean that all constitutional conventions would need to be recorded, on a subject-by-subject basis, before being enacted into law by Parliament. From all that has been said thus far about the difficulties in defining and identifying conventions, one can imagine how difficult it would be to have Parliament select and agree on all of the conventions that should be included in such an enactment. In fact, even if Parliament were able to agree and succeed in such a mammoth task, ultimately its efforts

cross reference

You may wish to refresh your memory of parliamentary privilege in Chapter 7.

thinking point

What do you think? Would putting conventions on a statutory footing and allowing the court to review potential breaches of conventions undermine parliamentary privilege, and also Parliament's role as a check on the executive?

could be regarded as futile. This is because further conventions could then develop over time to fill the voids created by the initial enactment and as new moral standards came to be expected from the governing institutions. Presumably, Parliament would then be called upon to further legislate on all such new conventions. The other issue that would need to be considered is whether all conventions, if codified, would become justiciable. Would the courts be able to consider all possible breaches of conventions? And if so, would this diminish Parliament's role in scrutinising the executive—and, for that matter, in regulating itself? It could be argued that this would erode elements of **parliamentary privilege**.

Another potential weakness of codification would be that the system could lose all its valuable flexibility. The major advantage of the system as it currently stands is that conventions are developed over time to reflect changes in the political and wider community. As a result, the functions and powers of the governing institutions have changed significantly over time. However, the fear would be that if all of the relevant conventions were to be placed on a statutory footing, all political flexibility would disappear. Would the system become far more rigid? Would it create a two-tiered conventional structure? Professor Munro again provides a clear summary of the pertinent issues.

● **C. R. Munro, *Studies in Constitutional Law*** (London: Butterworths, 1999), p. 77

Is there an argument here for legislating to replace all of the conventions of the constitution? As well as strengthening the obligations, this would lead to greater certainty, as they would have to be precisely formulated, and there could be authoritative judicial interpretation of them when necessary. However, conventions are adaptable to changing ideas and circumstances, and have been a useful means of evolving the constitution, so there would be losses as well as gains. As de Smith succinctly put it, the process 'would purchase certainty at the expense of flexibility' (SA de Smith and R Brazier *Constitutional and Administrative Law* [8th edn, 1998] p 34) …

An ad hoc approach is preferable … Therefore, when it is important to secure obedience to rules and there is often a danger of disobedience, the case for legislating is strong. Often, it is not.

Two further points may be made about legislating. First, we should realise that, by making conventions into laws, we would not avoid disputes about what the rules ought to be, but would merely have put a particular formulation into statutory form. Secondly, even if the attempt were made to incorporate all the conventions in legislation or into a constitution, this would not, in the nature of things, prevent the growth of further non-legal practices and rules.

If one accepts Professor Munro's doubts about the feasibility and desirability of collectively converting all conventions into law, one must also accept that these new laws would provide some advantages in certain circumstances. There is no doubt, for example, that it would be desirable to have some legal redress against an executive that failed to comply with a key constitutional convention now law. There is no doubt either that, in many circumstances, it would be desirable to be able to state exactly what the convention now law was. Nonetheless, it is unclear whether the advantages of change outweigh the potential disadvantages of converting all constitutional conventions into legal rules. As things stand at present, governments generally do respect conventions, as was noted in the previous section. Further, if all that is required is further clarification on the content of the conventions, maybe more use could be made of the non-legal codification of constitutional conventions, as has happened with the Ministerial Code, for example?

This is perhaps why successive governments have chosen to enact legislation to convert individual constitutional conventions on an ad hoc basis as and when needed for clarification and enforcement reasons. This reduces the flexibility of the particular convention (by virtue of the fact that it would need to be amended by legislation from that point onwards), but it also has distinct advantages. It has meant that Parliament has not had the difficult task of collating

cross reference

You may wish to look back at Chapter 6 for a recent discussion about codification and the varying views on this issue.

373

and classifying *all* conventions. It has provided a mechanism for legal redress, in the event of breach, for those (former) conventions that were considered to be particularly important, while preserving the political redress mechanisms for those that appear to work well or be considered to be of lesser importance. Lastly, it has provided more certainty about the content of particular conventions (now laws), because they have been set out in writing and thus can be analysed more effectively. Therefore, in situations in which a specific constitutional convention has needed to be set out on a more formal basis or those in which legal redress is deemed more appropriate than political redress, an ad hoc approach has been preferred.

One recent and topical example that demonstrates such an ad hoc enactment relates to the developing convention that the government will not deploy the armed forces without allowing the House of Commons the opportunity to debate and vote upon the issue. The Ministry of Justice Consultation Paper, *The Governance of Britain: War Powers and Treaties—Limiting Executive Powers* (CP 26/07, London: HMSO, October 2007), explored the possibility that this convention be made more formal by means of either House of Commons resolution or, significantly, by statutory enactment. The Ministry of Justice White Paper, *The Governance of Britain: Constitutional Renewal* (Cm 7342-I, London: HMSO, March 2008), appeared to make it more likely that the more informal House of Commons resolution would be chosen, whereby the convention will be written, but will not be legally enforceable (owing to the often urgent nature of troop deployment), rather than a statutory solution. The Constitutional Reform and Governance Act 2010 has confirmed this approach.

cross reference

Manuel v Attorney General *is discussed in Chapter 7.*

The UK and Commonwealth courts have consistently held that constitutional conventions do not give rise to common law obligations (see *Reference re Amendment of the Constitution of Canada*, cited above, and *Manuel v Attorney General* [1983] 1 Ch 77). As a result, if it is ever felt that a constitutional convention needs to be placed on a legally enforceable basis, it must be enacted by Parliament. This is what is usually meant by the 'codification' of conventions. However, as has been seen in this section, the codification and enactment of all constitutional conventions is far from easy, not least because of the rigidity that its adoption would introduce to the system. If political society were to demand that, say, a convention be made formal to limit the power of the executive, it is much more likely that it would be done through individual enactment or through a House of Commons resolution. In any case, as was emphasised in the previous section, the existing political or moral sanctions may be sufficient to ensure that there is no need to enact conventions in all but the most exceptional of circumstances.

summary points

Should constitutional conventions be codified and given the force of law?

- *In this context, codification refers either to:*
  1. *the recording and gathering of all constitutional conventions together in one written document, which would still have no legal effect; or*
  2. *the process of legislating to give legal effect to conventions, either collectively or on an ad hoc basis.*
- *Codification in the first sense can prove effective in providing certainty, as is shown by the Ministerial Code.*
- *The concerns about the prospect of enacting all constitutional conventions relate to the practical difficulties and the rigidity that would be introduced to the system.*
- *The advantages of enacting all constitutional conventions include the introduction of a legal remedy for compliance failure and of certainty to constitutional conventions.*
- *Ad hoc enactment of individual conventions has its advantages. It can provide legal redress for failure to comply, and certainty of content and extent. It can do this without the practical difficulties of enacting all conventions.*

How does individual ministerial responsibility operate?

As has been noted throughout the chapter, the doctrine of ministerial responsibility is one of the most important examples of constitutional conventions regulating the behaviour of the executive. There are two main branches of ministerial responsibility. One is individual ministerial responsibility—that is, a minister's obligation to account to Parliament for his or her words and actions, and for those of his or her civil servants. In theory, this branch of ministerial responsibility should preserve the strength of Parliament, because the convention provides a mechanism that assists it in holding the government to account. This will be the focus of this section of the chapter. The other branch of ministerial responsibility concerns ministers' obligation to account to the Prime Minister for their words and actions (and for those of their civil servants), and to support their colleagues against attack from others. This is collective ministerial responsibility, sometimes known as collective Cabinet responsibility. As was noted in the *Crossman Diaries case*, cited above, it incorporates the principles that Cabinet discussions should be kept confidential. This will be the focus of the next section of the chapter.

The convention of individual ministerial responsibility is really a series of individual conventions grouped under a single umbrella term. Under this general term, the convention is that ministers are accountable to Parliament and that civil servants are accountable to their minister. It is a form of explanatory accountability, whereby a minister should explain any given situation to Parliament (having consulted the relevant civil servants, where necessary). This ensures that the minister remains accountable to Parliament and to the general public through its elected representatives. As will be seen, under some circumstances, the convention can place the minister in question under an obligation to resign from office if a serious error has been made for which the minister is responsible.

● **Public Service Committee,** *Ministerial Accountability and Responsibility* [Second Report, Session 1995–96, HC 313, London: HMSO, 1996], para. 31

> The pursuit of Ministerial resignations is important as part of a process of enforcing political accountability, but too great a concentration on it obscures the wider importance of the day-to-day business of holding the executive to account in Parliament, to ensure that it is kept under proper democratic control. Dr Philip Giddings . . . argues that Parliamentary accountability has a 'variety of objectives'. At one level, its purpose is simply to secure information about and explanations of what has or has not occurred. But it may also be regarded as a way of exerting pressure for change, or a means of attributing blame or praise for government actions. It is seen as a means of influencing the decision-makers who are being held to account, so that they will act in a way which is responsive to the wishes of those who are holding them to account. Ministers, in short, have to give information; but they also have to ensure that they are sufficiently responsive to the concerns of Members of Parliament in order to maintain their confidence.

The above extract is useful because it attempts to reveal the main objectives of individual ministerial responsibility. A minister has a duty to provide information to Parliament about any particular act or omission within, or on behalf of, his or her government department. Parliament in general, and the House of Commons in particular, has an electoral mandate to represent the electorate and to hold the government to account for its mandate. Thus Parliament needs to be made aware of all relevant facts so that the minister in question can be held to account for any error. In some instances, it is apparent that the minister will have to take responsibility for any such error by resigning from office. However, that is not to say that the prime objective of individual ministerial responsibility today is to seek a ministerial resignation; rather, the emphasis is on the sharing of information and the maintenance of confidence in the government. Only where that confidence is lost will pressure be put on the minister in question to resign. One such circumstance is that in which a minister knowingly misleads Parliament. In this situation, convention dictates that the minister should offer his or her resignation to the Prime Minister; he or she should be sacked for failing to do so. This convention was expressly approved by House of Commons resolution in March 1997 and by the subsequent versions of the Ministerial Code. This also partly accounts for the debate surrounding former Prime Minister Tony Blair's comments in Parliament about alleged weapons of mass destruction in Iraq at the beginning of conflict in that country in 2003. Had there been evidence that the former Prime Minister had knowingly misled Parliament, he would have been under a duty to resign.

Apart from those circumstances in which Parliament has been misled deliberately, there is some doubt as to when the convention will demand a minister's resignation. The 2010 Ministerial Code states only that 'Ministers have a duty to Parliament to account, and be held to account, for the policies, decisions and actions of their departments and agencies' (at paragraph 1.2b). It does not state when an error in such policies, decisions, and actions will be considered grave enough to warrant holding the minister to account through his or her forced resignation. As a result, one has to look to the historical development of the convention to see under what circumstances ministers have been forced to resign in the past.

It could be argued that the traditional interpretation of individual ministerial responsibility was that all failures of departmental policy or administration were the personal responsibility of the minister. This was the case whether the failures were the personal fault of the minister *or* of the civil servants working in her or his department. If the failure was sufficiently serious, the minister had to resign without awaiting censure of Parliament. Thus a minister was 'held to account' for the workings of his or her department and was also held responsible too. Such an interpretation is supported by evidence given to the Public Service Committee.

● **Public Service Committee,** *Ministerial Accountability and Responsibility* [Second Report, Session 1995–96, HC 313, London: HMSO, 1996), para. 8

> In his evidence to the Committee, the Chancellor of the Duchy of Lancaster quoted as a summary of 'what may be called the classical doctrine' of Ministerial accountability the memorandum which was drawn up by Sir Edward Bridges, the then Permanent Secretary to the Treasury, in 1954, at the time of the Crichel Down affair. Bridges wrote:
>
> > 'Under our constitutional practice, executive powers are conferred by Parliament on Ministers of the Crown. Both in regard to these powers and to others which derive from the prerogative and not from statute, it has long been the established constitutional practice that the appropriate Minister of the Crown is responsible to Parliament for every action in pursuance of them . . .
> >
> > It is upon Ministers, and not upon civil servants that the powers of Government have been conferred: and it is Ministers—who are Members of one or other House of Parliament, whose dismissal from office Parliament can bring about if it so chooses—who are answerable to Parliament for the exercise of those powers . . .
> >
> > It follows that a civil servant, having no power conferred on him by Parliament, has no direct responsibility to Parliament cannot be called to account by Parliament. His acts, indeed, are not his own. All that he does is done on behalf of the Minister, with the Minister's authority express or implied: the civil servant's responsibility is solely to the Minister . . .'

At first glance, such a reading of the traditional interpretation could be justified by reference to the Crichel Down case of 1954. In that case, the Minister of Agriculture, Sir Thomas Dugdale, resigned from office for errors committed by civil servants within his department. The ministry in question had received and rejected repurchase requests from the original owner of a piece of land that had been requisitioned by the Air Ministry in 1937. Subsequent investigations found that there had been severe mismanagement within the department, but not by Mr Dugdale himself. Nonetheless, despite that fact, the minister promptly resigned. This could be viewed as adherence to the traditional interpretation of the convention. Alternatively, it could also be argued that the minister resigned on the basis that he had lost the support of his own **back-bench members of Parliament (MPs)** on various policies. If this was the case, it is clear that, as early as 1954, there was no strict convention as to when ministers should resign on such grounds. This view is propounded in the following extract, written in 1956.

● **S. E. Finer, 'The individual responsibility of ministers'** (1956) 33 Public Administration 377, 393

> The convention implies a form of punishment for a delinquent Minister. That punishment is no longer an act of attainder, or an impeachment, but simply loss of office.
>
> If each, or even very many charges of incompetence were habitually followed by the punishment, the remedy would be a very real one: its deterrent effect would be extremely great. In fact, that sequence is not only exceedingly rare, but arbitrary and unpredictable. Most charges never reach the stage of individualisation at all: they are stifled under the blanket of party solidarity . . .
>
> We may put the matter in this way: whether a Minister is forced to resign depends on three factors, on himself, his Prime Minister and his party . . .
>
> For a resignation to occur all three factors have to be just so: the Minister compliant, the Prime Minister firm, the party clamorous. This conjuncture is rare, and is in fact fortuitous. Above all, it is indiscriminate—which Ministers escape and which do not is decided neither by the circumstances of the offence nor its gravity . . .
>
> A remedy ought to be certain. A punishment, to be deterrent, ought to be certain. But whether the Minister should resign is simply the (necessarily) haphazard consequence of a fortuitous concomitance of personal, party and political temper.

In his article, Professor Finer noted his belief that Dugdale resigned on grounds other than compliance with convention. In his opinion, the numerous examples of ministers who had not been forced to resign for mismanagement within their departments during the preceding century were evidence that the convention operated in an extremely haphazard manner. In his view, the important factors were the minister's own attitude towards the situation and the support (or lack thereof) of the Prime Minister, and of the minister's party. Dugdale had resigned as the result of a combination of these factors.

Whatever the truth in the 1950s, it is clear that today's convention on ministerial resignations has evolved significantly. By way of illustration, there were no ministerial resignations on the grounds of departmental mismanagement between Crichel Down in 1954 and the 1980s, when both Lord Carrington (in 1982) and Leon Brittan (in 1986) resigned on such grounds. This was despite the fact that many instances had arisen that seemingly merited the minister's resignation under the 'traditional' interpretation of the convention. The same is true of the situation since the 1980s (an example of which will be given later in this section). This may be explained partly by reference to two relatively recent developments to the convention.

12.7.1 Accountability versus responsibility

Ministerial responsibility was reinterpreted by then Cabinet Secretary Sir Robin Butler in a memorandum to the Treasury and Civil Service Committee in 1993. In that memorandum, he stated that whilst ministers are always 'accountable to Parliament'—that is, liable to account for any problem in their department and to be held *to* account for such problems—they are only 'responsible'—that is, personally to blame and potentially liable to resign—when they were directly involved in the problem or mistake. If this were true, ministers would always remain accountable to Parliament, but would be regarded as responsible only in extremely limited circumstances. Any mismanagement by a department's civil servants, for example, may not warrant the minister's resignation, provided that he or she did not mislead Parliament knowingly or direct civil servants to act as they did.

Despite being rejected initially as being unrealistic by the Public Service Committee in its second report (at paragraph 21), the distinction was accepted by the Scott Inquiry in its *Report of the Inquiry into the Export of Defence Equipment and Dual-Use Goods to Iraq and Related Prosecutions* (HC 115, Session 1995–96, London: HMSO, February 1996). Provided that a minister gives full and accurate answers to Parliament's questions, he or she will not be expected to take personal responsibility for an error committed by a civil servant. The duty to provide full and accurate answers was subsequently placed in the Ministerial Code (see, for example, the 2010 Ministerial Code at paragraph 1.2c–d).

12.7.2 Policy versus operational issues

This distinction between 'accountability' and 'responsibility' has given rise to another distinction—that made between matters of policy and matters of operation. A minister will always be responsible for policy failures (and may have to resign for such failings), but will be accountable only for matters of its implementation, operation, and administration (by giving full and accurate answers to Parliament). This distinction became extremely pertinent in the 1990s when numerous 'Next Step agencies' were established to operate specific areas of government departments' policy responsibilities. In such instances, the agencies provided an additional layer of managerial control between the minister and his or her civil servants. In other words, the agency (and the civil servants within it) took a step further away from central government and the minister who is responsible for that area of work. The civil servants may never come into contact with the minister and the minister may not have knowledge of their day-to-day work. He or she will set the broad government policy within which the agency will operate, but the agency will be responsibility for putting the policy into practice, subject, of course, to funding constraints.

cross reference
You may wish to refresh your memory of the Next Steps initiative by reading Drewry's extract again in section 1.3.

example

Michael Howard, former Home Secretary (and Conservative Leader in Opposition), dismissed the head (Director General) of the Prison Service Agency in 1995 after a series of incidents involving prisoners escaping from prison. Mr Howard claimed that the problems were operational matters, not policy ones. As a result, whilst he was liable to 'give an account' to Parliament for the failures, personal responsibility lay with the Director General, Mr Derek Lewis, who was promptly dismissed from office. In effect, by stressing the distinction between responsibility for policy and accountability for its administration, Mr Howard saved his ministerial post.

The distinction is rarely as clear-cut as in the above example, however. And the level of funding provided by central government may have a real impact on how the policy can be put into practice by the agency. In some instances, as Diana Woodhouse suggests, a minister can artificially manufacture the distinction to keep his or her ministerial office.

● **D. Woodhouse, 'The reconstruction of constitutional accountability'** [2002] Public
Law 73, 75

The emphasis on causal responsibility has resulted in a general acceptance that resignation may be required for serious departmental errors in which ministers were involved, or of which they knew or should have known, and the corollary position that ministers 'cannot be expected to shoulder the blame for decisions of which they knew nothing or could be expected to know nothing'. However, this has raised questions about what a minister 'could be expected to know' and has resulted in attempts by ministers to minimise expectations and distance themselves from culpability. Hence the employment of the distinction between 'policy' and 'operations', which implies that ministers cannot be expected to know anything about operational matters, and that between 'responsibility' and 'accountability', which implies that they therefore cannot be blamed for any operational error or for a series of such errors.

Nowhere was the use of these distinctions more evident than when the Home Secretary, Michael Howard, dismissed the Director General of the Prison Service Agency in 1995 after a series of incidents concerning prison security. Howard insisted that these were the result of operational failures for which the Director General . . . was responsible and that while he, as minister, was accountable to Parliament, in terms of 'giving an account', responsibility, in the sense of culpability, lay with the Director General. Such a division assumes that in instances of serious departmental fault the requirements of ministerial responsibility are fulfilled by the minister accounting for what had happened . . . The division also allows ministers to escape blame for operational errors which may amount to negligence or mismanagement on the minister's part, on the basis that no individual mistake is his or her own. In this instance, as far as the Prison Service was concerned, the Home Secretary became responsible for virtually nothing, the 'cause' was tied to the responsibilities of the Director General, and managerial accountability was substituted for constitutional accountability.

The development of a distinction between a minister's responsibility for policy issues and his or her accountability for the policy's implementation is the most recent development to the convention of individual ministerial responsibility, and it continues to be controversial (see the note below giving a recent example of the controversy as regards Theresa May and Brodie Clark). It dictates that, nowadays, ministers will not be forced to resign where an error has been made in a policy's implementation by civil servants. However, it must be emphasised that this does not necessarily affect the convention's ability to enable Parliament to hold the executive to account. As has been stressed, ministers are always accountable to Parliament for any mistake committed by their government departments. In reality, this means that they will have to answer any parliamentary questions on the issue accurately and fully. If they fail to do so, the convention contained in the Ministerial Code stipulates that they should resign. Ministers will also be expected to resign where they have made a serious personal error, but this could and has included other aspects of their life. For example, David Laws MP resigned from his role when a question mark was paced over his parliamentary expenses claims. Resignations are, at least in theory, more likely to result from perceived errors of judgement in relation to a minister's running of a government department or the development of government policy. But such situations are quite rare nowadays, partly owing to the development of the distinctions between responsibility–accountability and policy–operational issues. Parliament's scrutiny role in relation to the executive remains vital so that Parliament may gain the information it needs so as to place pressure on the government to change policy direction where there are concerns by Parliament or the electorate in this regard.

NOTE

For a recent example of the policy–operational divide, consider the recent controversy about border control and the way in which Brodie Clark, a (now former) civil servant, was apparently made to take responsibility for decisions about immigration checks and allegations by the Labour opposition for which Home Secretary Theresa May may have taken responsibility.

---

summary points

How does individual ministerial responsibility operate?

- *Individual ministerial responsibility is an umbrella term for a series of key constitutional conventions that allow Parliament to regulate the behaviour of the executive.*

- *In effect, individual responsibility means that a government minister must account to Parliament, and will be held to account by it, for any errors committed by his or her department.*

- *Today's definitions of 'giving account' and 'being held to account' mean that a minister will always be accountable to Parliament, in the sense that he or she will have to answer any questions fully and accurately.*

- *However, the minister will be considered to be 'responsible', in the sense that he or she will have to resign, only in limited circumstances.*

- *It appears that ministers will have to resign only where they have knowingly misled Parliament or where they have made a serious personal error, usually in the creation of policy. As a result, a minister usually has to be only accountable for the errors of his or her civil servants unless the civil servant acted on the minister's direction.*

12.8 How does collective ministerial responsibility operate?

The second branch of ministerial responsibility is collective ministerial responsibility. As was the case with the first branch, this is a series of interlinking constitutional conventions. Some of these conventions have been incorporated into the terms of the Ministerial Code (in all versions up to and including the 2010 edition). Individual ministerial responsibility was regarded primarily as a method by which Parliament could scrutinise the behaviour of individual members of government, whereas collective ministerial responsibility is more to do with a minister's accountability to the Prime Minister.

Amongst other things, collective ministerial responsibility prescribes that decisions reached by the Cabinet or other ministerial committees are binding on all members of the government, regardless of whether or not the individual ministers agree with them. The decisions in question are then normally 'announced and explained as the decision of the minister concerned' (paragraph 2.3 of the 2010 Ministerial Code). Convention also dictates that the way in which a policy decision was reached must remain confidential. There may well be internal dispute within the Cabinet and various ministerial committees about the merits of a decision, but once that policy decision is announced, no individual minister can speak out against it. This is to ensure that the government appears to have a united front and to create the facade of solidarity. Any government minister who wishes to protest against a government decision is usually expected to resign from his or her government post before doing so, unless he or she is given special dispensation by the Prime Minister to permit this while still in office (which is very unusual).

One example of a government minister opting to do so is the late Robin Cook, who resigned from government in 2003 in order to speak out against the government's decision to go to war in Iraq (although the decision had been approved by Parliament). A counter-example is Clare Short, who remained in office for a considerable period while criticising the government's decision to go to war.

NOTE

The Ministerial Code is available online at http://webarchive.nationalarchives.gov.uk/+/ http://www.cabinetoffice.gov.uk/media/409215/ministerialcodemay2010.pdf

In this respect, all members of the government are answerable to the Prime Minister, who decides how rigidly the convention is to be enforced and whether ministers should resign for breaking it. This decision can be influenced by many factors, including the Prime Minister's strength of character, the magnitude of the convention breach, and the support for the Prime Minister from within his or her own government. Public opinion will also play an extremely important role. If it is felt that the general public has lost confidence in the Prime Minister or his or her government, partly or wholly as a result of a rebellious minister, it is very likely that the minister will be forced to resign or will be dismissed. This aspect of collective ministerial responsibility applies to Cabinet ministers, non-Cabinet ministers, and to parliamentary secretaries. It also applies to the shadow government (that is, the members of the opposition party with portfolios corresponding to ministerial departments), who also require the facade of solidarity to be kept. Despite rarely being involved in the decision-making processes, it is also very likely that the convention applies to shadow junior ministers. Breaches of the Ministerial Code, and even the suspicion that a minister may have breached the Code, may lead to calls for the minister's resignation. A recent example of this was the resignation of the (now former) Defence Minister Dr Liam Fox.

● **Cabinet Office, *Ministerial Code*** [London: HMSO, 2010], paras 2.1–2.8 and 8.9–8.10

2.1 Collective responsibility requires that Ministers should be able to express their views frankly in the expectation that they can argue freely in private while maintaining a united front when decisions have been reached. This in turn requires that the privacy of opinions expressed in Cabinet and Ministerial Committees, including in correspondence, should be maintained.

...

2.3 The internal process through which a decision has been made, or the level of Committee by which it was taken should not be disclosed. Decisions reached by the Cabinet or Ministerial Committees are binding on all members of the Government. They are, however, normally announced and explained as the decision of the Minister concerned. On occasion, it may be desirable to emphasise the importance of a decision by stating specifically that it is the decision of Her Majesty's Government. This, however, is the exception rather than the rule.

...

2.7 Ministers relinquishing office should hand back to their department any Cabinet documents and/or other departmental papers in their possession.

2.8 On a change in Government, the Cabinet Secretary on behalf of the outgoing Prime Minister issues special instructions about the disposal of Cabinet papers in the outgoing Administration.

...

8.9 Ministers may not, while in office, write and publish a book on their ministerial experience. Nor, while serving as a Minister, may they enter into any agreement to publish their memoirs on leaving ministerial position.

8.10 Former Ministers intending to publish their memoirs are required to submit the draft manuscript in good time before publication to the Cabinet Secretary...

The above extract highlights some of the most important conventions contained in the current edition of the Ministerial Code. Most of the above principles have survived from the original publication of the Ministerial Code's predecessor, *Questions of Procedure for Ministers*, in May 1992. It will be seen that the Code contains a series of conventions, including the fact that a minister must respect the principles of unanimity and confidentiality or secrecy. He or she must also respect the fact that all Cabinet or government documents are to be treated with the same confidential diligence. However, as has been stressed, the question of whether or not a minister will be forced to resign is, ultimately, a question of political judgement for the Prime Minister. A Prime Minister may wish to demote a government member via a reshuffle or simply warn him or her about his or her behaviour. There are no hard-and-fast rules to state when the Prime Minister will impose particular political sanctions. In turn, this has led some writers to doubt whether or not the conventions in question exist at all today.

● **E. Barendt, *An Introduction to Constitutional Law*** (Oxford: Oxford University Press, 1998), p. 121

> It is doubtful, however, whether all aspects of the doctrine of collective ministerial responsibility should now be regarded as regulated by conventions binding on the government and its ministers. One should distinguish, from other aspects of the doctrine, the rule requiring a government to resign if it is defeated in the House of Commons on a motion of censure or of no confidence: that is almost certainly a binding convention. It was illustrated most recently in 1979 ...
>
> Apart from the obligation to resign on a no confidence motion, the principles of Cabinet and ministerial solidarity and confidentiality now appear little more than political practices or usages which may be departed from whenever this is convenient to the government. For example, Harold Wilson as Prime Minister suspended the principle that Cabinet ministers must support its majority view when he allowed dissenters in the government to argue against membership of the European Community during the 1975 Referendum campaign.

In Professor Barendt's opinion, the only convention that forms a binding part of collective ministerial responsibility is that a government that loses a vote of no confidence on an opposition motion is bound to resign. To support his argument, Barendt refers to Harold Wilson's decision in 1975 effectively to suspend the convention that Cabinet discussions should be kept confidential. This was in order for a full and frank public discussion to be held on the merits of membership of the European Community. In essence, Barendt's argument is that the remainder of the 'conventions' are so dependent on the Prime Minister's interpretation of the situation that they are not true conventions. However, this viewpoint is regarded as being quite controversial. A second interpretation would be that the remainder (for example, the confidentiality of Cabinet discussions) *are* conventions, but are not binding. A third interpretation is that they are all conventions, but that those conventions include a significant amount of **discretion** for the Prime Minister. The conventions listed in the Ministerial Code do not state that a minister will be expected to resign for *all* breaches of convention, regardless of their magnitude. In reality, such a situation could be regarded as overly rigid. It is argued that this third interpretation is the most representative of today's reality. Not only are the conventions listed as such in the Ministerial Code, but there is also **judicial** evidence of the convention to keep Cabinet discussions confidential, as has already been highlighted in the chapter.

● *Attorney General v Jonathan Cape Ltd* [1975] 3 All ER 484

Widgery CJ at 495:

> It is convenient next to deal with the third submission of counsel for the Sunday Times, namely that the evidence does not prove the existence of a convention as to collective responsibility, or adequately define a sphere of secrecy.

I find overwhelming evidence that the doctrine of joint responsibility is generally understood and practised and equally strong evidence that it is on occasion ignored. The general effect of the evidence is that the doctrine is an established feature of the English form of government, and it follows that some matters leading up to a cabinet decision may be regarded as confidential. Furthermore, I am persuaded that the nature of the confidence is that spoken for by the Attorney General, namely that since the confidence is imposed to enable the efficient conduct of the Queen's business, the confidence is owed to the Queen and cannot be released by the members of cabinet themselves.

…

Applying those principles to the present case, what do we find?

…

2. The maintenance of the doctrine of joint responsibility within the cabinet is in [at 496] the public interest, and the application of that doctrine might be prejudiced by premature disclosure of the views of individual ministers.

As we discussed in the section on court recognition of conventions, in this case, the court recognised both the convention and its breach as evidence that there was an expectation that the information was imparted 'in confidence'. It may be taken as evidence that the courts respect the existence of the convention that ministers shall not disclose the nature of confidential Cabinet discussions (but cannot enforce it without an accompanying legal argument).

As was the case with individual ministerial responsibility, it is clear that collective ministerial responsibility is an umbrella term that covers many different constitutional conventions. As Professor Barendt highlighted and as was true of the first branch of ministerial responsibility, there is some doubt as to the nature of the breaches that could, or should, lead to a minister's resignation. This is mostly owing to the significant amount of discretion that the Prime Minister has in such a situation. But the Ministerial Code and the attitude of the courts suggest that key parts of the doctrine are conventions. Great importance is placed on the confidentiality of Cabinet discussions and the presentation of a united front to the general public, for example. Breaches of such conventions may not necessarily lead to indiscriminate resignations, but the Prime Minister would be required to ask the Queen to dissolve Parliament (and thus trigger a general election) if the government were to lose a vote of no confidence. This last convention is the only way in which Parliament can use the doctrine of collective ministerial responsibility to regulate the behaviour of the executive *in extremis*.

383

summary points

How does collective ministerial responsibility operate?

- *Collective ministerial responsibility is an umbrella term for many individual conventions, most of which ensure the accountability of ministers to the Prime Minister.*
- *They include, but are not confined to, the conventions that:*
  - *ministers cannot openly criticise government decisions;*
  - *Cabinet and ministerial discussions are to remain confidential;*
  - *the Prime Minister will ask the monarch to dissolve Parliament, triggering a general election, after losing a vote of no confidence in the House of Commons. (Once the result of the general election is known, there is further guidance on what the Prime Minister should then do.)*
- *Some of these conventions are contained in the Ministerial Code.*
- *Significant discretion is given to the Prime Minister where these conventions have been breached. There are no hard-and-fast rules relating to when a Minister will be expected to resign for breaching the conventions.*
- *This has led some, Professor Barendt included, to doubt whether some elements of ministerial responsibility are conventions at all, but are rather political practices.*

 # Summary

This chapter has considered constitutional conventions as a key piece of the constitutional jigsaw. As Sir Ivor Jennings noted (1959: 177), 'they provide the flesh which clothes the dry bones of the law'. In effect, this means that to truly understand the UK's constitution, you will need to appreciate the significance of its conventions. In the context of ensuring responsible government, these conventions play a key role in limiting the powers of the executive. This is evidenced by several key conventions, not least the series of conventions under the doctrine of ministerial responsibility. Despite the fact that the UK and Commonwealth courts have held consistently that they cannot be legally enforced, and the fact that conventions are relatively fluid and vague concepts, they are regarded as a relatively effective means of holding the government to account. In fact, their fluidity or flexibility is regarded as one of their main strengths. Over time, they can adapt to meet the challenges of contemporary society. This is illustrated by the way in which conventions have developed increasingly to limit the powers of the Crown (and the government). Despite valid arguments that, under some circumstances, it would be beneficial to have a legal redress for failing to comply with some such conventions, on the whole, the political sanctions that can follow convention breaches are sufficient to ensure that they assist in the task of securing responsible government. Where they have proved to be insufficient, there have been calls to place them on a statutory footing.

Questions

1 How can one define constitutional conventions? Why is it difficult to provide such a definition?

2 When are constitutional conventions 'created'? What is Sir Ivor Jennings' identification test?

3 List some of today's most important constitutional conventions. What are the consequences of non-compliance?

4 What are the advantages and disadvantages of using constitutional conventions as mechanisms for limiting the use of executive power? Why does the executive respect constitutional conventions if the sanctions are non-legal in nature?

5 How do conventions contained under the umbrella term of ministerial responsibility help to ensure a responsible government (if at all)?

 # Further reading

Drewry, G., 'The executive: towards accountable government and effective governance?', in J. Jowell and D. Oliver (eds) *The Changing Constitution* (7th edn, Oxford: Oxford University Press, 2011), pp. 187–212

This chapter sets out the way in which the executive may be called to account for its actions. It provides a review of the effectiveness of accountability mechanisms and has recently been updated.

Flinders, M., 'Shifting the balance? Parliament, the executive and the British constitution' (2002) 50 Political Studies 23

This article considers the way in which parliamentary scrutiny has developed and the extent to which Parliament is able to hold the government to account, particularly in situations in which the executive holds a large majority in the House of Commons. It provides historical context, as well as recent reforms.

Gay, O., 'The Ministerial Code' (House of Commons Library Standard Note PC/03750, 13 September 2010), available online at http://www.parliament.uk/commons/lib/research/briefings/snpc-03750.pdf

This note explains the background to the Ministerial Code, the way in which it operates, and how alleged breaches of the Code are investigated and dealt with. It is comprehensive, yet easy to read.

The Parliamentary Commissioner for Administration

Key points

This chapter will cover:

- The creation of the post of Parliamentary Ombudsman
- The role and constitutional position of the Parliamentary Ombudsman
- The difference between making a complaint to the Ombudsman and taking a case to court
- What bodies can the Parliamentary Ombudsman investigate?
- What is meant by 'maladministration' and 'injustice'?
- Limitations on the Parliamentary Ombudsman's powers
- The investigative procedure
- The Parliamentary Ombudsman and the courts
- Examples of investigations conducted by the Parliamentary Ombudsman
- Reform of the Parliamentary Ombudsman

Introduction

This chapter examines the role of the Parliamentary Commissioner for Administration (PCA), who is now also known as the Parliamentary Ombudsman. The Parliamentary Ombudsman is an officer who is independent of other government bodies and who has the power to investigate administrative complaints. The Parliamentary Commissioner Act 1967 introduced the office to the UK.

(13.1) The creation of the post of Parliamentary Ombudsman

The creation of the post of **Parliamentary Ombudsman** was a response to the growth in the administrative and regulatory powers of the **state** in areas such as finance, welfare, immigration, licensing, and many other areas of daily life. This meant that decisions made by **government** and administrative bodies affected the lives and well-being of citizens. As a consequence, there was a need to provide a complaints mechanism for those who felt that they had not been treated fairly and competently. The concern in the 1960s was that citizens were unable to have their complaints dealt with effectively by existing **judicial**, political, or administrative bodies. An explanation and development of the institution of the Ombudsman and its Swedish origin is explained in the following extract.

● **M. Seneviratne,** *Ombudsman in the Public Sector* (Buckingham: Open University Press, 1994), pp. 2–4

> The idea that citizens should be entitled to complain against specific acts of their rulers, and that their complaints should be independently investigated goes back thousands of years (see Bell, C. and Vaughan, J.W. (1988) 'Building Society Ombudsman: a customers' champion?, Solicitors Journal 132, 1478). However, the establishment of a specific office to investigate citizen complaints against public officials is relatively recent, having started in Sweden in the early nineteenth century. Indeed the word 'ombudsman' was originally a Swedish word, meaning a representative or agent of the people or a group of people. In relation to the public sector, the word is now used generally to refer to an officer appointed by the legislature to handle complaints against administrative and judicial action...
>
> ...
>
> Ombudsmen came to be seen as useful in helping to meet the problem of an expanded bureaucracy in the modern welfare state (Rowat, D. (1985) *The Ombudsman Plan*, London, University Press of America p. 3) the activities of which had grown in range and complexity. The increase in the powers of discretion given to the executive side of government led to a need for additional protection against administrative arbitrariness, particularly as there was often no redress for those aggrieved by administrative decisions (Rowat 1985, p49)
>
> The growth of ombudsmen in both the public and private sectors has been a feature of modern life. In this country, ombudsmen were introduced in the public sector in the 1960s and 1970s, with the Parliamentary Commissioner Act 1967, the National Health Service Reorganisation Act 1973 and the Local Government Act 1974. More recently ombudsmen have been introduced in the private sector. In 1981, the insurance industry created the Insurance Ombudsman Bureau. This was followed in 1986 by the banks, which established the Office of the Banking

Ombudsman. The Building Societies Act 1986 provided for an ombudsman scheme for that industry, and the use of ombudsmen has now been extended to legal services, pensions, estate agents and investments.

As the extract suggests, there are other public sector ombudsmen, such as the Health Service Ombudsman, who deals with administrative complaints in the health service, and the Local Government Ombudsman. The Parliamentary Ombudsman also holds the position of the Health Service Ombudsman, meaning that the same person holds both posts. The work of the Health Service Ombudsman is, however, governed by a separate statute and different procedures, and will not be dealt with here. There are also ombudsmen for the devolved regions. One reform that has been made to the ombudsman system was introduced in the Regulatory Reform Order 2007, which amends the Parliamentary Commissioner Act 1967 and other relevant legislation. This allows the Parliamentary Ombudsman, the Health Service Ombudsman, and the Local Government Ombudsman to share information, to work jointly on cases with the complainant's consent, and to issue joint reports. This means that the various offices can work together when a complaint involves an investigation into the different areas of jurisdiction.

As the extract above explains, the ombudsman model is one that has caught on in the private sector. There are many private organisations and industries that have set up ombudsman schemes to deal with complaints by customers. These are a matter for private law. This chapter focuses on the work of the first ombudsman, the Parliamentary Ombudsmen. The Law Commission has recently published a report on the work of the public services ombudsmen, in which it makes various recommendations on access to the ombudsmen, and on improving their relationship with courts and other administrative bodies (Law Commission, *Public Services Ombudsmen*, Law Com No 329, HC 1136, London: HMSO, June 2011).

(13.2) The role and constitutional position of the Parliamentary Ombudsman

The Parliamentary Ombudsman is appointed by the **Crown** and holds office during good behaviour, although the Ombudsman can be removed by the Crown following an address by both Houses of **Parliament** (under section 1 of the Parliamentary Commissioner Act 1967). The Ombudsman's independence is protected in the same way as that of a senior judge. The office of the Parliamentary Ombudsman and the Health Service Ombudsman has a staff of some 250 people.

In the following extract, Ann Abraham, Parliamentary Ombudsman at the time of writing, describes her position. She refers to some of the uncertainties about the ombudsman's place in the constitution, which will be discussed later.

. . . .

● **A. Abraham, 'The Ombudsman as part of the UK constitution: a contested role?'** (2008) 61(1) Parliamentary Affairs 206, 206

The office of 'Ombudsman' is of venerable and international pedigree. It was in 1809 that the Swedish Ombudsman institution was created, destined to be imitated in later years not just in Scandinavia but throughout the world. The etymology of the word entails for the Ombudsman a role as 'representative of the people', implying an advocacy function in enforcing the rights of aggrieved citizens. Throughout much of the world in the intervening years this is precisely the remit entrusted to national ombudsmen, for example, as '*defensor del pueblo*' in the Latin American countries or as protector of human rights in the new democracies of South Africa or Eastern Europe. In such instances, the popular mandate is clear and the trail of accountability directly democratic.

In the UK, the situation is rather different. Taking inspiration from the original Scandinavian model but far from slavishly bound by it, Parliament in 1967 in effect created an officeholder whose remit combined investigating complaints with the possibility of improving standards of administration, and assisting Parliament in its duties of protecting the rights of citizens and of holding the Executive to account. MPs at first baulked at the potential encroachment on their territory: surely it was their task, in weekend surgeries up and down the land, to take the constituency temperature and exert their personal influence in Whitehall and Westminster to remedy legitimate citizen grievance? In the end, the MP filter (the device by which MPs rather than their constituents make complaints to the Ombudsman) preserved MP autonomy and established a uniquely convoluted mechanism for delivering citizen redress.

The work of the Parliamentary Ombudsman is complementary to the role of members of Parliament (MPs) and it was hoped that the Ombudsman would help MPs to better perform their duties of holding government to account. As part of their work, MPs deal with complaints about the administration from their constituents. They may, for example, write letters on behalf of constituents or ask questions in Parliament. But MPs receive too many complaints to deal effectively with all of them. They also do not have the resources or the powers to carry out a thorough investigation into a complaint against a government department or agency. This is why it was necessary to introduce another complaints process that could provide a more detailed form of enquiry. However, there were concerns that the Parliamentary Ombudsman might take over the role of MPs, who see it as their job to hold the government to account in Parliament. There was also a fear that the ombudsman system might undermine ministerial responsibility to Parliament, because ministers and their departments might be seen as accountable to the Ombudsman rather than to Parliament as a whole.

thinking point
Do you think the Parliamentary Ombudsman should help MPs to hold ministers to account or should this job be left to MPs alone? You might want to refer to Chapter 12 on the convention of ministerial responsibility when you are thinking about this point.

It was because of constitutional concerns about diminishing the role of MPs as representatives of the people that the decision was made that complaints to the Parliamentary Ombudsman can be referred to her only by MPs. This procedure is known as the 'MP filter'. It was also decided that the Parliamentary Ombudsman should report annually to Parliament (under section 10(4) of the Parliamentary Commissioner Act 1967). A select committee of the House of Commons was established to consider the report. The committee that now performs this function is the Public Administration Select Committee. The Law Commission (2011: 81) has recommended that, to reinforce the link with Parliament, the Parliamentary Ombudsman should actually be nominated by Parliament and then appointed by the **Queen**. The relationship between the Ombudsman and Parliament is discussed in the next extract.

● **M. Seneviratne, *Ombudsman in the Public Sector*** (Buckingham: Open University Press, 1994), p. 19

Indeed, the White paper (1965) emphasized that the office was intended to enforce the existing constitutional arrangements for protecting individuals. The ombudsman is set very much in a Parliamentary context, with MPs referring cases, and the ombudsman presenting reports to MPs and the House of Commons. Gregory and Hutchesson[1] have concluded (1975: 88) that the ombudsman scheme introduced in Britain was transformed from a public institution readily and directly available to the citizen, to a 'wholly Parliamentary institution, in essence an instrument at the disposal of MPs and designed to help them carry out more effectively their traditional functions on behalf of the citizen'. The office is not a citizen's friend and protector, as it is in Scandinavia and New Zealand.

1 R. Gregory and P. Hutchesson, *The Parliamentary Ombudsman* (London: George Allen and Unwin, 1975).

The lack of direct access to the Ombudsman by citizens has been criticised and this will be discussed later in the chapter.

The Parliamentary Ombudsman at the time of writing has argued that her job has evolved beyond simply redressing individual complaints. The handling of individual grievances means that she is able to identify systemic failures and to recommend principles of good practice. She makes this point in the next extract.

● **A. Abraham, 'The Ombudsman as part of the UK constitution: a contested role?'** (2008) 61(1) Parliamentary Affairs 206, 211

The founding legislation of 1967 in effect established the Ombudsman as an aid to Parliament in its constitutional scrutiny of the Executive. That role has evolved to comprise the distinct but inter-related functions of dispute resolution, guardian of good public administration, and of systemic check on the Executive's effectiveness. It is the core activity of investigating complaints that makes operational those strategic priorities and makes possible the broader public interest remit that so characterises the role of Ombudsman.

The Parliamentary Ombudsman explains that, when examining individual cases, she can often see a pattern in the complaints or can identify a structural problem that has led to the difficulties leading to the complaint. She is able to report this to Parliament and the **executive**, but ultimately it is up to them to decide whether or not to change the system.

13.3 The difference between making a complaint to the Ombudsman and taking a case to court

Pursuing a complaint with the Parliamentary Ombudsman is different from challenging the decision of a **public authority** in the courts. The difference between court proceedings and making a complaint to the Parliamentary Ombudsman is discussed in the following extract.

● **A. Abraham, 'The Ombudsman as part of the UK constitution: a contested role?'** (2008) 61(1) Parliamentary Affairs 206, 208

Yet the performance of these quasi-judicial functions is marked by characteristics that put clear blue water between the Ombudsman approach and that of the courts and tribunals, especially those of a common law jurisdiction like that of England and Wales. First, my investigative process is inquisitorial, not adversarial; it is normally conducted in correspondence and by face to face or telephone interviews, rather than in the combative environment of a courtroom. Secondly, my findings are not confined by strict judicial precedent; instead I reach conclusions that are just and reasonable in the particular circumstances of the case, informed by principle no doubt, but far less overtly legalistic than the judgment of a court or tribunal. Thirdly, the remedy imposed will not be enforceable against the respondent by the complaint, but will instead derive its authority from its cogency and moral force; on the other hand, the remedy will very frequently extend beyond the sort of financial redress that is the staple fare of the courts and tribunals, effecting instead a degree of future prevention as well as retrospective cure.

The extract explains that the procedure adopted by the Ombudsman is inquisitorial rather than adversarial. 'Inquisitorial' means that the decision-maker plays an active role in collecting evidence and finding the facts. This is in contrast to the adversarial system practised in the common law courts. In an adversarial system, the judge or decision-maker is not responsible for gathering evidence; rather, the relevant parties present the evidence to the judge. The judge, acting impartially, decides between them. The Parliamentary Ombudsman, unlike a judge supervising a court case, conducts the investigation. This means that the Ombudsman questions the relevant parties, amasses the information, and decides the facts. The Parliamentary Ombudsman is not bound by strict rules of evidence, and the investigation is intended to be informal and flexible, as we shall see below.

13.4 What bodies can the Parliamentary Ombudsman investigate?

The Parliamentary Ombudsman has jurisdiction over government departments and quasi-governmental bodies. These bodies are listed in Schedule 2 to the Parliamentary Commissioner Act 1967. The list can be amended by Order in Council (a type of delegated legislation) and, over time, the number of bodies included in the Parliamentary Ombudsman's remit has risen to around 250. The following bodies are typical of the kind of authorities that the Parliamentary Ombudsman can investigate: the Border and Immigration Agency (part of the Home Office); Jobcentre Plus (part of the Department for Work and Pensions); the Ministry of Defence; and the Ministry of Justice.

The next extract gives information on the number of complaints considered by the Parliamentary Ombudsman and the departments that receive the highest number of complaints.

● **Parliamentary and Health Service Ombudsman,** *Annual Report 2010–11* (Fifth Report, Session 2010–12, HC 1404, London: HMSO, July 2011), pp. 7 and 8

During 2010–11 we resolved a total of 23,667 enquiries. Of these, 3,340 were about bodies or issues outside our jurisdiction or remit and we advised enquirers on where to complain about issues ranging from financial services and utilities to school admissions or advertising content …

The government departments we received the most complaints about were the Department for Work and Pensions (2,462 complaints), HM Revenue & Customs (1,671) and the Ministry of Justice (924) …

During the year we accepted 403 cases for formal investigation, and reported on 412 (this includes some investigations carried over from the previous year) …

As you will see, there are a large number of claims made each year to the Parliamentary and Health Service Ombudsman.

13.5 What is meant by 'maladministration' and 'injustice'?

The Parliamentary Ombudsman investigates complaints of injustice by reason of **maladministration** against government departments and other public authorities. Section 5(1) of the Parliamentary Commissioner Act is set out below.

Parliamentary Commissioner Act 1967

....

Section 5

(1) Subject to the provisions of this section, the Commissioner may investigate any action taken by or on behalf of a government department or other authority to which this Act applies, being action taken in the exercise of administrative functions of that department or authority, in any case where—

 (a) a written complaint is duly made to a member of the House of Commons by a member of the public who claims to have sustained injustice in consequence of maladministration in connection with the action so taken; and

 (b) the complaint is referred to the Commissioner, with the consent of the person who made it, by a member of that House with a request to conduct an investigation thereon.

 ...

The terms 'maladministration' and 'injustice' are explained below.

13.5.1 The meaning of 'maladministration'

As stated above, the Parliamentary Ombudsman investigates complaints of injustice caused by maladministration. The term 'maladministration' is not defined in the statute. However, Richard Crossman, the minister responsible for the legislation creating the Parliamentary Ombudsman, gave a definition in the House of Commons during a debate on the Bill. This definition is referred to as the 'Crossman catalogue' and was approved in *R v Local Commissioners for the North and East Area of England, ex p Bradford Metropolitan City Council* [1979] QB 287, as is illustrated in the next extract. Maladministration is not, strictly speaking, concerned with the merits of a decision, but rather with the process by which a decision is made. The case is relevant to the Parliamentary Ombudsman because the Local Commissioners also investigate complaints of injustice in consequence of maladministration.

....

● *R v Local Commissioners for the North and East Area of England, ex p Bradford Metropolitan City Council* [1979] QB 287

Lord Denning at 311:

So this is the guide suggested to the meaning of the word 'maladministration'. It will cover '*bias, neglect, inattention, delay, incompetence, ineptitude, perversity, turpitude, arbitrariness and*

> *so on*' [Crossman Catalogue] It 'would be a long and interesting list' clearly open-ended, covering the *manner* in which a decision is reached or discretion is exercised; but excluding the *merits* of the decision itself or of the discretion itself. It follows that 'discretionary decision, properly exercised, which the complainant dislikes but cannot fault the manner in which it was taken, is excluded': see Hansard, 734 H.C. Deb., col. 51.
>
> In other words, if there is no maladministration, the ombudsman may not question any decision taken by the authorities. He must not go into the merits of it or intimate any view as to whether it was right or wrong. This is explicitly declared in section 34 (3) of the Act of 1974. He can inquire whether there was maladministration or not. If he finds none, he must go no further. If he finds it, he can go on and inquire whether any person has suffered injustice thereby.

Maladministration may include failing to follow set procedures, offering a poor service, giving misleading advice, rudeness, failure to offer an apology, avoidable delay, and unfairness, bias, or prejudice.

NOTE

For case studies of complaints of maladministration, see the Parliamentary Ombudsman online at http://www.ombudsman.org.uk/annualreport/case-studies/case-study-12

The Parliamentary Ombudsman has laid down some principles that will lead to good administration. The hope is that if government departments and public authorities adopt these values, they will avoid or minimise complaints.

393

thinking point
Do you think that 'maladministration' should be defined in the statute or are there advantages in not having a definition? If so, what are the advantages?

Principles of good administration
....

Good administration by a public body means:

1. getting it right;

2. being customer-focused;

3. being open and accountable;

4. acting fairly and proportionately;

5. putting things right; and

6. seeking continuous improvement.

NOTE

A more detailed account of the principles of good administration can also be found online at http://www.ombudsman.org.uk/improving-public-service/ombudsmansprinciples/principles-of-good-administration

---

13.5.2 The meaning of 'injustice'

The maladministration must have led to injustice if the complaint is to be upheld.

The term 'injustice' has not been defined, but in *R v Parliamentary Commissioner for Administration, ex p Balchin (No 1)* (1996) EWHC Admin 152, Sedley J approved the definition of injustice given by the authors de Smith, Woolf, and Jowell.

● **R v Parliamentary Commissioner for Administration, ex p Balchin (No 1)** [1996] EWHC Admin 152

Sedley J:

> [15] Less judicial attention has been devoted so far to the meaning of 'injustice' in the legislation, but de Smith, Woolf and Jowell, *Judicial Review of Administrative Action* [5th edition] write at paragraph 1–102:
>
> > 'Injustice' has been widely interpreted so as to cover not merely injury redressible in a court of law, but also 'the sense of outrage aroused by unfair or incompetent administration, even where the complainant has suffered no actual loss' [citing Mr R H S Crossman, speaking as Leader of the House of Commons].
>
> [16] It follows that the defence familiar in legal proceedings, that because the outcome would have been the same in any event there has been no redressible wrong, does not run in an investigation by the Commissioner.

This broad definition of injustice means that there may be maladministration even when there is no actual loss, but there is anger and disappointment at being subject to incompetence and unfair treatment.

13.5.3 When investigating maladministration, the Parliamentary Ombudsman cannot investigate the merits of the decision

Parliamentary Commissioner Act 1967

. . . .

Section 12

...

(3)   ...nothing in this Act authorizes or requires the Commissioner to question the merits of a decision taken without maladministration by a government department or other authority in the exercise of a discretion vested in that department or authority.

This provision makes a distinction between the administrative process, which can be the subject of an investigation, and whether the decision made and policies applied are meritorious. In other words, the Parliamentary Ombudsman cannot investigate whether the policy and decision made are good or bad decisions, but only the decision-making process and the application of the policy. However, the distinction between merits and process is not always one that is easy to draw.

In *R v Local Commissioner for Administration, ex p Eastleigh Borough Council* [1988] 1 QB 855, Eastleigh Borough Council challenged a finding of maladministration in a report of the Local Commissioner (that is, the Local Government Ombudsman). The council argued that the Local Commissioner had exceeded his powers by considering the merits of the decision contrary to section 34(3) of the Local Government Act 1974 (the equivalent to section 12(3) of the Parliamentary Commissioner Act 1967). The case was about the allegedly poor inspection of drains during the construction process by the council. The individuals concerned complained that, because of the council's failure to inspect the drains properly, they were inadequate and did not work effectively. The council had decided it was unable to inspect at every point in the building process, and had limited its inspection to four stages during the course of the building works and to one particular type of test. The Local Commissioner's report was ambiguous and it was not clear whether the inspections that were carried out had been carried out satisfactorily. It was unclear whether this had led to the subsequent problems. The Court of Appeal discussed whether the Local Commissioner had acted unlawfully by considering the merits of the council's decision.

● **R v Local Commissioner for Administration, ex p Eastleigh Borough Council** [1988] 1 QB 855

Taylor LJ at 869:

> In my judgment its tenor [the Ombudsman's report] shows the ombudsman to be trespassing into the field of discretion by laying down what policy as to inspections the dictates of good administration require, and what tests the council ought to ensure are carried out. That is quite different from finding that a test specifically required by the council's policy has not been carried out or has been carried out inefficiently. I therefore agree…that the ombudsman was in breach of section 34(3) of the Local Government Act 1974 in his conclusion that maladministration was established.

Here, the finding of maladministration was held to be unlawful and one of the reasons was that the Local Commissioner had considered policy matters that were not his concern.

13.6 Limitations on the Parliamentary Ombudsman's powers

13.6.1 Excluded areas

Schedule 3 of the Parliamentary Commissioner Act 1967 lists the areas of administration excluded from the Parliamentary Ombudsman's jurisdiction. Some of the most important exclusions can be summarised as:

* matters certified by a minister as affecting international relations;

* action taken outside UK territory by representatives of the UK government;

* extradition proceedings taken by the Secretary of State under the Fugitive Offenders Act 1967 and the Extradition Act 1989;

* action taken by, or with the authority of, the Secretary of State to investigate crime and to protect national security, including action taken in relation to passports;

* the commencement or conduct of civil or criminal proceedings;

* the grant of honours; and

* the exercise of the prerogative of mercy.

The two most controversial exclusions are:

* action taken by an authority in matters relating to contractual or other commercial transactions; and

* action taken in relation to appointments, removals, pay, discipline, superannuation, or other personnel matters.

The next extract discusses the exclusion of commercial relations from the Ombudsman's remit.

● M. Seneviratne, *Ombudsman in the Public Sector* (Buckingham: Open University Press, 1994), p. 24

> The government has argued that commercial relations and grants to industry, using statutory powers that involve a wide measure of commercial discretion, should not be subject to review by the PCA (Government Observations (1979) Observations by the Government on the Fourth Report from the Select Committee on the PCA, Review of Access and Jurisdiction Session 1977–78, Cmnd 7449, London, HMSO). Clearly there are some contractual matters that are more appropriately dealt with by litigation, but this is not a valid reason for excluding the whole administrative side of contracting from the remit of the PCA…
>
> The government is, however, unwilling to have commercial and contractual relationships subjected to scrutiny by the PCA, because it does not consider that these affairs are of the very nature of government. However, it could be argued that it is the exercise of the power of government that is in question here, albeit a power that is exercised through the medium of contract, and that this power is inadequately supervised (see Birkinshaw, P. *Grievance, Remedies and the State*, London, Sweet and Maxwell, 1985: 133) Despite the criticisms of the exclusion, there has been little progress in this area…

The exclusion of government contracts may be justified in areas such as defence, which concern national security. However, private contractors carry out many of the functions of public authorities. It is argued that the award and administration of such contracts may give rise to complaints that should be subject to the Ombudsman's jurisdiction. However, there are no plans to change the law in this area.

13.6.2 Availability of an alternative remedy

Section 5(2) of the Parliamentary Commissioner Act 1967 states that the Ombudsman should not investigate a complaint if the complainant has the right to appeal to a tribunal or has a remedy in a court of law. However, if the Parliamentary Ombudsman thinks that, in the particular circumstances, it is not reasonable to expect the complainant to resort to the appeal or other legal process, then an investigation can be carried out (under section 5(2) of the Parliamentary Commissioner Act 1967).

If there has already been a court decision and a remedy granted, then the complainant cannot then ask the Parliamentary Ombudsman to investigate. However, the Parliamentary Ombudsman has interpreted these provisions liberally. The general approach appears to be that if there is an administrative appeal or review, then, unless there is a particular reason why it is unsuitable, it should be used. But the availability of judicial review does not usually prevent an investigation. This is because judicial review proceedings are often costly and may be complicated, requiring the services of a lawyer, and because the remedy may not be appropriate. In addition, judicial review is not a fact-finding process and is concerned only with the legality of the decision. By contrast, the Parliamentary Ombudsman is concerned more broadly with the administrative process and whether there has been maladministration.

The report by the Parliamentary Ombudsman on the wartime detainees (extracted below) illustrates the difficulties that can arise. The Parliamentary Ombudsman investigated a complaint by Professor Hayward against the Ministry of Defence. This concerned an enquiry into a decision of the Ministry of Defence, announced in the House of Commons in 2000, to compensate individuals who had been interned by the Japanese during the Second World War because they were British subjects. When the details of the scheme were revealed, individuals such as Professor Hayward found that they were not entitled to compensation. They were not considered to fall within the definition, adopted by the Ministry of Defence, of a British subject, because their parents or grandparents were not born in the UK. (This was referred to as the 'blood link'.) This was despite the fact that these individuals were interned by the Japanese because of the very fact that they were British subjects. Many of them were naturalised as British subjects and, after the end of the Second World War, had lived in the UK for many years.

An unsuccessful judicial review action had been brought by the Association of British Civilian Internees: Far Eastern Region (ABCIFER) challenging the decision to adopt such a narrow definition—*R (on the application of Association of British Civilian Internees: Far East Region) v Secretary of State for Defence* [2003] QB 1397 (the *Wartime Detainees case*). Professor Hayward had not been involved in this judicial review action and was not a member of the ABCIFER. The Parliamentary Ombudsman decided, despite objections from the Ministry of Defence, that she was entitled to investigate, even though there had been an action for judicial review by other detainees, which had discussed the same complaint. The following extract from the report shows how section 5(2) of the Parliamentary Commissioner Act 1967 operates in practice. It also highlights the difference between an investigation by the Parliamentary Ombudsman and a judicial review action.

cross reference

The Wartime Detainees case is discussed in Chapter 17.

● **Parliamentary Commissioner for Administration, 'A Debt of Honour': The Ex Gratia Scheme for British Groups Interned by the Japanese during the Second World War** (Fourth Report, Session 2004–05, HC 324, London: HMSO, July 2005), pp. 5–6

...

My decision to investigate

25. Professor Hayward's complaint, which my predecessor had received prior to the initiation of any proceedings, was not directed at whether the scheme was *lawful* but concerned the injustice he claimed to have suffered in consequence of *maladministration*. His complaint was in my view therefore not one that was wholly amenable to an application for judicial review, as maladministration is not synonymous with acting unlawfully. Thus I considered that in this case the availability of an alternative remedy was limited.

26. In any event, having regard to the circumstances of his case I did not consider it reasonable to expect Professor Hayward to exercise any alternative remedy—to the limited extent that he might have had such a remedy—by means of proceedings before a court of law. I believed that such proceedings might well have been costly to him—in both emotional and financial terms.

27. I also had regard to the fact that court proceedings are adversarial in nature and, given the particular circumstances of Professor Hayward's case, I did not consider it reasonable to expect him to have to resort to such a process when that could have been distressing and as he had firmly indicated that instead he wished me to investigate his complaint.

28. In addition, I considered that it would have been difficult for Professor Hayward to have obtained the evidence necessary to pursue legal proceedings as he did not have access to official files. I have considerable powers in relation to access to evidence. That being so, in the circumstances of this case I considered that my fact-finding powers made an investigation by me more appropriate than expecting Professor Hayward to initiate legal proceedings.

29. Finally, I considered whether the ABCIFER application for judicial review, and the judgments in relation to it, prevented me from carrying out an investigation into Professor Hayward's complaint.

30. In doing so, I considered his specific case in the wider context of the purpose of my Office as decided by Parliament, which is to investigate complaints about injustice caused by maladministration on the part of public bodies in my jurisdiction.

31. While it is for the courts to determine questions of *legality*, Parliament has determined that my role is to consider whether the administrative actions about which individuals complain constitute *maladministration* causing injustice to them. Professor Hayward had asked me to investigate such a complaint.

32. It was proper that I should have had regard to the challenge by others to the lawfulness of *some* of the actions about which Professor Hayward complained and it is also proper that I should not question the decisions of the courts about the scheme, some of which have upheld its lawfulness and others which have not.

33. However, I considered that these proceedings and decisions did not prevent me from investigating whether those actions constituted maladministration causing injustice to Professor Hayward. My investigation would be confined to determining whether the administrative actions of the MOD constituted *maladministration falling short of unlawfulness*.

34. For the reasons set out above, I decided that I should investigate Professor Hayward's complaint.

The Parliamentary Ombudsman decided that it was not reasonable to expect the complainant to initiate legal proceedings. This was because the court was limited in its remit, being able to consider only issues of legality. The Parliamentary Ombudsman has a broader jurisdiction, because maladministration includes decisions that are lawful, but where injustice is caused by an incompetent application of policy. The Parliamentary Ombudsman also considered that the applicant would have difficulty gathering the evidence to present to the court. By contrast, she would have access to witnesses and official information. She also thought that litigation would be emotionally draining and costly for the applicant.

The Law Commission (2011) has recommended that that this requirement to exhaust existing remedies be repealed and that the Ombudsman should decide whether or not a claim should be pursued. This would certainly give more flexibility to the Ombudsman to decide which complaints process is more appropriate—but there is no plan to pursue this course of action at present.

13.7 The investigative procedure

13.7.1 The MP filter

Members of the public have to ask an MP to refer the complaint to the Parliamentary Ombudsman rather than approach her directly. An MP is under no obligation to pass the complaint to the Parliamentary Ombudsman. However, the referral does not have to be by the MP who represents the complainant's constituency in Parliament. Any MP can refer a complaint. There is a twelve-month time limit. So if a complaint is referred, it must reach the Ombudsman within twelve months of the person having knowledge of the matter to which the complaint relates. The Ombudsman cannot initiate a complaint herself. The reasons for the MP filter were discussed earlier in this chapter.

13.7.2 The investigation

When the complaint is received, the Parliamentary Ombudsman decides whether it is suitable for investigation. Rather than immediately conducting a full investigation, she may make an initial attempt to resolve the dispute between the complainant and the department.

A decision of the Parliamentary Ombudsman not to investigate can be judicially reviewed, but the court is likely to exercise this power very sparingly. In the following case, Dyer challenged the decision of the Parliamentary Ombudsman to investigate only some, and not all, of her complaints.

● ***R v Parliamentary Commissioner for Administration, ex p Dyer*** [1994] 1 WLR 621

Simon Brown LJ at 625:

> Bearing in mind too that the exercise of these particular discretions inevitably involves a high degree of subjective judgment, it follows that it will always be difficult to mount an effective challenge...

If the Parliamentary Ombudsman decides to investigate, a copy of the complaint will be sent to the principal officer in charge of the department complained about and anyone who took or authorised the disputed action (section 7(1) of the Parliamentary Commissioner Act 1967). They must be given an opportunity to comment on the allegations made. Investigations are carried out in private and the Parliamentary Ombudsman has a great deal of **discretion** as to how to carry out the investigation (section 7(2) of the Parliamentary Commissioner Act 1967). The Parliamentary Ombudsman will gather the relevant evidence and question witnesses. The statute confers the same powers on the Parliamentary Ombudsman as those of a High Court judge. The Ombudsman can summon and examine witnesses, including ministers, and order the production of documents relevant to the investigation. Very wide powers are conferred by section 8 of the Parliamentary Commissioner Act 1967 and the only information that is exempt from disclosure is proceedings relating to Cabinet meetings. Obstructing the work of the Parliamentary Ombudsman is contempt of court and is punishable as such (under section 9 of the Parliamentary Commissioner Act 1967).

summary points

Key facts about the complaints procedure

- *A complaint must be made to an MP within twelve months of the person having knowledge of the matter to which the complaint relates.*

- *The Parliamentary Ombudsman may attempt to resolve the matter informally.*

- *The investigative process is inquisitorial, with the Parliamentary Ombudsman initiating and conducting the investigation.*

- *The relevant department and officers must have the opportunity to comment on the complaint.*

- *The Parliamentary Ombudsman has the same powers as a High Court judge to summon witnesses and to order the production of documents.*

- *Obstructing the work of the Parliamentary Ombudsman is contempt of court.*

13.7.3 Remedies

cross reference
Remember the role that select committees of the House of Commons play in holding government to account that we discussed in Chapter 11.

After the Parliamentary Ombudsman has conducted the investigation, a report must be sent to the MP who referred the complaint, explaining the result of the investigation (section 10(1) of the Parliamentary Commissioner Act 1967). A copy of the report must also be sent to the principal officer of the department and or authority concerned and any other person who has been the subject of a complaint (section 10(2) of the Parliamentary Commissioner Act 1967). The report will normally contain a recommendation as to the remedy that the government department should grant, such as a monetary remedy or an apology. The Parliamentary Ombudsman has no power to enforce the recommendation, but in most cases the recommendations are complied with. However, if there has been a finding of injustice due to maladministration and the Parliamentary Ombudsman believes that the injustice has not been, or will not be, remedied, then there is a power to lay a report before each House of Parliament (under section10(3) of the Parliamentary Commissioner Act 1967). Such a report is referred to as a 'special report'. This is a way of bringing the problem to the attention of Parliament in the hope that MPs will put pressure on the government to comply with the recommendation. Such a report will be examined by the Select Committee on Public Administration.

A special report was laid before Parliament, in accordance with section 10(3) of the Parliamentary Commissioner Act 1967, after the Ministry of Defence rejected the adverse findings of the Parliamentary Ombudsman on the wartime detainees imprisoned by *the Japanese* and refused to grant the recommended remedy. The report was examined by the Select Committee, which agreed with the Parliamentary Ombudsman's findings. Subsequently, the Ministry of Defence relented and extended the **ex gratia** scheme. An article by Kirkham analyses the events in this case and the effectiveness of making a report in the extract below.

● **R. Kirkham, 'Challenging the authority of the Ombudsman: the Parliamentary Ombudsman's special report on *Wartime Detainees*'** (2006) 69(5) Modern Law Review 792, 814

Fortunately, section 10(3) reports are rare, and the report on the ex gratia scheme was only the third such report ever to be submitted to Parliament. Indeed, until recently, the record of the PO in terms of securing her recommendations was one of almost total success. According to the PO herself[1] and from the information that can be gathered from past ombudsman reports, even where the government has refused to accept the findings of the PO, ultimately, it has almost always agreed to provide redress.[2] Acceptance by the government is sometimes grudging and qualified, as for instance with the response to the PO's recommendations in the *Barlow Clowes* affair in 1989.[3] Payments in that case of £150 million were made 'out of respect for the office of the Parliamentary Commissioner'[4] but 'without admission of fault or liability'.[5] A similar unwillingness to accept the reasoning of the PO was repeated by the government following the channel tunnel rail link investigation in 1994, a response which came after only the second ever section 10(3) special report.[6] In that case financial redress was eventually made available after another four years of debate and a change of government.[7]

Despite these occasional disagreements, the PO's overall track record is testament to the past strength of the office and, in a hearing before the Select Committee in October 2005, the PO expressed continuing confidence in the government's respect for the office.[8] It is doubtful that the PO could have achieved or maintained such a position of strength without the support of Parliament and, in particular, the Select Committee. The Select Committee brings to the process a degree of moral and political clout that would otherwise be absent. As one former ombudsman has put it:

> It was perhaps not fully appreciated when the Office was set up that the effect of a report to Parliament of unremedied maladministration by a government department was a potential depth-charge. The Commissioner's report had no party implications; the House tended to be united in demanding explanations from the department in a highly public manner. The relevant Secretary of State had to stand and deliver these. No sensible civil servant wants to put his minister in this situation … [I]t is wonderfully effective, because if ministers find themselves in difficulties in the House, one may depend upon it that when they get back to their departments some awkward questions are going to be asked there too.[9]

Thus the doctrine of ministerial responsibility provides the Select Committee with much scope to back up the PO.

1 Ann Abraham in oral evidence: Public Administration Select Committee, *Tax Credits: Putting Things Right* (Second Report, Session 2005–06, HC 577, London: HMSO, January 2006), Annex, qq 10–11.

2 The two major exceptions were in 2001 and 2003: Parliamentary Commissioner for Administration, *Access to Official Information* (Fourth Report, Session 2001–02, HC 353, London: HMSO, 2001), Investigation A28/01; and Parliamentary Commissioner for Administration, *Access to Official Information* (Fourth Report, Session 2002–03, HC 951, London: HMSO, 2003), Investigation A7/03. Both concerned the Parliamentary Ombudsman's former responsibility to investigate complaints under the Code of Practice on Access to Government Information. With the Freedom of Information Act 2000 coming into force in 2005, this area of responsibility has since passed to the Information Commissioner.

3 Parliamentary Commissioner for Administration, *The* Barlow Clowes *Affair* (Second Report, Session 1989–90, HC 76, London: HMSO, 1990); see R. Gregory and G. Drewry, '*Barlow Clowes* and the Ombudsman: Part 1' [1991] Public Law 192, and '*Barlow Clowes* and the Ombudsman: Part 2 [1991] Public Law 408.

4 Nicholas Ridley, Secretary of State for Trade and Industry (HC Deb, 19 December 1989), vol. 164, col. 201.

5 Home Office, *Observations by the Government on the Report of the PCA on* Barlow Clowes (Session 1989–90, HC 99, London: HMSO, 1990), para. 37.

6 Parliamentary Commissioner for Administration, *The Channel Tunnel Rail Link and Blight: Complaints against the Department of Transport* (Fifth Report, Session 1994–95, HC 193, London: HMSO, 1995). For an analysis, see R. James and D. Longley, 'The Channel Tunnel rail link, the Ombudsman and the Select Committee' [1996] Public Law 38.

7 Lord Whitty, Parliamentary Under-Secretary of State, Department of the Environment, Transport and the Regions (HL Deb, 17 December 1998), vol. 595, col. WA 166.

8 See n. 1.

9 C. Clothier, 'Fact finding in inquiries: the PCA's perspective' [1996] Public Law 384, 388–9.

The author stresses the political pressure that is generated by a special report. The political neutrality of the Parliamentary Ombudsman means that the findings are regarded with greater authority and legitimacy. Questioning and scrutiny of the minister responsible for the relevant department may lead the government to remedy the situation even if it does not accept the findings of the Parliamentary Ombudsman.

The recommendations of the Parliamentary Ombudsman are not legally binding and it is possible for the department to refuse to implement them. However, the Court of Appeal has held that the decision of a government department to reject the Ombudsman's findings must be justified on rational grounds. In *Bradley v Secretary of State for Work and Pensions* [2008] 3 WLR 1059, the Parliamentary Ombudsman upheld a complaint against the Department for Work and Pensions (DWP). The report made various findings of fact and pointed to flaws in the department's conduct. So, for example, one finding was that information provided by the DWP in a leaflet about the winding up of final-salary occupation schemes was misleading. This amounted to maladministration, which had led to injustice to those who suffered loss to their pensions when the final-salary schemes were wound up. It was recommended that the government should consider making arrangements to compensate those who had lost out financially. The findings and recommendations of the Parliamentary Ombudsman were rejected by the DWP. The claimants—members of occupational pensions schemes that had been wound up—challenged the decision of the DWP. The Court discussed the legal status of the Parliamentary Ombudsman's report.

● **Bradley v Secretary of State for Work and Pensions** [2008] 3 WLR 1059

Sir John Chadwick at 1106:

> [44] It is, I think, impossible to contend that there is anything in the 1967 Act which, in terms, requires the body whose conduct is the subject of an investigation under section 5(1) to accept the commissioner's findings of maladministration. Parliament could have enacted such a provision; but it did not. Had that been its intention, it might have been expected to say so; if only because it would have been necessary to make it clear whether it intended any element of reciprocity. If a finding that there had been maladministration was binding on the department—so as to preclude the minister from denying maladministration when called to account in Parliament—was a finding that there had not been maladministration be binding on the Member of the House of Commons who had referred the complaint to the commissioner—so as to preclude him from asserting maladministration in debate? It is not difficult to suppose a case in which the commissioner had found maladministration in one respect but rejected it in another...

At a later point in the judgment, at 1128, Chadwick LJ considered whether the Secretary of State could rationally reject the finding that the DWP had produced misleading information:

> [95] As I have said, the judge observed, at para 66 of his judgment, that no reasonable Secretary of State could rationally disagree with the ombudsman's view that the information... was incomplete and potentially misleading. I am satisfied that the judge was correct in that observation; but, for my part, I prefer to say that, in the circumstances of this case, it was irrational for the Secretary of State to reject the ombudsman's finding to that effect. For that reason I would hold that the judge was correct to conclude that the Secretary of State's decision to reject the first finding of maladministration should be quashed. It follows that I would dismiss the Secretary of State's appeal.

The Court of Appeal held that the relevant question was not whether it was rational for the Parliamentary Ombudsman to come to a particular factual conclusion, but rather the reaction of the Secretary of State. Was it rational for the Secretary of State to disagree with the Parliamentary Ombudsman's findings? In this instance, it was held that it was not. This case was followed in *R (on the application of Equitable Members Action Group) v HM Treasury* [2009] EWHC, 2495. The controversy over Equitable Life is discussed later in the chapter, but what concerns us here is the decision of the previous government to reject some of the findings of the Parliamentary Ombudsman and to refuse to establish a compensation scheme, for the Equitable Life investors, as was recommended. It was held that the government had acted unlawfully in rejecting some findings of the Parliamentary Ombudsman because it had failed to give rational and cogent reasons for the decision. The court also held that the government's decision not to follow the Parliamentary Ombudsman's recommendation to set up a compensation scheme was not irrational.

These judgments do not mean that the Parliamentary Ombudsman's findings are legally binding, but that if they are rejected, the government department must give rational and intelligible reasons for the decision to reject them.

summary points

Remedies: the consequences of a finding of maladministration.

- *The Parliamentary Ombudsman cannot grant a remedy and cannot force a government department to grant a remedy.*
- *The Parliamentary Ombudsman may recommend a remedy and the government usually accepts such recommendations.*
- *If the government rejects the findings of the Parliamentary Ombudsman, it must act rationally and give rational and cogent reasons for its rejections.*

- *The Parliamentary Ombudsman may lay a special report before Parliament if a complaint of maladministration has been upheld, but is not remedied. This may generate sufficient political pressure by MPs to persuade the government to provide compensation.*

13.8 The Parliamentary Ombudsman and the courts

The decisions of the Parliamentary Ombudsman are subject to judicial review by the courts. As we have seen in relation to *R v Parliamentary Commissioner for Administration, ex p Dyer* [1994] 1 WLR 621, the courts are reluctant to overturn decisions of the Parliamentary Ombudsman. But decisions have been successfully challenged where the courts have found that the Parliamentary Ombudsman's decisions are legally flawed. In *R v Parliamentary Commissioner for Administration, ex p Balchin (No 1)* (1996) EWHC Admin 152, the court quashed a decision of the Parliamentary Ombudsman because there was a failure to take into account a relevant consideration and therefore the power had not been exercised properly. In this case, the Parliamentary Ombudsman investigated an allegation of planning blight of a property owned by the Balchins. Their property had been severely reduced in value because of a decision to build a major road that ran adjacent to the property and, in effect, they suffered near financial ruin. The court held that the Parliamentary Ombudsman should have considered the role of the Department of Transport in informing the local authority of its statutory powers to help the Balchins. However, a subsequent decision of the Parliamentary Ombudsman that found that there was no maladministration was also quashed. In *R v Parliamentary Commissioner for Administration, ex p Balchin (No 2)* [2000] 2 LGLR 87, Dyson J held that this was not a reasonable conclusion based on the evidence. He also held that the Parliamentary Ombudsman had failed to consider whether the Balchins' sense of outrage at their treatment amounted to injustice. This case was later settled and the Balchins were granted an *ex gratia* payment of £200,000.

cross reference
The courts' role in reviewing the legality of the actions and inactions of those exercising public functions is explained more fully in Chapter 14.

403

13.9 Examples of investigations conducted by the Parliamentary Ombudsman

This section gives a sample of the kinds of case investigated by the Parliamentary Ombudsman. The first section gives examples of complaints that have attracted public attention and have been widely publicised in the media.

13.9.1 Examples of high-profile investigations

Sachsenhausen

Sachsenhausen was the first high-profile case investigated by the Parliamentary Ombudsman. It concerned the redistribution of a compensation scheme for **victims** of Nazi persecution based on an Anglo-German Agreement of 1964. The distribution of the money was organised by the British Foreign Office in accordance with rules drawn up by the Foreign Secretary. The complaint arose because some twelve applicants were excluded from the scheme on the ground that they had been detained at a separate unit within the Sachsenhausen camp. As a consequence, they were not considered victims of Nazi persecution in accordance with the definition in the Anglo-German Agreement. When they and various MPs complained about their treatment, they were informed that the funds had already been distributed. The Parliamentary Ombudsman found that there had been maladministration. He criticised the administrative process by which the decisions were made and then defended, when challenged by MPs and others. The Foreign Office rejected the criticisms made of it in the report, but nevertheless, out of respect for the Parliamentary Ombudsman, decided that compensation should be paid. The following extract is from a speech of the Secretary of State for Foreign Affairs making this point in the House of Commons.

● **Mr George Brown, Secretary of State for Foreign Affairs** (Hansard, HC Deb, 5 February 1968), vol 758, cols 107–70

> However, all the Ministers who have looked at this quite separately have come to one conclusion and the Parliamentary Commissioner has come to another. I repeat that no one has ever disputed that this was a borderline case. I am bound to say that I do not see any reason for thinking that the judgment of the Parliamentary Commissioner is necessarily better than that of all of us...
>
> Having quite firmly, and I hope quite honestly, explained my own view, I have nevertheless decided that compensation will be paid on the appropriate basis to all these claimants or, in a case of those who have died dependants...

Barlow Clowes

The next particularly notable case concerned the collapse of the Barlow Clowes investment company in 1988. This caused loss and hardship to many ordinary investors, including those in retirement. The Department of Trade and Industry (DTI) had licensed the company under the Prevention of Fraud Investment Act 1958. The Parliamentary Ombudsman found that there had been significant maladministration in five areas in the department's dealings with Barlow Clowes. These included failures to understand the impact of Barlow Clowes' interests in Jersey, which affected its financial viability. There were also failures to investigate the company even when there were suspicions about its status. The DTI refused to accept the findings of maladministration. However, it did agree to pay compensation, which provided for 99 per cent of investors to receive at least 85 per cent of their capital. In the light of this, the Parliamentary Ombudsman concluded as follows.

● **Parliamentary Commissioner for Administration, *Annual Report for 1989*** (Third Report, Session 1989–90, HC 353, London: HMSO, 1990), p. 24

> However, I saw ground for satisfaction that the Government-with whatever reservations-was prepared to act as it proposed in providing a fair remedy for what, as I had seen things, had been an injustice suffered by investors as a result of maladministration.

Equitable Life

The final case to be considered here concerned an investigation into the regulatory competence of various public authorities, including the (then) DTI, in their supervision of Equitable

Life. Equitable Life was found to have misled its investors about the value of their investments and to have made promises that it was unable to keep, which caused loss to many of them. Equitable Life was the subject of much publicity and various investigations were conducted. A report by the Parliamentary Ombudsman made findings of maladministration against the DTI, the Government Actuary's Department, and the Financial Services Authority. The Parliamentary Ombudsman also found that there had been a failure to regulate the company properly in the period before December 2000. She recommended that, as well as apologising, the government should establish a compensation scheme for Equitable Life policyholders who would not have suffered loss had they invested elsewhere.

NOTE

See Parliamentary and Health Service Ombudsman, *Equitable Life: A Decade of Regulatory Failure* (Fourth Report, HC 815, Session 2007–08, London: HMSO, July 2008).

The previous Labour government apologised to Equitable Life policyholders and accepted some, but not all, of the findings of maladministration in the Ombudsman's report, but rejected the compensation scheme recommended by the Ombudsman in favour of a less generous arrangement.

NOTE

See *The Prudential Regulation of the Equitable Life Assurance Society: The Government's Response to the Report of the Parliamentary Ombudsman's Investigation* (Cm 7538, London: HMSO, January 2009).

However, after the May 2010 election, the Conservative–Liberal **coalition government** decided to implement the Parliamentary Ombudsman's recommendations and the Equitable Life Payments Act 2011 goes some way towards doing this.

13.9.2 Examples of typical claims made to the Parliamentary Ombudsman

The following extracts comprise two case studies drawn from the Parliamentary Ombudsman's report. These extracts illustrate individual cases of maladministration. They do not concern such large-scale or high-profile investigations as the cases noted above, but such cases, involving smaller sums of money, are typical of the work of the Parliamentary Ombudsman.

● **Parliamentary and Health Service Ombudsman,** *Annual Report 2007–08* [Fifth Report, Session 2007–08, HC 1040, London: HMSO, October 2008], p. 21

Cessation of bank payments left income support claimant short of food

Mr L wrote to Jobcentre Plus on 11 February 2006 asking that the means by which his income support was paid be changed from payment direct into a bank account to payment by cheque. He instructed his bank to close his account and destroyed his bank card. Jobcentre Plus did not receive Mr L's letter until 14 February, by which time it had paid his weekly payment for 13 February into his bank account. On receipt of Mr L's letter, Jobcentre Plus suspended his payments, waiting for him to say if he was going to open a new bank or Post Office account.

When the next benefit payment did not arrive as expected Mr L contacted his MP (he said he did that because in the past Jobcentre Plus had ignored some of his letters until the MP had become involved). The MP contacted Jobcentre Plus, which lifted the suspension and sent Mr L a cheque for his missing payments. Jobcentre Plus apologised to Mr L and said that a consolatory payment would be considered. The referral for a consolatory payment included a letter from Mr L to his MP, in which he described the effects of being without income support: he had no electricity and hence no heat, light or hot water. He was also unable to afford food. Jobcentre Plus accepted that maladministration had interrupted Mr L's benefit payments, but concluded that the degree of inconvenience caused did not warrant compensation. It also took account of the fact that Mr L had not contacted it about the payment problem, but instead had approached his MP. Mr L complained to the Ombudsman that Jobcentre Plus had left him without payment for three weeks, for which it had apologised but refused to give compensation.

We partly upheld the complaint. It was maladministrative of Jobcentre Plus to stop paying Mr L's benefit into his bank account but not to start paying it by cheque. It was not at fault, however, for making the 13 February payment direct into Mr L's bank account, as it had not yet received his request to change the payment method. It was reasonable, given Mr L's history of interaction with Jobcentre Plus, for him to have initially sought his MP's help. For its part, Jobcentre Plus paid insufficient attention to the facts of Mr L's deprivation when considering the consolatory payment.

Jobcentre Plus reconsidered its decision and awarded Mr L £400 for inconvenience and distress. It also agreed to apologise to him for not making a payment in the first place. Jobcentre Plus also undertook to reply promptly to any future correspondence from Mr L in line with its service standards.

. . . .

● **Parliamentary and Health Service Ombudsman,** *Annual Report 2007–08* (Fifth Report, Session 2007–08, HC 1040, London: HMSO, October 2008), p. 29

Delay processing application caused woman to miss a funeral and wedding

In June 2004 Mrs F and her husband applied for leave for her to remain in the UK on the basis of her marriage to a UK resident. In June 2005 Mr F wrote to tell the Border and Immigration Agency (the Agency) that Mrs F needed to travel abroad as his father had recently died. The Agency received the letter but took no action. Nor did it respond to letters it received in February and March 2006 from Mrs F's solicitors querying the delay processing the application. Throughout July the solicitors sent further letters of complaint about the delay and requests for a reply. On 14 August the solicitors told the Agency that unless Mrs F's application was decided by 3 September, they would refer matters to the Ombudsman.

The solicitors and the Agency continued to exchange correspondence. In a letter dated 12 October, the solicitors complained that Mrs F's application had been handled appallingly. They said she had made plans to travel to Nigeria for urgent family reasons by 15 December and asked that her application be dealt with immediately. On 20 December the Agency noted that it was unable to make a decision because her application form and documents, including both her and her husband's passports, were not on the file.

Mrs F complained to the Ombudsman in January 2007 that the delays deciding her application for leave had led to her missing a funeral and her sister's wedding. Furthermore, the Agency had not responded to her solicitors' letters and had lost her passport and other documents. In June 2007 the Agency granted Mrs F two years' leave to remain as a spouse of a UK resident.

We upheld Mrs F's complaint. The Agency took no substantive action on her application between July 2004 and February 2007; it lost Mr and Mrs F's passports and other documents; and did not respond to the solicitors' correspondence. The Agency offered Mrs F consolatory payments totalling £250 for the delay and failure to reply to her solicitors' correspondence, and a further £1,250 for Mr and Mrs F being unable to attend the funeral. The Agency agreed to compensate them for the cost of replacing their passports, and to make a consolatory payment in respect of having missed the wedding, on receipt of suitable supporting evidence. It agreed to apologise to Mrs F for its failings.

These cases deal with a wide variety of issues. They illustrate the important role that the Parliamentary Ombudsman plays in redressing individual grievances. The Parliamentary Ombudsman's constitutional position, independence, and statutory ability to access documents and to question witnesses mean that the office can play an important part in helping people to pursue complaints against public authorities.

Reform of the Parliamentary Ombudsman

The ombudsman scheme introduced by the Parliamentary Commissioner Act 1967 has attracted criticisms and there have been various suggestions for reform over the years. In its 2011 report, the Law Commission makes seventeen recommendations, only some of which are relevant to the Parliamentary Ombudsman. It recommends that the government establish a wide-ranging review of the public service ombudsmen's role in providing administrative justice. Perhaps one of the most interesting recommendations is that there should be greater interaction between ombudsmen and the **Administrative Court**. So, for example, there is a recommendation that ombudsmen could refer points of law to the Administrative Court for decision. It also recommends that the Administrative Court be able to stay a case and send it to the ombudsman for resolution. These would be innovative changes and if you want to read further, then the report is listed in the further reading at the end of the chapter.

Some other criticisms and suggestions for reform include the following.

- Dissatisfaction has been expressed with the fact that the Parliamentary Ombudsman is prevented from investigating issues such as commercial transactions and personnel issues (as discussed above).

- It has also been argued that the definition of maladministration should be clarified. However, some commentators have argued that the vagueness of the definition is advantageous, because it allows for flexibility in deciding whether action or inaction amounts to maladministration.

- It has also been suggested that the Parliamentary Ombudsman should be able to grant a remedy or to force government authorities to provide a remedy. The main argument in favour of this change is that it would increase the authority of the office and raise public confidence, because citizens would understand that if there were a finding of maladministration, they would receive a remedy. But the arguments against such a move are that the proceedings are informal and inquisitorial, and do not necessarily give sufficient opportunity for the government authority to respond at every stage.

- The most serious criticism of the present system is that there is no direct access to the Parliamentary Ombudsman by the public because of the MP filter. As we have seen, this requires citizens' complaints to be referred by an MP. This practice is not one that is applied to other ombudsman services in the UK. Similarly, it is not the practice in most other countries where there are ombudsman-like complaints mechanisms. There have been many recommendations that the MP filter be abolished, as the next extract demonstrates.

● P. Collcutt and M. Hourihan, *Review of the Public Sector Ombudsman in England: A Report by the Cabinet Office* (London: HMSO, April 2000) (the Collcutt Report)

The Case for Change

3.42 During the course of this chapter we have set out a number of the arguments put forward in favour of or against the MP filter and the issue has been looked at in great depth in the past. We note in particular the inquiry by the PCA Select Committee in 1993 which summarised the benefits of the MP filter in words from a report by the Select Committee in 1978: '... the committee concluded that the filter worked to the advantage of:

a) the complainant, because his problem can often be resolved quickly through the intervention of a Member;

b) the Member, because he is kept in touch with the problems which his constituents are facing in their daily contact with the machinery of the state; and

c) the commissioner, because he is normally asked to investigate only complaints that the Member has been, or knows that he will be, unable to resolve himself'.

We have had difficulty, however, in seeing the consistency of these arguments with the evidence presented to us during the review. In the case of complainants, representative groups have argued that complainants' interests would be better served without the filter. Our survey and other evidence have shown that a very small proportion of MPs' contacts with their constituents is associated with use of the ombudsman. Both the current PCA and previous PCA have expressed the opinion that the MP filter should go.

It is argued that direct access would be beneficial because it would:

- allow greater direct publicity and more personal communication with the public;
- make it easier to complain by removing a layer of the procedure;
- allow other organisations that work with the public, such as volunteer organisations, to refer cases directly;
- end reliance on MPs who may not be familiar with the Parliamentary Ombudsman's work, who may be seen as partisan by citizens, or who may simply be unwilling to refer a case.

An alternative is the 'dual-track approach', which the Law Commission Report (2011) suggests. This is a compromise that would allow individuals to complain directly to the Parliamentary Ombudsman, while also preserving the right of MPs to refer complaints as well.

Despite the various recommendations in the Cabinet Office Review and other reports, the MP filter remains.

👁 Summary

The Parliamentary Ombudsman is an independent officer, appointed by the Crown, who investigates complaints against government and public authorities listed in Schedule 2 to the Parliamentary Commissioner Act 1967. She investigates injustice by reason of maladministration leading to injustice. Complaints have to be referred to the Parliamentary Ombudsman by an MP. This is known as the MP filter. The Parliamentary Ombudsman cannot start an investigation on her own without an MP referral. The enquiry process is inquisitorial and not adversarial.

It is different from going to court and having to prove a case in court. The investigation is informal and flexible, but the Ombudsman has the same powers as a court to demand documents and to summon witnesses. She cannot grant a remedy or compel public authorities to grant a remedy. She submits an annual report to Parliament and can also issue a special report to draw Parliament's attention to a finding of maladministration that has not been remedied. The decisions of the Parliamentary Ombudsman are subject to judicial review by the courts. She can conduct an investigation jointly with the Local Government Ombudsman and the Health Service Ombudsman. Most reform proposals have centred around the abolition of the MP filter, but the Law Commission Report (2011) recommends a 'dual-track approach', which would retain MPs right to refer cases, but give an additional opportunity to the public to access the Parliamentary Ombudsman's services directly. The Parliamentary Ombudsman is generally regarded as a useful mechanism for holding public authorities to account.

Questions

1 Write a memo describing the role and functions of the Parliamentary Ombudsman.

2 Describe the Parliamentary Ombudsman's relationship with Parliament and the executive.

3 What reforms, if any, do you think would help the Parliamentary Ombudsman to carry out the function of investigating maladministration?

Further reading

Abraham, A., 'The Ombudsman as part of the UK Constitution: a contested role?' (2008) 61(1) Parliamentary Affairs 206

This is an interesting article by the Parliamentary Ombudsman discussing the nature of her work.

Kirkham, R., 'Challenging the authority of the Ombudsman: the Parliamentary Ombudsman's special report on *Wartime Detainees*' (2008) 69(5) Modern Law Review 792

This provides an account of the Parliamentary Ombudsman's investigation in the *Wartime Detainees* case and her subsequent submission of a special report to Parliament. It also compares the effectiveness of making a complaint to the Parliamentary Ombudsman with making a claim for judicial review.

Kirkham, R., Thompson, B., and Buck, T., 'When putting things right goes wrong: enforcing the recommendations of the Ombudsman' [2008] Public Law 510

The article discusses the enforcement of the Ombudsman's recommendations and whether they should be legally enforceable. In particular, it discusses the implications of the Court of Appeal decision in *R (on the application of Bradley) v Secretary of State for Work and Pensions* [2007] EWHC 242 (Admin).

Law Commission, *Public Services Ombudsmen* (Law Com No 329/HC 1136, London: HMSO, June 2011)

This is an in-depth review of the statutory ombudsmen, including the Parliamentary and Health Service Ombudsman, the Local Government Ombudsman, and the Public Service Ombudsman for Wales. Part 3 deals with access to the Public Service Ombudsman, and Part 6 deals with the independence and accountability of the ombudsmen.

Seneviratne, M., *Ombudsmen in the Public Sector* (Buckingham: Open University Press, 1994)

The book is rather dated, but it does provide a sound detailed account of ombudsmen in the public sector and many of the policy issues that arise in relation to the redress of grievances.

Part 4
Judicial Review

14

The Role of the Courts, Judicial Review, and Human Rights

Key points

This chapter will cover:

- The role of the courts in holding the executive to account

- The history of judicial review

- What are the grounds of review?

- Judicial review and the constitution

- The difference between judicial review and appeal

- The role of the courts and the Human Rights Act 1998

- The judicial review procedure

- The judicial review procedure: an exclusive procedure

- Can the jurisdiction of the court be ousted or narrowed?

- To what extent does judicial review act as a check on executive power?

Introduction

This chapter is the fourth chapter considering responsible government and the first chapter on judicial review. The previous chapters focused on the role of government and the function of the Parliamentary Ombudsman. This chapter considers the role that the courts play as a check on executive power. It explains how the courts become involved in acting as a check on the exercise of executive power, principally through the mechanism of judicial review and more recently through the application of the Human Rights Act 1998. It examines the history and purpose of judicial review, and the facts that need to be present for a judicial review claim to proceed. It explains the extent to which the courts' power may be ousted or narrowed and the limits on the courts' power. It looks at the procedure for bringing a claim for judicial review and the factors that need to be considered in the context of a potential claim. Finally, the chapter examines to what extent judicial review acts as a safeguard against abuse of power by the executive. The chapter will close with a summary and a series of questions, so that you may test your understanding of the area.

14.1 The role of the courts in holding the executive to account

The courts act as a check on the **executive**. One of the main purposes of **judicial** review is to hold the **government** to account. In the introduction to his book on *Administrative Law*, Cane explains the meaning of the term 'accountability'.

● **P. Cane, *Administrative Law*** (4th edn, Oxford: Oxford University Press, 2004), pp. 7–8

> Our topic, then, is 'accountability' for the performance of public functions. Alternatives to the idea of 'accountability' include 'checking' 'controlling' and 'regulating'. The criteria of account-ability with which we are primarily concerned are the rules and principles of administrative law. Most of these rules and principles have been made by, and typically are enforced by, courts.[1] The main mechanism by which the courts control public decision-making is called 'ju-dicial review'. Judicial review is by no means the only form of accountability to which public decision-makers may be subject. Actions in tort, contract, and so on provide another form of 'legal' accountability, and there are various forms of 'non legal' accountability (such as inves-tigations by Parliamentary committees). The role and significance of judicial review cannot be understood without examining its relationship to such alternative methods of control.
>
> 1 In Australia, these principles have been codified in the Administrative Decisions (Judicial Review) Act 1977 (Cth). See T. H. Jones, 'Judicial review and codification' (2000) 20 Legal Studies 517.

The extract explains some key points about accountability, as follows, which will be explored throughout this chapter.

• Accountability includes the idea of checking, controlling, and regulating.

- Those exercising public functions are held accountable through various legal and political mechanisms.

- Political mechanisms include executive accountability to **Parliament** through parliamentary questions and select committees.

- Other important non-legal mechanisms include making a complaint to the **Parliamentary Ombudsman**, or the Local Government Ombudsman, etc.

- Legal mechanisms may include suing the government in contract or tort.

- The main legal mechanism for holding government to account is through judicial review.

So far, we have studied political mechanisms of accountability. We saw, in Chapter 12, that the convention of collective ministerial responsibility means that the government is responsible to Parliament. It must resign if it loses a vote of no confidence in the House of Commons. The convention of individual ministerial responsibility makes ministers individually responsible to Parliament for the work of their departments and other relevant bodies. Ministers and the **Prime Minister** must answer questions put to them by members of Parliament (MPs) in the House of Commons, they must account for their work before select committee inquiries, and the financial accounts of their departments are subject to scrutiny by the Public Accounts Committee and other parliamentary bodies. The merits of government policy are debated in Parliament, with government expected to defend and explain its decisions. The advantages and disadvantages of the government's strategy in areas such as the economy and foreign affairs are open to censure. The opposition parties will often compare their proposed policies with those of government and claim that their strategies would serve the country better. There are many criticisms of the way in which the political process works in practice and the weakness of Parliament in acting as a check on government is highlighted by many critics. But the system of political accountability does provide some degree of scrutiny of government.

The role of the courts in acting as a check on the government is quite different from that of Parliament. Judges, unlike most politicians, are not elected and are expected to be politically impartial. Judges, when deciding cases, do sometimes comment on the merits or consequences of government policy, but it is not part of their function to criticise government or to discuss the merits of particular policies. In particular, judges do not have the power to scrutinise the exercise of executive power in the absence of a claim being brought before them. In other words, the courts do not act like Parliament—judges cannot call the executive to account in the absence of an individual or an organisation bringing a matter to them.

The courts' role is to check the legality of government action. This is mainly done through the process known as judicial review. Judicial review is a special form of court process that calls the executive to account for its exercise of power. Part 54 of the Civil Procedure Rules defines judicial review as follows.

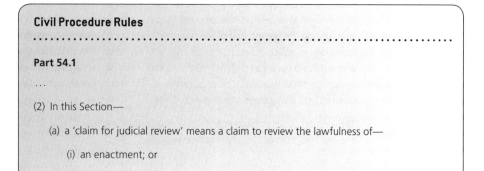

Civil Procedure Rules

Part 54.1

...

(2) In this Section—

   (a) a 'claim for judicial review' means a claim to review the lawfulness of—

      (i) an enactment; or

(ii) a decision, action or failure to act in relation to the exercise of a public function.

...

Judicial review is initiated through the **Administrative Court**, which is one of the divisions of the High Court. Judicial review actions are brought by individuals who, or by groups or organisations that, have been affected by the exercise of **state** (public) power, although there are limited exceptions that permit a claimant who is not personally affected by the exercise of power to bring a judicial review claim. These will be discussed in later chapters.

Judicial review aims to check that the executive has the power to act. This is the **rule of law** in operation, in that the state and its departments and authorities must act within the law. Judicial review also checks that the legal power is being used in a responsible way, or more specifically that the state is using its legal power rationally, reasonably, and proportionately. The courts imply that Parliament (legislation) or the **monarch (royal prerogative)** would permit the legal power that they have conferred on the executive to be used only rationally and reasonably. The court also examines the way in which power is used to make sure that the rules of **natural justice** (that is, the common law rules that have been developed by the courts over the centuries) have been adhered to, because these are the minimum guarantees put in place to ensure that the rule of law is applied fairly and free from bias. The court also reviews the exercise of power to ensure that the requirements of procedural propriety have been met, which once more are largely court-developed (although some are on a statutory footing), to ensure the fairness and integrity of the process. Finally, judicial review now looks at the exercise of power and the respect for minimum standards of human rights protection. In the absence of primary legislation passed by Parliament that states to the contrary, the courts will require that executive power is exercised in conformity with the rights and freedoms enshrined by the **European Convention on Human Rights (ECHR)**. Taken together, the purpose of judicial review is to protect the individual against the excessive use of power by the state, and to ensure that the state and its organs adhere to the rule of law. It is also important to note the need for certainty and speed: if the executive is acting outside of its powers, then this needs to be addressed quickly, because the situation may be affecting hundreds or thousands of people—hence the need for an application to be brought swiftly.

14.2 The history of judicial review

Many of the principles of judicial review have existed for centuries, but the modern law of judicial review has largely been developed by the judges in the post-war era. The reason for this is that, during the second half of the twentieth century, the role of government expanded rapidly into areas in which it had not previously intervened as intensely. There was greater provision and regulation of areas such as health, welfare, housing, immigration, and education. As a consequence, there was much more potential for conflict between individuals and the state, and a need to find a way to resolve these conflicts.

Tomkins describes the way in which the courts since the 1960s have refashioned and developed the law into a set of comprehensive principles.

● A. Tomkins, *Public Law* (Oxford: Oxford University Press, 2003), pp. 171–2

... [T]oday's judicial review law uses remedies that date from medieval times, and adopts rules of natural justice that had already become established by the sixteenth century. But such judicial review as there was before the 1960's was, in the words of the leading commentator of the time 'superficial' and little more than 'perfunctory'.[1]

During the 1960's what had been little more than an 'asymmetrical hotchpotch'-a bits and pieces, occasional approach to legal accountability-started to be transformed into something closer to a series of 'coherent principles' of judicial review.[2] The figure at the forefront of the legal transformation was Lord Reid who, in a string of revisionist judgments, led the House of Lords in its task of modernising judicial review. First the law of procedural fairness was reformed,[3] then substantive review[4] and aspects of the relationship between the law and the Crown[5] were reformulated and strengthened. Finally, the arcane but important area of jurisdictional review was revisited.[6] In each case Lord Reid approached the task of reform in the same basic way: his mission was to sweep away what he saw as the unnecessary, and out-moded restrictions and technicalities of the past, and to replace them not with a detailed series of rules, but rather with wide-ranging judicial discretion so that the law could be further developed and clarified on a case-by-case basis in the future. Thus, a significant characteristic of modern judicial review law is that it possesses a remarkable degree of judicial discretion ...

By 1984 the court had developed the law of judicial review to such a point that Lord Diplock was able to synthesize it, giving it a new and authoritative framework for analysis. In his seminal judgment in the *GCHQ* case of that year, Lord Diplock stated that there were three 'heads' or 'grounds of judicial review, which he labelled 'illegality' 'irrationality' and 'procedural impropriety.[7]

1 See S. de Smith, *Judicial Review of Administrative Action* (3rd edn, London: Stevens & Sons, 1973), p. 28.

2 Ibid, p. 4.

3 See *Ridge v Baldwin* [1964] AC 40.

4 See *Padfield v Minister of Agriculture, Fisheries and Food* [1968] AC 997.

5 See *Conway v Rimmer* [1968] AC 910.

6 *Anisminic v Foreign Compensation Commission* [1969] 2 AC 147.

7 *Council for the Civil Service Unions v Minister for the Civil Service Union* [1985] AC 374, 410.

Judicial review as a process has been through a number of reviews. The Law Commission's report on *Remedies in Administrative Law* (Law Com No 73, Cmnd 6407, London: HMSO, 1976) led to changes to Order 53 of the Rules of Supreme Court and subsequently to the Supreme Court Act 1981 (since renamed the Senior Courts Act 1981). These instruments governed the judicial review process until there was a general reform of civil procedure in the late 1990s when the new **Civil Procedure Rules (CPR) 1998** were introduced in April 1999. The CPR replaced the Rules of the Supreme Court. The CPR lay down the detailed procedures that have to be followed when bringing a claim in the High Court and Court of Appeal. The CPR were a consequence of the Woolf Report—Lord Woolf, *Access to Justice: The Final Report to the Lord Chancellor on the Civil Justice System in England and Wales* (London: HMSO, 1996)—and the changes to judicial review were also shaped by the Bowman Report—Lord Chancellor's Department, *Review of the Crown Office List* (London: HMSO, 2000). As a result of these changes, the most important legal instruments governing judicial review are the Senior Courts Act 1981 and the CPR, especially Part 54. We will turn to issues of procedure later in the chapter.

NOTE The Civil Procedure Rules are available online at http://www.justice.gov.uk/civil/procrules_fin/contents/parts/part54.htm

What are the grounds of review?

Claimants must show that at least one of the grounds of review is satisfied in order to be successful on judicial review, and/or that a **public authority** has acted in a way that is incompatible with a Convention right (see sections 6 and 7 of the Human Rights Act 1998 and later in this chapter). The grounds of review can be seen as a list of legal wrongs that will lead the court to intervene in the decision of those exercising public functions, as the extract from Fordham will shortly show. In the following landmark case, Lord Diplock tried to regroup or classify the various legal wrongs into three grounds of review, as he explains in the following extract.

● *Council of Civil Service Unions v Minister for the Civil Service* [1985] AC 374

Lord Diplock at 410:

> Judicial review has I think developed to a stage today when without reiterating any analysis of the steps by which the development has come about, one can conveniently classify under three heads the grounds upon which administrative action is subject to control by judicial review. The first ground I would call 'illegality' the second 'irrationality' and the third 'procedural impropriety'. That is not to say that further development on a case by case basis may not in course of time add further grounds. I have in mind particularly the possible adoption in the future of the principle of 'proportionality' which is recognised in the administrative law of several of our fellow members of the European Economic Community; but to dispose of the instant case the three already well-established heads that I have mentioned will suffice.
>
> By 'illegality' as a ground for judicial review I mean that the decision-maker must understand correctly the law that regulates his decision-making power and must give effect to it. Whether he has or not is par excellence a justiciable question to be decided, in the event of dispute, by those persons, the judges, by whom the judicial power of the state is exercisable.
>
> By 'irrationality' I mean what can by now be succinctly referred to as '*Wednesbury* unreasonableness' (*Associated Provincial Picture Houses Ltd. v. Wednesbury Corporation* [1948] 1 K.B. 223). It applies to a decision which is so outrageous in its defiance of logic or of accepted moral standards that no sensible person who had applied his mind to the question to be decided could have arrived at it. Whether a decision falls within this category is a question that judges by their training and experience should be well equipped to answer, or else there would be something badly wrong with our judicial system'… 'Irrationality' by now can stand upon its own feet as an accepted ground on which a decision may be attacked by judicial review.
>
> I have described the third head as 'procedural impropriety' rather than failure to observe basic rules of natural justice or failure to act with procedural fairness towards the person who will be affected by the decision. This is because susceptibility to judicial review under this head covers also failure by an administrative tribunal to observe procedural rules that are expressly laid down in the legislative instrument by which its jurisdiction is conferred, even where such failure does not involve any denial of natural justice. But the instant case is not concerned with the proceedings of an administrative tribunal at all.

cross reference
We will discuss proportionality and its application in Chapter 17.

In the forthcoming chapters, we will consider and explain each ground of review in some detail. Note that Lord Diplock states that there are three grounds of review, which he describes as **illegality**, **irrationality**, and **procedural impropriety**. He also indicates that other grounds of review may develop over time. In particular, he refers to proportionality, which is a concept familiar to many European legal systems. It is now very important in the application of the ECHR.

14.4 Judicial review and the constitution

When judges exercise the power of judicial review, they do so within the context of the constitution. Judges often refer to the rule of law, parliamentary supremacy, and the **separation of powers** when they are deciding cases. Ganz explains that although there are numerous mechanisms for holding those exercising public functions to account, the role of the courts is constitutionally significant.

● **G. Ganz, _Understanding Public Law_** (3rd edn, London: Sweet & Maxwell, 2001), p. 5

> The courts, though numerically they deal with only a small number of cases, are perhaps constitutionally the most significant because the subjection of public authorities to the ordinary courts is the cornerstone of the rule of law as formulated by Dicey in his _Law of the Constitution_ (1885, Chapter 1V)

Ganz emphasises the connection between judicial review and the rule of law. It is through the legal mechanism of judicial review that ordinary citizens can challenge the decisions of those exercising public functions in courts. When a claim for judicial review is brought, it forces the public authority to show that it is acting lawfully. In this sense, it provides a way in which ordinary citizens can demand that those exercising public functions explain the legal basis for their actions, whether it be refusing to provide Housing Benefit, making a tax demand, granting a licence with strict conditions, or deciding to build a new town or motorway.

The principle of parliamentary supremacy provides the setting for judicial review. The courts have to give effect to Acts of Parliament and are not able to repeal statutes even if they appear to conflict with constitutional principles (that is, they must abide by the doctrine of parliamentary supremacy). But the courts can ensure that those exercising public functions are acting lawfully and in accordance with Parliament's intention by applying the principles of judicial review. This has led some authors to argue that the constitutional basis for judicial review is the **ultra vires** principle. They see the courts' authority in judicial review cases as ensuring that public authorities act in accordance with Parliament's intent, as laid down by statute. The courts derive their powers from carrying out Parliament's intention by interpreting statutes, and ensuring that public authorities do not exceed their legal powers and act ultra vires. Other authors argue that the powers of the court in judicial review cases are derived from the common law rules developed by the judges when deciding cases. They do not approve of the ultra vires view, because Parliament rarely indicates its intention on the principles of judicial review. However, the common law theorists still acknowledge parliamentary sovereignty. They argue that if Parliament is displeased by the courts' development of the principles of the common law, it can change the law by passing an Act of Parliament. This theoretical debate is beyond the scope of this book, but you will find it discussed in the articles by Craig (1999) and Forsyth (1996) listed in the further reading at the end of this chapter.

cross reference
See Chapter 7 for a reminder on parliamentary supremacy.

The doctrine of the separation of powers also limits the extent to which the courts are willing to intervene in the decision-making of public authorities. It is the function of the executive to decide policy and to make decisions, and it is the function of Parliament to pass legislation. The courts should not interfere with these functions, but they do have the job of ensuring that those exercising public functions are acting lawfully. Fordham describes the courts as having to strike an 'intricate constitutional balance'.

● **M. Fordham, 'Surveying the grounds: key themes in judicial interventions', in P. Leyland and T. Woods (eds)** *Administrative Law Facing the Future: Old Constraints and New Horizons* (London: Blackstone, 1997), pp. 184–99, at 186

> The intricate balance was identified by Sir Thomas Bingham MR in the 'gays in the military' case, when he said:
>
> > 'It is not the constitutional role of the court to regulate the conditions of service in the armed forces of the Crown, nor has it the expertise to do so. But it has the constitutional role and duty of ensuring that the rights of citizens are not abused by the unlawful exercise of executive power. While the court must properly defer to the expertise of responsible decision-makers, it must not shrink from its fundamental duty to *do right for all manner of people* …'[1]
>
> The courts say, time and again, that they will not interfere on the basis that they simply 'disagree' with the 'merits' of an impugned decision. It is not enough that the decision appears to the court to be 'wrong'. Before the court will interfere, there must be a 'wrong' of a kind recognised by administrative law. The grounds for judicial review are simply a list of recognised 'public law wrongs'.
>
> 1 *R v Ministry of Defence, ex p Smith* [1996] QB 517, 556D–E.

cross reference
See Chapter 18 for more on the CCSU case.

NOTE

R v Ministry of Defence, ex p Smith [1996] QB 517, mentioned in the extract above by Fordham, is an important case on the ground of review referred to as irrationality. The case is explained more fully in Chapter 17. Many decisions on irrationality refer to this case.

cross reference
See Chapter 20 for a discussion of the anti-terror case law.

Fordham explains that the courts' jurisdiction is supervisory. They focus on the legality of the decision made by the public authority rather than on the merits of the decision. The decision must be legally wrong and not only a decision that the court thinks is wrong in principle or with which the court disagrees on policy grounds. This will be explained further below.

One of the consequences of the separation of powers is that there are some governmental powers that the courts are reluctant to review. The court may regard such issues as largely the province of the executive. Traditionally, issues of national security, defence, and foreign affairs have been treated with particular caution by the courts. These issues often arise in relation to prerogative powers. So, for example, in the *CCSU* case, national security considerations defeated the claim of the trade union to be consulted before a decision was made to withdraw its members' rights to belong to a trade union. However, there has been greater willingness for the courts to consider issues of national security. For example, in *A v Secretary of State for the Home Department* [2004] UKHL 56 (the **Belmarsh Detainees** case), the House of Lords reviewed the anti-terror laws. The Law Lords rejected the argument that they should not intervene because such issues were exclusively a matter for the executive. Nevertheless, despite being willing to intervene if appropriate, the courts still exercise extreme care when considering cases concerned with such issues.

thinking point
Why are the courts particularly cautious before intervening in cases concerned with national security and defence?

The difference between judicial review and appeal

14.5.1 Judicial review and appeal contrasted

A claim for judicial review is different from appealing against a decision. Statutes often provide for appeals to an administrative body, tribunal, or a court of law, but this can be distinguished from an appeal. Cane discusses some of the differences between an appeal and a judicial review in the next extract.

● **P. Cane, *Administrative Law*** (4th edn, Oxford: Oxford University Press, 2004), p. 29

What are the main differences between appeal and review? The first relates to the power of the court: in appeal proceedings the court may substitute its decision on the matters in issue for that of the body appealed from. For example, if an appeal court thinks that the victim of a motor accident has been awarded too small a sum of damages for injuries inflicted by the defendant's negligence, it can increase the award. In review proceedings, on the other hand, the court's basic power is to 'quash' the challenged decision, that is, to hold it to be invalid. If any of the matters in issue have to be decided again, this must be done by the original deciding authority and not by the supervising court. If the authority was under a duty to make a decision on the matters in issue between the parties, this duty will revive when the decision is quashed, and it will then be for the authority to make a fresh decision. It is also open to the court, in appropriate cases, to issue an order requiring the authority to go through the decision-making process again...

The second main distinction between appeal and review relates to the 'subject matter' of the court's jurisdiction. This distinction can be put briefly by saying that an appellate court has power to decide whether the decision under appeal was 'right or wrong', while a court exercising supervisory jurisdiction only has power to decide whether or not the decision under review was 'legal'...If the decision is illegal it can be quashed; otherwise the court cannot intervene, even if it thinks the decision to be wrong in some respect. Conversely, if a decision is illegal—for instance, because the decision-maker did not follow proper procedures—it may be quashed even if the court thinks that the decision was right as a matter of law and fact...

Appeals to courts constitute an important alternative to judicial review as a form of judicial control of public decision making. Very many statutes make provision for appeals from decisions of public functionaries. Commonly, such appeals are limited to 'points of law' but they may extend further—to issues of fact, for instance. Also, the concept of 'error of law' has been given a very wide meaning that includes, for instance, making perverse or irrational findings of fact and ignoring relevant considerations (both of which are 'grounds' of judicial review).

Footnotes omitted

This extract discusses several important points, as follows.

• On appeal, the court has the power to make the decision for the body in question. On judicial review, the matter is usually referred back to the decision-maker to take the decision again in accordance with law. This is explained more fully in Chapter 19 on remedies.

- On judicial review, the court is limited to considering the legality of the decision. It should not consider the merits or whether the decision is right or wrong. This is discussed later in the chapter, when examples will be given.

- Judicial review cases are usually concerned with questions of law rather than questions of fact, whereas an appeal can be on a question of fact or law depending on the relevant statute.

- Judicial review has traditionally been seen as an inherent power of the court. The courts developed the principles of judicial review through the common law. By contrast, a right of appeal is granted by statute. However, Parliament sometimes grants a right of appeal in a statute on a point of law. The grounds of appeal on a point of law may be similar to the grounds of review. If such a right of appeal is granted, then the claimant is expected to exercise this remedy rather than to make a claim for judicial review. This is the situation in relation to homelessness cases under the Housing Act 1996. Here, the public authority is concerned to establish whether or not individuals are homeless for the purpose of granting priority housing under the housing legislation. Before 1996, the number of these cases being judicially reviewed was of concern to the authorities. As a consequence, appeals on homelessness are now dealt with by way of appeal to the county court. The appeal grounds are very similar to the grounds of review (see Part 7 of the Housing Act 1996). The Administrative Court could still exercise the power of judicial review in relation to a homelessness case, but the Court has stated that it will do so only in exceptional circumstances (see Cane, 2004: 31–2).

- One very recent and innovative change made by section 15 of the Tribunals Courts and Enforcement Act 2007 has been to confer the power to judicially review a tribunal decision on the Upper Tribunal. This must be seen in the context of a complete reorganisation of the tribunal system following the recommendations of Sir Andrew Leggatt in *Tribunals for Users: One System, One Service—Report of the Review of Tribunals* (London: HMSO, 2001). Giving the power of judicial review to the Upper Tribunal means that it has the power to grant the same remedies as the Administrative Court. The power of judicial review is conferred by statute on the Upper Tribunal and can be exercised only if certain conditions are satisfied. The decisions of the Upper Tribunal may be judicially reviewed in very limited circumstances. This was discussed by the Supreme Court in *R (Cart) v Upper Tribunal* [2011] UKSC 28, which is explained later in the chapter.

NOTE If you would like to see a diagram and read more about the new tribunal system, then read the articles by Hickinbottom (2010) and Mitchell (2010) listed in the further reading at the end of the chapter.

14.5.2 The merits of a decision

When the courts are considering a claim for judicial review, as discussed above, they should not consider the merits of a decision. One case that is often used to illustrate this point is *R v Cambridge Health Authority, ex p B (No 1)* [1995] 1 WLR 898. In this case, B was a 10-year-old child who was suffering from leukaemia. She had received treatment, which had failed. The health authority refused to proceed with a third course of treatment, which had a low chance of success and was of an experimental nature. Her father wanted her to undergo the treatment, which, if fully carried out, would cost £75,000. The health authority refused on the grounds that it was not in B's best interest and not an appropriate use of its resources. On a claim for judicial review, the judge at first instance quashed the decision. However, the Court of Appeal upheld the decision of the health authority. Sir Thomas Bingham MR, as he then was, expressed sympathy for the plight of the child and her family, but explained why the court could not interfere with the decision.

● *R v Cambridge Health Authority, ex p B (No 1)* [1995] 1 WLR 898

Sir Thomas Bingham MR at 906:

> ... [T]he courts are not, contrary to what is sometimes believed, arbiters as to the merits of cases of this kind. Were we to express opinions as to the likelihood of the effectiveness of medical treatment, or as to the merits of medical judgment, then we should be straying far from the sphere which under our constitution is accorded to us. We have one function only, which is to rule upon the lawfulness of decisions. That is a function to which we should strictly confine ourselves.

The case neatly illustrates the point that the courts should not consider the merits of the decision. Ultimately, it is up to the public authority how to allocate its resources and decide whether it should fund the operation. The Court of Appeal reviewed the way in which the decision had been made and the factors that the authority had considered. Once the Court of Appeal had decided that the decision-making process was lawful, it held that it was unable to intervene. It did not express an opinion on the merits of the medical judgement or on the decision of the authority not to fund the operation.

However, as we have already noted, the principles of judicial review confer a high degree of **discretion** on judges when deciding cases. Sometimes, this leads to a blurring of the distinction between issues of legality and merits. Some commentators have argued that judges have taken an activist stance and intervened in decisions when they do not approve of the policy of the public authority.

14.6 The role of the courts and the Human Rights Act 1998

14.6.1 Responsible government, human rights, and the role of the courts

This section considers the role of the courts in applying the Human Rights Act 1998 (HRA 1998). Before we start this section, consider the following checklist points to remind yourself of some key facts about the Act.

Human Rights Act 1998 checklist

• The HRA 1998 gives effect to the European Convention on Human Rights (ECHR) in domestic law (see section 1 as to the Convention rights that can be enforced in the domestic courts).

• When interpreting the Convention, the court must take into account any judgment, decision, **declaration**, or advisory opinion of the European Court of Human Rights (section 2).

• The HRA 1998 grants a strong interpretive power to the courts. The courts must, in so far as it is possible to do so, read and give effect to legislation in a way that is compatible with the Convention (section 3).

- The courts are not permitted to repeal legislation that is incompatible with the Convention (section 3(2)).

- The higher courts may grant a declaration of incompatibility stating that a statutory provision is inconsistent with the ECHR. This is not binding on the parties to the case and has no legal effect. Its consequences are political (section 4).

- After a declaration of incompatibility has been made, a government minister can introduce legislation to Parliament to remedy the conflict with the Convention. A fast-track legislative process can be used in accordance with section 10 of the HRA 1998.

cross reference

See Chapter 20 for examples from the anti-terrorism case law of declarations of incompatibility.

The HRA 1998 has given the judges the task of applying the ECHR. This strengthens the judges' constitutional role of protecting the rights of individuals against the executive. This has led judges to make decisions that have been regarded as controversial. Sometimes, the judges have faced criticism when they have found against the government in human rights and judicial review cases. The authors of *De Smith* comment on some of the more robust criticisms that have been made of the judges.

● **H. Woolf, J. L. Jowell, and A. Le Sueur, *De Smith's Judicial Review*** (6th edn, London: Sweet & Maxwell, 2007), p. 31

From time to time senior ministers have thought it fit to encourage and engage in hostile political comment about particular judges, judgments or the role of judicial review in general. Criticisms of the judiciary by both Conservative and Labour Home Secretaries are discussed. The authors continue:... 'ill tempered outbursts' emanated from Labour Home Secretary Mr David Blunkett during 2003,[1] and again the tabloid press dispensed scorn on to some named judges and deplored 'unaccountable and unelected judges' who were 'usurping the role of Parliament, setting the wishes of the people at nought and pursuing a liberal, politically correct agenda of their own, in the zeal to interpret European legislation'.[2]

1 A. Bradley, 'Judicial independence under attack' [2003] Public Law 397. During a radio interview, Mr Blunkett said: 'Frankly, I'm personally fed up with having to deal with a situation where Parliament debates issues and the judges overturn them' (quoted in *The Independent*, 20 February 2003).

2 *Daily Mail*, 21 February 2003.

Whilst many judicial review cases may lead to tension between the executive and the **judiciary**, those involving human rights are often particularly sensitive.

The Supreme Court's decision in *R (on the application of F and Thompson) v Home Department* [2010] UKSC 17 attracted criticism from Prime Minister David Cameron in the House of Commons. The Supreme Court granted a declaration of incompatibility under section 4 of the HRA 1998 on the grounds that section 82 of the Sexual Offences Act 2003 was incompatible with the right to a private life in Article 8 of the Convention. Section 82 required someone who was sentenced to thirty months' imprisonment or more for a sexual offence to notify the police where he or she would subsequently be living and if he or she were to travel abroad. It was held to be incompatible with Article 8, because it imposed a lifetime ban without any possibility of review. When the Prime Minister was questioned on the decision in the House of Commons, he stated as follows.

● **Prime Minister David Cameron** (Hansard, HC, 16 February 2011), col. 955

My hon. Friend speaks for many people in saying how completely offensive it is, once again, to have a ruling by a court that flies in the face of common sense.... I am appalled by the Supreme

Court ruling. We will take the minimum possible approach to this ruling and use the opportunity to close some loopholes in the sex offenders register.

The Conservative Home Secretary, Theresa May, has also been critical of the courts' application of the HRA 1998. She gave a controversial speech at the Conservative Party Conference in October 2011 in which she claimed that the Act was being abused in immigration cases. She gave the example of the courts preventing the deportation of an illegal immigrant on the grounds that his right to family life under Article 8 of the Convention would be breached because he would be separated from his cat. Her comments were reportedly challenged by the Judicial Office, which represents the judiciary. It was pointed out that the decision to deport was held to be unlawful because the Home Office had failed to apply its own policy and had little to do with the cat. The Justice Secretary also criticised the Home Secretary, accusing her of misrepresenting the case. The incident which was referred to as 'Catgate' dominated the headlines for several days and underlines the divisive nature of human rights decisions.

thinking point
Do you think it is right for politicians to criticise decisions made by judges with which they do not agree?

NOTE

You can read more about the 'Catgate' incident online at http://ukhumanrightsblog.com/2011/10/10/catgate-and-some-other-things-that-happened-last-week/

14.6.2 Judicial review claims and the Human Rights Act 1998

Since the HRA 1998 was enacted, it has been possible for claimants to argue in the domestic courts that the action or inaction of a public authority is unlawful because it contravenes the ECHR. Sections 6(1) and 7(1) of the HRA 1998 state as follows.

> **Human Rights Act 1998**
> ·
>
> **Section 6**
>
> (1) It is unlawful for a public authority to act in a way which is incompatible with a Convention right.
>
> ...
>
> **Section 7**
>
> (1) A person who claims that a public authority has acted (or proposes to act) in a way which is made unlawful by section 6 (1) may—
>
> (a) bring proceedings against the authority under this Act in the appropriate court or tribunal, or
>
> (b) rely on the Convention right or rights concerned in any legal proceedings but only if he is (or would be) a victim of the unlawful act.
>
> ...

In accordance with sections 6 and 7, anyone who claims that a public authority has acted unlawfully because his or her Convention rights have been breached can bring a claim for judicial review, provided that he or she is a **victim** of the unlawful act.

cross reference

The victim test and the definition of a public authority will be discussed in Chapter 15.

The claimant must be able to show that there has been a breach of a Convention right. Not all Convention rights are given effect to in domestic law by the HRA 1998. Section 1 of the Act states which Articles and **protocols** of the Convention apply. Some notable exclusions include Article 13 (the right to a remedy) and Article 15 (derogations in times of emergency).

. . . .

protocols   These are additional rights that have been added to the original Convention, which are open to ratification by the state parties to the Convention.

. . . .

cross reference

See Chapter 19 for more on remedies.

There is a general time limit of one year in HRA 1998 cases. But if the claimant applies for judicial review, then the stricter time limit applies (section 7(5)(a)(b)). On judicial review, all claims must be brought promptly and in any event within three months.

If the court finds that the public authority has acted unlawfully, it can grant any remedy that it normally has the power to grant. The court has to believe it is just and appropriate to grant the remedy (section 8).

Bringing an action for judicial review for breach of a Convention right under the HRA 1998: points to consider

. . . .

- The claim must be brought against a public authority (section 6).

- The claimant must be a victim of the unlawful act (section 7).

- The claimant must show that there has been a breach of one of the Convention rights stated in section 1.

- The court can grant any remedy that it normally has the power to grant and, in addition, it can also grant **damages** under section 8.

14.6.3 The application of the HRA 1998: horizontal and vertical effect

The HRA 1998 is described as having **vertical effect**. This is because it directly binds public authorities only as defined in section 6 of the Act. The definition of a public authority includes private organisations if they carry out functions of a public nature. This will be explained more fully in Chapter 15.

Primarily, the HRA 1998 provides for claims to be brought against those who carry out public functions. It does not allow private individuals and organisations to sue each other directly for breach of a Convention right. This is because the Act does not have **horizontal effect**. This means that a claim cannot be brought directly against a private body exercising a private function.

The HRA 1998 may still be of relevance in cases involving only private parties. This is because the courts themselves are defined as public authorities (section 6(3)). They are therefore bound to apply the ECHR when they are deciding cases, including when they decide cases between private individuals. In addition, section 3 of the HRA 1998 requires the courts to interpret legislation consistently with Convention rights so far as possible and this applies equally to statutes affecting horizontal relationships, such as landlord and tenant. The Convention therefore has an impact on such cases. Once a case is before the courts, it has to be decided in a way that is consistent with the Convention. This is why the Convention is said to have **indirect horizontal effect**.

A case that illustrates the indirect horizontal effect of the HRA 1998 is *Campbell v MGN Ltd* [2004] UKHL 22. Naomi Campbell, the famous supermodel, brought an action for breach of confidence against the Mirror Group of Newspapers for publishing photographs of her attending a Narcotics Anonymous meeting. The court, in its application of the law of confidence between the private parties, applied Articles 8 and 10 of the Convention. Baroness Hale explains why the Convention is relevant to the case in the brief extract below.

● *Campbell v MGN Ltd* [2004] UKHL 22

Baroness Hale:

> [132] The 1998 Act does not create any new cause of action between private persons. But if there is a relevant cause of action applicable, the court as a public authority must act compatibly with both parties Convention rights. In a case such as this the relevant vehicle will normally be the action for breach of confidence...

So, in this case, the claim was brought against the newspaper as a tort claim for breach of confidence. This is because, as we have seen, the HRA 1998 does not create a right of action against private parties. The parties could not, therefore, rely directly on Articles 8 and 10 as the basis for the claims. The newspaper is a private body and therefore immune from a claim under the HRA 1998. But once the case was before the court, it applied Article 10 ECHR on freedom of expression and Article 8 on the right to family and private life. It ultimately decided by a majority in favour of the claimant that there had been a breach of confidence, after balancing the various rights in question.

summary points

Horizontal and vertical effect

- *The HRA 1998 applies vertically. This means it applies to public authorities, as defined in section 6 of the Act.*

- *The HRA 1998 does not apply horizontally between private parties. A claim for breach of a Convention right cannot be brought against a private individual or body exercising private functions.*

- *The HRA 1998 has indirect horizontal effect. The courts, as public authorities, have a duty to apply the Convention when deciding all cases, including cases between private individuals.*

14.6.4 Notable judicial review cases involving claims under the HRA 1998

Examples of judicial review cases involving claims under the HRA 1998 are discussed in subsequent chapters. Some notable cases include the following.

- *R (on the application of Daly) v Secretary of State for the Home Department* [2001] 2 AC 532   The court had to consider whether a prison policy on searching prisoners' cells was a breach of the right to private life in Article 8 ECHR. The court held in favour of the prisoners, because the policy failed to protect the confidentiality of legally privileged material, such as correspondence between the prisoners and their lawyers.

- *R (on the application of Begum) v Denbigh High School Governors* [2006] UKHL 15   The court had to consider whether a school's decision to prohibit a female student from wearing a jilbab (a type of religious dress) was a breach of her right to manifest her religion in accordance with Article 9 of the Convention. It held there was no breach of Article 9.

- *R (on the application of Farrakhan) v Secretary of State for the Home Department* [2002] QB 1391   The Court of Appeal upheld the decision of the Home Secretary to refuse entry to Farrakhan, the leader of a group called the Nation of Islam. It was held that there was no breach of Farrakhan's right to freedom of expression under Article 10 of the Convention. The Court accepted that the refusal was justifiable on the grounds that Farrakhan's presence might cause public disorder.

cross reference
These decisions are discussed in more detail in Chapter 17 on irrationality and proportionality.

The HRA 1998 has introduced the Convention into domestic law, reaffirming the role of judges in protecting individual rights. Claims that public authorities are acting in conflict with the Convention can be brought by judicial review. The procedure for bringing a claim for judicial review is discussed below.

(14.7) The judicial review procedure

The special procedure to be followed on judicial review is laid down in Part 54 of the Civil Procedure Rules, discussed earlier in the chapter. Judicial review is not an action that may be brought as of right; rather, a claimant requires the **permission** of the court to bring a judicial review of an action, omission, or decision. Permission was formerly known as **leave**, but the court terminology changed quite radically when the CPR were introduced and many of the old terms were translated from Latin or into plain English. Older texts may still use the old terms. A court is unlikely to grant permission for judicial review unless an individual has first exhausted other reasonable avenues to resolve the issue. These may include taking the case through the decision-maker's own internal appeal mechanism, or it may involve going to a designated tribunal. Since the introduction of the CPR, it is also necessary for a claimant to state whether he or she has complied with the **pre-action protocol**. This requires that the claimant write to the defendant identifying the disputed issues and seeing whether the matter can be resolved without litigation.

14.7.1 Initiating the action, time limits, and standing

There is a set procedure for initiating judicial review, which is set out in CPR Part 54. Firstly, a claimant should complete the claim form, including the facts, his or her legal submission to the court, and relevant citations to accompany his or her legal arguments. He or she will need to include written evidence to verify facts. The form must be submitted to the Administrative Court (High Court) before the time limit expires.

One of the features of the judicial review procedure is the strict time limit of three months. The relevant provisions are set out below.

Civil Procedure Rules

Part 54.5

(1) The claim form must be filed—

    (a) promptly; and

    (b) in any event not later than 3 months after the grounds to make the claim first arose.

...

Senior Courts Act 1981 (formerly the Supreme Court Act 1981)

Section 31

...

(6) Where the High Court considers that there has been undue delay in making an application for judicial review, the court may refuse to grant—

    (a) leave for the making of the application; or

    (b) any relief sought on the application, if it considers that the granting of the relief sought would be likely to cause substantial hardship to, or substantially prejudice the rights of, any person or would be detrimental to good administration.

(7) Subsection (6) is without prejudice to any enactment or rule of court which has the effect of limiting the time within which an application for judicial review may be made.

The outer time limit on judicial review is three months. But the application must be made promptly. So claims made within three months have been held not to have been made quickly enough and have been refused. This is in contrast to the time limit in private law, which, subject to any statutory restriction, is between three and six years. The reasons for the strict time limit in judicial review cases is explained by Lord Diplock in the next extract.

● *O'Reilly v Mackman* [1983] 2 AC 237

Lord Diplock at 281:

> The public interest in good administration requires that public authorities and third parties should not be kept in suspense as to the legal validity of a decision the authority has reached in purported exercise of decision-making powers for any longer period than is absolutely necessary in fairness to the person affected by the decision.

If there is going to be a challenge, it must be made quickly, so that the public authority does not experience the threat or uncertainty that litigation may pose.

If there has been undue delay, the court does have a discretion to extend the time limit, but this discretion is exercised very sparingly. An example of the strict way in which the courts interpret the provisions on time limits can be seen in *R v Dairy Produce Quota Tribunal for England and Wales, ex p Caswell* [1990] 2 AC 738. In this case, the court refused to allow a claim out of time because if the case were successful, it might lead to existing decisions being reopened. This was not in the interest of certainty or good administration. The court will also refuse to exercise its discretion to extend the time limit if it would be prejudicial to third parties. This was the situation in *R v Secretary of State for Health, ex p Furneaux* [1994] 2 All ER 652. The court refused to allow a late claim for judicial review even though there were breaches of natural justice in the original decision and the delay was not the fault of the claimants. However, the court has allowed late claims where there is a good reason for the delay. So, for example, in *R v Stratford on Avon District Council, ex p Jackson* [1985] 1 WLR 1319, the court exercised its discretion to allow the claim to proceed out of time. This was because the delay was caused by difficulties in obtaining legal aid.

The claimant will need to demonstrate a recognised interest in a decision, act, or omission in order to be permitted to apply for judicial review. **Standing** will not normally be dealt with at the permission stage, but at the full hearing stage, if the claimant has good grounds for seeking judicial review (see *R v Inland Revenue Commissioners, ex p National Federation of Self-Employed and Small Businesses Ltd* [1982] AC 617). Standing is ascertained using the **sufficient interest** test, as set out in section 31(3) of the Senior Courts Act 1981, unless a human rights issue is being raised, in which case the HRA 1998 and case law for the victim will apply, or the potential victim test as set out in section 7 of the HRA 1998.

cross reference
Standing will be discussed fully in Chapter 15.

14.7.2 Permission stage

The permission stage (CPR 54.10) is the point at which the court decides whether to permit the case to go on to a judicial review hearing. In *R v Inland Revenue Commissioners, ex p National Federation of Self-Employed and Small Businesses Limited* [1982] AC 617, 643, Lord Diplock explained that the purpose of permission is to 'prevent the time of the court being wasted by busybodies with misguided or trivial complaints of administrative error and to remove uncertainties'.

Claims for permission are dealt with on the papers by a judge. This means that there is no oral hearing, although changes introduced in 2000 now mean the defendant is notified and has a chance to respond in writing. However, if permission is refused, the claimant may request an oral hearing. If the court refuses to grant permission, then there is the possibility of an appeal to the Court of Appeal against the refusal of permission (CPR 54.12).

The test for permission is often stated to be whether there is an 'arguable case'. However, the authors of *De Smith's Judicial Review* note that 'No comprehensive statement for determining applications for permission exists'. The authors then go on to note that 'The most commonly given reason for refusing permission is that the claim is unarguable' (Woolf, Jowell, and Le Sueur, 2007: 840). In other words, permission will be refused if there is no real prospect of succeeding on the issues. Once permission is granted, the parties may take the opportunity to negotiate a settlement; otherwise, the case is likely to proceed to a full hearing.

A study of the permission stage (V. Bondy and M. Sunkin, 'Accessing judicial review' [2008] Public Law 647) found that whereas in 1981 71 per cent of claimants were given permission to proceed, in 2006 the figure was just 22 per cent. The research also noted that there was a wide variation between different judges. The researchers concluded that the decline in success rates was partly due to procedural reforms introduced in 2000 whereby the defendant public authority is more involved in the permission stage than it was in the past. This has also led to a higher rate of settlement before the permission stage than previously. The researchers do, however, express some concern at the inconsistent outcomes in claims for permission between the different judges.

14.7.3 The hearing

The hearing is usually conducted by one judge. The calling of witnesses and cross-examination are rare in judicial review cases, which nearly always focus on issues of law rather than fact. At the hearing, the claimant's and the respondent's legal teams will orally put forward their submissions, although they will have been required to provide written submissions prior to the hearing and to have produced the evidence on which they intend to rely in the action. The judge(s) may reach a decision on the day, or may retire to reach a decision. It is important to note that even if the claimant does succeed, he or she may not receive the remedy sought, because judicial review remedies are relatively narrow. Remedies are discretionary, meaning that the claimant does not get the remedy as of right even if he or she does succeed in proving the case.

cross reference
More detail on remedies is provided in Chapter 19.

14.8 The judicial review procedure: an exclusive procedure

14.8.1 Exclusivity

We have already seen that a number of changes were made in the 1970s to the procedure for applying for judicial review subsequent to the Law Commission's report (1976). These changes tried to make the judicial review process easier to use. For example, the process of **discovery** of documents was simplified.

....

discovery   Concerns the rules around the disclosure of documents before a trial.

....

Cross-examination was also permitted on judicial review, although in practice it is rarely necessary. The Law Commission had recommended many of these changes, but intended that those challenging the decision of a public authority would be allowed to use the judicial review procedure *or* the ordinary private law procedure. However, in the landmark case of *O'Reilly v Mackman* [1983] 2 AC 237, the House of Lords decided that judicial review, with a few exceptions, should be an exclusive procedure. This meant that it should be the *only* procedure available for those challenging the decision of a public authority. Consequently, a more rigid distinction developed between public law and private law, and if claimants used the wrong procedure, they faced the possibility that their claim might be struck out completely. Additionally, it has proved very difficult to distinguish between private law and public law issues. In recent years, the courts have been more flexible about the procedures used. This is partly a consequence of the introduction of the CPR. The exclusivity rule in *O'Reilly v Mackman*, the exceptions to the rule, and the more flexible approach are discussed below.

In *O' Reilly v Mackman*, the facts of the case were that the claimants were prisoners who had been disciplined by the Board of Prison Governors for various offences. They alleged that there had been breaches of the Prison Rules and the rules of natural justice. They asked the court for a declaration using private law proceedings rather than claiming for judicial review. The House of Lords agreed with the defendants that the claim was an abuse of procedure and should be struck out.

. . . .

● *O'Reilly v Mackman* [1983] 2 AC 237

Lord Diplock at 285:

> The position of applicants for judicial review has been drastically ameliorated by the new Order 53. It has removed all those disadvantages, particularly in relation to discovery, that were manifestly unfair to them and had, in many cases, made applications for prerogative orders an inadequate remedy if justice was to be done. This it was that justified the courts in not treating as an abuse of their powers resort to an alternative procedure by way of action for a declaration or injunction (not then obtainable on an application under Order 53), despite the fact that this procedure had the effect of depriving the defendants of the protection to statutory tribunals and public authorities for which for public policy reasons Order 53 provided.
>
> Now that those disadvantages to applicants have been removed and all remedies for infringements of rights protected by public law can be obtained upon an application for judicial review, as can also remedies for infringements of rights under private law if such infringements should also be involved, it would in my view as a general rule be contrary to public policy, and as such an abuse of the process of the court, to permit a person seeking to establish that a decision of a public authority infringed rights to which he was entitled to protection under public law to proceed by way of an ordinary action and by this means to evade the provisions of Order 53 for the protection of such authorities.
>
> My Lords, I have described this as a general rule; for though it may normally be appropriate to apply it by the summary process of striking out the action, there may be exceptions, particularly where the invalidity of the decision arises as a collateral issue in a claim for infringement of a right of the plaintiff arising under private law, or where none of the parties objects to the adoption of the procedure by writ or originating summons. Whether there should be other exceptions should, in my view, at this stage in the development of procedural public law, be left to be decided on a case to case basis—a process that your Lordships will be continuing in the next case in which judgment is to be delivered today [*Cocks v Thanet District Council* [1983] 2 AC 286].
>
> …I have no hesitation, in agreement with the Court of Appeal, in holding that to allow the actions to proceed would be an abuse of the process of the court. They are blatant attempts to avoid the protections for the defendants for which Order 53 provides.

Lord Diplock held that it would be an abuse of process to allow the case to proceed other than by judicial review. This was because there are various safeguards built into the judicial review system. These safeguards protect the public authority from unmeritorious claims, which are a waste of time and money, and include the permission requirement and the strict time limits (as discussed above). If the private law procedure is used, as in *O'Reilly v Mackman*, then the claimant does not have to seek permission and has a much longer period in which to bring the claim. The public authority is therefore deprived of the protections in the judicial review process. Lord Diplock held that it was contrary to public policy and an abuse of procedure for claimants to use private law procedures to challenge the decisions of public authorities.

However, this case has caused considerable difficulty. One problem has been distinguishing public law and private law cases; another has been dealing with public law issues that arise in other private law or criminal law proceedings. These are usually referred to as **collateral challenges**. This is because they are collateral, or incidental, to the main issue in the case.

14.8.2 Distinguishing private and public law

If the case against the public authority is essentially a private law action, such as a damages claim for negligence, then the action does not have to be brought by judicial review. So, in *Davy v Spelthorne Borough Council* [1984] AC 262, the claimant failed to appeal against an enforcement order in relation to his property. He alleged that this was because council officials had negligently failed to inform him of his rights. The House of Lords held that he was entitled to bring the action by private law proceedings. This was because he was not challenging the validity of the enforcement order, which would be a public law matter, but claiming damages for negligence, which was a private law matter. By contrast, in *Cocks v Thanet* [1983] 2 AC 286, the claimant alleged that he was unintentionally homeless in accordance with the Housing (Homeless Persons) Act 1977 and applied for an **injunction** ordering the authority to provide him with permanent accommodation; he also claimed damages. It was held that he must proceed by judicial review. This was because it was essential to his claim for the court to determine the legality of the authority's decision as to whether or not he was intentionally homeless. This was a public law decision and, following *O'Reilly v Mackman*, it would be an abuse of process to allow the claimant to make a claim in private law.

The difficulty of separating public law and private law was also apparent in *Roy v Kensington and Chelsea and Westminster Family Practitioner Committee* [1992] 1 AC 624. Dr Roy, a general practitioner (GP), brought an action in private law claiming payment for money due. The Kensington and Chelsea FPC refused to pay him the amount demanded, because, in accordance with the relevant National Health Service (NHS) regulations, it was claimed he had not spent sufficient time on his general practice. It was argued that he should have brought the action by judicial review rather than by private law. The House of Lords decided in his favour and held that he did not need to proceed by judicial review. The Lords held that it was undesirable for there to be unnecessary procedural barriers for claimants, that there was no abuse of process, and that the remedy claimed was an order for money owed and was not available on judicial review. Although public law issues may have been raised by the case, it was primarily concerned with the claimant's private law claim for money owed.

A decision of a body can be challenged collaterally in civil and criminal proceedings. This means that if a criminal or civil action is brought against an individual, he or she can, by way of defence, challenge the validity of the public authority's action or the delegated legislation on which it is based (see *Wandsworth London Borough Council v Winder* [1985] AC 461 on civil proceedings and *Boddington v British Transport Police* [1999] 2 AC 143 on criminal proceedings).

The enactment of the CPR has meant that the courts have taken a more flexible and pragmatic approach. This was exemplified by the Court of Appeal in *Clark v University of Lincolnshire and Humberside* [2000] 1 WLR 1988. This case concerned a student involved in a dispute about plagiarism, and the fairness of the university appeal process and regulations. She sued the university for breach of contract. It was argued by the university that, because it was a public authority, the proceedings should have been brought by judicial review and it was an abuse of process for the student to bring the claim outside the three-month time limit in a private law claim. The Court of Appeal held that she was entitled to proceed in private law by contract. In his judgment, Lord Woolf explained that the exclusivity principle should not be applied overly rigidly. Cases against a public authority should usually be brought by judicial review, but if, as in this case, the proceedings were commenced in private law, they may be allowed to proceed. This is because, since the introduction of the CPR, the court has greater power to supervise the case. If a private law case against a public authority were unmeritorious or there were an attempt to gain an unfair advantage by using the private law procedure, the court could now strike the case out. As the short extract below from Lord Woolf's judgment shows, the court is concerned to avoid procedural disputes.

. . . .

● **Clark v University of Lincolnshire and Humberside** [2000] 1 WLR 1988

Lord Woolf at 1998:

> The intention of the C.P.R. is to harmonise procedures as far as possible and to avoid barren procedural disputes which generate satellite litigation.
>
> 38 Where a student has, as here, a claim in contract, the court will not strike out a claim which could more appropriately be made under Order 53 [now Part 54] solely because of the procedure which has been adopted. It may however do so, if it comes to the conclusion that in all the circumstances, including the delay in initiating the proceedings, there has been an abuse of the process of the court under the C.P.R. The same approach will be adopted on an application under Part 24.
>
> 39 The emphasis can therefore be said to have changed since *O'Reilly v. Mackman* [1983] 2 AC 237. What is likely to be important when proceedings are not brought by a student against a new university under Order 53, will not be whether the right procedure has been adopted but whether the protection provided by Order 53 has been flouted in circumstances which are inconsistent with the proceedings being able to be conducted justly in accordance with the general principles contained in Part 1. Those principles are now central to determining what is due process.

The distinction between private and public law issues may, on occasion, be hard to draw. If there is doubt about which procedure to use, it is safer to use the judicial review procedure. But, as the decision in *Clark* shows, the courts will not automatically strike a case out if it is brought in the wrong court; they will, however, consider whether there has been an abuse of process. It should also be noted that the court does have a jurisdiction to transfer cases that have been started using the wrong procedure. So a case can be transferred from the Administrative Court in accordance with CPR 54.20, and the court can transfer a case to the Administrative Court if it raises issues of public law (CPR 54.20).

summary points

The judicial review procedure: an exclusive procedure

- *Judicial review is an exclusive procedure. Claims against a body or individual exercising public functions should be brought by judicial review*—O'Reilly v Mackman.

- *Public authorities are entitled to the procedural protections provided in judicial review.*

- *There are exceptions to the rule in* O'Reilly v Mackman. *If the claim against the public authority involves a private law matter, it need not be brought by judicial review*—Davey v Spelthorne.

- *Individuals can challenge the legality of public law decisions by way of a defence to criminal or civil proceedings.*

- *The rule in* O'Reilly v Mackman *is applied less rigidly since the introduction of the Civil Procedure Rules. A case brought using the wrong procedure may be allowed to continue provided that the court thinks there has been no abuse of process.*

- *The Civil Procedure Rules do provide for cases to be transferred to different courts (CPR 54.20).*

Can the jurisdiction of the court be ousted or narrowed?

Parliament has attempted to exclude or restrict access to judicial review in order to prevent excessive litigation, to reduce costs to allow specialist bodies to have the final say in decision-making, and to provide for speed and efficiency. It sometime does this by inserting an ouster clause in the relevant statute or by providing that another body, such as a tribunal, should appeal of review the decision. The courts have always been concerned to ensure that adminis-trative bodies act within their legal powers, that they act fairly, and that individual citizens are not denied access to the courts against an arbitrary decision-maker. The courts' attitude to-wards clauses limiting their jurisdiction can be seen in *R v Medical Appeal Tribunal, ex p Gilmore* [1957] 1 QB 574. The claimant in this case wanted to challenge the amount of compensation that he received from the Medical Appeal Tribunal for a work-related injury. Section 36(3) of the National Insurance (Industrial Injuries) Act 1946 stated that the decision of the Medical Appeal Tribunal 'shall be final'. The court held that such a clause prevented an appeal on fact or law—but it did not prohibit judicial review.

● ***R v Medical Appeal Tribunal, ex p Gilmore*** [1957] 1 QB 574

Lord Denning at 583:

> The word 'final' is not enough. That only means 'without appeal'. It does not mean without recourse to certiorari, it makes the decision final on the facts, but not final on the law. Notwithstanding that the decision is by a statute made final, certiorari can still issue...

cross reference

For further discussion of remedies, see Chapter 19.

Lord Denning held that the claimant could apply for a remedy by way of judicial review. He refers to the remedy of certiorari (now known as a **quashing order**). This would have invali-dated the tribunal's decision.

The courts have taken a similarly strict approach to ouster clauses. A typical ouster clause states that 'a decision shall not be questioned in any court of law'.

Before the landmark case of *Anisminic Ltd v Foreign Compensation Commission* [1969] 2 AC 147, the courts used to hold that only errors of law that went to jurisdiction were subject to judicial review. Jurisdiction refers to the power of the tribunal to make the decision. This meant that only errors of law that caused the tribunal to exceed its powers were reviewable; errors of law within jurisdiction were not reviewable if there were an ouster clause. The problem here was that it was almost impossible to distinguish between jurisdictional and non-jurisdictional errors of law. The House of Lords in *Anisminic* held that all errors of law were jurisdictional. If the tribunal had made an error of law, it would be considered to have gone beyond the powers granted to it by statute. Its decision was subject to review notwithstanding any ouster clause in the statute.

cross reference

Errors of law and jurisdiction are also discussed in Chapter 16.

The facts of *Anisminic* were as follows. Anisminic's claim to the Foreign Compensation Commission for compensation for the confiscation of its property in Egypt was rejected. Anisminic challenged the decision by judicial review on the grounds that the Commission had misinterpreted the statute. However, section 4(4) of the Foreign Compensation Act 1950 con-tained an ouster clause that stated 'the determination by the commission of any application made to them under this Act shall not be called in question in any court of law'. The Commission argued that its decisions were not subject to judicial review by the courts, which therefore had no jurisdiction to consider the case.

The House of Lords by a majority rejected this argument. It held that the Foreign Compensation Commission had misinterpreted the words 'successor in title' in the legislation. It had therefore not made a proper determination in law. It was a 'purported' determination or an erroneous one and so it could not stand. This error of law meant that it had exceeded its legal powers or jurisdiction, and that the courts were entitled to entertain the claim. The Lords granted a declaration to this effect.

● **_Anisminic Ltd v Foreign Compensation Commission_** [1969] 2 AC 147

Lord Reid at 170:

> Statutory provisions which seek to limit the ordinary jurisdiction of the court have a long history. No case has been cited in which any other form of words limiting the jurisdiction of the court has been held to protect a nullity...

Considering the issues in *Anisminic*, he went on to state:

> But I do not think that it is necessary or even reasonable to construe the word 'determination' as including everything which purports to be a determination but which is in fact no determination at all and there are no degrees of nullity. There are a number of reasons why the law will hold a purported decision to be a nullity. I do not see how it could be said that such a provision protects some kinds of nullity but not others: if that were intended it would be easy to say so.

Lord Wilberforce at 207:

> In every case, whatever the character of a tribunal, however wide the range of questions remitted to it, however great the permissible margin of mistake, the essential point remains that the tribunal has a derived authority, derived, that is, from statute: at some point, and to be found from a consideration of the legislation, the field within which it operates is marked out and limited. There is always an area, narrow or wide, which is the tribunal's area; a residual area, wide or narrow, in which the legislature has previously expressed its will and into which the tribunal may not enter...
>
> The question, what is the tribunal's proper area, is one which it has always been permissible to ask and to answer, and it must follow that examination of its extent is not precluded by a clause conferring conclusiveness, finality, or unquestionability upon its decisions. These clauses in their nature can only relate to decisions given within the field of operation entrusted to the tribunal. They may, according to the width and emphasis of their formulation, help to ascertain the extent of that field, to narrow it or to enlarge it, but unless one is to deny the statutory origin of the tribunal and of its powers, they cannot preclude examination of that extent.

NOTE

An error of law is a mistake of law made by the public authority or tribunal. An error of law is essentially a decision that can be challenged under one of the three heads of review, as formulated by Lord Diplock in the *CCSU case*. For more detailed discussion of errors of law and errors of fact, see Chapter 16.

During the course of the judgment, the House of Lords held that all ouster clauses were to be construed strictly. Lord Wilberforce stated that tribunals and inferior bodies should act within the statutory power that they have been granted by Parliament. The court needs to judicially review their decisions to prevent them going outside their jurisdiction and acting unlawfully. The effect of the judgment was that all errors or mistakes of law were jurisdictional or took the tribunal or public authority beyond the power that it had been granted by Parliament, and thus were subject to review whether or not there was an ouster clause.

In the later case of *Re Racal Communications* [1981] AC 374, Lord Diplock made it clear that the courts can judicially review decisions of inferior bodies or tribunals even if there is an ouster clause. If the claimant shows that there is an error of law, then that is sufficient reason for the court to engage in judicial review.

The *Anisminic* principle, which preserves access to the courts and provides for the courts' supervision of administrative bodies, is regarded as one of the most fundamental principles in constitutional and administrative law. The government tried to introduce legislation to override the *Anisminic* principle and to insert an ouster clause into the Asylum and Immigration (Treatment of Claimants) Bill 2003. This would have ousted the courts' power of judicial review of the then Asylum and Immigration Tribunal. There was outcry amongst the legal profession and the judiciary: Lord Woolf described the proposal as unconstitutional and contrary to the rule of law. The provision in the Bill was subsequently dropped. But the right to challenge immigration decisions by way of judicial review was curtailed by legislation and upheld by the courts in *R (on the application of G) v Immigration Appeal Tribunal* [2005] 1 WLR 1445.

NOTE For an account of this controversial issue, see Le Sueur (2004) listed in the further reading at the end of the chapter.

14.9.1 Time-limited ouster clauses

Time-limited ouster clauses are clauses that impose a time limit on the claimant. They do not attempt to oust the courts' jurisdiction completely, but require claimants to make their claim within a time limit of, say, six weeks. These ouster clauses are not subject to the principles in *Anisminic* and the courts have held that once the time limit has expired, they do prevent a claim for review. An example of this occurred in *R v Secretary of State for the Environment, ex p Ostler* [1977] QB 122. The claimant argued that he had not objected to plans to build a road in the town centre of Boston, Lincolnshire, because inaccurate plans had been published that did not show the effect that the road would have on his business.

He therefore alleged that there had been a breach of natural justice and bad faith, verging on fraud. He applied for judicial review to quash the order. However, Schedule 2 to the Highways Act 1959 stated that any challenge to an order had to be made within six weeks from the date on which the order was published; the claimant's challenge was outside of this time limit. It was argued unsuccessfully that, in accordance with the principles in *Anisminic*, the challenge should be allowed. However, the court upheld the clause in the interest of finality. If the decision could be challenged after six weeks, the delay and cost would, in the view of the court, be contrary to the public interest.

14.9.2 Alternative statutory procedures

Ouster clauses are not the only method used to limit judicial review claims. Parliament sometimes restricts the ability of individuals to bring a claim for judicial review by introducing an alternative statutory appeal or review process to a specially created tribunal or court. The alternative tribunal or court may have the power to consider the relevant decision in accordance with judicial review principles. In these situations, the ability to make an alternative or further claim for judicial review in the Administrative Court will be limited. The Supreme Court has recently had to consider two cases about access to judicial review. In *R (A) v Director of Establishments of the Security Service* [2009] UKSC 12, the claimant was an ex-member of the security services wanting to publish a book about his time in the service. The director of the security service refused him permission to publish certain portions of the book. A claimed that this was a breach of the right to freedom of expression, contrary to Article 10 ECHR, and he wanted to bring a claim for judicial review in the Administrative Court. It was successfully argued by the director of the security service that any such claim had to be heard in the Investigatory Powers Tribunal (IPT), which had the statutory power to hear evidence about state secrets. Section 65(2)(a) of the Regulation of Investigatory Powers Act 2000 stated that any claim under the HRA 1998 against the security services had to be heard in the IPT and that judicial review principles must be applied. The Supreme Court held that this case was different from *Anisminic* in which the statute removed all judicial supervision. It held that Parliament had not ousted judicial scrutiny of the security services; it had simply given the power of scrutiny to the IPT, which had similar status and authority to that of the Administrative Court, but had more appropriate procedures and expertise in dealing with sensitive information.

R (Cart) v Upper Tribunal [2011] UKSC 28 also restricted the circumstances in which a judicial review claim could be brought. The main question of law was whether the claimants, most of whom had been refused leave to appeal to the Upper Tribunal from the First-tier Tribunal, could make a claim for judicial review against the refusal of leave. This was a question of some importance, because the First-tier Tribunal deals with regulatory matters, immigration and asylum, health, education, social care, tax and social entitlement, and war pensions and armed forces compensation. There is the potential for a large number of judicial review claims to arise from these cases that are likely to be of profound importance to the individual concerned. The Supreme Court in *Cart* was trying to balance the need to ensure that errors of law could be corrected by the Administrative Court with the need to make sure that there were not an over-whelming number of judicial review claims that would stretch resources. The Supreme Court decided that judicial review would only be permitted where: the case raises some important point of principle or practice; or there is some compelling reason for the Administrative Court to review the decision. These are strict criteria that will limit the number of judicial reviews heard in the Administrative Court, but they are sufficiently flexible to allow the Court to intervene if it thinks that an important principle or issue is at stake.

These cases show that there are circumstances in which access to judicial review in the Administrative Court is restricted either because the matter is best dealt with in another court, or to make sure that the judicial review process is not used in all cases, but only when there is a matter of principle at stake.

summary points

Can the jurisdiction of the court be ousted or narrowed?

- *Following* Anisminic, *all errors of law are reviewable. Ouster clauses are not effective in preventing claimants from challenging decisions by judicial review. Claimants can bring an action for judicial review if there is an error of law.*

- *Time-limited ouster clauses are effective in preventing challenges by way of judicial review. Once the time limit has expired, a claim for judicial review cannot be brought*—R v Secretary of State for the Environment, ex p Ostler.

- *The courts construe all ouster clauses and finality clauses strictly as a matter of interpretation.*

- *The availability of judicial review will be limited if there is an alternative statutory review or appeal.*

(14.10) To what extent does judicial review act as a check on executive power?

The courts hold the executive to account for the legality of their decisions. This is achieved through the process of judicial review. The effectiveness of judicial review has to be considered in the light of the courts' limited powers within the constitution. The court is concerned with the legality of the decision and not the merits. When the court grants a remedy after a successful claim for judicial review, it often sends the case back to the public authority to retake the decision lawfully.

NOTE

See Chapter 19 for examples of cases in which the claimant won the judicial review case and forced the authority to reconsider the claim. But the ultimate decision was one that was adverse to the claimant.

In addition it is expensive to bring a claim for judicial review, with the average hearing in 2005 costing around £10,000 (Woolf, Jowell, and Le Sueur, 2007: 852). There is also the risk for the claimant of having to pay the defendant's costs if unsuccessful.

On judicial review, the courts' powers are further limited by being unable to challenge primary legislation even if the legislation conflicts with fundamental constitutional principles, although it should be remembered the courts do have the power to disapply a statutory provision that is contrary to European law (*R v Secretary of State for Transport, ex p Factortame (No 2)* 1991 AC 603). They can also make a declaration that a law is incompatible with the Convention under section 4 of the HRA 1998. This does not invalidate legislation, but may lead to the law being

cross reference

Factortame *is discussed in Chapter 8.*
changed by Parliament. Provided that the executive has the power to act and acts in conformity with the principles of legality developed by the courts through the judicial review jurisdiction, the courts cannot intervene. Parliament can also curtail the judicial review process by providing alternative statutory procedures, as discussed earlier in relation to *R (Cart) v Upper Tribunal* [2011] UKSC 28. Within the constitution, sovereignty resides with Parliament and the court must give effect to Acts of Parliament.

However, judicial review does perform an important role in the constitution. The strength of judicial review is its important constitutional function in acting as a check on the executive. Cane explains the symbolic importance of judicial review in the final extract in this chapter.

●●●

● **P. Cane,** *Administrative Law* [4th edn, Oxford: Oxford University Press, 2004], p. 456

> Law can be important not only on account of what it practically achieves but also on account of what it symbolically stands for. In law and politics, as in life, symbols can be important regardless of their actual impact on the world ... Judicial review is symbolically important for the values it embodies and protects. From this perspective, judicial enforcement of administrative-law norms may have value independently of its impact on public decision-making.

 # Summary

The emphasis in this chapter has been on the constitutional function of the courts in holding the executive to account and protecting the rights of the individual through the application of the Human Rights Act 1998. The grounds of review have been developed by the courts in order to check executive power. The grounds of review focus on the legality of the decision and not the merits. The courts are cautious in reviewing particular executive decisions on issues such as national security and are generally reluctant to intervene unless there is clear illegality. Ouster clauses trying to exclude the courts' jurisdiction are construed strictly. After *Anisminic*, it appears that most mistakes of law will lead to the decision of an inferior body or tribunal being reviewed by the courts even if there is an ouster clause. The right to make a claim for judicial review will also be limited if there is an alternative statutory appeal or review.

Judicial review can be brought only against someone exercising public functions. It has developed its own procedures with short time limits, a requirement that the court grant permission before the case can proceed, and a broad test of standing. The procedure has been held to be an exclusive one (*O'Reilly v Mackman*), so that public authorities can have the necessary procedural protection. However, the courts have subsequently adopted a more lenient approach, as shown by the case of *Clark*. And a case will not be struck out simply because it is brought in the wrong court, but only if the claimant is thought to be guilty of an abuse or process. Figure 14.1 is a reminder of the factors that need to be present to bring a claim for judicial review. It will be helpful as a brief overall summary as we look at these key factors in detail in the following chapters.

Figure 14.1

> *Judicial review*
>
> is
>
> a legal action to ask the Administrative Court to rule on whether
>
> *public functions are being exercised*
>
> and
>
> an *action*, failure to act (an omission), or a decision
>
> is
>
> contrary to the law on the ground(s) that the action, omission, or decision is
>
> illegal (contrary to the body's legal power)
>
> and/or
>
> irrational
>
> and/or
>
> *procedurally* improperor abreach of the rules of natural justice
>
> and/or
>
> a breach of the Human Rights Act 1998
>
> and
>
> is capable of remedy through one of the following remedies:
>
> *quashing, mandatory, or prohibiting orders, a declaration, an injunction,* and/or Human Rights Act damages
>
> and
>
> the claimant has a *sufficient* interest in the matter and, in a Human Rights Act claim, is a *victim* of the unlawful act
>
> and
>
> the claim is brought promptly and in any event within three months.

Questions

1 What is the purpose of judicial review?

2 To what extent may the jurisdiction of the court be limited or ousted?

3 To what extent do you believe that judicial review is able to ensure that the rule of law is respected by the executive?

4 Should the judicial review procedure be exclusive?

Further reading

Craig, P., 'Competing models of judicial review' [1999] Public Law 428

This explains the different theoretical approaches that underpin judicial review and supports the common law theory of judicial review.

Forsyth, C., 'Of fig leaves and fairy tales: the ultra vires doctrine, the sovereignty of parliament and judicial review' [1996] Cambridge Law Journal 122

The author discusses the ultra vires theory of judicial review and attempts to defend the theory from its critics.

Hickinbottom, Mr Justice, 'Tribunal reform: a new coherent system' [2010] Judicial Review 103

This article is an explanation of the new tribunal system introduced by the Tribunals, Courts and Enforcement Act 2007 and provides a useful diagram.

Le Sueur, A., 'Three strikes and its out? The UK government's strategy to oust judicial review from immigration and asylum decision making' [2004] Public Law 225

This article gives an account of the controversy over the proposed ouster clause in the Asylum and Immigration (Treatment of Claimants, etc.) Bill 2003.

Lord Woolf, 'The rule of law and a change in. the constitution' (2004) 63 Cambridge Law Journal 317

Lord Woolf discusses constitutional developments and the rule of law. He considers whether the controversy over the ouster clause in the Asylum and Immigration (Treatment of Claimants, etc.) Bill 2003 provides an argument in favour of the adoption of a written constitution.

Mitchell, G., 'Judicial review, but not as we know it: judicial review in the Upper Tribunal' [2010] Judicial Review 112

This article explains the Upper Tribunal's power of judicial review.

15

The Parties to a Judicial Review: who can make a claim for judicial review and against whom can a claim for judicial review be made?

Key points

This chapter will cover:

- Why can claims for judicial review be brought only against a body carrying out a public function?
- What is the difference between non-human-rights judicial review cases and human rights judicial review cases?

- Non-human-rights judicial review claims: functions of a public nature
- Public authorities exercising private functions and private authorities exercising public functions
- The meaning of a 'public authority' under the Human Rights Act 1998
- Is the law on public functions and public authorities in need of reform?
- The relevance of standing
- What are the rules of standing in HRA 1998 cases?
- Third-party interventions

Introduction

This chapter is the second substantive chapter on judicial review. It will focus on identifying the parties to a judicial review. It will consider what bodies and individuals can be the subject of a claim for judicial review *and* who can bring a claim for judicial review in the Administrative Court. The principle that a judicial review can be brought only against a body that is carrying out public functions will be explained. The next section will consider the 'rules' on standing (formerly known as *locus standi*), which determine who can bring a claim for judicial review.

15.1 Why can claims for judicial review be brought only against bodies carrying out a public function?

A **judicial** review action may be brought only against a body that is carrying out a public function. Usually, this body will be a public body, but, as we shall see, private organisations carrying out public functions are also subject to judicial review. Before bringing an action for judicial review, it is imperative to decide whether the body in question is exercising a public function, or, in human rights cases, whether the body has the elements associated with a **public authority**. This classification will be addressed in some detail.

The law treats public authorities differently from private authorities. This is because there is an expectation that public authorities and those exercising public functions will act in the public interest. Public authorities are often spending public money in order to meet their objectives and thus they must be accountable for their decisions. Public authorities and those exercising public functions often have powers over and above those of ordinary citizens. They may make decisions that affect the population as a whole or a section of the population. When the Department of Health exercises its power, it may make a decision that affects every hospital in England and Wales. A local authority may make a decision about parking enforcement or planning that affects many people in the area. The expectation is that each of these will act in the public interest and not in the individual interest of the hospital or the local authority members. This is unlike a commercial company, which may legitimately seek to further only its own commercial interests. Public authorities or those exercising public functions may also have the power to coerce citizens and to make decisions affecting fundamental rights, and it is very important that they be able to prove that they are acting lawfully. It is an integral aspect of the **rule of law** that those exercising public functions must abide by the law and that the legality of their decisions is subject to challenge by us—ordinary citizens—in the courts. In the next extract, Cane discusses some of the reasons why those exercising public functions are subject to a separate set of rules.

● **P. Cane, *An Introduction to Administrative Law*** (Oxford: Oxford University Press, 2004), pp. 13–14

> First, because institutions of governance have the job of running the country they must have some functions, powers, and duties which private citizens do not have; obvious examples are the waging of war and the issuing of passports. Secondly, because of the very great power governmental institutions can wield over its citizens (most particularly because government enjoys a monopoly of legitimate force), we may want to impose on them special duties of procedural fairness that do not normally apply to private citizens,[1] and special rules about what organs of governance may do and decide. Thirdly, because certain institutions of governance have a monopoly over certain activities and the provision of certain goods and services it might be thought that the exercise of such powers ought to be subject to forms of 'public accountability' to which the activities of private individuals are usually not subject.[2]
>
> 1 For example, *R v Legal Aid Board, ex p Donn & Co.* [1996] 3 All ER 1.
>
> 2 In economic terms, it is sometimes said that when there is no possibility of 'exit' (that is, choosing another supplier of a good or service), consumers/citizens should have a 'voice' about the way in which the good or service is provided. The possibility of exit is one of the hallmarks of a competitive market.

Not everyone agrees that there should be a different set of rules for those operating in the public sphere. A. V. Dicey thought that the **government** should be subject to the ordinary law in the ordinary courts, so that it would not have any unfair advantages. He famously stated: 'In England we know nothing of administrative law; and we wish to know nothing.' But this was at a time when the **state** was far less powerful and intruded less on the life of the individual than it does now. Harlow (1980; 2002) argues that the same rules that govern the relations between citizens in private law should apply between the individuals and the state. Oliver (2004) argues that a set of values and principles should be developed that apply to all cases, public and private, depending on the type of case. These sophisticated arguments can be explored in the articles by these scholars listed in the further reading at the end of the chapter, but suffice to stay that there is disagreement about the extent to which those exercising a public function should be assessed by a different legal standard from private bodies. For now, at least, judicial review relates to the public and not the private.

(15.2) What is the difference between non-human-rights judicial review cases and human rights judicial review cases?

In non-human-rights judicial review cases, the emphasis is on showing that the body or individual is exercising a public function. There is no statutory definition of a public function, but

Part 54 of the **Civil Procedure Rules (CPR) 1998** states that a claim for judicial review has the following meaning.

> **Civil Procedure Rules**
> . . . .
>
> **Part 54**
>
> ...a claim to review the lawfulness of a decision, action or failure to act in relation to the exercise of a public function.

There will be a full discussion of the case law on this term in the next section.

cross reference

See Chapter 16 for more on a public authority acting incompatibly with a Convention right.

In human rights cases, the emphasis is on ensuring that the body is a public authority. Section 6 of Human Rights Act 1998 (HRA 1998) states that 'it is unlawful for a public authority to act in a way which is incompatible with a Convention right'. Section 6 contains a partial definition that creates two kinds of public authority: **core public authorities**, **functional public authorities** (or **hybrid public authorities**). A person who claims that a public authority has acted incompatibly with a Convention right may bring an action in the appropriate court or tribunal (under section 7 of the HRA 1998). This normally excludes a direct action against private bodies and individuals. The definition has given rise to a considerable degree of controversy and will be explored below.

Note also that there is some overlap between the definition of a functional public authority under the HRA 1998 and the definition in non-human-rights judicial review cases.

summary points

What is the difference between non-human-rights judicial review cases and human rights judicial review cases?

- *On occasion the terminology can be confusing.*
- *The courts sometimes use the term public bodies, public authorities, or refer to the public functions of a body.*
- *Irrespective of the term used it is important to keep in mind that the courts are generally trying to decide whether the body's powers and functions are sufficiently public in nature to subject it to the judicial review process or whether the issues are essentially private in nature.*

15.3 Non-human-rights judicial review claims: functions of a public nature

15.3.1 What is a function of a public nature?

This section explains the test used by the courts in non-human-rights matters to determine whether a body is carrying out a public function. The case of *R v Panel on Takeovers and Mergers, ex p Datafin plc and another* [1987] 2 WLR 699 provides the most authoritative statement of the law and is therefore discussed in some detail. We shall then consider the development of the case law subsequent to *Datafin*. The section concludes with an explanation of the relevant factors taken into account by the courts when making its decisions.

Datafin established that when the court considers whether a body is exercising a public, as opposed to a private, function, the court has to consider the *nature* of the body's power and not only the *source* of the power. In relation to the source of the power, the court is concerned with from where the body's power is derived, for example from a contract (a private agreement between the parties), a statute (legislation that confers special power on the body), or the **royal prerogative** (a form of **executive** power, discussed in Chapter 6). The court is also concerned with the kind of work or activity in which the body is engaged and whether this work can be considered to have a public character. In previous case law, the source of the power was definitive. So if the source of the relationship were contractual, then the courts would regard the issue as a matter for the private law of contract and the use of judicial review would not be appropriate. If the relationship were largely governed by statute or prerogative powers, then the body would be subject to the public process of judicial review. However, this approach proved to be inadequate in *Datafin*, a case involving the Panel on Takeovers and Mergers, because, as is discussed below, the source of the body's power was neither contractual nor statutory.

It may help to explain a little about the body that was the subject of the judicial review action. The Panel on Takeovers and Mergers was an unincorporated association that oversaw and regulated the UK financial market. Lord Donaldson MR explained at 825: '[The Panel] has no statutory, prerogative or common law powers and it is not in contractual relationship with the financial market or with those who deal in that market.' It was part of a system of stock exchange and financial markets self-regulation. **Parliament** had left those who worked in the financial markets to regulate themselves rather than legislating. The Panel wrote, administered, and interpreted a non-legally binding code of practice that regulated the way in which takeovers and mergers could be conducted on the London Stock Exchange. It also exercised quasi-judicial functions (that is, it acted in a way similar to a court), and could receive and determine claims that the code had been breached. If the code was breached, the Panel could discipline the offender by expulsion from the Stock Exchange. This was done by a very complicated mechanism, which meant that the Panel's decisions were referred to the Department of Trade and Industry (DTI) or the Stock Exchange, which would use the relevant contractual or statutory powers to enforce the penalty imposed by the Panel; the Panel did not have the power to enforce the penalty directly. Although the code was not legally binding, it was referred to in various statutory instruments governing the financial markets. Anyone who wanted to use the Stock Exchange had to abide by the code whether or not they were members of bodies represented on the Panel of Takeovers and Mergers. The code of conduct and the decisions of the Panel were voluntary on paper, but were effectively mandatory and enforceable in practice.

The next question is the extent to which a decision reached by the Panel would be susceptible to judicial review. In this case, the Panel dismissed a complaint by Datafin that its rivals had breached the code of practice during a takeover bid and Datafin wished to challenge the decision via judicial review. The judge refused the application for judicial review on the grounds that the Panel was not carrying out a public function and the decision was consequently not susceptible to judicial review. The Court of Appeal reversed the judge's decision, and held that the Panel was carrying out a public function and subject to judicial review. However, it rejected Datafin's claim on the basis that the Panel had acted lawfully in determining the complaint.

The important point for the purposes of our discussion in this chapter is the Court of Appeal's reasoning in relation to whether a judicial review action may be brought against this type of body and the reasoning behind that decision. The Court decided that the regulation of a major national institution, like the Stock Exchange, was a public or governmental function. It held that the Panel's powers affected the rights of citizens and that those wanting to use the Stock Exchange were compelled to submit to its powers. It was therefore only right that individuals subject to the Panel's jurisdiction should have recourse to the courts for a remedy. In addition, the Panel was part of a system of self-regulation acknowledged and supported by the government. The Bank of England and the DTI supported and aided the enforcement of the code of practice administered by the Panel. Various statutory instruments governing the financial markets referred to the code. Finally, the Court of Appeal made it clear that were the Panel not to exist, it was likely that the government would intervene to create such a body and that would be a public body. On this basis, the Court of Appeal found that the nature of the Panel's functions was public.

In the following extract, the Court discusses the reasoning behind its decision that the Panel was exercising a public function.

● *R v Panel on Takeover and Mergers, ex p Datafin Plc and another* [1987] 2 WLR 699

Lord Donaldson MR at 838:

> It is without doubt performing a public duty and an important one. This is clear from the expressed willingness of the Secretary of State for Trade and Industry to limit legislation in the field of take-overs and mergers and to use the panel as the centrepiece of his regulation of that market. The rights of citizens are indirectly affected by its decisions, some, but by no means all of whom, may in a technical sense be said to have assented to this situation, e.g. the members of the Stock Exchange. At least in its determination of whether there has been a breach of the code, it has a duty to act judicially and it asserts that its raison d'être is to do equity between one shareholder and another. Its source of power is only partly based upon moral persuasion and the assent of institutions and their members, the bottom line being the statutory powers exercised by the Department of Trade and Industry and the Bank of England. In this context I should be very disappointed if the courts could not recognise the realities of executive power and allowed their vision to be clouded by the subtlety and sometimes complexity of the way in which it can be exerted.

The wording in this extract is relatively complicated, but it is expressed succinctly by Lloyd LJ a few pages further on, at 846: 'So long as there is a possibility, however remote, of the Panel abusing its great powers, then it would be wrong for the court to abdicate responsibility'—in other words, the Panel wielded enormous power that could have an impact on individual rights and had the quality of executive power. Lord Justice Lloyd rejected the Panel's argument that a body should be subject to judicial review only if the source of the power is based on statute or the prerogative.

The decision in *Datafin* makes it clear that there is no one factor that the courts will look at when deciding whether a body is exercising a public function. Some of the factors that the court has considered in deciding the nature of the function are discussed below.

15.3.2 What factors does the court consider when deciding whether the function is of a public nature?

The existence of a statutory power

Bodies that have been created, or are governed, by statute, or have been given special statutory powers, are usually considered to perform a public function, but this is not necessarily the case. The court may still consider that such a body is carrying out predominantly private functions. Lloyd's of London is incorporated by a private Act of Parliament and its powers are laid down in various private Acts of Parliament because of its significance in the insurance market. However, in *R (on the Application of West) v Lloyd's of London* [2004] EWCA Civ 506, the Court of Appeal held that Lloyd's was not carrying out a public function. The claimant, Dr West, challenged decisions of the Business Conduct Committee of Lloyd's concerned with the disposal of shares, which he argued had been sold at an undervalue, causing him to lose money. The Court of Appeal, upholding the decision of the **Administrative Court**, held that Lloyd's functions were of a commercial and not a public nature even though they were governed by statute. The following extract explains the reasoning of the Court of Appeal.

447

● **R (on the application of West) v Lloyd's of London** [2004] EWCA Civ 506

Brooke LJ:

> 30...The fact that Lloyd's corporate arrangements are underpinned by a private Act of Parliament and not by the Companies Acts makes it in no way unique and is certainly not dispositive of the matter...
>
> 31 The decisions under challenge were concerned solely with the commercial relationship between Dr West and the relevant managing agents, and this was governed by the contracts into which he had chosen to enter. Those decisions were of a private, not a public, nature. They have consequences for Dr West in private, not public, law...
>
> It seems to me that the functions of Lloyd's which are under review in this case are totally different from the functions of the Takeover Panel that were under consideration in *Ex p. Datafin*. The Panel exercised regulatory control in a public sphere where governmental regulatory control was absent. This case is concerned with the working out of private contractual arrangements at Lloyd's which is itself subject to external governmental regulation.

The Court distinguished *Datafin*, meaning that it judged the facts of *Datafin* to be sufficiently different from this case so that *Datafin* did not apply. In *Datafin*, the Panel was actually exercising the power to regulate the Stock Exchange in a situation in which there was no direct government regulation. In this case, the fact that there was statutory regulation of the insurance industry and of Lloyd's work meant that Lloyd's itself was not carrying out a public function. In addition, the Court held that Dr West's dispute was essentially about his contract with Lloyd's and was a commercial matter to be dealt with in private law, and so was not amenable to judicial review.

The existence of a contract

The presence of a contract is a very strong indication that the dispute is a commercial matter and private in nature, rather than a public law matter suitable for judicial review. The distinction is not always that clear, and the courts stress that it is the nature of the function that is important and not the source.

This situation is illustrated by the decision in *R v Insurance Ombudsman Bureau and another, ex p Aegon Life Assurance Ltd* [1994] CLC 88. This case concerned an application by an insurance company for judicial review of a decision of the Insurance Ombudsman Bureau (IOB). The IOB had been created by insurance companies to hear complaints by customers mainly arising from decisions made about insurance claims. The IOB scheme was governed by a contract between an individual insurance company and the IOB, and insurance companies had the contractual right to terminate membership of the scheme by giving six months' notice of their intention to leave the scheme. Under the terms of the scheme, the Insurance Ombudsman had the power to award compensation against insurance companies, but there was no enforcement mechanism if the insurance company refused to pay. Thereafter it gets quite complicated. The IOB was one of a number of complaints procedures that could be used by dissatisfied insurance company customers, including a scheme that had been recognised in the statute that regulated the insurance industry—the Financial Services Act 1986. Section 10 of the Act provided recognition by the Secretary of State for Trade and Industry for the Life Assurance and Unit Trust Regulatory Organisation (LAUTRO) as an organisation regulating the investment business. The IOB was not recognised in this way by the Act. However, the scheme with statutory recognition, LAUTRO, recognised the IOB as performing a complaints investigation function under the legislation. It had been established in a previous case that LAUTRO was subject to judicial review. Did the fact that LAUTRO was susceptible to judicial review and that LAUTRO recognised the IOB as performing a complaints investigation function under the terms of the Financial Services Act 1986 mean that the IOB was also susceptible to judicial review, even though insurance companies joined that scheme by way of a contract?

The claimant argued that the IOB was carrying out a public function similar to that of the Panel in the *Datafin* case, even though the relationship between the insurance companies and the IOB appeared, on the face of it, to be contractual and therefore private. It was argued that the IOB scheme was part of a system of insurance industry self-regulation. In turn, that scheme formed part of a larger system of government control that was ultimately underpinned by statute and approved by the government. The court, as stated in the extract below, rejected the argument on the grounds that the IOB's relationship with its members was based on contract, that its decisions were similar to those of an arbitrator in a private law contractual case, that its decisions could not be enforced, and that there was no mechanism by which the government could enforce the decision, unlike the enforcement of Panel decisions via the Secretary of State in *Datafin*.

• ***R v Insurance Ombudsman Bureau and another, ex p Aegon Life Assurance Ltd***
  [1994] CLC 88

Rose LJ at 94:

> The IOB's power over its members is, as it seems to me, still, despite the Act, solely derived from contract and it simply cannot be said that it exercises government functions. In a nut shell, even if it can be said that it has now been woven into a governmental system, the source of its power is still contractual, its decisions are of an arbitrative nature in private law and those decisions are not, save very remotely, supported by any public law sanction. In the light of all these factors, the IOB is not in my judgment a body susceptible to judicial review.

In this instance, by virtue of the fact that the relationship between the IOB and members of the scheme was governed by contract, and for the other reasons mentioned in the extract, the body was deemed to be exercising a private function.

Inherently private functions

There are functions that the courts appear to regard as private in nature and which they have consistently refused to review. The activities of sporting and religious organisations often fall into this category.

Sporting bodies

The courts have refused applications to review decisions of, for example, the Jockey Club, the Football Association (*R v Football Association Ltd, ex p Football League Ltd; Football Association Ltd v Football League Ltd* ([1993] 2 All ER 833), and the Greyhound Racing Association (*Law v National Greyhound Racing Club Ltd* [1983] 3 All ER 300). The courts are reluctant to submit bodies that regulate what are essentially recreational and commercial activities to the principles developed to prevent the abuse of executive (public) power.

R v Disciplinary Committee of the Jockey Club, ex p Aga Khan [1993] 1 WLR 909 illustrates that even where a body has a regulatory function that borders on the quasi-judicial, the courts still class the sporting body to be exercising a private function. In this instance, the claimant was the racehorse owner whose horse had, subsequent to disciplinary proceedings, been disqualified from competing by the Jockey Club. Further, the trainer had been fined after a prohibited substance had been found in the horse's urine during a routine drug test. It was argued by the claimant that, following the decision in *Datafin*, the Jockey Club should be considered as exercising public functions. The claimant's reasoning was that the Club had been created by royal charter, that it had an effective monopoly over horse racing (anyone who wanted to participate seriously in the sport had to subject itself to its regulations), and that the government would have to regulate horse-racing activity if the Jockey Club did not exist. The Court of Appeal held that the Jockey Club was not subject to judicial review, because the powers it exercised were not governmental, as illustrated in the next extract.

● *R v Disciplinary Committee of the Jockey Club, ex p Aga Khan* [1993] 1 WLR 909

Sir Thomas Bingham MR at 923–4:

> But the Jockey Club is not in its origin, its history, its constitution or (least of all) its membership a public body. While the grant of a Royal Charter was no doubt a mark of official approval, this did not in any way alter its essential nature, functions or standing. Statute provides for its representation on the Horserace Betting Levy Board, no doubt as a body with an obvious interest in racing, but it has otherwise escaped mention in the statute book. It has not been woven into any system of governmental control of horseracing, perhaps because it has itself controlled horseracing so successfully that there has been no need for any such governmental system and such does not therefore exist. This has the result that while the Jockey Club's powers may be described as, in many ways, public they are in no sense governmental...

This is not the only case that has considered the nature and functions of sporting bodies. Other cases such as *R v Jockey Club, ex p Massingberd-Mundy* [1993] 2 All ER 207 and *R v Jockey Club, ex p Ram Racecourses Ltd* [1993] 2 All ER 225 have been decided similarly, although with *obiter* comments suggesting that there may be limited situations in which sporting clubs could be susceptible to judicial review.

Religious bodies

The courts have refused to judicially review the decisions of religious organisations. In *R v Chief Rabbi of The United Hebrew Congregations of Great Britain and the Commonwealth, ex p Wachmann* [1992] 1 WLR 1036, there was an attempt to judicially review the Chief Rabbi's decision to declare a rabbi unfit to hold rabbinical office, based on accusations that he had been accused of adultery with his congregants. This declaration led to the rabbi's dismissal from his congregation. The court held that the decisions of the Chief Rabbi were not reviewable because his functions were 'spiritual and religious', and not public, in nature.

The court reached a similar conclusion in a case concerned with the management of a mosque. In *R v Imam of Bury Park Mosque, Luton, ex p Ali (Sulaimaman)* [1994] COD 142, an application to review a decision by an imam to leave the claimants off a list of those entitled to vote in a mosque committee election was not subject to review because it was not sufficiently governmental in nature.

thinking point
Do you think it is fair that the functions of religious bodies and sporting bodies are usually classified as private functions? Why are the courts reluctant to review these decisions?

NOTE

See also the comments of the House of Lords on the private nature of religious institutions in the *Aston Cantlow* case discussed later in the chapter in relation to the Human Rights Act 1998.

Functions that have been contracted out

Contracting out occurs when a public authority has a power or duty to provide a service. Instead of providing the service itself, the authority makes a contract with a private body to carry out the service. The question that has arisen is whether the private body is performing a 'public function' within the meaning of Part 54 of the Civil Procedure Rules and is therefore subject to judicial review. The case of *YL v Birmingham City Council* [2007] UKHL 27 has established that private bodies providing services to local authorities are also *not* usually considered public authorities for the purposes of the HRA 1998. We will discuss this case and section 145 of the Health and Social Care Act 2008 below. Contracting out raises complex issues of law and policy, and this practice is discussed in more detail later in the chapter.

This section has discussed the test used by the court to decide if a body is exercising a public or private function. The *Datafin* case established that the courts should focus on the functions of the body. So the courts will look at the nature of the work and activities of the body rather focus solely on the source of the body's power. When making the decision, the courts will take into account a number of factors, including the history of the body, whether it is publicly funded, and whether it has coercive powers, such as the power to punish or to enforce its decisions. If submission to the body's power is based on choice and consent, it is more likely to be carrying out private functions. The courts have consistently held the activities of some organisations to be private in nature. These include the activities of sporting and religious organisations, which are not suitable for judicial review.

summary points

Non-human rights judicial review claims: functions of a public nature

- *Factors the court considers when deciding whether a body is exercising a public function for the purposes of judicial review include:*
  - *the history of the body;*
  - *whether the body is financed by public funds; and*
  - *whether the body has coercive powers, such as the power to punish individuals or enforce its decisions.*
- *In addition, the court will consider the following questions.*
  - *Is submission to the body's power based on choice or compulsion?*
  - *Is there a contract between the parties that indicates that disputes should be resolved through private law?*
  - *Is the body exercising statutory powers?*
  - *Is there a policy reason why the body's powers should be considered to be private or public functions?*

451

15.4 Public authorities exercising private functions and private authorities exercising public functions

15.4.1 Public authorities exercising private functions

We have so far considered the extent to which public functions may be reviewed. In this section, we consider the extent to which the courts will review public authorities exercising private functions. We shall then consider the circumstances that may lead to the functions of a private body being subject to judicial review.

In judicial review cases that do not concern human rights issues, public authorities will only be subject to judicial review if the function that they are carrying out is a public function. If it is a private function, it will not be reviewable and instead a potential claimant will have to use private law proceedings (for example, a contract or a tort law claim) to seek any available legal remedy. The courts have found it hard to classify some public authority functions and this has generated a complex case law. It is not necessary to explore this case law in depth here, but it is important to be aware that employment relationships and commercial contracts cause particular problems.

Employment by a public or private body is usually considered to be a matter of private law that would be dealt with by an employment tribunal. However, some cases have been considered by the Administrative Court because individuals have sought to establish that their employment situation, or their dismissal, from a public authority means that the matter should be considered through judicial review. For the court to judicially review the decision, there has to be a 'public law' element. The Court of Appeal discussed this issue in the recent case of *R (on the application of Shoesmith) v Ofsted and others* [2011] EWCA Civ 642. Shoesmith was dismissed from Haringey Council after being removed from her post as director of children's services by the Secretary of State for Education. This was subsequent to the much-publicised death of Peter Connolly, 'Baby P', who was on the child protection register and subject to a child protection plan drawn up by Haringey Council. Shoesmith claimed that her removal as director was unlawful because there was a failure to follow fair procedures. The Court of Appeal rejected the argument that the case should be heard in an employment tribunal. The case was suitable for judicial review because the post of director of children's services was created and defined by statute (under section 11 of the Children Act 2004), and the post holder was the person within Children's Services with ultimate executive responsibility. In other words, there was a sufficient public law element and statutory underpinning to differentiate the case from a private employment dispute, and which made it suitable to be heard in the Administrative Court.

cross reference

The grounds on which the claimant brought the judicial review case in Shoesmith *are further discussed in Chapter 18.*

Similar issues have arisen in relation to the commercial activities of public authorities and, again, these have been subject to the same public law element test. For further information, you may wish to read the following two cases as an illustration of the courts' reasoning.

NOTE If you would like to read more about these issues, then it is recommended that you refer to Bailey (2007) listed in the further reading list at the end of the chapter.

- In *R v Bolsover District Council, ex p Pepper* [2001] LGA 43, it was held that a decision to sell land by a local authority pursuant to a statute was not subject to judicial review, because the local authority was simply acting as a landowner and was not performing a public function.

- An earlier decision in *R v Barnet LBC, ex p Pardes House School Ltd* [1989] COD 512, however, had held that a decision to sell a school playing field for non-recreational purposes was subject to judicial review, because the authority was exercising a statutory power.

It is not surprising that many commentators have criticised the law in this area as confusing and in need of reform.

15.4.2 Private authorities exercising public functions

An obviously private body may be subject to judicial review in certain circumstances if it were found to be exercising functions of a public nature. So, for example, in *R v Cobham Hall School, ex p G* [1998] ELR 389, a private school that participated in the assisted places scheme was held to be subject to judicial review. This was because the assisted places scheme, whereby the government paid the school fees of certain children to attend private schools rather than them to attend state schools, was a statutory scheme provided for in the Education Act 1996 and the Education (Assisted Places) Regulations 1995. This laid down the admission criteria and gave the Secretary of State the power to control funding. In general terms, private schools will be subject to a contractual relationship between the school and the parents/child that is a private law relationship, and any legal remedy would be defined through contract law. However, a private school will be exercising a public rather than a private function if the fees are being paid by the state under a statutory scheme. In this case, the head teacher decided to remove an assisted places student from the school on the grounds that the student's behaviour was unacceptable; this decision was subject to judicial review because the school was carrying out a statutory function—that is, it was behaving in a similar way to a state school because the education was effectively paid for by the state and the admission of the student to the school was regulated by statutory criteria.

The law for judicial review cases that do not involve human rights issues focuses on whether or not the body in question is exercising a function of a public nature. It follows that the public functions of private bodies may be subject to judicial review. The private functions of public authorities are not judicially reviewable, however, and the correct course is to bring a private law action. Employment relationships and decisions to contract with public authorities are generally considered as private law issues. However, if there is a 'public law element' to a seemingly private law function such as a commercial relationship, then it will be reviewable. The difficulty is that the case law on what constitutes a 'public law' element is complex and the cases discussed above give only limited guidance. This is an area of law ripe for reform or clarification by the courts.

summary points

Public authorities exercising private functions and private authorities exercising public functions

- *It is necessary to consider whether the body is exercising a public function.*
- *The actions, omissions, and decisions of public bodies and private bodies may both be subject to review as long as they relate to a public function.*
- *The actions, omissions, and decisions of public and private bodies will not be subject to review if they are considered to relate to private functions.*
- *The functions of some bodies are generally classed as private functions (sporting and religious bodies).*

453

15.5 The meaning of a 'public authority' under the Human Rights Act 1998

15.5.1 What is a public authority?

This section discusses the meaning of the term public authority in the HRA 1998. It explains that an action alleging a breach of the HRA 1998 can be brought only against a public authority; this is different from the functions-based approach to bodies discussed above in relation to non-human-rights-related matters. Section 6 of the HRA 1998 recognises two types of public authority: core public authorities and functional public authorities. We shall consider the courts' interpretation of these terms and provide examples of the relevant types of authority. We shall also explore the problems that the definition and its subsequent interpretation have caused. First, we shall consider the definition of a public authority, as set out in section 6 of the HRA 1998.

Human Rights Act 1998

Section 6

(1) It is unlawful for a public authority to act in a way which is incompatible with a Convention right.

(2) Subsection (1) does not apply to an act if—

(a) as the result of one or more provisions of primary legislation, the authority could not have acted differently; or

(b) in the case of one or more provisions of, or made under, primary legislation which cannot be read or given effect in a way which is compatible with the Convention rights, the authority was acting so as to give effect to or enforce those provisions.

(3) In this section 'public authority' includes—

(a) a court or tribunal, and

(b) any person certain of whose functions are functions of a public nature,

but does not include either House of Parliament or a person exercising functions in connection with proceedings in Parliament.

(4) In subsection (3) 'Parliament' does not include the House of Lords in its judicial capacity.

(5) In relation to a particular act, a person is not a public authority by virtue only of subsection (3)(b) if the nature of the act is private.

(6) 'An act' includes a failure to act but does not include a failure to—

(a) introduce in, or lay before, Parliament a proposal for legislation; or

(b) make any primary legislation or remedial order

---

cross reference

See Chapter 9 for a discussion of this in the context of parliamentary supremacy.

The HRA 1998 states that it is unlawful for a public authority to act in a way that is incompatible with a right under the **European Convention on Human Rights (ECHR)**, assuming that there is no UK primary legislation that requires a public authority to so act. A public authority includes the courts and tribunals, which are bound by the Act; it does not include Parliament, apart from the House of Lords when it acts in a judicial capacity. So it is not possible to take an action against Parliament on the grounds that it has acted unlawfully by passing legislation in conflict with the ECHR. This is because Parliament is not a public authority for the purposes of the HRA 1998. However, even if Parliament has passed legislation that requires a public authority to act in a way that is incompatible with a Convention right, it may be possible to bring a judicial review action to ask the court to rule on whether the law, as passed by Parliament, offends against the ECHR. This is done through applying to the court for a **declaration** of incompatibility under section 4 of the HRA 1998 on the basis that the statute in question is in conflict with a Convention right. For the purposes of this chapter, however, we shall focus on cases brought when it is alleged that a public authority may have acted contrary to the HRA 1998 by having unlawfully made a decision, or acted, or failed to act, in a way that breaches an individual's Convention rights. This requires us to consider when the court will allow an action to be brought and one of the criteria is that an action may only be brought against a public authority. As explained earlier, the courts have recognised different types of public authority and the effect of the HRA 1998 is a little different depending on whether an authority is considered to be a core or functional public authority.

Table 15.1

Core public authorities	Functional or hybrid public authorities
All acts of a core public authority are subject to the Human Rights Act 1998 whether the function in question is public or private.	All of the public functions, but not the private functions, of functional or hybrid public authorities are subject to the Human Rights Act 1998.

15.5.2 Core public authorities

Some bodies are clearly public authorities and, as Lord Nicholls explains in *Aston Cantlow and Wilmcote with Billesley Parochial Church Council v Wallbank and another* [2004] 1 AC 546, [7], 'the most obvious examples of core public authorities are government departments, local authorities, the police and the armed forces'. The HRA 1998 binds such bodies, whether their functions are public or private. This is because such bodies are governmental in nature. They are obliged to act in the public interest, they have special powers, they are democratically accountable, and they enjoy either full or partial public funding. But there are also some bodies that are less obviously public authorities: what about the Church of England, for example, which is the established official Church of England?

Aston Cantlow

The status of the Church of England, or rather one part of the Church of England, was considered in *Aston Cantlow,* in which the House of Lords had to decide whether a Church of England parochial church council (PCC) was a public authority for the purposes of section 6(1) of the HRA 1998. This case concerned a dispute between Mr and Mrs Wallbank, the owners of Glebe Farm, and Aston Cantlow Parish Church Council of the Church of England. The Wallbanks owned land, known as 'rectoral' land, which had a historic connection with the local church. It carried with it an ancient land law duty that ran with the land (that is, if the land were sold, then the new owner would also be under the duty) to repair the **chancel** of the church. This duty to repair could be enforced by section 2(3) of the Chancel Repairs Act 1932. When the Wallbanks refused to pay, the PCC took action against them in court to recover the sum owed. The Wallbanks, in their defence, argued that the PCC was a core public authority in accordance with section 6 of the HRA 1998, and had violated their right to property contrary to Article 1 of the First Protocol to the ECHR and their right not to be discriminated against contrary to Article 14. The court first had to determine whether the PCC was a public authority, because if it was not, then an action could not be brought in relation to the right to property.

. . . .

chancel   The area of the church around the altar; often enclosed by a railing, it is used by the clergy during services.

. . . .

The Wallbanks argued that the PCC, as an essential part of the Church of England, was a core public authority. This is because the Church of England is an established or official church. The **monarch** is the head of the Church of England, and it has a special status and various privileges that other churches do not enjoy. Although PCCs have a long history, their powers and functions are statutory and are set out in the Parochial Church Councils (Powers) Measure 1956. The House of Lords decided the case against the Wallbanks and held that the PCC was not a core public authority. It reversed the decision of the Court of Appeal in this respect and held that such a body was not a public authority, and therefore was not bound by the HRA 1998. The main reason for this decision was that the functions of the PCC were not public or governmental, and that Parliament did not intend the Church of England, and its constituent parts, to lose its right to make a claim under the HRA 1998. We shall examine both of these reasons in turn, because they provide good evidence of when a court will hold that an organisation is a core public authority.

The functions of a parochial church council were not public or governmental

The House of Lords held that a PCC was essentially part of a religious organisation and acted in the interest of the Church, not in the public interest. A PCC was composed of local members of the Church of England who promoted church teaching in their area, looked after the local church, and managed its finances. *These were private religious matters and not governmental in nature*. The PCC was not supervised, nor was it accountable to the government, as Lord Hope explains in the next extract.

● **Aston Cantlow and Wilmcote with Billesley Parochial Church Council v Wallbank and another** [2004] 1 AC 546

Lord Hope:

> [59] ... [A PCC] plainly has nothing whatever to do with the process of either central or local government. It is not accountable to the general public for what it does. It receives no public funding, apart from occasional grants from English Heritage for the preservation of its historic buildings. In that respect it is in a position which is no different from any private individual.

Parliament did not intend the Church of England, and its constituent parts, to lose its right to make a claim under the HRA 1998

If the PCC and the Church of England were core public authorities, they would not be able to bring an action under the HRA 1998 claiming that the Church and its members' rights of religious freedom, for example, had been breached by the state. Core public authorities are governmental bodies and are not permitted to bring actions as **victims**. In accordance with section 7 of the HRA 1998 and Article 34 ECHR, only non-governmental bodies can allege violations of Convention rights (as we will see later in the chapter). In reaching this decision, the House of Lords followed the case law of the European Court of Human Rights (ECtHR) in this regard. The House of Lords also referred to section 13 of the HRA 1998 to strengthen its reasoning that the PCC was not a core public authority. Section 13 requires the courts to have particular regard to the importance of the right to freedom of thought, conscience, and religion when considering questions affecting the exercise of rights by a religious organisation. As Lord Nicholls states at [15]: 'One would expect that these [rights] and other Convention rights would be enjoyed by the Church of England as much as other religious bodies.'

The following extract from the judgment explains the reasoning behind the Law Lords' decision that the PCC was not a public authority.

● **Aston Cantlow and Wilmcote with Billesley Parochial Church Council v Wallbank and another** [2004] 1 AC 546

Lord Nicholls at 554:

> 7 Conformably with this purpose, the phrase 'a public authority' in section 6(1) is essentially a reference to a body whose nature is governmental in a broad sense of that expression. It is in respect of organisations of this nature that the government is answerable under the European Convention on Human Rights. Hence, under the Human Rights Act 1998 a body of this nature is required to act compatibly with Convention rights in everything it does. The most obvious

examples are government departments, local authorities, the police and the armed forces. Behind the instinctive classification of these organisations as bodies whose nature is governmental lie factors such as the possession of special powers, democratic accountability, public funding in whole or in part, an obligation to act only in the public interest, and a statutory constitution: see the valuable article by Professor Dawn Oliver, 'The Frontiers of the State: Public Authorities and Public Functions under the Human Rights Act': [2000] PL 476.

8 A further, general point should be noted. One consequence of being a 'core' public authority, namely, an authority falling within section 6 without reference to section 6(3), is that the body in question does not itself enjoy Convention rights. It is difficult to see how a core public authority could ever claim to be a victim of an infringement of a Convention rights. A core public authority seems inherently incapable of satisfying the Convention description of a victim: 'any person, non-governmental organisation or group of individuals' (article 34 . . .). Only victims of an unlawful act may bring proceedings under section 7 of the Human Rights Act 1998, and the Convention description of a victim has been incorporated into the Act, by section 7(7). This feature, that a core public authority is incapable of having Convention rights of its own, is a matter to be borne in mind when considering whether or not a particular body is a core public authority. In itself this feature throws some light on how the expression 'public authority' should be understood and applied. It must always be relevant to consider whether Parliament can have been intended that the body in question should have no Convention rights.

9 In a modern developed state governmental functions extend far beyond maintenance of law and order and defence of the realm. Further, the manner in which wide ranging governmental functions are discharged varies considerably. In the interests of efficiency and economy, and for other reasons, functions of a governmental nature are frequently discharged by non-governmental bodies. Sometimes this will be a consequence of privatisation, sometimes not. One obvious example is the running of prisons by commercial organisations. Another is the discharge of regulatory functions by organisations in the private sector, for instance, the Law Society. Section 6(3)(b) gathers this type of case into the embrace of section 6 by including within the phrase 'public authority' any person whose functions include 'functions of a public nature'. This extension of the expression 'public authority' does not apply to a person if the nature of the act in question is 'private'.

. . .

12 What, then, is the touchstone to be used in deciding whether a function is public for this purpose? Clearly there is no single test of universal application. There cannot be, given the diverse nature of governmental functions and the variety of means by which these functions are discharged today. Factors to be taken into account include the extent to which in carrying out the relevant function the body is publicly funded, or is exercising statutory powers, or is taking the place of central government or local authorities, or is providing a public service . . .

13 Turning to the facts in the present case, I do not think parochial church councils are 'core' public authorities. Historically the Church of England has discharged an important and influential role in the life of this country. As the established church it still has special links with central government. But the Church of England remains essentially a religious organisation. This is so even though some of the emanations of the church discharge functions which may qualify as governmental. Church schools and the conduct of marriage services are two instances. The legislative powers of the General Synod of the Church of England are another. This should not be regarded as infecting the Church of England as a whole, or its emanations in general, with the character of a governmental organisation . . .

. . .

15 The contrary conclusion, that the church authorities in general and parochial church councils in particular are 'core' public authorities, would mean these bodies are not capable of being victims within the meaning of the Human Rights Act 1998. Accordingly they are not able to complain of infringements of Convention rights. That would be an extraordinary conclusion. The Human Rights Act goes out of its way, in section 13, to single out for express mention the exercise by religious organisations of the Convention right of freedom of thought, conscience

457

and religion. One would expect that these and other Convention rights would be enjoyed by the Church of England as much as other religious bodies.

The extract illustrates clearly that the House of Lords considers a number of factors when reaching a decision about whether a body is or is not a core public authority. The House of Lords also rejected the argument that the PCC was a functional public authority—the second type of public authority to be considered in this chapter. The Law Lords considered that the PCC was enforcing a debt, which is essentially a private and not a public function. Some members of the House of Lords did acknowledge that some functions of the Church of England, such as running a school or conducting a marriage ceremony, were public functions and likely to be subject to the HRA 1998, but private law functions were not. This distinction is an important one in relation to functional public authorities and will be discussed in detail in the next section.

When deciding whether a body is a core public authority, the following questions are likely to be relevant

. . . .

- Is the body publicly funded?

- Is the body accountable to the government?

- Is the body supervised by the government?

- Is the body carrying out an essentially private function?

- Is the body obliged to act in the public interest?

15.5.3 Functional public authorities

Functional public authorities carry out a combination of private and public functions, but only their public functions are subject to judicial review (in contrast to core public authorities, which we have just considered, the functions of which are always deemed to be judicially reviewable). When the government introduced the Human Rights Bill into Parliament, it indicated that the inclusion of the functions test was to make sure that a wide range of organisations was covered by the HRA 1998, not only organisations that were core public authorities.

. . . .

● **Lord Irvine, Lord Chancellor, Second reading of the Human Rights Bill** (HL Deb, 3 November 1997), col. 1241

We also decided that we should apply the Bill to a wide rather than a narrow range of public authorities so as to provide as much protection as possible to those who claim that their rights have been infringed.

The **Lord Chancellor** gave examples of what he considered were functional public authorities. He explained that a private security company that ran a prison is a functional authority; if the same security company were guarding commercial premises, then it would be acting privately. He also stated that a charity such as the National Society for the Prevention of Cruelty to Children (NSPCC) would be a functional public authority when it exercised its statutory powers, but not in other respects (Lord Chancellor, HL Deb, 24 November 1997, cols 811 and 800). This does add some complexity to the definition of a public authority and means that if an authority is not a core public authority, the courts will need to consider the function that the authority is performing in order to judge whether it can be the subject of an HRA 1998 claim.

As has probably become clear on reading this chapter, the definition of functional public authorities has been controversial. Contracting out, as discussed above, raises particularly difficult issues. Many public bodies such as local authorities make contracts with commercial companies, who aim to make a profit, and with non-profit organisations, such as charities and voluntary groups, which carry out functions on behalf of the public authority. These services can include running homes for the elderly and disabled, providing housing, enforcing parking regulations, and the disposal of rubbish. The question is whether such bodies are carrying out public functions and are bound by the HRA 1998? Once more, we have to consider the nature of the function and not only the nature of the body.

Several of the leading cases at which we will look concern care homes. It should be noted that recent legislation (section 145 of the Health and Social Care Act 2008, discussed further below) has classified care homes, in certain circumstances, as functional public authorities because they are carrying out functions of a public nature. This means that the outcome in the cases that we will consider would now be different. But it is still necessary to study this case law in some detail because the principles laid down by the courts in these cases is used to determine whether a body, other than a care home, is carrying out functions of a public nature.

The courts' interpretation of section 6(3)(b) has preferred a narrow definition of a public function and, therefore, the HRA 1998 does not cover many organisations, because they are not considered to be carrying out public functions. In *R (on the application of Heather) v Leonard Cheshire Foundation* [2002] EWCA Civ 366, one of the early cases decided under the Act, the Court of Appeal held that the Leonard Cheshire Foundation was not a functional public authority. The Leonard Cheshire Foundation is a charitable organisation that is the leading provider of voluntary care home facilities for the disabled in the UK. The majority of residents in its homes nationally are funded by local authorities or health services to meet their statutory duty to provide accommodation and/or medical care. In this case, the severely disabled claimants challenged the Leonard Cheshire Foundation's decision to close the care home in which they had been living for periods of at least seventeen years as contrary to their right to a home in accordance with Article 8 of the ECHR. The Court of Appeal decided that Leonard Cheshire was not a functional public authority under the HRA 1998 and was not carrying out a public function for the purposes of judicial review. This was because Leonard Cheshire was essentially a charitable organisation and was not subject to a high degree of statutory regulation. Just because it had a contract with a public authority did not mean that it was carrying out functions of a public nature. This is an interesting rationale and a difficult one for many commentators, because it appears that a core public authority may be able in some senses to delegate its statutory duties and to provide public funds to meet those duties, and yet that the body that is charged with carrying them out will not be subject to review.

This case should be contrasted with *Poplar Housing and Regeneration Community Association v Donoghue* [2001] EWCA Civ 595, in which the Court of Appeal held that Poplar Housing and Regeneration Community, a registered social landlord, was carrying out public functions. The Court of Appeal took into account the fact that Poplar Housing was closely associated with the local authority, because the authority had created Poplar Housing to take possession of its housing stock and five members of the local authority were members of its governing body. The claimant's tenancy was transferred from the local authority to Poplar Housing and, in providing her accommodation and then seeking possession, its role was so similar to the role of the authority that it could be said to be performing public functions.

The House of Lords considered the definition of functional public authorities for the first time in *YL v Birmingham City Council* [2007] UKHL 27. This was a controversial case and the House of Lords, by a majority of three to two, preferred the approach of the Court of Appeal in *Leonard Cheshire*. In other words, the House of Lords adopted a narrow approach to the definition of a public authority and excluded many bodies from the reach of the HRA 1998. The decision remains controversial, however.

It may help to provide some background on the case of *YL*. The claimant was an 84-year-old, who suffered from Alzheimer's disease and who was resident in a home run by a commercial company, Southern Cross Healthcare Ltd. At the time when the case was heard, Southern Cross had around 29,000 beds in the UK and about 80 per cent of its residents were wholly or partly supported by public funds. YL's place there was largely funded by Birmingham City Council pursuant to its duty under section 21 of the National Assistance Act 1948 to 'make arrange-ments for providing residential accommodation for persons in need of care and attention which is not otherwise available to them'. Birmingham City Council contracted with Southern Cross to provide the accommodation using its powers in section 26 of the National Assistance Act 1948, which allows the authority to contract with outside organisations. There was a three-way agreement between YL's family, Birmingham City Council, and Southern Cross as to pay-ment and care. The dispute arose when YL was given notice to leave the home because of a dispute between YL's family and the staff of the home. YL argued that this decision was in conflict with various Articles, including Article 8 of the Convention, which provides for the right to respect for family life, and therefore Southern Cross was acting unlawfully under the HRA 1998. Southern Cross argued that it was not subject to the Act because it was not exercising a public function under section 6(3)(b). The judge at first instance and the Court of Appeal agreed with Southern Cross.

The majority of the House of Lords upheld the decisions of the lower courts and agreed with Southern Cross that it was *not* carrying out public functions. The main reasons for its decisions were that the provision of care and accommodation, as opposed to the arrangement of the care, was not an inherently governmental function: the authority had a duty to arrange the care and the claimant could enforce her Convention rights against the local authority, but the care and accommodation themselves could actually be given by a private contractor without that contractor carrying out a public function. Other reasons included that Southern Cross was acting as a private, profit-making company and was acting in that capacity in this situation. Further, it was not a good argument to say that, just because some care facilities are provided by public authorities and those residents benefit from ECHR rights protection, this should be extended to all care homes regardless of their nature. Additionally, the fact that care homes were subject to extensive regulation did not mean that they were carrying out public functions. Many private and commercial activities are subject to regulation without their functions being considered public ones. And by contrast with other institutions, the care homes did not enjoy powers to compel or coerce residents, which are a feature or a power that many public au-thorities have at their disposal. Finally, that if it is thought desirable that care homes should be subject to the HRA 1998, then Parliament can always pass legislation to this effect. The extract from Lord Scott's judgment explains the reasoning behind the House of Lords' decision.

● *YL v Birmingham City Council* [2007] UKHL 27

Lord Scott:

> [26] My Lords...To express in summary terms my reason for so concluding, Southern Cross is a company carrying on a socially useful business for profit. It is neither a charity nor a phil-anthropist. It enters into private law contracts with the residents in its care homes and with the local authorities with whom it does business. It receives no public funding, enjoys no spe-cial statutory powers, and is at liberty to accept or reject residents as it chooses (subject, of course, to anti-discrimination legislation which affects everyone who offers a service to the public) and to charge whatever fees in its commercial judgment it thinks suitable. It is oper-ating in a commercial market with commercial competitors.

[27] A number of the features which have been relied on by YL and the intervenors seem to me to carry little weight. It is said, correctly, that most of the residents in the Southern Cross care homes, including YL, are placed there by local authorities pursuant to their statutory duty under section 21 of the 1948 Act and that their fees are, either wholly or partly, paid by the local authorities or, where special nursing is required, by health authorities. But the fees charged by Southern Cross and paid by local or health authorities are charged and paid for a service. There is no element whatever of subsidy from public funds. It is a misuse of language and misleading to describe Southern Cross as publicly funded. If an outside private contractor is engaged on ordinary commercial terms to provide the cleaning services, or the catering and cooking services, or any other essential services at a local authority owned care home, it seems to me absurd to suggest that the private contractor, in earning its commercial fee for its business services, is publicly funded or is carrying on a function of a public nature. It is simply carrying on its private business with a customer who happens to be a public authority. The owner of a private care home taking local authority funded residents is in no different position. It is simply providing a service or services for which it charges a commercial fee.

[28] The position might be different if the managers of privately owned care homes enjoyed special statutory powers over residents entitling them to restrain them or to discipline them in some way or to confine them to their rooms or to the care home premises. The managers do, of course, have private law duties of care to all their residents and these duties of care may sometimes require, for the protection of a resident, or of fellow residents, from harm, the exercise of a degree of control over the resident that might in other circumstances be tortious ...

[29] An argument heavily relied on in support of the appeal has been a comparison of the management by a local authority care home with the management of a privately owned care home. There is no relevant difference, it is pointed out, between the activities of a local authority in managing its own care homes and those of the managers of privately owned care homes. The function of the local authority is unquestionably a function of a public nature, so how, at least in relation to residents the charges for whom are being paid by the local authority, can the nature of the function of the managers of a privately owned care home be held to be different? So the argument goes. There are, in my opinion, very clear and fundamental differences. The local authority's activities are carried out pursuant to statutory duties and responsibilities imposed by public law. The costs of doing so are met by public funds, subject to the possibility of a means tested recovery from the resident. In the case of a privately owned care home the manager's duties to its residents are, whether contractual or tortious, duties governed by private law. In relation to those residents who are publicly funded, the local and health authorities become liable to pay charges agreed under private law contracts and for the recovery of which the care home has private law remedies. The recovery by the local authority of a means tested contribution from the resident is a matter of public law but is no concern of the care home.

[30] As it seems to me, the argument based on the alleged similarity of the nature of the function carried on by a local authority in running its own care home and that of a private person running a privately owned care home proves too much. If every contracting out by a local authority of a function that the local authority could, in exercise of a statutory power or the discharge of a statutory duty, have carried out itself, turns the contractor into a hybrid public authority for section 6(3)(b) purposes, where does this end? Is a contractor engaged by a local authority to provide lifeguard personnel at the municipal swimming pool a section 6(3)(b) public authority? If so, would a local authority employee engaged by the local authority as a lifeguard at the pool become a public authority? Could it be argued that his or her function was a function of a public nature? If Southern Cross is a section 6(3)(b) public authority, why does it not follow that each manager of each Southern Cross care home, and even each nurse or care worker at each care home would, by reason of his or her function at the care home, be a section 6(3)(b) public authority?

[31] These examples illustrate, I think, that it cannot be enough simply to compare the nature of the activities being carried out at privately owned care homes with those carried out at local authority owned care homes. It is necessary to look also at the reason why the person in question, whether an individual or corporate, is carrying out those activities. A local authority is doing so pursuant to public law obligations. A private person, including local authority

employees, is doing so pursuant to private law contractual obligations. The nature of the function of privately owned care homes, such as those owned by Southern Cross, no different for section 6 purposes from that of ordinary privately owned schools or privately owned hospitals (nb some schools and hospitals may have special statutory powers over some pupils and patients eg reformatories in the olden days and mental hospitals these days), seems to me essentially different from that of local authority care homes.

NOTE Lord Scott emphasises the commercial nature of Southern Cross, stating that it is operating in a commercial market with commercial competitors.

One of the reasons for the House of Lords' decision that the care home was not a public authority was to prevent essentially commercial bodies being burdened with the obligations of the human rights legislation. This might make it more difficult for them to operate in a commercial market and to make a profit. This might deter them from entering into contracts with local authorities, it may drive them out of the market, and, in the long run, it may make it harder to find care and accommodation for the elderly and the disabled. The House of Lords also used the 'floodgates' argument, as can be seen in the above extract. Lord Scott was worried that if a private care home contracting with a local authority is considered to be a private organisation, then other contractors, such as a company providing lifeguards for local swimming pools, might also be public authorities. This view has been criticised as being overly restrictive and not facilitating the development of a human rights culture, which encourages human rights to be respected and applied by all. These criticisms and the views of the minority in the case are discussed below in the section on whether the law is in need of reform.

Although the House of Lords in *YL* held that the care home was not a functional public authority and adopted a narrow test, it did approve two previous cases in which the lower courts had found that the body was a functional public authority. In *R (on the application of A and others) v Partnerships in Care Ltd* [2002] 1 WLR 2610, a private psychiatric hospital was held to be a functional public authority because the hospital had the power to coerce patients and there was a general public interest in ensuring that patients had the appropriate treatment. The power of coercion was viewed as particularly significant—the fact that a body has the power to make someone do something is seen as a feature of public power rather than private power, and so tipped the balance in favour of this body being viewed as a public authority. The Court of Appeal also held, in *R (on the application of Beer (trading as Hammer Trout Farm)) v Hampshire Farmer's Markets Ltd* [2004] 1 WLR 233, that a company that ran farmers' markets was a functional public authority. The local authority had established the farmers' markets using its statutory powers. It had then handed over the running of the scheme to a specially created private company, which the council continued to assist. These factors, plus the fact that the markets were held on publicly owned land, were held to make the company a functional public authority for purposes of the HRA 1998.

The principles laid down in *YL*, which determine how the courts decide whether a body is exercising public functions, remain good law and will be followed in future cases. However, the actual decision in *YL* in relation to care homes has now been reversed by section 145 of the Health and Social Care Act 2008.

Health and Social Care Act 2008

....

Section 145 Human Rights Act 1998: provision of certain social care to be public function

(1) A person ('P') who provides accommodation, together with nursing or personal care, in a care home for an individual under arrangements made with P under the relevant statutory provisions is to be taken for the purposes of subsection (3)(b) of section 6 of the Human Rights Act 1998 (c. 42) (acts of public authorities) to be exercising a function of a public nature in doing so.

...

Section 145 of the Health and Social Care Act 2008 deals with the situation in which a care home is providing accommodation, together with nursing or personal care, by agreement with a body acting in accordance with certain statutory provisions. In these circumstances, the person running the care home is considered to be exercising functions of a public nature for the purpose of section 6(3)(b) of the HRA 1998. The effect of this is, for example, that residents of a care home who are placed there by a local authority acting pursuant to statute will be able to bring a claim under the Act against the care home, alleging a breach of their Convention rights. However, those residents who pay their own fees and have their own contract with the care home will not be protected by the HRA 1998. This means that they will not be able to make a claim against the care home alleging a breach of their Convention rights. This is because they have a private arrangement with the care home, which cannot therefore be said to be carrying out a public function. Human rights organisations have criticised this as making an unfair distinction between residents of the same care home. But nevertheless the change in the law does provide human rights protection for those residents whose care is wholly or partly publicly funded.

15.5.4 The application of *YL* in subsequent cases

In *R (on the application of Weaver) v London and Quadrant Housing Trust* [2009] EWCA 585, the Court of Appeal considered whether the Quadrant Housing Trust, a registered social landlord under the Housing Act 1996, should be considered a functional public authority. Weaver, a tenant, of the trust, wanted to challenge a possession order made against her because she had not paid her rent. She argued that this was a breach of her rights under Article 8 ECHR. To put the case in context, it is important to understand what registered social landlords do: they provide subsidised housing below the market rent to poorer sections of the community. In accordance with the housing legislation, they work closely with local authorities to achieve their statutory duties in relation to housing. The Court of Appeal, by a majority, held that the trust was a functional public authority. It took a broad and generous approach to the application of section 6(3)(b) of the HRA 1998, and it took into account the following factors when deciding that the Trust was a functional public authority:

- it was not paid for services rendered, but was granted a substantial public subsidy;
- it had a statutory duty to cooperate with the local authority;
- the provision of subsidised housing is not a private commercial activity;
- the regulation to which it is subject goes beyond ensuring good standards of performance, but tries to make sure that the government's policy objective of providing low-cost housing to vulnerable people is achieved; and
- the Trust also had charitable objectives.

The Court stressed that no one of these factors on its own was enough to make the body a public authority, but when they were considered altogether, they established that the Trust was carrying out a public function.

An interesting example of a case following the principles laid down by the House of Lords in *YL* and concluding that a body was not a public authority is *R (on the application of Francis Boyle) v Haverhill Pub Watch* [2009] EWHC 2441. This case is not about contracting out, but raises some interesting points. It concerned pubs and other licensed premises in the Haverhill area that belonged to a Pub Watch scheme to discuss matters of mutual interest. The members of the Pub Watch scheme held meetings and shared information about troublemakers in their area. The police and local authority initiated and encouraged the scheme, and its representatives attended meetings. The claimant had been labelled as a troublemaker and barred by the members of the Pub Watch scheme. He argued that this was a breach of his Convention rights to a fair hearing, because he had not been given any opportunity to rebut the allegations against him contrary to Article 6. One issue that arose was whether the decision was subject to judicial review and whether the HRA 1998 applied to the members of the Pub Watch scheme. In other words, was it carrying out functions of a public nature and was it a functional public authority under section 6(3)(b) of the HRA 1998? It was held by the court that the scheme was not a functional public authority. The court noted that the police had not taken part in the decision to ban the claimant and that 'the decision . . . had no sufficient public element, flavour or character to bring it within the purview of public law' (Mackie J at [560]). The court stressed that the involvement of the police and the local authority in the scheme was not sufficient to make the body into a public authority.

thinking point

Do you think that this case was correctly decided? The decision meant that the claimant was unable to challenge his exclusion from the pubs in his area by judicial review principles or under the HRA 1998, and that, because it is unlikely that there are any private law rights at stake, he does not appear to have any legal remedy.

These cases show that, after *YL*, the courts will look closely at the functions of the body to decide whether or not it is a public authority under section 6(3)(b) of the HRA 1998. There is no one determining factor and the courts will look at the relevant points in the round.

This section has explained that a claim, under section 6 of the HRA 1998, that a body or individual has acted unlawfully in conflict with the ECHR can be brought only against a public authority. There are two kinds of public authority. A core public authority is an 'obvious' public authority, such as a government department, the police force, and a local authority. All of its functions, whether private or public, must be exercised compatibly with Convention rights. The second kind of public authority is a functional or hybrid public authority. This is a body exercising a combination of public and private functions. Only its public functions are subject to the HRA 1998 and not its private functions. This definition has been restrictively drawn, as discussed in the context of *YL*. This means that when a local authority contracts out its powers, the contractor does not become a public authority unless there is a sufficiently public element to its functions, such as a power of coercion as in *R (on the application of A and others) v Partnerships in Care Ltd* [2002] 1 WLR 2610.

summary points

The meaning of a 'public authority' under the Human Rights Act 1998

- *An action for breach of the HRA 1998 may be brought only against a public authority, as defined in section 6.*

- *There are two types of public authority: those defined as core public authorities; and those defined as functional or hybrid public authorities.*

- *Core public authorities are obvious public authorities that are clearly linked to the state—in other words, government departments and local authorities, for example. Their functions, whether public or private, are subject to review in relation to the terms of the HRA 1998.*

- *Functional or hybrid public authorities are those that are carrying out some private and some public functions. These may be subject to review under the terms of the HRA 1998 as regards the exercise of their public functions.*

- In accordance with section 145 of the Health and Social Care Act 2008, care homes are classified as functional public authorities when they take in residents pursuant to an agreement with an authority acting under its relevant statutory powers.

- Private bodies (not core or functional/hybrid public authorities) may never be judicially reviewed in the context of the HRA 1998.

(15.6) Is the law on public functions and public authorities in need of reform?

It could be argued that the different tests for judicial review cases that do not involve human rights issues and those that do are unnecessarily complicated and have little justification in logic. However, most of the criticism of the law has focused on the courts' approach to the meaning of a public authority under the HRA 1998.

Subsequent to the decision in *YL*, as we have seen, Parliament has now intervened. Those residents of a care home whose places are funded by a local authority, acting in pursuance of its statutory duty, can make a human rights claim against the care home, because it is now considered to be a public authority. But the reasoning in *YL* is still important in deciding cases and it is argued that the narrow approach taken in *YL* may cause difficulties. This is because of the many complex arrangements into which core public authorities enter with private service providers. The approach taken by the House of Lords has generated a considerable degree of uncertainty in determining whether a body working with a statutory authority is a functional public authority.

The reasoning in *YL* may lead to situations in which clients and customers who are provided with statutory services and benefits by private service providers cannot sue the service provider directly. It is argued that this would mean that the UK is in breach of Article 13 of the ECHR, which provides that individuals (victims) have the right to an effective remedy—that they may be able to get redress for a breach. Another consequence of the narrow definition of a public authority is that people who are victims of human rights abuses may find it difficult to bring a claim because they may claim only against a public authority. The more narrow the definition of the public authority, the less likely it is that an individual will find a body that is subject to review in this way. This is inconsistent with the government's aim of ensuring that the Convention rights are enforceable in the domestic courts.

One of the main criticisms of the courts' decision is that the enforceability of the HRA 1998 depends on whether the function has been contracted out to an outside body rather than carried out by the body that has the statutory duty to provide the service in the first place. This is not something over which individuals have control, and whether human rights protection is enjoyed may simply depend on where they live and whether the local authority directly provides the service or contracts it out.

A better approach to this would be to consider private contractors delivering public services to be part of a public framework for the delivery of services and therefore bound by the HRA 1998. This would mean that the function should be considered a public one if the government has taken responsibility for it. This is the view of the dissenting judges in the House of Lords in *YL*. They applied a different test to the majority. Baroness Hale, with whose judgment Lord

Bingham concurred, stated that the test as to whether the function was a public one should be 'whether the state has assumed responsibility for seeing that this task is performed' (at [66]). In the *YL* case, the state had taken responsibility for providing care for the elderly and had provided that care at public expense.

● *YL v Birmingham City Council* [2007] UKHL 27

Baroness Hale at [71]:

[It is] artificial and legalistic to draw a distinction between meeting those needs and the task of assessing and arranging them, when the state has assumed responsibility for seeing that both are done.

She also took into account the:

...strong public interest in having people who are unable to look after themselves, whether because of old age, infirmity, mental or physical disability or youth, looked after properly.

She also noted that there was a:

close connection between the service and the core values underlying the Convention rights and the undoubted risk that rights will be violated unless adequate steps are taken to protect them.

Baroness Hale clearly favours an approach that focuses on whether the service is funded or provided so as to meet a statutory or public function, rather than whether the service has been carried out by a body that is essentially public or essentially private.

This is some support for this assessment. Palmer, commenting on the *YL* case, argues as follows.

● S. Palmer, 'Public, private and the Human Rights Act 1998: an ideological divide' (2007) 66 Cambridge Law Journal 559, 572

[95] ...The consequence of the *YL* decision is that the delivery of many formerly public services by way of contractual arrangements with private bodies is beyond the reach of human rights law and regulated solely by the private law of contract. This decision creates a lacuna for many public recipients of services. Occasions may arise where there will be no direct contractual relationship between the private service provider and the users of services. The Joint Committee on Human Rights described such recipients as 'stranded victims'.[1]

1 Joint Committee on Human Rights, *The Meaning of 'Public Authority' under the Human Rights Act* (Seventh Report, Session 2003–04, HL 39/HC 382, London: HMSO, 2004), para. 84.

However, some commentators have argued that it would be wrong to extend the definition of public authority too far. Oliver has stated that it would be unfair to impose the burden of human rights protection on private bodies and that they should not be expected to maintain the same high standards that we expect of public bodies.

● D. Oliver, 'Functions of a public nature under the Human Rights Act' [2004] Public Law 329, 340

It is entirely consistent with constitutional principle that higher standards of consideration for others, selflessness and public service are demanded of public bodies[1] than of private individuals and bodies, even when the former are not performing functions of a public nature, and that these public bodies should give primacy to the rights of individuals and subordinate their own interests to those of others.

1 See, e.g., the 'Seven Principles of Public Life' elaborated by the Committee on Standards in Public Life and widely accepted by public bodies in their codes of conduct: *First Report of the Committee on Standards in Public Life* [Cm 2850, London: HMSO, 1995] [the Nolan Report].

There have been various suggestions made for reform of the law and these include amendment of the HRA 1998. This could be achieved by rewriting the definition of public authorities to make clear that a function of a public nature includes functions carried out pursuant to an agreement or contract with a public authority acting in accordance with its duty. Another option would be to add a Schedule to the Act that comprises a list of public authorities. The Freedom of Information Act 2000 takes this approach. The government could produce greater guidance on standard terms inserted by public authorities when contracting out their services to private providers. The advantages and disadvantages of these ideas are explored by the report of the Parliamentary Joint Committee on Human Rights (2004) listed in the further reading at the end of the chapter.

After having discussed what bodies can be the subject of a judicial review, the next section will consider who can make a claim for judicial review.

15.7 The relevance of standing

15.7.1 When may an individual or organisation bring a claim for judicial review?

An individual or organisation may bring a claim for judicial review only with the **permission** of the courts (this used to be referred to as **leave**). This means that **standing** restricts the people who and organisations that may bring a judicial review claim. Some judicial review claims include human rights issues as part of the claim; others do not. There are different tests for judicial review cases depending on whether there is a human rights element; in some instances, both tests for standing will need to be applied—the one for non-human rights issues and the one for human rights issues.

The standing requirement for non-human-rights cases is set out in section 31(3) of the Senior Courts Act 1981 and has been developed further by judges in the case law. It is referred to as the '**sufficient interest** test'.

Senior Courts Act 1981

. . . .

Section 31

...

(3) No application for judicial review shall be made unless the leave of the High Court has been obtained in accordance with rules of court; and the court shall not grant leave to make such an application unless it considers that the applicant has a sufficient interest in the matter to which the application relates.

The test for standing in human rights judicial review cases is stricter than in non-judicial review cases. It is set out in the HRA 1998 and is often referred to as 'the victim test' (see later in the chapter).

NOTE

It is important that, for each potential judicial review claim, you ask yourself: is there an element of **illegality**, **irrationality**, or **procedural impropriety**? If so, apply the 'sufficient interest test'. Is there a human rights issue being argued in the claim? If so, refer to the victim test contained in the HRA 1998. If there are both non-human-rights and human rights elements, then you must argue both.

Decisions made by public bodies often affect a large number of individuals or groups. They may affect individuals and groups in different ways, both positively and negatively, and directly and indirectly. There is the potential for very large numbers of cases to be brought if there is no restriction on the people and groups who may bring a claim. Sometimes, a decision will directly affect the individual concerned, for example someone may have his or her application for welfare benefit refused, or may be refused housing by the local authority. This decision will have an immediate and negative impact on that individual. On other occasions, the impact of a decision will be broader and may affect people differently. If, for example, a local authority grants planning permission for a housing development in an area of natural beauty in Dorset, this decision might cause concern to various categories of individuals and groups. It may anger nearby residents, whose view of the area of natural beauty is obscured, and upset people who walk their dogs in the area. Objections might come from environmental groups, such as Greenpeace or the National Trust, which will be concerned to preserve areas of natural beauty. A millionaire in Aberdeen, who has read about the development in the newspaper, may be willing to fund a court claim to challenge the decision. At the same time, the grant of planning permission may be approved of by a housing developer and local businesses, which may view the housing development as a way of providing homes for workers in local factories and out-of-town supermarkets. Different people may welcome and may object to the same decision.

One approach is to allow all citizens to bring a claim for judicial review. This is sometimes referred to as a 'citizens' claim'. In these circumstances, whether a claim for judicial review is successful will depend entirely on the merits of the case. Such an approach would make sure that the decisions of all government bodies were open to question in the courts even where no individual was affected by the decision. The rules of standing would be abolished.

Yet there are disadvantages to this approach. The main problem is that it could lead to an excessive amount of expensive litigation. The cost would be borne by the public purse and there might be unnecessary disruption to the work of public authorities. Other disadvantages to the abolition of standing or adopting a very broad test of standing are the over-involvement of judges in political and policy decisions that, it is argued, are best left to the democratically elected government to decide. Cases brought by public interest groups to further their causes are regarded as particularly problematic by some commentators and will be discussed below.

15.7.2 How do the courts deal with standing?

As stated earlier, a claimant applying for judicial review in a non-human-rights case must have a 'sufficient interest' in the claim. The introduction of this term led to the simplification of the previous laws whereby the rules of standing varied depending on the remedies sought. The case of *R v Inland Revenue Commissioners, ex p National Federation of Self-Employed and Small Businesses Ltd* [1982] AC 617 laid down the principles that the courts use to determine whether claimants have a sufficient interest. The case has also led to the development of a broader, more inclusive law on standing.

The National Federation of Self-Employed and Small Business Ltd (the Federation) challenged a decision of the Inland Revenue not to collect back taxes from a group of workers described as the 'Fleet Street casuals' (the case is often referred to as the *Fleet Street Casuals case* as a result). The Fleet Street casuals were workers in the printing industry who filled in false or imaginary names, such as 'Mickey Mouse' and 'Donald Duck', when collecting their pay. This meant that the Inland Revenue could not collect taxes from them, because they did not know who they were and could not match up their pay against tax records. When the Inland Revenue discovered this irregularity, it arranged, after negotiations with the employer and trade union, for the workers to register so that taxes could be collected for future earnings. It granted an 'amnesty' in relation to the lost taxes for previous years, meaning that it would not investigate or penalise any of the Fleet Street casuals who had not paid taxes previously, but it expected the taxes to be paid properly in future. A group known as the Federation of Small Businesses objected to this arrangement on the grounds that, in other cases involving its members, the Inland Revenue had not granted an amnesty. It challenged the Inland Revenue's decision and asked the court for a declaration that the Inland Revenue had acted unlawfully in failing to collect the back taxes. It also applied for an order of mandamus to assess and collect income tax from the casual workers. This order would have had the effect of requiring the Inland Revenue to collect the money that it was owed from the Fleet Street casuals.

The Divisional Court (the first-instance court) refused to grant the Federation permission to bring the case on the basis that it did not have a sufficient interest in the matter. It dealt with standing as a preliminary issue before it made a decision on the merits of the legal points raised by the Federation. The Court of Appeal allowed the appeal on the basis that the Federation did have a sufficient interest. The Inland Revenue then appealed to the House of Lords. The House of Lords decided in favour of the Inland Revenue. All five Law Lords held that the Inland Revenue had acted lawfully and that the Federation did not have a sufficient interest. However, the House of Lords went on to make significant comments on the law of standing.

The House of Lords criticised the lower courts for dealing with standing as a preliminary issue at the leave stage (now called the permission stage). Only obviously hopeless or unmeritorious cases should be weeded out at the beginning; others should be allowed to be heard in full. Generally, the sufficient interest questions should be decided in the context of the legal and factual issues in the case. An extract from Lord Wilberforce's judgment follows.

● ***R v Inland Revenue Commissioners, ex p National Federation of Self-Employed and Small Businesses Ltd*** [1982] AC 617 (the *Fleet Street Casuals case*)

Lord Wilberforce at 630:

> There may be simple cases in which it can be seen at the earliest stage that the person applying for judicial review has no interest at all, or no sufficient interest to support the application: then it would be quite correct at the threshold to refuse him leave to apply. The right to do so is an important safeguard against the courts being flooded and public bodies harassed by irresponsible applications. But in other cases this will not be so...the question of sufficient interest cannot, in such cases, be considered in the abstract, or as an isolated point: it must be taken together with the legal and factual context. The rule requires sufficient interest in the matter to which the application relates. This, in the present case, necessarily involves the whole question of the duties of the Inland Revenue and the breaches or failure of those duties of which the respondents complain...
>
> The Federation's case against the Inland Revenue was not hopeless. However, when the court examined the relevant statutory framework it concluded that it was lawful for the Inland Revenue to exercise a managerial discretion not to collect taxes. It had properly concluded that it would not be cost effective to try to collect the back taxes. In addition, the court noted

The Parties to a Judicial Review

that the legislation provided for confidentiality in the collection of taxes. It therefore followed, that in general, one taxpayer could not challenge the tax assessment of another.

After examining the law and facts, the House of Lords dismissed the Federation's case. However, several of the Law Lords went on to say that if there had been a serious breach of the law, then the courts might have found in favour of the Federation. This is interesting, because it suggests that standing is partly dependent upon how important or serious is the issue that has been brought before the court. This point of view was most clearly stated by Lord Diplock.

● *R v Inland Revenue Commissioners, ex p National Federation of Self-Employed and Small Businesses Ltd* [1982] AC 617

Lord Diplock at 644:

It would, in my view, be a grave lacuna in our system of public law if a pressure group, like the federation, or even a single public-spirited taxpayer, were prevented by outdated technical rules of locus standi from bringing the matter to the attention of the court to vindicate the rule of law and get the unlawful conduct stopped.

These statements indicate that, in some circumstances, the law of standing has merged with the merits of the case. This means that if the claimant can show that the body has acted unlawfully, the courts will review the case even though the claimant may have only a remote connection to the case. This broadens the test for standing in non-human-rights judicial review claims. The case brought by the World Development Movement discussed below is an example of this.

thinking point

Why does Lord Diplock think it would be wrong for the technical rules of standing to prevent people from bringing unlawful conduct to the attention of the court? Why does he mention the rule of law? Review Chapter 4 on the rule of law.

15.7.3 To what extent can public-spirited individuals and interest groups bring a judicial review claim?

There are examples of both public-spirited individuals and interest groups being granted permission to bring judicial review claims. In *R v Secretary of State for the Foreign and Commonwealth Affairs, ex p Rees-Mogg* [1994] QB 552, Lord Rees-Mogg was able to challenge the British government's ratification of the Maastricht Treaty. He was held to have a sufficient interest because the court accepted 'without question that Lord Rees-Mogg brings the proceedings because of his sincere concern for constitutional issues' (Lloyd LJ, at 564). Public-spirited citizens have also been able to challenge the grant of planning permission. In *R v Somerset County Council and ARC Southern Limited, ex p Dixon* [1998] Env LR 111, Dixon was held to have a sufficient interest to challenge the grant of conditional planning permission to ARC Southern Limited to extend its limestone extraction operation at a quarry in Somerset. Dixon was a local resident, a parish councillor, and a member of various local government and environmental associations. Sedley J rejected the argument that standing should be denied because Dixon had no interest as a landowner and possessed no personal right or interest threatened by the quarrying.

Interest groups (sometimes called 'pressure groups', or 'non-government organisations', or NGOs) have also been granted standing to bring claims for judicial review. A public interest group is an organisation that attempts to influence public policy or to promote a cause or a political position. After the House of Lords' decision in the *Fleet Street Casuals case*, there have been many cases in which public interest groups have been held by the courts to have a 'sufficient interest' in challenging the decision of a public body. In part, this is because pressure groups or NGOs may have a level of expertise that may be very useful to the court when trying to weigh evidence and reach a decision. The Child Poverty Action Group (CPAG) was granted standing to challenge a decision of the Secretary of State for Social Services that had an impact on a large number of claimants of supplementary benefits. In *R v Secretary of State for Social Services, ex p Child Poverty Action Group* [1989] 1 All ER 1047, Lord Woolf emphasised the importance of the issues being raised in the case, the fact that individual claimants were unlikely to bring a challenge themselves, and the fact that the CPAG had an interest in bringing this case, effectively in their place, because it played an important role in giving guidance and advice, and providing assistance to claimants in similar types of case. This is not an isolated instance. Standing has been granted to the environmental group Greenpeace in a number of cases to challenge public body decisions. In *R v Inspectorate of Pollution, ex p Greenpeace (No 2)* [1994] 4 All ER 329, Greenpeace challenged a decision to vary a licence given to British Nuclear Fuels Ltd (BNFL) to allow it to test a new method of reprocessing nuclear waste at its Sellafield Plant in Cumbria. Greenpeace argued that this variation was contrary to the Radioactive Substances Act 1960. The court rejected the challenge, but the judge held that Greenpeace did have standing to challenge the decision. The judge took into account the fact that Greenpeace was an 'entirely responsible and respected body within a genuine concern for the environment'. Its credentials were shown by its observer status at various international bodies. The worldwide membership of Greenpeace was noted, as well as the interest of the 2,500 members who lived in the Cumbria region. The judge also considered the expertise that Greenpeace could offer and that it would be difficult for individuals to mount a challenge.

Another notable case in which the court applied the 'sufficient interest' test in a broad way was *R v Secretary of State for Foreign and Commonwealth Affairs, ex p The World Development Movement Ltd*. The World Development Movement, an NGO, challenged the decision of the Secretary of State for Foreign and Commonwealth Affairs (the Foreign Secretary) to grant aid to the Malaysian government to build the Pergau Dam. The basis for its challenge was, it argued, that the Foreign Secretary's decision was contrary to section 1(1) of the Overseas Development and Co-operation Act 1980, which permitted aid to be granted only for economically viable projects. The Pergau Dam project had been described by economists as economically unsound. When deciding whether the World Development Movement had standing, the court placed emphasis on the merits of the case and the nature of the case against the Foreign Secretary. The court did not apparently focus on the World Development Movement's interest in the matter. The court stressed that the World Development Movement was a well-respected organisation with considerable expertise. If the claimant had not applied for judicial review, it was likely that the illegal decision would have gone unchallenged, because there did not appear to be any obvious group or individual to question the legality of the decision. The judge listed in detail the factors that led him to hold that the World Development Movement had a sufficient interest. Many of these relate to the organisation's breadth and depth of membership, the way in which it was financed, its role and functions both nationally and internationally, and its level of respect around the world.

However, it cannot be assumed that standing will automatically be granted in every case. In *R v Secretary of State for the Environment, ex p Rose Theatre Trust Company* [1990] 1 All ER 756, the Rose Theatre Trust Company was denied standing to challenge the refusal of the Secretary of State for the Environment to register the archaeological remains of the Rose Theatre on the schedule of monuments. This schedule was maintained under the Ancient Monuments and Archaeological Area Act 1979 and was intended to preserve monuments of national importance. The remains of the theatre, where two of Shakespeare's plays had first been performed, had been uncovered during the development of a site in London. The Rose Theatre Company included distinguished archaeologists, writers, and actors, who had formed a company specifically to preserve the remains of the theatre and to make it accessible to the public. The Trust had been formed after the theatre remains had been found and so was not a pre-existing group. This proved to be very important. The judge held that none of the individuals in their own right would have had the necessary standing to challenge the decision, and that consequently a trust created by individuals for the purposes of challenging the decision could not have standing either; the formation of a group did not change the fact that no one had standing. The group did not generate standing by virtue of being a group, but instead by being able to stand in the place of someone who did have standing. Schiemann J was not troubled that a potential illegality might go unchecked. He held that 'the law does not see it as the function of the courts to be there for every individual who is interested in having the legality of an administrative action litigated' (at 522). This case reflects a very narrow view of standing and has been much criticised. In general, the courts have adopted the broader approach illustrated by the decisions to grant Greenpeace and the World Development Movement standing—but be aware that the question of standing for groups is by no means certain.

summary points

The relevance of standing

- *Only hopeless claims will be rejected on the grounds of standing at the permission stage.*
- *Standing will be considered at the full hearing of the case and should not be considered to be a preliminary matter independent of the merits of the case.*
- *The court will consider the facts, the statute in question, the relevant case law, the claimant's interest in the matter, and whether the case raises general matters of public importance.*
- *The court may be prepared to grant standing if it is established that the public body has acted unlawfully.*
- *Standing will not depend on the remedy asked for, but on the claimant's interest in the case.*

15.8 # What are the rules of standing in HRA 1998 cases?

For judicial review cases that raise human rights issues, there is a different test for standing: the sufficient interest test is not applied for the aspect of any judicial review claim that relates to the operation of the HRA 1998 or the domestic application of the ECHR. Section 7 of the HRA 1998 sets out the test that is applied, commonly termed the 'victim test' because only victims can bring a claim against a public authority that has unlawfully breached their rights.

Human Rights Act 1998

Section 7

(1) A person who claims that a public authority has acted (or proposes to act) in a way which is made unlawful by section 6(1) may—

    (a) bring proceedings against the authority under this Act in the appropriate court or tribunal, or

(b) rely on the Convention right or rights concerned in any legal proceedings, but only if he is (or would be) a victim of the unlawful act.

…

(3) If the proceedings are brought on an application for judicial review, the applicant is to be taken to have a sufficient interest in relation to the unlawful act only if he is, or would be, a victim of that act.

…

(7) For the purposes of this section, a person is a victim of an unlawful act only if he would be a victim for the purposes of Article 34 of the Convention if proceedings were brought in the European Court of Human Rights in respect of that act.

The victim test mirrors the test for standing in Article 34 ECHR, from which the human rights are derived. Usually, this is a straightforward requirement to satisfy. A person will be a victim where they are actually affected by the violation of the Convention. But there are some areas of uncertainty. So, in the ECtHR case *Marckx v Belgium* (1979–80) 2 EHRR 330, the applicant, an unmarried mother, challenged Belgian laws that discriminated against illegitimate children contrary to Article 8 of the Convention. The Court rejected the government's argument that she and her child had not suffered as a result of such laws, and stated that an applicant is entitled to claim that 'a law violates their rights by itself, in the absence of an individual measure of implementation, if they run the risk of being directly affected by it'.

A recent example in which the courts denied standing in a human rights claim on the grounds that the claimant was not a victim was *JR1's Application* [2011] NIQB 5. It concerned a challenge to the decision of the Chief Constable of Northern Ireland to introduce taser guns to the police service. It was argued on behalf of the claimant, an 8-year-old child, that she was a victim in accordance with section 7 of the HRA 1998. She feared that there was a risk that her right to life under Article 2 of the Convention would be infringed if taser guns were used by the police in Northern Ireland. This was because she lived in an area of West Belfast where there was public disorder from time to time, making it more likely that taser guns would be used by the police to restore order. She was also the granddaughter of a woman who had been killed by a plastic bullet fired by the police in 1981 and, it was argued, as a child, she was more vulnerable to injury from a taser gun than an adult. The court rejected the argument that she was a victim, because she was not directly affected by the decision to use taser guns. A very brief extract from the judgment is set out below.

● *JR1's Application* [2011] NIQB 5

Morgan KCJ:

[41] In this case no factual scenario was put forward which raised any material risk that this applicant would be exposed to the possible use of a taser. I do not accept that it can be said that this applicant was directly affected by the decision to deploy and authorise the use of tasers either on a pilot basis or permanently and I conclude, therefore, that she is not a victim for the purpose of the Human Rights Act 1998.

The case shows that general challenges to a policy decision of a public authority cannot be brought under the HRA 1998. The claimant must show that he or she has been directly affected by the act or omission by the public authority.

There has been some uncertainty as to whether the victim test applies to those who make a claim for a declaration of incompatibility under section 4 of the HRA 1998 or to those who ask

These cases are described in more depth on the Online Resource Centre.

the courts to use their interpretive powers under section 3. The case law is conflicted here, with one case refusing to allow a claim for a declaration of incompatibility under section 4 because the claimant was not a victim (*Lancashire County Council v Taylor* [2005] EWCA 284), and another in which the House of Lords indicated that it would take a more flexible approach to standing (*R (on the application of Rusbridger) v Attorney General* [2003] UKHL 37). It is unlikely that this issue will be resolved until it is decided by the House of Lords.

---

thinking point

Review sections 3 and 4 of the HRA 1998 as set out in Chapter 9. Why there might be some doubt as to the application of the 'victim' test to these sections?

It is important to note that the victim test is narrower than the test of sufficient interest in non-human-rights judicial review cases. It excludes the possibility of interest groups directly challenging the decisions of public authorities under the HRA 1998 unless those groups are victims. As a consequence of this approach, an interest group or other organisation can bring a claim only if the group itself is alleging that it is the victim of the breach of the Convention—that the group has had its group rights breached by the action, omission, or decision. For an example of this, you may want to look at the case of *Open Door Counselling Ltd and Dublin Well Woman Centre v Ireland* (1993) 15 EHRR 244, which offers evidence that it is possible for an interest group to meet the victim test in relation to a breach of its 'own' rights.

---

summary points

What are the rules of standing in HRA 1998 cases?

- *To bring a claim under section 7 of the HRA 1998, the claimant must be a victim.*
- *A victim is someone directly affected by the act or omission, or someone who runs the risk of being directly affected.*
- *The test of standing in human rights judicial review cases is stricter than in non-human-rights judicial review cases.*
- *An interest group cannot bring a public interest group challenge under the HRA 1998 unless it is a victim of the act or omission.*
- *To bring a claim for a declaration of incompatibility under section 4 of the HRA 1998, the claimant does not have to be a victim, but has to have suffered some adverse affect.*

15.9 Third-party interventions

Interest groups and individuals who do not want to become involved in costly court proceedings, or who do not have full standing, may be able to use alternative methods to participate in court proceedings. Interest groups might support an individual who is a victim or who has an interest in bringing a case by giving advice or financial support. However, in recent years, it has become increasingly popular for interest groups to present their views to the court by making a third-party intervention—that is, a situation in which the court grants permission to a third party to give an opinion or to provide information to the court. The third party may usefully contribute advice, information, or expertise because of its work in the relevant area. Most third-party interventions are in the form of written opinions or briefs, but sometimes a third party might instruct counsel to present its views orally to the court. The court has **discretion** to grant applications for third-party interventions under the CPR Part 54. Interventions in the Supreme Court are dealt with by section 26 of the Supreme Court Rules 2009.

cross reference
See Chapter 16 for more on discretion.

discretion   The court's choice regarding a course of action.

One justification for allowing third-party interventions is that a decision in a case may not only affect the parties before the court, but may also have wider implications for those not present at the court hearing. Decisions may also have possible social, political, and economic consequences that are not immediately obvious to the court, especially decisions of the higher courts. Cases on terrorism or press freedom, for example, may establish important human rights principles that affect many different groups, and which are of concern to interest groups and society as a whole. The decision of the House of Lords in *YL (by her litigation friend the Official Solicitor) (FC) v Birmingham City Council and others* (cited above) involved the Lords in deciding whether a nursing home that cared for the elderly was a public authority for the purposes of the HRA 1998. The actual dispute in question was between the nursing home and a resident, supported by her family, who objected to her eviction and wanted to use the HRA 1998 to challenge the decision of the nursing home. However, the case raised important principles about the protection of the elderly and the disabled across the UK—namely, whether services contracted out by public bodies to private bodies were subject to the HRA 1998. There were oral interventions by groups including Justice, Liberty, and Help the Aged.

NOTE For more information about the Equality and Human Rights Commission, visit http://www.equality humanrights .com/

There may also be interventions by interested government departments and other quasi-government bodies, such as the Equality and Human Rights Commission. They will normally intervene where the case is one of importance, and when their knowledge and expertise may assist the court. The powers of the Commission are derived from the Equalities Act 2010.

475

summary points

Third-party interventions

- *Interest groups and individuals who lack standing can present their views, and provide expertise and information that may not otherwise be before the court.*
- *Individuals and interest groups may choose to make a third-party intervention in an on-going dispute rather than to bring an expensive action in their own names.*

👁 Summary

This chapter has considered against whom a judicial review claim can be brought and who can bring a claim for judicial review.

An action for judicial review can be brought only against a body exercising a public function (Part 54 of the Civil Procedure Rules). The *Datafin* case established that it is the nature of the power rather than the source of the power that is important. The courts take into account a variety of different factors when deciding whether the function is of a public nature, as illustrated by the cases discussed in this chapter. If public authorities are carrying out a private function, they are not subject to judicial review unless there is a public law element. Private bodies are, generally, not subject to judicial review unless it can be shown that they are carrying out a public function, such as administering a statutory scheme. Private bodies that contract with local authorities to provide services are not generally exercising public functions

If the judicial review concerns human rights, then the claim must be brought against a public authority (under section 6 of the HRA 1998). The HRA 1998 creates two kinds of public authorities: core public authorities and functional public authorities. Core public authorities are obvious public authorities, such as government departments and the police force (*Aston Cantlow*). Both the private and public functions of core authorities are subject to the HRA 1998. Functional public authorities have private and public functions, but, unlike core public authorities, only their public functions are subject to the Act. The courts have adopted a narrow test when deciding whether a public function exists. Therefore, when a private body contracts with a public authority to provide services, the private body is not usually bound by the HRA 1998 (*YL*). This means that such bodies are not subject to judicial review in either human rights or non-human-rights judicial review cases. As a result of the courts' decisions, the number of bodies that have to comply with the Act is reduced, and there has been a vigorous debate amongst politicians, lawyers, and academics as to whether and in what way the law should be changed.

The rules of standing in judicial review cases determine whether individuals or groups are permitted to challenge a decision of a public body. The rules of standing in non-human-rights judicial review cases are applied flexibly subsequent to the *Fleet Street Casuals case*. Individuals and interest groups which can show that there is merit in their case will, subject to the courts' discretion, be granted standing. As regards human rights issues raised in judicial review claims, only the victims or the potential victims of the act, the omission, or the decision may be granted standing. The victim test has its origins in Article 34 ECHR and the courts will follow the Strasbourg jurisprudence. Individuals and groups will be granted standing if they are directly affected by the alleged act or omission, or if they run the risk of being affected by it. Interest groups cannot bring public interest challenges as is sometimes possible in non-human rights judicial review cases. Third-party interventions provide an alternative mechanism for interest groups and interested individuals to present their views to the court, and enable the court to benefit from their expertise, albeit using the vehicle of a case brought by someone else. Although some commentators have criticised their use, they have become much more popular in recent years. The consequence of these changes is that it is much easier for public-spirited individuals and interest groups to access the courts.

This chapter has illustrated the special nature of judicial review proceedings. It has explained that a claim for judicial review may be brought only against a body exercising public functions or a public authority. It has also made clear that a claimant in a judicial review case must have a sufficient interest to bring the case. The following chapters will explain the grounds of review and the remedies that might be granted by the Administrative Court.

❓ Questions

1 Do you think that the law should make a distinction between the public and the private spheres?

2 Can you explain the meaning of a function of a public nature for the purposes of a non-human-rights judicial review case?

3 Can you give examples of bodies or powers that the courts regard as private and have refused to judicially review?

4 Explain the House of Lords' reasoning in the *YL* case.

5 Do you think the criticism of the courts' reasoning in the *YL* case is justified?

6 Why cannot any citizen challenge a decision with which he or she disagrees? After all, do not all citizens have an interest in ensuring that government and public bodies act lawfully?

7 Are the different tests of standing for judicial review cases and human rights judicial review cases justified? Refer to the relevant case law in your answer.

8 What are the arguments for and against allowing third parties to intervene in court proceedings?

9 Consider the following problem.

Reclaim is an imaginary organisation providing schooling for children excluded from mainstream school. Reclaim was created in 2004 by several local authorities in south-east England. Students at the school are funded by their local authority, although Reclaim also receives significant charitable donations. There are also some students whose fees are paid privately by their parents. Reclaim was intended to help local authorities who were having difficulties fulfilling their statutory obligation to provide a suitable education for all under-16-year-olds. Half of the members of the Reclaim board of management are also local authority officials. Reclaim has to comply with the Imaginary (Service Providers) Standards Act 2002. This provides detailed regulation about the running of such schools. All students and parents are asked to sign a 'home school agreement' by which students agree to attend all classes and to be of good behaviour. Samuel, a pupil at the school, has been excluded for poor behaviour. He wants to challenge his exclusion by way of judicial review. Samuel's lawyer, Miss Mina, thinks that the decision can be challenged on the grounds of procedural impropriety because Samuel was denied the opportunity to defend himself. She also thinks that he has been denied the right to education contrary to Article 2 of the First Protocol to the ECHR, and wants to make a claim under the HRA 1998. However, Miss Mina is not sure whether Reclaim's functions are private or public in nature.

Write a fully reasoned opinion for Miss Mina, giving your view as to whether or not Reclaim can be the subject of a claim for judicial review, including a claim under the HRA 1998. Refer to the relevant case law on the nature of public functions and public authorities discussed in this chapter.

Further reading

Arshi, M. and O'Cinneide, C., 'Third-party intervention: the public interest reaffirmed' [2004] Public Law 69

The authors discuss the use of third-party interventions and argue in support of their use in litigation.

Bailey, S. H., 'Judicial review of contracting decisions' (2007) Public Law 444

In this article, the author discusses the circumstances in which the decision of a public authority to exercise its contractual powers is subject to judicial review.

Cane, P., 'Standing up for the public' [1995] Public Law 276

The author discusses and categorises public-interest challenges in judicial review claims, as well as comments on the developing case law on standing and proposals for reform.

Hannett, S., 'Third-party interventions: in the public interest?' [2003] Public Law 128

The author presents her research on the increased use of third-party interventions in litigation and argues that interventions may distort judicial proceedings.

Harlow, C., ' "Public" and "private" law: definition without distinction' (1980) 43 Modern Law Review 241

This is an interesting historical article presenting an alternative viewpoint. It argues against the emerging distinction between private and public law.

Harlow, C., 'Popular law and popular justice' (2002) 65 Modern Law Review 1

This piece discusses the liberalisation of the rules of standing and the increased use of third-party interventions. It cautions against the blurring of the legal and political forums, arguing that courts must remain within legal boundaries.

Oliver, D., 'Functions of a public nature under the Human Rights Act' [2004] Public Law 329

Oliver discusses the definition of a 'public authority' under the Human Rights Act 1998 and is generally in favour of a narrow interpretation of the term.

Palmer, S., 'Public, private and the Human Rights Act 1998: an ideological divide' (2007) 66 Cambridge Law Journal 559

Palmer discusses the background to the House of Lords' decision in the case of *YL* and expresses concern at the decision of the court to avoid dealing with the human rights implications of the case by classifying it as private.

Parliamentary Joint Committee on Human Rights, *The Meaning of Public Authority under the Human Rights Act* (Seventh Report, 2003–04 Session, HL 39/HC 382, London: HMSO, March 2004)

The report provides a thorough analysis of the definition of a 'public authority' under the Human Rights Act 1998. It considers the consequences of the adoption by the courts of a consistently narrow approach and notes that this has led to a gap in human rights protection. It discusses how this situation might be remedied.

Schiemann, K., '*Locus standi*' [1990] Public Law 342

Although this is a rather dated article, it does provide a concise account of the advantages and disadvantages of widening the rules of standing.

Illegality

Introduction

This chapter is the third substantive chapter on judicial review. It will focus on illegality. Illegality is a very broad ground of review and covers a wide range of possible abuses of power by public authorities. Lord Diplock defined the term 'illegality' as one of the three possible grounds of review, alongside irrationality and procedural impropriety.

● *Council for the Civil Service Unions v Minister for the Civil Service* [1985] AC 374

Lord Diplock at 410:

> By 'illegality' as a ground for judicial review I mean that the decision-maker must understand correctly the law that regulates his decision-making power and must give effect to it. Whether he has or not is par excellence a justiciable question to be decided, in the event of dispute, by those persons, the judges, by whom the judicial power of the state is exercisable.

This is a very general description and covers a very wide range of possible wrongs that can be committed by a body exercising a public function. It brings them together under one heading. This chapter will give a detailed explanation of illegality and describe the circumstances in which illegality can be used as a ground of challenge. It will begin with a description of the simple ultra vires principle. The central role that discretion plays in administrative decision-making will be explained. It will then go on to illustrate the various ways in which abuse of discretion can occur. The chapter will also consider the issue of jurisdiction. In particular, the distinction between errors of law and errors of fact will be described and illustrated by considering the relevant case law.

16.1 Illegality and simple ultra vires

Public authorities must not go beyond their legal powers or they will be acting **ultra vires**, meaning without legal authority. This has already been discussed in Chapter 4 on the **rule of law**. Wade and Forsyth explain this principle clearly.

ultra vires

Latin meaning 'outside power'. To be lawful, a public authority must act intra vires ('within power').

● **H. W. R. Wade and C. F. Forsyth,** *Administrative Law* (8th edn, Oxford: Oxford University Press, 2000), p. 35

> The simple proposition that a public authority may not act outside its powers (ultra vires) might fitly be called the central principle of administrative law[1] . . . To a large extent the courts

The essence of the ultra vires rule is that the authority has gone beyond its legal powers or used its powers in a way that the court regards as unlawful. It is from this principle that the courts have built up a large body of principles that are covered by the three grounds of review restated by Lord Diplock in the *CCSU* case (above) and which are largely applied on an application for **judicial** review.

Ultra vires is a very general term and, in its most general sense, it means simply that the public authority has acted unlawfully. So once a claimant can show that one of the grounds of review is established, it is said that the authority has acted ultra vires or unlawfully. In the early case law, the term ultra vires was used more frequently. The term is still in use, but now the authority is often just said to have acted illegally, irrationally, or procedurally improperly, or there is said to have been a breach of the **European Convention on Human Rights (ECHR)** contrary to the Human Rights Act 1998 (HRA 1998). These individual terms are more precise, because they explain subsets of ultra vires, rather than the concept of judicial review itself.

16.1.1 Illegality and acting beyond power

Thus far, we have considered that ultra vires is a term used to describe unlawful actions by public authorities. Over time, judicial review developed to recognise different forms of ultra vires and these were gradually identified under different headings. These headings were developed by judges, because judicial review is primarily judge-made rather than a creature of parliamentary intervention. Consequently, with a number of judges developing the area over time, there is variation in the use of vocabulary. These different usages persist. For the remainder of this book, we shall use the individual terms of **illegality**, **irrationality**, **procedural impropriety**, and, where appropriate, 'breach of the rules of **natural justice**' and 'breach of the ECHR contrary to the HRA 1998'. This is in preference to ultra vires, which is the broad overarching heading that explains the concept of abuse or lack of power. But you will see the term 'ultra vires' being used in the case law to mean both the broad meaning and also a form of illegality—simple ultra vires. We shall consider this next before we move on to discuss other forms of illegality.

The most straightforward illustration of the simple ultra vires principle is demonstrated by cases in which public authorities are found to have undertaken activities for which they have no legal authority. A case from the early twentieth century is often referred to as an example. In *Attorney General v Fulham Corporation* [1921] 1 Ch 440, the local authority had the power to establish baths, wash-houses, and open bathing spaces pursuant to the Baths and Wash-houses Acts 1846–78. It set up a municipal laundry that everyone could use, but corporation employees operated the relevant machinery. It was held by the court that the authority had gone beyond the powers it had been granted in the statute. The court held that the statute permitted Fulham Corporation only to provide the facilities for people to wash their clothes; the statute did not permit the authority to create a facility where clothes were washed, totally or partially, by corporation employees. The court was called upon to consider the meaning of the statute, and its principal purpose and related purposes. If the activity of washing clothes had been found to be reasonably incidental or consequential to the main statutory power to create a bath and wash-house, then the court might have held that the corporation's decision to create the laundry was lawful under what has become known as the 'fairly incidental rule'. This rule allows the court to read into, or to imply, a secondary power where it is clearly linked to the primary power and does not overshadow the primary power. But here, the court held that this was not the case, as the following extract shows.

. . . .

● *Attorney General v Fulham Corporation* [1921] 1 Ch 440

Mr Justice Sargant at 454–5:

> ... [T]he matter turns on this, whether or not the Council has, either expressly or impliedly, power to conduct the operation which it is conducting. In my judgment, neither expressly nor impliedly, under the Acts on which it relies, has it that power, and accordingly the plaintiff is entitled to succeed.
>
> There will therefore be a declaration that the defendant corporation is not entitled to carry on any enterprise which carries into execution the report of the Committee, or which involves the total or partial washing of clothes for others by the defendant corporation, as distinguished from facilities for enabling others to come to the wash-house to wash their clothes;

16.1.2 Illegality and discretionary power

So far, we have considered situations in which a public authority has done something and there has not been the legal power to authorise that action. However, another situation that is fraught with danger in judicial review terms is that in which a public authority is given the power to do something, but is not required to act. Should the authority act, or should it choose not to act? This is what is known as having a **discretion**. Discretion is a central part of modern administration and it is therefore very important to understand the meaning of 'discretionary power'. Very often, applications for judicial review are complaints by individuals about the exercise of discretion by public authorities. Many statutes confer discretion on a public authority. This means that the public authority has a choice as to the action it takes. A local authority, for example, may grant or refuse a licence for a taxi service, or it may grant or refuse housing to a claimant. If a statute says that a public authority *must* do something, then the authority has no choice—it must do as the law requires. If it does not do as instructed, then it will be a simple ultra vires, because the authority does not have the legal power to refuse to act. But more often the public authority will be told that it *may* do something, meaning that it has a choice, because it has been conferred with a discretion. Some examples of discretionary powers are set out below.

> **Gambling Act 2005**
> . . . .
>
> (1) The [Gambling] Commission may issue operating licences in accordance with the provisions of this Part.
>
> (2) An operating licence is a licence which states that it authorises the licensee—
>
> (a) to operate a casino (a 'casino operating licence'),
>
> (b) to provide facilities for playing bingo (a 'bingo operating licence'), ...

> **Immigration Act 1971**
>
> . . . .
>
> **Section 3**
>
> ...
>
> (5) (a) A person who is not a British citizen is liable to deportation from the United Kingdom if—
>
>   ... The Secretary of State deems his deportation to be conducive to the public good; ...

Provisions such as the above indicate that the authority has to exercise discretion—in other words, it has to make a choice. Exercising discretion does not mean that the authority must do what is asked of it—that is, grant the licence—but it does mean that it must consider whether to act or not. It may grant the licence, but it may refuse it. The claimant does not have a right to the licence and the authority does not have a duty to grant it. The claimant has to apply and await the decision of the public authority. Cane explains the distinction between a discretionary power and a duty.

. . . .

● **P. Cane, *Administrative Law*** (Oxford: Oxford University Press, 2004), p. 185

> The essence of discretion is choice; the antithesis of discretion is duty. The idea of 'decision making' implies an element of choice: duty does away with the need to make decisions. Duty removes discretion; but discretion may also be limited without being entirely removed, by standards or guidelines or criteria which the decision maker is to take into account in exercising discretion. Discretion can also be limited by the specification of ends or purposes which the decision-maker is to pursue in exercising discretion. Duties impose rigid limits on the exercise of discretion whereas standards, guidelines, criteria and the specification of purposes to be achieved impose flexible limits which preserve some choice to the decision maker.

Cane explains that a duty imposes a rigid obligation, whereas discretion is more open-ended. However, the exercise of discretion may be constrained or structured. The relevant statute may lay down certain criteria that the public authority has to take into account when making its choice or exercising its discretion, or it may require the authority to draw up a code of practice explaining how choices are made between claimants. But on other occasions the wording is very vague and general. In the absence of statutory guidance, can the public authority decide the application in any way it wants, and who can check that the authority has exercised its power properly? So, for example, can the authority refuse or grant housing on any ground it pleases? Can it refuse housing to anyone who has red hair or who is an accountant? Can it take into account the fact that the claimant is a Labour Party voter or has a relation who works for the authority? These sorts of question have been considered by the courts and the principles of administrative law have emerged from the courts' decision on these questions.

Cane also discusses the advantages and disadvantages of the use of discretion.

. . . .

● **P. Cane, *Administrative Law*** (Oxford: Oxford University Press, 2004), p. 187

> Discretion has both advantages and disadvantages... Discretion has the advantage of flexibility; it allows the merits of individual cases to be taken into account. Discretion is concerned with the spirit, not the letter of the law, and it may allow government policies to be more effectively implemented by giving administrators freedom to adapt their methods of working in the light of experience. It is useful in new areas of government activity as it enables administrators to deal with novel and perhaps unforeseen circumstances as they arise.

He goes on to explain that discretion also has disadvantages.

● **P. Cane, _Administrative Law_** (Oxford: Oxford University Press, 2004), p. 187

On the other hand, discretion puts the citizen much more at the mercy of the administrator, especially if the latter is not required to tell the citizen the reason why the discretion was exercised in the particular way it was. Discretion also opens the way for inconsistent decisions, and demands a much higher level of care and attention on the part of the decision maker exercising it; discretion is expensive of time and money. In political terms, the conferral of discretion may be used as a technique for off-loading onto front-line administrators difficult and politically contentious policy choices as to the way a public programme ought to be carried out and as to the objectives of the programme. In this way political debate and opposition may be avoided...

As Cane explains, discretion confers flexibility and allows a public authority to deal with issues on a case-by-case basis. But if a public authority deals with each case differently, then it may be accused of acting inconsistently and of being unjust by some claimants who cannot understand why their case has been treated differently from that of another claimant. This puts public authorities in a difficult position and may lead them to draw up policies or guidelines to help their decision-makers to reach consistent decisions. But these policies cannot frustrate the intention of the legislation, which was to give power to a public authority to make choices on a case-by-case basis. Adopting policies to try to ensure that the decision-maker acts consistently and lawfully can also lead to other forms of illegality (such as fettering of discretion). In short, illegality is really a way in which the courts can say to the public authority: 'Use your power, and only your power, in an even-handed way.'

Public authorities are accountable for the way in which they exercise their discretion. This accountability can be through the legal or political process. Political accountability might include a member of **Parliament** (MP) asking the relevant **government** minister a question in Parliament about the exercise of power by a public authority, or a parliamentary committee setting up an inquiry to look at the way in which a public authority exercises its discretion. But public authorities are also legally accountable through the courts and, in particular, through the judicial review process. The judicial review case law has developed in response to the increasing use of discretion during the twentieth century. The Victorian legal theorist A. V. Dicey argued against the use of discretion, fearing that it would lead to the exercise of arbitrary power. But discretion is essential to the modern administrative **state**, in which almost all areas of life are subject to regulation. It is therefore necessary for discretion to be controlled. Administrative law has developed since the 1950s, partly to prevent the arbitrary or capricious exercise of discretion, as Jowell explains.

● **J. Jowell, 'The rule of law and its underlying values', in J. Jowell and D. Oliver (eds) _The Changing Constitution_** (6th edn, Oxford: Oxford University Press, 2007), pp. 5–24, at 18

During the first half of the twentieth century, a time of reaction to Dicey's Rule of Law, the courts rarely interfered with the exercise of discretionary powers. From that time on, however they began to require that power be exercised in accordance with three 'grounds' of judicial review, each of them resting in large part on the Rule of Law.

The courts now insist that, when public authorities exercise discretion, they comply with certain principles summarised by Lord Diplock in the _CCSU_ case when he restated the three grounds of review. This means that the decision of a public authority will be unlawful if the exercise of discretion is irrational, illegal, or there is procedural impropriety. In addition, since the introduction of the HRA 1998, by virtue of section 6 it is 'unlawful for a public authority to act in a way that is incompatible with a Convention right'. In other words, when acting or making decisions, a public authority must remain within its legal powers (be lawful), it must use its discretion rationally and properly (be procedurally proper and in keeping with the rules of natural justice), and it must not breach section 6 of the HRA 1998 in doing so.

We shall now consider another aspect of the exercise of discretion—that discretion is not unrestricted.

thinking point

Define discretion, and consider its advantages and disadvantages. Has a decision been made about you that involved the decision-maker in exercising a discretionary power? Consider when you applied to university or college, or if you have applied for a grant, a loan, or a licence.

16.1.3 Discretion is not unrestricted

The courts have developed rules about the application of discretion and the fact that, in using the discretion, the decision-maker must not undermine the purpose for which the discretion and the power was given. This means that 'discretion is not unfettered', which is a way of explaining that the decision-maker must exercise his or her choice according to the purpose of the law that gave rise to the discretion. Discretion is not without restriction. One of the earliest cases to establish that discretionary powers are not unrestricted—or, as the courts often say, unfettered—was *Padfield v Minister of Agriculture, Fisheries and Food* [1968] AC 997. This case concerned the organisation of the milk marketing scheme. Under this scheme farmers had to sell their milk to the Milk Marketing Board, which paid a fixed fee for the milk depending on the region in which the farmer lived. Farmers in the south-east claimed that the fee was too low because, as they lived near London, they could, if allowed, sell their milk at a higher price. Every time the south-east farmers tried to negotiate a raise, they were outvoted, because they were a minority on the Milk Marketing Board. The scheme was regulated by the Agricultural Marketing Act 1958, which provided for a committee of investigation to consider complaints. However, the committee could consider complaints only if the Minister for Agriculture directed them to do so.

Agricultural Marketing Act 1958

....

Section 19

...

(3)...[a] committee of investigation shall—

...

(b) be charged with the duty, if the Minister in any case so directs, of considering, and reporting to the Minister on...any complaint made to the Minister as to the operation of any scheme...

The minister had a discretion as to whether   to dismiss the complaint or to refer it to a committee to investigate.

In this case, the minister dismissed the complaint by the farmers in the south-east. He said that the complaint raised wide issues and that if the committee were to find in the farmers' favour, he would be expected to give effect to its decision. The implication was that this might place the minister in an embarrassing political situation if he refused to follow a committee of investigation's decision. The minister argued that the statute conferred a discretionary power on him. This meant that he alone should be able to decide as he personally thought fit and that the court must not intervene to change his decision. The House of Lords emphatically rejected this argument and granted an order of mandamus (what would now be a **mandatory order**). Lord Reid explained the nature of the discretion.

● *Padfield v Minister of Agriculture, Fisheries and Food* [1968] AC 997

Lord Reid at 1029–30:

> The respondent [the Minister] contends that his only duty is to consider a complaint fairly and that he is given an unfettered discretion with regard to every complaint either to refer it or not to refer it to the committee as he may think fit. The appellants [the farmers] contend that it is his duty to refer every genuine and substantial complaint, or alternatively that his discretion is not unfettered and that in this case he failed to exercise his discretion according to law because his refusal was caused or influenced by his having misdirected himself in law or by his having taken into account extraneous or irrelevant considerations.
>
> In my view, the appellants' first contention goes too far. There are a number of reasons which would justify the Minister in refusing to refer a complaint. For example, he might consider it more suitable for arbitration, or he might consider that in an earlier case the committee of investigation had already rejected a substantially similar complaint, or he might think the complaint to be frivolous or vexatious. So he must have at least some measure of discretion. But is it unfettered?
>
> It is implicit in the argument for the Minister that there are only two possible interpretations of this provision either he must refer every complaint or he has an unfettered discretion to refuse to refer in any case. I do not think that is right. Parliament must have conferred the discretion with the intention that it should be used to promote the policy and objects of the Act, the policy and objects of the Act must be determined by construing the Act as a whole and construction is always a matter of law for the court. In a matter of this kind it is not possible to draw a hard and fast line, but if the Minister, by reason of his having misconstrued the Act or for any other reason, so uses his discretion as to thwart or run counter to the policy and objects of the Act, then our law would be very defective if persons aggrieved were not entitled to the protection of the court.

The majority of the House of Lords concluded that the minister's actions were ultra vires, because he had not acted in accordance with the purpose of the statute. The reasons that the minister gave for rejecting the complaint were not legitimate. The statute required him to consider the farmers' grievances and to consider whether an investigation should be set up without considering the political consequences for him. Refusing to pursue the complaint for fear the complaint would be upheld frustrated the purpose of the scheme. The House of Lords granted an order of mandamus that the minister should consider the complaint in accordance with law. Terminology has changed: an order of mandamus is an order now referred to as a mandatory order. This means that the minister was ordered by the court to use his discretion properly, with the likely result that this would lead the minister to refer the farmers' complaint to a committee of investigation were he to find that they had a genuine grievance that needed to be examined further.

The case is extremely important because it is one of a number of cases decided in the 1960s and 1970s that illustrate the courts' willingness to call the **executive** to account for the way in which it exercised its discretionary powers. Even though the discretion conferred appeared extremely subjective and very broad, the courts were prepared to intervene. This sort of case would now be considered to be a form of illegality.

In summary, discretionary power means that an administrative body has to exercise a choice when making a decision. Discretion has the advantage of allowing decisions to be made on a case-by-case basis. However, this may lead to inconsistent decision-making or to power being exercised in an arbitrary way. In order to prevent arbitrary decisions being made, the rules of administrative law, as developed by the judges, provide that discretion is not unfettered or unrestricted. Cases such as *Padfield* illustrate that the courts will hold public authorities accountable for their decisions.

summary points

Illegality and simple ultra vires

- *A public authority that is conferred with a discretion must exercise its discretion.*

- *However, the discretion will not be unrestricted; instead, there may be statutory guidelines on its exercise.*

- *The courts may also imply restrictions on the exercise of discretion, which they have developed from the purpose of the Act that gave rise to the discretion.*

16.2 Illegality: discretion, policies, and contract

16.2.1 Fettering discretion: policy

When a public authority is exercising a discretion, it may adopt rules or a policy for guidance. This is often the case when the authority is dealing with large numbers of people and when the authority wants to be consistent. Cane describes the benefit of a policy in the next short extract.

• **P. Cane, *Administrative Law*** (4th edn, Oxford: Oxford University Press, 2004), p. 203

An obvious advantage of policies is that they save time and promote certainty and uniformity. But they must not be applied without regard to the individual case. If the claimant raises some relevant matter that the authority did not take into account in forming its policy, it must listen and be prepared not to apply its policy if it turns out to be irrelevant or inappropriate to the particular case. In other words, policies and non-statutory rules must be applied flexibly and not rigidly ... Policies and non statutory rules strike a compromise between unregulated discretion and rigid rules. They help the decision-maker by saving time and resources; and provided they are published, they can also help the citizen by giving guidance about how to present their case and about its likely outcome.

[Footnotes omitted]

cross reference

Daly is discussed further in Chapter 17.

A policy can be challenged because it is unlawful. For example, it might be argued that the policy is unlawful because it is irrational, or because it breaches a Convention right. The case of *R (on the application of Daly) v Secretary of State for the Home Department* [2001] 2 AC 532 is an example in which a policy was held to be unlawful because it was in conflict with Article 8 ECHR. However, even if the policy is legal, the public authority must *apply* the policy lawfully. The courts have held that policies are not incompatible with the free exercise of discretion provided that the public authority is willing to make exceptions and to listen to someone who thinks that the policy should not be applied in his or her case.

This issue is discussed in the leading case of *British Oxygen Company Ltd v Minister of Technology* [1971] AC 619. The British Oxygen Company manufactured medical gases that were kept in cylinders, which individually cost £20, although in total the company had spent £4 million on the cylinders. The Board of Trade had the power to make a grant for new plant (equipment) in accordance with the Industrial Development Act 1966. The Board of Trade refused a grant application from British Oxygen for the cylinders, because the Board had a policy that it would not consider applications for items that individually cost less than £25. It was argued that the Board of Trade had fettered its discretion by applying its policy too rigidly. However, the House of Lords found in favour of the Board of Trade. Lord Reid explained the approach the authority should take when applying its policy.

....

● **British Oxygen Company Ltd v Minister of Technology** [1971] AC 619

Lord Reid at 625:

> The general rule is that anyone who has to exercise a statutory discretion must not 'shut his ears to an application' ... I do not think there is any great difference between a policy and a rule. There may be cases where an officer or authority ought to listen to a substantial argument reasonably presented urging a change of policy. What the authority must not do is to refuse to listen at all. But a Ministry or large authority may have had to deal already with a multitude of similar applications and then they will almost certainly have evolved a policy so precise that it could well be called a rule. There can be no objection to that, provided the authority is always willing to listen to anyone with something new to say ...

In *British Oxygen*, the House of Lords upheld the policy because it could be applied flexibly. The following are some examples in which the courts have held that a public authority has acted unlawfully by applying a policy too rigidly. In *R v North West Lancashire Health Authority, ex p A and others* [2000] 1 WLR 977, the claimants wanted to undergo sex-change operations and had been diagnosed with gender identity dysphoria, with a clinical need for gender reassignment surgery. The North Lancashire Health Authority rejected their application for surgery. It stated that it had a policy of not funding such operations, except where there was evidence of an overriding clinical need or exceptional circumstances. The Court of Appeal upheld the policy as rational, but held that the authority had acted unlawfully because it had applied the policy too rigidly.

....

● **R v North West Lancashire Health Authority, ex p A and others** [2000] 1 WLR 977

Lord Justice Auld at 993:

> However, if a regional health authority devises a policy not to provide treatment save in cases of overriding clinical need, it makes a nonsense of the policy if, as a matter of its medical judgment, there is no effective treatment for it for which there could be an overriding clinical need ... In my view, the stance of the authority, coupled with the near uniformity of its reasons for rejecting each of the applicant's requests for funding was not a genuine application of a policy subject to individually determined exceptions of the sort considered acceptable ...

Auld LJ found that the policy had been applied too rigidly because the authority did not describe what was meant by 'exceptional circumstances' and it had rejected all of the applications for almost the same reasons. This convinced the Court that the authority was operating a blanket policy without considering the individual merits of each case. This can also be referred to as a form of fettering of discretion, which is discussed later in the chapter.

There are other examples of unlawful policies. The Prison Service was held to have applied its policy in an overly rigid fashion in *R (on the application of P) v Secretary of State for the Home Department; R (on the application of Q and another) v Secretary of State for the Home Department* [2001] EWCA 1151. Prison Service policy permitted mothers with newborn babies to remain together in prison, in special mother-and-baby units, only until the baby was 18 months old. The court upheld the policy as lawful and compatible with the right to family life in Article 8 ECHR. However, it held that the policy had to take account of individual circumstances, and it was unlawful to apply the policy of separating the mother and child irrespective of the affects of separation on the child and the difficulties of finding a placement for the child outside the prison. It upheld the decision of the prison authorities in relation to P, but held that the policy had been applied too rigidly in relation to Q.

. . . .

● ***R (on the application of P) v Secretary of State for the Home Department; R (on the application of Q and another) v Secretary of State for the Home Department*** [2001] 1 WLR 2002

Lord Phillips of Worth Matravers MR at 2032:

> The only question we have to decide is whether the Prison Service is entitled to operate its policy in a rigid fashion, insisting that all children leave by the age of 18 months at the latest (give or take a few weeks if their mother is about to be released), however catastrophic the separation may be in the case of a particular mother and child, however unsatisfactory the alternative placement available for the child, and however attractive the alternative solution of combining day care outside prison with remaining in prison with the mother.
>
> In our view the policy must admit of greater flexibility than that.

cross reference

Luton Borough Council *is discussed more fully in Chapters 17 and 18.*

The importance of the decision-maker considering each case individually in the light of the relevant rules or policy was stressed by the court in *R (on the application of Luton Borough Council and others) v Secretary of State for Education* [2011] EWHC 217 (Admin). In this case, the Secretary of State for Education exercised his statutory discretion to cancel the previous Labour government's school-building project. He applied a detailed policy that determined which school rebuilding works could go ahead and which were cancelled. One of the grounds on which the judge held that the Secretary of State had acted unlawfully was that he had fettered his discretion contrary to the principles laid down in the *British Oxygen* case. The Secretary of State had applied the rules in 'a hard-edged way, with no residual individual discretion' (Holman J at [61]), whereas he should have treated each relevant school-building project as an individual case and considered each separately.

A policy must generally be published or accessible. In *R (Lumba) v Secretary of State for the Home Department* [2011] 2 WLR 671, the Supreme Court held that the Home Secretary had unlawfully exercised her discretion under Schedule 3, paragraph 2, to the Immigration Act 1971. This allowed her to detain foreign prisoners who had completed their sentence of imprisonment in the UK pending their deportation. The Home Secretary was in an embarrassing political situation after the media revealed that foreigners who had committed crimes and were serving sentences in the UK were rarely deported to their own countries after they had finished their terms of imprisonment. This had led to criticism in the media and ultimately the resignation of a previous Home Secretary. The subsequent Home Secretary had a published policy stating that foreign prisoners who had served their sentences would be detained only when this was justified. However, she had introduced a secret unpublished and contradictory policy of always detaining foreign prisoners after they finished their sentences. The Supreme Court held by a majority that, firstly, a blanket policy that failed to provide for exceptions was unlawful; secondly, it was unlawful to apply a secret policy. The up-to-date policy that guided the exercise of the statutory discretion should be published unless there were exceptional reasons such as national security. The Court stressed that publication of the policy is important, so that the person concerned has the opportunity to make representations to the decision-maker before a decision is made about his or her case (Dyson LJ at [35]).

To conclude, a policy must be lawful. It must be publicly available, rational, and must not breach human rights. It must not be rigid. It must be applied flexibly and the authority must always listen to someone with something new to say. Finally, it should be noted that a policy may give rise to a legitimate expectation—which will be explained further in Chapter 18.

16.2.2 Fettering discretion by contract

When a public authority enters into a contract, it must not fetter or restrict its statutory discretion. The classic example of a case in which a public authority was held to have acted unlawfully because it fettered its discretion by contract was *Ayr Harbour Trustees v Oswald* (1883) 8 App Cas 323. The Ayr Harbour Trustees had a statutory power to acquire land for the construction of works connected to the harbour. The trustees made an agreement with Oswald, a landowner whose land was being compulsorily purchased. The trustees would reduce the amount of compensation in return for a covenant that they would not, in the future, construct works that blocked access to the harbour for Oswald's remaining land. The House of Lords held that this was unlawful for the following reason.

● **Ayr Harbour Trustees v Oswald** (1882–83) LR 8 App Cas 623

Lord Blackburn at 634:

> I think that where the legislature confer powers on any body to take lands compulsorily for a particular purpose, it is on the ground that the using of that land for that purpose will be for the public good . . . and, consequently, that a contract purporting to bind them and their successors not to use those powers is void.

This issue raises difficult questions because, as Wade and Forsyth (2000: 334) state, 'Since most contracts fetter freedom of action in some way, there may be difficult questions of degree in determining how far the authority may legally commit itself for the future'.

NOTE

The complexities of this subject are outside the scope of this text, but if you would like to explore this area further, then you will find that Wade and Forsythe (2000) and Craig (2008), listed in the further reading at the end of this chapter, offer full explanations of this topic.

16.3 Illegality: discretion and delegation, abdication, and dictation

This section will discuss unlawful delegation, abdication of power, and dictation. It is important to understand that these categories overlap and that one decision might give rise to a claim of delegation, abdication, and dictation, and other grounds of review, such as following an unlawful or rigid policy. We shall take each of them in turn, but do not be concerned if they appear very similar to each other as you read through them.

16.3.1 Unlawful delegation of power

The basic principle is that when a public authority or person is granted statutory powers, it must exercise those powers and not delegate them to anyone else. This is because Parliament has decided which individual or public authority is the most appropriate one to exercise the power. This may be because it has the necessary knowledge or expertise to make the decision. This principle is known by the Latin term *delegatus non potest delegare* ('a delegate is not allowed to delegate'). However, the delegation principle can, of course, be overridden by Parliament, because some statutes expressly permit delegation. So, for example, the Local Government Act 1972 and the Local Government Act 2000 provide that powers of the local authority can be delegated to executive officers and committees of the authority. There are also exceptions to the non-delegation principle for government departments, which, as we shall see, are not subject to the delegation principle.

NOTE

If in doubt, you should read the statute or statutory instrument that gives rise to the power to check what Parliament intended and be guided by that. This is why it is so important that you read the legislation in its original form rather than rely on extracts given to you by someone else. The answer is usually contained in the legislation itself.

The case of *Barnard v National Dock Labour Board* [1953] 3 QB 18 is the classic example of a case in which the court held that the public authority, the National Dock Labour Board, had unlawfully delegated its power to dismiss a dock worker. The Dock Workers (Regulation of Employment Scheme) 1947 granted the power to suspend a worker to the local dock labour board made up of equal numbers of representatives of workers and employers. The port manager suspended workers during a dispute without reference to the board. The board did not investigate, did not see the relevant report, and made no decision on the matter. The court held that the power had been granted to the board and could not be delegated to the port manager. This case was approved by the House of Lords in *Vine v National Dock Labour Board* [1957] AC 488, in which the Lords granted a **declaration** that the dismissal of a worker was invalid. This case concerned the same statutory scheme as in *Barnard*. The statutory power to dismiss a dock worker lay with the local dock labour board and had been unlawfully delegated to a disciplinary committee. In this case, the composition of the board, comprising of workers and employers, was meant to inspire confidence that decisions had been made fairly and it was held that it would undermine the statute if power were delegated. The power conferred by statute stipulated how that power had to be used and by whom.

However, the courts have held that it is not unlawful delegation for a public authority to assign some tasks to appropriate individuals or committees within the authority provided that it retains overall control. This is more likely to be the case where the court finds that the process is administrative, rather than judicial, in nature. This issue has arisen in relation to the investigative functions of some bodies. In *R v Race Relations Board, ex p Selvarajan* [1975] 1 WLR 1686, the Race Relations Board rejected the claimant's complaint of unlawful race discrimination contrary to the Race Relations Act 1968 and refused to exercise its powers to pursue an action against his employer. The claimant complained that there had been unlawful delegation because the employment committee, rather than the full Board, had investigated the complaint. The full Board then endorsed the committee's recommendation. However, only some members of the Board had access to all of the papers considered by the employment committee. The court held that the Board had acted lawfully. Lord Scarman explained that the Board had a degree of control over how it carried out its functions.

● **R v Race Relations Board, ex p Selvarajan** [1975] 1 WLR 1686

Lord Scarman at 1700:

> The [Race Relations] Board was created so that in the sensitive field of race relations compliance with the law and the resolution of differences could first be sought without recourse to the courts with their necessarily open and formalised judicial process. The board is an administrative agency charged with a number of critically important functions in the administration of the law: but it is not a judicial institution—nor is it the apex of a hierarchy of judicial institutions. The procedures are not adversarial but conciliatory: settlement, not litigation, is the business of the board; and it is left to the board to decide how best to perform the functions which the statute requires it to perform, namely, investigation, the formation of an opinion, conciliation, and, if all else fails, the taking of legal proceedings in the county court. I draw attention specifically to sections 14 and 15 of the Act.

Lord Scarman stresses that the Race Relations Board does not have to abide by the same sort of strict rules as a court, but is carrying out administrative functions. Provided that the Board retains overall control of the decision and there is sufficient information for the Board to form an opinion, then the court will not intervene. In essence, the public authority was still exercising the power and had not fully delegated it to another.

The non-delegation rule does not apply to the decisions of government ministers, who are permitted to delegate to civil servants working within their departments. This was established in *Carltona Ltd v Commissioners of Works* [1943] 2 All ER 560. The Commissioner of Works exercised statutory power to requisition (to compulsorily acquire) the claimant's factory in accordance with regulation 51(1) of the Defence (General) Regulations 1939. It was claimed that this was ultra vires because the decision had been taken by an assistant secretary and because the Commissioner did not personally direct his mind to the matter. The Court of Appeal held that the Commissioner could not be expected personally to consider every requisition, as Lord Greene explained.

● **Carltona Ltd v Commissioners of Works** [1943] 2 All ER 560

Lord Greene at 563:

> In the administration of government in this country the functions which are given to ministers (and constitutionally properly given to ministers because they are constitutionally responsible) are functions so multifarious that no minister could ever personally attend to them. To take the example of the present case no doubt there have been thousands of requisitions in this country by individual ministers. It cannot be supposed that this regulation meant that, in each case, the minister in person should direct his mind to the matter. The duties imposed upon ministers and the powers given to ministers are normally exercised under the authority of the ministers by responsible officials of the department. Public business could not be carried on if that were not the case. Constitutionally, the decision of such an official is, of course, the decision of the minister. The minister is responsible. It is he who must answer before Parliament for anything that his officials have done under his authority, and, if for an important matter he selected an official of such junior standing that he could not be expected competently to perform the work, the minister would have to answer for that in Parliament. The whole system of departmental organisation and administration is based on the view that ministers, being responsible to Parliament, will see that important duties are committed to experienced officials. If they do not do that, Parliament is the place where complaint must be made against them.

Lord Greene states that government ministers are entitled to delegate their powers. If they were not, then the government would not operate effectively. They are responsible to Parliament for the decisions of the officials in their departments. This approach was confirmed in *R v Secretary* of State for the Home Department, ex p Oladehinde and another [1991] 1 AC 254. The House of Lords upheld the decision of the Home Secretary to delegate his power to issue a deportation order under section 3(5)(a) of the Immigration Act 1971 to officers of at least inspector level in the Immigration Department. The House of Lords held that the immigration service was made up of a collection of public servants, including civil servants, who were answerable to the Home Secretary. Lord Griffiths explained.

● *R v Secretary of State for the Home Department, ex p Oladehinde and another* [1991] 1 AC 254

Lord Griffiths at 304:

> [The Secretary of State] is responsible and I can for myself see no reason why he should not authorise members of that service to take decisions under the *Carltona* principle providing they do not conflict with or embarrass them in the discharge of their specific statutory duties under the Act.

This clearly demonstrates that ministers are able to delegate their powers to appropriate people working within their departments, while retaining responsibility for the exercise of that power.

Hopefully, delegation appears relatively straightforward. The next issue to be considered is the abdication of discretion. We have considered this in brief earlier and will examine it in detail in the next section.

16.3.2 Abdicating discretion

A public authority will be abdicating its discretion if it does not exercise its discretion, but allows itself to follow another body's decision instead. This is sometimes referred to as fettering of discretion (which is not quite the same as a discretion that is unrestricted or unfettered, which we discussed above). *Lavender and Son Ltd v Minister of Housing and Local Government* [1970] 1 WLR 1231 is an example of an abdication of discretion. The claimants were refused planning permission to extract gravel from agricultural land at Walton on Thames. They exercised their statutory right to appeal to the Minister of Housing and Local Government in accordance with section 179 of the Town and Country Planning Act 1962. The Minister rejected the appeal on the grounds that it was his policy not to release such land for gravel extraction unless the Minister of Agriculture approved. The claimants challenged the decision on the basis that the Minister of Housing and Local Government had fettered his discretion. He had adopted a rigid policy—that of not granting permission unless the Minister of Agriculture agreed. It was also argued that the Minister of Housing had been entrusted by the statute to exercise the discretion, but he had effectively allowed the Minister of Agriculture to make the decision. The judge in the case held that the Minister of Housing had acted unlawfully.

● *Lavender and Son Ltd v Minister of Housing and Local Government* [1970] 1 WLR 1231

Willis J at 1241:

> On the main ground on which this case has been argued, however, I am satisfied that the applicants should succeed. I think the Minister failed to exercise a proper or indeed any discretion by reason of the fetter which he imposed upon its exercise in acting solely in accordance with

As the extract shows, the case was decided on the basis that the Minister had adopted a rigid policy that appeared to allow no exceptions. He had also effectively given his decision-making power to the Minister of Agriculture, who did not have the statutory power to make the decision. This is very similar to the cases described above of unlawful delegation, in which the decision-making power is given to someone other than the body or individual named in the statute. It is a fine, and not entirely clear, distinction. You should not be too concerned about pinpointing whether the discretion has been abdicated or delegated, but you should be aware of these two principles. The next one—acting under dictation—similarly overlaps with abdication and delegation of discretion.

16.3.3 Dictation

The person or body entrusted with the decision-making power must make the decision freely. The decision will be ultra vires if the decision-maker is dictated to or ordered to make the decision by another person. The case of *Roncarelli v Duplessis* [1959] SCR 12 illustrates this principle very well, even though it is a Canadian case from the mid 1950s. It is discussed here in brief. In this case, the Prime Minister of Quebec gave instructions to the Quebec Liquor Commission to withdraw the claimant's liquor licence for his restaurant in Montreal. This was because the claimant was a Jehovah's Witness who supported other Jehovah's Witnesses, who had been arrested, by helping them to obtain bail. The decision to revoke the licence had nothing to do with the claimant's fitness to hold the licence. The Supreme Court of Canada held that the licence had been wrongly revoked because the Liquor Commission had used its power to revoke a licence for an improper political purpose. But, more relevant to our discussion here, it held that the Liquor Commission had allowed itself to be dictated to by the Prime Minister; it had not independently exercised its statutory powers. The following short extract makes this point.

● ***Roncarelli v Duplessis*** [1959] SCR 121

Abbot J at 185:

> I have no doubt that in taking the action which he did, the respondent [Prime Minister] was convinced that he was acting in what he conceived to be the best interests of the people of his province but this, of course, has no relevance to the issue of his responsibility ... for any acts done in excess of his legal authority. I have no doubt also that respondent knew and was bound to know as Attorney-General that neither as Premier of the province nor as Attorney-General was he authorized in law to interfere with the administration of the Quebec Liquor Commission or to give an order or an authorization to any officer of that body to exercise a discretionary authority entrusted to such officer by the statute.

Exercising a discretion in response to a threat may also make the decision ultra vires. This is because it is argued that no real discretion has been exercised by the decision-maker. The case of *R v Coventry City Council, ex p Phoenix Aviation* [1995] 3 All ER 37, DC, illustrates this point. The public authorities that ran Coventry Airport and Dover Harbour refused to allow the export of livestock. This was because protestors objecting to the export of live animals disrupted the work of the airport and harbour. The companies involved in the livestock trade were inconvenienced because they could not use the port and airport. They claimed that this decision was unlawful. The court held that the authorities did not have the statutory power to

NOTE As a Canadian case of some standing, *Roncarelli* is said to have persuasive, rather than binding, precedent value. This means that it may be cited in court, but will not be binding on the **judiciary**.

refuse the claimant companies' trade. The court went on to hold that even if the authorities did have such a discretion, it would be unlawful to exercise it in response to unlawful threats made by the protestors, and that the police had ample powers to deal with disruption to the facilities in question.

Contrast this case with *R (on the application of Corner House Research and another) v Director of the Serious Fraud Office* [2008] 3 WLR 568. This concerned the validity of a decision by the director of the Serious Fraud Office (SFO) to discontinue an investigation that he had begun using his powers under section 1(3) of the Criminal Justice Act 1967. The two-year investigation involved allegations of corruption against British Aerospace in securing an arms contract with Saudi Arabia. The SFO started to investigate Swiss bank accounts to determine whether British Aerospace had made payments to Saudi Arabian officials. The Saudi Arabian government then threatened that it would withdraw its cooperation with the UK on counter-terrorism and other areas in which it had assisted the UK government if the investigation were to continue. The director of the SFO was informed of the Prime Minister's view, in a memo to the Attorney General, that continuing the investigation raised real risks to the UK's security. The director of the SFO also met with the UK's ambassador to Saudi Arabia who told him that 'British lives on British streets were at risk' if the Saudi Arabian government withdrew cooperation with the UK. Even though the director of the SFO thought there was sufficient evidence to proceed, he decided to discontinue the investigation because of the need to safeguard national and international security. The decision was challenged on a number of grounds. The House of Lords, reversing the decision of the lower court, held that the director of the SFO had acted lawfully. The *Phoenix Aviation* case was distinguished because, in that case the protestors, unlike the Saudi Arabian authorities, were subject to domestic law and could be dealt with by the police. Also, the *Corner House* case involved issues of national security. In the next brief extract, Lord Bingham explains why the House of Lords came to the conclusion that the director of the SFO acted lawfully.

●●

● **R (on the application of Corner House Research and another) v Director of the Serious Fraud Office** [2008] 3 WLR 568

Lord Bingham at 584:

> 41 The Director was confronted by an ugly and obviously unwelcome threat. He had to decide what, if anything, he should do. He did not surrender his discretionary power of decision to any third party, although he did consult the most expert source available to him in the person of the ambassador and he did, as he was entitled if not bound to do, consult the Attorney General who, however, properly left the decision to him. The issue in these proceedings is not whether his decision was right or wrong, nor whether the Divisional Court or the House agrees with it, but whether it was a decision which the Director was lawfully entitled to make. Such an approach involves no affront to the rule of law, to which the principles of judicial review give effect...

NOTE

For a discussion of other cases concerned with judicial review and national security issues, see Chapter 14. See also the discussion on judicial **deference** in Chapter 18.

Lord Bingham explains that the director of the SFO was entitled to consult and listen to the expert advice available to him. He had to balance the advice given to him on security issues against the general public interest in pursuing a criminal investigation. The director's decision to follow the advice given after due consideration was not the same as surrendering or giving up his discretion to a third party, and he had therefore acted lawfully.

thinking point

Do you think that the House of Lords was right to uphold the decision of the director of the SFO or do you prefer the view of Moses LJ in the Administrative Court? Try writing a dissenting judgment to the House of Lords' decision in Corner House.

There have, however, been many criticisms of the House of Lords' decision in the *Corner House* case. Giving the judgment of the **Administrative Court**, which was overturned by the House of Lords, Lord Justice Moses had stated as follows.

● **R (on the application of Corner House Research and Campaign against Arms Trade) v Director of the Serious Fraud Office**   [2008] EWHC 714 (Admin)

Moses LJ at [102]:

> The Director [of the SFO] failed to appreciate that protection of the rule of law demanded that he should not yield to the threat. Nor was adequate consideration given to the damage to national security and to the rule of law by submission to the threat.

This section emphasises that the discretionary power must be exercised by the public authority. Delegation is not permitted unless the statute expressly provides for it or the power in question belongs to a government minister. Decision-makers must not abdicate their discretion as a consequence of a policy or for other reasons. The authority should not be dictated to by an individual or another authority. However, public authorities are often required to consider guidance or to consult before a decision is made. Ultimately, the case law emphasises that the power in question must be exercised by the public authority that has been entrusted by Parliament to make the decision.

summary points

Illegality: discretion and delegation, abdication, and dictation

- *Power must be exercised by the public authority that has had the power conferred upon it.*
- *A public authority may be permitted to get another part of the authority to exercise the power, under its supervision, assuming that is not prohibited by the legislation.*
- *However, a public authority may not delegate its power to another body or person.*
- *A public authority must not abdicate its discretion. When given a discretionary power, it must use it, even though that does not mean that it must make a decision one way or another. It must make a choice if given the power to make one.*
- *A public authority must not allow itself to be ordered to use its power in a particular way. It must not allow someone else to dictate its choice.*

16.4 Illegality: discretion, improper purpose, and irrelevant considerations

It is unlawful for a public authority to exercise its discretion for an improper purpose. This section will explain what is meant by an 'improper purpose', give examples, and discuss the way in which the courts determine the purpose of the legislation. In addition, decisions must not be made on the basis of irrelevant considerations. Decision-makers are required to take into account relevant factors and exclude from their mind irrelevant factors. This section will explain how the courts determine what factors are relevant. This includes a discussion of the extent to which financial and other resource considerations are relevant considerations. We shall also explain the **fiduciary duty** between ratepayers (council taxpayers) and local authorities, because this is an issue that arises in the case law on illegality. There will also be an illustration of the overlap between irrelevant considerations and improper purposes.

16.4.1 Acting for an improper purpose

It is unlawful for a public authority to use its discretion to act for an ulterior or improper purpose. This was the main ground for the decision in *Padfield* (cited above). One of the most controversial decisions decided on the ground of improper purpose is *Wheeler v Leicester City Council* [1985] AC 1054. This was a challenge by Leicester Rugby Football Club to Leicester City Council's decision to suspend the club from using a recreation ground for matches in accordance with its statutory powers in the Open Spaces Act 1906 and the Public Health Act 1925. The reason for the suspension was that three members of the club had joined a rugby tour of South Africa. This was at a time when sporting links with South Africa were controversial because of the apartheid regime. This had led to some sporting boycotts, whereby sports people had refused to play competitive sport in South Africa against all-white teams, or had refused to play against South African teams on tour in other countries. Boycotts aimed to put international pressure on the South African state to end apartheid, and to give full civil and political rights to the black majority in the country. Leicester City Council's decision should be seen in this light.

The club condemned apartheid, but refused to condemn its individual members for participating in the tour. Leicester City Council, taking into account the fact that 25 per cent of the council's population were of Asian or Afro-Caribbean origin, claimed that, in accordance with section 71 of the Race Relations Act 1976, it was acting to promote good relations between persons of different racial groups. It argued that the tour of South Africa would endorse that regime's racist policies and that it was an insult to the local population. The House of Lords upheld the challenge to the council's decision. One of the reasons the House of Lords gave for the decision was that Leicester City Council had misused its statutory powers to punish the club. Lord Templeman explains, in the following extract, that the club had acted lawfully and that the council should not use its powers to punish the club because it disagreed with its decision.

● ●

● **Wheeler v Leicester City Council** [1985] AC 1054

Lord Templeman at 1080:

> The club having committed no wrong, the council could not use their statutory powers in the management of their property or any other statutory powers in order to punish the club. There is no doubt that the council intended to punish and have punished the club ... The council could not properly seek to use its statutory powers of management or any other statutory powers for the purposes of punishing the club when the club had done no wrong.

This is not the only illustration to which we could point. Another decision in which the House of Lords held that a public authority had acted for an improper purpose is *Porter v Magill* [2002] 2 AC 357. Westminster City Council, led by its Conservative leader Lady Porter, decided to sell off some of its council housing stock using its power under section 32 of the Housing Act 1985. This in itself was perfectly legal, because the council had the discretion to sell some of its local authority housing. The difficulty was the underlying reason for the council's sale. The main reason for the decision was to increase the potential number of Conservative voters in marginal areas to make it more likely that the Conservatives would be re-elected. It was believed that homeowners were more likely to vote Conservative than the council tenants, who tended to be Labour Party voters. The auditor challenged the decision to sell the housing, and held that Lady Porter and others were guilty of wilful misconduct that had caused the council financial loss, and that they were personally liable for this loss. This case raised many issues of procedure and, naturally, the defendants contested the allegations relating to the purpose of the sale. But the

House of Lords was asked to consider whether the council had acted for an improper purpose. In the next extract, Lord Bingham discusses this issue.

● **Porter v Magill** [2002] 2 AC 357

Lord Bingham at 466:

[21] Whatever the difficulties of application which may arise in a borderline case, I do not consider the overriding principle to be in doubt. Elected politicians of course wish to act in a manner which will commend them and their party (when, as is now usual, they belong to one) to the electorate. Such an ambition is the life blood of democracy and a potent spur to responsible decision-taking and administration. Councillors do not act improperly or unlawfully if, exercising public powers for a public purpose for which such powers were conferred, they hope that such exercise will earn the gratitude and support of the electorate and thus strengthen their electoral position. The law would indeed part company with the realities of party politics if it were to hold otherwise. But a public power is not exercised lawfully if it is exercised not for a public purpose for which the power was conferred but in order to promote the electoral advantage of a political party. The power at issue in the present case is section 32 of the Housing Act 1985, which conferred power on local authorities to dispose of land held by them subject to conditions specified in the Act. Thus a local authority could dispose of its property, subject to the provisions of the Act, to promote any public purpose for which such power was conferred, but could not lawfully do so for the purpose of promoting the electoral advantage of any party represented on the council.

NOTE Before Lord Bingham decides whether the power has been exercised properly, he briefly discusses the nature of the power in question and states its purpose.

Lord Bingham notes that local councils are political bodies and hope to earn the approval of the electorate when exercising power. However, they must still act for a public purpose and cannot use their powers to manipulate the housing stock blatantly to obtain a political advantage over their opponents. But how do the courts work out in each situation what is the public purpose? The next section will consider how the courts find the purpose behind the legislation and use this as a mechanism to determine how the public authority should use its legal power.

16.4.2 Finding the purpose of the legislation

The courts determine the purpose of the legislation by interpreting the statute. Sometimes, the statute will clearly state its purpose, but on other occasions the courts will have to find the purpose by implication after reading the statute carefully. In *R v Environment Secretary, ex p Spath Holme Ltd* [2001] 2 AC 249, the court discussed, amongst other things, how the purpose of an Act of Parliament could be determined. Spath Holme Ltd challenged the Rent Acts (Maximum Fair Rents) Order 1999. Spath Holme was the freehold owner of flats, the ability of which to raise rent from its tenants would be restricted as a result of the Order. The Order was a piece of delegated legislation made by the Secretary of State for the Environment in accordance with powers granted by Parliament in section 31 of the Landlord and Tenant Act 1985. Spath Holme Ltd challenged the delegated legislation, arguing that it was unlawful because it was made for an improper purpose and not for the purpose for which Parliament passed the Landlord and Tenant Act 1985. Spath Holme argued that the purpose of the 1985 Act was to control inflation, whereas the Order had been made in order to help tenants who had suffered steep rent increases as a result of the way in which their rents had been calculated. The House of Lords considered the purpose of the Landlord and Tenant Act 1985. The Law Lords held that the legislation's main concern was the relationship between landlord and tenant, and the protection of tenants from excessive rent increases. This was not restricted to rent increases caused by inflation, but was wide enough to include hardship caused by the present circumstances. Therefore the challenge by Spath Holme was rejected and the House of Lords found that the Secretary of State for the Environment had acted for a proper statutory purpose.

In the following extract, the House of Lords discusses the way in which courts should determine the purpose of the legislation. The judgment explains that the purpose might be stated in the statute, but if not, the court has to infer the meaning from the statute as a whole.

● *R v Environment Secretary, ex p Spath Holme Ltd* [2001] 2 AC 249

Lord Nicholls at 397:

> No statutory power is of unlimited scope. The discretion given by Parliament is never absolute or unfettered. Powers are conferred by Parliament for a purpose, and they may be lawfully exercised only in furtherance of that purpose: 'the policy and objects of the Act', in the oft-quoted words of Lord Reid in *Padfield v. Minister of Agriculture, Fisheries and Food* [1968] AC 997, 1030. The purpose for which a power is conferred, and hence its ambit, may be stated expressly in the statute. Or it may be implicit. Then the purpose has to be inferred from the language used, read in its statutory context and having regard to any aid to interpretation which assists in the particular case. In either event, whether the purpose is stated expressly or has to be inferred, the exercise is one of statutory interpretation.

This extract emphasises the principle that discretion must be exercised in accordance with the purpose intended by Parliament, as stated in the Act of Parliament.

16.4.3 Where there is more than one purpose

Public authorities may have more than one purpose or motive for their action. If one purpose is lawful and the other unlawful, then the courts have used more than one test to decide whether the discretion has been exercised lawfully, as Craig discusses.

● **P. Craig,** *Administrative Law* (London: Sweet & Maxwell, 2008), pp. 541–2

> It would be a simple world in which an authority always acted for one purpose only. Complex problems can arise where one of the purposes is lawful and one is regarded as unlawful. The courts have used various tests to resolve this problem. First, what was the true purpose for which the power was exercised? Provided that the legitimate statutory purpose was achieved it is irrelevant that a subsidiary object was also attained.[1] Second, what was the dominant purpose for which the power was exercised?[2] Third, were any of the purposes authorised? This has less support in the case law than the previous two tests. Fourthly, if any of the purposes was unauthorised and this had an effect upon decision taken, it will be overturned as being based upon irrelevant considerations.[3]
>
> 1 *Mayor, & C., of Westminster v London and North Western Railway Company* [1905] AC 426.
> 2 *R v Immigration Appeals Adjudicator, ex p Khan* [1972] 1 WLR 1058; *R v Greenwich London Borough Council, ex p Lovelace* [1991] 1 WLR 506.
> 3 *Hanks v Minister of Housing v Local Government* [1963] 1 QB 999, *R v Inner London Education Authority, ex p Westminster City Council* [1986] 1 WLR 28; *R v Broadcasting Complaints Commission, ex p Owen* [1985] QB 1153.

In *Mayor, & C., of Westminster v London and North Western Railway Company* [1905] AC 426, the local authority had the power to build public conveniences (toilets) in accordance with section 44 of the Public Health (London) Act 1891. It built the conveniences underground, in the middle of a road, with a subway for access. It was argued that the authority had acted unlawfully because it had used the statute to build a subway and this was not authorised by the statute. The House of Lords held that the authority had acted lawfully because the main purpose was the construction of the public conveniences. The courts will generally take a common-sense approach to interpreting legislation and the purposes for which public authorities may put their legal powers.

16.4.4 Irrelevant considerations

When a public authority exercises a statutory discretion, it must consider all of the relevant factors and exclude all of the irrelevant factors before reaching its decision. Parliament confers power for specific reasons and expects a public law decision-maker, often funded through public funds, to make use of its discretion fairly and sensibly, having regard to Parliament's intention in granting the power. If a public law decision-maker fails to take account of relevant considerations or takes into account irrelevant considerations, then the decision will be illegal. A now rather controversial example of a decision in which the public authority was held by the House of Lords to have taken into account irrelevant considerations is *Roberts v Hopwood* [1925] AC 578. Poplar Borough Council had the power, in accordance with section 62 of the Metropolis Management Act 1885, to pay its workers such wages as it may think fit. The council decided that it should act as a model employer and set an example to other employers. It therefore paid its lowest grade of workers, irrespective of sex, a minimum wage. This wage was above the market rate and the district auditor, who was responsible for checking the accounts of the council, decided that it had wasted ratepayers' money. He used his statutory powers to surcharge the council, which meant that the councillors were personally responsible for the overspend in the budget due to the extra amount paid in wages. The auditor argued that the council had abused its discretion. The House of Lords held against the council.

. . . .

● *Roberts v Hopwood* [1925] AC 578

Lord Atkinson at 594:

> Nobody has contended that the council should be bound by any of these things, but it is only what justice and common sense demand that, when dealing with funds contributed by the whole body of the ratepayers, they should take each and every one of these enumerated things into consideration in order to help them to determine what was a fair, just and reasonable wage to pay their employees for the services the latter rendered. The council would, in my view, fail in their duty if, in administering funds which did not belong to their members alone, they put aside all these aids to the ascertainment of what was just and reasonable remuneration to give for the services rendered to them, and allowed themselves to be guided in preference by some eccentric principles of socialistic philanthropy, or by a feminist ambition to secure the equality of the sexes in the matter of wages in the world of labour.

The House of Lords held that the council had failed to consider its duty to the ratepayers (the council taxpayers) to obtain value for money. The House of Lords stated that the council had taken into account factors that were regarded as irrelevant, such as the desire to secure equality and socialist principles. Of course, no court today would regard these factors as irrelevant, but in the 1920s societal views were very different. But the case makes the point very strongly that discretionary powers must be exercised in the context of the statute, and that the authority must consider all of the relevant factors and exclude from its mind all of the irrelevant factors. The case also raises the issue of the fiduciary duty to ratepayers (local council taxpayers), which will be discussed below.

A more modern-day example in which the Home Secretary was held to act unlawfully because he took into account irrelevant consideration is *R v Secretary of State for the Home Department, ex p Venables; R v Secretary of State for the Home Department, ex p Thompson* [1997] 3 WLR 23. This highly publicised case concerned the sentencing of two 10-year-old boys convicted of the murder of Jamie Bulger, a 2-year-old toddler. A young person sentenced by a judge to be detained at Her Majesty's pleasure in accordance with section 53(1) of the Children and Young Persons Act 1933 would remain in detention for a minimum number of years before being eligible for release under supervision. This minimum period was known as the tariff. The Home Secretary determined the tariff on the recommendation of the judge who presided over the trial. After the claimants' conviction for the murder of Jamie Bulger, the trial judge recommended a tariff of eight years, but this was increased to ten years by the **Lord Chief Justice**. The Home Secretary, acting under his powers under the Criminal Justice Act 1991, increased the tariff to fifteen years. He treated the claimants in the same way he would treat adults sentenced to life imprisonment. The Home Secretary informed the claimants that he had considered petitions from the public urging that the claimants spend a long period in detention. One petition had been organised by *The Sun* newspaper as part of a highly publicised campaign. The House of Lords found in favour of the claimants on a number of grounds. The ground of the most relevance here is discussed below in the judgment of Lord Steyn. He states that the Home Secretary, when fixing a tariff, is acting in a judicial capacity and that therefore it was wrong for him to take into account the various petitions. Judges are not permitted to take public opinion in relation to a specific case into account when reaching their decisions; they must remain impartial at all times.

● *R v Secretary of State for the Home Department, ex p Venables; R v Secretary of State for the Home Department, ex p Thompson* [1998] AC 407

Lord Steyn at 526:

> In fixing a tariff the Home Secretary is carrying out, contrary to the constitutional principle of separation of powers, a classic judicial function: see Lord Diplock's explanation of the importance of the separation of powers between the executive and the judiciary in *Hinds v. The Queen* [1977] A.C. 195, 212 and *Dupont Steels Ltd. v. Sirs* [1980] 1 W.L.R. 142, 157. Parliament entrusted the underlying statutory power, which entailed a discretion to adopt a policy of fixing a tariff, to the Home Secretary. But the power to fix a tariff is nevertheless equivalent to a judge's sentencing power. Parliament must be assumed to have entrusted the power to the Home Secretary on the supposition that, like a sentencing judge, the Home Secretary would not act contrary to fundamental principles governing the administration of justice. Plainly a sentencing judge must ignore a newspaper campaign designed to encourage him to increase a particular sentence. It would be an abdication of the rule of law for a judge to take into account such matters. The same reasoning must apply to the Home Secretary when he is exercising a sentencing function. He ought to concentrate on the facts of the case and balance considerations of public interest against the dictates of justice. Like a judge the Home Secretary ought not to be guided by a disposition to consult how popular a particular decision might be. He ought to ignore the high-voltage atmosphere of a newspaper campaign. The power given to him requires, above all, a detached approach. I would therefore hold that public protests about the level of a tariff to be fixed in a particular case are legally irrelevant and may not be taken into account by the Home Secretary in fixing the tariff. I conclude that the Home Secretary misdirected himself in giving weight to irrelevant considerations. It influenced his decisions. and it did so to the detriment of Venables and Thompson.
>
> For this further reason I conclude that his decisions were unlawful.

Lord Steyn makes the point that the information the Home Secretary took into account was irrelevant because it was not informed public opinion and was based on sensationalised newspaper accounts. He also found that, because setting a tariff was a judicial function, the Home Secretary had to act impartially and should not take into account the popularity of the decision with the public. It should be noted that, subsequent to the introduction of the HRA 1998, the power of the Home Secretary to fix a tariff has now been removed and the decision is now made by a judge.

16.4.5 Overlap between irrelevant considerations and improper purpose

Many of the decisions on irrelevant consideration and improper purpose could be decided under either heading. One case in which improper purpose and irrelevance were considered by the court was *R v Somerset County Council, ex p Fewings* [1995] 1 WLR 1037. Somerset County Council owned land in the Quantock hills where deer were hunted. In accordance with section 120(1)(b) of the Local Government Act 1972, the council had the power to manage land for the 'benefit, improvement or development of their area'. In 1993, Somerset County Council passed a resolution banning deer hunting with hounds on its land because a majority of councillors considered it to involve an unacceptable and unnecessary degree of cruelty. The Quantock Staghounds, an organisation that hunted deer for sport, challenged the decision. It was held by Laws J that the council had acted unlawfully because it had taken into account 'freestanding moral perceptions as opposed to an objective judgement about what will conduce to the better management of the estate' (at 529–30).

The Court of Appeal, by a majority, upheld the decision of Laws J. However, the Court of Appeal acknowledged that it was not necessarily unlawful to take into account the cruel nature of deer hunting. However, the council had not prohibited deer hunting in order to benefit, improve, or develop the land. At the relevant meeting at which the decision to ban deer hunting was taken, this was not considered. In other words, the council had not acted for the purposes stated in the statute and therefore its decision was unlawful.

● ***R v Somerset County Council, ex p Fewings*** [1995] 1 WLR 1037

Bingham LJ at 1046:

> The lack of reference [by the councillors] to the governing statutory test was not in my view a purely formal omission, for if councillors had been referred to it they would have had to attempt to define what benefit a ban would confer on the area and conversely what detriment the absence of a ban would cause. It may be that they could have done so, but as it was they did not need to try. The note certainly suggests that the debate ranged widely, and reference was made to 'economic grounds' and 'social damage' as well as to the cruelty argument and the contrary moral argument. But the note also suggests that expressions of purely personal opinion loomed large: 'rituals unwholesome instincts', 'systematically torture' 'barbaric and amusement', 'uniquely abhorrent', 'pleasure torturing animals'. In the absence of legal guidance, it was not, I think, appreciated that personal views, however strongly held, had to be related to the benefit of the area.
>
> I accordingly agree, although on much narrower grounds, that the county council were not entitled to make the decision they did on the grounds they relied on. I leave open, but express no view on, the possibility that the same decision could have been reached on proper grounds.

The case illustrates the principle that the public authority must act for the purpose stated in the statute. It also emphasises that the authority must consider only relevant factors. The statutory context determines whether the consideration is relevant. So the council could not prohibit deer hunting simply because it had a moral objection. However, Lord Justice Bingham indicates that it is lawful to consider moral arguments about the cruel nature of deer hunting when deciding whether prohibiting deer hunting was for the benefit, improvement, or development of the area. This is because to prohibit deer hunting for a reason stated in the statute is to act for a proper purpose rather than an improper one.

16.4.6 The relevance of resources

Whether a public authority can take into account its resources depends on whether the authority is exercising a discretionary power or is carrying out a statutory duty. If the authority has a duty to provide a service, then it cannot use resource arguments as a reason for not providing the service. If a discretionary power is being exercised, then resources may be a relevant factor in the decision-making process. In *R (on the application of G) v Barnet London Borough Council and others* [2003] UKHL 57, the House of Lords had to consider whether a local authority had to provide housing to homeless children with their parents, as opposed to other arrangements that would separate children from their parents, such as fostering the children or taking them into local authority care. The majority of the House of Lords construed the Children Act 1989 as imposing no such obligation. Lord Nicholls, in the next extract, describes the acute financial problems that local authorities face when trying to fulfil a wide range of functions without enough money to go around.

● *R (on the application of G) v Barnet London Borough Council and others* [2004] 2 AC 208

Lord Nicholls at 219:

> The ability of a local authority to decide how its limited resources are best spent in its area is displaced when the authority is discharging a statutory duty as distinct from exercising a power. A local authority is obliged to comply with a statutory duty regardless of whether, left to itself, it would prefer to spend its money on some other purpose. A power need not be exercised, but a duty must be discharged. That is the nature of a duty. That is the underlying purpose for which duties are imposed on local authorities. They leave the authority with no choice.
>
> [13] The extent to which a duty precludes a local authority from ordering its expenditure priorities for itself varies from one duty to another. The governing consideration is the proper interpretation of the statute in question. But identifying the precise content of a statutory duty in this respect is not always easy. This is perhaps especially so in the field of social welfare, where local authorities are required to provide services for those who need them. As a general proposition, the more specific and precise the duty the more readily the statute may be interpreted as imposing an obligation of an absolute character. Conversely, the broader and more general the terms of the duty, the more readily the statute may be construed as affording scope for a local authority to take into account matters such as cost when deciding how best to perform the duty in its own area. In such cases the local authority may have a wide measure of freedom over what steps to take in pursuance of its duty.

The extract explains that whether or not resources are a relevant consideration depends on whether the statute imposes a statutory duty. However, deciding on whether there is a duty or discretionary power is a matter of statutory interpretation. The next two House of Lords' decisions to be discussed illustrate that it is often a difficult and technical task to interpret the statute.

In the first case, *R v Gloucestershire CC, ex p Barry* [1997] AC 584, the claimant, Mr Barry, who was elderly and disabled, was assessed by the council in accordance with section 2(1) of the Chronically Sick and Disabled Persons Act 1970 as needing home care, including help with shopping, laundry, and cleaning. However, two years later, he was told that some of these services were being withdrawn because the authority no longer had enough money to pay for them. Barry argued that the council had acted unlawfully because it had taken into account its financial resources without reassessing his needs. By a majority, the House of Lords rejected his claim. It held that, when assessing Barry's needs, the council was entitled to consider its resources.

- -

● **R v Gloucestershire CC, ex p Barry** [1997] AC 584

Lord Nicholls at 604:

> A person's need for a particular type or level of service cannot be decided in a vacuum from which all considerations of cost have been expelled.

The House of Lords held that needs had to be assessed in the context of what would benefit the claimant, but this had to be balanced against the cost to the authority.

A different conclusion was reached in *R v East Sussex County Council, ex p Tandy* [1998] AC 714. The claimant, Beth Tandy, suffered from myalgic encephalomyelitis (ME, also known as chronic fatigue syndrome) and as a consequence was unable to attend school. The local authority provided her with five hours' home schooling per week, pursuant to its duty under section 19 of the Education Act 1996 to provide her with 'suitable education'. Suitable education was defined as 'in relation to the child or young person, means efficient education suitable to his age, ability aptitude and any special educational needs'. The local authority decided to cut Beth Tandy's home tuition to three hours per week for financial reasons. The House of Lords held that this was unlawful, because the local authority was not entitled to take into account its financial resources.

- -

● **R v East Sussex County Council, ex p Tandy** [1998] AC 714

Lord Brown-Wilkinson at 747:

> ...I can see no reason to treat the resources of the L.E.A. as a relevant factor in determining what constitutes 'suitable education'...

Later in the judgment, at 748, Lord Brown-Wilkinson stated that:

> The position in the present case is quite different [from *Barry*]. Under section 298 the L.E.A. is not required to make any prior determination of Beth's need for education nor of the necessity for making provision for such education. The statute imposes an immediate obligation to make arrangements to provide suitable education. Moreover it then expressly defines what is meant by 'suitable education' by reference to wholly objective educational criteria. For these reasons, in my judgment the decision in the *Barry* case [1997] A.C. 584 does not affect the present case.

The conflicting results in these cases show that the courts' decision on the nature of the statutory provision is crucial. Where the court finds that the power is wholly or partly discretionary, as in *Barry*, then resources are a relevant consideration and the authority may decide not to provide the benefit in question for financial reasons. In a later case, *R v Chief Constable of Sussex, ex p International Trader's Ferry Ltd* [1999] 2 AC 418, the House of Lords confirmed the view that resources can be a relevant consideration where the decision-maker has a discretion. In this case, animal rights protestors were making it difficult for ferry companies to export livestock on cross-Channel ferries. To prevent the demonstrators from interfering with the ferry crossings at the port required a high level of policing. The Chief Constable of Sussex took the decision to police the port two days a week only rather than five. This was because policing the port for five days was depleting resources and manpower, and having an impact on the efficient policing of the county. The House of Lords upheld the Chief Constable's decision on the grounds that, in carrying out his duty to uphold the law, he had a wide discretion and was entitled to take into account resources. It was therefore lawful to decide to reduce the amount of money spent on policing this one protest when deciding how best to meet the operational needs of the force.

NOTE

The courts are cautious about reviewing decisions when there are disputes centred on the allocation of resources. These issues are particularly sensitive during an economic downturn, when the government has a policy of reducing public expenditure. Consider the comments of Holman J in *R (on the application of Luton Borough Council and others) v Secretary of State for Education* [2011] EWHC 217 (Admin), noted above, which we will consider more fully in Chapters 17 and 18.

thinking point

Why do you think judicial review cases that challenge the way in which resources are allocated by public authorities cause particular difficulties for the courts? Reflect on the functions of Parliament, the executive, and the judiciary within the constitution when considering your answer. You may find it useful to reread Chapter 5 on the separation of powers.

16.4.7 Fiduciary duties

When local authorities exercise their discretion, they have to consider the fiduciary duty that they have to council taxpayers. This means that an authority has a special duty to its council taxpayers to spend money raised in a prudent or sensible way. This principle is a very controversial one. This is because it is argued that the principle prioritises the interests of local taxpayers above other interests. This is especially the case if the local authority has been elected on a mandate (an electoral promise) to introduce certain policies by local electors. *Roberts v Hopwood*, discussed above under the category of irrelevant political considerations, was also decided on the grounds of fiduciary duty. In that case, the House of Lords held that the local authority was acting unlawfully because it paid its workers what the district auditor and the court regarded as an excessive wage. This was not only considered to be unlawful on the grounds of irrelevant consideration, but also to be a breach of the local authority's duty to its ratepayers (now council taxpayers). Lord Atkinson explained why.

● *Roberts v Hopwood* [1925] AC 578

Lord Atkinson at 592:

> A body charged with the administration for definite purposes of funds contributed in whole or in part by persons other than the members of that body, owes, in my view, a duty to those latter persons to conduct that administration in a fairly businesslike manner with reasonable care, skill and caution, and with a due and alert regard to the interest of those contributors who are not members of the body. Towards these latter persons the body stands somewhat in the position of trustees or managers of the property of others.
>
> This duty is, I think, a legal duty as well as a moral one, and acts done in flagrant violation of it should, in my view, be properly held to have been done 'contrary to law'...

The reasoning in *Roberts v Hopwood* was applied in *Prescott v Birmingham Corporation* [1955] 1 Ch 210. The relevant statutory provision provided that the council could charge such fares as it thought fit for public transport. It was held that a scheme that provided for senior citizens to enjoy free travel was unlawful. This was because it generously benefited one section of the community at the expense of local taxpayers. This is an interesting decision, because it shows concerns that all (then) ratepayers should benefit from public funds, even though now it is well accepted by many taxpayers that particular provision should be made for the young, the elderly, and the infirm. Indeed, Parliament later enacted legislation that permits local authorities to provide concessionary fares to particular sections of the community.

Perhaps the most famous application of the principle was in *Bromley London Borough Council v Greater London Council* [1983] 1 AC 768. The Greater London Council (GLC) was elected after promising that it would cut transport fares in London by 25 per cent. In order to finance the fare cut, it issued a notice to the London borough councils (LBCs) to increase their rates. As a consequence of issuing the notice to increase the rates, the GLC would lose a rate support grant of £50 million. Bromley LBC, one of the London boroughs that had been told by the GLC to increase its rates, challenged the scheme as ultra vires. Section 1 of the Transport for London Act 1969 provided that the GLC had a duty to 'promote the provision of integrated efficient and economic transport facilities and services for London'. There were many arguments put forward in the case, including unreasonableness, irrelevant considerations, and breach of fiduciary duty. The House of Lords upheld the challenge of Bromley LBC on a number of grounds. On the issue of fiduciary duties to the ratepayers, the House of Lords held that, by funding the fare cut by increasing the rates and losing the rate support grant, the GLC had breached its fiduciary duty to ratepayers.

• •

● ***Bromley London Borough Council v Greater London Council*** [1983] 1 AC 768

Lord Diplock at 829:

> My Lords, the conflicting interests which the G.L.C. had to balance in deciding whether or not to go ahead with the 25 per cent reduction in fares, notwithstanding the loss of grant from central government funds that this would entail, were those of passengers and the ratepayers. It is well established by the authorities...that a local authority owes a fiduciary duty to the ratepayers from whom it obtains moneys needed to carry out its statutory functions, and that this includes a duty not to expend those moneys thriftlessly but to deploy the full financial resources available to it to the best advantage;...As I have already indicated I think that the G.L.C. had a discretion as to the proportions in which that total financial burden should be allocated between passengers and the ratepayers...So the total financial burden to be shared by passengers and the ratepayers for the provision of an integrated and efficient public passenger transport system was to be increased by an extra £50 million as a result of the decision, without any equivalent improvement in the efficiency of the system, and the whole of the extra £50 million was to be recovered from the ratepayers. That would, in my view, clearly be a thriftless use of moneys obtained by the G.L.C. from ratepayers and a deliberate failure to deploy to the best advantage the full financial resources available to it by avoiding any action that would involve forfeiting grants from central government funds. It was thus a breach of the fiduciary duty owed by the G.L.C. to the ratepayers. I accordingly agree with your Lordships that the precept issued pursuant to the decision was ultra vires and therefore void.

Lord Diplock held that imposing a heavy financial burden on the ratepayers in order to finance the reduction of 25 per cent in Tube and bus fares was unlawful. It was not a financially sound decision, in the view of the court, and therefore was a breach of the GLC's duty towards the ratepayers.

thinking point

It is worth noting that that this is one of the most controversial decisions in the history of administrative law. Many commentators argued that the judges had intervened in a decision of an elected authority on an issue of social policy as to the allocation of resources between ratepayers (council taxpayers) and electors. It has been seen as an example of judicial activism against a decision with which the court disagreed with. You should think about this decision in the context of what you have learnt about the separation of powers in constitutional law.

NOTE See Griffiths (1997: 126), listed in the further reading at the end of this chapter, for a discussion of this case and the role of the judiciary.

In this section, we have seen that discretionary powers must be exercised in accordance with the relevant statutory purpose. A public authority will be acting unlawfully if it acts for an improper purpose and this includes an improper political purpose. The courts will determine the statutory purpose by interpreting the statute. Public authorities must consider all relevant considerations and exclude from their mind all irrelevant factors. What is relevant will depend on the court's construction of the statute. Resources may be a relevant factor. Whether resources are relevant will depend on the statute in question. If the public authority is exercising a statutory duty, then resources are not relevant. If the power is discretionary, then resources may be a relevant factor. The courts have also held that local authorities have a fiduciary or special relationship with their ratepayers (council taxpayers) to act carefully when spending money and allocating resources.

summary points

Illegality: discretion, improper purpose, and irrelevant considerations

- *Public authorities must act in accordance with the statutory purpose.*

- *They must take into account relevant factors and exclude from their mind irrelevant factors. Resources may be a relevant factor depending on the statute in question.*

- *Local authorities must also consider their fiduciary relationship (that is, relationship of trust) with council taxpayers (previously ratepayers).*

507

16.5 Illegality and jurisdiction: error of law and error of fact

The issue of jurisdiction does not fit easily into any of the categories that we have studied so far. It is based on more classical doctrines of administrative law that are now used infrequently. But as Wade and Forsyth (2000: 285) note, 'It is not safe to say that the classical doctrines are wholly obsolete and that the broad and simple principles of review...will supplant them' (see the further reading listed at the end of the chapter). It is therefore important to have some understanding of jurisdictional issues, because the terminology is still used by the courts and, on occasion, jurisdiction is of real importance in judicial decision-making. This area of law also has particularly significance where the case concerns tribunals and other inferior courts created by statute, but jurisdiction is relevant to all public authorities.

When the court discusses the 'jurisdiction' of a public authority, it is discussing the power of that public authority to decide an issue of fact or law. The courts' main concern is that public authorities do not go beyond their powers or jurisdiction to decide issues that do not concern them and that they have no power to decide. So, for example, an employment tribunal would go beyond its jurisdiction if it were to decide immigration cases. Similarly, if a local authority had a statutory power to 'make a grant to school children in full-time education', it would be exceeding its jurisdiction if it were to make a grant to a university student. But who makes the decision as to what is an immigration case or who is a schoolchild? If, for example, the local authority were to define a 'schoolchild' as 'anyone in any kind of full-time education', it would extend its jurisdiction beyond the power granted to it in the statute. But should the courts have the power to correct such a decision?

The courts may be reluctant to intervene in a decision of a tribunal or public authority. Parliament may confer a power on an authority to make a decision because it is believed that body has a particular knowledge or expertise. Education, housing, and social security tribunals may be expert in their particular area. Specialist lawyers, lay experts, and judges may sit on the body, and may have acquired a better understanding and experience of the issues than the courts. If the court overturns its decisions on the grounds of error of law or fact, then it will interfere in areas in which Parliament intended the public authority to have the final say.

The courts have used many different methods to decide whether or not to intervene, and this has made this area of law legally and conceptually complex. One of the distinctions that need to be made is whether the body in question is said to have made an error of law or an error of fact. If a question is one of fact, then the courts are far less likely to intervene to overrule the decision. If the question is one of law, then judicial intervention to correct the decision is likely. This question is also important in many areas of law in which a statute may provide that an appeal is permitted only on a point of law and not fact.

16.5.1 What is the difference between a question of fact and a question of law?

There is no easy answer to the question of the difference between fact and law. Sometimes, the courts will decide that a question is a mixed question of fact, law, and degree. What follows aims to give the reader an idea of the courts' approach. Cane (2004, cited above: 229) argues that one approach is the analytic approach: the court decides whether a question is one of law or fact and then acts accordingly. So, for example, is the question of whether a young person is a schoolchild a question of law or fact? Such a straightforward question is likely to be one of fact and, as we will see below, the courts will rarely intervene to correct an error of fact.

One of the leading cases on the error of law/error of fact distinction is *Brutus v Cozens* [1972] 3 WLR 521. In that case, the appellant disrupted a tennis match by blowing a whistle and handing out leaflets to protest against apartheid as practised in South Africa at the time. He was charged with using insulting behaviour, contrary to section 5 of the Public Order Act 1936. He was acquitted, because the magistrates held that his behaviour was not insulting. On appeal, the House of Lords had to decide whether the question of whether behaviour was 'insulting' was a matter of fact or law. The House of Lords held that the question was one of fact.

● *Brutus v Cozens* [1973] AC 854

Lord Reid at 861:

The meaning of an ordinary word of the English language is not a question of law. The proper construction of a statute is a question of law. If the context shows that a word is used in an unusual sense the court will determine in other words what that unusual sense is. But here there is in my opinion no question of the word 'insulting' being used in any unusual sense. It appears to me . . . to be intended to have its ordinary meaning.

In this case, the classification was that the question was one of fact because 'insulting' is such a simple and straightforward word. Lord Reid stresses that unless a word has a technical or special meaning, it should be a question of fact and left to the decision-making body to decide. The consequence of the decision being classified as one of fact was that, unless there were exceptional circumstances, the court would not intervene and overturn the decision. In this case, the decision of the magistrates to acquit was upheld, because the House of Lords did not seek to overturn the facts as presented.

Another approach to the question of fact and law distinction, as suggested by Cane (2004: 230), is called the pragmatic approach. He argues that the court will classify an issue as one of law if the court wants to impose the courts' definition of the word on the body in question, for the sake of consistency, and to ensure that it is easy for the courts to intervene in decisions. There is evidence for Cane's pragmatic approach. In *Smith (Inspector of Taxes) v Abbott* [1994] 1 WLR 306, the majority of the House of Lords held that the question of whether expenditure by journalists on the purchase of newspapers and periodicals was incurred 'in the performance of the duties' of their employment so as to qualify as a deductible expense was a question of law. This enabled the House of Lords to unify conflicting decisions and to make sure that future decisions would be consistent. It appears that the traditional view that the courts make decisions on whether an issue is one of fact or law on principled grounds goes part way to explaining the courts' reasoning in this area. The courts use varying tests to decide whether an issue is one of fact or law. Decisions will vary depending on the statutory context and the answer to the question will often be found by studying previous case law dealing with the same statutory term in the area under consideration.

16.5.2 Errors of fact

The courts are reluctant to overturn decisions of fact for the reasons discussed above. In summary, these reasons are that, on judicial review, the courts do not want to take over the role of the main decision-maker and decide the merits of the case. Parliament has given the decision-making body the power to decide because of its special knowledge and expertise, and the original decision-maker may have actually examined the factual evidence, such as the relevant documents. It may also have heard witnesses and may be in a better position to decide on the weight given to the evidence. Judicial review is an examination of the legality of the decision and it is not appropriate to deal with factual questions on judicial review. Allowing claims based on errors of fact might lead the courts to be overwhelmed with applications. It can be seen that there are good reasons for restricting challenges to decisions based on the facts.

Nevertheless, the way in which the decision-making body deals with the facts may lead to real unfairness and therefore the courts will intervene in very limited circumstances. These are cases in which the fact is a precedent fact, in which there has been an irrational conclusion as fact, in which there is no evidence, and, more recently, in which there is a mistake of fact giving rise to unfairness. These categories overlap and cover many different situations, such as decisions made on no evidence and mistakes based on the evidence.

Precedent fact

The courts will intervene if the fact is a precedent or jurisdictional fact. This is a fact that has to be decided before the public authority has jurisdiction or power. An example of this is *White and Collins v Minister for Health* [1939] 2 KB 838. Section 74 of the Housing Act 1936 enabled a local authority to acquire land to provide houses for the working classes. But section 75 stated that the land must not form 'part of any park, garden or pleasure ground ...'. The legality of a compulsory purchase order was challenged by the owners of Highfield House. They claimed that the 35 acres around the house was a park. Therefore, according to the statute, it could not be the subject of the order, because parks could not be acquired under section 74 of the Act; section 75 specifically excluded them from it. The court had to determine, first of all, whether the land in issue was a park, because this would affect whether the authority had the power to acquire it, or not. The question of whether land was a park was a precedent or jurisdictional fact—precedent fact because it was a fact that had to be established first. The power to acquire the land depended on this finding of fact. If there were a mistake and the land in question were a park, then the local authority and the minister would have no power to order the compulsory purchase of the land. If the land were not a park (or a pleasure ground or a garden), then the authority would have the power to acquire it.

● ***White and Collins v Minister for Health*** [1939] 2 KB 838

Lord Justice MacKinnon at 856:

> The first and most important matter to bear in mind is that the jurisdiction to make the order is dependent on a finding of fact; for, unless the land can be held not to be part of a park or not to be required for amenity or convenience, there is no jurisdiction in the borough council to make, or in the Minister to confirm, the order. In such a case it seems almost self-evident that the Court which has to consider whether there is jurisdiction to make or confirm the order must be entitled to review the vital finding on which the existence of the jurisdiction relied upon depends. If this were not so, the right to apply to the Court would be illusory.

He goes on to conclude, at 859, that:

> I am satisfied that there was no evidence before the inspector sufficient to entitle the local authority or the Minister to come to a conclusion that the land in question was not part of the park of Highfield ...

The Court of Appeal found in favour of the owners. It held that the fact was a precedent or jurisdictional fact and the court was willing to invalidate the decision because the minister had concluded wrongly that the land was not a park. This meant that he was acquiring the land when he had no power or jurisdiction to do so.

The courts have been willing to hold that certain facts are jurisdictional or precedent facts, because if there is a mistake as to the fact, then the consequences for the claimant will be severe. This is one way of explaining why the courts have been willing to hold that certain facts are jurisdictional in a line of immigration cases concerned with the deportation of illegal entrants. The result of a finding that someone was an illegal entrant meant that a detention-and-removal order could be issued. This was considered in *Khawaja v Secretary of State for the Home Department* [1984] AC 74, in which the House of Lords held that the term 'illegal entrant' in the Immigration Act 1971 was a precedent or jurisdictional fact. This meant the Lords could review the evidence, which led to the conclusion that the claimants were illegal entrants. The House of Lords' justification for the decision was that the power concerned the liberty of the subject. Lord Wilberforce, in the extract below, explains that the decision whether someone is an illegal entrant is one of fact and he describes how the information is collected by the immigration department. He then goes on to discuss the nature of the review by the courts.

● **Khawaja v Secretary of State for the Home Department**   [1984] AC 74

Lord Wilberforce at 100:

> [T]he conclusion that a person is an illegal entrant is a conclusion of fact reached by immigration authorities upon the basis of investigations and interviews which they have power to conduct, including interviews of the person concerned, of an extensive character, often abroad, and of documents whose authenticity has to be verified by inquiries.

He continues at 105:

> Now there is no doubt that the courts have jurisdiction to review the facts on which the Home Office's conclusion was reached: there is no doubt that procedural means exist, whether under the head of habeas corpus or of judicial review, for findings of fact to be made, by the use of affidavit evidence or cross-examination upon them or oral evidence. There is no doubt that, questions of liberty and allegations of deception being involved, the court both can and should review the facts with care. The sole question is as to the nature of this review . . .

Lord Wilberforce then goes on to describe the way in which the court should approach a review of the facts in this type of case. He explains that the review of the facts is not a rehearing of the evidence, but instead a review to ensure that, on the basis of the evidence presented to the court, the decision-maker has reached a justifiable conclusion. This is not the same as looking at all of the evidence and coming to an initial conclusion; instead, the court considers whether the evidence is such that the decision-maker is entitled to reach the conclusion that it has reached. It does not substitute the court's conclusion, but considers whether the decision-maker's conclusion was acceptable, given the evidence that it considered in reaching it.

The Supreme Court decision in *R (A) v Croydon LBC (Secretary of State intervening)* [2009] 1 WLR 2557 provides a more recent illustration of how the Court decides whether a precedent fact exists. The local authority has a duty under section 20(1) of the Children Act 1989 to provide accommodation to 'any child in need within their area who appears to them to require accommodation'. The claimants were asylum seekers from Libya and Afghanistan, who claimed to be under the age of 18. But they were assessed by immigration officers and social services to be over the age of 18. The local authorities' duty to accommodate the claimants depended on them being classified as children. The local authorities owed no duty to accommodate adults. On a challenge for judicial review, the Court had to decide whether the question as to whether a person was a child or not was a precedent fact to be reviewed by the Court. The Supreme Court held that it was a precedent fact. Lady Hale explains why.

● **R (A) v Croydon LBC (Secretary of State intervening)**   [2009] 1 WLR 2557

Lady Hale:

> [32] The word 'child' is undoubtedly defined in wholly objective terms (however hard it may be to decide upon the facts of the particular case). With a few limited extensions, it defines the outer boundaries of the jurisdiction of both courts and local authorities under the 1989 Act. This is an Act for and about children. If ever there were a jurisdictional fact, it might be thought, this is it.

Lady Hale makes the point that the obligations to the individual under the relevant legislation are completely dependent on establishing that the individual is a child. If the individual is not a child, there is no statutory obligation by the local authority. So it is of the utmost importance that the question is decided correctly and therefore the public authorities' decision should be subject to supervision by way of judicial review.

Irrational conclusion of fact

If the conclusion as to fact is one that is irrational or based on no evidence, then the courts will be willing to intervene in the decision. In *Edwards v Bairstow* [1956] AC 14, Bairstow and others had purchased, for £12,000, a spinning machine; they had then sold it for £18,000. It was a one-off transaction and Bairstow had not undertaken any such business before. The question was whether it was 'an adventure in the nature of trade' so as to warrant assessment under Schedule D of the Income Tax Act 1918. The House of Lords held that the determination by the Inland Revenue Commissioners that it was not 'an adventure in the nature of trade' was wrong. Viscount Simonds stated that, even though it was a question of fact, the court could intervene.

● **Edwards v Bairstow** [1956] AC 14

Viscount Simonds at 29:

> For it is universally conceded that, though it is a pure finding of fact, it may be set aside on grounds which have been stated in various ways but are, I think, fairly summarized by saying that the court should take that course if it appears that the commissioners have acted without any evidence or upon a view of the facts which could not reasonably be entertained.

However, it is very difficult to convince the court that there has been an irrational conclusion on the facts. This is because, as discussed above, the courts are reluctant to interfere with the factual conclusions of the decision-making body. So, in *R v Monopolies and Mergers Commission, ex p South Yorkshire Transport* [1993] 1 WLR 23, the House of Lords refused to review the conclusion drawn by the Monopolies and Mergers Commission (MMC). The MMC had concluded that 'bus services' in an area that covered 1.65 per cent of the UK were carried out in a 'substantial part' of the UK in accordance with section 64(3) of the Fair Trading Act 1973. It thus investigated the merger between bus companies and found that the mergers were contrary to the public interest. The MMC stated that it had considered the social, economic, geographic, and political features of the area when deciding whether bus services covered a substantial part of the UK. The House of Lords discussed the decision in *Edwards v Bairstow*, but held that the decision in this case was a rational one, as can be seen in the following extract.

● **R v Monopolies and Mergers Commission, ex p South Yorkshire Transport** [1993] 1 WLR 23

Lord Mustill at 32:

> ... [T]he court is entitled to substitute its own opinion for that of the person to whom the decision has been entrusted only if the decision is so aberrant that it cannot be classed as rational: *Edwards v Bairstow* ... Approaching the matter in this light I am quite satisfied that there is no ground for interference by the court, since the conclusion at which the commission arrived was well within the permissible field of judgment ...

Mistake of fact giving rise to unfairness

It is now established that a mistake of fact giving rise to unfairness is a ground of challenge. In *E v Secretary of State for the Home Department* [2004] QB 1044, the Court of Appeal had to consider the impact of a mistake of fact in an immigration case. E was a foreign national, whose claim for asylum was rejected by the Home Secretary, which decision was upheld by adjudica-tors and the Immigration Appeal Tribunal. E wanted to put evidence before the Tribunal in the form of reports showing that membership of the Muslim Brotherhood in Egypt would lead to the risk of torture and detention, and that this should be considered as part of his asylum claim. These reports had become available after the hearing of the Immigration Appeal Tribunal, but before the decision was made. E was refused **leave** to appeal on the grounds that the Tribunal could determine the case only on the basis of the evidence before it at the hearing and could order a rehearing only if there was an error of law.

The claimant argued that the Tribunal had made a mistake of fact by not considering the new evidence. The Court of Appeal held that the law had now evolved to the stage at which it could be said that an error of fact giving rise to unfairness was a separate ground of review.

- **E v Secretary of State for the Home Department** [2004] QB 1044

Carnwath LJ at 1071:

[66] In our view, the time has now come to accept that a mistake of fact giving rise to unfair-ness is a separate head of challenge in an appeal on a point of law, at least in those statutory contexts where the parties share an interest in co-operating to achieve the correct result. Asylum law is undoubtedly such an area. Without seeking to lay down a precise code, the or-dinary requirements for a finding of unfairness are apparent...

First, there must have been a mistake as to an existing fact, including a mistake as to the availability of evidence on a particular matter. Secondly, the fact or evidence must have been 'established', in the sense that it was uncontentious and objectively verifiable. Thirdly, the appellant (or his advisers) must not been have been responsible for the mistake. Fourthly, the mistake must have played a material (not necessarily decisive) part in the tribunal's reasoning.

[67] Accordingly, we would accept the submissions of each of E and R, that, if the new evidence is admitted, the court will be entitled to consider whether it gives rise to an error of law in the sense outlined above.

thinking point
Review the case law on error of fact. Do you think the courts should review errors of fact in the same way as they review errors of law? What would be the consequence of such a change?

It went on to hold that the Immigration Appeal Tribunal had 'wrongly failed to consider the new evidence in the context of its discretion to direct a rehearing'.

The case is very significant in broadening the circumstances in which an error of fact can lead to the decision being challenged. It also blurs the distinction between error of law and error of fact. This is because the Court stated that the failure to consider a material fact is an error of law.

16.5.3 Error of law

An error of law is a mistake of law made by the public authority or tribunal. An error of law is essentially a decision that can be challenged under one of the three heads of review, as formulated by Lord Diplock in the *CCSU* case (outlined in the Introduction to this chapter). In other words, it is an error that comes within the grounds of irrationality, procedural impro-priety, and illegality. It would now also include a judicial review challenge under the Human Rights Act 1998.

cross reference
The decision in Anisminic and its significance for understand-ing ouster clauses is discussed in Chapter 14.

This area of law used to be extremely complicated. This was because the law used to distin-guish between different kinds of errors of law. Some errors of law were said to go to jurisdic-tion and could be reviewed; others were errors within jurisdiction and were regarded as not serious enough to be subject to review. However, in the landmark case of *Anisminic v Foreign*

513

Compensation Commission [1969] 2 AC 147 and subsequent cases, it has been established that all errors of law are subject to judicial review by the courts and the distinction is of less importance.

summary points

Illegality and jurisdiction: error of law and error of fact

- *Jurisdiction refers to the power of a public authority to decide a question of fact or law.*
- *The courts are reluctant to review errors of fact, preferring to leave such matters to the primary decision-maker.*
- *Errors of fact are reviewable if they are precedent facts.*
- *Irrational conclusions of fact or decisions based on no evidence may be reviewable.*
- *Mistakes of fact giving rise to unfairness are reviewable if there is a mistake as to an existing fact, if the evidence is uncontentious, and if the applicant is not responsible for the mistake.*
- *Errors of law are generally reviewable by the courts.*

👁 Summary

Illegality is largely concerned with errors of law, although, as we have seen, errors of fact may, in exceptional circumstances, be reviewable. Central to judicial review is the idea of ultra vires, which is the principle that public authorities have to act within their legal powers, and that if they act or fail to act consistently with their legal powers, they will be acting unlawfully. Much of the case law that we have discussed in this chapter has concerned challenges to the exercise of discretionary powers by public authorities. This is where the authority has had to exercise an element of choice when making a decision. Cases such as *Porter v Magill* and *Wheeler v Leicester City Council* demonstrate that the authority must act for a proper purpose. The authority must take into account all relevant factors and may not fetter or restrict its discretion by taking into account irrelevant considerations, as the cases of *Roberts v Hopwood* and *R v Somerset Council, ex p Fewings* show. Public authorities may adopt a policy when exercising a discretion, provided that they do not apply it rigidly and are willing to listen to someone with something new to say. The policy must also be in keeping with the purpose of the legislation that gave rise to the discretion. Resources can be taken into account provided that the statutory provision is construed as a discretionary power as opposed to a statutory duty. Local authorities are able to enter into contracts, although, in some circumstances, the courts have held that the nature of the contract is overly restrictive of their discretion. The courts have also held that public authorities or public officers must not delegate their power unless there is a statutory provision permitting delegation. The case of *Carltona* shows that this rule does not apply to government departments. Public authorities cannot allow themselves to be dictated to and may not abdicate their discretion by, in effect, allowing some other body to take the decision.

Illegality is a broad ground of judicial review that covers a wide range of possible wrongs by the authority by way of acting without legal authority, failing to act, and abusing discretion. Illegality is a ground of review that is frequently used by claimants challenging the decisions of those exercising public functions and it is likely that the case law in this area will continue to grow.

 **Questions**

1   What does 'ultra vires' mean?

2   Explain what is meant by 'discretionary power' and its significance to administrative decision-making.

3   Distinguish between errors of law and errors of fact, and explain in what circumstances the courts will review errors of fact.

4   Write a memorandum for a friend who has just taken up a job with a local authority that issues taxi licences. Explain in your memo how a discretionary power should be exercised. Also explain in what circumstances a court is likely to hold that a discretionary power has been exercised unlawfully.

5   The Imaginary Mobile Phone Mast Act 2003 gives power to a local council to grant applications for mobile phone masts and to attach conditions 'if it thinks fit'. Mobile L has made a successful application to Hill Town Council to erect a mobile phone mast outside Fairview Primary School on condition that it builds a new sports hall for the school. Mobile L objects to this condition being added on the basis that it has no obligation towards the school.

   Hill Town Council receives a letter from Fairview Primary School, and a petition signed by all of the parents and teachers at the school. They argue that it is a potential health hazard to place a mast so near a school and that the children's health should be paramount in such a decision. The school produces a report from an independent group of scientists about the cancer risk to children from such masts. The council refuses to consider the report. It simply says that it has a policy of approving such applications and it must follow its policy for the sake of consistency. The council also states that the mast is at least 5 metres from the school and is perfectly safe. In fact, the mast is only 3 metres from the school. The council has also received guidance from the Secretary of State for the Environment that, for commercial reasons, all mobile phone mast applications should be accepted. The Secretary of State has written to the council informing it that, if the council wants to receive funds in the next round of spending by central government, it must encourage commercial enterprises. The council leaders know that losing central government funds would have serious financial consequences for its budget.

   Advise Fairview Primary School and the parents of the chances of successfully challenging the decision on a claim for judicial review. Also consider whether Mobile L can object to the imposition of the condition that it builds a new sports hall for the school.

 **Further reading**

Craig, P., *Administrative Law* (6th edn, Sweet & Maxwell, 2008)
Chapters 14 and 15 provide an analysis of the case law on error of law and fact. Chapters 16 and 17 deal with the failure to exercise discretion and the abuse of discretion. The book is a detailed account, with analysis written in a scholarly, but readable, style.

Griffiths, J. A. G., *The Politics of the Judiciary* (5th edn, London: Fontana Press/Harper Collins, 1997)

This is Griffiths' controversial study of the judiciary, which highlights the class and social backgrounds of the judges. His analysis of the case law illustrates his argument about the political nature of judging. Chapter 4 discusses the control of discretionary powers by the courts.

Wade, H. W. R. and Forsyth, C. F., *Administrative Law* (8th edn, Oxford: Oxford University Press, 2000)

The authors provide a detailed account of administrative law principles in this frequently quoted text. Chapters 8–12 deal with illegality.

Irrationality and Proportionality

Key points

This chapter will cover:

- The history of irrationality
- The development of the irrationality test
- The application of irrationality as a ground of review
- Human rights judicial review: the proportionality test
- Human rights judicial review: the application of the proportionality test
- Non-human-rights judicial review: irrationality is the correct test
- Is there a need for reform?

Introduction

This chapter is the fourth substantive chapter on judicial review and it will focus on the circumstances in which the courts can review a decision of a public authority or a body exercising public functions on the grounds that it is irrational. This chapter will explain the history of irrationality and Wednesbury unreasonableness, to provide some background to the topic and to chart its development. It will then give examples of cases in which the courts have discussed different versions of the irrationality test. It will discuss the difference between irrationality and proportionality, and examine the development of proportionality and its use in judicial review cases. It will distinguish between proportionality and merits review, and discuss the use of judicial deference by the courts. It will explain that proportionality, and not irrationality, is the test used to determine whether a public authority has acted unlawfully when its decision is challenged by judicial review under section 6 of the Human Rights Act 1998. But the courts have insisted that, in non-human-rights cases, irrationality remains the correct ground on which to challenge a decision. The chapter will conclude by considering whether the irrationality test should be replaced by the test of proportionality across both types of case—traditional judicial review cases and those involving a human rights issue. To begin with, we shall focus on the history of irrationality as a ground for judicial review of public body and public authority decisions.

 ## 17.1 The history of irrationality

Historically, this ground of review was known as 'unreasonableness', or **Wednesbury unreasonableness** after the case in which the principle was most clearly laid down. Confusingly, the courts use both terms (unreasonableness and **irrationality**) interchangeably to refer to the same principle. Because there appears to be no agreed distinction between them, both terms will be used here. Irrationality is a controversial principle because it has been used by the courts on occasion to interfere in politically contentious **executive** decisions—in other words, to review policy decisions that may more properly be considered to be the domain of the executive rather than the **judiciary**. The leading case on unreasonableness is *Associated Provincial Picture Houses v Wednesbury Corporation* [1948] 1 KB 223—the case that gave rise to the term '*Wednesbury* unreasonableness'.

It may be helpful to set out the facts of the case, to illustrate the point. Associated Provincial Picture Houses ran a cinema in the Wednesbury area, in the Midlands. It wanted to open the cinema on Sundays. Sunday opening was controversial at this time, because many Christians believed the Sabbath should be given over to prayer and contemplation as opposed to entertainment. The licence application was made in accordance with section 1 of the Sunday Entertainments Act 1932. This gave the **public authority** the power to grant a licence for Sunday opening 'subject to such conditions as the authority think fit to impose'. Associated Provincial Picture Houses was granted the licence, but the Wednesbury Corporation imposed a condition that no children under the age of 15 should be admitted to Sunday performances, under any circumstances. This meant that children under 15 could not be admitted to the cinema even if they were accompanied by an adult. Associated Provincial Picture Houses sought a **judicial** review of the decision that imposed this condition, because it argued that the imposition of the condition was an unreasonable exercise of **discretion** and therefore **ultra vires**.

The Court of Appeal upheld the first-instance decision and rejected the claim that Wednesbury Corporation had acted unreasonably in imposing the condition. Lord Greene explained (at 230) that the Court might have a different opinion from Wednesbury Corporation as to whether children under 15 should be admitted to a cinema on a Sunday and in fact 'all over the country I have no doubt on a thing of that sort honest and sincere people have different views'. He explained that it was not for the courts to impose their view on the public authority; provided that the authority acted lawfully, then courts would not intervene to change a decision that was legally taken. However, Lord Greene made it clear that lawfulness was linked to reasonableness: in order to act lawfully, the authority had to act reasonably. In the following extract, Lord Greene describes what was meant by 'reasonable'.

● **Associated Provincial Picture Houses v Wednesbury Corporation** [1948] 1 KB 223

Lord Greene at 229:

> It is true the discretion must be exercised reasonably. Now what does that mean? Lawyers familiar with the phraseology commonly used in relation to exercise of statutory discretions often use the word 'unreasonable' in a rather comprehensive sense. It has frequently been used and is frequently used as a general description of the things that must not be done. For instance, a person entrusted with a discretion must, so to speak, direct himself properly in law. He must call his own attention to the matters which he is bound to consider. He must exclude from his consideration matters which are irrelevant to what he has to consider. If he does not obey those rules, he may truly be said, and often is said, to be acting 'unreasonably'. Similarly, there may be something so absurd that no sensible person could ever dream that it lay within the powers of the authority. Warrington L.J. in *Short v. Poole Corporation* gave the example of the red-haired teacher, dismissed because she had red hair. That is unreasonable in one sense. In another sense it is taking into consideration extraneous matters. It is so unreasonable that it might almost be described as being done in bad faith; and, in fact, all these things run into one another.

cross reference

Discretion is discussed further in Chapter 16.

Lord Greene mentions the term 'discretion', which denotes that the body has a choice in making its decision. Much legislation gives public bodies a discretion, or a choice, in how they exercise their legal power. One public body may come to one decision; another to a different one. Their decision must be lawful and reasonable, and must be made following the proper procedure, but assuming that this has been done, the decision will stand even if another decision-maker may have come to a different conclusion faced with the same power and the same facts. The question is when is a decision classed as reasonable? In this instance, Lord Greene held that it was reasonable for the public authority to be concerned with the moral and spiritual well-being of children when exercising its discretion as to whether to permit a cinema to be open on Sunday. There are several points that arise from the *Wednesbury* case. Firstly, the *Wednesbury* test is an objective test and the court cannot invalidate the decision because it disagrees with it or because it would have reached a different conclusion. In the words of Lord Greene, the decision has to be 'so absurd that no sensible person would ever dream that it lay within the power of the authority' before the court will hold the decision to be unreasonable. Secondly, it is not enough for the decision to be unreasonable; it has to be *so* unreasonable that *no* reasonable authority could come to such a conclusion. This is why the case has been said to introduce the idea of degrees of unreasonableness. Thirdly and finally, it is clear from the *Wednesbury* judgment that the judicial review grounds of **illegality** and irrationality overlap with each other.

The exercise of a power may be challenged on more than one ground of review. Lord Greene uses the example of a teacher who is dismissed simply because she has red hair. In one sense, this decision is invalid on the ground that we now call illegality because the decision-maker has taken into account an irrelevant consideration—but it is also an unreasonable decision because it is so unreasonable to dismiss a teacher because she has red hair that no reasonable person could make such a decision. This case provides the evidence that the grounds of illegality and irrationality are blurred.

However, this was not the end of the discussion on unreasonableness or irrationality. Nearly forty years later, the unreasonableness test was reformulated in *CCSU*, also known as the *GCHQ case*. The next extract sets out the classic restatement of irrationality as a ground for review.

thinking point

Could this case have been brought on the ground of review now called illegality? You might find it helpful to review the material in Chapter 16 before answering this question.

· ·

● **Council for the Civil Service Unions v Minister for the Civil Service** [1985] AC 374

Lord Diplock at 410:

> By 'irrationality' I mean what can now succinctly be referred to as *Wednesbury* unreasonableness... It applies to a decision which is so outrageous in its defiance of logic or of accepted moral standards that no sensible person who had applied his mind to the question to be decided could have arrived at it. Whether a decision falls within this category is a question that judges by their training and experience should be well equipped to answer, or else there would be something wrong with our judicial system... irrationality by now can stand on its own feet as an accepted ground on which a decision may be attacked by judicial review.

This statement of the test makes it clear that irrationality is a separate ground of review from illegality and **procedural impropriety**. Jowell and Lester point out the following.

· ·

● **A. Lester and J. Jowell, 'Beyond *Wednesbury*: substantive principles of administrative law'** [1987] Public Law 368, 369

> By separating irrationality from illegality he [Lord Diplock] made the point that even though a decision may be legal (in the sense of being within the scope of the legislative scheme), it may nevertheless be substantially unlawful.

So a decision that is not ultra vires on the grounds of illegality or procedural impropriety may be unlawful because it is irrational. We shall examine below the kind of decisions that the courts will hold to be irrational and the way in which the irrationality test has developed since the decision in *CCSU*.

summary points

The history of irrationality

- *The test of unreasonableness was stated by Lord Greene in* Associated Provincial Picture Houses v Wednesbury Corporation *[1948] 1 KB 223.*
- *It is an objective test that often overlaps with other grounds of review.*
- *It was restated in the CCSU case by Lord Diplock, who used the term 'irrationality' rather than 'unreasonableness'.*
- *The CCSU case stressed that irrationality could now be considered as a free-standing ground for review.*

17.2 The development of the irrationality test

Subsequent to the decision in *Wednesbury*, the unreasonableness/irrationality test has continued to play an important role in the development of administrative law, although it has often been used in combination with other grounds of review. Craig (2008: 621) describes it as having 'occupied centre stage in the control of discretion'. There have been various attempts to apply the irrationality test strictly, with the result that it is very difficult for the claimant to demonstrate that the public authority's decision is irrational. There have also been attempts by the courts to apply the test more leniently to make the irrationality test easier to satisfy. This section will consider the way in which the test has been applied since its development in *CCSU*.

17.2.1 The 'strict' application of the irrationality test

The strict approach to irrationality has sometimes been described as applying a 'super-*Wednesbury* test' because it is so hard to satisfy. An example of a strict approach to irrationality can be found in *Nottinghamshire County Council v Secretary of State for the Environment* [1986] AC 240. The facts of this case are extremely complex. Essentially, the case was brought by two local authorities against the Secretary of State for the Environment. The local authorities were very concerned that guidance issued by the Secretary of State pursuant to the Local Government Planning and Land Act 1980 meant that their authorities would suffer severe financial penalties if they were to overspend their budget. The guidance issued was bitterly opposed by many local authorities, which felt that they were being unfairly penalised. Central **government** was determined to ensure that local authorities remained within their key spending targets and it was a major part of the then Conservative government's economic policy. The guidance to the authorities was made by the Secretary of State for the Environment, but the statute provided for an extra safeguard and this was that the guidance had to be approved by the House of Commons in the form of a resolution, which, in this instance, it was. The authorities challenged the decision partly on the basis of illegality—it was claimed that the Secretary of State had exceeded his statutory powers—but it was also argued that the Secretary of State had acted unreasonably. The claimants argued that the burden imposed on some authorities compared with that on others was so disproportionate that it was perverse and unreasonable. The House of Lords rejected both arguments. Lord Scarman gave the leading judgment on irrationality. In the next extract, he explains his reasoning for rejecting the local authority's argument.

. . . .

● ***Nottinghamshire County Council v Secretary of State for the Environment***
   [1986] AC 240

Lord Scarman at 247–9:

> But I cannot accept that it is constitutionally appropriate, save in very exceptional circumstances, for the courts to intervene on the ground of 'unreasonableness' to quash guidance framed by the Secretary of State and by necessary implication approved by the House of Commons, the guidance being concerned with the limits of public expenditure by local authorities and the incidence of the tax burden as between taxpayers and ratepayers. Unless and until a statute provides otherwise, or it is established that the Secretary of State has abused his power, these are matters of political judgment for him and for the House of Commons. They are not for the judges or your Lordships' House in its judicial capacity.

For myself, I refuse in this case to examine the detail of the guidance or its consequences. My reasons are these. Such an examination by a court would be justified only if a **prima facie** case were to be shown for holding that the Secretary of State had acted in bad faith, or for an improper motive, or that the consequences of his guidance were so absurd that he must have taken leave of his senses. The evidence comes nowhere near establishing any of these propositions. Nobody in the case has ever suggested bad faith on the part of the Secretary of State. Nobody suggests, nor could it be suggested in the light of the evidence as to the matters he considered before reaching his decision, that he had acted for an improper motive.

prima facie   Latin meaning 'on the face of it'.

This extract shows that Lord Scarman was applying the irrationality test very strictly indeed. His rationale for this was that the guidance was based on a political judgement, which was endorsed by democratically elected representatives, and it was therefore not for the courts to question it unless it was so absurd that it must be wrong in principle. There are good public policy reasons for taking such a view. Lord Scarman explained why the courts should hesitate to review this kind of decision.

● ***Nottinghamshire County Council v Secretary of State for the Environment*** [1986] AC 240

Lord Scarman at 250–1:

The present case raises in acute form the constitutional problem of the separation of powers between Parliament, the executive, and the courts...

To sum it up, the levels of public expenditure and the incidence and distribution of taxation are matters for Parliament, and, within Parliament, especially for the House of Commons. If Parliament legislates, the courts have their interpretative role: they must, if called upon to do so, construe the statute. If a minister exercises a power conferred on him by the legislation, the courts can investigate whether he has abused his power. But if, as in this case, effect cannot be given to the Secretary of State's determination without the consent of the House of Commons and the House of Commons has consented, it is not open to the courts to intervene unless the minister and the House must have misconstrued the statute or the minister has—to put it bluntly—deceived the House. The courts can properly rule that a minister has acted unlawfully if he has erred in law as to the limits of his power even when his action has the approval of the House of Commons, itself acting not legislatively but within the limits set by a statute. But, if a statute, as in this case, requires the House of Commons to approve a minister's decision before he can lawfully enforce it, and if the action proposed complies with the terms of the statute (as your Lordships, I understand, are convinced that it does in the present case), it is not for the judges to say that the action has such unreasonable consequences that the guidance upon which the action is based and of which the House of Commons had notice was perverse and must be set aside. For that is a question of policy for the minister and the Commons, unless there has been bad faith or misconduct by the minister. Where Parliament has legislated that the action to be taken by the Secretary of State must, before it is taken, be approved by the House of Commons, it is no part of the judges' role to declare that the action proposed is unfair, unless it constitutes an abuse of power in the sense which I have explained; for Parliament has enacted that one of its Houses is responsible. Judicial review is a great weapon in the hands of the judges: but the judges must observe the constitutional limits set by our parliamentary system upon their exercise of this beneficent power.

The House of Lords was extremely reluctant to intervene, because it saw economic policy and political disputes as a matter for political forums such as **Parliament** and not an issue to be considered by the courts. Lord Scarman was exercising judicial restraint. This means that he was stating that the courts, in accordance with the constitutional doctrine of the **separation of powers**, should be wary of straying into areas that are better dealt with by the executive and Parliament. However, this is not always the case and the courts have been criticised for being willing to intervene in other equally controversial cases. The irrationality test has not been universally applied in its strict form, however, and the next subsection considers cases in which the test has been applied less strictly.

NOTE

For an example of a contentious decision in which the judiciary intervened to hold the decision of a public authority unlawful, see *Bromley London Borough Council v Greater London Council* [1983] 1 AC 768, which was discussed in Chapter 16.

thinking point

Why does Lord Scarman think that 'Judicial review is a great weapon in the hands of the judges'? Do you agree with him? You may find it helpful to revisit the reading in Chapter 14 when considering this question.

17.2.2 The 'lenient' application of the irrationality test

The *Nottinghamshire* case made it seem as though the irrationality test was very difficult to satisfy and would not be of much use to claimants seeking to challenge public authorities' decisions. However the courts have also developed a more lenient approach towards irrationality. This is referred to as the 'heightened scrutiny approach', because it requires a higher degree of investigation of the decision by the courts. As a result, it is this form of the test that claimants seek to use in their submissions and, in *R v Ministry of Defence, ex p Smith* [1996] 2 WLR 305, the Court of Appeal approved a less strict formulation of the irrationality test. This case concerned a challenge to a Ministry of Defence policy that prevented homosexuals from serving in the armed services. In this instance, the claimants had been dismissed from the armed services after their sexual orientation became known. They challenged the policy as an irrational exercise of discretion. This case occurred before the Human Rights Act 1998 was in force and therefore the claimants had to rely on the traditional grounds of review. The Court of Appeal rejected their challenge of irrationality and found in favour of the government—but the Court of Appeal approved the following application of the irrationality test.

● ***R v Ministry of Defence, ex p Smith*** [1996] QB 517

Sir Thomas Bingham MR at 554:

> Mr. David Pannick, who represented three of the applicants, and whose arguments were adopted by the fourth, submitted that the court should adopt the following approach to the issue of irrationality:
>
>> 'The court may not interfere with the exercise of an administrative discretion on substantive grounds save where the court is satisfied that the decision is unreasonable in the sense that it is beyond the range of responses open to a reasonable decision-maker. But in judging whether the decision-maker has exceeded this margin of appreciation the human rights context is important. The more substantial the interference with human rights, the more the court will require by way of justification before it is satisfied that the decision is reasonable in the sense outlined above.'
>
> This submission is in my judgment an accurate distillation of the principles...

The Court of Appeal reluctantly held that the Ministry of Defence's policy was not irrational even when applying the easier test. The decision-maker had a discretion and, in reaching the conclusion that homosexuals could not serve in the armed forces, it was a decision that was within the range of decisions that a reasonable decision-maker could make.

● *R v Ministry of Defence, ex p Smith* [1996] QB 517

Sir Thomas Bingham MR at 557:

> The existing policy cannot in my judgment be stigmatised as irrational at the time when these applicants were discharged. It was supported by both Houses of Parliament and by those to whom the ministry properly looked for professional advice. There was, to my knowledge, no evidence before the ministry which plainly invalidated that advice. Changes made by other countries were in some cases very recent. The Australian, New Zealand and Canadian codes had been adopted too recently to yield much valuable experience. The ministry did not have the opportunity to consider the full range of arguments developed before us. Major policy changes should be the product of mature reflection, not instant reaction. The threshold of irrationality is a high one. It was not crossed in this case.

This case reflects a much more flexible approach to irrationality and is easier to satisfy. It means that the more significant the issue at stake, the greater the courts' scrutiny of the decision. However, irrationality is an inherently difficult test to satisfy even in its more leniently applied form, and the claimants were still unable to show irrationality despite the blatant discrimination and prejudice displayed towards them. It is very important to understand that a case such as this would now engage the Human Rights Act 1998, and, as will be explained later in the chapter, the correct test in a human rights case is now proportionality and not irrationality. Indeed, the policy has since changed, in 2000, to reflect this. Nevertheless, *Smith* remains a very significant case because the irrationality test continues to be used in non-human-rights cases and this case shows that irrationality can be applied less strictly than in cases such as *Nottinghamshire*.

summary points

The development of the irrationality test

- *The irrationality test has continued to develop since the CCSU case.*
- *There are cases that demonstrate the courts will apply the test more leniently, particularly when the decision that is being challenged is one that will have a major impact on individuals' lives.*
- *In these situations, the courts may subject the decision to a high degree of scrutiny, to check that it is a rationale one.*
- *However, the test remains difficult to satisfy, as indicated by* R v Ministry of Defence, ex p Smith.

17.3 The application of irrationality as a ground of review

17.3.1 Successful claims based on irrationality or *Wednesbury* unreasonableness

The irrationality test has been much criticised, but it continues to be used as a ground of review for administrative decisions. The two cases set out below are illustrations of successful challenges to administrative decisions based on the irrationality ground. The first case we shall consider, *In Re Duffy (FC) (Northern Ireland)* [2008] UKHL 4, relates to the Public Processions (Northern Ireland) Act 1998. Public parades and processions are an important part of the life of Northern Ireland. The routes of processions have been contentious, and have led to public disorder and communal violence. The statute established a seven-member Parades Commission, the purpose of which was to resolve and mediate disputes concerned with public processions, and to issue a code of practice to guide them. It also had the power to impose conditions on public processions and to prescribe the route to be taken. This case concerned a challenge to the Secretary of State for Northern Ireland's decision to appoint two new commissioners to the Parades Commission. The objection was that the two new commissioners were members of Protestant loyalist organisations that had been involved in disputes with rival Catholic organisations about the routing of parades. This was a politically charged decision in the context of Northern Ireland, where there is a history of tension between the Catholic and Protestant communities. In this case, the House of Lords held that the appointments were ones that no reasonable Secretary of State could make.

. . . .

● ***In Re Duffy (FC) (Northern Ireland)*** [2008] UKHL 4

Lord Bingham of Cornhill:

> [27] Mr Burrows and Mr Mackay had both been very prominent and committed proponents of the loyalist parade from Drumcree along the Garvaghy Road to Portadown. When appointed neither had resigned from the bodies to which they belonged and neither gave any recorded indication that he had changed his allegiance. No reasonable person, knowing of the two appointees' background and activities, could have supposed that either would bring an objective or impartial judgment to bear on problems raised by the parade in Portadown and similar parades elsewhere.

Lord Bingham makes it clear that the political allegiances of the two appointees mean that they could not be viewed as impartial. In view of the Parades Commission's purpose as a mediator between the conflicting demands of the different communities in Northern Ireland, the Secretary of State's decision to appoint them could not be considered to be rational.

Another example of the successful application of the irrationality test can be seen in *R (on the application of Rogers) v Swindon NHS Primary Care Trust* [2006] 1 WLR 2649. The claimant challenged the policy of the Swindon NHS Primary Care Trust in relation to the prescription of the drug Herceptin®. Rogers sought to challenge the decision to refuse to prescribe her Herceptin for early-stage breast cancer. The drug had not yet been licensed for early-stage breast cancer, but there was medical evidence that it could be effective. Following much media publicity and guidance from the Secretary of State for Health, the authority decided to exclude consideration of its resources and to prescribe Herceptin in exceptional circumstances for those women who would benefit from the drug. The Court of Appeal held this policy to be irrational, because there was no logical way in which to distinguish between patients' circumstances so as to deem them exceptional.

. . . .

● ***R (Rogers) v Swindon NHS Primary Care Trust*** [2006] 1 WLR 2649

Sir Anthony Clarke MR at 2672:

> [81] All the clinical evidence is to the same effect. The PCT has not put any clinical or medical evidence before the court to suggest any such clinical distinction could be made. In these circumstances there is no rational basis for distinguishing between patients within the eligible group on the basis of exceptional clinical circumstances any more than on the basis of personal, let alone social, circumstances. In short, we accept . . . that once the PCT decided (as

it did) that it would fund Herceptin for some patients and that cost was irrelevant, the only reasonable approach was to focus on the patient's clinical needs and fund patients within the eligible group who were properly prescribed Herceptin by their physician. This would not open the floodgates to those suffering from breast cancer because only comparatively few satisfy the criteria so as to qualify for the eligible group.

[82] For these reasons we have reached the conclusion that the policy of the PCT is irrational...

This case demonstrates a number of things. Firstly, it suggests that the courts will require a decision to be clearly rational if the decision is liable to have a major impact on individuals—in this case, the prescription of a drug could be deemed to fall into this category. Secondly, it requires decision-makers to be clear and robust in their decision-making. The term 'exceptional circumstances' appears, on the face of it, to be a sensible basis upon which to found a decision—but the Court of Appeal required it to be capable of being put into practice in a rational manner, as well as to appear, on the face of it, to be rational.

17.3.2 Unsuccessful claims based on irrationality and *Wednesbury* unreasonableness

There are many examples of cases in which the courts have rejected a challenge to an administrative decision on the grounds of irrationality. The *Wednesbury* case itself is an example of a failed claim, as are the decisions in *Smith* and *Nottinghamshire*, discussed earlier in this chapter. The case of *R (Luton and others) v Secretary of State for Education* [2011] EWHC 217 (Admin), which was briefly mentioned in Chapter 16, is an example of a recent decision in which irrationality failed as a ground of review. The claimants were local authorities, which were planning to rebuild a number of schools in their area under the previous Labour government's Building Schools for the Future (BSF) programme. This programme aimed to refurbish or rebuild every secondary school in the UK over a fifteen-year period starting from 2005. The BSF procedure involved various complicated stages whereby the local authorities had to produce plans that were approved by central government. The claimant local authorities had got to the stage at which they had received what was called 'outline business case approval' from central government for their plans, but they had not yet received 'final business case approval', which would have provided them with funding.

After the May 2010 general election, Education Secretary Michael Gove announced the cancellation of the scheme. He provided a cut-off date and, put simply, he stated that all local authority plans for rebuilding schools that had not received final business case approval by that date could not go ahead. The claimant authorities all had some schools in their area that had their rebuilding cancelled because they fell outside the chosen cut-off date. The local authorities challenged the decision on several grounds; the one that concerns us here is irrationality. It was argued that the Education Secretary's decision overall was irrational, as was his choice of cut-off date. The judge rejected this argument.

● **R (Luton and others) v Secretary of State for Education** [2011] EWHC 217 (Admin)

Holman J:

[48] The present case concerns a very major decision with a patently political and heavy macroeconomic content, made at the highest level in the immediate aftermath of a general election and change of government, and patently intended to help achieve economic demands from the Treasury... By drawing the line so as to stop rather than save the claimants' projects,

> the Secretary of State 'saved' about £1 billion or more. The Secretary of State and the government are politically answerable for the decisions they have taken. Their reasons may or may not withstand political scrutiny and challenge; but, being satisfied that there is no inherent irrationality about them, I decline further to examine their rationality. To do so would, in my view, be a grave and exorbitant usurpation by the court of the minister's political role.

The judge stressed that it was not irrational for the Education Secretary to end the BSF programme to save money in line with government policy and to choose this cut-off date. He emphasised the highly political nature of the issue and stated that while the decision to save money in this way might be challenged politically in Parliament, it was not for the court to challenge a decision based on economic policy that concerned how the government used its resources.

cross reference

See Chapters 16 and 18 for more detail on Luton.

The claimants in this case did, however, succeed on other grounds of review and the court ordered the Education Secretary to reconsider his decision.

This section has shown that irrationality can be used successfully as a ground for reviewing the decisions of public authorities. The use of the term 'unreasonableness' by the House of Lords in *Re Duffy* confirms the interchangeability of the two terms 'irrationality' and 'unreasonableness'. It also confirms that unreasonableness/irrationality is an independent ground of review. The breadth of the subject matter of the three successful cases reflects the usefulness of irrationality often as a catch-all ground of review. The difficulties of establishing irrationality as a ground of review can be seen in cases such as *Smith* and *Nottinghamshire*. In the most recent case, *Luton*, the court stressed that it would be reluctant to quash a decision on the grounds of irrationality where it is concerned with the allocation of resources.

summary points

The application of irrationality as a ground of review

- *The irrationality test is a difficult test to satisfy.*
- *The terms 'unreasonableness' and 'irrationality' are now often used interchangeably.*
- *It is firmly established as a separate ground for review from illegality and procedural impropriety.*
- *The courts are reluctant to find a decision irrational if the decision has public funding and/or public resource allocation issues associated with it. This is because public funding and the allocation of resources are viewed as inherently political, rather than legal, decisions that should be made by elected representatives as opposed to the unelected judiciary.*

527

17.4 Human rights judicial review: the proportionality test

17.4.1 What is the difference between proportionality and irrationality?

At the beginning of this chapter, we mentioned the term 'proportionality' in the context of judicial review on grounds of irrationality. Thus far, we have concentrated on unreasonableness and irrationality. There are good reasons for this—not least because proportionality is a relatively new and developing concept in judicial review in the UK, by comparison with unreasonableness. The proportionality test has its origin in European law and has been imported into the UK legal system through European Union (EU) law and the **European Convention on Human Rights (ECHR)**. Writing over twenty years ago, Jowell and Lester noted that although the test is European in its origin, it does have features that are in accord with our own UK legal systems.

● **A. Lester and J. Jowell, 'Beyond *Wednesbury*: substantive principles of administrative law'** [1987] Public Law 368, 375

> It seems so characteristically English to require that the means employed by the decision-maker must be no more than is reasonably necessary to achieve his legitimate aims—that he should not use a sledgehammer to crack a nut—that there should be no difficulty in absorbing the concept of proportionality into the English judicial process.

We shall discuss the precise nature of the proportionality test as applied by the courts in more detail below, but it is necessary for you first to understand the basic idea that underpins the concept of proportionality and how it differs from the test of irrationality. Feldman provides the following definition of how the courts use the concept of proportionality.

● **D. Feldman, *Civil Liberties and Human Rights in England and Wales*** (Oxford: Oxford University Press, 2002), p. 57

> This involves balancing the seriousness of the interference against the seriousness of the threats to the interests which are protected within the purposes for which it is legitimate to interfere with the right. Part of that balancing exercise requires the court to consider whether the extent of the interference is greater than is reasonably necessary to achieve the legitimate aim.

Proportionality usually involves the court in considering whether it would have been possible to achieve the legitimate aim by a less intrusive means or whether the interference causes harm to the rights holder that is serious enough to outweigh any benefit that the interference might achieve through furthering a legitimate aim. It may be useful to think of this in concrete terms.

example

> In order to prevent military secrets being revealed and national security being compromised, the government might try to prevent any media reports on the war in Afghanistan by imposing a blanket ban on reports in the UK. But such a ban would restrict the right to freedom of expression set out in Article 10 ECHR and would deprive the public of information about the war. The government cannot be faulted for trying to protect national security and this is regarded as a proper or legitimate aim. But its blanket ban on reporting would be regarded as disproportionate to the aim of protecting national security. The government could protect military secrets by other measures that do not infringe the right to freedom of expression so drastically. One way in which it might do this would be to prevent the disclosure of the exact location of a military incident or to prevent details of military strategies being revealed in advance of action by the armed forces. The government does not need to go as far as banning all news reporting in order to protect national security and such a ban would be regarded as disproportionate.

Consequently, proportionality means that, assuming that the aim is a legitimate one (in the example, protecting national security by protecting military secrets), the means used to achieve that legitimate aim must be in proportion when one balances what is being lost or restricted in attempting to meet the aim.

There has been a long-running debate amongst administrative lawyers as to whether proportionality has become another ground of review independent of European law. The Court of Appeal decision in *R (on the application of Association of British Civilian Internees: Far East Region) v Secretary of State for Defence* [2003] QB 1397 (the *Wartime Detainees case*) established that this is not the case, and that the proportionality test is appropriate only in cases concerned with EU law and the Human Rights Act 1998 (HRA 1998). So, for cases that relate to pure domestic law, the irrationality test stands as the appropriate one; for cases that involve domestic law in fields regulated by EU law or the ECHR (and related international legal principles), or for the interpretation of EU and Council of Europe provisions, the proportionality test should be used. This will be discussed in more detail below.

The proportionality test allows the court to scrutinise a public authority's decision in greater depth than does the irrationality test. This means it is easier to show that a decision is not proportional than it is to show that it is irrational. The difference between the two tests is illustrated by the case of *R v Ministry of Defence, ex p Smith* (cited above). The claimants failed to show that the decision to exclude homosexuals from the armed forces was irrational. Because the HRA 1998 was not in force at this time, the claimants decided to challenge the decision in the European Court of Human Rights (ECtHR), as the final court responsible for the ECHR. In *Smith and Grady v United Kingdom* (2000) 29 EHRR 493, the claimants succeeded in their claim to the ECtHR on the basis that there was a breach of their right to a private life contrary to Article 8 ECHR. The Court was able to apply the proportionality test and this allowed it to probe more deeply into the British government's reasons for its decision. The Court found that the policy could not be justified on the grounds of national security or public order, and that the government could not demonstrate a legitimate aim that was capable of being protected by the measures that were being employed to meet it. However, that is not the issue of primary importance in relation to this discussion: what the Court did highlight was its view on the inadequacy of the irrationality test in relation to human rights issues in an ECHR context and held that it failed to provide the claimants with an effective remedy in breach of Article 13. This was because, at that time, the domestic court was unable to consider whether the interference with the claimant's rights was justified by a pressing social need or proportionate to the aims pursued by the government. One can see why it is important to weigh the legitimate aim against the means used to meet the aim, and the restrictions imposed on individuals and their rights by those means.

The difference between the test of irrationality and proportionality was discussed by the House of Lords in *R (on the application of Daly) v Secretary of State for the Home Department* [2001] 2 AC 532. This case is the leading case on human rights judicial review. It decided that the appropriate test to be applied in human rights judicial review cases is the test of proportionality and not irrationality. Daly was a prisoner who complained that a prison policy that required prisoners to absent themselves from their cell while searches were conducted by prison officers was ultra vires. The reason given for this was that, in the process of conducting the search, there was a danger that legally privileged correspondence between the prisoner and his legal adviser might be read by prison officers, and its confidentiality compromised. This would be contrary to the rights protected in Article 8 ECHR. The Home Department argued that the policy was necessary for various reasons, which included preventing prisoners intimidating officers, becoming familiar with search techniques, and making a scene. The House of Lords held that the Home Department had acted unlawfully by applying this policy. This was because although it had acted for a legitimate aim, the policy was disproportionate to the aim pursued. There were other ways in which prisons could achieve the aim in question without violating the prisoners' rights. There were alternative search procedures that could allow effective searches to take place that would ensure the confidentiality of the legally privileged material. During the course of the judgment, several members of the House of Lords discussed the difference between the proportionality test and the irrationality test. In the next extract, Lord Steyn describes the proportionality test. He compares the proportionality and irrationality tests using *Smith* to illustrate the difference, and he then cautions that the courts should not engage in merits review—an extension of these tests that considers the substance of the case rather than the more limited irrationality and proportionality points.

● ***R (on the application of Daly) v Secretary of State for the Home Department*** [2001] 2
   AC 532

Lord Steyn at 547:

[27] The contours of the principle of proportionality are familiar. In *de Freitas v Permanent Secretary of Ministry of Agriculture, Fisheries, Lands and Housing* [1999] 1 AC 69 the Privy Council adopted a three-stage test. Lord Clyde observed, at p 80, that in determining whether a limitation (by an act, rule or decision) is arbitrary or excessive the court should ask itself:

> 'whether: (I) the legislative objective is sufficiently important to justify limiting a fundamental right; (ii) the measures designed to meet the legislative objective are rationally connected to it; and (iii) the means used to impair the right or freedom are no more than is necessary to accomplish the objective.'

Clearly, these criteria are more precise and more sophisticated than the traditional grounds of review. What is the difference for the disposal of concrete cases? Academic public lawyers have in remarkably similar terms elucidated the difference between the traditional grounds of review and the proportionality approach: see Professor Jeffrey Jowell QC, 'Beyond the Rule of Law: Towards Constitutional Judicial Review' [2000] PL 671; Professor Paul Craig, *Administrative Law*, 4th ed (1999), pp 561–563; Professor David Feldman, 'Proportionality and the Human Rights Act 1998', essay in *The Principle of Proportionality in the Laws of Europe* edited by Evelyn Ellis (1999), pp 117, 127 et seq. The starting point is that there is an overlap between the traditional grounds of review and the approach of proportionality. Most cases would be decided in the same way whichever approach is adopted. But the intensity of review is somewhat greater under the proportionality approach. Making due allowance for important structural differences between various convention rights, which I do not propose to discuss, a few generalisations are perhaps permissible. I would mention three concrete differences without suggesting that my statement is exhaustive. First, the doctrine of proportionality may require the reviewing court to assess the balance which the decision maker has struck, not merely whether it is within the range of rational or reasonable decisions. Secondly, the proportionality test may go further than the traditional grounds of review inasmuch as it may require attention to be directed to the relative weight accorded to interests and considerations. Thirdly, even the heightened scrutiny test developed in *R v Ministry of Defence, Ex p Smith* [1996] QB 517, 554 is not necessarily appropriate to the protection of human rights. It will be recalled that in Smith the Court of Appeal reluctantly felt compelled to reject a limitation on homosexuals in the army. The challenge based on article 8 of the Convention for the Protection of Human Rights and Fundamental Freedoms (the right to respect for private and family life) foundered on the threshold required even by the anxious scrutiny test. The European Court of Human Rights came to the opposite conclusion: *Smith and Grady v United Kingdom* (1999) 29 EHRR 493. The court concluded, at p 543, para 138:

> 'the threshold at which the High Court and the Court of Appeal could find the Ministry of Defence policy irrational was placed so high that it effectively excluded any consideration by the domestic courts of the question of whether the interference with the applicants' rights answered a pressing social need or was proportionate to the national security and public order aims pursued, principles which lie at the heart of the court's analysis of complaints under article 8 of the Convention.'

In other words, the intensity of the review, in similar cases, is guaranteed by the twin requirements that the limitation of the right was necessary in a democratic society, in the sense of meeting a pressing social need, and the question whether the interference was really proportionate to the legitimate aim being pursued.

> [28] The differences in approach between the traditional grounds of review and the proportionality approach may therefore sometimes yield different results. It is therefore important that cases involving Convention rights must be analysed in the correct way. This does not mean that there has been a shift to merits review. On the contrary, as Professor Jowell [2000] PL 671, 681 has pointed out the respective roles of judges and administrators are fundamentally distinct and will remain so. To this extent the general tenor of the observations in *Mahmood* [2001] 1 WLR 840 are correct. And Laws LJ rightly emphasised in *Mahmood*, at p 847, para 18, 'that the intensity of review in a public law case will depend on the subject matter in hand'. That is so even in cases involving Convention rights. In law context is everything.

NOTE

Lord Steyn notes that there are important differences between the various Convention Articles, but says that it is possible to generalise about the application of the proportionality test to Convention rights.

thinking point

Would the outcome have been different if the irrationality test, and not the proportionality test, had been applied in Daly?

Lord Steyn acknowledges that the irrationality test is very difficult to satisfy and that the proportionality test allows the court to examine the decision more carefully. The court is not simply considering whether a rational decision-maker could have reached the relevant conclusion; the court will also look at how the decision-maker has balanced the various relevant interests and considerations. This means that the court will consider the importance the decision-maker has given various factors. The proportionality test also requires the court to consider whether the limitation on the right was necessary in a democratic society and whether the interference was disproportionate. Even the more intense heightened scrutiny irrationality test simply does not call for the court to consider these issues. It is a much more superficial, or light-touch, review that requires a far less detailed examination of the decision. The irrationality test requires that the decision-maker consider all of the relevant factors involved in the process. But it does not consider whether the decision-maker has properly balanced all of the factors and has given due weight to the more important considerations.

531

Lord Steyn is keen to emphasise that the proportionality test does not mean that the court is reviewing the merits of the decision. The decision may be proportional even if the court would have reached a different conclusion on the facts or thinks that the decision is a bad one. Even though the proportionality test gives the courts more power than the irrationality test, the courts must still respect the role of the primary decision-maker in deciding on the correct course of action to take.

Why is *R (on the application of Daly) v Secretary of State for the Home Department* [2001] 2 AC 532 the leading case on human rights judicial review?

· ·

- It makes it clear that the correct test to be applied in human rights judicial review cases is proportionality and not irrationality.

- It explains how courts should decide whether a decision is proportional. It does this by affirming the *de Freitas* test, which will be discussed later in the chapter.

- Lord Steyn compares the irrationality and proportionality test, and highlights the differences.

- Lord Steyn emphasises that the courts must not conduct a review of the merits; they must respect the role of the decision-maker and must show restraint. A decision should not be overturned simply because the court thinks that it is a poor decision. This raises questions of judicial **deference**, which will be discussed below.

Human rights judicial review: the application of the proportionality test

There are different ways of expressing the proportionality test and there are several versions of the test. Understanding proportionality is crucial, and it is therefore worth repeating the test and looking at it in more detail. The House of Lords stated in *Daly* that, when considering whether a decision is proportional, the court should consider:

1　the importance of the legitimate objective or aim;

2　whether the measures taken are rationally connected to the legitimate aim; and

3　whether the measures taken are no more than is necessary to achieve the legitimate aim.

This is the test of proportionality that the courts have repeatedly applied when they are considering the compatibility of legislation with the ECHR for the purposes of sections 3 and 4 of the HRA 1998 (*A v Secretary of State for the Home Department* (2004) UKHL 56, known as the **Belmarsh Detainees** case), and also for determining the legality of administrative action in accordance with section 6 of the HRA 1998.

cross reference
If you are unfamiliar with this process and its purpose, then you may wish to refer back to Chapter 9 before moving forward with this section.

The exact application of the proportionality test will vary in accordance with the Convention right that is the subject of the litigation. The Articles differ in their wording and the requirements needed to show a breach of the right before the proportionality test is applied may be different. The intensity of the application of the proportionality test may also vary depending on the subject matter in question. For example, in a case involving housing allocation, concerned with the distribution of resources, the courts will show greater deference to the decision-maker and scrutinise the decision less intensely than in an immigration case. The series of subsections that follow will examine each limb of the proportionality test, with the aid of key House of Lords' decisions. Even though each limb is discussed separately here, it should be remembered that there is an inevitable degree of overlap between them.

17.5.1　The importance of the legitimate aim

'The importance of the legitimate aim' refers to the aim that the authority hopes to achieve by restricting the right. The following are some examples.

- In *Daly* (cited above), the aim of the authority for introducing the search policy, and infringing Article 8 ECHR, was the prevention of crime.

- In *R (on the application of Begum) v Denbigh High School Governors* [2006] UKHL 15, discussed below, the aim of the school in prohibiting the claimant from wearing her jilbab to school was the protection of the rights of others.

- In *R (on the application of Farrakhan) v Secretary of State for the Home Department* [2002] QB 1391, also discussed below, the Home Secretary's aim in refusing Farrakhan entry to the UK was to prevent public disorder.

17.5.2 Are the measures rationally connected to the aim?

The measures taken must be rationally connected to the aim. If the court finds that they are unable to achieve the aim or that the steps taken are illogical, they will not be considered proportionate. The *Belmarsh Detainees case* provides an example of a case in which the court considered that the steps taken to achieve the aim were not capable of achieving the aim in question. The claimants were foreign nationals detained indefinitely in Belmarsh Prison in accordance with section 23 of the Anti-Terrorism, Crime and Security Act 2001. They were suspected of terrorist activity, but they had not been charged with any criminal offence and there were no plans to charge them. The legislation permitted the indefinite detention of foreign nationals suspected of terrorist activities. However, if the foreign nationals wanted to leave the UK, they were free to do so. The government argued that it needed such powers of detention on the ground that some foreign nationals could not lawfully be deported because it was feared that they would be subject to cruel and inhuman punishment in their country of origin. This placed foreign nationals in a different position from British citizens, because British citizens could not be detained in this way without trial; foreign nationals could be if they were not willing to leave the country.

It was clear that the provisions of the Anti-Terrorism, Crime and Security Act 2001 were an infringement of the right to liberty in Article 5 ECHR. Knowing this, the government decided to derogate from Article 5, as permitted by Article 15 ECHR. Article 15 allows the suspension of some Articles of the Convention during a state of emergency. The government, subsequent to the events of 11 September 2001 in New York, claimed that, in accordance with Article 15, there was a 'public emergency threatening the life of the nation' and that it was necessary to derogate from or suspend the right to liberty in Article 5. The claimant argued that the derogation from the Convention was unlawful because the government had not shown that there was a state of emergency, and because the relevant sections of the Anti-Terrorism, Crime and Security Act 2001 went further than was necessary to deal with the problem and were not, as Article 15 stated, 'strictly required by the situation'. Consequently, the issue of proportionality was raised.

The majority of the House of Lords found that there was a public emergency and deferred to the government on this point. However, the House of Lords accepted the claimants' argument that section 23 of the legislation was incompatible with Articles 5 and 14 of the Convention, and that the measures taken were not rational or proportional to achieve the end—namely, to address the security threat that had been identified by the executive. This was partly because the House of Lords held that it was not logical or rational to allow the suspected terrorists to leave the UK as an alternative to indefinite detention. Once such individuals had left the UK, they could carry on planning terrorist activities against UK interests. Secondly, the Lords accepted evidence that British nationals were also engaged in terrorism and that the legislation did not attempt to deal with this problem.

● ***A v Secretary of State for the Home Department*** (2004) UKHL 56 (the *Belmarsh Detainees case*)

Lord Hope:

> [133] As Mr Pannick QC put it for Liberty, section 23 of the 2001 Act is not rationally connected to the legislative objective. If the threat is as potent as the Secretary of State suggests, it is absurd to confine the measures intended to deal with it so that they do not apply to British nationals, however strong the suspicion and however grave the damage it is feared they may cause.

There is also the point that foreign nationals who present the same threat are permitted, if they can safely do so, to leave this country at any time. Here too there is a clear indication that the indefinite detention of those who remain here as a means of countering the same threat is disproportionate.

This case makes many important points about constitutional law and human rights. The extract above, however, is a very good example of the application of the proportionality test. It shows that the action taken to achieve the aim must be logically connected to it and that, if the measures taken are inconsistent and are not capable of achieving the aim, the court may well hold that they are not proportionate.

NOTE

The *Belmarsh Detainees case* is central to the explanation of the anti-terrorist legislation that will be considered in Chapter 20. It is consequently worth making sure that you understand the facts and law, and can explain what was decided by the House of Lords.

17.5.3 Are the measures taken no more than is necessary to achieve the legitimate aim?

The court may hold that an action is disproportionate if the aim of the government can be achieved by an alternate means that does not infringe the right or is less destructive of the right. *Daly* falls into this category, because in that case the House of Lords held that there were credible alternate search procedures that were just as effective that would not infringe the claimant's rights under Article 8 ECHR. Consequently, it is important to consider whether there are other measures that could be taken that would achieve the legitimate aim, and yet be less restrictive of individuals' rights and liberties.

17.5.4 Examples of the application of the proportionality test in judicial review cases

It may be useful to pull together all of these strands with a series of cases that combine the themes that we have considered in this section. In *Huang v Secretary of State for the Home Department; Kashmiri v Secretary of State for the Home Office* [2007] UKHL 11, the House of Lords considered the application of the proportionality test in two cases concerned with the right to family life under Article 8 ECHR. Two applications were joined together for the purposes of the appeal. Mrs Huang was a Chinese citizen whose husband (from whom she was separated), daughter, son-in-law, and grandsons lived in the UK. She was refused indefinite leave to remain in the UK. Mr Kashmiri was an Iranian citizen who was refused asylum, but whose father, wife, and brothers had been given indefinite leave to remain. His application for indefinite leave was refused. Indefinite leave to remain is not the same as being granted citizenship, but it does permit someone legally to remain living in the country even though he or she has not been granted citizenship. As a result of the refusal of indefinite leave to remain, both claimants had no right to remain under the immigration rules and they argued that the refusal of leave to remain was a breach of their right to family life under Article 8 ECHR. This is because they would have to leave the country while their families remained living here.

The case hinged on the correct application of the immigration legislation by an immigration adjudicator when considering an appeal from the primary decision-maker. The case proceeded all the way to the House of Lords, which made it plain that the job of an adjudicator or court when considering the decision made by the original decision-maker (the primary decision-maker) was to determine whether the claimants' Convention rights had been breached. It was not simply to review the decision to check whether the original decision-maker had taken the human rights of the claimant into account when making the decision.

Of equal importance was the House of Lords' discussion of the proportionality test more generally. It stated that, when it considers whether the government's action in interfering with a right is justified, it must keep in mind that the Convention requires that a fair balance should be struck between the rights of the individual and the interest of the community. These comments, although applied here in an immigration case engaging Article 8, are likely to be applied more widely by the courts when they are considering the issue of proportionality. The five Law Lords who heard the case gave one judgment, which expressed the view of all of them, of which the next extract sets out the relevant part.

. . . .

● **Huang v Secretary of State for the Home Department; Kashmiri v Secretary of State for the Home Office** [2007] UKHL 11

> [19] In *de Freitas v Permanent Secretary of Ministry of Agriculture, Fisheries, Lands and Housing* [1999] 1 AC 69, 80, the Privy Council, drawing on South African, Canadian and Zimbabwean authority, defined the questions generally to be asked in deciding whether a measure is proportionate:
>
> > 'whether: (i) the legislative objective is sufficiently important to justify limiting a fundamental right; (ii) the measures designed to meet the legislative objective are rationally connected to it; and (iii) the means used to impair the right or freedom are no more than is necessary to accomplish the objective.'
>
> This formulation has been widely cited and applied. But counsel for the applicants (with the support of Liberty, in a valuable written intervention) suggested that the formulation was deficient in omitting reference to an overriding requirement which featured in the judgment of Dickson CJ in *R v Oakes* [1986] 1 SCR 103, from which this approach to proportionality derives. This feature is (p 139) the need to balance the interests of society with those of individuals and groups. This is indeed an aspect which should never be overlooked or discounted. The House recognised as much in *R (Razgar) v Secretary of State for the Home Department* [2004] UKHL 27, [2004] 2 AC 368, paras 17–20, 26, 27, 60, 77, when, having suggested a series of questions which an adjudicator would have to ask and answer in deciding a Convention question, it said that the judgment on proportionality
>
> > 'must always involve the striking of a fair balance between the rights of the individual and the interests of the community which is inherent in the whole of the Convention. The severity and consequences of the interference will call for careful assessment at this stage' (see para 20).
>
> If, as counsel suggest, insufficient attention has been paid to this requirement, the failure should be made good.
>
> [20] In an article 8 case where this question is reached, the ultimate question for the appellate immigration authority is whether the refusal of leave to enter or remain, in circumstances where the life of the family cannot reasonably be expected to be enjoyed elsewhere, taking full account of all considerations weighing in favour of the refusal, prejudices the family life of the applicant in a manner sufficiently serious to amount to a breach of the fundamental right protected by article 8. If the answer to this question is affirmative, the refusal is unlawful and the authority must so decide.

The House of Lords was not satisfied that the proportionality test had been applied correctly and both cases were remitted to the Immigration Appeal Tribunal for reconsideration, meaning that a fresh panel of adjudicators in the Tribunal was required to rehear the case, taking into account the correct test for proportionality.

Another judicial review case that discussed the proportionality test in some detail is the decision in *R (on the application of Begum) v Denbigh High School Governors* [2006] UKHL 15. The claimant was a British Muslim schoolgirl who claimed that her school's refusal to allow her to wear a jilbab (a long flowing gown associated with the practice of Islam) was a breach of her right to manifest her religion contrary to Article 9 ECHR and of her right to education in Article 2 of the First Protocol to the Convention. Over 70 per cent of the students at the school were Muslim and female students were permitted to wear headscarves in keeping with some Islamic interpretations of appropriate dress. The school had also modified its uniform in consultation with religious leaders to comply with the religious beliefs of some students. The jilbab was prohibited, because the school was concerned that some girls may fear being pressured into wearing it if it were permitted. There had been demonstrations outside the school by an extreme Muslim group unconnected with the claimant's family protesting against the secular education of Muslim children and some pupils had complained about harassment. The school also argued that if the jilbab were permitted, then it may lead to differentiation between Muslim groups according to the strictness of their beliefs. This had led to conflict amongst students in the past and the school did not wish to act in a way that might inflame this further.

However, the student who sought the judicial review was unhappy that she was not permitted to wear the jilbab in conformity with her religious beliefs. She was unsuccessful at first instance, but was successful in the Court of Appeal on the grounds that the school had failed to consider her right to manifest her religion. However, Ms Begum lost her case in the House of Lords. The majority decided that there had been no interference with her right to manifest her religion. She could have chosen to attend another school at which she could have worn her jilbab—the ban on the jilbab was not one imposed by the **state**, but only by the state school that she had been attending. In addition, the House of Lords decided unanimously that even if there had been an interference with her right to manifest her religion, this would have been justified on the basis that it was necessary to protect the rights of others at the school. The House of Lords was critical of the Court of Appeal's approach. The Court of Appeal had decided in favour of Ms Begum because it considered that the school, when making its decision, had not considered sufficiently her right to manifest her religion. The House of Lords disapproved of this approach. It stressed that, in a human rights case, the court is not considering whether the decision-making body had followed the right procedure or considered the Convention right in question; instead, the court had to decide for itself whether the claimant's rights have been infringed by the public authority. The court had to undertake the balancing exercise and come to a decision, rather than leave that to the original decision-maker.

● *R (on the application of Begum) v Denbigh High School Governors* [2006] UKHL 15

Lord Bingham:

[32] It is therefore necessary to consider the proportionality of the school's interference with the respondent's right to manifest her religious belief by wearing the jilbab to the school . . .

[33] The respondent criticised the school for permitting the headscarf while refusing to permit the jilbab, for refusing permission to wear the jilbab when some other schools permitted it and for adhering to their own view of what Islamic dress required. None of these criticisms can in my opinion be sustained. The headscarf was permitted in 1993, following detailed consideration of the uniform policy, in response to requests by several girls. There was no evidence that this was opposed. But there was no pressure at any time, save by the respondent, to wear the jilbab, and that has been opposed. Different schools have different uniform policies, no doubt influenced by the composition of their pupil bodies and a range of other matters. Each school has to decide what uniform, if any, will best serve its wider educational purposes. The school did not reject the respondent's request out of hand: it took advice, and was told that its existing policy conformed with the requirements of mainstream Muslim opinion.

> [34] On the agreed facts, the school was in my opinion fully justified in acting as it did. It had taken immense pains to devise a uniform policy which respected Muslim beliefs but did so in an inclusive, unthreatening and uncompetitive way. The rules laid down were as far from being mindless as uniform rules could ever be. The school had enjoyed a period of harmony and success to which the uniform policy was thought to contribute. On further enquiry it still appeared that the rules were acceptable to mainstream Muslim opinion. It was feared that acceding to the respondent's request would or might have significant adverse repercussions. It would in my opinion be irresponsible of any court, lacking the experience, background and detailed knowledge of the head teacher, staff and governors, to overrule their judgment on a matter as sensitive as this. The power of decision has been given to them for the compelling reason that they are best placed to exercise it, and I see no reason to disturb their decision.

Lord Bingham set out the structured approach required by the test of proportionality, as indicated at the beginning of the extract. He accepted that the school acted in accordance with law and that it had a legitimate aim in refusing to allow the claimant to wear the jilbab. The question then was whether the restriction was proportionate to the aim. Lord Bingham rejected the argument that the school's decision was not related to the legitimate aim of protecting others' rights because it was not logical to permit headscarves yet not the jilbab. He noted that the headscarf was permitted in response to requests by students, but there had been no similar pressure to permit the jilbab.

He restated that the courts should not indulge in a merits review. The court had examined the school's reasoning in detail, including the fact that the school believed that having a uniform promoted harmony amongst the students. The House of Lords accepted the school's reasons for refusal and was impressed by the trouble the school had taken to consult with the local community to find a uniform that complied with Muslim requirements. Ultimately, Lord Bingham stated that the court was willing to defer to the school's judgement as the primary decision-maker, on the basis that the school was better placed to make the decision on such a sensitive matter. This is an example of the court deferring to the primary decision-maker and is discussed further below under the heading 'judicial deference'.

The cases of *Huang* and *Begum* demonstrate the approach the courts take when deciding issues of human rights on judicial review claims. Both cases stress that, on judicial review, the courts have to decide whether there has been a breach of a Convention right. They should not simply review the decision of the primary decision-maker to check that Convention rights have been considered. The proportionality test is applied in a structured way, as Figure 17.1 illustrates, and the decision is reviewed more intensely than the irrationality test would allow. However, judicial deference also plays an important part in both judgments, as does the concern of the House of Lords not to engage in merits review. This is discussed in the next section.

17.5.5 Proportionality and judicial deference

When the court is considering the justification for the limitation of a right, it may decide to defer to the judgement of the public authority. Lord Steyn has explained that he thinks that deference refers to the following.

● **Lord Steyn, 'Deference: a tangled story'** [2005] Public Law 346, 349

> ...the idea of a court, exceptionally out of respect for other branches of government and in recognition of their democratic decision-making role, declining to make its own independent judgment on a particular issue.

Lord Hoffmann stated, in *R (on the application of Pro Life Alliance) v BBC* [2003] UKHL 23, [75], that he dislikes the term 'deference', because it has 'overtones or servility and gracious concession'. But the term has been used extensively by the judiciary and academic commentators, and various justifications for its use have been given.

Justifications for judicial deference

- The courts lack democratic legitimacy.

- The judiciary lack expertise on socio-economic issues.

- The trial process is an inadequate forum in which to decide complex policy.

As we have seen, the proportionality test allows a higher degree of scrutiny than irrationality. But the courts must not usurp the role of the public authority, and must take into account its greater expertise and knowledge. It is also argued that the courts are not the best place in which to decide issues of policy—particularly economic and social policy. This is why the court will often defer to the decision of the public authority. This is a practical application of the doctrine of the separation of powers. The courts are mindful of their separate constitutional role of interpreting and applying the law, but do not want to overstep the boundary and decide government policy. This is something that is the function of the democratically elected government and not the courts. However, the boundary line between the different functions is not always easy to see, particularly because the HRA 1998 gives the courts greater power to ensure that individual rights are not infringed by the state. The danger is that if the courts defer and refuse to intervene, they will not be able to protect the rights of the individual against the state. However, if they overstep the mark and intervene too frequently, they will be accused of interfering too readily with functions that belong to the legislature and executive. This problem has given rise to some robust exchanges between the different branches of government and between members of the judiciary themselves.

cross reference
See the discussion of responsible government, human rights, and the role of the courts in Chapter 14 for some examples.

The issue of deference arises not only in judicial review cases, but is also a crucial factor when the court is exercising its powers of interpretation under section 3 and its power to issue a **declaration** of incompatibility under section 4 of the HRA 1998. It can be argued that the doctrine of deference is based on the doctrine of the margin of appreciation developed by the ECtHR—that is, where the Court allows the national courts considerable discretion in deciding what are the appropriate limits to a right.

There is no easy guide to deciding when the courts should exercise judicial deference. However, there are some indications in the case law and in the extrajudicial writing of the judges. One area in which the courts tend to defer is in the area of national security. In the *Belmarsh Detainees case*, the House of Lords deferred to the executive on the issue of whether there was a state of emergency threatening the life of the nation.

● *A v Secretary of State for the Home Department* (2004) UKHL 56 (the *Belmarsh Detainees case*)

Lord Bingham:

> [29] I would accept that great weight should be given to the judgment of the Home Secretary, his colleagues and Parliament on this question, because they were called on to exercise a pre-eminently political judgment. It involved making a factual prediction of what various people around the world might or might not do, and when (if at all) they might do it, and what the consequences might be if they did. Any prediction about the future behaviour of human beings

> (as opposed to the phases of the moon or high water at London Bridge) is necessarily problematical ... It would have been irresponsible not to err, if at all, on the side of safety ... The more purely political (in a broad or narrow sense) a question is, the more appropriate it will be for political resolution and the less likely it is to be an appropriate matter for judicial decision. The smaller, therefore, will be the potential role of the court. It is the function of political and not judicial bodies to resolve political questions. Conversely, the greater the legal content of any issue, the greater the potential role of the court, because under our constitution and subject to the sovereign power of Parliament it is the function of the courts and not of political bodies to resolve legal questions. The present question seems to me to be very much at the political end of the spectrum ...

By contrast, on the issue of the proportionality of the legislation, the House of Lords refused to defer. Lord Hope distinguished social and economic issues in which the court may have less expertise from an issue of liberty.

. . . .

● *A v Secretary of State for the Home Department* (2004) UKHL 56 (the *Belmarsh Detainees case*)

Lord Hope:

> [108] ... We are not dealing here with matters of social or economic policy, where opinions may reasonably differ in a democratic society and where choices on behalf the country as a whole are left to government and the legislature. We are dealing with actions taken on behalf of society as a whole which affect the rights and freedoms of the individual. This is where the courts may legitimately intervene to ensure that the actions taken are proportionate. It is an essential safeguard, if individual rights and freedoms are to be protected in a democratic society which respects the principle that minorities however unpopular, have the same rights as the majority.

Lord Bingham also rejected the argument made by the Attorney General that the judges should refuse to intervene because they are not elected. He stated that it was the proper constitutional functions of the court to interpret and apply the law.

. . . .

● *A v Secretary of State for the Home Department* (2004) UKHL 56 (the *Belmarsh Detainees case*)

Lord Bingham:

> [42] It is also of course true, as pointed out ... that Parliament, the executive and the courts have different functions. But the function of independent judges charged to interpret and apply the law is universally recognised as a cardinal feature of the modern democratic state, a cornerstone of the rule of law itself. The Attorney General is fully entitled to insist on the proper limits of judicial authority, but he is wrong to stigmatise judicial decision-making as in some way undemocratic.

Other judges, such as Lord Steyn, have argued that there should be no areas of law, such as social and economic policy, in which the courts should automatically be deferential. He has stated that each case depends on the particular context and that judges should not abdicate their responsibility. There is no settled view of the basis on which judges should defer to the executive and Parliament when they are applying the Convention rights. An example of a judicial review decision in which the Court of Appeal deferred to the Home Secretary on an issue concerning public order is *R (on the application of Farrakhan) v Secretary of State for the Home Department* [2002] QB 1391. Louis Farrakhan is the leader of the Nation of Islam, which is a 'religious, social and political movement whose aims include the regeneration of black self-esteem, dignity and self-discipline'. Farrakhan was refused entry to the UK to address his followers because the

Home Secretary decided that his presence in the UK was not conducive to the public good. This was because it would strain community relations, especially between Muslims and Jews, and there was a risk of public disorder at meetings addressed by Farrakhan. Farrakhan argued that the refusal to allow him to enter was a breach of his right to freedom of expression under Article 10 ECHR. The Court of Appeal rejected his claim, holding that it would defer to the decision of the Home Secretary. The Court does not use the term 'deference', but uses the interchangeable term the 'margin of discretion'. In the next extract, Lord Phillips explains the Court's reasons for deferring to the Home Secretary.

● *R (on the application of Farrakhan) v Secretary of State for the Home Department* [2002] QB 1391

Lord Phillips at 1418:

[71] … [It is] submitted that there were factors in the present case which made it appropriate to accord a particularly wide margin of discretion to the Secretary of State. We agree. We would identify these factors as follows. First and foremost is the fact that this case concerns an immigration decision. As we have pointed out, the European Court of Human Rights attaches considerable weight to the right under international law of a state to control immigration into its territory. And the weight that this carries in the present case is the greater because the Secretary of State is not motivated by the wish to prevent Mr Farrakhan from expressing his views, but by concern for public order within the United Kingdom.

[72] The second factor is the fact that the decision in question is the personal decision of the Secretary of State. Nor is it a decision that he has taken lightly. The history that we have set out at the beginning of this judgment demonstrates the very detailed consideration, involving widespread consultation, that the Secretary of State has given to his decision.

[73] The third factor is that the Secretary of State is far better placed to reach an informed decision as to the likely consequences of admitting Mr Farrakhan to this country than is the court.

[74] The fourth factor is that the Secretary of State is democratically accountable for this decision. This is underlined by the fact that section 60(9) of the 1999 Act precludes any right of appeal where the Secretary of State has certified that he has personally directed the exclusion of a person on the ground that this is conducive to the public good …

Farrakhan illustrates that the application of the proportionality test does not mean that the courts should engage in merits review. This means the courts should not make decisions on policy or otherwise take on the role of primary decision-making. They should not interfere too readily in the decisions of public authorities. The courts will therefore exercise judicial deference. This means that they will give considerable weight to the experience and expertise of the decision-maker before deciding that the actions of the public authority are unlawful. But as the *Belmarsh Detainees case* illustrates, it is difficult to predict accurately when the court will exercise deference. Some judges have suggested that it is most appropriate when the executive has special expertise, such as issues of national security, or areas such as economic and social policy. This continues to be a subject of intense debate amongst constitutional lawyers.

summary points

Human rights judicial review: the application of proportionality in human rights judicial review cases

* *The court is not only reviewing the way in which the decision-maker has dealt with human rights; the court itself must be satisfied that there is no infringement of the claimant's human rights.*

* *The proportionality test is stated in* de Freitas v Permanent Secretary of Ministry of Agriculture, Fisheries, Lands and Housing *[1999] 1 AC 69. The court will consider the importance*

of the legitimate objective, whether the measures taken are rationally connected to the legitimate aim, and whether the measures taken are no more than is necessary to achieve the legitimate objective.

- *In* Huang, *the House of Lords emphasised that the proportionality test involves balancing the rights of the individual and the interests of the community.*

- *The court should not engage in a 'merits review'. It should not hold that the decision is unlawful simply because it disagrees with the decision or it wishes that the issue had been dealt with differently.*

- *The courts may defer to the primary decision-maker in certain circumstances. This means that the court will respect the greater expertise and knowledge of the executive when it considers whether the decision is proportional.*

Figure 17.1

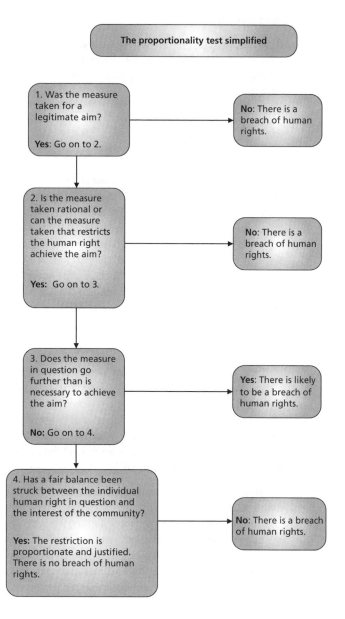

The proportionality test simplified

1. Was the measure taken for a legitimate aim?

Yes: Go on to 2.

No: There is a breach of human rights.

2. Is the measure taken rational or can the measure taken that restricts the human right achieve the aim?

Yes: Go on to 3.

No: There is a breach of human rights.

3. Does the measure in question go further than is necessary to achieve the aim?

No: Go on to 4.

Yes: There is likely to be a breach of human rights.

4. Has a fair balance been struck between the individual human right in question and the interest of the community?

Yes: The restriction is proportionate and justified. There is no breach of human rights.

No: There is a breach of human rights.

Non-human-rights judicial review: irrationality is the correct test

After the decision in *Daly*, many commentators hoped that the courts would abandon the irrationality test and apply the proportionality test in all appropriate judicial review cases. This was because of the negative comments that some members of the House of Lords made about the irrationality test. We have already studied Lord Steyn's comments on the limitations of the irrationality test. But Lord Cooke in *Daly* went even further in his criticism.

● *R (on the application of Daly) v Secretary of State for the Home Department* [2001] 2
    AC 532

Lord Cooke at 549:

> [32] And I think that the day will come when it will be more widely recognised that *Associated Provincial Picture Houses Ltd v Wednesbury Corpn* [1948] 1 KB 223 was an unfortunately retrogressive decision in English administrative law, in so far as it suggested that there are degrees of unreasonableness and that only a very extreme degree can bring an administrative decision within the legitimate scope of judicial invalidation. The depth of judicial review and the deference due to administrative discretion vary with the subject matter. It may well be, however, that the law can never be satisfied in any administrative field merely by a finding that the decision under review is not capricious or absurd.

The question that was asked was whether proportionality had become a free-standing ground of review that could be used in cases that did not involve the ECHR or EU law. Despite the House of Lords' acknowledgement of the limitations of the irrationality test, it has survived and is still the test to be used in non-human-rights judicial review cases. This was made clear by the Court of Appeal in *R (on the application of Association of British Civilian Internees: Far East Region) v Secretary of State for Defence* [2003] QB 1397 (the *Wartime Detainees case*). After many years of campaigning by veterans groups including the Royal British Legion, the British government decided that British civilians interned during the war by the Japanese should receive a single *ex gratia* payment of £10,000. This was announced by the Parliamentary Under-Secretary of State for Defence in the House of Commons in November 2000. In this statement, he said that the scheme would include members of the armed forces and British civilians who were interned. At the time of the Second World War, section 1(1) of the British Nationality and Status of Alien Act 1914 provided that any person born within His Majesty's dominions and allegiances was deemed to be a 'natural born British subject'. This meant that the potential number of British subjects was very large. In a response to a parliamentary question in July 2001, the Under-Secretary of State gave a more specific definition and stated that a British civilian was someone who was born in the UK, or someone who had a parent or grandparent born here. This was to fulfil its requirement that an internee should have had strong links with the UK. This led to the challenge being brought.

The claimants in the case represented a group interned by the Japanese because they were British subjects who did not satisfy the above criteria. One of the arguments made by the claimants was that the requirement of a strong link with the UK at the time of internment, and the birth criteria, were disproportionate and irrational. Japanese internment during the war pre-dated both the inception of the European Community and the Council of Europe, and the internment was carried out by a non-European country. Consequently, the Court of Appeal had to decide, as a preliminary issue, whether proportionality existed as a separate ground of review in a case such as this one, which did not involve an accusation that there had been a breach of the ECHR. The Court explains the issue in the following extract.

• **R (on the application of Association of British Civilian Internees: Far East Region) v Secretary of State for Defence** [2003] QB 1397 (the *Wartime Detainees* case)

Dyson LJ gave the judgment of the court at 1412:

> [32] Mr Pannick submits that the requirement of close links with the UK at the time of intern-ment and the birth criteria are disproportionate to the aims of the Government's policy and/or irrational, and that for this substantive reason the scheme in so far as it affects civilians should be declared to be unlawful. A preliminary question that arises is whether proportionality exists as a separate ground of review in a case which does not concern European Community law or human rights protected by the European Convention for the Protection of Human Rights and Fundamental Freedoms, as scheduled to the Human Rights Act 1998...
>
> [33] It is true that the result that follows will often be the same whether the test that is applied is proportionality or *Wednesbury* unreasonableness: see *Associated Provincial Picture Houses Ltd v Wednesbury Corpn* [1948] 1 KB 223. This is particularly so in a case in the field of social and economic policy. But the tests are different: see, for example, Lord Steyn in *R (Daly) v Secretary of State for the Home Department* [2001] 2 AC 532, 547a–g. It follows that the two tests will not always yield the same results...
>
> [34] Support for the recognition of proportionality as part of English domestic law in cases which do not involve Community law or the Convention is to be found in para 51 of the speech of Lord Slynn of Hadley in *R (Alconbury Developments Ltd) v Secretary of State for the Environment, Transport and the Regions* [2003] 2 AC 295, 320–321; and in the speech of Lord Cooke of Thorndon in *R (Daly) v Secretary of State for the Home Department* [2001] 2 AC 532, 548–549, para 32... It seems to us that the case for this is indeed a strong one. As Lord Slynn points out, trying to keep the *Wednesbury* principle and proportionality in separate compartments is un-necessary and confusing. The criteria of proportionality are more precise and sophisticated: see Lord Steyn in the *Daly* case, at pp 547–548, para 27. It is true that sometimes proportion-ality may require the reviewing court to assess for itself the balance that has been struck by the decision-maker, and that may produce a different result from one that would be arrived at on an application of the *Wednesbury* test. But the strictness of the *Wednesbury* test has been relaxed in recent years even in areas which have nothing to do with fundamental rights: see the discussion in Craig, *Administrative Law* 4th ed (1999), pp 582–584. The *Wednesbury* test is moving closer to proportionality and in some cases it is not possible to see any daylight between the two tests: see Lord Hoffmann's Third John Maurice Kelly Memorial Lecture 1996 'A Sense of Proportionality', at p 13. Although we did not hear argument on the point, we have difficulty in seeing what justification there now is for retaining the Wednesbury test.
>
> [35] But we consider that it is not for this court to perform its burial rites. The continuing ex-istence of the *Wednesbury* test has been acknowledged by the House of Lords on more than one occasion...
>
> [37] Finally, the passages in the speeches of Lord Slynn in *R (Alconbury Developments Ltd) v Secretary of State for the Environment, Transport and the Regions* [2003] 2 AC 295, 320–321 and Lord Cooke in the *Daly* case [2001] 2 AC 532, 548–549 to which we have referred, them-selves imply a recognition that the *Wednesbury* test survives, although their Lordships' clearly expressed view is that it should be laid to rest. It seems to us that this is a step which can only be taken by the House of Lords. We therefore approach the issues in the present appeal on the footing that the *Wednesbury* test does survive, and that this is the correct test to apply in a case such as the present which does not involve Community law and does not engage any question of rights under the Convention.

The Court of Appeal then went on to decide that the criteria used to determine eligibility for the payment were lawful. This was because there was a large number of potential claimants and it was an *ex gratia* scheme, because the government had no obligation to make the payments.

Therefore it was not irrational for the government to seek to limit claimants to those who had a close connection to the UK. This decision is very important because it makes it clear that the irrationality test is, at least for the time being, the correct test to apply when the case is not concerned with the ECHR or EU law. Proportionality has not been established as a ground of review except in cases concerned with EU law and the HRA 1998.

thinking point

*The decision of the Ministry of Defence to limit payments to only those internees who satisfied the birth criteria was the subject of an investigation by the **Parliamentary Ombudsman**. An individual internee who had not taken part in the judicial review proceedings instigated the complaint. The Parliamentary Ombudsman criticised the Ministry of Defence's handling of the scheme, including the late change to the criteria for making the payments. See Chapter 13 for more information and see Parliamentary Ombudsman, 'A Debt of Honour': The Ex Gratia Scheme for British Groups Interned by the Japanese during the Second World War (Fourth Report, HC 324, Session 2004–05, London: HMSO, July 2005).*

The House of Lords has also applied the irrationality test rather than the proportionality test in a decision concerned with non-human-rights judicial review. This case raises several important principles and the facts can be summarised as follows.

R (on the application of Bancoult) v Secretary of State for Foreign and Commonwealth Affairs (No 2) [2008] 3 WLR 955 (*Bancoult No 2*) concerned the forced removal of the Chagos islanders from their homes in the British Indian Ocean Island Territories in the Pacific Islands in 1971. The removal occurred because the main island, Diego Garcia, was leased by the UK to the US government as an airbase in the late 1960s. Because the islands were British colonies, the removal of the population was effected by the **Crown**'s prerogative power to legislate for its colonies. Sometime after these events, in *R (on the application of Bancoult) v Secretary of State for Foreign and Commonwealth Affairs* [2001] QB 1067 (*Bancoult No 1*), it was held by the Divisional Court that this removal of the islanders had been an ultra vires use of the relevant prerogative powers. The Foreign Secretary, recognising the injustice to the islanders, decided not to appeal from the Court's decision. He stated the government would continue with a feasibility study to consider the return of the islanders to the outer islands and a new prerogative order was made allowing the islanders to return to the outer islands without immigration controls. This meant that the islanders could visit, but because there were no facilities, they could not live there. Subsequent to concerns about activists landings on Diego Garcia to protest against the US airbase and security concerns in the post-2001 environment, a new Order in Council, The British Indian Ocean Territory (Constitution) Order 2004, was passed. This imposed immigration controls and the ex-residents of the Chagos Islands had to obtain visas to visit. The government also stated that it was impossible to let the islanders resettle on the islands. This was because the feasibility study had shown that it was impracticable for the outer islands to be inhabited.

cross reference

We will consider the point about the islanders' legitimate expectation in Chapter 18 when we discuss procedural impropriety.

This decision was challenged on the grounds that the 2004 Order was irrational. In addition, it was argued that there was a legitimate expectation created by the Foreign Secretary that the Chagos islanders would be able to return to live on the islands. After unanimously deciding that the Crown's prerogative power to legislate for its colonies was subject to judicial review, the majority of the House of Lords decided in favour of the Crown, upholding the legality of the Order.

The claimants had argued that the Order subjecting the islanders to immigration controls was irrational because the law was not made in the islanders' interest. The majority of the House of Lords rejected this argument, and held that the decision was not irrational and that the government was entitled to exercise the prerogative in the interest of the UK. This was the case even though this prevented the Chagossians living on the island. Lord Hoffmann stated that, because the case concerned the claimants' right to live in the Chagos Islands the anxious scrutiny test laid down by Lord Bingham MR in *R v Ministry of Defence, ex p Smith* [1996] QB 517, 554, should be applied. This meant that because the prerogative Order had interfered substantially with the claimants' right to live in Diego Garcia, the court would require more by way of explanation and justification from the Crown than might otherwise be the case. Lord Carswell also stated (at [131]) that because this was a situation in which the HRA 1998 did not apply, the irrationality test rather than the proportionality test was the correct test.

Lord Rodger explained his reasoning for deciding against the claimants as follows.

· ·

● **R (on the application of Bancoult) v Secretary of State for Foreign and Commonwealth Affairs (No 2)** [2008] 3 WLR 955

Lord Rodger at 992–3:

[113] The ministerial statement indicates that a decision to legislate was taken on the basis of the experts' (second) report on the difficulties and dangers of resettling the islands-these difficulties and dangers being dangers and difficulties which would affect the Chagossians themselves, if they were to try to live on the outer islands. Given the terms of that report alone, it could not, in my view, be said that no reasonable Government would have decided to legislate to prevent resettlement. In particular, the advice that the cost of any permanent resettlement would be 'prohibitive' was an entirely legitimate factor for the Government—which is responsible for the way that tax revenues are spent—to take into account. In addition, the Government had regard to defence considerations, the views of its close ally, the United States, and the changed security situation after 9/11. These additional factors reinforce the view that the decision to legislate was neither unreasonable nor irrational.

The House of Lords also noted that the original decision to remove the islanders in 1971 may have been irrational, but that the decision in 2004 to impose immigration controls was not. The government was entitled to consider security considerations, the concerns of the US about protecting the airbase at Diego Garcia, and the fact that the feasibility study had shown that it would have been prohibitively expensive and impracticable to allow the islanders to return. These concerns were matters for the executive and the court would be slow to intervene in such decisions.

thinking point

Do you think the case was rightly decided? What factors might make you think that the Order prohibiting the islanders to return was irrational? You might find it helpful to consider the dissenting judgments of Lord Bingham and Lord Mance in the case.

17.7 # Is there a need for reform?

The most pressing issue is whether the courts should use the test of proportionality rather than irrationality in all cases, even those that do not involve considering European law issues. The advantage of this would be that there would be more consistency in the courts' approach. The proportionality test, as we have seen, permits the courts a greater degree of scrutiny over administrative decision-making, and allows the courts to consider the way in which the decision-maker has balanced and weighed the various factors. Arguably, the irrationality test is very vague and difficult to apply, whereas proportionality provides for a more structured and reasoned form of investigation by the court. The arguments against using proportionality include that it might lead to the courts overreaching themselves and interfering too readily in decisions that are better made by the public authority, which has the experience and knowledge. Tomkins reflects on this problem.

● **A. Tomkins,** *Public Law* (Oxford: Oxford University Press, 2000), p. 199

> The new proportionality is not the old irrationality... Rather, it is a device which enables the judiciary to probe more deeply into government decision-making, but which also requires the courts to make clear the precise grounds on which they do so. Proportionality may therefore lead to greater transparency in judicial decision making. But it may also signal the abandonment of, or at least a substantial adjustment to the distinction, which has been central to the law of judicial review for forty years, between appeal and review...
>
> ... [W]hat is clear is that in embracing proportionality, the courts have significantly altered the law of judicial review, and have further shifted the relationship between the executive and the judiciary at the expense of the former and to the advantage of the latter.

thinking point

Explain why the Court of Appeal in the British Civilian Internees *case refused to apply the proportionality test. Do you agree with the Court's decision? Give full reasons for your answer*

Other writers acknowledge concerns about the use of the proportionality test, but argue that these problems can be overcome. Craig (2008: 632) notes that: 'It is right to acknowledge such difficulties, but they should be kept within perspective. The variability in the intensity with which proportionality is applied will itself be of assistance in this regard'. In cases in which the courts decide that the subject is one best left squarely in the hands of the public authority, the court can apply a less intense version of the proportionality test, which makes judicial intervention in the decision less likely. The court can achieve this by deferring to the executive when appropriate.

◉ Summary

The terms '*Wednesbury* unreasonableness' and 'irrationality' can be used interchangeably. In human rights judicial review cases, the correct test is the proportionality test; in non-human-rights judicial review cases, the irrationality test must be used.

The test of *Wednesbury* unreasonableness has been used as a ground of review to overturn administrative decisions that are 'so absurd that no sensible person could ever dream that it lay within the power of the authority'. In the *CCSU* case, Lord Diplock reformulated this ground of review and named it 'irrationality'. He also made it clear that irrationality was a separate ground of review from illegality and procedural impropriety. After the *CCSU* case, the irrationality test was applied very strictly in a number of cases, including *Nottinghamshire*, and some commentators argued that the courts had developed a 'super-*Wednesbury*' test that was almost impossible to satisfy. However, in *Smith*, the courts applied the irrationality test more flexibly and developed a heightened scrutiny test, which provided for a more careful study of the decision that was being challenged. But even using that test, the claimants in *Smith* were unable to show that excluding homosexuals from serving in the armed forces was irrational. It is more difficult to convince the court that a decision is irrational and the courts have warned that they will be slow to overturn a decision on this ground where a decision involves the allocation of resources. Nevertheless, this ground of review has been used successfully, as the case of *Re Duffy* shows.

After the introduction of the HRA 1998, the case of *Daly* established that the irrationality test had been replaced by the test of proportionality. However, this applies only to cases brought under section 6 of the Act in which the claimant is arguing that the public authority has acted unlawfully because it has breached a Convention right. In non-human-rights judicial review cases, the Court of Appeal stated in the *British Civilian Internees* case that the test of irrationality must be applied.

The proportionality test that should be used in judicial review cases was stated in *Daly*. The House of Lords acknowledged that there are differences between the application of the proportionality and irrationality criteria. The proportionality test provides for a more structured and probing investigation of the decision, which makes it easier for the court to intervene. Some commentators have expressed reservations about this, arguing that it has transferred too much power to the judiciary. Others reject this criticism and argue that the proportionality test should be applied to all administrative decisions on a judicial review claim, because this would lead to greater consistency and clarity in decision-making.

 # Questions

1   What is the difference between the test of irrationality and proportionality? Give examples from the case law to illustrate the difference.

2   Do you think that the courts should adopt proportionality as a free-standing ground of review in all claims for judicial review?

3   What is meant by 'merits review' and why does Lord Steyn state in *Daly* that the courts should not engage in it?

4   What is meant by 'judicial deference'? In what circumstances do you think the courts should defer to the executive?

5   Sonia, aged 18, is a sixth-form student at Avenue School, who is studying A-level politics. The school publishes an in-house newspaper for its staff and students. Sonya writes an article for the newspaper approving of the American invasion and occupation of Iran, and arguing that the Americans should invade Iran if it continues with its nuclear programme. The editor of the newspaper, who is the head of the politics department, initially accepts the article. He tells Sonia that it is very well written and that he is going to enter it for the 'UK National Best Student Journalist of the Year' competition. However, the head teacher refuses to approve its publication and he writes to Sonia informing her that the article is unsuitable. He explains that her views are controversial and provocative. Given that there are many students from different religious and cultural traditions at Avenue School, it will cause great offence and may lead to demonstrations, which will cause disruption. Sonia accepts that her views are controversial, but says that she is prepared to add a paragraph

cross reference
You may find it helpful to read the material on standing in Chapter 15 before answering this part of the question.

in bold letters at the top of the article stating that the views expressed are hers alone and in no way reflect the views of the school, its management, or staff. The head teacher refuses to reconsider his decision not to publish.

Sonia would like to make a claim for judicial review. She wants to argue that the school has violated her rights under Article 10 ECHR. The Campaign for Free Speech has also heard about the decision and wants to take legal action against Avenue School. Advise Sonia and the Campaign for Free Speech of their chances of success. Pay particular attention to the way in which the court will decide whether there are any justifications for interfering with the right to freedom of expression. You will find the discussion on proportionality particularly helpful. Also consider the issue of **standing** and advise whether Sonia and the Campaign for Free Speech would be allowed to make the claim.

Further reading

Allan, T. R. S., 'Judicial deference and judicial review: legal doctrine and legal theory' (2011) 127(1) Law Quarterly Review 96

Allan argues against the adoption of a doctrine of deference, stating that the courts must consider each case in context.

Craig, P., *Administrative Law* (6th edn, London: Sweet & Maxwell, 2008)

Chapter 19 provides an excellent analytical account of the principles and case law on rationality and proportionality.

Daly, P., '*Wednesbury*'s reason and structure' [2011] Public Law 238

Daly re-evaluates the *Wednesbury* principle and suggests how it might be used to greater effect by the courts.

Jowell, J. and Lester, A., 'Beyond *Wednesbury*: substantive principles of administrative law' [1987] Public Law 368

This is the landmark article by two leading scholars discussing the inadequacy of irrationality as a ground of review. It argues that the courts should develop more effective principles of review, including proportionality, when reviewing the decision of public authorities.

Steyn, Lord, 'Deference: a tangled story' [2005] Public Law 346

In this article, Lord Steyn discusses the circumstances in which the courts should defer to the other branches of government. He argues that there should be no areas in which the court should automatically defer.

Tomkins, A., *Public Law* (Oxford: Oxford University Press, 2003)

Tomkins provides a very short and easy-to-read history of the development of the grounds of review. He sees the development of the irrationality principle and the use of proportionality as a shift in the balance of power from the executive and Parliament towards the judiciary. See especially pp. 176–201.

Procedural Impropriety

Key points

This chapter will cover:

- Failure to follow a statutory procedure
- The rules of natural justice
- The right to be heard
- Legitimate expectation
- The detailed requirements of natural justice
- The rule against bias
- Article 6 of the European Convention on Human Rights (ECHR)

Introduction

This chapter is the fifth substantive chapter on judicial review and it focuses on the procedures that are required to be followed when a decision is made. Since the introduction of the Human Rights Act 1998, we also have to consider Article 6 of the European Convention on Human Rights, the right to a fair and impartial hearing, which has had an impact on the law in this area. The usual place to begin a discussion on procedural impropriety is with Lord Diplock's description of procedural impropriety in the *CCSU* case.

● *Council of Civil Service Unions and others v Minister for the Civil Service*
[1985] AC 374

Lord Diplock at 411:

> I have described the third head as 'procedural impropriety' rather than failure to observe basic rules of natural justice or failure to act with procedural fairness towards the person who will be affected by the decision. This is because susceptibility to judicial review under this head covers also failure by an administrative tribunal to observe procedural rules that are expressly laid down in the legislative instrument by which its jurisdiction is conferred, even where such failure does not involve any denial of natural justice.

Lord Diplock's definition is an expansive one, which includes both a breach of a statutory procedure and also a breach of the common law rules of natural justice. We have adopted his definition for the purposes of this chapter and you will sometimes see breaches of all three sets of procedural rules: statutory, common law, and those specified in the European Convention on Human Rights referred to as 'procedural impropriety' for ease of reference.

(18.1) Failure to follow a statutory procedure

As we discussed in the previous chapter, a **public authority** must have the legal power to act; if that power is conferred by statute, it may also specify the procedure that must be used prior to an action or a decision being taken. This is what is known as a 'statutory procedure', because it is specified in a statute. The statute may, for example, require the authority to give notice of its intention to take action in a certain way, to consult interested groups, or to tell individuals that they have the right to appeal from an adverse decision. If the authority does not comply, then this is a breach of the statutory procedure and may be reviewed as a **procedural impropriety**. The court may be reluctant to invalidate the decision that has been taken if the breach is of a minor procedural rule, for what is a small technicality. But the courts are also keen to ensure that public authorities follow procedural rules, particularly where the rule is one that ensures that rights are protected. As a consequence, the courts have developed the law so as to try to balance the interests of decision-makers, who need to make regular decisions often in short periods of time, against the interests of members of the public, who are entitled to have their rights protected.

Traditionally, the courts held that if the statutory provision was classified by the court as mandatory (compulsory), then the public authority was required to follow it and failure to do so would make the decision void. If the statutory provision was classified as directory (advisory, but with a high degree of expectation that it be followed), then strict compliance was not required and failure to follow the statutory procedure would not invalidate the decision. It may help to provide an example in the form of *Bradbury v Enfield London Borough Council* [1967] 1 WLR 1311. In this case, the local authority, following **government** policy, reorganised the schools in its areas from grammar and secondary modern schools to comprehensive schools. The statute provided that the local authority should give notice to existing schools of its intention to consult on this change. Owing to a misinterpretation of the statute by the local authority, it failed to consult eight of the relevant schools. These schools challenged the decision. The Court of Appeal held that the authority had acted unlawfully. Failing to give the required notice of consultation meant that parents and others lost the opportunity to object to the authority's decision to the Secretary of State for Education. By contrast, in *Coney v Choyce* [1975] 1 All ER 979, a reorganisation of schools to establish a comprehensive system was proposed. In accordance with the statute, notice of the proposed changes was given, but there was a failure to comply with the strict requirement in relation to two schools. This was because no notice was posted at or near the main entrance to the school. The argument that this failure invalidated the proposed reorganisation was rejected by the court. This was because there had been substantial compliance with the provision and there were only minor breaches. The proposals had been widely advertised in the local press and were well known. The judge commented as follows.

. . . .

● *Coney v Choyce and others* [1975] 1 WLR 422

Templeman J at 434:

> Asking myself whether any substantial prejudice has been suffered by those for whose benefit the requirements were introduced, I am quite satisfied the answer is 'No'. The plaintiffs, having lost the battle on the merits, are now fighting a battle purely on the technicalities. I make no criticism. If the Education Act 1944 is so full of technicalities that the proposals can be tripped up, well, the plaintiffs are entitled to do just that. But in my judgment this is not an Act where Parliament intended that the technicalities should rule rather than the spirit of the law. The object...has been achieved, and in those circumstances it seems to me that it would be quite wrong to hold that the technical defects in compliance with the regulations make the Minister's approval invalid.

Certain kinds of provisions are more likely to be classified as mandatory provisions than directory ones. As we have seen in the cases above, provisions that require consultation, as in *Bradbury*, tend to be mandatory requirements. Another example of a mandatory requirement can be seen in *London and Clydesdale Estates Ltd v Aberdeen District Council* [1980] 1 WLR 182, in which the House of Lords held that the planning authority had acted unlawfully. This was because it had failed to notify the claimants of the right to appeal against a planning decision on a planning certificate that the authority had issued. The statutory provision required that the information on the right to appeal must be included on the certificate. The court stressed the significance of the statutory provision, which was intended to inform individuals of their rights against the authority, and its importance explained why it was deemed to be mandatory.

More recent case law has emphasised the importance of looking at the consequences of the failure to follow the statutory procedure. In *R v Secretary of State for the Home Department, ex p Jeyeanthan* [2000] 1 WLR 354, Lord Woolf underlined the need for the court to consider the facts of each case, as well as the nature of the statutory requirement. In this case, a failed asylum seeker claimed that the Home Secretary had failed to act in accordance with the statutory procedure laid down in rule 13(3) of the Asylum Appeals (Procedure) Rules 1993. The Home Secretary had appealed against the adjudicator's decision by letter rather than by using the prescribed form. Lord Woolf stated that the non-compliance with the statutory requirements was a 'pure technicality' and explained the approach that the court should take.

● ***R v Secretary of State for the Home Department, ex p Jeyeanthan*** [2000] 1 WLR 354

Lord Woolf at 362:

> I suggest that the right approach is to regard the question of whether a requirement is directory or mandatory as only at most a first step. In the majority of cases there are other questions which have to be asked which are more likely to be of greater assistance than the application of the mandatory/directory test. The questions which are likely to arise are as follows.
>
> 1. Is the statutory requirement fulfilled if there has been substantial compliance with the requirement and, if so, has there been substantial compliance in the case in issue even though there has not been strict compliance? (The substantial compliance question.)
>
> 2. Is the non-compliance capable of being waived, and if so, has it, or can it and should it be waived in this particular case? (The discretionary question.) I treat the grant of an extension of time for compliance as a waiver.
>
> 3. If it is not capable of being waived or is not waived then what is the consequence of the non-compliance? (The consequences question.)
>
> Which questions arise will depend upon the facts of the case and the nature of the particular requirement. The advantage of focusing on these questions is that they should avoid the unjust and unintended consequences which can flow from an approach solely dependent on dividing requirements into mandatory..., or...directory...

Lord Woolf stresses that those inconsequential failures that have no impact, such as the one in this case, should not lead to the decision being quashed. In addition, if the claimant knows about the breach of procedure and does not object, then the court may consider the breach to have been waived. In general, it is fair to conclude that the failure of a public authority substantially to follow a statutory requirement that affects, for example, the right to be consulted, or to object, or to appeal, is likely to be regarded as invalidating the decision. Otherwise, the court is reluctant to quash the decision. But it will focus on the facts of the case and the nature of the statutory requirement.

summary points

Failure to follow a statutory procedure

- *The court will consider whether the procedure is mandatory or directory.*
- *Mandatory procedures are those that are deemed to be of significance in protecting an individual or a group of individuals' legal rights or in affording protection to them.*
- *The greater the impact that the decision has on an individual, the more likely it is to be deemed to be a breach of mandatory requirement, which may invalidate the decision.*
- *However, mere technical breaches are unlikely to lead to a decision being quashed.*

18.2 The rules of natural justice

The rules of **natural justice** are common law rules developed over the centuries to ensure that public authorities take decisions and actions in a manner that is deemed to be fair and transparent, while also allowing for relatively efficient decision-making. Some people find that the American definition sums up the purpose of the rules of natural justice rather neatly. Americans refer to natural justice as 'due process', because the emphasis is on the fairness of the decision-making process.

18.2.1 An introduction to the rules of natural justice

Natural justice provides a minimum standard of fairness and is implied by the courts into the statute or into the decision-making process that is not regulated by statute. It is used to supplement statutory procedures or is applied when the statute is silent on the kind of procedure to be used. However, sometimes statutes will also provide a higher standard than the common law rules of natural justice require. It should be noted that the rules of natural justice are also implied into certain types of contract. This is why some of the case law concerns relationships between private individuals, for example between trade unions and their members, or between members and sporting associations. However, in order to bring a claim for **judicial** review arguing that there has been a breach of natural justice, the claim must be brought against someone exercising a public function. Private law cases must be brought using the appropriate private law procedure. Before considering the detailed rules that have developed, it is important to keep in mind some of the issues that have arisen in cases concerned with natural justice.

cross reference
See Chapter 14 for more on the judicial review procedure.

Natural justice covers a very wide area of decision-making, which can include bodies that are more like a court, such as a disciplinary tribunal in a prison. But it can also include decisions such as licensing applications or applications to university, which are far more administrative in nature. Natural justice applies to many kinds of decision-making, but the requirements of natural justice are flexible. The type of procedure that will comply with the rules of natural justice will depend on the kind of decision and decision-making body. For example, if a taxi licence were being withdrawn from an individual who has been accused of misconduct, natural justice might require that the individual be granted an oral hearing at which cross-examination of witnesses is permitted and a lawyer is present. Conversely, when a candidate applies to university, an oral hearing, cross-examination, and legal representation are not required before the university makes its decision as to whether or not a place should be offered. But the university is still expected to act fairly and without bias. So the rules of natural justice will vary depending on the circumstances. The other general point to consider is that what natural justice requires will depend on the kind of right or interest at stake. The different kinds of interests will be discussed later in the chapter.

18.2.2 What are the reasons for the rules of natural justice?

Judges rarely discuss the reasons why the rules of natural justice are important. However, this is something considered by many of the commentators and legal theorists. There are three main justifications for the rules of natural justice. The first kind is that the rules of natural justice improve the quality of decision-making by public authorities. If an authority has acted without bias and heard representations from concerned parties, then it is more likely to make an accurate and fair decision. In addition, individuals who have been treated fairly by the decision-making process are more willing to accept the decision, whereas people may not respect decisions in which there are real or perceived procedural deficiencies and the decision will therefore lack credibility or legitimacy. The second set of justifications centres around principles of fairness and dignity. It is argued that human dignity requires that individuals whose interests may be affected by a decision should be consulted or able to participate in the process in some way. Jowell discusses this point in the next extract. He also argues that natural justice, or as he calls it 'fair process', is linked to the idea of the **rule of law**.

cross reference
You may wish to refer back to Chapter 4 on the rule of law.

● J. Jowell, 'The rule of law and its underlying values', in J. Jowell, and D. Oliver (eds) *The Changing Constitution* (6th edn, Oxford: Oxford University Press, 2007), pp. 5–24, at 12–13

> Another of Dicey's feature of the Rule of Law is that no person should be condemned unheard- that there should be no punishment without a trial. The requirement of 'due process' or natural justice (these days called 'procedural fairness') is associated with his notion of legality, as it assumes that the person will be able to challenge both the announced rule or the implementa- tion of the rule by the official. In order to do this, the claimant will need access to the courts. So access to justice is another feature of the Rule of Law.
>
> Once the claimant reaches the court, another aspect of the Rule of Law is engaged, namely the requirement that the decision-maker be unbiased ...
>
> [Jowell goes on to explain that:]
>
> ... [D]ue process is not merely a formal virtue. Its substantive dimensions emerges when we consider that it endorses the notion that every person is entitled to be treated with due regard to the proper merits of their cause. Failure to provide that treatment diminishes a person's sense of individual worth and impairs their dignity. The right to due process goes further than forbidding actual punishment without a trial. It extends to concern that individuals should not have decisions made about their vital interests without an opportunity to influence the out- come of those decisions. And it requires restrictions on rights, liberties and interests to be properly *justified*.
>
> [Footnotes omitted]

The third justification for the rules of natural justice is that they encourage participation in decision-making and therefore make it more democratic. This means that those who have an interest in decisions have an opportunity to participate.

● J. Jowell, 'The rule of law and its underlying values', in J. Jowell, and D. Oliver (eds) *The Changing Constitution* (6th edn, Oxford: Oxford University Press, 2007), pp. 5–24, at 13

> Some decisions decide not only rights between the individual and the public organisation but also questions of policy, such as whether a motorway should be built over a stretch of land. In those situations the decision may be structured by means of an inquiry or tribunal hearing, or may simply be made by an official within a government department. There has been a demand for public participation in those decisions. Even though those seeking participation have mere interests (rather than vested rights) in the decision's outcome, they ask for the right to par- ticipate in the process of making that decision. Neighbours want to be consulted about the application for planning permission on a local site, and people want to be consulted about the closure of hospitals, local railway lines or coal pits. If the rule of law is concerned to protect in- dividuals from being deprived of their rights without an opportunity to defend themselves, the concern is only narrowly stretched to protect group interests from being overridden without the opportunity to express views on the matter to be decided.
>
> [Footnotes omitted]

thinking point
Are you now able to outline how the rules of natural justice illustrate a key feature of Dicey's rule of law?

Jowell also emphasises that decisions made by public authorities, such as where to build a motorway, may affect a wide range of individuals and that a fair procedure should allow them to participate in decision-making. Thinking about the reasons why the rules of natural justice evolved will help you to understand the structure of some of the legislation that is being challenged, why claimants object to the way in which decisions have been made, how the principles of natural justice have evolved and continue to develop, and the reason for judges' decisions.

summary points

The rules of natural justice

- *The rules of natural justice are common law rules that may be in addition to statutory procedures or may operate in the absence of any statutory procedures.*

- *Because they are common law rules, they are to be found in cases rather than in statutes.*

- *They have been developed over the centuries to promote fair and transparent decision-making while allowing for efficient decision-making too.*

- *The first reason for the rules of natural justice is that a proper and fair decision-making process is likely to lead to a better standard of decision-making,*

- *The second reason for the rules of natural justice is that they promote human dignity and fairness by allowing those who are to be affected by decisions to provide their side of the case or to participate in the process through which their interests may be affected.*

- *The third justification for the rules of natural justice is that they promote participation in the decision-making process and thus encourage democracy.*

18.3 **The right to be heard**

We shall now turn to the detail of the content of the rules of natural justice, taking a number of the key rules in turn: the right to be heard; legitimate expectation; the right to know the case against you; the right to a decision-maker free from bias; and related rights that may apply, such as the right to legal representation and the right to cross-examine witnesses. As mentioned above, not all apply in all instances and not all in the same way. We shall turn first to one of the most important of those rights—the right to be heard.

This aspect of natural justice is sometimes referred to by the Latin term *audi alterem partem* (meaning 'hear the other side') and is a very ancient principle. In *John v Rees* [1970] Ch 345, Mr Justice Megarry explained that the right to be heard is vital. This is because unless the decision-maker hears both sides of a dispute, there is likely to be misunderstanding and misinterpretation.

. . . .

● *John v Rees* [1970] Ch 345

Megarry VC at 402:

> As everyone who has anything to do with the law well knows, the path of the law is strewn with examples of open and shut cases, which somehow, were not; of unanswerable charges which in the event, were completely answered; of inexplicable conduct which was fully explained; of fixed and unalterable determinations that by discussing suffered a change.

The judge emphasised that decision-makers may change their minds or have their suspicions dispelled if they hear relevant representations. However, the right to be heard fell into disuse, and was used only infrequently, until the House of Lords restated its importance and simplified the law in the landmark case of *Ridge v Baldwin* [1964] AC 40. The court swept away the distinction between administrative and judicial cases that limited the application of the rules of natural justice. It was made clear that the right to be heard is relevant in judicial and administrative cases. It is often said that the right to be heard was reasserted in this case because the House of Lords emphasised that this notion developed by the common law was of real relevance in the modern administrative **state**.

Ridge v Baldwin concerned the summary dismissal of the Chief Constable of Brighton, after thirty-three years' employment, by the committee responsible, which was known as the Watch Committee. The relevant statute gave the Watch Committee the power to dismiss 'any . . . constable whom they think negligent in the discharge of his duty, or otherwise unfit for the same'. The Chief Constable was dismissed because he had been tried with other members of his force for conspiring to obstruct the course of justice. Although he was acquitted, his officers were convicted, and the trial judge criticised the Chief Constable's leadership of the force. The trial judge claimed that, by dismissing the Chief Constable without a hearing, the Watch Committee had acted in breach of natural justice and the decision was **ultra vires**. This was because he had been denied the right to be heard in his defence. He wanted to be heard in person, so that he could persuade the Watch Committee to allow him to resign and thus to retain his pension rights. He claimed, more specifically, that he was not informed of the case against him and he had been given no opportunity to be heard in his own defence, although his solicitor had been allowed to address the committee. In other words, he complained that he did not know the details of the accusations against him and had no chance to persuade the committee, in person, to allow him to resign. The House of Lords reviewed the previous case law and concluded that the decision of the Watch Committee was in breach of natural justice. Lord Reid explains why in the following extracts from his judgment.

● ***Ridge v Baldwin*** [1964] AC 40

Lord Reid at 64:

> The principle *audi alteram partem* goes back many centuries in our law and appears in a multitude of judgments of judges of the highest authority. In modern times opinions have sometimes been expressed to the effect that natural justice is so vague as to be practically meaningless. But I would regard these as tainted by the perennial fallacy that because something cannot be cut and dried or nicely weighed or measured therefore it does not exist . . . It appears to me that one reason why the authorities on natural justice have been found difficult to reconcile is that insufficient attention has been paid to the great difference between various kinds of cases in which it has been sought to apply the principle. What a minister ought to do in considering objections to a scheme may be very different from what a watch committee ought to do in considering whether to dismiss a chief constable.

Lord Reid, at 66, then said that there were three different categories of case and that this case fell into the third category:

> So I come to the third class, which includes the present case. There I find an unbroken line of authority to the effect that an officer cannot lawfully be dismissed without first telling him what is alleged against him and hearing his defence or explanation . . .

Lord Reid reviewed the previous case law and concluded, at 68–9, that:

> Stopping there, I would think that authority was wholly in favour of the appellant, but the respondent's argument was mainly based on what has been said in a number of fairly recent cases dealing with different subject-matter. Those cases deal with decisions by ministers, officials and bodies of various kinds which adversely affected property rights or privileges of persons who had had no opportunity or no proper opportunity of presenting their cases before the decisions were given. and it is necessary to examine those cases for another reason. The question which was or ought to have been considered by the watch committee on March 7, 1958, was not a simple question whether or not the appellant should be dismissed. There were three possible courses open to the watch committee—reinstating the appellant as chief constable, dismissing him, or requiring him to resign. The difference between the latter two is that dismissal involved forfeiture of pension rights, whereas requiring him to resign did not. Indeed, it is now clear that the appellant's real interest in this appeal is to try to save his pension rights.

It may be convenient at this point to deal with an argument that, even if as a general rule a watch committee must hear a constable in his own defence before dismissing him, this case was so clear that nothing that the appellant could have said could have made any difference. It is at least very doubtful whether that could be accepted as an excuse. But, even if it could, the respondents would, in my view, fail on the facts. It may well be that no reasonable body of men could have reinstated the appellant. But as between the other two courses open to the watch committee the case is not so clear. Certainly on the facts, as we know them, the watch committee could reasonably have decided to forfeit the appellant's pension rights, but I could not hold that they would have acted wrongly or wholly unreasonably if they had in the exercise of their discretion decided to take a more lenient course.

I would start an examination of the authorities dealing with property rights and privileges with *Cooper v. Wandsworth Board of Works*. Where an owner had failed to give proper notice to the Board they had under an Act of 1855 authority to demolish any building he had erected and recover the cost from him. This action was brought against the board because they had used that power without giving the owner an opportunity of being heard. The board maintained that their discretion to order demolition was not a judicial discretion and that any appeal should have been to the Metropolitan Board of Works. But the court decided unanimously in favour of the owner. Erle C.J. held that the power was subject to a qualification repeatedly recognised that no man is to be deprived of his property without his having an opportunity of being heard and that this had been applied to 'many exercises of power which in common understanding would not be at all a more judicial proceeding than would be the act of the district board in ordering a house to be pulled down'. Willes J. said that the rule was 'of universal application, and founded upon the plainest principles of justice', and Byles J. said that 'although there are no positive words in a statute requiring that the party shall be heard, yet the justice of the common law will supply the omission of the legislature'...

Lord Reid then went on to say, at 72–3, that:

We do not have a developed system of administrative law—perhaps because until fairly recently we did not need it. So it is not surprising that in dealing with new types of cases the courts have had to grope for solutions, and have found that old powers, rules and procedure are largely inapplicable to cases which they were never designed or intended to deal with. But I see nothing in that to justify our thinking that our old methods are any less applicable today than ever they were to the older types of case. and if there are any dicta in modern authorities which point in that direction, then, in my judgment, they should not be followed...

His reasoning led him to decide, at 79, that:

So I would hold that the power of dismissal in the Act of 1882 could not then have been exercised and cannot now be exercised until the watch committee have informed the constable of the grounds on which they propose to proceed and have given him a proper opportunity to present his case in defence.

cross reference

Lord Reid refers to the case of Cooper v Wandsworth Board of Works *(1863) 14 CBNS 180, discussed later in this chapter.*

The principle that emerged from the decision in *Ridge v Baldwin* was that natural justice applies to decisions of public authorities that affect the interests of the individual. Although the case concerned the statutory dismissal of a chief constable, the principle has been applied to a wide variety of different administrative decisions.

Sometimes, the courts use the term 'fairness' when discussing the principles applied to administrative decisions. There is an academic debate about whether fairness is part of natural justice or a different principle. Perhaps the best approach is to consider the term 'fairness' to be interchangeable with natural justice. So natural justice and procedural fairness are relevant to all kinds of decision-making. But be aware that the courts often use the term 'fairness' rather than natural justice when the decision is an administrative one requiring that basic procedural rules are complied with by the decision-maker. An example of this, and a case in which the term 'fairness' is used by the court, is *Re HK (An Infant)* [1967] 2 WLR 962. An immigration officer at a London airport refused to grant permission to the claimant to enter the UK. The claimant claimed to be under 16 years of age and a dependant of a Commonwealth citizen resident in the UK. The immigration officer did not believe that the claimant was aged under 16. The claimant was given a medical examination and was interviewed twice by the immigration officer, who directed that he be returned to Pakistan. The claimant asked for judicial review of the decision, arguing that he should have been granted a hearing so that he could prove his age. The court rejected this argument. It held that the rules of natural justice or fairness did apply, but did not require an elaborate hearing. It was enough that the claimant and his father understood the nature of the immigration officer's concerns, and that they had an opportunity to address them.

The importance of the right to be heard was re-emphasised by the Court of Appeal in the high-profile case of *R (on the application of Shoesmith) v Ofsted and others* [2011] EWCA Civ 642. Ms Shoesmith was summarily dismissed as director of Children's Services by Haringey Council after the public controversy over the death of 'Baby P' at the hands of his carers. Baby P was on the child protection register and subject to a child protection plan drafted by Haringey London Borough Council. His death led to an inquiry into children's services in Haringey by the Office for Standards in Education, Children's Services and Skills (Ofsted). It was ordered by Ed Balls, the then Labour Secretary of State for Education. It was a general inquiry into the service, as opposed to a disciplinary hearing into the work of any individual. The report identified some serious problems with the operation of Haringey Children's Services, but did not identify any individuals as blameworthy. However, before the report was published, the members of the Ofsted team met with Mr Balls and were highly critical of Ms Shoesmith. Mr Balls then announced publicly that he was removing her from her statutory post as director of Children's Services. He also said that her employment relationship with Haringey LBC was a matter for the council, but that he did not think she should be awarded with any payoffs. She was subsequently summarily dismissed by Haringey LBC.

This is a rather complicated series of events, but what concerns us here is the claimant's allegation that she had not been treated fairly and had been denied the right to be heard, because she was not given the opportunity to make representations rebutting the allegations against her. The Court of Appeal found that Ofsted had acted fairly. She had the opportunity to respond to the gist of the criticisms made about the running of the service and, because the report had not criticised her personally, this was sufficiently fair. But the Court of Appeal found that the Secretary of State for Education had acted unlawfully. This was because he did not give Ms Shoesmith the opportunity to respond to the allegations that were made against her by the Ofsted team in its meeting with Mr Balls. Giving her the chance to respond would have led to only a short delay, and because she was not a front-line social worker dealing with children on a day-to-day basis, there was no danger to individual children. The Court stressed that although public servants were expected to take responsibility for their work, that did not deprive them of the opportunity of explaining themselves. The consequences of the Secretary of State's decision were described as 'catastrophic' for Ms Shoesmiths's career and reputation. She should therefore have had the opportunity to respond to the allegations against her. The Court of Appeal referred to the dicta of Megarry VC in *John v Rees* [1970] 1 Ch 345 and stressed that it was important that the Secretary of State for Education should have listened to her representations, because it was at least possible that this might have changed the outcome.

These cases show that the principles of natural justice and fairness often form an important basis for judicial review, and that the degree to which they apply will vary from case to case. The way in which natural justice is applied in different cases will be discussed further below.

18.3.1 Different interests and expectations

The rules of natural justice are applicable in different sorts of case concerned with different types of right, interest, and expectation. Natural justice is not limited to cases involving the deprivation of rights, such as property rights; it is also relevant in cases in which there is an application for a benefit, such as a planning or licensing application. There are also cases in which the courts have held that the claimant has a legitimate expectation of a substantive benefit (see below). A simple classification of the different types of case and interest was attempted by Megarry VC in *McInnes v Onslow-Fane and another* [1978] 1 WLR 1520. In this case, the British Boxing Board of Control refused an application for a boxer's management licence without giving the claimant an oral hearing or reasons. The court held in favour of the Board, rejecting the argument that there had been a breach of natural justice. This was partly because refusal of the licence did not cast doubt on the claimant's honesty and character. The judge went on to discuss the various kinds of interest that a claimant may have.

● *McInnes v Onslow-Fane and another* [1978] 1 WLR 1520

Megarry VC at 1529:

> First, there are what may be called the forfeiture cases. In these, there is a decision which takes away some existing right or position, as where a member of an organisation is expelled or a licence is revoked. Second, at the other extreme there are what may be called the application cases. These are cases where the decision merely refuses to grant the applicant the right or position that he seeks, such as membership of the organisation, or a licence to do certain acts. Third, there is an intermediate category, which may be called the expectation cases, which differ from the application cases only in that the applicant has some legitimate expectation from what has already happened that his application will be granted. This head includes cases where an existing licence-holder applies for a renewal of his licence or a person already elected or appointed to some position seeks confirmation from some confirming authority ...

Decisions that involve forfeiture or deprivation of a right require the administrator to apply a higher standard of procedural fairness than cases in which the individual is making an application. This is considered in more detail when we look at the requirements of natural justice later in the chapter. So, for example, an oral hearing may be required in a forfeiture case, but not in an application case. An example of a case in which the property rights of a claimant were at stake and an oral hearing was required was *Cooper v Wandsworth Board of Works* (1863) 14 CBNS 180. In this case, the claimant had started to build a house without giving the necessary notice. The Board then began to demolish the building without giving the claimant a hearing. It was held by the court that this was unlawful and that the right to be heard was implied into the relevant statute. This was because the demolition of the house would be a heavy loss to the claimant, whose right to property was at stake, and he should have a chance of explaining himself before such a drastic step was taken.

In addition to application and forfeiture cases, the courts have also developed another kind of interest, which is referred to as 'legitimate expectation'. The legitimate expectation might arise because of an expectation that a conferred benefit will continue, as in the case of an existing licence being renewed, as mentioned by Megarry VC in *McInnes v Onslow-Fane*. But legitimate expectations may arise in other circumstances based on a representation by a public authority. This concept of legitimate expectation, and the procedural and substantive benefits that it confers, has developed into an important area of administrative law that, in some ways, goes beyond its origins as a way of accessing procedural fairness.

● J. Jowell, 'The rule of law and its underlying values', in J. Jowell, and D. Oliver (eds) *The Changing Constitution* (6th edn, Oxford: Oxford University Press, 2007), pp. 5–24, at 13

cross reference
The requirements of natural justice will be discussed in depth later in the chapter.

We shall consider this in the next section.

summary points

The right to be heard

- *The right to be heard was reasserted in the case of* Ridge v Baldwin *when the House of Lords removed the distinction between administrative and judicial decision-making.*

- *The rules of natural justice are sometimes referred to as 'the duty to act fairly' in the context of administrative decision-making.*

- *Natural justice applies to different types of case concerned with different types of right, interest, and legitimate expectation.*

- *The requirements of natural justice vary depending on the type of case and interest involved in the decision.*

18.4 Legitimate expectation

This section will explain the concept of legitimate expectation and how the law has developed in this area. It will examine the elements that have to be present before the court holds that there is a legitimate expectation. It will then explain the difference between procedural and substantive expectations, and discuss in what circumstances the court will hold that the authority must give effect to the representation.

18.4.1 What is a legitimate expectation?

A policy, a statement, or the past practice of a public authority may create a legitimate expectation of a procedure being followed or a substantive benefit being conferred. There are some circumstances in which the courts have held that it is unlawful for the public authority to disappoint the claimant and have forced the authority to keep its promise. It is similar to the doctrine of estoppel in contract law. One of the early cases on legitimate expectation that illustrates the courts' insistence on following a certain procedure before a decision is made is *Attorney General v Ng Yuen Shiu* [1983] 2 AC 629.

The claimant was a Chinese national who had entered Hong Kong from Macau illegally in 1967 and had an interest in a factory in Hong Kong. In 1980, the Hong Kong government announced that it was ending the 'reached base' policy. This policy allowed illegal Chinese immigrants to remain in Hong Kong once they reached the urban areas without being arrested. Concerns were raised about the changes from those who had entered Hong Kong illegally from Macau. In response, the Immigration Department issued a statement that immigrants from Macau would be treated in the same way as illegal immigrants from other parts of China. This meant that there was no guarantee that they would not be subsequently removed. But the statement also said that each case would be treated on its merits. In this case, a removal order was made against the claimant without him being given the chance to make representations against his removal. It was held by the Privy Council that the Hong Kong government was bound by its undertaking to consider each case on the merits. It therefore had to give the claimant the opportunity to make representations. Lord Roskill explains the reasoning behind the decision in the following extract.

· ·

● **Attorney General of Hong Kong v Ng Yuen Shiu** [1983] 2 AC 629

Lord Roskill at 638–9:

> Their Lordships see no reason why the principle should not be applicable when the person who will be affected by the decision is an alien, just as much as when he is a British subject. The justification for it is primarily that, when a public authority has promised to follow a certain procedure, it is in the interest of good administration that it should act fairly and should implement its promise, so long as implementation does not interfere with its statutory duty. The principle is also justified by the further consideration that, when the promise was made, the authority must have considered that it would be assisted in discharging its duty fairly by any representations from interested parties and as a general rule that is correct.

Lord Roskill emphasised that the claimant had to be given the opportunity to put forward his case as to why he should be allowed to remain in Hong Kong. This expectation arose out of the government's statement that it would consider 'each case on the merits'. The public authority was not permitted to go back on its statement.

Another situation in which the court has held that there may be a legitimate expectation of a hearing is where the authority changes an established policy. This may occur where there is a general representation stating the policy, but the authority fails to apply the policy or changes the policy. This was the situation in *R v Secretary of State for the Home Department, ex p Khan* [1984] 1 WLR 1337. In this case, the claimants were a childless couple who wanted to adopt a nephew from Pakistan. After visiting a Citizens Advice Bureau, they were given a circular from the Home Department explaining its policy on adoption. A circular is a form of official guidance and, in this case, it set out the principles on which adoption decisions would be based. It was stated that, although the immigration rules made no specific mention of overseas adoption, the Home Secretary was likely to grant entry clearance if four criteria were met. However, entry clearance was refused to the couple in this case, despite compliance with the four criteria. This was because there was a fifth criterion, not stated in the circular, which was that in order for the adoption to go ahead, the birth parents had to be unable to care for the child.

How does this illustrate legitimate expectation? It was argued by the claimants that the circular had given them a legitimate expectation that the policy in the circular would be followed and that, on that basis, they should be permitted to adopt their nephew. The Court of Appeal held that the circular did create a legitimate expectation. It stated that the Home Secretary could either grant entry clearance in accordance with the policy in the circular, or he could apply the new policy with the fifth criterion that the birth parents were unable to look after the child. But if he did so, he had to give the claimants an opportunity to make representations that the new policy should not apply to them, as Lord Justice Parker explained.

● *R v Secretary of State for the Home Department, ex p Khan* [1984] 1 WLR 1337

Parker LJ at 1348:

> ...I have no doubt that the Home Office letter afforded the applicant a reasonable expectation that the procedures it set out, which were just as certain in their terms as the question and answer in Mr. Ng's case, would be followed; that if the result of the implementation of those procedures satisfied the Secretary of State of the four matters mentioned, a temporary entry clearance would be granted and that the ultimate fate of the child would then be decided by the adoption court of this country. I have equally no doubt that it was considered by the department at the time the letter was sent out that if those procedures were fully implemented they would be sufficient to safeguard the public interest. The letter can mean nothing else. This is not surprising. The adoption court will apply the law of this country and will thus protect all the interests which the law of this country considers should be protected. The Secretary of State is, of course, at liberty to change the policy but in my view, vis-a-vis the recipient of such a letter, a new policy can only be implemented after such recipient has been given a full and serious consideration whether there is some overriding public interest which justifies a departure from the procedures stated in the letter...
>
> I would allow the appeal and quash the refusal of entry clearance. This will leave the Secretary of State free either to proceed on the basis of the letter or, if he considers it desirable to operate the new policy, to afford the applicant a full opportunity to make representations why, in his case, it should not be followed.
>
> I would add only this. If the new policy is to continue in operation, the sooner the Home Office letter is redrafted and false hopes cease to be raised in those who may have a deep emotional need to adopt, the better it will be. To leave it in its present form is not only bad and grossly unfair administration but, in some instances at any rate, positively cruel.

As Lord Justice Parker explained, it was not fair that the couple were given false hope that they be permitted to adopt, based on official guidelines, only to find that the public authority decided to apply a further criterion that had not been communicated to them and of which they could have no knowledge. Once again, it can be seen that the rules of natural justice are based on the concept of fairness. A legitimate expectation can also arise from a past practice. So, for example, in the *CCSU* case, the expectation was that the union would be consulted based on a past practice of consultation. Were this case to relate to a more standard occupational group, teachers or doctors for example, then it is likely that the legitimate expectation would have been sustained, and the rules of natural justice would have been applied and the decision quashed. However, on the facts of this case, it was held that national security considerations outweighed considerations of natural justice, because the civil servants worked at the government listening centre GCHQ, which is involved in work that involves national security considerations.

● *Council for the Civil Service v Minister for the Civil Service* [1985] AC 374

Lord Fraser of Tullybellton at 401:

> Legitimate expectations such as are now under consideration will always relate to a benefit or privilege to which the claimant has no right in private law, and it may even be to one which conflicts with his private law rights. In the present case the evidence shows that, ever since GCHQ began in 1947, prior consultation has been the invariable rule when conditions of service were to be significantly altered. Accordingly in my opinion if there had been no question of national security involved, the appellants would have had a legitimate expectation that the minister would consult them before issuing the instruction of 22 December 1983. The next question, therefore, is whether it has been shown that consideration of national security supersedes the expectation.

This case illustrates that natural justice may have to give way to other weighty considerations in certain circumstances. The rules of natural justice are not rights to which one is entitled in all circumstances and at one level; instead they are balanced against the interests at stake. Having discussed how legitimate expectations are created, it is important to consider the different kinds of benefits that are produced.

18.4.2 Substantive and procedural benefits

In the above cases, the legitimate expectation concerned procedural benefits, such as being consulted before a decision is made. But there are some circumstances in which it has been argued that, as a result of the representation or practice, an actual benefit should be conferred as opposed to a procedural advantage, such as a hearing or consultation. In other words, the public authority may be deemed to have promised something concrete other than a process or procedure to be followed. And the courts may require the public authority to provide the benefit or the item that is deemed to have been promised. Some commentators have argued that this is part of the development of a doctrine of fairness. In other words, the public authority has promised to take certain action and it would be an abuse of its power and extremely unfair if it were then to let the claimant down by going back on its word. However, there are other factors to consider here. The courts generally insist that public authorities exercise their **discretion** in the public interest—but it may not always be in the public interest for the authority to be bound to confer the benefit. Granting the expectation may mean that others may lose out. The courts might then be accused of interfering in the work of the public authority.

There are only a few cases in which a claim of a legitimate expectation of a substantive benefit has been successful. *R v North and East Devon Health Authority, ex p Coughlan* [2001] QB 213 is the landmark decision on substantive legitimate expectations and the judgment of Lord Woolf is very helpful in explaining the development of the law in this area. Ms Coughlan had been severely injured in a road accident and was unable to look after herself or to live on her own. She moved from the care home in which she had lived for over twenty years to a new and more suitable care home, Mardon House. She was persuaded to move because the authority promised that she and other residents could live there for 'as long as they chose'. However, after some years, the authority decided that Mardon House should be closed, because it was very expensive to run, and the residents moved. Coughlan argued that, owing to the representation of the authority, she had been promised a home for life and that the authority could not go back on its word. The Court of Appeal, in a landmark judgment, held that the authority was bound by its representation. In the following extract, Lord Woolf explains that there are three different types of legitimate expectation.

● **R v North and East Devon Health Authority, ex p Coughlan** [2001] QB 213

Lord Woolf at 241–3:

> [57] There are at least three possible outcomes.
>
> (a) The court may decide that the public authority is only required to bear in mind its previous policy or other representation, giving it the weight it thinks right, but no more, before deciding whether to change course. Here the court is confined to reviewing the decision on *Wednesbury* grounds (*Associated Provincial Picture Houses Ltd v Wednesbury Corpn* [1948] 1 KB 223]. This has been held to be the effect of changes of policy in cases involving the early release of prisoners: see *In re Findlay* [1985] AC 318; *R v Secretary of State for the Home Department, ex p Hargreaves* [1997] 1 WLR 906.

(b) On the other hand the court may decide that the promise or practice induces a legitimate expectation of, for example, being consulted before a particular decision is taken. Here it is uncontentious that the court itself will require the opportunity for consultation to be given unless there is an overriding reason to resile from it (see *Attorney General of Hong Kong v Ng Yuen Shiu* [1983] 2 AC 629) in which case the court will itself judge the adequacy of the reason advanced for the change of policy, taking into account what fairness requires.

(c) Where the court considers that a lawful promise or practice has induced a legitimate expectation of a benefit which is substantive, not simply procedural, authority now establishes that here too the court will in a proper case decide whether to frustrate the expectation is so unfair that to take a new and different course will amount to an abuse of power. Here, once the legitimacy of the expectation is established, the court will have the task of weighing the requirements of fairness against any overriding interest relied upon for the change of policy.

[58] The court having decided which of the categories is appropriate, the court's role in the case of the second and third categories is different from that in the first. In the case of the first, the court is restricted to reviewing the decision on conventional grounds. The test will be rationality and whether the public body has given proper weight to the implications of not ful-filling the promise. In the case of the second category the court's task is the conventional one of determining whether the decision was procedurally fair. In the case of the third, the court has when necessary to determine whether there is a sufficient overriding interest to justify a departure from what has been previously promised...

[59] ... Nevertheless, most cases of an enforceable expectation of a substantive benefit (the third category) are likely in the nature of things to be cases where the expectation is confined to one person or a few people, giving the promise or representation the character of a contract. We recognise that the courts' role in relation to the third category is still controversial; but, as we hope to show, it is now clarified by authority.

Lord Woolf then explained that this case came within the third category and that only an 'over-riding public interest' would justify the authority going back on the promise. He held that the promise should be honoured:

Our reasons are as follows. First, the importance of what was promised to Miss Coughlan (as we will explain later, this is a matter underlined by the Human Rights Act 1998); second, the fact that promise was limited to a few individuals, and the fact that the consequences to the health authority of requiring it to honour its promise are likely to be financial only.

This case is extremely important because it holds that there can be a legitimate expectation of a substantive benefit. However, the Court makes it clear that such an expectation can be over-ridden in the public interest. The reason why this case was successful was that the promise was made only to a small number of individuals, it was similar to a contract, and the consequences of honouring the promise were financial only. It would have been less likely to have been suc-cessful were the benefit to have been open-ended or to have been made in relation to a large group of people, because this would have had severe resource implications.

The decision in *Coughlan* referred to the earlier Court of Appeal decision in *R v Inland Revenue Commissioners, ex p Unilever plc* [1996] STC 681. In this case, the Inland Revenue had allowed Unilever to submit its tax return in a certain form. The effect of this was that Unilever submitted its full tax return late. The Inland Revenue had accepted this breach of the time limit for over twenty years. However, a dispute arose between the parties and the Inland Revenue refused to allow Unilever to submit its claim late, which had financial consequences for the company. The Court of Appeal found in favour of Unilever. Although the Court of Appeal referred to the traditional grounds of judicial review, Lord Justice Bingham stated as follows.

● *R v Inland Revenue Commissioners, ex p Unilever plc* [1996] STC 681

Sir Thomas Bingham MR at 691:

> These points cumulatively persuade me that on the unique facts of this case the Revenue's argument should be rejected. On the history here, I consider that to reject Unilever's claims in reliance on the time-limit, without clear and general advance notice, is so unfair as to amount to an abuse of power.

The discussion of the *Unilever* case by Lord Woolf in *Coughlan* indicates that the rationale behind the upholding of a legitimate expectation is that the courts regard the frustration of a legitimate expectation by the public authority as an abuse of power. However, the post-*Coughlan* case law illustrates that there may be other competing public interests that make it difficult to give effect to the expectation.

18.4.3 Legitimate expectation after the *Coughlan* case

The courts have stressed that the three categories that Lord Woolf identified in *Coughlan* may overlap. The second category is concerned with natural justice and confers a procedural benefit, such as an oral hearing. The first and the third categories are not easily distinguishable, but reflect the notion that the weight the court will give to the legitimate expectation will depend on the circumstances. In general, if a legitimate expectation is made, then the court will insist that the representation be given effect only if it would be irrational not to do so. There will be very few cases that fall into the third category. This means the courts will rarely hold that frustration of the expectation will be an abuse of power. Claims of legitimate expectation have been made in many cases following *Coughlan*. But even if the court finds that the claimant has a legitimate expectation, it may simply require the authority to take this into account when making the relevant decision.

The distinction between substantive and procedural expectations was discussed in *R (Luton BC and others) v Secretary of State for Education* [2011] EWHC 217. The case concerned the cancellation of the Building Schools for the Future (BSF) programme by the Secretary of State for Education after the May 2010 general election. The court rejected the argument of the six claimant local authorities that they had a substantive legitimate expectation that the school-building projects in their area would go ahead. The judge pointed out the fact that although the claimants had passed important procedural milestones, they had not reached the crucial final binding stage of the process. He also held that there was always a chance in such a long-term project that it would be affected by available resources or a change of government after the May 2010 general election. Although there was no substantive legitimate expectation, the court held that there was a procedural legitimate expectation. This imposed a duty on the Secretary of State for Education to consult the claimant local authorities before he made a decision as to whether or not to cancel the rebuilding of the schools in question. The legitimate expectation arose because large sums of money were involved, there had been years of continuous and intense dialogue between the Education Department and the claimants, they had recently received the non-binding outline business case approval letters, and the claimants were acting and spending money in reliance on them. Any consultations could have been conducted swiftly and would not have delayed the final outcome. The next brief extract summarises the judge's reasons for the decision on this point.

cross reference
The facts of Luton *are explained more fully in Chapter 17.*

565

Holman J:

> [96] In my view, the way in which the Secretary of State abruptly stopped the projects in re-lation to which OBC approval had already been given, without any prior consultation with the five claimants, must be characterised as being so unfair as to amount to an abuse of power. However, pressing the economic problems, there was no 'overriding public interest' which pre-cluded any consultation; and insofar as it affects the five claimants the decision making pro-cess was unlawful.

cross reference

See the discussion on remedies in Chapter 19.

The claimants did not have a substantive legitimate expectation that the school-building pro-ject would go ahead, but, because of the history and size of the projects, they did have a pro-cedural expectation that they would be consulted before a decision was taken to cancel the projects.

The judge stressed that the Secretary of State must listen to the representations of the claimant local authorities with an open mind, but the final decision was his alone.

thinking point

Do you understand why the court in Coughlan said that it recognised that the court's role in upholding substantive expectations was controversial?

18.4.4 The representation made must be clear and unequivocal

One of the issues that the courts will consider when deciding upon whether a legitimate ex-pectation has arisen is the extent to which the statement or representation made was clear and unequivocal. This is important because the item or the procedure that is being relied upon will need to be clear and it will need to be similar to a promise in order for a public authority to be required to fulfil it. The statement or conduct relied on as constituting a representation must be clear and precise. If it is vague or ambiguous, then it will not be sufficient. In both *R v Secretary of State for Education and Employment, ex p Begbie* [2000] 1 WLR 1115 and *R (on the applica-tion of Association of British Civilian Internees: Far East Region) v Secretary of State for Defence* [2003] QB 1397, the statements relied on were not sufficient to constitute representations. It is worth studying the facts and judgments to understand when the court is likely to be reluctant to find that a legitimate expectation has been created.

In the first case, the claimant, Heather Begbie, attended an independent (non-state) junior school on the assisted places scheme whereby the government paid for pupils to attend pri-vate schools. The incoming Labour government in 1997 pledged to abolish the scheme so as to be able to divert the budget in order to fund a reduction in class sizes in state schools. The Education (Schools) Act 1997 was passed shortly after Labour's election to government in 1997. It abolished the assisted places scheme and made transitional arrangements for those children already on the scheme. These arrangements were consistent with statements the Labour Party had made prior to the election. Such statements were repeated in letters to interested par-ties and newspaper articles after the election. These statements stressed that children already funded through the scheme would not lose out and would be able to continue their education: primary children could continue until the end of primary school and those in senior schools could finish their secondary education. The claimant was in a different position. She was in an 'all-through' school for children aged 5–18, and she was informed that her funding under the scheme would cease once she reached the end of her primary education.

It was argued by the claimant that pre-election promises stating that 'no one' would lose out as a result of the scheme had created a legitimate expectation that she would be able to stay at her school until she was aged 18. The Court of Appeal rejected her claim. It held that the Education (Schools) Act 1997 had abolished the assisted places scheme and that to allow the claimant to continue from the junior school to the senior school would be inconsistent with the statute. This point is considered further below. But the Court also held that a legitimate expectation had not arisen because pre-election promises by members of the opposition were not made by a public body and a letter containing misleading information was corrected soon after it was sent. In addition, statements in newspapers about the status of children on the assisted places scheme were too vague and general to create a legitimate expectation.

- ● **R v Secretary of State for Education and Employment, ex p Begbie** [2000] 1 ELR 1115

Gibson LJ at 1125:

> Mr. Beloff argues that the statements of prominent Labour Party politicians both in opposition and in office created a legitimate expectation that Heather would enjoy the benefit of the A.P.S. until conclusion of her education...

The Court rejected this argument. Gibson LJ stated that:

> [I]t is obvious that a party in opposition will not know all the facts and ramifications of a promise until it achieves office. To hold that the pre-election promises bound a newly-elected government could well be inimical to good government. I intend no encouragement to politicians to be extravagant in their pre-election promises, but when a party elected into office fails to keep its election promises, the consequences should be political and not legal.

The Court held that representations made by politicians in opposition were not sufficient to found a legitimate expectation. Opposition leaders would not know all of the relevant facts and figures until they got into government. So any statement made by the opposition parties was not authoritative enough to form the basis of a legitimate expectation.

In the *British Civilian Internees* case, it was held that a representation made by a minister in **Parliament** was not sufficient to give rise to a legitimate expectation. The minister had announced that compensation would be paid to British subjects interned by the Japanese in the Second World War. The Court of Appeal (see below) held that the representation was not clear and unambiguous.

- ● **R (on the application of Association of British Civilian Internees: Far East Region) v Secretary of State for Defence** [2003] QB 1397

Dyson LJ at 1420:

> [62] Our conclusion is that the announcement did not contain a clear and unequivocal representation that all those civilians who were British subjects at the time of their internment would receive ex gratia payments under this scheme.

The Court of Appeal decided that the statement made by the minister was loosely worded and understood by the claimants as needing clarification at a later date. It could not therefore create a legitimate expectation.

18.4.5 Has there been reliance on the representation?

In some cases, the courts have held that there must be reliance on the legitimate expectation if it is to be enforced. In *Begbie*, one reason that Lord Justice Sedley gave for not enforcing the representation was that there was no evidence of detrimental reliance by Begbie and her family on the statement that she could stay at the school until the end of her education. 'Detrimental reliance' means that the person has relied upon a statement made and has done so in a way that has caused him or her a detriment, such as doing something that he or she would not have chosen to do but for the statement. Detrimental reliance is necessary only if the statement is made to an individual or a small group of people. If the representation is one that is made to the public generally, then the court will not require detrimental reliance. This is because there is an expectation that the government will keep its word. The following short extract from *Begbie* sums up this point.

● ***R v Secretary of State for Education and Employment, ex p Begbie*** [2000] 1 WLR 1115

Sedley LJ at 1333:

> I have no difficulty with the proposition that in cases where government has made known how it intends to exercise powers which affect the public at large it may be held to its word irrespective of whether the applicant had been relying specifically upon it. The legitimate expectation in such a case is that government will behave towards its citizens as it says it will. But where the basis of the claim is, as it is here, that a pupil-specific discretion should be exercised in certain pupil's favour, I find it difficult to see how a person who has not clearly understood and accepted a representation of the decision-maker to that effect can be said to have such an expectation at all. A hope no doubt, but not an expectation. Consequently, one must consider whether the representation has been made to the whole world or instead to an individual or a small group of individuals. If the former, then there is no need to demonstrate detrimental reliance. If the latter, then it will be necessary to demonstrate that the individual has relied upon the representation and has done so to his or her detriment.

The House of Lords approved this approach in *R (on the application of Bancoult) v Secretary of State for Foreign and Commonwealth Affairs (No 2)* [2008] 3 WLR 955. The claimants argued that the actions and statements of the Foreign Secretary gave rise to a legitimate expectation that they would be allowed to return to their home in the Chagos Islands. These statements were made subsequent to a finding by the **Administrative Court** in *R (on the application of Bancoult) v Secretary of State for Foreign and Commonwealth Affairs* [2001] QB 1067 (*Bancoult No 1*) that the claimants had been unlawfully removed from their home in the Chagos Islands by the UK government. However, the House of Lords held that the representations made were not clear and unambiguous, because the government was awaiting the outcome of a feasibility study on the islanders' return and made no promise about what would happen in the long term. Even if there had been a clear and unambiguous statement, it was held that there would be no abuse of power if there were a sufficiently good public policy reason for changing the policy. In addition, the claimants could not show that they had relied on the statement. Lord Carswell, in *Bancoult No 2* (at [135]), held that if a claimant had not relied on the statement to his or her detriment, that was a strong indication that there had been no abuse of power.

cross reference
Bancoult No 2 *is discussed further in Chapter 17.*

18.4.6 What is the position if there is an ultra vires representation?

If the representation promises a procedural or substantive benefit that cannot lawfully be given by the public authority, then the court will not uphold the representation. So, for example, in *Begbie*, the court stated it was unable to give effect to any representation that the claimant could remain at her current school because it would be inconsistent with the statute.

Legitimate expectation

- *A legitimate expectation can arise from a policy, a statement, or past practice.*

- *A legitimate expectation may be of a procedural benefit. This means that a certain procedure must be followed before a decision is reached*—Attorney General of Hong Kong v Ng Yuen Shiu; R v Secretary of State for the Home Department, ex p Khan.

- *A legitimate expectation may be of an actual substantive benefit being conferred, as in the case of* Coughlan.

- *The courts are more likely to give effect to a legitimate expectation of a certain procedure. The courts are less likely to give effect to a legitimate expectation of a substantive benefit unless it would be irrational or unfair to deny it, and it has been made to an individual or to a small group and is capable of being fulfilled.*

- *The representation must be clear and unambiguous to be capable of leading to a legitimate expectation.*

- *If the representation is aimed at an individual or a small group, then detrimental reliance must be shown, but not if the representation is made to the public at large.*

- *The court will not enforce the representation if it will lead to the action being ultra vires.*

18.5 The detailed requirements of natural justice

569

This section will focus on the content of the rules of natural justice. It will address the right to be heard, the right to know the opposing case, the right to an oral hearing, and the right to reasons. The rule against bias will be considered in a separate section.

18.5.1 The right to be heard

As we have seen, *Ridge v Baldwin* established the importance of the right to be heard. It cleared up the confusions of the previous case law. However, there is not much guidance in the case as to the content or requirements of the right to be heard, and this has been developed in subsequent case law. This is what we will look at next. The case law since *Ridge v Baldwin* has established that what natural justice requires in each case will be different depending on the circumstances. On some occasions, the procedural protections and requirements may almost be as rigorous as a court hearing; in other cases, the procedural protections will be minimal. Some writers refer to this as a 'sliding scale'. The dial on the sliding scale will move up towards a full hearing in some cases, but down towards minimal protection in others. And, of course, there are lots of situations in which the dial will stop in between. So it is necessary to know where a case sits on the sliding scale. As we have discussed above, this may depend on the type of case and interest at stake. So a prisoner whose liberty is at stake may have more procedural protections than someone applying for a licence to run a lap-dancing club or to obtain a taxi licence. If the situation is more like a judicial hearing, then natural justice may require more than if it is a straightforward administrative case. The flexible nature of the rules of natural justice are emphasised by Lord Bridge in the next extract.

● **Lloyd v McMahon** [1987] AC 625

Lord Bridge at 702–3:

> My Lords the so-called rules of natural justice are not engraved on tablets of stone. To use the phrase which better expresses the underlying concept, what the requirements of fairness demand when any body, domestic, administrative or judicial, has to make a decision which will affect the rights of individuals depends on the character of the decision-making body, the kind of decision it has to make and the statutory or other framework in which it operates. In particular, it is well-established that when a statute has conferred on any body the power to make decisions affecting individuals, the courts will not only require the procedure prescribed by the statute to be followed, but will readily imply so much and no more to be introduced by way of additional procedural safeguards as will ensure the attainment of fairness.

According to Lord Bridge, the key factors are the rights and interests of the individual concerned, the character of the decision-making body, the kind of decision that it has to make, and the statutory or other legal framework. Below, we will consider the requirements of natural justice by considering different possible procedural elements.

18.5.2 The right to know the opposing case

The individual in question has the right to know the opposing case or the case against them. This is especially so if the case involves forfeiture, for example a licence being withdrawn or, as in the case of *Ridge v Baldwin*, dismissal for reasons of misconduct. But even in cases in which an application is made for a licence, natural justice may require that individuals know factors that are troubling the licensing body or an indication of why the body is minded to decide the case against them. The case of *R v Secretary of State for the Home Department, ex p Fayed* [1998] 1 WLR 763 concerned an application for British nationality from the claimants who were born in Egypt, but had well-known business interests in the UK. The Home Secretary rejected their application under the British Nationality Act 1981. He had no duty to give reasons, but the claimants argued that they should have been given some notice or explanation as to the problems that the Home Secretary had with their application so that they could respond. You should note that giving reasons after a decision is made raises different issues, which will be discussed later in the chapter. But here the claimants wanted to know what the issues that were troubling the Secretary of State were before the decision was made. This would enable them to make arguments that could address the concerns in question. By a majority, the Court of Appeal found in their favour. Lord Woolf explains the reason for the decision.

● **R v Secretary of State for the Home Department, ex p Fayed** [1998] 1 WLR 763

Lord Woolf at 777:

> I appreciate there is also anxiety as to the administrative burden involved in giving notice of areas of concern. Administrative convenience cannot justify unfairness but I would emphasise that my remarks are limited to cases where an applicant would be in real difficulty in doing himself justice unless the area of concern is identified by notice. In many cases which are less complex than that of the Fayeds the issues may be obvious. If this is the position notice may well be superfluous because what the applicant needs to establish will be clear. If this is the position notice may well not be required. However, in the case of the Fayeds this is not the position because the extensive range of circumstances which could cause the Secretary of State concern mean that it is impractical for them to identify the target at which their representations should be aimed.

The Court emphasised here that the process would be unfair unless the claimants knew what areas were of concern to the Home Secretary. There were so many possible problems that the claimants could not make effective representations unless they knew what troubled the Home Secretary about their application. However, the purpose of knowing the opposing case is so that the claimants can have the opportunity to explain or to defend themselves. They do not necessarily have to be told all of the details of the case against them, as long as they understand the general idea. The Court has come to this conclusion in cases in which the information against the claimant is confidential, perhaps because it has been obtained by sources who want to remain anonymous. In *R v Gaming Board for Great Britain, ex p Benaim and Khaida* [1970] 2 QB 417, the claimants applied for a gaming licence in accordance with the Gaming Act 1968, but their application was refused. They were told of the issues troubling the Board about their application and given the opportunity to address them. However, the Board's decision not to disclose confidential information from anonymous sources was upheld. Lord Denning held that the claimants had an opportunity to deal with the general allegations and that the Board had therefore acted fairly.

NOTE

For the importance of the right to know the opposing case under Article 6 of the **European Convention on Human Rights (ECHR)**, which protects the right to a fair hearing, see the discussion on **control order** hearings and the anti-terrorist law in Chapter 20. In particular, see the comments of the House of Lords in *Secretary of State for the Home Department v AF (No 3)* [2010] 2 AC 269.

18.5.3 The right to an oral hearing

Statutes or administrative regulations may provide for an oral hearing where a dispute can be resolved or more general issues can be considered. However, problems may arise where there is no statute or regulation stating that an oral hearing is required. If a request for a hearing is refused, then the court has to consider whether natural justice requires an oral hearing. The basic principle is that there is no right to an oral hearing and, in many situations, one will not be considered necessary. Natural justice may be satisfied by making written representations that are considered by the public authority before it makes its decision. However, there are some circumstances in which the court has held that an oral hearing may be necessary. Sometimes, there are factual disputes that can be resolved sensibly only by listening to the evidence of witnesses; then, any questions or challenges can be put directly. This issue was considered by the House of Lords in *Lloyd v McMahon* [1987] AC 625. This case concerned a group of Liverpool City councillors who were surcharged for wilful misconduct by the district auditor in accordance with section 20 of the Local Government Finance Act 1982. This meant that they were made personally liable for the loss suffered by the council. The councillors had failed to set a valid rate to enable the rates (local taxes) to be collected. This was because of a dispute over a grant between the council and central government. The councillors had made full written representations that were responded to by the auditor and there had been an appeal on the merits in the Divisional Court that had upheld the auditor's decision. However, the councillors did not request an oral hearing. On an application for judicial review, it was argued that there was a breach of natural justice, because the councillors should have had the chance to make oral representations.

The House of Lords rejected this argument. This was because the councillors had not requested an oral hearing and they had been able to make full written representations answering all of the issues raised by the auditor. They chose to do this as a group, rather than to respond individually. However, Lord Bridge of Harwich did state that if the councillors had asked for an oral hearing, then one should have been given. This is because of the serious financial consequences to the councillors.

The failure of the Army Board to consider whether an oral hearing was required was the subject of the challenge in *R v Army Board for the Defence, ex p Anderson* [1991] 3 WLR 42. Anderson, the only black soldier in his regiment, had gone absent without leave from the army and claimed that he had suffered racial discrimination. As a member of the armed forces, his claim for racial discrimination was dealt with by the Army Board rather than by an employment tribunal. The Army Board rejected his claim, although Anderson was told that disciplinary action had been taken against two soldiers. The Army Board did not meet to consider his claim, but considered the papers individually and then passed them to the next board member. On judicial review, there were various procedural challenges. These included the argument that there had been a breach of natural justice because no oral hearing had been held. The court upheld the claim because the Army Board had not even considered whether an oral hearing would be appropriate. The court did not go so far as to hold that an oral hearing would be required in every situation. But the court explains, in the next extract, that there are some situations, especially where there is a dispute of fact, which cannot be resolved by reading the papers. In those circumstances, there will be a breach of natural justice if a hearing is not given.

● *R v Army Board for the Defence, ex p Anderson* [1991] 3 WLR 42

Taylor LJ at 187–8:

> [2] The hearing does not necessarily have to be an oral hearing in all cases. There is ample authority that decision-making bodies other than courts and bodies whose procedures are laid down by statute, are masters of their own procedure. Provided that they achieve the degree of fairness appropriate to their task it is for them to decide how they will proceed and there is no rule that fairness always requires an oral hearing...Whether an oral hearing is necessary will depend upon the subject matter and circumstances of the particular case and upon the nature of the decision to be made. It will also depend upon whether there are substantial issues of fact which cannot be satisfactorily resolved on the available written evidence. This does not mean that whenever there is a conflict of evidence in the statements taken, an oral hearing must be held to resolve it. Sometimes such a conflict can be resolved merely by the inherent unlikelihood of one version or the other. Sometimes the conflict is not central to the issue for determination and would not justify an oral hearing. Even when such a hearing is necessary, it may only require one or two witnesses to be called and cross-examined...

The Army Board had not considered whether an oral hearing was necessary, but had adopted an inflexible policy never to grant an oral hearing. This made the decision ultra vires.

The House of Lords had to consider a case concerned with prisoners whose parole had been revoked as a consequence of breach of parole conditions in *R (on the application of West) v Parole Board; R (on the application of Smith) v Parole Board* [2005] UKHL 1. The claimants disputed the facts and claimed that they should not be returned to prison. Their case was dealt with by way of written representations. The House of Lords held that although an oral hearing did not have to be granted in every case, fairness required an oral hearing in certain circumstances. This was the case even where the facts were not in dispute. The reasons are discussed by Lord Bingham.

● *R (on the application of West) v Parole Board; R (on the application of Smith) v Parole Board* [2005] UKHL 1

Lord Bingham:

> [35] The common law duty of procedural fairness does not, in my opinion, require the board to hold an oral hearing in every case where a determinate sentence prisoner resists recall, if he does not decline the offer of such a hearing. But I do not think the duty is as constricted as

has hitherto been held and assumed. Even if important facts are not in dispute, they may be open to explanation or mitigation, or may lose some of their significance in the light of other new facts. While the board's task certainly is to assess risk, it may well be greatly assisted in discharging it (one way or the other) by exposure to the prisoner or the questioning of those who have dealt with him. It may often be very difficult to address effective representations without knowing the points which are troubling the decision-maker. The prisoner should have the benefit of a procedure which fairly reflects, on the facts of his particular case, the importance of what is at stake for him, as for society.

The court took into account the fact that the claimants' liberty was at stake. It also considered the nature of the process and the fact that an oral hearing would, in some circumstances, help the Parole Board to make a better decision. However, subsequent case law has made it clear that oral hearings are not required in every case. The courts highlight the flexibility of the rules of natural justice. In each case, the court considers the statutory context, the claimant's interest, and the nature of the decision-making body.

Requirements of an oral hearing

If an oral hearing is held, then various other procedural safeguards have to be considered. What is required will depend on the type of hearing. But the courts have stressed that such proceedings do not have to be conducted as court proceedings with all the technical rules of evidence. So, for example, evidence not permitted in court, such as hearsay evidence, may be admitted, provided that there are sufficient safeguards. But the proceedings do have to be conducted fairly. Some of the important elements of an oral hearing are discussed below.

> **Oral hearings**
> ....
>
> • Consider the need to allow cross-examination.
>
> • Consider the need to call witnesses.
>
> • Consider the need to permit legal representation.

Cross-examination

Often, the purpose of an oral hearing is to provide for the cross-examination of witnesses. This is because cross-examination allows the witness's version of the facts to be challenged and for the decision-maker to decide between competing versions of the facts. In other words, it enables the decision-maker to decide whose story to believe. Whether or not cross-examination is permitted will depend on the type of hearing. If the hearing is a fact-gathering or fact-finding exercise, such as a public inquiry, then cross-examination of witnesses may not be required. But there may be a breach of natural justice if cross-examination is not permitted during a disciplinary hearing at which the liberty of the individual is at stake.

In *R v Board of Visitors of Hull Prison, ex p St Germain (No 2)* [1979] 1 WLR 1401, it was held there was a breach of natural justice when prisoners were denied the opportunity to cross-examine witnesses during a prison disciplinary hearing. The prisoners in question were accused of serious disciplinary offences that, if proved, would lead to a loss of remission, whereby they would spend longer in prison. At the hearing, the prisoners were not allowed to call or cross-examine key witnesses in their defence. The court held that this was a breach of natural justice.

● *R v Board of Visitors of Hull Prison, ex p St Germain (No 2)* [1979] 1 WLR 1401

Geoffrey Lane LJ at 1419:

> To deprive him of the opportunity of cross-examination would be tantamount to depriving him of a fair hearing.

The court also held that the applicants should have been given the chance to call witnesses in their defence. The court also said that hearsay evidence could be admitted provided the applicants were able to challenge the evidence.

By contrast, in *Bushell v Secretary of State for the Environment* [1981] AC 75, it was held that the refusal to allow cross-examination of expert witnesses during a public inquiry into the building of a motorway was not a breach of natural justice. The objectors had been allowed to voice their objections, but did not have the opportunity to cross-examine the expert witnesses on their traffic predictions. Lord Diplock stated that a public inquiry did not have to adopt the same procedures as a court.

● *Bushell v Secretary of State for the Environment* [1981] AC 75

Lord Diplock at 97:

> Here the relevant circumstances in considering whether fairness requires that cross-examination should be allowed include the nature of the topic upon which the opinion is expressed, the qualifications of the maker of the statement to deal with that topic, the forensic competence of the proposed cross-examiner, and, most important, the inspector's own views as to whether the likelihood that cross-examination will enable him to make a report which will be more useful to the minister in reaching his decision than it otherwise would be is sufficient to justify any expense and inconvenience to other parties to the inquiry which would be caused by any resulting prolongation of it.

In this case, because it involved technical evidence during a fact-finding hearing, the court held that the inspector conducting the inquiry was justified in taking into account the expense and delay in deciding whether to allow cross-examination. The court held that, provided that the procedure was fair, there was no breach of natural justice.

The cases make the point that what natural justice requires depends on the type of hearing. In *ex p St Germain*, the hearing was adversarial, the claimant's credibility was challenged, and the right to liberty of the claimants was at stake; so cross-examination was necessary in the interest of fairness. However, in *Bushel*, the hearing was a fact-finding exercise and the cross-examination was of technical evidence. The inspector was therefore entitled to prohibit the cross-examination of expert witnesses.

The right to call witnesses

In certain circumstances, there may be a breach of natural justice if the claimant is not allowed to call witnesses. So, in *ex p St Germain (No 2)*, it was held that the failure to allow the claimants to call witnesses in their defence was a breach of natural justice.

Legal representation

It should be remembered that, in many circumstances, the relevant statute will permit legal representation at a hearing or allow the claimant to be accompanied by a legal adviser. Where the statute or rules are silent, then the general principle is that there is no right to legal representation, but there may be a breach of natural justice where legal representation is denied. In *Enderby Town Football Club Ltd v Football Association Ltd* [1971] Ch 591, the

Court of Appeal held that there was no breach of natural justice when a football club was denied legal representation at a disciplinary hearing by the Football Association. The Court stated that proceedings at a tribunal may be speedier and less costly if conducted without a lawyer present. However, in *R v Secretary of State for the Home Department and Another, ex p Tarrant* [1985] QB 251, it was held that there was a breach of natural justice where the claimants, prisoners charged with serious offences against prison discipline including mutiny, were denied legal representation by the Board of Prison Visitors. The court stated that, when considering whether legal representation should be permitted, the following factors should be considered.

● **R v Secretary of State for the Home Department and another, ex p Tarrant** [1985] QB 251

Webster J at 285:

(1) The seriousness of the charge and of the potential penalty.

(2) Whether any points of law are likely to arise...

(3) The capacity of a particular prisoner to present his own case...

(4) Procedural difficulties.

(5) The need for reasonable speed in making their adjudication, which is clearly an important consideration.

(6) The need for fairness as between prisoners and as between prisoners and prison officers.

In this case, the Board's failure to consider whether or not legal representation should be permitted made the decision ultra vires. The House of Lords approved this decision in *R v Board of Visitors of HM Prison, the Maze, ex p Hone* [1988] AC 379. However, it was decided, in this case, that prisoners charged with assault were not entitled to legal representation in a hearing before the prison governor. Applying the criteria in *Tarrant*, it was held that assault was a simple offence, that no legal questions arose, and that the prisoners were capable of representing themselves.

Two recent decisions have considered whether Article 6 of the ECHR requires that legal representation be allowed at a disciplinary tribunal. The relevant part of Article 6 provides that 'in the determination of his civil rights and obligations...everyone is entitled to a fair and public hearing'. In order for Article 6 to apply and for there to be a right to legal representation, the case must concern 'the determination of the civil rights and obligations' of the claimant. This is a very technical term at which we will look at again a little later in the chapter. An ordinary workplace disciplinary tribunal that leads to dismissal from employment does not determine civil rights and obligations. For Article 6 to apply, the decision of the tribunal would have to go further than this and lead to the loss of a livelihood. So, for example, a tribunal decision preventing a doctor from practising medicine ever again would determine the civil rights and obligations of the claimant. The following two contrasting cases illustrate this.

In *Kulkarni v Milton Keynes Hospital NHS Foundation Trust* [2009] EWCA Civ 789, the claimant doctor had been disciplined by the National Health Service (NHS) trust for inappropriately touching a patient. His right to legal representation was restricted by the relevant regulations governing the disciplinary tribunal. The Court of Appeal held *obiter* that he should be allowed legal representation. This was because a finding of guilt would not only lead to the loss of his job, but would effectively prevent him from completing his training and working again within the NHS. Because the NHS was a single employer for the whole country, he would not only be deprived of his job, but of his livelihood as a doctor. In this situation, the disciplinary tribunal was determining the civil rights and obligations of the claimant. What was at stake was so serious for the claimant that legal representation was required.

But the Supreme Court came to a different conclusion in *R (G) v Governors of X School* [2011] UKSC 30. In this case, a teaching assistant was subject to a disciplinary hearing before the school governors at a state primary school for an alleged inappropriate relationship with a child. It was held that Article 6 did not apply here and that he was not entitled to legal representation at the hearing. This was because his civil rights and obligations were not determined by a finding of guilt by the school governors. This decision would not in itself deprive him of his livelihood as a teaching assistant. The governors would refer his case to the Independent Safeguarding Authority, a statutory body, which did have the power to bar him from working with children. Lord Hope was concerned (at [94]) that if legal representation were allowed, disciplinary proceedings in the workplace might become too complicated and formal to be administered by laypersons without knowledge of the law.

NOTE

For Article 6 to apply to disciplinary hearings, the decision must go beyond the loss of employment; it must actually lead to the loss of the claimant's livelihood, for example by preventing the individual from working again in his or her chosen profession.

Article 6 does complicate matters slightly, because, for it to apply, the dispute must involve the 'determination of civil rights and obligations'. But keep in mind that, for natural justice or for Article 6 to require legal representation, the cases indicate that it will depend on the nature of the interest at stake, the nature of the decision-making body, and the need for speed and efficiency in the decision-making process.

18.5.4 The right to reasons for a decision

Statutes will often require that reasons be given. If reasons are given for a decision, then the reasons should provide an adequate explanation of the decision. The common law does not recognise that there is always a right to reasons for a decision. However, the courts have accepted that, in certain circumstances, there may be a breach of natural justice where reasons are not given. So, in *R v Civil Service Appeal Board, ex p Cunningham* [1992] ICR 816, the claimant was unfairly dismissed from the Prison Service. As a civil servant, his case was dealt with by the Civil Service Appeal Board rather than by an employment tribunal. He was awarded £6,000 in compensation, but no reasons were given as to how this sum was calculated. The claimant was disgruntled because this was considerably less than he would receive in an ordinary tribunal and there was no explanation for the difference. The Court of Appeal decided in his favour. This was because fairness required that the claimant know the issues that the Board had considered when making its decision. This was so it could be seen that it had acted lawfully. Lord Justice McCowan listed the factors that led him to hold that the Board should give reasons for its decision.

● *R v Civil Service Appeal Board, ex p Cunningham* [1992] ICR 816

McCowan LJ at 831:

1. There is no appeal from the board's determination of the amount of compensation.
2. In making that determination the board is carrying out a judicial function.
3. The board is susceptible to judicial review.
4. The procedure provided for by the code, that is to say the provision of a recommendation without reasons, is insufficient to achieve justice.
5. There is no statute which requires the courts to tolerate that unfairness.
6. The giving of short reasons would not frustrate the apparent purpose of the code.

7. It is not a case where the giving of reasons would be harmful to the public interest.

These considerations drive me to the view that this is a case where the board should have given reasons and I would, therefore, dismiss the appeal.

This decision was upheld in the House of Lords in *R v Secretary of State for the Home Department, ex p Doody* [1994] 1 AC 531. In this case, the claimants were mandatory life prisoners. In accordance with his powers under section 61 of the Criminal Justice Act 1967, the Home Secretary, in consultation with the **Lord Chief Justice** and the trial judge, set a minimum period that the claimants had to spend in prison before they could be considered for parole. This period is known as the 'tariff', and satisfies the requirements of retribution and deterrence. The claimants were not allowed to make representations to the Home Secretary before the tariff was set. They did not know the period recommended by the judges and were not given reasons for the decision. In this case, the House of Lords held that the claimants should be allowed to make representations and that, in order to do this, they had to have reasons for the decision.

Reasons were also necessary so that the claimants could ensure that the decision was made lawfully and that they had the opportunity to challenge the decision by way of judicial review. Lord Mustill explained that the law requires reasons to be given in certain circumstances in the interest of fairness.

. . . .

● *R v Secretary of State for the Home Department, ex p Doody* [1994] 1 AC 531

Lord Mustill at 564–6:

I accept without hesitation, and mention it only to avoid misunderstanding, that the law does not at present recognise a general duty to give reasons for an administrative decision. Nevertheless, it is equally beyond question that such a duty may in appropriate circumstances be implied, and I agree with the analyses by the Court of Appeal in *Reg. v. Civil Service Appeal Board, Ex parte Cunningham* [1991] 4 All E.R. 310 of the factors which will often be material to such an implication.

. . . The giving of reasons may be inconvenient, but I can see no ground at all why it should be against the public interest: indeed, rather the reverse. This being so, I would ask simply: Is refusal to give reasons fair? I would answer without hesitation that it is not. As soon as the jury returns its verdict the offender knows that he will be locked up for a very long time. For just how long immediately becomes the most important thing in the prisoner's life . . . Where a defendant is convicted of, say, several armed robberies he knows that he faces a stiff sentence: he can be advised by reference to a public tariff of the range of sentences he must expect; he hears counsel address the judge on the relationship between his offences and the tariff; he will often hear the judge give an indication during exchanges with counsel of how his mind is working; and when sentence is pronounced he will always be told the reasons for it. So also when a discretionary life sentence is imposed, coupled with an order under section 34. Contrast this with the position of the prisoner sentenced for murder. He never sees the Home Secretary; he has no dialogue with him: he cannot fathom how his mind is working. There is no true tariff, or at least no tariff exposed to public view which might give the prisoner an idea of what to expect. The announcement of his first review date arrives out of thin air, wholly without explanation. The distant oracle has spoken, and that is that.

My Lords, I am not aware that there still exists anywhere else in the penal system a procedure remotely resembling this. The beginnings of an explanation for its unique character might perhaps be found if the executive had still been putting into practice the theory that the tariff sentence for murder is confinement for life, subject only to a wholly discretionary release on licence: although even in such a case I doubt whether in the modern climate of administrative law such an entirely secret process could be justified. As I hope to have shown, however, this is no longer the practice, and can hardly be sustained any longer as the theory. I therefore simply ask, is it fair that the mandatory life prisoner should be wholly deprived of the information which all other prisoners receive as a matter of course. I am clearly of the opinion that it is not.

My Lords, I can moreover arrive at the same conclusion by a different and more familiar route, of which *Ex parte Cunningham* [1991] 4 All E.R. 310 provides a recent example. It is not, as I understand it, questioned that the decision of the Home Secretary on the penal element is susceptible to judicial review. To mount an effective attack on the decision, given no more material than the facts of the offence and the length of the penal element, the prisoner has virtually no means of ascertaining whether this is an instance where the decision-making process has gone astray. I think it important that there should be an effective means of detecting the kind of error which would entitle the court to intervene, and in practice I regard it as necessary for this purpose that the reasoning of the Home Secretary should be disclosed. If there is any difference between the penal element recommended by the judges and actually imposed by the Home Secretary, this reasoning is bound to include, either explicitly or implicitly, a reason why the Home Secretary has taken a different view. Accordingly, I consider that the respondents are entitled to an affirmative answer on the third issue.

NOTE Lord Mustill's judgment seems to place considerable stress on the fact that, without reasons, the prisoner has no idea how the length of the sentence has been determined.

Doody emphasised that the key issue is one of fairness. Lord Mustill recognises that there is a trend towards the giving of reasons in administrative law. Reasons must be given when fairness requires it, but reasons are not required in all cases. In *R v Higher Education Funding Council, ex p the Institute of Dental Surgery* [1994] 1 WLR 242 (the *Institute of Dental Surgery case*), Sedley J attempted to make sense of the case law by considering when reasons would be required. He said that reasons would generally be required where the subject matter of the decision is of particular importance. So, for example, reasons were required in *Doody* because the claimants' personal liberty was at stake. The other situation in which reasons may be required is where the decision is 'aberrant'—by which he meant that the decision is unusual in some way or appears to be contrary to the evidence.

However, in other cases, reasons may not be required. So, for example, in the *Institute of Dental Surgery case*, the claimant, the Institute of Dental Surgery, applied to review the decision of the Universities Funding Council. The Council, after an in-depth review process, had reduced the claimant's research rating and, in consequence, the claimant's funding was cut. The court held that the assessment process had been fair and open. But the claimants were not entitled to reasons for the decision because the decision was based on an academic judgement. Sedley J explained his decision and some of the general principles concerning when reasons will be required.

● ***R v Higher Education Funding Council, ex p the Institute of Dental Surgery*** [1994] 1 WLR 242 (the *Institute of Dental Surgery case*)

Sedley J at 251:

But purely academic judgments, in our view, will as a rule not be in the class of case exemplified, though by no means exhausted, by *Ex parte Doody* [1993] 3 W.L.R. 154, where the nature and impact of the decision itself call for reasons as a routine aspect of procedural fairness. They will be in the *Ex parte Cunningham* [1992] I.C.R. 816 class where some trigger factor is required to show that, in the circumstances of the particular decision, fairness calls for reasons to be given...

The judgment then goes on to give a general summary of the law on reasons, at 263:

In summary, then: (1) there is no general duty to give reasons for a decision, but there are classes of case where there is such a duty. (2) One such class is where the subject matter is an interest so highly regarded by the law (for example, personal liberty), that fairness requires that reasons, at least for particular decisions, be given as of right. (3) (a) Another such class is where the decision appears aberrant. Here fairness may require reasons so that the recipient

Sedley J explains that reasons were not required in this case because the interest at stake was not as serious as that in *Doody*. There was nothing suspicious about the decision, which indicated that it was 'aberrant' or made in error, as in *Cunningham*. In *Cunningham*, one of the grounds on which the case was decided was that the amount of compensation awarded was much lower than expected. This alerted the court to the fact that the decision was probably wrong. However, in subsequent cases, Sedley J has commented that the categories of decision that require reasons to be given are not closed. He has also said that the *Institute of Dental Surgery* case may not be decided the same way today. However, the case does provide a useful starting point when considering the circumstances in which reasons may be required.

Cases in which reasons have been required

There are some instances in which a decision-maker is required to give reasons for its decision. One case that illustrates this effectively is *R (on the application of Wooder) v Feggetter and another* [2003] QB 219, in which the claimant was a convicted mental patient at a secure hospital. His doctors decided that he should receive anti-psychotic medication, but the claimant refused to consent. In accordance with the provisions of the Mental Health Act 1983, a doctor, appointed to give a second opinion, granted a certificate approving the medication. No reasons were given for the decision. It was held by the court that reasons were required.

. . . .

● *R (on the application of Wooder) v Feggetter and another* [2003] QB 219

Brooke LJ at 226:

> ...that one of the classes of case where the common law implies a duty to give reasons is where the subject matter is an interest so highly regarded by the law (for example, personal liberty) that fairness requires that reasons, at least for particular decisions, be given as of right...I have no hesitation in holding that a decision to administer medical treatment to a competent non-consenting adult patient falls into this category...The fact that the critical decision is made by a doctor in the exercise of his clinical judgment and not by a tribunal following a more formal process cannot, in my judgment, be allowed to diminish the significance of the doctor's decision.

A further illustration is provided by *R v Ministry of Defence, ex p Murray* [1998] COD 134, in which reasons were required where a member of the armed forces was sentenced to imprisonment, for an offence of wounding, after a court martial. The claimant had given evidence that the crime in question was completely out of character and committed because he had taken anti-malarial drugs. This evidence was rejected without reasons being given. The court held that fairness required that reasons should be given for concluding that there was no causal connection between taking the drugs and the offence.

Cases in which reasons were not required

However, a decision-maker will not always be required to give reasons. Following the *Institute of Dental Surgery* case, the court held in *R (on the application of the Asha Foundation) v The Millennium Commission* [2003] EWCA Civ 88 that reasons were not required. The Asha Foundation applied for a grant from the Millennium Commission. The application criteria were very broad and gave the Commission a wide discretion. The Commission told the Foundation that its application met the criteria, but that it had been rejected because other applications were more attractive. It was argued unsuccessfully that reasons should have been given for the decision.

● **R (on the application of the Asha Foundation) v The Millennium Commission** [2003] EWCA Civ 88

Lord Woolf:

[32] Here the Commission exercised their judgment. It was not an academic judgment; it was a similar but more difficult judgment to make than that of the Higher Education Funding Council (*Institute of Dental Surgery Case*). This is because the Commission were required to make a selection from the eligible applications.

[33] In his reasoning Sedley J pointed to the fact that there may be special circumstances in a particular case why reasons are required because the decision is otherwise inexplicable. That special situation does not apply in the circumstances which are before us.

[34] ...As I have already explained this does not in my view require the Commission to do more than, first, to make it clear that they regarded the application as eligible (which was done at the first stage), and secondly, to say that on the basis of a collective decision the application of Asha was trumped by the other applications which were preferred.

This case indicates that where a value judgement is made by a decision-maker, reasons will not normally be required unless the decision would otherwise appear to be inexplicable. The simple assertion that the candidate was considered, was considered eligible, but was considered not as strong as other applications, was sufficient by way of an explanation.

Adequate reasons

Sometimes, Parliament will require reasons to be given when a decision-maker makes use of a statutory power during the decision-making process. If a statute requires that reasons should be given for a decision, then the reasons given must be adequate. In *South Bucks District Council and another v Porter (No 2)* [2004] UKHL 33, the House of Lords dismissed the claim of a local authority that a planning inspector had given inadequate reasons for a decision. Lord Brown of Eaton-Under-Heywood explained that although reasons could be brief, they should be intelligible and adequate. The amount of detail needed would vary depending on the issue in question.

thinking point
Do you think that the law should require reasons be given for all administrative decisions?

This area of law is still developing and there is a degree of uncertainty. The general principles are that natural justice does not always require that reasons be given for a decision. However, the courts will require reasons to be given in cases in which the interest at stake is very serious, such as a case involving the right to liberty, as in *Doody* and *Fegetter*. In other cases, the court will consider various factors, such as the nature of the body, whether there is an appeal, whether the decision is contrary to the evidence, issues of administrative convenience, and the overall fairness of the decision-making process.

section summary

The right to reasons for a decision

- *The common law does not recognise a right to reasons for a decision.*
- *There may be a breach of natural justice if reasons are not given in some circumstances.*
- *Natural justice may require reasons if a decision appears perverse or if the decision concerns a right or interest such as the right to liberty.*
- *If reasons are required by a statute, then they must be adequate and intelligible.*
- *It is likely that the law will develop further in this area.*

The rule against bias

The rule against bias reflects the fundamental principle that the decision-maker should not have an interest in the outcome of the decision. The law is concerned with the appearance of bias and actual bias does not have to be shown. This is because the law is concerned that justice is not only done, but is also seen to be done. This is so that people will have confidence in the decision-making process. This is expressed by the famous dicta of Lord Hewart in *R v Sussex Justices, ex p McCarthy* [1924] 1 KB 256. He was stressing that a clerk who had a conflict of interest with one of the parties to the case was unlikely to be biased, but nevertheless had to be disqualified, because there was an appearance of bias.

● *R v Sussex Justices, ex p McCarthy* [1924] 1 KB 256

Lord Hewart CJ at 259:

> It is not merely of some importance, but of fundamental importance that justice should not only be done, but should manifestly and undoubtedly be seen to be done.

Bias can be divided into two main categories: cases concerned with direct bias and other cases in which there is apparent bias. This area of law has also been influenced by Article 6 ECHR. The impact of Article 6, more generally, will be considered in the next section; the emphasis here is on the requirement in Article 6 that the decision-maker is 'independent and impartial'.

18.6.1 What is bias?

A useful summary of what is meant by 'bias' is provided by Lord Phillips in the following case. Although he uses the term 'judge', the comments apply widely to any decision-maker.

● *Re Medicaments and Related Classes of Goods (No 2)* [2001] 1 WLR 700

Lord Phillips at 711:

> Bias is an attitude of mind which prevents the judge from making an objective determination of the issues that he has to resolve. A judge may be biased because he has reason to prefer one outcome of the case to another. He may be biased because he has reason to favour one party rather than another. He may be biased not in favour of one outcome of the dispute but because of a prejudice in favour of or against a particular witness which prevents an impartial assessment of the evidence of that witness. Bias can come in many forms. It may consist of irrational prejudice or it may arise from particular circumstances which, for logical reasons, predispose a judge towards a particular view of the evidence or issues before him.

Thus bias relates to a decision-maker's mindset and the decision-maker's ability to reach an objective decision.

18.6.2 Direct bias

If the court finds that there has been direct bias, then this automatically disqualifies the decision-maker and the decision will be set aside. Most direct bias is concerned with pecuniary (financial) interests. The classic case of bias is *Dimes v Grand Junction Canal Proprietors* (1852) 3 HL Cas 759. In this case, there was a dispute between the Grand Junction Canal Proprietors and Dimes over a strip of land adjacent to a canal. The case had involved a considerable amount of litigation. The **Lord Chancellor**, Lord Cottenham, had affirmed judgments made by the Vice Chancellor in favour of the canal company. It was subsequently discovered that Lord Cottenham had several thousand pounds' worth of shares in the company. Dimes appealed to the House of Lords, arguing that the judgments should be set aside because Lord Cottenham was biased. The House of Lords held in favour of Dimes.

● ***Dimes v Grand Junction Canal Proprietors*** (1852) 3 HL Cas 759

Lord Campbell at 793:

> No one can suppose that Lord Cottenham could be, in the remotest degree, influenced by the interest that he had in this concern; but my Lords, it is of the last importance that the maxim that no man is to be a judge in his own cause should be held sacred. And that is not be confined to a cause in which he is a party but applies to a cause in which he has an interest...
>
> This will be a lesson to all inferior tribunals to take care not only that in their decrees they are not influenced by their personal interest, but to avoid the appearance of labouring under such an influence...

There are some qualifications to the direct bias rule. For example, there is a *de minimis* rule. This means that if the interest is minor or remotely connected to the decision, then the rule will not apply. The direct bias principle was applied in a case concerned with a non-pecuniary interest in *R v Bow Street Metropolitan Stipendiary Magistrate, ex p Pinochet Ugarte (No 2)* [2000] 1 AC 119. This case concerned the extradition of President Pinochet of Chile to Spain. The House of Lords decided that he was not entitled to immunity as a head of state and could be extradited to Spain. Amnesty International, a human rights organisation, was an intervener in the appeal. It had put in submissions against granting Pinochet immunity and was represented by counsel. Lord Hoffmann, who sat in the House of Lords, was accused of bias in a challenge to the original decision. This was because he was a director and chair of Amnesty International Charity Limited. It was held by the House of Lords, following *Dimes*, that Lord Hoffmann was a judge in his own cause. Lord Hope explained the reasoning for the decision.

● ***R v Bow Street Metropolitan Stipendiary Magistrate, ex p Pinochet Ugarte (No 2)*** [2000] 1 AC 119

Lord Hope at 141–3:

> The ground of objection which has invariably been taken until now in criminal cases is based on that other principle which has its origin in the requirement of impartiality. This is that justice must not only be done; it must also be seen to be done. It covers a wider range of situations than that which is covered by the maxim that no one may be a judge in his own cause. But it would be surprising if the application of that principle were to result in a test which was less exacting than that resulting from the application of the *nemo judex in sua causa* principle. Public confidence in the integrity of the administration of justice is just as important, perhaps even more so, in criminal cases. Article 6(1) of the European Convention on Fundamental Rights and Freedoms makes no distinction between civil and criminal cases in its expression of the right of everyone to a fair and public hearing within a reasonable time by an independent and impartial tribunal established by law...
>
> As for the facts of the present case, it seems to me that the conclusion is inescapable that Amnesty International has associated itself in these proceedings with the position of the prosecutor. The prosecution is not being brought in its name, but its interest in the case is to achieve the same result because it also seeks to bring Senator Pinochet to justice. This distinguishes its position fundamentally from that of other bodies which seek to uphold human rights without extending their objects to issues concerning personal responsibility. It has for many years conducted an international campaign against those individuals whom it has

identified as having been responsible for torture, extra-judicial executions and disappearances. Its aim is that they should be made to suffer criminal penalties for such gross violations of human rights. It has chosen, by its intervention in these proceedings, to bring itself face to face with one of those individuals against whom it has for so long campaigned...

... I think that the connections which existed between Lord Hoffmann and Amnesty International were of such a character, in view of their duration and proximity, as to disqualify him on this ground. In view of his links with Amnesty International as the chairman and a director of Amnesty International Charity Ltd. he could not be seen to be impartial. There has been no suggestion that he was actually biased. He had no financial or pecuniary interest in the outcome. But his relationship with Amnesty International was such that he was, in effect, acting as a judge in his own cause. I consider that his failure to disclose these connections leads inevitably to the conclusion that the decision to which he was a party must be set aside.

NOTE The House of Lords subsequently reheard the appeal without Lord Hoffmann sitting as a Law Lord.

Lord Hope states that Lord Hoffmann did not have a financial interest in the case, but had a direct interest to establish that there is no immunity for ex-heads of state in relation to crimes against humanity. As a director of the charitable arm of Amnesty International, he was an active member and was automatically disqualified from hearing the case.

18.6.3 Apparent bias

cross reference
The facts of Porter v Magill are discussed in Chapter 16.

There may still be apparent bias, even if there is no direct financial or other bias: for example, the decision-makers may have an association with one of the parties, or there may be a conflict of interest. There has been a long-standing debate in the case law and academic literature about the test for bias. But, in the case of *Porter v Magill* [2002] 2 AC 357, the House of Lords considered the impact of Article 6 ECHR, reviewed the case law, and settled the issue. The test for bias was stated as 'whether a fair-minded and informed observer having considered the facts would conclude that there was a real possibility that the tribunal (decision-maker) was biased'.

The auditor conducted an investigation into the decision of Westminster Council to sell its housing stock. The decision was made in order to increase the number of homeowners. The hope was that homeowners were more likely to re-elect the Conservative council than those who rented property who tended to vote Labour. It was alleged that this decision was wilful misconduct, which meant that three councillors could be surcharged and would have to repay personally any loss. The auditor found that the councillors had acted unlawfully, because they had acted for an improper political purpose. The auditor's decision was challenged unsuccessfully. However, one of the grounds of challenge was that the auditor was biased. This was because, after the first stage of the investigation, but before its conclusion, he held a press conference to present his preliminary findings. He was said to have used 'florid' language, indicating that he thought at this stage that the claimants were guilty of misconduct. The press conference generated prejudicial publicity against the claimants. The House of Lords agreed with the findings of the lower court that the actions of the auditor were unfortunate, but held that he was not biased.

● *Porter v Magill* [2002] 2 AC 357

Lord Hope at 495:

[105] The question is what the fair-minded and informed observer would have thought, and whether his conclusion would have been that there was real possibility of bias. The auditor's conduct must be seen in the context of the investigation which he was carrying out, which had generated a great deal of public interest. A statement as to his progress would not have

been inappropriate. His error was to make it at a press conference. This created the risk of unfair reporting, but there was nothing in the words he used to indicate that there was a real possibility that he was biased. He was at pains to point out to the press that his findings were provisional. There is no reason to doubt his word on this point, as his subsequent conduct demonstrates. I would hold, looking at the matter objectively, that a real possibility that he was biased has not been demonstrated.

The House of Lords considered the auditor's conduct overall, including the fact that he had stressed the preliminary nature of his findings at the press conference. It concluded that a fair-minded and informed observer, knowing all of the facts, would think that the auditor had acted unwisely, but that a real possibility of bias had not been shown.

The House of Lords approved in *Porter v Magill* the approach of the Court of Appeal in *Re Medicaments and Related Classes of Goods (No 2)* [2001] 1 WLR 700. This case provides an example in which a conflict of interest led to a finding of bias. It concerned a decision before the Restrictive Practices Court, in which a judge sits with two lay (that is, non-legally trained) members who are economic experts. There was an allegation of bias against one of the lay members, Dr Rowlatt. This was because she had applied for a job with a company called Frontier, which employed one of the main expert witnesses in the case. The evidence of the expert witnesses was crucial to one of the key issues to be decided by the Restrictive Practices Court. Soon after the case began, Dr Rowlatt told the judge of her application and wrote Frontier a letter, stating that she would not pursue the application until the case concluded. It was held that the decision could not stand because there was an appearance of bias.

· ·

● **Re Medicaments and Related Classes of Goods (No 2)** [2001] 1 WLR 700

Lord Phillips at 728:

What concerns would the remarkable facts that we have set out above raise in the mind of a fair-minded observer? The Restrictive Practices Court is, in this case, going to have to resolve a fundamental conflict of economic analysis between rival economic consultants ... Dr Rowlatt had, by making her application for employment to one of these consultants, indicated a partiality to them which could not be undone. We consider that the fair-minded observer would be concerned that, if Dr Rowlatt esteemed Frontier sufficiently to wish to be employed by them, she might consciously or unconsciously be inclined to consider them a more reliable source of expert opinion than their rivals.

A related issue arose in *Lawal v Northern Spirit Ltd* [2003] UKHL 25. In this case, counsel for one of the parties before the Employment Appeal Tribunal (EAT) also sat as a part-time judge in the EAT. He had sat as a judge with one of the lay members of the EAT hearing the claimant's case. Applying the test in *Porter v Magill*, it was held, by the House of Lords, that the fair-minded and informed observer would think that the lay member's previous relationship with counsel, in his capacity as a part-time judge, was likely to make him unconsciously biased in his favour.

This should be contrasted with the decision in *Gillies v Secretary of State for Work and Pensions* [2006] UKHL 2. This concerned a claim that the medical member of the Disability Appeals Tribunal was biased. This was because she was on a list of doctors that provided reports to the Benefits Agency on claimants for various disability allowances. Appeals involving Benefit Agency decisions would be heard by the tribunal and it was argued that, because she acted as an assessor for the Benefits Agency, she would be seen as biased in its favour and unable to assess impartially the evidence of other doctors on the list of experts. The House of Lords rejected this argument on the basis that the medical member acted as an independent adviser to the Benefits Agency, and that an independent and fair-minded observer would not think that she was likely to be unconsciously biased in favour of other experts. The difference between this case and *Lawal* is that the doctor's relationship with the Benefits Agency was very remote, because she was just one of a number of experts on its list and she would be expected to have a degree of detachment from the agency. The court also took into account the nature of the tribunal system, which benefited from expert knowledge, and held that the medical member's knowledge and experience was likely to be of value in assessing evidence.

A more blatant conflict of interest occurred in the case of *R (on the application of Al-Hassan) v Secretary of State for the Home Department* [2005] UKHL 1. In this case, a deputy prison governor, Mr Copple, found the claimant prisoners guilty of refusing to squat for a search contrary to the Prison Rules. He rejected the argument, made by the claimants, that the order by the governor to authorise the search was unlawful. It was claimed that there was a breach of natural justice because the deputy prison governor had been present when the governor gave the order authorising the search. The House of Lords found in favour of the claimant.

● ***R (on the application of Al-Hassan) v Secretary of State for the Home Department*** [2005] UKHL 1

Lord Brown:

> [39] I return therefore, against the background of the relevant case law, to the critical question: how would a fair-minded observer regard these appellants' adjudications? …
>
> …At the end of the day it seems to me that by the very fact of his presence when the search order was confirmed, Mr Copple gave it his tacit assent and endorsement. When thereafter the order was disobeyed and he had to rule upon its lawfulness, a fair-minded observer could all too easily think him predisposed to find it lawful. After all, for him to have decided otherwise would have been to acknowledge that the governor ought not to have confirmed the order and that he himself had been wrong to acquiesce in it.

The courts have also applied the fair-minded observer tests where there have been allegations of bias on the grounds that the decision-maker belongs to an association that leads him or her to favour a particular viewpoint. In *Helow v Secretary of State for the Home Department* [2008] UKHL 62, there was a challenge, on the grounds of bias, to the decision of a Scottish Court of Session judge who had dismissed an immigration appeal from a Palestinian asylum seeker. The judge was a member of the International Association of Jewish Lawyers, which produced a magazine, some of the articles of which were pro-Israel. It was held by the House of Lords that the fair-minded and informed observer would not have held that there was a real possibility of bias. This was because membership of the association alone did not mean that the judge supported all of the views expressed in its publications. The aims of the association were unobjectionable and the judge had not said or done anything to associate herself with the more extreme views expressed by some of its members.

It follows that, generally, membership of a respectable association will not alone lead to an appearance of bias, but if there is anything said or done by the decision-maker to associate himself or herself with a particular viewpoint or political position, then the fair-minded observer is more likely to find that there is a real possibility of bias.

The recent case law applies the fair-minded observer test, but the different results in these cases show that much depends on the context in which the decision is taken.

18.6.4 Conflict of roles

As we have seen, the rule against bias has also been used to invalidate decisions in which decision-makers have a conflict of interest with another role that they perform. This is particularly the case where the decision-maker has been involved in bringing the case against the claimant. If there is involvement in the decision-making process, then there will be confusion between the role of prosecutor and judge in the case. One example of this is *R v Barnsley MBC, ex p Hook* [1976] 1 WLR 1052. In this case, a market trader's licence was withdrawn after he urinated in a side street and argued with a security officer who rebuked him. There was a complaint to the market manager, who reported him to the relevant committee and wrote a letter to the trader revoking his licence. He was given the opportunity to contest the decision before a council committee, which upheld the decision. However, the market manager was present throughout the committee's proceedings. It was held that this made the decision ultra vires. One of the main reasons was the presence of the market manager, who had brought the complaint, at the proceedings at which the decision was made.

. . . .

● ***R v Barnsley Metropolitan Borough Council, ex p Hook*** [1976] 1 WLR 1052

Lord Scarman at 1061–2:

> It was the revocation of a licence because of misconduct that they had under consideration—not merely the man's fitness or capacity for the grant of a licence. There was, therefore, a situation here in which (using the terms broadly) Mr. Hook was on trial, and on trial for his livelihood. There was a complainant, the market manager. The market manager had a professional interest in the matter since he was concerned to protect his employees, or the employees for whom he was responsible, from abuse and misconduct by stallholders in the market. Mr. Fretwell was a prosecutor, a complainant; Mr. Hook was a man, albeit in an administrative field, who was on trial not for his life but for his livelihood.
>
> If ever there was a case in which it was imperative that the complainant or the prosecutor should not participate in the adjudication, I should have thought it was this one . . .

This rule applies where the decision-maker is a member of the body that brings complaints or prosecutions even if the individual is not involved in the decision. So, in *Re P (a barrister)* [2005] 1 WLR 3019, a lay member of the Professional Conduct and Complaints Committee (PCCC) of the Bar Council sat on a disciplinary tribunal of the Inns of Court. It decided that a decision of the tribunal that the claimant was guilty of breaches of the Bar code of conduct could not stand. This was because although the lay member of the PCCC had not taken part in the decision to bring the case against the claimant, she was a judge in her own cause, because she might be unconsciously biased in favour of the PCCC.

18.6.5 Institutional bias

As discussed at the beginning of this chapter, natural justice is concerned with a wide range of different bodies. The courts have recognised that some bodies, such as elected local authorities or government ministers, have an inevitable interest in politics that may form part of their decision-making. However, such bodies are also subject to the bias rules and the courts have held that they are expected to act impartially when exercising their discretion. But they are not expected to act in the same way as a judge or other quasi-judicial agency. This is illustrated by the classic case of *Franklin v Minister of Town and Country Planning* [1948] AC 87. This involved a dispute over the building of Stevenage, a new town under the New Towns Act 1946. There were objections that were heard at the planning inquiry, but a subsequent order that permitted the building was confirmed by the minister. At a meeting, the minister had stated to protestors: 'It is no good your jeering, it is going to be done.' It was argued that this showed that the minister had already made up his mind before making the statutory order confirming the building of the new town. The House of Lords rejected the allegations of bias, stating that he

NOTE For a further
discussion of this
issue and recent
developments, see
the article by Havers
and Henderson
(2011) listed in the
further reading
at the end of this
chapter.

did not have a judicial or quasi-judicial function and that, as long as he genuinely considered the inspector's report resulting from the inquiry, the minister's decision could be upheld.

18.6.6 Exceptions to the bias rule

A claimant may waive his or her right to claim bias. This may be the case if the claimant knows that a decision-maker has an interest in the decision or if there is a potential conflict. This point is made in *Locabail (UK) Ltd v Bayfield Properties Ltd* [2000] 2 WLR 870. This was a case in which the Court of Appeal consolidated five cases concerned with bias and heard them together. One of the points made in the case concerned waiver. The Court states that waiver cannot be established unless the claimant knows all of the facts.

● *Locabail (UK) Ltd v Bayfield Properties Ltd* [2000] QB 451

Lord Bingham of Cornhill CJ, Lord Woolf MR, and Sir Richard Scott VC at 475:

> [15] Although disqualification under the rule in the *Dimes* case, 3 H.L.Cas. 759 and *Ex parte Pinochet (No. 2)* is properly described as automatic, a party with an irresistible right to object to a judge hearing or continuing to hear a case may, as in other cases to which we refer below, waive his right to object. It is however clear that any waiver must be clear and unequivocal, and made with full knowledge of all the facts relevant to the decision whether to waive or not.

There may be rare occasions on which there is a conflict of interest that offends the bias rule and there is no alternative decision-maker. The court may then apply the 'necessity' exception. In the *Dimes* case (cited above), it was held that the Lord Chancellor should not have heard the case because of his pecuniary interest. However, he had signed the relevant orders to allow the case to be heard by the House of Lords. It was held that this was a valid exercise of his power because it was a matter of necessity.

If the necessity exception applies, then there may be a conflict with Article 6(1) ECHR, which requires that the decision-maker be 'independent and impartial'. *Kingsley v UK* (2002) 35 EHRR 10 was concerned with a decision by the Gaming Board that the claimant's licence should be withdrawn. This was because he was not considered a fit and proper person to hold a gaming licence, in accordance with section 19 of the Gaming Act 1968. The decision was held to be in breach of Article 6(1), because the Gaming Board had already formed an adverse view of the claimant before it had heard his case. The Court of Appeal had rejected the judicial review of the claimant's claim on the ground of bias. It held that the doctrine of necessity applied and that the Gaming Board had the statutory power to make the decision, and that this could not be delegated to another more impartial body. The European Court of Human Rights held that this was a breach of the claimant's right to have his case heard by an 'independent and impartial tribunal'. This means that although the common law rules of bias provide for an exception based on necessity, if Article 6(1) is applicable, then the claimant may argue that there has been a breach of the Convention right.

summary points

The rule against bias

- *The rule against bias prohibits the decision-maker from having an interest in the outcome of the decision.*
- *It is not necessary to prove actual bias, but only the appearance of bias.*
- *Direct bias occurs when the decision-maker has a direct interest in the outcome.*

- *Direct bias normally concerns pecuniary interests, but it can also concern non-pecuniary interests, as in the* Pinochet *case.*
- *Apparent bias can include cases in which decision-makers have already made up their minds or have a conflict of interest.*
- *Apparent bias occurs when a fair-minded and informed observer, having considered the facts, would conclude that there was a real possibility that the tribunal (decision-maker) was biased.*

18.7 Article 6 of the European Convention on Human Rights (ECHR)

Article 6 ECHR also deals with procedural issues. Since the introduction of the Human Rights Act 1998 (HRA 1998), Article 6 has been used by claimants in cases concerned with natural justice to supplement their arguments before the courts for procedural fairness. But, for the most part, Article 6 has conferred only a few additional safeguards. However, Article 6 has had an impact on the bias rule and, as we have discussed, the courts in *Porter v Magill* took into account the requirements of Article 6 when deciding on the correct test for bias. This is because Article 6 states that the decision-maker must be 'independent and impartial'. This requirement has been used to challenge administrative decision-making on the grounds that it conflicts with the **separation of powers** between different institutions of government. This will be discussed below.

NOTE

The procedural requirements of Article 6 ECHR have also been applied by the courts in cases concerned with the anti-terrorist laws, most notably in relation to control orders, as we will see in Chapter 20.

18.7.1 The application of Article 6(1)

European Convention on Human Rights

....

Article 6

(1) In the determination of his civil rights and obligations...everyone is entitled to a fair and public hearing within a reasonable time by an independent and impartial tribunal established by law.

...

Article 6(1) does not apply in all cases; it applies only in cases that are concerned with 'the determination of civil rights and obligations'. The problem is that not all administrative decisions are concerned with civil rights and obligations. They often involve decisions that are not private law rights. When interpreting this term, the European Court of Human Rights (ECtHR)

cross reference

See the discussion on Article 6 and legal representation at disciplinary tribunals earlier in this chapter.

has stated that Article 6 does apply to some administrative decisions, such as the conferral of welfare benefits.

This is the case even though such benefits do not typically fall within the definition of civil rights and obligations, and go beyond the determination of rights in private law. This complex area was discussed by the Supreme Court in *Ali v Birmingham City Council* [2010] UKSC 8. In this case, the Supreme Court reviewed the UK and ECtHR case law, and concluded that a claim to housing under the homelessness legislation was not a civil right. This was because the local authority had to make 'evaluative judgements' before the right to housing was established. This means that the authority had a high degree of discretion in deciding whether the statutory criteria were met before granting housing. This is a difficult area of law that goes beyond the scope of this book, but the following examples indicate the types of case in which the courts have held that the matter is one in which civil rights and obligations are being determined:

- the grant by the state of contributory social benefits—*Feldbrugge v The Netherlands* (1986) 8 EHRR 425;
- some non-contributory social benefits—*Salesi v Italy* (1993) 26 EHRR 187;
- planning decisions—*R (on the application of Alconbury Developments Ltd) v Secretary of State for the Environment Transport and Regions* [2001] UKHL 23;
- a claim for Housing Benefit payments—*Tsfayo v United Kingdom* (2006) 48 EHRR 457; and
- the right to practise one's profession—*Kulkarni v Milton Keynes Hospital NHS Foundation Trust and another* [2009] EWCA Civ 789.

NOTE If you want to explore this issue further, then you should read the article by Cross (2010) listed in the further reading at the end of this chapter.

18.7.2 Impartial and independent decisions

589

When the HRA 1998 was introduced, there was some concern that the requirement of an impartial and independent decision-maker in Article 6 ECHR might lead to many administrative processes, particularly in relation to planning and housing, being declared incompatible with the Convention. This is because politicians, who have some policy or political interest in the outcome, make many administrative decisions. There are often safeguards to try to make such decisions as fair as possible. Nevertheless, such cases raise issues of what is referred to as 'institutional bias', which may offend against the principle of the separation of powers. This is because there is an **executive**/political and quasi-judicial type of power being exercised. On other occasions, a decision-maker may not be completely independent because someone in the same department as the original decision-maker may decide an appeal or review the original decision.

However, the courts have been very unwilling to find that there is bias in these types of case. They have held that, as long as the overall procedure is fair and there is an opportunity to bring an action for judicial review to correct any errors, then the process is likely to be compatible with Article 6. The decision in *R (on the application of Alconbury Developments Ltd) v Secretary of State for the Environment Transport and Regions* [2001] UKHL 23 decided that planning decisions heard by the Secretary of State were compatible with Article 6. In this case, the claimant, Alconbury, agreed with the owners of a disused airfield, the Ministry of Defence, that if planning permission were granted, it would develop the site. It applied to the local authority for planning permission. However, in this case, the Secretary of State decided to 'recover' the application. This meant that rather than the application being decided by a planning inspector, the inspector would conduct an inquiry and make a recommendation to the Secretary of State, who would make the final decision. This was often done in complex cases or cases that raised issues of public interest or importance. This process was in accordance with the Town and Country Planning Act 1990.

It was argued that the Secretary of State was not impartial, and that these provisions were incompatible with Article 6 and a **declaration** of incompatibility should be granted in accordance with section 4 of the HRA 1998. It was claimed that the Secretary of State was not independent, because he was responsible for policy and deciding on the most efficient use of land. His department creates policies and guidance followed in planning decisions. In addition, the Ministry of Defence, another branch of government, owned the land. The House of Lords, reversing the decision of the Divisional Court, held that even though the Secretary of State was not independent, the process was fair overall. This was because planning law inevitably involved executive decisions and it was not like a decision made by a judge. The Secretary of State was accountable to Parliament for his decision and the courts should be slow to intervene. There were also sufficient safeguards, because there was an inquiry by a planning inspector and an opportunity to judicially review the decision. Even though judicial review did not allow a complete rehearing of all of the issues, it did provide sufficient supervision of the decision and could deal with many complaints, as Lord Hoffmann explained.

● *R (on the application of Alconbury Developments Ltd) v Secretary of State for the Environment Transport and Regions* [2001] UKHL 23

Lord Hoffmann:

[159] As I indicated at the outset, Parliament, democratically elected, has entrusted the making of planning decisions to local authorities and to the Secretary of State with a general power of supervision and control in the latter. Thereby it is intended that some overall coherence and uniformity in national planning can be achieved in the public interest and that major decisions can be taken by a minister answerable to Parliament. Planning matters are essentially matters of policy and expediency, not of law. They are primarily matters for the executive and not for the courts to determine. Moreover, as a matter of generality the right of access to a court is not absolute. Limitations may be imposed so long as they do not so restrict or reduce the access that the very essence of the right is impaired ... Moreover the limitation must pursue a legitimate aim and the relationship between the means employed and the aim sought to be achieved must be reasonably proportionate: *Ashingdane v United Kingdom* [1985] 7 EHRR 528. In the context of the present case the aim of reserving to a minister answerable to Parliament the determination of cases which will often be of very considerable public interest and importance is plainly a legitimate one. In light of the considerations which I have already canvassed it seems to me that there exists a reasonable balance between the scope of matters left to his decision and the scope of the control possessed by the courts over the exercise of his discretionary power.

In this extract, Lord Hoffmann recognised that planning decisions often involved matters of public policy and that the input of the Secretary of State may be necessary to ensure consistency. Provided that the procedure was fair and the decision could be judicially reviewed, the procedure was compatible with Article 6(1).

NOTE

Alconbury can be seen as an example of a case in which the House of Lords deferred to the executive and Parliament. Lord Hoffmann accepted that the democratically elected Parliament had entrusted planning decisions to the executive, which was best placed to deal with them. For a discussion of **deference**, see Chapter 17.

summary points

Article 6 of the European Convention on Human Rights (ECHR)

* *Article 6(1) ECHR applies in cases that are concerned with the claimant's civil rights and obligations.*

- *This means that not all administrative law decisions are covered by Article 6(1), but the House of Lords has applied the term widely enough to include some administrative decisions.*

- *Most of the procedural protections required by Article 6 are already provided by the common law rules of natural justice.*

- *The requirement of an independent and impartial tribunal does not apply at every stage of the administrative proceedings, provided that there is access to judicial review and the decision is fair overall.*

 # Summary

Procedural impropriety is concerned with the administrative process. Fair procedures ensure a better quality of decision-making, and that decisions are more likely to be understood and respected. Statutes often provide procedural safeguards, such as requiring consultation or informing individuals of their appeal rights. When public authorities fail to follow the statutory proceedings, the decision may be invalid, but this depends on the courts' assessment of the statutory provision in question. If the provision is considered to be mandatory and there has not been substantial compliance, then the decision will be invalid. If the provision is directory, then the court will be unwilling to invalidate the decision. Recent case law has emphasised that the courts will focus on the consequences of the failure to comply with the statutory provision rather than on whether it is a mandatory or directory provision.

Procedural impropriety also includes a failure to observe the rules of natural justice. These common law rules are implied into the statute by the court. They include the right to be heard and the rule against bias. The courts have stressed the flexible nature of the rules of natural justice and the fact that their application is different depending on the type of circumstances in question. The circumstances include the statutory framework, the nature of the decision-making body, and the kind of interest at stake. The right to be heard may require a full oral hearing with a right to cross-examination and legal representation, as in the case of a prison disciplinary hearing. But in other circumstances it may simply require the decision-maker to explain the case against the claimant and to provide an opportunity for him or her to make representations. This was what was expected of the immigration officer in *Re HK*. The right to be heard has also developed in favour of reasons being given in the interest of fairness. But, as we have seen, there is no right to reasons for all administrative decisions. In addition, if the claimant has a legitimate expectation, then this may give rise to certain additional procedural protections being given. However, the legitimate expectation may, in certain rare circumstances, go beyond conferring procedural protection and give rise to an expectation of a substantive benefit, as in *Coughlan*.

The rule against bias means that a decision will be invalid if there is an appearance of bias, even if there is no actual bias. Direct bias usually involves the decision-maker having a direct pecuniary interest in the outcome, as in *Dimes*. Occasionally, it can include direct non-financial interests, as in *Pinochet*. Direct bias will lead to the decision-maker being automatically disqualified. Most cases of bias involve apparent bias. In *Porter v Magill*, the House of Lords decided that there is bias if a fair-minded and informed observer would think that there was a real possibility of bias. Bias can be alleged in many different circumstances, but the courts have stressed that it is not acceptable for a member of the decision-making body to have been involved with the authority bringing the case.

Article 6(1) ECHR adds another dimension to the law on procedural fairness. It applies only where the decision determines 'civil rights and obligations'. It has been argued that decision-makers involved in administrative schemes such as planning are not 'independent and impartial', as required by Article 6. The courts have applied what is referred to as the 'curative principle'. This means that not every decision in the administrative scheme has to be made by an 'independent and impartial' decision-maker. Provided that a decision can be reviewed by the court and any lack of impartiality remedied, the process will be compatible with Article 6.

Procedural impropriety deals with a very wide range of administrative decision-making, but the courts have attempted to lay down a framework of rules to ensure that those exercising public functions abide by minimum standards of fairness.

Questions

1 Davenport School for the Gifted is run by Hampstead Local Council in accordance with its powers under the Imaginary Gifted Schools Act 2006. The school can admit or exclude students 'as it thinks fit'. The school has a policy of expelling students after they have had two written warning for misconduct.

Marina, aged 16, a gifted pupil, has been accused of misbehaviour after swearing at her English teacher, Miss January, during an argument about her grade for an English essay. Because she now has two written warnings, Marina is asked to appear before a disciplinary tribunal to decide whether or not she should be allowed to remain at the school. Marina is not allowed to cross-examine Miss January, because the teacher would find it too upsetting and she is prohibited from calling the only witness, another student, named Melissa. She is also not allowed to have a lawyer present. When Marina gives evidence, she admits to raising her voice, but denies swearing. She also produces medical evidence that she is taking medication for clinical depression that has the side effect of causing mood swings and which may cause her to act out of character. She apologises to Miss January if she caused offence. Miss January remains with the disciplinary committee when it retires to consider its decision about Marina. The committee decides that it must follow the school policy and expel Marina, and refuses to give any further reasons for its decision.

Advise Marina, who would like to make a claim for judicial review against Davenport School.

2 Explain the development of the case law on legitimate expectation. Do you think that the Court of Appeal was right in *Coughlan* to decide that there could be a legitimate expectation of a substantive benefit? Give full reasons for your answer.

Further reading

Craig, P., *Administrative Law* (London: Sweet & Maxwell, 2008)

Chapters 12 and 13 set out the principles of natural justice in considerable detail, and Chapter 13 also discusses Article 6 of the Convention.

Cross, T., 'Is there a "civil right" under Article 6? Ten principles for public lawyers' [2010] Judicial Review 366

This article refers to the recent case law and explains the principles by which the court decides whether there is a civil right for the purposes of Article 6.

Havers, P. and Henderson, A., 'Recent developments (and problems) in the law on bias' [2011] Judicial Review 80

This is a handy guide to some of the recent decisions on bias.

Leigh, I., 'Bias, necessity and the Convention' [2002] Public Law 407

This is an analysis of the implications of the decision of the European Court of Human Rights in *Kingsley v UK* (2001) 33 EHRR 288 on Article 6 and the problematic nature of the necessity defence in cases concerned with bias.

Steele, I., 'Substantive legitimate expectations; striking the right balance?' (2005) 121 Law Quarterly Review 300

This article considers whether the case law on substantive legitimate expectation is based on a well-thought-out set of principles that are capable of dealing effectively with the conflicting interests that underlie these decisions.

Remedies

Introduction

This chapter is concerned with the grant of remedies by the court. It will consider the different remedies that are available on judicial review, the difference between the remedies, and the factors that the court takes into account when deciding which remedy to award. This chapter also discusses the courts' powers to grant a remedy under the Human Rights Act 1998.

19.1 What remedies are available and what is the purpose of a remedy?

19.1.1 What is the purpose of a remedy?

If the claimant successfully establishes that the **public authority** has acted in contravention of one of the grounds of review, then the court may grant a remedy. As the following extract states, the purpose of a remedy is to tell the public authority what it has to do to comply with the judgment and to ensure, as far as possible, that it obeys the courts' decision.

● P. Cane, 'The constitutional basis of judicial remedies in public law', in P. Leyland and T. Woods (eds) *Administrative Law Facing the Future: Old Constraints and New Horizons* (London: Blackstone, 1997), pp. 242–70, at 242

> Remedies are the means by which the courts enforce compliance by public bodies with the rules and principles of administrative law, and they are important regulators of the relationship between the courts and the other branches of government.

From the claimant's point of view, the remedy is extremely important, because the whole point of bringing the case is usually to overturn or change the decision of the public authority. However, remedies available on **judicial** review are discretionary and there are circumstances in which the court may refuse a remedy. Even if a remedy is granted by the court, the public authority may be obliged only to reconsider the decision and may arrive at the same decision again. *R (Luton BC and others) v Secretary of State for Education* [2011] EWHC 217, discussed later in the chapter, is an example of just such a situation.

So the claimant needs to consider carefully the purpose of applying for judicial review. All of these issues will be considered below.

19.1.2 What remedies are available?

There are two main types of remedy available in judicial review cases: ordinary remedies and prerogative remedies. The *ordinary remedies* are:

- **injunction**;
- **declaration**; and
- **damages** (available only where there is an additional private law wrong, such as a tort or in accordance with the Human Rights Act 1998).

NOTE The **Civil Procedure Rules (CPR) 1998** renamed these remedies and the former name of each is noted in parentheses.

NOTE The CPR direct the way in which the High Court and Court of Appeal operate, and, as discussed in Chapter 14, CPR Part 54 regulates the judicial review procedure.

The *prerogative remedies* are as follows:

• a **mandatory order** (formerly mandamus);

• a **prohibiting order** (formerly prohibition); and

• a **quashing order** (formerly certiorari).

Some writers, such as Cane, use the term 'private law remedies' to describe injunctions and declarations, because of their origin in private law. Wade and Forsyth, *Administrative Law* (8th edn, Oxford: Oxford University Press, 2000) use the term 'ordinary law remedies' to describe these remedies and that is the term adopted here. You may, however, find Cane's brief summary of the function of the key remedies useful to keep in mind as a reference point.

● **P. Cane, *Administrative Law*** (4th edn, Oxford: Oxford University Press, 2004), p. 82

Leaving damages aside, these remedies perform four main functions: ordering something to be done is the function of the mandatory order and the (mandatory) injunction; ordering that something not be done is the function of the prohibiting order and the (prohibitory) injunction; depriving a decision of legal effect is the function of the quashing order and stating legal rights or obligations is the function of the declaration.

The ordinary remedies were developed to provide redress in cases involving private law, such as contract, tort, and trust law. Historically, only the prerogative law remedies were available on judicial review, because these were special remedies generally granted against bodies carrying out public functions. If a claimant wanted to obtain an injunction or declaration, this had to be done in separate private law proceedings. However, in 1977, a number of changes were made that simplified the application for judicial review. These changes can now be found in section 31 of the Senior Courts Act 1981.

Senior Courts Act 1981

Section 31

(1) An application to the High Court for one or more of the following forms of relief, namely—

(a) a mandatory prohibiting, or quashing order;

(b) a declaration or injunction under subsection (2) or

(c) an injunction under section 30 restraining a person not entitled to do so from acting in an office to which that section applies,

shall be made in accordance with the rules of court by a procedure to be known as an application for judicial review.

(2) A declaration may be made or an injunction granted under this subsection in any case where an application for judicial review, seeking that relief, has been made and the High Court considers that, having regard to—

(a) the nature of the matters in respect of which relief may be granted by mandatory, prohibiting or quashing orders;

(b) the nature of the persons and bodies against whom relief may be granted by such orders and

(c) all the circumstances of the case,

it would be just and convenient for the declaration to be made or the injunction to be granted, as the case may be.

As a consequence of the changes made in section 31 of the Senior Courts Act 1981, the ordinary law remedies were, for the first time, available on judicial review. This made it easier for claimants to combine different types of remedy in one application.

19.1.3 The effect of a remedy on judicial review

When the court grants a remedy on judicial review, it may invalidate the decision or grant a declaration that the decision is unlawful. It may also grant a remedy ordering an authority to make a decision in accordance with its statutory duty or to implement a decision properly. It is not unusual for the court to grant a quashing order (formerly certiorari), quashing the decision, combined with a mandatory order (formerly mandamus) directing the authority to reconsider the decision in accordance with the law. This is because the court does not want to appropriate the decision-making power of the public authority. In some circumstances, this means that the authority may make a fresh decision, which is also unfavourable to the claimant. This may be the case if, for example, the court has held that the original decision is in breach of **natural justice**. In this situation, the public authority may make the same decision again after it has given the claimant a hearing.

This possibility was acknowledged by the court in *Attorney General of Hong Kong v Ng Yuen Shiu* [1983] 2 AC 629. In this case, the House of Lords quashed the decision to remove the claimant from Hong Kong by certiorari (a quashing order) because he had a legitimate expectation of a hearing. However, the court stated that, after there had been a full inquiry, it was then open to the authorities to remove him.

• **Attorney General of Hong Kong v Ng Yuen Shiu** [1983] 2 AC 629

Lord Fraser of Tullybellton at 636:

> That order of certiorari is of course entirely without prejudice to the making of a fresh removal order ... after a fair inquiry has been held at which the applicant has been given an opportunity to make such representations as he may see fit as to why he should not be removed.

A more recent example of this occurred in *R (Luton BC and others) v Secretary of State for Education* [2011] EWHC 217, in which six local authorities successfully challenged the cancellation of the schools-building project by the Secretary of State for Education. The claim succeeded on various grounds. These included the application by the Secretary of State of the rules in an overly rigid way and a failure to give effect to a legitimate expectation by the local authorities to be consulted.

cross reference
For the grounds of review discussed in this case, see Chapters 16 (overly rigid policy), 17 (irrationality), and 18 (legitimate expectation).

But Mr Justice Holman made it clear that although the Secretary of State had a duty to consider the local authorities' representations, he was under no obligation to change his mind.

• **R (Luton BC and others) v Secretary of State for Education** [2011] EWHC 217

Holman J at [126]:

> ... the final decision on any given school or project still rests with [the Secretary of State]. He may save all, some, a few, or none. No one should gain false hope from this decision.

The Secretary of State for Education, Michael Gove, then reconsidered the decisions in the light of the representations made by the local authorities. But he announced in the House of

Commons on 19 July 2011 that while he would indemnify the authorities for contractual liabilities, the schools in question would not be rebuilt, because he would not be restoring the specific Building Schools for the Future (BSF) projects (Hansard HC, 19 July 2011, col. 794). So the local authorities were successful on judicial review, but ultimately failed in their objective of persuading the Secretary of State to allow the school-building projects to go ahead.

Nevertheless, it is also possible that, after having granted a hearing, a public authority will make a decision favourable to the claimant.

There are also other occasions on which, as a result of the court decision, the authority is unable to proceed in the way in which it intended and it will have to change its policy or decision. This is more likely to be the case where the court has held that a decision is irrational or is in breach of the Human Rights Act 1998. In *R (on the application of Daly) v Secretary of State for the Home Department* [2001] 2 AC 532, the House of Lords held that the policy of the prison on searching prisoners' cells was in breach of Article 8 of the **European Convention on Human Rights (ECHR)**, which protects the right to respect for private and family life. As a consequence of the decision, the prison authorities had to revise their policy so that legally privileged material was protected.

cross reference
For a full discussion of Daly, see Chapter 17.

The court does have the power in section 141 of the Tribunals, Courts and Services Act 2007 not to refer the decision back to the tribunal, but to substitute its own decision. This means that the court makes the actual decision rather than the tribunal. Only a decision of an inferior court or tribunal may be substituted and not that of a public authority. There must be an error of law and, in addition, the court must find that there was only one decision that the tribunal or court could have reached. This power is not used frequently. But on those occasions on which it is used, it provides a speedy decision for the claimant, who does not have to return to the court or tribunal for a fresh decision.

The following sections will discuss the nature of the individual remedies.

19.2 The ordinary remedies: injunction, declaration, and damages

As stated above, the ordinary remedies are available on judicial review, but the natures of the remedies are different. It is important to understand the distinction between them and which one is most appropriately applied for when challenging a decision.

19.2.1 Injunction

The short extract that follows explains that an injunction is a command from the court to the public authority and that there are different kinds of injunction. Injunctions are not normally available against the **Crown**, as we will see later in the chapter.

● H. Woolf, J. L. Jowell, and A. Le Sueur, *De Smith's Judicial Review* (6th edn, London: Sweet & Maxwell, 2007), p. 705

An injunction is an order of a court addressed to a party requiring that party to do or refrain from doing a particular act. A *mandatory injunction* is an order of the court requiring the public authority to take a particular action usually to carry out a public duty. A *prohibitory injunction* orders the authority to refrain from a particular act. Injunctions are equitable and discretionary remedies and applications can be refused by the court. Failure to obey an injunction is a contempt of court.

An example of an injunction preventing unlawful action was granted in *Attorney General v Fulham Corporation* [1921] 1 Ch 440. The injunction ordered Fulham Corporation to cease running a wash-house where the corporation employees washed clothes for customers. The injunction was coupled with a declaration stating that the scheme was unlawful. The terms of the order were as follows..

● ***Attorney General v Fulham Corporation*** [1921] 1 Ch 440

Sargant J at 454:

> There will therefore be a declaration that the defendant corporation is not entitled to carry on any enterprise which carries into execution the report of the Committee, or which involves the total or partial washing of clothes for others by the defendant corporation, as distinguished from facilities for enabling others to come to the wash-house to wash their clothes; and there will be an injunction to restrain the defendant corporation, its officers, servants and agents, acting in contravention of this declaration.

In *Bradbury and others v Enfield London Borough Council* [1967] 1 WLR 1311, an injunction was granted preventing Enfield London Borough Council from changing its schools to comprehensives, because the authority had failed to comply with mandatory statutory procedures requiring consultation. The court rejected the argument that chaos would be caused by the injunction, as the extract from Lord Denning's judgment shows.

cross reference
See Chapter 18 for more on Bradbury.

● ***Bradbury and others v Enfield London Borough Council*** [1967] 1 WLR 1311

Lord Denning at 1324:

> I must say this: If a local authority does not fulfil the requirements of the law, this court will see that it does fulfil them. It will not listen readily to suggestions of 'chaos'. The Department of Education and the local education authority are subject to the rule of law and must comply with it, just like everyone else. Even if chaos should result, still the law must be obeyed. But I do not think that chaos will result. The evidence convinces me that the 'chaos' is much overstated.

Note that, once the statutory requirements had been complied with, the council would, in accordance with the statutory procedures, be able to implement the comprehensive school system.

Interim injunction

An **interim injunction** is a temporary injunction that is granted by the court to preserve the position of the parties until the trial date. For example, a claimant may challenge the legality of a decision of the local authority to demolish a property because it is in breach of planning regulations. The claimant will want to prevent the destruction of the house until the court has had the opportunity to hear the case. In these circumstances, the court may grant an interim injunction to prevent the local authority from taking any action until the case is decided. The interim injunction is often used in private law cases and the court applies a test of the balance of convenience. One example of a public law case in which the court refused an interim injunction is *R v Ministry of Agriculture, Fisheries and Food, ex p Monsanto* [1999] 2 WLR 599. Monsanto plc challenged a decision of the Ministry of Agriculture to grant a rival company, C, permission to manufacture and supply a herbicide. Questions of law were referred to the European Court of Justice (ECJ). The Court refused an interim injunction to suspend approval until the issues of law were decided at trial. This was the case even though damages were unlikely to be an adequate remedy for Monsanto. Balancing the various factors, the Court decided that there was a presumption against providing interim relief where it would restrict free competition unless there was another overriding interest, such as concerns about public health. Because no such concerns arose in this case, the interim injunction was refused.

Injunctions against the Crown

Injunctions may be granted against Crown servants, such as **government** ministers, but not against the Crown itself. This is a confusing area of law with a complex history partly because of uncertainty over the meaning of 'the Crown'. It is clear from section 21 of the Crown Proceedings Act 1947 that injunctions cannot be granted directly against the Crown. However, it is now established that injunctions may be granted against servants of the Crown, usually government ministers. This is a consequence of two important House of Lords' decisions.

In *R v Secretary of State for Transport, ex p Factortame Ltd (No 2)* [1991] 1 AC 603, after a reference to the ECJ, it was held that the claimants were entitled to an interim injunction against a minister of the Crown suspending certain provisions of the Merchant Shipping Act 1988 until the compatibility of the legislation with European law was determined.

cross reference
Factortame also raises important issues of parliamentary sovereignty—see Chapter 7.

In *M v Home Office* [1994] 1 AC 377, the House of Lords discussed whether the court had power to grant injunctive relief against the Crown and, if the injunction was breached, whether the Crown could be held in contempt of court. The case concerned the deportation of an asylum seeker to Zaire while judicial proceedings were ongoing. The Home Secretary had given an undertaking that M would be allowed to remain until the judicial review was complete. M's lawyers argued that the Home Secretary had acted in contempt of court. Lord Woolf reaffirmed the principle that injunctive relief was not available against the Crown, but held that section 31 of the Senior Courts Act 1981 did permit interim and full injunctions to be granted against ministers and other officers of the Crown, and that ministers in their official capacity could be held to be in contempt. However, he did state that such injunctions should be granted sparingly.

. . . .

● *M v Home Office* [1994] 1 AC 377

Lord Woolf at 423:

> The fact that, in my view, the court should be regarded as having jurisdiction to grant interim and final injunctions against officers of the Crown does not mean that that jurisdiction should be exercised except in the most limited circumstances. In the majority of situations so far as final relief is concerned, a declaration will continue to be the appropriate remedy on an application for judicial review involving officers of the Crown.

thinking point

*Do you think that the court was right to hold that injunctions are available against ministers of the Crown? What implications does this case have for the **rule of law**? Reread Chapter 4 before you attempt an answer.*

Relator actions

The Attorney General has a general capacity to apply for injunctions against any group or individual in the public interest to prevent them acting unlawfully. He or she can also take action against public authorities to stop **illegality**. This may be useful if there is no individual who is able or willing to take legal action. The Attorney General can also bring an action at the relation (that is, on the initiative of) of another person claiming a declaration or injunction. The Attorney General can be described as lending the name and authority of the office to the legal action, but handing over the conduct of the litigation to a private individual who is the real claimant. In the past, **relator actions** tended to be used by individuals wanting to challenge the decision of local authorities, but who lacked a **sufficient interest** in the case. The decision of the Attorney General as to whether or not to bring a relator action cannot be challenged by way of judicial review. This was established in *Gouriet v Union of Post Office Workers* [1978] AC 435.

Injunctions

- A mandatory injunction orders the authority to carry out a particular action.

- A prohibitory injunction orders the authority to stop carrying out a particular action.

- An interim injunction is a temporary injunction that preserves the litigants' position until the trial takes place.

- Injunctions may be granted against servants and ministers of the Crown, but the court will exercise this power sparingly.

- The Attorney General may permit a relator action to be brought using his name.

19.2.2 Declaration

A declaration is a formal statement of the law by the court. Breach of a declaration is not in itself a contempt of court, but because public authorities are expected to abide by court decisions, this does not usually present any difficulties. Consider the above statement of Lord Woolf, in *M v Home Office* [1994] 1 AC 377, 423, where he states that a declaration rather than an injunction is the appropriate remedy in cases involving ministers of the Crown. An interim declaration can also be granted by the court to state the position of the parties before the full trial of the issues.

Declarations may be used to clarify the legal position of the parties, although the issue must be in the context of a real dispute; it should not be a purely hypothetical or academic matter.

Royal College of Nursing v Department of Health and Social Security [1981] AC 800 concerned a dispute between the Royal College of Nursing (RCN) and the government. The RCN applied to the court for a declaration that a circular sent to the medical authorities by the Department of Health and Social Security (DHSS) was unlawful. The circular advised that nurses could administer abortion-inducing drugs, provided that the overall procedure was supervised by a medical practitioner. The RCN argued that this advice was wrong in law, because it was contrary to section 1(1) of the Abortion Act 1967, which provided that only a medical practitioner could terminate a pregnancy. The House of Lords held that the circular issued by the DHSS was lawful and refused the declaration asked for by the RCN. Instead, it upheld the declaration of the judge in the High Court that nurses who followed the advice in the circular would be acting lawfully.

In *Gillick v West Norfolk and Wisbech Area Health Authority* [1985] 3 WLR 830; [1986] AC 112, Mrs Gillick applied for a declaration that advice issued by the DHSS to local health authorities was unlawful. The advice permitted doctors in certain circumstances to counsel and prescribe contraception to children under the age of 16 without parental consent. The House of Lords, by a majority, refused her a declaration. However, the Law Lords accepted that the remedy of declaration would have been an appropriate one.

● ***Gillick v West Norfolk and Wisbech Area Health Authority*** [1985] 3 WLR 830; [1986] AC 112

Lord Bridge at 115:

> We must now say that if a government department, in a field of administration in which it exercises responsibility, promulgates in a public document, albeit non-statutory in form, advice which is erroneous in law, then the court, in proceedings in appropriate form commenced by an applicant or plaintiff who possesses the necessary locus standi, has jurisdiction to correct the error of law by an appropriate declaration.

In the next short extract, the authors note that the courts may prefer to grant a declaration rather than an injunction. This is because it states the legal position and is less intrusive than an injunction. Public authorities can generally be relied on to comply with the law and a stronger remedy is not always necessary.

● **H. Woolf, J. L. Jowell, and A. Le Sueur, *De Smith's Judicial Review*** (6th edn, London: Sweet & Maxwell, 2007), pp. 899–900

> The fact that a declaration is not coercive is one of its advantages as a public law remedy. Because it merely pronounces upon the legal position it is well suited to the supervisory role of administrative law in England. In addition . . . the declaration can be tailored so as not to interfere with the activities of public authorities more than is necessary to ensure that they comply with the law. In many situations all that is required is for the legal position to be clearly set out in a declaration for a dispute of considerable public importance to be resolved.

Since the introduction of the Civil Procedure Rules 1998, it is now possible to obtain an interim declaration (see CPR 25.1(1)(b)). This means that the court can make a declaration stating the legal position. So, in *X NHS Trust v T (Adult Patient: Refusal of Medical Treatment)* [2004] EWHC 1279 (Fam), the court granted an interim declaration applied for by a National Health Service (NHS) trust. The declaration stated that T lacked the mental capacity to consent to treatment and could lawfully be given a blood transfusion against her wishes.

19.2.3 Damages

There is no right to damages for an administrative wrong at common law. Loss suffered as a consequence of the unlawful action of the authority does not attract damages. The claimant has to show that a private law wrong has also been committed, such as a breach of contract or a tort. If such a claim can be made out, then damages may be claimed as an additional remedy on judicial review.

The lack of administrative law damages can cause hardship to individuals, for example if they have wrongfully been refused a licence and have been unable to work as a consequence. However, there are various alternative methods of claiming compensation by making a complaint to a non-judicial body, such as the **Parliamentary Ombudsman**, who does have the power to recommend that compensation be paid for administrative wrongs. The legal group JUSTICE has explained the defects in the present system and has recommended that the law be changed to allow the court to grant damages for administrative wrongs.

cross reference
See Chapter 13 for more on the powers of the Parliamentary Ombudsman.

● **Patrick Neill, JUSTICE, and All Souls College (University of Oxford),** *Administrative Justice: Some Necessary Reforms—Report of the Committee of the JUSTICE–All Souls Review of Administrative Law in the United Kingdom* (Oxford: Clarendon Press, 1988), p. 344

11.33 When a citizen has been adversely affected by administrative action which he considers to be wrong, the primary redress which he seeks will often be the reversal of the offending decision; thus, he will wish to secure the payment of a grant which has been withheld, the repayment of money wrongfully demanded, the abandonment of an excessive claim for tax, the granting of a licence which has been refused, the withdrawal of an order requiring him to discontinue his business activities, and so on. Yet in many cases the offending administrative act may cause the citizen pecuniary loss before it is reversed; for example, the market stall holder whose licence is revoked in breach of natural justice may succeed in getting his licence restored by the court, but on the law as it stands, he cannot recover in respect of the loss of income which he suffered while he had no licence, unless he can prove a tort such as negligence...

After an examination of the law, the authors conclude as follow.

● **Patrick Neill, JUSTICE, and All Souls College (University of Oxford),** *Administrative Justice: Some Necessary Reforms—Report of the Committee of the JUSTICE–All Souls Review of Administrative Law in the United Kingdom* (Oxford: Clarendon Press, 1988), p. 361

11.81 So we take the view that where wrongful administrative action injures the citizen he should have a remedy in damages...

A Consultation Paper produced by the Law Commission, examining administrative remedies, has also commented on the absence of damages for administrative wrong.

● **Law Commission,** *Administrative Redress: Public Bodies and the Citizen—Summary of Consultation Paper 187* (London: HMSO, July 2008), para. 1.21

Having regard to examples drawn from existing case law, our preliminary view is that this situation is clearly problematic. The addition of a monetary remedy for those already available may be required to provide a satisfactory set of remedies in an individual citizen's case.

NOTE

For a full discussion of the complexities of introducing administrative damages and the system of administrative redress, see the full text of the Law Commission Consultation Paper available online at http://www.justice.gov.uk/lawcommission/docs/cp187_Administrative_Redress_Consultation.pdf

---

19.3 The prerogative remedies: quashing order, prohibiting order, and mandatory order

As we have seen above, the prerogative remedies are mandatory orders, prohibiting orders, and quashing orders. These remedies were traditionally exercised by the courts as a way of controlling inferior courts, tribunals, and public authorities. In *R v Electricity Commissioners, ex p London Electricity Joint Committee* [1924] 1 KB 171, Atkin LJ stated as follows.

• *R v Electricity Commissioners, ex p London Electricity Joint Committee* [1924] 1 KB 171

Atkin LJ at 205:

> Whenever any body of persons having legal authority to determine questions affecting the rights of subjects, and having the duty to act judicially, act in excess of their legal authority, they are subject to the controlling jurisdiction of the King's Bench Division exercised in these writs.

This statement was made in the 1920s and seems dated. This is because judicial review has developed since this time and phrases such as 'acting judicially' are no longer very helpful. The courts will now judicially review a wide range of decisions and the term 'rights' is interpreted very broadly to include many different interests. However, this dictum remains the starting point for the discussion in major texts on quashing orders and prohibition. It does convey the courts' determination to assert its authority over administrative bodies.

19.3.1 A quashing order

A quashing order invalidates a decision that has already been made. Traditionally, a quashing order (formerly certiorari) was used by the courts to quash (invalidate) the decision of inferior courts and tribunals.

• C. Lewis, *Judicial Remedies in Public Law* (London: Sweet & Maxwell, 2004), pp. 205–6

> The primary purpose of a quashing order in modern administrative law is to quash an ultra vires decision. The order is technically an order bringing a decision of a public body to the High Court

so that the court may determine whether the decision is valid. Where the decision is ultra vires a quashing order will issue to quash the decision. By quashing the decision, the order confirms that the decision is a nullity and is to be deprived of all legal effect. In modern terms, quashing orders are the means of controlling unlawful exercises of power by setting aside decisions reached in excess or abuse of power. The House of Lords has said that a quashing order is the primary and most appropriate remedy for achieving the nullification of a public law decision (*Cocks v Thanet District Council*).

cross reference
See Chapter 18 for more on Barnsley.

The following are examples of cases in which a quashing order (certiorari) has been used.

- *R v Barnsley MBC, ex p Hook* [1976] 1 WLR 1052   Certiorari (a quashing order) was granted to invalidate the decision of a local authority committee, which had revoked the market trader's licence. It was held that there had been a breach of the rule against bias.

- *Re Duffy (FC) (Northern Ireland)* [2008] UKHL 4   The decision of the Secretary of State for Northern Ireland to appoint certain individuals with well-known partisan views to the Parades Commission was held to be unreasonable. The House of Lords granted a quashing order to nullify the decision.

cross reference
See Chapter 17 for more on Duffy.

A quashing order overturns the decision of the public authority. It may also be combined with another remedy, such as a mandatory order, demanding that the authority reconsider the decision. A failure to comply with a quashing order, for example by pursuing the decision that has been quashed, is a contempt of court.

19.3.2 A prohibiting order

A prohibiting order forbids the authority from carrying out a proposed course of action. Failure to obey a prohibiting order is a contempt of court and the rules for its application are similar to those relating to a quashing order. A quashing order invalidates a decision that has already been made, whereas prohibition is usually used to prevent a proposed course of action, as Lewis explains.

● **C. Lewis,** *Judicial Remedies in Public Law* (London: Sweet & Maxwell, 2004), p. 224

> A quashing order issues to quash a decision that has already been reached and is unlawful. A prohibiting order may operate at an earlier stage to prevent the body from acting unlawfully and reaching flawed decisions.

Prohibition was granted by the court in *R v Electricity Commissioners, ex p London Electricity Joint Committee Co* [1924] 1 KB 171. The Electricity Commissioners were a statutory body empowered, in accordance with the Electricity (Supply) Act 1919, to organise the supply of electricity. The Commissioners proposed to reorganise the bodies supplying electricity in London by creating a joint authority with two committees, to which different powers were delegated. Such a scheme would then be submitted to **Parliament** for approval. Two existing electricity companies claimed that the scheme was unlawful and applied to the court for various remedies, including prohibition. The court granted the order, stating that prohibition was the most sensible remedy, because it would prevent further expenditure on an unlawful scheme.

● *R v Electricity Commissioners, ex p London Electricity Joint Committee Co* [1924] 1 KB 171

Atkin LJ at 206:

> If the proceedings establish that the body complained of is exceeding its jurisdiction by entertaining matters which would result in its final decision being subject to being brought

up and quashed on certiorari, I think that prohibition will lie to restrain it from so exceeding its jurisdiction...

...All we say is that it is not a scheme within the provisions of the Act of 1919. That it is convenient to have the point of law decided before further expense and trouble are incurred seems beyond controversy. I think therefore that the appeal should be allowed, so far as the writ of prohibition is concerned, and that the rule for the issue of the writ should be made absolute.

Another use of prohibition occurred in the case of *R v Liverpool Corporation, ex p Taxi Fleet Operators' Association* [1972] 2 QB 299. Liverpool Corporation was proposing to increase substantially the number of taxi licences in Liverpool. It failed to consult with existing licence holders despite having represented that it would not act without conferring with them. The Court of Appeal granted prohibition (prohibiting order) to prevent Liverpool Corporation from increasing the number of taxi licences without consulting with existing licence holders. Lord Denning explains the impact of the order.

● *R v Liverpool Corporation, ex p Taxi Fleet Operators' Association* [1972] 2 QB 299

Lord Denning at 308:

The order should prohibit the corporation or their committee or sub-committee from acting on the resolutions of November 16, 1971, December 8, 1971, and December 22, 1971; in particular, from granting any further number of licences pursuant to section 37 of the Town Police Clauses Act 1847 over and above the 300 currently existing, without first hearing any representations which may be made by or on behalf of any persons interested therein, including the applicants in this case and any other matters relevant thereto, including the undertaking recorded in the town clerk's letter of August 11. If prohibition goes in those terms, it means that the relevant committee, subcommittee and the corporation themselves can look at the matter afresh. They will hear all those interested and come to a right conclusion as to what is to be done about the number of taxicabs on the streets of Liverpool.

In effect, the corporation was prohibited from going ahead with the scheme until it had consulted with the interested parties about the appropriate number of taxi cabs.

19.3.3 A mandatory order

Mandatory orders are used to command a public authority to carry out its statutory duty.

● H. Woolf, J. L. Jowell, and A. Le Sueur, *De Smith's Judicial Review* (6th edn, London: Sweet & Maxwell, 2007), para. 18–024

If the court has found there to be a breach of a duty, a mandatory order may be granted if in all the circumstances that appears to the court to be the appropriate form of relief...

cross reference
See Chapter 15 for more on the Fleet Street Casuals *case.*

The mandatory order is very similar in its effect to a mandatory injunction. It is usually used by individuals asking the court to order the authority to take particular action. So, for example, in *R v Inland Revenue Commissioners, ex p National Federation of Self-Employed and Small Businesses Ltd* [1982] AC 617 (the *Fleet Street Casuals* case), the claimants demanded that mandamus be granted to order the Inland Revenue to carry out its statutory duty to collect taxes. The court refused to grant a remedy, because it held that the Inland Revenue had lawfully exercised its **discretion**. But the case is a good example of the potential use of mandamus.

A mandatory order can also be used by one public body against another. For example, in the historic case of *R v Poplar Borough Council, ex p London County Council (No 1)* [1922] KB 72, London County Council obtained an order of mandamus against Poplar Borough Council compelling it to pay its portion of the rates to London County Council in accordance with the statute. Failure to obey an order of mandamus is a contempt of court, and when Poplar Borough Council refused to pay, the councillors were jailed for contempt of court.

A mandatory order may be used to order an authority to exercise its discretion in accordance with law. In *Padfield v Minister of Agriculture, Fisheries and Food* [1968] AC 997, the House of Lords upheld the decision of the judge at first instance. He had made an order of mandamus ordering the minister to consider an application to refer a complaint about the Milk Marketing Board 'according to law and upon relevant considerations to the exclusion of irrelevant considerations'.

cross reference

See Chapter 16 for more on *Padfield*.

A mandatory order is often combined with a quashing order. The quashing order will invalidate the original decision and a mandatory order will command the authority to consider the decision or to exercise its discretion in accordance with law. In *R v Tower Hamlets London Borough Council, ex p Chetnik Developments Ltd* [1988] AC 858, the claimant alleged that the local authority had unlawfully failed to refund an overpayment of rates (local taxes). The House of Lords held that none of the reasons given by the local authority justified the retention of the money in accordance with the relevant statute. The original decision not to refund the rates was quashed by certiorari and the court then made an order for mandamus, directing the authority to hear and determine an application for a refund of rates.

A mandatory order is an effective and powerful remedy, because it directs the public authority to take action. It is often used to direct the public authority to carry out its statutory decision or to reconsider a decision that has been quashed.

19.4 Refusal of a remedy

The ordinary remedies of injunction and declaration are equitable remedies, which means that they are discretionary. The prerogative remedies are also discretionary and can be refused by the court. This is so even if the claimant shows that the public authority has acted unlawfully and the claim for judicial review has been made within the strict time limit imposed in judicial review cases. Because each remedy is different and has various consequences, there is case law on each remedy. So, we have seen, for example, that the courts are often more reluctant to grant mandatory injunctions or mandatory orders that compel public authorities to take particular action. This is because doing so may be viewed as too great an interference with the power of the authority. The court may prefer to grant a declaration instead. This enables the authority to consider the law, as stated by the court, and to decide how best to proceed.

cross reference

See Chapter 14 for more on the time limit imposed in judicial review cases.

Over the years, a large body of case law has built up attached to the grant of each remedy and the circumstances under which each remedy may be refused may vary. The following discussion attempts to explain the general type of situation that may cause the court to refuse a remedy.

Usually, the courts will grant an appropriate remedy when the claimant has shown that one of the grounds of review is satisfied and that the authority has acted unlawfully. However, there are some occasions on which the court has refused to grant a remedy. This may be because invalidation of the decision may cause a high degree of disruption. So, for example, in *R v Secretary of State for Social Services, ex p Association of Metropolitan Authorities* [1986] 1 WLR

1, the minister had failed to consult with interested groups, as required by the Housing Benefits Act 1982, before drafting regulations. The court held that he had acted unlawfully. But in this instance the court decided not to quash the regulations, as would normally be the case. This was because the complaint was about the failure to consult rather than the substance of the regulations; because the regulations had been in force for six months, it would be disruptive to invalidate them. The court was, however, prepared to grant a declaration stating that the failure to consult was unlawful.

Another important case in which a remedy was refused was *R v Monopolies and Mergers Commission, ex p Argyll Group plc* [1986] 1 WLR 763. The case concerned a dispute between two companies over a takeover bid for a company. The Monopolies and Mergers Commission decided not to pursue an investigation in its early stages after controversial aspects of the bid had been abandoned. The court held that the chairman should not have taken the decision alone, because this was contrary to the statutory provisions. However, the court refused to grant a remedy. This was because third parties may have relied on the decision, it was likely the Commission would take the same decision again, and, as Lord Donaldson stated (at 774), 'good public administration requires decisiveness and finality'.

There are some older cases in which the courts have taken into account the claimant's conduct in deciding not to grant a remedy. In *Glynn v Keele University* [1971] 1 WLR 487, a student disciplined for parading naked on campus was excluded from residence at the university. There had been a breach of natural justice, but the court exercised its discretion and refused to grant an injunction. This was because there was no dispute on the facts, it was a serious offence, and in the view of the judge there had been no injustice to the claimant.

If there is an alternative remedy available to the claimant, then the court will usually expect this to be pursued. So, for example, in *R v Secretary of State for the Home Department, ex p Swati* [1986] 1 WLR 477, the claimant challenged the refusal of temporary entry to the UK by an immigration officer at Heathrow Airport. The official was not satisfied that the claimant intended to leave at the end of his visit. The court held that there were no grounds to review the decision.

. . . .

● *R v Secretary of State for the Home Department, ex p Swati* [1986] 1 WLR 477

Sir John Donaldson at 485:

> However, the matter does not stop there, because it is well established that in giving or refusing leave to apply for judicial review, account must be taken of alternative remedies available to the applicant. This aspect was considered by this court very recently . . . and it was held that the jurisdiction would not be exercised where there was an alternative remedy by way of appeal, save in exceptional circumstances. By definition, exceptional circumstances defy definition, but where Parliament provides an appeal procedure, judicial review will have no place, unless the applicant can distinguish his case from the type of case for which the appeal procedure was provided.

cross reference
See the fuller discussion on alternative statutory procedures to judicial review in Chapter 14.

The court then stated that the claimant should have appealed using the statutory appeal procedure rather than applied for judicial review. This should normally be the case unless there are exceptional circumstances. This means that the court reserves the discretion to allow claims for judicial review, when there is a statutory appeal process, but it will be exercised sparingly.

summary points

Refusal of a remedy

- *The courts generally grant a remedy if the claimant can show that the public authority has acted unlawfully.*
- *The courts do have a discretion to refuse to grant a remedy.*

- *The courts have refused remedies where:*
  - *granting a remedy would cause a high degree of disruption;*
  - *a third party has relied on the decision;*
  - *the claimant has been guilty of misconduct; and*
  - *there is an effective alternative remedy available.*

Remedies and the Human Rights Act 1998 (HRA 1998)

19.5.1 Remedies available under the HRA 1998

The Human Rights Act 1998 (HRA 1998) provides that remedies may be granted if a breach of a Convention right is established (section 8). But the court must have the authority to grant the remedy in question. So, for example, a magistrates' court will not award damages for breach of a Convention right because such courts do not generally have the power to award damages. However, the **Administrative Court** can grant remedies, such as damages, or an injunction, or any of the prerogative orders, in pursuance of a human rights claim. In other words, the Administrative Court is able to grant all of the remedies at its disposal for a breach of the HRA 1998, including damages if this is appropriate.

If a court is considering granting a remedy that might affect the exercise of freedom of expression, usually an injunction, then it must have particular regard to the significance of freedom of expression. This might arise, for example, where a court is asked for an injunction by government to protect confidential information that a newspaper wants to publish or where individuals ask the court to grant an injunction to prevent the disclosure of confidential information. These sorts of claim are not brought by judicial review and will not be considered further here.

cross reference
See section 12 of the HRA 1998 for more details of these sorts of claim.

Section 8 of the HRA 1998 outlines the relevant principles on remedies.

609

Human Rights Act 1998

Section 8 Judicial remedies

(1) In relation to any act (or proposed act) of a public authority which the court finds is (or would be) unlawful, it may grant such relief or remedy, or make such order, within its powers as it considers just and appropriate.

(2) But damages may be awarded only by a court which has power to award damages, or to order the payment of compensation, in civil proceedings.

(3) No award of damages is to be made unless, taking account of all the circumstances of the case, including—

(a) any other relief or remedy granted, or order made, in relation to the act in question (by that or any other court), and

(b) the consequences of any decision (of that or any other court) in respect of that act, the court is satisfied that the award is necessary to afford just satisfaction to the person in whose favour it is made.

(4) In determining—

(a) whether to award damages, or

(b) the amount of an award,

the court must take into account the principles applied by the European Court of Human Rights in relation to the award of compensation under Article 41 of the Convention.

...

(6) In this section—

'court' includes a tribunal;

'damages' means damages for an unlawful act of a public authority; and

'unlawful' means unlawful under section 6(1).

19.5.2 Damages

The courts have a general discretion to award damages if the public authority has acted unlawfully under section 6(1) of the HRA 1998. This means that a claim for damages may be made in a non-judicial-review tort claim. However, the Administrative Court can also grant damages on judicial review. The Court may grant damages only if it thinks that it is just and appropriate to do so, and if it is satisfied that the award is necessary to afford just satisfaction. When the Court considers the amount of damages to award, it must apply the principles established by the European Court of Human Rights (ECtHR) when it awards compensation under Article 41 ECHR. These principles aim to put the claimant in the position in which he or she would have been had the unlawful act not occurred. The House of Lords has stressed that damages are not the primary award under the HRA 1998 and that generally they should be awarded sparingly. On some occasions, a simple acknowledgement of the wrong done or an apology will be sufficient.

In *R (on the application of Greenfield) v Secretary of State for the Home Department* [2005] 1 WLR 673, it was held that the claimant, a prisoner, had been subject to disciplinary proceedings in breach of his rights under Article 6, because he was denied legal representation. As a consequence, he had to spend an additional twenty-one days in prison. The Home Secretary acknowledged that there had been a breach of the claimant's rights, but declined to pay damages. The House of Lords refused to grant damages and, following the ECtHR case law, held that, in general, damages would not be awarded for breaches of Article 6. It noted that, in most Article 6 cases, the finding that there had been an infringement of the claimant's right was itself just satisfaction without an award of damages being made. This reflects the focus of the Convention being on just satisfaction rather than on the award of damages.

In the earlier decision of *Anufrijeva v Southwark Borough Council* [2004] QB 1124, the Court of Appeal stressed that the award of damages in cases involving **maladministration** (poor administrative practice) should be modest. This decision involved three different cases in which it was argued that there was a breach of the right to family life in Article 8 ECHR because of various failings in the asylum process and, in one of the cases, a failure to provide suitable housing. The claims were rejected on the merits, but the Court went on to discuss the correct approach to an award of damages.

● **Anufrijeva v Southwark Borough Council** [2004] QB 1124

Lord Woolf:

> [75] We have indicated that a finding of a breach of a positive obligation under article 8 to provide support will be rare, and will be likely to occur only where this impacts severely on family life. Where such a breach does occur, it is unlikely that there will be any ready comparator to assist in the assessment of damages. There are good reasons why, where the breach arises from maladministration, in those cases where an award of damages is appropriate, the scale of such damages should be modest. The cost of supporting those in need falls on society as a whole. Resources are limited and payments of substantial damages will deplete the resources available for other needs of the public including primary care. If the impression is created that asylum seekers whether genuine or not are profiting from their status, this could bring the HRA into disrepute.

The Court was keen to stress that an award of damages under the HRA 1998 should be modest. Public authorities have limited funds and if excessive amounts were to be paid in damages, this would reduce the amount that the authority has to spend on other services.

cross reference
For a discussion of the office of ombudsmen, see Chapter 13.

An example of a case in which damages were awarded under the HRA 1998 is *R (on the application of Bernard) v Enfield London Borough Council* [2002] EWHC 2282. Damages were awarded against a local authority for a breach of the right to family life contrary to Article 8 ECHR. In this case, the authority had failed to provide suitable accommodation for a seriously disabled woman and her family, and £10,000 was awarded. The judge assessed damages based on the awards of the Local Government Ombudsman.

● **R (on the application of Bernard) v Enfield London Borough Council)** [2002] EWHC 2282

611

Sullivan J:

> [60] The Local Government Ombudsman's recommended awards are the best available United Kingdom comparables. Although I am awarding damages under s.8 as just satisfaction for a breach of the claimants' Art.8 rights, this case is, in essence, an extreme example of maladministration which has deprived the ... claimant of much needed social services care (suitably adapted accommodation) for a lengthy period: some 20 months.

Thinking point
Why do you think damages are granted sparingly in human rights cases?

Damages

- The court in question must have the power to award damages.

- The Administrative Court has the power to award damages in judicial review cases in which the claimant establishes that a Convention right has been breached.

- The public authority must have acted unlawfully.

- The court must think that it is just and appropriate to grant damages, and that the award is necessary to afford just satisfaction.

- The court must take into account the principles applied by the European Court of Human Rights. These principles aim to put the party in the position in which he or she would have been had the illegality not occurred.

- Damages are granted sparingly and, on some occasions, an apology will be sufficient.

19.5.3 Section 4 of the HRA 1998: a declaration of incompatibility

A declaration of incompatibility is a statement by the court that a statutory provision is in conflict with the ECHR. It is a unique order and only those courts listed in section 4(5) of the HRA 1998 can make such an order. These are the higher courts and include the High Court, Court of Appeal, and Supreme Court. Section 4 of the HRA 1998 is set out below.

Human Rights Act 1998

Section 4 Declaration of incompatibility

(1) Subsection (2) applies in any proceedings in which a court determines whether a provision of primary legislation is compatible with a Convention right.

(2) If the court is satisfied that the provision is incompatible with a Convention right, it may make a declaration of that incompatibility.

(3) Subsection (4) applies in any proceedings in which a court determines whether a provision of subordinate legislation, made in the exercise of a power conferred by primary legislation, is compatible with a Convention right.

(4) If the court is satisfied—

    (a) that the provision is incompatible with a Convention right, and

    (b) that (disregarding any possibility of revocation) the primary legislation concerned prevents removal of the incompatibility,

it may make a declaration of that incompatibility.

(5) In this section 'court' means—

    (a) the Supreme Court;

    (b) the Judicial Committee of the Privy Council;

    (c) the Court Martial Appeal Court;

    (d) in Scotland, the High Court of Justiciary sitting otherwise than as a trial court or the Court of Session;

    (e) in England and Wales or Northern Ireland, the High Court or the Court of Appeal;

    (f) the Court of Protection, in any matter being dealt with by the President of the Family Division, the Vice-Chancellor or a puisne judge of the High Court.

(6) A declaration under this section ('a declaration of incompatibility')—

    (a) does not affect the validity, continuing operation or enforcement of the provision in respect of which it is given; and

    (b) is not binding on the parties to the proceedings in which it is made.

If a claimant argues that there is an apparent incompatibility between a statutory provision and the ECHR, the court will try to reconcile the difference using its interpretive powers provided in section 3 of the HRA 1998.

> **Human Rights Act 1998**
>
> ●
>
> **Section 3 Interpretation of legislation**
>
> (1) So far as it is possible to do so, primary legislation and subordinate legislation must be read and given effect in a way which is compatible with the Convention rights.
>
> …

cross reference
See Chapter 9 for the full text of section 3 of the HRA 1998.

However, if the court finds that it is not possible to reconcile the statute with the Convention, then the court has no power to invalidate the statute, because section 3(2) states that this 'does not affect the validity, continuing operation or enforcement of any incompatible primary legislation'. But the court can grant a declaration of incompatibility stating its view that the relevant provision of the statute is contrary to the ECHR.

The effect of a declaration of incompatibility is largely political. This is because the court does not have the power to invalidate the law in question. The declaration is not binding on the parties to the case and this means it does not have an impact on those involved in the decision. So if the court grants a declaration of incompatibility, it does not affect the legal position of the parties to the case.

However, the declaration of incompatibility may have political consequences, because the government may then decide to introduce legislation to correct the inconsistency. It can either introduce a Bill amending the law using the normal parliamentary proceedings, or it can amend the law by introducing a **remedial order** to Parliament under section 10 of the HRA 1998.

> **Human Rights Act 1998**
>
> ●
>
> **Section 10 Power to take remedial action**
>
> (1) This section applies if—
>
> (a) a provision of legislation has been declared under section 4 to be incompatible with a Convention right and, if an appeal lies—
>
> (i) all persons who may appeal have stated in writing that they do not intend to do so;
>
> (ii) the time for bringing an appeal has expired and no appeal has been brought within that time; or
>
> (iii) an appeal brought within that time has been determined or abandoned; or
>
> (b) it appears to a Minister of the Crown or Her Majesty in Council that, having regard to a finding of the European Court of Human Rights made after the coming into force of this section in proceedings against the United Kingdom, a provision of legislation is incompatible with an obligation of the United Kingdom arising from the Convention.
>
> (2) If a Minister of the Crown considers that there are compelling reasons for proceeding under this section, he may by order make such amendments to the legislation as he considers necessary to remove the incompatibility…

Section 10, together with Schedule 2, provide a fast-track method for amending legislation. Essentially, they allow legislation that has been held to be incompatible to be changed

cross reference

See Chapter 9 for more on declarations of incompatibility.

using the speedier process normally used for subordinate legislation. This procedure can also be used where the ECtHR rules that a provision in UK law is incompatible with the Convention.

Below are examples of cases in which the courts have made declarations of incompatibility under section 4 of the HRA 1998. In some cases, they have led to an amendment of the law by way of remedial order under section 10 of the HRA 1998.

summary points

Section 4 of the HRA 1998: a declaration of incompatibility

- *A declaration of incompatibility is a statement from the court that statutory provisions are in conflict with the ECHR.*

- *A declaration of incompatibility may be used if the court is unable to exercise its interpretive powers under section 3 of the HRA 1998 to reconcile the statutory provisions with the Convention.*

- *The HRA 1998 does not give the courts the power to invalidate legislation.*

- *A declaration of incompatibility is not binding on the parties to the case and does not change their legal position.*

- *The declaration of incompatibility may have political consequences, because the government may decide to introduce legislation to Parliament to change the law.*

- *The government may use section 10 of the HRA 1998 to fast-track legislation through Parliament in order to remove the offending provisions.*

19.5.4 Examples of declarations of incompatibility

One of the most well-known human rights cases is *A v Secretary of State for the Home Department* [2004] UKHL 56 (the **Belmarsh Detainees** case). The House of Lords held that the indefinite detention of the claimants, foreign nationals suspected of terrorist activities who could not be deported, was in breach of the Convention. The court granted a declaration of incompatibility, stating that section 23 of the Anti-Terrorism, Crime and Security Act 2001 was in breach of Articles 5 and 14 of the Convention. Baroness Hale explained the impact of a declaration of incompatibility.

● *A and others v Secretary of State for the Home Department* [2004] UKHL 56 [the *Belmarsh Detainees case*]

Baroness Hale:

[220] We do not have power in these proceedings to order that the detainees be released. This is not a challenge to the individual decisions to detain them ... Before us is a challenge to the validity of the law under which the detainees are detained. That law is contained in an Act of Parliament, the Anti-terrorism, Crime and Security Act 2001. The Human Rights Act 1998 is careful to preserve the sovereignty of Parliament. The courts cannot strike down the laws which the Queen in Parliament has passed. However, if the court is satisfied that a provision in an Act of Parliament is incompatible with a Convention right, it may make a declaration of that incompatibility (under section 4 of the 1998 Act). This does not invalidate the provision or anything done under it. But Government and Parliament then have to decide what action to take to remedy the matter.

thinking point

Why are the courts unable to invalidate legislation? You may want to reread Chapter 9 before you answer this question.

cross reference

For a more detailed explanation of the Prevention of Terrorism Act 2005, see Chapter 20.

NOTE

Baroness Hale emphasises the limited powers of the courts under section 4 of the HRA 1998, and stresses that it is up to the government and Parliament to remedy any breach of the Convention. The facts of this case are stated more fully in Chapter 17 and the implications of this case, in the context of the anti-terror laws, are explored in Chapter 20.

After the decision, the government introduced new legislation to Parliament that later became the Prevention of Terrorism Act 2005. This addressed the issues raised by the House of Lords in the case and introduced a controversial system of **control orders** that avoided detention, but restricted individuals' movements and communication within their homes.

A declaration of incompatibility was also granted by the House of Lords in *Bellinger v Bellinger* [2003] UKHL 21. In this case, a male-to-female transsexual who wanted to marry in her acquired sex was prevented from doing so by section 11 of the Matrimonial Causes Act 1973. The legislation required marriage to be between a man and a woman, which sex was to be determined at birth. The House of Lords refused to use its powers under section 3 of the HRA 1998 to interpret the term 'woman' as including a man who had undergone a sex change to become a woman. The House of Lords issued a declaration of incompatibility under section 4 of the HRA 1998 on the grounds that section 11 of the Matrimonial Causes Act 1973 was incompatible with the right to family and private life under Article 8 ECHR and the right to marry under Article 12. The Gender Recognition Act 2004 was subsequently passed to enable transsexuals to marry in their acquired sex. The short extract that follows discusses the court's reasons for granting the declaration of incompatibility rather than using its interpretive powers under section 3 of the HRA 1998.

● **Bellinger v Bellinger** [2003] UKHL 21

Lord Nicholls:

> [36] Despite this, I am firmly of the view that your Lordships' House, sitting in its judicial capacity, ought not to accede to the submissions made on behalf of Mrs Bellinger. Recognition of Mrs Bellinger as female for the purposes of section 11(c) of the Matrimonial Causes Act 1973 would necessitate giving the expressions 'male' and 'female' in that Act a novel, extended meaning: that a person may be born with one sex but later become, or become regarded as, a person of the opposite sex.
>
> [37] This would represent a major change in the law, having far reaching ramifications. It raises issues whose solution calls for extensive enquiry and the widest public consultation and discussion. Questions of social policy and administrative feasibility arise at several points, and their interaction has to be evaluated and balanced. The issues are altogether ill-suited for determination by courts and court procedures. They are pre-eminently a matter for Parliament, the more especially when the government, in unequivocal terms, has already announced its intention to introduce comprehensive primary legislation on this difficult and sensitive subject.

Here, the House of Lords chose not to use its interpretive powers under section 3 of the HRA 1998 to try to reconcile the statute with Articles 8 and 12 ECHR; instead, the court granted a declaration of incompatibility under section 4 of the HRA 1998. The court's reasoning includes the fact that the issues are too complex to be dealt with by way of interpretation by the courts; it is Parliament's job to pass legislation in this difficult area.

# Summary

When applying for judicial review, it is important to consider what remedies will be most effective. A quashing order will invalidate a decision that has already been made, whilst a prohibiting order will prevent an authority from going ahead with a plan of action that is unlawful. A mandatory order will order the authority to take a particular action, such as to carry out a statutory duty that it has neglected; it can also be used to order an authority to reconsider its decision after it has been quashed by the court. Breach of any of the prerogative orders is a contempt of court. The ordinary remedies of injunction, declaration, and damages are available on judicial review. Injunctions can be granted against a minister of the Crown and interim injunctions can be granted to preserve the parties' legal position until the full judicial review has been heard. The Attorney General has the power to apply for an injunction against any public authority and can also lend his or her name to a claimant who wants to apply for an injunction in a relator action. Breach of an injunction is a contempt of court. Another very useful remedy is a declaration: this simply declares the legal position between the parties and may be all that is necessary to clarify a legal dispute. There must be an actual dispute between the parties and a declaration cannot be used for a purely academic question. Breach of a declaration is not a contempt of court, but this is not generally problematic, because public authorities will respect a court order. Damages can be claimed on judicial review if the claimant can show that there has been a private law wrong, such as a breach of contract or tort. Damages can also be claimed under section 8 of the HRA 1998, as explained above. Otherwise, the court has no power to allow a claim for damages for an administrative wrong, such as incompetence or delay.

The court has the power to refuse the prerogative remedies, and a declaration and an injunction, even if it has been shown that the public authority or inferior body has acted unlawfully. Remedies have been refused on the grounds that the claimant should have pursued an alternative remedy, that it would be too disruptive, and that the claimant has been guilty of misconduct.

The HRA 1998 provides that the court can grant any remedy for a breach of a Convention right that the court ordinarily has power to grant. On judicial review, this means that the Administrative Court can grant all of the remedies discussed above. In addition, the Court can award damages for breach of a Convention right by a public authority contrary to section 6 of the HRA 1998. The courts must follow the principles laid down by the European Court of Human Rights for damages claims. Case law subsequent to the HRA 1998 shows that the courts take a cautious approach to the grant of damages and that they are awarded sparingly. A declaration that the action was unlawful and/or an apology has been held by the courts to be sufficient in some cases.

One remedy unique to the HRA 1998 is a declaration of incompatibility under section 4 that a statutory provision is incompatible with a Convention right. It does not alter the legal position of the parties to the case, but it may have political consequences. The government has the option, under section 10 of the HRA 1998, of introducing legislation to Parliament using a fast-track process to amend the offending provision. It can also introduce a Bill to Parliament to deal with the inconsistency. Such a declaration is not binding on the parties to the case and does not invalidate the legislation.

Questions

1 Do you think that damages should be available for administrative wrongs?

2 Do you think that it is right that the court has a discretion to refuse a remedy?

3 Explain the various remedies that the court can grant and what the impact of each remedy is on the public authority.

4 If a declaration of incompatibility does not have a legal effect, then what is the point of applying for one?

 # Further reading

Cane, P., 'The constitutional basis of judicial remedies in public law', in P. Leyland and T. Woods (eds) *Administrative Law Facing the Future: Old Constraints and New Horizons* (London: Blackstone, 1997), pp. 242–70

Cane explains how the courts decide which remedy to grant in the context of constitutional principles such as the **separation of powers**.

Craig, P., *Administrative Law* (6th edn, London: Sweet & Maxwell, 2008)

See especially Chapter 25, which provides a comprehensive and analytical account of the remedies available on judicial review.

Horne, A., 'The substitutionary remedy under CPR 54.19(3): a final word' [2007] Judicial Review 135

This article discusses section 141 of the Tribunals, Courts and Services Act 2007 and CPR 54.19(3), which allows the court, in certain limited circumstances, to substitute its own decision for that of the relevant decision-maker.

Lewis, C., *Judicial Remedies in Public Law* (London: Sweet & Maxwell, 2004)

A very detailed practitioners' text on remedies that is written in an accessible way and which may be useful for reference purposes.

Lewis, C., 'Current issues in remedies in judicial review' [2010] Judicial Review 144

This provides an update on recent developments in the law on remedies.

20

A Case Study: human rights, terrorism, and public law principles

Key points

This chapter will cover

- The background to the law on terrorism in the UK

- What is the definition of 'terrorism'?

- An outline of the recent legislation on terrorism

- Accountability and anti-terrorist powers

- Extraordinary powers: indefinite detention, control orders, and terrorism prevention and investigation measures (TPIMs)

Introduction

This chapter will consider the challenges that recent terrorist activity has posed in the UK. It will provide an opportunity for you to see how principles such as the rule of law, the separation of powers, and the sovereignty of parliament work in practice.

The prevention, investigation, and prosecution of terrorism have presented enormous difficulties for constitutional democracies like the UK. Special legal powers are often required because of the loss of life and fear caused by terrorism. If the compatibility of these laws with the European Convention of Human Rights (ECHR) is challenged, the judges will have to make difficult decisions. They will have to decide whether breaches of human rights can be justified in accordance with the ECHR. Often, the courts will apply the principle of proportionality, and will have to decide whether to defer or not to the executive or Parliament. This may lead judges into conflict with the executive, which may believe that the anti-terrorist laws in question are necessary to protect the public. Judges might also be accused of failing to respect parliamentary sovereignty. Alternatively, judges may be criticised for being too timid and for not protecting human rights sufficiently. This raises difficult questions about the role of judges in upholding the rule of law and their correct functions within the framework of the separation of powers.

We will focus on the government's attempt to deal with the problem of those suspected of terrorist activity, but who cannot be deported or prosecuted. We will consider the background to the anti-terrorist laws, the definition of terrorism, and methods of legal and political accountability. We will then look more closely at some of the important case law on indefinite detention and control orders. Finally, we will discuss the introduction of terrorist prevention and investigation measures (TPIMs). However, there have been many other legal controversies generated by anti-terrorist legislation. These include, for example, the police power to stop and search at random, and pre-charge detention in terrorist cases. There is further reading at the end of the chapter if you want to find a more detailed account of other aspects of these laws. If you find this subject particularly interesting, you may be able to consider it further in relation to human rights later in your course of study.

NOTE

You may find it helpful to reread the material in Chapter 14 on the role of the courts and the Human Rights Act 1998, and the discussion of **judicial deference** in Chapter 17. These explain how tensions between the **executive** and the courts may arise in human rights cases.

20.1 The background to the law on terrorism in the UK

The UK has experienced a considerable degree of terrorist activity since the end of the Second World War. The main terrorist threat arose from the Troubles in Northern Ireland. During this conflict, there were terrorist attacks both in Northern Ireland and in Great Britain. The first terrorist law was the Prevention of Terrorism (Temporary Provisions) Act 1974. There were several other terrorist statutes passed after this and, because the legislation had the potential to severely limit people's human rights, it was decided, as a precaution, that it had to be renewed by **Parliament** on an annual basis. This legislation was eventually consolidated (that is, put together in one piece of legislation) in the Terrorism Act 2000, which was permanent and did not have to be renewed annually. This period in the history of the UK presented many human rights problems and the activities of the UK **government** were challenged in the European Court of Human Rights (ECtHR) by individuals arguing that their rights had been violated. During this period, the UK derogated from Article 5(3) of the **European Convention on Human Rights (ECHR)**, which protects the right to liberty and security of individuals under arrest. By following a specific procedure, Article 15 allows a **state** to suspend the application of some Convention rights in times of war or other public emergency threatening the life of the nation.

cross reference
The Troubles are discussed further in Chapter 10.

cross reference
See the discussion of different types of rights in Chapter 9.

It was the attack by Al-Qaeda on the World Trade Center in New York on 11 September 2001 (referred to as '9/11') that marked the beginning of a new phase in the history of terrorism. The subsequent attacks in Europe, including the bombings on 7 July 2005 in London, led to new legislation granting special and controversial powers to the executive to deal with the threat of terrorism.

thinking point

How can democracies like the UK protect themselves from terrorism without giving up the openness, human rights, and freedoms that they need to flourish? If we abandon human rights, are we letting the terrorists win?

20.2 What is the definition of 'terrorism'?

Terrorism is an international problem and one might expect that there is an authoritative definition on which all states agree. Unfortunately, this is not the case. The definition of 'terrorism' is important because, once an activity or a person is labelled a 'terrorist', there may be very serious consequences. The definition of terrorism in the UK is set out in section 1 of the Terrorism Act 2000.

Terrorism Act 2000

. . . .

Section 1 Terrorism: interpretation

(1) In this Act "terrorism" means the use or threat of action where—

(a) the action falls within subsection (2),

(b) the use or threat is designed to influence the government [or an international organisation] or to intimidate the public or a section of the public, and

(c) the use or threat is made for the purpose of advancing a political, religious, racial or ideological cause.

(2) Action falls within this subsection if it—

(a) involves serious violence against a person,

(b) involves serious damage to property,

(c) endangers a person's life, other than that of the person committing the action,

(d) creates a serious risk to the health or safety of the public or a section of the public, or

(e) is designed seriously to interfere with or seriously to disrupt an electronic system.

(3) The use or threat of action falling within subsection (2) which involves the use of firearms or explosive is terrorism whether or not subsection (1)(b) is satisfied.

(4) In this section—

(a) "action" includes action outside the United Kingdom,

(b) a reference to any person or to property is a reference to an person, or to property wherever situated,

(c) a reference to the public includes a reference to the public of a country other than the United Kingdom, and

(d) "the government" means the government of the United Kingdom, of a part of the United Kingdom or of a country other than the United Kingdom.

(5) In this Act a reference to action taken for the purposes of terrorism includes a reference to action taken for the benefit of a proscribed organisation.

The definition shows that terrorism is distinct from ordinary criminal offences, such as robbing a bank or defrauding an insurance company. This is because terrorism, unlike other offences, is committed in order to advance a political, racial, religious or ideological cause. As discussed above, much terrorism in the UK has arisen from the conflict in Northern Ireland and also from attacks by Al-Qaeda-inspired groups or individuals. But actions of, for example, animal liberation groups that cause serious damage to property could come within the definition.

The definition of terrorism

. . . .

1. There must be a use or threat of action that involves serious violence against a person, or serious damage to property, or endangers the life of any person, or creates a serious risk

to the health or safety of the public, or a section of the public, or is designed seriously to interfere with an electronic system.

2. The use or threat must be made in order to further a political, religious, racial or ideological cause.

3. The use or threat must be designed to influence the government or an international governmental organisation, or to intimidate the public or a section of the public. (This element is not needed if firearms or explosives are used.)

The definition of terrorism includes action taken against a foreign government and/or in a foreign state. This has been criticised by some commentators, who have argued that this means that individuals taking action against states that are totalitarian in nature may be labelled as terrorist. Harding discusses the main reason why there is no agreed definition.

● **C. Harding, 'The problem of definition of terrorism in international law', in P. Eden and T. O'Donnell [eds] *September 11, 2001: A Turning Point in International and Domestic Law?* [New York: Transnational Publishers, 2005], pp. 187–205, at 188**

One person's freedom fighter is another's terrorist. For Mrs Thatcher, Mr Cheney and the apartheid regime, Nelson Mandela was a terrorist; for many others he was a freedom fighter … It is largely a problem of perception. Those who perceive matters from the perspective of the state, see state violence as lawful, however much terror it may induce in the minds of the population. For them, individuals or organizations who oppose the authority of the state must do so within the limits of the law prescribed by the state, or, at most, by peaceful protest and action. Once they take up arms and resort to violence to overthrow the authority of the state, they become terrorists. If they seek to widen the conflict by directing their violence at public places that attract foreigners or at international transportation systems, they become international terrorists …

Harding explains that there is no consensus on whether violence in a just cause is morally permissible. He points out that Nelson Mandela was regarded as a terrorist by the South African state for advocating the violent overthrow of the racist apartheid regime. But, in 1991, he became the President of South Africa and is now held in high esteem around the world. The definition of terrorism in the UK was reviewed by Lord Carlisle in 2007. In his report, *The Definition of Terrorism: A Report by Lord Carlile of Berriew QC, Independent Reviewer of Terrorism Legislation* (Cm 7052, London: HMSO, 2007), at paragraph 50, he rejected the argument that violence in a just cause against an oppressive regime should not be considered terrorism. He thought that trying to distinguish between different kinds of violence was impractical. He also rejected the argument that offences against property should not be included as terrorism. He stated that acts that, for example, disrupted the gas or electricity system of a city could cause the loss of life and induce panic.

There are still some concerns that the definition of 'terrorism' is too wide and it is generally accepted that the prosecution has to exercise its **discretion** carefully when it decides whether or not to prosecute actions as 'terrorist'. It should not prosecute offences as terrorist unless they are sufficiently grave to deserve that label.

thinking point

Should someone who makes plans in London to use violence against persons or property abroad to overthrow a dictator such as (formerly) Saddam Hussein in Iraq or (formerly) Colonel Gaddafi in Libya be considered a terrorist?

An outline of the recent legislation on terrorism

As a response to the events of 9/11, Parliament passed the Anti-Terrorism, Crime and Security Act 2001. This was followed by more legislation against terrorism, including:

- the Prevention of Terrorism Act 2005;
- the Terrorism Act 2006;
- the Justice and Security (Northern Ireland) Act 2007;
- the Counter-Terrorism Act 2008;
- the Terrorist Prevention and Investigations Measures Act 2011 (the TPIM Act 2011);
- the Protection of Freedom Act 2011, which also has significant provisions on terrorism.

NOTE Action taken against terrorism is sometimes referred to as counter-terrorism.

NOTE

At the time of writing, the TPIMs Bill 2011 was before Parliament and had passed its second reading in the House of Lords. As explained below, it abolishes the system of **control orders** and replaces them by **terrorist prevention and investigations measures (TPIMs)**. The new legislation is intended to come into effect in January 2012 and it is consequently referred to here as the TPIM Act 2011.

In the next extract, McKeever comments on the reason why so much legislation on terrorism has appeared and briefly summarises the main provisions of some of the legislation.

● **D. McKeever, 'The Human Rights Act and anti-terrorism in the UK: one great leap forward by Parliament, but are the courts able to slow the steady retreat that has followed?'** (2010) Public Law 110, 116–19

Recent legislation in this field has brought about a rapid increase in the sheer number of terrorism-related offences. Between 2000 and 2005, new legislation resulted in the creation of 40 new terrorism-related offences.[1] This trend continued with the Terrorism Act 2006 (five new offences)[2] and the Counter-Terrorism Act 2008 (one new offence).[3]

Considering that new anti-terrorism legislation was introduced in 2000, 2001, 2005, 2006 and 2008, it is difficult to disagree with those who present these as largely 'panic measures'[4] designed to assuage public fears and prevent the perception of government inaction, rather than necessary, considered and proportionate responses to the actual threats that exist.

With new legislation being introduced so frequently, it can be difficult to keep track of the many dimensions of the current legal framework for combating terrorism. Some of the notable provisions of anti-terrorism legislation adopted since 2000 are as follows.

The Terrorism Act 2000 introduced the broad definition of 'terrorism' described above, gave the Home Secretary power to proscribe organisations 'concerned in terrorism' and criminalised various actions related to membership of, or support for, these organisations[5] (including, notably, wearing an item of clothing so as to 'arouse reasonable suspicion' of membership).[6] Section 41 of the Act provided for pre-charge detention of suspected terrorists of up to 48 hours, extendable up to seven days with judicial authorisation. The Act also created offences related to 'terrorist property'[7] and introduced new stop-and-search powers.[8] Other new offences related to weapons training, directing terrorist organisations, the possession of an article 'for terrorist purposes',[9] and the collection of information likely to be useful for terrorist purposes.[10] According to statistics provided by the Home Office to a Parliamentary Select Committee, as of October 2005 over 750 people had been arrested under the TA 2000, though only 22 of these individuals were subsequently convicted of offences under the Act.[11]

The Anti-Terrorism, Crime and Security Act (ATCSA) 2001 was introduced shortly after 9/11. Part 1 relates to the seizure of assets at the start of an investigation into possible terrorism, and created a new offence where financial institutions fail to report knowledge or suspicion of terrorist financing.[12] Part 2 expanded powers for the freezing of overseas assets, in case of threat to the UK economy and/or to the life or property of a UK resident.[13] The Act also created new offences relating to the use of nuclear, chemical and biological weapons.[14] Notably, Pt 4 of this Act allowed the indefinite detention, without charge, of any foreign national whom the Home Secretary had certified as a suspected international terrorist but who could not be deported from the United Kingdom.[15] As this detention regime would clearly violate art.5 ECHR, the Act provided that the United Kingdom could derogate from that article on the basis of a 'public emergency threatening the life of the nation'.[16] In terms of litigation relating to the provisions of the ATCSA 2001, 18 cases have so far reached the higher courts; two of these reached the House of Lords (HL) and are discussed below.

In response to a HL ruling in December 2004…, the Government introduced the Prevention of Terrorism Act (PTA) 2005. This empowered the Home Secretary to impose 'control orders' on persons suspected of terrorism. The 'non-derogating control orders' imposed a range of restrictions, relating not only to freedom of movement but also communication with others, work arrangements, use of telephone and internet services, electronic tagging, etc.[17] Where necessary, the Home Secretary can also apply to the court to make control orders which impose conditions incompatible with art.5 ECHR ('derogating control orders').[18] As of June 2009, 38 individuals have been subjected to non-derogating control orders under the PTA.[19] In terms of litigation relating to the provisions of the PTA, 23 cases have so far reached the higher courts. All but two of these cases related to control orders: indeed in just over four years the HL has already ruled four times on control orders.[20] As Lords Philips of Worth Matravers remarked in the most recent judgment, the control order regime has generated 'an extraordinary volume of litigation'.[21]

The UK Terrorism Act (TA) 2006 was introduced, at least in part, as a response to the London bombings of July 2005.[22] As discussed, it broadened the definition of terrorism slightly. Part 1 of the Act created a range of new offences including encouragement of terrorism (s.1), disseminating terrorist publications (s.2), preparation of terrorist acts (s.5), training for terrorism (s.6), and attendance at a place used for terrorist training (s.8), etc. Part 2 extended the powers of the Home Secretary to proscribe terrorist organisations (s.21). Most controversially, this Act sought to extend the period for pre-charge detention of persons suspected of terrorism. Following extended debates, the maximum period[23] was extended from 14 to 28 days.[24]

The 2008 Counter-Terrorism Act provides for post-charge questioning of terrorist suspects (s.22), and provides police with new powers for gathering and sharing terrorism-related information (Pt 1). As mentioned above, it also provides that a 'terrorist connection' must be considered as an aggravating factor in sentencing for a range of offences (ss.30–31). Individuals convicted of terrorism-related offences are required to notify the police of their whereabouts (Pt 4). Part 5 confers powers on the Treasury in respect of transactions with terrorism-related concerns.

1 P. Mendelle and A. N. Bajwa, 'Human rights and terrorism' (2008) 172 Justice of the Peace and Local Government Law 486, at p. 2 of the version published on Westlaw UK.

2 Encouragement of terrorism (s. 1), dissemination of terrorist publications (s. 2), preparation of terrorist acts (s. 5), training for terrorism (s. 6), and attendance at a place used for terrorist training (s. 8).

3 Eliciting, publishing or communicating information about members of armed forces etc. (s. 76).

4 C. Walker, 'Clamping down on terrorism in the United Kingdom' (2006) 4 Journal of International Criminal Justice 1137.

5 Terrorism Act 2000, ss. 3, 11 and 12.

6 Ibid, s. 13.

7 Ibid, ss. 14–18.

8 Ibid, s. 44.

9 Ibid, s. 57.

10 Ibid, s. 58.

11 According to the (then) Home Secretary, this statistic merely confirmed the difficulty of 'getting evidence to bring prosecution' for such offences (Select Committee on Home Affairs, *Draft Terrorism Bill: Minutes of Evidence—Examination of Witness, Rt Hon. Charles Clarke MP*, 11 October 2005, Q73 (Session 2005–06, HC Paper No. 515-I), available online at http://www.publications.parliament.uk/pa/cm200506/cmselect/cmhaff/515/5101105.htm [accessed 28 October 2009].

12 Anti-Terrorism, Crime and Security Act 2001, ss. 1–3.

13 Ibid, ss. 4–5.

14 Ibid, ss. 43, 47, 50 and 67.

15 Ibid, ss. 21–23.

16 Pursuant to ECHR Art. 15, see s. 30 of the 2001 Act. This derogation order came into force on 13 November 2001 (the Human Rights Act 1998 (Designated Derogation) Order 2001, SI 2001/3644), and was repealed on 8 April 2005 (the Human Rights Act 1998 (Amendment) Order 2005, SI 2005/1071).

17 Prevention of Terrorism Act 2005, s. 1.

18 Ibid, s. 4.

19 *AF* [2009] UKHL 28; The Times, 11 June 2009, [6]. To date, seven of the thirty-eight individuals have absconded. At time of writing, no derogating control orders have yet been imposed.

20 The four judgments in question are: *MB* [2007] UKHL 46, [2008] 1 AC 440; *Secretary of State for the Home Department v E* [2007] UKHL 47, [2008] 1 AC 499; and *Secretary of State for the Home Department v JJ* [2007] UKHL 45, [2008] 1 AC 385; *AF* (see n. 19).

21 *AF*, at [6].

22 Walker (see n. 4).

23 The Terrorism Act 2000 had provided for a maximum of seven days' pre-charge detention. The Criminal Justice Act 2003 (s. 306) had extended this to fourteen days.

24 Terrorism Act 2006, ss. 23–24.

McKeever summarises the powers that the executive has gathered under the terrorism legislation. He is critical of the amount of legislation, implying that much of it was passed in a panic after terrorist incidents and is not well thought-out. He explains, in brief, the notable features of the anti-terrorist legislation passed since 2000. If you read this extract carefully, you will understand what each piece of legislation has contributed. The powers range from allowing the police to stop and search people on the streets at random, to banning certain organisations, allowing assets to be seized at the start of a terrorist investigation, and detaining and controlling terrorist suspects.

Other criticisms of the terrorist legislation are of particular interest to constitutional lawyers. Bogdanor discusses the scrutiny of this legislation by Parliament.

● **V. Bogdanor,** *The New British Constitution* (Oxford: Hart, 2009), p. 56

> The progress through Parliament of the 2001 Anti-Terrorism, Crime and Security Act and of the 2005 Prevention of Terrorism Act shows that parliamentary scrutiny of legislation bearing on human rights can be somewhat perfunctory during a period of moral panic. The Anti-Terrorism, Crime and Security Act provided for the indefinite detention of suspected terrorists, who were not British citizens, if the Home Secretary had reasonable grounds to suspect that they were a threat to national security. The bill was debated for just 16 hours in the House of Commons and for an even shorter time in the House of Lords. It received the royal assent in December 2001, just one month after being introduced into the Commons, insufficient time surely for the proper scrutiny of legislation bearing so closely on human rights and civil liberties.

thinking point
Refer back to Chapter 11, which considers **legislative** *scrutiny by Parliament. Do you think the examples given by Bogdanor reinforce some of the criticisms of parliamentary scrutiny of legislation?*

He then goes on to describe how this legislation was repealed and replaced by the Prevention of Terrorism Act 2005, which was also rushed through Parliament.

Bogdanor makes the point that this legislation made some very serious inroads into human rights. If Parliament is doing its job of holding the government to account, it should study such legislation very carefully to ensure that the executive is acting properly in introducing such a drastic Bill. But, in fact, this law was passed more quickly and with far less debate than other less important Bills.

20.4 Accountability and anti-terrorist powers

The executive has been granted sweeping powers to use against terrorists. The accompanying infringement of human rights is justified on the grounds that the government has a duty to make sure that its people are secure and that their right to life is protected (under Article 2 ECHR). Lord Bingham explains how the balance between liberty and security changed after 9/11.

● **T. Bingham,** *The Rule of Law* (London: Allen Lane, 2010), p. 136

> In Britain also the mood music changed. This was reflected in the then Prime Minister Tony Blair's observation at his monthly press conference on 5 August 2005, after the July bombings, when he said: 'Let no one be in any doubt, the rules of the game are changing …' This was not, perhaps, a happy choice of phrase, since no responsible person had ever supposed there was a game. A learned author, having examined the matter at length, has concluded that the only rule-change has been found on the greater willingness of the courts to uphold civil liberties and hold government to account for its breaches of the law.[1]
>
> 1 D. Bonner, *Executive Measures, Terrorism and National Security: Have the Rules of the Game Changed?* (Aldershot: Ashgate, 2007), pp. 4 and 352.

Lord Bingham is referring to former **Prime Minister** Tony Blair's view that greater legal powers were needed to counter the new threat posed by modern terrorism. Tony Blair suggested that government should not be held back by human rights law. Lord Bingham seems to doubt this view and makes it clear that he thinks it is the courts' duty to uphold civil liberties.

The wide powers held by the executive, with the potential for the abuse of human rights, make it essential that the executive are accountable for the way in which these powers are used. As we have discussed throughout the book, the executive is politically accountable to Parliament for the exercise of its powers. It is also legally accountable to the courts, where its actions can be challenged as unlawful. Accountability means that the government has to justify its use of power. The courts, Parliament, or other bodies act as a check on the way in which the executive exercises its authority. Accountability is complex, because some anti-terrorist activity involves the security services and other national security matters that the government does not want to make public. The executive may refuse to provide information to Parliament or the courts on the grounds that it is sensitive information, perhaps obtained from legally intercepting phone calls or emails (intercept evidence), or from secret informants. Revealing the source of secret information might damage the defence of the country, interfere with international relations, or endanger members of the security services. But there are occasions on which the court may reject government claims as exaggerated, and hold that the **rule of law** and the public interest require disclosure. This was partly the subject of the dispute in the highly publicised case of *R (Mohamed) v Secretary of State for Foreign and Commonwealth Affairs* [2010] EWCA Civ 65. The Court of Appeal approved the disclosure of information that was relevant to deciding how much the UK security services knew about the torture of the claimant by a foreign government.

20.4.1 Legal accountability

There have been many claims against the government questioning the legality of its actions in the courts. The Human Rights Act 1998 (HRA 1998) has been used repeatedly to challenge the decisions of the executive on terrorism.

cross reference
You should reread the sections in Chapter 14 that explain the meaning of legal accountability, and the role of the courts and the HRA 1998.

- Sections 6 and 7 of the HRA 1998 permit a **victim** to bring proceedings against a **public authority** claiming that it has acted unlawfully by breaching a Convention right. Many of the cases discussed in this chapter come within this category: see, for example, *Secretary of State for Home Department v JJ* [2007] UKHL 45.

- Section 4 of the HRA 1998 has been relied on by terrorist suspects to argue that legislation (section 23 of the Anti-Terrorism, Crime and Security Act 2001) was incompatible with Convention rights: see *A v Secretary of State for the Home Department* [2004] UKHL 56 (the **Belmarsh Detainees** case), considered later in the chapter.

- Section 7 of the HRA 1998 also states that a victim can rely on a convention right in any legal proceedings against a public authority. This includes criminal cases in which it may be argued that the law or the rules of evidence have violated the defendant's rights. For example, in *Attorney General's Reference (No 4 of 2002)* [2005] 1 AC 264, the defendant was charged with being a member of a proscribed (banned) terrorist organisation contrary to section 11 of the Terrorism Act 2000. The House of Lords decided that the legislation must be interpreted in accordance with section 3 of the HRA 1998. It would therefore be read to ensure that the legal burden of proof was on the prosecution to prove that the organisation was banned at the time when the defendant was a member. Otherwise, there was a potential breach of the presumption of innocence contrary to the right to a fair trial in Article 6 ECHR.

- The HRA 1998 can be relied on in civil cases in which the government has been sued for compensation. Section 8 provides that **damages** may be granted in these circumstances. The UK government has been sued by individuals claiming that they have been tortured by foreign governments with the knowledge of the UK authorities in various locations, including at Guantanamo Bay. The claimants used ordinary civil law proceedings to claim damages from the UK government for false imprisonment, torture, and breaches of the HRA 1998. Many of these claims were settled in a mutually confidential settlement agreement announced by the Minister for Justice in the House of Commons (Statement by the Lord Chancellor and

Secretary of State for Justice, Hansard HC, 16 November 2010, col. 752). Some evidential aspects of the litigation were decided by the Supreme Court in *Al Rawi and others v Security Services and others* [2011] UKSC 34.

- However, the HRA 1998 is not the only form of legal accountability and ordinary common law principles, including those of judicial review, have been used to challenge the decisions of the executive. In *Ahmed and others v Her Majesty's Treasury* [2010] 2 AC 534, the claimants used the principles of administrative law, the common law, and the HRA 1998 to argue successfully that the Terrorism (United Nations Measures) Order 2006 and the Al-Qaida and Taliban (United Nations Measures) Order 2006 were unlawful. The orders were a form of delegated legislation passed under the United Nations Act 1946 and allowed for the assets of terrorist organisations to be seized. The Supreme Court held that the statute did not give the executive the power to override fundamental rights by delegated legislation.

NOTE

You should remind yourself of the other powers of the court under section 3 of the HRA 1998 to interpret legislation consistently with the Convention and the right to make a **declaration** of incompatibility under section 4 of the HRA 1998, as discussed in Chapter 9. We will see how the courts have used these powers in terrorism cases later in this chapter.

20.4.2 Political accountability

Political accountability to Parliament takes place through the normal mechanisms: for example, the Home Secretary and other ministers must answer questions during Question Time, participate in debates, and give evidence to the relevant scrutiny committees, such as the Home Affairs Committee. The work of the Joint Committee on Human Rights is also worthy of note. This is a joint committee of the House of Commons and House of Lords, which scrutinises parliamentary Bills and comments on the human rights implications. It usually does this by hearing evidence and producing reports, which are debated in Parliament and responded to by government. It has produced detailed reports on the anti-terror laws. In addition to these parliamentary mechanisms, there are also other methods of accountability that have been built into the terrorism legislation, such as requiring the Home Secretary to report on her TPIMs powers to Parliament every three months (section 19 of the TPIM Act 2011). Other mechanisms include the creation of the office of the Independent Reviewer of Terrorism Legislation. This office was created by statute, currently under section 36 of the Terrorism Act 2006. This provides for a power to review the terrorist legislation and to make a report to Parliament on an annual basis. Lord Carlile QC held this post from 2001 to 2011, when he was replaced by David Anderson QC.

summary points

Accountability and anti-terrorist powers

- *Legal accountability can be summarised as follows.*
  - *Judicial review may be based on administrative law principles.*
  - *Judicial review may be based on the Human Rights Act 1998 under section 7 of that Act.*
  - *Reliance may be placed on the common law and the HRA 1998 in criminal cases.*
  - *Actions may be taken against the executive in contract or tort.*
- *Political accountability can be summarised as follows.*
  - *Ministers answer questions and give evidence to scrutiny committees.*

- *Debates are held in Parliament on terrorism.*
- *The Joint Committee on Human Rights holds inquiries and produces reports on human rights, of which there have been several.*
- *The Independent Reviewer of Terrorism Legislation (appointed under section 36 of the Terrorism Act 2006) produces annual reports to Parliament reviewing the terrorist legislation.*
- *The Home Secretary has to report to Parliament every three months on the exercise of the TPIMs powers (under section 19 of the TPIM Act 2011).*

NOTE

For more on the Joint Committee on Human Rights, see http://www.parliament.uk/business/committees/committees-a-z/joint-select/human-rights-committee/

NOTE

For more on the Independent Reviewer of Terrorism Legislation, see http://terrorismlegislation reviewer.independent.gov.uk/

20.5 Extraordinary powers: indefinite detention, control orders, and terrorism prevention and investigation measures (TPIMs)

The subject of this section is probably the most controversial aspect of the anti-terrorist legislation. It concerns the restriction of the liberty of those suspected of terrorist activity, but who cannot, for reasons explained below, be prosecuted or deported from the UK. Many of the challenges to the terrorist legislation have been brought using Article 5 ECHR (the right to liberty and security) and Article 6 (the right to a fair trial). As we shall see, these successful legal challenges using the HRA 1998 have led Parliament to change the law. The courts have had to apply the Act and answer profound constitutional questions about their role in the protection of human rights, and the relationship between the courts, Parliament, and the executive.

Much of the law in this area has been generated by the attempt to try to control the activities of those suspected of terrorism to prevent them from preparing terrorist acts. The government has been faced with two problems, as follows.

- Foreign nationals suspected of terrorism cannot be deported to a country where they may be subject to torture, or inhuman or degrading treatment. The ECtHR, in *Chahal v UK* (1997) 23 EHRR 413, has held that this would put the UK in breach of Article 3 of the Convention.
- There is not always sufficient evidence to prosecute either British or foreign nationals for terrorist offences. This is on the ground that the government will not reveal the evidence against them, because it has often been gathered by the security services and to disclose it may damage national security.

There have been three main attempts to deal with the problem.

1 Parliament passed section 23 of the Anti-Terrorism, Crime and Security Act 2001, which allowed the detention of foreign nationals. This was repealed after the decision in the *Belmarsh Detainees case* (cited above).

2 The system of control orders was introduced by the Terrorism Act 2005. (Control orders are now being abolished.)

3 Terrorist investigation and prevention measures (TPIMs) are introduced by the TPIM Act 2011.

20.5.1 Indefinite detention of foreign nationals

cross reference

The Belmarsh Detainees *case is dealt with in some depth in Chapter 17.*

The provisions of section 23 of the Anti-Terrorism, Crime and Security Act 2001 were considered by the House of Lords in *the Belmarsh Detainees case.* To recap, the majority of the House of Lords accepted the government's argument that there was a public emergency affecting the life of the nation. However, they found in favour of the claimants on the grounds that that section 23 was incompatible with Articles 14 and 5 of the Convention. It was neither rational nor proportionate to detain foreign nationals indefinitely if they remained, but to allow them to leave the UK given that they could then carry on their terrorist activities abroad. It was also discriminatory to detain only foreign nationals when there was evidence to suggest that British citizens might also be involved in terrorism.

cross reference

See Chapter 9 for more on parliamentary sovereignty and the Human Rights Act.

The court issued a declaration of incompatibility under section 4 of the HRA 1998. This is not binding on the parties to the case and, because Parliament is sovereign, the court does not have the power to set aside the law. So the claimants were not immediately released from detention in Belmarsh prison, but remained there for some time. As a consequence of this decision, the Prevention of Terrorism Act 2005 was enacted, which introduced the system of control orders discussed below. Several of the detainees in the case were then released, but subject to control orders.

NOTE

We studied the *Belmarsh Detainees case* in Chapter 17 when we considered the proportionality test, which is the method used by the court to decide whether there has been a breach of a convention right. This case illustrates the importance of judicial independence and the **separation of powers**. The court acted as a check on the other branches of government; it was not deferential and held that the government had acted unlawfully in the sensitive area of national security.

> **The impact of the *Belmarsh Detainees case***
>
> ....
>
> This case is regarded as one of the most constitutionally significant decisions in recent history. The following are quotes from three commentators on the case.
>
> • D. Feldman, 'Proportionality and discrimination in anti-terrorism legislation' (2005) Cambridge Law Journal 271, 273, declares the case 'perhaps the most powerful judicial defence of liberty' since the 1700s.

- S. Foster, The fight against terrorism: detention without trial and human rights' (2009) Coventry Law Journal 4, 8, has stated that 'The majority decision of the House of Lords represents a robust judicial approach towards the protection of fundamental constitutional rights'.

- Keith Ewing, *Bonfire of the Liberties: New Labour, Human Rights and the Rule of Law* (Oxford: Oxford University Press, 2010), p. 283, has a different opinion. He argues that much of the positive commentary is 'an exaggerated reading of the decision…it was reached with due deference to the judgment of the government that there was a public emergency threatening the life of the nation'.

20.5.2 Control orders

The Prevention of Terrorism Act 2005 abandoned the scheme of detaining foreign nationals and introduced a system of control orders. Control orders were an attempt at overcoming the objections of the House of Lords in the *Belmarsh Detainees* decision to the indefinite detention of foreign nationals. Control orders were non-discriminatory, because they applied both to British and to foreign nationals. Those subject to a control order were sometimes referred to as 'controlees'. Control orders tried to prevent individuals from plotting or preparing for terrorist acts by restricting their actions rather than by keeping them in prison. Even so, control orders may conflict with the right to liberty in Article 5 ECHR. Control order hearings raised issues of procedural fairness under Article 6. Breaching a control order was a criminal offence. The legislation provided for two kinds of control order: derogating and non-derogating. A derogating control order restricted the liberty of the individual under Article 5 of the Convention and would require the government to derogate from the Convention. No derogating control orders have been made since the legislation came into force and they will not be discussed further here. Control orders were criticised for limiting the freedom of individuals without their having been convicted of a criminal offence.

Control orders were made where the Home Secretary had reasonable grounds for suspecting that the individual was involved in terrorist-related activity and it was necessary to protect members of the public from terrorism (section 2(1)(a) and (b) of the Prevention of Terrorism Act 2005). The Home Secretary had the power to make a control order, but she had to seek **permission** from the court unless the situation was urgent. In this case, the control order was made immediately and later referred to the court. The court had very narrow powers over the control order. It could refuse permission or quash the making of the order only if it was 'obviously flawed'. It could be imposed for only twelve months, but could be renewed an unlimited number of times.

As explained above, the individual subject to a control order was not imprisoned, but had restrictions placed on his or her activities. Any obligation could be imposed that was deemed necessary to prevent or restrict that individual from participating in terrorist-related activity (section 1(3) of the Prevention of Terrorism Act 2005). However, section 1(4) lists seventeen of the obligations that may be included. Some of the restrictions are described in the cases below. The recent Home Office review on control orders described the way in which they have been used.

● **Home Office, *Review of Counter Terrorism and Security Powers: Review Findings and Recommendations*** (Cm 8004, London: HMSO, January 2011), p. 36

3. The activities intended to be controlled by these orders have included the planning of mass casualty attacks in the UK, providing financial, material or other logistical support for

631

terrorism-related activity, travelling overseas to attack British or allied military forces or travelling to attend a terrorist training camp.

...

5. Since they were introduced, 48 people have been made subject to a control order. 28 of the orders have been imposed on foreign nationals. 10 of those foreign nationals were on a control order until the necessary arrangements were in place to begin deportation proceedings. Most of those who have been subject to a control order have been on an order for less than 2 years. Two foreign nationals spent more than 4 years on an order before their orders were revoked.

6. As of 10 December 2010, there were 8 people all British citizens on control orders. Of these 2 had been on orders for over 2 years (one between 3–4 years, the other between 2–3 years); 4 had been on orders for between 1–2 years; and the remaining 2 had been on orders for less than a year.

This extract explains that control orders have been imposed on both British and foreign nationals. The restrictions were flexible and some control orders were severe, whilst others only imposed a few limitations. There has been a constant stream of case law that has challenged the Home Secretary's decision to impose control orders.

Although control orders are being replaced by TPIMs (see later in the chapter), the case law on control orders has influenced the drafting of the new legislation and will continue to be of significance when the courts have to decide the compatibility of TPIMs with the Convention. The case law will also guide the procedures used to impose them. The landmark case law that centred on the right to liberty and security protected by Article 5 is the subject of the next section.

Article 5 and control orders

The House of Lords considered the issue of control orders in *Secretary of State for Home Department v JJ* [2007] UKHL 45. In this case, six individuals challenged as unlawful the control orders that had been made against them. They argued that they had been unlawfully deprived of their liberty, contrary to Article 5. Lord Bingham outlines the nature of the control orders.

● ***Secretary of State for Home Department v JJ*** [2007] UKHL 45

Lord Bingham:

[20] Each respondent is required to remain within his 'residence' at all times, save for a period of six hours between 10 a m and 4 p m ... During the curfew period the respondents are confined in their small flats and are not even allowed into the common parts of the buildings in which these flats are situated. Visitors must be authorised by the Home Office ... During the six hours when they are permitted to leave their residences, the respondents are confined to restricted urban areas, the largest of which is 72 square kilometres. These deliberately do not extend, save in the case of GG, to any area in which they lived before. Each area contains a mosque, a hospital, primary health care facilities, shops and entertainment and sporting facilities. The respondents are prohibited from meeting anyone by pre-arrangement who has not been given the same Home Office clearance as a visitor to the residence.

It may be added that the controlled persons were required to wear an electronic tag ... They were forbidden to use or possess any communications equipment of any kind save for one fixed telephone ...

The House of Lords went on to hold, by a majority of five to three, that the control orders did deprive the claimants of their liberty in contravention of Article 5 of the Convention. This was partly because the individuals were required to remain at home for eighteen hours each day.

The House of Lords held that whether there was a deprivation of liberty was a matter of fact and degree: it would depend on the conditions imposed in each case. Lord Bingham explained why the control orders in this case were a breach of Article 5.

· ·

● *Secretary of State for Home Department v JJ* [2007] UKHL 45

Lord Bingham:

> [24] The effect of the 18-hour curfew, coupled with the effective exclusion of social visitors, meant that the controlled persons were in practice in solitary confinement for this lengthy period every day for an indefinite duration, with very little opportunity for contact with the outside world, with means insufficient to permit provision of significant facilities for self-entertainment and with knowledge that their flats were liable to be entered and searched at any time … they were (save for GG) located in an unfamiliar area where they had no family, friends or contacts, and which was no doubt chosen for that reason. The requirement to obtain prior Home Office clearance of any social meeting outside the flat in practice isolated the controlled persons during the non-curfew hours also. Their lives were wholly regulated by the Home Office, as a prisoner's would be, although breaches were much more severely punishable. The judge's analogy with detention in an open prison was apt, save that the controlled persons did not enjoy the association with others and the access to entertainment facilities which a prisoner in an open prison would expect to enjoy.

Lord Bingham held that the nature and extent of the restrictions was a deprivation of liberty contrary to Article 5 because:

- being forced to remain at home on their own for such long periods meant that the claimants were, in effect, being kept in solitary confinement;
- all but one of the claimants lived in an unfamiliar area in which it was hard to socialise; and
- the conditions to which they were consequently subjected were harsher than those in an open prison.

Lord Brown also agreed that the control orders in this case were unlawful. He went on to state that control orders that confined individuals to their homes for more than eighteen hours would breach Article 5. However, in other cases in which the restrictions are less severe, the control orders have been held to be lawful. In *Secretary of State for the Home Department v E and another* [2008] 1 AC 499, a judgment given at the same time as *JJ*, a control order with a twelve-hour night-time curfew and less harsh conditions was held not to breach Article 5. The House of Lords distinguished it from *JJ* as follows.

· ·

● *Secretary of State for the Home Department v E and another* [2008] 1 AC 499

Lord Bingham:

> [7] The obligations imposed on E do, however, differ from those imposed on JJ and others in respects accepted by the courts below as material. The curfew to which he is subject is of 12 hours' duration, from 7 p m to 7 a m, not 18 hours. The residence specified in the order is his own home, where he had lived for some years, in a part of London with which he is familiar … his residence is defined to include his garden, to which he thus has access at any time. He lives at his home with his wife and family … Five members of his wider family live in the area, and have been approved as visitors. He is subject to no geographical restriction during non-curfew hours, is free to attend a mosque of his choice, and is not prohibited from associating with named individuals. The judge found, at para 231, that E does not lack a social network, goes to the mosque, takes his older children to school, picks them up, goes shopping and sees family members who live in the area.

In this case, the length, nature, and extent of the restriction were far less oppressive and did not breach Article 5.

Further, in *Secretary of State for the Home Department v AF* [2007] UKHL 46, it was held that a fourteen-hour curfew in a flat in which AF was already living, a requirement to wear an electronic tag, restrictions on visitors during curfew hours, and various other prohibitions on places that AF could visit and individuals whom he could meet did not breach Article 5.

Finally, in *Secretary of State for the Home Department v AP* [2010] UKSC 24, the Supreme Court held that forcing controlees to relocate to a different part of the country (internal exile) was unlawful.

This brief look at the case law shows the courts performing their important constitutional function of acting as a check on the executive. Unlike the *Belmarsh Detainees* decision, the cases on control orders did not lead the courts to grant declarations of incompatibility under section 4 of the HRA 1998 that the law itself was contrary to the Convention. By insisting that the executive use its powers to impose control orders consistently with Article 5 of the Convention, it is making the executive legally accountable and attempting to ensure that the rights of the controlees are not abused.

Control orders and Article 6

Article 6 requires that: 'In the determination of his civil rights and obligations or of any criminal charge against him, everyone is entitled to a fair and public hearing ...' Control order proceedings were closed proceedings from which the public and press were usually excluded. The courts have held that the proceedings are not concerned with a criminal charge, but they do engage Article 6 because they determine civil rights and obligations.

cross reference

For a discussion of Article 6 in the context of administrative proceedings, see Chapter 18.

There are two main areas of concern about the hearings:

- the use of secret evidence (usually referred to as 'closed material'); and
- the use of special advocates.

The rules provided that, at control order proceedings, the Home Secretary can apply to the court to refuse to disclose relevant information to the individual and his or her legal representatives if it endangers national security or other important public interests (under the Schedule to the Terrorism Act 2005). However, the secret or closed information could be disclosed to the court in the absence of the individual and his or her lawyer. The court could then appoint a special advocate from an approved list of lawyers who have security clearance. The drawback is that the special advocate is not allowed to contact the individual or his or her legal representative once he or she has been shown the closed information (paragraph 7 of the Schedule to the Prevention of Terrorism Act 2005). So the special advocate has to try to represent the interests of the individual without talking to, or taking instructions from, him or her. The use of special advocates is intended to mitigate the unfairness of depriving the individual of the opportunity to see the evidence against him or her and to respond to it. However, some critics have argued that special advocates cannot be effective representatives, and do not make up for the deprivation of the right to know and challenge hostile evidence.

The House of Lords had to consider whether control order procedures were compatible with Article 6 in *Secretary of State for the Home Department v MB; Secretary of State for the Home Department v AF* [2007] UKHL 46. The House of Lords indicated that the use of special advocates could help to overcome some of the problems of using secret evidence and satisfy the fair procedure requirements of Article 6, but it would depend on the facts of the case. The court, using its interpretive powers in section 3 of the HRA 1998, held that the relevant sections of the Prevention of Terrorism Act 2005 should be read so far as is possible to do so consistently with Article 6.

NOTE

Notice the way in which section 3 of the HRA 1998 is used here. Rather than declare these provisions incompatible under section 4 of the HRA 1998, the House of Lords is trying to interpret the legislation in a way that makes the proceedings fair and thus compatible with Article 6 of the Convention.

---

cross reference
See Chapter 9 for more on declarations of incompatibility.

However, this was not the end of the matter: the ECtHR considered the procedure in the case of *A v United Kingdom* (2009) 49 EHRR 625. It held that the system of special advocates did go some way towards making the procedure fair when secret material was used, but the Court held that it could not totally make up for the fundamental problem that much of the material against the claimant was in the unseen closed material. It held that there was a core irreducible minimum of procedural fairness with which the courts had to be comply. Following the ECtHR decision, this issue returned to the House of Lords in *Secretary of State for the Home Department v AF (No 3)* [2010] 2 AC 269. This case involved a number of individuals who were subject to control orders based on closed material that was not disclosed to them at the relevant hearing, but who had been represented by special advocates. The House of Lords sent the cases back to the High Court to be reconsidered. But the Law Lords laid down the principles of fairness that had to be followed.

. . . .

● ***Secretary of State for the Home Department v AF (No 3)*** [2010] 2 AC 269

Lord Bingham:

> [59] …the controlee must be given sufficient information about the allegations against him to enable him to give effective instructions in relation to those allegations. Provided that this requirement is satisfied there can be a fair trial notwithstanding that the controlee is not provided with the detail or the sources of the evidence forming the basis of the allegations. Where, however, the open material consists purely of general assertions and the case against the controlee is based solely or to a decisive degree on closed materials the requirements of a fair trial will not be satisfied, however cogent the case based on the closed materials may be.
>
> The Grand Chamber has now made clear that non-disclosure cannot go so far as to deny a party knowledge of the essence of the case against him, at least where he is at risk of consequences as severe as those normally imposed under a control order.

Lord Hope:

> [84] The consequences of a successful terrorist attack are likely to be so appalling that there is an understandable wish to support the system that keeps those who are considered to be most dangerous out of circulation for as long as possible. But the slow creep of complacency must be resisted. If the rule of law is to mean anything, it is in cases such as these that the court must stand by principle. It must insist that the person affected be told what is alleged against him.

The consequence of these decisions is that unless the most important evidence against the individual can be disclosed, a control order cannot be made.

In the cases concerned with Article 6, the courts have used their powers to check and balance both the powers of Parliament and those of the executive. By using their interpretive powers under section 3 of the HRA 1998, the courts are ensuring that legislation passed by Parliament is interpreted as far as possible consistently with the Convention. So the executive, when seeking to impose the control order, has to disclose the essence of the case against the individual or drop the proceedings. It means that the individuals' rights are upheld and he or she is treated more fairly by the court.

NOTE

The House of Lords refers to the decision of the Grand Chamber of the ECtHR in its judgment in *AF (No 3)*. Three points to consider are as follows.

- In accordance with section 2 of the HRA 1998, the UK courts have to take into account the judgments of the ECtHR when it decides cases and normally follows its decisions.

- The ECtHR provides an extra layer of human rights protection for the individual. If a claimant loses a human rights case in the Supreme Court, he or she still has the opportunity to take his or her case to the Strasbourg Court.

- The House of Lords also refers to the constitutional principles of the rule of law in its decision. At [83], Lord Hope states that failure to tell someone of the case against him or her is 'the stuff of nightmares'.

Control orders and evidence obtained by torture

The question of whether evidence obtained by torture could be lawfully admitted in court was decided in *A v Secretary of State for the Home Department (No 2)* [2005] UKHL 71. The law has long prohibited evidence obtained by torture by law enforcement agencies in the UK being admitted in court. But the question that arose here was whether evidence obtained by torture in a third country by foreign officials could be admitted in a UK court. This case arose at hearings connected with the detention of foreign nationals under section 23 of the Anti-Terrorism, Crime and Security Act 2003, but it lays down general principles that are of continuing importance, particularly in judicial proceedings concerned with control orders. The House of Lords unanimously held that such evidence could not be admitted.

● *A and others v Secretary of State for the Home Department (No 2)* [2005] UKHL 71

Lord Bingham:

> [51] The issue is one of constitutional principle, whether evidence obtained by torturing another human being may lawfully be admitted against a party to proceedings in a British court, irrespective of where, or by whom, or on whose authority the torture was inflicted. To that question I would give a very clear negative answer.
>
> I accept the broad thrust of the appellants' argument on the common law. The principles of the common law, standing alone, in my opinion compel the exclusion of third party torture evidence as unreliable, unfair, offensive to ordinary standards of humanity and decency and incompatible with the principles which should animate a tribunal seeking to administer justice. But the principles of the common law do not stand alone.

Lord Hope:

> [101] Torture, one of most evil practices known to man, is resorted to for a variety of purposes...The temptation to use it in times of emergency will be controlled by the law wherever the rule of law is allowed to operate.

The House of Lords unanimously held that the common law, the ECHR, and international law all prohibited the admission of evidence based on torture. It emphasised that the admission of such evidence is contrary to the rule of law. The House of Lords decided by a majority that evidence should not be admitted if it were concluded, on a balance of probabilities, that it was obtained by torture.

The courts and control orders

The case law shows that the courts have tried to ensure that the control order system is consistent with the convention and the government has suffered many defeats. But the courts have not held that control order legislation is incompatible with the Convention and have not used section 4 of the HRA 1998 as they did in the *Belmarsh Detainees* decision.

● **C. Walker, *Blackstone's Guide to the Anti-terrorism Legislation*** (Oxford: Oxford University Press, 2009), p. 238

Perhaps they wished to avoid another spectacular showdown with the politicians. Perhaps control orders are of a lower order of threat to basic rights and can be compatible as Article 5 and 6 jurisprudence suggests

The courts have made a significant impact on the way in which control orders operate and, as we shall see, the principles laid down in this case law are of continuing significance.

20.5.3 The Terrorism Prevention and Investigation Measures Act 2011

The assumption of power by the **coalition government** in May 2010 led to a review of the counter-terrorism law and the publication of a policy document by the Home Office: *Review of Counter-Terrorism and Security Powers: Review Findings and Recommendations* (Cm 8004, London: HMSO, January 2011). Apart from the problems identified by the various legal challenges discussed above, control orders have also been criticised because:

- a number of controlees have absconded;
- they have been imposed for very long periods; and
- they distract the authorities from pursuing prosecutions in the criminal courts.

Following the recommendations in the review, the government decided to change the system of control orders and replace them with TPIMs. The TPIM Act 2011 makes these changes. It abolishes the system of control orders and replaces it with the new measures. The TPIMs are very similar to control orders and have been described as 'control orders lite'. Like control orders, they restrict the liberty of those suspected of terrorist activity where there is insufficient evidence to charge an individual with criminal activity or it is impossible to legally deport him or her. But there are some significant differences from control orders, which we will discuss below.

NOTE

You should also note that, at the time of writing, the government has published in draft the Enhanced Terrorism Prevention and Investigation Measures Bill 2011 (ETPIM Bill 2011). If this becomes law, it will give the Home Secretary the power, if exceptional circumstances arise, to impose more severe restrictions on terrorist suspects than the TPIM Act 2011 allows.

How is a TPIM imposed?

The Home Secretary has the power to impose a TPIM, but she must generally first seek the permission of the court. The court is limited to reviewing her decision on judicial review principles and can only overturn it if it is obviously flawed (section 6(3) of the TPIM Act 2011). So the role of the courts in imposing TPIMs is still very limited. In order to impose a TPIM, the Home Secretary has to reasonably believe that the individual is, or has been, involved in terrorist-related activity (section 3(1) of the TPIM Act 2011). The new legislation raises the standard of proof from reasonable suspicion to reasonable belief. Raising the standard of proof to a higher level means that the Home Secretary has to have an even firmer belief that the person is involved in terrorist activity. It makes only a small difference, but making the test slightly harder has some symbolic importance in stressing the seriousness of imposing a TPIM. Secret evidence and special advocates still remain a problem at TPIM hearings. The procedure to be followed at the court hearings is laid down in Schedule 4 to the TPIM Act 2011. There has been no sub-stantial change to the proceedings, but the process is governed by the control order case law on Articles 5 and 6 ECHR at which we looked earlier in the chapter.

What restrictions can be imposed under a TPIM?

When the Home Secretary imposes a TPIM, she will specify certain measures on the individual, such as requirements as to where he or she must stay, or restrictions on with whom he or she may communicate. Under the system of control orders, this list of measures was non-exhaustive, leaving it open to the Home Secretary to create new measures. Under the TPIM Act 2011, these measures are set out in an exhaustive list in Schedule 1 to the TPIM Act 2011. This means that the Home Secretary can impose only the measures on the list. The measures include: overnight residence; travel; exclusion from specified areas or places; movement directions (such as being allowed to go to certain places only accompanied by a police constable); restrictions on the transfer and use of property; association conditions (preventing or restricting association with specified persons); work or studies restrictions; and reporting, photograph, and monitoring requirements.

The new legislation tries to ensure that the individual is not treated unduly harshly. So for example, paragraph 7 of Schedule 1 states that the Home Secretary may impose restrictions and requirements on the possession and use of electronic communications. But she must allow the individual to possess and use a landline telephone, a computer with Internet connection via a fixed line, and a mobile phone that does not provide access to the Internet. The Home Secretary can, however, monitor and impose restrictions on their use. A TPIM is subject to stricter time limits than a control order. It is initially imposed for one year, but can be extended to two by the Home Secretary if there is a continuing necessity for it to remain in force (section 5). But, after this time, no further TPIM can be made unless the Home Secretary reasonably believes that the individual has engaged in further terrorism-related activity since the imposition of the TPIM (section 3 of the TPIM Act 2011).

Changes made by the TPIM Act 2011 in comparison with control orders

- A higher standard of proof has to be satisfied before a TPIM can be imposed.

- The TPIMs are subject to stricter time limits and are more difficult to renew.

- The measures that can be imposed are more tightly prescribed in an attempt to prevent undue hardship to the individual.

Enhanced TPIMs

When the TPIM Act 2011 was going through Parliament, the government decided that if there were exceptional circumstances, it might be necessary to impose greater restrictions on terrorist suspects than the TPIM Act 2011 allowed. So it has now published in draft the ETPIM Bill 2011. The procedures for imposing the enhanced TPIMs are similar to standard TPIMs, but there are some significant differences. The Bill allows the Home Secretary to impose an enhanced TPIM if she is satisfied, on the balance of probabilities, that the individual is, or has been, involved in terrorist activities. This is a stricter burden of proof than for an ordinary TPIM. The measures imposed under the enhanced TPIM must be ones that cannot be imposed under the TPIM Act 2011. Apart from these two factors, the conditions for imposing an enhanced TPIM are the same as those for a regular TPIM (clause 2 of the ETPIM Bill 2011). If the Bill were to become law, it would mean that there would be two kinds of TPIM that the Home Secretary could choose to impose:

- a standard TPIM (under the TPIM Act 2011); or
- an enhanced TPIM (under the ETPIM Bill 2011).

The Home Secretary is able to impose stricter conditions in an enhanced TPIM: for example, she is able to require the individual to relocate and to reside at a specific residence. She is also able to restrict the use of all electronic devices and does not have to provide minimal access.

Paragraph 6 of the Explanatory Note to the Bill does, however, assert that this is considered to be draft emergency legislation and is likely to become law only if there is a serious terrorist risk that could not be managed in any other way (Enhanced Terrorism and Prevention and Investigation Measures Bill 2011: Explanatory Note, Cm 8166, London: HMSO, September 2011).

Criticisms of TPIMs

The new TPIMs system has retained many of the features of control orders. It is an executive-led process that imposes restrictions on the freedom of the individual without charge or conviction of a crime in a court of law. It has been suggested that there should be a greater focus on gathering evidence that will secure criminal convictions of those suspected of terrorism. This might be helped if the law of evidence were changed so that evidence obtained through the use of surveillance could be admitted in court; the government has so far rejected this suggestion. Other reform proposals can be found in the further reading listed at the end of the chapter.

Summary

This chapter has illustrated the way in which constitutional law principles work in practice. We have seen many illustrations of their important functions and some key examples include the following.

- The separation of powers requires Parliament to check and balance the powers of the executive. It is Parliament's function to ensure that anti-terrorist legislation is closely scrutinised before it becomes law. How well Parliament does this is questionable. Consistent with the separation of powers, the courts also ensure that the executive acts within the law.
- The HRA 1998 has been used by the courts to ensure that the executive and Parliament act consistently with the ECHR. But, as we have seen, the courts cannot repeal legislation because Parliament is sovereign. The courts have, however, exercised the power in section 4 of the HRA 1998 to grant a declaration of incompatibility, as in the *Belmarsh Detainees* case. The courts have also used the power in section 3 to hold that control order procedures were consistent with the Convention only if they provided certain safeguards.

- The courts have upheld challenges to control orders in some cases. They have held that certain restrictions, such as an eighteen-hour curfew and a requirement that an individual relocate to a different area, are incompatible with Article 5 and that some of the procedures in control order hearings conflict with Article 6.

- The rule of law has been relied on by the courts in cases concerned with the anti-terror laws to hold that evidence obtained by torture must be excluded and that individuals must be informed of adverse evidence in control order proceedings.

Terrorism tests the limits of constitutional democracies such as the UK. Democracies are based on freedom and respect for human rights; in order to prevent terrorist activity, rights must be balanced against public safety and national security. The constitutional principles that we have studied throughout this book have been apparent in the discussion of the anti-terrorist laws. There are different views as to whether the British constitution has provided a strong enough framework to make sure that the executive has not exceeded its powers and interfered excessively with human rights. There are many different checks on executive power, but how effective they are will continue to be a matter of debate for some time.

? Questions

1 What problems does terrorism pose to a constitutional democracy?

2 How do constitutional principles such as the rule of law and the separation of powers guide the way in which terrorism is dealt with?

3 How have the various powers granted to the courts in sections 3 and 4 of the HRA 1998 been used by the **judiciary** to ensure that the ECHR is observed in the UK?

4 What role has the European Court of Human Rights played in helping to uphold human rights in the UK?

5 What is the relationship between the Supreme Court, the ECtHR, and Parliament?

6 How useful has the HRA 1998 been in helping Parliament, the executive, and the judges to get the balance right between preserving individual liberty and protecting the security of individuals and the state?

📖 Further reading

Ewing, K., *Bonfire of the Liberties: New Labour, Human Rights and the Rule of Law* (Oxford: Oxford University Press, 2010)

This book is Ewing's analysis of the state of civil liberties during the term of the New Labour government. He discusses the terrorist legislation in Chapter 7. He is sceptical of the capacity of the courts to protect civil liberties and prefers to focus on reform to the political process as a way of upholding basic rights.

Feldman, D., 'Proportionality and discrimination in anti-terrorism legislation' (2005) 64(2) Cambridge Law Journal 271

This is an important analysis of the decision in the *Belmarsh Detainees* case.

Foster, S., 'The fight against terrorism, detention without trial and human rights' (2009) 14(1) Coventry Law Journal 4

Foster analyses the House of Lords' decision in the *Belmarsh Detainees case*. He also discusses the subsequent challenge in the same case in the European Court of Human Rights in *A v United Kingdom* (2009) 49 EHRR 625.

Walker, C., *Blackstone's Guide to the Anti-terrorism Legislation* (Oxford: Oxford University Press, 2009)

This is a thorough description and analysis of the terrorist legislation. It is very well set out and is an excellent reference point.

Welch, J. and Chakrabarti, S., 'The war on terror without the Human Rights Act: what difference has it made' (2010) 6 European Human Rights Law Review 593

The article focuses on the use of the Human Rights Act 1998 in legal challenges to decisions made by the government in the war on terror. This includes decisions that have led to the detention of foreign nationals and the imposition of control orders.

Further reading

21

Judicial Review: putting it all together in problem answers

Key points

This chapter will cover:

- What are judicial review problem questions designed to test?

- How does one approach a judicial review problem question?

- How does one approach whether the body may be judicially reviewed?

- How does one approach whether the client has standing or may intervene in an action?

- How does one approach whether the other preconditions are met?

- Some general points to check before you consider the grounds of review

- How does one approach the grounds for review?

- How does one deal with issues of remedy?

- How does one provide a final assessment to the client?

Introduction

This chapter attempts to pull together all of the judicial review strands, to provide a checklist of issues that you will need to consider to diagnose a judicial review problem and then to provide a legal opinion for a client. It is, in part, a revision of the previous judicial review chapters. It is also a way in which you can test your knowledge and understanding of judicial review, by considering the extent to which you are able to apply the principles that you have learnt throughout your study of judicial review.

21.1 What are judicial review problem questions designed to test?

Judicial review problem questions, as other problem questions, are designed to test a range of skills and substantive areas of knowledge. You are being assessed on the extent to which you are able to diagnose the relevant legal issues from the facts presented. You are also being assessed on your ability systematically to describe and explain the applicable law, to apply the law to the facts, and to determine what more you would need to do prior to making a final determination. Your application of the law to the facts is your analysis. You are also being judged on your ability to weigh up the factual and legal evidence, and to provide an assessment of the likely chances of success on each of the grounds that you discuss, as well as likely remedies.

In general terms, problem questions are designed so that each piece of information within them is of relevance. They are complex scenarios that aim to put you through your legal paces. You will need to consider each of the legal issues that you have covered in the judicial review section of your course or module, even if you do not need to include all of them, because they are not relevant to the scenario. Different modules and courses will measure students against a different set of criteria, but most will adopt some of the following as the basis for measurement.

Assessment criteria

The question is likely to be structured so as to assess the student's ability to:

- identify the relevant legal (and in some courses/modules, the non-legal) issues and principles raised by the question;

- demonstrate knowledge of the relevant legal principles;

- apply the relevant legal principles (statutory, common law, and case law) to the facts in the scenario;

- provide an analysis of the strengths of the client's case with reference to law and case law;

- provide an analysis of the weaknesses of the client's case with reference to law and case law;

- provide an analysis of any remedies that may result from an action and the likely chances of success;

- provide an analysis of issues that require further investigation, why, and to what end;

- demonstrate an ability to conduct relevant research (coursework) or to answer questions in timed conditions (exams);

- provide full and accurate citations in relation to the evidence provided in support of each point (coursework); and

- communicate in good English.

Consequently, it is clear that a strong answer to a problem question will involve the use of case law and statutory evidence in support of the points being made. It is not sufficient to know the general legal principles and to apply those to the question; you will also need to provide evidence in support of each one.

21.2 How does one approach a judicial review problem question?

When answering a judicial review problem question, you are acting in a similar role to a barrister providing a legal opinion to the solicitor, and an assessment of chances of success and appropriate action to the client. Therefore you must include the relevant legal points, but also explain their significance for the benefit of the solicitor's client. You are advising a named party or parties, rather than writing an essay on the points of law. Remember, too, that a good lawyer does not give a one-sided viewpoint. You have to be realistic about the client's chances. If there is case law that weakens the client's case, then say so, as well as provide case law that supports it.

You are trying to make a point about the client's case in each paragraph. It may help you to focus your discussion if you begin each paragraph by raising the issue that you will address in that paragraph, prior to moving on to the detail and evidence associated with it. Therefore do not start a paragraph with a case, because cases are evidence of the law, as are references to legislation. Make your point first; then use the case(s) to back it up. You must provide evidence to back up your points in problem questions and this is evidence that could be cited in court. Judges will generally allow only primary and secondary legislation and common law, plus European Union (EU) law and, in some cases, international law—the **European Convention on Human Rights (ECHR)**, for example. Cases from courts in England and Wales that have precedent value will be binding according to the rules of precedent. These are evidence of how the law has been interpreted previously. European Court of Justice (ECJ) and European Court of Human Rights (ECtHR) cases are evidence of how EU law and the ECHR are interpreted, and are authoritative in respect of these sources of law. The judgments from other cases in England and Wales may not have a binding precedent authority, but may be considered to be persuasive in the absence of binding precedent on the point. The judgments of Commonwealth jurisdictions may also be persuasive in the same way as non-precedent cases. No other sources are classed as 'legal sources'. Occasionally, academic texts are referred to as evidence of the law, if there is no case law on the point or if the case law is terribly confused. Certain sections of Hansard may be referred to as an aid to the interpretation of legislation by judges. Generally, you will be referring to cases that have been raised in the lectures and in your textbook reading, or which you have found via databases such as Lexis, Westlaw, and Lawtel. You should have a legal source to back up each point you are making.

It is important to structure your answer so that it provides a logical explanation of the client's case. Your answer should contain: an introduction; a middle section made up of a series of paragraphs; and a conclusion. The introduction simply sets out what you are advising on (briefly) and the issues with which you will deal in your answer. It is usually a single paragraph in an exam or in a short piece of coursework. The middle section of your problem question answer is when you provide the substance of your advice, set out in a series of paragraphs. Each paragraph should deal with one point or issue. Those matters that must be demonstrated in a judicial review action (such as public function/**standing** issues) must be mentioned in your answer. However, you are not usually required to mention everything that you have considered and discounted in relation to the substantive elements of the case, such as each rule of **natural justice**. Do check with your tutor about this, though, if you are in any way unsure about your institution's policy on this. You do, however, need to work through your checklists (set out below) in order to diagnose the relevant issues. Finally, your conclusion should provide an assessment of the likely chances of success in the matter. You may need to refer matters back to the solicitor and client, for example, if there is missing information that may have bearing on the case.

The next issue is how you go about dissecting and reviewing a problem question before determining your advice. You may wish to pursue the steps outlined in this chapter, or to develop your own approach.

The figure that appears in the next extract is only one way of approaching a problem question, but it may help you in the early stages of your law studies until such time as you have developed your own approach to dissecting and answering problem questions. The extract sums up the factual analysis part of the process prior to your proceeding on to the application of law to the facts.

· ·

● **Lisa Webley,** *Legal Writing* [London: Routledge-Cavendish, 2010], pp. 30–1

Problem questions are relatively easy to approach, although the law that you need to apply may be complicated. Firstly, read the scenario—obvious yes, but it is tempting to jump in when you recognise something that you think you can write about. Next, read it again. You will not pick up on all the facts and the importance of the facts on the first reading. You may find it useful to write a list of events in chronological order, or, if you prefer, to draw a diagram showing who did what to whom, when and apparently why . . .

Summary Chapter 3 Legal Writing

The following stages may assist in approaching, structuring, and writing answers to problem questions.

Figure 21.1

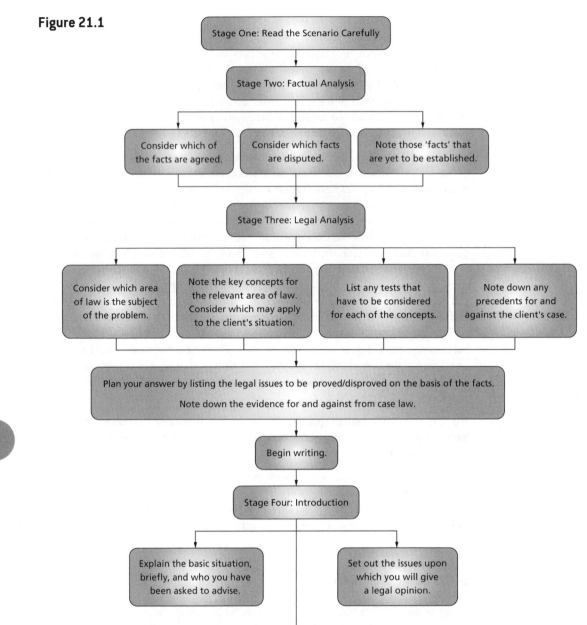

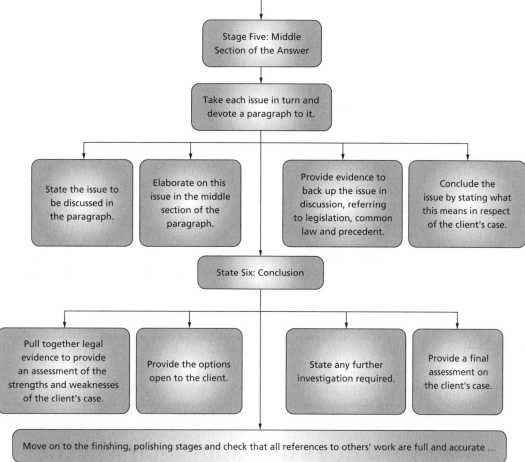

Hopefully, by now, you will have a good factual basis from which to work. Make sure that you identify for whom you are working—in other words, who is the client seeking advice. This will be important once you come to write up your opinion and it may also help you to bear this in mind when you are trying to work out the legal basis of the case. This is the factual analysis of the problem.

You should now be ready to consider the relevant legal points, and to provide your analysis of each main issue in the question with reference to the relevant law.

21.3 How does one approach whether the body may be judicially reviewed?

You should initially determine the decision, the action, or the omission that gives rise to concern, because this is the issue that will be the subject of the review. Judicial review is a review of a decision, action, or omission, and not a review of the body itself. Secondly, you should determine the parties and for whom you act: are you acting for the defendant or the claimant(s)?

Make sure that you know for whom you are acting and whether he or she is, or they are, bringing the action or defending it.

Initial considerations

....

1 Pinpoint the decision, action, or omission that gives rise to legal concern. This will be the issue to be reviewed.

2 Who made that decision, performed that act, or did not act? This will be the defendant.

3 Who is the person who was affected by the decision, action, or omission, and who wishes to bring the action? This is the claimant.

Once you have determined the parties, you then need to make sure that the defending body is susceptible to judicial review, meaning that the body must be a **public authority** or a body carrying out a public function.

For the traditional grounds of judicial review, the body in question must be exercising a public function. For the human rights ground, the body must be a public authority under the terms of the Human Rights Act 1998 (HRA 1998). Assuming that these requirements are met, then you should address the question of the claimant's standing.

Table 21.1

Traditional grounds	Human rights ground
Is the body exercising a public function?	Is the body a public authority according to the terms of section 6 of the HRA 1998 and related case law?

(21.4) How does one approach whether the client has standing or may intervene in an action?

The claimant must have an interest in the matter in order to be permitted to bring the judicial review action. This is known as 'standing'. The standing requirements differ for traditional judicial review grounds and those associated with the HRA 1998. You will need to make sure that the claimant meets both of these requirements, if both traditional and human rights issues are present in the problem question.

Standing

....

1 Does the claimant meet the **sufficient interest** test in section 31(3) of the Senior Courts Act 1981 in relation to traditional judicial review grounds?

2 Does the client meet the **victim** (or potential victim test), as outlined in section 7 of the HRA 1998 in relation to human rights grounds?

3 If the client is a group rather than an individual, check the extent to which the case law suggests that this group is likely to be granted standing.

Groups and associations are a little more difficult in relation to being granted standing and you will need to be familiar with the case law outlined in Chapter 15 in relation to these. In some situations, groups will be granted standing in relation to the traditional grounds for judicial review. However, this is much less likely in relation to human rights issues. If the group does not have standing, consider whether it can make a third-party intervention.

21.5 How does one approach whether the other preconditions are met?

There are a number of other precursor issues that need to be established before a judicial review may be brought, as follows. Check whether these conditions are met, or may be successfully argued at the **permission** stage.

> **Preconditions that must be met**
>
> ·
>
> 1 Time limits—normally three months for traditional judicial review grounds, under the **Civil Procedure Rules (CPR) 1998**, Part 54.5, this may be foreshortened by a time limit clause. This also applies to human rights cases brought by judicial review.
>
> 2 Is there an ouster clause present and, if so, would the court consider that it had jurisdiction to hear the matter?
>
> 3 Has the claimant exhausted all alternative routes to redress, such as internal appeal procedures?
>
> 4 Is this a public law or a private law matter? If the claimant is asking only for **damages** by way of a remedy, then it may be a private law matter, such as a breach of contract or a tort, rather than a judicial review case. If so, follow the private law route rather than this one.

Once you are reasonably confident on each of these issues, you may then address the substantive grounds for review.

21.6 Some general points to check before you consider the grounds of review

Before you consider the grounds of review and the HRA 1998, you might find it helpful to identify the legal source of the power being exercised. This is because specific issues might arise, for example, in relation to the prerogative or you might want to consider matters of general statutory interpretation.

You should also look at the nature or kind of power that is being exercised, because this might also raise special issues. So, for example, in some problem questions, you may be told that a public authority 'may grant a licence if it thinks fit'. In this sort of case, you should identify the power as a discretionary power and you would need to consider some points specific to **discretion**, such as the rule that discretion should not be fettered. If the question concerns a statutory duty that has not been exercised or has been used improperly, you might ask for a specific remedy, such as a **mandatory order** instructing the authority to carry out its duty. But no matter whether the law is based on the prerogative or statute, or is a matter of discretion or duty, you should consider all of the grounds of review and the HRA 1998 to check whether the authority has exercised its power properly.

What is the nature of the power being exercised?

General points to check before you consider the grounds of review include the following.

1 What is the basis for the body's action? Is it a statute or the **royal prerogative**?

2 Check the nature of the power that is being exercised. Is it a discretionary power or a statutory duty? You may want to comment on the general rules on the exercise of discretion in your answer.

3 If it is a statutory duty, then decide whether the duty has been exercised lawfully by considering the grounds of review and any human rights issues that arise.

4 If it is a discretion, then consider whether the discretion has been exercised lawfully by considering the grounds of review and the human rights issues.

You are now ready to move on to the substantive grounds for review.

(21.7) How does one approach the grounds for review?

21.7.1 Illegality

Illegality covers a wide range of sub-issues, ranging from the obvious ones, such as an error of law, through to delegating legal power unlawfully to someone else. The following is a checklist of issues that you should consider for each problem question.

Does the body have the legal power to do what it has done and has it exercised its powers correctly?

1 How has the body used its legal power?

• Has it misinterpreted the relevant statute?

• Has it used its power in bad faith?

• Has it used its power for an improper purpose?

• Has it taken into account an irrelevant consideration?

• Has it considered all of the relevant considerations?

- Has it applied any policy correctly?

- Has the body made an error of fact that is reviewable?

2 Has the correct person or office holder exercised the power as required by law?

- Has the decision-maker acted under dictation?

- Has the decision-maker abdicated the power?

- Has the decision-maker unlawfully delegated the power to someone else?

Work your way through the checklist and consider each of the issues in the light of the facts in the problem question. Which ones do appear to apply? Which ones may apply, but you would need more information to be sure either way? You will need to note this in your answer, to demonstrate that there is a potential ground for review, but that you need more information. Turn your attention to the issues that do apply. Refresh your memory of the relevant principles and evidence for those principles (case law and statute). Consider the law and precedent, and how they fit with your client's case. Does your client look to have a strong case on this ground? If so, why? If not, why not? Explain this with reference to the principles, providing case law and statutory evidence for your answer. Write up your analysis of this ground for the client, then move on to the next one.

21.7.2 Irrationality

The next ground that you may wish to consider is that of **irrationality**. Some of the issues overlap with the illegality ground, above, so be sure that you have covered all of them under one or other of these grounds. It is important to distinguish between the more traditional irrationality test for non-human-rights-related matters, and the proportionality test for human-rights-related ones.

Has the body acted rationally, reasonably, and/or proportionately?
. . . .

1 Has the body reached a decision that no rational body could have reached? (Non-human-rights judicial review)

2 Is this a situation in which the decision is going to be scrutinised more strictly because it will have a major impact on the individual? (Non-human-rights judicial review)

3 Has the body acted proportionately in respect of human rights issues? (Human rights judicial review—see below)

This ground is heavily reliant on case law, and you should refresh your memory of the relevant cases, consider the extent to which they are similar or different from the facts in the problem question, and apply them accordingly.

21.7.3 Procedural impropriety

You should review the decision-making procedure (or the procedure adopted prior to the action or the failure to act) to ensure that it complies with procedural requirements and the rules of natural justice. In other words, has the proper procedure been followed? Failure to follow the proper procedure—that is, **procedural impropriety**—may mean that the public body is required to reconsider its decision. This may have the effect of changing the decision that it reaches, or the action that it takes or chooses not to take. It may also reaffirm the original decision and that the claimant may not be in a better position than he or she was when bringing the judicial review. You should work your way through your checklist of issues to consider whether any of them are relevant to your client's case.

Table 21.2

Failure to follow the statutory procedure	Breach of the rules of natural justice
Is there a mandatory statutory procedure and has it been followed?	Did the claimant know the case against him or her?
Is there a statutory procedure that ought to be followed (directory) and has it been followed?	Has the right to be heard been respected? (This may include the right to make written representations or an oral hearing.)
Has the Article 6 ECHR right to a fair hearing, if applicable, been respected?	Is an oral hearing required? If so there may be a right to cross-examine witnesses, to call witnesses, and to have legal representation.
	Is this a situation in which natural justice requires that reasons be given for the decision?
	Has the rule against bias been breached? If so, is this a case of direct or apparent bias?
	Has the public body created a legitimate expectation that a particular procedure will be followed?
	Has the public body created a legitimate expectation that the claimant will receive a substantive benefit?

It is important to remember that the rules of natural justice are not absolute and some will not be applicable to a claimant. You should consider each one in turn, and then, if you find one or more that may be relevant to the claimant's case, discuss them in the light of the claimant's factual situation and the relevant case law. You should draw the reader's attention to factual similarities between the cases that you are citing and the claimant's case, and likewise distinguish cases that have a very different factual basis, explaining why the legal principle may not apply given the lack of factual symmetry.

21.7.4 Human rights issues

This is quite a complex area of judicial review. There are a number of things that you need to bear in mind when providing advice. It is important to distinguish between the two human-rights-based grounds for review, because students often confuse the two. This can be confusing in the context of a problem question, particularly if it is set under time-constrained conditions during which it is easy to mix up domestic law and international law—the HRA 1998 and the ECHR. The first ground for review in the context of human rights matters is that a public authority has breached the terms of the HRA 1998 by taking a decision, acting, or failing to act in a way that unlawfully infringes the ECHR. The second is that UK law itself (primary legislation) breaches the terms of the ECHR. This may seem like a minor distinction, but in the first instance a court may grant a 'useful' remedy to the client if the breach is upheld. This may have the effect of preventing the breach of human rights from continuing. In the second case, the court is not able to remedy the breach actively, because the UK **Parliament** is supreme and may legally pass primary legislation that infringes the ECHR. The courts are not able to set this aside, but instead may only issue a **declaration** of incompatibility to declare that the UK primary legislation infringes the ECHR. They may not go further to prevent the continued application of the law.

Table 21.3

Human rights ground for review	Remedy
The public authority has acted, taken a decision, or failed to act in breach of a Convention right contrary to section 6 of the HRA 1998.	Potential remedy available to the claimant.
UK primary legislation breaches a Convention right, thus infringing the ECHR.	No remedy available to the claimant. The court may issue a declaration of incompatibility to declare UK law to be in breach of the ECHR, if proved.

In order to determine whether the claimant has a viable case in relation to the first ground, it is important to work through the following steps systematically.

Breach of an ECHR right by a public authority

1 Which is the ECHR right that it is claimed has been breached?

2 Considering the ECHR case law, does the claimant's situation appear to fall within the terms of this right?

- If no, then there is no human rights ground in this instance.

- If yes, then proceed to the next step.

3 Were the restrictions that were made proportionate to meet the purpose?

4 Was the restriction made for a legitimate aim? In other words, was the restriction placed on the right one that the law considers legitimate and important? If yes, then move onto the next step.

- Were the measures taken rationally connected to the aim?

If yes:

- Were the measures taken no more than is necessary to achieve the legitimate objective? To put it another way, were there any other restrictions that could have been put on the right that would have been less destructive of the right?

If yes:

- Has a fair balance been struck between the individual human right and the interest of the community?

If yes:

- Is this a situation in which the court will defer to the **executive**?

If no, then it is likely that the court will consider the restriction to be proportionate.

5 What remedies would the claimant seek if the case were to be allowed?

Were the public authority to have breached the terms of the HRA 1998 by unlawfully infringing a Convention right (without authorisation by an Act of Parliament), then the judge may grant a remedy. However, it may be that the public authority has acted lawfully, even if the claimant's Convention right has been breached. This situation would arise if UK primary legislation were to require the public authority to act in a way that breached an individual's Convention rights: the court cannot set aside primary legislation in favour of the ECHR. Run through the following steps if you think that it may be UK primary legislation, rather than the public authority, that is infringing the ECHR right.

UK law incompatible with a Convention right

. . . .

1 Which is the ECHR right that it is claimed has been breached?

2 Considering the ECHR case law, does the claimant's situation appear to fall within the terms of this right?

- If no, then there is no human rights ground in this instance.

- If yes, then proceed to the next step.

3 Were the restrictions that were made proportionate to meet the purpose?

- What is the aim of the public authority in restricting the right? Is the restriction placed on the right one that the law considers legitimate and important? If yes, then move onto the next step.

- Were the measures taken rationally connected to the aim?

If yes:

- Were the measures taken no more than is necessary to achieve the legitimate objective? In other words, were there any other restrictions that could have been put on the right that would have been less destructive of the right?

- Has a fair balance been struck between the individual human right and the interest of the community?

If yes:

- Is this a situation in which the court will defer to the executive?

If no, then it is likely that the court will consider the restriction to be proportionate.

4 Is there any primary legislation that requires or authorises the public authority to restrict the right in question?

- If yes, check whether it is possible to reinterpret UK law so that it may comply with the ECHR, and if that is not possible, then the court may declare UK law to be incompatible with the EHCR.

- If no, then check whether the public authority is acting in breach of the ECHR, as set out in the checklist above.

Were you to decide that UK primary legislation infringes a Convention right, then you should explain that a judge of High Court level or above may issue a declaration of incompatibility that UK primary legislation breaches the ECHR. However, a judge cannot override a UK Act of Parliament in this situation. It would then be for the client to decide whether to attempt to take the UK to the ECtHR in Strasbourg, for failure to respect the ECHR. Once you have worked your way through the substantive grounds, you should then consider available remedies, plus the claimant's likely chances of success.

21.8 How does one deal with issues of remedy?

What remedies is the client seeking? If the client is seeking purely private law remedies, then check again that this is a public law matter and not a private law matter. Does the client require a **quashing order**, a mandatory order, a **prohibiting order**, **injunction**, or damages? If there is a decision in place that needs to be set aside, then a quashing order may well be the most appropriate remedy.

Remedies

. . . .

1 Is there a *decision* in place that needs to be set aside? If so, consider a *quashing order* first.

2 Are you arguing that the public body ought *not to act* in a particular way? If so, request a *prohibiting order* or an *injunction*.

3 Are you arguing that the public body ought *to do something* in particular or ought to carry out its statutory duty? If so, request a *mandatory order* or a *mandatory injunction*.

4 Do you want the court to declare that the authority has acted unlawfully and/or to state the legal position? If so, request a *declaration*.

5 Are you claiming that, in addition, there has been a private law wrong, such as a breach of contract or a tort? If so, claim *damages*.

6 Are you arguing that UK primary legislation is in breach of the ECHR? If so, you need to request a declaration of incompatibility.

You should set out what remedies are realistic and why, as well as the limitations of those remedies: for example, a quashing order followed by an order that the public authority rehear the issue prior to reaching a fresh decision may not result in a substantially different decision being reached. However, the defending body should have followed the proper procedure the second time around.

21.9 How does one provide a final assessment to the client?

This is your opportunity to provide your professional assessment of the claimant's likely chances of success if the matter were to proceed to judicial review. You should consider which grounds, if any, are strong and which are weak. You should also note anything that the legal adviser (solicitor) needs to check in order to be sure of any of the outstanding or ambiguous issues. Finally, you should advise the solicitor and his or her client on the best course of action.

Summary

Your problem question answer should provide a fictional solicitor and his or her client with your assessment of the client's case, along with an assessment of what more information, if any, you would need in order to finalise your opinion. You should set out the legal issues that are relevant to the client's case, how they relate to it, your analysis, and the legal evidence that you have in support. You should not begin your paragraphs with the evidence, but instead you should provide the evidence after setting out your points. Your written style should be clear and concise. However, unlike a real barrister's opinion, your opinion should also show sufficient 'working out' so that the marker may see the areas that you have considered and rejected (in brief), as well as those that you have selected and discussed. This is not a licence for you to discuss everything that you know about judicial review, but instead indicates to the marker that you have grounds that could be relevant, but which you have ultimately rejected. In short, the marker may give you marks only for what appears on the paper and cannot read into your answer something that is not present.

Questions

Now have a go at one of the problem questions set out at Chapters 16, 17, and 18 with the aid of these checklists. Then turn to the Online Resource Centre to see an example of strong answers and some feedback on common mistakes that may be made in answer to questions like these.

Glossary

absolute right A human right that cannot be curtailed under any circumstances, such as the right to be free from torture, but which right is given a legal definition, meaning that a right such as the right to be free from torture is subject to the definition of what constitutes 'torture'.

Administrative Court Part of the Queen's Bench Division of the High Court, the Administrative Court hears claims for judicial review.

Assembly Measure A law enacted by the National Assembly of Wales that is classified at the level of an Act of Parliament; it applies only to Wales and not to the other countries that make up the United Kingdom.

backbench member of Parliament (MP) An MP who is not a member of the government or the shadow government; so-called because he or she does not sit on the front benches (seats) in the chambers, which are reserved for members of the government and shadow government.

bicameral A legislative system that involves two chambers, such as the Westminster Parliament, which comprises the House of Commons and the House of Lords.

Belmarsh Detainees The name given to the landmark decision of the House of Lords in *A v Secretary of State for the Home Department* [2004] UKHL 56, which concerned a Human Rights Act 1998 challenge to the indefinite detention of foreign nationals under the Anti-Terrorism, Crime and Security Act 2001.

bill of rights A constitutionally guaranteed statement of rights that may be enforced through the courts; usually overrides primary legislation, because it is considered to be of higher constitutional standing, and often appears in written constitutions.

Civil Procedure Rules (CPR) 1998 With some exceptions, rules that regulate proceedings in the High Court, the Court of Appeal (civil division), and the County Court; Part 54 of which lays down the procedures to be followed in judicial review cases.

coalition government Arises when two or more parties form a government together because one party alone does not hold a majority of seats in Parliament (House of Commons).

collateral challenge A challenge to the legality of the decision of a public authority that arises incidentally in legal proceedings not involving a claim for judicial review, although of a type that would normally have to be brought by judicial review, because the public law matter has arisen incidentally during private law or criminal proceedings, it can usually be dealt with by the relevant court.

constitutional convention A non-legal, yet binding, rule that regulates the way in which the royal prerogative should be exercised, such as the constitutional convention that the monarch, in all but the most exceptional circumstances, should not refuse the royal assent to a Bill that has been passed by the House of Commons and the House of Lords.

control order Imposed by the Home Secretary in accordance with the Prevention of Terrorism Act 2005, restricting the activity of an individual, for example by requiring him or her to live at a particular address or to observe a curfew, and limiting his or her access to the Internet or other communications; applies to British and foreign nationals suspected of terrorist activity, but, at time of writing, control orders are being abolished and replaced by the terrorism investigation and prevention measure (TPIM).

core public authority For the purposes of the Human Rights Act 1998, an 'obvious' public authority, such as a local authority, government department, or the police force, which is bound by the 1998 Act in all aspects of its work.

Crown A term used to refer to: (1) the monarch's crown; (2) the Monarch herself or himself; and (3) the state.

damages The money awarded by a court to a claimant for loss or injury that he or she has suffered.

declaration An ordinary remedy—which can be granted on judicial review, that provides an authoritative statement of the legal position between the parties; often granted to resolve a dispute about the correct interpretation of the law.

deference The action whereby a court declines to make its own independent judgment on an issue, usually out of respect for the democratic nature of another branch of government; an extremely controversial area of law, deference has generated considerable academic and judicial discussion.

derogable right A human right that may be subject to some limitation in times of emergency, as long as the derogation meets the Article 15 ECHR requirements.

devolution The delegation of powers from central state institutions to regional or local institutions.

direct applicability The term often used in a constitutional law context in relation to the way in which some forms of EU law, such as some treaty articles, automatically apply within the UK legal system without further translation, which means that these provisions may give rise to rights and duties in the domestic legal system without Parliament passing law to bring them into effect in the UK; they may be enforced against the state, and also against private bodies and individuals.

direct effect Another term often used in respect of EU law provisions, some of which, such as some directives, may be enforced against the state through the UK courts even though they are not directly applicable and even if Parliament has not enacted legislation to translate them into the UK jurisdiction; not usually enforceable against private individuals or private bodies, but only against the state and related public authorities.

direct horizontal effect The application of a legal instrument, such as a statute, between private individuals and organisations, as well as between the individual and public authorities; the Human Rights Act 1998 does not have direct horizontal effect, which means that one private individual is not entitled to bring a claim directly against another private individual.

discretion A power that gives the decision-maker a choice of action or decision; there is no discretion if a public authority is required to act in a particular way, but there is a discretion if a public authority has the power to act if it so chooses.

dualist state A state, common in systems that are based on parliamentary supremacy, in which international law (treaties) does not apply automatically within the domestic jurisdiction (that country); instead, international law becomes applicable domestically only if the state translates it into the domestic jurisdiction—in a UK context, through passing an Act of Parliament to that effect.

entrenched (entrenching) Legislation that is relatively fixed, meaning that it is very hard to amend, and into which category written constitutions usually fall, because they often require the approval of the legislature, the executive, and the people (through a referendum) prior to a change being made; the term 'semi-entrenched' is used to denote legislation that is harder to amend than standard legislation (for example, the legislature may be permitted to amend or repeal this legislation if two-thirds vote in favour of the change, rather than a simple majority).

European Convention for the Protection of Human Rights and Fundamental Freedoms, or European Convention on Human Rights (ECHR) The key international treaty that members agree to respect on joining the Council of Europe; often referred to simply as the 'European Convention', or even 'the Convention'.

ex gratia Latin meaning 'as a favour', this usually refers to payments made by government for which there is no legal obligation.

executive The branch of the state that governs the country; sometimes referred to as the 'narrow' or 'political' executive (to denote the MPs and peers), or the 'wider' executive (which includes the political executive, and civil servants and other public officials who help to run the country), and sometimes as the government.

fiduciary duty A relationship of trust between the relevant individuals; in public law, it is usually used to refer to the special relationship between local authorities and council taxpayers (that is, local authorities are said to have to take particular care about the way in which money collected from council taxpayers is spent and should make sure that money is not wasted).

formal school, the A group of theorists who believe that the rule of law is a doctrine that requires law to be clear and transparent, relatively stable in nature (that is, not changing so rapidly that it is impossible to keep up with it), and made according to the proper procedure and respected by the state, as well as by individuals.

free vote An issue (such as a Bill) on which an MP or peer has a free choice as to which way to vote in the Commons or the Lords; cf. **whipped vote**

functional public authority A body that has a combination of private and public functions against which a claim under the Human Rights Act 1998 can be brought only when it is carrying out functions of a public nature.

government The party (or parties, in the case of a hung parliament) in power, which has the tasks of running the country; sometimes referred to as the political executive, or the executive.

hereditary peerage A peerage that has been granted to an individual for his or her lifetime, but which is then passed down through the generations according to the rules that govern hereditary peerages.

horizontal effect See **direct horizontal effect**

hybrid public authority A term sometimes used to describe a functional public authority for the purposes of the Human Rights Act 1998; see **functional public authority**

illegality A broad ground of review named by Lord Diplock in the *CCSU* case that refers to a number of wrongs that a body exercising public functions can commit, including simple ultra vires, misinterpreting a statutory power, and abuse of discretion (*Council for the Civil Service Unions v Minister for the Civil Service* [1985] AC 374).

indirect horizontal effect The term used to explain the indirect impact of the Human Rights Act 1998 on cases concerned with private individuals; the Act does not have direct horizontal effect and a claim under the Act cannot be brought against a private individual (see above), but if a dispute between private individuals is being heard by the court, then the 1998 Act may be applied indirectly; this is because the courts are considered to be public authorities under section 6(3) and have to act compatibly with the Convention through their development of the common law; in addition, courts have a duty under section 3 of the Human Rights Act 1998 to interpret legislation consistently with the Convention in so far as it is possible to do so.

injunction   A remedy granted by the court ordering the public authority to carry out a particular act, such as an order to perform its statutory duty, or to refrain from doing some act; it is an ordinary remedy, but can be granted on judicial review.

interim injunction   A temporary order granted by the court before the full hearing on the merits of the case has taken place, intending to preserve the parties' position before the court makes its final decision at the full hearing.

irrationality   One of the grounds or review referred to by Lord Diplock in the *CCSU* case, this means a decision that is 'so outrageous in its defiance of logic or of accepted moral standards that no sensible person who had applied his mind to the question to be decided could have arrived at it' (*Council for the Civil Service Unions v Minister for the Civil Service* [1985] AC 374, 410).

judicial   The branch of the state, independent of the others, which adjudicates on legal matters by applying the law; it is made up of judges (and some would include jurors) who sit in tribunals and courts.

Judicial Appointments Commission (JAC)   Established as a result of the Constitutional Reform Act 2005, the JAC selects candidates for judicial office (judges) for England and Wales, and recommends appropriate candidates for appointment; prior to its inception, judges were selected by the Lord Chancellor.

judiciary   The judicial branch of the state, which is made up of judges, whether in courts or tribunals.

leave   *See* **permission**

legislative   The branch of the state that makes the law—in the UK, the Westminster Parliament; in the UK, the legislative also scrutinises the executive.

life peerage   A peerage that has been granted to an individual for life, but which will die with the peer rather than be passed down through the family via inheritance.

locus standi   The Latin term that describes the legal right to bring an action. *See* **standing**

Lord Chancellor   Also known as the Justice Secretary, or Secretary of State for Justice, the government minister in charge of the Ministry of Justice (a government department) who has the duty of ensuring the independence of the judiciary and the functioning of the court system; also a politician who sits either in the House of Commons (as an MP) or the House of Lords (as a peer); the Lord Chancellor was formerly also the head of the judiciary and a serving judge, plus speaker of the

House of Lords—but the Constitutional Reform Act 2005 removed this role from the Lord Chancellor and granted it to the Lord Chief Justice.

Lord Chief Justice   The head of the judiciary in England and Wales since the Constitutional Reform Act 2005 removed this role from the Lord Chancellor; also the senior judge in the Court of Appeal Criminal Division.

maladministration   Poor administrative practices that do not necessarily make a decision of a public authority unlawful; the *Crossman* definition states that maladministration includes 'bias, neglect, inattention, delay, incompetence, ineptitude, perversity, turpitude, arbitrariness and so on' (*R v Local Commissioners for the North and East Area of England, ex p Bradford Metropolitan City Council* [1979] QB 287).

mandatory order   Formerly an order of mandamus, this prerogative remedy available on judicial review requires the public authority, tribunal, or other body executing a public function to carry out its public duty.

monarch   The (apolitical) head of state in a system that is based on a constitutional monarchy.

monist state   A state in which international law does not need to be translated into the domestic jurisdiction in order for it to be applicable; instead, it applies automatically once the state has ratified the treaty in question.

natural justice   The common law rules of procedural fairness developed by the judges.

Parliament   The legislative body exercising the legislative function, the full title of which is the 'Queen in Parliament'; Parliament may also have the duty to scrutinise the executive; the Westminster (UK) Parliament is made up of the House of Commons, the House of Lords, and the Queen (whose royal assent is required before Bills become Acts).

Parliamentary Ombudsman   The name given to the Parliamentary Commissioner for Administration, who independently investigates complaints of maladministration leading to injustice against central government departments and other public bodies listed in the Parliamentary Commissioner Act 1967; complaints made by members of the public have to be referred to the Ombudsman by an MP.

parliamentary privilege   Parliament's power to regulate itself free from outside interference, which precludes the courts from regulating Parliament and is said to strengthen parliamentary supremacy. NOTE: Do not confuse Parliament with the government, because the courts have the power of judicial review in relation to executive acts.

permission   Formerly known as 'leave', but renamed under the Civil Procedure Rules 1998, the requirement, in judicial review cases, that the claimant must obtain the consent of the court before the case can be heard in full; in order to consent, the court must be convinced that there is an arguable case.

pre-action protocol A procedure laid down in the Civil Procedure Rules that encourages the parties to resolve their dispute without recourse to judicial review, but which may not be appropriate in all cases; where it is relevant, the pre-action protocol will involve an exchange of letters between the parties to attempt to settle the matter.

Prime Minister The leader of the government—usually, the leader of the party in power; he or she is also usually the leader of the party that has the most seats in the House of Commons following a general election and is appointed by the monarch under the royal prerogative in accordance with constitutional convention.

procedural impropriety The third ground of review discussed by Lord Diplock in the *CCSU* case, this includes both a breach of a statutory procedure and also a breach of the common law rules of natural justice (*Council for the Civil Service Unions v Minister for the Civil Service* [1985] AC 374).

prohibiting order Formerly known as an order of prohibition, this prerogative remedy available on judicial review requires the public authority, tribunal, or other body carrying out a public function to refrain from acting unlawfully; usually used to prevent a public authority from carrying out a planned action that the court has determined to be unlawful.

public authority The only type of body against which a claim relating to a breach of a Convention right may be brought in accordance with section 6 of the Human Rights Act 1998; includes both a core public authority and a functional public authority.

qualified right A right that is subject to limitation by a range of interests that are usually expressly stated in the relevant Article of the Convention—for example, Article 10 states that the right to freedom of expression may be subject to necessary restriction as provided by law; justifications for restrictions include protecting national security, public order, public health, or morals, and respecting the rights and reputations of others; the courts will decide whether a restriction on a right is necessary by applying the proportionality test; rights may also be qualified when they are balanced against each other, taking into account whether any restriction is lawful and proportionate—for example, the right to freedom of expression in Article 10 might be balanced against the right to a private and family life in Article 8 (see, for example, *Campbell v MGN Ltd* [2004] UKHL 22).

quashing order Formerly an order of certiorari, a prerogative remedy available on judicial review requiring that the decision of a public authority, tribunal, or other body carrying out a public function be set aside or invalidating that decision.

Queen The current monarch—but not necessarily so, if she is married to the king; the wife of a male monarch (a king) is usually referred to as a queen, whereas the husband of a female monarch (the queen) is usually referred to as a prince (although there are some exceptions to these general rules).

referendum A motion, usually on one issue, that is put to the electorate to decide rather than left solely to members of the legislature, such as the referendum on the European Economic Community in 1975 in which the British people voted to remain in Europe.

relator action An action in which the Attorney General allows a private individual to bring a claim in his or her name.

remedial order A power granted to ministers under section 10 of the Human Rights Act 1998 to make amendments to legislation subsequent to a declaration of incompatibility by a court under section 4 of the Act, the order allows the amendments to be fast-tracked through Parliament relying on similar procedures to those used for delegated legislation.

royal prerogative A special branch of the common law that is enjoyed by the monarch, but which may be delegated, by constitutional convention, to members of the political executive.

rule of law A theory or doctrine that describes the principles that underscore the legal system; there are, however, different views about what values and principles should be considered to be part of the rule of law.

separation of powers The way in which the powers of the state (executive, legislative, and judicial) are divided in the state, which separation may be complete or partial; it may also be a separation of power, function, or personnel.

stakeholder A person or body that has an interest (a stake) in the matter under consideration.

standing The test that determines whether the claimant is able to become a party to the case so as to bring the claim before the court: on judicial review, the claimant has to show 'a sufficient interest' in the matter in order to be a party to the case; in cases brought under the Human Rights Act 1998, a claimant has to satisfy a stricter test and must show that he or she is the victim of the alleged breach of the Convention right.

state The nation, for the purposes of legal definition; the UK is made up of four countries and yet is one state, which clarifies that 'country' and 'state' are not necessarily the same entity.

substantive school, the A group of theorists who believe that the rule of law should meet the formal school requirements, but also adhere to key standards in relation to its substance, such as respect for morality, respect for human rights standards, etc.

sufficient interest A test for standing in judicial review cases, under which the claimant must show that he or she has an interest or connection to the decision that has been made; after the House of Lords' decision in *Inland Revenue Commissioners Appellants v National Federation of Self-Employed and Small Businesses Ltd* [1982] AC 617, it has become much easier to apply for standing.

terrorism prevention and investigation measure (TPIM) Introduced by the Terrorism Prevention and Investigation Measures Act 2011 to replace the control order, a TPIM will restrict the activities of British and foreign nationals suspected of terrorist activity, for example by imposing curfews and residence requirements, and by restricting Internet access; although similar to control orders, TPIMs impose stricter time limits, an exhaustive list of restrictions, and provide some safeguards so that suspects are not treated excessively harshly.

ultra vires The Latin term used to describe the situation in which a body acts beyond or outside its legal powers.

unicameral A legislative system that involves only one chamber, such as the Scottish Parliament, the National Assembly of Wales, and the Northern Ireland Assembly.

universal suffrage Electoral rules that do not discriminate against people on the basic characteristics such as gender, ethnicity, property ownership, wealth, etc.; it does not mean that everyone has to be permitted to vote (non-British citizens, minors, for example), but rather that the eligibility criteria should be as broad as possible so as to permit democratic engagement and that all adult citizens should be entitled to vote, subject to very limited exceptions.

vertical effect A term used to describe the ability of an individual to bring a claim against a public authority as opposed to a private body or individual: for example, the Human Rights Act 1998 has a vertical effect because it provides that claims may be brought against a public authority.

victim Defined by the courts as any person directly affected by the unlawful action, omission, or decision that is at issue in a case brought under section 7(1)(b) of the Human Rights Act 1998.

***Wednesbury* unreasonableness** A decision that is so unreasonable—that is, so beyond the range of reasonable outcomes available to the decision-maker—that no reasonable person could have to come to the conclusion in question; most famously stated in *Associated Provincial Picture Houses v Wednesbury Corporation* [1948] 1 KB 223, 229, from which it takes its name, it was reformulated by Lord Diplock in *CCSU* as a test of irrationality, and the two terms are now frequently used interchangeably.

whipped vote An issue (such as a Bill) in the Commons or Lords on which the party whips instruct members of Parliament or peers in which way they should vote; cf. **free vote**

Index

663

K

L

complete: law solution

Reading and making sense of original case extracts is a vital part of understanding how law works. But how do you know which sections of **which** cases to read?

Books in the **complete** series combine extracts from a wide range of primary materials with clear explanatory text to provide students with a complete introductory resource.

Each author carefully unfolds the complexities of the subject, exposing the reader to relevant case extracts and supporting them with illuminating commentary. Helpful learning features are clearly presented and effectively employed, ensuring each **complete** title provides students with a **stimulating** introduction to the subject.

For further details about titles in the series, visit

www.oxfordtextbooks.co.uk/law/complete